Admiralty Record®

Volume 2

PUBLISHED ADMIRALTY OPINIONS OF
THE SUPREME COURT OF THE UNITED STATES AND
THE UNITED STATES COURTS OF APPEALS ISSUED DURING
THE CALENDAR YEAR

2014

Cite as: 2 Adm. R. _____

REPORTED BY KIRK N. AURANDT, ESQ.
MEMBER OF THE BAR IN LOUISIANA AND PENNSYLVANIA

ADMIRALTY RECORD PUBLISHING COMPANY, L.L.C.
MANDEVILLE, LOUISIANA, U.S.A.

ISSN 2334-5411
ISBN 978-0-9983853-2-7

Admiralty record: published admiralty opinions of the
Supreme Court of the United States and the United
States Courts of Appeals issued during the calendar
year ... Mandeville, Louisiana, U.S.A.: Admiralty
Record Publishing Company, LLC, 2014-

     KF1104 .A75
     ISSN: 2334-5411

https://lccn.loc.gov/2014200303

PREFACE

Volume 2—the second annual edition of the Admiralty Record®—reports published admiralty opinions of the United States Courts of Appeals that were issued during the calendar year 2014. There were no admiralty opinions from the Supreme Court of the United States in 2014. The opinions reported are the original majority, concurring, and dissenting opinions of the Court, with only minor changes in formatting to better suit a dual-column presentation. The pagination found in the original opinion is indicated by the number contained inside of black brackets. Also, where applicable, I have added parallel citations to opinions reported in Volumes 1 and 2 of the Admiralty Record®.

The decision to select an opinion to appear in Volume 2 of the Admiralty Record® was made solely by me following an examination of those opinions that each of the above-named courts designated for publication in 2014. Every effort has been made to ensure inclusion of all 2014 federal appellate court admiralty opinions that were designated for publication; however, to the extent that a relevant admiralty opinion has been inadvertently overlooked or otherwise mistakenly omitted, the error is regretted and is solely my own. A few opinions from appeals in civil cases that technically may not have fallen under a federal district court's admiralty or maritime jurisdiction have been reported if they touched upon admiralty matters, or were otherwise deemed to be of potential interest to the admiralty practitioner. Additionally, several opinions from criminal cases involving maritime crimes, and civil cases arising under the Federal Employers' Liability Act have been included.

To assist the reader in locating those opinions from 2014 involving subject matters of interest, I have prepared an Index to the opinions. I have also prepared Tables of Authority, which supply page references to the cases, statutes, and rules cited in each opinion. Prior to relying upon any of the opinions reported herein, the reader is reminded to verify the current status of any particular case as valid precedent by checking the case with a reliable citator.

Additional copies of Volume 1 (covering 2013), Volume 2 (covering 2014), and succeeding-year volumes may be ordered at www.admiraltyrecord.com. I hope that the Admiralty Record® will become a valuable and ready reference source for not only the admiralty practitioner, but for anyone who is interested in reading the published admiralty opinions of the federal appellate courts.

KIRK N. AURANDT, ESQ.

This page intentionally left blank

Table of Contents[1]

(Cases arranged chronologically by Court)

---

[1] In 2014, there were no published admiralty opinions from the Supreme Court of the United States and the United States Courts of Appeals for the Third and Tenth Circuits.

This page intentionally left blank

United States Court of Appeals for the First Circuit

United States Court of Appeals
for the First Circuit

No. 12-2174

CRACCHIOLO
vs.
EASTERN FISHERIES, INC.

Appeal from the United States District Court for the District of Massachusetts

Decided: January 15, 2014

Citation: 740 F.3d 64, 2 Adm. R. 2 (1st Cir. 2014).

Before **LYNCH**, Chief Judge, **STAHL**, and **LIPEZ**, Circuit Judges.

[—2—] **LYNCH**, Chief Judge:

Shortly after midnight on January 28, 2011, Giuseppe Cracchiolo fell and drowned after slipping from an obviously hazardous place on a pier at a New Bedford fishery while attempting to return to the commercial fishing boat on which he was working. His wife Carla Cracchiolo, acting individually and as administratrix of the estate, sued defendants RCP Realty and Eastern Fisheries, Inc. for damages for wrongful death based on a negligence theory. These defendants are, respectively, the owner and the leaseholder of the facility where the ship was docked. They were alleged to have failed to use due care in the inspection, maintenance, and repair of the premises and to have failed to provide Cracchiolo with a safe and reasonable egress from and ingress to the boat, particularly with respect to the ice and snow conditions on the pier that night.

The district court granted the defendants' motion for summary judgment on the basis that the defendants owed no duty of care to remedy the hazard under the circumstances of this case. We reverse and remand. We do not decide the duty of care issue. We write narrowly and conclude the issue cannot be decided on the undisputed facts in this summary judgment record.

I.

Plaintiff filed suit against O'Hara Corporation, which owned the boat, under the Jones Act, 46 U.S.C. § 30104, and general maritime law. She also brought tort claims under Massachusetts's [—3—] wrongful death statute, Mass. Gen. Laws ch. 229, § 2, against Eastern Fisheries, which operated the property where the boat was docked, and RCP Realty, which owned the property.

All three defendants moved for summary judgment on July 2, 2012. Plaintiff opposed the motions, and the court held a hearing on the motions on August 15, 2012. Trial was scheduled for September 17, 2012. On September 6, 2012, at the final pretrial conference, the district court, in an oral order, denied O'Hara's summary judgment motion but granted Eastern Fisheries and RCP's. On September 11, 2012, plaintiff filed a motion for reconsideration, which was denied.[1] Plaintiff appeals.

II.

For purposes of summary judgment, we describe the facts in the light most favorable to the nonmovant, drawing all reasonable inferences in her favor. *See, e.g., Barclays Bank PLC v. Poynter*, 710 F.3d 16, 19 (1st Cir. 2013).

A. *Layout of the Defendants' Property*

Giuseppe Cracchiolo worked as a commercial fisherman and engineer on the *F/V Sunlight*, a herring boat. During the winter, the *Sunlight* operated out of the defendants' fish processing facility in New Bedford, Massachusetts, and docked at the facility's pier. The *Sunlight* paid a fee for use of that facility; [—4—] the facility was used both for processing fish and for berthing vessels. At least thirteen vessels used the facility in 2010 and 2011.

---

[1] On September 13, 2012, Plaintiff and O'Hara settled their case. The district court retained supplemental jurisdiction over the claims against Eastern Fisheries and RCP.

The roughly rectangular waterfront property is enclosed by a chain link fence on its north, west, and south sides; the east side abuts the water. The property contains a fish processing plant, the front door of which faces the western side of the property, where there is a parking lot. At the back of the plant is a pier on the east side, where fishing vessels dock and in some instances offload their catches. The pier runs from north to south and a wooden cap board, about a foot wide, runs its length. There are bollards, for the boats to tie off their lines, located at various points along the pier, including near the south end. In the ordinary course, the entire length of the pier is used, including to tie the lines to the southern bollard. Scallop boats also unloaded near the southern end and occasionally stored nets in the area.

There are several feet of space between the plant and the fence on the north side, and a smaller grass-covered space of just a few feet between the plant and the fence on the south side. Between the fence on the western side, which has a large gate with a padlock, and the western door of the plant is a parking lot.

The fence along the south side did not go all the way to the water's edge; rather, it stopped two to three feet short of the [—5—] water's edge. Importantly, the end of the fence had been folded back deliberately, leaving an obvious gap in the fence. Access to the south side of the property, from the adjacent property, was easily obtained through the use of this gap. This was the most direct way for crew members to get to the boats if the gate to the property was locked and they did not have keys.

The grass on the building's south side extends about ten feet north of the fence in the southeast corner. Immediately to the north of the grassy area, an asphalt surface begins. It goes across the pier from the south to the northeast corner of the property. Along the eastern edge of the property, where the pier runs along the water, is a retaining wall. The easternmost edge of the pier was covered by a wooden cap log.

Fishing vessels, including the *Sunlight*, tied off next to the plant at its pier and unloaded their fish catch into the building. Sometimes another fishing vessel would be tied to the vessel tied to the dock. This was true of the *Sunlight* and its companion vessel. The *Sunlight* had used the pier since 2009. The *Sunlight* always tied off with its bow to the south and its stern to the north. The boat would tie off using a bollard at the southern end of the pier near the bow. The stern sat lower on the water than the bow and was roughly level with the pier. As a result, crew members leaving the boat would ordinarily step off the *Sunlight*'s stern onto the pier. By contrast, at the south end of [—6—] the boat, the bow rose an additional several feet above the pier. Crew members tying off the boat with the bow lines would walk to the southern end of the pier to do so. Scallop boats also unloaded their catches at the southern end of the pier. After leaving from the stern, crew members wanting to leave the property typically walked along a wide path on the north side of the property, between the processing plant and the fence, until reaching the parking lot on the western half of the property. They left through the gate. The reverse route, from the parking lot, along the north side of the property, and to the stern, would allow the crew to reboard the boat.

Apart from the gate at the front entrance, the other way into the property was through the obvious gap in the fence at the southeast corner. As the *Sunlight*'s captain, Joseph Martin, testified, "[e]verybody knows you can go that way." Another crew member, Craig Lazaro, explained that the gap was "easy to see."[2] Captain Martin stated that although they knew the gap in the southeast corner existed, crew members would, "most of the time," enter the property through the main gate on the west side of the property. [—7—]

---

[2] Eastern Fisheries' corporate representative, however, asserted that the company did not even know that the gap existed, much less that anyone walked through it to access the defendants' property. We disregard that denial of knowledge of access through the gap, as we must take the evidence in favor of the plaintiff.

Upon entering through the gap in the southeast corner of the fence, crew members could turn left and walk in the area between the fence and the fish processing building, back to the parking lot, past the building's front door, then take the path along the north side of the building to the stern of the boat. This was the longer of the two possible routes from the southeast corner.

Alternatively, a few crew members chose a shorter but more hazardous route. Instead of turning left, they walked straight ahead to the asphalt and continued along the waterfront retaining wall, to walk along the pier from the bow to the stern of the boat. Of necessity, those taking this route would have to walk for part of the way on the wooden cap log on the retaining wall alongside a raised platform attached to the rear of the building (known as a "takeout platform") used for scallop vessels. One of the defendants' security cameras covered the area.

In that particular area, the takeout platform extended out toward the water, leaving only a narrow space along the pier. That space was estimated to be about a foot in width. An individual taking this path would, on reaching the platform, turn sideways, try to hold on to the wall of the takeout platform, and step or shimmy alongside it on the retaining wall of the pier until past the platform and near the boat's stern. This route was significantly shorter than the option of turning left and walking [—8—] around the building to reach the boat's stern. It was defendants' policy and practice to remove snow from the parking lot, but the snow and ice removal ended there. Snow and ice were not removed from the pier, most of the adjacent northern walkway, or the grounds around the building.

Although it is clear that it was more dangerous to cross the retaining wall than to walk around the building, a jury could assess the degree of risk involved in doing so, as part of its assessment of the foreseeability that a seaman would use the route. It could consider the testimony of Captain Martin, who found the increased danger of use of the retaining wall so self-evident that he did not even

consider walking along it. It could also consider the contrasting testimony of crew member Craig Lazaro, who testified that he twice crossed the retaining wall and "never even thought about" taking the alternate route around the building. In doing so, it could also consider the relative risks posed by ice and snow along the two routes.

B. *Crew Members' Past Patterns of Accessing the Property*

Cracchiolo died after he took the route through the gap in the southeastern corner of the fence when he found the western gate locked and he did not have a key. There are a great number of facts in dispute as to how often such situations, which caused crew members to use the gap to enter the property, arose. It is unclear what Eastern Fisheries' policy was with respect to who would lock [—9—] the gate and when, as well as whether different policies applied when crew members were sleeping aboard boats docked at the facility. The evidence shows that the gate was locked sporadically at best, and may even have been unlocked the vast majority of the time. It further shows that crew members lost or broke their keys with some frequency, as Eastern Fisheries had to provide about twenty-five replacement keys per year to crew members of boats using its facility. It is also disputed how many spare keys, if any, were kept aboard the *Sunlight*, and whether Cracchiolo personally had one. We think it foreseeable that some crew members would not have keys with them and would enter the property through the gap in the fence when the gate was locked.

More important is the connection between foreseeable use of the gap in the fence to enter the property and the foreseeability, under the conditions that night, that seamen would choose not to turn left and go around the building, but to try to access the boat by walking straight from the southeast corner to the asphalt and along the pier's retaining wall to get to the stern of the boat on the pier's north side despite the obvious hazards. The record contains evidence of at least five instances in which crew members chose to use the southeast gap in the fence to enter the property. Captain Martin did so once. Significantly, when he did, he elected to turn left, walk along the south side of the processing plant to the parking lot, and then take the customary [—10—] route around the north side of the plant to the boat's stern. On the other hand, the record shows that on two of the five occasions when crew members used the gap in the fence, they accessed the boat via the retaining wall. Besides the night of Cracchiolo's death, in early January 2011, Lazaro and Dale Moore, a crew member of the companion ship to the *Sunlight*, had used the southeast gap, continued straight, and walked directly along the pier's retaining wall past the takeout platform to board the boat. Finally, later that month, Lazaro and Cracchiolo used that same route along the retaining wall on the night Cracchiolo died. We think it fair to infer the security cameras probably captured the uses of the hazardous route before the night Cracchiolo died.

C. *Particulars Regarding Cracchiolo's Death*

The *Sunlight* docked at the New Bedford facility on January 26, 2011, after a fishing trip. A pipe on the boat had broken, and the crew decided to keep the boat docked at the plant for at least a few days while it was being repaired. Lazaro and Cracchiolo, the engineer, stayed on board to oversee the repairs. Defendants were aware that the boat would remain docked with crew members aboard during that period, and that the crew members would come and go from the property.

The defendants' property was covered in snow and ice on January 27, 2011. Photographs show that the parking lot had been plowed, and that the entire pier and the grassy areas were covered [—11—] in ice and snow. The retaining wall on the pier was likewise covered in ice and snow. In addition, there is some evidence that Eastern Fisheries workers also hosed down the takeout platform and parts of the pier that night, adding to the ice. The area between the processing plant and the fence along the entire southern side of the building was also covered in snow.

On the night of January 27, Cracchiolo and Lazaro left the facility together for dinner and drinks around 7:30 p.m. The main gate was open when they left but was locked when they separately returned, and neither brought with him a key to the gate. At some point in the night, the two men separated, and Lazaro took a cab back to the *Sunlight*. Lazaro wanted to return to the boat to get money to pay the cab driver. He found the gate locked and decided to walk in through the gap in the southeast corner of the fence. Once through the gap, Lazaro continued straight and walked along the waterfront retaining wall rather than turning left and walking around the fish processing building. The security footage shows Lazaro reaching the takeout platform, holding onto it, and side-stepping alongside it on the one-footwide retaining wall to get to the boat's stern. After getting past the takeout platform, Lazaro boarded the *Sunlight*, retrieved his money, walked back to the main gate along the northern route, and paid the cab driver through the fence. He returned to the boat [—12—] along the northern route he had just taken to the gate; that route was icy.

Some time later that night, Lazaro called Cracchiolo, who had not yet returned. He told Cracchiolo that the gate was locked. Cracchiolo asked how, then, to return to the boat. A jury could infer he did not have a key. Lazaro responded that Cracchiolo should come up into the property from the southeastern corner and he should continue walking along the retaining wall, the same way Lazaro had, to get to the boat. He also warned Cracchiolo that the path was icy. Cracchiolo told Lazaro that he was staying at a bar to watch the end of a basketball game and that Lazaro should not wait for him.

Cracchiolo eventually returned to the property just after midnight. The security footage shows that Cracchiolo entered from the southeastern side through the gap in the fence. Once inside, he continued straight ahead and began to walk along the pier to the retaining wall and takeout platform, as Lazaro had done. Security footage shows that as Cracchiolo was holding on to the takeout platform and trying to step sidewise along the retaining wall between the takeout platform and the *Sunlight*, he slipped and fell from the pier into the water. He drowned. Lazaro found Cracchiolo's body in the water the next morning and called the police. A later forensic examination measured Cracchiolo's blood alcohol level at 0.21 in one sample and 0.18 in another. [—13—]

III.

We review the district court's summary judgment decision de novo. *See Barclays Bank PLC v. Poynter*, 710 F.3d 16, 19 (1st Cir. 2013).

A. *Wrongful Death and Negligence*

The Massachusetts wrongful death statute imposes liability against a "person who . . . by his negligence causes the death of a person." Mass. Gen. Laws ch. 229, § 2. Plaintiff's negligence theory in this case is that Eastern Fisheries and RCP violated their duty to remedy the hazard of snow and ice on the pier, particularly on the retaining wall at the takeout platform, from which Cracchiolo fell.

"To prevail on a negligence claim, a plaintiff must prove that the defendant owed the plaintiff a duty of reasonable care, that the defendant breached this duty, that damage resulted, and that there was a causal relation between the breach of the duty and the damage." *Jupin v. Kask*, 849 N.E.2d 829, 834-35 (Mass. 2006). The questions of breach, damages, and causation are "the special province of the jury." *Id.* at 835. However, the question of whether the defendant owed a duty of care in the first instance is an issue of law, and may be settled on summary judgment if (on the undisputed facts) the risks posed by the defendant's actions were not "foreseeable." *Id.* Massachusetts courts may also make this determination after trial, in light of all of the evidence. *See* [—14—] *Dos Santos v. Coleta*, 987 N.E.2d 1187, 1198 (Mass. 2013) (finding evidence sufficient to allow jury to impose duty of care based "[o]n the[ ] facts" established at trial).

B. *Massachusetts Snow and Ice Cases*

The Massachusetts courts have established fairly clearly the obligations of landowners to remove snow and ice accumulations on their property. In *Soederberg v. Concord Greene Condominium Ass'n*, 921 N.E.2d 1020 (Mass. App. Ct. 2010), the Massachusetts Appeals Court concluded that landowners do have a duty to remove snow and ice accumulations even though those accumulations present open and obvious hazards to visitors. The court explained that the open and obvious nature of the hazard does not "negate[ ] an owner's duty to remedy the hazard." *Id.* at 1024. Rather, a landowner must remedy snow and ice hazards where he "can and should anticipate that the dangerous condition will cause physical harm to the invitee notwithstanding its known or obvious danger." *Id.* (quoting *Restatement (Second) of Torts* § 343A cmt. f) (internal quotation marks omitted). The court further explained that a plaintiff's unreasonable decision to encounter an ice hazard could bear on the issue of comparative negligence, *see id.* at 1025, but that this is a jury question and that the plaintiff's unreasonable behavior will not bar recovery as a matter of law even where other options that avoided the ice hazard were available, *see id.* at 1024. [—15—]

The SJC further developed the law in this field in *Papadopoulos v. Target Corp.*, 930 N.E.2d 142 (Mass. 2010). In *Papadopoulos*, a customer in the defendant's parking lot slipped and fell on a patch of ice that either fell from a snow pile or melted off the pile and refroze. The customer sued for negligence, and the trial court granted summary judgment in favor of defendants on the ground that the ice was a natural accumulation. *Id.* at 144. The SJC reversed and remanded. It held that the proper consideration was not whether the snow and ice accumulation was natural or unnatural, but rather whether the landowner had made the premises reasonably safe for lawful visitors. *See id.* at 150. In reaching that holding, the SJC emphasized the distinction between the duty to warn of dangers and the duty to remedy them. The duty to warn, the court reasoned, was typically obviated in snow and ice cases by the fact that the hazard was open and obvious, so a warning "would be superfluous." *Id.* at 151. It then explained, citing *Soederberg*, that the duty to remedy the danger remained when it was foreseeable that visitors would choose to encounter a hazard despite the open and obvious risks it posed. *Id.* The court reiterated:

> It is not reasonable for a property owner to leave snow or ice on a walkway where it is reasonable to expect that a hardy New England visitor would choose to risk crossing the snow or ice rather than turn back or attempt an equally or more perilous walk around it. [—16—]

Id. (citing *Soederberg*, 921 N.E.2d at 1025). The court concluded by holding that snow and ice accumulations trigger the same duty to remedy as other dangerous conditions—namely, the duty to "make reasonable efforts to protect lawful visitors against the danger." *Id.* at 154.

C. *Massachusetts Duty of Care Cases*

Dos Santos, though not a snow and ice case, provides further guidance for us here.[3] Like *Dos Santos*, this case alleges not a duty to warn,[4] but a duty to remedy a hazardous condition. *Dos Santos* involved a question not merely of foreseeability of a risk posed by a hazard, but the foreseeability of a risk posed by an open and obvious hazard. *Dos Santos* explained that a landowner "is not relieved from remedying an open and obvious danger where [the landowner] can and should anticipate that the dangerous condition will cause physical harm to the [lawful visitor] notwithstanding its known or obvious danger." 987 N.E.2d at 1192 (alterations in original) (quoting *Papadopoulos*, 930 N.E.2d

---

[3] *Dos Santos*, we should note, was decided after the parties in this case submitted their summary judgment papers. In fact, *Dos Santos* was decided after defendants had already been granted summary judgment and plaintiff had moved for reconsideration, but one week before the district court denied that motion.

[4] Landowners ordinarily have no duty to *warn* of hazards where the warning "would be superfluous for an ordinary intelligent" visitor. *Papadopoulos*, 930 N.E.2d at 151.

at 151) [—17—] (internal quotation marks omitted). In this, Massachusetts has adopted the Restatement (Second) of Torts § 343A, comment f.[5]

In *Dos Santos*, the court considered the scope of a landowner's duty to remedy under §343A of the Restatement. The *Dos Santos* court endorsed the conclusion that a landowner can and should anticipate a particular harm on a finding that a reasonable man in plaintiff's position would conclude the advantages of encountering the danger would outweigh the apparent risk. 987 [—18—] N.E.2d at 1193. But it went on to say that "application of § 343A is not limited to

---

[5] This comment in the Restatement provides:

> There are, however, cases in which the possessor of land can and should anticipate that the dangerous condition will cause physical harm to the invitee notwithstanding its known or obvious danger. In such cases the possessor is not relieved of the duty of reasonable care which he owes to the invitee for his protection. This duty may require him to warn the invitee, or to take other reasonable steps to protect him, against the known or obvious condition or activity, if the possessor has reason to expect that the invitee will nevertheless suffer physical harm.

> Such reason to expect harm to the visitor from known or obvious dangers may arise, for example, where the possessor has reason to expect that the invitee's attention may be distracted, so that he will not discover what is obvious, or will forget what he has discovered, or fail to protect himself against it. Such reason may also arise where the possessor has reason to expect that the invitee will proceed to encounter the known or obvious danger because to a reasonable man in his position the advantages of doing so would outweigh the apparent risk. In such cases the fact that the danger is known, or is obvious, is important in determining whether the invitee is to be charged with contributory negligence, or assumption of risk. (*See* §§ 466 and 496D.) It is not, however, conclusive in determining the duty of the possessor, or whether he has acted reasonably under the circumstances.

Restatement (Second) of Torts § 343A cmt. f.

situations where the plaintiff encounters the danger only after concluding the benefit of doing so outweighs the risk." *Id.*

The court recognized that § 343A contemplates that a lawful entrant's encounter with an open or obvious hazard may in some instances be a result of the entrant's own negligence. But even if the plaintiff was negligent, "[a] plaintiff's own negligence in encountering the danger does not relieve the landowner of a duty to remedy that danger where the plaintiff's negligent act can and should be anticipated by the landowner." *Id.* at 1195. While Massachusetts recognizes comparative negligence, that does not necessarily negate a defendant's duty of care. *See, e.g.*, *Soederberg*, 921 N.E.2d at 1025.

Dos Santos held it was error for the trial court to instruct the jury that there was no duty of care merely because the risk of injury was obvious to visitors. It explained that the defendant had set up a trampoline next to a shallow inflatable pool with the specific intent to enable the use that resulted in the injury, *and* the defendant knew both that the trampoline and pool were in fact being used in this manner and that the use was dangerous. *Dos Santos*, 987 N.E.2d at 1189-90. The SJC remanded the case with directions to the trial judge to instruct the jury that "a landowner is not 'relieved from remedying open and obvious [—19—] dangers where he [or she] can or should anticipate that the dangerous condition will cause physical harm to the [lawful entrant] notwithstanding its known or obvious danger.'" *Id.* at 1198 (alterations in original) (quoting *Soederberg*, 921 N.E.2d at 1024).

We agree with defendants that unlike *Dos Santos*, this is not a case in which the landowner expressly created a hazard in the form of the narrowing of the space caused by the takeout platform to induce activity which foreseeably would cause injury. It is clear that the defendants did not intend this route to be a pathway and in fact had an established pathway to the pier and the boat along the northern side of the property. This is an important distinction. But we do not think

this distinction entitles defendants to summary judgment for at least three reasons.

First, even though the property owner in *Dos Santos* expressly created the hazard (hoping to benefit from it) and obviously knew of the hazard, the SJC did not itself declare there was a duty of care in that case but remanded for a new jury trial, considering the issues to be ones for a jury to resolve under particular instructions. Thus, the intentional placement of the trampoline in *Dos Santos* was not dispositive.

Second, defendants would be wrong to distinguish *Dos Santos*'s emphasis on the defendant's own conduct as eliminating the foreseeability analysis aspect of duty of care cases. The *Dos* [—20—] *Santos* court did not treat the landowner's specific intent that visitors would use the trampoline as a separate element of its holding. *Dos Santos* continued to focus on foreseeability and not on intent as the ultimate issue. That is particularly so given *Dos Santos*'s reliance on § 343A of the Restatement, which does not discuss intent at all and focuses solely on whether the landowner "should anticipate the harm" despite its obviousness. *Restatement (Second) of Torts* § 343A; *see also id.* cmt. f (explaining that landowner "is not relieved of the duty of reasonable care" when he "can and should anticipate that the dangerous condition will cause physical harm" despite its obviousness). *Dos Santos* used the intent of the landowner as a means to show that the landowner there "would surely have reason to anticipate that persons would use" the hazardous condition "despite the danger." 987 N.E.2d at 1197.

Third, such a reading would be inconsistent with prior Massachusetts case law, cited in *Dos Santos*. We draw guidance from *Jupin*, 849 N.E.2d at 829, and from *Quinn v. Morganelli*, 895 N.E.2d 507 (Mass. App. Ct. 2008), *cited by Dos Santos*, 987 N.E.2d at 1192-93, 1195, 1196. In *Jupin*, the court reversed the entry of summary judgment for the defendant, rejecting the holding that the defendant did not have a duty of care. There, the property owner was held to owe a duty of care to a police officer shot with a gun taken from the owner's property when she had not ensured proper storage of the gun despite knowing that an individual with a [—21—] history of violence and mental instability had a key to her house. 849 N.E.2d at 837-38. The court stressed foreseeability, *id.* at 836, and that there was no public policy reason not to impose a duty of care.

In *Quinn*, the plaintiff sued defendant landowners after falling from a hallway into a sunken living room. The hallway and the living room were covered in the same color tile, which plaintiff alleged created a hazard that the landowners had a duty to warn of or to remedy. The Massachusetts Appeals Court reversed the trial court's grant of summary judgment to the defendants. *Quinn*, 895 N.E.2d at 511. It explained that a jury would be able to conclude that the step created a foreseeable hazard, even though the record contained evidence of only one other person having ever fallen on it in the roughly twenty years since it was constructed. *Id.* at 508-09. The court went on to note that the jury could find the hazard open and obvious, that the record was "insufficiently developed" on that issue, and that the proper solution was to reverse the entry of summary judgment and remand for further proceedings, which could include a special verdict or interrogatories submitted to the jury. *Id.* at 511. Further, in *Soederberg*, the court explained that "whether a plaintiff's own conduct in encountering an ice hazard should bar recovery [is] generally a question for the jury to decide." 921 N.E.2d at 1024. [—22—]

IV.

With these principles in mind, although the question is close, we conclude that this case is not suitable for resolution on summary judgment. The record contains too many disputes of fact and too many disputed inferences, as in *Quinn*. The record does not establish that the defendants did not have any reason to anticipate crew members would attempt to cross the icy pier in this manner as the shortest way to get back to the boat. A factfinder could infer that the landowners here knew the gap in the fence existed and knew the gap was used: it was obvious to

observers. It was also foreseeable that the front gate would sometimes be locked and prevent crew members without keys from entering that way. Indeed, Eastern Fisheries had to provide some twenty-five replacement keys per year to crew members who needed a key to enter the property by means other than the gap.

The most difficult issue is whether the defendants knew or should have known that crew members would use the more hazardous route, particularly in these conditions—that is, whether it was insufficiently foreseeable such that we may say as a matter of law there was no duty of care.

Defendants argue that the record contains evidence of only two prior uses before the night in question, and that this is insufficient as a matter of law to put them on notice that crew members might use it to cross the pier. We disagree with [—23—] defendants for three reasons. The first is that as a matter of law in Massachusetts, notice of even a single instance years before was relevant to defeat summary judgment in the *Quinn* case. *See Quinn*, 895 N.E.2d at 511. The record here on prior use goes farther than that in *Quinn*. For example, the two prior uses of the route across the pier involved crew members of two different vessels, who may have told others. The prior uses were also during the winter, and they were recent, occurring roughly one month before the night of Cracchiolo's death. Additionally, a factfinder could infer that the two instances in the record were only a partial sampling. Lazaro alone had entered through the gap twice in two winter seasons at the facility, and other crew members on both the *Sunlight* and the dozen or more other vessels that used the facility might have done the same. A factfinder could also consider that the individuals entering through the gap were crew members on commercial fishing vessels, who would have had experience and confidence walking along slippery, waterside conditions, as that was inherent in their jobs.

Second, while actual knowledge of a particular prior use is surely sufficient to prove that a landowner had "reason to anticipate" that use, *Dos Santos*, 987 N.E.2d at 1197, actual knowledge is not necessary; liability exists if the defendant should have known about the use. *See, e.g., Papadopoulos*, 930 N.E.2d at 154 (imposing duty to remedy "[i]f a property owner knows [—24—] or reasonably should know of a dangerous condition"). A factfinder could infer that the landowners knew or should have known the gap in the fence existed and was used, and that no obstacle except self-restraint prevented crew members from taking the risky route to the boat that Cracchiolo took. A factfinder might also conclude that the defendants were not negligent in relying on crew members to exercise such self-restraint.

Third, the disputes as to inferences and insufficient development of the record counsel against resolution of the duty of care issue on summary judgment. *See Quinn*, 895 N.E.2d at 511; *see also Am. Steel Erectors, Inc. v. Local Union No. 7, Int'l Ass'n of Bridge, Structural, Ornamental & Reinforcing Iron Workers*, 536 F.3d 68, 80-81 (1st Cir. 2008); *Merino Calenti v. Boto*, 24 F.3d 335, 340 (1st Cir. 1994) (reversing summary judgment where record was inadequate to allow determination of issues). In light of *Dos Santos, Jupin,* and *Quinn* and the many disputes of fact and of inferences to be drawn, and acknowledging the difficulty of the issues, we think the landowners are not entitled to summary judgment, as a matter of law, on this record.

On remand, the district court has discretion to submit the issue of foreseeability to the factfinder by using a special verdict, *cf. Quinn*, 895 N.E.2d at 511, or to allow further development of the record. [—25—]

V.

For the reasons stated above, we *reverse* and *remand*. No costs are awarded.

United States Court of Appeals
for the First Circuit

No. 13-2000

ARDENTE

vs.

STANDARD FIRE INS. CO.

Appeal from the United States District Court for the District of Rhode Island

Decided: March 12, 2014

Citation: 744 F.3d 815, 2 Adm. R. 11 (1st Cir. 2014).

Before **TORRUELLA,** Circuit Judge, **SOUTER,** * Associate Justice, and **SELYA,** Circuit Judge.

 * Hon. David H. Souter, Associate Justice (Ret.) of the Supreme Court of the United States, sitting by designation.

[—2—] **TORRUELLA,** Circuit Judge:

Standard Fire Insurance Company appeals from a district court order awarding Evan Ardente summary judgment on his claim for breach of a yacht insurance policy. Because the policy does not cover the type of damage sustained by Ardente's yacht, we reverse.

I. *Background*

Standard Fire insured Ardente's yacht. At some point after purchasing the boat, Ardente noticed that its top speed had decreased and that it was not navigating properly. The parties agree that these were symptoms of water damage to the yacht's hull. They also agree about how water was getting into the hull. A ship's hull has holes for the installation of fixtures, such as port lights. Normally, the material surrounding these so-called "installation holes" is solid laminate, which is waterproof. But in Ardente's yacht, the installation holes are surrounded by balsa wood, which is not waterproof. Water seeping into the balsa wood around the installation holes then spread throughout the hull.

Ardente presented a claim to Standard Fire, which denied coverage on the ground that the claim fell within an exclusion for manufacturing defects. Ardente sued in state court, alleging, among other claims, breach of contract, whereafter Standard Fire removed the case to federal court. The parties then filed cross motions for summary judgment. [—3—]

The district court granted summary judgment in favor of Standard Fire on all of Ardente's claims except for the breach of contract allegation. *Ardente v. Standard Fire Ins. Co.*, 906 F. Supp. 2d 22 (D.R.I. 2012). On that claim, the district court granted Ardente summary judgment with respect to liability, interpreting the policy in such a way that the damage fell within an exception to the exclusion for manufacturing defects. The issue of damages was reserved for trial, but the parties reached a stipulation with respect to damages, and the district court entered judgment. Standard Fire appealed.

II. *Discussion*

We review de novo both the district court's grant of summary judgment and its interpretation of the insurance policy. *Penn-Am. Ins. Co. v. Lavigne*, 617 F.3d 82, 84 (1st Cir. 2010). Summary judgment is appropriate when the record, viewed in the light most favorable to the nonmovant, reveals no genuine issue of material fact and that the movant is entitled to judgment as a matter of law. *See id*. This case presents no factual issues and asks only whether Ardente's loss is covered by the policy, a legal question properly resolved by summary judgment. *See Littlefield v. Acadia Ins. Co.*, 392 F.3d 1, 6 (1st Cir. 2004).

The parties agree that Rhode Island law governs the interpretation of the policy. Under Rhode Island law, if the terms of an insurance policy are unambiguous, there is no further need [—4—] for judicial construction. *Amica Mut. Ins. Co. v. Streicker*, 583 A.2d 550, 551 (R.I. 1990). To determine whether ambiguity exists, the policy must be viewed in its entirety and the language must be given its plain, everyday meaning. *Id.* at 552. Where a policy is ambiguous, it will be construed against the insurer. *Id.* But "[a] policy is not to be described as ambiguous because a word is viewed in isolation or a phrase is taken out of context. A court should not, through an effort to seek out ambiguity when there is no ambiguity, make an insurer assume a liability not imposed by the policy." *McGowan v. Conn. Gen. Life Ins. Co.*, 289 A.2d 428, 429 (R.I. 1972).

Ardente's Standard Fire policy explicitly disclaims coverage for "loss or damage caused by or resulting from . . . [d]efects in manufacture, including defects in construction, workmanship and design *other than* latent defects as defined in the policy" (emphasis added). This provision is referred to as the "manufacture-defect exclusion," and the emphasized exception to that exclusion is referred to as the "latent-defect exception." The parties agree that use of balsa wood instead of solid laminate constitutes a manufacturing defect, but they disagree over whether the defect falls within the latent-defect exception.

The policy defines "latent defect" as "a hidden flaw inherent in the material existing at the time of the original building of the yacht, which is not discoverable by ordinary [—5—] observation or methods of testing." The parties agree that the use of balsa wood was a flaw that existed at the time of the original building of the yacht and that it was not discoverable by ordinary observation or methods of testing. The only dispute is whether the balsa wood constitutes "a hidden flaw inherent in the material." Standard Fire claims that the material, in this case the balsa wood, was not flawed in any way; that it was perfectly good balsa wood, and that it did what balsa wood does -- absorb water. Unsurprisingly, Ardente takes the opposite tack and argues that while the balsa wood itself was not flawed, the *use* of balsa wood, instead of solid laminate, was certainly a flaw.[1]

The district court sided with Ardente. It first determined that the phrase, "flaw inherent in the material" – part of the

---

[1] The opinion responds to the case as presented by the arguments to us. It should not be read as holding that no reading of the latent defect exception other than the one applied here is possible in the context of this policy.

definition of "latent defect" -- contained a contradiction. According to the district court:

> The word "inherent" requires that a latent defect be characteristic of or intrinsic to the material. The word "flaw" imposes the exact opposite requirement. It includes problems with a specific piece of material, but not problems characteristic of the material itself. In short, giving the terms their plain and reasonable meaning, there can be no such thing as an inherent flaw.

Ardente, 906 F. Supp. 2d at 27. Because ambiguity in an insurance policy is interpreted against the insurer, the district court refused to let this apparent contradiction render the entire latent-defect exception meaningless. Instead, to reflect the [—6—] reasonable expectations of the insured, the district court interpreted "latent defect" to include the flawed *use* of unflawed material. Said the district court, "The use of balsa wood in these areas was a flaw in the construction of the Yacht, even if it was not a flaw in the underlying material itself." *Id.* at 28.

We fear that the district court committed the error against which *McGowan* warns: deeming a policy ambiguous, and thus making an insurer liable, by taking a term out of context and viewing it in insolation. *See* 289 A.2d at 429. The policy's definition of "latent defect" -- "a hidden flaw inherent in the material existing at the time of the original building of the yacht, which is not discoverable by ordinary observation or methods of testing" -- while not a model of precision, is not self-contradictory. Viewing the definition in its entirety and giving the language its plain, everyday meaning, *see Streicker*, 583 A.2d at 552, the gist is clear. The phrase refers to flaws in the material used to build the boat that were not noticeable. A quintessential example, we imagine, is a piece of wood with a hairline fracture or with an undetectable termite infestation.

If anything, the definition could be criticized not as self-contradictory but as redundant. It mentions flaws that are "hidden" but goes on to add that they must be "not discoverable by ordinary observation or methods of testing," which is another way of saying "hidden." Indeed, the word "inherent" is yet a third [—7—] means of emphasizing this same quality: In this context, inherent means "within" and conveys that the flaw must impugn the material in a way that evaded observation at the time it was handled. While "inherent" may not have been the best choice of words, and reiterated an already redundant aspect of the definition, the district court failed to give that term its everyday meaning by reading it to require that the flaw inhere in every piece of the type of material under consideration.

We acknowledge that redundancy may itself be a form of ambiguity; indeed, one canon of interpretation urges courts to give each word meaning, thereby avoiding surplusage. *See Andrukiewicz v. Andrukiewicz*, 860 A.2d 235, 239 (R.I. 2004). But we offer two responses. First, we note a general point -- colorfully made by the Sixth Circuit -- about redundancy in insurance policies:

> [The] label ["redundancy"] surely is not a fatal one when it comes to insurance contracts . . . where redundancies abound. In just this one provision of the 80-page insurance contract, there are at least three truly redundant phrases . . . : (1) "loss or damage"; (2) "caused by or resulting from"; and (3) "faulty, inadequate or defective." As in so many insurance contracts, iteration is afoot throughout--from an exclusion for "war and military action" to one for "fraudulent, dishonest or criminal acts or omissions" to one for flooding of "lakes, reservoirs, ponds, brooks, rivers, streams, harbors, oceans or any other body of water or watercourse" to numerous others.

> . . . .

All of this helps to reveal the limits of the interpretive canon . . . that courts [—8—] must avoid interpreting contracts to contain superfluous words.

The canon is one among many tools for dealing with ambiguity, not a tool for creating ambiguity in the first place. Where there are two ways to read the text--and the one that avoids surplusage makes the text ambiguous--applying the rule against surplusage is, absent other indications, inappropriate.

TMW Enterprises, Inc. v. Fed. Ins. Co., 619 F.3d 574, 577-78 (6th Cir. 2010) (Sutton, J.) (citations and internal quotation marks omitted).

Second, accepting that "inherent" in the policy's definition is redundant, we fail to see how this redundancy invites the reading adopted by the district court and urged by Ardente. Granting that ambiguity should be interpreted against the insurer and in light of the reasonable expectations of the insured, if ambiguity lives in the phrase "inherent flaw," *that phrase*, and not another, should be so construed. That remedy might, for example, entail striking the word "inherent" so that the definition would read, "a hidden flaw ~~inherent~~ in the material existing at the time of the original building of the yacht, which is not discoverable by ordinary observation or methods of testing." But instead of doing that, the district court changed the word "material" to "yacht," such that "latent defect" referred to a "hidden flaw in the yacht." This might have been proper had ambiguity marred the word "material," but the district court found ambiguity not in that term but in the term "inherent flaw." [—9—]

For his part, Ardente does argue that the term "material" is ambiguous. He urges us to interpret "material" to mean not the balsa wood, but something like, "all of the stuff that is near the installation holes." Part of that "stuff" is the balsa wood, and it is that fact -- the fact that balsa wood makes up some of the "stuff" surrounding the installation holes -- that, according to Ardente, constitutes the flaw.

Ardente's interpretation would create surplusage, and not that of the relatively benign variety that comes with describing a flaw as both "hidden" and "inherent." His interpretation of the word "material" would allow the latent-defect exception to swallow the manufacture-defect exclusion, rendering the exclusion superfluous and doing violence to the policy. The policy expressly excludes from coverage damage caused by "[d]efects in manufacture, including defects in construction, workmanship, and design other than latent defects." To say that "material" in the definition of "latent defect" refers not to an individual raw ingredient used in constructing the yacht, but rather to a composite of various raw ingredients that appear in close proximity in a particular area of the ship, yields the following result: If a carpenter building the yacht accidentally affixes balsa wood instead of solid laminate around the installation holes, we could refer to the defect as a "latent defect" instead of a "defect in construction or workmanship." Similarly, if an engineer drawing the blueprints of [—10—] the yacht accidentally calls for balsa wood instead of solid laminate to be placed around the installation holes, we could refer to that defect as a "latent defect" instead of a "defect in design." But it is clear that the policy meant to exclude from coverage precisely those types of defects.

As a last ditch effort to support affirmance, Ardente makes two arguments based on sources that are irrelevant here. First, Ardente argues that the policy's definition of "latent defect" guts the term of a broader meaning that it allegedly enjoys under Rhode Island common law. Citing one Rhode Island case and Black's Law Dictionary, Ardente contends that, at common law, "latent defect" would mean a hidden flaw in the yacht, as opposed to a hidden flaw in the balsa wood. But in the case cited, the policy did not define "latent defect," *see Neri v. Nationwide Mut. Fire Ins. Co.*, 719 A.2d 1150, 1153-54 (R.I. 1998), and whatever interpretation courts might adopt in the absence of an explicit policy definition has no bearing on this case, where Ardente's policy defines the term.

Second, Ardente accuses Standard Fire of defining "latent defect" to include flaws that some other insurance policies capture with a separate "faulty materials" exception. Ardente cites *TRAVCO Insurance Co. v. Ward*, 715 F.

Supp. 2d 699, 710 (E.D. Va. 2010), *aff'd*, 504 F. App'x 251 (4th Cir. 2013), where, because the policy explicitly excluded loss caused by both "latent defects" and [—11—] "faulty materials," the court avoided surplusage by interpreting the undefined term "latent defect" not to include faulty materials. *Id.* But Standard Fire was free to define "latent defect" to include faulty materials and, given that its policy contains no separate exclusion for "faulty materials," that seems to be precisely what Standard Fire did.

Because the damage to Ardente's yacht does not fall within the latent-defect exception to the manufacture-defect exclusion, Standard Fire -- not Ardente -- was entitled to summary judgment on the breach of contract claim. We need not reach Standard Fire's alternative arguments supporting reversal.

III. *Conclusion*

For the foregoing reasons, the district court's order granting Ardente summary judgment on his breach of contract claim is **REVERSED**, the judgment in favor of Ardente is **VACATED**, and the district court is directed to grant Standard Fire's cross motion for summary judgment and to enter judgment in Standard Fire's favor. No costs are awarded.

United States Court of Appeals
for the First Circuit

No. 13-1947

YACUBIAN
vs.
UNITED STATES

Appeal from the United States District Court for the
District of Massachusetts

Decided: April 30, 2014

Citation: 750 F.3d 100, 2 Adm. 15 (1st Cir. 2014).

Before **LYNCH**, Chief Judge, **SOUTER,*** Associate
Justice, and **LIPEZ**, Circuit Judge.

* Hon. David H. Souter, Associate Justice (Ret.) of the
Supreme Court of the United States, sitting by
designation.

[—2—] **LYNCH**, Chief Judge:

Lawrence M. Yacubian, a former scallop fisherman, filed suit in July 2012 alleging his prior prosecution by the National Oceanic and Atmospheric Administration ("NOAA") constituted malicious prosecution and abuse of process under the Federal Tort Claims Act ("FTCA"), 28 U.S.C. §§ 1346(b), 2671-2680. He did so after official reports stated that there had been abuses by NOAA.

The 2012 suit arises out of Yacubian's prosecution in 2000 by the enforcement arm of NOAA. The Administrative Law Judge ("ALJ") sustained all charges against Yacubian. On judicial review of the ALJ's decision in 2004, the district court sustained findings of liability on two charges of fishing in a prohibited area, vacated a false statement charge against him, and remanded for adjustment of penalties. *Lobsters, Inc. v. Evans*, 346 F. Supp. 2d 340 (D. Mass. 2004). On remand, Yacubian reached a settlement with the government.

The district court, in this later FTCA case, dismissed both of Yacubian's claims on two independent grounds, *see Yacubian v. United States*, 952 F. Supp. 2d 334 (D. Mass. 2013), and Yacubian now appeals.

The waiver of immunity under the FTCA for the causes of action Yacubian has chosen to pursue is itself limited in scope. As a matter of federal statute and case law, there can be no FTCA recovery for the actions of the prosecutors who bring such [—3—] enforcement actions but only for the actions of investigative or law enforcement officers who have committed the wrongful acts specified. *See* 28 U.S.C. § 2680(h); *cf. Limone v. United States*, 579 F.3d 79, 88 (1st Cir. 2009).

We agree with the district court that Yacubian has failed to state a claim that any law enforcement officer in any way wrongfully induced a malicious prosecution or acted to abuse process. We affirm the district court on those limited grounds. We need not get into thorny limitations period and accrual issues regarding the timing of Yacubian's claims.

I.

On an appeal from a grant of a motion to dismiss, we recite the facts as alleged in Yacubian's complaint, *Ocasio-Hernández v. Fortuño-Burset*, 640 F.3d 1, 4 (1st Cir. 2011), and as not contradicted by the official documents attached to his complaint, *Young v. Wells Fargo Bank, N.A.*, 717 F.3d 224, 229 n.1 (1st Cir. 2013). Yacubian appended to his complaint other documents, including the Offense Investigation Report from when NOAA officials first boarded his vessel and the 2011 Special Master Report concerning NOAA enforcement actions. He also references the record in the prior proceedings in this case. We consider all of these documents as well. *See Trans-Spec Truck Serv., Inc. v. Caterpillar, Inc.*, 524 F.3d 315, 321 (1st Cir. 2008) ("Exhibits attached to the complaint are properly considered part of the [—4—] pleading 'for all purposes,' including Rule 12(b)(6)." (quoting Fed. R. Civ. P. 10(c))).

A. *Background and Initial NOAA Proceedings*

Lawrence M. Yacubian took his fishing vessel *F/V Independence* on a scalloping trip on December 4, 1998. Coast Guard Officers Timothy Brown and Chris Mooradian, aboard the *USCGC Wrangell* at the time, observed via radar that the *Independence* had entered a

"Closed Area" where fishing was prohibited. After concluding, based on its "courses and speeds," as tracked on Boatracs, a satellite-based monitoring system, that the *Independence* appeared to be "engaged in fishing inside the closed area," Officer Brown led a boarding of the vessel.

During the boarding, Officer Brown informed Yacubian that the team was "onboard to ensure that he and the vessel were in compliance with all applicable federal laws and regulations." Brown did not tell Yacubian at the time that the *Independence* had been plotted inside of the Closed Area.

Officer Brown spoke with Yacubian about his navigational practices and his vessel's equipment, which included a Boatracs unit, as required by applicable fisheries regulations. *Lobsters, Inc.*, 346 F. Supp. 2d at 341-42. Officer Brown asked Yacubian if he had been having trouble with the Boatracs equipment on board, and Yacubian responded that he was not aware of any problems. The two "visually confirmed" that the status of the Boatracs system was [—5—] "good." Officer Brown's report of the boarding noted that Yacubian and his crew were "as cooperative as could be expected" throughout.

Officer Brown also asked Yacubian how many scallops he had on board, both on deck and in the ship's hold. After making clear that he had no way of knowing the exact amount, Yacubian provided an estimate. Officer Brown also made an estimate, and it was higher than Yacubian's. Officer Brown's write-up of the boarding noted the discrepancies between his estimate and Yacubian's but did not indicate that he suspected Yacubian of intentionally making a false statement as to these estimates.

On June 14, 2000, NOAA Enforcement Attorney (EA) Charles Juliand issued Yacubian a Notice of Violation and Assessment (NOVA) and a Notice of Permit Sanctions (NOPS). The NOVA included two counts for fishing in a restricted area (the "prohibited fishing" counts) and one count of making a false statement to an officer about the estimated number of scallops on board.

The NOPS, which was issued with the NOVA, revoked Yacubian's vessel and operating permits but did not take effect until all agency action on the matter became final. *See* 15 C.F.R. § 904.273(c) ("If a party files a timely petition for discretionary [agency] review, . . . the effectiveness of the initial decision is stayed . . . until the initial decision becomes final . . . ."). Yacubian has pled in his complaint that negotiation of a settlement is typical in this type of case, but that in this instance, "EA Juliand was [—6—] uncharacteristically unwilling to negotiate a settlement." Yacubian admittedly had prior violations on his record.

Yacubian had an evidentiary hearing before an ALJ, Edwin M. Bladen, on the NOVA/NOPS from about June 19 through June 22, 2001. The government was represented by EA Juliand and EA Mitch MacDonald.

The government introduced data from the Boatracs system to support the two prohibited fishing charges. Indeed, Yacubian's case was the first one in which Boatracs data was used as the entire basis for such a charge. His defense was to challenge the reliability of the Boatracs system. To this end, Yacubian's attorney contacted a Massachusetts Environmental Police (MEP) officer, Lieutenant Peter Hanlon, to obtain evidence as to the inaccuracy of Boatracs, and then to testify voluntarily on Yacubian's behalf.

At some point well before the ALJ hearing, Lt. Hanlon was informed that his superiors were displeased with his decision to testify for Yacubian's defense. The complaint alleges his superiors applied pressure to Lt. Hanlon not to testify. This caused him to ask to be excused from testifying. He did not orally testify.

Special Agent in Charge at NOAA (SAC) Andy Cohen was one of several enforcement officers who was "involved in the [—7—] investigation and prosecution" of Yacubian.[1]

---

[1] In addition to Enforcement Attorneys Juliand and MacDonald, Officers Brown and Mooradian, and Special Agent in Charge Cohen, Yacubian states that Special Agent Louis Jachimcyzk of

The complaint alleges that it was SAC Cohen whose actions caused Lt. Hanlon's superiors to put pressure on Lt. Hanlon to ask to be excused from testifying. Specifically, Yacubian alleges, again on information and belief, that SAC Cohen called Lt. Hanlon's superiors at the MEP to express displeasure at Lt. Hanlon's initial decision to testify on Yacubian's behalf.[2]

We describe below the Special Master's report, appended to the Complaint, as to the incident with SAC Cohen. According to that report, Lt. Hanlon did provide a written report to Yacubian's counsel in support of Yacubian's position, and that report was [—8—] submitted by the defense as part of the official record before the ALJ. Yacubian maintains that he was harmed because the ALJ never heard Lt. Hanlon's oral testimony.

On December 5, 2001, ALJ Bladen issued an Initial Decision that sustained the NOVA/NOPS on both counts and imposed

---

NOAA Fisheries Office for Law Enforcement was also "involved in the investigation and prosecution." Special Agent Jachimcyzk is only mentioned again in the complaint to note his comments in a NOAA press release about Yacubian's case: he said that satellite-based Boatracs information "had never been used, on its own, to prove a closed-area case." Yacubian makes no allegations that SA Jachimcyzk engaged in wrongdoing, or that Mooradian or Brown did.

[2] Yacubian supports this allegation with a reference to the hearing testimony. At the June 19 ALJ hearing, Yacubian's counsel stated:

> I was advised by Lieutenant Hanlon that he had been -- how shall I say this? I want to be very cautious of the way that I say this. His commander, Captain O'Donnell, called him and advised him that she had received phone calls from [National Marine Fisheries Service] enforcement and that it was pursuant to his employment he now -- now a subpoena was necessary.

> Up until that point, I had no idea -- I was understanding that he was going to come voluntarily. He then advised me that he had been called, that he was instructed that a subpoena had to issue.

fines and sanctions as proposed by NOAA. The fines totaled $250,000, including a $110,000 civil penalty for each of the two prohibited fishing counts and a $30,000 civil penalty for the false statement charge. Yacubian sought discretionary review within NOAA, which was denied on July 2, 2003. According to Yacubian, this denial constituted a final agency action and triggered the revocation of Yacubian's permits at that time. *Lobsters, Inc.*, 346 F. Supp. 2d at 342-43; *see* 15 C.F.R. § 904.273(c).

B. *2003 Appeal to the District Court and Post-Remand ALJ Proceeding*

On August 1, 2003, Yacubian filed suit in federal district court under the Administrative Procedure Act, 5 U.S.C. § 702, challenging the ALJ's decision on the NOVA/NOPS. He did not ask to stay the revocation of his permit pending judicial review. While that case was pending, Yacubian tried to sell the *Independence* to finance his ongoing legal expenses; however, the complaint in this case alleges that on three separate occasions, EA [—9—] Juliand blocked the sale of the vessel by refusing to agree to allow Yacubian to sell his vessel permit along with the boat.[3]

The parties filed cross-motions for summary judgment in the district court based on the administrative record. On November 29, 2004, the district court (Gorton, J.) (1) sustained the finding of liability as to the two prohibited fishing counts; (2) vacated the finding of liability as to the false statement (about scallops caught) charge,[4] ruling that as a matter of law no false statement could be

---

[3] EA Juliand later explained to the Special Master investigating this series of events that he blocked the sales attempts because one of the proposed buyers of the vessel was a former employee of Yacubian's, and because EA Juliand feared that Yacubian would simply become a silent partner in the ongoing fishing venture. He also stated that he denied these sales offers because he believed that Yacubian did not have a "rightful claim" to sell the *Independence* along with its permits. When Yacubian eventually entered a settlement agreement with NOAA, EA Juliand allowed the sale of the boat to a buyer whom he had blocked from purchasing the boat earlier.

[4] The false statement charge was not based on statements about the two prohibited fishing counts.

based on the expression of Yacubian's estimation of how many scallops were on board; (3) vacated the civil penalties and permit sanctions assessed against Yacubian because the penalties were calculated incorrectly and were too high in light of the court's rulings;[5] and (4) remanded the case to NOAA "for *de novo* [—10—] reconsideration of *civil penalties and permit sanctions.*" *Lobsters, Inc.*, 346 F. Supp. 2d at 349 (emphasis added). The court further ordered that "NOAA is directed to assess an appropriate penalty . . . based on [the] violations of Count I and II and, when considering [Yacubian's] history of prior offenses, should recognize only two prior offenses . . . or, in the alternative, should explain its departure from the Agency's five year 'look back' policy." *Id.*

On remand, on or around May 5, 2005, the agency filed a motion for an expedited hearing to reconsider the penalties and permit sanctions.[6] Yacubian opposed the motion, arguing that Judge Gorton's order mandated an entirely new agency proceeding. On June 15, 2005, a new ALJ granted NOAA's motion for an expedited hearing, reasoning that "the original NOVA and NOPS dated June 14, 2000 satisfied the due process requirements embodied in the [Administrative Procedure Act]. On remand, the original NOVA and NOPS still govern unless agency counsel seeks an amendment." The new ALJ made clear

that only the penalties as to the prohibited [—11—] fishing counts were at issue because the false statement charge had been vacated entirely.[7]

Around June 24, 2005, before any further proceedings, Yacubian signed a settlement agreement with NOAA. Under the agreement, which Yacubian asserts was coercive and excessive, he agreed to (1) pay a $430,000 civil penalty; (2) forfeit $25,972 in profits from fish seized from the *Independence* in December 1998; and (3) permanently forfeit his commercial fishing permits and privileges. The agreement also made explicit that the transfer to Amber Nicole, Inc. was contingent upon Yacubian signing the settlement agreement. The civil penalties imposed by the settlement were substantially higher than the initial $250,000 fine imposed by the NOVA. Yacubian maintains that EA Juliand's continued efforts to block his sale of the *Independence* ultimately coerced him into assenting to this settlement.

C. *The 2010 OIG Reports, 2011 Special Master Report, and 2013 Secretary's Memorandum*

In 2010, the Office of the Inspector General (OIG) completed an investigation of alleged improprieties in NOAA's fisheries enforcement programs and issued several reports on its findings. The OIG audited NOAA's Asset Forfeiture Fund (AFF), the fund into which Yacubian's fines were paid. The OIG's audit [—12—] report, released on July 1, 2010, found mismanagement in the expenditure and use of AFF funds. OIG concluded that the AFF was improperly used to finance the purchase of various luxury vessels and trips around the world that were generally unrelated to NOAA enforcement proceedings.

The OIG final report, issued on September 23, 2010, found that NOAA assessed excessive fines in order to force settlements in several cases. Yacubian's case and the matter of Lt. Hanlon being pressured not to testify were

---

[5] Adjustments were required because the false statement count was reversed and because the court excluded certain past violations from Yacubian's violation history in light of the agency's five-year look back policy and ruled that the agency abused its discretion in failing to provide any reasoned explanation for its departure from its established policy. *Lobsters, Inc.*, 346 F. [—10—] Supp. 2d at 347-48.

[6] Before the motion for an expedited hearing was filed with the agency, Yacubian filed a Motion for Order in Aid of Enforcement of the Judgment in the district court, and the government opposed it. The focus of these opposing motions was the dispute over whether the agency was required to reinstate Yacubian's fishing permits while his case was pending before the agency on remand. The underlying liability for the prohibited fishing charges was not contested, nor was the fact that the false statement charge had been vacated entirely.

[7] Yacubian pled that the ALJ "reinstated the false statement charge vacated by Judge Gorton." The ALJ's opinion belies this assertion and we do not credit it.

two of many that were identified for further review by a Special Master.

The Special Master issued his report in April 2011. Yacubian appended a portion of the report to his complaint in this case. In the report on Lt. Hanlon's case, the Special Master found that SAC Cohen had talked to Lt. Hanlon's superiors, and after the superiors learned Lt. Hanlon had been subpoenaed to testify, they told him that he could not go to court while he was on state duty, nor could he use his cruiser to get there.[8] The report found that Lt. Hanlon asked Yacubian's counsel to excuse him from appearing in court as a result of pressure from his superiors and others.

Ultimately, the report concluded that Lt. Hanlon "was not prevented from testifying by SAC Cohen," but SAC Cohen's actions [—13—] were "sufficient to put enough pressure" on Lt. Hanlon to "request that he be excused from testifying." The report labeled SAC Cohen's conduct as "inappropriate."

As to the prosecution against Yacubian, the Master found that "money was NOAA's motivating objective in this case," and that "EA Juliand had no right to extract an oppressive penalty for the sale of the permits because EA Juliand and others at NOAA completely ignored the plain meaning of Judge Gorton's decision." The Master found that the assessed penalties were excessive, and that NOAA had improperly coerced the settlement. The Special Master recommended that Yacubian be reimbursed $330,000.

On May 17, 2011, Gary Locke, then Secretary of Commerce, issued a "Secretarial Decision Memorandum" which followed up on the Special Master Report. Secretary Locke categorized his view of the various NOAA actions as follows:

In light of this systemic failing [described in the Master's Report], I find after legal review that none of the

conduct described in the report undertaken by any individual NOAA lawyer or law enforcement officer warrants disciplinary action against any employee mentioned in [the Special Master's] report. At bottom, these problems were not the product of individual bad acts, but rather the result of conduct enabled and even encouraged by the management and enforcement culture in place at the time.

As to Yacubian's case specifically, Secretary Locke directed NOAA to remit $400,000 to Yacubian. The affirmance of Yacubian's liability for the two prohibited fishing counts was not mentioned [—14—] in the Secretary's Memorandum or in the Master's Report, nor was the permanent forfeiture of Yacubian's operating permits as part of the settlement agreement.

D. *This Case*

On January 19, 2012, Yacubian, relying on the Special Master's Report, filed FTCA administrative claims with the Department of Commerce and the Coast Guard. After the Coast Guard denied his claim,[9] Yacubian filed a complaint in the district court on July 30, 2012. He alleged that NOAA engaged in abuse of process and malicious prosecution in initiating the 2000 NOVA/NOPS and in negotiating the 2005 settlement agreement.

On October 11, 2012, the United States filed a motion to dismiss the case for lack of subject matter jurisdiction and for failure to state a claim. On July 8, 2013, the district court (Tauro, J.) granted the motion on two independent grounds. It held that Yacubian's claims accrued, at the very latest, by June 27, 2005, when he signed the settlement agreement, and that his FTCA claims were time-barred as a result. *Yacubian*, 952 F. Supp. 2d at 339-40. The district court also

---

[8] The report also found that in the months before the ALJ hearing, SAC Cohen asked another Special Agent how to "initiate paperwork" to remove Lt. Hanlon from the agency's list of deputized state officers.

[9] The Department of Commerce had indicated that it intended to deny his FTCA claim but had not yet officially done so. Because the six-month period for administrative consideration of the claim lapsed on July 19, 2012, Yacubian's claim was deemed denied under 28 U.S.C. § 2675(a) as of that date.

made an alternative and independent holding, dismissing both the malicious prosecution and abuse of process counts pursuant to Federal Rule of Civil Procedure [—15—] 12(b)(6). *Id.* at 340-42. It relied on the intentional torts exception to the FTCA, under which the United States is immune from prosecution for malicious prosecution and abuse of process claims unless these torts are committed by an "investigative or law enforcement officer." 28 U.S.C. § 2680(h). The district court found that the NOAA Enforcement Attorneys, who brought and pursued the prosecution and obtained the settlement, were not "investigative or law enforcement officers" within the meaning of the statute, and that Yacubian's complaint failed to state a claim for malicious prosecution or abuse of process as to SAC Cohen, who is a law enforcement officer. *Yacubian*, 952 F. Supp. 2d at 341-42. This appeal followed. We deal only with the second holding.

II.

We review a district court's dismissal under Rule 12(b)(6) de novo, construing the facts of the complaint in the light most favorable to the plaintiff. *Ocasio-Hernández v. Fortuño-Burset*, 640 F.3d 1, 7 (1st Cir. 2011). We indulge in all reasonable inferences in Yacubian's favor. *McCloskey v. Mueller*, 446 F.3d 262, 266 (1st Cir. 2006). However, "[i]t is a well-settled rule that when a written instrument contradicts allegations in the complaint to which it is attached, the exhibit trumps the allegations." *Young v. Wells Fargo Bank, N.A.*, 717 F.3d 224, 229 n.1 (1st Cir. 2013) (quoting *Clorox Co. P.R. v. Proctor & Gamble* [—16—] *Commercial Co.*, 228 F.3d 24, 32 (1st Cir. 2000)) (internal quotation marks omitted).

To survive a motion to dismiss, Yacubian's complaint "must state a plausible, not a merely conceivable, case for relief." *Sepúlveda-Villarini v. Dep't of Educ. of P.R.*, 628 F.3d 25, 29 (1st Cir. 2010). This threshold requires that the factual allegations support the "reasonable inference that the defendant is liable for the misconduct alleged." *Haley v. City of Boston*, 657 F.3d 39, 46 (1st Cir. 2011)

(quoting *Ashcroft v. Iqbal*, 556 U.S. 662, 678 (2009)) (internal quotation mark omitted).

The FTCA gives jurisdiction over tort claims only "if a private person[] would be liable to the claimant in accordance with the law of the place where the act or omission occurred." 28 U.S.C. § 1346(b)(1). The FTCA is a limited waiver of the federal government's sovereign immunity, *McCloskey*, 446 F.3d at 266, and, as with all such waivers, it must be "construed strictly in favor of the federal government." *Bolduc v. United States*, 402 F.3d 50, 56 (1st Cir. 2005) (quoting *United States v. Horn*, 29 F.3d 754, 762 (1st Cir. 1994)) (internal quotation marks omitted).

The FTCA permits suits against the government for torts "caused by the . . . wrongful act[s] . . . of any employee of the Government while acting within the scope of his office or employment." 28 U.S.C. §1346(b)(1). This waiver is limited further for the torts of malicious prosecution and abuse of [—17—] process. As to these two torts, suits are permitted to proceed only with respect to actions by "investigative or law enforcement officers." *Id.* § 2680(h). It is undisputed here that the actions of federal prosecutors are outside the ambit of § 2680(h) and are accordingly immune from this type of suit under the FTCA. *See, e.g., Limone v. United States*, 579 F.3d 79, 88-89 (1st Cir. 2009); *Bernard v. United States*, 25 F.3d 98, 104 (2d Cir. 1994) ("[T]he FTCA does not authorize suits for intentional torts based upon the actions of Government prosecutors . . . .").

Yacubian does not dispute the government's assertion that the actions of Enforcement Attorneys Juliand and MacDonald, who brought the charges and were the prosecutors in the ALJ proceedings, are, like those of other federal prosecutors, immune in this context. That leaves only whether the complaint and appended documents plausibly allege that SAC Cohen himself wrongfully engaged in malicious prosecution or abuse of process. We agree with the district court that they do not.[10]

---

[10] On appeal, Yacubian does not mount a serious argument that he should be allowed to amend his complaint if we affirm the district court

To discern the elements of a claim under the FTCA, we look to the law of the place where the alleged wrongful act [—18—] occurred. *See González-Rucci v. U.S. I.N.S.*, 539 F.3d 66, 69 (1st Cir. 2008).

A. *Malicious Prosecution*

Under Massachusetts law, there are three elements of a malicious prosecution claim. A plaintiff must establish that he was damaged because (1) the defendant commenced an original action without probable cause, (2) with malice, and (3) that the original action terminated in his favor. *Chervin v. Travelers Ins. Co.*, 858 N.E.2d 746, 753 (Mass. 2006).

The two prohibited fishing charges cannot possibly form the basis of Yacubian's malicious prosecution claim because the findings of liability mean that those aspects of the proceedings did not terminate in his favor. The underlying liability as to those counts was affirmed. *Lobsters, Inc.*, 346 F. Supp. 2d at 349.

This leaves only a claim for malicious prosecution based on the initiation of the false statement charge.[11] We address whether the allegations against SAC Cohen plausibly state a claim as to that matter.

As to the first element, there is no allegation at all that SAC Cohen in any way initiated the prosecution of any charge, [—19—] much less the false statement charge. The only specific allegation of SAC Cohen's involvement related to activities after the

---

on a Rule 12(b)(6) theory and so we do not consider that option. *See United States v. Zannino*, 895 F.2d 1, 17 (1st Cir. 1990) ("[I]ssues adverted to in a perfunctory manner, unaccompanied by some effort at developed argumentation, are deemed waived.").

[11] We do not need to reach the argument by the United States that there was no termination of any part of the enforcement proceedings which was in Yacubian's favor. The government says the claims were settled, and that the Secretarial Decision Memorandum did not terminate or invalidate the 2000 NOVA/NOPS or vacate the operative terms of the Settlement Agreement, including the relinquishment of permits and forfeiture of profits.

charges were brought.[12] In particular, the only wrongdoing alleged is SAC Cohen inducing Lt. Hanlon's superiors into pressuring Lt. Hanlon not to testify as to the prohibited fishing charges.[13] But Lt. Hanlon had no knowledge relevant to the false statement charge and was not a witness as to that charge. As the district court noted, the Complaint does not allege "that any of the investigative or law enforcement officers named in the Complaint induced or caused EA Juliand to issue the 2000 NOVA/NOPS. Nor does plaintiff allege that any of the officers exercised control or influence over EA Juliand's decisions in prosecuting the case." *Yacubian*, 952 F. [—20—] Supp. 2d at 342 (footnote omitted). Without such allegations, the complaint cannot state a claim for malicious prosecution.

The complaint must permit the "reasonable inference" that SAC Cohen in some sense caused the bringing of the NOAA false statement charges, and it requires "more than a sheer possibility" that he acted unlawfully. *Iqbal*, 556 U.S. at 678. The bare allegation that SAC Cohen was "involved" in the

---

[12] Yacubian's "continuation of a prosecution" theory fails for a number of reasons, including that there plainly was at least probable cause for the prohibited fishing charges and because merely taking steps to strengthen a case does not make agents "continuers" of a prosecution. *Limone*, 579 F.3d at 91.

[13] Even accepting the proposition that SAC Cohen acted improperly in this regard, that does not aid Yacubian's case. *Limone*, 579 F.3d at 90 (even where record leaves no doubt federal agents acted deplorably, that does not mean they can be said to have instituted wrongful prosecution).

To the extent Yacubian suggests an inference can be drawn that this action after the charges were brought suggests that SAC Cohen somehow maliciously induced the initial prosecution or service of the complaint, the inference is neither reasonable nor plausible. *See Bernard*, 25 F.3d at 104 (holding that actions by agent after prosecution is brought cannot support claim of malicious prosecution in bringing the charges).

To the extent Yacubian suggests SAC Cohen applied pressure by protesting Lt. Hanlon's testimony absent a subpoena, such a protest would be unremarkable. There is nothing inherently illegitimate or malicious in the federal government's request for a subpoena to minimize the likelihood of giving a false impression.

investigation of Yacubian's case simply does not permit any plausible inference that he, and not the Enforcement Attorneys, was responsible in any way for the institution or maintenance of the prosecution.[14] *See Limone*, 579 F.3d at 89. He was obviously not present at the time the false statements were made. Indeed there is no assertion that SAC Cohen had any knowledge pertinent to the false statement charge. That dooms Yacubian's malicious prosecution claim. [—21—]

B. *Abuse of Process*

Under Massachusetts law, an abuse of process claim requires a plaintiff to show that "process" was used for an ulterior or illegitimate purpose and resulted in damages. *Vittands v. Sudduth*, 730 N.E.2d 325, 332 (Mass. App. Ct. 2000). We begin and end here with the first requirement: the use of "process." That term "means causing papers to be issued by a court to bring a party or property within its jurisdiction." *Id.* at 332 n.9 (quoting *Silvia v. Bldg. Inspector of W. Bridgewater*, 621 N.E.2d 686, 687 n.4 (Mass. App. Ct. 1993)) (internal quotation mark omitted). One can "use process" under Massachusetts law by providing information that causes process to be used improperly. *See Gutierrez v. Mass. Bay Transp. Auth.*, 772 N.E.2d 552, 563-64 (Mass. 2002) (holding that where plaintiffs presented evidence that officers falsified arrest reports which provided the basis for criminal complaints, a jury could conclude those officers "caused papers to

issue" by a court). The parties agree that the only "process" at issue in this case is the original NOVA/NOPS.

As we have said, Yacubian does not plausibly allege that SAC Cohen had any involvement in EA Juliand's initial decision to file the NOVA/NOPS and serve it on Yacubian. Under *Iqbal*, that is insufficient.

Yacubian, on appeal, urges us to infer from his complaint that SAC Cohen "used process" in "supplying the basis for the [—22—] Enforcement Attorneys to secure the NOVA/NOPS with an ulterior purpose." His complaint does not so plead, and we have no need to discuss this further.

III.

The judgment of the district court is *affirmed.*

---

14 The Special Master's report on two other matters, unrelated to Yacubian's case, noted that SAC Cohen was involved in and caused process (in those cases, an Administrative Inspection Warrant) to issue. The Master made no express conclusions as to SAC Cohen's actions in those other cases. Yacubian urges us to infer from these other two cases that SAC Cohen "supplied and further influenced the prosecution with respect to all of the charges" in this case. That is not a plausible inference. The Special Master made no such findings as to SAC Cohen in Yacubian's case. First, the Special Master did not make any conclusions that SAC Cohen acted improperly in those other two cases. Second, there are no allegations in the complaint to support the link Yacubian suggests, and SAC Cohen's actions in two unrelated cases are not germane to the events here.

United States Court of Appeals
for the First Circuit

No. 13-2109

RAMIREZ

VS.

CAROLINA DREAM, INC.

Appeal from the United States District Court for the
District of Massachusetts

Decided: July 28, 2014

Citation: 760 F.3d 119, 2 Adm. R. 23 (1st Cir. 2014).

Before **HOWARD, STAHL,** and **LIPEZ,** Circuit Judges.

[—2—] **LIPEZ,** Circuit Judge:

Appellant Santos Ramirez, a seaman, became ill while working aboard a fishing vessel and was immediately hospitalized when he returned to shore. Shortly thereafter, he was diagnosed with aplastic anemia, a serious blood condition that prevented him from returning to work as a seaman. He subsequently brought this personal injury action against his employer, seeking a remedy under the Jones Act, 46 U.S.C. § 30104, and general maritime law. The district court granted summary judgment for the defendant, Carolina Dream, Inc., on each of appellant's alleged causes of action. On appeal, Ramirez challenges only dismissal of his maritime claim for maintenance and cure, arguing that he is entitled to that remedy until he reaches "maximum medical recovery." *Vaughan v. Atkinson*, 369 U.S. 527, 531 (1962). Because we agree that the record would permit a factfinder to find that appellant is entitled to maintenance and cure, we vacate the district court's ruling and remand for further proceedings.

I.

A. Factual Background

In recounting the facts, which we present in the light most favorable to appellant Ramirez, see, e.g., *Adamson v. Walgreens Co.*, 750 F.3d 73, 76 (1st Cir. 2014), we borrow liberally from the district court's clear and succinct recitation. [—3—]

Ramirez had been a crew member on the commercial fishing boat F/V DEFIANT for about eight years when, in December 2008, rough seas during a scallop fishing trip off the New Jersey coast bounced the vessel and caused him to strike his jaw against his bunk. He sustained a laceration inside his mouth, felt dizzy the next day, and began to feel weak and sick to his stomach about three days after the incident. Although appellant asked to be brought ashore, the captain refused and instructed him to perform his duties until the end of the trip.

Appellant's condition worsened before the vessel returned to its home port in Seaford, Virginia, several days later, and his wife took him directly from the dock to a hospital emergency room for treatment. He remained hospitalized for about a month, was discharged in mid-January 2009, but then was readmitted to a different hospital a week later because of continuing symptoms.[1] He was then diagnosed with aplastic anemia, "[a] rare and serious condition" that occurs when the body stops producing sufficient new [—4—] blood cells. *See* Mayo Clinic Staff, "Aplastic Anemia, Definition," http://www.mayoclinic.org/diseases-conditions/aplasticanemia/basics/definition/con-20019296 (last visited July 9, 2014).

One of appellant's treating doctors reported that the exact cause of appellant's disease would likely remain unknown—"as is the case in many occurrences of aplastic anemia"—but the doctor noted his history of hepatitis C, a typical "culprit of aplastic anemia." Before the trip during which he became ill, appellant had

---

[1] The district court noted appellant's assertion that he was admitted to the first hospital "due to a serious infection," although none of the medical reports submitted in this case explicitly identify his problem as an infection. Appellant's records from the first hospital, the Sentara Careplex Hospital in Hampton, Virginia, were not introduced in the district court, although two documents reporting his treatment at that hospital are included in his appendix on appeal. Reports from doctors at the second facility, the Medical Center of Virginia Commonwealth University in Richmond, focused on his blood disorder. In reaching our decision, we have not relied on the records submitted for the first time on appeal.

experienced no symptoms and "was doing [his] work well." Ramirez states in his brief that he continues to undergo treatment for aplastic anemia and remains unable to work.

Ramirez filed this action in August 2011 alleging negligence under the Jones Act, 46 U.S.C. § 30104, and maritime claims of unseaworthiness and maintenance and cure. He asserts that his injury "and the delay in receiving the proper medical treatment" caused "a serious infection that lead to [a]plastic [a]nemia." In opposing summary judgment, he averred that a factfinder could reasonably infer "manifestation of [his] aplastic anemia during his service to the FV DEFIANT." As noted above, appellant on appeal has challenged only the summary judgment for Carolina Dream on his cause of action for maintenance and cure. We thus limit our analysis to that claim. [—5—]

B. The Doctrine of Maintenance and Cure

The owner of a vessel has a duty to pay maintenance and cure to a seaman "who [is] injured or fall[s] ill while 'in service of the ship.'" *Whitman v. Miles*, 387 F.3d 68, 72 (1st Cir. 2004)(quoting *LeBlanc v. B.G.T. Corp.*, 992 F.2d 394, 396 (1st Cir. 1993)); *see also Atl. Sounding Co. v. Townsend*, 557 U.S. 404, 413 (2009); *Vaughan*, 369 U.S. at 531.[2] "Maintenance" refers to the cost of food and lodging during the period of illness or recovery from injury, and "cure" covers the reasonable medical expenses incurred for the seaman's treatment. *Atl. Sounding*, 557 U.S. at 413; *Whitman*, 387 F.3d at 71.

---

[2] The requirement that a seaman be "serving the ship" at the time of his illness or injury, *Lewis v. Lewis & Clark Marine, Inc.*, 531 U.S. 438, 441 (2001), means that he must be "generally answerable to its call to duty rather than actually in performance of routine tasks or specific orders." *Farrell v. United States*, 336 U.S. 511, 516 (1949). Hence, a seaman who is injured or taken ill while off the ship may nonetheless be eligible for maintenance and cure. *Cf. Haskell v. Socony Mobil Oil Co.*, 237 F.2d 707, 709-10 (1st Cir. 1956) (distinguishing between brief shore leaves and "protracted vacations" in holding that maintenance and cure is inapplicable to the latter).

The remedy of maintenance and cure is deliberately expansive, *see Vella v. Ford Motor Co.*, 421 U.S. 1, 4 (1975) (noting the "breadth and inclusiveness of the shipowner's duty"), and it is not "restricted to those cases where the seaman's employment is the cause of the injury or illness," *Calmar S.S. Corp. v. Taylor*, 303 U.S. 525, 527 (1938) ["*Taylor*"]. "[T]he obligation can arise out of a medical condition such as a heart [—6—] problem, a prior illness that recurs during the seaman's employment, or an injury suffered on shore." 1 Thomas J. Schoenbaum, *Admiralty & Maritime Law* § 6-29, at 380 (4th ed. 2001); *see also Haskell v. Socony Mobil Oil Co.*, 237 F.2d 707, 709 (1st Cir. 1956) ("[I]t arises when [the seaman] is taken ill from whatever cause during a voyage.").

The doctrine is "so broad" that the seaman's "negligence or acts short of culpable misconduct . . . will not relieve the shipowner of the responsibility." *Vella*, 421 U.S. at 4 (alterations omitted) (internal quotation marks omitted); *see also Messier v. Bouchard Transp.*, 688 F.3d 78, 82 (2d Cir. 2012) (noting that maintenance and cure "is a far more expansive remedy" than workers' compensation); *DiBenedetto v. Williams*, 880 F. Supp. 80, 86 (D.R.I. 1995) ("[M]aintenance and cure may still be awarded plaintiff notwithstanding a pre-existing condition as long as that condition is not deliberately concealed and is not disabling at the time the seaman signs on for the voyage."). The wide scope of the duty springs from the status of seamen as "emphatically the wards of the admiralty," *Harden v. Gordon*, 11 F. Cas. 480, 485 (C.C.D. Me. 1823) (No. 6,047) (Story, J.), and advances multiple purposes, among them to protect seamen "from the hazards of illness and abandonment while ill in foreign ports" and to induce maritime employers to guard against safety and health risks. *Taylor*, 303 U.S. at 528 (citing *Harden*, 11 F. Cas. at 483). [—7—]

The shipowner's ancient duty to provide maintenance and cure for the seaman who becomes ill or is injured while in the service of the ship derives from the "unique hazards (which) attend the work of seamen," and fosters the "combined object of encouraging marine commerce and assuring the well-being of seamen." . . . [The shipowner's duty] "has few exceptions or conditions to stir contentions, cause delays, and invite litigations."

Vella, 421 U.S. at 3-4 (quoting *Aguilar v. Standard Oil Co.*, 318 U.S. 724, 727 (1943); *Farrell v. United States*, 336 U.S. 511, 516 (1949)).

The duty of maintenance and cure applies until the seaman has fully recovered or is "so far cured as possible," *Farrell*, 336 U.S. at 518—the latter alternative taking into account that the seaman's condition might stabilize short of full health. The obligation to pay maintenance and cure is thus described as extending until the seaman "reaches maximum medical recovery." *Vaughan*, 369 U.S. at 531; *see also, e.g., Haskell*, 237 F.2d at 709 (explaining that "cure" is "cure in the sense of care until medical science can do no more"); Robert Force, Federal Judicial Center, *Admiralty & Maritime Law* 94 (2d ed. 2013) (defining the cutoff point as "when the condition is cured or declared to be incurable or of a permanent character").

With these legal principles in mind, we now examine the district court's conclusion that appellant did not adduce sufficient evidence to support a claim for maintenance and cure. [—8—]

II.

Summary judgment is appropriate only if the record shows no genuine dispute of material fact and the moving party is entitled to judgment as a matter of law. Fed. R. Civ. P. 56(a); *Hicks v. Johnson*, No. 13-1741, 2014 WL 2793806, at *2 (1st Cir. June 20, 2014). Our review of the district court's grant of summary judgment is de novo. *Hicks*, 2014 WL 2793806, at *2.

Appellant asserts that he is entitled to maintenance and cure until he has reached maximum recovery from aplastic anemia, which he contends has not yet occurred. The district court rejected his entitlement to *any*

maintenance and cure on the ground that appellant failed to produce evidence that the disease arose during his service on the F/V DEFIANT—"[o]ther than asserting that he was in 'normal health' prior to the fishing voyage and hospitalized upon returning to port." The court's rationale reflects a too-narrow view of both the facts and the vessel owner's responsibility.

As detailed above, appellant began feeling weak and dizzy shortly after he sustained an injury onboard the F/V DEFIANT, and he required more than a month's hospitalization immediately after disembarking. A doctor's report stated that he was admitted to a second hospital "due to continued symptoms" a week after he was initially discharged, at which time he was diagnosed with aplastic anemia. Hence, the record shows that appellant became ill during [—9—] the December 2008 fishing voyage and remained ill continuously through the time he was determined to have the blood condition. Before that voyage, appellant had been working regularly and without symptoms, notwithstanding a history of hepatitis C.

As appellant emphasizes, the facts here resemble those considered by the Supreme Court in *Taylor*. In that case, a seaman who obtained medical treatment after stubbing his toe in the ship's boiler room was diagnosed with Buerger's disease, an incurable illness that affects the arteries and veins. 303 U.S. at 526. The Court took for granted that the seaman was entitled to maintenance and cure even though the disease was found to be unrelated to the foot injury. *See id.* at 528-29. The Court focused, instead, on the duration of the duty. It noted widespread recognition that a seaman who is hurt or becomes ill while serving the ship may receive maintenance and cure "for a reasonable time after the voyage," but it acknowledged that most cases so holding involved a work-related disability. *Id.*

The Court nonetheless held that the right to maintenance and cure "may outlast the voyage" even when "the efficient cause of the injury or illness was [not] some proven act of the seaman in the service of the ship." *Id.* at 529. Among its rationales, the Court invoked "the liberality" that admiralty courts give to rules "devised for the benefit and protection of seamen who are its wards," and it noted the undesirable consequences of a contrary [—10—] conclusion: "The practical inconvenience and attendant danger to seamen in the application of a rule which would encourage the attempt by master or owner to determine in advance of any maintenance and cure, whether the illness was caused by the employment, are manifest." *Id*. at 529-30.

The Supreme Court thus confirmed that maintenance and cure is available for a disabling illness whether or not that illness, though discovered during treatment for an onboard injury, resulted from the injury. Moreover, as noted above, it does not matter if an incapacitating illness preexisted the seaman's maritime employment, so long as the condition was not deliberately concealed or disabling when the seaman joined the ship's service. *See Messier*, 688 F.3d at 84; Schoenbaum, *supra*, at 380. The inquiry is not one of causation, but of timing: did the illness for which the seaman seeks maintenance and cure begin or become aggravated while he was "serving the ship"? *Lewis v. Lewis & Clark Marine, Inc.*, 531 U.S. 438, 441 (2001).[3] Here, then, the question for purposes of summary judgment is whether a factfinder could [—11—] conclude that Ramirez suffered from aplastic anemia while still in service to the FV/DEFIANT.

The facts outlined above readily permit such an inference. Ramirez presented evidence that he boarded the ship feeling well and able to work, but left very ill. His medical history includes a known trigger for aplastic anemia. Given his deteriorating health while

in the ship's service, his history of hepatitis C, and the short interval between the onset of illness and the diagnosis, a factfinder reasonably could conclude that the dizziness and weakness that appellant experienced on the vessel were the first noticeable and debilitating symptoms of the aplastic anemia. Although the record does not contain medical evidence substantiating appellant's contention that the delay in treatment for his mouth laceration caused "a serious infection" that in turn triggered the aplastic anemia, he is not obliged to prove a cause-and-effect medical basis for the disease. *See Taylor*, 303 U.S. at 527. Rather, as we have explained, the duty to pay maintenance and cure "arises when [the seaman] is taken ill from whatever cause during a voyage." *Haskell*, 237 F.2d at 709.

Moreover, in keeping with the breadth of the duty to provide maintenance and cure, the Supreme Court has stated that, in evaluating the shipowner's liability, "ambiguities or doubts . . . are resolved in favor of the seaman." *Vaughan*, 369 U.S. at 532. At a minimum, a factfinder could conclude on the record before us [—12—] that aplastic anemia was the most likely reason for appellant's deteriorating condition while on the ship, with the disease manifesting as a result of the injury to appellant's jaw or happening to coincide with the injury.

Our decision in *Whitman v. Miles*, cited by the district court, is not to the contrary. The plaintiff in that case was diagnosed with multiple sclerosis ("MS") after experiencing various physical symptoms (including fatigue, numbness, and incontinence) while working as a cook on a ship. The vessel owner conceded his general duty to provide maintenance and cure, but the parties disputed the duration of the duty and its application to the seaman's specific treatment for depression. *See* 387 F.3d at 71-74.

We declined to determine whether the depression was a symptom of MS or a separate ailment because, regardless, the seaman would not be entitled to maintenance and cure based on that disorder. *Id*. at 74. We explained that, if depression were viewed as a distinct ailment, it did not provide a basis for

---

[3] The Court in *Taylor* went on to consider the proper duration for the maintenance-and-cure duty in such instances and settled on the now well established principle of maximum medical recovery. *See* 303 U.S. at 530 ("We can find no basis for saying that, if the disease proves to be incurable, the duty extends beyond a fair time after the voyage in which to effect such improvement in the seaman's condition as reasonably may be expected to result from nursing, care, and medical treatment.").

maintenance and cure because the seaman had "failed to produce any evidence that she began to suffer from depression while in the service of the ship." *Id.* Alternatively, if the depression were treated as a symptom of MS, she would have no claim for additional compensation because the employer already had paid maintenance and cure up to the point of maximum medical recovery. *Id.*; *see also id.* at 72 ("The testimony of the doctors for both parties leaves no [—13—] genuine issue of material fact that [the plaintiff's] treatment . . . would not reverse her symptoms or improve her condition beyond the point of maximum medical recovery.").

Thus, in *Whitman*, the maintenance and cure claim that we rejected for evidentiary insufficiency involved either a second, possibly separate medical condition or an attempt to extend benefits beyond the previously identified cutoff point for the remedy. Here, by contrast, the recognized triggers for aplastic anemia, together with the evidence of physical symptoms experienced by appellant onboard the vessel, provide sufficient support for a finding that his aplastic anemia arose or became aggravated during his service on the ship and, hence, triggered the duty of maintenance and cure.

The impact of our decision, however, may be modest. At oral argument, appellant's counsel reported that appellee Carolina Dream paid maintenance and cure to his client through the date of the district court's summary judgment ruling in August 2013. As we have explained, appellant is entitled to maintenance and cure only while he is "moving toward recovery," *In re RJF Int'l Corp. for Exoneration from or Limitation of Liab.*, 354 F.3d 104, 106 (1st Cir. 2004), up to the point of "maximum medical recovery," *Vaughan*, 369 U.S. at 531. Although Ramirez asserts that his condition has not yet stabilized, the record on that issue is undeveloped and our decision here does not foreclose summary judgment on the ground [—14—] that the employer has satisfied its obligation. We note, however, that even after achieving maximum medical cure, a seaman may "reinstitute a demand for maintenance and cure where subsequent new curative medical treatments become available." *Force, supra,* at 94; *see also Farrell*, 336 U.S. at 519 (noting that the seaman may be able to recover, "in a new proceeding," the costs of "future treatment of a curative nature" and "for maintenance while receiving it"); *Messier*, 688 F.3d at 82 (quoting Force and citing *Farrell*).

Accordingly, we remand this case to the district court for further proceedings consistent with this opinion.

So ordered.

United States Court of Appeals
for the First Circuit

No. 13-1066

UNITED STATES
vs.
BRESIL

Appeal from the United States District Court for the
District of Puerto Rico

Decided: September 24, 2014

Citation: 767 F.3d 124, 2 Adm. R. 28 (1st Cir. 2014).

Before **LYNCH**, Chief Judge, **HOWARD**, and **KAYATTA**,
Circuit Judges.

[—2—] **KAYATTA**, Circuit Judge:

John Wenor Bresil was convicted of illegally reentering the United States after he was found in the middle of the night by Coast Guard and Border Patrol officials in an open boat with seventeen others twenty-three nautical miles off the coast of Puerto Rico. On appeal he argues that he was wrongly prevented from showing at trial that he did not intend to enter the United States but instead was passing Puerto Rico on his way to the island of St. Maarten. Specifically, he argues that: (1) the district court wrongly denied him a continuance after the government announced its intention to call an expert witness only five days before trial; (2) the government violated his due process rights by sinking his boat after it took him into custody, preventing a conclusive determination of whether it contained enough fuel to make it to St. Maarten, and by deporting others found in the boat with him who would have testified that the boat was traveling to St. Maarten; and (3) there was insufficient evidence to support his conviction. Though we find that the government plainly violated Federal Rule of Criminal Procedure 16, we affirm because that violation did not prejudice Bresil, and his other claims are without merit.

I. Background

The basic facts leading to Bresil's conviction are not disputed. On the evening of March 19th, 2012, a border patrol aircraft was patrolling the Mona Passage, the body of water that [—3—] lies between the islands of Hispaniola (which contains Haiti and the Dominican Republic), to the west, and Puerto Rico, to the east. At around 9:40 P.M., the aircraft detected a vessel about 30 miles southwest of Puerto Rico traveling toward that island. Border patrol agents tracked the vessel as it traveled northeast toward Puerto Rico until it came to a stop twenty-three nautical miles off the coast at approximately 1:00 A.M.

Only then did a Coast Guard vessel intercept the boat, which was twenty-six feet long and six feet wide with a forty horsepower outboard engine and eighteen people aboard. The boat had taken on two feet of water by the time the Coast Guard reached it. From their vessel, the Coast Guard officials reported seeing in the bottom of the boat a number of empty fuel containers and one fifteen gallon container that was 75 percent full. The boat's outboard engine did not have an internal fuel tank, instead drawing fuel from a container. After the passengers were taken onto a Coast Guard vessel, the Coast Guard set fire to the boat in order to sink it because, government witnesses testified, it was a hazard to navigation if it remained where it was and they were unable to safely tow it somewhere else. When interviewed, all eighteen passengers on the boat said that they had departed from Miches in the Dominican Republic.

Bresil was indicted on one count of illegally attempting to return to the United States after being deported for commission [—4—] of an aggravated felony. 8 U.S.C. § 1326(a)(2), (b)(2). Bresil was convicted on the sole count of the indictment and sentenced to 78 months' imprisonment and 36 months' supervised release. This appeal of his conviction followed.

II. Discussion

A. Timing of the Government's Rule 16 Disclosure

The Government first informed Bresil of its intention to call an expert witness who could testify about the boat's fuel consumption five days before trial. The expert proposed to testify, and eventually testified, that, based on the type of boat, the number of people in it, and the weight of fuel, it would have traveled at most two and a half to three nautical miles per gallon of gasoline. St. Maarten is approximately 175 nautical miles from the eastern coast of Puerto Rico.

Federal Rule of Criminal Procedure 16(a)(1)(G) provides that "[a]t the defendant's request, the government must give to the defendant a written summary of any [expert] testimony that the government intends to use . . . during its case-in-chief at trial." Bresil had timely requested such a disclosure over a month previously. In response to the government's disclosure, Bresil filed an emergency motion seeking a continuance to obtain his own expert and to further investigate other facts included in the government's disclosure which he claimed were new to him. The district court denied Bresil's motion the same day he filed it on [—5—] the grounds that "[a]ll the facts movant claims as requiring additional investigative efforts were easily discernible from day one."

The government claims that Bresil waived any objection to its late notice under Rule 16 by not mentioning the rule by name in his motion seeking a continuance based on the government's notice that itself referred to Rule 16(a)(1)(G) explicitly. Not surprisingly, the government cites no precedent for this contention that a party need expressly cite a rule when that rule's application is obviously the point of the motion. Bresil made clear that he was seeking a continuance because he "need[ed], at least, the services of an expert in navigation/captain to analyze the evidence and inform us about the capacity of this boat to travel to St. Maarten." One reason he needed such testimony, his motion explained,

was that the government intended to address this question with its expert. In sum, Bresil clearly raised and preserved his argument that the government's designation was filed at a time that warranted a remedy to avoid prejudice to Bresil. Because Bresil raised the issue before the district court we review for abuse of discretion. *See United States v. Espinal-Almeida*, 699 F.3d 588, 614 (1st Cir. 2012).[1] [—6—]

Rule 16(a)(1)(G) "is intended to minimize surprise that often results from unexpected expert testimony, [to] reduce the need for continuances, and to provide the opponent with a fair opportunity to test the merit of the expert's testimony through focused cross-examination." Fed. R. Crim. P. 16 advisory committee's note (1993 Amendment). The fact that Bresil knew that the boat's fuel usage would be at issue at trial does not excuse the government of its duty under Rule 16(a)(1)(G) to give timely notice of its intent to call an expert who would marshal evidence on that issue in service of the government's case. It is one thing to be prepared to argue about a fact at trial, but quite another to prepare to rebut an expert who can testify about implications of that fact in a way different from a lay witness. Prior to the government's notice, the government gave no indication that it would be presenting evidence to the jury that, if the government witnesses were right about the amount of fuel on board, the boat had only a fraction of the fuel it needed to make it to St. Maarten.

The government's notice was plainly untimely because it is unreasonable to expect a defense attorney in the midst of trial preparation to drop everything and try to obtain an expert five days before trial. *See United States v. Martinez*, 657 F.3d 811,

---

[1] Bresil also suggests that the government's notice, in addition to being untimely, did not provide a sufficient summary of the "witness's opinions, the bases and reasons for those opinions, and the witness's qualifications." Fed. R. Crim. P. 16(a)(1)(G). He does not explain how the government's notice was insufficient, [—6—] however, and our review of that notice does not show any obvious omissions, much less omissions which could have prejudiced Bresil.

[—7—] 817 (9th Cir. 2011) (government disclosure of expert five days before trial not "timely" but district court was within its discretion to deny a continuance where expert's testimony was a month away); *United States v. Hoffecker*, 530 F.3d 137, 184-88 (3d Cir. 2008) (defendant's disclosure of expert three business days before jury selection untimely); *United States v. Johnson*, 228 F.3d 920, 922, 926 (8th Cir. 2000) (government's disclosure of expert six days before trial in violation of district court order untimely). Not knowing when to fold a losing hand, the government nevertheless suggested at oral argument that because "Puerto Rico is an island and it's surrounded by ocean" and one of the island's largest marinas was located "forty-five minutes away" (from the courthouse, presumably) it would have been "easy" for Bresil's counsel to obtain an expert on short notice. The government provides no evidence for its claim that this would be easy, however, and, having no experience trawling marinas for experts on outboard motorboat fuel efficiency, we can hardly presume it to be so. More to the point, the government should not be able to send defense counsel on such a hunt when defense counsel is trying to get ready for trial.

The government also suggested at oral argument that denying the motion for a continuance was appropriate because, by the time the motion was filed, the government had already flown in its witnesses, so granting a continuance would have caused [—8—] inconvenience for the government and the agencies for which its witnesses work. In other words, the government claims that it can create a last minute exigency by violating a rule, and then block a remedy for the defendant merely because a remedy would be inconvenient for the government. This argument falls of its own weight and suggests that the government does not take its obligations under Rule 16 seriously.

Nonetheless we affirm because "[t]o obtain a reversal based on a Rule 16 claim, a defendant has to show prejudice." *Espinal-Almeida*, 699 F.3d at 614; *see United States v. Melucci*, 888 F.2d 200, 203 (1st Cir. 1989) (where results and identity of handwriting

expert were not disclosed until four days before expert testified at trial, the district court did not abuse its discretion by admitting the testimony because the defendant did not explain how late disclosure prejudiced him). With the benefit of hindsight (and time), it turns out that, when pressed to explain after the trial what an expert actually could have said that might have helped his defense, Bresil makes no claim that any expert could have materially challenged (or, indeed, challenged at all) the technical claims upon which the testimony of the government's expert was based. In other words, no defense expert would have challenged the opinion that, given the factual assumptions made by the government expert, the boat could not have traveled more than two-and-one-half to three nautical miles per gallon. [—9—]

Instead, Bresil suggests that presenting his own expert would have allowed him to challenge the government expert's assumptions (about, for instance, the weight of the passengers) that were incorporated into his calculations about the distance the boat could travel on a given amount of fuel. But those assumptions were just that— assumptions dependent on facts to which lay witnesses testified. No expert—and Bresil does not say he would have called any additional non-expert witnesses if granted a continuance—could testify to such facts. And if it is facts, not expert testimony, that Bresil wishes to have explained, then as the district court observed in denying the motion to continue, Bresil had long had ample incentive to challenge the facts. Moreover, as it turned out, it was highly improbable that any changes in the facts could have materially changed the conclusion. The type and size of the boat and its motor were undisputed, as was the number of passengers. Bresil says that the weight estimates the government's expert used were high, but there is no claim that lesser estimates on the margins would have made a material difference.[2]

For these reasons, this is an instance of foul, but no harm. We caution the

---

[2] One would need to increase the boat's fuel efficiency six-fold to make it plausible that the boat had enough fuel to make it to St. Maarten.

government, however, that our holding arises from the particular facts of this case and we do not lightly find [—10—] harmless such a clear violation of Rule 16. By failing to disclose experts in a timely fashion parties risk not only undesired and inconvenient continuances but also the exclusion of their expert's testimony entirely. *See* Fed. R. of Crim. P. 16(d)(2) ("If a party fails to comply with this rule, the court may . . . prohibit that party from introducing the undisclosed evidence . . . .").

B. Due Process Claims

Bresil argues that the government violated his due process rights by destroying the boat, which contained evidence of whether or not it had enough fuel to travel to St. Maarten, and by deporting other passengers who, he argues, would have testified in his defense that the boat was traveling to St. Maarten. Because Bresil raised both arguments in the district court, we review de novo the district court's legal conclusion that Bresil's due process rights were not violated. *See United States v. Teague*, 469 F.3d 205, 210 (1st Cir. 2006).

Bresil's argument concerning the destruction of the boat fails because he does not show that there was anything else the Coast Guard could have safely done. He provides no reason to doubt testimony of government witnesses that it was unsafe for them to board the boat to conduct a more thorough inventory of its contents; that, had the boat been left where it was, it would have been a "hazard of navigation;" and that the Coast Guard vessel was not technically capable of safely towing it to another location. [—11—] Absent any reason to doubt these claims, it is hard to understand what Bresil thinks the government should have done. Moreover, because the evidence in the boat was "no more than 'potentially exculpatory evidence,'" he is only entitled to a new trial if he can show that the government acted in bad faith by destroying the boat. *Magraw v. Roden*, 743 F.3d 1, 8 (1st Cir. 2014) (quoting *Arizona v. Youngblood*, 488 U.S. 51 (1988)). Bresil does not argue, nor would the record support an argument, that the government acted in bad faith and so his due process

argument concerning the destruction of his boat fails. *See id.*

Bresil also argues that the government violated his due process rights by deporting the other people on the boat who, he says, would have testified that they were going to St. Maarten. The boat contained eighteen people when stopped by the Coast Guard. The record reflects that five of those eighteen people, including Bresil, gave sworn statements that they were heading to St. Maarten, while a sixth passenger gave a sworn statement that he was heading to Puerto Rico. Of the twelve remaining passengers, one, Bresil's sister, was prosecuted for illegally attempting to enter the United Sates, but charges against her were dropped (the record does not reveal why). It is unclear if she was then deported but, even if she was, she was in the United States, apparently legally, at the time of Bresil's trial. The parties agree that the remaining eleven passengers, about whose stated destination the [—12—] record is silent, were deported the day the boat was stopped and there is no reason to think they reentered the United States.

Of the five passengers who claimed to be going to St. Maarten, one later recanted and pled guilty to illegally attempting to reenter the United States, expressly admitting that he was going to Puerto Rico. Excluding Bresil, that left three passengers who made un-retracted claims that they were headed to St. Maarten. At some point before Bresil's trial and before Bresil's counsel interviewed them, the government deported all three.

Bresil argues on appeal that all the deportations violated his due process rights. However, he limited his argument in the district court to the deportation of four passengers who initially gave sworn statements that they were headed to St. Maarten[3] and so review of his due process

---

[3] He also argued that the government shouldn't have deported his sister, one of the twelve passengers who did not give sworn statements, who, he says, would also have testified that she was going to St. Maarten. But since the record shows

argument with regard to the other passengers would, at best, be for plain error. We first discuss Bresil's preserved due process argument and, finding that it fails, need not reach his unpreserved argument as it must fail for the same reason.

Our assessment of Bresil's complaint that the deportation of the four passengers who initially claimed they were going to St. Maarten violated his due process rights begins with the Supreme [—13—] Court's decision in *United States v. Valenzuela-Bernal*, 458 U.S. 858 (1982). In that case the Court found that the government did not violate the due process rights of a man prosecuted for transporting an illegal alien into the United States when it deported two other people he transported. *Id.* at 874. *Valenzuela-Bernal* could be read as applying a single-prong test under which a defendant's due process rights are violated when witnesses are deported "only if the criminal defendant makes a plausible showing that the testimony of the deported witnesses would have been material and favorable to his defense, in ways not merely cumulative to the testimony of available witnesses" such that there is "a reasonable likelihood that the testimony could have affected the judgment of the trier of fact." *Id.* at 873-74.

Other circuits, however, have added a second, bad-faith prong to the test by drawing on the Court's statement in *Valenzuela-Bernal* that "the responsibility of the Executive Branch faithfully to execute the immigration policy adopted by Congress justifies the prompt deportation of illegal-alien witnesses upon the Executive's good-faith determination that they possess no evidence favorable to the defendant in a criminal prosecution," *id.* at 872, and on *Youngblood*'s characterization, 488 U.S. at 57, of *Valenzuela-Bernal* as a case in which the government's good faith is relevant. *See United States v. Damra*, 621 F.3d 474, 485-90 (6th Cir. 2010); *United States v. Chaparro-Alcantara*, 226 F.3d 616, 623-24 (7th Cir. 2000); *United States v. Dring*, 930 F.2d 687, 693 (9th [—14—] Cir. 1991); *United*

States *v. Iribe-Perez*, 129 F.3d 1167, 1173 (10th Cir. 1997).[4] Under this view, if the government deports a person with no reason to believe the person would give exculpatory testimony in some case, the prosecution of that case does not violate the defendant's due process rights.

We need not decide in this case whether an absence of government bad faith can defeat Bresil's argument that the deportations violated his due process rights. At the time the government deported the other passengers, it presumably knew that it might charge Bresil with illegally reentering the United States and that his defense would likely be that he was going to St. Maarten and not attempting to enter Puerto Rico. It also knew that four passengers had, at least at one point, claimed to support that assertion. We therefore assume that Bresil has satisfied any bad [—15—] faith prong by showing the government's awareness of the potential exculpatory value of the testimony of the people it was deporting.[5]

---

that she was in the United States at the time of his trial this claim was moot.

[4] While we have never explicitly discussed the role of good faith in applying *Valenzuela-Bernal*, we have done so in interpreting *Youngblood*. *See United States v. Garza*, 435 F.3d 73, 75-76 (1st Cir. 2006). We have also described "the Supreme Court's jurisprudence [as] divid[ing] cases involving nondisclosure of evidence into two distinct universes . . . ," *United States v. Femia*, 9 F.3d 990, 993 (1st Cir. 1993), one beginning with *Brady v. Maryland*, 373 U.S. 83 (1963), and the other enunciated in *Youngblood* and *California v. Trombetta*, 467 U.S. 479, 485 (1984). In grouping *Youngblood* and *Trombetta* together we noted, *see Fermia*, 9 F.3d at 993, that both rely on *Valenzuela-Bernal*. *See Youngblood*, 488 U.S. at 55; *Trombetta*, 467 U.S. 485. Unlike *Youngblood* and *Trombetta*, *Brady* has no good faith requirement. *Brady*, 373 U.S. at 87. Declining to read a bad-faith prong into *Valenzuela-Bernal* when we have read one into *Youngblood* and made clear that *Youngblood* and *Valenzuela-Bernal* apply the same principle would thus be, at minimum, in tension with our precedent.

[5] Because we find that Bresil's argument fails on other grounds, we also need not decide precisely how much knowledge by the government of a witness's exculpatory value would be sufficient to satisfy the defendant's burden under a bad-faith prong.

Bresil's appeal therefore turns on whether he has also established that testimony by those passengers deported to the Dominican Republic to a "reasonable likelihood . . . could have affected the judgment of the trier of fact." *Valenzuela-Bernal*, 458 U.S. at 873-74. We think not, for four reasons.

First, and most importantly, given the direction in which the boat was traveling (north-east toward Puerto Rico rather than straight east toward St. Maarten), the location in which it was intercepted (23 nautical miles from Puerto Rico and more than 175 nautical miles from St. Maarten), the limited fuel on board, and the fact that it was traveling at night without lights, it is highly unlikely that any reasonable jury would have believed any claim that the boat was headed to St. Maarten based merely on self-serving assertions to that effect from other passengers.[6]

Second, if it had retained the four passengers Bresil says it should have retained, a prudent government would also likely have retained the other passenger who said from the start that he was going to Puerto Rico and the government would have [—16—] likely waited until Bresil's trial to deport the passenger who pled guilty to attempting to reenter the United States. The credibility of the testimony of the three passengers who consistently said they were going to St. Maarten would have been undercut by the testimony of the other two passengers who admitted to attempting to enter the United States. In this respect, no passenger testimony was likely better for Bresil than conflicting passenger testimony.

Third, Bresil could have called as a witness his sister, who was on the boat and in the United States at the time of his trial. That he did not suggests he thought her "going to St. Maarten" story would not have held up to cross-examination.

Fourth, if Bresil is correct that the deportation wrongfully deprived him of relevant testimony, he could have put into

evidence the favorable hearsay statements of the other passengers under Federal Rule of Evidence 804(b)(6). True, the testimony would not have been live for the jury, but it also would not have been subject to cross-examination by the government. Nor would the government have likely been able to offer the conflicting statements.

In short, it is hard to see how Bresil would have been better off if the five passengers (other than Bresil's sister) whose stated destinations we know (three St. Maartens and two Puerto Ricos) had testified. No one of these reasons alone necessarily defeats Bresil's argument. All four considered together, though, are sufficient to establish the absence of a [—17—] reasonable likelihood that testimony by the deported witnesses could have affected the judgment of the jury in a manner favorable to Bresil.

C. Sufficiency of the Evidence

Bresil's final argument is that there was insufficient evidence to convict him of attempting to reenter the United States. For the reasons we have stated above, far from being insufficient, the evidence was compelling that the boat and its passengers had embarked for and were heading to Puerto Rico. Bresil, moreover, owned property in Puerto Rico and demonstrated no ties to St. Maarten. In short, the circumstances of his capture were such that a rational factfinder could have found beyond a reasonable doubt that he intended to reenter the United States.

III. Conclusion

For the foregoing reasons the judgment of the district court is *affirmed*.

So ordered.

---

[6] Bresil does not argue that the passengers, had they been called, would have claimed anything other than they were headed to St. Maarten.

United States Court of Appeals
for the First Circuit

No. 13-1776

FRONTIER FISHING CORP.
vs.
PRITZKER

Appeal from the United States District Court for the
District of Massachusetts

Decided: October 24, 2014

Citation: 770 F.3d 58, 2 Adm. R. 34 (1st Cir. 2014).

Before **THOMAS**, **KAYATTA**, and **BARRON**, Circuit
Judges.

[—2—] **KAYATTA**, Circuit Judge:

The National Oceanic and Atmospheric
Administration ("NOAA") determined
Frontier Fishing liable for trawling in a
restricted gear area in violation of regulations
promulgated under the Magnuson-Stevens
Fishing Conservation and Management Act,
16 U.S.C. §§ 1801-1891d. NOAA fined
Frontier Fishing $10,000 and suspended one-
quarter of Frontier Fishing's seasonal fishing
days under its Northeast Scallop Days-at-Sea
Permit. Frontier Fishing appeals, arguing
that the record lacks substantial evidence for
a rational finding that its vessel trawled in
the restricted area, and challenging other
aspects of the agency proceedings. Largely for
reasons given by the district court, we affirm.

I. Background

The lengthy background out of which this
appeal arises covers nearly seventeen years
and is impressively reviewed in the most
recent district court opinion. *See Frontier
Fishing Corp. v. Locke*, No. 10-10162, 2013
WL 2090551 (D. Mass. May 13, 2013). We
repeat only as much as is necessary to explain
our ruling.

A. The Night of the Violation

On the evening of October 16, 1997, the
crew of the Coast Guard cutter *Spencer*
detected a radar contact up to one mile inside
Restricted Gear Area 1, southeast of
Nantucket. From October 1 to June 15,
Restricted Gear Area 1 was open only to fixed
fishing [—3—] gear, like lobster traps marked
with "high flyers."[1] The applicable regulations
prohibited the use of mobile fishing gear, like
trawl nets. *See* 50 C.F.R. § 648.14(a)(98)
(1997).

Following the crew's initial report of a
contact in the restricted area, *Spencer*'s
commander, Charley Diaz, verified the contact
on bridge radar, and assigned identification
number 8174 to the object indicated by the
radar. At 21:30, a Coast Guard lookout
observed a white light on the horizon. Crew
members thereafter maintained visual contact
with the lit object using oversized binoculars
known as "big eyes." As the Coast Guard
cutter got closer, crew members observed
green over white lights, indicating a fishing
vessel trawling at night. Commander Diaz
then directed his crew to plot the radar
contact's location. At 21:40, the Coast Guard
proceeded to record the following data:
Spencer's own position using its navigational
system and DGPS, which determines and
records location in longitude and latitude; the
radar range and bearing of target 8174; and
the course and speed of target 8174 as
determined by the Command Display and
Control system. Using this data, the Coast
Guard plotted the location of radar contact
8174 at 21:40 approximately seven-tenths of a
mile inside the restricted area. [—4—]

In addition to recording data on electronic
equipment, other members of *Spencer*'s crew
simultaneously used an alidade[2] to determine
by sight the bearing of the observed lights.
Commander Diaz himself checked the
approximate position of the contact both
visually and through radar equipment. The
Coast Guard crew did not detect by sight or
radar any other vessels in the area at that
time. Shortly after determining that the 21:40
radar contact was within the restricted gear

---

[1] A high flyer is a radar reflector, attached to a
lobster trap buoy, that assists lobster boats locating
their traps.

[2] "A telescope mounted on a compass repeater
and used as part of a ship's navigational equipment
for taking bearings." WEBSTER'S THIRD NEW
INTERNATIONAL DICTIONARY at 53 (1986).

area, the Coast Guard altered course to intercept the target at a high rate of speed. The Coast Guard ultimately recorded range and bearing data for radar contact 8174 three additional times showing it within the restricted area, at 21:47, 21:52, and 21:58. We note that the various readings estimate location at the time of the reading without implying that contact 8174 moved in a straight line from one location to the other.

At 22:00, *Spencer* closed on a fishing vessel that all parties agree was *Settler*, a 90-foot trawler owned by Frontier Fishing, which had departed New Bedford, Massachusetts earlier that day on a monkfish trawling expedition. Commander Diaz estimated that *Settler* was 1,000 yards off *Spencer*'s starboard side at 22:00. Commander Diaz visually confirmed that *Settler* had mobile fishing gear deployed off its stern. *Spencer* then quickly turned around *Settler* and ended up on its port quarter, where *Spencer* remained [—5—] parallel to *Settler* for several minutes. It is undisputed that this interception occurred just outside the restricted gear area, at approximately 22:08. The Coast Guard maintained continuous visual contact with the lit object it had observed throughout its approach that night.

The Coast Guard subsequently issued *Settler* a citation for violating regulations promulgated under the Magnuson-Stevens Act. *See* 50 C.F.R. § 648.14(a)(98) (1997). Two years later, NOAA issued Frontier Fishing a Notice of Violation and Assessment and a Notice of Permit Sanction.

B. Frontier Fishing's Challenges to the Finding of Liability

During the seventeen years since the Coast Guard cited *Settler*, Frontier Fishing has consistently denied that *Settler* was actually in the restricted area. Central to Frontier Fishing's position is the radar contact recorded at 21:58 just inside the restricted area. That location is simply too far from the location that *Spencer*'s captain estimated observing *Settler* two minutes later, at 22:00 (approximately 1,000 yards from *Spencer*). Frontier Fishing built two arguments based

on this discrepancy: it must have been another vessel that the Coast Guard was tracking by radar (the phantom vessel theory); or, in any event, any unreliability of the 21:58 readings rendered unreliable the other range and bearing readings, most crucially those used to plot the 21:40 contact upon which the citation rests. [—6—]

The adjudication of Frontier Fishing's challenge based on these arguments worked its way through an administrative law judge, to the NOAA administrator, to the district court (which remanded for de novo review), *Frontier Fishing Corp. v. Evans*, 429 F. Supp. 2d 316, 335 (D. Mass. 2006), back through the same administrative law judge, to the administrator again, back for a de novo review by a different administrative law judge, to the administrator for a third time, and finally to the district court again, which this time affirmed NOAA's ultimate finding of liability.

In finding Frontier Fishing liable, NOAA rested largely on the fact that the evidence was clear that a vessel was in the restricted area at 21:40, and *Settler*, viewed in the direction of the radar sightings and eventually intercepted just outside the restricted area, was the only vessel that could have been the contact identified at 21:40. In reaching that finding, NOAA agreed with Frontier Fishing that the 21:58 contact could not have represented an accurate depiction of where *Settler* was located at that time. NOAA nevertheless rejected the hypothetical explanation for the 21:58 contact proffered by Frontier Fishing: that there was a second phantom vessel visible to radar but not by sight, and that *Settler* itself was invisible to radar although visible by sight. Instead, NOAA opted for the explanation that the 21:58 contact was *Settler*, albeit erroneously located. In so reasoning, NOAA noted that the 21:40 plot placed a vessel well inside the area, that the [—7—] parties agreed that "something" spotted by the radar was in the area at the time, that the Coast Guard crew visually observed a lighted vessel in the direction of the 21:40 contact, and that any suggestion that the Coast Guard somehow missed a second vessel throughout the entire sequence of events was simply not credible given *Spencer*'s radar capabilities and the observations of both the *Settler* and *Spencer* crews.

II. Standard of Review

The Magnuson-Stevens Act incorporates the standard of review from the Administrative Procedure Act (APA), and thus we look for substantial evidence to support the agency's final decision. *See* 16 U.S.C. §1858(b); 5 U.S.C. § 706(2); *N. Wind, Inc. v. Daley*, 200 F.3d 13, 17 (1st Cir. 1999). Under the substantial evidence test, "the agency's decision is presumed valid." *N. Wind*, 200 F.3d at 17. "'[I]t requires not the degree of evidence which satisfies the *court* that the requisite fact exists, but merely the degree that *could* satisfy a reasonable factfinder.'" *Penobscot Air Servs., Ltd. v. Fed. Aviation Admin.*, 164 F.3d 713, 718 (1st Cir. 1999) (quoting *Allentown Mack Sales & Serv., Inc. v. N.L.R.B.*, 522 U.S. 359, 377 (1998)). The agency's findings must be set aside when the record before the court "'clearly precludes the [agency's] decision from being justified by a fair estimate of the worth of the testimony of witnesses or its informed judgment on matters within its special competence.'" *Penobscot*, 164 F.3d at 718 [—8—] (quoting *Universal Camera Corp. v. N.L.R.B.*, 340 U.S. 474, 490 (1951)).

Our review of the district court's decision is de novo, because the district court reviewed only the administrative record and thus was "in no better position to review the agency than the court of appeals." *Puerto Rico v. United States*, 490 F.3d 50, 61 (1st Cir. 2007) (internal quotations and citations omitted).

III. Analysis

A. Frontier Fishing's Procedural Complaints

Before addressing the substance of Frontier Fishing's arguments on the matter of *Settler*'s location, we address two procedural arguments preserved by Frontier Fishing and pressed on appeal.

1. Refusal to Supplement the Administrative Record

During discovery prior to the very first hearing, NOAA produced to Frontier Fishing a one-page document that consisted of a single handwritten entry on a form like the Coast Guard's radar tracking log form. Dated October 16, 1997, with a time entry of "10:19", the document listed a "track" of "8174", "remarks" of "*Settler* Pts" and navigation data that Frontier Fishing's expert claimed shows contact 8174 at 22:19 located well inside the restricted area and a long way off from where *Settler* was admittedly located post-intercept by *Spencer*. Due to the passage of [—9—] time, discovery shed no light on what exactly this document was, or who created it.

At the first hearing, in August 2001, Frontier Fishing did not offer this document into evidence. Subsequently, it sought to introduce it in its first appeal to the district court. The district court rejected the attempt to supplement the record before the court. *Frontier Fishing*, 429 F. Supp. 2d at 325. In remanding, however, the district court did not preclude "such further development of the record . . . as appears advisable to the ALJ." *Id.* at 335.

ALJ Devine denied Frontier Fishing's request to supplement the record compiled at the first hearing by adding Exhibit 15. The ALJ questioned the relevance of the document, noting that it was unsigned and was not annotated in standard form. Most significantly, the document could not have any relevance unless the time entry of "10:19" were construed as 10:19 p.m. (i.e., 22:19), which would suggest no one accustomed to use of military time on such documents wrote it. Finally, the ALJ observed that Frontier Fishing had a full and fair opportunity to offer the document at the original hearing, and did not do so.

In so ruling, the ALJ did not abuse the discretion left to him on remand. His observations regarding the questionable materiality and provenance of the document speak for themselves. Frontier Fishing fails, also, to offer any good cause for why it

[—10—] did not offer the document at the first hearing, claiming only negligence by prior counsel (whom the ALJ found to have presented a vigorous defense).

2. Denial of Request for Additional Discovery

Frontier Fishing argues on appeal that the NOAA and the district court erred in denying requests for additional discovery. "We disturb a district court's management of discovery 'only upon a clear showing of manifest injustice, that is, where the lower court's discovery order was plainly wrong and resulted in substantial prejudice to the aggrieved party.'" *Olsen v. United States*, 414 F.3d 144, 156 (1st Cir. 2005) (quoting *Mack v. Great Atl. & Pac. Tea Co.*, 871 F.2d 179, 186 (1st Cir. 1989)). Generally, further discovery is not allowed in an action for judicial review upon an administrative record for the same reasons that supplementation is generally not permitted. *Id.* at 155-56. "It is almost inherent in the idea of reviewing agency or other administrative action for reasonableness; how could an administrator act unreasonably by ignoring information never presented to it?" *Liston v. Unum Corp. Officer Severance Plan*, 330 F.3d 19, 23 (1st Cir. 2003). As for NOAA's denial of additional discovery, the applicable agency rule gave the ALJ the discretion to "allow additional discovery only upon a showing of relevance, need, and reasonable scope of the evidence sought." 15 C.F.R. §904.240(b). For the reasons stated by the ALJ and the district [—11—] court, we find that this is not one of those unusual cases in which a district court or an agency must allow additional discovery. Frontier Fishing (1) was given ample opportunity to conduct reasonable discovery throughout the various administrative proceedings; (2) was able to move for summary judgment without the information it now seeks through further discovery; and (3) received all of the information the agency used to make its determination. *Frontier Fishing Corp.*, 429 F. Supp. 2d at 326.

B. The Merits

We begin our analysis of the merits with several observations amply supported by the record. First, prior to 21:40, the cutter's crew spotted one set of lights in the general direction of the restricted area, prompting the taking of a plotted radar contact at 21:40. Second, Frontier Fishing, by conceding that the Coast Guard reliably plotted 'something' in the restricted gear area, agreed that the position of radar contact 8174 at 21:40 was .69 nautical miles inside the restricted gear area.[3] Third, there is no claim that the distance between that location and the location where *Spencer* intercepted *Settler* just outside the area was too far for *Settler* to travel between 21:40 and 22:08. Fourth, during the entire incident, no crew member of either vessel observed any other lights or vessels, nor did *Spencer*'s radar [—12—] detect two vessels at any point during the relevant events. Fifth, *Settler* could not have been in the location of the radar contact as recorded at 21:58 because that location was too far from the location at which Commander Diaz estimated *Settler* at 22:00, approximately 1,000 yards away from *Spencer*.

NOAA's take on the foregoing information was that radar contact 8174 was *Settler*, and that the 21:58 radar contact was erroneously recorded. The primary alternative explanation tendered by Frontier Fishing is that there was a phantom vessel that moved from the site of the 21:40 plot to the sites of the 21:47, 21:52, and 21:58 contacts, and then disappeared from the radar. This explanation presumes that *Settler* itself was invisible to the radar until after 21:58, while the phantom vessel by coincidence remained visible to the radar until after 21:58 but invisible to the eyes of those on both *Settler* and *Spencer* on an evening when visibility was eight miles.

NOAA, which plainly has much more expertise with such matters than do we, rejected this explanation as not credible. Substantial evidence supports this conclusion. *Spencer*'s radar was set to pick up vessels

---

[3] *Spencer*'s quartermaster placed it approximately 200 yards further inside the area.

within twelve nautical miles. Frontier Fishing's claim that "radar clutter" from "high flyers" in the area may have blinded *Spencer*'s radar does not persuasively explain how *Spencer*'s radar would repeatedly detect one moving vessel and not the other over the course of a half hour. And the commanders of [—13—] both *Spencer* and *Settler* testified that they could tell the difference on radar between high flyers and a vessel.

Frontier Fishing claims that the Coast Guard never visually correlated radar target 8174 to the lighted vessel, and that *Spencer*'s steady approach to the lighted vessel was actually consistent with Frontier Fishing's claim that *Settler* maintained a straight, southerly trawl path outside the restricted area, and was not consistent with target 8174's radar plots. Frontier Fishing's expert testified that "the heading and maneuvering of [*Spencer*] was always directed at the trawler lights and at no time was [*Spencer*'s] maneuvering or heading directed toward any of the radar points purported to be [*Settler*]." Of course the alidade readings cut against this theory, so Frontier Fishing points to an absence of any written reference to those readings in some reports, as implying that the crew of *Spencer* actually took no such visual bearings.

NOAA considered Frontier Fishing's expert analysis on this point and rejected it. NOAA found that "there is no evidence of a continuous navigational track for [*Settler*]," as assumed by Frontier Fishing's expert. The ALJ noted that Frontier Fishing's expert relied on *Settler*'s manually inputted 21:30 waypoint position to support his analysis, and that no corroborating evidence supports Frontier Fishing's allegation that *Settler* actually began trawling at the manually inputted waypoint position. [—14—] Further, nothing in the record conclusively established that *Spencer*'s approach angles, cited by Frontier Fishing's expert, would be unreasonable for intercepting another vessel at high speed. Contrary to Frontier Fishing's claim, we also note multiple instances in the record that show the crew did correlate radar readings with its visual sightings using an alidade. For example, in the offense

investigation report, Commander Diaz noted that he himself at one point "shot a bearing" of *Settler* using *Spencer*'s starboard alidade. He also testified that Coast Guard crew determined target 8174's location at 21:40 using "an alidade bearing, a radar range and [*Spencer*'s] electronic DGPS position." A quartermaster also testified to the use of an alidade that night. While not supported by all the evidence in the record—acknowledging that several crew member reports do lack specific reference to alidade use—NOAA's conclusion that Coast Guard crew properly correlated the 21:40 radar reading and visual sightings was supported by substantial evidence, given the testimony by crew members at the hearings. The ALJ's decision to credit the testimony from Coast Guard crew on this point, and not Frontier Fishing's expert's analysis, based on uncorroborated assertions, constituted a reasonable resolution of the record.

Substantial evidence also amply supports the finding that the presumed location of the 21:58 radar contact was simply an error. The 21:58 reading was taken after the chase was on, as [—15—] *Spencer* traveled at high speed in the direction of *Settler*. The quartermaster recorded the reading by hand, based on information relayed to him verbally by other crew members. The measurement's baseline margin of error was as much as 200 yards, although that was not enough, even doubled, to account for the discrepancy between the 21:58 location and the 22:00 estimated position. The ALJ, however, cited as well the fact that, once the 21:40 plot was confirmed as a vessel within the restricted area, the crew would have devoted attention to the law enforcement and safety considerations manifest in the visually observed rapid pursuit of that vessel. And, in affirming the ALJ's decision, NOAA pointed to the fact that the 21:58 bearings were "taken when the vessels were closing in on each other at high speed." In short, the record supports the conclusion that human error provided an additional reason, beyond random error, to distinguish the 21:58 readings from the 21:40 plot. So, too, once one concludes that the convincing and reinforcing radar and visual evidence placed *Settler* at the 21:40 plot and that it was unbelievable that *Settler* remained invisible to radar while another visually invisible vessel was detectable by radar in a peek-a-boo manner, it follows, as Sherlock Holmes might observe, that the 21:58 location must have been wrong for the reasons suggested. And given the undisputed fact that the vessel detected at 21:40 was inside the area, it matters not that the 21:58 reading of that same vessel was itself erroneous. [—16—]

We also recognize that Frontier Fishing, throughout its brief, makes a series of objections to NOAA's handling of this case. None of these objections leads inexorably to the conclusion that substantial evidence does not support the finding that *Settler* trawled illegally at 21:40. Frontier Fishing claims in essence that both ALJs and the Administrator all joined together with the Coast Guard in overzealous enforcement, in such a manner to render the NOAA's decisions unreliable. We have reviewed the record as a whole and find nothing that would support such a claim. The record here contained a complicated set of facts. That these extensive and complicated facts do not all neatly fit together does not thereby support a finding that NOAA proceeded in a manner that would allow its conclusions to be disregarded as biased. *See N.L.R.B. v. Hosp. San Pablo, Inc.*, 207 F.3d 67, 70 (1st Cir. 2000) (internal quotations and citation omitted)("[T]he possibility of drawing two inconsistent conclusions from the evidence does not prevent an administrative agency's finding from being supported by substantial evidence.")

In so concluding, we do not suggest that the case against Frontier Fishing was ironclad. The vessels' relative locations in relationship to the restricted area boundaries potentially rendered location by visual sighting insufficiently precise. And the point of interception was outside the area. Perhaps *Settler* was in the wrong (but legal) place at exactly the wrong time when unusual [—17—] radar conditions masked the visually obvious *Settler* even as the radar clearly and repeatedly detected an inexplicably unlit vessel moving nearby, but in the restricted area. Just as the district court did, we hold only that, in rejecting this interpretation of the evidence, NOAA acted neither irrationally nor without minimally sufficient support in the record to conclude that *Settler* was the vessel plotted in the restricted area at 21:40. In short, the record here does not "clearly preclude[] the [agency's] decision from being justified by a fair estimate of the worth of the testimony of witnesses or its informed judgment on matters within its special competence." *Penobscot*, 164 F.3d at 718 (quoting *Universal Camera Corp.*, 340 U.S. at 490) (internal quotation marks omitted).

IV. Conclusion

Substantial evidence supports NOAA's finding. Consequently, and for the reasons outlined above, we *affirm* the district court's decision upholding the NOAA Administrator's final decision. *So ordered.*

United States Court of Appeals
for the First Circuit

No. 14-1380

LYMAN MORSE BOATBUILDING, INC.
vs.
NORTHERN ASSURANCE CO. OF AM.

Appeal from the United States District Court for the
District of Maine

Decided: December 2, 2014

Citation: 772 F.3d 960, 2 Adm. R. 40 (1st Cir. 2014).

Before **LYNCH**, Chief Judge, **STAHL**, and **KAYATTA**, Circuit Judges.

[—2—] **LYNCH**, Chief Judge:

Lyman Morse Boatbuilding, Inc. (LMB) of Maine contracted to build a luxury yacht for Russ Irwin. Unhappy with the completed yacht, in 2011 Irwin brought an arbitration proceeding against LMB and Cabot Lyman, the controlling owner of LMB, alleging that the vessel had numerous defects. LMB and Cabot Lyman tendered defense of the arbitration complaint to their insurer, Northern Assurance Company of America, but Northern Assurance refused to defend the insureds. So the insureds filed this federal suit in 2012 seeking to recover the costs and attorneys' fees that they incurred in the arbitration proceeding.

The district court held that Northern Assurance had a duty to defend Cabot Lyman, the individual, but not LMB, the corporation; it then awarded to Cabot Lyman 50 percent of the attorneys' fees incurred during the arbitration by the two insureds together. Each side was unhappy and we are faced with appeals and cross-appeals. We conclude that on the pertinent facts Northern Assurance owed neither insured a defense under Maine law. Thus, we affirm in part, reverse in part, and remand for entry of judgment in favor of Northern Assurance.

I.

A. *The Arbitration Demand*

On July 22, 2011, Irwin filed an arbitration complaint against LMB and Cabot Lyman, claiming damages related to the allegedly defective construction of a 52-foot custom sailing [—3—] vessel.[1] Irwin alleged that LMB and Cabot Lyman had agreed to build the vessel "with the 'best practices for quality yacht construction' using the 'highest quality materials'" for a price of $2,155,000. However, there were cost overruns, and Irwin eventually ended up paying over $3,400,000 for the completed vessel. Moreover, upon LMB's delivery of the vessel to Irwin, Irwin allegedly discovered multiple defects, which necessitated a series of rejections and repairs. As of the date of filing of the arbitration complaint, the quality of the vessel was still unsatisfactory to Irwin.

That complaint alleged eight causes of action: intentional fraud, negligent misrepresentation, constructive fraud, breach of contract, rejection and revocation of acceptance under the Uniform Commercial Code, breach of the implied warranty of fitness for a particular purpose, breach of the implied warranty of merchantability, and violations of Maine's unfair trade practices laws. Irwin requested rescission of the agreement and a refund and damages for the time he spent and the expenses he incurred during the period when he repeatedly rejected the yacht because of its defects, as well as "the return . . . of the amounts overpaid to [LMB and Cabot Lyman] and the difference between the value of the [—4—] 'highest quality' version of the Vessel that [LMB and Cabot Lyman] represented that [Irwin] would receive and the actual version [Irwin] received." He also requested punitive damages, attorneys' fees and costs, interest, and "such other and further relief as the Court deems just and proper."

---

[1] The "Yacht Construction Contract" applicable to the transaction contains an arbitration clause providing that "[a]ny dispute arising from this agreement will be resolved via binding arbitration."

The arbitration complaint contained two paragraphs naming Cabot Lyman. First, Irwin alleged that Cabot Lyman, the controlling owner of LMB, was the alter ego of the corporation, and alleged that "[a] unity of interest exists between [Cabot] Lyman and [LMB] and injustice and fraud can only be avoided by piercing the corporate veil" and holding Cabot Lyman jointly and severally liable for the wrongs alleged.

Second, in the course of alleging violations of Maine's unfair trade practices laws, the complaint stated that LMB and Cabot Lyman

made further repeated representations and promises to [Irwin] about "best practices" and "highest quality" construction that they guaranteed for the completion of the Vessel . . .; for example, [Cabot] Lyman expressly represented to [Irwin] that he had extensive experience sailing worldwide including in the Caribbean and he was aware of the most common problems [Irwin] would encounter during his travels in tropical and other varying conditions . . .; as such he assured the Vessel would be completed to withstand these issues.

After the insurer refused their request for defense, LMB hired a law firm, Thompson & Bowie, LLP, to represent both it and [—5—] Cabot Lyman in the arbitration. That firm then filed this lawsuit on behalf of the insureds, seeking to recover from Northern Assurance the costs and attorneys' fees incurred in the arbitration.[2] LMB and Cabot Lyman also brought a claim for unfair claims settlement practices, contending that Northern Assurance had not made a coverage decision in a timely manner.

B. *The CGL Insurance Policy*

On January 4, 2008, Northern Assurance had issued a package insurance policy to LMB and Cabot Lyman. The named insureds listed in the Declarations of the policy are "Lyman Morse Boatbuilding Co., Inc." and "Cabot & Heidi Lyman ATIMA." "ATIMA" stands for "as their interests may appear." Section III of the package policy provides the insureds with Commercial General Liability (CGL) insurance. It states in relevant part as follows:

Throughout this policy the words "you" and "your" refer to the Named Insured shown in the Declarations, and any other person or organization qualifying as a Named Insured under this policy. . . .

. . . .

a. We will pay those sums that the Insured becomes legally obligated to pay as damages because of "bodily injury" or "property damage" to which this insurance applies. We will have the right and duty to defend the Insured against any "suit" seeking those damages. However, we will have no duty to defend the insured against [—6—] any "suit" seeking damages for "bodily injury" or "property damage" to which this insurance does not apply. . . .

b. This insurance applies to "bodily injury" and "property damage" only if:
(1) The "bodily injury" or "property damage" is caused by an "occurrence" . . . .

"Property damage" is defined as "[p]hysical injury to tangible property, including all resulting loss of use of that property" or "[l]oss of use of tangible property that is not physically injured." "Occurrence" is defined as "an accident, including continuous or repeated exposure to substantially the same general harmful conditions." "'Suit' means a civil proceeding in which damages because of . . . 'property damage' . . . to which this insurance applies are alleged," and includes "[a]n arbitration proceeding in which such damages are claimed and to which the Insured must submit."

---

[2] The district court found that LMB paid or reimbursed all of Cabot Lyman's attorneys' fees.

Importantly, the policy excludes from coverage "'[p]roperty damage' to 'your product' arising out of it or any part of it." This exclusion, common to CGL policies, is generally called the "your product" exclusion. "Your product," in turn,

a. Means:
  (1) Any goods or products, other than real property, manufactured, sold, handled, distributed or disposed of by:
    (a) You;
    (b) Others trading under your name; or [—7—]
    (c) A person or organization whose business or assets you have acquired; and
  (2) Containers (other than vehicles), materials, parts or equipment furnished in connection with such goods or products.

b. Includes
  (1) Warranties or representations made at any time with respect to the fitness, quality, durability, performance or use of "your product"; and
  (2) The providing of or failure to provide warnings or instructions.

C. *The Proceedings in the District Court*

On cross-motions for summary judgment, the district court held that Northern Assurance had no duty to defend LMB, but that it did have an obligation to defend Cabot Lyman in the arbitration proceeding. *Lyman Morse Boatbuilding, Inc. v. N. Assurance Co. of Am., Inc.*, No. 2:12-cv-313-DBH, 2013 WL 5435204, at *1 (D. Me. Sept. 27, 2013) [hereinafter *Lyman I*]. The court held that the "your product" exclusion excused Northern Assurance from any duty to defend LMB because the only "property damage" alleged by the arbitration demand was to the yacht built by LMB. *Id.* at *4. "There is no suggestion" in the arbitration demand, the court explained, "that somehow the yacht's defects damaged *other* property." *Id.*

However, the court determined that Northern Assurance did have a duty to defend Cabot Lyman, the individual, notwithstanding [—8—] the "your product" exclusion, because "[t]he yacht was the boatyard's product, not Cabot Lyman's product." *Id.* at *5.[3]

In a separate order on the issue of damages, the district court held that Cabot Lyman was entitled to recover 50 percent of the attorneys' fees that LMB and Cabot Lyman jointly incurred in defending the arbitration proceeding. *Lyman Morse Boatbuilding, Inc. v. N. Assurance Co. of Am., Inc.*, No. 2:12-cv-313-DBH, 2014 WL 901445, at *1, *4 (D. Me. Mar. 6, 2014) [hereinafter *Lyman II*]. Reasoning that "[b]oth the corporation and the individual needed a defense, [and that] the nature of their defenses overlapped substantially, albeit not entirely," the court concluded that an equal division of fees between the corporation and the individual was appropriate. *Id.* at *3-4.

D. *This Appeal*

Northern Assurance has appealed, arguing that it did not owe a duty to defend Cabot Lyman in the arbitration proceeding, and LMB and Cabot Lyman have cross-appealed, arguing that Northern Assurance did owe a duty to defend LMB. Both parties contend that the district court's ruling on the duty to defend and the damages issue was error. [—9—]

II.

"The district court's conclusion on the duty to defend is reviewed de novo." *Metro. Prop. & Cas. Ins. Co. v. McCarthy*, 754 F.3d 47, 49 (1st Cir. 2014) (citing *Bucci v. Essex Ins. Co.*, 393 F.3d 285, 290 (1st Cir. 2005)); *see also Mitchell v. Allstate Ins. Co.*, 36 A.3d 876, 879 (Me. 2011) (analysis of insurer's duty to defend

---

[3] The court also held that Irwin's claims for economic loss were not covered by the policy, *see Lyman I*, 2013 WL 5435204, at *2, *4 & n.10, and that Northern Assurance was entitled to summary judgment on the insureds' claim of unfair claims settlement practices, *see id.* at *5-6. Those rulings are not at issue on appeal.

under Maine law is a pure question of law reviewed de novo).

The parties agree that Maine law applies to this dispute. To determine whether an insurer owes its insured a duty to defend, Maine courts apply the "comparison test," which involves a "comparison of the allegations in the underlying complaint with the provisions of the insurance policy" to determine if the claims alleged are within the coverage of the policy. *Mitchell*, 36 A.3d at 879. "[A]n insurer must provide a defense if there is any *potential* that facts ultimately proved could result in coverage." *Id.*; *accord Howe v. MMG Ins. Co.*, 95 A.3d 79, 81 (Me. 2014) (quoting *Cox v. Commonwealth Land Title Ins. Co.*, 59 A.3d 1280, 1283 (Me. 2013)). "Because the duty to defend is broad, any ambiguity in the policy regarding the insurer's duty to defend is resolved against the insurer, and policy exclusions are construed strictly against the insurer." *Mitchell*, 36 A.3d at 879 (citations omitted). At the same time, courts may "not speculate about causes of action that were not stated" in the complaint. *York Golf & Tennis Club v. Tudor Ins. Co.*, 845 A.2d 1173, 1175 (Me. 2004). **[—10—]**

We first address whether Northern Assurance had a duty to defend LMB in the arbitration proceeding. LMB concedes that "the 'your product' exclusion serves to exclude coverage for any property sold, handled, distributed or disposed of by" LMB, which includes the allegedly defective yacht. But, LMB argues, Northern Assurance nonetheless owed a duty to defend it in the arbitration proceeding because "the allegations in the Arbitration Complaint provide a basis for Russ Irwin to prove damage to his own or others' personal property, which would fall within the ambit of coverage under the Policy as unexcluded 'property damage.'"

This argument fails. As the district court correctly observed,

> [Irwin's] Arbitration Demand is strident, but simple. It complains about the failure to build the yacht as promised, as well as overbilling. . . . [T]he claims for economic damage . . . . all have to do

with what the buyer paid, the difference in value between the yacht as promised and actually delivered, and the value of the buyer's time, expense and burdens in dealing with the boatyard while trying to obtain satisfaction. There is no suggestion that somehow the yacht's defects damaged *other* property. There is no suggestion, for example, that the buyer put cushions and equipment on the yacht that were damaged on account of defects.

Lyman I, 2013 WL 5435204, at *4. Thus the complaint did not allege any facts that even suggest the potential for a covered claim.

Plaintiffs resist this conclusion, pointing out that, in the course of alleging constructive fraud, Irwin alleged that LMB **[—11—]** and Cabot Lyman "breached the trust and confidence which [Irwin] entrusted with them in the failed construction and completion of the Vessel and in putting [Irwin]'s life, limb and property and those of his family and loved ones at risk on the oceans and at sea." But this passing reference to a "risk" to property is not sufficient to trigger a duty to defend under Maine law.

In *Baywood Corp. v. Maine Bonding & Casualty Co.*, 628 A.2d 1029 (Me. 1993), the Maine Law Court found that a complaint alleging that the insured inadequately designed a sewer system for a condominium complex did not fall within the coverage of a CGL policy because it sought only "the cost to replace or upgrade the [sewer] system." *Id.* at 1031. Although "the complaint refer[red] generally to property damage," the Law Court explained, it "allege[d] no physical damage to the [condominium] units." *Id.* Thus, the insurer had no duty to defend. *Id.*

So it is here. While referring generally to a "risk" to personal property, Irwin's arbitration complaint did not allege any damage to such property or request any relief for personal property damage. Instead, the complaint requested several specific items of relief related to the damage sustained by the defective vessel itself and the expense that Irwin went to in discovering and attempting to rectify its defects. "[B]ecause [Irwin's] complaint d[id] not allege actual damage to property but rather s[ought] damages for replacing defective workmanship, which is a business [—12—] risk specifically excluded from the policy, [Northern Assurance] ha[d] no obligation to defend the underlying action." *Id.*

Plaintiffs erroneously argue that because the arbitration complaint did not *foreclose* the possibility that Irwin's personal property was damaged, LMB was entitled to a defense. That is not a correct statement of the law. If plaintiffs' articulation of the duty to defend were correct, that would make the duty virtually limitless.[4] More specifically, it would run afoul of the Maine Law Court's admonition that courts adjudicating the duty to defend may "not speculate about causes of action that were not stated" in the complaint. *York Golf & Tennis Club*, 845 A.2d at 1175.

The cases upon which plaintiffs rely do not in fact support plaintiffs' overly broad articulation of the duty to defend. They are readily distinguishable from this case. In *Auto Europe, LLC v. Connecticut Indemnity Co.*, 321 F.3d 60 (1st Cir. 2003), the underlying complaint alleged that Auto Europe had fraudulently overcharged its customers in violation of the Maine Unfair Trade Practices Act (UTPA). *Id.* at 63, 66-67. The court held that Auto Europe was entitled to a defense from its insurance company notwithstanding a policy exclusion for "willfully dishonest [—13—] or fraudulent acts" because the Maine UTPA "permit[ted] liability in the absence of an intent to deceive," so "it [was] possible . . . that the facts as developed at trial would reveal an improper practice that was unaccompanied by an intent to deceive." *Id.* at 67-68. Similarly, in *Mitchell*, the Maine Law Court held that Mitchell was entitled to a

defense against a complaint that alleged that he converted lobster fishing equipment, notwithstanding a policy exclusion for intentional acts, because the complainant, Ames, could have established that Mitchell committed conversion by "accidentally interfer[ing] with Ames's rights." 36 A.3d at 880-81. Finally, in *Howe*, the Law Court held that the insurer had a duty to defend a nuisance and negligence lawsuit arising out of the conduct of the insured condominium owner's dog because the complaint alleged that the dog had "bitten people" and that other "unit owners ha[d] been assaulted" by the dog, and thus alleged "bodily injury" potentially covered by the insurance policy. *See* 95 A.3d at 81.[5] Thus, in *Auto Europe*, *Mitchell*, and *Howe*, the court found a duty to defend because there [—14—] was a theory of liability under a cause of action *actually pleaded* that would have afforded insurance coverage. Here, in contrast, Irwin's complaint—while specifying in considerable detail the relief sought—made no claim whatsoever for damage to personal property. The district court correctly found that Northern Assurance had no duty to defend LMB.

We conclude otherwise as to the court's ruling that Northern Assurance did have a duty to defend Cabot Lyman in the arbitration proceeding because the "your product" exclusion did not apply to him. We find that the exclusion does apply to Cabot Lyman and thus hold that Northern Assurance had no duty to defend him in the arbitration proceeding.

---

[4] The same goes for plaintiffs' contention at oral argument that Northern Assurance owed a duty to defend based on the complaint's request "[f]or such other and further relief as the Court deems just and proper." If an insurer were required to defend simply because a complaint includes a catchall request for all "just and proper" relief, the duty to defend would be triggered in virtually every case, contrary to the contours of Maine law.

[5] Counsel for LMB stated at oral argument that, in *Howe*, the Law Court determined that "there was a duty to defend because it [was] possible, though never alleged in the complaint, that the dog could have done property damage to [condominium] Association property." This was an argument that Howe's counsel made in her brief, *see Howe*, 95 A.3d at 81, but the court did not explicitly accept (or reject) it. The court explicitly found a duty to defend because the complaint "outline[d] a claim of *bodily injury* for which Howe might be answerable to the [condominium] Association, depending on the facts developed as the case proceeds." *Id.* (emphasis added).

In interpreting this insurance contract, our task is to "'effect the parties' intentions . . . construed with regard for the subject matter, motive, and purpose of the agreement, as well as the object to be accomplished.'" *State v. Murphy*, 861 A.2d 657, 661 (Me. 2004) (alteration in original) (quoting *Handy Boat Serv., Inc. v. Prof'l Servs., Inc.*, 711 A.2d 1306, 1308 (Me. 1998)). We must examine the entire agreement, giving the language its plain meaning. *Id.* (citing *Am. Prot. Ins. Co. v. Acadia Ins. Co.*, 814 A.2d 989, 993-94 (Me. 2003)).

The insurance policy defines "your product" as "goods or products . . . manufactured, sold, handled, distributed or disposed of by . . . [y]ou." The term "[i]ncludes . . . [w]arranties or [—15—] representations made at any time with respect to the fitness, quality, durability, performance or use of 'your product.'" "[T]he words 'you' and 'your' refer to the Named Insured" listed on the policy, and those Named Insureds are LMB, Cabot Lyman, and Heidi Lyman. Thus, the "your product" exclusion, by its plain terms, applies to the products of LMB, Cabot Lyman, or Heidi Lyman, and to damages arising out of warranties or representations made "with respect to the fitness, quality, durability, performance or use" of such products. *Cf. Am. First Credit Union v. Kier Constr. Corp.*, 314 P.3d 1055, 1059 (Utah Ct. App. 2013) (holding that "your product" exclusion in CGL policy on which Broberg was the named insured was properly read to "exclude[] coverage for '[p]roperty damage to [Broberg's] product arising out of it or any part of it'" (second and third alterations in original) (internal quotation marks omitted)). The term "your product" includes the yacht (because it is LMB's product) and the allegedly fraudulent misrepresentations made by Cabot Lyman as president and officer of LMB (because they concerned the quality of the yacht).

Northern Assurance argues that the "your product" exclusion is "not insured-specific"— the operation of the exclusion does not depend on the identity of the insured against whom the suit is brought. It adds that this must at least be true here, where the other insured, as a corporate officer, has allegedly acted as an

alter ego of the corporation that designed [—16—] the product, and the policy explicitly precludes coverage for representations made with respect to the quality of the corporate insured's products.[6] The provision does not exclude property damage to "the insured's product"; it excludes property damage to "your product," a term that, on these facts, includes the yacht even with respect to the suit against Cabot Lyman.

Cabot Lyman and LMB cite no case or policy language that refutes that interpretation of the insurance contract on the facts here. Instead, they rely on the rule that ambiguities in insurance contracts should be resolved against the insurer. That rule is inapplicable. The "your product" exclusion is not ambiguous in its application here. Irwin's complaint alleged damages to the yacht; the policy excludes damages to "your product"; "you" is defined as, *inter alia*, LMB; the yacht is LMB's product; thus, the policy unambiguously excludes the allegations of the complaint. Accordingly, on these facts, we find that Northern Assurance had no duty to defend Cabot Lyman in the arbitration proceeding.

To hold otherwise would undercut the well-recognized purpose of CGL insurance policies, as articulated by the Maine Law Court. CGL policies are designed to cover "occurrence of harm [—17—] risks" but not "business risks." *Peerless Ins. Co. v. Brennon*, 564 A.2d 383, 386 (Me. 1989). As the Law Court explained,

[a]n "occurrence of harm risk" is a risk that a person or property other than the product itself will be damaged through the fault of the [insured]. A "business risk" is a risk that the [insured] will not do his job competently, and thus will be obligated to replace or repair his faulty work. The distinction between the two risks is critical to understanding a CGL policy. A CGL policy covers an

---

[6] We need not address whether the "your product" exclusion would preclude coverage for a claim against an individual officer that is not explicitly included in the policy's definition of "your product."

occurrence of harm risk but specifically excludes a business risk.

Id. (quoting Note, *Baybutt Construction Corp. v. Commercial Union Insurance Co.: A Question of Ambiguity in Comprehensive General Liability Insurance Policies*, 36 Me. L. Rev. 179, 182 (1984)). The type of harm alleged in Irwin's complaint is, by contrast, a "business risk" that is excluded under the terms of the CGL policy Northern Assurance issued to LMB and Cabot Lyman. There is no principled reason why that result would change because Irwin named Cabot Lyman as a defendant on an alter ego theory and for representations he made as a director and president of LMB about a yacht manufactured by LMB. As was recognized in *Cle Elum Bowl, Inc. v. N. Pac. Ins. Co.*, 981 P.2d 872 (Wash. Ct. App. 1999), "an insured director and officer . . . is subject to the same exclusions that deny coverage to the corporation." *Id.* at 877.

We note that a contrary holding would also create perverse incentives when plaintiffs sue a corporation for defective workmanship. If these plaintiffs could trigger a duty to defend on [—18—] the part of the corporation's CGL insurer not otherwise obligated to provide a defense by simply adding a corporate officer or employee as a defendant, they would often have the incentive to do so in order to add another pocket to the other side of the negotiating table. As a consequence, the "your product" exclusion, long a staple of CGL policies, would be rendered a dead letter. We decline to read the policy to allow such a result, absent any evidence, of which there is none, that this was the parties' intent.

III.

We hold that Northern Assurance did not owe a duty to defend LMB or Cabot Lyman in the underlying arbitration proceeding. The decision of the district court is affirmed in part and reversed in part. We remand for entry of judgment in favor of Northern Assurance. Costs are awarded to Northern Assurance Company of America.

United States Court of Appeals for the Second Circuit

United States Court of Appeals
for the Second Circuit

No. 13-0254

BARLOW

vs.

LIBERTY MARITIME CORP.

Appeal from the United States District Court for the
Eastern District of New York

Decided: March 4, 2014

Citation: 746 F.3d 518, 2 Adm. R. 48 (2d Cir. 2014).

Before **POOLER**, **RAGGI**, and **WESLEY**, Circuit Judges.

[—2—] **WESLEY**, Circuit Judge:

George Barlow started going to sea as a deck hand in 1974. He was twenty-three. In 1986, after working aboard ships for more than a decade, and without ever having attended college, he passed the merchant marine officer's exam, licensing him to serve as an officer aboard U.S. flagged cargo vessels. In 1992 he received his master's license, the merchant marine equivalent of a captain's qualification. Now retired, Barlow never actually took command of a ship, but did spend his whole career at sea aboard various vessels. In March [—3—] 2007, Barlow took a job as third mate on the last of these vessels, the Motor Vessel Liberty Sun, a 33,000-ton, 738-foot-long cargo ship.

Two months after Barlow took the job, the Liberty Sun steamed up the Amazon River to the Hermasa floating grain elevator in the port of Itacoatiara, Brazil. Feeder barges bring grain, or in this case soy beans, from shore to the [—4—] terminal to be loaded onto larger seagoing vessels like the Liberty Sun, which moor in the river alongside the terminal.[1] [—5—]

---

[1] As we shall see, this case involves a number of technical nautical terms. We offer a few definitions below to help our lubberly readers.

To "moor" a ship, is to "attach a vessel to a buoy, or buoys" or to "secure a vessel by attaching ropes to positions ashore." C. W. T. Layton, Dictionary of Nautical Terms and Words 229 (Peter Clissold ed. 4th ed. 1994). Aboard ships, ropes or metal cables used for mooring (or any other purpose) are called

On May 21, 2007 the Liberty Sun tied-up alongside Hermasa. To control her fore and aft movement, the Liberty Sun had three lines forward secured to mooring buoys, two lines aft to mooring buoys, and one line off the port quarter,[2] also to a mooring buoy. She also had two starboard breast lines—lines perpendicular to the ship that control distance from the pier—that were married[3] to lines from the shore. Additionally, there was one tug boat on the starboard bow at all times to fend the ship off the terminal.[4] [—6—]

"lines." *See id.* at 205. A mooring buoy is a buoy "carrying a large ring or shackle, securely moored so that a vessel can be attached to it and ride in safety." *Id.* at 232. To "tie up" a ship is to secure it to a pier or mooring. It is synonymous with "to moor." *See* American Association of Port Authorities, Glossary of Maritime Terms (2013) *available at* http://www.aapa-ports.org/Industry/content.cfm?ItemNumber=1077 (defining "to dock" as "To bring in a vessel *to tie up* at a wharf berth.") (emphasis added).

"Fore" and "aft" are terms for forwards and backwards. Layton *supra* at 145, 10. Aft, can also refer to the rear portion of the ship, *id.* at 10, and "bow" is the forward portion of the hull. *Id.* at 55.

A line "pays out" when it runs out or spools out. *Id.* at 252. For example, if one ship is towing another, the towing ship can increase the distance between the ships by "paying out" additional line. A line can also pay out rapidly or uncontrollably, if, as here, it is under tension and the tension is suddenly released. [—5—]

Upon entering port, ships are often secured using multiple lines to more finely control their movement. For example, in tying a ship to a pier, lines that run perpendicular to the ship and the pier ("breast lines"), *id.* at 58, will control the ship's distance from the pier, but may not adequately control its fore and aft movements. Additional lines, that run diagonally, from an aft portion of the ship to a part of the pier further forward, or from a forward part of the ship, aft, may also be used. These are called "spring lines." *Id.* at 328. In this case, the Liberty Sun had breast lines to control her distance from the grain terminal, and various lines from the bow and stern to prevent her from moving forwards and backwards.

[2] The port quarter is the rear left portion of the ship. Arthur Young, Nautical Dictionary 298 (2d ed. 1863).

[3] To marry two lines is "[t]o join [them] together . . . ." Young, *supra* at 253.

[4] Tug boats, or simply "tugs," are used in ports to help put a ship in position for mooring. *See* Layton, *supra* at 369. In this case, the tug was in

Three days after mooring, at about 5:15 AM, the forward breast line parted. There was no wind or wave action at the time. The only forces acting on the ship were the four-knot current moving from bow to stern[5] and the forward tug. The tug was pushing away from the shore, exactly opposite to the now-parted breast line.[6]

The second mate, Timothy Schloemer, was the watch officer when the line parted. He immediately notified Captain Donald Grosse who instructed Schloemer to assemble the crew and re-attach the line. The Captain also ordered the Chief Engineer to start the engines. Meanwhile, the remaining lines came under additional strain and approximately five minutes after the breast line parted, the starboard bow line parted.

Schloemer noted that the remaining forward lines were also in danger of snapping. He described them as "running against brake[s]." We understand him to mean that the winches used to control the lines were turning as a result of [—7—] the increased tension and that the lines were paying out slowly in spite of the fact that the winch brakes were engaged. Schloemer ordered the boatswain to slacken the lines. In the meantime, the rest of the crew began to assemble.

Barlow was the last crew member to arrive on the scene. He was outranked by Schloemer. Nonetheless, Barlow tried to take charge. First, he argued with Schloemer about how best to slacken the line. Schloemer told him that others were dealing with the problem and ordered him to do nothing.[7] Barlow initially

tried to get the captain to intervene, but was unable to reach him on the ship's internal telephone system. He then sought to take matters into his own hands, and proceeded to one of the winches that controlled the forward mooring lines.

The standard method for operating a winch is to first start the motor, and next put it in gear. *Only then* does one release the brake, and either pay out or take in line *using the motor* to control the rate at which the line pays out. Barlow [—8—] decided to use his own method of operation, which he calls "bumping the brake." Barlow "bumped" the brake handle to loosen the brake's grip on the winch, without first engaging the motor. He hoped that, freed from the brake's grip, the line would slacken and that he would then be able to re-engage the brake. In Barlow's mind, "bumping the brake" was quicker than the standard operation of the winch, and would save him from greater danger by making it unnecessary to reach under the winch—near the dangerously taut line—to engage the motor.

Alas, even the best-laid plans of mariners go awry. After Barlow bumped the brake, the line paid out uncontrollably. As it did, it whipped around the winch and hit him. After the injury, Barlow remained aboard the Liberty Sun for a week, receiving treatment locally. His wound soon became infected, however, and he returned to the United States in great pain.

In November 2008, Barlow commenced this action in the United States District Court for the Eastern District of New York, against his employer, the Liberty Sun *in rem*, and the various entities associated with its ownership, management, and operation, *in personam*. Barlow asserts claims for damages [—9—] under a negligence theory and an admiralty cause of action against the owners of "unseaworthy" vessels.

---

place to provide an occasional push to the Liberty Sun if she came too close to the grain terminal.

[5] Front to back. Layton, *supra* at 335.

[6] The breast line was pulling the ship in towards the shore and the tug was pushing away from it. Ideally, the two forces would have counter acted each other to keep the Liberty Sun in place. A diagram from the record best captures the ship's mooring configuration. It is included at the end of this opinion.

[7] Barlow does not dispute that he was told to stand down, but characterizes Schloemer's words to him as a "polite request" rather than an order. Pl. Br. at 23. Directions from an officer to a

---

subordinate in an emergency are not requests, but orders to be obeyed, however phrased. *See* 46 U.S.C. § 11501(5) (permitting ship masters to confine disobedient sailors within the ship and place them on a diet of 1,000 calories per day "until the disobedience ends").

Before trial, and in response to Liberty's contention that Barlow's actions contributed to his own injuries, Barlow submitted proposed jury instructions adopting the Fourth Circuit's "maritime rescue doctrine." Barlow argued that the maritime rescue doctrine applied because he was acting under emergency circumstances and in bumping the brake he was attempting to rescue the ship and crew from the dangers of parting lines. Under Barlow's proposed instruction, the jury would have been required to find that his conduct was "wanton and reckless" before apportioning him any fault for his injuries. The district court rejected this proposal and instead gave an "emergency" instruction. The court instructed the jury to consider the fact that Barlow was in a position where he must act quickly without opportunity for reflection, and that it should [—10—] hold him to the standard of a "reasonably prudent [seaman] . . . faced with the same emergency." Dist. Ct. Op. at 7 n. 3.[8]

---

[8] In full, the court instructed the jury:

A person faced with an emergency and who acts without opportunity to consider the alternatives is not negligent if he acts as a reasonably prudent person would act in the same emergency, even if it later appears that he did not make the safest choice or exercise the best judgment. A mistake in judgment or wrong choice of action is not negligence if the person is required to act quickly because of danger. This rule applies where a person is faced with a sudden condition which could not have been reasonably anticipated, provided that the person did not cause or contribute to the emergency by his own negligence.

If you find that the plaintiff was faced with an emergency and that his response to the emergency was that of a reasonably prudent seaman, then you will conclude that the plaintiff was not negligent. If, however, you find that the situation facing the plaintiff was not sudden or should reasonably have been foreseen, or was created or contributed to by the plaintiff's own negligence, or that the plaintiff's conduct in response to the emergency was not that of a reasonable seamen, then you may find that the plaintiff was negligent.

Dist. Ct. Op. at 7 n.3.

With respect to his seaworthiness claim, Barlow also sought an instruction clarifying that the mooring lines were part of the ship. The court rejected this [—11—] instruction, because Barlow made this request for the first time mid-trial at the pre-charging conference. The court further found his request unnecessary and concluded that the "jury would reasonably understand from the extensive testimony in the case regarding the ship's use and operation of the mooring lines that they were part of the 'equipment' referenced in the charge." Dist. Ct. Op. at 18.

Following trial in November 2011, the jury returned a verdict for Defendants on Barlow's unseaworthiness claim and, on the negligence claim, apportioned ten percent of the fault to Defendants and ninety percent to Barlow. The jury totaled damages at $446,000.

Following trial, Barlow timely moved for judgment as a matter of law under Federal Rule of Civil Procedure 50(b) as to his unseaworthiness claim; in the alternative he moved for a new trial under Federal Rule of Civil Procedure 59(a), again requesting his proposed jury instructions. The district court denied these motions by memorandum order on December 26, 2012. Barlow now appeals. [—12—]

Discussion

A. The Negligence Claim

1. The Jury Instruction

This case presents us anew with a question that is nearly as old as tort law itself: How does one judge the conduct of a man in physical peril? Barlow asserts that acts of those in danger should be measured in light of the danger and not in spite of it. The exigencies of circumstance may prompt even the coolest heads to miscalculate and do otherwise than they would in calmer moments. In this much, Barlow is correct. Yet, this much does not tell us how to instruct a jury.

Litigants are entitled to a jury instruction on any theory of liability supported by law and the evidence.[9] Here we must choose between two possible standards of care for maritime torts. Under the maritime rescue doctrine, a would-be rescuer, faced with an emergency, can only be held contributorily liable for injuries resulting from his rescue attempt, if his conduct was reckless [—13—] and wanton. Under the district court's jury charge, a rescuer may be held liable for actions that were merely unreasonable under the circumstances. We adopt the latter.

In the Nineteenth and early Twentieth Centuries, American courts generally assumed that

> liability for risk-creating conduct should not attach unless the person creating the risk had been "at fault." "Fault" was used as a label by which "blameworthy" conduct was admonished; the party "at fault" was forced to pay for injuries he had caused. It followed from this conception of civil responsibility that a person who was himself "at fault" should not be able to recover for his injuries, even if the risk of those injuries had been created by another blameworthy person.

G. Edward White, Tort Law in America: An Intellectual History 164 (2d ed. 2003). We have come to know this as the doctrine of contributory negligence: "In cases where both parties were blameworthy, [courts] let losses lie where they fell." *Id.*

But the doctrine of contributory negligence was a harsh one. An injured plaintiff was unable to recover—and the defendant went unpunished—even if the plaintiff's actions were much less blameworthy than those of the defendant. To mitigate the harshness of this rule, courts developed devices to avoid its application. *See Dole v. Dow Chem. Co.*, 30 N.Y.2d 143, 147-48, 153 (1972); *see also* N.Y. CPLR § 1411. [—14—]

---

[9] We review the district court's instructions *de novo* and will order a new trial if the instruction "[misled] the jury as to the correct legal standard or [did] not adequately inform the jury on the law." *Boyce v. Soundview Tech. Grp., Inc.,* 464 F.3d 376, 390 (2d Cir. 2006) (internal quotations omitted).

One was the so-called "rescue doctrine." Persons faced with emergencies must act quickly and are prone to mistakes that a jury, with the benefit of hindsight, might consider negligent. Although courts applying the doctrine of contributory negligence may have been willing to deny recovery to a person whose negligence precipitated an emergency, they hesitated before applying it to someone who voluntarily exposed himself to danger in order to rescue others from it. To protect would-be rescuers, courts created the rescue doctrine. Under the doctrine, defendants asserting the defense of contributory fault were required to show that a rescuer acted not just negligently, but recklessly, thus providing additional leeway to claims of rescuers. *See, e.g.,* N.Y. Pattern Jury Instr. Civil 2:41.

In the maritime context, the rescue doctrine is articulated most clearly by the Fourth Circuit in *Furka v. Great Lakes Dredge & Dock Co., Inc.,* 755 F.2d 1085, 1088 (4th Cir. 1985) (*Furka I*) and *Furka v. Great Lakes Dredge & Dock Co.,* 824 F.2d 330, 332 (4th Cir. 1987) (*Furka II*). In the *Furka* cases, a tug owned by the Great Lakes Dredge & Dock Company was engaged in dredging operations on a rough January day on the Chesapeake Bay. The tug radioed for help. The evidence conflicted, however, about whether the call for help indicated that human lives [—15—] were in peril or that the tug was merely having mechanical difficulties. Regardless, Paul Furka, one of Great Lake's employees, quickly responded to the distress call in a small power boat. When he arrived at the tug, the tug's captain refused to return to shore with him; Furka turned back. On the return journey, however, Furka's boat took on water and he drowned. His widow then brought suit. *Furka I*, 755 F.2 at 1087.

At trial the defendant argued that Furka was contributorily negligent both in assessing the need for a rescue and in executing it. In *Furka I*, the Fourth Circuit, sitting in admiralty, applied the rescue doctrine. It held that Furka could not be found contributorily liable unless his rescue attempt was wanton or reckless. *Furka I,* 755 F.2d at 1088. The court reasoned that of all branches of jurisprudence, the admiralty must be the one most hospitable to the impulses of man and law to save life and limb and property. The best traditions of seafaring men demand that we honor attempts to rescue, unless the rescuer acts beyond the bounds that even the exigencies of the moment would allow. The wanton and reckless standard reflects the value society places upon rescue as much as any desire to avoid a total defeat of recovery under common law. Law must encourage an environment where human instinct is not insular but responds to the plight of another in peril.

Id. at 1089 (internal citations and quotations omitted). After a new trial and a second appeal, the Fourth Circuit held that this standard also applied to a rescuer's assessment of whether the rescue was required. *Furka II*, 824 F.2d at [—16—] 332. The Ninth Circuit has explicitly followed *Furka* and the Fifth Circuit has adopted a similar rule. *Wharf v. Burlington N. R.R. Co.*, 60 F.3d 631, 635 (9th Cir. 1995); *Grigsby v. Coastal Marine Serv. of Tex., Inc.*, 412 F.2d 1011, 1021 (5th Cir. 1969).

Barlow would have us, too, adopt *Furka*. As an initial matter, we agree with Barlow that, if *Furka* were the law in this Circuit, it would have been appropriate to give an instruction on its rescue doctrine. Under the *Furka* doctrine, Barlow need not show that there was an emergency that required a rescue, he need only show that he actually believed a rescue was needed and that this belief was not reckless.

Every witness who testified on the matter said that a line under tension has the potential to snap back and kill anyone in its path. Here, a jury could conclude from Barlow and Schloemer's testimony that the lines were about to part. The Captain himself said that the sailors on the forecastle were "at risk" and that this was an "emergency situation." Although some evidence indicates that the danger was subsiding by the time Barlow acted, Barlow's belief that immediate action

was required cannot be ruled "reckless" as a matter of law. [—17—] Accordingly, we find ourselves squarely presented with the question of whether to follow *Furka*.

As noted above, the rescue doctrine originated at a time when contributory negligence was an absolute bar to recovery. *Furka I*, 755 F.2d at 1088-89. But maritime law has long used comparative fault in resolving competing claims of negligence between the injured and the tortfeasor,[10] and today a majority of the states do the same.[11] Under comparative negligence, of course, even a negligent rescuer can recover, as Barlow did here. Consequently, the principle justification for the rescue doctrine—encouraging rescue—has largely disappeared. Under the reasonable person standard and comparative negligence, rescuers can be confident that even if they misstep, the emergency will be taken into account, and even if, under that circumstance, a jury finds their actions unreasonable, they will not necessarily be denied any recovery. Not surprisingly, then, the majority [—18—] rule in comparative negligence jurisdictions is that rescuers must act reasonably under emergency circumstances. 57B Am. Jur. 2d Negligence § 1015.[12]

We find no authority within our case law to support the application of the maritime rescue doctrine and our few holdings in this area apply the reasonable person standard. *Pedersen v. United States*, 224 F.2d 212, 215 (2d Cir. 1955) presents one example. There, plaintiff was on an oil barge attached to defendant's ship. Plaintiff saw that one of the breast lines that connected the barge to the ship was chaffing on the block. Since fuel and steam lines also ran between the ship and

---

[10] *Socony-Vacuum Oil Co. v. Smith*, 305 U.S. 424, 431-32 (1939). The abrogation of the contributory negligence defense in admiralty has a venerable pedigree. As early as the Seventeenth Century, in cases of collisions at sea, where both parties were at fault, damages were divided evenly. *See The North Star*, 106 U.S. 17, 20-22 (1882).

[11] 1 Comparative Negligence Manual § 1:1 (3d ed.).

[12] New York, for example, has adopted this rule. *See Rodriguez v. New York State Thruway Auth.*, 82 A.D.2d 853 (2d Dep't 1981).

barge, a parting of the line and separation of the vessels could have been dangerous. Plaintiff shouted to the ship for help, but to no result. He then managed to grab hold of a Jacob's ladder[13] that was hanging from the ship about eight feet above the barge deck. After plaintiff had proceeded up several rungs of the ladder, the ladder came loose from the ship and plaintiff fell. The district court held that plaintiff was contributorily negligent for failing to test the ladder before putting his weight on it. On appeal, [—19—] we applied a regular negligence standard and explained, much like the district court here, that the "emergency and possibility of harm to others were factors to be considered" in the analysis. *Id.* at 215; *see also The Cape Race*, 18 F.2d 79 (2d Cir. 1927) (applying a regular negligence standard in a maritime salvage case).

Barlow, nonetheless, argues that we adopted an "early formulation" of the rescue doctrine in *Badalamenti v. United States*, 160 F.2d 422, 426 (2d Cir. 1947). We disagree. Contrary to Barlow's claim, *Badalamenti* applied the reasonable mariner standard. In that case, a longshoreman was walking through a ship in an unlighted area when he fell through an open hatch. A second longshoreman came looking for him and also fell. We held that the second longshoreman was not contributorily negligent, even though the disappearance of his colleague gave him reason to be cautious. We quoted Judge Cardozo: "The risk of rescue, if only it be not wanton, is born of the occasion. The emergency begets the man. The wrongdoer may not have foreseen the coming of a deliverer. He is accountable as if he had." *Id.* at 426 (quoting *Wagner v. Int'l Ry. Co.*, 232 N.Y. 176, 180 (1921)). Barlow, seizing on the word "wanton," argues that in *Badalamenti* we adopted a *Furka*-like standard. He misreads the case. [—20—]

In the sentence just before we quoted Judge Cardozo, we wrote that the facts did not suggest the plaintiff "to have been *unreasonable* or *negligent*" in proceeding to the rescue. *Id.* (emphasis added). We quoted

Judge Cardozo because, as further review of *Wagner* reveals, he was applying a reasonableness standard. Judge Cardozo makes the "wanton" reference when discussing the "normal" and "probable" urge to rescue. *Wagner*, 232 N.Y. at 180. These words, associated with a reasonableness standard, reflect the actual substance of Judge Cardozo's holding. Subsequent New York courts have similarly interpreted *Wagner* as applying a reasonableness standard. *See Rodriguez*, 82 A.D.2d at 854.[14] [—21—]

Barlow finally argues that the unique perils of life at sea favor the *Furka* standard. Rescues at sea are different than those on land, he argues, because there is often no fire department or even coast guard to call. Because deliverance can only come from other

---

[14] We also find Barlow's reliance on New York's pattern jury instructions unpersuasive. In cases where a plaintiff has attempted the rescue of a human life, New York Civil Pattern Jury Instruction 2:41 charges the jury that:

A person who is injured while attempting to rescue someone else from danger in an emergency is not negligent simply because the rescue attempt itself involved danger to the rescuer. The law has a high regard for human life and efforts to save it. Danger invites rescue, meaning that the impulse to respond to an urgent need for assistance, without complete regard for one's own safety, is recognized as normal. The law will not view an attempt to preserve life as negligent unless the attempt, under the circumstances, was reckless. [—21—]

New York law is, of course, not binding on us when we sit in admiralty, but even if it were, we think this instruction misstates New York law. All but the most ancient cases cited in the jury instruction's commentary support a reasonable person standard. *See, e.g., Provenzo v. Sam*, 23 N.Y.2d 256, 260 (1968) (requiring the plaintiff to "show that in attempting the rescue he acted as a reasonable man under the circumstances"); *Rucker v. Andress*, 38 A.D.2d 684, 685 (4th Dep't 1971) (asking "whether plaintiff, in going to the rescue . . . was foolhardy or reasonable in the light of the emergency confronting him . . . ."); *Tassone v. Johannemann*, 232 A.D.2d 627, 628 (2d Dep't 1996) ("There is nothing in the record to suggest that the plaintiff reasonably could have believed that" a rescue was necessary).

---

[13] "Ladder with wooden rungs, or treads, and rope sides." Layton, *supra* at 187 (cross-referencing "jack's ladder").

sailors, Barlow contends, we must not hold rescuers liable, absent recklessness, lest they hesitate.

It is true that life at sea is generally more dangerous than life on land, but that is no reason to adopt Barlow's rule. As this case demonstrates, unreasonable rescues injure people just as surely as the emergency that begets them. Barlow would have us hold the defendant liable for injuries resulting from actions that *no reasonable mariner* would have taken. Indeed, under his rule, defendant would [—22—] be liable even if no reasonable mariner would have even thought there was an emergency, let alone taken the actions Barlow did.

Of course, we should not hold rescuers to the same standard as those acting with time to plan. But the reasonable seaman standard is quite forgiving, while recognizing that mariners may have particular skills for responding to emergencies.[15] Here, the district court's instruction properly emphasized that when acting quickly and under stress, even prudent seamen will make mistakes. Under a reasonable mariner standard, a rescuer is forgiven his mistakes, because of the circumstances in which he acted. And under a comparative negligence regime, even if the rescuer acts unreasonably, he can still recover in proportion to his caution, as Barlow did here. As *Furka* admits, the rescue doctrine came from a time when the rescuer's slightest misstep could cost him any recovery whatsoever. That is no longer the case. [—23—]

2. The Jury's Apportionment of Fault

Barlow also argues that, even under the district court's instruction, the jury's finding of ninety percent fault was excessive as a matter of law. This argument is easily dismissed. Barlow admits he operated the winch improperly and that this caused it to

pay out. There was also evidence that Barlow was specifically ordered not to operate the winch at all because others were addressing the problem. A reasonable jury could easily have concluded that Barlow was acting contrary to orders in a way that disrupted the efforts of those in charge to safely re-moor the ship. This jury did conclude that he was thus primarily responsible for his own injuries.

B. Unseaworthiness Claim

In admiralty, ship owners are strictly liable for injury resulting from the unseaworthiness of their vessel and the vessel's appurtenances. *Mitchell v. Trawler Racer, Inc.*, 362 U.S. 539, 550 (1960). Nonetheless, ship owners do not have a duty "to furnish an accident-free ship." *Id.* "The standard is not perfection, but reasonable fitness; not a ship that will weather every conceivable storm or withstand every imaginable peril of the sea, but a vessel reasonably suitable for her intended service." *Id.* The liability is absolute in the sense that [—24—] owners may be strictly liable, but relative in the sense that seaworthiness is determined by the purpose for which the ship is used. The same vessel may be adequate sitting in port, or on a calm river, but unseaworthy if taken on a transoceanic voyage. *See Lester v. United States*, 234 F.2d 625, 628 (2d Cir. 1956).

Barlow argues that because the Liberty Sun broke free from her moorings, a presumption arises that she was unseaworthy. We disagree. In several cases where a ship— or her mooring lines—have broken, we have applied a presumption of unseaworthiness against the owners. In *Martinez v. United States*, for example, the fuel tanker, Arabian Sea, was moored in a New Hampshire river to unload jet fuel. 705 F.2d 658, 659-60 (2d Cir. 1983). She was expected to face strong currents for that stretch of river and was tied up with eighteen mooring lines, more than double her usual number. Nonetheless, all eighteen mooring lines parted and the vessel floated free. As the lines were parting, one of the ship's sailors was injured while scrambling to secure her fuel lines. He later brought suit. With respect to his seaworthiness claim, we held that "[t]he fact

---

[15] We note that the district court applied the standard of a reasonably prudent *seaman*, not that of a reasonably prudent *person*. This was correct. Those with special skills are expected to use their special skills. *See Toth v. Cmty. Hosp. at Glen Cove*, 22 N.Y.2d 255, 262 (1968).

that the ship broke loose from her moorings raised a presumption of unseaworthiness which the defendant" could only overcome with a showing of *vis major*. *Id*. at 662. We held that the defendant had not met this burden because [—25—] "[t]he currents, even if three or four knots stronger than predicted by tables, were not so great that the vessel should not have been equipped to encounter them." *Id*.

We likewise applied this presumption in *Oliveras v. Am. Exp. Isbrandtsen Lines, Inc.*, 431 F.2d 814 (2d Cir. 1970). As the motor vessel Export Buyer rolled in "moderately heavy weather," a hatch that had been pinned open slammed shut, injuring a sailor. We held that the vessel was unseaworthy as a matter of law because "[t]here [was] no evidence that the weather conditions encountered at the time of plaintiff's injury were the least bit unusual or unexpected." *Id*. at 816. There was no evidence of any other condition that forced the hatch shut except normal North Atlantic swells. "Nothing more need be shown except that the device in question failed under conditions when it should have functioned properly." *Id*.

As these cases reflect, the fact that equipment fails is some evidence that it was unfit for the duties it was undertaking. But it is not conclusive. Forces beyond the reasonably foreseeable—*vis major*—may intervene. In both *Martinez* and *Oliveras* we presumed that the ship was unseaworthy, because the forces acting on the ship were those normally expected. [—26—]

In this case, however, there was evidence of the unexpected. Defendants argued that the tug fending the Liberty Sun off the grain terminal gave a sudden and unexpected surge that caused the lines to part. There was evidence to support this theory.[16] By contrast, Barlow offered no evidence to support his claim that the Liberty Sun was unseaworthy other than the mere fact that the lines parted.

---

[16] Barlow responds that since the crew knew the tug was there, it was not an *unexpected* force. It is true the tug was expected, but it does not follow that everything the tug would do was expected.

The fact that the lines broke is relevant to whether the ship was defective, but, given the tug's unforeseen push, it was insufficient to render the Liberty Sun defective as a matter of law. As the Seventh Circuit has explained, "[a]lthough the doctrine of unseaworthiness entails liability without fault, there must still be a defect in the vessel." *Hughes v. ContiCarriers & Terminals, Inc.*, 6 F.3d 1195, 1197 (7th Cir. 1993). The jury might have found for Barlow, but it did not. We will not disturb this finding. [—27—]

C. Barlow's Remaining Arguments

We need not linger over Barlow's remaining contentions. First, he argues in a few conclusory sentences that the testimony of Defendants' expert should have been excluded under *Daubert*. Barlow raised this objection *in limine*, but failed to raise it at trial, and specifically withdrew his objection in his post-trial briefing. We therefore need not consider it. *United States v. Bilzerian*, 926 F.2d 1285, 1295 (2d Cir. 1991).

Finally, Barlow asserts that it was error for the district court to fail to mention specifically in its seaworthiness instruction that mooring lines are considered part of the vessel's equipment. District courts exercise broad discretion in formulating jury instructions and we think the court's instruction was adequate. *Parker v. Sony Pictures Entm't, Inc.*, 260 F.3d 100, 106-07 (2d Cir. 2001). Since the whole case was about the mooring lines, we have no reason to think that the jury was confused. [—28—]

Conclusion

To summarize, we hold that (1) the correct standard of care in maritime injury cases is that of a reasonable mariner under the circumstances and (2) since evidence supported the conclusion that abnormal forces were acting on the Liberty Sun at the time the lines parted, she was not unseaworthy as a matter of law. We have considered Barlow's remaining arguments find them without merit.

The judgment of the district court is
AFFIRMED. [—29—]

United States Court of Appeals
for the Second Circuit

No. 13-461

TANDON
vs.
CAPTAIN'S COVE MARINA OF BRIDGEPORT, INC.

Appeal from the United States District Court for the
District of Connecticut

Decided: May 19, 2014

Citation: 752 F.3d 239, 2 Adm. R. 57 (2d Cir. 2014).

Before **KATZMANN**, Chief Judge, **LIVINGSTON**, Circuit
Judge, and **CARTER**, District Judge.*

* The Honorable Andrew L. Carter, Jr., United States District Judge for the Southern District of New York, sitting by designation.

[—3—] KATZMANN, Chief Judge:

This case calls upon us to determine whether federal admiralty jurisdiction extends to tort claims arising from a physical altercation among recreational visitors on and around a permanent dock surrounded by navigable water. We hold that federal admiralty jurisdiction does not reach the claims at issue here, because this type of incident does not have a potentially disruptive effect on maritime commerce.

Petitioners-Appellants Sapna Tandon and Robert Doohan, III, are the owners of the *Up and Over*, a thirty-nine-foot fiberglass powerboat designed for recreational purposes. On May 28, 2010, visitors on the *Up and Over* were involved in a fistfight on a floating dock operated by Claimant-Appellee Captain's Cove Marina of Bridgeport, Inc. ("Captain's Cove"). At least one person was seriously injured in the fight. Tandon and Doohan subsequently filed a petition for limitation of liability[1] in the

[1] In 1966, the procedural rules governing federal civil cases and federal admiralty cases were unified, and the former Federal Rules of Practice in Admiralty and Maritime Cases were superseded by the Supplemental Rules for Admiralty or Maritime Claims and Asset Forfeiture Actions ("Supp. R."). *See* Supp. R. Rule A, 1966 advisory committee's note. As part of this unification, the Supplemental Rules adopted certain terminology from the Federal

United States District Court for the [—4—] District of Connecticut (Hall, *J.*), seeking to limit their tort liability for the incident. The district court dismissed their petition for lack of subject matter jurisdiction, holding that this case falls outside the general grant of admiralty jurisdiction in 28 U.S.C. § 1333. We now affirm.

BACKGROUND

A. Factual Background

Captain's Cove operates a marina in Bridgeport, Connecticut, on the waters of Black Rock Harbor and Cedar Creek, which open onto Long Island Sound. The marina facilities include a dockside restaurant, several docks extending from the dry land into the harbor, and a floating dock (the "South Dock") accessible only by water. A water taxi runs from the South Dock to the restaurant and other facilities. [—5—]

On May 28, 2010, Tandon and Doohan took several passengers[2] on the *Up and Over* on a social trip to Captain's Cove. They docked the *Up and Over* by the marina restaurant, and

Rules of Civil Procedure; they refer to a "complaint" for limitation of liability, and they call the person filing that pleading a "plaintiff." In order to minimize confusion, we adhere to the more common practice of using the terms "petition" and "petitioner." *See* 3 Benedict on Admiralty § 1 (7th ed. rev. 2009).

[2] We use the term "passenger" throughout in its broad general sense of "a person who travels in a conveyance . . . without participating in its operation." *passenger, n.*, The American Heritage Dictionary 1285 (4th ed. 2000). We do not mean to invoke the special admiralty usage of this term for "a person who travels in a public conveyance *by virtue of a contract, express or implied, which involves paying a fare or some other consideration.*" 1 Thomas J. Schoenbaum, Admiralty and Maritime Law, § 5-5, at 269–70 (5th ed. 2011) (emphasis added). Nothing in the record indicates that the passengers on board the *Up and Over* paid any consideration for their voyage; to the contrary, the available evidence indicates that they were social guests, and so likely "visitors" under admiralty law. *See id.* at 270 ("A visitor is a person other than a passenger or a member of the crew who is on board with the express or implied consent of the shipowner or operator of the vessel.").

proceeded inside for food and drinks. Claimant-Appellee Ryan Ulbrick, who had also been invited along, arrived at Captain's Cove by car and met the others there.

At about the same time, Third-Party Defendant–Appellee Frank Genna and two companions also made a social visit to Captain's Cove. They arrived in a boat owned by one of Genna's companions, moored at the South Dock, and then took a water taxi to the marina restaurant. Genna and his companions were not previously acquainted with Tandon, Doohan, or their companions.

Both parties left the restaurant at about the same time. As Tandon, Doohan, and their passengers were boarding the *Up and Over*, one of those passengers fell [—6—] into the water and injured himself. Genna and his companions laughed at the mishap, leading the passengers on the *Up and Over* to yell unspecified but presumably unfriendly comments in response. Genna and his companions then boarded the water taxi to return to the South Dock, and both the *Up and Over* and the water taxi left the main docks.

At that point, the parties' accounts diverge somewhat. According to an affidavit filed by Ulbrick, the water taxi headed slightly northeast, toward the north end of the South Dock, while the *Up and Over* headed southwest down the channel toward Long Island Sound. As the *Up and Over* was making its way down the channel, Tandon noticed that the passenger who fell while boarding the *Up and Over* was bleeding from a scalp wound. She therefore asked Doohan, who was piloting the boat, to pull over and moor so that she could examine the passenger's injuries. According to the state court complaint filed by Genna, on the other hand, the *Up and Over* followed in hot pursuit of the water taxi toward the South Dock. Meanwhile, its passengers yelled and screamed at Genna and his companions, and at one point threw a beer bottle at them.

The parties agree that both the *Up and Over* and the water taxi docked at the South Dock, where a fistfight broke out between Genna's party and the [—7—] passengers of the *Up and Over*. During the fight, one passenger from the *Up and Over* hit Genna, knocking him off of the South Dock into the water. According to Ulbrick, Genna landed face-down in the water and appeared unconscious; according to Genna, he was physically held underwater to the point of asphyxia. Genna claims that he suffered severe injuries from the lack of oxygen, including "cardiac arrest, respiratory failure, hypoxic encephalopathy resulting in permanent brain damage[,] and multi-organ failure." J.A. 40.

B. Procedural Background

Genna and his wife Donna Genna (together, "the Gennas") filed suit in Connecticut state court against Captain's Cove and several persons affiliated with it (together, "the Captain's Cove defendants").[3] They alleged that the Captain's Cove defendants were liable for Genna's injuries, and for Donna Genna's resulting loss of consortium, under theories of negligent supervision, negligence, and reckless dispensing of liquor, and also under the Connecticut [—8—] Dram Shop Act.[4] The Captain's Cove defendants responded by filing a third-party complaint against Tandon, Doohan, and their passengers on the *Up and Over* (including Ulbrick). In that third-party complaint, the Captain's Cove defendants sought contribution and indemnity for any damages they might be required to pay the Gennas. The Gennas then filed a second

---

[3] Specifically, the Gennas named as defendants "Captain's Cove Marina of Bridgeport, Inc. a/k/a The Restaurant at Captain's Cove, Inc. a/k/a Restaurant at Captain's Cove"; Jill Williams, as the "[p]ermittee" of Captain's Cove; and Kaye Williams and Bruce Williams, as the "backers" of Captain's Cove. J.A. 81–82. Captain's Cove Marina of Bridgeport, Inc. and The Restaurant at Captain's Cove Inc., a/k/a Restaurant at Captain's Cove, are apparently separate entities and are represented by different counsel in the present appeal.

[4] The Connecticut Dram Shop Act, Conn. Gen. Stat. § 30-102, makes a person who "sells any alcoholic liquor to an intoxicated person" liable to any other person injured as a consequence of the buyer's intoxication. *See Zucker v. Vogt*, 329 F.2d 426, 427–28 (2d Cir. 1964).

amended complaint adding Tandon, Doohan, and the passengers on the *Up and Over* as third-party defendants, and asserting claims against them for negligence, recklessness, assault and battery, and conspiracy.[5]

Tandon and Doohan proceeded to file a petition for limitation of liability in the United States District Court for the District of Connecticut, initiating the present case. That petition asked the district court to either exonerate Tandon and Doohan from liability for the incident at Captain's Cove, or else limit their liability to the value of the *Up and Over* (appraised at $285,000). In accordance with the normal rules governing limitation proceedings, the district court stayed [—9—] the pending state court proceedings and ordered that notice be sent to all persons asserting claims with respect to the incident. The Gennas, the Captain's Cove defendants, and Ulbrick all filed claims in the limitation proceeding; two other passengers on the *Up and Over*, Michael Hermann and Robert Barbieri, also filed notices of potential claims.

Ulbrick then moved to dismiss the petition under Federal Rule of Civil Procedure 12(b)(1), asserting that the district court lacked subject matter jurisdiction. The district court agreed. Applying the jurisdictional analysis laid out in *Jerome B. Grubart, Inc. v. Great Lakes Dredge & Dock Co.*, 513 U.S. 527 (1995), the district court held that the alleged torts at issue in this case failed both the "location" test and the "connection" test for federal admiralty jurisdiction. It held the location test was not met because the fight in which Genna was injured took place primarily on the South Dock, and this floating dock was properly considered an extension of land because it remained permanently in a fixed location. It also held that the connection test was not met because the type of incident involved—which the district court characterized as "[a] fight on a dock"—did not have a potentially disruptive impact on maritime commerce. J.A. 130. The district

---

[5] Along with Tandon, Doohan, and Ulbrick, this second amended complaint named Jose Guzman, Brandon McNeal, Ziba Guy, Michael Hermann, Stacy Romano, Robert Barbieri, and Michael Sprague as third-party defendants.

court therefore dismissed the petition for lack of subject matter jurisdiction. [—10—]

Tandon and Doohan then filed the present appeal. We have jurisdiction under 28 U.S.C. § 1291, and now affirm.

DISCUSSION

A. Standard of Review

"When reviewing a district court's determination of subject matter jurisdiction pursuant to [Rule] 12(b)(1), we review factual findings for clear error and legal conclusions *de novo*." *Close v. New York*, 125 F.3d 31, 35 (2d Cir. 1997). In resolving a motion to dismiss under Rule 12(b)(1), the district court must take all uncontroverted facts in the complaint (or petition) as true, and draw all reasonable inferences in favor of the party asserting jurisdiction. *See Amidax Trading Grp. v. S.W.I.F.T. SCRL*, 671 F.3d 140, 145 (2d Cir. 2011) (per curiam). But "[w]here jurisdictional facts are placed in dispute, the court has the power and obligation to decide issues of fact by reference to evidence outside the pleadings, such as affidavits." *APWU v. Potter*, 343 F.3d 619, 627 (2d Cir. 2003) (quoting *LeBlanc v. Cleveland*, 198 F.3d 353, 356 (2d Cir. 1999)). In that case, the party asserting subject matter jurisdiction "has the burden of proving by a preponderance of the evidence that it exists." *Makarova v. United States*, 201 F.3d 110, 113 (2d Cir. 2000). [—11—]

B. Admiralty Jurisdiction

Under our Constitution, the federal judicial power extends "to all Cases of admiralty and maritime Jurisdiction." U.S. Const. art. III, §2, cl. 1. Congress has codified that jurisdiction at 28 U.S.C. § 1333(1), which gives federal district courts original jurisdiction over "[a]ny civil case of admiralty or maritime jurisdiction." *See Vasquez v. GMD Shipyard Corp.*, 582 F.3d 293, 298 (2d Cir. 2009). "The primary purpose of federal admiralty jurisdiction is to protect commercial shipping with uniform rules of conduct." *MLC Fishing, Inc. v. Velez*, 667 F.3d 140, 141–42

(2d Cir. 2011) (per curiam) (quoting *Vasquez*, 582 F.3d at 298).

In this case, Tandon and Doohan invoked the district court's admiralty jurisdiction by filing a petition for exoneration from or limitation of liability. That petition is a form of action peculiar to the admiralty and maritime context. It seeks the protection of the Limitation of Liability Act, first enacted by Congress in 1851 "to encourage ship-building and to induce capitalists to invest money in this branch of industry." *Lewis v. Lewis & Clark Marine, Inc.*, 531 U.S. 438, 446 (2001) (quoting *Norwich Co. v. Wright*, 80 U.S. (13 Wall.) 104, 121 (1872)). Under the present version of this statute, "the liability of the owner of a vessel for any claim, debt, or liability [covered by the Act] shall not exceed the value of the vessel and [—12—] pending freight." 46 U.S.C. § 30505(a). It applies broadly, limiting the owner's liability for any claims arising from "embezzlement, loss, or destruction of any property, goods, or merchandise shipped or put on board the vessel, any loss, damage, or injury by collision, or any act, matter, or thing, loss, damage, or forfeiture, done, occasioned, or incurred, without the privity or knowledge of the owner." *Id.* § 30505(b). The Act thus protects the owner of a vessel from unlimited vicarious liability for damages caused by the negligence of his captain or crew. *See In re City of N.Y.*, 522 F.3d 279, 283 (2d Cir. 2008).

To take advantage of this statute, "[t]he owner of a vessel may bring a civil action in a district court of the United States for limitation of liability." 46 U.S.C. § 30511(a). The owner may also seek total exoneration from liability in the same action (for instance, by asserting an affirmative defense that bars potential claims). *See* Supplemental Rules for Admiralty or Maritime Claims and Asset Forfeiture Actions ("Supp. R.") Rule F(2). Once the owner files a petition for limitation, "all [other] claims and proceedings against the owner related to the matter in question shall cease." 46 U.S.C. § 30511(c). The district court then "issue[s] a notice to all persons asserting claims with respect to which the [petition] seeks limitation," instructing such claimants to file their claims in the [—13—] limitation proceeding before a specified deadline. Supp. R. Rule F(4). Claimants may also file an answer challenging the petitioner's right to exoneration from or limitation of liability. *Id.* Rule F(5). If the petition for limitation of liability is granted, the owner can be liable on the covered claims only up to the total value of his vessel and its pending freight; that amount will then be distributed pro rata among the proven claims. *Id.* Rule F(8).

Although the Limitation of Liability Act provides a federal cause of action for a vessel owner seeking exoneration or limitation, it "does not provide an independent foundation for federal admiralty jurisdiction." *MLC Fishing*, 667 F.3d at 143. That is, the fact that a vessel owner may file a petition for limitation does not mean the district court necessarily has jurisdiction to hear it. Instead, the district court will only have admiralty jurisdiction to hear a petition for limitation if it already has admiralty jurisdiction over the underlying claims that the petition seeks to limit. *See id.* at 143–44. We therefore ask whether the underlying claims raise a "civil case of admiralty or maritime jurisdiction" that the district court could hear under 28 U.S.C. § 1333(1). [—14—]

Here, the petition seeks to limit liability on underlying claims that sound in tort. We therefore turn to examine the scope of federal admiralty jurisdiction over maritime tort claims.

1. Legal Standard

"The traditional test for admiralty tort jurisdiction asked only whether the tort occurred on navigable waters. If it did, admiralty jurisdiction followed; if it did not, admiralty jurisdiction did not exist." *Jerome B. Grubart, Inc. v. Great Lakes Dredge & Dock Co.*, 513 U.S. 527, 531–32 (1995). The location of the tort normally depended on where the plaintiff was harmed—or to use a more lawyerly phrase, where "the substance and consummation of the injury" took place. *The Plymouth*, 70 U.S. (3 Wall.) 20, 33 (1866). This could occasionally lead to odd results. For instance, the Supreme Court held on multiple occasions that when negligently piloted ships rammed structures on the land, the resulting claims were outside the law of admiralty, because the structures harmed were on the land and not in the water. *See, e.g., Martin v. West*, 222 U.S. 191, 195–97 (1911) (collision between a steamship and the pier of a drawbridge); *Cleveland Terminal & Valley R.R. Co. v. Cleveland S.S. Co.*, 208 U.S. 316, 319–21 (1908) (collision involving multiple vessels and causing damage to a shore dock, bridge, protection piling, and pier); *Johnson* [—15—] *v. Chi. & Pac. Elevator Co.*, 119 U.S. 388, 389, 397 (1886) (collision between a schooner and a warehouse, in which the jibboom of the schooner went through the wall of the warehouse and caused a large quantity of shelled corn to run out and be lost in the Chicago River).

These ship-to-shore collision cases were superseded in 1948 by the Extension of Admiralty Jurisdiction Act, which extended admiralty jurisdiction to all "cases of injury or damage, to person or property, caused by a vessel on navigable waters, even though the injury or damage is done or consummated on land." 46 U.S.C. § 30101(a); *see Grubart*, 513 U.S. at 532. But outside of cases covered by that Act, the jurisdictional test continued to focus solely on whether the tort at issue occurred on navigable water. *See, e.g., Victory Carriers, Inc. v. Law*, 404 U.S. 202, 203–05 (1971) (reiterating the "historic view . . . that the maritime tort jurisdiction of the federal courts is determined by the locality of the accident," and finding no admiralty jurisdiction over an accident suffered by a longshoreman driving a forklift on a pier).

The Supreme Court first turned away from the traditional location-based rule in *Executive Jet Aviation, Inc. v. City of Cleveland*, 409 U.S. 249 (1972). *Executive Jet* involved an airplane that took off from a Cleveland, Ohio airport bound for [—16—] Portland, Maine. Shortly after takeoff, the plane hit a flock of seagulls and crashed into the navigable waters of Lake Erie. *Id.* at 250. The owners of the airplane alleged that the air traffic controller and other airport employees had been negligent in failing to keep the runway free of seagulls or to adequately warn the plane's pilot about the birds. *Id.* at 251.

The Court declined to decide whether the alleged tort was consummated when the plane hit the birds (over land) or when it hit the water. *Id.* at 266–67. Instead, it held that the location of the tort alone was not enough to give rise to admiralty jurisdiction. At least in the aviation context, the Court declared, admiralty jurisdiction also required that the underlying incident bear a "significant relationship" to "traditional maritime activity involving navigation and commerce on navigable waters." *Id.* at 272. The Court held that a flight between two airports in the continental United States had no such significant relationship to traditional maritime activity, and therefore found no admiralty jurisdiction over the case. *Id.* at 272–74.

In *Foremost Insurance Co. v. Richardson*, 457 U.S. 668 (1982), the Court clarified that the "significant relationship" or "connection" requirement announced in *Executive Jet* was a general rule of admiralty jurisdiction, not [—17—] limited to the aviation context. *Id.* at 674. *Foremost* involved a collision between two noncommercial vessels—pleasure boats—in navigable water on the Amite River in Louisiana. *Id.* at 669. The Court found that the connection test was satisfied, even though neither boat was engaged in commercial maritime activity, because this type of incident had a significant potential effect on maritime commerce: "For example, if these two boats collided at the mouth of the St. Lawrence Seaway, there would be a substantial effect on maritime commerce, without regard to whether either boat was actively, or had been previously, engaged in commercial activity." *Id.* at 675. The Court determined that this potential effect on maritime commerce, "when coupled with the traditional concern that admiralty law holds for navigation," demonstrated the significant relationship necessary to support admiralty jurisdiction. *Id.*

The Court next considered the scope of admiralty tort jurisdiction in *Sisson v. Ruby*, 497 U.S. 358 (1990). In that case, a vessel owner filed a petition for limitation of liability after a fire broke out on his pleasure yacht while it was docked at a marina on Lake

Michigan. The fire destroyed the yacht and damaged several nearby vessels, but no commercial vessels were affected. *Id.* at 360, 363. [—18—] Nevertheless, the Court held that this incident had a sufficiently significant relationship to traditional maritime activity to sustain admiralty jurisdiction.

The Court applied a two-part test in *Sisson* to determine whether the case before it had a significant connection to maritime affairs. First, the Court looked to whether the underlying incident had a potentially disruptive effect on maritime commerce. It described the underlying incident as "a fire on a vessel docked at a marina on navigable waters," *id.* at 363, and held that such a fire has a potentially disruptive effect, because it "can spread to nearby commercial vessels or make the marina inaccessible to such vessels," *id.* at 362. The Court explained, moreover, that this potential effect does not depend on "the particular facts of the incident in this case," but on "the general features of the type of incident involved." *Id.* at 363. The jurisdictional inquiry therefore turned on whether fires at marinas would generally disrupt maritime commerce, rather than on whether the particular fire at issue actually disrupted maritime commerce.

Second, the *Sisson* Court looked to whether there was a "substantial relationship between the activity giving rise to the incident and traditional maritime activity." *Id.* at 364. Again, the Court emphasized that the relevant [—19—] "activity giving rise to the incident" is defined by the general type of conduct from which the incident arose, not by the specific facts of the case. "In *Executive Jet*, for example, the relevant activity was not a plane sinking in Lake Erie, but air travel generally." *Id.* Likewise, in *Sisson*, the Court described the relevant activity as "the storage and maintenance of a vessel at a marina on navigable waters." *Id.* at 365. The Court found this conduct was substantially related to traditional maritime activity, *id.* at 367, and so concluded that admiralty jurisdiction was appropriate.

Finally, the Court restated and formalized the current test for admiralty tort jurisdiction in *Jerome B. Grubart, Inc. v. Great Lakes Dredge & Dock Co.*, 513 U.S. 527 (1995). That case involved a tort claim arising from construction work in the Chicago River. A construction company had used a crane sitting on a barge in the river to drive wooden pilings into the riverbed; it thereby (allegedly) cracked a freight tunnel running under the river, causing water to pour down into the tunnel and flood buildings in downtown Chicago. The flood victims filed a number of tort actions in state court; in response, the construction company filed a petition for limitation of liability in federal district court, invoking the court's admiralty jurisdiction. *Id.* at 529–31. [—20—]

The Supreme Court held that this case fell within the scope of federal admiralty jurisdiction. It began by laying out its analytical framework:

> [A] party seeking to invoke federal admiralty jurisdiction pursuant to 28 U.S.C. § 1333(1) over a tort claim must satisfy conditions both of location and of connection with maritime activity. A court applying the location test must determine whether the tort occurred on navigable water or whether injury suffered on land was caused by a vessel on navigable water. The connection test raises two issues. A court, first, must assess the general features of the type of incident involved to determine whether the incident has a potentially disruptive impact on maritime commerce. Second, a court must determine whether the general character of the activity giving rise to the incident shows a substantial relationship to traditional maritime activity.

Id. at 534 (internal quotation marks and citations omitted).

The Court then proceeded to apply that analysis to the facts before it. It held that the location test was met because the alleged injury, though occurring on land, was proximately caused by a vessel on navigable water; the location of the tort was therefore within the bounds of admiralty as defined by the Extension of Admiralty Jurisdiction Act. *Id.* at 534–37; *see* 46 U.S.C. § 30101(a). It also held that both parts of the connection test were met: i.e., that this type of incident had a potentially disruptive impact on maritime commerce, and that the general [—21—] character of the activity giving rise to the incident showed a substantial relationship to maritime commerce. *Grubart*, 513 U.S. at 538–43.

In assessing whether this type of incident had a potentially disruptive effect on maritime commerce, the Court explained that the type of incident should be described "at an intermediate level of possible generality," neither too general to distinguish different cases nor too specific to the unique facts of the particular case. *Id.* at 538–39. It thus characterized the type of incident at issue in *Grubart* as "damage by a vessel in navigable water to an underwater structure." *Id.* at 539. The Court found this type of incident could easily have a disruptive effect on maritime commerce, by disrupting the course of the waterway itself or by restricting the use of the waterway during necessary repairs. *Id.*

In applying the second part of the connection test, the Court recognized that there was "inevitably some play in the joints in selecting the right level of generality" in describing the general character of the activity giving rise to the incident. *Id.* at 542. But that "inevitable imprecision," it warned, "is not an excuse for whimsy." *Id.* The Court therefore rejected the idea that the relevant activity could be described as simply "repair and maintenance" or "pile driving," since [—22—] those descriptions would artificially eliminate the maritime character of the construction company's activity. *Id.* at 541.

Instead, the Court described the activity giving rise to the incident as "repair or maintenance work on a navigable waterway performed from a vessel." *Id.* at 540. It found that this activity did bear a substantial relationship to traditional maritime activity, since barges and similar vessels have traditionally been used to engage in similar repair work. *Id.* (citing cases involving repair work carried out from barges). The Court

clarified that although other non-maritime activities might have contributed to the ultimate injury—for instance, the city of Chicago's alleged failure to maintain and operate the tunnel system—the substantial relationship test requires only that "one of the arguably proximate causes of the incident originate[] in the maritime activity of a tortfeasor." *Id.* at 541. Consequently, as the location test and both parts of the connection test were met, the Court held that there was federal admiralty jurisdiction over the petition for limitation of liability arising from the incident.

The test established in *Grubart* remains the current test for admiralty jurisdiction over claims sounding in tort. *See MLC Fishing*, 667 F.3d at 142; *Vasquez*, 582 F.3d at 298. To restate: First, we ask whether the alleged tort meets [—23—] the location test: that is, whether it occurred on navigable water or was caused by a vessel on navigable water. Second, we ask whether the alleged tort meets both subparts of the connection test: that is, whether the general type of incident involved has a potentially disruptive effect on maritime commerce, and whether the general character of the activity giving rise to the incident bears a substantial relationship to traditional maritime activity. *See Grubart*, 513 U.S. at 534. Only if the location test and both subparts of the connection test are met will admiralty tort jurisdiction be proper under 28 U.S.C. § 1333(1).

2. Analysis

We begin our analysis with the location test, evaluating whether the underlying torts at issue in this case occurred on land or on navigable water. But the facts here present one of those "perverse and casuistic borderline situations," *Executive Jet*, 409 U.S. at 255, that have always bedeviled the traditional location test. The fistfight at issue took place on and around a floating dock surrounded by navigable water, and so one might think the tort occurred on navigable water. That dock, however, was connected by pilings to the harbor floor, making it "technically land, through a connection at the bottom of the sea." *The Blackheath*, 195 U.S. 361, 367 (1904). It also remained permanently situated in its existing [—24—] location, according to the district court's factual findings, and so it cannot be described as a vessel for admiralty purposes. *See Stewart v. Dutra Constr. Co.*, 543 U.S. 481, 493–94 (2005) (holding that a watercraft that "has been permanently moored" is no longer a "vessel" for admiralty purposes).[6] Moreover, the fight occurred both on the floating dock and in the surrounding water. According to the facts recited in the district court's opinion, Genna was struck on the dock and knocked into the water. He was then held underwater to the point of asphyxiation. He consequently suffered injury both on the dock, where he was struck, and in the water, where he landed and where he was suffocated.

Like the Supreme Court in *Executive Jet*, we see no reason to resolve the difficult question of where the underlying tort (or torts) here occurred. Even assuming *arguendo* that the location test is met, admiralty jurisdiction cannot attach because the connection test is not met. In particular, we conclude that the [—25—] first subpart of the connection test is not met, as this type of incident does not have a potentially disruptive effect on maritime commerce.

a. Potential Effect on Maritime Commerce

In assessing the potential effect of this type of incident on maritime commerce, we begin by describing the incident "at an intermediate level of possible generality." *Grubart*, 513 U.S. at 538. Our description should be general enough to capture the possible effects of similar incidents on maritime commerce, but specific enough to exclude irrelevant cases. We

---

[6] At oral argument, counsel for Tandon and Doohan conceded that sections of the South Dock were moored by pilings to the floor of the harbor. However, he stated that floating docks like the South Dock are sometimes detached and taken by boat to the shore to be stored for the winter. We see no evidence in the record that the South Dock was ever detached from its existing position, and therefore see no clear error in the district court's determination that the South Dock was permanently situated in its current location.

then determine whether that type of incident is "likely to disrupt [maritime] commercial activity." *Id.* (quoting *Sisson*, 497 U.S. at 363). In so doing, we look not to the particular facts of the case before us—i.e., whether maritime commerce was actually disrupted here—but to whether similar occurrences are likely to be disruptive. The overall purpose of the exercise is to determine "whether the incident could be seen within a class of incidents that pose[] more than a fanciful risk to commercial shipping." *Id.* at 539.

We conclude that the incident at issue in this case is best described as a physical altercation among recreational visitors on and around a permanent dock surrounded by navigable water. This description accurately captures the nature of the event giving rise to this suit, and the type of risks that the incident could [—26—] pose to maritime commerce. Like the descriptions the Court has used in its cases, our description focuses on the direct and immediate cause of the injuries suffered, rather than the alleged negligence underlying the suit. *See Grubart*, 513 U.S. at 538–39 (considering "damage by a vessel in navigable water to an underwater structure"); *Sisson*, 497 U.S. at 362–63 (considering "a fire on a vessel docked at a marina on navigable waters"). It also takes into account the general location of the incident and the roles of the persons involved, both of which can be relevant to the potential effect on maritime commerce. *See Sisson*, 497 U.S. at 363 (including in its description the general location of the fire); *Vasquez*, 582 F.3d at 300 (describing the type of incident as "the death of *persons repairing and refitting a vessel*" (emphasis added)).

We conclude that this type of incident does not realistically pose a threat to maritime commerce. First, a fistfight on and around a dock cannot immediately disrupt navigation. Unlike a sinking plane (as in *Executive Jet*), a collision between vessels (as in *Foremost*), or a collision between a vessel and an underwater structure (as in *Grubart*), it does not create any obstruction to the free passage of commercial ships along navigable waterways. Nor can it lead to a disruption in the course of the waterway itself. *See Grubart*, 513 U.S. at

539. **[—27—]** Second, a fistfight on a dock cannot immediately damage nearby commercial vessels. The fire considered in *Sisson* threatened the safety of all other boats nearby; a fistfight threatens only its participants. As the district court correctly pointed out, "[a] fight is unlikely to spread the entire length of a dock, as a fire would, and, therefore, there is little risk that a fight would make the marina inaccessible or impact other boats." J.A. 130.

Third, the class of incidents we consider here includes only fights on permanent docks—that is, docks that are connected in a permanent fashion to the land underneath or beside navigable water, and that do not move relative to the shore (except perhaps by rising and falling with the tide). This type of incident does not pose the same risks to maritime commerce as a fistfight occurring on a vessel on navigable water. A fight on a vessel may distract the crew from their duties, endangering the safety of the vessel and risking collision with others on the same waterway. If a fight injures someone on a vessel that is at sea, moreover, that vessel may be forced to divert from its course to obtain medical care for the injured person. By contrast, a fistfight on a permanent dock does not endanger the safety of the dock itself or risk a collision between that dock and nearby vessels. And it obviously cannot require the dock to move or change course. **[—28—]**

Fourth, the class of incidents we consider here involves only physical altercations among recreational visitors, not persons engaged in maritime employment. This type of incident therefore cannot have a potential effect on maritime commerce by injuring those who are employed in maritime commerce. *Cf. Vasquez*, 582 F.3d at 300 (holding there is "little question" that "the death of persons repairing and refitting a vessel" can potentially disrupt maritime commerce); *Gruver v. Lesman Fisheries Inc.*, 489 F.3d 978, 982–83 (9th Cir. 2007) (finding a potential effect on maritime commerce from "an assault on a seaman by his former maritime employer aboard a vessel in navigable waters"); *Coats v. Penrod Drilling Corp.*, 61 F.3d 1113, 1119 (5th Cir. 1995) ("Without a doubt, worker injuries,

particularly to those involved in repair and maintenance, can have a disruptive impact on maritime commerce by stalling or delaying the primary activity of the vessel.").[7] **[—29—]**

We therefore conclude that the type of incident involved here—a physical altercation among recreational visitors on and around a permanent dock surrounded by navigable water—presents no realistic threat to maritime commerce.

b. Counterarguments

Tandon and Doohan raise several counterarguments, none of which we find persuasive. First, they claim that the "type of incident" involved should include the actions leading up to the fistfight—including their alleged negligence in piloting the *Up and Over* in hot pursuit of the water taxi. That argument confuses the first and second parts of the connection test. The first part of the connection test looks to the nature of the incident that immediately caused the underlying injury; the second part, by contrast, looks to the nature of the broader activity giving rise to that incident. To take a few concrete examples: the type of incident at issue in *Executive Jet* was an airplane crash in navigable water, while the nature of the activity giving rise to that incident was air

---

[7] There is a substantial difference for admiralty purposes between an occasional visitor or passenger on a vessel and a person whose employment revolves around that vessel. *See Chandris, Inc. v. Latsis*, 515 U.S. 347, 376 (1995) (defining a "seaman" for purposes of the Jones Act as an employee whose duties "contribute to the function of the vessel or to the accomplishment of its mission," and whose "connection to a vessel in navigation . . . is substantial in terms of both its duration and its nature"). For instance, the duty of seaworthiness is owed only to seamen, not to passengers and visitors. *See* 1 Thomas J. Schoenbaum, Admiralty and Maritime Law, § 6-27, at 501 (5th ed. 2011). Likewise, because the relation between seamen and their employers is central to maritime commerce, it is well established that federal admiralty jurisdiction extends **[—29—]** to claims by seamen against their employers even for injuries on land. *See O'Donnell v. Great Lakes Dredge & Dock Co.*, 318 U.S. 36, 42–43 (1943); *see also* Schoenbaum, *supra*, § 3-7, at 160–62 & n.3.

travel generally. *See Sisson*, 497 U.S. at 363–64 (describing *Executive Jet*). The type of incident at issue in [—30—] *Foremost* was a collision between two boats on navigable water, while the nature of the activity giving rise to that incident was the navigation of vessels generally. *Id.* (describing *Foremost*). The type of incident at issue in *Sisson* was a fire on a vessel docked at a marina on navigable waters, while the activity giving rise to that incident was the storage and maintenance of a vessel at a marina on navigable waters. *Id.* at 363–65. In each case, the first part of the connection test looked more narrowly at the event that directly caused the injury at issue; the second part of the connection test looked more broadly at the proximate causes of that event. *Cf. Grubart*, 513 U.S. at 541 (asking, in applying the second part of the connection test, "whether one of the arguably proximate causes of the incident originated in the maritime activity of a tortfeasor"). Here, the event that immediately caused Genna's injuries was the physical altercation on and around the South Dock. It is that "incident" to which we look in determining the "type of incident" at issue and its potential effect on maritime commerce.

Tandon and Doohan next emphasize that the fight took place not only on the dock itself, but also in the water beside the dock. We agree that in considering the type of incident involved, the location of the incident may be relevant. And we agree that on the facts found by the district court, it appears some harm was [—31—] done in the water as well as on the dock. That is why we characterize the type of incident at issue as a physical altercation *on and around* a permanent dock surrounded by navigable water.

But we are not convinced by the conclusion Tandon and Doohan seek to draw: that because the incident involved some harm suffered on navigable water, it necessarily had a potential effect on maritime commerce. Not all torts that happen on or over navigable water have the potential to disrupt commercial shipping. Otherwise, there would be no need for the potential effect test at all; we could simply apply the location test in its place. *Cf. Foremost*, 457 U.S. at 675 n.5

(noting that the substantial relationship test is necessary because "[n]ot every accident in navigable waters that might disrupt maritime commerce will support federal admiralty jurisdiction").

Tandon and Doohan speculate that when a fight occurs partly in navigable water, the struggling bodies could themselves pose a navigational hazard. Because the class of incidents we are considering is limited to fights on and around permanent docks, however, we do not worry that the combatants might present an obstacle to commercial navigation in open sea lanes. Unlike the "collision between two pleasure boats in navigable waters" considered in [—32—] *Foremost*, the type of incident described here could not disrupt commerce by occurring at the mouth of the St. Lawrence Seaway, because there are no permanent docks stationed in the middle of that major shipping route. (If there were, it would be the docks themselves rather than the altercation that would threaten commercial navigation.) We thus think that the scenario Tandon and Doohan pose presents only a fanciful risk to commercial shipping. *See Grubart*, 513 U.S. at 539.

At worst, an incident of this sort might temporarily prevent commercial vessels from mooring at the permanent dock around which the fight occurred. *Cf. Sisson*, 497 U.S. at 362 (noting that a fire on a boat at a marina can "make the marina inaccessible to [commercial] vessels"). But the potential impact of such a temporary disruption is simply too meager to support jurisdiction. The fire considered in *Sisson* might have damaged a marina enough to close it for days or weeks, or even permanently; a fistfight presents no similar danger. At worst, it might prevent commercial ships from using part of a dock for a few hours. We do not think that this slight possibility of a temporary inconvenience is the "potentially disruptive impact on maritime commerce" envisioned by the Supreme Court's test. *Grubart*, 513 U.S. at 538. [—33—]

Alternatively, Tandon and Doohan suggest that a fight on a dock surrounded by navigable water may require emergency responders to come to the dock by boat and leave by boat, potentially snarling naval traffic in nearby waters. We recognize that other courts have found the potentially disruptive impact of a maritime emergency response enough to satisfy the first part of the connection test in some cases. *See, e.g.*, *In re Mission Bay Jet Sports, LLC*, 570 F.3d 1124, 1129 (9th Cir. 2009); *Ayers v. United States*, 277 F.3d 821, 827–28 (6th Cir. 2002); *Sinclair v. Soniform, Inc.*, 935 F.2d 599, 602 (3d Cir. 1991). Those cases, however, have generally dealt with incidents occurring either aboard a vessel or else in open water. *See, e.g.*, *Mission Bay*, 570 F.3d at 1129 (considering "harm by a vessel in navigable waters to a passenger"); *Ayers*, 277 F.3d at 827 (considering "a drowning which occurred a short distance downstream from a lock on navigable waters"). Where such an incident takes place on a vessel or in open water far from the shore, the potential danger to commercial shipping posed by a maritime emergency response may be more significant. *Cf. Roane v. Greenwich Swim Comm.*, 330 F. Supp. 2d 306, 315 (S.D.N.Y. 2004) ("[T]hose on board a boat . . . giving their full attention to the saving of the life of a swimmer in difficulty may well be **[—34—]** distracted from hazards posed by the approach of other boats unaware of the rescue in progress, or coming at speed in an effort to assist.").

But the type of incident at issue in this case is a fight on and around a permanent dock, not a fight on a vessel or in open water. The risks to maritime commerce posed by a rescue operation at a dock are substantially lower than the risks to maritime commerce posed by a rescue operation at sea. Emergency responders may have to travel by boat to reach persons injured near a permanent dock, but they will never have to travel far. And once the emergency responders arrive at the scene, they can moor their vessel at the permanent dock, rather than having to focus simultaneously on navigating their vessel and rescuing the injured. An emergency response to an incident on and around a floating dock is consequently much less likely to "ensnarl maritime traffic," *Mission Bay*, 570 F.3d at 1129, than an emergency response to an

incident on a vessel or an incident in open water.[8] **[—35—]**

Indeed, accepting the argument that Tandon and Doohan advance would effectively eviscerate the first part of the connection test. If the possibility of a maritime emergency response is alone enough to show a potential impact on maritime commerce, then almost any tort occurring anywhere on or near navigable water would satisfy this requirement.[9] We do not think this part of the connection test is so easily evaded.

Because the type of incident at issue in this case poses only "a fanciful risk to commercial shipping," *Grubart*, 513 U.S. at 539, it is outside the admiralty and maritime jurisdiction extended by 28 U.S.C. §1333(1).[10] The district court was therefore correct to dismiss the petition for lack of subject matter jurisdiction. **[—36—]**

---

[8] Tandon and Doohan also cite a number of specific facts about this incident that they claim increased the risk of disruption to maritime commerce. Those facts include, for instance, that the incident occurred on Memorial Day weekend, and that the *Up and Over* allegedly left the South Dock after the incident at a high rate of speed. To the extent their argument rests on specific aspects of the incident that actually occurred, it clearly fails, because our analysis looks only to the general type of incident at issue rather than particular facts about that incident. *See Grubart*, 513 U.S. at 538. To the extent they simply raise these facts to show that this type of incident has a potential disruptive **[—35—]** effect on maritime commerce, we remain unconvinced that the potential risk is anything more than fanciful.

[9] Perhaps the requirement might still rule out, for example, a defamation claim, *see Wells v. Liddy*, 186 F.3d 505, 523–27 & n.16 (4th Cir. 1999), or a claim for tortious interference with contract, *see Wiedemann & Fransen, A.P.L.C. v. Hollywood Marine, Inc.*, 811 F.2d 864, 865–66 & n.1 (5th Cir. 1987) (per curiam). We need not consider such questions here.

[10] As this incident does not satisfy the first part of the connection test, we do not reach the second part, and thus need not decide whether the "activity giving rise to the incident shows a substantial relationship to traditional maritime activity." *Grubart*, 513 U.S. at 534 (internal quotation marks omitted).

c. Coda

In developing the modern test for admiralty tort jurisdiction, the Supreme Court "aimed at keeping a . . . class of odd cases out." *Grubart*, 513 U.S. at 532. It sought to realign the jurisdictional inquiry toward the primary purpose that supports admiralty jurisdiction—namely, "the federal interest in the protection of maritime commerce." *Sisson*, 497 U.S. at 364 n.2. We are quite convinced that this case does not implicate that underlying purpose.

In the eloquent words of Justice Stewart:

> The law of admiralty has evolved over many centuries, designed and molded to handle problems of vessels relegated to ply the waterways of the world, beyond whose shores they cannot go. That law deals with navigational rules—rules that govern the manner and direction those vessels may rightly move upon the waters. . . . Through long experience, the law of the sea knows how to determine whether a particular ship is seaworthy, and it knows the nature of maintenance and cure. It is concerned with maritime liens, the general average, captures and prizes, limitation of liability, cargo damage, and claims for salvage.

Executive Jet, 409 U.S. at 269–70. As that description shows, the scope of admiralty law has little or nothing to do with the issues that are likely to appear in cases like this one. On the contrary, state courts have long dealt with similar fistfights under state tort law, without any need for interference from federal courts sitting [—37—] in admiralty. Given the traditional role of state courts in adjudicating such torts, "[w]e are not inclined at this juncture to disturb the existing precedents and to extend shoreward the reach of the maritime law further than Congress has approved." *Victory Carriers, Inc. v. Law*, 404 U.S. 202, 211 (1971).[11]

---

[11] We recognize that "[a]dmiralty jurisdiction and federal maritime law need not go hand-in-hand." *Blue Whale Corp. v. Grand China Shipping Dev. Co.*, 722 F.3d 488, 497, 1 Adm. R. 38, 43 (2d Cir. 2013). But we remain unwilling to encourage federal courts to take admiralty jurisdiction over cases better heard in state court.

CONCLUSION

For the reasons above, the judgment of the district court is **AFFIRMED**.

United States Court of Appeals
for the Second Circuit

No. 11-3473

D'AMICO DRY LTD.
vs.
PRIMERA MARITIME (HELLAS) LTD.

Appeal from the United States District Court for the
Southern District of New York

Decided: June 12, 2014

Citation: 756 F.3d 151, 2 Adm. R. 69 (2d Cir. 2014).

Before **KATZMANN**, Chief Judge, **LEVAL**, and **CABRANES**, Circuit Judges.

[—3—] **LEVAL**, Circuit Judge:

Plaintiff D'Amico Dry Limited ("D'Amico") appeals from the judgment of the United States District Court for the Southern District of New York (Koeltl, *J.*) dismissing its complaint for lack of subject matter jurisdiction. D'Amico brought this suit to enforce an English court's judgment on a forward freight agreement ("FFA") between D'Amico and Defendant Primera Maritime (Hellas) Limited ("Primera").[1] Under this contract, Primera was obligated to pay D'Amico if the market freight rates for a specified shipping route on agreed future dates were lower than the price specified in the contract. At the agreed future dates, the rates were indeed lower, which obligated Primera to pay D'Amico. Primera refused to pay. D'Amico sued Primera in an English court, which ruled for D'Amico, rendering judgment in its favor. The suit was heard in the commercial division, not the admiralty division, of the English court.

D'Amico then brought this suit in the United States district court to enforce the English judgment, asserting entitlement to federal jurisdiction under 28 U.S.C. [—4—] § 1333, which provides the maritime jurisdiction of the federal courts. Primera moved to dismiss for lack of subject matter jurisdiction. The district court granted Primera's motion to dismiss, holding that the suit did not fall under the federal courts' admiralty jurisdiction because the English judgment was not rendered by an admiralty court and the claim underlying the judgment was not deemed to be maritime under English law.

D'Amico moved for reconsideration, arguing that enforcement of the English judgment lies within the federal court's admiralty jurisdiction because the claim on which the judgment was rendered would have come within federal admiralty jurisdiction if brought in the United States courts. The district court rejected the contention that the maritime classification of the claim under U.S. law is pertinent to the question whether the suit may be brought in the admiralty jurisdiction of the federal courts. The court therefore denied D'Amico's motion for relief from the judgment. D'Amico now appeals from the denial of the Rule 60(b) motion, as well as from the judgment dismissing the complaint.

We conclude that, under § 1333, United States courts have jurisdiction to enforce a judgment of a foreign non-admiralty court if the claim underlying that [—5—] judgment would be deemed maritime under the standards of U.S. law. We therefore vacate the judgment and remand.

BACKGROUND

A. The Forward Freight Agreement

D'Amico operates Panamax dry bulk cargo vessels, among others, in the business of carriage of goods by sea. A major risk of an ocean carrier's business is that a slowdown in worldwide commercial activity will lead to diminution in shipments of cargo, causing vessels to make expensive voyages partially empty or, in more extreme circumstances, to lay idle. The rates carriers charge for carriage of goods fall during such slowdowns. The cost of maintaining one of D'Amico's Panamax dry bulk cargo vessels in an unemployed, idle state is roughly $12,000 per day on average. As a way of offsetting losses from its vessels being underemployed or idle during such a slowdown, D'Amico enters into futures

---

[1] The remaining Defendants are alleged to be alter egos of Primera.

contracts on international shipping rates. These contracts, sometimes called "forward freight agreements" or "FFAs," specify a base rate (the "contract rate") for a hypothetical shipment of specified goods over specified routes and future dates for comparison of the contract rate with the market rates on such [—6—] future dates. If on a specified future date the market rate is above the contract rate, then the party that took the downside of the agreement must pay the other party the difference. If on the future date the market rate is below the contract rate, the party that took the upside of the contract must pay the other party the difference. Profits realized from such contracts as rates fall will increase D'Amico's revenues when demand is low, counteracting its losses from under-employment. Conversely, the losses on such contracts will decrease D'Amico's net revenues when demand is high and rates rise.

At the beginning of September 2008, Luciano Bonaso, D'Amico's Chief Executive Officer, ascertained that for the first quarter of 2009, 280 vessel days remained unchartered. Believing, based on market projections, that D'Amico would be unable to book cargo filling those days, Bonaso decided that D'Amico should hedge against the underemployment by entering into an FFA, taking the downside. On September 2, 2008, through the service of broker IFCHOR, S.A., D'Amico entered into an FFA with Primera, taking the downside of freight rates for forty-five Panamax vessel days over four "Baltic Exchange" charter routes. The FFA used a contract rate of $55,750 per day to be compared to market rates [—7—] for the Baltic Panamax Index ("BPI"), as published by the Baltic Exchange, at specified dates during the first quarter of 2009. Under the FFA contract, Primera was to pay D'Amico if the market rates published in the BPI for the later dates were below the contract rate, and D'Amico to pay Primera if the market rates on the later dates were higher. The FFA provided that all disputes arising under it would be submitted to the English High Court of Justice. By early 2009, as D'Amico had predicted, the market rate had declined significantly, so that Primera was obligated by the FFA to pay the difference. On January 30,

2009, D'Amico invoiced Primera for $795,963.20 under the terms of the FFA. Primera failed to pay.

B. The Prior Proceedings

D'Amico brought suit in England at the High Court of Justice, Queen's Bench Division, to enforce the agreement. The Queen's Bench Division of the High Court of Justice is subdivided into multiple divisions, including the Admiralty Court and the Commercial Court. The case was heard by the Commercial Court, and not the Admiralty Court. The English court entered a judgment in D'Amico's favor in the amount of $1,766,278.54, including, in [—8—] addition to D'Amico's contract entitlement, interest and other components. Primera did not pay the judgment.

It appears that FFAs are not considered to be maritime contracts under English law because they involve a theoretical, rather than an actual shipment of goods by sea. *See* Senior Courts Act, 1981, c. 54 § 20(2)(h) (vesting English courts with admiralty jurisdiction over "any claim arising out of any agreement relating to the carriage of goods in a ship or to the use or hire of a ship"); *The Sandrina*, [1985] A.C. 255 (H.L.) 271 (appeal taken from Scot.) (interpreting the phrase "arising out of" in the identically worded Scottish equivalent of § 20(2)(h) to require a "reasonably direct connection" with the carriage of goods or hire of a ship, and holding that a claim on a shipping insurance contract did not qualify); *The "Lloyd Pacifico"*, [1995] 1 Lloyd's Rep. 54 (Q.B.) 57 (holding that for admiralty jurisdiction to apply, a claim must relate to an identifiable ship).

D'Amico then brought this action in the U.S. district court to enforce the English judgment, asserting federal subject matter jurisdiction under § 1333. That statute gives the federal district courts exclusive jurisdiction to hear "[a]ny civil case of admiralty or maritime jurisdiction." Primera moved to dismiss for lack of [—9—] subject matter jurisdiction. The district court granted Primera's motion to dismiss, concluding that it lacked admiralty jurisdiction to enforce the

English court's judgment because the English judgment was not rendered by an admiralty court and the claim underlying the judgment was not deemed maritime in English law. D'Amico then moved for reconsideration pursuant to Rules 59(e) and 60(b) of the Federal Rules of Civil Procedure, arguing that a suit to enforce a foreign judgment falls under federal admiralty jurisdiction if the underlying claim would be maritime under U.S. law, irrespective of whether the foreign court that entered the judgment was sitting in admiralty. The district court rejected this argument and denied D'Amico's motion for reconsideration. D'Amico now appeals from both the judgment of dismissal and the denial of the post-judgment motion. [—10—]

DISCUSSION[2]

The federal admiralty jurisdiction is as old as the federal courts themselves. Article III section 2 of the U.S. Constitution provides that "[t]he judicial Power shall extend . . . to all Cases of admiralty and maritime Jurisdiction . . . ." Congress first gave effect to this constitutional grant of jurisdiction in the Judiciary Act of 1789, which provided:

> That the district courts shall have . . . exclusive original cognizance of all civil causes of admiralty and maritime jurisdiction, including all seizures under laws of impost, navigation or trade of the United States, where the seizures are made, on waters which are navigable from sea by vessels of ten or more tons of burthen, within their respective districts as well as upon the high seas; saving to suitors, in all cases, the right of a common law remedy, where the common law is competent to give it . . . .

---

[2] Whether a suit falls within federal subject matter jurisdiction is a question of law, which is reviewed de novo. *Atl. Mut. Ins. Co. v. Balfour Maclaine Int'l Ltd.*, 968 F.2d 196, 198 (2d Cir. 1992). A district court's denial of a motion for reconsideration is generally reviewed for abuse of discretion. *L-7 Designs, Inc. v. Old Navy, LLC*, 647 F.3d 419, 435 (2d Cir. 2011).

Judiciary Act of 1789, § 9, Ch. 20, 1 Stat. 73, 76-77. The jurisdictional statute now provides that "[t]he district courts shall have original jurisdiction, exclusive of the [—11—] courts of the States, of . . . [a]ny civil case of admiralty or maritime jurisdiction, saving to suitors in all cases all other remedies to which they are otherwise entitled." 28 U.S.C. § 1333.

It is well established that the law governing federal jurisdiction under § 1333 to enforce admiralty judgments of foreign courts differs substantially from the law governing jurisdiction to enforce judgments rendered by federal courts exercising federal question jurisdiction under 28 U.S.C. § 1331. A suit to enforce a judgment rendered by a federal court exercising federal question jurisdiction may not be brought in federal court unless the enforcement suit has a basis of federal jurisdiction independent of the fact that the original suit was on a federal question. *See Stiller v. Hardman*, 324 F.2d 626, 628 (2d Cir. 1963) ("[A] suit on a judgment [rendered by a federal court exercising federal question jurisdiction] does not involve a federal question, however important federal questions may have been to the resolution of the original controversy."). In contrast, some judgments of foreign admiralty courts are enforceable in the admiralty or maritime jurisdiction of the United States courts. *See Penhallow v. Doane's Adm'rs*, 3 U.S. (3 Dall.) 54, 97 (1795) (opinion of Iredell, *J.*); *Victrix S.S. Co. v. Salen Dry Cargo* [—12—] *A.B.*, 825 F.2d 709, 713 (2d Cir. 1987); *Int'l Sea Food Ltd. v. M/V Campeche*, 566 F.2d 482 (5th Cir. 1978).

The rule providing federal admiralty jurisdiction for suits to enforce judgments of foreign admiralty courts has been recognized since the birth of the Nation. In *Penhallow v. Doane's Administrators*, 3 U.S. (3 Dall.) 54 (1795), Supreme Court Justice Iredell declared that "a Court of Admiralty in one nation, can carry into effect the determination of the Court of Admiralty of another." *Id.* at 97. Justice Cushing wrote separately that it "seems to be settled law and usage" that "courts of Admiralty can carry into execution decrees of foreign Admiralties." *Id.* at 118. This principle has been reaffirmed many times in the subsequent decades. *See Hilton v. Guyot*, 159 U.S. 113, 186 (1895) ("The respect which is due to judgments, sentences, and decrees of courts in a foreign state, by the law of nations, seems to be the same which is due to those of our own courts. Hence the decree of an admiralty court abroad is equally conclusive with decrees of our admiralty courts. Indeed, both courts proceed by the same rule, are governed by the same law— the maritime law of nations, which is the universal law of nations, except where treaties alter it." (citation and internal quotation marks omitted)); [—13—] *Int'l Sea Food*, 566 F.2d at 484 (affirming "the existence of a general principle that admiralty courts of this nation are empowered to carry into effect the maritime decrees of foreign admiralty courts"); *Penn. R.R. Co. v. Gilhooley*, 9 F. 618, 619 (E.D. Pa. 1881) (stating, in the context of an action to enforce a judgment of another district court, that the court "had a general jurisdiction which would enable it in its discretion to enforce the decree of a foreign admiralty court"); *Otis v. The Rio Grande*, 18 F. Cas. 902, 903 (C.C.D. La. 1872) (No. 10,613) ("This court is in duty bound to carry into effect the sentences and decrees, not only of other federal courts, but even of the admiralty courts of foreign countries . . . ."), *aff'd*, 90 U.S. 458 (1874); *The Jerusalem*, 13 F. Cas. 559, 563 (C.C.D. Mass. 1814) (Story, J.) (No. 7,293) (stating in dicta that an admiralty court "will enforce a foreign maritime judgment between foreigners, where either the property or the person is within its jurisdiction").

A. Admiralty Jurisdiction Extends to Suits to Enforce Foreign Judgments on Maritime *Claims*, Even if Those Judgments Were Not Rendered by Specialized Admiralty *Courts*.

In addition to the narrowest conception of the *Penhallow* rule opening the federal admiralty jurisdiction to suits to enforce judgments of foreign admiralty [—14—] courts, there is some recent, but scant, precedent supporting a related proposition that the federal admiralty jurisdiction provided by § 1333 should also accommodate suits to enforce foreign judgments based on claims of maritime character. In *Victrix*, we said in dictum that "an admiralty court has

jurisdiction of a claim to enforce a foreign judgment that is itself based on a maritime claim." *Victrix*, 825 F.2d at 713. And in *Vitol, S.A. v. Primerose Shipping Co.*, 708 F.3d 527, 1 Adm. R. 106 (4th Cir. 2013), the Fourth Circuit approvingly construed the *Victrix* dictum as meaning that "the dispositive question is not whether the English Judgment issued from an 'admiralty court,' but rather, whether the claim itself is maritime in nature." *Id.* at 535, 1 Adm. R. at 110; *see also* Harold K. Watson, *Transnational Maritime Litigation: Selected Problems*, 8 Mar. Law. 87, 104 n.102 (1983) (arguing that whether there is jurisdiction to recognize foreign judgments per *International Sea Food* should turn on the substantive nature of the foreign case, and not on whether the foreign court "was an 'admiralty court' in the sense of a specialized court").

Extending federal admiralty jurisdiction to suits to enforce foreign judgments adjudicating maritime claims undoubtedly serves the purposes intended by the *Penhallow* rule. That rule reflects numerous related policies that [—15—] shape admiralty jurisdiction in the United States. First, the rule reflects a preference for specialized admiralty courts for the resolution of maritime disputes because of their expertise in the arcane rules, nomenclatures, and traditions of the sea. Second, it promotes a desirable uniformity in matters of international trade. Third, it promotes international comity by facilitating the recognition of foreign judgments. Fourth, it reflects a constitutionally endorsed distribution of power between state and federal courts, which offers a forum for international disputes, which is—at least theoretically—less likely to be influenced by local bias. *See* Wythe Holt, *"To Establish Justice": Politics, the Judiciary Act of 1789, and the Invention of Federal Courts*, 1989 DUKE L.J. 1421, 1427-30 (describing the problem of local bias in state court admiralty proceedings in the 1770s). In combination, these policies all tend to promote international maritime commerce by facilitating the enforcement of the law of the sea—simplifying the enforcement of judgments (including enforcement of in rem jurisdiction against vessels), and protecting vulnerable parties such as foreign litigants and seamen (who are considered the "wards of admiralty," entitled to special solicitude because of the daily hazards of their work, *see Truehart v. Blandon*, 672 F. Supp. 929, 937 (E.D. La. 1987)). [—16—]

These policies all relate far more to the maritime character of the underlying dispute than to the classification of the court that rendered the judgment. Thus, take for example, British and French seamen who suffer injury by reason of the unseaworthiness of a Greek vessel and obtain judgments against the vessel owner in their local courts. If the seamen subsequently sue in the United States to enforce their judgments, the policies underlying *Penhallow* argue in favor of allowing both of them to bring their suit in federal court under § 1333, rather than admitting the British plaintiff because the judgment in his favor was rendered by an admiralty tribunal while excluding the French plaintiff because his judgment was rendered by a court not specialized in maritime matters.[3] We accordingly have no hesitation in reaffirming the proposition of the *Victrix* dictum that federal admiralty jurisdiction extends to suits to enforce the judgments of [—17—] foreign courts deciding maritime claims, regardless of whether the judgments were rendered by specialized admiralty courts.

B. U.S. Law Appropriately Determines Whether a Foreign Judgment Was Rendered on an Admiralty Claim.

The district court accepted the view that federal admiralty jurisdiction applies to suits to enforce foreign judgments, not only when the judgment was rendered by an admiralty court, but also when the claim upon which the judgment was rendered was maritime. The district court construed our *Victrix* dictum as meaning that the maritime nature of the claim must be determined by reference to the law of the nation that rendered the judgment. *See D'Amico Dry Ltd. v. Primera Maritime (Hellas) Ltd.*, No. 09 Civ. 7840, 2011 WL 1239861, at *3 (S.D.N.Y. Mar. 28, 2011) ("The question, then, is whether the English judgment was rendered in an exercise of the admiralty jurisdiction of the English court— that is, whether the claim adjudicated was, under English law, maritime in nature. As the Second Circuit Court of Appeals described in dicta in *Victrix S.S. Co., S.A. v. Salen Dry Cargo A.B.*, 'an admiralty court has jurisdiction of a claim to enforce a foreign judgment that is itself based on a maritime claim.'"). The court rejected [—18—] the plaintiff's contention that federal admiralty jurisdiction encompasses suits to enforce foreign judgments when the claim recognized in the foreign judgment would have been deemed an admiralty claim under U.S. law. The court said:

> D'Amico argues, in essence, that a district court has admiralty jurisdiction to enforce a foreign judgment where the court would have had admiralty jurisdiction over the subject matter of the foreign dispute. That is not the case. An action to enforce a foreign judgment is a separate civil action imposing its own jurisdictional requirements, and a suit to enforce a judgment rendered on a maritime claim is not itself maritime in nature.

D'Amico Dry Ltd. v. Primera Maritime (Hellas) Ltd., No. 09 Civ. 7840, 2011 WL 3273208, at *4 (S.D.N.Y. Aug. 1, 2011). The district court assumed that, because the claim was not maritime under English law, it was not maritime for purposes of determining admiralty jurisdiction.

We respectfully disagree. As noted above, had the district court been speaking of federal question jurisdiction under 28 U.S.C. § 1331, the court would undoubtedly have been

---

[3] Indeed, the *Vitol* court faced a similar situation, where the English Commercial Court and Admiralty Court had concurrent jurisdiction over the claim underlying the judgment that the plaintiff sought to enforce in federal court. *Vitol*, 708 F.3d at 531-32, 1 Adm. R. at 107. The Fourth Circuit reasonably concluded that making federal subject matter jurisdiction turn on the happenstance of whether the parties had asked the English court to exercise its admiralty or commercial jurisdiction to adjudicate the concededly maritime claim would elevate form over substance. *See id.* at 535, 1 Adm. R. at 110.

correct. *See Stiller*, 324 F.2d at 628. But *Penhallow* imported different considerations for determining whether a suit to enforce a foreign judgment may be brought within the admiralty jurisdiction of the federal courts. As these issues have arisen infrequently in cases where the foreign judgment was [—19—] *not* rendered by specialized admiralty court, there is no governing authority on whether the maritime nature of the underlying claim is more appropriately determined under the standards of U.S. or foreign law. We believe there are compelling reasons to find federal admiralty jurisdiction if a claim is maritime under the standards of U.S. law. We first address the issue of existing authority on the question.

While the District Court read our dictum in *Victrix* to mean that the maritime or non-maritime nature of the claim must be determined under the standards of the laws of the nation that rendered the judgment, as we read *Victrix*, it did not address which nation's law should be consulted to decide whether the claim underlying the foreign judgment of a non-admiralty court should be deemed maritime, and thus whether a suit to enforce that judgment lies within the federal admiralty jurisdiction. While arguments may be advanced on both sides as to the meaning of the opaque statement in *Victrix* that "an admiralty court has jurisdiction of a claim to enforce a foreign judgment that is itself based on a maritime claim," it certainly does not constitute precedential authority that the standards of U.S. law are *not* pertinent to the inquiry. [—20—]

In contrast, when the Fourth Circuit considered this issue in *Vitol*, it was clear the court looked to the maritime characterization of the claim under foreign law. Nonetheless, the *Vitol* decision did not constitute a precedent on the question whether the maritime character of the claim under U.S. law is pertinent, both because the *Vitol* court never considered the question whether U.S. law should be consulted, and because the answer would have been the same under either British or U.S. law, as the underlying claim (breach of the warranty of seaworthiness) is maritime in both nations.

Vitol never considered whether the maritime character of the underlying claim under U.S. law standards justifies the exercise of federal admiralty jurisdiction.[4]

We know of no other appellate level precedents addressing the question of the pertinence of U.S. law in deciding whether the claim underlying the foreign judgment is of maritime nature, so as to justify the exercise of federal admiralty [—21—] jurisdiction over a suit to enforce the foreign judgment.

In rejecting the pertinence of U.S. law, the district court relied on two other strands of authority, which we do not believe are apposite. The court relied in part on an unpublished opinion of the United States District Court for the Western District of Washington, ruling that it lacked subject matter jurisdiction to enforce an English judgment on a contract of charter because the suit to enforce the judgment needed to satisfy federal jurisdictional requirements and was "untouched" by the substantive law supporting the judgment. *Bergen Indus. & Fishing Corp. v. Joint Stock Holding Co.*, No. 01-cv-1994, 2002 WL 1587179, at *1 (W.D. Wash. Feb. 25, 2002). However the *Bergen* court relied for this proposition on a misinterpretation of the Restatement (Third) of Foreign Relations § 481 cmts. g, h (1987). The Restatement commentary cited by the *Bergen* court focuses on the issue of personal jurisdiction "over the judgment debtor or his property." It does not address the separate issue whether a federal court has subject matter jurisdiction over the suit.

The district court also relied on cases holding that an action to enforce a *settlement agreement* cannot be heard in admiralty even where the underlying [—22—] dispute was brought in admiralty. *See Fednav, Ltd. v.*

---

[4] A district court in the Fourth Circuit, when confronted with a substantially similar question to the one we face here, construed *Vitol* (as do we) to have not addressed the question and concluded that U.S. rather than foreign law should determine whether the claim underlying a foreign judgment is maritime. *See Flame S.A. v. Indus. Carriers, Inc.*, No. 2:13-cv-658, 2014 WL 108897, at *3 (E.D. Va. Jan. 10, 2014).

Isoramar, S.A., 925 F.2d 599, 601 (2d Cir. 1991); *Pac. Sur. Co. v. Leatham & Smith Towing & Wrecking Co.*, 151 F. 440, 443 (7th Cir. 1907) (cited in dicta in *Kossick v. United Fruit Co.*, 365 U.S. 731, 735 (1961)). The reasoning of this line of cases is that *an agreement* to pay damages "neither involves maritime service nor maritime transactions." *Pacific Sur. Co.*, 151 F. at 443. Thus an agreement to pay to resolve a maritime claim is not itself a maritime contract and does not confer admiralty jurisdiction over a subsequent suit on that agreement to resolve the underlying maritime claim.

The considerations are different, in our view, when a court has adjudicated the underlying claim in the plaintiff's favor. In the settlement context, agreement between the parties does not legitimate the original maritime claim. There is no telling whether the defendant who agrees to pay money in settlement of the claim is in any way by doing so acknowledging validity of the claim, or in contrast is continuing to deny it categorically while agreeing to pay some money to avoid the inconvenience, expense, and risk of further litigation. The settlement extinguishes that claim through private contract without validating it. In contrast, where a court has rendered a final judgment on the claim, the claim has been [—23—] validated. If that claim was of maritime nature, the maritime nature of the claim has been validated, furnishing good reason for the dispute over the enforceability of the judgment to be heard as a maritime matter in the admiralty jurisdiction of the federal court.

Further, the district court's reasoning with respect to its analogy to settlement agreements is in conflict with the *Penhallow* rule. *Penhallow* posits that the question of the enforceability of the judgment of a foreign maritime court is itself a maritime matter to be heard in the admiralty jurisdiction of United States courts, like a suit on a maritime claim. The district court accepted that the *Penhallow* principle should extend not only to the judgments of foreign admiralty courts but also to the judgments of foreign courts enforcing claims deemed maritime under the law of that nation. We do not see how that

principle is compatible with the district court's reasoning that suits to enforce foreign judgments may not be brought in federal courts absent a separate source of federal jurisdiction. The question at issue is the proper scope of the *Penhallow* rule.

Accordingly we do not agree with the district court's conclusion that existing precedent—although authorizing suits to enforce foreign judgments of [—24—] non-admiralty courts if the underlying claim was maritime under the law of the nation that rendered the judgment—does not authorize extending admiralty jurisdiction to such suits when the claim was maritime according to U.S. law standards. We know no precedent for that proposition.

Finally, if the principle is to be extended, as we stated in *Victrix*, to open federal admiralty jurisdiction not only to suits to enforce the judgments of foreign admiralty courts, but also to suits to enforce the judgments of foreign non-admiralty courts when the underlying claim validated by the judgment was maritime, we think that there are strong theoretical and practical reasons for assessing the maritime nature of the claim under U.S. admiralty standards. The reasons are numerous.

Of the theoretical reasons, the first is a principal enshrined in the Constitution that the jurisdiction of the federal courts should extend to maritime matters. Thus, Article III provides that "[t]he judicial Power shall extend . . . to all Cases of admiralty and maritime Jurisdiction." U.S. Const. art. III, § 2. And the policy of the United States to place maritime matters in the federal courts is so strong that § 1333 makes federal court jurisdiction exclusive. Although, as a [—25—] general proposition, there is widespread agreement throughout the world which kinds of matters are maritime and which are not, there is no assurance that some other nation might not define its own maritime jurisdiction more broadly, or more narrowly, than we do. It seems reasonable to assume that the Framers of the Constitution and Congress wanted to ensure that matters deemed maritime *under our laws* have access to our federal courts. There is no reason to suppose that the Founders or Congress would have wished to exclude from the admiralty jurisdiction matters that U.S. law deems maritime, merely because another nation does not consider them maritime. The fact that some nation, unlike ours, does not reserve a special jurisdiction for maritime matters, or classify maritime matters as subject to a discrete body of laws, does not derogate from the policies of our law to provide for the adjudication of matters we regard as maritime in our federal courts.

Second, choice of law principles support using U.S. law's characterization. The question whether a claim belongs in one or another court is jurisdictional and procedural. Under choice of law principles, the law of the forum state is used for such a question. *See* Restatement (Second) of Conflict of Laws § 123 (1971) ("Each [—26—] state determines which of its courts or systems of courts, if any, are competent to hear a particular case over which the state has judicial jurisdiction. So it is for each state to decide whether an action on a given claim shall be brought in a court of law, of equity, of probate or of admiralty.").[5]

Third, international comity favors allowing federal jurisdiction over suits to enforce foreign maritime judgments to the extent that

---

[5] This analysis is supported by our recent analogous discussion in *Blue Whale Corp. v. Grand China Shipping Development Co.*, 722 F.3d 488, 1 Adm. R. 38 (2d Cir. 2013). There, we faced the question which nation's law should apply when deciding whether a plaintiff "'has a valid prima facie admiralty claim'" for purposes of attachments under Rule B of the Supplemental Rules for Certain Admiralty and Maritime Claims. *See id.* at 493, 1 Adm. R. at 40 (quoting *Aqua Stoli Shipping Ltd. v. Gardner Smith Pty Ltd.*, 460 F.3d 434, 445 (2d Cir. 2006), *overruled on other grounds by Shipping Corp. of India Ltd. v. Jaldhi Overseas Pte Ltd.*, 585 F.3d 58 (2d Cir. 2009)). In deciding the choice of law issue, we noted: "[W]hat is clear is that federal law controls the procedural inquiry, namely, whether a plaintiff's claim sounds in admiralty. This question is inherently procedural by virtue of its relationship to the courts' subject matter jurisdiction and, thus, is controlled by federal maritime law." *Id.* at 494, 1 Adm. R. at 41 (citation omitted).

we would wish for reciprocal enforcement of U.S. judgments in foreign courts. The concern for the enforceability of the foreign judgment is of far greater importance to international comity than whether the U.S. court agrees with the foreign nation as to the [—27—] maritime nature of the claim. Foreign interests seeking to enforce a foreign judgment, who are denied access to federal court will not take comfort in (or believe that comity has been served by) the fact that the U.S. court followed their nation's law to determine whether the claim was maritime.

Finally, some nations neither have specialized admiralty courts nor classify maritime matters as distinct from other areas of commerce. The fact that a foreign nation does not recognize in its laws a categorical distinction which U.S. law deems so important should not frustrate the policy of U.S. law to place maritime disputes in federal courts.

There are also *practical* reasons that strongly favor using U.S. law to determine whether the claim underlying a foreign judgment was maritime, so that the suit to enforce the judgment should be allowed within the federal admiralty jurisdiction.

First, questions of subject matter jurisdiction should be amenable to quick and relatively certain resolution. If the characterization of the claim under foreign law is controlling, the parties will be compelled in many cases to carry on an expensive, cumbersome litigation involving dueling experts on foreign law, [—28—] merely to determine whether the suit belongs in federal or state court.

Federal courts have a duty to inquire into their subject matter jurisdiction sua sponte, even when the parties do not contest the issue. Especially as the foreign law may be in a foreign language, it is not clear how a federal court would go about determining whether it has jurisdiction. If federal subject matter jurisdiction is not raised until the appeal, it is unclear how the court of appeals would deal with the question (foreign law being a question of fact) without remanding to the district court. Moreover, because subject matter jurisdiction cannot be waived, if a defect in the court's subject matter jurisdiction becomes apparent only after the litigation, that defect will render the prior litigation useless. The need for certainty is all the greater here, as § 1333 vests admiralty jurisdiction *exclusively* in the federal courts. 28 U.S.C. § 1333. Thus, parties concerned about uncertain federal jurisdiction cannot, as is generally the case, avoid the problem by bringing suit in a state court of concurrent (and unquestionable) jurisdiction. Regardless whether the litigation is conducted in federal or state court, the losing party would be able to attack the judgment after **[—29—]** the fact merely by offering expert evidence that the claim was or was not deemed maritime under the foreign law.[6]

We therefore conclude that a suit to enforce a foreign judgment may be heard in the federal admiralty jurisdiction under § 1333 if the claim underlying the judgment would be deemed maritime under U.S. law.[7]

---

[6] Enforcing foreign judgments rendered on claims considered maritime under U.S. law has the additional salutary effect of clearly establishing federal jurisdiction as a matter of law where complicated factfinding might otherwise be necessary, even under the literal terms of *Penhallow*'s rule of enforcing the judgments of foreign admiralty courts. Thus, for example, a foreign court might have jurisdiction over maritime and other non-maritime commercial claims. Or it might have jurisdiction over personal injuries suffered by workers employed in motor, air, rail, and sea transportation. Whether such a court is a foreign admiralty court may not be obvious. But if the foreign court renders a judgment on a claim for personal injury suffered by a seaman as a result of the unseaworthiness of a vessel, the use of U.S. law to conclude that the claim is maritime obviates the need under *Penhallow* (or otherwise) to inquire into the intricacies of the foreign judicial system.

[7] We have outlined reasons why we believe that admiralty jurisdiction under § 1333 includes the authority to enforce foreign judgments on claims that would be considered maritime under U.S. law. We have no reason in this case to decide whether the maritime nature of the claim under the law of the nation that rendered the judgment would also suffice to bring a suit on the judgment within the jurisdiction established by § 1333. Our ruling today would remain the same regardless of whether the maritime classification of the underlying claim

Accordingly, this suit **[—30—]** to enforce an English judgment comes within the admiralty jurisdiction of § 1333 if the underlying claim on the FFA is deemed maritime under the standards of U.S. law. Because the district court did not consider that question below, we remand to the district court to make that determination in the first instance.[8]

CONCLUSION

For the above reasons, the judgment of the district court is VACATED, and the case is REMANDED.

---

under the foreign substantive law is sufficient to bring the suit within § 1333 jurisdiction.

[8] We note that Primera also contends that D'Amico forfeited the argument that U.S. law should determine the maritime nature of the claim. We disagree. We believe this was adequately raised by D'Amico in the proceedings prior to the entry of judgment. *See* Pl.'s Mem. Opp'n Def.'s Mot. Dismiss 6-13, Nov. 20, 2009, S.D.N.Y. ECF No. 16 (arguing that the district court had admiralty jurisdiction because FFAs are maritime under both U.S. and English law).

United States Court of Appeals
for the Second Circuit

No. 13-3416

SOMPO JAPAN INS. CO. OF AM.
VS.
NORFOLK S. RY. CO.

Appeal from the United States District Court for the
Southern District of New York

Decided: August 6, 2014

Citation: 762 F.3d 165, 2 Adm. R. 78 (2d Cir. 2014).

Before **JACOBS, SACK,** and **LYNCH,** Circuit Judges.

[—3—] **LYNCH,** Circuit Judge:

In April 2006, a train derailed near Dallas, Texas, destroying much of the [—4—] train's cargo—a variety of manufactured goods ranging from tractors to copy machines. The derailment precipitated these actions, which are on appeal before this Court for the second time. Before taking their fateful train ride, the manufactured goods had traveled across the Pacific Ocean from various parts of Asia. Their entire international journey was governed by through bills of lading—essentially, contracts—issued by ocean carriers to the cargo owners or their intermediaries. In the aftermath of the derailment, the plaintiffs Sompo Japan Insurance Company of America ("Sompo") and Nipponkoa Insurance Company ("Nipponkoa") (collectively, "plaintiffs")—subrogees of the cargo owners/shippers—filed suit against Norfolk Southern Railway Company, Norfolk Southern Corporation (together, "Norfolk Southern"),[1] and the Kansas City Southern Railway Company ("KCSR") (collectively, "defendants" or "the Railroads") to recover for the damage sustained to the cargo by the derailment.

The litigation was originally pursued based on plaintiffs' federal causes of action under the framework of the Carmack Amendment, legislation that addresses carrier liability for goods lost or damaged during an interstate [—5—] shipment. Following the Supreme Court's decision in *Kawasaki Kisen Kaisha Ltd. v. Regal-Beloit Corp.*, 561 U.S. 89 (2010) ("*Regal-Beloit*"), which made clear that the Carmack Amendment does not apply to the shipments at issue, the ground shifted, and the cases were remanded to the United States District Court for the Southern District of New York (Denny Chin, *Judge*) for further proceedings on plaintiffs' state law claims. In these appeals, heard in tandem, plaintiffs ask us to decide the meaning and enforceability of provisions found in the bills that purport to designate the ocean carrier as the sole entity responsible to the cargo owners for damage to the cargo. In addition, the appeal in *Nipponkoa Insurance Co. v. Norfolk Southern Railway* challenges Nipponkoa's ability to maintain its claim for contractual indemnification—a claim assigned to it by the upstream ocean carrier—against Norfolk Southern and KCSR. For the reasons described below, we affirm the judgments of the district court in full.

BACKGROUND

I. *The Underlying Facts*

In March and April 2006, a number of manufacturers arranged to have their products shipped from places in Asia to locations in the southern United States. Two of the manufacturers sought to ship automotive parts from Japan to [—6—] Georgia, and hired Nippon Express U.S.A. ("Nippon Express"), a non-vessel owning common carrier ("NVOCC"),[2] to arrange for the transportation of the shipments.[3] Nippon

---

[1] Sompo, but not Nipponkoa, sued Norfolk Southern Corporation. For ease of reference, we will refer to the Norfolk entities that the plaintiffs have respectively sued simply as Norfolk Southern.

[2] "An NVOCC will issue a bill of lading to the shipper but does not undertake the actual transportation of the cargo. Instead, the NVOCC delivers the shipment to an ocean carrier for transportation." *Royal & Sun Alliance Ins., PLC v. Ocean World Lines, Inc.*, 612 F.3d 138, 140 n.2 (2d Cir. 2010) (internal quotation marks omitted).

[3] The two shipments governed by the Nippon Express bill of lading that are relevant to these appeals are the Unisia Shipment and the Enplas Shipment. Sompo is pursuing a claim for damage to the Unisia Shipment, while Nipponkoa has

Express issued a through bill of lading to the manufacturers ("Nippon Express bill of lading"). A through bill of lading is essentially a contract that describes the terms that will govern both the ocean and land portions of the shipments' transport.[4] Because Nippon Express does not itself provide transportation services, it hired Yang Ming—an ocean carrier—to provide the ocean transport and arrange the land leg of the shipments' journey. Accordingly, Yang Ming issued through bills of lading of its own to Nippon Express ("Yang Ming bill of lading"), detailing the terms under which the [—7—] transportation would be undertaken.[5] A third manufacturer sought to ship tractors from Japan to Georgia, and contracted directly with Yang Ming to arrange for the entirety of the shipment's transportation.[6] Yang Ming again issued a through bill of lading.

With respect to each of the shipments, Yang Ming subcontracted responsibility for a portion of the inland transport to defendant Norfolk Southern and Norfolk Southern enlisted the assistance of defendant KCSR. Norfolk Southern undertook to transport the shipments pursuant to an Intermodal Transport Agreement ("ITA") that it had entered into with Yang Ming. The plaintiffs Sompo and Nipponkoa are the subrogees of the owners of the destroyed cargo.

The bills of lading contain a number of terms that, in the event of damage to or loss of the cargo, serve to limit the carriers' liability—for instance, provisions that cap the amount of damages to be paid per package of goods, and [—8—] that limit the time for filing suit. The bills also contain Himalaya clauses[7]—clauses that extend the benefit of the bills' liability-limiting provisions to downstream carriers that are engaged by an upstream carrier to assist in the carriage of goods.[8] Most importantly, the Yang Ming bill of lading contains a provision that Sompo and Nipponkoa refer to as an "Exoneration Clause."[9] The Exoneration Clause reads:

It is understood and agreed that, other than the Carrier, no Person, firm or corporation or other legal entity whatsoever (Including the Master, officers and crew of [—9—] the vessel, agents, Underlying Carriers, Sub-Contractors and/or any other independent contractors whatsoever utilized in the Carriage) is, or shall be deemed to be, liable with respect to the Goods as Carrier, bailee or otherwise.

Sompo J.A. 241.

---

secured a judgment for damage to the Enplas Shipment.

[4] "A through bill of lading covers both the ocean and inland portions of the transport in a single document." *Regal-Beloit*, 561 U.S at 94.

[5] The parties have provided the court with a copy of the terms of the Yang Ming and Nippon Express bills of lading, as well as typed excerpts from those bills. Because the parties have not argued otherwise, we assume that the terms in each bill of lading issued by Yang Ming are identical in all material respects, and that the terms in each bill of lading issued by Nippon Express are similarly identical.

[6] This shipment is referred to as the Kubota Shipment; it is one of the two shipments that are the subject of Sompo's appeal.

[7] "Clauses extending liability limitations take their name from an English case involving a steamship called *Himalaya. See Adler v. Dickson*, [1955] 1 Q.B. 158 (C.A.)." *Norfolk S. Ry Co. v. Kirby*, 543 U.S. 14, 20 n.2 (2004).

[8] The Himalaya Clause in the Nippon Express bill of lading reads: "If an action for loss or damage to the goods is brought against a person referred to in Clause 4.2, such person shall be entitled to avail himself of the defenses and the limits of liability which the Carrier is entitled to invoke under these conditions." Nipponkoa J.A. 73. The Himalaya Clause in the Yang Ming bill of lading provides: "If, however, it shall be adjudged that any Person other than the Carrier is Carrier or bailee of the Goods, or under responsibility with respect thereto, then all exemptions and limitations of, and exonerations from, liability provided by law or by the terms in this Bill shall be available to such Person." *Id*. at 76; 136.

[9] The Railroads refer to the provision as a "covenant not to sue." Although the provision is not phrased or labeled as a covenant not to sue, because it purports to relieve the Railroads from liability to anyone other than Yang Ming, it renders suit against the Railroads by any such person futile. We will refer to the clause as an Exoneration Clause, but the clause's appellation does not affect our analysis.

Consistent with the arrangements described above, the manufactured goods traveled from Asia to California by ocean vessel. In California, the shipments were loaded onto the trains of non-party Burlington Northern Santa Fe Railway Company, and transported to Texas, where they were transferred to the railcars of Norfolk Southern, which were operated by KCSR. The derailment took place just outside Dallas, Texas.

II. *The Litigation: Round I*

In the aftermath of the derailment, Sompo and Nipponkoa filed suit against the defendants. Both plaintiffs asserted claims under the Carmack Amendment, as well as claims for breach of contract, negligence, and bailment. In addition, in its amended complaint, Nipponkoa asserted a claim based on an assignment it received from Yang Ming of Yang Ming's rights against the defendants arising out of loss or damage to the Enplas Shipment. The defendants [—10—] answered without asserting that the Yang Ming bill of lading's Exoneration Clause prevented them from being liable to the plaintiffs.

Although the complaints asserted state law causes of action against the defendants, the litigation centered on plaintiffs' claims under the Carmack Amendment. The Carmack Amendment amended the Interstate Commerce Act ("ICA") in 1906. Act of June 29, 1906, ch. 3591, 34 Stat. 584 (1906) (current version at 49 U.S.C. § 11706). The ICA, itself enacted in 1887, created the Interstate Commerce Commission, which was responsible for regulating railroad rates.[10] The Carmack Amendment "addresses the subject of carrier liability for goods lost or damaged during shipment, and most importantly provides shippers with the statutory right to recover for the actual loss or injury to their property caused by any of the carriers involved in the shipment." *Cleveland v. Beltman N. Am. Co.*, 30 F.3d 373, 377 (2d Cir. 1994) (emphasis omitted). It establishes

"a single uniform regime for recovery by shippers" from any receiving or delivering carriers involved in the shipment of the goods, and preempts the "shipper's state and common law claims against a carrier for loss or damage to goods during [—11—] shipment." *Project Hope v. M/V IBN SINA*, 250 F.3d 67, 73-74 n.6 (2d Cir. 2001); *see also Adams Express Co. v. Croninger*, 226 U.S. 491, 505-06 (1913). Prior to the initiation of these actions, this Circuit had held that the Carmack Amendment applied to the domestic rail leg of a continuous intermodal shipment originating in a foreign country and traveling under a through bill of lading like the shipments at issue here. *See Sompo Japan Ins. Co. of Am. v. Union Pac. R. Co.*, 456 F.3d 54, 59 (2d Cir. 2006) ("*Sompo Japan*"). That holding has since been abrogated by the Supreme Court's decision in *Regal-Beloit*.

The Carmack Amendment is a favorite among shippers because it imposes something close to strict liability on covered carriers, *see Sompo Japan*, 456 F.3d at 59, *abrogated on other grounds by Regal-Beloit*, 561 U.S. at 100, and it "imposes upon receiving rail carriers and delivering rail carriers liability for damage caused during the rail route under the bill of lading, regardless of which carrier caused the damage." *Regal-Beloit*, 561 U.S. at 98 (internal quotation marks and alterations omitted). "Once the shipper establishes a prima facie case of Carmack liability by showing delivery in good condition, arrival in damaged condition, and the amount of damages, the carrier is liable for the actual loss or injury to the property it transports," unless the carrier can establish that it was [—12—] free of negligence and that the loss or damage was caused by one of five excusable factors.[11] *Sompo Japan*, 456 F.3d at 59 & n.8 (internal quotation marks and citations omitted). The Amendment also "constrains carriers' ability to limit liability by contract." *Regal-Beloit*, 561 U.S. at 98 (citing 49 U.S.C. § 11706). Suffice it to say that, ordinarily, a

---

[10] In 1995, the Interstate Commerce Commission Termination Act replaced the Interstate Commerce Commission with the Surface Transportation Board. 49 U.S.C. § 702.

[11] Specifically, the defendant may avoid liability by proving that the loss or damage was caused by "(a) an act of God, (b) the public enemy, (c) an act of the shipper himself, (d) public authority, or (e) the inherent vice or nature of the goods." *Sompo Japan*, 456 F.3d at 59 n.8.

carrier may not limit its liability to a shipper without first offering the shipper full Carmack liability. *Sompo Japan*, 456 F.3d at 59-60 (internal citations omitted).

Although the Carmack Amendment did not leave the defendants without defenses to the plaintiffs' suits, it circumscribed the field of litigable issues. Accordingly, only a few months after filing suit, Sompo moved for partial summary judgment, seeking to strike the defendants' defenses based on liability limitations in the pertinent through bills of lading and other contracts. Because our then-controlling decision in *Sompo Japan* made clear that the Carmack Amendment applied to the domestic rail leg of a continuous intermodal shipment originating in a foreign country, the litigation of this summary judgment motion focused on a slightly different issue—whether Norfolk [—13—] Southern, in its contract with Yang Ming, had entered into a type of private contract that might make the Carmack Amendment inapplicable. *Cf. Regal-Beloit Corp.*, 561 U.S. at 98-99 ("The parties argue about whether they may contract out of Carmack's venue provisions and other requirements, see [49 U.S.C.] §§ 10502, 10709; but in light of the disposition and ruling to follow, those matters need not be discussed or further explored.").

The district court determined that Norfolk had not entered into such a contract,[12] that Carmack accordingly applied, and that because Norfolk had not offered the shippers the option of full Carmack liability, the

defendants could not rely on any alternative terms limiting their liability for the damage to the cargo. *Norfolk S. Ry.*, 540 F. Supp. 2d at 497-500. In a subsequent round of summary judgment practice, the plaintiffs' common law claims were dismissed as preempted by the Carmack Amendment. The parties disputed only whether the [—14—] plaintiffs had established all of the elements of a prima facie Carmack claim. Because the district court determined that they had, that no reasonable jury could conclude otherwise, and that no reasonable jury could find that the defendants had established a viable defense, the court granted summary judgment in the plaintiffs' favor.[13] *Sompo Japan Ins. Co. of Am. v. Norfolk S. Ry. Co.*, 652 F. Supp. 2d 537, 542-45 (S.D.N.Y. 2009).

The defendants appealed. While the appeal was pending, however, the Supreme Court decided *Regal-Beloit*, 561 U.S. 89 (2010), holding that the Carmack Amendment "does not apply to a shipment originating overseas under a single through bill of lading," *id.* at 100, thereby abrogating our contrary holding in *Sompo Japan*. In light of this change in the governing law, we remanded these cases, explaining as follows:

> The district court granted summary judgment to the plaintiffs in these two related cases based on what was then binding Second Circuit precedent. The parties agree that the Supreme Court, in *Kawasaki Kisen Kaisha Ltd. v. Regal-Beloit Corp.*, 561 U.S. —, 130 S.Ct. 2433 (2010), has abrogated the precedent upon which [—15—] the district court relied. The plaintiffs-appellees have raised further grounds they claim would support the judgment regardless of *Regal-Beloit*, but concede that they did not present these grounds below because of the state of

---

[12] The district court also held that even if Norfolk Southern's contract with Yang Ming could be construed as such a private contract, it should not be so construed. *Sompo Japan Ins. Co. v. Norfolk S. Ry. Co.*, 540 F. Supp. 2d 486, 498 (S.D.N.Y. 2008) ("*Norfolk S. Ry.*") ("I conclude that rail contracts for the movement of cargo traveling on the domestic rail leg of a continuous intermodal movement, such as the ITAs in this case, should be read as § 10502 and not § 10709 contracts."). For that conclusion, the court relied in part on *Sompo Japan*'s holding that "Carmack applies to the domestic rail portion of an international shipment originating in a foreign country and traveling under a through bill of lading." *Norfolk S. Ry.*, 540 F. Supp. 2d at 499 (internal quotation marks omitted).

[13] Initially, Sompo, but not Nipponkoa, moved for summary judgment on its Carmack Amendment claim. After the district court granted summary judgment in Sompo's favor on that claim, Nipponkoa moved for and was granted summary judgment on the same basis. *Nipponkoa Ins. Co. Ltd. v. Norfolk S. Ry. Co.*, No. 07 Civ. 10498, 2009 WL 3734068 (S.D.N.Y. Nov. 9, 2009).

the law at the time. The parties therefore have agreed that we should decline to reach these issues so that the district court may have the first opportunity to address them on remand.

The judgment is VACATED and REMANDED for further proceedings.

Nipponkoa Ins. Co. v. Norfolk S. Ry. Co., 394 F. App'x 751, 751-52 (2d Cir. 2010) (internal citations omitted).

III. *The Litigation: Round II*

When the case returned to the district court, the plaintiffs' state law claims—no longer preempted by the Carmack Amendment—were reinstated. After an additional period of discovery, a third round of summary judgment practice ensued, now focused on the viability of the plaintiffs' state law claims. For the first time, the defendants argued that provisions in the Yang Ming and Nippon Express bills of lading—the Exoneration Clauses—prevented the defendants from being liable to the plaintiffs because those clauses designated the issuing carrier as the sole entity responsible to the cargo owners for damage to the cargo. Plaintiffs contested this argument on multiple fronts. In addition to arguing that [—16—] the defendants' assertion of the Exoneration Clauses was untimely, they contended that the clauses should not be interpreted to relieve the defendants of liability to the plaintiffs, and that if so interpreted the clauses would violate statutory law[14] and public policy.

The district court initially granted in part and denied in part the defendants' summary judgment motion. Because the court construed the Yang Ming bill of lading's Exoneration Clause as relieving the defendants of liability to the plaintiffs, and found that clause to be enforceable, the court granted summary judgment to the defendants with respect to the shipments covered by the Yang Ming bill of lading alone. With respect to the shipment that was covered by both the Yang Ming and Nippon Express bills of lading, however, the court ruled differently. Because the court determined that the putative Exoneration Clause in the Nippon Express bill of lading was ambiguous, it denied summary judgment, and instructed the parties to offer extrinsic evidence of the clause's intended meaning. *See Sompo Japan Ins. Co. of Am.*, 891 F. Supp. 2d at 496-503. [—17—]

Following the district court's decision, both sides moved for reconsideration. The defendants argued that it was unnecessary for the court to interpret the putative Exoneration Clause in the Nippon Express bill of lading because the shipment governed by that bill of lading was also governed by the Yang Ming bill of lading, which the court had already ruled contained an enforceable and unambiguous Exoneration Clause. In accordance with the Supreme Court's decision in *Norfolk So. Ry. Co. v. James N. Kirby, Pty Ltd.*, 543 U.S. 14 (2004),[15] the defendants argued that they were entitled to invoke the Exoneration Clause in the Yang Ming bill of lading against the plaintiffs even though, with respect to the shipments at issue, the Yang Ming bill of lading was issued to Nippon Express, and not to the cargo owners in whose shoes the plaintiffs stood. For their part, plaintiffs argued that extrinsic evidence demonstrated that the terms of the Nippon Express bill of lading were not intended to bar the cargo owners from suing the defendants. In support of this [—18—] argument, the plaintiffs submitted affidavits from a Nippon

---

[14] In the district court, plaintiffs argued that enforcement of the Exoneration Clauses would violate the Carriage of Goods by Sea Act, 46 U.S.C. § 30701 note, and the Harter Act, 46 U.S.C. §§ 30702 *et seq. Sompo Japan Ins. Co. of Am. v. Norfolk S. Ry. Co.*, 891 F.Supp. 2d 489, 499-500 (S.D.N.Y. 2012). The district court rejected those arguments, and plaintiffs have not contested that ruling on appeal.

[15] In *Kirby*, the Supreme Court decided that the bills of lading at issue were maritime contracts governed by federal law, that Himalaya Clauses in bills of lading are subject to ordinary contract interpretation principles, and that the downstream rail carrier in that case was entitled to invoke the liability limitations contained in the bills of lading issued by upstream carriers to the cargo owner and to the cargo owner's intermediary. 543 U.S. at 24, 30-35.

Express executive and an expert in the transportation industry.

Additionally, Nipponkoa argued that, irrespective of the meaning or enforceability of the Exoneration Clauses, it should prevail on its claim for damage to the Enplas Shipment, which it asserted as assignee of Yang Ming. In support of this claim, Nipponkoa relied on an indemnification provision in the ITA between Norfolk Southern and Yang Ming, which states that:

> [Norfolk Southern] will be liable for and will hold [Yang Ming] harmless against loss of or damage to freight in containers transported at the rates and charges provided in this Agreement and Exhibit 1 only to the extent that the sole proximate cause of said loss or damage is a railroad accident, derailment, or collision between railroad equipment negligently caused by [Norfolk Southern].

Nipponkoa J.A. 51. In opposing this claim, defendants argued that Nipponkoa was not entitled to summary judgment on its assigned claim for contractual indemnification because there was no evidence that Yang Ming had paid damages to anyone for damage to the Enplas Shipment.[16] [—19—]

Upon reconsideration, the district court granted summary judgment in defendants' favor on all claims with the exception of Nipponkoa's claim for damage to the Enplas Shipment. On that claim, the district court granted summary judgment for Nipponkoa. *See Sompo Japan Ins. Co. of Am. v. Norfolk S. Ry. Co.*, 966 F. Supp. 2d 270, 279-82 (S.D.N.Y. 2013). Defendants again sought reconsideration of the district court's judgment. This time defendants argued that

Nipponkoa's claim for contractual indemnification must fail because Yang Ming—the assignor of the claim—had no claim for contractual indemnification since, by the time Nipponkoa obtained the assignment, Yang Ming no longer had any potential liability for damage to the Enplas Shipment. The district court denied defendants' motion for reconsideration on the ground that it raised new arguments that could have been raised earlier.

IV. *The Appeals*

Sompo appeals the grant of summary judgment in defendants' favor, and defendants appeal the grant of summary judgment in Nipponkoa's favor on its [—20—] claim for damage to the Enplas Shipment.[17] For the reasons discussed below, we affirm the judgments of the district court.

DISCUSSION

"We review a district court's grant of summary judgment *de novo.*" *Gould v. Winstar Commc'ns, Inc.*, 692 F.3d 148, 157 (2d Cir. 2012). Summary judgment is appropriate only when, construing the evidence in the light most favorable to the non-moving party, "there is no genuine dispute as to any material fact and the movant is entitled to judgment as a matter of law." Fed. R. Civ. P. 56(a). Where, as here, cross-motions for summary judgment are appealed, "each party's motion must be examined on its own merits, and in each case all reasonable inferences must be drawn against the party whose motion is under consideration." *Morales v. Quintel Entm't, Inc.*, 249 F.3d 115, 121 (2d Cir. 2001).

We consider each of the summary judgment decisions being appealed in turn. First, we consider whether the district court properly

---

[16] The defendants also argued that the ITA required any suit pertaining to the agreement to be brought in specific venues that do not include New York City. The district court concluded that the defendants were estopped from pressing that argument by virtue of their prior admission that venue was proper in the Southern District of New York. The defendants do not renew their venue argument on appeal.

[17] Nipponkoa does not separately appeal the district court's grant of summary judgment to defendants on Nipponkoa's other claims. It does, however, join in Sompo's arguments and presses those arguments as an alternative basis for affirming the district court's grant of summary judgment in Nipponkoa's favor on its claim pertaining to the Enplas Shipment.

granted summary judgment to the defendants on Sompo's claims. Next, we consider whether the [—21—] district court properly granted summary judgment to Nipponkoa on Nipponkoa's claim for contractual indemnification arising out of damage to the Enplas Shipment.

I. *Sompo*

The district court granted summary judgment in favor of defendants and against Sompo on the ground that the Exoneration Clause in the Yang Ming bill of lading unambiguously and validly relieved the Railroads of liability to the cargo owners in whose shoes Sompo stands. On appeal, Sompo presses roughly five objections to that ruling. Specifically, Sompo argues that (1) the district court exceeded the mandate issued by this Court in connection with the prior appeal when, on remand, the district court permitted the Railroads to raise defenses to Sompo's common law claims; (2) the Railroads waived their defense based on the Exoneration Clauses by failing to plead it in their answer to Sompo's complaint and by failing to raise it at any point in the litigation prior to the summary judgment practice that ensued upon remand; (3) the Exoneration Clause in the Yang Ming bill of lading is ambiguous and should be construed against the Railroads; (4) insofar as the Exoneration Clause is construed as relieving the Railroads from liability to the cargo owners, that construction is contrary to the [—22—] intent of the parties that executed the bill of lading, industry practice, and public policy; and (5) Nippon Express did not have authority to bind a cargo owner—and thus Sompo—to the Exoneration Clause in the Yang Ming bill of lading.[18] We consider each of these arguments in turn.

---

[18] In a letter submitted pursuant to Federal Rule of Appellate Procedure 28(j), Sompo and Nipponkoa point the Court to the Sixth Circuit's decision in *CNA Insurance Co. v. Hyundai Merchant Marine Co.*, 747 F.3d 339, 2 Adm. R. 410 (6th Cir. 2014), and claim that it supports their point that "when the intermodal bill of lading incorporates the Carmack Amendment by reference, then the through bill of lading must offer a full Carmack option or a carrier cannot limit its liability." Dkt No. 13-3416, ECF No. 69. That

A. *Mandate Rule*

"Under the law-of-the-case doctrine, where a case has been decided by an appellate court and remanded, the court to which it is remanded must proceed in accordance with the mandate and such law of the case as was established by the appellate court." *Kerman v. City of New York*, 374 F.3d 93, 109 (2d Cir. 2004) (internal quotation marks and brackets omitted). The "mandate rule prevents relitigation in the district court not only of matters expressly decided by the appellate court, but also precludes re-litigation of issues impliedly resolved by the appellate court's mandate." *Brown v. City of Syracuse*, 673 F.3d 141, 147 (2d Cir. 2012) (internal quotation marks omitted). Furthermore, where the mandate [—23—] limits the issues open for consideration on remand, the district court ordinarily may not deviate from the specific dictates or spirit of the mandate by considering additional issues on remand. *See Riley v. MEBA Pension Trust*, 586 F.2d 968, 970-71 (2d Cir. 1978).

We conclude that the district court did not violate the mandate rule when it considered the Railroads' defenses based on the Exoneration Clauses in the pertinent bills of lading. To begin, Sompo does not, and cannot, contend that this Court addressed the merits of those defenses. The Railroads' original appeal challenged the district court's determination that the Carmack Amendment applied to the shipments it carried. The Supreme Court's decision in *Regal-Beloit* revealed that determination to be erroneous. The Railroads' appeal did not raise, and we did not address, whether certain defenses that might be viable against Sompo's state law claims were they not preempted, but that would not have been available if the Carmack Amendment applied, would succeed. Thus the district court did not violate the mandate rule by addressing on remand an issue that was not decided by this Court in the original appeal. *See New England Ins. Co. v. Healthcare Underwriters Mut. Ins. Co.*, 352 F.3d 599, 606 (2d Cir. 2003) ("[A] mandate is

---

argument is made nowhere in the plaintiffs' briefs and is therefore waived.

controlling only as to matters within its compass . . . . Put simply, the [—24—] law of the case does not extend to issues an appellate court did not address." (internal quotation marks and citations omitted)).

Nor are we persuaded that our remand order instructed the district court not to consider the Railroads' defenses. Sompo insists that the remand order required the district court to consider only plaintiffs' "further grounds" for relief, and not any defenses the Railroads might have to those grounds. Sompo's Br. at 21. Sompo's interpretation of our remand order is utterly implausible. While the order acknowledged that "[t]he parties . . . have agreed that we should decline to reach these issues so that the district court may have the first opportunity to address them on remand," it did not instruct the district court to limit its consideration to the prima facie elements of additional claims the plaintiffs might seek to pursue on remand. *Nipponkoa Ins. Co.*, 394 F. App'x at 751-52. Instead, we simply vacated the judgment and remanded "for further proceedings," leaving it to the district court to determine how the case ought to proceed. *See United States v. Salameh*, 84 F.3d 47, 49 (2d Cir. 1996) (remand order that "specified only that the case was remanded 'for further proceedings' . . . permitted the District Court itself to determine the appropriate course of 'further proceedings.'"). Furthermore, the remand order itself acknowledged that the [—25—] plaintiffs "did not present [their further] grounds [for relief] below because of the state of the law at the time." 394 F. App'x at 752. It is illogical to suppose that we instructed the district court to consider claims that were not previously pursued by the plaintiff, but prohibited the district court from considering defenses to those claims.

B. *Waiver*

As a separate matter, a party may waive an argument by failing to raise it in a timely manner, making consideration of that argument by the district court inappropriate in certain circumstances even if consideration is not barred by the appellate court's mandate.

No such waiver prevents consideration of the Railroads' defenses.

The district court did not exceed its discretion by considering the defenses despite the defendants' failure to plead them in their answers. It is true that a party responding to a pleading "must affirmatively state any avoidance or affirmative defense," Fed. R. Civ. P. 8(c)(1), and that generally, "[f]ailure to plead an affirmative defense in the answer results in the waiver of that defense and its exclusion from the case." *Satchell v. Dilworth*, 745 F.2d 781, 784 (2d Cir. 1984) (internal quotation marks omitted). Nonetheless, "a district court may entertain [—26—] unpleaded affirmative defenses at the summary judgment stage in the absence of undue prejudice to the plaintiff, bad faith or dilatory motive on the part of the defendant, futility, or undue delay of the proceedings." *Rose v. AmSouth Bank of Fla.*, 391 F.3d 63, 65 (2d Cir. 2004) (internal quotation marks, ellipsis, and alteration omitted). Those are precisely the circumstances here.

We reject Sompo's contention that the Railroads waived the Exoneration Clause defense by failing to raise it in the initial rounds of summary judgment practice that preceded the Railroads' prior appeal, or on appeal to this Court. The Exoneration Clause defense would have been irrelevant in those contexts. It is undisputed that if the Carmack Amendment applied to the shipments carried by the Railroads, and if the Railroads had not entered into the type of private contract that might make Carmack inapplicable, the Exoneration Clauses would be unenforceable against the plaintiffs because the cargo owners were not offered the option of full Carmack liability. The initial rounds of summary judgment, and the Railroads' first appeal, focused on questions about the applicability of Carmack to the shipments at issue and on plaintiffs' ability to establish a prima facie case under the Amendment. Neither of those questions could be answered, or in any way influenced, by reference to the existence of putative Exoneration [—27—] Clauses in the Yang Ming and Nippon Express bills of lading. It is thus entirely appropriate, and unremarkable, that the

Railroads did not seek to press that defense at those stages of the litigation. But the Supreme Court's decision in *Regal-Beloit* marked a sea change in the case. The Carmack Amendment—formerly the focus of the litigation—was rendered inapplicable to the shipments at issue. The parties took stock of their changed circumstances, and plaintiffs elected to continue the litigation on claims previously believed to be preempted. The summary judgment practice that ensued upon remand was, for all practical purposes, the Railroads' first opportunity to litigate the viability of their Exoneration Clause defense.

For the same reason, we are unpersuaded that Sompo has suffered any prejudice as a result of the Railroads' failure to raise the Exoneration Clauses prior to summary judgment practice on remand. Although Sompo deplores the time and money wasted on the initial phase of litigation in the trial court and on the first appeal to this Court, none of that waste was attributable to the Railroads' failure to assert the Exoneration Clauses at an earlier stage. Rather, Sompo's misfortunes are the result of its own, entirely reasonable, decision to pursue this litigation under the framework of the Carmack Amendment, and of a change in [—28—] the law that rendered plaintiffs' efforts on that front for naught. In short, we are not convinced that the district court's consideration of the Railroads' defense was in any way improper.

This Court's decision in *Parmalat Capital Financial Ltd. v. Bank of America Corp.*, 671 F.3d 261 (2d Cir. 2012) is not to the contrary. In a prior appeal of the consolidated cases involved in *Parmalat*, the plaintiffs there had challenged the district court's decision not to abstain from deciding the cases pursuant to the mandatory abstention provision in 28 U.S.C. § 1334(c)(2) that applies to bankruptcy-related proceedings.[19] We vacated those decisions in part and remanded for a determination of whether the cases could be "timely adjudicated" in Illinois state court in accordance with factors set out in our opinion. *Id.* at 264. On remand, the district court ruled that even if the cases could be "'timely adjudicated' in the Illinois state courts, mandatory abstention did not apply because these cases 'could have been commenced' in federal court." *Id.* at 270 (ellipsis omitted). We concluded that "[i]t was error [for the district court] to consider this argument, because it had been waived, and because it was outside [—29—] the scope of the mandate set forth in our previous Opinion." *Id.* In so ruling, the court explained that "this argument was waived in the initial appeal, because it had not been raised with the District Court as a basis to avoid mandatory abstention," and consideration of the argument exceeded the court's mandate, which "focused specifically and exclusively on the question of 'timely adjudication.'" *Id.*

Parmalat is far removed from the circumstances of this case. Unlike in *Parmalat*, where the new argument considered on remand would have been determinative of the issue decided by the district court in the initial phase of litigation, in this case the Railroads' Exoneration Clause defense would have been irrelevant to the issues litigated before the district court and the court of appeals during the initial phase of litigation. Furthermore, while the opinion remanding the cases to the district court in *Parmalat* focused specifically and exclusively on the question of timely adjudication, our order was not so focused, instead recognizing that whatever further grounds for relief the plaintiff might have, those grounds had not previously been presented to the district court. Under the circumstances, the district court properly considered the Railroads' defenses to the plaintiffs' common law claims. Because the district court's consideration of [—30—] the Exoneration Clause defense was proper, we proceed to consider the merits of that defense.

---

[19] "Section 1334(c)(2) provides that, in certain circumstances, a district court must abstain from hearing state law claims that are related to a bankruptcy case when those proceedings can be 'timely adjudicated' in state court." *Parmalat*, 671 F.3d at 266.

C. *Interpretation of the Yang Ming Bill of Lading's Exoneration Clause*

Sompo next argues that the Exoneration Clause in the Yang Ming bill of lading—which the Railroads argue prevents them from being held liable to Sompo—is ambiguous and should be construed against the Railroads.[20] The alleged ambiguity in the putative Exoneration Clause is created by the interaction of the Exoneration Clause itself and the Yang Ming bill of lading's definitions of the terms "Carrier" and "Underlying Carrier."

As described above, the Exoneration Clause provides:

> It is understood and agreed that, other than *the Carrier*, no Person, firm or corporation or other legal entity whatsoever (Including the Master, officers and crew of the vessel, agents, *Underlying Carriers*, Sub-Contractors and/or any other independent contractors whatsoever [—31—] utilized in the Carriage) is, or shall be deemed to be, liable with respect to the Goods as Carrier, bailee or otherwise.

Sompo J.A. 241 (emphasis added). Meanwhile, however, the bill defines the term "Carrier" as "the party on whose behalf this Bill is issued, as well as the Vessel and/or her Owner, demise charterer (if bound hereby), the time charterer and an[y] substituted or *Underlying Carrier* whether any of them is acting as a Carrier or bailee." *Id.* (emphasis supplied).

The bill further defines the term "Underlying Carrier" to "include[] any water, rail, motor, air or other carrier utilized by the Carrier for any parts of the transportation [of] the shipment covered by this Bill." *Id.* The parties agree that the Railroads are "Underlying Carriers" within the meaning of the Yang Ming bill of lading.

Because "Underlying Carriers" are included within the bill's definition of "Carrier," the Railroads are also "Carriers" per the definition of that term. As a result, although the Exoneration Clause purports to state that *only* "the Carrier" shall be liable, and that no one else—including any Underlying Carrier—shall be, because of the inclusive definition of the term "Carrier," the Exoneration Clause simultaneously states that the Railroads *can* be held liable and that they *cannot* be. Relying on this odd result, Sompo argues that the clause is ambiguous and must [—32—] be construed against the parties seeking its benefit, here the Railroads. We cannot agree.

To be sure, "[t]he traditional rule of construction, applied in admiralty cases, is to construe contract language most strongly against its drafter." *Navieros Oceanikos, S.A. v. S.T. Mobil Trader*, 554 F.2d 43, 47 (2d Cir. 1977) (internal quotation marks and ellipsis omitted).[21] "That maxim only applies, however, where the contract language is ambiguous—where it is *susceptible of two reasonable and practical interpretations*." *Id.* (internal quotation marks omitted) (emphasis supplied). Here, the only reasonable interpretation of the clause is that the carrier that issued the bill of lading—Yang Ming—and no one else, shall be liable to the cargo owners and those subrogated to the cargo owners' interests. Sompo's proposed interpretation, which is to read the clause as inherently contradictory, is not reasonable

---

[20] In the district court, the parties agreed that the bills of lading of two other ocean carriers responsible for some of the shipments "contain[ed] covenants not to sue any party other than the carrier that issued the bill." *Sompo Japan Ins. Co. of Am.*, 891 F. Supp. 2d at 496. The parties only disputed whether the Yang Ming and Nippon Express bills of lading contained such provisions. The district court ruled that the Yang Ming bill of lading, but not the Nippon Express bill of lading, unambiguously prevented the Railroads from being held liable to the plaintiffs. Because of our disposition of the issues pertaining to the Yang Ming bill of lading, we need not address the putative Exoneration Clause in the Nippon Express bill of lading.

[21] "[S]o long as a bill requires substantial carriage of goods by sea, its purpose is to effectuate maritime commerce—and thus it is a maritime contract. Its character as a maritime contract is not defeated simply because it also provides for some land carriage." *Kirby*, 543 U.S. at 27. The parties do not dispute that the Yang Ming bill of lading is a maritime contract.

because it renders the clause nonsensical. In contrast, the interpretation that we adopt, although requiring us to the read the term "Carrier" more restrictively for purposes of the Exoneration Clause than the [—33—] bill's definition would seemingly require for the contract generally, gives the Exoneration Clause a comprehensible meaning and does not render any other clause meaningless. The bill's expansive definition of "Carrier" is not rendered meaningless by our interpretation because that broader definition may govern application of other sections of the bill.[22] *See Hartford Fire Ins. Co. v. Orient Overseas Containers Lines (UK), Ltd.*, 230 F.3d 549, 558 (2d Cir. 2000) ("In a situation of potential contract ambiguity, an interpretation that gives a reasonable and effective meaning to all terms of a contract is preferable to one that leaves a portion of the writing useless or inexplicable.").

Our interpretation is also supported by the rule of construction that a specific contract provision should prevail over a general one. *See J. Aron & Co. v. The Askvin*, 267 F.2d 276, 277 (2d Cir. 1959) ("Effect should be given to all the contract terms and the specific controls the general."). While the Yang Ming bill of lading's definition section provides definitions of terms that are generally [—34—] applicable throughout the bill, the Exoneration Clause specifically withdraws "Underlying Carriers" from the group of entities considered to be the "Carrier" in the context of that clause. The Exoneration Clause thus expressly contrasts "Underlying Carriers," who are *not* to be deemed liable "as Carrier[s]," with "the Carrier," which bears exclusive liability. Sompo J.A. 244. Accordingly, we conclude that the Exoneration Clause in the Yang Ming bill

of lading unambiguously prevents the Railroads from being held liable to Sompo.

Sompo next argues that our interpretation contravenes the intent of the parties to the bill of lading and industry practice. In support of its argument, Sompo points to the affidavits of Atsushi Maeda, an executive of Nippon Express, and Peter J. Zambito, an expert on transportation industry custom and practice. In his affidavit, Maeda explains that the Nippon Express bill of lading was "intended to ensure that any carrier in the chain could be claimed against or litigated against, should they be the carrier who caused the loss or damage." Sompo J.A. 510. For his part, Zambito avers that "it . . . has always been routine and common for the offending party [in a case like this] to settle directly with cargo interests, regardless of whether there is a direct contract between the two and whether or not the bill of lading contains a so-called covenant not to sue a [—35—] subcontractor, such as are at issue in this case." *Id.* at 514. He further opines that "it has been the understanding in the industry for decades that an exoneration of liability or covenant not to sue in a bill of lading would not be enforced in favor of a subcontractor." *Id.* at 516. Sompo's evidence of contractual intent and industry practice is unpersuasive.

To begin, Sompo's reliance on the Maeda affidavit is flawed in at least two respects. First, because the Exoneration Clause unambiguously relieves the Railroads of liability to Sompo, we may not consider extrinsic evidence of the contracting parties' intent to vary the meaning of that clause. *See Garza v. Marine Transp. Lines, Inc.*, 861 F.2d 23, 26-27 (2d Cir. 1988) ("In the absence of ambiguity, the effect of admitting extrinsic evidence would be to allow one party to substitute his view of his obligations for those clearly stated." (internal quotation marks omitted)). Second, even if extrinsic evidence of the contracting parties' intent were admissible, extrinsic evidence of intent would only be relevant insofar as it clarified what the contracting parties intended the Exoneration Clause in the Yang Ming bill of lading to mean. But, Maeda—an executive of Nippon Express—testified only to his

---

[22] The broader definition of Carrier may be applicable, for example, in Section 2 of the Yang Ming bill of lading, which incorporates the terms and conditions of the "Carrier's" tariffs as part of the bill of lading, and Section 25, which provides that the Carrier "shall have a lien on the Goods" being shipped under the bill of lading. Sompo J.A. 244. As the Railroads point out, unlike the Exoneration Clause, Sections 2 and 25 function normally with the broader definition of "Carrier" applied.

understanding of the meaning of the terms in the Nippon Express bill of lading. He did not express any view on [—36—] the meaning of the putative Exoneration Clause in the Yang Ming bill of lading. Furthermore, even if we assumed that Maeda understood the Exoneration Clause in the Yang Ming bill of lading to permit the cargo owners to hold underlying carriers liable for damage to their cargo, that hardly suggests that Yang Ming, the contractual counterparty, held such a view of the clause's effect.

Sompo's evidence of industry practice (essentially, the Zambito affidavit) is also unavailing. Evidence of trade practice and custom may assist a court in determining whether a contract provision is ambiguous in the first instance. *See Kerin v. U.S. Postal Serv.*, 116 F.3d 988, 992 & n.2 (2d Cir. 1997) (considering evidence of trade usage to determine that contract's reference to "sewerage service" was ambiguous). Terms that have an apparently unambiguous meaning to lay persons may in fact have a specialized meaning in a particular industry. But Sompo does not contend that terms in the Exoneration Clause have a specialized meaning in the transportation industry distinct from the ordinary or common meaning that would otherwise be ascribed to them. Instead, the industry practice evidence that Sompo offers is expert testimony that, regardless of what the exoneration clauses mean, they simply are not enforced. In other words, Sompo is asking us to consider evidence of industry practice and custom [—37—] in order to persuade us to ignore the Exoneration Clause, not to help us interpret it. As one of our sister circuits has explained,

> Consideration of trade practice may be a useful interpretation aid where there is a term in the contract that has an accepted industry meaning different from its ordinary meaning or where there is a term with an accepted industry meaning that was omitted from the contract. But [appellant] does not claim that there is such a term of art included or omitted here. Trade practice is therefore irrelevant in this case, and

the contract's unambiguous terms govern.

Hunt Constr. Grp, Inc. v. United States, 281 F.3d 1369, 1373 (Fed. Cir. 2002) (internal quotation marks and first alteration omitted).

In sum, Sompo has presented no evidence to suggest that the Exoneration Clause in the Yang Ming bill of lading was intended to have a meaning different from the one we have given it.

D. *Enforceability of the Exoneration Clause*

Because we have determined that the Exoneration Clause in the Yang Ming bill of lading unambiguously relieves the Railroads of liability to Sompo, we must next consider Sompo's arguments that the clause is unenforceable.

Sompo first argues that the Exoneration Clause is unenforceable because it violates the public policy against permitting a common carrier to stipulate to [—38—] immunity for the negligence of itself or its agents. Sompo contends that the principle has been established for over a century by Supreme Court precedent, and lower federal court cases. *See, e.g., United States v. Atl. Mut. Ins. Co.*, 343 U.S. 236, 239 (1952); *Adams Express Co.*, 226 U.S. at 509-12; *Hart v. Pa. R. Co.*, 112 U.S. 331, 338, 340-41 (1884); *Bank of Ky. v. Adams Express Co.*, 93 U.S. 174, 181, 183 (1876); *N.Y Cent. R.R. Co. v. Lockwood*, 84 U.S. (17 Wall) 357, 374-81, 384 (1873); *York Co. v. Cent. R.R.*, 70 U.S. (3 Wall.) 107, 111 (1865); *Klicker v. Nw. Airlines, Inc.*, 563 F.2d 1310, 1312-13 (9th Cir. 1977); *Demel v. Am. Airlines, Inc.*, No. 09 Civ. 5524(PKC), 2011 WL 497930, at *4, *6 (S.D.N.Y. Feb. 10, 2011); *Associated Metals and Minerals Corp. v. M/V Kilmelford*, No. B-81-3085, 1983 WL 595, at *4 (D. Md. Sept. 23, 1983). While that principle is as well-established as Sompo claims, its application to a clause like the instant one is not. Indeed, with the exception of a single district court case,[23] none of the cases cited by

_____

[23] That case is *Associated Metals and Minerals Corp. v. M/V Kilmelford*, No. B- 81-3085, 1983 WL 595, at *4 (D. Md. Sept. 23, 1983). In *Associated Metals*, the shipper and subrogated insurer sought

to recover against a stevedore for damage to a shipment of steel. The stevedore argued that it was not liable to the plaintiffs, relying on a provision of the governing bill of lading that stated: "It is hereby expressly agreed that no servant or agent of the Carrier (including every independent contractor from time to time employed by the Carrier) shall in any circumstances whatsoever be under any liability whatsoever to the Shipper, Consignee, Receiver or Owner of the goods or to any holder of this Bill of Lading for any loss, damage or delay of whatsoever kind arising or resulting directly or indirectly from any act, neglect or default on his part while acting in the course or [—39—] in connection with his employment." *Id.* at *1. The district court rejected the stevedore's argument, concluding that the provision was "null and void, both under COGSA and common law." *Id.* at *2. The district court relied on the Fifth Circuit's decision in *Brown & Root, Inc v. M/V Peisander*, 648 F.2d 415, 419 (5th Cir. 1981), which stated that "at most, all the Himalaya clause does is extend to Stevedore whatever and only such 'defenses' as Carrier has. This leads to the natural conclusion . . . that whatever rights Stevedore has to limit liability are necessarily limited to those which Carrier had, [and] . . . if [the defense would be] unavailable to the Carrier [against the Shipper] it is automatically unavailable to the Stevedore." *Brown & Root*, 648 F.2d at 419. The district court extended the Fifth Circuit's reasoning to hold that "[b]ecause COGSA does not permit a carrier to enforce a provision for total exoneration," the stevedore could not enforce a provision for total exoneration through the carrier's contract with the shipper. *Associated Metals*, 1983 WL 595, at *4.

Associated Metals, which is not binding on us in any event, is unpersuasive. First, the case does not address the fact that the exoneration clause, as applied to the stevedore, would not in fact result in complete exoneration since the stevedore remained liable to the common carrier that issued the bill of lading. Furthermore, the court's decision is premised on the principle that a Himalaya Clause cannot extend to subcontractors defenses that would not be available to the issuing carrier itself. Although the language of a particular Himalaya Clause might limit the types of defenses that are extended to subcontractors, we see no reason why a Himalaya Clause could not extend to subcontractors defenses that are not available to the issuing carrier itself. The operation of a Himalaya Clause is after all, as the Supreme Court has instructed, simply a matter of contract. *Kirby*, 543 U.S. at 31-32. Here, the Himalaya Clause in the Yang Ming bill of lading broadly provides that "[i]f . . . it shall be adjudged that any Person other than the Carrier is Carrier or bailee of the Goods,

[—39—] Sompo involve provisions even remotely similar to the Exoneration Clause in the Yang Ming bill of lading. [—40—]

Furthermore, we are not convinced—despite the clause's appellation—that it in fact exonerates a common carrier or its agent from liability for damages caused by their negligence. Considered carefully, the Exoneration Clause does no such thing. Instead, the clause designates Yang Ming, and only Yang Ming, as the entity responsible for loss of or damage to a shipment caused by itself or any entity involved in the transportation of the cargo. It thereby concentrates all liability to the cargo owner in the issuing carrier, essentially requiring the cargo owner to sue the issuing carrier, and no one else, for damage to or loss of the cargo. The clause correspondingly prevents underlying carriers, like the Railroads, from being held liable for the damage they cause by their negligence *to any entity other than Yang Ming*. The Railroads are not, however, relieved of liability for their negligence. They remain liable, as Sompo concedes, to Yang Ming.[24]

Understood in context, the clause is simply an ordering mechanism. *Cf. Fed. Ins. Co. v. Union Pac. R.R. Co.*, 651 F.3d 1175, 1180 (9th Cir. 2011) ("The [—41—] requirement that all suits be brought against [the ocean carrier] is an enforcement mechanism rather than a reduction of the carrier's obligations to the cargo owner below what COGSA guarantees." (internal quotation marks omitted)). It serves to regulate who will be responsible to whom. Thus, Sompo concedes that it could sue Yang Ming for the damage to the cargo, and Yang

---

or under responsibility with respect thereto, then *all exemptions and limitations of, and exonerations from, liability* provided by law *or by the terms in this Bill* shall be available to such Person." Sompo J.A. 241 (emphasis supplied).

[24] The Yang Ming bill of lading provides that "[i]t is also agreed that each of the aforementioned Persons referred to in the [Exoneration Clause] are intended beneficiaries, but nothing herein contained shall be construed to limit or relieve them from liability to the Carrier for acts arising or resulting from their fault or negligent [sic]." Sompo J.A. 241.

Ming could then sue the Railroads.[25] It can fairly be assumed, as Sompo argues, that by requiring the cargo owner, or its subrogee, to sue the issuing carrier even when an underlying carrier is the party at fault for the damage to the cargo, the Exoneration Clause makes litigation of the claim for damage more challenging in some respects. We see no reason, however, why parties to a shipping contract should be prohibited, as a matter of public policy, from channeling claims for damage to cargo through the carrier that issues the through bill of lading. [—42—]

For similar reasons, we do not believe that the Exoneration Clause violates the letter or the spirit of the Supreme Court precedent on which Sompo relies. As Sompo points out, at common law, it is the general rule that "a common carrier may, by special contract, limit his common-law liability; but . . . he cannot stipulate for exemption from the consequences of his own negligence or that of his servants." *Hart*, 112 U.S. at 338. Examination of the precedent enforcing this principle, particularly in the context of cargo damaged by a common carrier, reveals that the general rule is animated principally by two concerns: (1) a desire to ensure that the cargo owner obtains full compensation for damage to its cargo, *see Atl. Mut. Ins. Co.*, 343 U.S. at 241-42 ("[I]t would be 'anomalous' to hold that a cargo owner, who has an unquestioned right under the law to recover full damages from a noncarrying vessel, can be compelled to give up a portion of that recovery to his carrier because of a stipulation exacted in a bill of lading."); and (2) concern that a contrary rule would induce the carrier to exercise less care, *see Hart*, 112 U.S. at 340 (upholding provision

limiting amount of loss recoverable because it "does not induce want of care" but rather "exacts from the carrier the measure of care due to the value agreed on"). [—43—]

Enforcement of the Exoneration Clause does not conflict with either of these concerns. As explained, the cargo owner, or its subrogee, can still sue the issuing carrier for damage caused by underlying carriers and thereby obtain the recovery to which it is entitled. Furthermore, the clause should not induce want of care on the part of the underlying carrier because that carrier remains liable for the consequences of its negligence to the issuing carrier. Accordingly, we conclude that the Exoneration Clause is not void as against public policy, and may therefore be enforced by the Railroads against Sompo.

E. *Authority of Intermediary to Bind Cargo Owner*

With respect to the Unisia shipment, which is governed by both the Nippon Express bill of lading and the Yang Ming bill of lading,[26] Sompo argues that because the Nippon Express bill of lading does not unambiguously contain an Exoneration Clause, and because Nippon Express was not authorized by the cargo owner to agree to the Exoneration Clause in the Yang Ming bill of lading, it is entitled to sue the Railroads for damage to that shipment.

As explained above, the cargo owner of the Unisia Shipment contracted with Nippon Express to arrange the transportation of the cargo. We assume [—44—] arguendo that the bill of lading issued by Nippon Express to the owner does not contain an Exoneration Clause. Nippon Express, a NVOCC, does not itself transport goods. It therefore contracted with Yang Ming to perform part, and arrange the remainder, of the transportation of the Unisia Shipment. The Yang Ming bill of lading issued to Nippon Express contains the Exoneration Clause at issue. Sompo, standing in the shoes of the cargo owner, argues that Nippon Express had no authority to agree to

---

[25] We do not mean to suggest that it is currently possible for Sompo to sue Yang Ming, merely that the Exoneration Clause does not preclude such a suit. We need not decide whether a suit by Sompo against Yang Ming would be time-barred, or frustrated by other circumstances. Furthermore, we acknowledge that, if the Railroads were correct that the Nippon Express bill of lading contains an Exoneration Clause, that clause would prohibit Sompo from suing Yang Ming for damage to the particular shipment governed by the Nippon Express bill of lading. But in that case, Sompo's remedy would be to sue Nippon Express for the damage to the cargo.

[26] The Enplas Shipment, which is the subject of Nipponkoa's judgment, is also governed by both the Yang Ming and Nippon Express bills of lading.

the Exoneration Clause in the Yang Ming bill of lading, and that the clause is therefore not enforceable with respect to Sompo's claim for damage to the Unisia Shipment. Guided by the Supreme Court's decision in *Kirby*, we are compelled to disagree.

While it is certainly true that an intermediary like Nippon Express "is . . . not automatically empowered to be the cargo owner's agent in every sense . . . when it comes to liability limitations for negligence resulting in damage, an intermediary can negotiate reliable and enforceable agreements with the carriers it engages." *Kirby*, 543 U.S. at 33. The facts of *Kirby* were strikingly similar to those here. In *Kirby*, the cargo owner hired a freight forwarding company, International Cargo Control ("ICC"), to arrange for the transportation of goods from Australia to Alabama. ICC issued a bill of lading to the cargo owner that [—45—] limited the carrier's liability for any loss or damage to the goods occurring during the land leg of the journey to a specified amount that was higher than $500 per package. Subsequently, ICC hired Hamburg Süd, an ocean shipping company, to transport the goods. Hamburg Süd issued a bill of lading to ICC that limited recovery for any loss or damage to the cargo to $500 per package. When the train carrying the cargo derailed, the cargo interest and its insurer sued the railroad (coincidentally, Norfolk Southern) for $1.5 million in damages.

Norfolk argued that it was entitled to invoke the less generous $500 per package damages limitation in the Hamburg Süd bill of lading to limit its liability.[27] The plaintiffs argued that they could not be bound by a liability limitation contained in a bill of lading to which they were not parties. The Supreme Court disagreed, ruling that "[w]hen an intermediary contracts with a carrier to transport goods, the cargo owner's recovery against the carrier is limited by the liability limitation to which the intermediary and carrier agreed." *Kirby*, 543 U.S. at 33. The Court explained that while a shipper hired by a cargo [—46—] owner to arrange transportation of cargo is not the cargo owner's agent in "the classic sense," it is nonetheless the cargo owner's agent for the "single, limited purpose" of contracting with "subsequent carriers for limitation on liability." *Id.* at 34 (emphasis omitted).

The Court offered three reasons in support of the rule it adopted. First, a contrary rule would be unworkable because carriers, who may not know whether they are dealing with an intermediary or a cargo owner, would be required to track down that information—a nearly impossible task in international shipping—in order to assure themselves that their contractual liability limitations would be enforceable. Second, a contrary rule would induce discrimination in common carriage, contrary to the goals of statutory and decisional law, because "if liability limitations negotiated with cargo owners were reliable while limitations negotiated with intermediaries were not, carriers would likely want to charge the latter higher rates." *Id.* at 35. And finally, holding a cargo owner to the terms agreed upon by its intermediary is equitable because the cargo owner retains the option to sue the intermediary carrier that is responsible "for any gap between the liability limitations" in the bill issued by the intermediary and the bill issued by the subsequent carrier. *Id.* [—47—]

Kirby controls this case. Nippon Express was the agent of the cargo owner, in the limited sense articulated in *Kirby*, when it contracted with Yang Ming for the liability limitations, including the Exoneration Clause, contained in the Yang Ming bill of lading. Accordingly, Sompo is bound by the Exoneration Clause, which the Railroads are entitled to invoke by virtue of the bill's Himalaya Clause. Sompo protests that *Kirby* is limited to provisions that limit a carrier's liability to a specified dollar amount, and does not apply to provisions that exonerate a

---

[27] Norfolk also argued, and the Supreme Court held, that it was entitled to invoke the liability limitations contained in the ICC bill of lading by virtue of that bill's Himalaya Clause. Because the Hamburg Süd bill of lading included a less generous package limitation that Norfolk was keen to invoke, the Court also had to decide whether Norfolk was entitled to invoke that bill's liability limitations against the cargo interests. *Id.* at 30-32.

remote carrier from any liability.[28] We see nothing in the reasoning of the Supreme Court's decision that would support that distinction. The Exoneration Clause is simply another form of liability limitation. While the package limits at issue in *Kirby* limited the amount per package that the plaintiff could recover, the Exoneration Clause limits the entities against which the plaintiff may recover. Moreover, the reasons supporting the Supreme Court's rule in *Kirby* apply with equal force to a clause that exonerates a remote carrier from liability to the cargo interests. The downstream carrier that contracts with an intermediary to [—48—] exonerate a remote carrier from liability is just as unlikely to know whether it is dealing with an intermediary or cargo owner as the downstream carrier that contracts with an intermediary for a package limitation. Thus, the information-gathering costs are just as onerous. Furthermore, it is fairer to place responsibility "for any gap between the liability limitations" in the Nippon Express and Yang Ming bills of lading on Nippon Express, the only entity in a position to know that such a gap exists.

F. *Conclusion*

Having carefully considered all of Sompo's objections to the district court's decision, we conclude that summary judgment for defendants was properly entered. Accordingly, we reject Sompo's appeal and affirm the judgment in Docket No. 13-3416.

II. *Nipponkoa*

The district court granted summary judgment in Nipponkoa's favor on its claim for contractual indemnification arising out of the destruction of a shipment of automotive parts manufactured by a company called Enplas Corporation. Unlike Nipponkoa's other

claims, which it asserted in its role as the subrogee of the cargo interests, and which fail for the same reasons discussed above in [—49—] connection with Sompo's appeal, Nipponkoa asserted this claim as the assignee of Yang Ming.

In order to explain the nature of Nipponkoa's claim and how Nipponkoa obtained the assignment of the claim, some background is necessary. As described above, Yang Ming engaged Norfolk Southern to carry the various shipments of manufactured goods by train to locations in the southern United States. Norfolk Southern undertook the carriage of the goods pursuant to a preexisting contract between itself and Yang Ming, known as the Intermodal Transportation Agreement ("ITA"). The ITA lays out the rates and terms that govern transportation services Norfolk Southern has agreed to provide Yang Ming. The ITA contains a number of indemnification provisions under which either Norfolk Southern or Yang Ming agreed to indemnify the other for certain losses or damage that might be sustained by one party during the course of transporting shipments. As relevant here, Norfolk Southern agreed to indemnify Yang Ming for loss of or damage to freight under certain circumstances:

> [Norfolk Southern] will be liable for and will hold [Yang Ming] harmless against loss of or damage to freight in containers . . . only to the extent that the sole proximate cause of said loss or damage is a railroad accident, [—50—] derailment, or collision between railroad equipment negligently caused by [Norfolk Southern].

Nipponkoa J.A. 51.

Under the terms of the ITA, Yang Ming is permitted "[u]pon written notice to [Norfolk Southern], [to] assign to third parties its right to make claims against [Norfolk Southern] for freight loss and damage." Nipponkoa J.A. 52. In February 2007, Yang Ming wrote to Norfolk informing it that a claim had been filed relating to the Enplas Shipment, and that Yang Ming intended to assign the claim to either TM Claims Services (Enplas

---

[28] Sompo urges us to adopt the reasoning of *Royal & Sun Alliance Ins. PLC v. Ocean World Lines, Inc.*, 572 F. Supp. 2d 379 (S.D.N.Y. 2008), *affirmed on other grounds* 612 F.3d 138 (2d Cir. 2010), which interpreted *Kirby* as "ruling that the agent's authority extended only to accepted package limitations." *Id.* at 398. For the reasons described in the text, we decline to do so.

Corporation's underwriter) or WK Webster (Nipponkoa's claims agent) to deal with Norfolk directly. Norfolk Southern does not allege that it made any objection at that time. Moreover, shortly before the assignment was executed in October 2007, Nipponkoa, through its claims agent, corresponded with Norfolk Southern about the assignment. During their correspondence, Norfolk Southern confirmed that the contractual limitations period for claims by Yang Ming had not yet run, and provided Nipponkoa with an assignment form to be executed by Yang Ming.[29] Against [—51—] this background, in October 2007, Yang Ming assigned to Nipponkoa any rights Yang Ming might have had against Norfolk Southern for recovery of money pertaining to the destruction of the Enplas Shipment.[30]

After the assignment was executed, Nipponkoa emailed the completed assignment to Norfolk Southern and indicated its belief that the assignment was sufficient to entitle Nipponkoa to payment of $ 118,173.60.

---

[29] Nipponkoa's claims agent asked Norfolk Southern to "confirm by return e-mail that the contractual Time Bar for the cargo claim against Norfolk Southern under [Norfolk Southern's] terms and conditions will not expire until February 2008 and that we are NOT time barred at present," and whether Norfolk Southern had "standard wording for a 'Letter of Assignment' that meets [Norfolk [—51—] Southern's] needs." Nipponkoa J.A. 107 (emphasis omitted). Norfolk responded that "[p]er the Intermodal Circular: claimant has 1 year from date of declination to amend claim," and that "[b]ased on the date of declination, February 2008, [Nipponkoa] is within legal limits to amend the claim." Id. Norfolk also attached an assignment form, asked the claims agent to have Yang Ming execute it, and advised that Norfolk Southern would "proceed with the investigation." Id.

[30] The assignment states: "That Yang Ming America, as agent of Yang Ming Marine Transport . . . does hereby give over and assign to [Nipponkoa], all title interest and rights which it has or may have in any claim or claims against each and every transportation subsidiary of Norfolk Southern Corporation or any other transportation company for the recovery of money or for other redress on account of Yang Ming America, as agent of Yang Ming Marine Transport against the [Enplas Shipment or other shipments] described below." Nipponkoa J.A. 99; Appellee Nipponkoa's Br. at 5-6.

Nipponkoa also indicated that it was copying Yang Ming on the email and stated that "[Nipponkoa] and Norfolk Southern will now conclude this case directly." Nipponkoa J.A. 98. [—52—]

As explained above, Nipponkoa's claim for contractual indemnification for damage to the Enplas Shipment was not originally the focus of Nipponkoa's suit. In its motion for reconsideration following remand, however, Nipponkoa asserted its entitlement to indemnification as the assignee of Yang Ming. In opposition, the Railroads argued that in order for Yang Ming, and thus its assignee Nipponkoa, to have a claim for contractual indemnification, Yang Ming must have paid claims related to the damaged freight, which Yang Ming was not alleged to have done. The district court rejected this argument, reasoning that "[n]othing in the ITA . . . requires Yang Ming to first have made a payment on damages related to the Enplas shipment," and that the indemnification provision in question was "broadly worded, holding [Norfolk Southern] liable and Yang Ming harmless for damages to the Enplas shipment." *Sompo Japan Ins. Co. of Am.*, 966 F. Supp. 2d at 281. The district court accordingly granted summary judgment in Nipponkoa's favor on its claim for contractual indemnification.

The Railroads moved for reconsideration of this decision, arguing that Yang Ming had no claim for contractual indemnification to assign because, at the time of the assignment to Nipponkoa, Yang Ming had no potential liability for damage to the Enplas Shipment since, by virtue of the time limit for filing suit [—53—] specified in the Yang Ming bill of lading, any claim for damages against Yang Ming would be time barred. The Railroads pointed out that the time limit provision of the Yang Ming bill of lading specifically provides that "[Yang Ming] shall be discharged from any and all liability in respect of non-delivery, misdelivery, delay, loss or damage unless suit is brought within one year after delivery of the Goods or the date when the Goods should have been delivered."[31] Nipponkoa J.A. 77-78. Thus, the Railroads argued, Yang Ming, and therefore its assignee, could not seek indemnification for damages that Yang Ming had not incurred, and never would. The district court denied the Railroads' motion for reconsideration on the ground that they had waived the argument about Yang Ming's lack of potential liability by failing to raise it earlier, and entered judgment in favor of Nipponkoa against Norfolk Southern and KCSR.

On appeal, the Railroads argue that the judgment in Nipponkoa's favor cannot be sustained because at the time Yang Ming assigned its claims to Nipponkoa, Yang Ming could not have incurred damages for which it would be entitled to indemnification. Additionally, KCSR argues that the judgment against it should be vacated because it was not a party to the ITA and therefore had no [—54—] obligation to indemnify Yang Ming. In opposition, Nipponkoa argues that the Railroads have either waived or are estopped from making the arguments they seek to present and that those arguments fail on their merits.[32]

A. *Indemnification*

Ordinarily, a claim for contractual indemnification only accrues once the indemnitee has suffered a loss, i.e., made a payment. *See Cont'l Cas. Co. v. Stronghold Ins. Co.*, 77 F.3d 16, 19 (2d Cir. 1996) (stating that a claim founded on an express contract for indemnity against loss "generally accrues when the indemnitee actually suffers a loss"); *Schneider v. Nat'l R.R. Passenger Corp.*, 987 F.2d 132, 138 (2d Cir. 1993) ("A party must sustain a loss in order to assert an indemnification claim."). Additionally, a claim for indemnification generally will not lie

where the indemnitee has no potential liability requiring indemnification. *See In re Agent Orange Prod. Liab. Litig.*, 818 F.2d 204, 209 (2d Cir. 1987) ("If appellants have a valid claim against the Government, [then they also have a valid Government contractor defense, and] there can be no liability on their part, potential or actual, against which the Government should be required to [—55—] indemnify them."); *Atl. Richfield Co. v. Interstate Oil Transp. Co.*, 784 F.2d 106, 112 (2d Cir. 1986) ("[In *The Toledo*, 122 F.2d 255 (2d Cir. 1941),] we ruled that the trial court correctly denied the charterer's claim for damages [on its indemnification theory] because it acted as a 'volunteer' when it compensated the cargo owners, since it was not even potentially liable for the delay caused by the latent defect in the crankshaft web."). Nonetheless, because an express contract for indemnity remains a contract, it is ultimately a question of contract interpretation whether the indemnitee is required to make a payment prior to seeking indemnification. *See Cont'l Cas. Co.*, 77 F.3d at 19 ("An express contract for indemnity, however, remains a contract. Hence the parties are free, within limits of public policy, to agree upon conditions precedent to suit.").

We need not decide whether the language of the ITA's indemnification provision somehow removes this case from the purview of those general principles, or whether Yang Ming was even potentially liable to anyone at the time of the assignment, because we conclude that the Railroads have waived the arguments they press on appeal.

The Railroads waived their principal argument—that, by the time of the assignment to Nipponkoa, Yang Ming had been discharged of all liability for [—56—] damage to the Enplas Shipment by operation of the time bar provision in its bill of lading—because they raised that argument for the first time in their second motion for reconsideration. "Generally, we will not consider an argument on appeal that was raised for the first time below in a motion for reconsideration." *Official Comm. of Unsecured Creditors of Color Tile, Inc. v. Coopers & Lybrand, LLP*, 322 F.3d 147, 159 (2d Cir.

---

[31] The parties stipulated that the Enplas Shipment would have been delivered on May 1, 2006.

[32] Nipponkoa also argues that the district court's judgment can be affirmed on the alternative ground that the Railroads should not have prevailed on their Exoneration Clause defense for the reasons raised in Sompo's appeal. For the reasons stated above, we reject that argument.

2003). While we have discretion to excuse such untimeliness, we see no reason to exercise that discretion in this case. The Railroads argue, however, that they in fact raised this argument prior to their second motion for reconsideration, in opposition to Nipponkoa's motion for summary judgment on remand. Upon review of the Railroads' motion papers before the district court, we cannot agree that the Railroads timely raised the argument they now make on appeal.

Despite the Railroads' efforts to minimize the differences between the argument they made in opposition to Nipponkoa's motion for summary judgment and the argument they made in their second motion for reconsideration, a careful review of the record reveals that those arguments are meaningfully different. In their opposition, the Railroads did *not* argue, as they do now, that Nipponkoa's assigned claim for contractual indemnification failed [—57—] because Yang Ming (the assignor), having been discharged of liability by virtue of the fact that no entity had filed suit against it within the one year time limit permitted by the bill of lading, could incur no damages, an arguably essential element of a claim for contractual indemnification.

Instead, they made a much more straightforward argument. Specifically, they argued that Nipponkoa's claim *against the Railroads* was time-barred because, under the Yang Ming bill of lading, Nipponkoa was required to file suit within one year of the anticipated delivery of the cargo and, by virtue of the bill's Himalaya Clause, the Railroads were entitled to invoke that time limit to bar Nipponkoa's suit.[33] That

argument—an argument about the timeliness of Nipponkoa's suit against the Railroads—is substantively different from the defendants' current argument—an argument about whether Nipponkoa can prove the damages element of its contractual indemnification claim because no [—58—] claim was filed *against Yang Ming* within the limitations period. Because the argument that the Railroads actually made in opposition to Nipponkoa's motion for summary judgment is completely different from the argument they made in their second motion for reconsideration, and press now on appeal, the Railroads' current argument was not properly preserved.

The Railroads also argue, however, that Nipponkoa's claim for contractual indemnification fails because, at the time of the assignment, Yang Ming had incurred no damages, i.e., paid no claims for damage to the Enplas Shipment. That argument was timely raised in opposition to Nipponkoa's motion for reconsideration. Nonetheless, we conclude that to the extent the ITA's indemnification provision can be read as requiring Yang Ming to pay claims before seeking indemnification, Norfolk Southern waived that requirement. While Norfolk Southern might have originally been entitled to insist upon strict compliance with the payment requirement—requiring Yang Ming to first make a payment to the cargo owner's subrogee for damage to the freight and then file a claim for indemnification with Norfolk Southern—we think Norfolk Southern's conduct demonstrated an unequivocal intent not to insist upon such formalities.[34] [—59—]

---

[33] Whatever the merit of that argument with respect to the claims Nipponkoa pursued as subrogee of the cargo owners, it is meritless as pertains to the claim Nipponkoa pursued as assignee of Yang Ming. As Yang Ming's assignee, Nipponkoa stands in the shoes of Yang Ming. The Yang Ming bill of lading expressly provides that nothing in the bill shall be construed to relieve any underlying carrier, such as the Railroads, "from liability to [Yang Ming] for acts arising or resulting from their fault or negligent [sic]." Nipponkoa J.A. 76. In other words, while the bill's Himalaya Clause permits the Railroads to invoke the bill's

liability limitations against the cargo owners, it does not permit the Railroads to rely on those limitations against Yang Ming or its assignee.

[34] While the payment prerequisite might be more than a mere formality in some cases, this is not such a case. As the district court correctly held, there is no [—59—] colorable argument that the freight was not damaged, or that the damage, having been caused by the derailment, is not attributable to the defendants' negligence. In addition, with the exception of the argument that any suit against Yang Ming was time barred—an argument that was waived—there is no good faith contention that if Nipponkoa had sought compensation from Yang Ming, instead of Norfolk

See, e.g., Wolff & Munier, Inc. v. Whiting-Turner Contracting Co., 946 F.2d 1003, 1009 (2d Cir. 1991) ("[A] party to a contract may be precluded from insisting on strict compliance by conduct amounting to a waiver or estoppel." (citing New York law)); *Goldstein v. Old Dominion Peanut Corp.*, 177 Va. 716, 728-29 (1941) ("[C]ovenants and stipulations made by a covenantor for his benefit may be waived by him, either by express terms or by a course of dealing . . . [and a] covenantor may, by his conduct, so lull his covenantee into a sense of security as thereby to estop himself from the exercise of a right for which he had contracted.").[35] [—60—]

As set forth in detail above, upon receiving a claim for damage to the Enplas Shipment, Yang Ming communicated that fact to Norfolk Southern and expressed its intent to have Nipponkoa resolve its claim with Norfolk Southern directly. Norfolk Southern's response is telling. Rather than object, Norfolk Southern affirmatively provided Nipponkoa with an assignment form, tacitly encouraging Nipponkoa to proceed directly with Norfolk Southern, rather than first obtain a payment from Yang Ming.

Southern, Yang Ming would have had any legitimate basis to deny the claim. Indeed, the Railroads' argument about why the Exoneration Clause in the Yang Ming bill of lading does *not* exonerate the Railroads from liability for their negligence relies on the proposition that the subrogees would be able to recover damages from Yang Ming and that Yang Ming would, in turn, be able to sue the Railroads. Thus, Norfolk Southern's decision not to insist upon the formal payment requirement is entirely understandable, as that decision merely cuts out the middleman, permitting Norfolk Southern to deal directly with the injured party.

[35] On appeal, the Railroads insist that Nipponkoa's claim for contractual indemnification is governed by Virginia law. But in the district court, the Railroads relied on the law of multiple jurisdictions, including New York, in [—60—] opposition to Nipponkoa's claim. Furthermore, the Railroads identify no way in which Virginia law differs from New York law, or federal common law, in any material respects. As the cases cited in the text indicate, we too see no significant difference in the principles applicable under the laws of New York and Virginia.

Additionally, when Nipponkoa provided the completed assignment to Norfolk Southern and indicated its understanding that the assignment would permit Nipponkoa to resolve its claim with Norfolk Southern directly, Norfolk Southern merely responded that it would investigate the claim. It gave no hint that Nipponkoa could not resolve its claim with Norfolk Southern directly because Nipponkoa needed to obtain a payment for the damages to the Enplas Shipment from Yang Ming in order for Yang Ming's right to indemnification to arise. [—61—]

Norfolk Southern's conduct in the face of Yang Ming and Nipponkoa's expressed intention to have Nipponkoa resolve its claim with Norfolk Southern directly, without having to proceed against Yang Ming first, is inconsistent with any intention on Norfolk Southern's part to insist upon its now-claimed contractual right to a contrary prolonged process. *See, e.g., Voest-Alpine Int'l Corp. v. Chase Manhattan Bank, N.A.*, 707 F.2d 680, 685 (2d Cir. 1983) ("The intention to relinquish a right may be established . . . as a matter of law . . . where the party's undisputed acts or language are so inconsistent with his purpose to stand upon his rights as to leave no opportunity for a reasonable inference to the contrary." (internal quotation marks omitted)). Accordingly, because Norfolk Southern waived the alleged contractual requirement that Yang Ming pay for the damages to the Enplas Shipment before its contractual indemnification claim could become viable, that putative requirement does not defeat Nipponkoa's claim.[36] [—62—]

---

[36] The Railroads argue that they cannot be estopped from relying on this requirement because Nipponkoa did not rely to its detriment on Norfolk Southern's implicit representation that it would not insist upon it. We need not address Nipponkoa's estoppel argument since we hold that Norfolk Southern unambiguously waived any contractual right to have Nipponkoa proceed first against Yang Ming. Reliance is not an element of waiver, which is the intentional relinquishment of a known right. *See Waldman v. Cohen*, 125 A.D.2d 116, 122 (2d Dep't 1987) ("Although waiver and estoppel are sometimes used [—62—] interchangeably, a waiver is an intentional abandonment of a right without

B. *KCSR*

Finally, we reject KCSR's contention that judgment should not have been entered against it on Nipponkoa's claim because it was not a party to the ITA, and therefore had no contractual obligation to indemnify Yang Ming. KCSR failed to make this argument at any point before the district court. Furthermore, while the Railroads jointly opposed Nipponkoa's motion for reconsideration and summary judgment, they offered no reason why, if the motion were otherwise meritorious, it should be granted only as to Norfolk and not as to KCSR.[37] Accordingly, KCSR will not now be heard to complain that the district court failed to distinguish between the Railroads when entering judgment on Nipponkoa's claim. [—63—]

C. *Conclusion*

Because the Railroads' argument for reversal of Nipponkoa's judgment against them are all either waived or without merit, we affirm the judgment in Docket No. 13-3501.

CONCLUSION

For the foregoing reasons, the judgments of the district court are AFFIRMED.

---

need to show reliance or detriment to the asserting party.").

[37] While we have discretion to address arguments not presented to the district court where necessary to avoid manifest injustice, we see no reason to do so here. "[T]he circumstances normally do not militate in favor of an exercise of discretion to address . . . new arguments on appeal where those arguments were available to the [party] below and [it] proffer[s] no reasons for [its] failure to raise the argument below." *In re Nortel Networks Corp. Sec. Litig.*, 539 F.3d 129, 133 (2d Cir. 2008) (internal quotation marks omitted) (ellipsis in original); *see also In re Johns-Manville Corp.*, — F.3d —, 2014 WL 3583780, at *11 (2d Cir. July 22, 2014)(same).

United States Court of Appeals for the Fourth Circuit

United States Court of Appeals
for the Fourth Circuit

No. 13-1594

STEVE LINCOLN

vs.

DIRECTOR, OFFICE OF WORKERS' COMPENSATION
PROGRAMS

On Petition for Review of an Order of the Benefits
Review Board

Decided: March 11, 2014

Citation: 744 F.3d 911, 2 Adm. R. 100 (4ᵗʰ Cir. 2014).

Before **WILKINSON**, **KEENAN**, and **DIAZ**, Circuit Judges.

[—2—] **WILKINSON**, Circuit Judge:

Petitioner Steven Lincoln seeks attorney's fees from Ceres Marine Terminals, Inc. (Ceres) for his pursuit of a claim for disability benefits under the Longshore and Harbor Workers' Compensation Act (LHWCA). Lincoln contends that he is entitled to attorney's fees because Ceres did not pay "any compensation" within the meaning of the fee-shifting mechanism in 33 U.S.C. § 928(a) or, in the alternative, because Ceres's notice of controversion irrevocably triggered the same provision. We reject his arguments and deny his petition.

I.

A.

On May 24, 2011, Lincoln filed a claim with the District Director of the Office of Workers' Compensation Programs (OWCP) for benefits under the LHWCA, alleging that he had sustained binaural hearing loss (hearing loss in both ears) as a result of his work as a longshoreman in Charleston, South Carolina. The basis of Lincoln's claim was an April 11, 2011 audiogram. Lincoln, like many longshoremen, worked for several different companies over the course of his career, but he alleged that he was employed by Ceres at the time of his injury. Therefore, on May 26, Ceres responded by filing forms with the OWCP, one of which was a notice of controversion. [—3—]

In the notice, Ceres explained that it was controverting Lincoln's claim because, while it accepted the fact that "claimant's hearing loss [was] noise-induced," J.A. 5, additional information was needed before Ceres could determine what it believed was the correct disability payment. The information Ceres sought included whether Ceres was the last employer before Lincoln's audiogram and the amount of Lincoln's average weekly wage (calculated from wage records collected from the various employers for which Lincoln had worked). On June 2, Lincoln gave Ceres a copy of his April 11 audiogram along with a paystub from his time working for Ceres. Several days later, on June 6, Ceres submitted subpoenas requesting wage records from the other companies for which Lincoln had worked and medical records from the doctor who had conducted Lincoln's April 11 audiogram.

The OWCP formally served notice of Lincoln's claim on Ceres on June 14. After receiving the official notice of the claim, on July 7, Ceres "voluntarily paid" Lincoln $1,256.84, amounting to compensation for "0.5% [binaural] hearing loss" and the equivalent of one week of permanent partial disability pay under the maximum compensation rate. J.A. 25. Ceres also requested that Lincoln submit to an independent medical examination. In accordance with that request, Lincoln completed a second [—4—] audiogram on July 15 that demonstrated he had sustained a 10% binaural hearing loss.

On October 4, after negotiations, the District Director of the OWCP entered a settlement compensation order agreed to by both Lincoln and Ceres. The settlement acknowledged that Lincoln allegedly sustained a 10% binaural hearing loss and awarded benefits to Lincoln totaling $23,879.96 in compensation and $4,000 in medical benefits. Ceres did not pay any money to Lincoln between the July 7 disability payment and the October 4 settlement.

B.

Lincoln filed a petition with the OWCP on August 18, 2011, requesting that the Director award him $3,460 in attorney's fees under § 928(a) of the LHWCA, which shifts fees from a successful claimant to the employer when the employer "declines to pay any compensation on or before the thirtieth day after receiving written notice of a claim." 33 U.S.C. § 928(a). Ceres opposed the petition, and on April 24, 2012, the Director notified both parties that, because Ceres had paid Lincoln one week's worth of disability benefits within 30 days of receiving official notice of his claim, it was not liable for Lincoln's attorney's fees under § 928(a). He also found that Ceres was not liable for attorney's fees under § 928(b), the LHWCA's alternative fee-shifting provision. [—5—]

On May 15, 2012, the Director entered a Compensation Order ruling Ceres not liable for Lincoln's attorney's fees and denying the petition. Lincoln appealed to the Benefits Review Board (BRB), which found that the Director acted within his discretion in denying Lincoln's petition under §§ 928(a) and (b). Lincoln thereafter filed this timely petition for review.

II.

Lincoln maintains that the Director erred in denying his fee petition under § 928(a) for three independent reasons: (1) Ceres's July 7 payment was only a partial payment and thus not "any compensation"; (2) the payment did not technically constitute "compensation" for the purposes of that provision; and (3) Ceres's notice of controversion automatically triggered fee-shifting. We review the BRB's decision both for errors of law and to determine whether it properly found that the District Director's relevant factual findings were supported by substantial evidence. *Sidwell v. Va. Int'l Terminals, Inc.*, 372 F.3d 238, 241 (4th Cir. 2004). Our review of the BRB's interpretation of the LHWCA is *de novo*. *Wheeler v. Newport News Shipbuilding & Dry Dock Co.*, 637 F.3d 280, 283 (4th Cir. 2011).

A.

Lincoln first claims that the term "any compensation" in § 928(a) means all compensation due, and therefore cannot

[—6—] include Ceres's payment of a mere one week of disability benefits to Lincoln. To interpret this provision, we begin by examining the statutory text. If the language is plain, "we apply it according to its terms." *Newport News Shipbuilding & Dry Dock Co. v. Brown*, 376 F.3d 245, 248 (4th Cir. 2004) (internal quotation marks omitted). When determining whether or not statutory language is plain, we consider "the language itself, the specific context in which that language is used, and the broader context of the statute as a whole." *Holland v. Big River Minerals Corp.*, 181 F.3d 597, 603 (4th Cir. 1999) (internal quotation marks omitted).

The LHWCA establishes a reticulated scheme providing for fee-shifting in two specific contexts. "In all other cases any claim for legal services shall not be assessed against the employer or carrier." 33 U.S.C. § 928(b). Section 928(a) covers the first of these situations:

> If the employer or carrier declines to pay any compensation on or before the thirtieth day after receiving written notice of a claim for compensation having been filed from the deputy commissioner, on the ground that there is no liability for compensation within the provisions of this chapter and the person seeking benefits shall thereafter have utilized the services of an attorney at law in the successful prosecution of his claim, there shall be awarded, in addition to the award of compensation, in a compensation order, a reasonable attorney's fee against the employer or carrier . . . .

33 U.S.C. § 928(a). [—7—]

In Lincoln's view, the phrase "any compensation" means "all compensation," to the effect that an employer that fails to pay the entire claim within 30 days is liable for attorney's fees under § 928(a). We do not agree. The term "any compensation" is unambiguous and plainly encompasses an employer's partial payment of compensation. Thus, the most natural reading of the provision is that an employer that pays the claimant something by way of compensation is not liable for attorney's fees.

The surrounding context of § 928(a) buttresses this interpretation. It states that the employer's refusal to pay must be "on the ground that there is no liability for compensation within the provisions of this chapter." 33 U.S.C. § 928(a). This language is unequivocal, and demonstrates that an employer's refusal to pay compensation must be absolute in order for it to face possible fee liability under § 928(a).

To construe "any compensation" in § 928(a) as "all compensation" would mean that employers must pay the full claim within 30 days of receiving the official notice to avoid potential fee liability. But, as Lincoln's claim demonstrates, the medical evidence establishing the extent of the claimant's injury, and thus the amount of his benefits, is often in flux and cannot be ascertained with any degree of certainty within 30 days of his claim. Section 928 provides an employer a safe harbor: if it admits liability for the claim by paying some [—8—] compensation to the claimant for a work-related injury and only contests the total amount of the benefits, it is sheltered from fee liability under § 928(a). *Andrepont v. Murphy Exploration & Prod. Co.*, 566 F.3d 415, 418-19 (5th Cir. 2009); *Day v. James Marine, Inc.*, 518 F.3d 411, 419 (6th Cir. 2008). Therefore, fee-shifting under § 928(a) may not occur if the employer agrees that some amount is due the claimant for a work-related injury and "tenders any compensation." *Andrepont*, 566 F.3d at 418. This safe harbor provision serves to protect "the employers' interest in having their contingent liabilities identified as precisely and as early as possible." *Brown*, 376 F.3d at 250 (internal quotation marks omitted).

But the safe harbor is not permanently safe, because § 928(b) provides a mechanism by which the claimant could still recover attorney's fees. *Andrepont*, 566 F.3d at 419 (finding that § 928(b) applies when "the employer and claimant agree that some compensation is due but disagree as to what amount") (internal quotation marks omitted); *Va. Int'l Terminals, Inc. v. Edwards*, 398 F.3d

313, 317-18 (4th Cir. 2005). This alternative provision is only operative when "the employer initially pays voluntary compensation and a subsequent dispute arises about total amount of compensation due" and, additionally, four requirements are satisfied. *Id.* at 316. These requirements are: "(1) an informal conference, (2) a written recommendation [—9—] from the deputy or Board, (3) the employer's refusal to adopt the written recommendation, and (4) the employee's procuring of the services of a lawyer to achieve a greater award than what the employer was willing to pay after the written recommendation." *Newport News Shipbuilding & Dry Dock Co. v. Dir., OWCP*, 477 F.3d 123, 126 (4th Cir. 2007) (internal quotation marks omitted).

When taken together, §§ 928(a) and (b) mandate fee-shifting in certain defined circumstances, but plainly do "not provide for attorneys' fee awards in every case in which the claimant is successful." *Andrepont*, 566 F.3d at 420 (internal quotation marks omitted). This interpretation is consistent with the purposes of the LHWCA, one of which is to lessen the occasions where attorney's fees are incurred by encouraging claimants to resolve their disputes "without the necessity of relying on assistance other than that provided by the Secretary of Labor." *Kemp v. Newport News Shipbuilding & Dry Dock Co.*, 805 F.2d 1152, 1153 (4th Cir. 1986) (per curiam). Therefore, the structure of § 928 establishes that, until the claimant has exhausted the non-adversarial avenues for resolving his claim, he cannot avail himself of the fee-shifting provisions. *Day*, 518 F.3d at 416-17.

In sum, § 928(a)'s plain language requires fee-shifting only when an employer has paid no compensation within 30 days of [—10—] receiving the official claim. Applying this interpretation to Lincoln's case shows that his claim under § 928(a) fails. Ceres voluntarily paid Lincoln one week's compensation on July 7, which was within 30 days of receiving his claim, "thereby admitting to liability for the injury" for the purposes of § 928(a). *Andrepont*, 566 F.3d at 419. Ceres met the requirement of § 928(a), moving the dispute to

§ 928(b). Lincoln then had the right to request an informal conference, *see Pittsburgh & Conneaut Dock Co. v. Dir., OWCP*, 473 F.3d 253, 264 (6th Cir. 2007), but he did not and instead proceeded to settlement negotiations that ultimately produced an agreement. Lincoln was entitled to the services of an attorney but, under the LHWCA's fee-shifting scheme, he is not entitled to have that attorney paid for by Ceres.

B.

Lincoln's second contention is that Ceres's July 7 payment was not "compensation" in any true sense under § 928(a) because it was merely an attempt by Ceres to avoid fee liability. To support his argument, he relies on *Green v. Ceres Marine Terminals, Inc.*, 43 BRBS 173 (2010), *rev'd on other grounds*, 656 F.3d 235 (4th Cir. 2011). In *Green*, the BRB reviewed a ruling by an administrative law judge (ALJ) finding that the employer's $1 payment to the claimant did not constitute "compensation" for the purposes of § 928(a). *Id*. at 177. The BRB affirmed and [—11—] found § 928(a) applicable because the ALJ "rationally found that employer's payment of $1 was merely an attempt to avoid fee liability rather than the payment of compensation for claimant's injury." *Id*.

Lincoln contends that Ceres's payment of $1,256.84, corresponding to an injury of 0.5% binaural hearing loss, constitutes a "farce to avoid paying attorney's fees" in the same vein as in *Green*. Appellant's Br. at 10. However, Lincoln's case differs dramatically from *Green*, and we consequently do not find it applicable here. Ceres's counsel noted at oral argument that Ceres based its calculation of the July 7 payment on Lincoln's alleged disability. That is in stark contrast to the $1 payment in *Green*, which was clearly untethered to the underlying claim and therefore was not "compensation" at all. *See Andrepont*, 566 F.3d at 419 (holding that an employer's partial benefits payment constituted "compensation" under § 928(a)); *Pittsburgh & Conneaut Dock Co.*, 473 F.3d at 263-64 (ruling that an employer's initial payments of temporary disability benefits were sufficient

to meet § 928(a)'s "compensation" requirement).[1] [—12—]

We hold that Ceres's payment of one week's benefits at the maximum compensation rate, being directly tied as it was to Lincoln's alleged injury, qualifies as "compensation" within the meaning of § 928(a).

C.

Lastly, Lincoln maintains that, when Ceres filed a notice of controversion prior to the July 7 payment, it signaled that it was controverting his claim and, by doing so, irrevocably triggered § 928(a). Lincoln cites to the controversion procedure in § 914(d) of the LHWCA, which requires that an employer seeking to challenge an employee's benefits claim file a notice "on or before the fourteenth day after [it] has knowledge of the alleged injury or death." 33 U.S.C. § 914(d).

Lincoln did not raise this issue before the BRB, and thus the BRB did not have the opportunity to consider or rule on it. But even if we were to address the merits of his claim, we would find it wanting. Section 928(a) nowhere incorporates § 914(d) or its 14 day time limit specifically, or references notices of controversion generally. Rather, § 928(a) contains only one explicit trigger: the payment of "any compensation" within 30 days of the employer's receipt of official notice of the claim. Ceres met this requirement and consequently was entitled to the protections afford by § 928(a). [—13—]

III.

The LHWCA is one of those statutes that adjust employer and employee interests through multiple tradeoffs and compromises. Far be it from courts to disturb the balance. The petition for review is hereby denied.

PETITION DENIED

---

[1] We likewise find unavailing Lincoln's reference to *Roberts v. Sea-Land Services, Inc.*, 132 S. Ct. 1350 (2012). Nowhere in *Roberts* did the Supreme Court analyze the meaning of "any compensation" in § 928(a), the central issue in this case.

No. 13-2112

IN RE NORFOLK S. RY. CO.

Appeal from the United States District Court for the Eastern District of Virginia, at Norfolk

Decided: June 23, 2014

Citation: 756 F.3d 282, 2 Adm. R. 104 (4th Cir. 2014).

Before **TRAXLER,** Chief Judge, and **NIEMEYER,** and **DUNCAN,** Circuit Judges.

[—3—] **TRAXLER,** Chief Judge:

Norfolk Southern Railway Company ("Norfolk Southern") appeals a district court order remanding to state court a claim brought against it pursuant to the Federal Employers' Liability Act ("FELA"), 45 U.S.C. §§ 51-60. Norfolk also petitions for a writ of mandamus vacating the district court's order and either dismissing the case or, alternatively, remanding to the district court to address the merits of its federal defense to the FELA claim. We conclude that we lack jurisdiction to review the district court's order on appeal and therefore dismiss the appeal. We also deny mandamus relief.

I.

Gilbert Bynum was employed by Norfolk Southern as a control operator and brakeman at Lamberts Point Coal Terminal. The terminal, which was created for the purpose of loading coal from railroad cars onto ocean-bound vessels, was located on the Elizabeth River in Norfolk, Virginia. It was Bynum's job to release the brakes of loaded coal cars so that the cars would roll downhill into a rotary dumper, which would in turn "rotate the coal car 180 degrees and dump the coal onto conveyors, which move the coal onto [the pier] for deposit into the holds of coal ships." J.A. 43. On November 22, 2010, Bynum was injured when, while walking to recover a radio transmitter, "he tripped and fell on coal dust and debris that had been allowed to accumulate [—4—] between and aside the railroad tracks." J.A. 10. Bynum subsequently

applied for, and was awarded, federal workers' compensation benefits under the Longshore and Harbor Workers' Compensation Act ("LHWCA"), 33 U.S.C. §§ 901-950.

Bynum later filed suit in state court on May 29, 2013, under FELA, which, as is relevant here, provides railway employees with the right to recovery for injury or death caused in whole or in part by the negligence of the railroad's officers, agents, or employees.[1] *See* 45 U.S.C. § 51; *see Hernandez v. Trawler Miss Vertie Mae, Inc.,* 187 F.3d 432, 436 (4th Cir. 1999). Bynum alleged negligence on the part of Norfolk Southern and sought $30 million in damages.

On July 3, 2013, Norfolk Southern filed a notice of removal to federal court, arguing that Bynum had applied for and received benefits under the LHWCA, that the LHWCA in fact covered his injury, and that the LHWCA barred any recovery under FELA. *See Chesapeake & Ohio Ry. Co. v. Schwalb,* 493 U.S. 40, 42 (1989). The Railroad contended that whether Bynum's injury was covered by the LHWCA was "'exclusively a federal question which Congress never intended for state courts to resolve.'" J.A. 6 (quoting *Shives v. CSX Transp., Inc.,* 151 F.3d 164, 167 [—5—] (4th Cir. 1998)). On this basis, Norfolk Southern maintained that removal was proper under 28 U.S.C. §§ 1441 and 1446.

On July 15, 2013, Bynum moved to remand the matter to state court. Bynum cited 33 U.S.C. §§ 919 and 921, which provide that LHWCA claims are adjudicated in the first instance by the Department of Labor ("DOL"), with appeals considered by the Benefits Review Board, and appeals from those decisions considered by the United States Courts of Appeals. Bynum alleged that the district court lacked "jurisdiction to determine coverage under the LHWCA because Congress has specifically eliminated the jurisdiction of the federal district court concerning the LHWCA." J.A. 18. Bynum's motion also asserted that his "claim is not removable

---

[1] FELA provides for concurrent federal and state jurisdiction over FELA claims. *See* 45 U.S.C. § 56.

pursuant to 28 U.S.C. § 1445(a)"—which bars removal of FELA claims brought in state court[2]—"and [that] it is not removable under 28 U.S.C. § 1441 or § 1446."[3] J.A. 18. [—6—]

That same day, July 15, 2013, Norfolk Southern filed a motion in federal district court to dismiss Bynum's complaint, arguing that, although his claim was filed under FELA, his injury actually fell within the scope of the LHWCA's coverage and the LHWCA therefore provided the exclusive remedy for his injury. *See* 33 U.S.C. § 905(a). On that basis, Norfolk Southern maintained that Bynum's claim should have been filed with the DOL, *see* 33 U.S.C. § 919, and that both the district court and the state court lacked jurisdiction over the claim.

On July 18, 2013, Bynum filed a response to Norfolk Southern's motion to dismiss. He noted that he did "not concede that the exclusivity provisions of the LHWCA apply in this case." J.A. 55. He argued that 33 U.S.C. § 905(a), applying to suits against employers, would not bar a negligence claim under § 905(b) against a vessel owner in his capacity as owner rather than employer. He also maintained that "[t]he courts have not decided whether a railroad worker may sue his employer under 33 U.S.C. § 905(a) in its railroad capacity, where as in this case, the defendant admits Bynum was retrieving a

---

[2] Section 1445(a) provides that "[a] civil action in any State court against a railroad or its receivers or trustees, arising under sections 1-4 and 5-10 of the Act of April 22, 1908 (45 U.S.C. §§ 51-54, 55-60) may not be removed to any district court of the United States."

[3] As is relevant here, 28 U.S.C. § 1441(a) provides that

[e]xcept as otherwise expressly provided by Act of Congress, any civil action brought in a State court of which the district courts of the United States have original jurisdiction, may be removed by the defendant or the defendants, to the district court of the United (Continued) [—6—]
States for the district and division embracing the place where such action is pending.

28 U.S.C. § 1441(a). Section 1446 outlines the applicable procedure for removal of civil actions.

radio transmitter at the time of his injury." J.A. 55. Bynum noted that his remand [—7—] motion remained pending and that the state court would have jurisdiction to resolve the question of whether the exclusivity provisions of the LHWCA barred his FELA claim.

On July 24, 2013, Norfolk Southern responded to Bynum's motion to remand. Conceding that "§ 1445(a) prevents removal of an FELA action filed in state court," Norfolk Southern nonetheless contended that it had "not removed this case to litigate Bynum's FELA claim, but to determine whether that claim is barred" by virtue of the fact that Bynum's injury fell within the scope of LHWCA's coverage. J.A. 59. Norfolk Southern argued that Bynum's injury was covered by the LHWCA under the facts of this case and that the LHWCA therefore provided the exclusive remedy.

The district court granted Bynum's remand motion and denied as moot Norfolk Southern's motion to dismiss. The court noted that 28 U.S.C. § 1441(a) allows removal of any civil action that was brought in state court but which the district court had jurisdiction over "'[e]xcept as otherwise expressly provided by Act of Congress.'" J.A. 90 (emphasis in original). Recognizing that "[s]ection 1445(a) prohibits the removal of a civil action arising under FELA[] which is filed in state court against a railroad," the district court concluded that Bynum's FELA "claim must be remanded to state court." J.A. 90. [—8—]

The district court acknowledged Norfolk Southern's argument that because Bynum "has already received LHWCA benefits, the exclusivity provisions of the LHWCA bar *further* recovery under FELA." J.A. 91. However, the district court did not determine whether Bynum's injury actually fell within the scope of LHWCA's coverage or whether the LHWCA otherwise barred recovery under FELA. Rather, the district court concluded that the mere facts that Bynum brought his action in state court, that he asserted a claim under FELA (and that he timely moved to remand his action to state court once Norfolk Southern filed a notice of removal) were sufficient to trigger the § 1445(a) removal bar.

The court therefore remanded Bynum's claim to state court without considering the merits of Norfolk Southern's motion to dismiss.

Norfolk Southern timely appealed to us, and it also filed a petition for a writ of mandamus requesting us to vacate the district court's order and either dismiss the case or alternatively remand to the district court to address the merits of its federal defense to the FELA claim. We agreed to consider the mandamus petition together with the related appeal, and thus the two cases were consolidated. Bynum subsequently moved to dismiss the appeal as barred by 28 U.S.C. § 1447(d) and to have the mandamus petition denied for the same reason.

II. [—9—]

We first address the question of whether we are authorized to review the merits of the district court's remand order. We conclude that we are not.

A. Applicable Legal Principles

The removal statute prohibits appellate review of district courts' orders "remanding a case to the State court from which it was removed." 28 U.S.C. § 1447(d). The statute serves to "neutralize 'prolonged litigation on threshold nonmeritorious questions.'" *Barlow v. Colgate Palmolive Co.*, 2014 WL 1689002, at *4 (4th Cir. 2014) (quoting *Powerex Corp. v. Reliant Energy Servs., Inc.*, 551 U.S. 224, 237 (2007)). We have explained that this policy is so strong that § 1447(d) bars our review "even if the remand order is manifestly, inarguably erroneous." *Lisenby v. Lear*, 674 F.3d 259, 261 (4th Cir. 2012) (internal quotation marks omitted).

Nevertheless, § 1447(d)'s prohibition on appellate review has itself been limited, first in *Thermtron Products, Inc. v. Hermansdorfer*, 423 U.S. 336, 346 (1976). In that case, the Supreme Court held that § 1447(d) only restricts appellate review of remand orders that are "based on grounds in § 1447(c)" and that "invoked the grounds specified therein." *E.D. ex rel. Darcy v. Pfizer, Inc.*, 722 F.3d 574, 579 (4th Cir. 2013) (alteration and internal quotation marks omitted). Section 1447(c) provides in relevant part that "[a] motion to remand the [—10—] case on the basis of any defect other than lack of subject matter jurisdiction must be made within 30 days after the filing of the notice of removal under section 1446(a)." Thus, § 1447(c) allows a district court to remand "based on: (1) a district court's lack of subject matter jurisdiction or (2) a defect in removal 'other than lack of subject matter jurisdiction' that was raised by the motion of a party within 30 days after the notice of removal was filed." *Ellenburg v. Spartan Motors Chassis, Inc.*, 519 F.3d 192, 196 (4th Cir. 2008) (quoting 28 U.S.C. § 1447(c)). And, § 1447(d) generally bars our review of a remand that is ordered on one of these bases. *See id.*

The § 1447(d) prohibition on appellate review was further limited by this court in *Borneman v. United States*, 213 F.3d 819, 826 (4th Cir. 2000), wherein we held that district courts did not have authority to remand on a basis generally authorized by § 1447(c) when a more specific statute would prohibit remand. In such a case, § 1447(d) does not bar our review. *See id.*

Finally, even when § 1447(d) prohibits our review of a remand order itself, the severability exception fashioned by the Supreme Court in *City of Waco v. U.S. Fidelity & Guaranty Co.*, 293 U.S. 140 (1934), can authorize our review of issues collateral to the remand order. *See Palmer v. City Nat. Bank of W. Va.*, 498 F.3d 236, 240 (4th Cir. 2007). However, we [—11—] "restrict[] the applicability of the *Waco* exception to purportedly reviewable orders that (1) have a preclusive effect upon the parties in subsequent proceedings and (2) are severable, both logically and factually, from the remand order." *Id.* The exception does not allow reversal of the remand order itself. *See Powerex Corp.*, 551 U.S. at 236.

Two of our decisions, *Shives v. CSX Transportation, Inc.*, 151 F.3d 164 (4th Cir. 1998), and *In re Blackwater Security Consulting, LLC*, 460 F.3d 576 (4th Cir. 2006), figure prominently in our analysis of

§ 1447(d), and we therefore begin by discussing them in some detail.

B. *Shives*

In *Shives*, a railroad employee injured in a work-related accident ("Shives") filed a negligence suit against his employer in state court under FELA and also filed a protective claim with the DOL under the LHWCA. *See Shives*, 151 F.3d at 166. Contending that Shives was engaged in maritime employment and therefore entitled only to workers compensation under the LHWCA, the employer removed the case to federal district court and moved to dismiss the case to allow Shives's administrative claim to proceed before the DOL. *See id.* Shives moved to remand the case to state court, arguing that he was not engaged in maritime employment and thus had the right to litigate his negligence claim in state court under FELA. *See id.* The district court [—12—] concluded that Shives's injury was actually not covered by the LHWCA and thus remanded the case to state court. *See id.* The employer appealed the remand order and also filed a petition for writ of mandamus seeking review of the order. *See id.*

We began with the question of whether we possessed jurisdiction to consider the merits of the appeal. We determined that the district court had not remanded based on a conclusion that it lacked subject-matter jurisdiction, but instead on the basis that § 1445(a) prohibited removal. *See id.* at 167. However, we noted that the district court's conclusion that § 1445(a) prohibited removal was in turn based on the court's substantive ruling that Shives's injury fell outside the scope of LHWCA coverage. *See id.* We expressed some doubt as to whether that ruling was of the type included in § 1447(c). *See id.* In the end, however, we determined, apparently on the basis of the *Waco* severability exception to § 1447(d), that whether remand was on a basis included in § 1447(c) was immaterial since the conclusion that the LHWCA did not provide coverage was a "conceptual antecedent" to the court's ruling that § 1445(a) barred removal. *Id.*; *see Blackwater*, 460 F.3d at 588. We reasoned that the LHWCA-

coverage question was "exclusively a federal question which Congress never intended for state courts to resolve" and that insofar as the basis for the remand order "did not fall precisely under the grounds identified in" [—13—] § 1447(c), we could exercise appellate jurisdiction. *Shives*, 151 F.3d at 167.[4] Alternatively, we concluded that even if our analysis of the appellate jurisdiction issue were incorrect, we would vacate the remand order via mandamus in order "[t]o avoid forfeiting the federal courts' role of reviewing LHWCA coverage issues." *Id.*

We then addressed the merits of the issue of whether the LHWCA provided coverage, concluding that it did. *See id.* at 168-71. We further reasoned that "LHWCA coverage is exclusive and preempts Shives from pursuing an FELA claim." *Id.* at 171.

Having determined that LHWCA covered Shives's injury and that it barred Shives's FELA claim, we were "left with a procedural conundrum" regarding the remedy to be applied. *Id.* Although the district court had incorrectly determined that the LHWCA did not cover Shives's injury, its determination that removal was improper was nevertheless correct for two reasons: First, § 1445(a) prohibits the removal of FELA cases brought in state court, and second, district courts do not have original jurisdiction over LHWCA cases and § 1441 allows removal only of cases that could have been brought in district court in the first instance. *See id.* At the same time, the state court [—14—] would not have jurisdiction over Shives's (now recharacterized) claim because state courts do not have jurisdiction over LHWCA claims. *See id.* We concluded "[i]n the peculiarities of th[at] case," that had the district court correctly analyzed the LHWCA-coverage question and determined that the LHWCA covered Shives's injuries, the proper remedy would have been to simply dismiss the action and allow Shives to proceed through the appropriate administrative process. *See id.* We noted that dismissing would have allowed the district court to avoid "committing the federal

---

[4] Our opinion actually refers to 1445(c) rather than § 1447(c), but that appears to be the result of a typographical error.

question of LHWCA coverage to the state court when Congress intended that it be decided exclusively in federal court." *Id.* We therefore vacated the district court's remand order and remanded the case to the district court with instructions to dismiss for lack of subject-matter jurisdiction. *See id.*

C. *Blackwater*

Now we turn to *Blackwater*. In that case, according to the complaint, several men ("the decedents") entered into independent-contractor service agreements with two companies (collectively, "Blackwater") to provide services supporting Blackwater's contracts with third parties. *See Blackwater*, 460 F.3d at 580. Blackwater assigned the decedents to provide security for a company that had an agreement to provide various forms of support to a defense contractor that was providing services for the United States Armed Forces in support of its [—15—] operations in Iraq. *See id.* According to the complaint, Blackwater had represented to the decedents when they entered into their independent-contractor agreements that certain precautionary measures would be taken, but that in fact those measures were not taken and the decedents were ultimately killed as a result. *See id.* at 580-81. The administrator of the decedents' estates sued Blackwater as well as the man who had been the decedents' supervisor (hereinafter, collectively, "Blackwater") in North Carolina state court alleging state-law claims for wrongful death and fraud. *See id.* at 581. Blackwater subsequently removed the action to federal district court, asserting that the Defense Base Act ("DBA"), 42 U.S.C. §§ 1651 – 1654, completely preempted the state-law claims and that the case presented issues concerning unique federal interests that created a federal question.[5] *See id.* Blackwater then moved the district court to dismiss the action on the basis of lack of

subject-matter jurisdiction because the claims were covered by the DBA and thus could be litigated only in the DOL, which has jurisdiction over DBA claims in the first instance. *See id.* [—16—]

The district court determined that it lacked subject-matter jurisdiction over the case, concluding that the DBA did not completely preempt the state-law claims and that Blackwater's assertion of a unique federal interest in the claims was based on the incorrect assumption that the district court had jurisdiction to determine whether the decedents were covered under the DBA. *See id.* at 581. Based on its conclusion that it lacked subject-matter jurisdiction, the district court remanded the case to state court under § 1447(c). *See id.* Blackwater had urged the district court to instead remedy the lack of jurisdiction by dismissing the case as barred by the DBA. *See id.* at 581-82. However, the district court determined that it lacked jurisdiction to decide whether the DBA covered the claims. *See id.* at 582.

Blackwater appealed the remand order to this court and petitioned for a writ of mandamus. *See id.* We held that we lacked appellate jurisdiction and we declined to order mandamus relief. *See id.* In analyzing the appellate-jurisdiction question, we began by noting that the district court had clearly remanded the case on a basis included in § 1447(c) insofar as remand was based on the district court's determination that it lacked subject-matter jurisdiction. *See id.* at 585; *see also id.* at 591-92. Accordingly, we concluded that § 1447(d) [—17—] prohibited us from reviewing the merits of the appeal. *See id.* at 585.

We also considered an argument by Blackwater that the *Waco* severability exception allowed us to review the district court's mootness-based denial of Blackwater's motion to dismiss. We concluded that the exception did not allow our review because the denial of the motion on mootness grounds had no preclusive effect and because it was not logically and factually severable from the remand order. *See id.* at 588-90. Regarding the preclusive effect, we noted that "[o]ne of

---

[5] "The DBA is a federal statute that incorporates and extends the [LHWCA] to select forms of employment outside of the United States." *Nordan v. Blackwater Sec. Consulting, LLC*, 382 F. Supp. 2d 801, 807 (E.D.N.C. 2005), *appeal dismissed, mandamus denied by In re Blackwater Sec. Consulting, LLC*, 460 F.3d 576 (4th Cir. 2006).

the first principles of preclusion . . . is that the precluding order either actually determined the issue sought to be precluded (in the case of issue preclusion) or issued a final judgment on the merits (in the case of claims preclusion)." *Id.* at 589 (citing *Martin v. American Bancorporation Ret. Plan*, 407 F.3d 643, 650, 653 (4th Cir. 2005)). We also specifically distinguished our severability-exception analysis in *Shives* on the basis of two differences in procedural posture between the cases. First, unlike in *Shives*, wherein we expressed doubt regarding whether the district court had remanded on a basis included in § 1447(c)—and thus whether § 1447(d) applied—the remand in *Blackwater* was clearly based on lack of subject-matter jurisdiction, which is plainly a ground included in § 1447(c). *See id.* at 587-88. Second, the district court in *Blackwater* did not reach the [—18—] question of whether the DBA covered the alleged injuries, whereas the district court in *Shives* did determine that the LHWCA covered the plaintiff injury and that determination was a "conceptual antecedent" to the court's remand decision. *See id.* at 588.

We also considered whether we had jurisdiction under the *Waco* severability exception to review the district court's determinations that the DBA did not completely preempt the state-law claims and that no unique federal interest created a federal question that would provide removal jurisdiction. *See id.* at 590. We concluded that neither ruling could be reviewed under *Waco* because neither would have any preclusive effect on Blackwater and neither could be disengaged from the remand order. *See id.*[6]

We next considered whether we could review the remand order via mandamus. Noting that the Supreme Court has interpreted § 1447(d) to prohibit not only appellate review but also review via

---

[6] Although it is not relevant to the present case, we also declined Blackwater's request to create a new exception to § 1447(d)'s prohibition for cases "undermin[ing] the constitutional sequestration of foreign affairs and war powers within the political branches of the federal government, out of reach of both the federal and the state judiciaries." *Blackwater*, 460 F.3d at 592.

mandamus, we concluded we were precluded from granting mandamus relief. *See id.* at 593. [—19—]

We further determined that there was no tension between the DBA and § 1447(d) of the type that could authorize mandamus relief. *See id.* at 593-94 (distinguishing *Borneman*, 213 F.3d at 826). We noted that "the statute 'in tension' with § 1447(d) in *Borneman* declared that certain state-court actions against federal employees 'shall be removed.' 28 U.S.C. § 2679(d)(2)." *Blackwater*, 460 F.3d at 593. Accordingly, we observed:

> That statute thus directly and specifically addressed the removability of the relevant class of claims and contained language that channeled the district court's authority to remand in such cases. This absence of discretion to remand created the tension of which we spoke in *Borneman*. By contrast, Blackwater has not identified any portion of the DBA that similarly addresses either the removability to federal district court of state court actions purportedly preempted by the DBA or the district court's peculiar lack of discretion with respect to remand of such cases.

Id. at 593-94 (citation omitted).

We also rejected the notion that the DBA defense presented such "extraordinarily important question[s] of federal law" that mandamus relief would be appropriate to prevent the state court from adjudicating it. *Id.* at 594. In this regard, we noted that neither the Supreme Court's decision in *Thermtron* nor our prior decisions provided a basis for circumventing 1447(d)'s prohibition in order to avoid having a state court decide a federal issue. *See id.* Distinguishing *Shives* specifically, we noted that *Shives* "presented the court of appeals with an order in which the district court actually decided . . . as part of [—20—] its inquiry into the permissibility of removal, whether the LHWCA covered the plaintiff's claims" whereas in *Blackwater* "we ha[d] no coverage question to review—and rightfully so, as the district court did not need to reach that issue as part of its removal jurisdiction analysis." *Id*. at 594-95. We also distinguished *Shives* on the basis that *Shives* presented "an uncontested factual record" on which to decide the coverage question, whereas in *Blackwater*, we had only the pleadings to consider. *Id*. at 594-95. In light of both of these distinctions, we concluded that "mandamus is not only not compelled by *Shives* but is also particularly inappropriate." *Id*. at 595.

D. Appellate Review Analysis

Having outlined the applicable legal principles, we now turn to the facts of the case before us. The district court's decision in the present case was based on the simple fact that a FELA claim brought in state court cannot be removed to a federal court, *see* 28 U.S.C. § 1445(a), a point that Bynum had timely raised in his motion to remand. As we have explained, § 1447(c) authorizes remand based on a "lack[of] subject matter jurisdiction" and remand based on "any defect other than lack of subject matter jurisdiction" that was raised by a party "within 30 days after the filing of the notice of removal." 28 U.S.C. [—21—] § 1447(c).⁷ The § 1445(a) bar does not deprive courts of subject-matter jurisdiction over cases to which it applies. *See Shives*, 151 F.3d at 167 (explaining that "the district court could not rule . . . that it was without jurisdiction because federal courts have concurrent jurisdiction over FELA claims"). We are thus faced with the question that we did not answer in *Shives*, namely whether nonremovability based on § 1445(a) is a "defect other than lack of subject matter

---

⁷ Prior to 1996, § 1447(c) provided as follows:

A motion to remand the case on the basis of any defect *in removal procedure* must be made within 30 days after the filing of the notice of removal under section 1446(a). If at any time before final judgment it appears that the district court lacks subject matter jurisdiction, the case shall be remanded.

28 U.S.C. § 1447(c) (1995) (emphasis added). In 1996, the statute was amended to substitute the words "any defect other than lack of subject matter jurisdiction" for "any defect in removal procedure." Pub. L. No. 104-219, 110 Stat. 3022 (1996).

jurisdiction" within the meaning of § 1447(c). We conclude that it is.

The word "defect" is not defined in § 1447 or the associated statutes. However, the sixth edition of *Black's Law Dictionary*, which was the edition that was current when § 1447(c) was amended, defines "defect" as "[t]he want or absence of some legal requisite; deficiency; imperfection; insufficiency." *Black's Law Dictionary* 418 (6th ed. 1990). "Defect" is similarly defined in *Webster's Third New* [—22—] *International Dictionary* as "want or absence of something necessary for completeness, perfection, or adequacy in form or function." *Webster's Third New International Dictionary* 591 (1981).

From the context of § 1447, it is apparent "that 'defect' refers to a failure to comply with the statutory requirements for removal provided in 28 U.S.C. §§ 1441-1453." *Kamm v. ITEX Corp.*, 568 F.3d 752, 755 (9th Cir. 2009); *see Cook v. Wikler*, 320 F.3d 431, 435 (3d Cir. 2003) (holding that "the plain language of [§ 1447(c)] now applies broadly to include all removals that are not authorized by law" (internal quotation marks omitted)). That scope certainly encompasses § 1445(a). *See Albarado v. Southern Pac. Transp. Co.*, 199 F.3d 762, 766 (5th Cir. 1999) (holding that "remand based upon § 1445(a)'s statutory restriction against removal is a procedural defect under § 1447(c), and the district court's remand order based thereupon is not subject to appellate review"); *see also Vasquez v. North Cnty. Transit Dist.*, 292 F.3d 1049, 1062 (9th Cir. 2002) (holding that nonremovability under 28 U.S.C. § 1445(c), which prohibits removal of civil cases arising under state workmen's compensation law, is a "defect other than lack of subject matter jurisdiction" within the meaning of § 1447(c)); *Pierpoint v. Barnes*, 94 F.3d 813, 816-21 (2d Cir. 1996) (applying pre-1996-amendment version of 28 U.S.C. § 1447(c) and [—23—] holding that court of appeals lacked jurisdiction to review remand to state court based on district court's determination that claims brought in state court under the Death on the High Seas Act were not removable).[8] As such, the § 1447(d) bar applies, and we lack jurisdiction to review the remand order on appeal.[9] [—24—]

Although Norfolk Southern relies on *Shives* in asserting that we possess appellate jurisdiction, *Shives* does not warrant that conclusion. As we have noted, in *Shives* we did not decide whether a remand according to § 1445(a) was the type of ruling that § 1447(c) includes. *See Shives*, 151 F.3d at 167 (explaining that the district court's "ministerial application of § 1445(a) depended

---

[8] *In re Norfolk Southern Railway Co.*, 592 F.3d 907 (8th Cir. 2010), cited by Norfolk Southern, does little to advance its cause. In that case, the plaintiff brought a FELA claim in state court. *See id.* at 910. The defendant removed the action based on the contention that the LHWCA covered the injury and barred recovery under the FELA. *See id.* However, the district court concluded that the LHWCA did not cover the plaintiff's injury, and thus that the claim was properly brought under FELA. *See id.* Accordingly, the district court remanded to state court based on the conclusion that § 1445(a) barred removal of the claim. *See id.* at 910-11. The defendant appealed and petitioned for mandamus relief. *See id.* The plaintiff argued that § 1447(d) barred review of the remand order because the order was based on a lack of subject-matter jurisdiction. *See id.* at 910. Concluding that a § 1445(a) defect is not jurisdictional, the Eighth Circuit held that § 1447(d) did not bar appellate review of the remand order. *See id.* at 912. However, the court did not specifically address whether nonremovability under § 1445(a), if timely raised, qualifies as a "defect other than lack of subject matter jurisdiction" within the meaning of § 1447(c).

[9] For the same reasons that we held that there was no tension-creating statute in *Blackwater* that would bar the district court from remanding to state court and negate the application of § 1447(d), *see* 460 F.3d at 593-94 (distinguishing *Borneman v. United States*, 213 F.3d 819, 826 (4th Cir. 2000)), there is no such tension-creating statute here. After all, the federal defense asserted by the employer in *Blackwater*, that the LHWCA provided the exclusive remedy for the plaintiffs' injuries, is the same defense that Norfolk Southern asserts here except for the fact that Blackwater asserted a defense under the DBA, which "extends the [LHWCA] to select forms of employment (Continued) [—24—] outside of the United States," *Nordan*, 382 F. Supp. 2d at 807, whereas Norfolk Southern simply asserts an LHWCA defense directly.

on its substantive ruling that Shives was not engaged in maritime employment" and noting that "[t]his determination is probably not of the type of ruling included in 28 U.S.C. § 1447(c)" although "[t]his conclusion . . . is not entirely without doubt").

As we noted in *Blackwater*, our appellate review in *Shives* was based on the fact that the district court's decision that the LHWCA covered Shives's injury was a "conceptual antecedent" to the remand order. *Blackwater*, 460 F.3d at 587, 588 (internal quotation marks omitted). Here, in contrast, the district court did not reach the merits of the coverage question as it denied Norfolk Southern's motion to dismiss on mootness grounds. Thus, for the same reasons we articulated in *Blackwater*, the *Waco* severability exception does not allow our review of that ruling. Namely, the district court's dismissal of the motion to dismiss [—25—] on mootness grounds had no preclusive effect since the court did not resolve the merits of the issue and there was no final judgment on the merits; nor was the denial of that motion logically and factually severable from the remand order. *See id.* at 588-90. Furthermore, since our decision in *Shives*, the Supreme Court has further clarified the scope of the *Waco* severability exception by holding that it "does not permit an appeal when there is no *order* separate from the unreviewable remand order." *Powerex*, 551 U.S. at 236 (emphasis in original)). The fact that there is no such separate order here is yet another reason why the *Waco* exception does not provide us with jurisdiction over Norfolk Southern's appeal.

E. Mandamus Analysis

Because § 1447(d) deprives us of appellate jurisdiction, we also lack authority to grant mandamus relief. Congress's restriction on review of remand orders applies to review "on appeal or otherwise." 28 U.S.C. § 1447(d). "The Supreme Court has interpreted this language to forbid the use of mandamus to circumvent the requirements of § 1447(d)." *Blackwater*, 460 F.3d at 593 (citing *Thermtron*, 423 U.S. at 343)); *see Borneman*, 213 F.3d at 824.

Norfolk Southern asserts that unless we vacate the remand order, a state court will be left to decide the question of whether the LHWCA provides a defense to Bynum's claims. But [—26—] that is the very circumstance we faced in *Blackwater*, wherein we held that mandamus relief was not warranted. *See* 460 F.3d at 592-95. In distinguishing the facts that were before us in that case from those in *Shives*—wherein we concluded that we could grant mandamus relief regardless of whether § 1447(d) barred review on appeal, *see* 151 F.3d at 167—we noted that the fact that the district court in *Shives* actually decided the question that the LHWCA covered the alleged injury was "a key difference." *Blackwater*, 460 F.3d at 594. We conclude as well here that with the district court not having reached the merits of Norfolk Southern's LHWCA defense, *Shives* does not warrant our granting mandamus relief.

Moreover, granting mandamus relief here would also be inappropriate because Norfolk Southern has not made the requisite showing that its "right to the issuance of the writ is clear and indisputable." *Media Gen. Operations, Inc. v. Buchanan*, 417 F.3d 424, 433 (4th Cir. 2005); *see also In re Grand Jury Subpoena*, 596 F.2d 630, 632 (4th Cir. 1979) (per curiam) (holding that there was no showing of "a clear and indisputable right" when the issue was "close"). Specifically, Norfolk Southern has not shown that it was clearly entitled to have the district court dismiss Bynum's FELA claim rather than remand it to the state court. [—27—]

The facts of this case, after all, are quite different than those that were before us in *Shives*. In *Shives*, the district court's decision to remand was based on its conclusion that the LHWCA did not cover Shives's injury, *see Shives*, 151 F.3d at 166, and there is no indication that Shives had disputed that his FELA claim would be barred if the LHWCA covered his injury. On appeal, we concluded that the LHWCA in fact did cover Shives's injury and therefore that his FELA claim was barred. *See id.* at 168-71. Having determined that Shives actually had no FELA claim, we concluded that remand to state court was not a possibility as "[s]tate courts . . . do not have

jurisdiction over LHWCA cases." *Id.* at 171; *see id.* ("[W]e are faced with an LHWCA case over which neither the state court nor the district court had jurisdiction."). We also decided against remanding to state court to avoid "committing the federal question of LHWCA coverage to the state court when Congress intended that it be decided exclusively in the federal court." *Id.*

In this case, neither of these considerations stands in the way of a remand to state court. First, neither the district court nor our court has addressed the LHWCA coverage question;[10] [—28—] thus, Bynum's FELA claim continues to exist and the state court would have jurisdiction to adjudicate that claim, *see* 45 U.S.C. § 56. Second, the-scope-of-LHWCA coverage issue on which we were focused in *Shives* is not even likely to be an issue in the state court on remand because Bynum has already received LHWCA benefits. The primary question remaining will be whether his prior receipt of LHWCA benefits bars his FELA claim. Thus, in the absence of any clear barrier to remanding to state court, it simply cannot be said that Norfolk Southern has a clear and indisputable right not to have the case remanded to state court.

III.

In sum, we conclude that § 1447(d) bars review of the district court's order by appeal or via mandamus. We also conclude that Norfolk Southern has not established entitlement to mandamus relief because it has not shown a clear and indisputable right to such relief. Accordingly, we dismiss Norfolk Southern's appeal and deny its mandamus petition.

APPEAL DISMISSED AND PETITION FOR WRIT OF MANDAMUS DENIED

---

[10] Norfolk Southern had no clear and undisputable right even to have the district court decide the merits of the LHWCA coverage question. Indeed, in *Blackwater*, we noted that we "rightfully" had "no coverage question to review" when "the (Continued) [—28—] district court did not need to reach that issue as part of its removal jurisdiction analysis." 460 F.3d at 595.

United States Court of Appeals
for the Fourth Circuit

No. 13-1495

**AMERICAN S.S. OWNERS MUT. PROTECTION AND
INDEM. ASS'N, INC.**
vs.
DANN OCEAN TOWING, INC.

Appeal from the United States District Court for the
District of Maryland, at Baltimore

Decided: June 26, 2014

Citation: 756 F.3d 314, 2 Adm. R. 113 (4th Cir. 2014).

Before **WILKINSON, KEENAN,** and **DIAZ,** Circuit
Judges.

[—2—] **KEENAN,** Circuit Judge:

In this appeal, we consider whether the district court erred in concluding that a choice-of-law provision in a maritime insurance contract required use of New York's six-year statute of limitations, rather than the equitable doctrine of laches ordinarily applied under maritime law, to determine the timeliness of certain claims brought under the insurance contract. Upon our review, we hold that the district court properly determined that the choice-of-law provision in the parties' contract required application of New York's statute of limitations to the claims at issue. Therefore, we affirm the district court's judgment.

I.

The American Steamship Owners Mutual Protection and Indemnity Association, Inc. (the Club) is a non-profit provider of protection and indemnity insurance, which insurance covers vessel owners and charterers against third-party liabilities arising from the ownership and operation of insured vessels. Members of the Club pay insurance premiums and assessments, which the Club uses to reimburse members for covered losses. The Club issues to each of its members a Certificate of Entry, which reflects that the member has entered into a marine [—3—] insurance contract with the Club subject to the Club's By-Laws and Rules (Rules).

The Club's Rules include a choice-of-law provision selecting New York law and a two-year statute of limitations for claims against the Club, in addition to requirements for exhausting insurance disputes and selecting a forum for litigation. The relevant section of the Rules reads as follows:

If any difference or dispute shall arise between a Member and the [Club] concerning the construction of these Rules, or the insurance afforded by the [Club] under these Rules, or any amount due from the [Club] to the Member, such difference or dispute shall in the first instance be referred to and adjudicated by the Board of Directors. No Member shall be entitled to maintain any action, suit or other legal proceedings against the [Club] upon any such difference or dispute unless and until the same has been submitted to the Directors and they shall have given their decision thereto, or shall have been in default for three months in so doing. *These Rules and any contract of insurance between the [Club] and a Member shall be governed by and construed in accordance with the law of the State of New York. In no event shall suit on any claim be maintainable against the [Club] unless commenced within two years after the loss, damage or expense resulting from liabilities, risks, events, occurrences and expenditures specified under this Rule shall have been paid by the Member.* Any such suit against the [Club] shall be brought in the United States District Court for the Southern District of New York. (Emphasis added.)

Dann Ocean Towing, Inc. (Dann) was a member of the Club between 1995 and 2001. Dann obtained insurance through the Club for a tugboat, which damaged a barge when the tugboat ran [—4—] aground on a coral reef in 1998. The barge's owner asserted a claim against Dann for property damage, and the United States asserted a claim against Dann for environmental damage to the reef. Dann settled both parties' claims in November 2001 for a total amount of $2,170,000.

The Club originally agreed to contribute $1,170,000 toward the settlement. However, one of the underwriters for Dann's liability insurance became insolvent and could not pay its portion of the settlement, in the amount of $278,552.55 (the shortfall). Although both Dann and the Club denied responsibility for the shortfall, the Club paid the shortfall to preserve a settlement offer that it considered "extremely favorable," but indicated that the Club would seek reimbursement from Dann.

Dann refused to reimburse the Club for the shortfall. In response, the Club declined to reimburse Dann for certain insurance claims that otherwise would have been payable to Dann, and withheld a total amount of $131,085.43 in covered losses that the Club later used to offset the shortfall. Thereafter, Dann refused to pay its insurance premiums to the Club for the policy years 1999, 2000, and 2001. The total amount of Dann's unpaid premiums was $452,610.23.

In August 2008, the Club filed a civil action against Dann and the tugboat, alleging that Dann breached the insurance [—5—] contract by failing to reimburse the Club for the shortfall and by failing to pay the overdue insurance premiums. Dann filed a counterclaim against the Club, alleging that the Club breached the insurance contract by failing to indemnify Dann for covered losses. The Club and Dann each alleged that the respective claims against them were time-barred, posted $500,000 bonds as security and counter-security for the various claims,[1] and filed cross-motions for summary judgment.

In August 2010, the district court initially ruled that the equitable doctrine of laches, rather than New York's six-year statute of limitations for contract claims, governed the timeliness of the Club's claims against Dann. The court found that all the Club's claims, except one involving an unpaid insurance premium in the amount of $76,925.56, accrued more than six years before the Club filed suit. In its laches analysis, the court concluded that

---

[1] Dann posted a $500,000 vessel release bond as security for the claims against the tugboat, and the Club posted a $500,000 bond as counter-security for Dann's claims.

the Club's claim relating to the shortfall was not barred because the Club's delay in filing suit was reasonable, in that the Club made various out-of-court attempts to obtain reimbursement from Dann and the delay did not prejudice Dann. [—6—]

In May 2012, however, upon further briefing by the parties, the district court reconsidered its ruling. The court observed that although there is a "typical presumption that courts sitting in admiralty jurisdiction apply the equitable doctrine of laches rather than a specific statute of limitations," the choice-of-law clause in the parties' contract "compels the application of the elected jurisdiction's statute of limitations." Accordingly, the district court held that "claims arising from the maritime insurance contract between [Dann] and the Club are subject to New York's six-year statute of limitations," which barred all the Club's claims except for the one concerning the $76,925.56 premium.

Because the parties' contract expressly provided that claims brought *against* the Club were subject to an even shorter two-year limitation, the court ruled that Dann's indemnity claims against the Club were time-barred under the parties' contract, but that those claims could be employed defensively under the doctrine of recoupment to offset the entirety of the Club's surviving claim for the $76,925.56 unpaid insurance premium. Thus, although the court granted summary judgment to the Club on its surviving unpaid insurance claim and dismissed the parties' other claims, the court ultimately held that "neither party can recover against the other," granted Dann's motion to reduce the amount of its bond from $500,000 to [—7—] $100,000, and directed that the case be closed. The Club timely appealed.

II.

We consider on appeal whether the district court erred in concluding that the timeliness of the Club's contract claims against Dann is governed by New York's six-year statute of limitations for contract actions, based on the parties' agreement that the insurance contract "shall be governed by and construed in accordance with the law of the State of New York." The Club contends that because this case arises under admiralty jurisdiction, the district court was required to apply the doctrine of laches as the procedural law of the maritime forum, rather than New York's statute of limitations. We disagree with the Club's argument.

Laches is an equitable doctrine that can be raised by a defendant as an affirmative defense to a claim, and requires that the defendant show "(1) lack of diligence by the party against whom the defense is asserted, and (2) prejudice to the party asserting the defense." *Giddens v. Isbrandtsen Co.*, 355 F.2d 125, 127 (4th Cir. 1966) (citation and internal quotation marks omitted). In assessing the timeliness of a maritime claim, the doctrine of laches typically applies rather than any fixed statute of limitations. *See id.* at 126-27. However, [—8—] there are many examples of exceptions to this general rule, such as statutory provisions that impose time bars on personal injury actions arising out of maritime torts, *see* 46 U.S.C. § 30106, on certain cargo loss contract claims under the Carriage of Goods by Sea Act, *see* 49 Stat. 1207, 1209 (1936) (codified at 46 U.S.C. § 30701 note), and on maritime salvage actions, *see* 46 U.S.C. § 80107(c).

In this case, the district court ultimately agreed with Dann that parties to a maritime insurance contract may elect to avoid the doctrine of laches by including in their contract an enforceable choice-of-law provision that requires application of another jurisdiction's law and, implicitly, that jurisdiction's statute of limitations. The court based its analysis on two cases, namely, *Cooper v. Meridian Yachts, Ltd.*, 575 F.3d 1151 (11th Cir. 2009), and *Italia Marittima, S.P.A. v. Seaside Transportation Services, LLC*, 2010 WL 3504834 (N.D. Cal. Sept. 7, 2010) (unpublished).

In *Cooper*, the Eleventh Circuit considered a claim for indemnification and contribution brought by a ship owner against a ship builder for injuries sustained by a worker on the ship. The parties' contract provided that "all

disputes arising out of or in connection with [the contract] . . . shall be construed in accordance with and shall be governed by the Dutch law." 575 F.3d at 1162. The court held that this provision was "clearly [—9—] meant to be read broadly" and that the parties' choice of Dutch law governed not only the timeliness of pure contract claims, but also the timeliness of the indemnification and contribution action for related tort claims. *Id.*

Similarly, in *Italia Marittima*, a district court considered claims for negligence and breach of contract arising from the performance of stevedoring services aboard a vessel that sustained a loss of cargo during inclement weather. 2010 WL 3504834, at *1-3. The court held that California's statutes of limitations applied to both the breach of contract claims and the negligence claims based on a choice-of-law provision in the parties' contract stating that the contract "shall be construed, interpreted and enforced in accordance with the laws of the State of California without reference to the laws of any other jurisdiction, except to the extent that the laws, rules and regulations of the United States of America shall apply." *Id.* at *8. Because the choice-of-law clause clearly "promote[d] California law," and because laches is a common law doctrine rather than codified federal law, the court reasoned that the contract required application of California's statutes of limitations. *Id.*

We do not discern any contrary authority preventing a federal court sitting in admiralty from enforcing a valid choice-of-law provision in a maritime contract incorporating a [—10—] statute of limitations, in place of the traditional doctrine of laches. Accordingly, we agree with the district court, and with the reasoning of the decisions in *Cooper* and *Italia Marittima*, that an otherwise valid choice-of-law provision in a maritime contract is enforceable and may require application of a jurisdiction's statute of limitations, in lieu of the doctrine of laches, to govern issues regarding the timeliness of claims asserted under that agreement.

We find no merit in the Club's alternative argument that the decisions in *Cooper* and

Italia Marittima are distinguishable because, in contrast to the provision before us, the choice-of-law clauses interpreted in those cases were sufficiently detailed to incorporate the "procedural" rules in addition to the "substantive" rules of the chosen jurisdictions. Even assuming that New York's statute of limitations constitutes a "procedural" rule of law in this context, the Club's argument is unpersuasive because, under New York law, we must accord unambiguous provisions of an insurance contract their plain and ordinary meaning. *See, e.g., White v. Cont'l Cas. Co.,* 878 N.E.2d 1019, 1021 (N.Y. 2007). The plain language of the contract before us unambiguously provides that the contract shall be "governed by" New York law. This phrase clearly signals the parties' intent that, subject to any exceptions stated in the contract, New York law will be applied as [—11—] "governing" the timeliness of claims asserted under the contract. Because the claims at issue in this case are contractual in nature and are not subject to the stated exception for claims brought against the Club, the parties' choice-of-law clause amply encompasses the present claims. Thus, the plain language of the parties' contract fails to contain any indication that the parties intended to preserve application of the doctrine of laches for any claims brought under the contract.

Additionally, even if we were to assume, without deciding, that the choice-of-law provision is ambiguous regarding the parties' intent to incorporate New York's statute of limitations for contract actions, we would, under basic principles of contract interpretation, resolve any such ambiguity against the insurer and in favor of the insured party. *See id.* (stating that if the terms in an insurance contract are ambiguous, any ambiguity must be construed in favor of the insured and against the insurer); *see also McCarthy v. Am. Int'l Grp., Inc.,* 283 F.3d 121, 124 (2d Cir. 2002) (observing that under New York law, courts construe ambiguities in insurance contracts against the drafter). Here, it is undisputed that the Club, as insurer, supplied Dann with the contract of insurance and drafted the Rules governing the parties' insurance contract. Therefore, we construe any ambiguity regarding the intended breadth of the [—12—] choice-of-law provision against the Club and in favor of applying New York's statute of limitations to the Club's claims against Dann.

III.

Accordingly, we hold that the district court correctly applied New York's six-year statute of limitations to the Club's claims arising under its maritime insurance contract with Dann. We therefore affirm the district court's judgment.[2]

AFFIRMED

---

[2] In affirming the district court's judgment, we also affirm the court's decision granting Dann's motion to reduce the amount of its bond. Although Dann requested in its brief that we discharge the bonds posted by both parties, we do not address this issue because Dann did not seek a full discharge of the bonds from the district court in the first instance, and did not appeal the district court's order. Therefore, Dann's request for relief is not properly before us on appeal.

United States Court of Appeals
for the Fourth Circuit

No. 14-1189

FLAME S.A.
vs.
FREIGHT BULK PTE. LTD.

Appeal from the United States District Court for the
Eastern District of Virginia, at Norfolk

Decided: August 5, 2014

Citation: 762 F.3d 352, 2 Adm. R. 117 (4th Cir. 2014).

Before **WILKINSON, AGEE,** and **DIAZ,** Circuit Judges.

[—3—] **AGEE,** Circuit Judge:

Freight Bulk Pte. Ltd. ("Freight Bulk") appeals from the district court's order denying its motion to vacate a writ of maritime attachment previously issued in favor of Flame S.A. ("Flame") under Supplemental Rule B of the Federal Rules of Civil Procedure ("Rule B"). Flame filed a verified complaint in the Eastern District of Virginia seeking attachment of a shipping vessel for purposes of satisfying an English judgment, the underlying basis of which was a claim for breach of certain Forward Freight Swap Agreements ("FFAs"). The district court denied Freight Bulk's motion to vacate after concluding that its jurisdiction was determined by reference to federal, rather than English, law and that the FFAs are maritime contracts under federal law. For the reasons set forth below, we affirm the decision of the district court.

I.

In 2008, Flame, an integrated shipping and trading company organized under the laws of Switzerland and headquartered in Lugano, Switzerland, entered into four FFAs with Industrial Carriers, Inc. ("ICI"), a corporation organized under the laws [—4—] of a foreign country and registered to do business in the state of New York.[1]

FFAs are similar to futures or hedging contracts tied to the spread between a specified rate and market shipping prices at a future date. To act as a diversification against the vagaries of future maritime price fluctuations, shippers like Flame may enter into FFAs with another party although any entity could be a contracting party even if unrelated to the maritime industry. The FFAs in this case identified particular shipping routes listed in a specified maritime freight index, the Baltic Panamax Index, which provides market freight rates for the maritime industry. The shipping services contemplated in an FFA would likely never be performed by the parties who would usually settle the contract by exchanging cash, as the parties intended in this case.

FFAs can be complicated financial transactions, but we found the Second Circuit's description of how FFAs work in *D'Amico Dry Ltd. v. Primera Maritime (Hellas) Ltd.*, No. 11-3473-cv, 2014 WL 2609648, 2 Adm. R. 69 (2d Cir. June 12, 2014), an easy to follow narrative of the type of agreement at issue here: [—5—]

A major risk of an ocean carrier's business is that a slowdown in worldwide commercial activity will lead to diminution in shipments of cargo, causing vessels to make expensive voyages partially empty or, in more extreme circumstances, to lay idle. The rates carriers charge for carriage of goods fall during such slowdowns. . . . As a way of offsetting losses from its vessels being underemployed or idle during such a slowdown, [a carrier may] enter[] into futures contracts on international shipping rates. These contracts, sometimes called "forward freight agreements" or "FFAs," specify a base rate (the "contract rate") for a hypothetical shipment of specified goods over specified routes and future dates for comparison of the contract rate with the market rates on such future dates. If on a specified future date the market

---

[1] Three of the FFAs specified Flame as the seller and ICI as the buyer. The fourth was the reverse, with ICI as seller and Flame as the buyer. The record reflects only that ICI was a foreign corporation, but does not identify its country of origin.

rate is above the contract rate, then the party that took the downside of the agreement must pay the other party the difference. If on the future date the market rate is below the contract rate, the party that took the upside of the contract must pay the other party the difference. Profits realized from such contracts as rates fall will increase [the carrier's] revenues when demand is low, counteracting its losses from underemployment. Conversely, the losses on such contracts will decrease [the carrier's] net revenues when demand is high and rates rise.

D'Amico, 2014 WL 2609648, at *1, 2 Adm. R. at 69–70.

In September 2008, freight rates in the international shipping market entered a steep decline, causing ICI to become financially distressed. In October 2008, ICI voluntarily petitioned for bankruptcy in Greece, which constituted an Event of Default under the terms of the FFAs. Under the FFAs, ICI owed [—6—] Flame a substantial amount based on the difference between the contract and market rates.

In November 2010, Flame brought suit against ICI in the High Court of Justice, Queen's Bench Division, Commercial Court in London, England (the "English Court"), alleging breaches of the FFAs and seeking monetary damages. The English Court entered judgment against ICI on December 13, 2010 in the amount of $19,907,118.36 (the "English judgment").

After obtaining the English judgment against ICI, Flame moved for recognition and enforcement of that judgment in the United States District Court for the Southern District of New York.[2] ICI appeared before the district court and moved to dismiss for failure to state a claim, arguing that it did not have notice of the action in the English Court. The district

court denied ICI's motion. ICI's counsel subsequently filed a motion to withdraw as counsel, which the district court granted. When granting the withdrawal motion, the district court warned ICI that it must obtain new counsel or face a default judgment. ICI failed to obtain substitute counsel, and the court entered [—7—] default judgment on October 4, 2011,[3] recognizing the English judgment in favor of Flame.

On October 17, 2013, Flame registered the judgment of the Southern District of New York in the United States District Court for the Eastern District of Virginia pursuant to 28 U.S.C. § 1963. Flame then filed a verified complaint seeking an Order of Attachment against the shipping vessel M/V CAPE VIEWER (the "CAPE VIEWER"), docked at Norfolk, Virginia, pursuant to Rule B. Flame sought attachment of the CAPE VIEWER, which is owned by Freight Bulk, on the theory that Freight Bulk is the alter ego of ICI. The district court issued an attachment order, which was timely served on Freight Bulk.

Freight Bulk then appeared and moved the district court to vacate the Order of Attachment pursuant to supplemental Rule E(4)(f), arguing that the court lacked subject matter jurisdiction to enter the order. In particular, Freight Bulk contended that (1) the district court should apply English law in determining whether the FFAs are maritime contracts; and (2) regardless of the court's choice of law, FFAs are not maritime contracts. Because Flame invoked only the court's maritime [—8—] jurisdiction in its complaint, Freight Bulk argued that in the absence of a valid maritime claim the district court lacked subject matter jurisdiction and had no authority to enter the Rule B Order of Attachment.

After several hearings on Freight Bulk's motion to vacate, the district court denied that motion with respect to Freight Bulk's

---

[2] No federal statute provides for the recognition of foreign judgments. Instead, federal courts generally recognize judgments of foreign courts out of comity. *See Hilton v. Guyot*, 159 U.S. 113, 163–64, 202–03 (1895).

[3] The United States District Court for the Southern District of New York entered default judgment in recognition of the well-established rule that "'a corporation may appear in the federal courts only through licensed counsel.'" *See In re Under Seal*, 749 F.3d 276, 290 n.17 (4th Cir. 2014).

jurisdictional arguments.[4] Specifically, the district court concluded that it had properly exercised its admiralty jurisdiction over the case because federal law, rather than English law, controlled that issue. The district court determined that FFAs are maritime contracts under federal law. "However, considering the complexities and uncertainties involved . . . and the importance of clarifying the procedural issues presented," the district court certified the matter for expedited appeal to this Court. *Flame S.A. v. Industrial Carriers, Inc.*, No. 2:13-cv-658, 2014 WL 108897, at *4 (E.D. Va. [—9—] Jan. 10, 2014). Freight Bulk then sought permission to file an interlocutory appeal, which this Court granted.[5]

II.

This case presents two distinct issues on appeal, both of which concern the court's subject matter jurisdiction. First, we must determine whether federal law or foreign law controls our jurisdictional inquiry. Second, we must consider whether the FFAs at issue in this case are maritime contracts under the controlling law, establishing whether the district court could properly exercise admiralty jurisdiction in this case. We review the district court's legal conclusions regarding its own subject matter jurisdiction de novo. *See Vitol, S.A. v. Primerose Shipping Co.*, 708 F.3d 527, 533, 1 Adm. R. 106, 108 (4th Cir. 2013). "We review the district court's factual findings with respect to jurisdiction for clear

---

[4] In its Rule E(4)(f) motion to vacate, Freight Bulk also asserted that Flame's Complaint failed to set forth a legally sufficient basis upon which to pierce Freight Bulk's corporate veil. The district court withheld ruling on this separate issue of whether Flame properly pled that Freight Bulk is the corporate alter ego of ICI. As that question was not decided by the district court, it is not before us on appeal, and we offer no opinion on the issue.

[5] Section 1292(b) of 28 U.S.C. allows for the interlocutory appeal of an otherwise unappealable order when a district court judge certifies that the order "involves a controlling question of law as to which there is substantial ground for difference of opinion and that an immediate appeal from the order may materially advance the ultimate termination of the litigation."

error." *Velasco v. Gov't of Indon.*, 370 F.3d 392, 398 (4th Cir. 2004). [—10—]

III.

A.

"The judicial Power [of the United States] extend[s] . . . to all Cases of admiralty and maritime Jurisdiction." U.S. Const. art. III, § 2. In addition to this constitutional grant of original jurisdiction to the federal courts over admiralty matters, Congress has made plain the federal courts' exclusive authority over admiralty cases first with the Judiciary Act of 1789 and presently in 28 U.S.C. § 1333. That statute provides that "The district courts shall have original jurisdiction, exclusive of the courts of the States, of: (1) Any civil case of admiralty or maritime jurisdiction, saving to suitors in all cases all other remedies to which they are otherwise entitled." 28 U.S.C. § 1333; *see* Judiciary Act of 1789, § 9, Ch. 20, 1 Stat. 73, 76–77.

Since the Founding, the Supreme Court has made clear the authority and primacy of the federal courts in matters of admiralty particularly as relates to the recognition of foreign admiralty judgments.

It is well recognized that federal courts in the United States possess jurisdiction in admiralty over claims to enforce a foreign admiralty judgment. See, e.g., 1 Benedict on Admiralty § 106 ("[A]dmiralty jurisdiction in the United States may be broadly stated as extending to ... any claim to enforce a judgment of a foreign admiralty court."). Even in the [—11—] earliest days of the Republic, the Supreme Court *534 confirmed that the courts of the United States possess jurisdiction to recognize the admiralty decrees of foreign admiralty courts. *See Penhallow v. Doane's Adm'rs*, 3 U.S. (3 Dall.) 53, 97, 1 L. Ed. 507 (1795) (Iredell, J.) ("It was clearly shown at the bar, that a Court of Admiralty, in one nation, can carry into effect the determination of the [C]ourt of Admiralty of another.").

Vitol, 708 F.3d at 533–34, 1 Adm. R. at 108.

To proceed on a request for a Rule B writ of maritime attachment, the plaintiff must have a claim against the defendant that is cognizable in admiralty. *See Vitol*, 708 F.3d at 533–34, 1 Adm. R. at 108–09 (considering whether the court had admiralty jurisdiction over a request for attachment under Rule B). In the case before us, the initial issue is whether United States courts apply the law of the foreign jurisdiction that rendered the judgment to determine if the claim is cognizable in admiralty or whether the maritime law of the United States determines the admiralty status of that claim.

As the district court recognized, the distinction between English and American law is determinative in the case at bar.

It is apparent to the Court that under English law the [FFAs] would not be maritime contracts and as a result the English judgment in this matter would not be an admiralty judgment. Therefore, if English law were used in addressing this Rule B attachment, no admiralty jurisdiction would exist. [—12—]

Under federal law, however, it appears that the [FFAs] in question would certainly be maritime contracts.

Flame, 2014 WL 108897, at *3. Thus, the district court concluded "if federal law is applied, then this Court has admiralty jurisdiction. If English law is applied, there is no admiralty jurisdiction." *Id.* at *1.

Both before the district court and on appeal, Freight Bulk has argued that a claim to enforce a foreign judgment falls within a federal court's admiralty and maritime jurisdiction only if the claim underlying the foreign judgment would be considered a maritime claim under the laws of the foreign jurisdiction that rendered the judgment. The district court rejected Freight Bulk's argument and concluded that the maritime nature of a claim to enforce a foreign judgment must be determined under the laws

of the United States. The district court characterized the issue as "a question of choice of law on a procedural issue" and noted that "[g]enerally, procedural questions in federal court are governed by federal law," which led it to its ultimate conclusion that "federal law should inform this Court's determination of whether it has admiralty jurisdiction." *Flame*, 2014 WL 108897, at *2, *3.

The district court determined that there was no directly applicable Fourth Circuit precedent on the issue despite Freight Bulk's argument that our prior decision in *Vitol* dictated a [—13—] result in its favor. In the absence of controlling authority, the district court looked to analogous precedent from the Supreme Court in *Norfolk Southern Railway v. Kirby*, 543 U.S. 14 (2004), and the Second Circuit's opinion in *Blue Whale Corp. v. Grand China Shipping Development Co.*, 722 F.3d 488, 1 Adm. R. 38 (2d Cir. 2013). In our review of the district court's decision and the arguments presented to us, we first examine the impact of *Vitol* and then consider the application of other precedent.

B.

Freight Bulk contends that our prior opinion in *Vitol* requires holding that a claim's characterization under foreign law controls our jurisdictional inquiry. We disagree. Freight Bulk's reliance on *Vitol* is misplaced.

In *Vitol*, we considered whether a district court's Rule B attachment order to enforce a foreign admiralty judgment was properly issued. 708 F.3d at 533, 1 Adm. R. at 108. The defendants-appellees in *Vitol* (the companies owning or controlling the vessel) argued that the district court lacked admiralty jurisdiction because the plaintiff-appellant (the company seeking Rule B attachment and judgment holder) elected to pursue its cause of action in the English Commercial Court rather than the Admiralty Court (both part of the English High Court of Justice). In the *Vitol* appellants' view this choice of forum in England made the [—14—] foreign judgment obtained a non-admiralty judgment.[6] *Id.* at 534, 1 Adm. R. at 109. We rejected that argument:

> [The appellee ship owners] ask this Court to hold that the choice of forum in England, not the subject matter of the underlying claim, is dispositive of whether jurisdiction lies with the district court pursuant to 28 U.S.C. § 1333. In other words, [appellees] contend that [the] choice of forum in the English Commercial Court for an otherwise valid admiralty claim there divests any resulting judgment of its admiralty character in this country so it can no longer be considered as an admiralty matter. We find this argument unpersuasive and unsupported.
>
> The approach advocated by [appellees], which looks purely to form at the expense of substance, is unsupported by citation to any case as authority for its position. Indeed, the dispositive question is not whether the English Judgment issued from an "admiralty court," but *rather, whether the claim itself is maritime in nature.*

Id. at 535, 1 Adm. R. at 109–10 (emphasis added).

The issue Freight Bulk now raises, whether federal or foreign law applies when characterizing a foreign judgment as an admiralty judgment for purposes of federal jurisdiction, was not an issue in *Vitol*. As the Second Circuit recognized in *D'Amico*:

> the *Vitol* decision did not constitute a precedent on the question whether the maritime character of the claim under U.S. [—15—] law is pertinent, both because the *Vitol* court never considered the question whether U.S. law should be consulted, and because the answer would have been the same under either British or U.S. law, as the underlying claim (breach of the warranty of seaworthiness) is maritime in both nations. *Vitol* never considered whether the maritime character of the underlying claim under U.S. law standards justifies the exercise of federal admiralty jurisdiction.

2014 WL 2609648, at *6, 2 Adm. R. at 74. *Vitol* resolved the isolated issue raised in that case and no more. Freight Bulk's argument to the contrary is without merit.

C.

Supreme Court precedent strongly indicates that federal law should control our determination of whether a claim, such as the FFA dispute in this case, sounds in admiralty. Although the Supreme Court has not directly addressed the issue, its opinion in *Kirby* offers guidance.

In *Kirby*, the Supreme Court considered whether federal or state law governed the interpretation of two maritime contracts. 543 U.S. at 22–23. The Court concluded that "[w]hen a contract is a maritime one, and the dispute is not inherently local, federal law controls the contract interpretation." *Id.* In reaching this conclusion, the Supreme Court explained that Article III's purpose in granting admiralty jurisdiction to the federal courts was to provide for the uniformity of maritime law [—16—] throughout the country, including the uniform interpretation of maritime contracts. *Id.* at 28.

> It certainly could not have been the intention [of Article III] to place the rule and limits of maritime law under the disposal and regulation of the several States, as that would have defeated the uniformity and consistency at which the Constitution aimed on all subjects of a commercial character affecting the intercourse of the States with each other or with foreign states.

Id. at 28–29; *see also Ins. Co. v. Dunham*, 78 U.S. (11 Wall.) 1, 24 (1870) (holding that "the admiralty and maritime jurisdiction of the

---

[6] The parties in *Vitol* did not dispute that the claim at issue was a maritime claim under either federal law or English law or that the English court had jurisdiction to render its judgment. *See Vitol*, 708 F.3d at 533–35, 1 Adm. R. at 108–10.

United States is not limited either by the restraining statutes or the judicial prohibitions of England, but is to be interpreted by a more enlarged view of its essential nature and objects"). As the district court observed, based upon the constitutional principle of uniformity in the maritime context, "it could not have been the intention of Article III's grant of admiralty jurisdiction to place the rules and limits of maritime law under the disposal and regulation of foreign states." *Flame*, 2014 WL 108897, at *2 n.2.

This conclusion was bolstered by the Second Circuit's opinion in *Blue Whale*, which is instructive in part. While seemingly on point, the *Blue Whale* decision discusses the similar, but ultimately distinct, issue of whether a plaintiff "has a valid prima facie admiralty claim" for purposes of [—17—] satisfying the four-factor test for issuing a Rule B attachment adopted in *Aqua Stoli Shipping Ltd. v. Gardner Smith Pty Ltd.*, 460 F.3d 434 (2d Cir. 2006). *Blue Whale*, 722 F.3d at 493, 1 Adm. R. at 40. The Second Circuit split its inquiry into two parts: (1) whether the plaintiff alleged a claim sounding in admiralty, and (2) whether that claim is prima facie valid. *Id.*, 1 Adm. R. at 40. Recognizing a "split of authority" in the Southern District of New York, the Second Circuit reached the choice-of-law issue even though "[n]either party disputed that [the plaintiff] had alleged a claim sounding in admiralty and that the court had maritime jurisdiction." *Id.* at 491, 1 Adm. R. at 39. The court explained:

> Despite the divide, what is clear is that federal law controls the procedural inquiry, namely, whether a plaintiff's claim sounds in admiralty. This question is inherently procedural by virtue of its relationship to the courts' subject matter jurisdiction and, thus, is controlled by federal maritime law. . . . We hold that federal maritime law governs whether a claim sounds in admiralty.

Id. at 494–95, 1 Adm. R. at 41.[7] Thus, while helpful, the Second Circuit's treatment of the issue in *Blue Whale* is only analogous precedent.

After briefing and oral argument in the case at bar, the Second Circuit decided *D'Amico* which does directly address the jurisdictional question before us. In *D'Amico*, the holder of an [—18—] English judgment sought attachment under Rule B invoking the district court's admiralty jurisdiction. 2014 WL 2609648, at *1, 2 Adm. R. at 69. The district court concluded that it lacked jurisdiction because "the maritime nature of [a] claim must be determined by reference to the law of the nation that rendered the judgment," and under the laws of England, "the claim underlying the judgment was not deemed maritime in English law." *Id.* at *2, 2 Adm. R. at 71, 73.

The Second Circuit vacated the judgment of the district court, holding that "a suit to enforce a foreign judgment may be heard in the federal admiralty jurisdiction under § 1333 if the claim underlying the judgment would be deemed maritime under U.S. law." *Id.* at *9, 2 Adm. R. at 77. In a thorough analysis, the *D'Amico* court persuasively concluded that choice of law principles support using federal law because "[t]he question whether a claim belongs in one or another court is jurisdictional and procedural," and "[u]nder choice of law principles, the law of the forum state is used for such a question." *Id.* at *8, 2 Adm. R. at 76.[8]

The Second Circuit in *D'Amico* reached the same conclusion that *Kirby* leads us to: that by extending federal jurisdiction to "all Cases of admiralty and maritime Jurisdiction," "the Framers of the Constitution and Congress wanted to ensure that [—19—] matters deemed maritime *under our laws* have access

---

[7] The court then proceeded to the second part of its inquiry, which is not relevant to this case.

[8] In the district court and before us, Freight Bulk relied on the decision from the Southern District of New York in *D'Amico*. Now that the Second Circuit has reversed that decision, Freight Bulk is left with scant authority for its argument.

to our federal courts." *Id.* at *7, 2 Adm. R. at 75–76. As the *D'Amico* court explained:

> The policy of the United States to place maritime matters in the federal courts is so strong that § 1333 makes federal court jurisdiction exclusive. Although, as a general proposition, there is widespread agreement throughout the world which kinds of matters are maritime and which are not, there is no assurance that some other nation might not define its own maritime jurisdiction more broadly, or more narrowly, than we do. It seems reasonable to assume that the Framers of the Constitution and Congress wanted to ensure that matters deemed maritime under our laws have access to our federal courts. There is no reason to suppose that the Founders or Congress would have wished to exclude from the admiralty jurisdiction matters that U.S. law deems maritime, merely because another nation does not consider them maritime. The fact that some nation, unlike ours, does not reserve a special jurisdiction for maritime matters, or classify maritime matters as subject to a discrete body of laws, does not derogate from the policies of our law to provide for the adjudication of matters we regard as maritime in our federal courts.

Id. at *7, 2 Adm. R. at 75–76.

Based on the Supreme Court's reasoning in *Kirby* and the on-point and persuasive opinion in *D'Amico*, we hold that federal law, rather than foreign law, controls the procedural inquiry into whether a foreign judgment is a maritime judgment. Thus, a claim to enforce a foreign maritime judgment is within the admiralty subject matter jurisdiction of United States courts [—20—] when the claim underlying the judgment would be an admiralty or maritime claim under federal law.

IV.

A.

Having determined that federal law controls our jurisdictional inquiry, we must now consider whether the FFAs at issue in this case are maritime contracts under federal law. If the FFAs are not maritime contracts, then the district court's admiralty jurisdiction could not be invoked.

"The boundaries of admiralty jurisdiction over contracts—as opposed to torts or crimes—being conceptual rather than spatial, have always been difficult to draw." *Kossick v. United Fruit Co.*, 365 U.S. 731, 735 (1961). Whether a contract is maritime depends not upon "whether a ship or other vessel was involved in the dispute." *Kirby*, 543 U.S. at 23. "Instead, the answer 'depends upon . . . the nature and character of the contract,' and the true criterion is whether it has 'reference to maritime service or maritime transactions.'" *Id.* at 24; *see* 1-XII *Benedict on Admiralty* § 182 (providing that "a contract relating to a ship in its use as such, or to commerce or navigation on navigable waters, or to transportation by sea or to maritime employment is subject to maritime law and the case is one of admiralty jurisdiction"). [—21—]

In consideration of this question, the district court stated, "Under federal law, it is clear that the question of whether the [FFAs] are maritime contracts is answered in the affirmative," citing a number of decisions holding that certain FFAs are maritime contracts. *Flame*, 2014 WL 108897, at *3. Thus, the district court seemingly made a broad holding that all FFAs are maritime contracts under federal law.

However, other language in the district court's opinion indicates that its holding is more nuanced and specific to the FFAs in this case. For example, the district court observed that "Flame's use of [FFAs] appears to have been primarily for hedging the risks inherent in their shipping business" and that "the [FFAs] *in question* would certainly be maritime contracts," which Freight Bulk also challenges. *Id.* (emphasis added). The district court then seemed to express a case-specific holding that "the FFAs in question (and Flame's underlying claim) are maritime contracts." *Id.*

Ultimately, we need not resolve whether all FFAs are maritime contracts as a matter of law or remand the case for further consideration. Instead, because the district court made factual findings limited to the FFAs involved here, we affirm the district court's judgment with respect to the FFAs at issue in this case. We leave to another case the issue of whether all FFAs are maritime contracts as a matter of law. [—22—]

B.

On appeal, Freight Bulk argues that the FFAs cannot be maritime contracts because they have no connection to any particular vessel or to the transport of any particular cargo. Freight Bulk points out that the FFAs at issue in this case could be settled only with cash and not by delivery (i.e., performance of an actual shipment across the designated route). And Freight Bulk posits that FFAs cannot be maritime contracts because they are nothing more than financial bets on the direction of the freight shipping market.

First, with respect to Freight Bulk's argument that the FFAs have no connection to any particular vessel or shipment, the Supreme Court has directly held that a maritime contract need not refer to any particular vessel. *See Kirby*, 543 U.S. at 23 ("To ascertain whether a contract is a maritime one, we cannot look to whether a ship or other vessel was involved in the dispute."). Nor do maritime contracts need to refer to any particular shipment. *See generally Folksam. Reinsurance Co. v. Clean Water of N.Y., Inc.*, 413 F.3d 307 (2d Cir. 2005) (holding that an insurance contract providing coverage for losses sustained to vessels while undergoing repairs is a maritime contract). In fact, several district courts have concluded that FFAs are maritime contracts regardless of the fact that they do not refer to any particular vessels or shipments because "the [—23—] purpose of the [FFA] is to facilitate

maritime commerce." *Flame S.A. v. M/V Lynx*, No. 10-00278, 2010 U.S. Dist. LEXIS 145880, at *9 (E.D. Tex. June 22, 2010); *see Transfield ER Futures Ltd. v. Deiulemar Shipping S.P.A.*, Nos. 11-00099, 11-00754, 2012 WL 123286, at *3 (E.D. La. Jan. 17, 2012) (concluding that "the very essence of these FFAs concerns commitments to perform shipping services in the future" and that the FFA contracts, like those at issue in this case, provided "contract routes, contract months, contract quantity, the date upon which payment was due for such services and contract rates that would govern each particular contract"). Thus, the fact that the FFAs in this case did not refer to a particular vessel or a particular voyage is not dispositive.

Second, the fact that the FFAs could be settled only with cash also does not defeat the conclusion that these FFAs are maritime contracts. Again, marine insurance contracts are usually maritime contracts as a matter of law. *See Dunham*, 78 U.S. (11 Wall.) at 30-36. Marine insurance contracts cover risks inherent in maritime transportation, and, like the FFAs in this case, marine insurance contracts call for the payment of cash rather than the execution of a maritime shipment. *See Int'l Sea Food Ltd. v. M/V Campeche*, 566 F.2d 482, 485 (5th Cir. 1978); 16 *Williston on Contracts* § 49:28 (4th ed. 2014 supp.). Thus, that [—24—] the FFAs call for cash settlement does not preclude the conclusion that they are maritime contracts.

Lastly, as Freight Bulk points out, while in some cases financial speculators could enter into an FFA on either side of the transaction, we need not resolve the global issue of whether all FFAs are maritime contracts. In this case, there is no dispute that both Flame and ICI are shipping companies principally engaged in maritime commerce. It thus follows, as the district court found, that Flame and ICI did not create the FFAs as mere financial speculators, but as a component of their shipping businesses. The district court expressly found that the parties entered into the FFAs "primarily for hedging the risks inherent in their shipping business," a finding that Freight Bulk fails to demonstrate is clearly erroneous.[9] *Flame*, 2014 WL 108897, at *3.

We therefore hold that the district court did not err in concluding that the FFAs at issue in this case are maritime [—25—] contracts. Accordingly, the district court had subject matter jurisdiction to adjudicate the matter before it.[10]

V.

For the foregoing reasons, we affirm the district court's decision.

AFFIRMED

(Reporter's Note: Concurring opinion on p. 126).

---

[9] Freight Bulk contests this finding by arguing that Flame was listed as the seller on some of the FFAs and thus could not have been using the FFAs as a hedge. However, Freight Bulk does not contest that the FFAs listing Flame as the seller were used by the parties as hedges in their shipping businesses or that both Flame and ICI are chiefly engaged in the business of international shipping. Thus, consistent with the district court's finding, all of the FFAs here were used "primarily for hedging the risks inherent in" international shipping regardless of which party was listed as the buyer or seller on each instrument.

[10] We note that our holding is consistent with that of a number of out-of-circuit district courts that have considered whether similar FFAs are maritime contracts under federal law. *See Transfield*, 2012 WL 123286, at *3; *Flame*, 2010 U.S. Dist. LEXIS 145880, at *12; *Primera*, 2010 WL 481075, at *2; *Brave Bulk Transport Ltd. v. Spot On Shipping Ltd.*, No. 07 Civ. 4546 (CM), 2007 WL 3255823, at *2 (S.D.N.Y. Oct. 30, 2007).

[—26—] WILKINSON, Circuit Judge, concurring:

I readily concur in Judge Agee's fine opinion in this case. Notwithstanding my respect for English law, and in full agreement with the majority opinion, I write to underscore my conviction that the availability of federal admiralty jurisdiction simply must be determined by domestic, rather than foreign, law.

First, applying the law of the forum—here, federal court—accords with basic choice-of-law principles. In *Blue Whale Corp. v. Grand China Shipping Development Co.*, 722 F.3d 488, 494, 1 Adm. R. 38, 41 (2d Cir. 2013), the Second Circuit held that the question of whether a claim "sounds in admiralty" is "inherently procedural by virtue of its relationship to the courts' subject matter jurisdiction," that jurisdiction being, in the Second Circuit's view, a procedural matter. Because courts generally apply their own procedural law, the jurisdictional issue "is controlled" by the law of the forum: federal maritime law.

In fact, the argument for applying domestic law is even stronger than the Second Circuit suggested. Rules of jurisdiction are conceptually distinct from rules of procedure; the former determine *whether* a court is competent to hear a particular case, whereas the latter govern *how* the court is to hear it. *See Bowles v. Russell*, 551 U.S. 205, 210-11 (2007); [—27—] Scott Dodson, *In Search of Removal Jurisdiction*, 102 Nw. U. L. Rev. 55, 59-60 (2008).

Therefore, a court could theoretically import foreign procedure, just as it might use foreign substantive law as its rule of decision. Strictly speaking, however, it is incoherent to speak of adopting foreign law to decide the jurisdictional question. Jurisdiction is the sovereign grant of authority to make legally binding rules or determinations in a particular situation. To allow foreign law to dictate the availability of subject-matter jurisdiction would be to divest the Constitution and Congress of their sovereign authority to decide the extent of the power of the judicial branch. In other words, federal courts would no longer be acting as courts of the United States, since their power would be exercised pursuant to a grant of authority from a different sovereign—here, the foreign jurisdiction. It would, as Justice Story recognized in a related context, "annihilate the sovereignty and equality of the nations," and violate the principle that "every nation must judge for itself, what is its true duty in the administration of justice." Joseph Story, *Commentaries on the Conflict of Laws* §§ 32, 34 (1834).

Second, considerations of administrability counsel in favor of using domestic, rather than foreign, law to determine subject-matter jurisdiction. Even if we limit ourselves to the [—28—] many major maritime commercial powers, that would still require courts seeking to determine jurisdiction to analyze a different body of foreign law every time a contract with a different choice-of-forum or -law clause or every time a judgment from a different rendering jurisdiction came before them. *See D'Amico Dry Ltd. v. Primera Maritime (Hellas) Ltd.*, No. 11-3473-cv, 2014 WL 2609648, at *8, 2 Adm. R. 69, 76 (2d Cir. June 12, 2014). To make matters worse, other countries may not have the same conceptual frameworks for determining jurisdiction or maritime status as we do. This will often make asking whether a contract or judgment is maritime under *their* law for the purposes of *our* requirements of subject-matter jurisdiction anything but an apples-to-apples analysis, if not entirely meaningless.

Not only would this inquiry be incongruous, it would also impose an immense administrative burden on the judicial process. Our own law distinguishing maritime from non-maritime contracts has frequently been pilloried as opaque and arbitrary. *See, e.g.*, Charles L. Black, Jr., *Admiralty Jurisdiction: Critique and Suggestions*, 50 Colum. L. Rev. 259, 264 (1950) ("The attempt to project some 'principle' is best left alone. There is about as much 'principle' as there is in a list of irregular verbs."). To force courts and litigants down the rabbit hole of incorporating the law of various foreign countries at the jurisdictional stage would only make matters worse. *See* [—29—] *D'Amico*, 2014 WL 2609648, at *8. 2 Adm. R. at 76. Limiting the inquiry to the maritime status of a contract or judgment under domestic law is the best and most administrable option.

Third, applying domestic law in this case accords with the Constitution's and Congress's vesting of admiralty jurisdiction in federal courts. Imagine what would happen if we held that foreign law controlled the jurisdictional inquiry here. The federal court would lack admiralty jurisdiction and appellee would likely thus have to file suit in state court. (The same situation would occur if the parties were U.S. but non-diverse.) Thus, the state court would probably be the only available forum to hear the claim and the special procedures associated with federal admiralty jurisdiction might not be available.

None of this is to say that state courts are incapable of properly adjudicating maritime issues. But it does fly in the face of the Constitution's vesting of subject-matter jurisdiction in Article III courts over *all Cases of admiralty and maritime Jurisdiction,*" U.S. Const. art. III, § 2, cl. 1 (emphasis added), and Congress's grant to federal district courts, virtually unchanged since the Judiciary Act of 1789, of subject-matter jurisdiction over *[a]ny* civil case of admiralty or maritime jurisdiction," 28 U.S.C. § 1333(1) (emphasis added). Whether to promote greater uniformity in maritime law or to ensure the vindication of American maritime interests, the [—30—] Framers clearly wanted federal courts to possess admiralty jurisdiction over those cases that the courts believed to be maritime in nature. *See D'Amico,* 2014 WL 2609648, at *7, 2 Adm. R. at 75–76. Allowing foreign law to control the jurisdictional inquiry would subvert this goal and constrict the space that federal courts, already sandwiched between foreign and state law, possess to sit in admiralty.

Fourth and finally, applying domestic rather than foreign law in determining subject-matter jurisdiction advances the national policy goals of the Constitution's grant of admiralty jurisdiction to federal courts: the "advantages resulting to the commerce and navigation of the United States." *DeLovio v. Boit,* 7 F. Cas. 418, 443 (C.C.D. Mass. 1815) (No. 3776) (Story, J.); *see also Sisson v. Ruby,* 497 U.S. 358, 367 (1990) ("The fundamental interest giving rise to maritime jurisdiction is the protection of maritime commerce . . . .") (internal quotation marks omitted). This is because, in determining what counts as advancing the United States' maritime interests, we must by necessity refer to our *own* conception of what counts as "maritime"; after all, "we have a maritime law of our own." *The Lottawanna,* 88 U.S. 558, 574 (1874). Although this particular contract is between two non-U.S. parties engaging in a private financial transaction, the United States still has an interest in providing a forum for this type of contract, especially since [—31—] U.S. parties to a similar arrangement would benefit from being able to seek enforcement.

Appellant argues that international comity requires us to use foreign law to determine subject-matter jurisdiction. *See* Appellant's Br. at 18 & n.6. It notes that, in the interests of international comity, federal courts exercise admiralty jurisdiction over judgments issued by foreign tribunals sitting in admiralty, even if the judgments would not otherwise be treated as maritime under U.S. law. *See Int'l Sea Food Ltd. v. M/V Campeche,* 566 F.2d 482, 485 (5th Cir. 1978); *see also Vitol, S.A. v. Primrose Shipping Co.,* 708 F.3d 527, 536 & n.4, 1 Adm. R. 106, 110 & n. 4 (4th Cir. 2013).

Appellant would have us extend this rule and declare that federal courts must refuse to assert admiralty jurisdiction over contracts or judgments characterized as non-maritime by their rendering forums. Neither logic nor comity dictates this result. Just because we accept the foreign characterization of a dispute for the purpose of exercising admiralty jurisdiction—a jurisdictional *expansion*—does not mean that we must also accept it for the purpose of refusing to hear a case in admiralty—a jurisdictional *contraction*. The former accommodation is supported by considerations of international comity; the latter is not. [—32—]

Comity is satisfied as long as one court enforces the judgment of another court. Thus, it should not matter to the rendering court under what technical head of jurisdiction its judgment is ultimately enforced, at least where, as here, there is no indication that the rendering forum intended its judgment to be effectuated in only a particular way. *See D'Amico*, 2014 WL 2609648, at *8, 2 Adm. R. at 76. It is hard to fathom the British High Court of Justice caring what jurisdictional subclause of Article III, Section 2 the federal court invokes to enforce the judgment. It should be enough that a plaintiff in possession of a favorable English judgment is given the maximum constitutionally permissible freedom to choose his preferred forum—here, a federal court sitting in admiralty. If anything, such a rule enhances, rather than diminishes, comity. It may also make it easier for U.S. parties to enforce contracts such as the one here in foreign maritime courts.

To be sure, foreign law is not irrelevant to the determination of whether federal admiralty jurisdiction exists. The status of the contract or judgment under foreign law informs the inquiry in important ways. The question of whether a legal issue is maritime in nature is not an exercise in logic chopping wholly internal to the conceptual schemas of American jurisprudence; instead, it asks whether, as a practical matter, the "principal objective of [the] contract is maritime [—33—] commerce." *Norfolk S. Ry. Co. v. Kirby*, 543 U.S. 14, 25 (2004). The reasoned judgments of experienced jurists, foreign or domestic, on this issue are due respectful consideration by federal courts. Additionally, whether other countries characterize a contract as maritime might have collateral consequences that may affect its real-world impact on maritime commerce—for example, in terms of how the contract is interpreted overseas or what procedures its interpretations are afforded.

Nevertheless, the ultimate question of whether a contract or judgment is maritime for the purpose of supporting federal admiralty jurisdiction must, for the reasons explained above, be answered by reference to domestic rather than foreign law. While foreign law may or may not be instructive under the circumstances, it cannot determine the subject matter jurisdiction of an American court. And, as ably demonstrated in Judge

Agee's majority opinion, the contract here has a "genuinely salty flavor." *Kossick v. United Fruit Co.*, 365 U.S. 731, 742 (1961). Thus, federal admiralty jurisdiction properly lies.

United States Court of Appeals
for the Fourth Circuit

No. 13-1960

AMERICAN WHITEWATER
VS.
TIDWELL

Appeal from the United States District Court for the
District of South Carolina, at Anderson

Decided: November 5, 2014

Citation: 770 F.3d 1108, 2 Adm. R. 129 (4th Cir. 2014).

Before **KING** and **HARRIS,** Circuit Judges, and
HAMILTON, Senior Circuit Judge.

[—5—] **HARRIS,** Circuit Judge:

In 1974, Congress selected the 57 miles of the Chattooga River (the "Chattooga" or the "River") and 15,432 acres of adjacent land for preservation under the Wild and Scenic Rivers Act (the "WSRA" or the "Act"), 16 U.S.C. § 1274 et seq. (2006). Since then, the United States Forest Service (the "Forest Service") has managed the Chattooga under the WSRA.

Prior to 2012, longstanding Forest Service policy allowed non-motorized rafting or "floating"[1] on the lower portions of the Chattooga, but prohibited the practice on the 21-mile northernmost section of the River (the "Headwaters"). In 2012, after a lengthy review, the Forest Service revised its management plan for the Chattooga to allow floating on most of the Headwaters during the winter months, when flows are highest and conditions are best.

American Whitewater,[2] Plaintiff-Appellant, argues that the revised plan does not go far enough and that the remaining limits on floating are inconsistent with the WSRA and arbitrary and capricious in violation of the

Administrative Procedure Act [—6—] (the "APA"). 5 U.S.C. § 702 et seq. (2006). On the other hand, two intervening parties, Georgia ForestWatch ("ForestWatch"), a not-for-profit environmental group, and the Rust family (the "Rusts"), argue that the Forest Service's decision to allow any floating already goes too far. They contend that the WSRA prohibits any floating on the Headwaters whatsoever, and that the Forest Service violated the National Environmental Policy Act ("NEPA"), 42 U.S.C. § 4321 et seq. (2006), in the course of reaching its decision.

The district court rejected both sets of challenges and found that the Forest Service's revised plan "carefully balance[s] the wide-ranging interests advocated by the several parties and participants." *American Whitewater v. Tidwell*, 959 F. Supp. 2d 839, 860 (D.S.C. 2013) ("*Tidwell*"). We agree with the district court's well-reasoned opinion and affirm.

I.

A.

The WSRA establishes a national policy to preserve rivers of "outstandingly remarkable value." Once designated under the WSRA, rivers are managed by an administrative agency—in this case, the Forest Service—to prevent degradation of their condition and preserve their pristine quality for future generations. See 16 U.S.C. §§ 1271, 1274, 1281(a) (2006). The [—7—] statutory command is twofold: the outstandingly remarkable values, or "ORVs," that led Congress to designate the river must be "protecte[d] and enhance[d]," while other uses may be limited if they substantially interfere with the public's use of those ORVs. 16 U.S.C. §§ 1271, 1281(a).

The Forest Service manages the Chattooga through the Chattooga Wild and Scenic Development Plan. As relevant here, the original 1976 version of the plan—as well as each of the subsequent versions published in 1985, 2002 and 2004—limited floating to the lower portions of the Chattooga.

---

[1] We use the term "floating" throughout to refer to the class of hand-powered, river-going recreational activities that includes canoeing, kayaking, and whitewater rafting.

[2] Together with several other not-for-profit hobbyist organizations and interested individuals, "American Whitewater."

American Whitewater first challenged the Forest Service's ban on floating on the Headwaters in 2002. In 2005, a Forest Service Reviewing Officer agreed with American Whitewater and found that the 2004 development plan did not "provide an adequate basis for continuing the ban" on floating on the Headwaters. J.A. at 587.[3] He directed the Forest Service to study the issue and prepare a new plan in accordance with its results. *Id.*

To comply with the Reviewing Officer's ruling, the Forest Service began by preparing an action plan to establish capacity limits for use of the Chattooga and to measure the expected [—8—] impact of Headwaters floating on the Chattooga's ORVs. It then integrated a wide range of data on compatible recreational uses of the Headwaters in a 2007 report entitled *Capacity & Conflict on the Upper Chattooga River* (the "2007 Report"). The Forest Service also actively involved the public. It held six well-attended meetings to explain the review process and solicit feedback. Over seven years, members of the public submitted more than 4,300 responses and comments.

These efforts culminated in a 2012 Environmental Assessment presenting the Forest Service's findings. The Forest Service reached three conclusions of note here. First, it found that solitude, the "opportunit[y] for remoteness . . . in a spectacular scenic setting," was important to many users of the Headwaters. J.A. at 962. Second, it found that there was a significant likelihood of user conflict between floaters and anglers were the Headwaters floating ban to be lifted completely. J.A. at 981-82, 1273. Third, it determined that floating conditions are optimal during the winter months when flows are heavy, and that fishing conditions are less ideal during that same time period. J.A. at 974-76.

In connection with these findings, the Forest Service analyzed several alternative plans for the Headwaters, ranging from

leaving the ban on floating in place and unchanged to lifting the ban completely. The alternative it selected, [—9—] numbered Alternative 13A, falls in the middle of that range. It permits floating on the Headwaters, an activity that the Forest Service had not allowed since 1976, but subjects that floating to certain limits. Specifically, floating is permitted on most of the Headwaters between December 1 and April 30, on days when flows are greater than 350 cubic feet per second. The Forest Service explained that this would allow for floating "in the section of the Chattooga . . . that boaters rated highest for creek boating" and at the time of year "historically offer[ing] the best flows for these types of boating opportunities," while also preserving "opportunities for year round boat-free, cold water angling" in the reach that "attracts the highest angling use" and "provides the least challenging area for whitewater boating." J.A. at 1402-03.

Because the Forest Service determined that Alternative 13A would not have a "significant impact on the human environment," it found that NEPA did not require preparation of an Environmental Impact Statement. Instead, the Forest Service released its decision through a Decision Notice and Finding of No Significant Impact (together with the 2012 Environmental Assessment, the "2012 Decision").

B.

American Whitewater filed its first complaint in this action on October 14, 2009, while the study process was still [—10—] ongoing and before the Forest Service decided to partially lift the restrictions on floating. The Rusts, who own approximately 1.7 miles of the Headwaters' shoreline, intervened, seeking a declaratory judgment that the portion of the Headwaters running through their property is not navigable and thus outside the Forest Service's authority, and an injunction against any future attempt by the Forest Service to manage this portion of the Chattooga. American Whitewater filed an amended complaint, eliminating the allegations related to the portion of the Chattooga running through the Rusts'

---

[3] Citations herein to "J.A. at __" refer to the contents of the Joint Appendix filed by the parties in this matter.

property, and the district court dismissed the Rusts' claims for lack of a "case or controversy" under Article III of the Constitution. *American Whitewater v. Tidwell,* No. 8:09-cv-02665-JMC, ECF No. 151 (Feb. 22, 2012).

ForestWatch moved to intervene in August of 2011, in support of the Forest Service's then-existing ban on Headwaters floating. The district court granted ForestWatch's motion on May 1, 2012, after publication of the 2012 Decision partially lifting the floating ban. However, the district court limited the scope of ForestWatch's intervention to defending the Forest Service against American Whitewater's challenge to the remaining floating restrictions. *American Whitewater v. Tidwell,* No. 8:09-cv-02665-JMC, ECF No. 168 (May 1, 2012). [—11—]

After publication of the 2012 Decision, American Whitewater filed its second amended complaint, arguing that the remaining limits on floating violate the WSRA. In the alternative, American Whitewater argued that the Forest Service's decision violates the APA because the Forest Service did not have an adequate basis for its conclusion that restrictions on floating are needed to balance competing recreational uses on the Chattooga. *See* 5 U.S.C. § 706(2)(A) (2006).

ForestWatch and the Rusts also were dissatisfied with the 2012 Decision. ForestWatch, arguing that the remaining limits on floating are insufficiently strict to meet the WSRA's mandate, filed a separate action in the district court. *See Georgia ForestWatch v. Bradley,* No. 8:12-cv-3455-MGL (Dec. 6, 2012). The district court denied a motion to consolidate the two actions, and ForestWatch's lawsuit remains pending today. The Rusts also refiled their cross-claims, seeking a declaration that the Headwaters running through their property are non-navigable and asserting that the Forest Service's analysis did not satisfy NEPA.

The district court granted the Forest Service's motion for judgment on the administrative record on April 16, 2013. It rejected each of American Whitewater's claims, as well as the Rusts' NEPA claims, holding that the record provided ample support for the Forest Service's determination that conflicts [—12—] between floaters and other recreational users justified the remaining floating restrictions and that the Forest Service complied with NEPA. It also dismissed the Rusts' request for declaratory judgment as premature, and refused to consider ForestWatch's claims against the Forest Service because they went beyond the limited scope of its intervention. These timely appeals followed.

II.

The crux of American Whitewater's claim is that the Forest Service struck the wrong balance when it opened the Headwaters to floating partially but not entirely, maintaining some restrictions on floating in order to avoid conflicts with other recreational users. According to American Whitewater, there is no basis in the record for the Forest Service's concern about potential conflicts, and the remaining restrictions are arbitrary and capricious under the APA as well as contrary to the WSRA. Like the district court, we disagree.

A.

We review the district court's grant of judgment on the administrative record *de novo. Crutchfield v. Cnty. of Hanover,* 325 F.3d 211, 217 (4th Cir. 2003). But like the district court's, our review under the APA is "ultimately narrow and highly deferential." *Webster v. U.S. Dep't of Agric.,* 685 F.3d [—13—] 411, 422 (4th Cir. 2012). We may set aside an agency's action under the APA only if it is "arbitrary, capricious, an abuse of discretion, or otherwise not in accordance with law." 5 U.S.C. § 706(2)(A) (2006). In determining whether an agency action is arbitrary, capricious, or otherwise an abuse of discretion under the APA, a reviewing court must ensure that the agency has "examine[d] the relevant data and articulate[d] a satisfactory explanation for its action." *N.C. Wildlife Fed'n v. N.C. Dep't of Transp.,* 677 F.3d 596, 601 (4th Cir. 2012) (alteration in original) (*quoting F.C.C. v. Fox Television Stations, Inc.*, 556 U.S. 502, 513 (2009)). But so long as the agency "provide[s] an explanation of its decision that includes a rational connection between the facts found and the choice made," its decision should be sustained. *Ohio Valley Envtl. Coal. v. Aracoma Coal Co.*, 556 F.3d 177, 192 (4th Cir. 2009) (*quoting Motor Vehicle Mfrs. Ass'n v. State Farm Mut. Auto. Ins. Co.*, 463 U.S. 29, 43 (1983)) (internal quotation marks omitted). Our review is particularly deferential when, as is the case here, "resolution of th[e] dispute involves primarily issues of fact" that implicate "substantial agency expertise," *Marsh v. Or. Natural Res. Council*, 490 U.S. 360, 376-77 (1989), and the agency is tasked with balancing often-competing interests. *See Hells Canyon Alliance v. U.S. Forest Serv.*, 227 F.3d 1170, 1182 (9th Cir. 2000). [—14—]

We do not doubt that in this case there is a "rational connection between the facts found and the choice made," *Ohio Valley Envtl. Coal.*, 556 F.3d at 192. The alternative selected by the Forest Service opens substantial portions of the Headwaters for the first time to floating, from the months of December to April on days when flows exceed 350 cubic feet per second. As the 2012 Decision explains, this option allows for floating when water conditions are best, and also easiest to predict, so that users can plan ahead to take advantage of the best opportunities for Headwaters floating. J.A. at 1459. At the same time, by retaining the ban on floating during the spring and summer months, the Forest Service has addressed the documented concerns expressed by other recreational users of the Headwaters, providing for a floater-free environment when conditions are best for fishing and hiking. J.A. at 1460-61. The Forest Service also tailored the remaining restrictions by reach, reserving four miles of the Headwaters with the least challenging floating conditions, but some of the best angling opportunities, for fishermen. J.A. at 1460. Finally, as described in the 2012 Decision, the Forest Service's balance between competing uses also complies with the maximum capacities for the Headwaters as set out in the 2007 Report. J.A. at 1458.

Contrary to American Whitewater's assertions, the record amply supports the Forest Service's conclusions regarding [—15—] potential conflicts among recreational users. The Forest Service relied in part on a history of previous conflicts between recreational users, reviewing evidence from the Headwaters prior to the floating ban, from the lower portion of the Chattooga where floating always has been permitted, and from several proxy rivers. And it assembled significant data pointing to the potential for future conflicts, counting cars to estimate usage, developing expected encounter estimates, and analyzing a wealth of public comments including many from current users who expressed a preference for solitude and an isolated experience. J.A. at 966, 959-1038, 1031-32, 960-62, 1273-74; *see also Tidwell*, 959 F. Supp. 2d at 853.

American Whitewater argues that the Forest Service was required to authorize floating during the study period before it could accurately assess the likelihood of conflicts on the Headwaters. In other words, in order to justify maintenance of its existing restrictions, the Forest Service first would have to eliminate them so that recreational users could experience actual conflicts. Br. for American Whitewater at 35. We cannot accept this counter-intuitive argument. Where the agency's conclusion otherwise rests on a firm factual basis, nothing in the APA requires it to experiment with a practice before continuing preexisting policies. We will not second guess an agency's reasonable choice of methodology. *See Hughes River* [—16—] *Watershed Conservancy v. Johnson*, 165 F.3d 283, 289 (4th Cir. 1999).

At bottom, American Whitewater disagrees with the Forest Service's factual conclusions and the balance it chose to strike. But the APA does not give us license to second-guess an agency's well-reasoned decision simply because a party disagrees with the outcome. The Forest Service has provided a cogent justification for the remaining limits on Headwaters floating, supported by the record, and that is sufficient to sustain its decision under the APA.

B.

American Whitewater also contends that the Forest Service's remaining restrictions on Headwaters floating violate § 1281 of the WSRA, which requires the Forest Service to "protect and enhance the values which caused" the Chattooga to be designated for preservation "without, insofar as is consistent therewith, limiting other uses that do not substantially interfere with public use and enjoyment of these values." 16 U.S.C. § 1281(a). American Whitewater argues, first, that "floating" is a value that led Congress to designate the Chattooga, and that under the "protect and enhance" standard, the Forest Service has no choice but to lift all restrictions on floating. Second, American Whitewater argues that floating cannot be limited because it does not "substantially interfere" with any protected [—17—] recreational use of the Headwaters. Like the district court, we disagree on both counts.

1.

When Congress designated the Chattooga for preservation under the WSRA, it did not expressly identify the River's ORVs. In such cases, that task falls to the relevant administrative agency, which must define a river's "values" in accordance with published interagency guidelines. See Interagency Wild and Scenic Rivers Coordinating Council, *The Wild & Scenic River Study Process* 12-15 (1999). Here, the Forest Service identified "recreation" generally, as opposed to specific recreational uses such as floating or fishing, as an ORV of the Chattooga. J.A. at 915. American Whitewater argues that the Forest Service erred, and that floating itself is an ORV subject to the Act's "protect and enhance" standard. Like the district court, we find that the Forest Service's decision to designate "recreation" as the relevant ORV was entirely reasonable, and that floating is not a Chattooga River value that must be "protecte[d] and enhance[d]" under the WSRA.

To begin with, although the WSRA does not define "outstandingly remarkable values," its text seems to contemplate general categories such as "recreational value," rather than specific uses such as "hiking" and "fishing." Section 1271 of the WSRA lists the "outstandingly remarkable" values that are to [—18—] be protected by the Act: "scenic, recreational, geologic, fish and wildlife, historic, cultural, or other similar values." 16 U.S.C. § 1271 (2006). "Floating value" is not "similar" to, say, "historical value"; it is pitched at an entirely different level of specificity. The phrase "other similar values" is most naturally read to refer to ORVs at the same level of categorical generality as the examples listed before it. *See Washington State Dep't of Soc. & Health Servs. v. Guardianship Estate of Keffeler*, 537 U.S. 371, 384 (2003) ("[W]here general words follow specific words in a statutory enumeration, the general words are construed to embrace only objects similar in nature to those objects enumerated by the preceding specific words.") (citations omitted); *Sokol v. Kennedy*, 210 F.3d 876, 879 n.5 (8th Cir. 2000) (reading "values" in § 1281(a) together with the list of enumerated values in § 1271).

Notwithstanding the awkward textual fit, American Whitewater insists that Congress intended to identify floating as a protected value when it designated the Chattooga under the WSRA. In fact, the Forest Service's decision to identify "recreation" as the relevant value is fully consistent with the congressional record. For example, the 1971 Forest Service report that led to Congress's designation of the Chattooga as a protected river does not single out floating from other forms of recreation; instead, it identifies "hiking, floating—including [—19—] canoeing and rafting—and primitive camping" as potential uses of the Chattooga "recreation resource." Designation would be desirable, according to the 1971 report, because it would preserve not just one particular form of recreation, but rather "full enjoyment of river-related recreation activities" in general. The Senate and House Reports accompanying the Chattooga's designation under the WSRA likewise refer to a variety of "recreational" possibilities without giving special status to any one recreational use or pursuit.

The out-of-context references to floating cited by American Whitewater do not persuade us otherwise. For example, American Whitewater quotes this passage from the 1971 report: "To see and enjoy much of the river requires considerable time and effort from the recreationist, whether he be fisherman, canoeist, hiker or camper." But this passage, like the others cited by American Whitewater, actually is more consistent with the Forest Service's identification of recreation writ large as the relevant ORV, in its description of floating as only one recreational use among many.

American Whitewater has not challenged the Forest Service's discretion to identify ORVs when Congress has not done so. *Cf.* Interagency Wild and Scenic Rivers Coordinating Council, *supra*, at 12-15; *Sokol*, 210 F.3d at 879-80 (in setting boundaries for protected river areas, agencies must identify and seek to [—20—] protect ORVs). In this case, the Forest Service made its determination after careful consideration of relevant administrative guidance and voluminous reports describing the Chattooga's characteristics. J.A. at 913-19. We find that the Forest Service reasonably and lawfully identified "recreational value" as the relevant ORV, and that floating is not a value of the Chattooga that must be protected and enhanced under § 1281.

2.

As the Forest Service recognized, its determinations about how best to protect and enhance the Chattooga's recreational ORV necessarily involve "trade-offs" among competing recreational uses. J.A. at 915. Congress left the requisite calibration to the Forest Service, providing in § 1281 that agency management plans "may establish varying degrees of intensity" for protection based on "special attributes" of a river, 16 U.S.C. § 1281(a), and the balance struck by the Forest Service here is entitled to substantial deference. *See Hells Canyon Alliance,* 227 F.3d at 1174-75.

Nevertheless, American Whitewater argues that under the terms of § 1281, the Forest Service may not restrict floating in any way because it has not shown that floating

"substantially interferes" with other recreational uses. The district court rejected this claim, holding that the record supported a finding of "substantial interference." *Tidwell*, 959 F. Supp. 2d at 852- [—21—] 54. While we agree with that assessment, we also think that American Whitewater's argument is flawed in its premise: Floating is itself a "public use" of the recreational value, not an "other use" subject to the substantial interference standard.

Section 1281(a) divides "uses" of designated rivers into two mutually exclusive categories: There are "public use[s]" of ORVs, like the recreational value identified in this case; and then there are "other use[s]," to be limited when they interfere substantially with public use and enjoyment of an ORV. For instance, hiking would be a "public use" of the Chattooga's recreational value; operating a highway, on the other hand, might be an "other use" subject to restriction if it substantially interfered with hiking or any other component of the recreational ORV. Floating clearly is a form of "public use and enjoyment" of the Chattooga's recreational value. It cannot also be an "other use" or the statutory scheme would make no sense, directing the Forest Service to limit floating in order to protect it. Because floating is not an "other use" for purposes of § 1281(a), limits on floating are not governed by the substantial interference standard.[4] [—22—]

In any event, we agree with the district court that the record evidence of user conflict developed by the Forest Service, discussed above, is sufficient to show that floating can interfere substantially with other recreational uses. *Tidwell*, 959 F. Supp. 2d at 853-54. For that reason, as well, we hold that the

---

[4] In its brief, the Forest Service addressed this claim by defending the record on "substantial interference," which we address in turn. At oral argument, however, the Forest Service made clear that it was not conceding American Whitewater's (Continued) [—22—] reading of the statute or application of the substantial interference standard.

remaining restrictions on floating on the Headwaters are consistent with the WSRA.[5]

III.

The Rusts present a narrower challenge to the 2012 Decision, intended to protect what they see as their private property rights in land along the Headwaters. First, they ask us to declare the 1.7-mile portion of the Headwaters running through their land non-navigable, which would make it private property rather than a public waterway and preclude any Forest Service attempt to provide public access. Second, the Rusts argue that the 2012 Decision is invalid under NEPA because the [—23—] Forest Service failed to provide a sufficiently detailed analysis of the risk that floaters would trespass across their land to reach newly opened portions of the Headwaters.

A.

To be clear, the 2012 Decision does not authorize any floating on the Rusts' property. It does not cover the portion of the Headwaters that concerns the Rusts at all, in accordance with Forest Service policy treating rivers as non-navigable and private until found otherwise. J.A. at 943. Nor has the Forest Service taken any steps toward a determination of navigability. Absent any attempt by the Forest Service even to lay the groundwork for an exercise of its regulatory authority, the Rusts' request for a declaratory judgment fails to present a justiciable controversy.

We may address only disputes that are "definite and concrete, touching the legal relations of parties having adverse interests." *Aetna Life Ins. Co. v. Haworth,* 300 U.S. 227, 240-41 (1937). The same standard applies to a

request for declaratory relief and requires a controversy of "sufficient immediacy and reality [as] to warrant the issuance of a declaratory judgment." *White v. Nat'l Union Fire Ins. Co. of Pittsburgh, Pa.,* 913 F.2d 165, 167-68 (4th Cir. 1990) (*quoting Maryland Cas. Co. v. Pac. Coal & Oil Co.,* 312 U.S. 270, 273 (1941)). [—24—]

The Rusts' claims do not meet this standard. The Rusts acknowledge that the Forest Service would need to take additional action before it could manage this portion of the Chattooga. The Forest Service has not done so. Nor has it argued that this portion of the Chattooga is subject to Forest Service oversight. In fact, the Rusts agree that the Forest Service has consistently treated this segment of the Chattooga as non-navigable, private, and outside its authority. J.A. at 943; S.J.A. at 2199. To the extent that American Whitewater could be considered an adverse party in this context—which we doubt—it too disavows any attempt to declare this section of the Chattooga navigable. Reply Br. for American Whitewater at 21, 22.

We will not issue an advisory opinion, addressing a question that is not in actual dispute. *Flast v. Cohen,* 392 U.S. 83, 96 (1968) ("[T]he oldest and most consistent thread in the federal law of justiciability is that the federal courts will not give advisory opinions."); *Shenandoah Valley Network v. Capka,* 669 F.3d 194, 202 (4th Cir. 2012) ("[A] dispute is lacking here—and because we cannot issue an advisory opinion—we have no authority to adjudicate this suit."). The Rusts' declaratory judgment claim is dismissed. [—25—]

B.

The Rusts also argue that the Forest Service violated NEPA by failing to analyze the risk that opening portions of the Headwaters to floating could lead to trespass on Rust property. They insist that floaters are likely to attempt to reach the River by crossing their property illicitly, instead of using the trails and parking lots already available to the public. The district court correctly held that this prospect is so

---

[5] We reject American Whitewater's remaining claims for the reasons given by the district court. The record adequately supports the continued ban on floating on the Chattooga's tributaries. *Tidwell,* 959 F. Supp. 2d at 857-58. And American Whitewater's challenges based on the Forest Service's policy manual fail at the outset because the policy manual does not have the force of law. *Id.* at 864.

speculative that no NEPA analysis is required.

NEPA encourages conservation not by imposing substantive obligations on agencies, but by requiring that agencies consider the environmental consequences of their actions and present them to the public for debate. *Nat'l Audubon Soc'y v. Dep't of Navy*, 422 F.3d 174, 184, 185 (4th Cir. 2005). Accordingly, our review under NEPA is limited to ensuring that an agency has taken a "hard look" at the environmental impacts of a proposed action. *Id.* at 185. Moreover—and dispositive here—an agency need consider only the "reasonably foreseeable" effects of its decisions. *See Webster*, 685 F.3d at 429 ("[A]lthough agencies must take into account effects that are reasonably foreseeable, they generally need not do so with effects that are merely speculative."); *see also* 40 C.F.R. § 1508.8 (2008).

Any possible increase in the risk of trespass on the Rusts' land does not meet this standard. As the Forest Service points [—26—] out, the uppermost portion of the Headwaters opened to floating by the 2012 Decision is downstream from the Rusts' property line. The uppermost put-in location is another quarter-mile further downstream and easily accessible to the public via a trail from the existing Green's Creek parking lot. Nothing in the record gives us reason to think that floaters would prefer a less direct path across the Rusts' uncleared land. The situation might be different if the Forest Service had allowed floating upstream of the Rusts' land—but the agency rejected that option, precisely because it might present an increased risk of trespass. J.A. at 779, 911, 943.

The Rusts' response to this common-sense proposition is unconvincing. They rely on a few comments submitted by American Whitewater during the review process predicting that floaters would prefer to and eventually would launch from Grimshawe's Bridge, north of the Rusts' property. That, however, is a far cry from expressing an intent to trespass illegally, and American Whitewater has denied repeatedly that it

intends to violate the law. Otherwise, the Rusts point to a trespasser's account from forty years ago and a stray newspaper report. Neither explains why floaters might be expected to trespass under the Headwaters' present conditions.

Even assuming that a heightened risk of trespass was reasonably foreseeable, the Forest Service's discussion of that [—27—] risk satisfies NEPA. The Forest Service presented the Rusts' concerns to the public and explained that they were addressed by the continued ban on floating above Green's Creek, and the Rusts' property. J.A. at 911, 943. In this context, that discussion was sufficient; agencies have discretion to determine which issues merit detailed discussion, and here the risk of trespass or any associated environmental impact was not so significant that more was required. *See Nat'l Audubon Soc'y*, 422 F.3d at 186 ("A 'hard look' is necessarily contextual."); *Izaak Walton League of Am. v. Marsh*, 655 F.2d 346, 377 (D.C. Cir. 1981) ("Detailed analysis is required only where impacts are likely."). Review under NEPA is not a vehicle for "flyspeck[ing]" agency analysis and discussion, *Nat'l Audubon Soc'y*, 422 F.3d at 186, and we find that the Forest Service has met its NEPA obligations.[6]

IV.

Finally, we have the claims of ForestWatch, which, like the Rusts, intervened in this case below. The district court [—28—] limited the scope of ForestWatch's intervention to defending the Forest Service's remaining restrictions on floating on the Headwaters. ForestWatch now takes a different tack, arguing that the Forest Service erred by permitting any floating at all, and raising claims against the partial lifting

---

[6] In light of our disposition of the Rusts' claims we need not address the Rusts' motion to strike from the record certain features of maps included in the Forest Service's brief. *American Whitewater v. Tidwell*, Case No. 13-1960, ECF No. 112 (Sept. 11, 2014). We have not relied on the contested features and they have played no role in our decision. Accordingly, the Rusts' motion to strike is dismissed.

of the floating ban under NEPA and the WSRA. These claims, the subject of a separate ForestWatch action against the Forest Service now pending before the district court, go well beyond the scope of ForestWatch's clearly delineated interest in this litigation and are dismissed.

The district court carefully cabined ForestWatch's involvement in this litigation to the terms of its intervention order, striking ForestWatch's plea for relief against the Forest Service as beyond the scope of its intervention. *See American Whitewater v. Tidwell,* No. 8:09-cv-02665-MGL, ECF No. 254 (Feb. 25, 2013) (text order). It did not reach ForestWatch's arguments against the Forest Service and the partial opening of the Headwaters to floating, instead explicitly "limit[ing] its findings to the parties with claims pending" in the case. *Tidwell,* 959 F. Supp. 2d at 850. The merits of ForestWatch's claims against the Forest Service will be considered by the district court in ForestWatch's separate action, not by this court for the first time on appeal. *See Karpel v. Inova Health Sys. Servs.,* 134 F.3d 1222, 1227 (4th Cir. 1998) ("[I]ssues [—29—] raised for the first time on appeal generally will not be considered.") (internal quotation marks omitted).

What ForestWatch may appeal, however, is the underlying district court ruling on its motion to intervene. The district court granted ForestWatch's motion to intervene as of right but also limited ForestWatch to "[d]efending against [American Whitewater's] claim for declaratory and injunctive relief." *American Whitewater v. Tidwell,* No. 8:09-cv-02665-JMC, ECF No. 168 (May 1, 2012). ForestWatch now argues that the district court erred in imposing that limit on the scope of its intervention. Finding no reversible error, we affirm.

The parties dispute the appropriate standard for our review of the limits on ForestWatch's intervention, with ForestWatch arguing for *de novo* review and the Forest Service for an abuse of discretion standard. We need not reach this question because, as ForestWatch's counsel candidly admitted at oral argument, our review ultimately hinges on whether the district court's decision to limit intervention was fundamentally unfair. *See Columbus-America Discovery Grp. v. Atlanta Mut. Ins. Co.,* 974 F.2d 450, 470 (4th Cir. 1992). Under any standard of review, there has been no fundamental unfairness here.

ForestWatch's argument to the contrary is that the district court did in fact address its claims against the Forest Service in resolving this case, so that ForestWatch will be denied the [—30—] opportunity to raise them again in its separate suit. We read the record differently, and believe that the district court amply preserved ForestWatch's opportunity to assert its claims in its pending lawsuit. First, in denying a motion to consolidate ForestWatch's action with the present case, the district court expressly found that "the outcome or result in one case i[s] not dispositive or dependent on the outcome of the other." J.A. at 1886-88.[7] It then proceeded to insulate one case from the other by explicitly limiting its decision below so as to exclude ForestWatch's claims against the Forest Service. *Tidwell,* 959 F. Supp. 2d at 850 ("[A]lthough the court has considered Georgia ForestWatch's arguments and will discuss them herein, the court limits its findings to the parties with claims pending in this case.").

ForestWatch points to snippets of language in the district court opinion affirming the 2012 Decision as evidence that its claims against that decision already have been decided against it. But read in context, those passages uphold the 2012 [—31—] Decision only as against the Rusts' or American Whitewater's claims, referenced in each case on the same page, if not in the same paragraph, as the cited language. We are confident that nothing

---

[7] To the extent that ForestWatch appeals from the district court's denial of its motion to consolidate, we affirm. The district court ably managed the range of parties and interests involved in this case, and we see no basis for disturbing its judgment about how best to manage its docket. *See Arnold v. E. Airlines, Inc.,* 681 F.2d 186, 192 (4th Cir. 1982) (consolidation decisions are "necessarily committed to trial court discretion" and reviewed only for abuse of discretion).

in the district court's careful opinion will preclude ForestWatch from pressing its claims in its separate suit. Nor, we should note, should anything in our opinion today be understood as resolving ForestWatch's separate claims against the Forest Service.

V.

For the reasons set forth above, we affirm the judgment of the district court.

AFFIRMED

United States Court of Appeals for the Fifth Circuit

United States Court of Appeals
for the Fifth Circuit

No. 13-30095

IN RE DEEPWATER HORIZON— APPEALS OF THE ECONOMIC AND PROPERTY DAMAGE CLASS ACTION SETTLEMENT

Appeals from the United States District Court for the Eastern District of Louisiana

Decided: January 10, 2014

Citation: 739 F.3d 790, 2 Adm. R. 140 (5th Cir. 2014).

Before **DAVIS, GARZA,** and **DENNIS,** Circuit Judges.

[—1—] **DAVIS,** Circuit Judge:

This is an interlocutory appeal from the district court's order certifying a class action and approving a settlement under Rule 23 of the Federal Rules of Civil Procedure.[1] The ongoing litigation before the district court encompasses claims against British Petroleum Exploration & Production, Inc. ("BP") and numerous other entities. All these claims are related to the 2010 explosion aboard the *Deepwater Horizon*, an offshore drilling rig, and the consequent discharge of oil into the Gulf of Mexico.

Several of the original appellants in this case have moved to dismiss their appeals voluntarily, and we have granted those motions. We accordingly do not consider the arguments unique to those appellants. The three groups of appellants remaining before us—the "Allpar Objectors," the "Cobb Objectors," and the "BCA Objectors"—all filed objections with the district court opposing class certification and settlement approval based on various [—2—] provisions of Rule 23. The Objectors' arguments were each addressed and rejected by the district court in its order of December 21, 2012. The Objectors have now appealed the district court's order and ask this court to remand with instructions to decertify the class and withdraw approval from the Settlement Agreement.

BP also now asks this court to vacate the district court's order, although BP is not formally an appellant and, in fact, BP originally supported both class certification and settlement approval before the district court. In addition to its own set of new arguments under Rule 23, BP also raises additional arguments regarding the Article III standing of certain class members to make claims under the Settlement Agreement. Unlike the Objectors, however, BP argues that the Settlement Agreement can be salvaged if "properly construed and implemented." In BP's view, all of the problems that invalidate the class settlement under Article III and Rule 23 result from two Policy Announcements issued by the Claims Administrator, Patrick Juneau, who was appointed under the Settlement Agreement by the district court.

As set forth below, we cannot agree with the arguments raised by the Objectors or BP. The district court was correct to conclude that the applicable requirements of Rule 23 are satisfied in this case. Additionally, whether or not BP's arguments regarding Exhibits 4B and 4C are correct as a matter of contract interpretation, neither class certification nor settlement approval are contrary to Article III in this case. Accordingly, the district court's order is affirmed.

I.

The factual background of this case is described in more extensive detail in the district court's opinion, *In re Oil Spill by Oil Rig Deepwater Horizon in Gulf of Mexico, on April 20, 2010,* 910 F. Supp. 2d 891 (E.D. La. 2012), and in a previous decision by a different panel of this court, *In re Deepwater Horizon,* [—3—] 732 F.3d 326, 1 Adm. R. 287 (5th Cir. 2013) ("*Deepwater Horizon I*"). As explained in *Deepwater Horizon I*, BP leased the *Deepwater Horizon* drilling vessel to drill its Macondo prospect off the Louisiana coast. On April 20, 2010, an exploratory well associated with the drilling vessel blew out. After the initial explosion and during the ensuing fire, the vessel sank, causing millions of barrels of oil to spill into the Gulf of Mexico. Numerous lawsuits were filed against a variety of

---

[1] *See In re Oil Spill by Oil Rig Deepwater Horizon in Gulf of Mexico, on April 20, 2010,* 910 F. Supp. 2d 891 (E.D. La. 2012).

entities, and many of these lawsuits were transferred by the Judicial Panel on Multidistrict Litigation to the United States District Court for the Eastern District of Louisiana pursuant to 28 U.S.C. § 1407.

To satisfy its obligations under the Oil Pollution Act ("OPA"), BP initially established its own claims process and later funded the claims process administered by the Gulf Coast Claims Facility ("GCCF") in order to begin paying out claims immediately rather than at the conclusion of litigation. BP then began negotiating a class settlement in February 2011 and jointly worked with the Plaintiffs' Steering Committee ("PSC") to transfer claims from the GCCF to a program supervised directly by the district court.

On April 16, 2012, the PSC filed an Amended Class Action Complaint and a proposed Settlement Agreement for the district court's preliminary approval. In accordance with the terms of the Settlement Agreement, the district court appointed Patrick Juneau as Claims Administrator of the settlement program. Although the Settlement Agreement had not yet received the district court's final approval under Rule 23 of the Federal Rules of Civil Procedure, the Claims Administrator began reviewing claims left unresolved by the GCCF and processing new claims in June 2012 as provided for in Section 4 of the parties' Settlement Agreement, entitled "Implementation of the Settlement."

On August 13, 2012, after a preliminary hearing and the distribution of notifications to the absent members of the proposed class, BP and the PSC [—4—] moved for final approval of the Settlement Agreement and certification of the class defined at paragraph 306 of the Amended Class Action Complaint. The Allpar Objectors, Cobb Objectors, and BCA Objectors all filed objections with the district court opposing class certification and settlement approval based on various provisions of Rule 23. After conducting a fairness hearing on November 8, 2012, to consider the views of these Objectors and numerous others in accordance with Rule 23(e), the district court issued a final order certifying the class and

approving the parties' Settlement Agreement on December 21, 2012. The district court emphasized in particular that the "uncapped compensation" available under the Settlement Agreement would "ensure that a benefit paid to one member of the class will in no way reduce or interfere with a benefit obtained by another member."[2] The Objectors appealed.

BP supported the Settlement Agreement during the proceedings leading up to and including the district court's order of December 21, 2012. BP now argues that two Policy Announcements issued by the Claims Administrator regarding the interpretation and application of the Settlement Agreement—both of which were adopted in orders by the district court—have subsequently brought the Settlement Agreement into violation of Rule 23, the Rules Enabling Act, and Article III of the U.S. Constitution.

One of these two Policy Announcements by the Claims Administrator addresses the interpretation and application of the Settlement Agreement's Exhibit 4C, entitled "Compensation Framework for Business Economic Loss Claims." The Policy Announcement was endorsed on March 5, 2013, by the district court in an order that became the subject of the appeal heard by Judges Dennis, Clement, and Southwick in *Deepwater Horizon I*. The Settlement [—5—] Agreement's Exhibit 4C establishes a formula for measuring the payments made to class members as compensation for business-related economic loss. The text of Exhibit 4C, however, does not explicitly identify the accounting methodology that the Claims Administrator should apply when interpreting this payment formula. BP argued before the other panel that the Claims Administrator's interpretation of Exhibit 4C fails to reflect the parties' intent to apply the accrual method of accounting, rather than the cash method, when evaluating the financial records of all prospective claimants. The PSC disagreed and argued that the cash method of accounting could also be used by the Claims Administrator if a prospective claimant

---

[2] *Id.* at 918.

ordinarily used the cash method in its own business accounting and bookkeeping.

After considering the parties' arguments, a majority of the panel in *Deepwater Horizon I* remanded the case for further proceedings to reexamine the contractual interpretation questions arising under Exhibit 4C.[3] The district court issued an additional ruling on December 24, 2013,[4] which BP has appealed once again.[5]

The second Policy Announcement by the Claims Administrator addresses the interpretation and application of Exhibit 4B of the Settlement Agreement, entitled "Causation Requirements for Businesses [*sic*] Economic Loss Claims." Whereas the Settlement Agreement's Exhibit 4C established a formula for the measurement of economic loss, Exhibit 4B set forth criteria for prospective claimants to demonstrate to the Claims Administrator that their losses were caused by the *Deepwater Horizon* oil spill. In the Policy Announcement, the Claims Administrator explained: [—6—]

> The Settlement Agreement does not contemplate that the Claims Administrator will undertake additional analysis of causation issues beyond those criteria that are specifically set out in the Settlement Agreement. Both Class Counsel and BP have in response to the Claims Administrator's inquiry confirmed that this is in fact a correct statement of their intent and of the terms of the Settlement Agreement. The Claims Administrator will thus compensate eligible Business Economic Loss and Individual Economic Loss claimants for all losses payable under the terms of the Economic Loss frameworks in the Settlement Agreement, without regard to whether such losses resulted or may have resulted from a cause other than the

Deepwater Horizon oil spill provided such claimants have satisfied the specific causation requirements set out in the Settlement Agreement.[6]

The record reflects that no party ever formally objected to this second Policy Announcement, and the district court adopted this Policy Announcement in an order docketed on April 9, 2013. That order was never independently appealed to this court. In the initial brief that BP filed in this appeal on August 30, 2013, BP took "no position on the relevance *vel non*" of the second Policy Announcement with respect to the lawfulness of class certification and settlement approval in this case.

BP also has never suggested that the Claims Administrator was incorrect to state that "[b]oth Class Counsel and BP have . . . confirmed that [the second Policy Announcement] is in fact a correct statement of their intent and of the terms of the Settlement Agreement." In fact, the record contains an e-mail message from Judge Barbier to a number of participants in this litigation documenting a "discussion" on December 12, 2012, during which it [—7—] was confirmed that "Counsel for BP and the PSC agree with the Claims Administrator's objective analysis of causation with respect to his evaluation of economic damage claims," as set forth in the second Policy Announcement.[7] The record reflects no declared objection or disagreement with the district court's e-mail. This e-mail was later cited in the district court's order adopting the Policy Announcement on April 9, 2013.

In the supplemental brief that BP filed in this appeal on October 11, 2013, however, BP argued that the lawfulness of the Settlement Agreement was equally threatened by both Policy Announcements' effects on the interpretation and application of Exhibits 4B and 4C. According to BP, both of these Policy Announcements by the Claims Administrator permit claimants without any actual injuries caused by the oil spill to participate in the class settlement and receive payments.

---

[3] *Deepwater Horizon I*, 732 F.3d at 346, 1 Adm. R. at 301–02.

[4] Order of December 24, 2013 (Rec. Doc. 12055) ("Responding to Remand of Business Economic Loss Issues").

[5] BP's Notice of Appeal (Rec. Doc. 12066).

[6] *See* Declaration of Andrew T. Karron, Ex. 19-R, at 2 (Rec. Doc. 8963-71).

[7] *See id.*, Ex. 19-V (Rec. Doc. 8963-75).

According to BP, this result brings the class settlement into violation of Rule 23, the Rules Enabling Act, and Article III.

II.

Before we reach the questions regarding class certification and settlement approval under Rule 23, we must resolve the Article III question as a threshold matter of jurisdiction.[8] Questions of law relating to constitutional standing are reviewed *de novo*.[9] "Facts expressly or impliedly found by the district court in the course of determining jurisdiction are reviewed for clear error."[10] "An appellate court may not consider new evidence furnished for the first time on appeal and may not consider facts which were not before the [—8—] district court at the time of the challenged ruling."[11]

The abuse-of-discretion standard governs this court's review of both the district court's certification of the class and its approval of the settlement under Rule 23.[12] This court exercises *de novo* review as to whether the district court applied the correct legal standard.[13] Importantly, "Rule 23 grants courts no license to engage in free-ranging merits inquiries at the certification stage. Merits questions may be considered to the extent—but only to the extent—that they are relevant to determining whether the Rule 23 prerequisites for class certification are satisfied."[14]

III.

As explained in its supplemental brief, the crux of BP's standing argument is that Article III "preclude[s] certification of a settlement class that includes members that have suffered no injury" or "who suffered no harm caused by the *Deepwater Horizon* incident." In BP's view, because an unidentified number of such individuals have received and may continue to receive payments under the class settlement, Article III requires this court to reverse the district court's order of December 21, 2012.

In two respects, BP is correct. First, the elements of Article III standing do indeed include both an injury in fact and a causal connection to the defendant's conduct.[15] Second, under the previous decisions of this circuit, both of these elements must be present as a threshold matter of jurisdiction [—9—] whenever a district court certifies a class under Rule 23.[16]

It is striking, however, that BP makes no attempt to identify a standard that we should apply to determine whether these elements are satisfied in this case. The frequent references in BP's briefs to the "vast numbers of members who suffered no Article III injury" are disconnected from any discussion of pleading requirements, competent evidence, or the standards of proof by which the parties' contentions are evaluated during different stages of litigation. In particular, BP's arguments fail to explain how this court or the district court should identify or even discern the existence of "claimants that have suffered no cognizable injury" for purposes of the standing inquiry during class certification and settlement approval.

In the following sections, therefore, we review the law governing the standard applicable to Article III questions in the specific context of Rule 23, and then turn to examine the facts of the present case. As

---

[8] *Rivera v. Wyeth–Ayerst Labs.*, 283 F.3d 315, 319 (5th Cir. 2002).

[9] *Bonds v. Tandy*, 457 F.3d 409, 411 (5th Cir. 2006).

[10] *Cole v. Gen. Motors Corp.*, 484 F.3d 717, 721 (5th Cir. 2007).

[11] *Quesada v. Napolitano*, 701 F.3d 1080, 1084 n.9 (5th Cir. 2012); *Ramchandani v. Gonzales*, 434 F.3d 337, 339 n.1 (5th Cir. 2005); *Theriot v. Parish of Jefferson*, 185 F.3d 477, 491 n.26 (5th Cir. 1999).

[12] *Cole*, 484 F.3d at 723; *see Spence v. Glock, Ges.m.b.H.*, 227 F.3d 308, 310 (5th Cir. 2000); *In re Chicken Antitrust Litig. Am. Poultry*, 669 F.2d 228, 238 (5th Cir. 1982).

[13] *Mims v. Stewart Title Guar. Co.*, 590 F.3d 298, 304 (5th Cir. 2009).

[14] *Amgen Inc. v. Conn. Ret. Plans & Trust Funds*, 133 S. Ct. 1184, 1194-95 (2013).

---

[15] *See Lujan v. Defenders of Wildlife*, 504 U.S. 555, 560-61 (1992).

[16] *See Cole*, 484 F.3d at 721-22; *Rivera*, 283 F.3d at 318-19.

explained below, although the relevant authorities suggest two possible approaches to Article III questions at the class certification stage, both of these approaches require us to reject BP's standing argument. Whichever test is applied, therefore, Article III does not mandate reversal in this case.

A.

As the Supreme Court explained in *Lujan v. Defenders of Wildlife*, 504 U.S. 555, 560-61 (1992), the elements of Article III standing are constant throughout litigation: injury in fact, the injury's traceability to the defendant's conduct, and the potential for the injury to be redressed by the relief requested. As *Lujan* emphasized, however, the standard used to establish these three elements is not constant but becomes gradually stricter as the parties proceed through "the successive stages of the litigation." In *Lewis v. Casey*, 518 U.S. [—10—] 343, 358 (1996), the Supreme Court reaffirmed this formulation:

> Since they are not mere pleading requirements, but rather an indispensable part of the plaintiff's case, each element of standing must be supported in the same way as any other matter on which the plaintiff bears the burden of proof, *i.e.*, with the manner and degree of evidence required at the successive stages of the litigation. At the pleading stage, general factual allegations of injury resulting from the defendant's conduct may suffice, for on a motion to dismiss we presume that general allegations embrace those specific facts that are necessary to support the claim. In response to a summary judgment motion, however, the plaintiff can no longer rest on such mere allegations, but must set forth by affidavit or other evidence specific facts, which for purposes of the summary judgment motion will be taken to be true. And at the final stage, those facts (if controverted) must be supported

adequately by the evidence adduced at trial.[17]

Lujan and *Lewis* provide a useful blueprint, therefore, but do not comprehensively address all conceivable stages of litigation in which Article III standing may need to be addressed. This quoted passage does not explain, in particular, how courts are to evaluate standing for the purposes of class certification and settlement approval under Rule 23.

In attempting to answer this question, courts have followed two analytical approaches. According to one approach, which has been endorsed by three Justices concurring in *Lewis*,[18] several circuits, and an influential [—11—] treatise,[19] the inquiry hinges exclusively on the Article III standing of the "named plaintiffs" or "class representatives." This test requires courts to ignore the absent class members entirely:

> Unnamed plaintiffs need not make any individual showing of standing in order to obtain relief, because the standing issue focuses on whether the plaintiff is properly before the court, not whether represented parties or absent class members are properly before the court. Whether or not the named plaintiff who meets individual standing requirements may assert the rights of absent class members is neither a standing issue nor an Article III case or controversy issue but depends rather on meeting the prerequisites of Rule 23 governing class actions.[20]

---

[17] *Lewis*, 518 U.S. at 358 (quoting *Lujan*, 504 U.S. at 561) (alterations and internal quotation marks omitted).

[18] *Id.* at 395-96 (Souter, J., concurring in part, dissenting in part, and concurring in the judgment; joined by Ginsburg, J., and Breyer, J.).

[19] W. Rubenstein, A. Conte & H. Newberg, Newberg on Class Actions § 2:3 (5th ed. 2011) ("These passive members need not make any individual showing of standing because the standing issue focuses on whether the named plaintiff is properly before the court, not whether represented parties or absent class members are properly before the court.").

[20] *Lewis*, 518 U.S. at 395-96 (Souter, J., concurring in part, dissenting in part, and

In the years since *Lewis*, this approach to the standing inquiry during class certification has been followed by the Seventh,[21] Ninth,[22] and Third Circuits.[23] Additionally, the Tenth Circuit has adopted this test at least in "class action[s] seeking prospective injunctive relief" and arguably also in class actions for damages as well.[24] As stated in a frequently cited decision by the Seventh [—12—] Circuit, *Kohen v. Pacific Investment Management Co. LLC*, 571 F.3d 672, 677 (7th Cir. 2009), it is "almost inevitable" that "a class will . . . include persons who have not been injured by the defendant's conduct[] . . . because at the outset of the case many of the members of the class may be unknown, or if they are known still the facts bearing on their claims may be unknown." According to *Kohen*, however, even this "inevitability" does not preclude Article III standing during the Rule 23 stage.[25]

Other circuit decisions have not necessarily ignored absent class members. According to these decisions, courts must ensure that absent class members possess Article III standing by examining the class definition. Importantly, however, this approach does not contemplate scrutinizing or weighing any evidence of absent class members' standing or lack of standing during the Rule 23 stage. The most frequently cited formulation of this test is found in the Second Circuit's decision in *Denney v. Deutsche Bank AG*, 443 F.3d 253, 263-64 (2d Cir. 2006): "We do not require that each member of a class submit evidence of personal standing. At the same time, no class may be certified that contains members lacking Article III standing. The class must therefore be defined in such a way that anyone within it would have standing."[26] The Eighth Circuit has also applied this test,[27] as have the [—13—] Seventh[28] and Ninth Circuits,[29] despite both these latter circuits' statements in other decisions that absent class members are irrelevant to the Article III inquiry.[30]

If this case actually required us to do so, it might not be a simple task to choose between the *Kohen* test and the *Denney* test based on this roughly even split of circuit authority.[31]

---

concurring in the judgment) (alterations and internal quotation marks omitted).

[21] *Kohen v. Pac. Inv. Mgmt. Co. LLC*, 571 F.3d 672, 676-78 (7th Cir. 2009).

[22] *Stearns v. Ticketmaster Corp.*, 655 F.3d 1013, 1020-21 (9th Cir. 2011) ("On the contrary, our law keys on the representative party, not all of the class members, and has done so for many years . . . . In a class action, standing is satisfied if at least one named plaintiff meets the requirements . . . ." (internal quotation marks and citations omitted)).

[23] *In re Prudential Ins. Co. Am. Sales Practice Litig. Agent Actions*, 148 F.3d 283, 306-07 (3d Cir. 1998) ("There is also ample evidence that each named party has suffered an 'injury in fact' . . . . Thus, the named plaintiffs satisfy Article III. The absentee class members are not required to make a similar showing . . . .").

[24] *DG ex rel. Stricklin v. Devaughn*, 594 F.3d 1188, 1197-98 (10th Cir. 2010) ("First, only named plaintiffs in a class action seeking prospective injunctive relief must demonstrate [—12—] standing by establishing they are suffering a continuing injury or are under an imminent threat of being injured in the future. . . . '[A] class will often include persons who have not been injured by the defendant's conduct. . . . Such a possibility or indeed inevitability does not preclude class certification.'" (quoting *Kohen*, 571 F.3d at 677)).

[25] *Kohen*, 571 F.3d at 677.

[26] *Denney*, 443 F.3d at 263-64 (citations omitted).

[27] *Avritt v. Reliastar Life Ins. Co.*, 615 F.3d 1023, 1034 (8th Cir. 2010) (citing *Denney*, 443 F.3d at 263-64).

[28] *Adashunas v. Negley*, 626 F.2d 600, 603 (7th Cir. 1980) ("In order to state a class action claim upon which relief can be granted, there must be alleged at the minimum (1) a reasonably defined class of plaintiffs, (2) all of whom have suffered a constitutional or statutory violation (3) inflicted by the defendants.").

[29] *Mazza v. Am. Honda Motor Co., Inc.*, 666 F.3d 581, 594 (9th Cir. 2012) (citing *Denney*, 443 F.3d at 263-64).

[30] *See Kohen*, 571 F.3d at 677; *Stearns*, 655 F.3d at 1020-21.

[31] No clear guidance is provided by the Supreme Court's decision with the greatest relevance to Article III questions arising due to a class settlement, *Amchem Products, Inc. v. Windsor*, 521 U.S. 591, 612-13 (1997). The Supreme Court implied in that case that a district court could not approve a class settlement containing class members who had not yet manifested any health problems from their past exposures to asbestos. If these "exposure-only" plaintiffs' claims were not yet ripe, the Supreme Court suggested, then their inclusion in a class action would not be "in keeping

It is also perhaps unclear whether our circuit has already adopted the *Kohen* test in *Mims v. Stewart Title Guaranty Co.*, 590 F.3d 298 (5th Cir. 2009). Citing *Kohen*, we stated in *Mims* that "[c]lass certification is not precluded simply because a class may include persons who have not been injured by the defendant's conduct."[32] Although this particular statement was made in the context of analyzing Rule 23 rather than Article III, we elsewhere concluded in *Mims* that "[t]here is no serious question that the plaintiffs have standing" after explicitly analyzing only "the named plaintiffs."[33] [—14—]

Judge Clement's opinion in *Deepwater Horizon I*, however, did not mention *Mims*, distinguished *Kohen* on its facts, and instead applied the *Denney* test.[34] In Part II of her opinion, which Judge Southwick did not join and from which Judge Dennis dissented, Judge Clement explained that absent class members' standing is indeed relevant to jurisdiction over a class action. She also agreed with *Denney* that absent class members' standing should be evaluated based on how a class is "defined" and on whether the absent class members are "alleged" to have colorable claims.[35] As Judge Clement emphasized several times, when an absent

class member is "unable to plead the causation element," the absent class member's "non-colorable claims do not constitute Article III cases or controversies."[36] In Judge Clement's view, if absent class members include persons who "concede" that they have no "causally related injury," then a district court lacks jurisdiction to certify the class.[37] Judge Clement also agreed with *Denney* that Article III does not require a showing that an absent class member "can *prove* his case" at the Rule 23 stage, so long as the absent class member "can *allege* standing."[38]

This case is not a vehicle, however, for us to choose whether *Kohen* or *Denney* articulated the correct test. Nor does this case require us to decide whether *Mims* has already adopted the *Kohen* test as a matter of Fifth Circuit law. For the purposes of the present case, these questions are entirely [—15—] academic because BP's standing argument fails under both the *Kohen* test and the *Denney* test. As explained in the next section, both the named plaintiffs and the absent class members contemplated by the class definition include only persons and entities who can allege causation and injury in accordance with Article III.

B.

Looking first to the *Kohen* test for standing, it is clear that the class action in this case survives Article III because the named plaintiffs have each alleged injury in fact, traceability to the defendant's conduct, and redressability by the relief requested.[39] The named plaintiffs set forth their allegations in the operative pleading in this case, the Amended Class Action Complaint for Private Economic Losses and Property Damages, which was filed with the district court on May 2, 2012.[40] The Amended Class Action Complaint explains that "Plaintiffs are

---

with Article III constraints." *Amchem*, 521 U.S. at 612-13. The Supreme Court did not ultimately reach the ripeness question, however, because the asbestos-litigation class failed under a Rule 23 inquiry that the Supreme Court considered "logically antecedent to the existence of any Article III issues." *Id.* It is therefore unclear how the Supreme Court would eventually have approached its ripeness determination.

[32] *See Mims*, 590 F.3d at 308.

[33] *See id.* at 302.

[34] *See Deepwater Horizon I*, 732 F.3d at 340-42, 344 & n.12, 1 Adm. R. at 296–98, 300 & n. 12 (describing the "judicial role to ensure that *class definitions* comply with statutory and constitutional strictures" (emphasis added)).

[35] *Id.* at 340-42, 1 Adm. R. at 296–98 (quoting *Adashunas*, 626 F.2d at 603, and *Denney*, 443 F.3d at 263-64). Judge Clement also cited frequently to Judge Jordan's dissent in *Sullivan v. DB Investments, Inc.*, 667 F.3d 273, 346 (3d Cir. 2011) (en banc) (Jordan, J., dissenting), which proposed a test that could be applied to "a class complaint requesting relief" without looking to any additional items of proof.

[36] *Deepwater Horizon I*, 732 F.3d at 340-42, 1 Adm. R. at 296–98.

[37] *See id.* at 343, 1 Adm. R. at 299.

[38] *Id.* at 340-42, 1 Adm. R. at 296–98.

[39] *See Kohen*, 571 F.3d at 677.

[40] *See In re Oil Spill*, 910 F. Supp. 2d at 902 (citing Amended Class Action Complaint (Rec. Doc. 6412)).

individuals and/or entities who have suffered economic and property damages *as a result of the Deepwater Horizon Incident.*"[41] This document thereafter identifies each of the fifteen named plaintiffs individually and explains in detail how each has suffered economic damages due to the "lack of adequate supplies of seafood to process and sell," a "severe reduction in tourist-related bookings," a drop in "demand for marine tourism," "a loss on the sale of . . . residential property," and numerous other types of economic injury and property damage.[42]

Each one of these named plaintiffs satisfies the elements of standing by identifying an injury in fact that is traceable to the oil spill and susceptible to redress by an award of monetary damages. Under the *Kohen* test, that is the [—16—] end of the inquiry. As explained in *Cole v. General Motors Corp.*, 484 F.3d 717 (5th Cir. 2007), which addressed the Article III standing of named plaintiffs during class certification under Rule 23, we found it "sufficient for standing purposes that the plaintiffs seek recovery for an economic harm that they *allege* they have suffered."[43] At the Rule 23 stage, *Cole* provides that "a federal court must assume *arguendo* the merits of [each named plaintiff's] legal claim."[44] Indeed, BP has never argued that any of the named plaintiffs lack Article III standing. Accordingly, there is no question that the *Kohen* test is satisfied in this case.[45]

Applying the *Denney* test to the definition of the class proposed for certification, we come to the same conclusion. The Class Definition is set forth in paragraph 306 of the Amended Class Action Complaint and is reproduced in its entirety in Appendix B of the district court's order. Under the plain terms of the Class Definition, a "person or entity" is included "in the Economic Class only if their Claims meet the descriptions of one or more of the Damage Categories described" in Section 1.3.1 of the Class Definition. Of these "Damage Categories," the only category that BP has identified as giving rise to Article III difficulties is the "Economic Damage Category" under Section 1.3.1.2.[46] This section of the Settlement Agreement, however, explicitly limits claims to those based on "[l]oss of income, earnings or profits suffered by Natural Persons or Entities *as a result of* the DEEPWATER HORIZON INCIDENT," subject to exclusions for participants in certain industries.[47] As contemplated by the Class Definition, therefore, the class contains only [—17—] persons and entities that possess Article III standing.

Even if the "definition" of the class were interpreted for the purposes of the *Denney* test to include the entire Amended Class Action Complaint, rather than just the provisions set forth in paragraph 306, the result would be no different. The Amended Class Action Complaint includes numerous allegations of injuries to the absent class members caused by the oil spill. For example, the sections of the Amended Class Action Complaint directed toward the satisfaction of the Rule 23(a) requirements for numerosity, commonality, and typicality each emphasize causation and actual damages with respect to each member of the class:

> The Class consists of tens of thousands of individuals and businesses that have been economically damaged by the spill. . . . Each Class member's claim arises from the same course of planning, decisions, and events, and each Class member will make similar legal and factual arguments to prove Defendants' outrageous, willful, reckless, wanton, and deplorable conduct and liability . . . . The claims in this Second Amended Master Class Action Complaint are typical of the claims of the E&PD Class in that they represent the various types of non-governmental economic losses

---

[41] Amended Class Action Complaint 6-13 (Rec. Doc. 6412) (emphasis added).

[42] *Id.*

[43] *Cole*, 484 F.3d at 723 (emphasis added).

[44] *Id.* (quoting *Parker v. District of Columbia*, 478 F.3d 370, 377 (D.C. Cir. 2007) (internal quotation marks omitted)).

[45] *See Kohen*, 571 F.3d at 677.

[46] *See In re Oil Spill*, 910 F. Supp. 2d at 965-67.

[47] *Id.* (emphasis added).

and property damage caused by the Deepwater Horizon Incident.[48]

Accordingly, using Judge Clement's formulation of the standard, the class in this case does not include any members who "concede" that they lack any "causally related injury."[49] This ends the Article III inquiry under the *Denney* test, which does "not require that each member of a class submit evidence of personal standing"[50] so long as every class member contemplated by the class [—18—] definition "can *allege* standing."[51]

Our decision in *Cole* confirms that "it is sufficient for standing purposes that the plaintiffs seek recovery for an economic harm that they *allege* they have suffered" because for each class member we "must assume *arguendo* the merits of his or her legal claim" at the Rule 23 stage.[52] Although *Cole* addressed the standing of named plaintiffs rather than absent class members, it would make no sense to apply a higher evidentiary standard to absent class members than to named plaintiffs. We also stated in *In re Rodriguez*, 695 F.3d 360, 370 (5th Cir. 2012), that even the absent class members are "linked" under Rule 23 to the "common complaint, and the possibility that some may fail to prevail on their individual claims will not defeat class membership." Whether the *Kohen* test or the *Denney* test is applied, therefore, we find that Article III and the Rules Enabling Act[53] are satisfied in this case. [—19—]

C.

In concluding this analysis, we note the possibility that the application of a stricter evidentiary standard might reveal persons or entities who have received payments under Exhibits 4B and 4C and yet have suffered no loss resulting from the oil spill. But courts are not authorized to apply such a standard for this purpose at the Rule 23 stage. Under *Lujan* and *Lewis*, of course, this is precisely what the district judge must do at summary judgment and what the finder of fact must do at trial.[54] Without ever saying so explicitly, BP implies that we should also resolve Article III questions at the Rule 23 stage by looking to evidence of certain prospective claimants' standing. That is, BP cites to items of evidence—in particular, a series of declarations by economists, Henry H. Fishkind, A. Mitchell Polinsky, J. Richard Dietrich, and Hal Sider. These economists' declarations, in BP's view, demonstrate that the Claims Administrator has awarded payments under his interpretations of Exhibits 4B and 4C to persons and entities that likely were not injured by the *Deepwater Horizon* incident. It is unclear from BP's submissions during this appeal whether BP

---

[48] Amended Class Action Complaint 108-10 (Rec. Doc. 6412).

[49] *Deepwater Horizon I*, 732 F.3d at 343, 1 Adm. R. at 299.

[50] *Denney*, 443 F.3d at 263.

[51] *Deepwater Horizon I*, 732 F.3d at 340-42, 1 Adm. R. at 296–98.

[52] *Cole*, 484 F.3d at 721-23 (emphasis added) (quoting *Parker*, 478 F.3d at 377 (internal quotation marks omitted)).

[53] Under the Rules Enabling Act, 28 U.S.C. §2072(b), "[t]he Federal Rules of Civil Procedure cannot work as substantive law." *Klier v. Elf Atochem N. Am., Inc.*, 658 F.3d 468, 474 (5th Cir. 2011). In this case, the substantive law is neither Rule 23 nor any other Federal Rule of Civil Procedure, but the OPA and federal maritime law, under which the named plaintiffs raised a variety

of different claims in the Amended Class Action Complaint. Despite making several references to the Rules Enabling Act in their supplemental briefs, neither BP nor the Objectors have contested this basic point. The Rules Enabling Act therefore is not violated. *See Shady Grove Orthopedic Assocs., P.A. v. Allstate Ins. Co.*, 559 U.S. 393, 406-08 (2010) (plurality opinion) ("A class action, no less than traditional joinder (of which it is a species), merely enables a federal court to adjudicate claims of multiple parties at once, instead of in separate suits. And like traditional joinder, it leaves the parties' legal rights and duties intact and the rules of decision unchanged."); *id.* at 431-36 (Stevens, J., concurring in part and concurring in the judgment) (agreeing that Rule 23 does not violate the Rules Enabling Act so long as no substantive state law is displaced in a diversity case); *Sullivan v. DB Invs., Inc.*, 667 F.3d 273, 312-13 (3d Cir. 2011) (en banc) (concluding that a district court's "approval of the parties' settlement should not be considered a recognition or expansion of substantive rights" under the Rules Enabling Act).

[54] *Lewis v. Casey*, 518 U.S. at 358 (citing *Lujan*, 504 U.S. at 560-61).

asks us to evaluate this proof by applying a summary-judgment standard or a preponderance-of-the-evidence standard. Ultimately, we can do neither in this case.

With respect to the evidence cited by BP regarding these claimant's standing, we emphasize two points. First, and most obviously, none of this evidence was ever considered by the district court prior to December 21, 2012, the date when the district court certified the class and approved the settlement.[55] The cited versions of these economists' declarations were filed [—20—] with the district court on March 20, 2013, and none of them is dated earlier than January 15, 2013. Even though standing is a jurisdictional matter, any "facts expressly or impliedly found by the district court" in the course of "making its jurisdictional findings" must be accepted on appeal unless they are clearly erroneous.[56] Additionally, under the settled law of this circuit, "an appellate court may not consider new evidence furnished for the first time on appeal and may not consider facts which were not before the district court at the time of the challenged ruling."[57] We therefore cannot consider the economists' declarations cited by BP or draw any conclusions from them.

Second, BP has cited no authority—and we are aware of none—that would permit an

evidentiary inquiry into the Article III standing of absent class members during class certification and settlement approval under Rule 23. It is true that a district court may "probe behind the pleadings" when examining whether a specific case meets the requirements of Rule 23, such as numerosity, commonality, typicality, and adequacy.[58] But the Supreme Court cautioned in *Amgen Inc. v. Connecticut Retirement Plans & Trust Funds*, 133 S. Ct. 1184, 1194-95 (2013), that "Rule 23 grants courts no license to engage in free-ranging merits inquiries at the certification stage. Merits questions may [—21—] be considered to the extent—but only to the extent—that they are relevant to determining whether the Rule 23 prerequisites for class certification are satisfied."

Relevant circuit authority confirms the inappropriateness of reviewing evidence of absent class members' standing at the Rule 23 stage. *Mims* and *Kohen* suggest that such evidence is simply irrelevant, inasmuch as "[c]lass certification is not precluded simply because a class may include persons who have not been injured by the defendant's conduct."[59] *Denney* and Judge Clement's opinion in *Deepwater Horizon I*, for their part, also "do not require that each member of a class submit evidence of personal standing"[60] so long as the class is defined so that every absent class member "can *allege* standing."[61] Our older decision in *Cole* confirms that it would be improper to look for proof of injuries beyond what the claimants identified in the class definition can "*allege* they have suffered" at this stage.[62] Despite BP's urging, therefore, even a district court could not consider the evidence regarding absent class members' standing at the Rule 23 stage.

---

[55] The record contains an e-mail message from Judge Barbier documenting a "discussion" on December 12, 2012, during which it was confirmed that "Counsel for BP and [—20—] the PSC agree with the Claims Administrator's objective analysis of causation with respect to his evaluation of economic damage claims," as set forth in the second Policy Announcement. *See* Declaration of Andrew T. Karron, Ex. 19-V (Rec. Doc. 8963-75). But no party has suggested that any of the expert declarations that have been presented to this court were considered by Judge Barbier either during this "discussion" or at any time previously. In fact, given that BP and the named plaintiffs were both still in agreement with the Claims Administrator on that date, it seems more likely that the expert declarations were not shared with Judge Barbier.

[56] *Cole*, 484 F.3d at 721; *Pederson v. La. State Univ.*, 213 F.3d 858, 869 (5th Cir. 2000).

[57] *Quesada*, 701 F.3d at 1084 n.9; *Ramchandani*, 434 F.3d at 339 n.1; *Theriot*, 185 F.3d at 491 n.26.

[58] *Wal-Mart Stores, Inc. v. Dukes*, 131 S. Ct. 2541, 2551 (2011) (quoting *Gen. Tel. Co. of Sw. v. Falcon*, 457 U.S. 147, 160 (1982)).

[59] *See Mims*, 590 F.3d at 302, 308.

[60] *Denney*, 443 F.3d at 263-64.

[61] *Deepwater Horizon I*, 732 F.3d at 340-42, 1 Adm. R. at 296–98.

[62] *See Cole*, 484 F.3d at 721-23 (emphasis added) (quoting *Parker*, 478 F.3d at 377 (internal quotation marks omitted)).

Of course, had the class in this case been certified under Rule 23 for further proceedings on the merits rather than for settlement, the district court might ultimately have had occasion to apply a stricter evidentiary standard. As the district court said explicitly, "certain causation issues . . . would have to be decided on an individual basis were the cases not being settled," including "for example, the extent to which the *Deepwater Horizon* incident versus other [—22—] factors caused a decline in the income of an individual or business."[63] As early as October 6, 2010, the district court anticipated that "issues relating to damages" could and would be "severed and tried separately" from other issues relating to liability,[64] in accordance with this court's previous case law[65] and Rule 23(c)(4).[66] In its submissions to the district court, BP also contemplated the possibility of "a trial of an economic damage test case" and "presentations of proof and comparative responsibility."[67] Such proceedings would have provided opportunities for BP to inquire more deeply into individual claimants' evidence of Article III standing under the applicable evidentiary standards described in *Lujan* and *Lewis*.[68] In the absence of any motion for summary judgment or trial predicated upon the Article III standing of those absent class members, however, it would be premature and improper for a court to apply evidentiary standards corresponding to those later stages of litigation.

Indeed, it would make no practical sense for a court to require evidence of a party's claims when the parties themselves seek settlement under Rule 23(e). Logically, requiring absent class members to prove their claims prior to settlement under Rule 23(e) would eliminate class settlement because there would be no need to settle a claim that was already proven. Such a rule would [—23—] thwart the "overriding public interest in favor of settlement" that we have recognized "[p]articularly in class action suits."[69] The legitimacy of class settlements is reflected not only in Rule 23(e) but also in the special regime that Congress has created to govern class settlements under 28 U.S.C. §§ 1711-15. Through the procedural mechanism of a class settlement, defendants "are entitled to settle claims pending against them on a class-wide basis even if a court believes that those claims may be meritless, provided that the class is properly certified under Rules 23(a) and (b) and the settlement is fair under Rule 23(e)."[70] By entering into class-wide settlements, defendants "obtain[] releases from all those who might wish to assert claims, meritorious or not" and protect themselves from even those "plaintiffs with non-viable claims [who] do nonetheless commence legal action."[71]

This is certainly not to say, on the other hand, that the Claims Administrator must afford the same deference to the absent class members' allegations that we apply when addressing Article III issues at the Rule 23 stage. Naturally, the Claims Administrator is not bound to apply the *Denney* test or the

---

[63] *In re Oil Spill*, 910 F. Supp. 2d at 924.

[64] Scheduling Order of October 6, 2010, at 3 (Rec. Doc. 473).

[65] This court has previously "approved mass tort or mass accident class actions when the district court was able to rely on a manageable trial plan— including bifurcation" of "class-wide liability issues" and issues of individual damages. *Steering Comm. v. Exxon Mobil Corp.*, 461 F.3d 598, 603 (5th Cir. 2006) (analyzing *Watson v. Shell Oil Co.*, 979 F.2d 1014, 1017-18, 1024 & n.9 (5th Cir. 1992)).

[66] *See Butler v. Sears, Roebuck & Co.*, 727 F.3d 796, 800 (7th Cir. 2013) ("[A] class action limited to determining liability on a class-wide basis, with separate hearings to determine—if liability is established—the damages of individual class members, or homogeneous groups of class members, is permitted by Rule 23(c)(4) and will often be the sensible way to proceed.").

[67] Defs.' Memorandum of October 6, 2010, at 6, 8 (Rec. Doc. 488).

[68] *Lewis*, 518 U.S. at 358 (citing *Lujan*, 504 U.S. at 560-61).

[69] *Kincade v. Gen. Tire & Rubber Co.*, 635 F.2d 501, 507 (5th Cir. 1981) (quoting *Cotton v. Hinton*, 559 F.2d 1326, 1331 (5th Cir. 1977)); *see also Smith v. Crystian*, 91 F. App'x 952, 955 (5th Cir. 2004) (acknowledging the "strong judicial policy favoring the resolution of disputes through settlement" and affirming both class certification and settlement approval (internal citation and quotation marks omitted)).

[70] *In re Am. Int'l Grp., Inc. Sec. Litig.*, 689 F.3d 229, 243-44 (2d Cir. 2012).

[71] *Sullivan*, 667 F.3d at 310.

Kohen test but must follow whatever instructions are set forth in Exhibit 4B, Exhibit 4C, and the other provisions of the parties' detailed Settlement Agreement. In his concurrence to *Deepwater Horizon I*, Judge Southwick succinctly observed that Exhibits 4B and 4C created an evidentiary framework intended to "simplif[y] the claims process by making proof of loss a [—24—] substitute for proof of factual causation."[72] The parties now vigorously dispute how this evidentiary framework was intended to work. For its part, BP has argued in its subsequent submissions to the *Deepwater Horizon I* panel that "the Claims Administrator must make a threshold determination whether the claimant has suffered loss as a result of the spill" and that under footnote 1 of Exhibit 4B this "threshold determination must be made *before* applying the causation criteria outlined in Exhibit 4B." The named plaintiffs hold a different view.

The evidentiary standard to be applied by the Claims Administrator, however, is not a matter of Article III standing. It is a question of interpreting the Settlement Agreement and applying it to each individual claim, and we are not called upon to address those issues in this appeal.

IV.

We turn now to examine the Rule 23 arguments raised by BP, the Allpar Objectors, the Cobb Objectors, and the BCA Objectors. In addressing Rule 23, BP and the Allpar Objectors have made nearly identical arguments. They challenge class certification and settlement approval under a variety of provisions of Rule 23 based on the same central premise discussed above in the context of Article III—that a class cannot be certified when it includes persons who have not actually been injured. The Cobb Objectors also expressly adopt BP's arguments by reference and add only a single additional argument. According to the Cobb Objectors, the named plaintiffs did not adequately represent the class under Rule 23(a)(4) because there were no subclasses formed to represent residents of

different states, particularly residents of Texas, and no subclass formed to represent those potential claimants who [—25—] would have been "better off under the GCCF claims process." As explained below, the objections of the Allpar Objectors, the Cobb Objectors, and BP have no merit.

For their part, the BCA Objectors—who refer to themselves in this way because they are represented by Brent Coon & Associates—were among the 12,970 objectors who "failed to comply with the requirements of the Preliminary Approval Order in that they failed to provide written proof of class membership and, therefore, forfeited and waived their objections."[73] The district court's Preliminary Approval Order provided that any class member who wished to object to the Settlement Agreement must do so in writing by August 31, 2012, and include "written proof of class membership" with his or her objection, "such as proof of residency, ownership of property and the location thereof, and/or business operation and the location thereof."[74] As the record shows, the BCA Objectors' objection was filed timely but was incomplete. This submission included thousands of claimants' names listed in a chart spanning more than 150 pages but lacked even a single claimant's proof of residency, property ownership, or business operation.[75]

On November 7, 2012, the night before the fairness hearing and two months after the

---

[72] *Deepwater Horizon I*, 732 F.3d at 346, 1 Adm. R. at 302 (Southwick, J., concurring in Parts I and III of the majority opinion).

[73] *See In re Oil Spill*, 910 F. Supp. 2d at 936 (citing Report on Objections to and Opt-Outs from the Economic and Property Damages Settlement as Amended on May 2, 2012 (Rec. Doc. 8001)).

[74] *Id.* at 935-36 (internal quotation marks omitted).

[75] *See id.* (citing Report on Objections to and Opt-Outs from the Economic and Property Damages Settlement as Amended on May 2, 2012 (Rec. Doc. 8001)); *see also* Report on Objections to and Opt-Outs from the Economic and Property Damages Settlement as Amended on May 2, 2012, Ex. L, at 3-538 (Rec. Doc. 8001-18) (identifying each one of the 11,245 objectors represented by Brent Coon & Associates as lacking "Standing Proof"); Plaintiffs Represented by Brent Coon & Associates' Motion in Opposition and Objections to the Economic Class Settlement, Ex. 1 (Rec. Doc. 7224-2).

deadline for filing written objections, the BCA Objectors filed a Motion for Leave to File Reply Memorandum Late and in Excess of Ordinary [—26—] Page Limitations. On November 8, 2012—the morning of the fairness hearing—the district court issued an order striking this filing for untimeliness. The result of this, according to the district court's order of December 21, 2012, was that the BCA Objectors' challenges to class certification and settlement approval were therefore forfeited and waived. In the notice of appeal filed with this court, the BCA Objectors have once again appended a lengthy list including thousands of names listed alphabetically on a chart, but no written proof of residency, property ownership, or business operation.

The district court's instruction to provide proof of class membership was a legitimate exercise of its discretion under Rule 23(d)(1)(A) and Rule 23(d)(1)(C) to "issue orders that[] . . . determine the course of proceedings" and "impose conditions . . . on intervenors" in a class action. As the Supreme Court recognized in *Gulf Oil Co. v. Bernard*, 452 U.S. 89 (1981), a district court presiding over a class action "has both the duty and the broad authority" to enter such orders to minimize "the potential for abuse" during such proceedings.[76] Although a district court's discretion under Rule 23(d) is "not unlimited,"[77] the district court plainly acted within its discretion in finding that the BCA Objectors forfeited and waived their objections by disobeying the reasonable requirements of the Preliminary Approval Order. Moreover, in an unpublished case with equivalent facts, *Feder v. Electronic Data Systems Corp.*, 248 F. App'x 579, 580 (5th Cir. 2007), we dismissed an appeal from a district court's order on class certification and settlement approval based on [—27—] the objector's failure to "prove his membership in the class" in accordance with

the district court's reasonable documentation requirements. We see no meaningful difference between the present case and the facts of *Feder*. As we explained in *Feder*, "the right to object to settlement in a . . . class action must rest on something more than the sort of bare assertions" now offered by the BCA Objectors.[78]

Accordingly, because the BCA Objectors did not substantiate their membership in this class, the district court did not abuse its discretion under Rule 23(d)(1)(A) and Rule 23(d)(1)(C) in finding that the BCA Objectors "forfeited and waived" their objections to the class certification and settlement approval.[79] We therefore will not consider the merits of their objections.

In the remaining sections, we address the arguments raised by BP, the Allpar Objectors, and the Cobb Objectors in relation to the individual provisions of Rule 23.

A.

BP, the Allpar Objectors, and (by reference) the Cobb Objectors have all challenged certification of the class under Rule 23(a)(2), which requires a demonstration that "there are questions of law or fact common to the class." These arguments rest entirely on a selective quotation from *Wal-Mart Stores, Inc. v. Dukes*, 131 S. Ct. 2541 (2011), and must be rejected. As the Supreme Court stated in *Wal-Mart*, "[c]ommonality requires the plaintiff to demonstrate that the class members 'have suffered the same injury.'"[80] Based on this single sentence, it is now suggested that either the diversity of the class members' [—28—] economic injuries or the inclusion of members who "have suffered no injury at all" might preclude class certification.

---

[76] *Gulf Oil Co.*, 452 U.S. at 100; *see also Moulton v. U.S. Steel Corp.*, 581 F.3d 344, 353 (6th Cir. 2009) ("Rule 23 gives the district court broad discretion in handling class actions, authorizing 'orders that . . . impose conditions on the representative parties or on intervenors.'") (alteration in original); *Williams v. Chartwell Fin. Servs., Ltd.*, 204 F.3d 748, 759 (7th Cir. 2000).

[77] *Gulf Oil Co.*, 452 U.S. at 100.

[78] *See Feder*, 248 F. App'x at 581; *see also Union Asset Mgmt. Holding A.G. v. Dell, Inc.*, 669 F.3d 632, 639 (5th Cir. 2012) (holding that objectors had standing to object specifically because they had "complied" with the requirements of the settlement notice).

[79] *See In re Oil Spill*, 910 F. Supp. 2d at 936.

[80] *Wal-Mart*, 131 S. Ct. at 2551 (quoting *Gen. Tel. Co. of Sw. v. Falcon*, 457 U.S. 147, 157 (1982)).

When quoted in its entirety, however, the relevant passage from *Wal-Mart* demonstrates why both of these arguments are meritless:

> Commonality requires the plaintiff to demonstrate that the class members "have suffered the same injury." This does not mean merely that they have all suffered a violation of the same provision of law. Title VII, for example, can be violated in many ways—by intentional discrimination, or by hiring and promotion criteria that result in disparate impact, and by the use of these practices on the part of many different superiors in a single company. Quite obviously, the mere claim by employees of the same company that they have suffered a Title VII injury, or even a disparate-impact Title VII injury, gives no cause to believe that all their claims can productively be litigated at once. Their claims must depend upon a common contention—for example, the assertion of discriminatory bias on the part of the same supervisor. That common contention, moreover, must be of such a nature that it is capable of classwide resolution—which means that determination of its truth or falsity will resolve an issue that is central to the validity of each one of the claims in one stroke.[81]

As this passage shows, the Supreme Court's use of the phrase, "the same injury," in *Wal-Mart* (and decades previously in *General Telephone Co. of Southwest v. Falcon*, 457 U.S. 147, 157 (1982)) does not support BP's argument. To satisfy the commonality requirement under Rule 23(a)(2), class members must raise at least one contention that is central to the validity of each class member's claims. But this contention need not relate specifically to the damages component of the class members' claims. Even an instance of [—29—] injurious conduct, which would usually relate more directly to the defendant's liability than to the claimant's damages, may constitute "the same injury."

This is confirmed by the example given by the Supreme Court in the above passage from *Wal-Mart*, "discriminatory bias on the part of the same supervisor," which is itself not a type of damages, but an instance of injurious conduct that violates Title VII. Later in the same decision, the Supreme Court stated that another type of injurious conduct on the part of the defendant, "a companywide discriminatory pay and promotion policy," would also have satisfied the "same injury" test for commonality under Rule 23(a)(2).[82]

Accordingly, as these two examples from *Wal-Mart* demonstrate, the legal requirement that class members have all "suffered the same injury" can be satisfied by an instance of the defendant's injurious conduct, even when the resulting injurious effects—the damages—are diverse. This aspect of the law is therefore unchanged since our decision in *Bertulli v. Independent Association of Continental Pilots*, 242 F.3d 290, 298 (5th Cir. 2001), in which we upheld certification of a class action because "virtually every issue prior to damages [wa]s a common issue." As we indicated in *M.D. ex rel. Stukenberg v. Perry*, 675 F.3d 832, 840 (5th Cir. 2012), the principal requirement of *Wal-Mart* is merely a single common contention that enables the class action "to generate common *answers* apt to drive the resolution of the litigation." These "common answers" may indeed relate to the injurious effects experienced by the class members, but they may also relate to the defendant's injurious conduct. "[E]ven a single common question will do."[83]

The above passage from *Wal-Mart* also demonstrates that district courts do not err by failing to ascertain at the Rule 23 stage whether the class [—30—] members include persons and entities who have suffered "no injury at all." As the Supreme Court explained, a "contention" regarding the class members' injury is sufficient to satisfy Rule 23, so long as the party seeking certification can show that this contention is "common" to all the class members, is "central" to the validity of their claims, and is "capable" of

---

[81] *Wal-Mart*, 131 S. Ct. at 2551 (citation omitted) (quoting *Falcon*, 457 U.S. at 157).

[82] *Id.* at 2556.

[83] *Id.* (alterations and internal quotation marks omitted).

classwide resolution. There is no need to resolve the merits of the common contention at the Rule 23 stage or to attempt prematurely the "determination of its truth or falsity."[84] Although Rule 23 "does not set forth a mere pleading standard" and a court may need to "probe behind the pleadings before coming to rest on the certification,"[85] Rule 23 does not therefore become a dress rehearsal for the merits.[86] As the Supreme Court repeated last term in *Amgen*, "[m]erits questions may be considered to the extent— but only to the extent—that they are relevant to determining whether the Rule 23 prerequisites for class certification are satisfied."[87] In other words, to satisfy the commonality requirement under Rule 23(a)(2), the parties may potentially need to provide evidence to demonstrate that a particular contention is common, but not that it is correct.

The district court's certification of this class, therefore, did not violate Rule 23(a)(2). After reviewing expert evidence, the district court found that numerous factual and legal issues were central to the validity of all the class members' claims. These included "[w]hether BP had a valid superseding cause defense," "[w]hether BP used an improper well design that unreasonably heightened the risk," "[w]hether the cement mixture was unstable, and, if so, whether BP should have prevented its use," "[w]hether BP took appropriate [—31—] and timely steps to stop the release of hydrocarbons from the well," "whether these decisions (individually or collectively) constitute negligence, gross negligence, or willful misconduct," "[w]hether BP is a responsible party under OPA," "[w]hether BP could limit its liability under § 2704 of OPA," "[w]hether punitive damages are available as a matter of law," and whether BP "failed to mitigate the damages of the class."[88] Neither BP nor the remaining

Objectors find fault with any of the items on the district court's long list of common issues. Because "even a single common question will do" under *Wal-Mart*, this list was more than sufficient.[89]

Accordingly, the commonality arguments raised by BP, the Allpar Objectors, and the Cobb Objectors do not require decertification of the class. Although all of the factual and legal questions identified by the district court are more closely related to BP's injurious conduct than to the injurious effects experienced by the class members, they nonetheless demonstrate that the class members claim to have suffered the "same injury" in the sense that *Wal-Mart* used this phrase.[90] Additionally, the district court did not err by failing to determine whether the class contained individuals who have not actually suffered any injury, because this would have amounted to a determination of the truth or falsity of the parties' contentions, rather than an evaluation of those contentions' commonality. This was not required by *Wal-Mart*, and was expressly ruled out in *Amgen*.[91] We therefore reject the challenges raised by BP, the Allpar Objectors, and the Cobb Objectors under Rule 23(a)(2).[92] [—32—]

---

[84] *See id.* at 2551.

[85] *See id.* (quoting *Falcon*, 457 U.S. at 160).

[86] *In re Whirlpool Corp. Front-Loading Washer Prods. Liab. Litig.*, 722 F.3d 838, 851-52 (6th Cir. 2013); *Messner v. Northshore Univ. HealthSys.*, 669 F.3d 802, 811 (7th Cir. 2012).

[87] *Amgen*, 133 S. Ct. at 1195.

[88] *In re Oil Spill*, 910 F. Supp. 2d at 922-23.

[89] *See Wal-Mart*, 131 S. Ct. at 2556 (alterations and internal quotation marks omitted).

[90] *Id.* at 2551 (quoting *Falcon*, 457 U.S. at 157).

[91] *Amgen*, 133 S. Ct. at 1194-95.

[92] In a one-sentence footnote in its initial brief, BP adds that "the claims of the representative parties are no longer typical of the claims of the class" in light of the Claims Administrator's interpretations and directs our attention to the Supreme Court's statement [—32—] that "[t]he commonality and typicality requirements of Rule 23(a) tend to merge." *See Wal-Mart*, 131 S. Ct. at 2551 n.5 (alteration in original) (internal quotation marks omitted). The Allpar Objectors also have not differentiated in any way between their commonality argument under Rule 23(a)(2) and their typicality argument under Rule 23(a)(3). To the extent that the references to "typicality" by BP and the Allpar Objectors constitute a separate argument under Rule 23(a)(3), that argument is rejected. For the same reasons given with respect to their commonality argument, neither BP nor the Allpar Objectors have demonstrated that the district court abused its discretion in finding that "[t]ypicality is satisfied here, as the class

B.

BP and the Objectors also challenge class certification and settlement approval under Rule 23(a)(4), which requires a demonstration that "the representative parties will fairly and adequately protect the interests of the class." According to this argument, an impermissible "intraclass conflict" is created by the Claims Administrator's interpretation of Exhibits 4B and 4C because the claimants now include some persons and entities that have suffered injuries, and other persons and entities that allegedly have not. As it has been interpreted, BP argues, the Settlement Agreement "would almost necessarily make injured members worse off than they might have been had non-injured members been excluded from the class." According to BP, had the injured class members been represented by named plaintiffs negotiating exclusively on their behalf, they could have used their increased bargaining power during settlement negotiations to demand a more favorable formula for awarding payments.

The district court must be upheld, however, unless its decision constituted an abuse of discretion. In this case, the district court found that the named plaintiffs were "clearly adequate" to protect the interests of the class as they included "individuals and businesses asserting each category of loss" [—33—] and were assisted by adequate counsel.[93] After reviewing declarations by each of the named plaintiffs, the district court found that they had "participated in the settlement negotiations" and taken "an active role in the prosecution of this class action."[94] After reviewing expert testimony, the district court also found that the class action was structured to assure adequate representation of all interests within the class and to prevent intraclass conflict. Finally, the district court concluded that the "uncapped compensation" available under the Settlement Agreement would "ensure that a benefit paid to one member of the class will in no way reduce or interfere with a benefit obtained by another member."[95]

Although BP made no objection to the district court's order certifying the class and approving the Settlement Agreement, BP asks this court to find an intraclass conflict of interest because the claimants allegedly include persons and entities that have suffered no injury. In support of this allegation, BP presents us with a series of economists' declarations that had not been provided to the district court when the class was certified. But our previous decisions prevent us from considering this evidence for the first time on appeal.[96] Moreover, even if we were to accept BP's contention that the class does include uninjured persons, *Mims* and *Rodriguez* would foreclose decertification of the class on this basis. As we stated in *Mims* in the context of the Rule 23 requirements, "[c]lass certification is not precluded simply because a class may include persons who have not been injured by the [—34—] defendant's conduct."[97] As we stated in *Rodriguez*, "the possibility that some [absent class members] may fail to prevail on their individual claims will not defeat class membership."[98]

By contrast, we can consider the argument that the Cobb Objectors have raised under Rule 23(a)(4), which was passed upon by the district court. The Cobb Objectors argue that "class members from Texas, Louisiana, Alabama, Florida and Mississippi" should have been divided into their own subclasses, as should those class members who "were better off under the GCCF claims process."

Although the creation of subclasses is sometimes necessary under Rule 23(a)(4) to avoid a "fundamental conflict," there is no need to create subclasses to accommodate every instance of "differently weighted

---

representatives—like all class members—allege economic and/or property damage stemming directly from the *Deepwater Horizon* spill." *In re Oil Spill*, 910 F. Supp. 2d at 915.

[93] *In re Oil Spill*, 910 F. Supp. 2d at 916-17.

[94] *Id.* at 916 (quoting *Stott v. Capital Fin. Servs., Inc.*, 277 F.R.D. 316, 325 (N.D. Tex. 2011)).

[95] *Id.* at 918.

[96] *Quesada*, 701 F.3d at 1084 n.9; *Ramchandani*, 434 F.3d at 339 n.1; *Theriot*, 185 F.3d at 491 n.26.

[97] *Mims*, 590 F.3d at 308.

[98] *Rodriguez*, 695 F.3d at 370 (internal quotation marks omitted).

interests."[99] In this case, because the class members' claims arise under federal law rather than state law, we are not persuaded that there is any fundamental conflict between the "differently weighted interests" of class members from different geographical regions. Although geographical criteria were indeed incorporated into the Settlement Agreement, the reason for this is both obvious and acknowledged in the Cobb Objectors' brief. That is, "causation becomes more [—35—] difficult" for a claimant to establish "the further one moves from the coast" and, in particular, the further one moves from the Macondo reservoir where the *Deepwater Horizon* incident occurred.

As the district court expressly found, the differences between the formulas applicable in the different geographic zones were "rationally related to the relative strengths and merits of similarly situated claims."[100] The identification of objective, geographically-based criteria therefore easily distinguishes this case from *In re Katrina Canal Breaches Litigation*, 628 F.3d 185, 194 (5th Cir. 2010), in which the district court improperly approved a class settlement that sought simply to "punt[] the difficult question of equitable distribution from the court to the special master, without providing any more clarity as to how fairness will be achieved." The district court's rigorous consideration of

the expert evidence demonstrates that it did not abuse its discretion in declining to require subclasses for claimants based in Texas, Louisiana, Alabama, Florida, and Mississippi.

We also must reject the Cobb Objectors' argument that an intraclass conflict exists between class members who were "better off under the GCCF claims process" and those who were not. Most critically, the Cobb Objectors have failed to provide any details about the cause of these claimants' current disadvantage. In their brief, the Cobb Objectors repeat several times that some number of claimants are now "forced to meet arbitrary loss and recovery benchmarks" under the Settlement Agreement, whereas these same claimants apparently could have recovered under the GCCF without doing so. After considering substantial expert testimony, however, the district court found explicitly that the Settlement Agreement's compensation criteria were not [—36—] arbitrary, but "detailed" and "objective."[101] Nothing in the Cobb Objectors' arguments demonstrates that the district court's conclusions on this question constituted an abuse of discretion. Finally, even if some claimants were practically disadvantaged by the procedures of the court-administered claims process in comparison to the procedures of the GCCF, this mechanical discrepancy is only another example of "differently weighted interests" rather than a "fundamental conflict" of interests.[102] As the Sixth and Third Circuits have held, "each class member naturally derives different amounts of utility from any class-wide settlement" based on his or her unique circumstances, but this does not put all such class members in fundamental conflict with one another.[103] Without a more detailed description of the disadvantage experienced by the group that was supposedly "better off" under the GCCF, we cannot agree with the Cobb Objectors that the district court's certification of this class was an abuse of discretion.

---

[99] *Dewey v. Volkswagen Aktiengesellschaft*, 681 F.3d 170, 186 (3d Cir. 2012) (quoting *Gooch v. Life Investors Ins. Co. of Am.*, 672 F.3d 402, 429 (6th Cir. 2012)); *see also In re Literary Works in Elec. Databases Copyright Litig.*, 654 F.3d 242, 249 (2d Cir. 2011); *Ward v. Dixie Nat'l Life Ins. Co.*, 595 F.3d 164, 180 (4th Cir. 2010) ("For a conflict of interest to defeat the adequacy requirement, that conflict must be fundamental." (internal quotation marks omitted)); *Rodriguez v. W. Publ'g Corp.*, 563 F.3d 948, 959 (9th Cir. 2009) ("An absence of *material* conflicts of interest between the named plaintiffs and their counsel with other class members is central to adequacy . . . ." (emphasis added)); *Valley Drug Co. v. Geneva Pharms., Inc.*, 350 F.3d 1181, 1189 (11th Cir. 2003) ("Significantly, the existence of minor conflicts alone will not defeat a party's claim to class certification: the conflict must be a 'fundamental' one going to the specific issues in controversy.").

[100] *See In re Oil Spill*, 910 F. Supp. 2d at 917-18.

[101] *Id.*

[102] *Dewey*, 681 F.3d at 186 (quoting *Gooch*, 672 F.3d at 429).

[103] *See id.*

C.

BP and the Objectors also argue that class certification was improper under Rule 23(b)(3), which requires that "the questions of law or fact common to class members predominate over any questions affecting only individual members." According to BP and the Objectors, the Supreme Court's recent decision in *Comcast Corp. v. Behrend*, 133 S. Ct. 1426 (2013)—which was decided three months after the district court certified the class—precludes certification under Rule 23(b)(3) in any case where the class members' damages are not susceptible to a formula for classwide measurement.

This is a misreading of *Comcast*, however, which has already been [—37—] rejected by three other circuits.[104] As explained in greater detail below, *Comcast* held that a district court errs by premising its Rule 23(b)(3) decision on a formula for classwide measurement of damages whenever the damages measured by that formula are incompatible with the class action's theory of liability. As the court explained, "[t]he first step in a damages study is the translation of the legal theory of the harmful event into an analysis of the economic impact of that event."[105] This rule may reveal an important defect in many formulas for classwide measurement of damages. But nothing in *Comcast* mandates a formula for classwide measurement of damages in all cases. Even after *Comcast*, therefore, this holding has no impact on cases such as the present one, in which predominance was based not on common issues of damages but on the numerous common issues of liability. In the present case, the district court did not include a formula for classwide measurement of damages among its extensive listing of the "common issues" that weighed in favor of certification. The district court always recognized that the class members' damages

"would have to be decided on an individual basis were the cases not being settled," as would "the extent to which the *Deepwater Horizon* incident versus other factors caused a decline in the income of an individual or business."[106] The holding of *Comcast* cited by BP and the Objectors, therefore, is simply inapplicable here.

As recalled above, the district court set forth a considerable list of issues that were common to all the class members' claims. Nearly all of these issues related to either the complicated factual questions surrounding BP's involvement in the well design, explosion, discharge of oil, and cleanup efforts [—38—] or the uncertain legal questions surrounding interpretation and application of the OPA. Accordingly, BP and the Objectors are quite correct to suggest that, although the analysis of BP's injurious conduct gives rise to numerous common questions, the class members' damage calculations give rise primarily to individual questions that are not capable of classwide resolution.

But this is not fatal to class certification. As we stated in *Bell Atlantic Corp. v. AT&T Corp.*, 339 F.3d 294, 306 (5th Cir. 2003), "[e]ven wide disparity among class members as to the amount of damages" does not preclude class certification "and courts, therefore, have certified classes even in light of the need for individualized calculations of damages." Accordingly, as we recognized in *Steering Committee v. Exxon Mobil Corp.*, 461 F.3d 598, 603 (5th Cir. 2006), it is indeed "possible to satisfy the predominance . . . requirements of Rule 23(b)(3) in a mass tort or mass accident class action" despite the particular need in such cases for individualized damages calculations. On this basis, therefore, we have previously affirmed class certification in mass accident cases,[107] as in other cases in which "virtually every issue prior to damages is a common issue."[108]

104 *See Butler*, 727 F.3d at 800; *In re Whirlpool Corp.*, 722 F.3d at 860; *Leyva v. Medline Indus. Inc.*, 716 F.3d 510, 514 (9th Cir. 2013).

105 *Comcast Corp. v. Behrend*, 133 S. Ct. 1426, 1435 (2013) (quoting FED. JUDICIAL CTR., REFERENCE MANUAL ON SCIENTIFIC EVIDENCE 432 (3D ED. 2011) (emphasis omitted)).

106 *In re Oil Spill*, 910 F. Supp. 2d at 924.

107 *See Steering Comm.*, 461 F.3d at 603 (analyzing *Watson v. Shell Oil Co.*, 979 F.2d 1014, 1022-23 (5th Cir. 1992)).

108 *Bertulli*, 242 F.3d at 298.

In particular, as we explained in *Madison v. Chalmette Refining, L.L.C.*, 637 F.3d 551, 556 (5th Cir. 2011), predominance may be ensured in a mass accident case when a district court performs a sufficiently "rigorous analysis" of the means by which common and individual issues will be divided and tried. In many circuits, this has been accomplished by means of multi-phase trials under Rule 23(c)(4), which permits district courts to limit class treatment to [—39—] "particular issues" and reserve other issues for individual determination.[109] Accordingly, *Chalmette Refining* instructed district courts to consider rigorously how they plan to "adjudicate common class issues in the first phase and then later adjudicate individualized issues in other phases" of the multi-phase trial before the final decision is made to certify a class.[110]

Heeding our instruction in *Chalmette Refining*, therefore, the district court planned "to manage such litigation by breaking it down into separate phases, as the [district court] was prepared to do prior to the parties' reaching a settlement."[111] From the beginning of the litigation, the district court had anticipated that "issues relating to damages" would be "severed and tried separately" from other issues relating to liability.[112] The initial phases of this litigation would therefore have focused on common questions, including which defendants bore responsibility for the well blowout, how much oil escaped from the Macondo reservoir, who bore responsibility for the inability of the defendants to contain the flow earlier, where the oil finally came to rest, and how the efforts to disperse the oil were conducted.[113] "[A]bsent the Settlement," the district court would then have been obliged to determine in later phases how "responsible party status would translate into compensation" under the OPA.[114]

The district court was well aware, therefore, that the class members' damages "would have to be decided on an individual basis were the cases not being settled," as would "the extent to which the *Deepwater Horizon* incident [—40—] versus other factors caused a decline in the income of an individual or business."[115] Accordingly, the district court did not list the calculation of the claimants' damages either in its list of "common questions of fact" or in its list of "common questions of law."[116] But even without a common means of measuring damages, in the district court's view, these common issues nonetheless predominated over the issues unique to individual claimants. As the district court explained, "[t]he phased trial structure selected by the Court prior to the parties' arrival at a settlement agreement reflected the central importance of common issues to this case."[117]

In rendering this conclusion, the district court did not abuse its discretion. The phased trial of common issues in this case would undoubtedly prevent the repetitious re-litigation of these common issues by each individual claimant in thousands of separate lawsuits. In accordance with our directive in *Chalmette Refining*, the district court also rigorously analyzed how it would adjudicate "common class issues in the first phase" and "individualized issues in other phases."[118] As required by *Amchem Products, Inc. v. Windsor*, 521 U.S. 591, 615 (1997), this class action would indeed "achieve economies of time, effort, and expense, and promote . . . uniformity of decision as to persons similarly situated, without sacrificing procedural fairness or bringing about other undesirable results." This class action therefore satisfies Rule 23(b)(3).

This analysis is not changed by the Supreme Court's recent decision in *Comcast*. BP and the Objectors suggest that, three months after the district court certified the class and approved the settlement, *Comcast* brought about a revolution in the application

---

[109] *Butler*, 727 F.3d at 800; *In re Whirlpool Corp.*, 722 F.3d at 860; *Leyva*, 716 F.3d at 514.

[110] *Chalmette Ref.*, 637 F.3d at 556.

[111] *In re Oil Spill*, 910 F. Supp. 2d at 932.

[112] Scheduling Order of October 6, 2010, at 3 (Rec. Doc. 473).

[113] *In re Oil Spill*, 910 F. Supp. 2d at 921-23.

[114] *Id.* at 924.

[115] *Id.*

[116] *Id.* at 921-23.

[117] *Id.* at 921.

[118] *See Chalmette Ref.*, 637 F.3d at 556.

of Rule 23(b)(3). According to this argument, [—41—] *Comcast* declared "that certification under Rule 23(b)(3) requires a reliable, common methodology for measuring classwide damages." This reading is a significant distortion of *Comcast*, and has already been considered and rejected by the Seventh Circuit, the Sixth Circuit, and the Ninth Circuit in the months since *Comcast* was decided.[119]

The principal holding of *Comcast* was that a "model purporting to serve as evidence of damages . . . must measure only those damages attributable to th[e] theory" of liability on which the class action is premised.[120] "If the model does not even attempt to do that, it cannot possibly establish that damages are susceptible of measurement across the entire class for purposes of Rule 23(b)(3)."[121] In this case, however, the district court's inquiry into predominance was never premised on such a formula. As our three fellow circuits have already concluded, we agree that the rule of *Comcast* is largely irrelevant "[w]here determinations on liability and damages have been bifurcated" in accordance with Rule 23(c)(4) and the district court has "reserved all issues concerning damages for individual determination."[122] Even after *Comcast*, the predominance inquiry can still be satisfied under Rule 23(b)(3) if the proceedings are structured to establish "liability on a class-wide basis, with separate hearings to determine—if liability is established—the damages of individual class members."[123] As explained above, this is precisely how the district court planned to calculate the claimants' damages, which [—42—] "would have to be decided on an individual basis were the cases not being settled."[124] The principal holding of *Comcast* therefore has no application here.

As an additional matter relating to the predominance inquiry, we also address BP's suggestion that *Comcast* prohibits class certification in the present case because payments are made under the Settlement Agreement's Exhibits 4B and 4C to claimants "who have suffered no injury." In BP's view, payments made under such a formula are not "attributable" to the class action's theory of liability and therefore violate *Comcast*. In support of this argument, BP also has cited our decision in *Bell Atlantic*, which stated (very similarly to *Comcast*) that the predominance inquiry under Rule 23(b)(3) cannot be satisfied when it is premised on a formula for classwide measurement of damages that "is clearly inadequate."[125]

This argument must also be rejected. Neither *Comcast* nor *Bell Atlantic*, nor any other decision that BP has identified, has suggested that predominance under Rule 23(b)(3) can be defeated by a formula for making voluntary payments under a settlement agreement. Both *Comcast* and *Bell Atlantic* addressed formulas for measuring damages in class actions that had been certified for further proceedings on the merits, and neither made any mention of a settlement agreement. The *Amchem* decision, moreover, which did involve a settlement class proposed for certification under Rule 23(b)(3), explained that the predominance inquiry "trains on the legal or factual questions that qualify each class member's case as a genuine controversy, *questions that preexist any settlement.*"[126] Indeed, as stated elsewhere in *Amchem*, the existence of a settlement agreement allows the district court to dispense altogether with considering at least one of the Rule 23(b)(3) concerns: [—43—] "the likely difficulties in managing a class action." Under *Amchem*, when "[c]onfronted with a request for settlement-only class certification, a district court need not inquire whether the case, if tried, would present intractable management

---

[119] *See Butler*, 727 F.3d at 800; *In re Whirlpool Corp.*, 722 F.3d at 860; *Leyva*, 716 F.3d at 514.

[120] *Comcast Corp.*, 133 S. Ct. at 1433.

[121] *Id.*

[122] *In re Whirlpool Corp.*, 722 F.3d at 860; *see also Butler*, 727 F.3d at 800; *Leyva*, 716 F.3d at 514.

[123] *Butler*, 727 F.3d at 800; *see also In re Whirlpool Corp.*, 722 F.3d at 860; *Leyva*, 716 F.3d at 514.

---

[124] *In re Oil Spill*, 910 F. Supp. 2d at 924.

[125] *Bell Atl.*, 339 F.3d at 307.

[126] *Amchem*, 521 U.S. at 623 (emphasis added).

problems, see Fed. Rule Civ. Proc. 23(b)(3)(D), for the proposal is that there be no trial."[127]

We cannot therefore conceive of why or how a formula for making voluntary payments under a settlement agreement could threaten the predominance of common questions over individual questions in litigation. Indeed, the reason that BP has identified no authority for this proposition is that it is nonsensical. A question of law or fact that is "common" under Rule 23 is one that enables the class action "to generate common answers apt to drive the resolution of the litigation."[128] But after a class action has been settled, by definition the litigation has been resolved and the questions have been answered. For the commonality and predominance inquiries to have any meaning at all, therefore, they must be considered independently from the resolution provided in a settlement—which is precisely what *Amchem* instructs.[129] The arguments raised by BP and the Objectors regarding Rule 23(b)(3) must therefore be rejected.[130] [—44—]

---

[127] *Id.* at 620.

[128] *Wal-Mart*, 131 S. Ct. at 2551 (emphasis omitted); *M.D.*, 675 F.3d at 840.

[129] *Amchem*, 521 U.S. at 623 (explaining that the predominance inquiry "trains on the legal or factual questions that qualify each class member's case as a genuine controversy, questions that preexist any settlement."). It is worth recalling here that even though the settlement class in *Amchem* failed the predominance inquiry, this was not due to any feature of the settlement. This was because, rather, the district court had impermissibly taken into consideration factors such as the class members' "interest in receiving prompt and fair compensation," which was a factor unrelated to the case or controversy that they hypothetically would have litigated had the class action not been settled. Such factors are external to the predominance inquiry. *See id.*

[130] Neither the Cobb Objectors nor the Allpar Objectors have made any arguments under the second requirement of Rule 23(b)(3), that "a class action is superior to other available methods for fairly and efficiently adjudicating the controversy." BP has raised this [—44—] argument but has not differentiated in any meaningful way between its "predominance" argument and "superiority" argument. Citing *Amchem*, BP argues essentially that the class action would not be superior to individual lawsuits because a class action only satisfies Rule 23(b)(3) when it "would achieve

D.

BP and the Objectors have also argued that, by virtue of the Class Administrator's interpretations of Exhibits 4B and 4C, the class notice distributed to absent class members has been rendered deficient. Under Rule 23(c)(2)(B), "[t]he notice must clearly and concisely state in plain, easily understood language . . . the nature of the action," "the definition of the class certified," "the class claims, issues, or defenses," and other items of information relating to opting out, making objections, and the consequences of the judgment. Without tying their argument to any particular provision of Rule 23(c)(2)(B), BP and the Objectors contend that class members should have been informed of the likelihood that the prospective claimants would include uninjured persons and entities.

In our circuit, however, "[i]t is not required[] . . . that class members be made cognizant of every material fact that has taken place prior to the notice."[131] Moreover, as we held in *In re Nissan Motor Corp. Antitrust Litigation*, 552 F.2d 1088, 1104 (5th Cir. 1977), and as at least four of our fellow circuits have agreed, the class notice must describe the proceedings in [—45—] "objective, neutral terms."[132] The contention that BP and

---

economies of time, effort, and expense, and promote uniformity of decision as to persons similarly situated, without sacrificing procedural fairness or bringing about other undesirable results." *Amchem*, 521 U.S. at 615. As we already have decided in the context of the predominance inquiry, however, the district court did not abuse its discretion in finding that this requirement was met in this case. *See In re Oil Spill*, 910 F. Supp. 2d at 928. Accordingly, BP's argument as to superiority under Rule 23(b)(3) is also rejected.

[131] *In re Corrugated Container Antitrust Litig.*, 611 F.2d 86, 88 (5th Cir. 1980) (quoting *In re Nissan Motor Corp. Antitrust Litig.*, 552 F.2d 1088, 1104 (5th Cir. 1977)) (original alterations, quotation marks, and parentheses omitted).

[132] *See Int'l Union, United Auto., Aerospace, & Agric. Implement Workers of Am. v. Gen. Motors Corp.*, 497 F.3d 615, 630 (6th Cir. 2007) ("Rule 23(e) does not require the notice to set forth every ground on which class members might object to the settlement . . . ."); *see also Rodriguez v. W. Publ'g Corp.*, 563 F.3d 948, 962-63 & n.7 (9th Cir. 2009) (requiring the class notice to be "scrupulously

the Objectors now suggest should have been incorporated into the class notice is neither "objective" nor "neutral" but is an adversarial position that would have been inappropriate for inclusion in a class notice.

Additionally, in *Katrina Canal Breaches*, in which we found a statement in a class notice to be "slightly misleading" regarding a point of Louisiana law, we held that the notice was not rendered deficient because "the statement as written [wa]s accurate in its essential point."[133] Here, the class definition was explained in the notice to include persons and entities with economic loss and property damage "arising out of the 'Deepwater Horizon Incident.'" Accordingly, even if we were to accept that the class notice could have been improved by adding the word, "allegedly," this minor legal ambiguity would not be enough to render the class notice deficient. The district court therefore did not abuse its discretion in finding the class notice sufficient under Rule 23(c)(2)(B).

E.

BP and the Objectors also argue that the Claims Administrator's interpretations of Exhibits 4B and 4C preclude approval of the Settlement Agreement under Rule 23(e), which requires a district court to ensure that all class settlements are "fair, reasonable, and adequate." Even the cases cited by BP, however, emphasize that the purpose of Rule 23(e) is "to protect the [—46—] nonparty members of the class."[134] No case cited by BP or the Objectors suggests that a district court must also safeguard the interests of the defendant, which in most settlements can protect its own interests at the negotiating table. As we stated in *Newby v. Enron Corp.*, 394 F.3d 296, 301 (5th Cir. 2004), "[t]he gravamen of an approvable proposed settlement is that it be fair, adequate, and reasonable and is not the product of collusion between the parties."[135] As is abundantly clear from the current controversy surrounding the proper interpretation of Exhibits 4B and 4C, and as the district court expressly found,[136] the Settlement Agreement was concluded in an arms-length negotiation that was free of collusion.

BP also makes a novel argument regarding our decision in *Reed v. General Motors Corp.*, 703 F.2d 170 (5th Cir. 1983), in which we explained that the application of Rule 23(e) should hinge on the analysis of six factors. These factors are: (1) the existence of fraud or collusion behind the settlement; (2) the complexity, expense, and likely duration of the litigation; (3) the stage of the proceedings and the amount of discovery completed; (4) the probability of plaintiffs' success on the merits; (5) the range of possible recovery; and (6) the opinions of the class counsel, class representatives, and absent class members.[137] In the present case, the district court conducted a lengthy and detailed analysis of the proposed settlement under each of the six *Reed* factors.[138] In the district court's view, none of the *Reed* factors counseled [—47—] against approving the settlement.

BP's argument ignores the six *Reed* factors altogether. Rather, BP relies on a short quotation from *Reed* to suggest that district courts should also ensure that settlement agreements are based on a "fair approximation of [class members'] relative entitlement." This quotation is clearly taken out of context.[139] No other decision by our court or by any district court has ever cited *Reed* for such a proposition. Nor can any of the six *Reed* factors be easily related to the "fair approximation" analysis that BP proposes. Even attempting to analyze BP's argument

---

neutral"); *In re Traffic Exec. Ass'n E. R.R.*, 627 F.2d 631, 634 (2d Cir. 1980) (same); *Grunin v. Int'l House of Pancakes*, 513 F.2d 114, 122 (8th Cir. 1975) (same).

[133] *See In re Katrina Canal Breaches Litig.*, 628 F.3d 185, 199 (5th Cir. 2010).

[134] *Wilson v. Sw. Airlines, Inc.*, 880 F.2d 807, 818 (5th Cir. 1989) (quoting *Piambino v. Bailey*, 610 F.2d 1306, 1327 (5th Cir. 1980)); *see also All Plaintiffs v. All Defendants*, 645 F.3d 329, 334 (5th Cir. 2011) (citing *Strong v. BellSouth Telecomm'cns, Inc.*, 137 F.3d 844, 849 (5th Cir. 1998)).

[135] *Newby*, 394 F.3d at 301 (internal quotation marks omitted).

[136] *In re Oil Spill*, 910 F. Supp. 2d at 931.

[137] *Reed*, 703 F.2d at 172.

[138] *In re Oil Spill*, 910 F. Supp. 2d at 931-39.

[139] *See Reed*, 703 F.2d at 175.

under the fifth factor discussed in *Reed*, "the range of possible recovery," BP has identified no reason to believe that the payments made under the Settlement Agreement fall outside the class members' range of "possible" recovery in litigation.

F.

Last of all, BP and the Objectors have argued that, by virtue of the Class Administrator's interpretations of Exhibits 4B and 4C, Rule 23's implicit "ascertainability" requirement is not satisfied. As we held in *Union Asset Management Holding A.G. v. Dell, Inc.*, 669 F.3d 632 (5th Cir. 2012): "[I]n order to maintain a class action, the class sought to be represented must be adequately defined and clearly ascertainable."[140] According to this argument, the Claims Administrator's two Policy Announcements render the class definition irrational and therefore violate the ascertainability requirement. However, as we found in *Rodriguez*, "the possibility that some [claimants] may fail to prevail on their individual claims will not defeat class membership" on the basis of the ascertainability requirement.[141] Accordingly, this final [—48—] argument by BP and the Objectors is rejected. In the absence of any other arguments addressing this implicit component of Rule 23, we find that the district court did not abuse its discretion in finding that the settlement class satisfies the ascertainability requirement.

V.

To conclude, the numerous arguments that BP and the Objectors have raised with respect to each of the provisions of Rule 23 are variants, for the most part, of a single argument. Based on our previous decisions, we would reject this argument even if we could consider BP's evidence and accept its factual premise, which we cannot. Under *Mims* and *Rodriguez*, "[c]lass certification is

not precluded simply because a class may include persons who have not been injured by the defendant's conduct."[142] The result is no different, moreover, under Article III. As we wrote in *Cole*, "it is sufficient for standing purposes that the plaintiffs seek recovery for an economic harm that they *allege* they have suffered," because we "assume *arguendo* the merits" of their claims at the Rule 23 stage.[143]

For the foregoing reasons, therefore, we AFFIRM the district court's order of December 21, 2012.

AFFIRMED.

(Reporter's Note: Dissenting opinion follows on p. 163).

---

[140] *Dell*, 669 F.3d at 639 (5th Cir. 2012) (quoting *DeBremaecker v. Short*, 433 F.2d 733, 734 (5th Cir. 1970) (per curiam)).

[141] *Rodriguez*, 695 F.3d at 370 (internal quotation marks omitted).

[142] *Mims*, 590 F.3d at 308; *see Rodriguez*, 695 F.3d at 370 ("[T]he possibility that some [absent class members] may fail to prevail on their individual claims will not defeat class membership.").

[143] *Cole*, 484 F.3d at 723 (emphasis added) (quoting *Parker*, 478 F.3d at 377 (internal quotation marks omitted)).

[—49—] GARZA, Circuit Judge, dissenting:

The majority finds Article III causation satisfied by language in the complaint and Settlement Agreement, notwithstanding the Claims Administrator's controlling interpretation rendering this language void, eliminating all causation requirements for a broad swath of the class and allowing individuals or entities to participate in the settlement even though they lack a justiciable claim. "Rule 23's requirements must be interpreted in keeping with Article III . . . ." *Amchem Products, Inc., v. Windsor*, 521 U.S. 591, 613 (1997). Standing is an essential component of Article III's case-or-controversy requirement, and it mandates that "there must be a causal connection between the injury and the conduct complained of." *Lujan v. Defenders of Wildlife*, 504 U.S. 555, 560 (1992). That is, whether a class member was economically injured is immaterial if that loss was not caused by the oil spill. Absent an actual causation requirement for all class members, Rule 23 is not being used to simply aggregate similar cases and controversies, but rather to impermissibly extend the judicial power of the United States into administering a private handout program. Because Article III does not permit this, I respectfully dissent.

I

While the three elements of Article III standing—injury, causation, and redressability—remain constant throughout the litigation, the standard of proof necessary to demonstrate these elements becomes progressively more demanding through "the successive stages of the litigation." *Lujan*, 504 U.S. at 560; *ante*, at 9. I agree with the majority we must evaluate standing according to the standard of proof for the Rule 23 class certification and settlement approval stage. I disagree with the majority, however, that Article III standing is satisfied in this case under the *Denney* test. I also disagree that *Kohen*, [—50—] which by its facts addresses only pre-trial certification of a litigation class, applies to the certification of a settlement class.

A

In *Denney v. Deutsche Bank AG*, 443 F.3d 253, 264 (2d Cir. 2006), a class action settlement case like ours, the Second Circuit determined that "[n]o class may be certified that contains members lacking Article III standing. The class must therefore be defined in such a way that *anyone within it* would have standing." *Id.* (internal citations omitted) (emphasis added). The *Denney* test fundamentally recognizes that a class certification decision opens the doors of federal court to all members of that class. The federal courts are only open to justiciable cases.[1] Thus, *Denney* correctly appreciates that, at the end of litigation, settlement class certification stage, courts should verify that the class definition is limited to those with justiciable cases, that is, to those that would have standing. As the majority notes, the touchstone of this test is whether the class definition encompasses only persons and entities that possess Article III Standing. *Ante* at 16.

The majority holds that the extant settlement class is necessarily limited to those class members with claims causally connected to the oil spill, that is, to those with standing. *Id.* It bases this holding exclusively upon Section 1.3.1.2 of the Class Definition, which is contained in both the Amended Complaint and the Settlement Agreement. It totally, and erroneously, ignores language in other documents, including Exhibit 4B and the Claims Administrator's Policy Announcement, which materially affects the status of the causation requirement. Section 1.3.1.2 summarizes an economic damage [—51—] category for "[l]oss of income, earnings or profits suffered by Natural Persons or Entities *as a result of* the DEEPWATER HORIZON INCIDENT." (emphasis added). Certainly, this language encompasses a causation

---

[1] *See, e.g., Warth v. Seldin*, 422 U.S. 490, 498 (1975) ("[Standing] is founded in concern about the proper—and properly limited—role of the courts in a democratic society. [It] is the threshold question in every federal case, determining the power of the court to entertain the suit.").

requirement.[2] However, the inquiry does not end there. Other documents with significant bearing on the Class Definition's treatment of causation must also be examined.

Section 1.3.1 of the Class Definition incorporates by reference Exhibit 4B: "Causation Requirements for Business Economic Loss Claims." Section 1 of Exhibit 4B establishes that certain individuals and entities, based on their location or the nature of their enterprise, "are not required to provide any evidence of causation."[3] These groups are entitled to a presumption of causation.[4] Construed together, Section 1.3.1.2 of the Class Definition and Section 1 of Exhibit 4B establish that individuals and entities alleging a loss *caused by* the oil spill need not submit evidence of that causation when making a claim for payment.[5] Such a construction seemingly preserves a threshold [—52—] causation requirement while simply eliminating the need for specific evidence to

prove it when making a settlement claim. In other words, causation ostensibly remains an *element* of a claim even though *proof* is not a central feature of the claims process. Significantly, Section 1.3.1.2 and Section I of Exhibit 4B does not end our inquiry: The Claims Administrator has issued a controlling interpretation of the Class Definition's causation requirements.

The Claims Administrator is specifically charged with implementing and administering the Settlement in Section 4.3.1 of the Settlement Agreement. Pursuant to this charge he issued an interpretive decision about causation for economic losses, in which he explained that he would:

> "compensate eligible Business Economic Loss and Individual Economic Loss claimants for all losses payable under the terms of the Economic Loss frameworks in the Settlement Agreement, *without regard to whether such losses resulted or may have resulted from a cause other than the Deepwater Horizon oil spill* provided such claimants have satisfied the specific causation requirements set out in the Settlement Agreement." (emphasis added).

The Claims Administrator further determined that "the Settlement Agreement does not contemplate that the Claims Administrator will undertake additional analysis of causation issues beyond those criteria that are specifically set out in the Settlement Agreement." In short, the Claims Administrator established that the Settlement Agreement requires no proof of causation, beyond the specific requirements of Exhibit 4B. And, the district court has repeatedly affirmed this determination.[6] Essentially, this

---

[2] Under the Oil Pollution Act, 33 U.S.C. §2702(a), liability extends to removal costs and specified damages categories "that result" from an oil discharge incident.

[3] For example, Section I.1 states, "If you are a business in Zone A, you are not required to provide any evidence of causation unless you fall into one of the exceptions agreed to by the parties, and listed in footnote (1)." Section I.5 states, "If you are in Zone A, B, or C, and you meet the "Charter Fishing Definition" you are not required to provide any evidence of causation." *See infra* Part II (explaining why geographic and enterprise-based requirements alone do not comply with the cause-in-fact requirement of Article III and the substantive law governing the class claims).

[4] These groups are in contrast to other groups of claimants that must provide evidence of causation according to the requirements of one of several revenue loss models defined in the Settlement Agreement—e.g., the "Modified V-Shaped Revenue Pattern," or "Proof of Spill-Related Cancellations."

[5] Exhibit 4B's presumption of causation substitutes a claimant's geographical location, or the nature of a claimant's enterprise, for proof of causation. There is an open question as to whether this substitution, even in conjunction with Section 1.3.1.2, would satisfy Article [—52—] III's cause-in-fact element. However, on the facts before us, the Claims Administrator's interpretation has effectively eliminated Section 1.3.1.2's "as a result of" language.

[6] The Claims Administrator issued the Policy Announcement on October 10, 2012, just over two months *before* the District Court entered the final class certification order. On December 12, 2012, the district court acknowledged awareness of the interpretation in an email to the parties. And, on April 9, 2013, the district court issued an order adopting the [—53—] interpretation. On December 24, 2013, responding to the remand in No. 13-30315

interpretation renders Section [—53—] 1.3.1.2's causation language nugatory—all that matters is Exhibit 4B. There is no longer a threshold requirement that the economic losses stand "as a result of" the Deepwater Horizon incident, and at least five groups[7] of Business Economic Loss claimants will never be required to provide any proof of causation. That is, there is no causation requirement in the Settlement Agreement—*as actually implemented*—for a significant segment of the class. Surely, the words "as a result of" remain in the text of the Class Definition, the Amended Complaint, and the Settlement Agreement, but, in truth, they have no significance to determining who is eligible to participate in the settlement.

Consequently, this class can encompass individuals or entities who could never truthfully allege or establish standing, at any stage of the litigation. Thus, it fails under *Denney*. As explained in *Lujan*, Article III standing irreducibly requires that the injury be "fairly traceable to the challenged *action of the defendant*, and not the result of the independent action of some third party not before the court." 504 U.S. at 660 (internal quotations and alterations omitted). The elimination of a causation requirement for these Business Economic Loss claimants renders the Settlement Agreement unconstitutional in this respect.

At the settlement class certification stage, *Denney* does "not require that each member of a class submit evidence of personal standing." *Denney* 443 F.3d at 263. The test is whether each member contemplated by the definition can *allege* standing. *Ante* at 21. And for the purposes of standing allegations, we [—54—] "assume *arguendo* the merits of [the] legal claim." *Cole v. General Motors Corp.*, 484 F.3d 717, 723 (5th Cir. 2007). But here, at the

---

(Before Judges Dennis, Clement, and Southwick), the district court issued an order finding "that whether a business economic loss is "as a result of" the Deepwater Horizon incident for purposes of the Settlement is determined exclusively and conclusively by Exhibit 4B." *See* Order and Reasons [Responding to Remand of Business Economic Loss issues], 2:10-MD-2179, ECF No. 12055, at 18.

[7] *See* Exhibit 4B, §§ I.1–5.

settlement class certification stage, these standards are not met. Because the interpretation has nullified the causation language of Section 1.3.1.2 of the complaint, there is no guarantee that each member of the class meets the standing requirements of Article III. Thus, it is quite possible that claimants eligible for Exhibit 4B's presumption of causation can fully participate in the settlement even though their injuries, if any, are not fairly traceable to the Deepwater Horizon incident. *Cf. Lujan*, 504 U.S. at 560. *Denney* requires that the class must "be defined in such a way that *anyone* within it would have standing." *Denney*, 443 F.3d at 264 (emphasis added). Absent a causation requirement for certain segments of Business Economic Loss claimants, this Class Definition includes those who would not.[8]

The majority avoids the fatal impact of the Policy Announcement by concluding that "the evidentiary standard to be applied by the Claims Administrator [ ] is not a matter of Article III standing," but rather "a question of interpreting the Settlement Agreement and applying it to each individual claim . . . ." *Ante* at 24. If this case involved only a question of degree—say, what evidence is sufficient to establish causation—I might agree with this [—55—] conclusion. In that case, *some* form of

---

[8] On appeal, BP has presented particular evidence that the Administrator has made awards to persons and entities that "likely were not injured" by the oil spill. *Ante,* at 19. The majority holds that this evidence cannot be considered on appeal because it was not presented to the district court. *Id.* Taking this as true, there is no need to evaluate specific evidence to determine that the class definition, as currently interpreted, can include individuals or entities that cannot trace their injury to the oil spill. Looking at the totality of the relevant documents, it is clear that the Class Definition is overbroad. Exhibit 4B creates a presumption of causation for those that work in a specific area or occupation, and the "as a result of" language, stripped of meaning by the Claims Administrator, no longer bounds these individuals or entities. Thus, the class definition directly includes business claimants for which there is no causation requirement. Geographic and enterprise-based factors alone, all that are required under Section I of Exhibit 4B, are insufficient to satisfy the causal connection required by Article III. *See infra* Part II.

causation would remain intact. However, the issue here is not what evidence is sufficient, but rather whether causation has been entirely written out of the settlement. Certainly, this is within the bounds of an Article III inquiry. *See Lujan*, 504 U.S. at 560 (holding that a causal connection is [a]n irreducible component of Article III standing).

Furthermore, the majority strongly suggests that the Claims Administrator's interpretation is not before us in this appeal. *Ante* at 23. While the policy interpretation is not literally part of the district court's December 21, 2012 certification order, the document directly before us, it is clearly an integral aspect of how the Class Definition and the Settlement Agreement operate. The *Denney* test for verifying Article III standing at the class settlement stage of litigation requires the reviewing court to analyze the class definition. It is not possible to perform a true and accurate analysis while ignoring the controlling interpretation of this definition.[9]

The Claims Administrator's interpretation must be treated as part and parcel of the Settlement Agreement and Class Definition for several reasons. First, the very district court that certified the class and oversees the settlement's implementation has repeatedly affirmed this interpretation.[10] Second, the interpretation issued before the district court entered the final certification order and the record demonstrates the district court was aware of this.[11] Third, the Settlement Agreement provides that the Claims [—56—] Administrator will have authority to make policy decisions and to issue guidance. It is illogical to disregard a pronouncement on the meaning of the Settlement issuing from the very entity the Settlement established for this purpose.

Lastly, Article III cannot be so easily duped by sleight of hand. Here, the district court certified a class based on the written Class Definition in the Amended Complaint and Settlement Agreement. This definition initially included "as a result of"—a clear causation requirement. Because of the Claims Administrator's interpretation, it no longer does. The district court certified a class settlement agreement that, in pertinent part, no longer exists. And now, on appeal, the majority limits its standing analysis to the defunct text of Section 1.3.1.2. In essence, this analysis finds Article III satisfied by what has been transformed into an empty pleading allegation. But Article III demands more. A key function of the standing requirement is to "identify those disputes which are appropriately resolved through the judicial process." *Whitmore v. Arkansas*, 496 U.S. 149, 155 (1990). Claims for damages that are not "fairly traceable to the defendant's conduct," *Lujan*, 504 U.S. at 660, are not such disputes. Today's opinion improperly welcomes them into federal court.

B

The majority further determines that this settlement class certification satisfies Article III standing under the *Kohen* test, which requires that the named plaintiffs—as opposed to absent class members—can satisfy Article III's standing requirements. *Kohen*, 571 F.3d at 676; *ante* at 15. While I agree that the named plaintiffs' standing is uncontested in this case, *Kohen* does not apply. As also observed by Judge Clement in *Deepwater Horizon I*, 732 F.3d at 344 n.12, 1 Adm. R. at 300 n. 12, *Kohen* does not concern an end of litigation settlement class certification. This distinguishing factor is crucial. [—57—]

In *Kohen*, the court determined that the "possibility or indeed inevitability" that the defined class will "often include persons who have not been injured by the defendant's conduct" does not preclude class certification. Thus, the court looked only to the named plaintiffs to satisfy Article III standing.

---

[9] The majority further suggests that the Claims Administrator's interpretation of causation in the class definition has been waived on appeal because "no party ever formally objected" to it, and because BP initially took "no position on the relevance *vel non*" of the policy interpretation. *Ante* at 6–7. Be this as it may, "we are certainly free ourselves to raise an issue of standing as going to Article III jurisdiction . . . ." *Lewis v.* Casey, 518 U.S. 343, 394 (1996) (quoting *Mount Healthy City Bd. of Ed. v. Doyle*, 429 U.S. 274, 278, (1977)).

[10] *See supra* note 6.

[11] *Id.*

However, *Kohen* concerns a pre-trial litigation class certification, not a final settlement class certification, and in this presupposes that there will be a further stage where the Article III standing requirements will be proven up. *Kohen*, 571 F.3d at 677 ("If the case goes to trial, this plaintiff may fail to prove injury."). The *Kohen* opinion relies on the fact that jurisdiction alleged at the pleading stage of a class action litigation must eventually be substantiated. *Id*. But, in a settlement class certification, like that at bar, there will be no additional stages for substantiating standing. The settlement ends the litigation. Accordingly, the *Kohen* "named plaintiffs only" formula for evaluating Article III standing is inapplicable here.

Additionally, the *Kohen* court actually embraces *Denney's* focus on the class definition for verifying Article III standing. *Kohen* specifically rejected defendant-appellant' PIMCO's argument that the district court needed to verify each class members' individual standing before certifying the class—that is, absent class members needed to *prove* standing before certification. *Id*. at 676. According to the *Kohen* court, the burden of proving standing at the pre-trial class certification stage lies with the named plaintiffs alone. But *Kohen* simultaneously recognizes that a "class should not be certified if it is *apparent* that it contains a great many persons who have suffered no injury at the hands of the defendant . . . ." *Id*. at 677. (emphasis added). The court specifically noted that "if the class definition *clearly were overbroad*, this would be a compelling reason to require that it be narrowed." *Id*. at 678. So, without concern for proof of standing, *Kohen* recognizes that, even at the pre-trial class certification stage, a certification does not comply with Article III if it embraces [—58—] a swath of claimants who cannot claim injury-in-fact, causation, or redressability. Here, in light of the controlling interpretation, the class definition does exactly that for certain groups of Business Economic Loss claimants. *See supra* Part I.A.

C

In conclusion, this interpretation creates an overbroad class definition, which "includes people who have no legal claim whatsoever." *Sullivan v. DB Investments, Inc.*, 667 F.3d 273, 340 (3d Cir. 2011) (Jordan, J. dissenting). Under its terms, a segment of claimants could enter federal court and receive redress for injuries that need not have been caused by the defendant's conduct. Without a causation requirement for class membership, this Settlement Agreement encompasses individuals and entities that do not possess the requisite justiciable case or controversy. From an administrative perspective the elimination of causation may be more efficient, but it is also violates Article III, which does not permit the federal courts to administer private handout programs. Accordingly, the district court's Rule 23 certification is not in keeping with Article III constraints. *See Amchem*, 521 U.S. at 613.

II

In addition to straying beyond Article III jurisdictional constraints, the Claims Administrator's interpretation, by eliminating the causation requirement, violates at least two aspects of Rule 23, and runs afoul of the Rules Enabling Act, 28 U.S.C. § 2702(b).

A

Rule 23(a)(2) requires, as a necessary prerequisite to class certification, that "there are questions of law or fact common to the class." In *Wal-Mart Stores, Inc. v. Dukes*, 131 S. Ct. 2541, 2551 (2011), the Supreme Court interpreted this provision to require that the members of the class have "suffered the same injury." This requires that the class members' claims [—59—] "depend upon a common contention," the "truth or falsity [of which] will resolve an issue that is central to the validity of *each one of the claims* in one stroke." *Id*. (emphasis added). The majority asserts that the commonality requirement is satisfied by myriad questions of law and fact about BP's injurious conduct. *See ante*, at 30–31 (listing common questions). Certainly, these contentions are central to *many* class member's claims. But Rule 23(a)(2) and *Wal-Mart* require more—the common contentions must go to the validity of *each one of the claims*. Because this class includes a segment of claimants whose injuries need not have been caused by the oil spill, this cannot be so. For example, "[w]hether BP used an improper well design that unreasonably heightened the risk [of an incident]" says nothing about the validity of a claim for economic injuries caused by factors other than the oil spill. As long as the class impermissibly aggregates those whose injuries were purportedly caused by the oil spill with those without any arguable claim of such causation, questions concerning BP's liability are insufficient to satisfy Rule 23(a) commonality.

The same argument applies with full force to the Rule 23(a)(3) requirement that "the claims or defenses of the representative parties are typical of the claims or defenses of the class." *Cf. ante*, at 31 n.92. The Supreme Court has observed that the "commonality and typicality requirements of Rule 23(a) tend to merge." *Wal-Mart*, 131 S. Ct. at 2550–51 n.5. The majority holds that typicality is satisfied because "the class representatives—like all class members—allege economic and/or property damage stemming directly from the Deepwater Horizon spill." *Ante*, at 31 n.92. (quoting *In re Oil Spill by Oil Rig Deepwater Horizon in Gulf of Mexico, on April 20, 2010*, 910 F. Supp. 2d 891, 915 (E.D. La. 2012)). This disregards the unavoidable fact that causation, initially alleged in Section 1.3.1.2, has been effectively written out by the Claims Administrator. Given the Claims Administrator's controlling **[—60—]** interpretation, all class members do not allege injury "stemming directly" from the oil spill. *Cf. id.*

Rule 23 certification requires that the proposed class meets all the prerequisite requirements of Rule 23(a). *See* W. Rubenstein, A. Conte & H. Newberg, Newberg on Class Actions § 3:1 (5th ed. 2011). Commonality and typicality are absent here.

B

The Rules Enabling Act requires that that the rules of procedure "shall not abridge, enlarge or modify any substantive right." 28 U.S.C. § 2702(b). The class action rules must be applied in keeping with this mandate. *See Amchem*, 521 U.S. at 613. It follows that Rule 23's aggregation function cannot be used to "create new rights and then settle claims brought under them." *Deepwater Horizon I*, 732 F.3d at 342, 1 Adm. R. at 298; *see Sullivan*, 667 F.3d at 343 (Jordan, J. dissenting) ("Rule 23 [serves] to efficiently handle claims recognized by law, not to create new claims.").

This Settlement Agreement resolves claims arising under General Maritime Law (tort principles of federal common law) and the Oil Pollution Act, 33 U.S.C. § 2702(a). Each of these claims contains some sort of causation element. In order to prevail in a negligence action, a plaintiff must establish that the defendant's breach of duty is the but-for and proximate cause of the injury complained of.[12] Under the Oil Pollution Act, a plaintiff must demonstrate that the costs and damages sought "result from" an oil spill incident. Thus, under the controlling substantive law, there is no right to recover damages for injuries not caused by the defendant's breach. This **[—61—]** settlement, however, allows individuals and entities whose injuries were not caused by the oil spill to claim and receive damage payments. *See supra*, Part I.A. That is, the set of eligible claimants is not congruent with the set of actual (those injured by the spill) claimants, the latter being merely a subset of the former. Thus, the settlement eliminates an essential component of the underlying cause of action, creating a legal right for some class members where none exists at law. This violates the Rules Enabling Act—by bringing claimants without causally related injuries into the class, Rule 23's

---

[12] The Amended Class Action complaint asserts claims for negligence, gross negligence and willful misconduct, and breach of contract under general maritime law. The breach of contract claims pertain only to Vessels of Opportunity ("VoO") claimants.

aggregation function has been improperly used to expand substantive rights.[13]

III

What makes this case unique, perhaps, is that causation is contemplated on the face of the core documents—the Amended Complaint, Class Definition, and the Settlement Agreement—but eliminated in application by the Claims Administrator's interpretation. In evaluating whether Article III's causation requirement for standing has been properly demonstrated at the settlement class certification stage, I would look to the class definition as it has been authoritatively interpreted, not simply as it is ostensibly written. Today, the majority takes another path, turning a blind eye to the Claims Administrator's interpretation.

The concerns identified in this dissent each stem from a common problem: causation has been eliminated for a broad swath of Business Economic Loss claimants. For the foregoing reasons, this requires that the class be decertified. However, this does not necessarily mean that a Settlement Agreement, writ large, is entirely unworkable or that Rule 23 is inapplicable. I simply observe that this attempted global settlement fails in a narrow, but [—62—] significant, regard. I would vacate the class certification and Settlement Agreement, and remand to allow the parties and the district court to design a solution that complies with Article III, Rule 23, and the Rules Enabling Act.

Respectfully, I dissent.

---

[13] *See Deepwater Horizon I*, 732 F.3d at 339–44, 1 Adm. R. at 295–300 (offering additional insights into the impact of the causation policy on Article III, Rule 23 and the Rules Enabling Act).

United States Court of Appeals
for the Fifth Circuit

No. 12-30714

MCBRIDE
vs.
ESTIS WELL SERVICE, L.L.C.

Appeal from the United States District Court for the
Western District of Louisiana, Lafayette

Decided: February 24, 2014

Citation: 743 F.3d 458, 2 Adm. R. 170 (5th Cir. 2014).

ON PETITION FOR REHEARING EN BANC
(Opinion October 2, 2013, 5 Cir., 2013, 731 F.3d 505, 1 Adm.
R. 316)

Before **STEWART,** Chief Judge, **JOLLY, DAVIS, JONES, SMITH, DENNIS, CLEMENT, PRADO, OWEN, ELROD, SOUTHWICK, HAYNES, GRAVES** and **HIGGINSON,** Circuit Judges.

[—1—] BY THE COURT:

A member of the court having requested a poll on the petition for rehearing en banc, and a majority of the circuit judges in regular active service and not disqualified having voted in favor,

IT IS ORDERED that this cause shall be reheard by the court en banc with oral argument on a date hereafter to be fixed. The Clerk will specify a briefing schedule for the filing of supplemental briefs.

United States Court of Appeals
for the Fifth Circuit

No. 12-30012

IN RE DEEPWATER HORIZON

Appeals from the United States District Court for the
Eastern District of Louisiana

Decided: February 24, 2014

Citation: 745 F.3d 157, 2 Adm. R. 171 (5th Cir. 2014).

Before **JONES**, **BARKSDALE**, and **SOUTHWICK**,
Circuit Judges.

[—1—] **JONES**, Circuit Judge:

Eleven Louisiana coastal parishes (the "Parishes") filed suits against BP and other defendants ("Appellees")[1] involved in the DEEPWATER HORIZON oil spill to recover penalties under The Louisiana Wildlife Protection Statute ("Wildlife Statute") for the pollution-related loss of aquatic life and wildlife. La. R.S. 56:40.1.[2] Suits filed

---

[1] The Parishes filed suit against BP Exploration & Production, Inc.; BP Products North America, Inc.; BP America Production Company; and BP p.l.c. (collectively "BP"); Transocean Ltd.; Transocean Offshore; Transocean Deepwater; and Transocean Holdings (collectively "Transocean"); Halliburton Energy Services, Inc. and its related entities (collectively "Halliburton"); M-I, LLC; Cameron International Corp.; Weatherford U.S., L.P.; Anadarko Petroleum Corporation Co. and Anadarko E & P Company LP (collectively "Anadarko"); MOEX Offshore 2007 LLC and MOEX USA Corp. (collectively "MOEX"); Mitsui Oil Exploration Co., Ltd. ("MOECO").

On June 18, 2012, the district court entered a Consent Decree in MDL No. 2179 between the United States and MOEX defendants. Among other things, the Consent Decree provided for the payment of civil penalties to the State of Louisiana, conditioned on the State timely providing a Release to MOEX. The State timely provided the Release. Accordingly, the district court dismissed the Parishes' claims against MOEX.

[2] La. R.S. 56:40.1 *et seq.* authorizes civil penalties against any "person who . . . through the violation of any other state or federal law or regulation, kills or injures any fish, wild birds, [—2—] wild quadrupeds, and other wildlife and aquatic life."

originally in state court were removed to federal [—2—] court, which denied the Parishes' motions to remand and then dismissed all of the Parishes' claims as preempted by federal law. Both decisions are challenged in the Parishes' appeal. We concur with the district court that the state law claims were removable pursuant to the jurisdictional provision of the Outer Continental Shelf Lands Act ("OCSLA"). We also affirm their dismissal as preempted by federal law.

BACKGROUND

The Macondo well, which was being drilled by the mobile offshore drilling rig DEEPWATER HORIZON, experienced a catastrophic blowout and explosion in April 2010 and caused hydrocarbon, mineral, and other contaminant pollution all along the shores and estuaries of the Gulf Coast states, inflicting billions of dollars in property and environmental damage and spawning a litigation frenzy. Among the thousands of cases transferred for consolidated management by the Judicial Panel on Multidistrict Litigation to the Eastern District of Louisiana were the Parishes' lawsuits, some of which had been removed from state court. The district court handled cases filed by government entities, like the Parishes, in various groups according to their common issues. Considering first the remand motions filed by three of these Parishes, the court upheld its removal jurisdiction notwithstanding that the cases alleged only penalties accruing under state law for pollution damage that occurred in state waters or along the coastline.[3] The court predicated federal court jurisdiction on 43 U.S.C. § 1349(b)(1)(A). *See In re: Oil Spill by the Oil Rig "Deepwater Horizon" in the Gulf of Mex., on April 20, 2010 (In re: Oil Spill)*, 747 F. Supp. 2d 704, [—3—] 708-09 (E.D. La. 2010). Next, considering various defendants'

---

[3] At least three Parishes filed motions to remand (St. Bernard, Terrebonne, Plaquemines), and the court's pertinent order was issued on October 6, 2010. The docket sheets are somewhat ambiguous about which Parishes are included in the ruling and order, but all have appealed the refusal to remand.

Motions to Dismiss the "B1" pleading bundle cases, filed for private or "non-governmental economic loss and property damages," the district court held that admiralty jurisdiction was present because the alleged tort occurred upon navigable waters and disrupted maritime commerce, and the operations of the DEEPWATER HORIZON, the vessel, bore a substantial relationship to maritime activity. *In re: Oil Spill*, 808 F. Supp. 2d 943, 951 (E.D. La. 2011). The district court also held that state law was preempted by maritime law. *Id.* at 953-55. In a subsequent order concerning the "C" pleading bundle cases, brought by the states of Alabama and Louisiana, the court drew from its decision concerning the "B1" pleading bundle to hold that the states' wildlife actions are preempted by federal law. *See In re: Oil Spill*, MDL No. 2179, 2011 WL 5520295, at *3, 8 (E.D. La. Nov. 14, 2011). Finally, when considering the Local Government Entity Master Complaint and certain other cases within pleading bundle "C," the district court held, *inter alia*, that because the Parishes only asserted state law claims, which the district court already deemed preempted, the cases failed to state claims upon which relief could be granted and must be dismissed. *In re: Oil Spill*, 835 F. Supp. 2d 175, 179-80 (E.D. La. 2011).

STANDARD OF REVIEW

"The district court's denial of the motion to remand, the propriety of removal under the various governing statutes, and the existence of subject matter jurisdiction here are all interrelated questions of law subject to *de novo* review." *Oviedo v. Hallbauer*, 655 F.3d 419, 422 (5th Cir. 2011) (emphasis added). Further, "[w]e review the district court's grant of summary judgment on preemption grounds *de novo*." *O'Hara v. Gen. Motors Corp.*, 508 F.3d 753, 757 (5th Cir. 2007). [—4—]

DISCUSSION

I. Removal Jurisdiction

The Appellees principally rely on OCSLA's broad jurisdictional grant in petitioning for federal court removal jurisdiction.[4] Defendants may generally remove a case from state court if the federal court would have had original jurisdiction over it. 28 U.S.C. §1441(a). The defendants bear the burden of establishing the basis for removal, and operative facts and pleadings are evaluated at the time of removal. *City of Chicago v. Int'l Coll. of Surgeons*, 522 U.S. 156, 163, 118 S. Ct. 523, 529 (1997). The pertinent provision, OCSLA § 23(b)(1), states:

. . the district courts of the United States shall have jurisdiction of cases and controversies arising out of, or in connection with . . . any operation conducted on the outer Continental Shelf which involves exploration, development, or production of the minerals, of the subsoil and seabed of the outer Continental Shelf, or which involves rights to such minerals . . ..

The Fifth Circuit has interpreted this language as straightforward and broad. *See Tenn. Gas Pipeline v. Hous. Cas. Ins. Co.*, 87 F.3d 150, 154 (5th Cir. 1996); *EP Operating Ltd. P'ship v. Placid Oil Co.*, 26 F.3d 563, 569 (5th Cir. 1994) ("[A] broad reading of the jurisdictional grant of section 1349 is supported by the expansive substantive reach of the OCSLA."). Moreover, because jurisdiction is invested in the district courts by this statute, "[a] plaintiff does not need to expressly invoke OCSLA in order for it to apply." *Barker v. Hercules Offshore, Inc.*, 713 F.3d 208, 213, 1 Adm. R. 206, 208 (5th Cir. 2013). Courts typically assess [—5—] jurisdiction under this provision in terms of whether (1) the activities that caused the injury constituted an "operation" "conducted

---

[4] Appellees' reliance on 28 U.S.C. § 1331 "arising under" jurisdiction is unpersuasive because no claim based on federal law appeared on the face of the Parishes' well-pled complaints. *McKnight v. Dresser, Inc.*, 676 F.3d 426, 430 (5th Cir. 2012). Further, we need not decide (a) whether the Parishes, whose recovery is "in the name of the State, and who will share proceeds of any statutory recovery with the State," are nonetheless "citizens" for diversity purposes; or (b) whether the fact that the State, if the real party in interest, is a plaintiff means that it cannot raise an Eleventh Amendment bar to removal.

on the outer Continental Shelf" that involved the exploration and production of minerals, and (2) the case "arises out of, or in connection with" the operation. *See, e.g., EP Operating Ltd. P'ship*, 26 F.3d at 568-69. As the district court noted, the fact that the oil spill occurred because of the Appellees' "operations" in exploring for and producing oil on the Outer Continental Shelf ("OCS") cannot be contested.

The Parishes do not concede, however, that, under the second half of the inquiry, their statutory wildlife claims arose out of or in connection with the oil production operation. Following the migration of contaminants from the well, the injury to wildlife and aquatic life was wholly situated in state territorial waters and on land. The statutory wildlife claims, they assert, have no effect on the "efficient exploitation of resources from the OCS," nor do they "threaten the total recovery of federally-owned resources." *Id.* at 570. "Mere connection" to activities on the OCS, in other words, is insufficient to meet the jurisdictional test.

This argument, however, cannot be squared with applicable Fifth Circuit law or the facts before us. Even though one can hypothesize a "mere connection" between the cause of action and the OCS operation too remote to establish federal jurisdiction, this court deems § 1349 to require only a "but-for" connection. *See, e.g., Hufnagel v. Omega Serv. Indus., Inc.*, 182 F.3d 340, 350 (5th Cir. 1999) (applying the "but-for" test and finding § 1349 jurisdiction where a worker on a stationary drilling platform in the OCS was injured); *Tenn. Gas Pipeline*, 87 F.3d at 155 (using "but-for" test to find jurisdiction when a boat collided with a platform, even though the accident was argued to be a "navigational" error and the mineral operation in question did nothing to cause the accident); *Recar v. CNG Producing Co.*, 853 F.2d 367, 369 (5th Cir. 1988) (applying OCSLA to a personal injury suit when a platform worker was injured [—6—] because a rope broke and caused him to fall to the deck of an adjacent transport vessel). The but-for test does not include a purposive element as the Parishes advocate. It is undeniable that "the oil and

other contaminants would not have entered into the State of Louisiana's territorial waters 'but for' [Appellees'] drilling and exploration operation." *In re: Oil Spill*, 747 F. Supp. 2d at 708. This is not, in short, a challenging case for asserting original federal jurisdiction, and therefore removal jurisdiction, under OCSLA.

Undeterred by this reasoning, the Parishes raise additional but flawed arguments. First, their attempt to intertwine the Section 1349 jurisdictional inquiry with OCSLA's choice of law provision, 43 U.S.C. § 1333, fails because the provisions and the issues they raise are distinct. *See, e.g., Dahlen v. Gulf Crews, Inc.*, 281 F.3d 487, 491-92 (5th Cir. 2002); *Recar*, 853 F.2d at 368-70. Federal courts may have jurisdiction to adjudicate a dispute under OCSLA, but they must then turn to the OCSLA choice of law provision to ascertain whether state, federal, or maritime law applies to a particular case. (Choice of law will be addressed in the next section of this opinion.) Any contrary implication in *Golden v. Omni Energy Servs. Corp.*, 242 Fed. App'x 965, 967 (5th Cir. 2007), is not precedential because the case was unpublished; we reference *Golden* here only because the Parishes erroneously relied on it.[5] Second, the Parishes contend that there is a situs requirement for OCSLA jurisdiction under the language of Section 1349. We disagree. Because federal jurisdiction exists for cases "arising out of, or in connection with" OCS operations, 43 U.S.C. § 1349, the statute precludes an artificial limit based on situs and the Parishes' formulation conflicts with this court's but-for test. *See cases cited supra.* Third, [—7—] the Parishes misapprehend 28 U.S.C. § 1441(b) in urging that diversity of citizenship is necessary to support the removal of an OCSLA claim. The version of Section 1441(b) in effect at the time of the district court's ruling required instead that a federal basis for original jurisdiction exist

---

[5] *Golden* has been criticized and is in any event factually distinguishable from this case, as the injury there originated in the land-based operation of the helicopter. *See, e.g.,* David W. Robertson & Michael F. Sturley, *Recent Developments in Admiralty & Maritime Law at the National Level & in the Fifth & Eleventh Circuits*, 33 Tul. Mar. L.J. 381, 464 (2009).

(OCSLA) and that no defendant be a citizen of the forum state.[6] Because both of those preconditions were met here, removal jurisdiction existed.

II. Choice of Law

The more difficult question in this appeal is whether the Wildlife Statute's penalties can be applied against the Appellees. The Parishes' arguments are easily summarized. Both briefs submitted by the Parishes (authored on behalf of Orleans Parish, et al. and New Iberia Parish, et al.) acknowledge that the mobile offshore drilling unit DEEPWATER HORIZON is a vessel. *Demette v. Falcon Drilling Co.*, 280 F.3d 492, 498-99 (5th Cir. 2002), *overruled in part, on other grounds, by Grand Isle Shipyard, Inc. v. Seacor Marine, LLC*, 589 F.3d 778 (5th Cir. 2009) (en banc); *Offshore Co. v. Robison*, 266 F.2d 769, 776 (5th Cir. 1959). Both briefs assert that, for this reason, the OCSLA choice of law provisions cannot apply to their claims. ("Since, as the District Attorneys have consistently maintained, OCSLA situs is lacking, OCSLA cannot apply.") The Parishes thus foreswear any reliance on 43 U.S.C. § 1333(a)(2)(A), which [—8—] borrows state law as surrogate federal law to regulate certain OCSLA activity.[7] As Orleans Parish

puts it, "[i]t is not the adoption of state law as federal surrogate law that allows for penalties under Title 56, but the fact that the harm to wildlife made subject of the District Attorneys' suit occurred exclusively within Louisiana state waters, and Louisiana has the right to exercise its traditional police power . . . by pursuing penalty claims under Louisiana state law."[8]

While they purport to abjure the application of federal law, however, the Parishes also rely on savings clauses in federal statutes that regulate water pollution (Clean Water Act ("CWA")), 33 U.S.C. § 1321(o),[9] and oil pollution (Oil Pollution Act ("OPA")), 33 U.S.C. § 2718(c), and preserve some state remedies. Of course, if the in-state location of wildlife injury alone suffices to support Louisiana's exercise of its police power, why resort to federal savings clauses?

The Parishes' inconsistent positions reveal a basic flaw. The question here is not whether federal law plays a role in remediating the effects of the Macondo well blowout, but how extensive the role is. The Parishes cannot prove Appellees' responsibility, or respective shares of responsibility, for wildlife injuries without alluding to the blowout's physical source, emissions from a well [—9—] drilled in the OCS, or its human source, errors or omissions related to the DEEPWATER HORIZON'S production activity on the high seas above the OCS. The Parishes' pleadings expressly allege, *inter alia*, that Appellees

---

[6] Section 1441(b) was amended effective only for actions commenced after January 6, 2012. The Parishes' claims commenced prior to that date. The language of Section 1441(b) applicable to the Parishes' claims provides:

> Any civil action of which the district courts have original jurisdiction founded on a claim or right arising under the Constitution, treaties or laws of the United States shall be removeable without regard to the citizenship or residence of the parties. Any other such action shall be removeable only if none of the parties in interest properly joined and served as defendants is a citizen of the State in which such action is brought.

28 U.S.C. § 1441(b).

[7] Of course, the Parishes cannot prevent the application of OCSLA as a litigation choice any more than they could agree to a contract choice of law provision mandating admiralty law in these circumstances. *Alleman v. Omni Energy Servs. Corp.*, 580 F.3d 280, 283 n.2 (5th Cir. 2009)

("parties cannot choose to be governed by maritime law when OCSLA applies").

[8] The crux of the Parishes' argument is this analogy: "If someone commits murder on the navigable waters within the State of Louisiana, admiralty law might apply to any civil claim arising from that death, but Louisiana would undoubtedly be able to prosecute the murder under Louisiana law." It is a bad analogy because it assumes the murder was committed in Louisiana waters, unlike the pollution that simply migrated into state waters. It is also an inapt basis for considering federal preemption, a subject that demands close textual analysis of case law and statutes.

[9] The district court referred to this provision by Section number of the Clean Water Act (§ 311), rather than by the U.S.C. number (§ 1321).

caused the Macondo well oil spill and violated federal regulations in so doing.

Analysis of federal law thus inevitably precedes the Parishes' simplistic *lex loci delicti* theory. Federal law covers the disaster in two ways. First, pursuant to OCSLA, "[a]ll law applicable to the outer Continental Shelf is federal law," and all cases "involving events occurring on the Shelf [are] governed by federal law . . .." *Gulf Offshore Co. v. Mobil Oil Corp.*, 453 U.S. 473, 480-81, 101 S. Ct. 2870, 2876 (1981); *see* 43 U.S.C. § 1333(a)(1) ("The . . . laws . . . of the United States are extended to the subsoil and seabed of the outer Continental Shelf and to all . . . devices permanently or temporarily attached to the seabed . . . [for the purpose of resource exploitation].") Federal law governs injuries arising from activity on an OCSLA situs even if the injury occurs elsewhere. *See Alleman*, 580 F.3d at 286 (OCSLA applies to helicopter accident although victims fell into the sea after the helicopter crashed into an offshore platform). OCSLA allows the borrowing of state law as surrogate federal law only when state law is "not inconsistent with . . . other Federal laws and regulations . . .." 43 U.S.C. § 1333(a)(2)(A). The borrowing provision does not apply here, however, either because, as the district court stated, the disaster is governed by maritime law or because the broader language of Section 1333(a)(1), which extends explicitly to devices temporarily attached to the OCS (as Section 1333(a)(2)(A) does not), clearly controls.[10] In sum, even if the Parishes had not attempted to waive reliance on OCSLA, the federal law articulated by [—10—] OCSLA displaces state law. Further, as the Supreme Court has ruled, Section 1333(a) "supersede[s] the normal choice-of-law rules that the forum would apply." *Gulf Offshore*, 453 U.S. at 482 n.8, 101 S. Ct. at 2877 n.8.

---

[10] This Court's "*PLT* test," which we have used to determine when state law may apply to an OCSLA activity, is a misfit for the present case. *See Union Tex. Petroleum Corp. v. PLT Eng'g, Inc.*, 895 F.2d 1043, 1047 (5th Cir. 1990). *PLT* may suit cases under Section 1331(a)(2), but it is hard to square with Section 1333(a)(1), where state law has no role.

Alternatively, maritime law applies here because the DEEPWATER HORIZON is a vessel. A strong argument exists for the proposition that the disaster occurred while the vessel was engaged in the maritime activity of conducting offshore drilling operations, and the disaster had a significant effect on maritime commerce. *Cf. Jerome B. Grubart, Inc. v. Great Lakes Dredge & Dock Co.*, 513 U.S. 527 *passim*, 115 S. Ct. 1043 *passim* (1995) (maritime law applies to damages where drill barge flooded underwater tunnel and buildings on river bank); *Theriot v. Bay Drilling Corp.*, 783 F.2d 527, 538-39 (5th Cir. 1986).

OSCLA Section 1333(a)(1) and admiralty law constitute alternative, not overlapping, regimes of federal law. *See Rodrigue v. Aetna Cas. & Sur. Co.*, 395 U.S. 352, 361, 89 S. Ct. 1835, 1840 (1969); *Texaco Exploration & Prod., Inc. v. AmClyde Engineered Prods. Co.*, 448 F.3d 760, 772-73 (5th Cir. 2006). For present purposes, however, the exact dichotomy is irrelevant as either regime includes the federal statutes regulating water pollution and oil pollution, to which we now turn.

A. General Principles

The Federal Water Pollution Control Act (*aka* Clean Water Act, "CWA"), 33 U.S.C. §1251-1376, and its implementing regulations comprehensively govern oil exploration and development on the OCS, including BP's conduct of the Macondo well operations pursuant to National Pollutant Discharge Elimination System ("NPDES") Permit No. GMG290000. *Gulf Restoration Network v. Salazar*, 683 F.3d 158, 164-66 (5th Cir. 2012). Under the regulations, states like Louisiana that might be affected by offshore pollutant discharges may offer comments before permits are issued, but they have no other [—11—] express regulatory role. *Id.* at 165. Nevertheless, the Parishes assert the right to pursue state law penalties against the Appellees for pollution that migrated from nearly fifty miles offshore. We will examine their arguments in detail but first explain further the pertinent background law.

Put in starkest terms, had the blowout occurred in Texas state waters and caused pollution in Louisiana, the Parishes' Louisiana law claims would be squarely foreclosed. Federal preemption of interstate water pollution claims has been a feature of United States law for over a hundred years. *See, e.g., Missouri v. Illinois*, 200 U.S. 496, 26 S. Ct. 268 (1906). Since 1987, the issue has been settled by the Supreme Court's decision in *International Paper Co. v. Ouellette*, 479 U.S. 481, 107 S. Ct. 805 (1987). In *Ouellette*, the Court resolved conflicting circuit court decisions on the question whether a state could enforce its laws against pollution that migrated into its environment from a neighboring state. *Compare Illinois v. City of Milwaukee*, 731 F.2d 403, 410-11 (7th Cir. 1984), *with Ouellette v. Int'l Paper Co.*, 776 F.2d 55, 55-56 (2d Cir. 1985). The Court explained that federal common law had, until 1971, governed "the use and misuse of interstate waters," and the Court reaffirmed the preemption of state law by federal common law articulated in *Illinois v. City of Milwaukee (Milwaukee I)*, 406 U.S. 91, 92 S. Ct. 1385 (1972). *Ouellette*, 479 U.S. at 487, 107 S. Ct. at 809. The Court described how the enactment of the federal CWA displaced federal common law with a complex scheme of cooperative federalism, delegating to states the authority to issue NPDES effluent discharge permits to point sources within their borders while retaining primary federal responsibility to eliminate water pollution. *Ouellette*, 479 U.S. at 488-91, 107 S. Ct. at 809-11. The Court then applied the standards of conflict preemption, concluding that the "CWA precludes a court from applying the law of an affected State against an out-of-state source." 479 U.S. at 494, 107 S. Ct. at 813. The Court stated: [—12—]

> After examining the CWA as a whole, its purposes and its history, we are convinced that if affected States were allowed to impose separate discharge standards on a single point source, the inevitable result would be a serious interference with the achievement of the "full purposes and objectives of Congress."

479 U.S. at 493, 107 S. Ct. at 812 (citation omitted).

Among its reasons, the Court noted that factors such as the impact of discharges on a waterway, the types of effluents, and the schedule for compliance may vary widely among sources. Point source states may require stricter controls than the federal government. Complex policy, scientific, and technological decisions are required. Lawsuits based on affected states' common law of nuisance would upset this "balance of public and private interests." 479 U.S. at 494, 107 S. Ct. at 813. Such suits could "effectively override both the permit requirements and the policy choices made by the source State." 479 U.S. at 495, 107 S. Ct. at 813. The efficiency and predictability of the permit system would be undermined, to the disadvantage of private regulated entities. Chaotic confrontations among states could erupt over conflicting standards imposed on a single point source. In sum,

> It would be extraordinary for Congress, after devising an elaborate permit system that sets clear standards, to tolerate common-law suits that have the potential to undermine this regulatory structure.

479 U.S. at 497, 107 S. Ct. at 814.

Notably, *Ouellette* also confronted and rejected the contention that two provisions of the CWA, which preserved a State's right to regulate its waters and an injured party's right to seek relief under "any statute or common law," authorized the nuisance suit under the affected state's law rather than that of the point source state. According to the Court, neither savings clause, carefully read, would stand for so broad a proposition. 479 U.S. at 492-93, 107 S. Ct. at 812. The citizen suit savings clause was preceded by the qualifier, [—13—] "[n]othing in this section," while the states' authority was saved for regulation only of their own waters. *Id.*

Ouellette's interpretation of preemption under the CWA has not been superseded by any later Supreme Court decision nor, as we shall see, by statute. Indeed, its principles were affirmed by the Court in *Arkansas v. Oklahoma*, 503 U.S. 91, 100, 112 S. Ct. 1046, 1053-54 (1992).

Because the CWA was inadequate to provide complete remedies for the Valdez, Alaska oil spill catastrophe, Congress passed the Oil Pollution Act ("OPA") in 1990. 33 U.S.C. §§ 2701-62. Congress intended that the OPA would "build[] upon section 311 of the Clean Water Act [§ 1321] to create a single Federal law providing cleanup authority, penalties, and liability for oil pollution." S. Rep. No. 101-94, at 9 (1989), *reprinted in* 1990 U.S.C.C.A.N. 722, 730. The OPA prescribes a supplemental, comprehensive federal plan for handling oil spill responses, allocating responsibility among participants and prescribing reimbursement for cleanup costs and injuries to third parties. The remedial efforts for the Macondo well blowout occurred under the auspices of both the CWA, 33 U.S.C. § 1321(b)(1) (the CWA applies to oil discharges in connection with activities above the OCS), and the OPA, 33 U.S.C. § 2701(32)(C) (extending the OPA to offshore facilities above the OCS).

Both the CWA and the OPA contain provisions that save state law causes of action, including penalty claims, under certain circumstances. The CWA clause involved in this case is 33 U.S.C. § 1321(o), which states in pertinent part:

> (o) Obligation for damages unaffected, local authority not preempted; existing Federal authority not modified or affected
>
> (1) Nothing in this section shall affect or modify in any way the obligations of any owner or operator . . . or offshore facility to any person or agency under any provision of law for damages to any publicly owned [—14—] or privately owned property resulting from a discharge of any oil or hazardous substance . . ..

> (2) Nothing in this section shall be construed as preempting any State or political subdivision thereof from imposing any requirement or liability with respect to the discharge of oil or hazardous substance *into any waters within such State*, or with respect to any removal activities related to such discharge.

> (3) Nothing in this section shall be construed . . . to affect any State or local law not in conflict with this section.

(Emphasis added).

The OPA's provision is differently worded:

> Section 2718(a). Relationship to Other Law
>
> (a) Preservation of State authorities; Solid Waste Disposal Act
>
> Nothing in this Act . . . shall–
>
> (1) affect, or be construed or interpreted as preempting, the authority of any State or political subdivision thereof from imposing any additional liability or requirements with respect to—
>
> > (A) the discharge of oil or other pollution by oil *within such State*; or
> > (B) any removal activities in connection with such a discharge; or
>
> (2) affect, or be construed or interpreted to affect or modify in any way the obligations or liabilities of any person under . . . State law, including common law.
>
> . . . .
>
> (c) Additional requirements and liabilities; penalties [—15—]

Nothing in this Act . . . shall in any way affect, or be construed to affect, the authority of the United States or . . . any State or political subdivision thereof–

(1) to impose additional liability or additional requirements; or
(2) to impose, or to determine the amount of, any fine or penalty (whether criminal or civil in nature) for any violation of law;

relating to the discharge . . . of oil.

33 U.S.C. § 2718(a), (c) (emphasis added).

B. Application of General Principles

The Parishes make two basic arguments. First, they assert that their historic police powers to deter oil pollution in their waters and protect their aquatic life and wildlife are preserved notwithstanding the application of federal law. Second, they assert that both above-cited federal savings clauses expressly protect their ability to levy Wildlife Statute fines. Each argument must be carefully considered.

1. Does *Ouellette* control?

The Parishes' first proposition depends on whether the states maintained historic police powers to apply their local law to interstate water pollution even if the pollution originated outside the state. The Supreme Court's discussion of the issue in *Milwaukee I* contradicts the Parishes' position. 406 U.S. at 105-06, 92 S. Ct. at 1393-94. A federal common law of nuisance, not the competing laws of each affected jurisdiction, was applied to interstate water pollution cases from an early period. 406 U.S. at 106-07, 92 S. Ct. at 1394-95. This is not to say the states were deprived of rights and remedies in such cases, but only that they had to rely on the common body of federal law to do so. The claim by the states (and [—16—] their localities) to apply their historic police power in these situations is therefore dubious.

Even assuming the Parishes have some residual police power to apply local law to this

OCSLA-originated discharge, however, they must overcome federal preemption under the CWA. As the Supreme Court predicted in *Milwaukee I*, 406 U.S. at 107, 92 S. Ct. at 1395, Congress could and did supplant federal common law with an overarching regulatory framework to protect the nation's waters. To effectuate the full purposes of the regulations, *Ouellette* held that the states' ability to apply local law to out-of-state point sources of alleged water pollution was in conflict with the CWA. 479 U.S. at 494, 107 S. Ct. at 812-13.

The Parishes contend that *Ouellette* is distinguishable. First, it applies only to the CWA's permitting provision (33 U.S.C. §1342), not to the oildischarge prohibition (33 U.S.C. §1321(o)). Relatedly, the savings provisions that *Ouellette* found inapposite are different from the provisions the Parishes rely on. Second, since *Ouellette* considered only interstate water pollution, the decision has no bearing on discharges from the OCS. We find these distinctions unpersuasive.

The Supreme Court's subsequent interpretation of *Oullette* substantially undermines any cramped reading of the case. The Court reiterated *Ouellette*'s holding that "the Clean Water Act taken 'as a whole, its purposes and its history' pre-empted an action based on the law of the affected State and that the *only* state law applicable to an interstate discharge is 'the law of the State in which the point source is located.'" *Arkansas*, 503 U.S. at 100, 112 S. Ct. at 1053 (citing *Ouellette*, 479 U.S. at 493, 487, 107 S. Ct. at 812, 809) (emphasis added). This statement is not limited to the specific provisions of the CWA at issue in *Ouellette*; in fact, *Arkansas* refers to "interstate discharge" irrespective of type or permit status. The Fourth Circuit confirmed *Ouellette*'s reach by applying it to an interstate pollution dispute arising under the Clean Air Act. *North [—17—] Carolina ex rel. Cooper v. Tenn. Valley Auth.*, 615 F.3d 291, 306-07 (4th Cir. 2010). That court concluded, "[t]here is no question that the law of the states where emissions sources are located . . . applies in an interstate nuisance suit. The Supreme Court's decision in *Ouellette* is explicit: a 'court must apply the law of the

State in which the point source is located.'" *Id.* at 306 (citation omitted).

Hoping to confine *Ouellette* to NPDES permitting cases and the specific savings provisions the Court considered, the Parishes contend that the Court's goal in *Ouellette* was to prevent disruption of the point-source effluent permitting system by redundant or conflicting state legal regimes. 33 U.S.C. §1342. On the other hand, they contend, because the CWA essentially prohibits "discharges" of "oil or hazardous substances" into the nation's navigable waters and the waters of the OCS, 33 U.S.C. 1321(b), allowing all affected states to impose their laws on the illegal activity creates not conflict, but reinforcement of federal law.

The Court's opinion, however, resists such limitation. In the paragraph that introduces the Court's reasoning, *Ouellette* speaks plainly: "We hold that when a court considers a State-law claim concerning interstate water pollution that is subject to the CWA, the court must apply the law of the state in which the point source is located." 479 U.S. at 487, 107 S. Ct. at 809. There is no mincing about the precise preemptive provisions of the federal CWA. Later, the Court responds to the plaintiffs' allegations that the point source violated the terms of its NPDES permit by noting the availability of a citizen suit under the CWA in lieu of the law of the affected state. 479 U.S. at 498 n.18, 107 S. Ct. at 814 n. 18. A permit violation constitutes a "discharge" prohibited by Section 1321(b). 33 U.S.C. § 1321(a)(definition of "discharge"), (b)(3). The Court's logic must extend to oil discharges, which are illegal under the same provision. With respect to oil pollution originating from the OCS, *Ouellette* offers an analogous [—18—] answer: the affected parties can sue for the generous remedies, including for loss of wildlife, that the OPA offers. OPA, 33 U.S.C. § 2702(b)(2)(D).

A weaker argument against *Ouellette* urges that it quelled disputes over the application of competing state laws to interstate water pollution but has no impact on the overlay of state laws on a federally controlled point source. On the contrary, the federal

responsibility for the OCS is clear. The Macondo well site was developed under a plethora of federal regulations, including an NPDES permit. *See generally Gulf Restoration Network*, 683 F.3d at 165-66. The federal government's interest is no different from that of point-source states, which aim to encourage economic development while preserving optimal environmental conditions for their citizens. Allowing up to five states along the Gulf Coast to apply their individual laws to discharges arising on the Shelf would foster the legal chaos described by *Ouellette*. That three Gulf coast states submitted amicus briefs in this appeal, and all five Gulf Coast states filed suits[11] to recover damages based on particular state laws testifies to the problem. Moreover, just as with entities operating in point-source states, if entities engaged in developing the OCS were subjected to a multiplicity of state laws in addition to federal regulations, they could be forced to adopt entirely different operational plans or in the worst case be deterred by the redundancy and lack of regulatory clarity from even pursuing their OCS plans. The reasons for avoiding redundant or conflicting legal regimes are equally potent whether the point source is located in a state or a federal enclave.

In sum, *Ouellette* forms a controlling backdrop for resolving claims caused by the blowout. Federal law, the law of the point source, exclusively applies to the claims generated by the oil spill in any affected state or locality. [—19—]

2. Effect of Savings Clauses

With *Ouellette* as the controlling law, there are no state remedies to "save." The OPA applies as the law of the OCSLA point source and, along with the CWA penalties, furnishes a comprehensive remedial regime for affected states' governmental and private claims. Just because the Parishes are located in the most closely adjacent state, they fare no better than the "down-current" states of Texas,

---

[11] The Local Government Entity Master Complaint alleges breach of tort duties under the laws of Florida, Alabama, Mississippi, Louisiana, and Texas.

Mississippi, Alabama, and Florida. The CWA and the OPA "savings" clauses preserve but do not create state law claims. *Knickerbocker Ice Co. v. Stewart*, 253 U.S. 149, 162, 40 S. Ct. 438, 441 (1920); *Offshore Logistics, Inc. v. Tallentire*, 477 U.S. 207, 224-25, 106 S. Ct. 2485, 2495 (1986) (Death on the High Seas Act savings clause only preserves state courts' jurisdiction to provide remedies for fatalities in state waters).[12]

Nevertheless, for additional reasons, each savings clause is powerless to "save" the Parishes' claims under the Wildlife Statute. In general, the savings clauses must be read with particularity and, as *Ouellette* demonstrates, a savings clause does not disrupt the ordinary operation of conflict preemption. *See Ouellette*, 479 U.S. at 492-93, 107 S. Ct. at 812 (rejecting application of two savings provisions of the CWA); *Geier v. Am. Honda Motor Co.*, 529 U.S. 861, 869, 120 S. Ct. 1913, 1919 (2000).

a. CWA § 1321(o)

Most closely on point in the CWA is Section 1321(o)(2), which provides that, "[n]othing in this Section shall [preempt any state or local] requirement or liability with respect to the discharge of oil . . . into any waters within such state . . . ." The provision only saves state laws imposing liability or additional requirements with respect to the "discharge" of oil "into any waters within such [—20—] State." The provision does not save a state's laws where the discharge did not occur "within" the state. The Parishes contend that the term "discharge" should be read to include "any means by which oil enters state waters." According to the statute, however, "discharge" "includes, but is not limited to, any spilling, leaking, pumping, pouring, emitting, emptying or dumping . . . ." 33 U.S.C. § 1321(a)(2). These gerunds connote active conduct or movement from a point source to a place within the state rather than the mere passive migration or floating of oil into state waters. Contrary to the Parishes' view, the word "emitting" does not change this analysis. "Emit" means to send out or release. *Webster's Third New International Dictionary* 742 (3d ed. 1986). The principle of *noscitur a sociis*, that words grouped in a list should be given related meaning, reinforces our interpretation because, taken in context with the other gerunds, "emitting" must take on an active cast. *See Third Nat'l Bank in Nashville v. Impac Ltd., Inc.*, 432 U.S. 312, 322-23, 97 S. Ct. 2307, 2313-14 (1977).[13]

The other subsections of Section 1321(o) afford no benefit to the Parishes. Section 1321(o)(1) expressly saves damage claims, not penalties under the Wildlife Statute. Section 1321(o)(3), a catch-all provision, saves state laws *not in conflict* with the section itself. To construe the catch-all harmoniously with Section 1321(o)(2), which is limited to discharges within state waters, and avoid rendering the companion provision superfluous, the catch-all must be similarly limited.

b. Section 2718(c)

The Parishes place the most emphasis on this savings clause from the OPA. The section states that "[n]othing in this Act [OPA] . . . shall in any way [—21—] affect . . . the authority of the United States or any State [or locality] . . . to impose . . . any fine or penalty . . ." relating to an oil discharge. 33 U.S.C. §2718(c). First, they assert, the OPA was enacted to supplement the older CWA apparatus for redressing the consequences of oil pollution. Second, the Parishes urge that the OPA, being specific with regard to oil pollution, controls over the more general requirements of the CWA, which applies to both illegal oil and hazardous substance discharges into navigable waters. Third, the exact language of Section 2718(c) differs critically from the CWA's Section 1321(o) because it lacks the narrowing reference to state waters. Finally, a construction of

---

[12] We reject the assertion in Alabama's amicus brief that "effects jurisdiction" or the "objective territorial principle," theories associated only with international law, apply to the federal preemption issues here.

[13] *Askew v. Am. Waterways Operators, Inc.*, 411 U.S. 325, 93 S. Ct. 1590 (1973), does not support the Parishes' interpretation of Section 1321 as preserving state law regulation of oil pollution that originated outside state waters. The spill in that case occurred adjacent to Florida's shore.

Section 2718(c) that limits its effect to discharges within state waters would allegedly render the OPA savings clause superfluous. Section 2718(c), from their standpoint, preserves "all state penalty provisions 'relating to' oil spills in any way, not just those originating in state waters." On balance, however, we conclude that the Parishes place more weight on this savings provision than it can bear.

To begin, the canon of construction that mandates application of a specific over a general statutory provision is not easily adapted to this statutory scheme. As all parties acknowledge, the CWA, the fountainhead of clean water regulation, contains the provisions that prohibit oil discharges and set penalties for illegal discharges. 33 U.S.C. § 1321(b)(3),(6) ("Administrative penalties"), (7) ("Civil penalty actions"), (f) ("Liability for actual costs of removal"). These provisions led the district court to declare the CWA's savings provision more specific than those in the OPA. The Parishes, in contrast, characterize Section 2718(c) as plainly more specific both because it resides in the OPA and it preserves state penalty actions. We do not, however, perceive the applicability of these provisions to be an either/or proposition. Instead, each requires interpretation within a statutory framework in which the OPA was designed to complement, not compete with the CWA. That the OPA was enacted more [—22—] recently than the CWA means little where there is no fundamental conflict with provisions of the CWA. The statutes, in other words, must be construed, as the district court noted, in *pari materia*.

Moving to the specific language of Section 2718(c), the provision more precisely states, "Nothing in this Act, the Act of March 3, 1851 (46 U.S.C. § 183 *et seq.*), or § 9509 of Title 26, [shall affect] the authority of the United States or any State or political subdivision thereof . . .." Statutory construction begins with the language of the statute, *Hardt v. Reliance Standard Life Ins. Co.*, 560 U.S. 242, 251, 130 S. Ct. 2149, 2156 (2010), and, in the absence of ambiguity, often ends there. Two features of this prefatory language are

notable. The savings provision does not apply beyond the OPA itself and two other laws. Further, Congress did not refer to the CWA. Courts are not at liberty to expand the language chosen by Congress, and the omission here is telling. Thus, while Section 2718(c) saves from the OPA's diminution the ability of the United States or state entities to impose requirements relating to oil discharges, it does not save those powers from the effects of the CWA or any other non-identified federal law. Consistent with this conclusion, the Supreme Court in *Ouellette* held that a savings clause commencing with "nothing in this section" is by its terms limited to preemption caused by that section alone. *See* 479 U.S. at 493, 107 S. Ct. at 812 (such a clause "does not purport to preclude pre-emption of state law by other provisions of the Act"); *see also United States v. Locke*, 529 U.S. 89, 106, 120 S. Ct. 1135, 1146-47 (Section 2718 does not extend to subjects addressed in other Titles of the OPA or other acts).

Other principles of statutory construction are relevant because of the prefatory language here. If Section 2718(c) were interpreted, as the Parishes contend, to "supersede" the CWA and *Ouellette* by allowing all affected states to layer their unique penalty and regulatory laws on top of those governing this OCSLA blowout, the result would be an implied repeal of CWA preemption. [—23—] Implied repeals, however, are disfavored. *Crawford Fitting Co. v. J.T. Gibbons, Inc.*, 482 U.S. 437, 442, 107 S. Ct. 2494, 2497 (1987); *Ysleta del Sur Pueblo v. Texas*, 36 F.3d 1325, 1335 (5th Cir. 1994). Apart from omitting reference to waters within the state, however, there is no indication in Section 2718(c) or the OPA that Congress intended to repeal the point-source primacy ordained by the CWA. That the OPA in fact amended CWA Section 1321(o)(2) to add the phrase "or with respect to any removal activities related to such discharge" without also amending the immediately preceding phrase "into any waters within such State" signals Congressional intent not to modify this portion of the CWA. *See* OPA Sec. 4202, Pub. L. No. 101-380, 104 Stat. 484, 532 (codified as 33 U.S.C. § 1321(o)(2)). Courts cannot, without any textual warrant, expand the operation of Section 2718(c) to, in effect, modify the scope of preemption under the CWA.

It is also possible to understand why Section 2718(c) omits a reference to waters within the affected state. Simply, the provision saves remedies available to the United States as well as the states, rendering a geographic limitation to state waters meaningless. Viewed in light of Congress' presumed awareness of *Ouellette* when the OPA was passed, and Congress' failure to change the scope of CWA preemption despite its intent generally to broaden remedies against oil pollution, this omission cannot be controlling on the scope of this savings provision.

Nor does this construction deprive the savings provision of utility, as the Parishes assert. For any oil pollution whose point source is on the land or navigable waters within a state, Section 2718(c) authorizes the point source state and its political subdivisions to impose any additional liability, requirements, fines, and penalties. Preemption is limited to situations in which [—24—] the affected state is not the point source jurisdiction; affected states may still pursue relief based on the OPA and the CWA or the law of the point-source.[14]

Finally, we note that this interpretation does not diminish the incentives for compliance with the CWA or the OPA or the point source states' additional laws concerning oil pollution. The federal laws' extravagant penalties, fines, criminal liability, and damage exposure that may be imposed on entities associated with oil pollution, even in the absence of the layering of multiple affected states' laws, evidence a clear congressional policy of deterrence and retribution.[15]

CONCLUSION

For the reasons stated above, the district court had removal jurisdiction over the Parishes' Wildlife Statute claims. Further, it correctly concluded that the claims are preempted by the CWA as interpreted in *Ouellette*, and that Congress did not reject that interpretation explicitly or by negative implication in the CWA or when it passed the OPA. The judgment of the court dismissing the Parishes' claims is **AFFIRMED**.

---

[14] The argument is also briefly made that the Parishes' Wildlife Statute claims are preserved by Section 2718(a)(1)(A), which allows any state or political subdivision thereof to impose additional liability or requirements with respect to "the discharge of oil or other pollution by oil within such State . . .." The Parishes would limit "within such State" to modifying "pollution by oil." This does not wash grammatically; the geographic limitation applies to both means of pollution.

[15] From this discussion, it is clear that we reject a Tenth Amendment argument on behalf of the Parishes and need not reach Appellees' contention that the OPA's proscription of certain duplicative damages preempts the Wildlife Statute claims.

United States Court of Appeals
for the Fifth Circuit

No. 13-30315

IN RE DEEPWATER HORIZON

LAKE EUGENIE LAND & DEV., INC.
vs.
BP EXPLORATION & PROD., INC.

Appeals from the United States District Court for the
Eastern District of Louisiana

Decided: March 3, 2014

Citation: 744 F.3d 370, 2 Adm. R. 183 (5th Cir. 2014).

Before **DENNIS, CLEMENT,** and **SOUTHWICK,** Circuit Judges.

[—4—] SOUTHWICK, Circuit Judge:

This appeal concerns issues arising under a Settlement Agreement approved by the district court in December 2012. Relevant to us today is that the settlement provided a mechanism for presenting and processing claims for business losses caused by the April 2010 *Deepwater Horizon* disaster in the Gulf of Mexico. The district court made two rulings as directed by our October 2013 remand. One concerned an accounting question, which was resolved in a sufficiently satisfactory manner as not to be appealed by any party. The other ruling was that the Settlement Agreement did not require those submitting claims for certain business losses to provide evidence of causation. BP Exploration and Production, Inc. appeals that ruling and also argues that an injunction is required to stop payments on such claims. We AFFIRM.

FACTUAL AND PROCEDURAL BACKGROUND

This appeal was originally briefed in May and June of 2013 and orally argued in July. BP's argument at that time concerned contract interpretation. Its appeal was from an order of the district court entered on March 5, 2013. [—5—] That order affirmed a Policy Statement issued by the claims administrator on January 15, 2013. BP asserted that the district court and claims administrator's interpretations of Exhibit 4C of the Settlement Agreement were erroneous because they did not require matching of revenues and expenses in claims processing. On October 2, 2013, this panel, writing three separate opinions, remanded with guidance to the district court for reconsidering the necessity of matching revenues and expenses when processing Business and Economic Loss ("BEL") claims. *See In re Deepwater Horizon*, 732 F.3d 326, 332-39, 1 Adm. R. 287, 289–96 (5th Cir. 2013) ("*Deepwater Horizon I*").

Additionally, in a part of the opinion for the court that no other panel member joined, Judge Clement wrote on a separate but related issue. She determined that if the Settlement Agreement's causation evidentiary framework was interpreted not to require proof of a nexus between the *Deepwater Horizon* disaster and a claimant's damages, the Settlement Agreement would violate Article III, Federal Rule of Civil Procedure 23, and the Rules Enabling Act. *Id.* at 342-43, 1 Adm. R. at 298–300. Because that issue had not been briefed or argued, Judge Southwick wrote that it was inappropriate to resolve it. *Id.* at 346, 1 Adm. R. at 302 (Southwick, J. concurring). Nonetheless, he called the analysis "logical" and joined in requiring the district court to consider, on remand, the relevance of causation to the extent the parties argued the point. *Id.*, 1 Adm. R. at 302.

On remand, the district court, in three different orders spread over several weeks, indicated that it did not believe this court had required an evaluation of the causation issue. On December 2, 2013, we clarified that Judges Clement and Southwick had agreed in their separate October opinions that, if raised, the district court must consider the Article III and other causation arguments on remand. We acknowledged that our issuance of multiple "opinions may have created interpretive difficulties on the remand, [—6—] but the district court erred by not considering the arguments on causation." Yet again today, we each express ourselves individually. Two of us do at least say in tandem, clearly we trust, "affirm."

On December 24, the district court held that the Settlement Agreement requires matching of revenues and expenses. The court directed the claims administrator to implement that interpretation. As of that ruling, the entirety of BP's initial argument, namely, that the initial interpretations of Exhibit 4C were incorrect, was successful. Also at that point, though, the district court rejected BP's arguments with respect to the new issue of whether Article III, Rule 23, and the Rules Enabling Act permitted the parties to agree to a settlement that dealt with causation in this manner. To answer that second question, the district court analyzed the terms of the Settlement Agreement and an October 10, 2012, Policy Statement by the claims administrator to which BP had not objected. The district court concluded that the language of the Settlement Agreement did not require extrinsic inquiry into causation and that the Settlement Agreement had not violated Article III, Rule 23, or the Rules Enabling Act by eschewing the need for evidence of causation.

BP renewed its emergency motion for an injunction with this court on December 30, challenging only the district court's rejection of its causation arguments. No party appealed the district court's instruction to the claims administrator to implement the district court's interpretation of the Settlement Agreement with respect to matching.

While this panel has been addressing questions arising out of the claims administrator's interpretation of the Settlement Agreement, another panel considered the chronologically earlier question of the validity of the certification of the class by the district court on December 21, 2012, and the approval of the Settlement Agreement. In a January 10, 2014, decision, what [—7—] we will refer to as the "certification panel" determined the class certification and settlement approval did not contravene Article III, Rule 23, or the Rules Enabling Act. *See In re Deepwater Horizon*, 739 F.3d 790, 795, 2 Adm. R. 140, 140 (5th Cir. 2014) (*Deepwater Horizon II*).

The certification panel declined to analyze issues arising from the interpretation and implementation of the settlement after its approval by the district court, but the panel held that all Article III, Rule 23, and Rules Enabling Act concerns were resolved at the class certification and settlement approval stage. *Id.* at 804. We directed letter briefing on the impact of that decision on the remaining issues before this panel for resolution. We now consider the issues that we conclude remain before us.

DISCUSSION

Contract interpretation is a question of law we review *de novo*. *Waterfowl L.L.C. v. United States*, 473 F.3d 135, 141 (5th Cir. 2006). BP argues that the district court erred in concluding that the Settlement Agreement's causation framework did not violate Article III, Federal Rule of Civil Procedure 23, and the Rules Enabling Act. Only part of this issue was resolved on January 10 by the certification panel when it concluded that the certification of a class and the approval of the Settlement Agreement were proper. What this panel now must decide is whether the implementation of the Settlement Agreement is defective.

BP contends that Section 1.3.1.2 of the class definition and footnote 1 of Exhibit 4B establish a requirement that claimants prove with evidence that they are proper class members. Section 1.3.1.2 states: "Economic Damage Category. Loss of income, earnings or profits suffered by Natural Persons or Entities as a result of the **DEEPWATER HORIZON INCIDENT**." Footnote [—8—] 1 of Exhibit 4B states: "This Causation Requirements for Business Economic Loss Claims does not apply to . . . Entities, Individuals, or Claims not included within the Economic Class definition." We will discuss the referenced footnote later.

The class definition was relied upon by the certification panel when it concluded that the Settlement Agreement complied with Article III:

Under the plain terms of the Class Definition, a "person or entity" is included "in the Economic Class only if their Claims meet the descriptions of one or more of the Damage Categories described" in Section 1.3.1 of the Class Definition. Of these "Damage Categories," the only category that BP has identified as giving rise to Article III difficulties is the "Economic Damage Category" under Section 1.3.1.2. This section of the Settlement Agreement, however, explicitly limits claims to those based on "[l]oss of income, earnings or profits suffered by Natural Persons or Entities as a result of the DEEPWATER HORIZON INCIDENT," subject to exclusions for participants in certain industries. As contemplated by the Class Definition, therefore, the class contains only persons and entities that possess Article III standing.

Deepwater Horizon II, 739 F.3d at 803, 2 Adm. R. at 147 (footnotes omitted). The panel also determined that the class definition and the amended complaint satisfied the requirements of Rule 23 and the Rules Enabling Act. *Id.* at 804 & n.53, 2 Adm. R. at 148 & n. 53.

The Settlement Agreement was approved in the same December 2012 district court order that certified the class. The certification panel's opinion notes that the terms of this settlement substitute for at least some of the contested factual development that occurs in cases that do not have simultaneous certification and settlement. *Id.* at 806-08, 2 Adm. R. at 149–51. Despite the settlement, the individual claims still had to be processed. Thus, we now examine the methodology for presenting and processing those claims, as written in the Settlement Agreement and as interpreted by the claims administrator in the October 10, 2012, Policy Statement. [—9—]

Causation for BEL claims is primarily addressed in Exhibit 4B to the Settlement Agreement. It provides for the use of proof of loss as a substitute for proof of causation. Exhibit 4B exempts claimants located within certain geographic regions and in certain industries from presenting any evidence of causation. That exemption appears in a section under the heading "Business Claimants for Which There is No Causation Requirement." It continues: "If you are a business in [geographic] Zone A, you are not required to provide any evidence of causation unless you fall into one of the exceptions agreed to by the parties, and listed in footnote (1)." Claimants not within the exempt criteria must only meet one of a set of quantitative tests based on their revenue patterns during the pre- and post- *Deepwater Horizon* disaster periods.

BP seeks to override the explicit language disclaiming the need for evidence of causation by focusing on this footnote that appears in Exhibit 4B: "This Causation Requirements for Business Economic Loss Claims does not apply to . . . Entities, Individuals, or Claims not included within the Economic Class definition." Wielding this footnote, BP seeks to dismantle the complex framework of exemptions, presumptions, and formulas that allow business claimants to submit evidence of their income and expenses before and after the BP-caused disaster. BP, in essence, is arguing that only if a claimant can prove its injuries are traceable to BP's conduct will Exhibit 4B's forswearing of the need for proof of traceability to BP's conduct apply. There likely is a more nuanced manner in which BP would characterize its argument, but this fairly captures its essence. We reject the argument, of course.

We acknowledge, though, that BP is pointing out a possible inconsistency between what the certification panel says it found to satisfy Article III—namely, a requirement that class members be able to trace their claims to the defendant's conduct—and the way the Settlement Agreement is written and [—10—] has been implemented. In effect, BP argues that Exhibit 4B cannot be interpreted to exclude a requirement of causation because the certification panel held that requirement to be a feature of the class definition. BP argues, then, that even if the class were properly certified under Article III based upon this definition, a settlement that abandons such a requirement, or at least a settlement later interpreted and implemented as not including such a requirement, was simultaneously approved. This, according to BP, reanimates Article III, Rule 23, and Rules Enabling Act issues put to rest by the certification panel. We disagree with the premise of abandonment and therefore we never reach the applicability of these fundamental issues to the questions that remain before us.[1] Neither the Settlement Agreement's terms nor its implementation ignore causation. Instead, the parties explicitly contracted that traceability between the defendant's conduct and a claimant's injury would be satisfied at the proof stage, that is, in the submission of a claim, by a certification on the document that the claimant was injured by the *Deepwater Horizon* disaster. We explain.

The parties agreed to a form that BEL claimants would submit to make a claim. The introductory section of the form states: "The **Business Economic Loss Claim** is for businesses . . . that assert economic loss *due to the spill.*" (Italics added). The end of the form requires the claimant "certify and declare under penalty of perjury" that all of the information in the claim form is "true and accurate to the best of my knowledge." The claimant further attests "I understand that false statements or claims made in connection with this Claim Form may result in fines, imprisonment, and/or any other remedy [—11—] available by law . . . and that suspicious claims will be forwarded . . . for possible investigation and prosecution." Every claim BP argues suffers from some causal-nexus infirmity should have with it an attestation from the claimant or an attorney that the economic loss was caused by the spill.

In light of our reading of the Settlement Agreement, claim form, letter briefing, and the voluminous record in this appeal, we conclude the Settlement Agreement does not

require a claimant to submit *evidence* that the claim arose as a result of the oil spill. Each claimant does attest, though, under penalty of perjury, that the claim in fact was due to the *Deepwater Horizon* disaster. The attestation, of course, applies to all assertions on the claims form, including the financial figures and other details. Suspicious forms would be subject to investigation. These requirements are not as protective of BP's present concerns as might have been achievable, but they are the protections that were accepted by the parties and approved by the district court. It was a contractual concession by BP to limit the issue of factual causation in the processing of claims. Causation, or in Rule 23 terms, traceability, was not abandoned but it was certainly subordinated.

There is nothing fundamentally unreasonable about what BP accepted but now wishes it had not.[2] One event during negotiations in the fall of 2012 suggests reasons for just requiring a certification. The claims administrator, in working through how the proposed claims processing would apply in specific situations, submitted a hypothetical to BP and others. It posited three accountants being partners in a small firm located in a relevant geographic region. One of the three partners takes medical leave in the period immediately following the disaster, thus reducing profits in that period [—12—] because that partner is not performing services for the firm. At least some of the firm's loss, then, would have resulted from the absence of the partner during his medical leave. BP responded that such a claim should be paid. We raise this not for the purpose of analyzing an issue we conclude is not relevant to our decision, namely, whether BP is estopped from its current arguments. Instead, we mention it in order to identify the practical problem mass processing of claims such as these presents, a problem that supports the logic of the terms of the Settlement Agreement. These are business loss claims. Why businesses fail or, why one year is less or more profitable than another, are questions

---

[1] We observe that the difficulties that BP points out as to causation are outgrowths of the definition of the class and the terms of the Settlement Agreement that were sustained by the Certification panel. We do not perceive any basis for saying Article III, Rule 23, and the Rules Enabling Act are violated at the claims processing stage that has not already been addressed by the prior panel.

[2] Though the approach may have been reasonable, that fact does not make it legally valid. As we have already held, though, the Certification panel precedentially resolved validity.

often rigorously analyzed by highly-paid consultants, who may still reach mistaken conclusions. There may be multiple causes for a loss. As with the hypothetical accountants, all of the loss may be attributable to the missing partner, or some of the loss may be traceable to the *Deepwater Horizon* disaster. The difficulties of a claimant's providing evidentiary support and the claims administrator's investigating the existence and degree of nexus between the loss and the disaster in the Gulf could be overwhelming. The inherent limitations in mass claims processing may have suggested substituting certification for evidence, just as proof of loss substituted for proof of causation. Because the Settlement Agreement at least requires a formal assertion of the causal nexus, we conclude that what the certification panel relied upon in approving the class definition and Settlement Agreement remained in place during the processing of claims.

The dissent concludes we require too little as to causation. We see the extent of our colleague's disagreement to be as follows. All of us accept that the class definition and Settlement Agreement require that membership in the class be based on harm from BP's conduct, as the Certification Panel previously held. We also agree that the provision in Exhibit 4B that disclaims the need [—13—] for evidence of causation is at least generally applicable. We part analytical ways when identifying the role of the claims administrator regarding suspicious or implausible claims. The dissent would require the claims administrator to "ensure that claims are not paid that are not plausibly traceable to the spill," thus placing the onus on the claims administrator to ensure that implausible claims are adequately scrutinized such that those lacking a causal nexus are rejected.

We do not agree that we should order the claims administrator to perform that gatekeeping function. There is no language in the Settlement Agreement nor in BP's briefing, supplemental submissions, or emergency motions, about a procedure to be followed when an attestation of a nexus seems at odds with the specifics of the claim. Far

from proposing a specific procedure or even guidelines for crafting one, the entirety of BP's requested relief, exemplified in its Renewed Motion for Injunction, is "a permanent injunction barring the [claims administrator] from issuing or paying awards to claimants whose alleged injuries are not traceable to the spill." BP identifies its desired relief but does not identify a part of the Settlement Agreement that in any way suggests that each submitted claim would be examined as to whether it satisfies a traceability requirement.

Relevant to this concern is that BP did not object in this appeal to a decision made in October 2012 that the claims administrator was not to look at potential alternative causes for claimants' losses. Though we are reluctant to say that all claims must be accepted no matter how clear the absence of the required nexus may be, no one has concerned itself in this appeal with the when, by whom, and how of analyzing such suspicious claims after they are submitted. It seems to us that absent any specific provision in the Settlement Agreement, and no one suggests there is one, such concerns are to be addressed [—14—] in the usual course of processing individual claims. The Settlement Agreement contained many compromises. One of them was to provide in only a limited way for connecting the claim to the cause. The claims administrator, parties, and district court can resolve real examples of implausible claims as they resolve other questions that arise in the handling of specific claims.

We affirm the district court's December 24, 2013, order interpreting the Settlement Agreement. An injunction has been in place preventing payment of BEL claims pending the resolution of all of these issues. Between the certification panel's decision of January 10 and ours today, all issues presented to this panel have been resolved. On the other hand, petitions for rehearing *en banc* of the certification panel's decision on which we have relied have been filed. We can anticipate that our decision might not persuade all parties either. We conclude that the injunction should be dissolved, but the injunction remains in place until the mandate of the court is issued.

The December 24, 2013, ruling of the district court is AFFIRMED. The injunction prohibiting payment of the relevant claims is VACATED.

(Reporter's Note: Concurring opinion follows on p. 189).

[—15—] DENNIS, Circuit Judge, concurring in part and concurring in the judgment:

The Oil Pollution Act of 1990 ("OPA"), 33 U.S.C. § 2701 *et seq.*, imposes strict liability on those responsible for oil spills "into or upon the navigable waters or adjoining shorelines" of the United States. *Id.* § 2702. It provides for recovery of removal costs and of six categories of damages that "result from" such incidents, including damages for "loss of profits or impairment of earning capacity due to the injury, destruction, or loss of real property, personal property, or natural resources." *Id.* § 2702(b)(2)(E).

The oil spill from BP's Macondo oil well and Deepwater Horizon drilling rig into the Gulf of Mexico, which continued from April 20 to July 15, 2010, caused damages in all of the six OPA categories. Following the unprecedented spill that affected thousands of businesses across the Gulf Coast and surrounding regions, it seemed apparent that BP's liability for business economic loss (*viz.*, "loss of profits or impairment of earning capacity") could be enormous. However, the full scope of § 2702(b)(2)(E) liability, which is defined as affording recompense for business economic loss "due to" property and environmental damage that "result[s] from" a covered oil spill, had not yet been, and still has not been, judicially construed. Furthermore, the scope of such liability was, and still is, subject to intense scholarly debate.[1]

For these and other reasons, BP and the economic-loss claimants entered a settlement agreement adopting clearer definitions and formulas for the **[—16—]** payment of such claims. At their request, the district court

approved the settlement agreement as a class-action settlement in its consent decree.

Within days of the district court's judgment, however, BP brought this litigation, which has evolved into BP asking the courts to interpret the settlement agreement and consent decree to require certain economic-loss claimants to prove, with trial-type evidence, that their losses were caused by the oil spill, regardless of whether they have met the definitions and formulas provided by the settlement agreement and consent decree. The district court rejected BP's demands, and BP appealed. The majority of this panel, first, addressing an issue of how damages should be calculated, vacated the district court's judgment and remanded with instructions to determine whether the claims administrator was converting claimants' accrual-method accounting data into cash-method data. Second, addressing whether claimants must satisfy causation requirements external to the settlement agreement's text, the majority of this panel ordered the district court to "expeditiously craft" a "narrowly-tailored injunction" that would allow "those who experienced actual injury traceable to loss from the Deepwater Horizon accident to continue to receive recovery but those who did not do not receive their payments" pending further decision of the court. *In re Deepwater Horizon*, 732 F.3d 326, 345-46, 1 Adm. R. 287, 301 (5th Cir. 2013) (Clement, J.). I dissented from the panel majority's vacatur and remand because, in my view, BP's action was an unwarranted attempt to change the terms of the settlement agreement and the district court's judgment rejecting that attempt should have been affirmed. *Id.* at 361, 1 Adm. R. at 315. (Dennis, J., concurring in part and dissenting in part).

Next, after the district court issued an injunction, BP filed an "emergency motion" in this court seeking to have this panel order the district court to expand the injunction's scope. BP's Mot. (Doc. No. 195, filed Nov. 21, **[—17—]** 2013). A majority of this panel remanded to the district court and ordered it to give further "expeditious consideration" in the first instance to the "issue of causation" and to revise the injunction as found needed. *In re*

---

[1] *See* John C. P. Goldberg, *Liability for Economic Loss in Connection with the Deepwater Horizon Spill*, 30 Miss. C. L. Rev. 335 (2011); David W. Robertson, *The Oil Pollution Act's Provisions on Damages for Economic Loss*, 30 Miss. C. L. Rev. 157 (2011); John C. P. Goldberg, *OPA and Economic Loss: A Reply to Professor Robertson*, 30 Miss. C. L. Rev. 203 (2011); David W. Robertson, *OPA and Economic Loss: A Response to Professor Goldberg*, 30 Miss. C. L. Rev. 217 (2011).

Deepwater Horizon, No. 13-30315 (5th Cir. filed Dec. 2, 2013). I dissented from the panel's remand and order because I thought the district court had acted correctly and I agreed with the reasons it had assigned; moreover, I stated that BP's belated attempt to raise the issue of causation of damages under the OPA clearly did not survive BP's entering voluntarily into the settlement agreement and consent decree and failing to raise the causation issue in the initial proceedings in the district court and appeal. *Id.* (Dennis, J., dissenting).

After this second remand, the district court, first, granted BP certain partial relief it sought regarding the court's interpretation of the settlement agreement's provisions for calculating damages and ordered the claims administrator to adopt and implement a policy for matching revenue and corresponding variable expenses when calculating business-economic-loss claims. Second, the district court held that the settlement agreement would be interpreted as written without any judicial gloss. Third, the district court held that BP was judicially estopped from pursuing its causation arguments because those arguments contradicted numerous representations BP had made to the district court and this circuit court regarding how the settlement agreement should be interpreted and implemented. The district court explained, essentially, that BP had long maintained that the settlement agreement's definitions and formulas were the sole relevant provisions for processing claims, and such statements on BP's part clearly contradicted BP's new arguments that claimants must also prove causation with supporting evidence. And the district court rejected BP's arguments under Article III, Rule 23, and the Rules Enabling Act. *In re: Oil Spill by the Oil Rig "Deepwater* [—18—] *Horizon" in the Gulf of Mexico, on April 20, 2010*, No. 10-MD-2179 (E.D. La. filed Dec. 24, 2013).

BP has now lodged another appeal and motion with this panel, seeking to have this court, not the district court, "permanently enjoin" the claims administrator from processing claims from claimants who have not proven with trial-type evidence that their "alleged injuries" are "traceable to the Deepwater Horizon oil spill." BP's Mot. (Doc. No. 231, filed Dec. 30, 2013).

Although I continue to adhere to the views I expressed previously in this case, I now join Judge Southwick in affirming the district court's December 24, 2013 order interpreting the settlement agreement as written and declining to add, by judicial gloss, any additional requirements, procedures, or other provisions not contained in the text of the settlement agreement and consent decree and its attached exhibits. I agree with Judge Southwick that BP's renewed motion for an injunction should be denied and that no injunction against the payment of business-economic-loss claims shall continue. I also agree that we are bound by the certification panel's Article III, Rule 23, and Rules Enabling Act rulings in its January 10, 2014 opinion and decision. Accordingly, for these reasons, I concur in the above-described conclusions reached by Judge Southwick and in the judgment he has written for the majority of this panel.

(Reporter's Note: Dissenting opinion follows on p. 191).

[—19—] **CLEMENT,** Circuit Judge, dissenting:

A majority of this panel (1) affirms the district court's December 24, 2013 order, (2) denies BP's motion for a permanent injunction against the issuance or payment of awards to claimants whose injuries are not traceable to the Deepwater Horizon oil spill, and (3) holds that this panel is bound by the certification panel's rulings on Article III, Rule 23, and the Rules Enabling Act.[1] I respectfully dissent.

The judicial power of federal courts extends only to cases and controversies. There are but three irreducible constitutional requirements: an injury in fact, a causal connection between the injury and the conduct complained of, and that the injury is likely to be redressed by a favorable decision. *Lujan v. Defenders of Wildlife*, 504 U.S. 555, 560-61 (1992). Despite the modern development of class actions under our law, the extent of our judicial power remains unchanged. It extends only to cases and controversies—redressable injuries with a causal connection. *Lewis v. Casey*, 518 U.S. 343, 349 (1996).

The Deepwater Horizon tragedy took eleven lives and caused great damage to our environment and region. Cases and controversies abounded. In light of this, the parties sought to negotiate a settlement agreement that would resolve these issues on an enormous, class-wide basis, one of the largest settlements in history. This was a settlement that would compensate claimants for "[l]oss of income, earnings or profits . . . as a result of the" spill. Settlement Agreement § 1.3.1.2. The agreement was signed and the class was certified on December 21, 2012, with the support of the parties. [—20—]

Two subsequent decisions of the Claims Administrator brought the parties into

conflict. One was the Policy Statement endorsed by the district court in an order of March 5, 2013, that established the accounting methodology to be used to measure payments for Business Economic Loss claims under Exhibit 4C of the Settlement Agreement. The other was a Policy Statement that was issued on October 10, 2012, and adopted by the district court on April 9, 2013, that laid out a position on "Causation Requirements" in Exhibit 4B. It stated:

> The Claims Administrator will thus compensate eligible Business Economic Loss and Individual Economic Loss claimants for all losses payable under the terms of the Economic Loss frameworks in the Settlement Agreement, without regard to whether such losses resulted or may have resulted from a cause other than the Deepwater Horizon oil spill provided such claimants have satisfied the specific causation requirements set out in the Settlement Agreement.

On October 2, 2013, a majority of our panel agreed that Exhibit 4C required matching of revenues and expenses, and remanded to the district court with the additional instruction to consider the issue of causation if raised by the parties. *In re Deepwater Horizon*, 732 F.3d 326, 1 Adm. R. 287 (5th Cir. 2013) (*"Deepwater Horizon I"*). On remand, the district court declined to address the causation issues, and after a renewed motion to our panel, we remanded again on December 2, 2013, with instructions to consider the causation issues BP raised.

On December 24, 2013, the district court issued an order requiring the Claims Administrator to match revenue and expenses as directed by our October 2 opinion and subsequent order of December 2. This resolved the first dispute raised by the Claims Administrator's Policy Statement, and no party has appealed this issue. [—21—]

The district court also addressed the second disputed issue in an order that analyzed the causation issues we directed the court to consider. It held that BP was judicially

---

[1] Judge Dennis "concur[s] in the above-described conclusions reached by Judge Southwick and in the judgment he has written for the majority of this panel." While this opinion refers to Judge Southwick's opinion as speaking for the "majority," it is worth noting that little of his analysis and reasoning carries the support of two panel members.

estopped from arguing that individuals and entities whose injuries were not fairly traceable to the oil spill should not be able to recover. BP responded with an additional motion asking this court to put in place a permanent injunction to ensure that the Claims Administrator considers causation before paying out claims.

Meanwhile, another panel of this court heard challenges to the certification of the class action in this case and released an opinion on January 10, 2014, upholding the district court's certification of the Settlement Agreement.[2] The majority of that panel found no issue with upholding the certification of the Settlement Agreement, because the agreement as written "explicitly limits claims to those based on '[l]oss of income, earnings or profits suffered by Natural Persons or Entities *as a result of* the DEEPWATER HORIZON INCIDENT,' . . . . As contemplated by the Class Definition, therefore, the class contains only persons and entities that possess Article III standing." *In re Deepwater Horizon*, 739 F.3d 790, 803, 2 Adm. R. 140, 147 (5th Cir. 2014) ("*Deepwater Horizon II*").

The certification panel declined to address the Claims Administrator's interpretation of the Settlement Agreement, leaving that issue for our panel's consideration in light of our retention of jurisdiction. As the certification panel stated, "[t]he evidentiary standard to be applied by the Claims Administrator . . . is a question of interpreting the Settlement Agreement and applying it to [—22—] each individual claim, and we are not called upon to address those issues in this appeal." *Id.* at 808, 2 Adm. R. at 151. The opinion further acknowledged:

The parties now vigorously dispute how this evidentiary framework was intended to work. For its part, BP has argued in its subsequent submissions to the *Deepwater Horizon I* panel that "the Claims Administrator must make a threshold determination whether the claimant has suffered loss as a result of the spill" and that under footnote 1 of Exhibit 4B this "threshold determination must be made *before* applying the causation criteria outlined in Exhibit 4B." The named plaintiffs hold a different view.

Id. at 807–08, 2 Adm. R. at 151.

While the certification panel majority does not address what occurred after class certification, Judge Garza's dissent traces the ostensible elimination of the causation requirement to the Policy Statement of the Claims Administrator. That interpretation stated that the program would "compensate . . . claimants . . . *without regard to whether such losses resulted or may have resulted from a cause other than the Deepwater Horizon oil spill.*" *Id.* at 823, 2 Adm. R. at 164 (Garza, J., dissenting). This reading "effectively eliminated" the language requiring causation. *Id.* at 823 n.5, 2 Adm. R. at 164 n. 5.

The majority adopts the view that the agreement as written does not eliminate causation or traceability, but "subordinate[s]" it. Specifically, Judge Southwick agrees with the certification panel that causation was contemplated by the Settlement Agreement. He points to the Business Economic Loss claim form informing claimants that, "[t]he Business Economic Loss Claim is for businesses . . . that assert economic loss due to the spill." Deepwater Horizon Economic and Property Settlement Business Economic Loss Claim Form (Purple Form) 1. Nine pages later, the form requires the claimant to certify under penalty of perjury "that the information provided in this Claim Form is true and accurate to the best of my knowledge." *Id.* at 9. "Every claim BP [—23—] argues suffers from some causal-nexus infirmity should have with it an attestation from the claimant or an attorney that the economic loss was caused by

---

[2] While the decision of the certification panel is binding under our circuit's rule of orderliness, that opinion was careful to limit its holding to the class certification and settlement approval context. In addition, it was arguably premature for that panel to rule on the certification issue before ours had issued a final ruling on the proper interpretation of the Settlement Agreement. Much of the confusion, delay, and additional briefing in these cases could have been avoided if the cases had been consolidated into one panel.

the spill." To the majority, this attestation satisfies any concerns about causation.

The form certainly provides further evidence that causation was a critical part of the Settlement Agreement. The difficulty is that the interpretation and implementation of the agreement eliminated this requirement when the Exhibit 4B Policy Statement informed claimants that they would be compensated whether or not their injuries "resulted . . . from a cause other than the Deepwater Horizon oil spill." These decisions and pronouncements may not have been relevant for the certification panel majority, which declined to analyze issues that arose from the interpretation and implementation of the settlement after its approval by the district court, but they are crucial in assessing "whether the implementation of the Settlement Agreement is defective." This interpretation that submitting forms that lack colorable causation was acceptable under the agreement was relied upon by attorneys, who urged uninjured plaintiffs to file claims "[i]f the numbers work." BP Br. 77, Doc. 00512230427 (May 5, 2013) (citing R.16719). These attorneys were not urging perjury: they were merely interpreting the agreement in light of the Claims Administrator's interpretation that was upheld by the district court. How can they be pursued for false statements for relying on these legally binding pronouncements, much less an individual, unrepresented claimant who lacks even this level of legal sophistication? This Policy Statement effectively eliminated the need for a claimant to allege injury traceable to BP's conduct, and therefore raises once again the Constitutional concerns that the majority claims were "put to rest by the certification panel." [—24—]

The elements of standing do not end at certification, but continue to be vital throughout "the successive stages of litigation." *Lewis*, 518 U.S. at 358. Because this is a settlement class action, there are no successive stages of litigation: the certification stage and the proof stage have been combined. If someone is a member of the class, they recover. But while the certification panel analyzed the agreement as written, the subsequent implementation has expanded those who can recover even to those who cannot trace their injuries to BP's conduct. This agreement, as implemented, is using the powers of the federal courts to enforce obligations unrelated to actual cases or controversies.

Judge Southwick's opinion points out the challenge of proving causation when multiple causes are at stake by offering the hypothetical of an accounting firm that experienced economic loss after the disaster in part because one of its three partners took medical leave. It is admittedly difficult to isolate multiple causes, and that is not what Article III requires. Even in that example, an argument can be made that the disaster impacted part of the firm's losses. If so, these claimants can colorably assert injury due to the spill and are appropriate members of this class. A more fitting example here would be an accounting firm in Zone A where all three partners went on medical leave for several months after the disaster. The profits of their firm drop precipitously, but in no way due to the negligence of BP. Under Judge Southwick's reasoning, the Settlement Agreement requires BP to pay these losses as well so long as they sign a claim form. But these plaintiffs have no injury traceable to BP's actions, and would not have standing to maintain a suit individually under *Lujan*. Nonetheless, because of the majority's ruling here, these claimants will recover.

Perhaps recognizing that its ruling would lead to absurd results in at least a small number of cases, the majority states that the "[t]he claims [—25—] administrator, parties, and district court can resolve real examples of implausible claims as they resolve other questions that arise in the handling of specific claims." But I do not see how this statement provides any comfort in light of the district court's ruling that BP is judicially estopped from arguing causation. And the majority declines to rule one way or the other on judicial estoppel, which it inexplicably concludes is "an issue . . . not relevant to our decision." In the end, we are left with the majority's holding that the Claims Administrator does not need to perform the "gatekeeping function" of ensuring that claims are not paid that are not plausibly traceable to the spill. Claimants whose losses had absolutely nothing to do with Deepwater Horizon or BP's conduct will recover as a result of this ruling.

The number of claimants ultimately affected by this issue may well be small, but the constitutional principles are important because they assure the vigorous and fair resolution of disputes and respect the limitations on the power of the federal judiciary. I would reverse the district court's holding on judicial estoppel and permanently enjoin the Claims Administrator from paying awards to claimants whose injuries are not traceable to the Deepwater Horizon oil spill.

I respectfully dissent.

United States Court of Appeals
for the Fifth Circuit

No. 13-60119

CHENEVERT

vs.

TRAVELERS INDEM. CO.

Appeals from the United States District Court for the
Northern District of Mississippi

Decided: March 7, 2014

Citation: 746 F.3d 581, 2 Adm. R. 195 (5th Cir. 2014).

Before JONES, WIENER, and GRAVES, Circuit Judges.

[—1—] GRAVES, Circuit Judge:

In *Massey v. Williams-McWilliams, Inc.*, 414 F.2d 675 (1969), we considered the case of a shipowner/employer who made voluntary payments to an injured employee under the Longshore and Harbor Workers' Compensation Act ("LHWCA") and who was later held liable to the worker in a Jones Act claim. We held that the shipowner/employer was entitled to "a credit against those items of [Jones Act] damages . . . that bear a reasonable relation to the items of loss compensated by [LHWCA] benefits." *Id.* at 680. The present case requires us to answer a related question: whether an insurer who makes voluntary LHWCA payments to an injured employee on behalf of a shipowner/employer is entitled to recover these payments from the employee's settlement of a Jones Act claim against the shipowner/employer based on the [—2—] same injuries for which the insurer has already compensated him. We hold that such an insurer acquires a subrogation lien on the employee's Jones Act recovery for the amount of LHWCA benefits paid. Accordingly, we REVERSE the district court's denial of the motion to intervene filed by Travelers Indemnity Company ("Travelers") and REMAND with instructions.[1]

---

[1] Travelers was incorrectly characterized as a defendant in the district court, and is therefore incorrectly characterized as a defendant in the caption for this opinion. Travelers is in fact a movant that is currently appealing the denial of its motion to intervene.

BACKGROUND

Gary Chenevert was employed by GC Constructors ("GC") as a crane operator. In May 2007, Chenevert fell and was injured while working on a barge with a mounted crane. At the time of Chenevert's accident, Travelers provided coverage to GC for, among other things, its workers' compensation exposure to injured longshore and harbor workers. Travelers provided no coverage for "bodily injury to a master or member of the crew of any vessel." Between May 2007 and May 2010, Travelers voluntarily paid Chenevert a total of $277,728.72 in indemnity and medical benefits under the LHWCA.

In May 2010, Chenevert sued GC in federal court, alleging that he was working as a seaman at the time of his accident and seeking damages under the Jones Act for GC's negligence. Based on Chenevert's claim that he was a "seaman" (rather than a "longshoreman"), Travelers stopped making payments under the LHWCA. In November 2010, GC filed a notice of lien claiming that, in the event judgment is rendered in favor of Chenevert on his Jones Act claim, GC "has a lien against any funds due and payable to Travelers Insurance Company who is the insurer under the U.S. Longshore and Harbor Workers' Compensation Act."

Although Chenevert, through counsel, initially represented to Travelers that he did not contest Travelers's lien, he explained in August 2011 that he [—3—] intended to oppose any effort by Travelers to recover from his pending settlement with GC. In October 2011, Travelers was granted permission to file an untimely motion to intervene.[2] On October 27, 2011, Travelers moved to intervene in Chenevert's suit for the purpose of asserting its subrogation rights against any money recovered by Chenevert.

At some time between October 18, 2011, and October 27, 2011, Chenevert and GC agreed on a settlement. In November 2011, GC notified the district court that it had

---

[2] Under the scheduling order in place, motions were required to be filed no later than May 16, 2011.

reached a settlement with Chenevert and requested that $277,782.22 of the settlement funds be deposited into the court's registry pending the outcome of the dispute between Chenevert and Travelers. The district court granted this motion.[3] Chenevert and GC ultimately settled for $1,725,000, with $277.728.72 of this amount deposited into the district court's registry. In December 2011, the district court granted Chenevert and GC's joint motion for dismissal of Chenevert's claims against GC, with the case remaining open to allow resolution of Travelers's pending motion to intervene.

After the death of U.S. District Judge W. Allen Pepper, Jr., who had been presiding over the case, the case was randomly reassigned to a different district judge. However, for reasons that are not clear, a magistrate judge entered an order approximately two months later denying Travelers's motion to intervene. Travelers filed a motion to reconsider, arguing that the magistrate judge had no authority to enter the order because the parties had not consented to the magistrate judge's jurisdiction, and the district court had never referred the [—4—] motion to the magistrate judge for a proposed ruling. Travelers also objected to the substance of the magistrate judge's order.

In response to Travelers's motion, the magistrate judge withdrew his earlier order and submitted a somewhat expanded analysis as a report and recommendation to the district court. Travelers filed objections to this report and recommendation. The district court adopted the magistrate judge's recommendation in a memorandum opinion, denying Travelers's motion to intervene. The district court held that Travelers has no right of subrogation as to the settlement proceeds, and therefore no interest in the property in the case. The district court also held that Travelers's interests in the litigation had been adequately represented by GC. Travelers now appeals.

---

[3] GC's motion stated an incorrect amount to be deposited; the amount was later corrected to $277,728.72.

DISCUSSION

Under Federal Rule of Civil Procedure 24(a)(2), a party is entitled to intervene if:

(1) the motion is timely; (2) the putative intervenor asserts an interest related to the property or transaction that forms the basis of the controversy in the action into which he seeks to intervene; (3) the disposition of the action may impair or impede his ability to protect that interest; and (4) it is not adequately represented by the existing parties.

Effjohn Int'l Cruise Holdings, Inc. v. A&L Sales, Inc., 346 F.3d 552, 560 (5th Cir. 2003). A district court's ruling under Rule 24(a)(2) is reviewed *de novo. Ceres Gulf v. Cooper*, 957 F.2d 1199, 1202 (5th Cir. 1992). We discuss below whether Travelers has an interest in the settlement fund and whether its interest was adequately represented; the remaining elements are not disputed.

I. Double Recoveries Involving the LHWCA

A. *The LHWCA and Third-Party Vessel Suits*

The LHWCA, like other workers' compensation schemes, embodies a compromise between workers and employers: workers injured on the job receive quick, certain compensation from their employers regardless of fault, [—5—] but employers are generally absolved from any further liability in relation to such injuries. *See, e.g.*, 1 The Law of Maritime Personal Injuries § 2:1 (5th ed. 2012). However, the LHWCA generally preserves an injured worker's remedies against third parties who may have caused the injury. For example, a worker covered by the LHWCA whose injury is "caused by the negligence of a vessel" may bring an action against the vessel. 33 U.S.C. § 905(b).

It is therefore possible for an injured worker to obtain a tort recovery from a third party based on injuries for which he has already been compensated by his employer under the LHWCA. Although the LHWCA "does not expressly provide for reimbursement from a judgment or settlement obtained by the worker from a third party of compensation benefits that an employer has already paid," courts "have uniformly held . . . that an employer has a subrogation right to be reimbursed from the worker's net recovery from a third party for the full amount of compensation benefits already paid." *Peters v. North River Ins. Co.*, 764 F.2d 306, 312 (5th Cir. 1985). Furthermore, if compensation benefits are paid by an employer's insurer, that insurer is subrogated to the employer's reimbursement rights under the LHWCA. *See id.* at 308 n.1 (citing 33 U.S.C. § 933(h)).

In *Taylor v. Bunge Corp.*, 845 F.2d 1323, 1324 (5th Cir. 1988), this court considered a case in which a longshoreman was injured by a vessel owned by his employer. The worker received LHWCA benefits from his employer's insurer and later sued the vessel for negligence pursuant to 33 U.S.C. § 905(b). *Id.* The worker and the vessel settled for $700,000 "over and above the worker's compensation benefits already paid," in effect trying to settle around the insurer's lien. *Id.* at 1325. The insurer intervened and attempted to enforce the employer's lien against the settlement fund to recover the benefits [—6—] it had paid.[4] *Id.* We recognized circuit precedent holding that "an injured longshoreman and a third party defendant cannot settle around the employer's lien." *Id.* at 1324 (citing *Peters*); *see Peters*, 764 F.2d at 308 (holding that "settlement of the worker's claim necessarily settled the employer's subrogation claim and entitled the employer to reimbursement to the extent of the funds that the third party has agreed to pay in settlement"). We considered "whether this principle survives when [the] employer wears two hats as employer and as

vessel." *Id.* at 1324-25. We concluded that the same principle is fully applicable and held that "the worker's compensation carrier's ability to recover under the employer's lien against the settlement fund is not affected . . . by the fact that [the insured employer] was both employer and owner of the Vessel." *Id.* at 1330.

B. The LHWCA and Jones Act Suits

A worker who has received LHWCA benefits may also obtain a double recovery for the same injury by suing his employer for negligence under the Jones Act. The Jones Act provides that "[a] seaman injured in the course of employment . . . may elect to bring a civil action at law . . . against the employer." 46 U.S.C. § 30104. "[T]he Jones Act and the LHWCA are complementary regimes that work in tandem: The Jones Act provides tort remedies to *sea*-based maritime workers, while the LHWCA provides workers' compensation to *land*-based maritime employees." *Stewart v. Dutra* [—7—] *Construction Co.*, 543 U.S. 481, 488 (2005).[5] As the Supreme Court has recognized, a worker whose job title fits within one of the enumerated occupations of the LHWCA (such as a longshoreman or a ship repairman) may nevertheless be a "seaman" excluded from LHWCA coverage and entitled to bring a claim against his employer under the Jones Act. *See Southwest Marine, Inc. v. Gizoni*, 502 U.S. 81 (1991). This is a "fact-specific" question that "depend[s] on the nature of the vessel, and the employee's precise relation to it." *Id.* at 88 (quotations omitted). Furthermore, "an employee who receives voluntary payments under the LHWCA without a formal award is not barred from subsequently seeking relief under the Jones Act" because "the question of coverage [under

---

[4] The employer argued that allowing an insurer to exercise the employer's lien would "conflict[] with the basic principle of insurance law that an insurer may not subrogate against its own insured," because the employer had agreed to indemnify the worker for any attempt by the insurer to exercise the lien against the settlement fund. *Taylor*, 845 F.2d at 1329, 1325 n.6. The panel rejected this argument for two reasons. *Id.* at 1329-30. This issue does not arise in the present case because GC did not agree to indemnify Chenevert against Travelers's attempt to enforce the lien.

[5] The LHWCA provides that an "employee" covered by the Act does not include "a master or member of a crew of any vessel." 33 U.S.C. § 902(3)(G). The Supreme Court has explained: "[M]aster or member of a crew" is a refinement of the term "seaman" in the Jones Act; it excludes from LHWCA coverage those properly covered under the Jones Act." *McDermott Int'l, Inc. v. Wilander*, 498 U.S. 337, 347 (1991).

the LHWCA] has never actually been litigated." *Id.* at 91.

As the Supreme Court noted in *Gizoni*, the LHWCA "specifically provides that any amounts paid to an employee for the same injury, disability, or death pursuant to the Jones Act shall be credited against any liability imposed by the LHWCA." 502 U.S. at 91 (citing 33 U.S.C. § 903(e)). We have previously held that the reverse is also true; *i.e.*, that a shipowner-employer who voluntarily pays LHWCA benefits to an injured employee and is later found liable under the Jones Act is entitled to "a credit against those items of damages . . . that bear a reasonable relation to the items of loss compensated by workmen's compensation benefits." *Massey v. Williams-McWilliams, Inc.*, 414 F.2d 675, 679-80 (5th Cir. 1969). The question presented by this case is whether the principles of *Peters* and *Taylor* are applicable in the context of a Jones Act settlement. In other words, does an insurer who has made voluntary [—8—] LHWCA payments to an injured employee on behalf of the employer have a right to be reimbursed from the employee's settlement of a Jones Act claim against the employer based on the same injuries?

II. Travelers's Subrogation Right

We perceive no sound reason why an insurer's right of reimbursement against a Jones Act recovery should be different from its right of reimbursement against a § 905(b) recovery. Arguably, the insurer has an even stronger equitable claim to repayment from a Jones Act recovery. A worker who recovers against a third party under § 905(b) is necessarily covered by the LHWCA and therefore entitled to compensation benefits; nevertheless, the worker must still use the proceeds of the recovery to repay the employer or insurer for the benefits. On the other hand, a worker who succeeds in a Jones Act claim is necessarily a seaman, and therefore not entitled to LHWCA benefits. It would be particularly unfair to deny the insurer the

right to recover the benefits it has paid in such a situation.[6]

The district court appears to have viewed Travelers's attempt to assert a lien on settlement funds paid by GC (who is insured by Travelers) as an attempt to subrogate against its own insured. As the district court recognized, as a general rule "no right of subrogation can arise in favor of an insurer against its own insured." 16 Couch on Insurance 3d § 224:1 (2013). However, this broad statement "leave[s] out a crucial boundary of the rule: the prohibition of insurers' subrogation against their own insureds applies to claims arising from the very risk for which the insured was covered by that insurer." *Id.* Assuming Travelers's assertion of its repayment lien against [—9—] Chenevert's Jones Act settlement fund may be construed in some way as asserting a right of subrogation against GC, this would be unproblematic because Travelers did not insure GC against Jones Act liability. *See also Taylor*, 845 F.2d at 1329-30 ("[B]y enforcing the employer's lien against the settlement fund, [the insurer] is not trying to avoid the risk against which it insured.").

As explained above, an insurer's right of reimbursement from an employee's tort recovery is derived from the employer's right of reimbursement; that is, by paying LHWCA benefits to the injured employee on behalf of the employer, the insurer is subrogated to the employer's right of reimbursement. *See Peters*, 764 F.2d at 308 n.1. The magistrate judge, in his report and recommendation, reasoned that "[t]o suggest that an employer has a lien on a portion of the funds *the employer itself* agreed to pay in settlement the moment it settled the case is nonsense." However, at the time of settlement, it is the insurer, not the employer, who has the lien. The insurer, by satisfying

---

[6] Two district courts have considered the issue and held that an insurer who has paid LHWCA benefits to an injured worker may intervene in the worker's Jones Act suit against his employer to preserve the insurer's subrogation rights in the event the worker obtains a recovery. *Kahue v. Pacific Envtl. Corp.*, 834 F. Supp. 2d 1039, 1060-61 (D. Haw. 2011); *Lewis v. United States*, 812 F. Supp. 629, 633-34 (E.D. Va. 1993).

the employer's payment obligations under the LHWCA, becomes subrogated to all of the employer's repayment rights.

Along the same lines, Chenevert argues that allowing GC to assert a repayment lien against a portion of a settlement that it agreed to pay (without any provision for repayment of the lien) would in some sense abrogate the settlement. But again, it is Travelers that is asserting the lien, not GC. Chenevert argues that "Travelers would have no greater right to recover money from Gary Chenevert than GC Constructors itself would possess," but this is incorrect. By paying LHWCA benefits on behalf of GC, Travelers acquired a repayment lien that is independent of, and cannot be nullified by, GC. If this were not so, an employer and employee could easily settle around the insurer's lien and prevent any possibility of recovery by the insurer. [—10—]

We hold that an insurer who makes voluntary LHWCA payments to an injured employee on behalf of the employer acquires a subrogation lien on any recovery by the employee in a Jones Act suit against the employer based on the injuries for which the insurer has already compensated him. We therefore conclude that Travelers is entitled to the disputed funds in the district court's registry, and that Travelers may intervene for the purpose of collecting these funds. *See McDonald v. E.J. Lavino Co.*, 430 F.2d 1065, 1071 (5th Cir. 1970) (insurer's intervention to protect its subrogation interest in a plaintiff's recovery is cognizable as intervention of right under Rule 24(a)).

CONCLUSION

For the reasons explained above, we REVERSE the district court's denial of Travelers's motion to intervene and REMAND the case for the purpose of distributing the disputed funds in the district court's registry to Travelers.

United States Court of Appeals
for the Fifth Circuit

No. 12-31258

NAQUIN
vs.
ELEVATING BOATS, L.L.C.

Appeals from the United States District Court for the
Eastern District of Louisiana

Decided: March 10, 2014

Citation: 744 F.3d 927, 2 Adm. R. 200 (5th Cir. 2014).

Before **DAVIS** and **JONES**, Circuit Judges, and **MILAZZO**, District Judge.*

*District Judge of the Eastern District of Louisiana sitting by designation

[—1—] **DAVIS,** Circuit Judge:

Defendant-Appellant Elevating Boats, LLC ("EBI") employed Plaintiff-Appellee Larry Naquin, Sr. ("Naquin") as a vessel repair supervisor at its shipyard facility in Houma, Louisiana. After Naquin was severely injured in an accident in the shipyard, a jury found that EBI was negligent, found that Naquin qualified for seaman status, and awarded him money damages under the Jones Act. Because the evidence supports the jury's determination of seaman status and liability, we AFFIRM the district court's judgment on liability; because the damages determination was erroneously based upon emotional [—2—] anguish resulting from the death of a third party, we VACATE the damages award and REMAND for a new trial on damages.

I.

EBI manufactures, operates, and maintains a fleet of specialty lift-boats[1] and marine cranes out of several Louisiana port facilities. EBI employed Naquin at its shipyard in Houma, Louisiana, where he had served as a vessel repair supervisor since 2005. Naquin's primary responsibility as a vessel repair supervisor was the maintenance and repair of EBI's fleet of lift-boat vessels. Ordinarily, Naquin worked aboard the lift-boats while they were moored, jacked up, or docked in EBI's shipyard canal. Naquin's spent approximately 70 percent of his total time working aboard these vessels, including inspecting them for repairs, cleaning them, painting them, replacing defective or damaged parts, performing engine repairs, going on test runs, securing equipment, and operating the vessel's marine cranes and jack-up legs. Two to three times per week, Naquin would do his work while the vessel was being moved to another position in the canal. Occasionally, EBI dispatched Naquin to repair a vessel or fill in as a vessel crane operator while the vessel was operating in open water. Naquin spent the remaining 30 percent of his time working in the shipyard's fabrication shop or operating the shipyard's LC-400 land-based crane.

On November 17, 2009, Naquin was using the shipyard crane, which had been designed and constructed by EBI, to relocate a test-block, a heavy iron weight used to test the lifting capacity of cranes. Although the test-block was well within the LC-400's rated capacity, the crane suddenly failed, causing the boom and crane house to separate from the crane pedestal. As the crane toppled [—3—] over onto a nearby building, Naquin was able to jump from the crane house. However, he did not avoid injury; he sustained a broken left foot, a severely broken right foot, and a lower abdominal hernia. Naquin's cousin's husband, who happened to be another EBI employee, was working in the building and was crushed by the crane and killed. Naquin learned of his death while in the hospital after the accident, either later that same day or the next day.[2]

---

[1] A lift-boat is a self-propelled, self-elevating, offshore supply vessel. Although it functions and navigates much like any other supply vessel, a typical lift-boat is equipped with three column-like legs that can be quickly lowered to the seafloor to raise the vessel out of the water and stabilize it for marine operations.

[2] During his testimony on direct examination, Naquin stated that paramedics told him immediately after the accident that the workers in the building were "doing all right." He continued to say that he thought the information regarding their injuries, specifically the death of his cousin's husband, was kept from him "for [his] own good."

Following the accident, Naquin underwent one surgery for his hernia and one surgery to repair his right foot. Because Naquin's right foot was fractured in several places, a plate and screws were required to repair the damage. Despite Naquin's reparative surgeries and 70 physical therapy sessions, he was not able to return to physical work. EBI subsequently offered Naquin a "desk job" at the shipyard, but he declined, asserting that he was too emotionally upset to return to work. Although Naquin's medical treatment had ceased, at the time of trial, he continued to complain of chronic pain in his feet, difficulty walking, and chronic depression.

In November 2010, Naquin filed the instant Jones Act suit, alleging that EBI was negligent in the construction and/or maintenance of the LC-400 shipyard crane. After a three-day trial, a jury concluded that Naquin was a Jones Act seaman and that EBI's negligence caused his injury. The jury awarded Naquin $1,000,000 for past and future physical pain and suffering, $1,000,000 for past and future mental pain and suffering, and $400,000 for future lost wages. EBI immediately filed motions requesting a judgment as a matter of law, a new trial, a new trial on damages, and remittitur. The district court denied all of EBI's motions, and EBI now appeals. [—4—]

II.

"The determination of whether an injured worker is a seaman under the Jones Act is a mixed question of law and fact and it is usually inappropriate to take the question from the jury."[3] Accordingly, we will not disturb a jury's finding of seaman status unless the facts and the law do not "reasonably support" its conclusion.[4]

Conversely, the appropriate standard of review to test a jury's factual findings is whether there is "reasonable evidentiary basis for the jury's verdict."[5] We therefore review

the evidence "in the light most favorable to the verdict. 'Only when there is a complete absence of probative facts to support the conclusion reached does a reversible error appear.'"[6] As always, conclusions of law are reviewed de novo.

III.

On appeal, EBI challenges multiple legal conclusions and factual determinations of the district court. We now address, in order, EBI's contentions (1) that Naquin was not a Jones Act seaman, (2) that the district court provided the jury with erroneous seaman status instructions, (3) that the evidence is insufficient to establish EBI's negligence, and (4) that the district court erred by admitting evidence of Naquin's relative's death to support Naquin's emotional damages claim.

A.

EBI first argues that the jury erred in its determination that Naquin was a seaman entitled to Jones Act coverage. Specifically, EBI argues that because [—5—] Naquin is a land-based ship-repairman, he is not connected to vessels in navigation and cannot qualify as a seaman.

In support of its argument that Naquin is not a seaman, EBI primarily argues that Naquin is a land-based repairman who performs classic land-based harbor worker duties. As EBI points out, the Jones Act's land-based worker counterpart, the Longshore and Harbor Worker's Compensation Act ("LHWCA") expressly identifies "ship repairm[e]n" as subject to its coverage.[7] Because the LHWCA and Jones Act are mutually exclusive compensation schemes, EBI argues, Naquin's coverage under the LHWCA precludes his coverage under the Jones Act.

A few years ago we agreed with EBI's position.[8] However, the Supreme Court

---

[3] *Becker v. Tidewater, Inc.*, 335 F.3d 376, 386 (5th Cir. 2003).
[4] *See id.*
[5] *See Loehr v. Offshore Logisitics, Inc.*, 691 F.2d 758, 760 (5th Cir. 1982).

[6] *Huffman v. Union Pacific R.R.*, 675 F.3d 412, 425 (5th Cir. 2012) (citation omitted).
[7] *See* 33 U.S.C. § 902(3).
[8] *See Pizzitolo v. Electro-Coal Transfer Corp.*, 812 F.2d 977, 982–84 (5th Cir. 1987).

rejected this position and overruled our decision in *Pizzotolo* in *Southwest Marine, Inc. v. Gizoni*.[9] There, the Court clarified that the Jones Act covers any worker who qualifies as a "seaman," without regard to whether a worker may also qualify for coverage under the LHWCA.[10] This is true even in the case where a worker's job is specifically identified for coverage under the LHWCA.[11] Thus, the fact that Naquin performed ship repair duties (identified as covered by the LHWCA) cannot distract us from the threshold inquiry: whether Naquin first qualifies as a seaman.[12] [—6—]

Though the Jones Act does not define "seaman," Congress has elsewhere defined it as the "master or member of a crew of any vessel."[13] To determine if a worker is a seaman or member of a vessel's crew, the Supreme Court has established a two-prong test: "First, 'an employee's duties must contribute to the function of the vessel or to the accomplishment of its mission.' Second, 'a seaman must have a connection to a vessel in navigation (or to an identifiable group of such vessels) that is substantial in terms of both duration and nature.'"[14] Importantly, an individual can still qualify for seaman status even if he divides his time among multiple vessels under common ownership or control.[15] The relevant question is whether, in the course of his current job, he substantially contributes to the vessels' functions and maintains a substantial connection with the fleet.[16]

"[S]atisfying the first prong of the [seaman] test is relatively easy: the claimant need only show that he does the ship's work."[17] Under this standard, there can be little doubt that Naquin did the ship's work and contributed to the function of EBI's vessels. As EBI concedes, Naquin spent the majority of his time repairing, cleaning, painting, and maintaining the 26–30 lift-boat vessels that EBI operated out of the Houma shipyard. Moreover, the remainder of Naquin's hours aboard EBI lift-boats was spent operating the marine crane and securing [—7—] the deck for voyage. Equipment operators and mechanics performing such tasks are necessary to the function and operation of any vessel.[18]

Turning to the second prong of the seaman test, Naquin is only eligible for Jones Act coverage if his connection to the EBI lift-boat fleet is "substantial in terms of both duration and nature."[19] As the Supreme Court has explained, the fundamental purpose of the substantial connection requirement is "to separate the sea-based maritime employees who are entitled to Jones Act protection from those land-based workers who have only a transitory or sporadic connection to a vessel in navigation, and therefore whose employment does not regularly expose them to the perils of the sea."[20] Thus, a worker seeking seaman status must separately demonstrate that his connection to a vessel or fleet of vessels is, temporally, more than fleeting, and, substantively, more than incidental.[21] These inquiries are not always distinct, but are

---

[9] 502 U.S. 81, 87–88 (1991).

[10] *See id.*

[11] *See In re Endeavor Marine Inc.*, 234 F.3d 287, 291 (5th Cir. 2000).

[12] *See id.* ("[E]ven a ship repairman (which is traditional longshoreman work and is one of the enumerated occupations under the LHWCA) may qualify for seaman status if he has the requisite employment-related connection to the vessel.").

[13] *See Chandris v. Latsis*, 515 U.S. 347, 355–56 (1995); 33 U.S.C. § 902(3)(G).

[14] *Becker*, 335 F.3d at 387 (quoting *Chandris*, 515 U.S. at 368).

[15] *See Harbor Tug & Barge Co. v. Papai*, 520 U.S. 548, 558 (1997).

[16] *See id.*; *Bertrand v. Int'l Mooring & Marine, Inc.*, 700 F.2d 240, 245–46 (5th Cir. 1983).

[17] *Becker*, 335 F.3d at 387–88 (internal quotation marks and citation omitted).

[18] *See, e.g., id.* at 388. *See also Endeavor Marine Inc.*, 234 F.3d at 291 (finding barge crane operator to be a seaman, because "even a ship repairman (which is traditional longshoreman work and is one of the enumerated occupations under the LHWCA) may qualify for seaman status if he has the requisite employment-related connection to the vessel."); *Boatel, Inc. v. Delamore*, 379 F.2d 850, 853–54, 859 (5th Cir. 1967) (finding diesel "motorman" to be a seaman); *and Braniff v. Jackson Ave.-Gretna Ferry, Inc.*, 280 F.2d 523 (5th Cir. 1960) (finding ferry's maintenance superintendent to be a seaman).

[19] *See Chandris*, 515 U.S. at 368.

[20] *Id.*

[21] *See id.* at 369–71.

interrelated elements of the same substantial connection requirement.[22]

Weighing in on the durational aspect of the vessel-connection requirement, the Supreme Court has endorsed this Court's general rule of thumb: "A worker who spends less than about 30 percent of his time in the service of a vessel in [—8—] navigation should not qualify as a seaman under the Jones Act."[23] "Indeed, application of the 30 percent test is the very means by which a substantial temporal connection is determined, regardless whether a single vessel or group of vessels is at issue."[24] In the instant case, Naquin spent approximately 70 percent of his time repairing and operating cranes and other equipment on EBI's fleet of lift-boats. The evidence therefore clearly supported the jury's implicit finding that Naquin had a connection to the EBI fleet that was substantial in terms of duration.[25]

Although vessel repair is classic seaman's work, EBI argues that Naquin does not qualify as a seaman because his duties do not "regularly expose[him] to the perils of the sea."[26] The purpose of this requirement is to distinguish between land-based workers who do not face maritime dangers and the sea-based workers who do face those dangers.[27]

To support its argument that Naquin was not sufficiently exposed to maritime perils to merit seaman status, EBI emphasizes that Naquin was rarely required to spend the night aboard a vessel, that the vessels he worked upon were ordinarily docked, and that he almost never ventured beyond the immediate canal area or onto the open sea. However, courts have consistently rejected the categorical assertion that workers who spend their time aboard vessels near the shore do not face maritime perils. While these near-shore workers may face fewer risks, they still remain exposed to the perils of a [—9—]

maritime work environment.[28] As the Supreme Court explained in *Stewart v. Dutra*:

> [I]t seems a stretch of the imagination to class the deck hands of a mud dredge in the quiet waters of a Potomac creek with the bold and skillful mariners who breast the angry waves of the Atlantic; but such and so far-reaching are the principles which underlie the jurisdiction of the courts of admiralty that they adapt themselves to all the new kinds of property and new sets of operatives and new conditions which are brought into existence in the progress of the world.[29]

This court's decision in *Endeavor Marine* is particularly instructive. There, we considered whether a derrick barge crane operator had the requisite connection to a vessel that was substantial in terms of nature.[30] The crane operator worked exclusively on a stationary crane barge used to load and unload cargo at a Mississippi River dock facility.[31] He was rarely required to board a moving vessel and he never traveled beyond the immediate dock area.[32] Moreover, his primary job was to operate the crane on the barge and to repair and maintain the equipment on the barge.[33] The district court found the employee's connection to the barge was not substantial in nature because "it did not take him to sea. His work brought him aboard the barge only after the vessel [—10—] was moored or in the process of mooring."[34] We reversed. Despite the fact that the crane operator was not literally "taken to sea" and did not face some of the maritime dangers faced by seamen on moving vessels in the open sea, we still concluded that he was regularly exposed to

---

[22] *See id.*

[23] *See id.* at 371.

[24] *Roberts v. Cardinal Servs., Inc.*, 266 F.3d 368, 376 (5th Cir. 2011).

[25] *See Endeavor Marine*, 234 F.3d at 291.

[26] *See id.* at 292.

[27] *See Papai*, 520 U.S. at 560.

[28] *See Stewart v. Dutra Constr. Co.*, 543 U.S. 481, 497 (2005); *Endeavor Marine*, 234 F.3d at 291. *See also Grab v. Boh Bros. Constr. Co., L.L.C.*, 506 F. App'x 271, 276 (5th Cir. 2013) (unpublished) ("[T]he fact that [the injured employee] returned home daily did not remove him from his exposure to cognizable dangers of the sea.").

[29] 543 U.S. at 497 (internal citation omitted).

[30] 234 F.3d 287.

[31] *Id.* at 289.

[32] *Id.*

[33] *Id.* at 292 n.4.

[34] *Id.* at 291.

the perils of the sea and qualified as a seaman.[35]

We see no basis to distinguish *Endeavor Marine* from the instant case.[36] Like the crane operator in that case, Naquin's primary job duties were performed doing the ship's work on vessels docked or at anchor in navigable water. In doing this work, Naquin faced precisely the same type and degree of maritime perils faced by the port-bound derrick barge crane operator in *Endeavor Marine*. Additionally, we have dozens of cases finding oilfield workers and other "brown-water" workers on drilling barges and other vessels qualified as seamen even though they spent all their work time on these vessels submerged in quiet inland canals and waterways.[37] Accordingly, we conclude [—11—] that Naquin's connection to the EBI vessel fleet was substantial in terms of nature.

The record demonstrates that Naquin contributes to the function of a discrete fleet of vessels and has a connection with the fleet that is substantial in terms of both duration and nature. We therefore hold that the evidence supports the jury's finding that Naquin is a seaman.[38]

B.

EBI next argues that the district court abused its discretion by erroneously instructing the jury on the issue of seaman status. We apply a two-part test in considering a challenge to the district court's jury instructions: (1) First, the party challenging the instructions must "demonstrate that the charge as a whole creates substantial and ineradicable doubt whether the jury has been properly guided in its deliberations; and (2) Second, even where a jury instruction was erroneous, "we will not reverse if we determine, based upon the entire record, that the challenged instruction could not have affected the outcome of the case."[39] EBI levels a very specific complaint against the district court's instruction: That the district court erred by presenting the two prongs of the seaman test in reverse order, by "garbling" the separate requirements of the test, and failing to emphasize that a seaman's connection to vessels must be substantial in terms of *nature*.

In the instant case, the district court charged the jury as follows:

> Under the governing law the plaintiff is a seaman if he proves by a preponderance of the evidence the following: A, or first, that he has a connection to a vessel in navigation, or to an identifiable group of [—12—] vessels, that is substantial in terms of both its duration and nature, and secondly that his duty contributed to the function of a vessel or identifiable group

---

[35] *Id.* at 292.

[36] In *Endeavor Marine* the employee suffered his injury while working aboard a vessel, whereas Naquin was injured as he performed land-based duties. This distinction is not relevant to our analysis of whether Naquin qualifies as a Jones Act seaman because that inquiry is status-based, and does not focus solely upon the employee's activity at the time of the injury. *See Chandris*, 515 U.S. at 361 ("It is therefore well settled . . . that the Jones Act inquiry is fundamentally status based: Land-based maritime workers do not become seamen because they happen to be working on board a vessel when they are injured, and seamen do not lose Jones Act protection when the course of their service to a vessel [or group of vessels] takes them ashore.").

[37] *See, e.g., Producers Drilling Co. v. Gray*, 361 F.2d 432 (5th Cir. 1966) (employee performed maintenance work on submersible drilling barge in a navigable canal); *Colomb v. Texaco, Inc.*, 736 F.2d 218 (5th Cir. 1984) (employee worked aboard inland submersible barge at the end of a canal off inland waters which were eight feet deep); *Landry v. Amoco Production Co.*, 595 F.2d 1070 (5th Cir. 1979) (employee was a roustabout who worked aboard barges in inland waters and marshes); *Grab v. Boh Bros. Const. Co., LLC*, 506 F. App'x 271 (5th Cir. 2013) (per curiam) (unpublished) (employees worked aboard a crane barge in Lake Ponchartrain.

[38] Because the jury's seaman status finding was supported by the evidence, it follows that the district court did not err in denying EBI's motions for summary judgment, judgment as a matter of law, or a new trial. *See* FED. R. CIV. PROC. 56(a).

[39] *Navigant Consulting, Inc. v. Wilkinson*, 508 F.3d 277, 293 (5th Cir. 2007) (internal citation omitted).

of vessels, or to the accomplishment of its mission.

Despite a reversal of the test's normal organization, the above instruction is wholly consistent with our own articulation of the seaman test.[40] After reviewing the relevant jury charge in its entirety, we do not agree that the charge was confusing or misleading. Quite the opposite, a careful review of the district court's explanation reveals a careful attempt to explain a difficult-to-define concept to a jury of laymen. The court's explanation points out that Naquin's connection to the EBI fleet is only substantial if it was "an actual, regular connection"; that the connection must be "more than a temporary or occasional connection"; and that the jury should "focus on the nature and location of [Naquin's] work." In fact, the court's instruction mirrors the Supreme Court's explanation of the seaman status test in *Chandris v. Latsis*.[41]

Because the district court's seaman status instruction was clear and consistent with the usual articulation, we conclude that the district court did not err in its instruction on the issue of seaman status.

C.

EBI next argues that the evidence is insufficient to support the jury's finding of negligence. Specifically, EBI contends that it cannot be negligent because there is no evidence indicating that EBI caused or could have foreseen the accident.

The law of employer negligence is clear: Every employer has a duty to provide its employees with a reasonably safe work environment and work [—13—] equipment.[42] Because EBI designed, constructed, operated, and maintained the defective LC-400 crane which injured Naquin, EBI is liable if its negligent performance of any of those activities caused Naquin's injuries.

In this case, the testimony at trial established that the crane, which was manufactured by EBI, fell when the weld which bound the crane to its base failed. EBI's witness testified that the test block being moved by the crane was well within the rated capacity of the LC-400 crane. Although Naquin was unable to prove precisely why the weld failed, it is undisputed that EBI was the party who was responsible for the design of the crane' and the integrity of the weld and who could have implemented more stringent weld safety standards. Relying upon this circumstantial evidence, the jury determined that EBI was negligent.

On appeal, EBI argues that the exclusive reliance upon circumstantial evidence in this case is essentially a dependence on the doctrine of *res ipsa loquitur*.[43] Because *res ipsa* was never specifically pled or asserted, EBI argues, the argument has been waived and Naquin cannot rely exclusively on the fact that EBI was responsible for the weld to establish its negligence.

This court considered this precise argument on nearly identical facts in *Watz v. Zapata Off-Shore Co.*[44] Sitting in admiralty, the *Watz* court considered whether a chain manufacturer had been negligent when a defective weld in the chain caused it to snap, injuring a shipyard worker below.[45] At a bench trial, the district court inferred from the defective weld that chain manufacturer was [—14—] negligent.[46] On appeal to this court, the chain manufacturer argued that the district court could not rely on what amounted to a theory of *res ipsa* when no such theory had been pled.[47] However, we rejected the chain manufacturer's contention, stating:

---

[40] *See, e.g.*, *Becker*, 335 F.3d at 387–88.

[41] 515 U.S. at 370–71.

[42] *See Strong v. B.P. Exploration & Prod., Inc.*, 440 F.3d 665, 669 (5th Cir. 2006).

---

[43] Under *res ipsa loquitur*, a jury is permitted to infer negligence on the part of the one who exercised control over an item where that item has caused the damage and other plausible explanations have been reasonably ruled out. *See Brown v. Olin Chem. Corp.*, 231 F.3d 197 (5th Cir. 2000).

[44] 431 F.2d 100 (5th Cir. 1970).

[45] *Id.* at 103.

[46] *Id.* at 119.

[47] *Id.*

Certainly [the plaintiff] bore the burden of proof to show Campbell's [(the chain manufacturer)] negligence. But once it was proved that a defective weld had occurred during the manufacture of the chain by Campbell, we believe that the district court sitting as a finder of fact could reasonably infer negligence from that circumstantial evidence. Campbell objects that the pleadings and evidence did not specifically raise the doctrine of *res ipsa loquitur* and the district court did not refer to it. The evidence credibly established that responsible chain manufacturers attempt to avoid defective welds in the knowledge that they are dangerous. The finder of fact could reasonably infer that a defective weld would ordinarily not occur in the absence of negligence. We see no reason to invoke the Latin phrase here. We simply apply a rule of circumstantial evidence, not changing the burden of proof or casting presumptions against the defendant.[48]

There is no basis on which to distinguish this case from the holding of *Watz*. EBI was the only party responsible for welding the LC-400 crane to its base, a weld which was indisputably defective and the direct cause of Naquin's injuries. We therefore hold that this evidence, though circumstantial, is sufficient to support the jury's finding of negligence. [—15—]

D.

EBI next argues that the district court abused its discretion when it admitted evidence of the death of Naquin's cousin's husband ("the relative") because it found such evidence to be relevant to Naquin's claim for emotional damages. The relative was killed when the collapsing crane crushed part of the building in which he was working. Arguing that the relative's death was irrelevant to any of the issues at the trial, EBI filed a motion in limine to exclude any references to the death as prejudicial. The district court denied the motion, concluding that though potentially prejudicial, the evidence was relevant to Naquin's claims for emotional damages. At the trial, much of Naquin's claim for his emotional damages focused on his relative's death, and the jury ultimately awarded him $1,000,000 for past and future emotional suffering.

Because the death of Naquin's relative is unquestionably irrelevant to the issues of seaman status and EBI negligence, the only issue to which it might have been relevant is Naquin's emotional damages. However, the Jones Act does not indiscriminately permit compensation for emotional damages resulting from the death of another person.

In *Consolidated Rail Corp. v. Gottshall*,[49] the Supreme Court was called upon to determine the extent to which an employer is liable for emotional damages under the Federal Employers' Liability Act ("FELA").[50] The negligence provision of FELA is expressly incorporated into the Jones Act. Specifically, the *Gottshall* Court considered whether an employee could recover for emotional distress from his employer after witnessing a co-worker die due to the employer's negligence.[51] Recognizing that the emotional harm caused by an accident is [—16—] potentially limitless, the Court observed the need for limits on those who can recover such damages.[52] The Court then surveyed the common law on the issue, identifying three major limiting tests for evaluating claims of negligent infliction of emotional distress: (1) the "physical impact" test, which only permits recovery for emotional damages if the plaintiff sustains a physical impact; (2) the "zone of danger" test, which permits recovery if the plaintiff was physically impacted *or* within the zone of

---

[48] *Id.* EBI points out that its practice was to hire a third party to inspect and test crane welds, but that the records documenting who had inspected the instant crane had been destroyed by Hurricane Katrina. However, this does not distinguish the instant case from *Watz*, where the chain manufacturer similarly insisted that it had conducted tests on the defective chain but had destroyed the documentation in the ordinary course of business.

[49] 512 U.S. 532 (1994).

[50] 45 U.S.C. §§ 51–60.

[51] *Id.* at 536.

[52] *Id.* at 546.

potential impact; and (3) the "relative bystander" test, which extends recovery to those in the zone of danger as well as close relatives of a victim who are physically near and who observe the injury.[53] Concluding that "FELA's central focus [is] on physical perils," the Court also recognized that "a near miss may be as frightening as a direct hit."[54] Therefore, the Court reasoned, the appropriate test for awarding emotional damages under FELA—and by extension, the Jones Act—is whether the plaintiff was in the "zone of danger."[55]

Turning to the instant case, there is no question that Naquin was in the zone of danger and may therefore claim damages for his emotional harm. However, we are still left with the question of whether Naquin may assert a claim for emotional harm arising from the injury *to his relative*. In other words, Naquin contends that a Jones Act plaintiff, once physically injured and entitled to emotional damages, is entitled to the full spectrum of emotional damages, including those arising from an injury to someone else.

Despite the simplistic appeal of Naquin's argument, there is no caselaw or reasoning to support it. Instead, the Supreme Court's discussion of emotional [—17—] damages in *Gottshall* emphasizes the limited scope of damages available to individuals within the zone of danger: the emotional harm suffered from being physically injured or the emotional harm suffered from *almost* being physically injured.[56] As described by the Supreme Court, the zone of danger test allows a Jones Act plaintiff "to recover for emotional injury caused by *fear of physical injury to himself*."[57] More tellingly, the *Gottshall* Court explicitly rejected the relative bystander test, which would have permitted certain relatives to recover for emotional damages caused by witnessing an injury to someone else.[58] As our

own court has previously recognized, it would be a "major departure from the existing jurisprudence" to "allow recovery for injuries resulting not from physical trauma, or the fear of physical trauma, to the plaintiff but from witnessing a 'bad sight,' *i.e.*, harm to another."[59]

Several other considerations bolster this conclusion. If multiple people witness an injury to someone else, it would be arbitrary to award emotional damages for seeing that person's injury only to those people who also happened to suffer an injury at the same time. Moreover, the Jones Act only extends an action to recover for the death of a seaman to his immediate family.[60] It would thus be inconsistent with the Jones Act's wrongful death provision to permit anyone else to recover for the negligent death of a coworker. [—18—]

This conclusion is also most consistent with this court's decision in *Gaston v. Flowers Transp.*[61] In that case, we rejected an emotional damage claim by a Jones Act plaintiff who watched his half-brother get crushed to death between two vessels.[62] Although the *Gaston* plaintiff had not been physically injured, we nonetheless distinguished between plaintiffs who suffer emotional harm from an event "directly affecting *him*" and plaintiffs who suffer harm from "witnessing the death of *another*."[63] We finally concluded, "whatever merit allowing recovery for purely emotional injury may have or may lack, we see none in allowing mere crewmen-bystanders to recover for witnessing the misfortune of another."[64]

---

[53] *Id*. at 547–49.
[54] *Id*. at 547, 555 (internal citation omitted).
[55] *See id*. at 555.
[56] *Id*. at 555–56.
[57] *Id*. at 556 (emphasis added).
[58] Even if the Supreme Court had adopted the "relative bystander" test, that test ordinarily requires a relationship closer than that of victim's

spouse's cousin. *See, e.g.,* La. Civ. Code Art. 2315.6 (limiting bystander emotional damage claims to a spouse, child, grandchild, parent, sibling, or grandparent).
[59] *See Plaisance v. Texaco, Inc.*, 966 F.2d 166, 169 (5th Cir. 1992) (en banc).
[60] *See* 45 U.S.C. § 51.
[61] 866 F.2d 816 (5th Cir. 1989).
[62] *Id*. at 819–21.
[63] *Id*. at 819.
[64] *Id*. at 821. *See also Barker v. Hercules Offshore, Inc.*, 713 F.3d 208, 225, 1 Adm. R. 206, 217 (5th Cir. 2013) (finding that, because platform worker who was present when co-worker fell to his

The Supreme Court's decision in *Gottshall* and our own reasoning in similar cases compel us to conclude that emotional damages resulting purely from another person's injury, and not a fear of injury to one's self, are not compensable under the Jones Act. Such is the case even when the plaintiff has also been injured. To award damages for observing a "bad sight," even one which involves a family member, would contravene the zone of danger test's intent to compensate for physical dangers. Accordingly, we hold that Naquin's emotional damages arising from the death of his relative are not compensable under the Jones Act and the evidence regarding those damages should have been excluded from the trial.

Because we cannot discern to what extent Naquin's $1,000,000 award for emotional suffering was based upon the non-compensable harm caused by the [—19—] relative's death, the emotional portion of his damages is tainted.[65] Moreover, most reported decisions do not distinguish between physical and emotional pain and suffering awards,[66] so

we cannot utilize our usual comparative framework for evaluating the reasonableness of Naquin's *physical* damage award in isolation.[67] The record also reveals that counsel for Naquin in his closing argument leaned heavily on the emotional damages Naquin suffered as a result [—20—] of his relative's death.[68] Because Naquin's lost wages claim is also founded partially upon his non-compensable emotional injury, it too is tainted.[69]

Aucoin v. State through Dep't of Transp. and Dev., 712 So.2d 62 (La. 1998).

[67] Under this circuit's "maximum recovery rule," we will uphold a jury award if there is a damage award in at least one "factually similar case from the relevant jurisdiction" that, when increased by 50%, equals or exceeds the challenged jury award. *See Moore v. M/V ANGELA*, 353 F.3d 376, 384 (5th Cir. 2003).

[68] During his closing argument, counsel for Naquin said the following regarding Naquin's emotional damages due to the death of his relative:

> . . . He has tremendous issues because of [the accident]. I don't know that you could write anything more horrific than killing one of your relatives in an accident. You know, I hope Larry gets a lot out of that.
>
> I think when you assign a value to that, I think one thing you're signalling (sic) to him is whether you've understood it or not. I don't know how you put a value on a person's well-being mentally. I don't know how you sit down and try to get your head around someone who is actually going to kill themselves. That is extremely hard.
>
> I would suggest one comparison again to his past wages and future wages. If that little $550,000 is what his pocketbook is hurt, then what can you imagine his mind has been through and his experiences have been hurt. I would suggest, again, two to three times that is very fair for this man. Some of you may feel that's a low figure. You may think who is this lawyer who is trivializing what this man has been through. That's up for you all to decide.

[69] Naquin's claim for future lost wages stems solely from his inability to accept EBI's offer of sedentary work due to his continuing emotional distress. However, the lost wage consequences of Naquin's emotional distress are only compensable to the extent his distress is compensable. Because a substantial portion of his emotional damages are

---

death was not "in immediate risk of physical harm," he was not entitled to emotional damages).

[65] EBI also complains that the jury erred by awarding mental anguish damages to Naquin for his depression despite the lack of corroborating medical testimony. "Any award for emotional injury greater than nominal damages must be supported by evidence of the character and severity of the injury to the plaintiff's emotional well-being." *Salinas v. O'Neill*, 286 F.3d 827, 830 (5th Cir. 2002). Nonetheless, we have also previously recognized our unwillingness to "hold that medical evidence or corroborating testimony is always required for an award of mental anguish damages." *See Migis v. Pearle Vision, Inc.*, 135 F.3d 1041, 1046 (5th Cir. 1998). Instead, where a plaintiff's mental anguish testimony is corroborated by other witnesses, circumstances, and facts, we do not necessarily require expert medical testimony. *See id.* Although no expert testified concerning Naquin's depression, Naquin's own testimony regarding his mental anguish was supported by the testimony of his wife, his visits to doctors and social workers, and his prescription use of an anti-depressant drug following the accident.

[66] *See, e.g., Simeon v. T. Smith & Son, Inc.*, 852 F.2d 1421, 1427 (5th Cir. 1988); *Bernard v. United States*, 794 F. Supp. 608, 611 (E.D. La. 1991);

Even putting these concerns aside, serious practical problems would be presented at trial if we were to save some elements of the damage award and retry only other elements of damage. "[W]here, as here, the jury's findings on questions relating to liability were based on sufficient evidence and made in accordance with law, it [i]s proper to order a new trial only as to damages."[70] We therefore retain the jury's liability finding but order a new trial on damages.[71] [—21—]

IV.

For the reasons stated above, we AFFIRM the judgment of the district court as it relates to liability, but VACATE the judgment of the district court as it relates to damages and REMAND for proceedings consistent with this opinion.

AFFIRMED in part, VACATED and REMANDED in part.

(Reporter's Note: Dissenting opinion follows on p. 210).

---

based upon noncompensable emotional distress arising from the death of his relative, future wages lost because of that non-compensable emotional distress are likewise non-compensable.

As the issue has been raised by EBI, we separately note the proper work-life expectancy basis for calculating future lost wages on remand: "It may be shown by evidence that a particular person, by virtue of his health or occupation or other factors, is likely to live and work a longer, or shorter, period than the average. Absent such evidence, however, computations should be based on the statistical average." *Madore v. Ingram Tank Ships, Inc.*, 732 F.2d 475, 478 (5th Cir. 1984).

[70] *Hadra v. Herman Blum Consulting Engineers*, 632 F.2d 1242, 1246 (5th Cir. 1980).

[71] Because we remand the case for a new trial on damages, we need not consider EBI's final point of error, which alleges that the jury's emotional damage award was tainted by an [—21—] inadvertent discussion of previously-excluded testimony.

[—22—] JONES, Circuit Judge, dissenting:

I concur in all of this good opinion except the decision affirming Naquin's status as a seaman. On this issue, I respectfully disagree.

I. Seaman Status Elements

To be a seaman, Naquin must satisfy the two-prong test established in *Chandris v. Latsis*: (1) his duties must contribute to the function of the vessel or to the accomplishment of its mission; and (2) he must have a connection to a vessel in navigation (or to an identifiable group of such vessels) that is substantial in terms of both duration and nature. *Chandris v. Latsis*, 515 U.S. 347, 368 (1997). I agree with the majority that Naquin passes the first prong of the *Chandris* test. In my view, however, Naquin does not satisfy the duration or nature components of *Chandris*'s second prong. Indeed, if a jury could hold Naquin is a seaman, then it could so conclude as to any shore-based worker who maintained EBI's on-board computers or went aboard the lift-boats to gas them up before they left the repair yard. *Chandris* and *Sw. Marine, Inc. v. Gizoni*, 502 U.S. 81 (1991), broadly commit these cases to the jury, but they do not prevent courts from ever distinguishing seamen from harbor workers as a matter of law.

II. Duration Component

As a general rule, the duration component of *Chandris*'s second prong is satisfied when an employee spends 30 percent or more of his time in service of a "vessel in navigation." *Chandris*, 515 U.S. at 371. (The Supreme Court adopted this circuit's opinion in *Barrett v. Chevron, U.S.A.*, 781 F.2d 1067 (5th Cir. 1986) (en banc) on this rule of thumb.) But the Court noted,

This figure [30%] serves as no more than a guideline . . . and departure from it will certainly be justified in appropriate [—23—] cases . . . . And where undisputed facts reveal that a maritime worker has a clearly inadequate temporal connection to vessels in navigation, the court may take the question from the jury . . . .

Chandris, 515 U.S. at 371.

The sole issue here is whether Naquin's work as a repair supervisor on vessels docked in a canal or in drydock counts as service of a vessel in navigation. Naquin spent 70 percent of his time employed in this capacity.[1] In denying EBI's motion for summary judgment, the district court took a statement from *Chandris* out of context to reach a conclusion that runs contrary to the "fundamental distinction" that *Chandris* recognized between land-based and sea-based maritime workers. *Cf. id.* at 358. According to the district court, Naquin's land-based repair time was connected to a vessel in navigation because, as *Chandris* noted, a vessel remains in navigation even when it is temporarily moored or docked for repairs. *Naquin v. Elevating Boats, LLC*, 842 F. Supp. 2d 1008, 1017 (E.D. La. 2012) (citing *Chandris*, 515 U.S. at 373-74). The majority concludes without further discussion that Naquin's time repairing the lift-boat cranes satisfies the duration component.

In my view, this conclusion is irreconcilable with *Chandris*'s "basic point," which is that land-based employees like Naquin are not seamen. *Chandris*, 515 U.S. at 370 ("The Jones Act remedy is reserved for *sea-based* maritime employees whose work regularly exposes them [to maritime peril]" . . . . [T]he ultimate inquiry is whether the worker in question is a member of the vessel's crew or *simply a land-based employee*.") (emphasis added); *see also Heise v. Fishing Co. of Alaska*, 79 F.3d 903, 906 (9th Cir. 1996) (holding that a land-based repairman assigned to perform routine, off-season [—24—] maintenance on a fishing vessel did not satisfy *Chandris*'s first prong where the "first basic principle" behind *Chandris*'s definition of seaman is that the term does "not include land-based workers"). Moreover, the passage in *Chandris* regarding temporarily moored or docked vessels is

---

[1] The rest of Naquin's hours were not connected with a vessel in navigation. He divided nearly all of his remaining time between the fabrication shop and operating a land-based crane in the shipyard.

inapplicable to the present facts. Unlike the plaintiff in *Chandris*, Naquin did not sail on a ship that was temporarily docked. He worked almost exclusively on vessels that were moored, jacked up, or docked in the shipyard undergoing repair, and found himself on a navigable vessel only on rare occasions.[2] To allow Naquin to accrue the 30 percent minimum temporal connection while solely working on docked vessels under repair essentially removes the duration component for other land-based repairmen who are fortunate enough to work on vessels that do not require long-term repairs. According to the majority, these repairmen could always claim that they spent their time working on vessels "in navigation" despite the fact they do all of their work on or tied to land, safely removed from maritime dangers. To me, this outcome defies logic and disregards the overarching purpose of the Jones Act as stated in *Chandris*.

III. Nature Component

I also disagree with the majority's analysis of the nature component of *Chandris*'s second prong. The majority characterizes the facts that support the conclusion that Naquin spent all of his time dockside as a "categorical assertion" that does not demonstrate that Naquin was protected from maritime perils. But in the next sentence, the majority categorically asserts that near-shore workers "still remain exposed to the perils of the sea," citing no facts showing that Naquin, who spent nearly all of his time on boats [—25—] *moored to a dock*, faced any maritime perils in the ordinary course of his duties. This "moving right along" approach to the particulars of Naquin's employment runs contrary to the fact-specific inquiry that the Supreme Court has recommended for determining seaman status. *See, e.g., McDermott Int'l, Inc. v. Wilander*, 498 U.S. 337, 356 (1991) (holding that Jones Act status turns on the employee's "precise relation" to the vessel).

The majority then references several cases to support Naquin's claim to seaman's status,

but they have no bearing on what circumstances, if any, entitle a dockside worker like Naquin to Jones Act coverage. The sole issue in *Stewart v. Dutra Constr. Co.* was whether the dredge was a vessel for the purposes of the Jones Act. The court did not address whether the harbor-bound worker, much less the land-based repair supervisor suing in our case, faced maritime peril. *Stewart v. Dutra Const. Co.*, 543 U.S. 481, 485 (2005). Similarly, the dispositive factor in *Grab v. Boh Bros. Constr. Co., L.L.C.*, was not that the workers operated near the shore but that their work exposed them to sea-related dangers. The plaintiffs travelled daily to their worksite by crewboat and helped navigate a barge, which routinely had to be moved along the length of the Lake Pontchartrain bridge. *Grab v. Boh Bros. Constr. Co., L.L.C*, 506 F. App'x 271, 274, 276 (5th Cir. 2013). Naquin's shore-side duties exposed him to no such maritime perils.

In my view, the majority also misapplies *Endeavor Marine*. In that case, the district court held that plaintiff was not a seaman under *Harbor Tug and Barge Co. v. Papai* because his job did not literally "take him to sea." *In re Endeavor Marine Inc.*, 234 F.3d 287, 289 (5th Cir. 2000) (per curiam). We reversed, holding that the "going to sea" requirement is satisfied whenever the employee's connection to the vessel regularly exposes him to maritime [—26—] perils. *Id.* at 291. Further, we ruled that the plaintiff faced such perils. *Id.* at 292. The contrast between the work performed by the *Endeavor Marine* plaintiff and Naquin, however, seems clear. The *Endeavor Marine* plaintiff was a derrick barge crane operator who loaded and unloaded cargo vessels *in the Mississippi River* (not a canal). *Id.* at 288. His job required him to travel over water to his worksite and exposed him to the uniquely maritime dangers that arose when his barge was moored to the cargo vessels that he was assigned to load or unload. *Id.* at 289. He was injured, moreover, when struck by a mooring cable as he was handling the lines while waiting for his barge to be positioned alongside the cargo vessel. *Id.* Naquin, on the other hand, spent nearly all of his time dockside, repairing boats that were secured in the shipyard canal, or operating a

---

[2] Naquin testified that he was aboard on a moving vessel less than one percent of his time at work.

land-based crane, or working in the shipyard fabrication shop. His employment, in sum, was substantially similar to that of other land-based employees whose seaman status has been denied by federal and state courts.[3]

Finally, the majority refers to our "brown water" cases to show that employees who work on quiet waterways may recover under the Jones Act. All of these cases, however, involve employees who performed their work [—27—] while their vessel was operating on water.[4] Thus, they offer no help to Naquin, who worked nearly always in the shipyard.

IV. Conclusion

With all respect to the majority, I would hold that Naquin is not entitled to seaman status and, therefore, reverse the district court's ruling that EBI was liable under the Jones Act.

---

[3] *See, e.g., Clark v. Am. Marine & Salvage, LLC,* 494 Fed. App'x 32 (11th Cir. 2012) (unpublished) (affirming dismissal of Jones Act claim brought by crane operator who performed most of his repairs on land); *Schultz v. Louisiana Dock Co.* 94 F. Supp. 2d 746 (E.D. La. 2000) (ruling that repairman who inspected and repaired moored barges was not a seaman); *Richard v. Mike Hooks, Inc.,* 799 So.2d 462 (La. 2001) (reversing lower courts and dismissing land-based repairman's Jones Act claim).

[4] *See Producers Drilling Co. v. Gray,* 361 F.2d 432 (5th Cir. 1966) (affirming seaman status where employee worked on barge that traveled through navigable waters); *Colomb v. Texaco, Inc.,* 736 F.2d 218 (5th Cir. 1984) (holding that oilfield worker assigned to inland, submersible barge was a seaman); *Landry v. Amoco Production Co.,* 595 F.2d 1070 (5th Cir. 1979) (providing that worker employed as roustabout aboard barges on inland waters is a seaman); *Boh Bros. Const. Co., LLC, supra* (ruling that employees who worked aboard a crane barge on Lake Ponchartrain were seamen).

United States Court of Appeals
for the Fifth Circuit

No. 13-30315

IN RE DEEPWATER HORIZON

LAKE EUGENIE LAND & DEV., INC.
vs.
BP EXPLORATION & PROD., INC.

Appeals from the United States District Court for the
Eastern District of Louisiana

Decided: May 19, 2014

Citation: 753 F.3d 516, 2 Adm. R. 213 (5th Cir. 2014).

ON PETITION FOR REHEARING EN BANC
(Opinions 732 F.3d 326, 1 Adm. R. 287; 744 F.3d 370,
2 Adm. R. 183)

Before **DENNIS, CLEMENT,** and **SOUTHWICK,** Circuit
Judges.

[—4—] ORDER:

The court having been polled at the request of one of its members, and a majority of the judges who are in regular active service and not disqualified not having voted in favor (FED. R. APP. P.35 and 5TH CIR. R. 35), the Petition for Rehearing En Banc is DENIED.[1]

In the en banc poll, five judges voted in favor of rehearing (Judges Jolly, Jones, Clement, Owen, and Elrod) and eight judges voted against (Chief Judge Stewart and Judges Davis, Dennis, Prado, Southwick, Haynes, Graves, and Higginson).

ENTERED FOR THE COURT:

/s/ Leslie H. Southwick
Leslie H. Southwick
United States Circuit Judge

(Reporter's Note: Dissenting opinion follows on p. 214).

---

[1] Judge Smith is recused and did not participate in the consideration of the petition for rehearing en banc.

[—5—] **CLEMENT,** Circuit Judge, dissenting from Denial of Rehearing En Banc, joined by **JOLLY** and **JONES,** Circuit Judges:[1]

This court's denial of the petition for rehearing the Business Economic Loss panel decision en banc misses the last opportunity for this court to clarify its prior *Deepwater Horizon* decisions and to enforce a proper application of standing and causation. The panel opinion conflicts with prior precedent, and "the proceeding involves . . . questions of exceptional importance." Fed. R. App. P. 35(b)(1). En banc rehearing should have been granted. We respectfully dissent.

I

While this court may convert a petition for rehearing en banc into a petition for panel rehearing, the approach is typically reserved to grant some requested relief to the petitioner. *See In re Scopac*, 649 F.3d 320 (5th Cir. 2011). Judge Southwick's new order essentially serves as a second opportunity to extrapolate on his rejection of BP's position, apparently in an attempt to coalesce the reasoning between his and Judge Dennis's prior opinions in our latest take on this tortuous case. *See In re Deepwater Horizon*, No. 13-30315, 2014 WL 841313, 2 Adm. R. 183 (5th Cir. Mar. 3, 2014) ("*Deepwater Horizon III*"). The new order does not withdraw the panel's opinion or provide different legal analysis, it merely adds additional discussion. This discussion is not responsive to any motions filed by BP and does not change any holding from the prior panel opinion. It also has no effect on the related panel opinion in 13-30095. The failure to consolidate these cases has led to continued confusion in appeals that are inextricably intertwined and related. [—6—]

II

This court's decisions thus far have suffered from divided reasoning and a complete refusal to address the critical decision of the district court. Our first decision

remanded to the district court to address the issue of matching of revenues and expenses and for consideration of "the issue of causation." *In re Deepwater Horizon*, 732 F.3d 326, 347, 1 Adm. R. 287, 303 (5th Cir. 2013) ("*Deepwater Horizon I*") (Southwick, J., concurring). On remand, the district court addressed the matching issue but not causation. Order at 1, *In re Oil Spill by Oil Rig Deepwater Horizon in Gulf of Mexico, on April 20, 2010*, MDL No. 2179 (E.D. La. Oct. 3, 2013). BP appealed this refusal to address causation on November 21, 2013.

On December 2, 2013, we held that the district court erred by not considering arguments on causation. The district court proceeded to address those arguments and released an order on December 24, 2013. Order, *In re Oil Spill by Oil Rig Deepwater Horizon in Gulf of Mexico, on April 20, 2010*, MDL No. 2179 (E.D. La. Dec. 24, 2013). In that order, the district court held "that judicial estoppel bars BP from advancing its current interpretation of the Settlement Agreement." *Id.* at 12. The lower court, broadly and unambiguously, found that BP's prior statements barred it from raising any arguments concerning causation, or even "similar arguments."[2] [—7—]

---

[1] Judge Garza would join this dissent if he had been able to vote as an active member of the en banc panel.

[2] The district court held,

that BP is judicially estopped from arguing (1) that Exhibit 4B is not the exclusive means of determining whether a business economic loss is "as a result of" of [sic] the Deepwater Horizon incident for purposes of the Settlement, including the Class Definition; (2) or that the Settlement contains, implicitly or explicitly, a causation requirement other than Exhibit 4B; (3) or that satisfying Exhibit 4B does not establish under the Settlement an irrebuttable presumption that a business' economic loss was "as a result of" the Deepwater Horizon Incident; (4) or making similar arguments. As a corollary to this ruling, the Court finds that whether a business economic loss is "as a result of" the Deepwater Horizon Incident for purposes of the [—7—] Settlement is determined exclusively and conclusively by Exhibit 4B.

Id. at 18.

Over my objection, the panel declined to come to a definitive ruling on this critical issue. *See Deepwater Horizon III.* Instead, Judge Southwick's opinion relied on an attestation form that the lower court never discussed or addressed in the entirety of its 43-page order. But this analysis was never explicitly agreed to by Judge Dennis, whose concurrence described the procedural history and then essentially concurred in the judgment only.[3] While by implication Judge Southwick's consideration of the merits of BP's arguments signified a rejection of the judicial estoppel ruling, Judge Dennis apparently wanted to affirm the district court's ruling on estoppel alone. Reading the published opinions together with the district court's orders, it was clear that no two judges agreed on any legal basis for affirming. Because there was no definitive ruling on judicial estoppel in the panel opinion there was clear legal error that it was the duty of this court en banc to address. After a close vote, this court declined to do so.

Judge Southwick now submits yet another revised order, styled a denial of a petition for panel rehearing. This apparent attempt to

---

[3] The operative portion of Judge Dennis's concurrence reads,

Although I continue to adhere to the views I expressed previously in this case, I now join Judge Southwick in affirming the district court's December 24, 2013 order interpreting the settlement agreement as written and declining to add, by judicial gloss, any additional requirements, procedures, or other provisions not contained in the text of the settlement agreement and consent decree and its attached exhibits. I agree with Judge Southwick that BP's renewed motion for an injunction should be denied and that no injunction against the payment of business-economic-loss claims shall continue. I also agree that we are bound by the certification panel's Article III, Rule 23, and Rules Enabling Act rulings in its January 10, 2014 opinion and decision. Accordingly, for these reasons, I concur in the above described conclusions reached by Judge Southwick and in the judgment he has written for the majority of this panel.

Id. at *8.

meld the reasoning [—8—] between his and Judge Dennis's prior opinions is too little too late and leaves the essential results unchanged: the class of people who will recover from this settlement continues to include significant numbers of people whose losses, if any, were not caused by BP. Our court's decisions would allow payments to "victims" such as a wireless phone company store that burned down and a RV park owner that was foreclosed on before the spill.[4] Left intact, our holdings funnel BP's cash into the pockets of undeserving non-victims.

These are certainly absurd results. And despite our colleagues' continued efforts to shift the blame for these absurdities to BP's lawyers, it remains the fact that we are party to this fraud by (1) adopting an unreasonable interpretation of the Settlement Agreement to remove any requirement of causation, and (2) certifying a class by ignoring the fact that although causation and traceability were initially written into the Settlement Agreement, the Claim's Administrator's interpretation governing what would *actually happen* meant that Article III requirements would be ignored in the class settlement's execution.[5] The dissent to the denial of panel rehearing for the certification panel, 13-30095, explains in greater detail this elimination of causation.

---

[4] *60 Minutes: BP cries foul in massive oil spill settlement* (CBS television broadcast May 4, 2014) *available at* http://www.cbsnews.com/videos/bp-cries-foul-in-massive-oil-spill-settlement/.

[5] However, Judge Southwick's order "conclude[s] that causation is never abandoned as a requirement" and BP is thus implicitly *not* judicially estopped from continuing to argue causation in the district court, or to the Claims Administrator, for the settlement globally or against individual fraudulent claims. As I read this latest opinion, BP may seek recovery for losses due to fraud in individual actions, and government prosecutors may pursue those who submit fraudulent claims. Although not as protective as making clear that the Claims Administrator should not pay claims that were not "a result of" the Deepwater Horizon spill, a majority of the en banc court apparently seems to believe that those protections are still in place.

The judicial power extends only to actual cases and controversies even in a class action and even in a settlement. *Lewis v. Casey*, 518 U.S. 343, 349 [—9—] (1996). Judge Southwick's analogy to a stipulation supports an argument for judicial scrutiny, not judicial abdication. Even with the assent of all parties, judges still have the obligation to reject stipulations that are not factually true. *See People v. Marling*, 172 Cal. Rptr. 109 (Ct. App. 1981) ("Although a rose is a rose, a cactus is not and a stipulation does not make it so.") They may also do so because the parties cannot stipulate to law: they cannot force a court through stipulation "to decide a case according to a body of law that is nowhere in force." *Cent'l Soya Co. Inc. v. Epstein Fisheries, Inc.*, 676 F.2d 939, 941 (7th Cir. 1982) (Posner, J.); *see also Reeg v. Shaughnessy*, 570 F.2d 309, 314 (10th Cir. 1978) ("It is settled that parties cannot stipulate that the law of a forum will not control, but that other law will control.") This purported stipulation has ended up being either factually or legally untrue. It either trumpets one lie (businesses operating hundreds of miles from any sign of befouled water had injury "caused by" BP) or another (a party can stipulate away the legal requirement of causation). But parties cannot stipulate to force courts to decide cases based on "a body of law that is nowhere in force" or to declare a cactus a rose. There are limits on party autonomy and judicial efficiency, because a stipulation, like any other judicially enforced agreement, derives its force from the power of the court and its enforcement should not "discredit the judiciary." Charles Alan Wright and Kenneth W. Graham, Fed. Prac. & Proc. Evid. § 5194.

III

"The party invoking federal jurisdiction bears the burden of establishing [the elements of standing] . . . with the manner and degree of evidence required at the successive stages of litigation." *Lujan v. Defenders of Wildlife*, 504 U.S. 555, 561 (1992). While in the certification of a class action that will proceed to trial a lesser inquiry into standing may be required, *Kohen v. Pacific* [—10—] *Investment Management Co.*, 571 F.3d 672 (7th Cir. 2009),

in a settlement class such as this one, the standing inquiry must take into account the fact that inclusion in the class means recovery. *Denney v. Deutsche Bank AG*, 443 F.3d 253, 264 (2d Cir. 2006) ("[N]o class may be certified that contains members lacking Article III standing. The class must therefore be defined in such a way that anyone within it would have standing"). While the *Kohen* approach to standing has been used in the Seventh, Ninth, and Third Circuits, other cases in the Eighth, Seventh, and Ninth have assessed cases under the *Denney* formulation. *In re Deepwater Horizon*, 739 F.3d 790, 800-01, 2 Adm. R. 140, 144–46 (5th Cir. 2014) ("*Deepwater Horizon II*"). These different approaches, sometimes used by the same circuit, reveal the deep confusion in this area of class action standing. While our en banc court had the opportunity to address and clarify this issue for our circuit, confused as it was by two separate panel opinions on one essential, constitutional issue, it has declined to do so. Admittedly, even this articulation would not have been enough for our sister circuits considering the deep split on this issue. Another court surely must resolve this.

We respectfully dissent.

United States Court of Appeals
for the Fifth Circuit

No. 13-30315

IN RE DEEPWATER HORIZON

LAKE EUGENIE LAND & DEV., INC.
VS.
BP EXPLORATION & PROD., INC.

Appeals from the United States District Court for the
Eastern District of Louisiana

Decided: May 19, 2014

Citation: 753 F.3d 509, 2 Adm. R. 217 (5th Cir. 2014).

ORDER ON PETITION FOR PANEL REHEARING

Before **DENNIS, CLEMENT,** and **SOUTHWICK,** Circuit
Judges.

[—4—] **SOUTHWICK,** Circuit Judge:

BP Exploration & Production, Inc. petitions for rehearing of our March 3, 2014 decision in *In re Deepwater Horizon*, 744 F.3d 370, 2 Adm. R. 183 (5th Cir. 2014). We upheld the district court's opinion that because of the terms of the parties' settlement, claimants need not present direct evidence of causation during the processing of claims. On rehearing, BP argues that if the settlement is interpreted as not requiring evidence of causation at the claims-processing stage, that effectively "permit[s] the expansion of class membership during the claims-processing stage, resulting in awards to claimants whose injuries lack any causal nexus to the defendant's conduct." We disagree. What follows is a response to the rehearing argument, and our prior opinion remains fully in effect. The petition for rehearing is DENIED.

Judge CLEMENT dissents from this denial of panel rehearing for the reasons stated in her panel dissent of March 3, 2014, *In re Deepwater Horizon*, 744 F.3d 370, 380-84, 2 Adm. R. 183, 191–94 (5th Cir. 2014) (Clement, J., dissenting), and in the dissent from rehearing en banc. [—5—]

FACTUAL AND PROCEDURAL BACKGROUND

A thorough discussion of the relevant background of this case may be found in this panel's opinion of October 2013, *In re Deepwater Horizon*, 732 F.3d 326, 332-39, 1 Adm. R. 287, 289–96 (5th Cir. 2013) ("*Deepwater Horizon I*"), and that of March 2014, 744 F.3d 370, 2 Adm. R. 183 ("*Deepwater Horizon III*"). A different panel's opinion of January 2014, affirmed the district court's approval of the Class Definition and the Class Settlement. *See In re Deepwater Horizon*, 739 F.3d 790, 795, 2 Adm. R. 140, 140 (5th Cir. 2014) ("*Deepwater Horizon II*").

On rehearing in the current case, BP seeks reconsideration of whether the Claims Administrator's interpretation of the Settlement Agreement expands the settlement class beyond its certified definition. We had based our conclusions in part on *Deepwater Horizon II*. We noted that the earlier decision had held that Article III, the Rules Enabling Act, and Rule 23 requirements were fully met at the class certification stage. *See* 744 F.3d at 374-75, 2 Adm. R. at 183–85. We concluded that no new potential constitutional or other deficiencies existed in the procedures for resolving individual claims. *See* 744 F.3d at 376 n.1, 2 Adm. R. at 186 n. 1. In light of the petition for rehearing, we will analyze why the manner in which claims are presented and resolved is not fundamentally flawed.

The principal objection on rehearing focuses on the Claims Administrator's interpretation of the Settlement Agreement, exemplified by a Policy Statement issued by the Claims Administrator on October 10, 2012, and approved by the district court on April 9, 2013. The Policy Statement was developed because of questions that arose after a proposed Settlement Agreement was agreed upon by the parties in April 2012. As discussed more thoroughly below, the Policy Statement was issued with input and assent from BP. The proposed settlement contained an Exhibit 4B (which was later approved by the district court), entitled "Causation Requirements for [—6—] Businesses Economic Loss Claims." Instead of direct evidence of a causal connection between the *Deepwater Horizon* disaster and the claimant's business losses, the Exhibit described four geographic zones, several types of businesses, formulae for presenting economic losses, and various presumptions regarding causation that apply to specific combinations of those criteria. The parties agreed that a claimant's satisfaction of those criteria would establish causation for the purposes of the Settlement Agreement.

Agreement occurred after all parties had an opportunity to decide whether these indicia of causation were sufficient equivalents to direct evidence of causation to satisfy their respective evidentiary concerns. The factors set out in Exhibit 4B were acceptable to the parties at the time, and remained so through approval of the Settlement Agreement in December 2012.

After the proposed settlement was filed in April 2012, the Claims Administrator asked the parties what should be done with claims in which payment under the terms of Exhibit 4B would be permissible, but a cause for the business losses other than or in addition to the *Deepwater Horizon* disaster seemed possible. The Policy Statement expressed the agreement by all participants, including BP, on the answer to the Claims Administrator's question. We will discuss that answer in detail below. We say now, though, that BP argues it unconstitutionally allows the Claims Administrator to pay claims regardless of whether those losses were actually caused by BP's conduct. We conclude that causation is never abandoned as a requirement.

DISCUSSION

The elements of Article III standing "are not mere pleading requirements but rather an indispensable part of the plaintiff's case [and] each element must be supported . . . with the manner and degree of evidence required at the [—7—] successive stages of the litigation." *Lujan v. Defenders of Wildlife*, 504 U.S. 555, 561 (1992). The element of standing being contested in this case is traceability, *i.e.*, the causal connection between a plaintiff's injury and a defendant's conduct. Allegations of

causation are sufficient to satisfy Article III in a class action complaint and in a class definition.[1] Exhibit 4B and the October 10, 2012 Policy Statement are evidentiary frameworks that have no effect on the claimants' allegations or on the class definition. They are an agreed-upon methodology for presenting proof establishing that a claimant's loss was caused by the *Deepwater Horizon* disaster. Any claim not meeting the requirements of Exhibit 4B is precluded from recovery. Through Exhibit 4B, the parties agreed that claims would be governed by an objective formulae. BP argues that an additional duty on the Claims Administrator exists to ensure that every claim contains a direct causal nexus to BP's conduct. That requirement does not arise under the agreed terms of Exhibit 4B, and it does not arise under constitutional or other requirements for a class action.

I. Exhibit 4B

Exhibit 4B does not negate the claimants' allegations of Article III causation. Indeed, BP has never challenged Exhibit 4B. It has not argued, for example, that the approach of the exhibit violates Article III, such as not being [—8—] protective enough of causation or

---

[1] *See Cole v. Gen. Motors Corp.*, 484 F.3d 717, 723 (5th Cir. 2007) (concluding that during Rule 23 proceedings it is "sufficient for standing purposes that the plaintiffs seek recovery for an economic harm that they allege they have suffered," because "a federal court must assume *arguendo* the merits of [each claimant's] legal claim" (citation and quotation marks omitted)); *see also Kohen v. Pac. Inv. Mgmt. Co.*, 571 F.3d 672, 677 (7th Cir. 2009) (concluding that "one named plaintiff with standing . . . is all that is necessary" even where "[i]f the case goes to trial, this plaintiff may fail to prove injury . . . . [A]t the outset of the case many of the members of the class may be unknown, or if they are known still the facts bearing on their claims may be unknown. Such a possibility or indeed inevitability does not preclude class certification . . . ." (citation omitted)); *Denney v. Deutsche Bank AG*, 443 F.3d 253, 263-64 (2d Cir. 2006) ("We do not require that each member of a class submit evidence of personal standing. At the same time, no class may be certified that contains members lacking Article III standing. The class must therefore be defined in such a way that anyone within it would have standing." (citations omitted)).

allowing too many questionable claims to receive damage awards. Exhibit 4B explicitly contains no requirement that the Claims Administrator perform an additional calculation or take an additional step to ensure that each paid claim has a direct causal nexus to BP's conduct. In fact, it says the opposite: "If you are a business [meeting certain criteria], you are not required to provide *any evidence of causation.*" It continues: "If you are not entitled to a presumption as set forth . . . above [and you meet other criteria] you must satisfy the requirements of one of the following" formula. BP has not argued that Exhibit 4B itself is unconstitutional, but it maintains that the Constitution has been violated when the Claims Administrator applies it.

The dissent in *Deepwater Horizon II* identified the Policy Statement as the source of the constitutional defect. *See In re Deepwater Horizon*, 739 F.3d at 823, 2 Adm. R. at 164 (Garza, J., dissenting). The dissent stated that Exhibit 4B "seemingly preserves a threshold causation requirement while simply eliminating the need for specific evidence to prove it when making a settlement claim. In other words, causation ostensibly remains an element of a claim even though proof is not a central feature of the claims process." *Id.*, 2 Adm. R. at 164. The Policy Statement, the dissent argued, then eliminated the requirement of causation. *Id.*, 2 Adm. R. at 164. We disagree. As we will explain, the Policy Statement was at most a clarification or an application of the terms of the exhibit to a specific factual situation. It did not amend the basic approach. BP has not even argued, much less shown, that Exhibit 4B is constitutionally infirm. We conclude that it is not.

BP has urged in multiple filings in this case that the Claims Administrator's interpretation of the Settlement Agreement has expanded the class beyond its certified definition. We read BP's arguments to say that the Claims Administrator has interpreted the evidentiary framework in such a [—9—] way as to expand the settlement class. In other words, BP argues that there are certain claimants who, while they meet every explicit evidentiary standard in Exhibit 4B, should be denied recovery by the Claims Administrator if their claim lacks an actual causal nexus to the *Deepwater Horizon* disaster. The October 10, 2012 Policy Statement was developed in order to address that scenario. We discuss it next.

II. The October 10, 2012 Policy Statement

As a part of claims processing, the Claims Administrator issues occasional policy statements on various issues. The October 10, 2012 Policy Statement addressed a specific issue relevant to causation. As that Policy Statement explains, it was agreed after discussions among the parties and the Claims Administrator that a claimant establishes causation by satisfying the criteria set forth in Exhibit 4B even if additional or alternative explanations for a claimant's loss might exist:

> The Settlement Agreement represents the Parties' negotiated agreement on the criteria that must be satisfied in order for a claimant to establish causation. Once causation is established, the Settlement Agreement further provides specific formulae by which compensation is to be measured. All such matters are negotiated terms that are an integral part of the Settlement Agreement. The Settlement Agreement does not contemplate that the Claims Administrator will undertake additional analysis of causation issues beyond those criteria that are specifically set out in the Settlement Agreement. Both Class Counsel and BP have in response to the Claims Administrator's inquiry confirmed that this is in fact a correct statement of their intent and of the terms of the Settlement Agreement. The Claims Administrator will thus compensate eligible Business Economic Loss and Individual Economic Loss claimants for all losses payable under the terms of the Economic Loss frameworks in the Settlement Agreement, without regard to whether such losses resulted or may have resulted from a cause other than the Deepwater Horizon oil spill [—10—] provided such claimants have satisfied

the specific causation requirements set out in the Settlement Agreement. Further, the Claims Administrator will not evaluate potential alternative causes of the claimant's economic injury, other than the analysis required by Exhibit 8A of whether an Individual Economic Loss claimant was terminated from a Claiming Job for cause.

The above language does not abandon any claimant's allegation of Article III causation. Left in place is that the Claims Administrator must establish causation for settlement purposes with respect to every claim under the specific criteria and formulae that BP and Class Counsel agreed would be utilized for that purpose. The Policy Statement makes clear that there is no "additional analysis of causation issues beyond those criteria" in Exhibit 4B. It is true that the phrase appears that claims will be paid "without regard to whether such losses resulted or may have resulted from a cause other than" the *Deepwater Horizon* disaster. This language, though, is not an assertion by the Claims Administrator that he will pay claimants regardless of whether their losses are alleged to be traceable to BP's conduct. We cannot ignore the context for the language. The Policy Statement states this: *"Once causation is established"* under the approach of Exhibit 4B, the Claims Administrator will not be concerned with the possibility that a particular claimed injury might have been caused in whole or part by other events.

To summarize, causation is established by certain factors set out in Exhibit 4B that the parties agreed were a sufficient indirect way to satisfy the goal of connecting a claim to BP's conduct in the Gulf. The parties did not reject the need to establish a connection. Instead, they agreed to a means for doing so that sufficiently satisfied each party's litigation interests. The Policy Statement itself explains that its treatment of possible alternative causes was "a correct statement of their intent and the terms of the Settlement Agreement." Exhibit 4B can be analogized to a stipulation at trial. If parties [—11—] stipulate to an element of a claim, no proof at trial will be needed. Here, they stipulated to

the form of the proof that would demonstrate causation.

We do not accept that the phrasing of the October 2012 Policy Statement, particularly the "without regard to whether such losses resulted" from other causes, either discards the carefully crafted approach of Exhibit 4B or creates an unconstitutional breach in the boundaries of the Class Definition. It also does not negate the claimants' allegations of Article III causation.

We reach these conclusions, first, because neither the Policy Statement nor Exhibit 4B has anything to do with allegations in the complaint or with the Class Definition. *Deepwater Horizon II* held that Article III standing in this case has been met at the pleading stage and in the Class Definition. 739 F.3d at 804-805, 2 Adm. R. at 147–49. We accept that conclusion. The Policy Statement and Exhibit 4B apply later during settlement administration when the Claims Administrator examines the claimants' documentation. Second, the parties agreed that the evidentiary criteria of Exhibit 4B were a sufficient substitute for a full trial of factual causation by a preponderance of the evidence. Finally, the Policy Statement does not alter Exhibit 4B. The "without regard" language is inartful but not invalidating. In fact, there was substantial regard given to causation in the creation of the elaborate criteria that substituted for proof of factual causation as a separate element of the claim.

The Policy Statement did nothing more than state the most reasonable explanation of what Exhibit 4B meant if some other cause might appear during claims processing to have been a factor. The accepted conclusion follows readily from Exhibit 4B, which explicitly does not require direct evidence of causation but instead requires each claimant to present documentation that substituted for proof by a preponderance of the evidence at trial. The Claims Administrator did not thereby expand the class beyond its definition. Exhibit [—12—] 4B was the compromise reached by the parties on how an extremely difficult part of the claims process was to be handled. The Policy Statement simply states

that the compromise still controls even when
its accuracy as a substitute for direct evidence
of causation as to a particular claim is
questionable.

In settling this lawsuit, the parties agreed
on a substitute for direct proof of causation by
a preponderance of the evidence. By settling
this lawsuit and agreeing to the evidentiary
framework for submitting claims, the
claimants did not abandon their allegations of
Article III causation.

The petition for rehearing is DENIED.

United States Court of Appeals
for the Fifth Circuit

No. 13-30095

IN RE DEEPWATER HORIZON— APPEALS OF THE ECONOMIC AND PROPERTY DAMAGE CLASS ACTION SETTLEMENT

Appeals from the United States District Court for the Eastern District of Louisiana

Decided: May 19, 2014

Citation: 756 F.3d 320, 2 Adm. R. 222 (5th Cir. 2014).

ON PETITION FOR REHEARING EN BANC

Before **DAVIS, GARZA,** and **DENNIS,** Circuit Judges.

[—1—] ORDER:

The court having been polled at the request of one of its members, and a majority of the judges who are in regular active service and not disqualified not having voted in favor (Fed. R. App. P. 35 and 5TH Cir. R. 35), the petition for rehearing en banc is DENIED.[1]

In the en banc poll, five judges voted in favor of rehearing (Judges Jolly, Jones, Clement, Owen and Elrod) and eight judges voted against rehearing (Chief Judge Stewart and Judges Davis, Dennis, Prado, Southwick, Haynes, Graves and Higginson).

ENTERED FOR THE COURT:

/s/ W. Eugene Davis
United States Circuit Judge

(Reporter's Note: Dissenting opinion follows on p. 223).

---

[1] Judge Smith is recused and did not participate in the consideration of the petition for rehearing en banc.

[—2—] **CLEMENT**, Circuit Judge, dissenting from Denial of Rehearing En Banc, joined by **JOLLY** and **JONES**, Circuit Judges:[1]

Today the court approves a class action settlement agreement that permits payment for economic losses "without regard to whether such losses resulted or may have resulted from a cause other than the Deepwater Horizon oil spill." This violates the fundamental Article III requirement that "there must be a causal connection between the injury and the conduct complained of," *Lujan v. Defenders of Wildlife*, 504 U.S. 555, 560 (1992), and the principle that Rule 23 "must be interpreted in keeping with Article III," *Amchem Products, Inc., v. Windsor*, 521 U.S. 591, 613 (1997). In this class settlement, Rule 23 is not being used to aggregate similar constitutional cases and controversies, but to impermissibly extend the judicial power of the United States into administering a private handout program. We dissent from denial of rehearing en banc.[2]

I

The Claims Administrator's policy interpretation, permitting payment "without regard" to whether an injury was caused by the oil spill, creates the principal defect in this case.[3] The interpretation yields an irreconcilable conflict with Section 1.3.1.2 of the Class Definition (which appears identically in the Settlement Agreement and Complaint), requiring that Business [—3—]

---

[1] Judge Garza would join this dissent if he had been able to vote as an active member of the en banc panel.

[2] Here, the focus is on the Article III standing deficiency resulting from the Claims Administrator's interpretation. Judge Garza's initial dissent for this, the certification panel, identifies several additional problems with the court's treatment of Rule 23(a) and the Rules Enabling Act. These remain significant issues in this case, and are incorporated by reference. *See In re Deepwater Horizon*, 739 F.3d 790, 821–29, 2 Adm. R. 140, 163–69 (5th Cir. 2014) (Garza, J., dissenting).

[3] This Claims Administrator issued the interpretation on October 10, 2012. On April 9, 2013, the district court formally adopted the interpretation. *See* Order of April 9, 2013, 2:10-MD-2179, ECF No. 9232.

Economic Loss class members suffered injuries "*as a result of* the Deepwater Horizon incident." (emphasis added). Moreover, it creates an irreconcilable conflict with Article III. The federal courts are not limited by the parties' contentions when acting on Article III jurisdiction. *Steel Co. v. Citizens for a Better Env't*, 523 U.S. 83, 94 (1998) ("On every writ of error or appeal, the first and fundamental question is that of jurisdiction, first, of this court, and then of the court from which the record comes. This question the court is bound to ask and answer *for itself, even when not otherwise suggested, and without respect to the relation of the parties to it.*") (emphasis added). Accordingly, whether BP previously supported the Claims Administrator's interpretation, or whether it previously believed Article III standing to be satisfied, is not germane. To maintain the role of the courts in our system of divided powers, we have the independent duty to enforce the limitations of Article III.

The Settlement Agreement operates through a series of interconnected legal documents, one of which is Exhibit 4B— "Causation Requirements for Business Economic Loss Claims." Section I of Exhibit 4B establishes that certain individuals and entities, based solely on their geographical location or the nature of their enterprise, "are not required to provide *any evidence* of causation."[4] This subset of claimants is entitled to a presumption of causation. Standing alone, geographical proximity, or the nature of one's enterprise, is insufficient to satisfy Article III causation, which requires a "causal connection between the injury and the conduct complained of." *Lujan*, 504 U.S. at 560. However, but for the Claims Administrator's interpretation, Exhibit 4B's relationship to the Class Definition would have kept causation as an element [—4—] of class members' claims—claimants would have

---

[4] For example, Section I.1 states, "If you are a business in Zone A, *you are not required to provide any evidence of causation* unless you fall into one of the exceptions agreed to by the parties, and listed in footnote (1)." Section I.5 states, "If you are in Zone A, B, or C, and you meet the 'Charter Fishing Definition' *you are not required to provide any evidence of causation.*" (emphases added).

been required to have suffered injury "as a result of" the oil spill.

The Claims Administrator's interpretation fundamentally changed this balance, establishing that he would:

> "compensate eligible Business Economic Loss and Individual Economic Loss claimants for all losses payable under the terms of the Economic Loss frameworks in the Settlement Agreement, *without regard to whether such losses resulted or may have resulted from a cause other than the Deepwater Horizon oil spill* provided such claimants have satisfied the specific causation requirements set out in the Settlement Agreement." (emphasis added).

This decision effectively negates the requirement that injuries be "as a result of" the oil spill. These two positions—that injury must be "as a result of" the oil spill, and that compensation is available "without regard to whether such losses resulted" from the oil spill—are plainly irreconcilable. Thus, the Claims Administrator's interpretation renders Section 1.3.1.2's causation language nugatory—all that remains are the terms of Exhibit 4B. The district court confirmed this understanding. On December 24, 2013, responding to a remand order in No. 13-30315, the district court established "that whether a business economic loss is 'as a result of' the Deepwater Horizon incident for purposes of the Settlement is determined exclusively and conclusively by Exhibit 4B."[5]

Beyond geographical proximity or the nature of a claimant's enterprise, Exhibit 4B provides no specific causation requirements for a subset of the class.[6] Because the Claims Administrator will pay claims to this subset "without regard" to whether their injuries were caused by the oil spill, the class includes

members for which there is absolutely no requirement of causation. [—5—] Consequently, this settlement class may include individuals or entities who could never truthfully allege or establish an injury "fairly traceable to the challenged action of the defendant, and not the result of the independent action of some third party not before the court." *Lujan*, 504 U.S at 660 (internal quotations and alterations omitted).[7]

The Claims Administrator's interpretation of the Settlement's causation requirement is essential to determining whether this class certification is "in keeping with Article III." *Amchem*, 521 U.S. at 613. Notwithstanding this significance, the certification panel majority did not address the interpretation in concluding that Article III is satisfied.[8] This position is untenable.

While the interpretation does not directly reference Section 1.3.1.2's requirement that class members suffer losses "as a result of" the oil spill, it has the clear effect of rendering that language void. The interpretation addresses the requirements of Exhibit 4B, which is incorporated into the Class Definition—a key portion of the Complaint.[9] Moreover, Exhibit 4B begins by noting that it does not apply to "Entities, Individuals or Claims not included within the Economic Class definition."[10] So, when the Claims

---

[5] *See* Order and Reasons [Responding to Remand of Business Economic Loss issues], 2:10-MD2179, ECF No. 12055, at 18.").

[6] In fact, the section header in Exhibit 4B for this group of claimants makes plain that, "There is No Causation Requirement."

[7] Because the class definition can include those without allegations of causation sufficient to satisfy Article III, it cannot be certified under the test for Article III standing at the settlement class certification stage established in *Denney v. Deutsche Bank AG*, 443 F.3d 253, 263–64 (2d Cir. 2006). *Deepwater Horizon*, 739 F.3d at 822–26, 2 Adm. R. at 163–67 (Garza, J., dissenting) (citing *Lujan*, 504 U.S. at 560). *See infra* Part II.

[8] *In re Deepwater Horizon*, 739 F.3d at 808, 2 Adm. R. at 151 ("[T]he evidentiary standard to be applied by the Claims Administrator . . . is not a matter of Article III standing," but rather "a question of interpreting the Settlement Agreement and applying it to each individual claim . . . .").

[9] Section 1.3.1 of the Class Definition states: "The following are summaries of the Damage Categories, which are fully described in the attached Exhibits 1A-15."

[10] Footnote 1 of Exhibit 4B states: "This Causation Requirements for Business Economic

Administrator interprets the Settlement Agreement to allow compensation *"without regard to whether such losses resulted . . . from a cause other than the Deepwater Horizon* [—6—] *oil spill,"* its application is no longer limited to those within the class definition—that is, to those with injury "as a result of" the oil spill. To the contrary, claimants can participate "without regard" to the cause of their claimed injuries. This defies the Article III requirement there must be an injury "fairly traceable to the challenged action of the defendant." *Lujan,* 504 U.S. at 560.

II

The Claims Administrator's interpretation yields a settlement class that may include individuals and entities without any ability to allege or establish an injury fairly traceable to the oil spill. Whether this violates Article III standing turns on the "manner and degree of evidence required at [this] stage of the litigation." *Id.* at 561. The elements of Article III standing, including causation, "are not mere pleading requirements but rather an indispensable part of the plaintiff's case, [which] must be supported in the same way as any other matter on which the plaintiff bears the burden of proof." *Id.* In *Lujan,* the Supreme Court identified three "stages of litigation" during which the standing elements must be supported: pleading, summary judgment, and trial. *Id. Lujan* does not identify the requisite standards for establishing standing during a Rule 23 class certification, and the Courts of Appeals have now adopted conflicting approaches on this important matter.[11]

In *Denney v. Deutsche Bank AG,* 443 F.3d 253 (2d Cir. 2006), the district court certified a *settlement class* and approved a settlement agreement resolving claims arising from the defendant's allegedly fraudulent marketing of foreign currency options. In considering whether the certification satisfied Article III standing, the Second Circuit held that "no class may be certified that [—7—] contains members lacking Article III standing," and that Article III requires the class to "be defined in such a way that anyone within it would have standing." *Denney,* 443 F.3d at 264. *Denney* requires courts to ensure that the composition of the proposed class includes only those with claims that would satisfy the standing elements—injury, causation, and redressability.

In *Kohen v. Pacific Investment Management Co.,* 571 F.3d 672 (7th Cir. 2009), the Seventh Circuit adopted a different approach. The district court had certified a *pre-trial class* to pursue claims alleging the defendant-investment firm violated the Commodity Exchange Act by cornering a futures market for Treasury Notes. The Seventh Circuit evaluated Article III standing by analyzing the status of the named plaintiffs alone. *Id.* at 676. The *Kohen* test evaluates Article III standing for a pre-trial class certification by looking only at the status of the named plaintiffs.[12]

Here, the panel opinion did not adopt either of these approaches, holding that the settlement class certification satisfies Article III under either test. *See In re Deepwater Horizon,* 739 F.3d at 802, 2 Adm. R. at 146. There is no dispute that the named plaintiffs have sufficiently alleged standing, and that the certification could pass muster under *Kohen.* However, because the Claims Administrator's interpretation expands the class beyond those with plausible allegations of causation, the certification fails the *Denney* test—the class now "contains members lacking Article III standing." *Denney,* 443 F.3d at 264. Because the relevant stage of litigation

---

Loss Claims does not apply to (1) Start-up Businesses; (ii) Failed Businesses; (iii) Entities, Individuals or Claims not included within the Economic Class definition; and (iv) Claims covered under the Seafood Program."

[11] *See In re Deepwater Horizon,* 739 F.3d at 799–802, 2 Adm. R. at 143–46 (describing "two analytical approaches" for evaluating Article III standing for the purposes of class certification under Rule 23).

---

[12] Showing further division among the Circuits, in *In re Prudential Ins. Co. Am. Sales Practice Litig. Agent Actions,* 148 F.3d 283, 306-07 (3d Cir. 1998), the Third Circuit evaluated Article III standing for a settlement class by looking to the status of named plaintiffs alone.

in this case is the certification of a settlement class, *Denney* provides the correct test.

There are sound reasons to evaluate Article III standing differently for pre-trial and settlement class certifications under Rule 23. Primarily, the **[—8—]** settlement certification stage is more advanced in the life cycle of a class action than the pre-trial certification stage. When a settlement class is certified, all is resolved at the point of certification. However, in a pre-trial certification, the class must reach additional waypoints in the litigation—summary judgment, trial on the merits, or ultimately a settlement—to resolve the dispute. Accordingly, *Lujan*'s graduated approach for demonstrating the standing elements compels holding settlement class certifications to a higher standard than pre-trial certifications—the settlement certification stage has progressed further into the "successive stages of the litigation." *Lujan*, 504 U.S. at 561.

On its facts, *Denney* addresses Article III standing for a settlement class, whereas *Kohen* concerns a pre-trial class. Furthermore, the nature of the test adopted in each case reflects a distinction between these stages. At the pre-trial certification stage, *Kohen* focuses exclusively on the status of named plaintiffs, and explicitly assumes the standing elements will be held to greater scrutiny at subsequent stages of the litigation. *Kohen*, 571 F.3d at 677 ("If the case goes to trial, this plaintiff may fail to prove [Article III] injury."). But *Denney* checks compliance with Article III by looking to the entire composition of the proposed class. In this, *Denney* requires the certifying court to carefully scrutinize the class definition and project its potential makeup to determine whether it could contain members without injury fairly traceable to the defendant's conduct. It is entirely appropriate that the two tests have different focal points. This difference in focus shows judicial recognition that there are no additional opportunities to address standing after a settlement class is certified—settlement fully resolves the legal proceedings, leaving only administrative processing. The *Denney* approach appreciates that Article III **[—9—]** standing is a central component of a federal court's power and,

accordingly, provides a more robust test for the conclusive settlement certification stage.[13]

Accordingly, determining whether this Settlement Agreement complies with the tenets of Article III standing required the panel to adopt the *Denney* approach. It did not do so. And, to the extent it purported to apply *Denney* in the alternative, it failed to evaluate the class definition as actually implemented pursuant to the Claims Administrator's interpretation. The en banc court has refused to correct these jurisdictional errors.

III

The Claims Administrator and the District Court have established that Exhibit 4B provides the sole methodology for determining which claimants are eligible to recover. So long as the Settlement is interpreted to permit compensation "without regard" to the cause of a claimant's injuries, it is insufficient to ensure that all members of the proposed class have adequately alleged constitutional standing, a necessary component of our jurisdiction. *See Lujan*, 504 U.S. at 560 ("[S]tanding is an essential and unchanging part of the case-or-controversy requirement of Article III."). Causation has been entirely eliminated for a broad swath of Business Economic Loss claimants. The en banc court could have easily corrected this error by decertifying the offending segment of the Business Economic Loss class, or reversing the Claims Administrator's interpretation. However, it has eschewed both courses of action. We respectfully dissent.

---

[13] *Denney* and *Kohen* provided different tests for Article III standing under Rule 23. The conflict between these approaches can be patently resolved by applying them to different stages of a class action litigation—settlement class certification and pre-trial certification. However, no court has yet harmonized the cases in this way, and they remain in clear conflict.

United States Court of Appeals
for the Fifth Circuit

No. 13-30095

IN RE DEEPWATER HORIZON— APPEALS OF THE
ECONOMIC AND PROPERTY DAMAGE CLASS
ACTION SETTLEMENT

Appeal from the United States District Court for the
Eastern District of Louisiana

Decided: May 19, 2014

Citation: 2 Adm. R. 227 (5th Cir. 2014).

ON PETITION FOR PANEL REHEARING

Before **DAVIS, GARZA,** and **DENNIS,** Circuit Judges.

[—1—] **DAVIS,** Circuit Judge:

The petition for panel rehearing is denied. The majority of the panel notes its complete agreement with the reasoning set forth in Judge Southwick's order on petition for panel rehearing in *In re Deepwater Horizon*, No. 13-30315.

Judge Garza dissents from the denial of panel rehearing for the reasons stated in his panel dissent of January 10, 2014, *In re Deepwater Horizon*, 739 F.3d 790, 821-29, 2 Adm. R. 140, 163–69 (5th Cir. 2014) (Garza, J., dissenting), and the dissent from the court's denial of rehearing en banc.

DENIED.

United States Court of Appeals
for the Fifth Circuit

No. 13-30739

AMERICAN COMMERCIAL LINES, L.L.C.
vs.
D.R.D. TOWING CO., L.L.C.

Appeal from the United States District Court for the
Eastern District of Louisiana

Decided: May 21, 2014

Citation: 753 F.3d 550, 2 Adm. R. 228 (5ᵗʰ Cir. 2014).

Before **JOLLY**, **GARZA**, and **HIGGINSON**, Circuit Judges.

[—2—] **GARZA**, Circuit Judge:

American Commercial Lines ("ACL") sought a declaratory judgment that certain vessel chartering agreements with D.R.D. Towing Company, LLC ("DRD") were void *ab initio*. The district court dismissed the action pursuant to the equitable doctrine of judicial estoppel. It found that ACL's position in the declaratory judgment action—that the charters were void *ab initio*—clearly contradicted its earlier position in a related proceeding that the charters were valid, which had been accepted by the district court. ACL appeals from the district court's dismissal and seeks remand with instructions to declare the charters void *ab initio*.

I

ACL is a marine transportation enterprise that operates a fleet of barges and tugboats. ACL contracted with DRD to operate some of its tugs, including the MEL OLIVER.[1] This contractual relationship was created and governed by two charter agreements. Under the "Bareboat Charter," ACL chartered its tugboat to DRD at the rate of $1 per day. Then, under the "Fully Found Charter," DRD agreed to crew the tug and charter its services to ACL.

In the early morning of July 23, 2008, the MEL OLIVER was pushing an ACL barge, loaded with fuel oil, along the Mississippi River near the City of New Orleans. The DRD steersman operating the tug was unlicensed, in violation of Coast Guard regulations. As it moved towards its destination, the MEL OLIVER veered off course and collided with the tanker M/V TINTOMARA. The force of the impact separated the tug from the barge, which floated downriver and sank upstream of the Crescent City Connection Bridge. Three hundred thousand gallons of fuel oil were discharged into the Mississippi. [—3—]

Several lawsuits followed. The United States brought an action against ACL under the Oil Pollution Act, 33 U.S.C. § 2701, *et seq.* DRD pleaded guilty to criminal charges for its role in the collision. ACL, DRD, and entities with interests in the M/V TINTOMARA ("the TINTOMARA interests") each filed interpleader actions to limit, or preclude, their liability arising out of the collision under general maritime law. These limitations actions were consolidated and tried together ("the limitations action"). Lastly, ACL filed the instant declaratory judgment action to have the charter agreements with DRD declared void *ab initio*. Relying on DRD's admissions in its criminal guilty plea, ACL sought to prove that DRD entered into the charters with the intent to violate their terms, thereby perpetrating fraud in the inducement.

Initially, the declaratory judgment action and the limitations action proceeded in parallel. The district court denied ACL's motion for partial summary judgment in the declaratory judgment action, finding a dispute of material fact concerning DRD's intent to deceive ACL when forming the charters. Then, over ACL's objection, the district court granted two motions: it consolidated the declaratory judgment action into the limitations action, and it stayed the declaratory judgment action pending resolution of the limitations action. The stay order was entered pursuant to 28 U.S.C. § 2361, which permits a federal court to stay actions in state and federal courts during the pendency of a related interpleader. The district court's stay order stated that "the

---

[1] An amendment to the initial charter substituted the MEL OLIVER for the PAM D, the vessel originally listed in the agreement.

declaratory judgment action should be stayed pending resolution of the instant action."

The limitations action was tried to the bench. Among the arguments offered to the court, ACL asserted that, pursuant to the valid charters, DRD was the owner *pro hac vice* of the MEL OLIVER. The district court accepted this argument, finding that fault for the collision lay solely with DRD, *in personam*, and with the MEL OLIVER, under DRD's control, *in rem*. [—4—]

Following judgment in the limitations action, with the parties' consent, the district court proceeded to try the declaratory judgment action on the bench trial record from the limitations action. The court then granted the United States permissive intervention, as its interests in the Oil Pollution Act suit could be affected by a declaration that the charters were void *ab initio*.[2] After further briefing, in which the United States urged judicial estoppel, the district court dismissed the declaratory judgment action with prejudice, determining that "ACL's complaint seeking declaratory judgment to void the charters between itself and DRD is barred by judicial estoppel." The court determined that it could not declare the charters void *ab initio* because it had "already accepted ACL's argument that valid bareboat charters existed . . . ." ACL appeals from the dismissal, and from the district court's earlier denial of partial summary judgment.

II

We review a district court's decision to invoke judicial estoppel for abuse of discretion. *Hall v. GE Plastic Pac. PTE Ltd.*, 327 F.3d 391, 396 (5th Cir. 2003). "A trial court abuses its discretion when it bases its decision on an erroneous view of the law or a clearly erroneous assessment of the evidence." *United States v. Caldwell*, 586 F.3d 338, 341 (5th Cir. 2009).

A

Judicial estoppel is an equitable doctrine that defies "inflexible prerequisites or an exhaustive formula." *New Hampshire v. Maine*, 532 U.S. 742, 751 (2001). The doctrine "prevents a party from asserting a position in a legal proceeding that is contrary to a position previously taken in the same or [—5—] some earlier proceeding." *Ergo Science, Inc. v. Martin*, 73 F.3d 595, 598 (5th Cir. 1996); *see also New Hampshire*, 532 U.S. at 749 ("The doctrine of judicial estoppel prevents a party from asserting a claim in a legal proceeding that is inconsistent with a claim taken by that party in a previous proceeding.") (quoting 18 Moore's Federal Practice § 134.30, p. 134–62 (3d ed. 2000)). One of the doctrine's purposes is "to prevent litigants from playing fast and loose with the courts." *Hall*, 327 F.3d at 396. And, ultimately, judicial estoppel protects "the integrity of the judicial process." *United States ex rel. American Bank v. C.I.T. Constr. Inc. of Texas*, 944 F.2d 253, 258 (5th Cir. 1991). In this circuit, at least two requirements must be met before a party's argument may be judicially estopped. *Id.* First, the estopped party's position must be "clearly inconsistent with its previous one," and second, "that party must have convinced the court to accept that previous position." *Hall*, 327 F.3d at 396.[3]

---

[2] In seeking to void the charters, ACL's apparent objective is to defeat the United States' ability to recover from ACL under the Oil Pollution Act, believing that such recovery is only possible if ACL was in contractual privity with DRD.

DRD filed for bankruptcy and did not oppose ACL in the declaratory judgment action. Nor has DRD submitted briefing in this appeal.

[3] ACL asserts that there are three requirements for judicial estoppel applicable in this case, relying on our precedent in *In re Superior Crewboats, Inc.*, 374 F.3d 330, 335 (5th Cir. 2004). The purported third element is that "the non-disclosure must not have been inadvertent." *Id.* This element is not applicable in the instant case; we apply it only when the judicial estoppel is based on the non-disclosure of a claim in a prior bankruptcy proceeding. ACL has not directed us to any non-bankruptcy case that applied this factor. *Superior Crewboats* is a bankruptcy case. And, indeed, this requirement does not logically apply outside of the bankruptcy code's disclosure procedures—the requirement necessarily presumes that a "non-disclosure" has occurred, and it is concerned with the party's intent behind the non-disclosure. In *New Hampshire v. Maine*, the Supreme Court did

B

In the limitations action, ACL claimed that the charter agreements made DRD the owner *pro hac vice* of the MEL OLIVER. The validity of the charters is a necessary predicate to this claim. The district court adopted ACL's position [—6—] in deciding that DRD was solely liable for the collision. After lift of the stay order in the declaratory judgment action, ACL then asserted that the charters were void *ab initio*—that is, they never came into existence because of DRD's alleged fraud in the inducement. These two positions are clearly inconsistent, and, moreover, the district court adopted the first position in its judgment resolving the limitations action. *See Hall*, 327 F.3d at 396.

Here, ACL argues that its two positions are not inconsistent, claiming that, in the limitations actions, it only posited the "agreements were *intended* to be valid charters." Simultaneously, ACL asserts that the district court's actual holding in the limitations action was that "there was no act or omission of ACL which caused or contributed to the collision"—not that the charters were actually valid instruments. Under ACL's reasoning, the district court's judgment in the limitations actions established that ACL "intended" and "expected" that the charters would be valid, not that they were actually binding. Accordingly, under ACL's view, there is no inconsistency between its positions.

ACL's characterizations of its previous argument and the district court's holding are unavailing. In the limitations actions, ACL did not argue that the charters were merely

indicate that judicial estoppel might be inappropriate "when a party's prior position was based on inadvertence or mistake." *New Hampshire*, 532 U.S. at 753. However, the facts of *New Hampshire* and this case are distinct. In *New Hampshire*, inadvertence is addressed in conjunction with the Court's analysis of whether New Hampshire fully understood the significance of its previous position as to its border with Maine. Here, there is no question that ACL understood the significance of asserting that the charter agreements were, or were not, valid.

"intended" to be valid. Rather, it actively opposed the TINTOMARA interests' position that the charters were "crewing agreements," which did not render DRD owner *pro hac vice* of the tug. ACL asserted that "there is no evidence that [the charters] were anything other than what they purported to be, *valid and customary charters.*" Most significantly, throughout the limitations action, ACL argued the position that, pursuant to the charters, "DRD became owner *pro hac vice*" of the MEL OLIVER. This legal fiction of general maritime law is only tenable if the charters were in fact valid agreements. Accordingly, we reject ACL's claim that its positions in the two actions are not inconsistent. Similarly, we reject ACL's assertion that the [—7—] district court did not accept its position in the limitations action. The district court's judgment establishes that it found "there was a valid bareboat charter that invested DRD with ownership *pro hac vice* along with a valid time charter that recognized DRD's status as 'owner' vis-à-vis ACL's charter position in the latter charter." It is clear that the validity of the charters was central to the district court's judgment.

Next, ACL contends that its positions in the limitations action and the declaratory judgment action are not inconsistent because, in the limitations action, its position that the charters were valid was one of several alternative arguments. In addition to arguing the charters were valid, ACL also asserted the affirmative defense that the charters were void *ab initio*. Under this theory of the case, ACL claimed that there was no agreement between ACL and DRD for use of the tug, which DRD possessed illegally. It is true that alternative arguments are widely permitted, even if they are inconsistent. *See* Fed. R. Civ. P. 8(d)(3) ("A party may state as many separate claims or defenses as it has, regardless of consistency."). But, in the context of judicial estoppel, the fact that a party's previous position was an alternative argument is not determinative. The second prong of our judicial estoppel analysis requires that the party "must have convinced the court to accept that previous position." *Hall*, 327 F.3d at 396. This makes all the difference. Once a court has accepted and relied upon one of a party's several alternative positions, any argument inconsistent with that position may be subject to judicial estoppel in subsequent proceedings.

We take guidance from *New Hampshire v. Maine*, in which the Supreme Court estopped New Hampshire from making an argument about its maritime border with Maine that had been one of New Hampshire's alternative arguments in a previous proceeding. In the previous proceeding, litigated in the Supreme Court during the 1970's, "New Hampshire offered two [—8—] interpretations" of its border with Maine based upon language from King George II's 1740 decree fixing the boundary at the "Middle of the River." *New Hampshire*, 532 U.S. at 751–52. First, in the terms of a proposed consent decree, New Hampshire claimed that the "Middle of the River" was the center of the river's main navigable channel. *Id.* at 751. Second, New Hampshire asserted that the charter referred to the geographic middle of the river. *Id.* Ultimately, the 1970's dispute was resolved by the consent decree. The Court "accepted New Hampshire's agreement with Maine" that the charter indicated the center of the navigable channel—accepting one of the State's two alternative arguments. In the subsequent proceeding in 2001, the Court applied judicial estoppel notwithstanding the fact that New Hampshire had taken alternate positions in the 1970's proceeding. The relevant focus was that the "record of the 1970's dispute makes clear that this Court accepted New Hampshire's [position]." *Id.* at 752.

Lastly, ACL asserts that there is no inconsistency because its argument in the limitations action, that the charters were valid, "leads to the same result as ACL's position" in the declaratory judgment action. Certainly, ACL might obtain similar results with inconsistent arguments in these two cases—avoiding liability for the collision and liability for clean up costs. But judicial estoppel is not controlled by consistency of a party's desired objectives. The doctrine focuses on the consistency of a party's arguments as accepted by the court, and seeks to "prevent[ ] internal inconsistency." *Ergo Science, Inc., v. Martin*, 73 F.3d 595, 598 (5th Cir. 1996).

C

Next, ACL contends that judicial estoppel is inapplicable because the district court's order staying the declaratory judgment action prevented it from arguing that the charters were void *ab initio*. ACL asserts that "[i]t is merely trying to make the arguments that were stayed during the trial" of the [—9—] limitations action, and that it "never had the opportunity to address the other defense that the charters were void *ab initio*." In ACL's view, the district court's stay order obliged it to argue that the charters were valid in the limitations action, and, accordingly, applying judicial estoppel would be inequitable.

Judicial estoppel is not permitted "if it was the court, not the party, that instigated the first position that the party later chose to abandon."[4] In *Zedner v. United States*, 547 U.S. 489, 503 (2006), a criminal defendant signed the District Court's waiver form purporting to prospectively waive his rights under the Speedy Trial Act to secure a continuance. In a subsequent appeal, the defendant argued that prospective waivers are invalid. The government asserted a judicial estoppel defense because "petitioner's [prospective] express waiver induced the district court to grant a continuance . . . ." *Id.* The Court refused to apply judicial estoppel, in part, because, "it was the District Court that requested the waiver and produced the form for petitioner to sign." *Id.* at 505. In fact, the District Court's prospective waiver form was "apparently of its own devising." *Id.* at 494. Thus, the Court found that the "[p]etitioner did not succeed in persuading the District Court to accept the proposition that prospective waivers of the Speedy Trial Act are valid," the position later contradicted. *Id.* at 505 (alterations and internal quotations omitted). *Zedner* establishes that judicial estoppel is inapplicable when the court requires the party to adopt the position it later seeks to contradict.

Here, the district court's stay order did not require ACL to adopt the position that the

---

4 18B Charles Alan Wright & Arthur Miller, Federal Practice & Procedure, Jurisdiction § 4477 (2d ed. 2014).

charters were valid. Unlike the waiver form in *Zedner*, which **[—10—]** articulated a particular position, the instant stay order only delayed resolution of the declaratory judgment action until the limitations actions concluded.

The stay issued pursuant to 28 U.S.C. § 2361, which permits a federal court to stay pending actions when exercising jurisdiction over an interpleader action. The statute provides that "a district court may issue its process for all claimants and enter its order restraining them from instituting or prosecuting *any proceeding* in any State or United States court affecting the property, instrument or obligation involved in the interpleader action until further order of the court." 28 U.S.C. § 2361 (emphasis added). This statute only permits a court to restrain "a proceeding", it provides no authority to control the course of other proceedings, or to require a party to take certain positions in other proceedings.[5] Under this authority, the district court's stay order provided simply that "the declaratory judgment action should be stayed pending resolution of the instant action." Nothing in the text of this order restricts the scope of ACL's potential arguments in the limitations action. While the order stayed the declaratory judgment action, in which ACL sought to have the charters declared void *ab initio*, it did not prevent that argument from being raised in the limitations action, nor did it compel the argument that the charters were valid.

In addition to the limited statutory authority and the particular language of the district court's stay order, ACL's claim that the stay prevented **[—11—]** it from arguing

the charters were void *ab initio* in the limitations action is belied by the fact that it did make that argument. In the limitations action, one of ACL's alternative positions, "was that the Bareboat and Fully Found Charters and the amendment were void *ab initio* and DRD was illegally in possession of the MEL OLIVER at the time of the collision." Under this theory, ACL alleged that it was not liable for the collision because it had no connection to the tug at the time of the accident—DRD was the true possessor, though unlawfully. In short, ACL was able to take this position in the limitations action. The declaratory judgment stay order did not foreclose this position, or require the argument that the charters were valid.

Rather, it appears that ACL chose to assert that the charters were valid in the limitations action. This is not the same as a district court requiring a party to take a specific position, as in *Zedner*. In complex litigation such as this, litigants must routinely make strategic choices and weigh for themselves the consequences of each option. While the stay order put ACL to a choice, it neither forced ACL to argue that the charters were valid, nor prevented it from arguing that the charters were void *ab initio*. Accordingly, the district court did not require ACL to adopt the position it later sought to contradict, and it is not inequitable to apply judicial estoppel.

III

For the foregoing reasons, we hold that the district court did not abuse its discretion in dismissing the declaratory judgment action on grounds of judicial estoppel.

AFFIRMED.

---

[5] Similarly, FED. R. CIV. P. SUPP. R. F(3), which addresses limitation of liability in admiralty and maritime claims, such as the instant case, supports this understanding of the statute's scope. The rule provides that, "[o]n application of the plaintiff the court shall enjoin the further prosecution of any *action or proceeding* against the plaintiff or the plaintiff's property with respect to any claim subject to limitation in the action" (emphasis added). Like § 2361, Supplemental Rule F(3) only empowers a court to enjoin the prosecution of other actions. The rule does not permit a court to foreclose particular arguments in cases not subject to the stay.

United States Court of Appeals
for the Fifth Circuit

No. 12-30883

IN RE DEEPWATER HORIZON

UNITED STATES
VS.
BP EXPLORATION & PROD., INC.

Appeals from the United States District Court for the
Eastern District of Louisiana

Decided: June 4, 2014

Citation: 753 F.3d 570, 2 Adm. R. 233 (5th Cir. 2014).

Before **KING, BENAVIDES,** and **DENNIS,** Circuit Judges.

[—1—] BENAVIDES, Circuit Judge:

Before the Court is the federal government's civil enforcement action for Clean Water Act violations associated with the 2010 *Deepwater Horizon* oil spill in the Gulf of Mexico. Defendants BP Exploration & Production, Inc. ("BP") and Anadarko Petroleum Corporation ("Anadarko") appeal summary judgment in favor of the government on the question of their liability for civil penalties under 33 U.S.C. § 1321(b)(7)(A) (2006), which imposes mandatory penalties upon the owners of facilities "from which oil or a hazardous substance is discharged." The district court held that discharge is the point where "uncontrolled movement" begins. *In re Oil Spill by the Oil Rig "Deepwater* [—2—] *Horizon" in the Gulf of Mexico, on April 20, 2010*, 844 F. Supp. 2d 746, 758 (E.D. La. 2012). Applying this standard, the court concluded that oil flowing from the well through the *Deepwater Horizon*'s riser was a discharge from the well. *Id.* at 761. The court then entered summary judgment on the issue of BP's and Anadarko's liability as co-owners of that well. *Id.* at 762. Because we agree that there is no dispute of material fact regarding the discharge of oil from the well, we affirm.

I.

The Macondo Well ("the well") was an exploratory well located about fifty miles off the Louisiana coast in the Gulf of Mexico. Anadarko and BP (together, "the defendants" or "the well owners") were co-owners of the well and co-lessees of the continental shelf block in which the well was located.[1] The well itself was drilled by the *Deepwater Horizon*, a mobile offshore drilling vessel owned and operated by several Transocean entities.[2] The *Deepwater Horizon* was connected to the well by a riser. At the junction of the well and the riser was a blowout preventer that could be used automatically or manually to interrupt an impending blowout. Both the blowout preventer and riser were appurtenances of the *Deepwater Horizon*.

The blowout occurred on April 20, 2010, while the *Deepwater Horizon* was preparing to depart from the site in anticipation of the permanent extraction operation. As part of this preparation, the well had been lined and sealed with cement. Before the *Deepwater Horizon* departed, this cement failed, resulting in the high-pressure release of gas, oil, and other fluids. The [—3—] blowout preventer also failed, thus allowing these fluids to burst from the well, flowing up through the riser and onto the deck of the *Deepwater Horizon*. The oil and gas subsequently caught fire, and the ensuing blaze capsized the *Deepwater Horizon*, which was still connected to the well via the riser. The strain from the sinking vessel severed the riser, and for nearly three months oil flowed continuously through the broken riser and into the Gulf of Mexico. Authorities eventually installed a cap over what remained of the

---

[1] The well was also co-owned by MOEX Offshore 2007, LLC, which has settled with the government and is not party to this appeal.

[2] The vessel was owned or operated by various Transocean entities, including Transocean Deepwater, Inc., Transocean Offshore Deepwater Drilling, Inc., Transocean Holdings, LLC, and Triton Asset Leasing GmbH (collectively "Transocean"). These entities were originally named as defendants, but have settled with the government.

riser, and oil continued to leak for two days, with the well finally sealed on July 15, 2010.

Following the incident, the federal government filed the present action, seeking civil penalties under § 311 of the Clean Water Act, which mandates the assessment of fines on the owners or operators of any vessel or facility "from which oil or a hazardous substance is discharged."[3] The government then moved for summary judgment on several issues, including the well owners' civil-penalty liability for any "subsurface" discharge of oil. Anadarko filed a cross-motion for summary judgment on the same issue, arguing that the subsurface discharge emanated from the riser owned by Transocean, and thus that the oil was not discharged from any facility owned or operated by Anadarko or BP. Holding that discharge is the point where "uncontrolled movement" begins, the court concluded that the oil released from the well via the third party's broken riser was a discharge from the well. *In re Oil Spill*, 844 F. Supp. 2d at 758, 761. Because Anadarko and BP did not contest their ownership of the well, the district court then entered summary judgment in favor of the Government. *Id.* at 762. Anadarko and BP filed a timely appeal. [—4—]

II.

We review summary judgment *de novo*, applying the same standard as the district court. *Bd. of Miss. Levee Comm'rs v. United States EPA*, 674 F.3d 409, 417 (5th Cir. 2012); *see also Matsushita Elec. Indus. Co. v. Zenith Radio Corp.*, 475 U.S. 574, 587 (1986). Summary judgment is proper when the pleadings and other materials on file indicate that "there is no genuine dispute as to any material fact and that the moving party is entitled to judgment as a matter of law." Fed. R. Civ. P. 56(a); *see also Celotex Corp. v. Catrett*, 477 U.S. 317, 323–25 (1986). We are

not bound by the district court's analysis, and are free to affirm on any basis raised below and supported by the record. *United States v. Ho*, 311 F.3d 589, 602 n.12 (5th Cir. 2002).

III.

The Clean Water Act is "not a model of clarity."[4] In its current form, the Act is the result of over a century of successive statutory schemes and amendments.[5] Yet it is, in some respects, not overly complex. The legislation attempts to eliminate the introduction of any kind of pollutant—everything from paint and pesticides to rocks and dirt—into the waters of the United States. 33 U.S.C. §§ 1251(a), 1362(6). The Act does so by creating a regulatory framework and then prohibiting any discharge in violation of the regulations. *See* 33 U.S.C. §§ 1252, 1311–1313, 1316–17, 1319, 1329, 1342. Because of the heightened potential for "environmental disaster" resulting from the release of oil or hazardous waste, 33 U.S.C. § 1321 establishes increased fines for the discharge of these pollutants. *See* S. Rep. No. 92-414 (1972), *reprinted in* 1972 U.S.C.C.A.N. 3668, 3732 (referring to possible disaster). [—5—]

Specifically, the section prohibits the "discharge of oil or hazardous substances (i) into or upon the navigable waters of the United States, adjoining shorelines, or into or upon the waters of the contiguous zone . . . in such quantities as may be harmful," except under circumstances not implicated by the present case. 33 U.S.C. § 1321(b)(3). The section further provides that:

> Any person who is the owner, operator, or person in charge of any vessel, onshore facility, or offshore facility from which oil or a hazardous substance is discharged in violation of [33 U.S.C. § 1321(b)(3)] shall be subject to a civil

---

[3] 33 U.S.C. § 1321(a)(7)(A). All statutory references are to the 2006 edition of the U.S. Code. The government named a total of eight defendants and also sought reimbursement for clean-up costs pursuant to the Oil Pollution Act, 33 U.S.C. § 2702. These other parties and claims are not presently at bar.

[4] *Atl. States Legal Found., Inc. v. Tyson Foods, Inc.*, 897 F.2d 1128, 1137 (11th Cir. 1990); *accord Platte Pipe Line Co. v. United States*, 846 F.2d 610, 611 (10th Cir. 1988).

[5] Discharge into U.S. waters was first prohibited by the Rivers and Harbors Appropriation Act of 1899, 30 Stat. 1121 (codified as amended at 33 U.S.C. § 401, *et seq.*).

penalty in an amount up to $25,000 per day of violation or an amount up to $1,000 per barrel of oil or unit of reportable quantity of hazardous substances discharged.

Id. § 1321(b)(7)(A); *see also* 33 C.F.R. § 27.3 (2006) (indicating dollar amounts as increased by regulation). In the instant case, no one denies that there has been a discharge of harmful quantities of oil into navigable waters. Anadarko and BP further stipulate that the well is an offshore facility, and that they are the owners of that facility.[6] The only question, then, is whether it is beyond factual dispute that the well is a facility "from which" the harmful quantity of oil was discharged. We find no dispute as to the question.

Discharge is not defined for the purposes of this section, but is instead illustrated by a list of examples. Discharge "includes, but is not limited to, any spilling, leaking, pumping, pouring, emitting, emptying or dumping[.]" 33 U.S.C. § 1321(a)(2). Each of these statutory examples denotes the loss of controlled confinement. Similarly, the ordinary use of "discharge" refers to a fluid "flow[ing] out from where it has been confined."[7] Accordingly, a vessel or [—6—] facility is a point "from which oil or a hazardous substance is discharged" if it is a point at which controlled confinement is

lost. Turning to the facts, we find no dispute as to whether the well is such a facility. The parties stipulate that cement had been deposited at the well. There is no genuine dispute that controlled confinement was lost when this cement failed—the defendants do not contest the cement's failure, and they concede that oil then "escaped" and "flowed freely" from the well and ultimately into navigable waters. And although the defendants argue that the blowout preventer should have engaged and prevented the progression of the blowout, the need for this intervention only underscores the extent to which the oil was already unconfined and flowing freely. Accordingly, we find that the well is a facility from which oil was discharged in violation of 33 U.S.C. § 1321(b)(3).

It is immaterial that the oil flowed through parts of the vessel before entering the Gulf of Mexico. Anadarko argues that discharge is the point at which oil "enters the marine environment."[8] Yet Anadarko provides no relevant legal authority in support of the proffered interpretation. Nor does our research reveal any. On the contrary, it seems well settled that the section proscribes any discharge of oil that ultimately flows "into or upon . . . navigable waters," irrespective of the path traversed by the discharged oil.[9] For example, [—7—] a discharge of oil violates the

---

[6] The government argues that BP was also an operator of the *Deepwater Horizon*. BP disagrees. Because we find Anadarko and BP liable as owners of the well, we do not reach this question.

[7] *Discharge*, Oxford Dictionaries Online, U.S. Edition, http://www.oxforddictionaries.com/us/definition/american_english/discharge (last visited Feb. 24, 2014). We further note that Congress intended for the section to apply to "classic spill" situations, 124 Cong. Rec. 37502 (1978), and dictionaries generally define a spill in [—6—] terms of a loss or exit from a container. *See, e.g.*, *Spill*, Oxford English Dictionary Online, http://www.oed.com/view/Entry/186634 (subscription required) (last visited February 20, 2014) ("to allow or cause (a liquid) to fall, pour, or run out (esp. over the edge of the containing vessel)"); *Spill*, Merriam-Webster Online, http://www.merriam-webster.com/dictionary/spill (last visited February 24, 2014) ("to cause or allow (something) to fall, flow, or run over the edge of a container").

[8] Counsel used this phrase at oral argument. Similarly, the briefs argue that discharge denotes "direct" or "immediate" release into water. None of these proposed standards is consistent with existing law.

[9] 33 U.S.C. § 1321(b)(3); *see also Pepperell Assocs. v. United States EPA*, 246 F.3d 15 (1st Cir. 2001) (administrative penalties under 33 U.S.C. § 1321) (oil traversed third-party culvert); *Union Petroleum Corp. v. United States*, 651 F.2d 734 (Ct. Cl. 1981) (reimbursement provision under 33 U.S.C. § 1321) (oil ran across third-party rail line); *Pryor Oil Co., Inc. v.* [—7—] *United States*, 299 F. Supp. 2d 804 (E.D. Tenn. 2003) (action under 33 U.S.C. § 1321(c)) (oil "ran down hillside"); *In re D&L Energy, Inc.*, V-W-13 C-006 (EPA ALJ Feb. 27, 2013) (administrative penalties under 33 U.S.C. § 1321) (unpublished) (pollutant traversed storm sewer); *In re Philadelphia Macaroni Co.*, CWA-III-187 (EPA ALJ May 28, 1998) (administrative penalties under 33 U.S.C. § 1321) (unpublished) (oil traversed field and ran into unnamed creek).

section even where the oil flows over a rail yard or hillside before reaching water. *See generally Union Petroleum Corp. v. United States*, 651 F.2d 734 (Ct. Cl. 1981); *Pryor Oil Co., Inc. v. United States*, 299 F. Supp. 2d 804 (E.D. Tenn. 2003). Similarly, the Environmental Protection Agency fined a factory owner for oil that spilled from a boiler gasket, into an industrial drain, through a conduit, and eventually into a creek. *See generally Pepperell Assocs. v. United States EPA*, 246 F.3d 15 (1st Cir. 2001). The First Circuit ultimately denied review of the case, finding the agency's decision reasonable. *Id.* at 30. So oil need not flow from a facility directly into navigable waters to give rise to civil-penalty liability under 33 U.S.C. § 1321.

Nor is liability precluded by the fact that the property traversed by the oil was owned by a third party. The *Pepperell* factory owner was held liable for his facility's discharge even though the oil had traveled through a third party's conduit before reaching water. *Id.* at 20. Likewise, when spilled oil subsequently traverses municipal sewers or ditches, liability is imposed upon the owner of the facility where the oil was first discharged, and not on the owner of the municipal facilities. *See generally In re D&L Energy, Inc.*, V-W-13 C-006 (EPA ALJ Feb. 27, 2013) (unpublished). In one recent incident, EPA authorities discovered that oil and brine were being released from an oil exploration site. *In re D&L Energy, Inc.*, V-W-13 C-006, at 2. Authorities found that a nearby river was polluted with oil and that a tributary was "impacted with oil at least a foot deep." *Id.* Upon further investigation, they realized that fluids from the drilling site were flowing through a municipal [—8—] sewer, into a creek, and eventually to the Mahoning River. *Id.* The agency found the drilling site's owner liable, notwithstanding the fact that the oil flowed through third-party facilities before reaching water. *Id.* Indeed, we are aware of no case in which a court or administrative agency exempted a defendant from liability on account of the path traversed by discharged oil. The well owners' liability is thus unaffected by the fact that the oil traversed part of Transocean's vessel before entering the Gulf of Mexico.

We recognize that the aforementioned incidents involved blameless third parties, whereas here the owner or operator of the *Deepwater Horizon* might have contributed to the discharge. By all accounts, if the vessel's blowout preventer had functioned properly, the oil would not have entered navigable waters in violation of the Clean Water Act. The defendants therefore reason that liability is properly imposed upon the owner or operator of the *Deepwater Horizon*. Yet it is well established that this section of the Clean Water Act leaves no room for civil-penalty defendants to shift liability via allegations of third-party fault. *See United States v. Tex-Tow, Inc.*, 589 F.2d 1310, 1314 (7th Cir. 1978) (holding defendant liable for penalty notwithstanding fault of a third party). Early in the implementation of the Act's regulatory framework, there was some uncertainty as to where and how the law should apply. It was not uncommon for defendants to argue that the statute should not apply where a pollutant is accidentally discharged, or where a third party causes the discharge. *See Sierra Club v. Abston Const. Co., Inc.*, 620 F.2d 41, 45 (5th Cir. 1980) (summarizing early cases). Courts, however, now acknowledge that civil-penalty liability under 33 U.S.C. § 1321 arises irrespective of knowledge, intent, or fault.[10] In fact, courts have consistently rejected attempts to shift [—9—] liability on the basis of shared fault, instead choosing to consider any contributing cause as a mitigating factor at penalty calculation.[11]   This Court, in

---

[10] *Kelly v. United States EPA*, 203 F.3d 519, 522 (7th Cir. 2000) ("Civil liability under the Clean Water Act, therefore, is strict."); *United States v. Coastal States Crude Gathering Co.*, 643 F.2d 1125, 1127 (5th Cir. Unit A Apr. 1981) (referring to civil penalties in what is [—9—] now 33 U.S.C. § 1321(b)(6), which uses the same liability standard as § 1321(b)(7)); *Sierra Club, Mineral Policy Ctr. v. El Paso Gold Mines, Inc.*, No. A. 01 PC 2163 OES, 2002 WL 33932715, at *11 (D. Colo. Nov. 15, 2002) (rejecting argument that a defendant must "actively" contribute to a spill before liability may be imposed).

[11] *E.g., Coastal States Crude*, 643 F.2d at 1128 (reducing penalty in enforcement order due to lack of fault); *United States v. Egan Marine Corp.*, No. 08 C 3160, 2011 WL 8144393, at *5–6 (N.D. Ill. Oct. 13, 2011) (explaining that the majority of circuits have concluded that the imposition of penalties is

particular, recognizes the section as "an absolute liability system with limited exceptions, which are to be narrowly construed." *United States v. W. of Eng. Ship Owner's Mut. Prot. & Indem.*, 872 F.2d 1192, 1196 (5th Cir. 1989). And although 33 U.S.C. § 1321 includes a third-party-fault exception for removal-cost liability, it includes no such exception for civil-penalty liability.[12] That being the case, any culpability on the part of the *Deepwater Horizon*'s operators does not exempt the well owners from the liability at issue here.

After reviewing the record and the law, we find no genuine dispute as to the defendants' liability for civil penalties pursuant to § 311 of the Clean Water Act. As explained herein, it is undisputed that the well's cement failed, resulting in the loss of controlled confinement of oil such that the oil ultimately entered navigable waters. The well is therefore a facility "from which oil or a hazardous substance was discharged" "into or upon the navigable waters of the United States." 33 U.S.C. §§ 1321(a)(2), (b)(3), (b)(7)(A). Anadarko and BP do not dispute their ownership of the well. Therefore, by the express terms of the statute, Anadarko and BP "shall be subject to a civil penalty" calculated in **[—10—]** accordance with statutory and regulatory guidelines. *Id.* § 1321(b)(7)(A). This liability is unaffected by the path traversed by the discharged oil. Nor is liability precluded by any culpability on the part of the vessel's owner or operator.

---

mandatory); *United States v. General Motors Corp.*, 403 F. Supp. 1151, 1165 (D. Conn. 1975) (finding that liability was mandatory but fine of $1 was appropriate where no fault shown); *cf. United States v. Scruggs*, No. G-06-776, 2009 WL 500608, at *6 (S.D. Tex. Feb. 26 2009) (imposing fine of $65,000 where over $1 million was authorized by statute).

[12] *Compare* 33 U.S.C. § 1321(g) (allowing subrogation of removal costs where discharge was "caused solely by an act or omission of a third party"), *with id.* § 1321(b) (making no mention that such an option is available vis-à-vis civil-penalty liability).

IV.

For the reasons stated, we AFFIRM the grant of partial summary judgment with respect to the well owners' liability for civil penalties pursuant to 33 U.S.C. § 1321(b)(7)(A).[13]

---

[13] We do not adopt the district court's interpretation of § 1321(b)(7)(A) to the extent that such an interpretation differs from our own. Further, we express no opinion as to any other issues addressed in the district court's order.

United States Court of Appeals
for the Fifth Circuit

No. 13-30516

TETRA TECHNOLOGIES, INC.
vs.
CONTINENTAL INS. CO.

Appeal from the United States District Court for the
Eastern District of Louisiana

Decided: June 10, 2014

Citation: 755 F.3d 222, 2 Adm. R. 238 (5ᵗʰ Cir. 2014).

Before **SMITH**, **DeMOSS**, and **HIGGINSON**, Circuit
Judges.

[—1—] DeMOSS, Circuit Judge:

I.

This appeal arises from an insurance coverage dispute concerning an industrial accident that occurred on a decommissioned platform in the Outer Continental Shelf, approximately 34 miles off the coast of Louisiana. Appellant Continental Insurance Co. ("Continental") is the insurer of Vertex Services, LLC ("Vertex"), an oilfield services contractor. Pursuant to a Master Services Agreement (the "MSA"), Vertex employees performed work for Appellees Tetra Technologies, Inc. ("Tetra") and its subsidiary Maritech Resources, Inc. ("Maritech"). The MSA provides that Vertex must indemnify Tetra and Maritech for any injuries sustained by Vertex employees while [—2—] working for Tetra or Maritech, including any injuries caused by Tetra or Maritech's own negligence. The MSA also requires Vertex to make Tetra and Maritech additional insureds on Vertex's general liability insurance policy.

In May of 2011, Tetra and Maritech were involved in salvaging a decommissioned off-shore platform and engaged Vertex to assist in the operation. Abraham Mayorga, a Vertex employee, was assigned to work on the project as a rigger. He worked from the *D/B Arapaho*, a Tetra-owned barge with a large crane. According to the complaint he later filed against Tetra and Maritech, on May 22, 2011, Mayorga's supervisors instructed him to assist several other workers in making cuts to the structures supporting a bridge connecting two sections of the off-shore platform so that the crane on the *D/B Arapaho* could remove it. Mayorga and his co-workers made the cuts and then attached four nylon straps to the bridge, so that the crane could lift it. But, when the crane operator attempted to separate the bridge from the platform, the bridge would not come loose. Mayorga's supervisors directed him and the other workers to walk out on the bridge to determine why it would not come loose, while the crane operator would keep tension on the straps to prevent the bridge from collapsing. While Mayorga and the others were on the bridge, however, one end of the bridge separated from the platform, causing Mayorga and the other workers to fall 70-80 feet into the Gulf of Mexico.

Mayorga and the other workers sued Tetra and Maritech, alleging that both companies had been negligent in the planning and execution of the salvage operation. The complaint also alleged an unseaworthiness claim as to the *D/P Arapaho*. Tetra tendered Mayorga's claim to Vertex for indemnification pursuant to the MSA, which referred the claim to Continental, its insurer. Continental, however, denied coverage. After initiating the proceedings that are the subject of the instant appeal, Tetra and Maritech [—3—] settled Mayorga's claim. Continental chose not to participate in the settlement discussions.

II.

A.

On November 11, 2012, Tetra and Maritech filed a "Complaint for Indemnity" against Vertex and Continental. The complaint alleges that pursuant to "the terms of the MSA, VERTEX is obligated to defend and indemnify TETRA and MARITECH from and against the claims asserted by Mayorga." The complaint further alleges that, "TETRA and MARITECH are additional insureds under Continental Insurance Company General Liability Policy No. ML 0872815." The complaint additionally states that Tetra and Maritech "made formal demand upon VERTEX and CONTINENTAL to defend, indemnify, and hold TETRA and MARITECH harmless from and against the claims asserted by the plaintiff in the Mayorga action, and to indemnify Plaintiffs for any liability, damages, loss, cost, or expense arising out of the Mayorga action, . . . to no avail." The complaint concludes by seeking a judgment declaring that Vertex and Continental

are obligated to defend and indemnify Plaintiffs from and against the claims asserted in the Mayorga civil action, and to indemnify Plaintiffs for any liability, damages, loss, cost, or expense arising out of the Mayorga action, and this action including payment and reimbursement of attorneys' fees, costs, and expenses incurred by Plaintiffs in: (a) defending the principal demand in the Mayorga action; (b) in [sic] enforcing the contractual obligation of Defendants; and (c) in [sic] prosecuting this action.

Continental answered the complaint and asserted several affirmative defenses based on the terms of the insurance policy. Although an attorney entered an appearance for Vertex, it never answered Tetra and Maritech's complaint and did not meaningfully participate in the district court proceedings. [—4—]

On January 31, 2013, Continental moved for summary judgment. It asserted numerous arguments, only three of which it continues to press on appeal. First, Continental argued that the provision of the MSA requiring Vertex to indemnify Tetra and Maritech for their own negligence is void under the Louisiana Oilfield Indemnity Act ("LOIA" or "the Act"), and that, as a result, the additional insured provision of the MSA does not apply to claims by Vertex employees alleging negligence on the part of Tetra and Maritech. Second, Continental argued that, even if the LOIA does not void the indemnification and additional insured provisions of the MSA, Mayorga's claims fall within Exclusion (d) to the insurance policy, which provides that the Continental policy does not extend to "[a]ny obligation of the insured under a workers[sic] compensation, United States Longshoremen's [sic] and Harbor Workers' Compensation Act, Jones Act, Death on the High Seas Act, General Maritime Law, Federal Employers' Liability Act, disability benefits or unemployment compensation law or any similar law." Third, Continental argued that because Mayorga's injury occurred when the crane of the *D/B Arapaho* failed to keep tension on the straps supporting the bridge, his claims also fall within Exclusion (g), which provides that the policy does not provide coverage for claims for "bodily injury . . . arising out of: (1) [t]he ownership, maintenance, use or entrustment to others of any watercraft owned, leased, rented or chartered to any insured."

Tetra and Maritech opposed Continental's motion for summary judgment and filed a summary judgment motion of their own. They argued that the LOIA does not void the indemnity agreement because Vertex's work for Tetra and Maritech related to salvaging a decommissioned, non-producing off-shore platform and therefore did not "pertain to a well," as required by the Act. *See Lloyds of London v. Transcon. Gas Pipe Line Corp.*, 38 F.3d 193, 196 (5th Cir. 1994) (citing *Transcon. Gas Pipe Line Corp. v. Transp. Ins. Co.*, 953 [—5—] F.2d 985, 991 (5th Cir. 1992)). Tetra and Maritech also argued that Mayorga's claim does not fall within the scope of Exclusion (d). They asserted that, although Exclusion (d) references claims under "General Maritime Law," it should be construed to exclude coverage only for General Maritime Law claims based on workers' compensation-type employer liability. Finally, Tetra and Maritech argued that Exclusion (g) does not bar coverage because, while Mayorga's complaint alleged an unseaworthiness claim as to the *D/B Arapaho*, it also alleged several other negligence-based theories of liability that do not depend on Tetra's ownership of the *D/B Arapaho*.

B.

The district court agreed with Tetra and Maritech that the LOIA does not void Vertex's indemnification obligations. Specifically, the court found that Continental had failed to "offer any evidence that would tend to establish a functional or geographic nexus between any well and the platforms in question." The district court also agreed with Tetra and Maritech that Mayorga's claim does not fall within Exclusion (d). It found that because Exclusion (d) refers to General Maritime Law in the context of other laws that provide "for some form of worker compensation or employer liability," it was reasonable to read the provision "as excluding coverage for any form of employer's liability, but not for general liability claims under general maritime law, such [as] those of Mayorga against Tetra and Maritech."

Finally, with respect to Exclusion (g), the court found that Mayorga's complaint alleged liability based both on Tetra's ownership of the *D/B Arapaho* and on actions by Tetra and Meritech that were "completely independent of Tetra's ownership" of the barge. The court further found that based on the summary judgment record, it was "impossible to determine what if any of Tetra and/or Maritech's liability arises from ownership and/or use of the *D/B Tetra Arapaho* versus other independent sources of liability." [—6—] Accordingly, the court held that summary judgment was "not appropriate on th[e] issue."

The court then ruled as follows: it denied Continental's summary judgment motion and granted Tetra and Maritech's summary judgment motion, except "with respect to additional insured coverage under the Policy to the extent that Abraham Mayorga's injuries arose out of Tetra's and/or Maritech's ownership, maintenance, or use of the *D/B Tetra Arapaho*." The court later clarified its holding concerning Exclusion (g), stating: "Although the Court has held (and maintains its holding) that coverage may be excluded to the extent that liability is ultimately shown to arise from ownership, maintenance, or use of the *D/B Tetra Arapaho*, this holding cannot result in judgment dismissing any part of the plaintiffs' claim, as questions of fact exist which preclude such dismissal, as stated in the Order and Reasons."

C.

Subsequent to the court's summary judgment ruling, Continental filed an unopposed motion seeking either certification of an interlocutory appeal pursuant to 28 U.S.C. § 1292(b) or entry of final judgment pursuant to Federal Rule of Civil Procedure 54(b). Section 1292(b) permits a district court to certify for appeal an "order not otherwise appealable," when the court is "of the opinion that such order involves a controlling question of law as to which there is substantial ground for difference of opinion and that an immediate appeal from the order may materially advance the ultimate termination of the litigation." 28 U.S.C. § 1292(b). Rule 54(b), on the other hand, provides that "[w]hen an action presents more than one claim for relief . . . or when multiple parties are involved, the court may direct entry of a final judgment as to one or more, but fewer than all, claims or parties only if the court expressly determines that there is no just reason for delay." FED. R. CIV. P. 54(b). [—7—]

The district court denied Continental's motion for § 1292(b) certification on the ground that there was no "substantial ground for difference of opinion on the questions addressed" in its summary judgment order. The district court agreed, however, to enter judgment pursuant to Rule 54(b). The court explained:

In this case, the Court finds that there is no just reason for delay. Litigating the factual issues necessary to determine the applicability of the watercraft exclusion will be expensive for all concerned. Given that the personal injury plaintiffs have settled their claims, the parties to this indemnity action would be required to litigate the cause(s) of the bridge collapse in order to determine whether Mayorga's injuries arise out of Tetra's ownership, maintenance, or use of the barge or from some other source. If the Court were to decline to enter final judgment, the parties would be required to proceed to such a trial in order to preserve their right to appeal to the issues ruled upon on summary judgment. Moreover, regardless of the Circuit's decision on this appeal, there is virtually no danger that the Court of Appeals would be presented with the same issue twice. Thus, the Court finds that the equities favoring immediate appeal outweigh the danger of piecemeal appeals.

On April 15, 2013, the court entered judgment "in favor of Tetra Technologies, Inc. and Maritech Resources, Inc. and against Continental Insurance Company." In relevant part, the "Final Judgment" states as follows:

(1) The contractual obligation of Vertex Services, LLC and Continental Insurance Company to defend and indemnify Tetra and Maritech against the claims asserted by Abraham Mayorga in Civil Action No. 11-2493 (E.D. La.) is not voided by the Louisiana Oilfield Anti-Indemnity Act;

(2) Vertex Services, LLC is obligated to indemnify Tetra and Maritech for any liability, damages, loss, cost, or expense incurred by Tetra or Maritech in defending and settling Mayorga's claims, and in enforcing Vertex's contractual obligations, including but not limited to attorneys' fees and expenses; [—8—]

(3) Liability coverage for Tetra and Maritech as additional insureds under Continental Policy No. ML 0872815 for the claims asserted by Mayorga is not precluded by Exclusion (d);

(4) Liability coverage for Vertex' contractual obligation to defend and indemnify Tetra and Maritech pursuant to the Master Services Agreement (MSA) between Vertex and Tetra is not precluded by Exclusion (d).

The court's judgment makes no mention of its holdings conerning Exclusion (g).

Continental filed a timely notice of appeal. It argues that the district court erred in finding that the LOIA does not void the provisions of the MSA requiring Vertex to indemnify Tetra and Maritech for their own negligence and to provide insurance coverage for claims alleging the same. It also asserts that the district court erred in finding that Exclusion (d) does not bar coverage. Finally, Continental argues that the district court erred in finding that Mayorga's complaint alleges liability on any ground other than Tetra's ownership of the *D/B Arapaho* and that, as a result, Exclusion (g) also bars coverage for Mayorga's claim. Vertex did not contest Tetra and Maritech's summary judgment motion. It has not filed a notice of appeal and is not an appellant here.

III.

A.

This court is "duty-bound to examine the basis of subject matter jurisdiction" in all cases before it, whether or not the parties raise the issue. *Union Planters Bank Nat'l Ass'n v. Salih*, 369 F.3d 457, 460 (5th Cir. 2004). Federal Rule of Civil Procedure 54(b) permits a district court to enter final judgment on "one or more . . . claims." FED. R. CIV. P. 54(b). A district court's rulings concerning a particular claim may be appealed under Rule 54(b) only if the district court has "dispose[d] of that claim *entirely*." *Monument Mgmt.* [—9—] *Ltd. P'ship I v. City of Pearl, Miss.*, 952 F.2d 883, 885 (5th Cir. 1992). "The partial adjudication of a single claim is not appealable, despite a Rule 54(b) certification." *Ariz. State Carpenters Pension Trust Fund v. Miller*, 938 F.2d 1038, 1039-40 (9th Cir. 1991). Thus, unless a district court's rulings "sound the 'death knell' of litigation in the federal courts" concerning a particular claim, the court cannot enter judgment on that claim pursuant to Rule 54(b). *Baker v. Bray*, 701 F.2d 119, 121 (10th Cir. 1983) (quoting *Korgich v. Regents of N.M. Sch. of Mines*, 582 F.2d 549, 550 (10th Cir. 1979)).

The requirement that the district court must have completely disposed of a claim in order to enter final judgment under Rule 54(b) is jurisdictional and must be "met as to each party." *Eldredge v. Martin Marietta Corp.*, 207 F.3d 737, 740 (5th Cir. 2000). Whether the district court completely disposed of a claim is a question we review de novo and, implicating our jurisdiction, one that we may raise at any time. *Id.* None of the parties addressed in their principal briefs whether the district court fully disposed of any one claim before entering judgment on its summary judgment holdings. In accordance with our duty to ensure that subject matter jurisdiction exists in each case before us, we requested additional briefing from the parties on that issue.

B.

1.

Both sides agree that this case involves multiple parties, with Tetra and Maritech as plaintiffs and Vertex and Continental as defendants. Both sides also assert that Tetra and Maritech alleged only a single claim against Vertex—for indemnification—and that the district court fully disposed of that indemnification claim. Tetra and Maritech argue that the only claim the district court fully disposed of was their indemnification claim against Vertex, while Continental maintains that the district court also entirely disposed of at least one of Tetra and Maritech's claims against it. [—10—]

The judgment states that Vertex "is obligated to indemnify Tetra and Maritech for any liability, damages, loss, cost, or expense incurred by Tetra or Maritech in defending and settling Mayorga's claims, and in enforcing Vertex's contractual obligations, including but not limited to attorneys' fees and expenses." On the one hand, the judgment appears to definitively answer the question of whether Vertex is required to indemnify Tetra and Maritech for Mayorga's claim. On the other hand, the actual amount Vertex must pay to Tetra and Maritech is notably absent from the district court's judgment. It is therefore questionable whether, as both sides contend, the district court entirely disposed of Tetra and Maritech's indemnification claim against Vertex. *See Pemberton v. State Farm*

Mut. Auto. Ins. Co., 996 F.2d 789, 791-92 (5th Cir. 1993) (dismissing for lack of jurisdiction where district court certified for appeal under Rule 54(b) ruling that insurance company owed coverage without stating in final judgment precise amount insurance company was to pay insured in damages). We need not decide that question, however, since Vertex did not appeal the judgment entered by the district court and is not an appellant here. *See Eldredge*, 207 F.3d at 740. We therefore turn to the key issue in this appeal: whether the district court entirely disposed of any one claim against Continental.

2.

Continental's supplemental briefing suggests that Tetra and Maritech alleged two discrete claims against it: (1) a claim seeking a declaration that Continental was required to defend and indemnify Tetra and Maritech against Mayorga's claims and (2) a claim seeking money damages for any losses sustained by Tetra and Maritech resulting from Mayorga's claim, including the fees and costs they incurred in prosecuting the instant action against Continental. It is doubtful at best, however, that Tetra and Maritech's complaint asserts two distinct claims because it seeks both a declaration that [—11—] Continental must indemnify them for Mayorga's claims and a money judgment against Continental. *See Pemberton*, 996 F.2d at 791-92. Continental cites us to *St. Paul Mercury Ins. Co. v. Fair Grounds Corp.*, 123 F.3d 336, 338 (5th Cir. 1997), in which we found that we had jurisdiction to review the district court's holding that a policy exception identified by an insurance company did not void coverage. In that case, however, the insurance company initiated the litigation by seeking a declaration of non-coverage. *Id.* at 337. Further, the district court's decision finding that the policy exclusion was inapplicable was dispositive of the question of whether the insurance company owed coverage. *Id.* 337-38. Continental also cites *Jackson v. O'Shields*, 101 F.3d 1083, 1084-85 & n.2 (5th Cir. 1996) as an example of an appeal from a ruling on insurance coverage in a multi-party action. In *Jackson*, however, not only did the insurance company initiate a declaratory judgment action, but the lower court had held that the insurance company had no indemnity obligations at all, which terminated the insurer's involvement with the case. *Id.* at 1084-85.

In any event, we need not conclusively determine whether Tetra and Maritech have asserted one claim or two against Continental because, even if we were to construe their request for a declaration on Continental's indemnity obligations as a single claim, it is clear that the district court did not fully dispose of that one "claim."

3.

The Fifth Circuit "has not expressly adopted a method for determining what constitutes a distinct 'claim for relief' under Rule 54(b)." *Tubos de Acero de Mex., S.A. v. Am. Int'l Inv. Corp.*, 292 F.3d 471, 485 (5th Cir. 2002). Indeed, "[t]here is no generally accepted test that is used to determine whether more than one claim for relief is before the court." 10 CHARLES ALAN WRIGHT & ARTHUR R. MILLER, FEDERAL PRACTICE AND PROCEDURE § 2657 (3d. ed. 2014). Rather, in determining what constitutes a "claim for relief" within the meaning [—12—] of Rule 54(b), "various courts focus upon different things but are reluctant to articulate hard-and-fast tests." *Samaad v. City of Dallas*, 940 F.2d 925, 931 (5th Cir. 1991), *abrogated on other grounds by Stop the Beach Renourishment, Inc. v. Fla. Dep't of Envtl. Prot.*, 560 U.S. 702, 728 (2010). The few Supreme Court decisions concerning Rule 54(b) "have failed to lead the circuit courts to a consensus as to the handling of this confusing area of law." *Eldredge*, 207 F.3d at 740 (discussing *Liberty Mut. Ins. Co. v. Wetzel*, 424 U.S. 737 n. 4 (1976) and *Cold Metal Process Co. v. United Eng'g & Foundry Co.*, 351 U.S. 445 (1956)).

The lack of an articulable standard notwithstanding, our previous decisions provide sufficient guidance for us to determine that the district court did not fully dispose of Tetra and Maritech's indemnification claim against Continental. Specifically, we have held that where a court disposes of an affirmative defense, or even every affirmative defense raised by the defendant, the court still has not disposed of a "claim" for Rule 54(b) purposes unless it makes an express holding as to liability. *See Exxon Corp. v. Oxxford Clothes, Inc.*, 109 F.3d 1069, 1070 (5th Cir. 1997). Additionally, we have held that where the district court rules on some issues concerning a claim, but "decline[s] to complete the analysis" because there are "fact issues extant," the court may not certify the issues it has ruled on for appeal under Rule 54(b). *N.W. Enters. Inc. v. City of Houston*, 352 F.3d 162, 179 (5th Cir. 2003). Finally, it is clear from our case law that a district court does not resolve a "claim" merely by ruling on a threshold legal issue relevant to that claim. *See Eldredge*, 207 F.3d at 740-42; *see also Halliburton Co. Benefits Comm. v. Graves*, 191 F. App'x 248, 249 (5th Cir. 2006).

Here, the district court's determination that the LOIA does not void the Vertex indemnity agreement and associated additional insured provisions resolves a legal issue antecedent to Tetra and Maritech's indemnity claim [—13—] against Continental; it does not resolve the claim itself. Similarly, the district court's holding that Exclusion (d) does not bar coverage disposed of one of Continental's affirmative defenses, not the claim against which Continental asserted the defense. Finally, and most importantly, the district court did not make a final determination as to whether Exclusion (g) bars coverage for Mayorga's claim. As matters stood after the district court entered judgment, it was possible for Tetra and Maritech to prevail completely or not at all on their indemnification claim against Continental, depending on the resolution of certain "factual issues." Given those circumstances, the district court had hardly "sounded the death knell" of the litigation between Continental and Tetra and Maritech concerning Continental's indemnity obligations and therefore did not completely dispose of the claim. *N.W. Enters. Inc.*, 352 F.3d at 179; *Baker*, 701 F.2d at 121.

Continental responds by arguing that the questions concerning the applicability of the LOIA and Exclusion (d) were potentially case dispositive and, however we might have ruled, it was unlikely we would be faced with the same issue in successive appeals. Continental additionally points to the district court's finding that litigating the applicability of Exclusion (g) will be a potentially long and expensive process. Continental's arguments are better suited to a § 1292(b) certification, which "is designed to allow for early appeal of a legal ruling when resolution of the issue may provide more efficient disposition of the litigation." *Ford Motor Credit Co. v. S.E. Barnhart & Sons, Inc.*, 664 F.2d 377, 380 (3d Cir. 1981). Sensibly, however, §1292(b) certification is only available when there "is substantial ground for difference of opinion," which the district court found was lacking in this case. 18 U.S.C. §1292(b). Thus, what we are presented with here is a request by the district court for us to sign-off mid-litigation on legal questions it considers non-contentions. Since the inception of the federal judiciary, however, our role has been to review final [—14—] decisions of the trial courts, not to tinker with ongoing cases through piecemeal appeals, which waste "judicial energy," create unnecessary delays, and obstruct the pursuit of meritorious claims. *Sherri A.D. v. Kirby*, 975 F.2d 193, 201 (5th Cir. 1992) (citation omitted); *see also Ali v. Quaterman*, 607 F.3d 1046, 1048 (5th Cir. 2010). Indeed, were we to affirm the district court, we would no doubt be required to endure a second appeal concerning the same claim between the same parties, this time reviewing the district court's holdings concerning Exclusion (g). Rule 54(b) does not permit such piecemeal appeals, but rather was "created specifically to avoid" them. *Swope v. Columbian Chems. Co.*, 281 F.3d 185, 192 (5th Cir. 2002). Accordingly, the district court erred in entering judgment under Rule 54(b) against Continental.

For the foregoing reasons, the appeal is DISMISSED for want of jurisdiction.

United States Court of Appeals
for the Fifth Circuit

No. 13-60049

GREEN

vs.

LIFE INS. CO. OF N. AM.

Appeal from the United States District Court for the
Southern District of Mississippi

Decided: June 11, 2014

Citation: 754 F.3d 324, 2 Adm. R. 245 (5th Cir. 2014).

Before **STEWART,** Chief Judge, and **DEMOSS** and
CLEMENT, Circuit Judges.

[—1—] STEWART, Chief Judge:

Lindsey Green and Brenda Green (collectively "Plaintiffs") appeal the district court's grant of summary judgment in favor of Life Insurance of North America ("LINA") upholding LINA's denial of life insurance benefits to Plaintiffs, beneficiaries of the two policies at issue. Plaintiffs also appeal the modification of a discovery order. We AFFIRM both of these decisions. [—2—]

FACTS AND PROCEDURAL HISTORY

Joshua Green ("Green"), husband of Lindsey Green and son of Brenda Green, died while operating a boat on July 16, 2010. Around 8:20 p.m, he called his wife to say he was on his way home. When he did not arrive, she called the police. The Coast Guard found Green in his boat the next morning. He had died because of a head injury sustained when his boat struck the support legs of a landing light at Keesler Air Force Base.[1] The police report and radio log on the incident noted that Green had a blood alcohol content of .243, there were empty beer bottles and cans in the boat, he had not been using his running lights,[2] and when he had spoken to his wife he

sounded intoxicated. Sunset on July 16, 2010 occurred at 7:59 p.m. and civil twilight, the point at which terrestrial objects become indistinguishable, was 8:26 p.m. The official death certificate declared the death to be accidental, occurring when Green struck a concrete piling. It listed the immediate causes of death as (1) contusions of the brain, (2) depressed skull fracture, and (3) violent impact to the top of the head. It listed as a significant other condition acute alcohol intoxication.

A. Green's Life Insurance Policies

Plaintiffs sought to recover on two Accidental Death and Dismemberment ("AD&D") policies Green held with Life Insurance Company of North America ("LINA") through his employer, Northrop Grumman Corporation. The policies are governed by the Employee Retirement Income Security Act, 29 U.S.C. § 1001, *et seq.* ("ERISA"). LINA is the issuer, insurer, claims administrator, and plan administrator[3] of the two policies. The [—3—] policyholder is the Trustee of the Group Insurance Trust for Employers in the Manufacturing Industry, and Northrop Grumman is the subscriber of the policy. The policies defined a "Covered Accident" as:

[A] sudden, unforeseeable, external event that results, directly and independently of all other causes, in a Covered Injury or Covered Loss and meets all of the following conditions: 1. occurs while the Covered Person is insured under the policy; 2. is not contributed to by disease, Sickness, mental or bodily infirmity; 3. is not otherwise excluded under the terms of this policy.

The policies included as a "Common Exclusion" from recovery number 8:

---

[1] Both parties agree the light was not lit.

[2] Both parties agree that running lights are merely navigational, indicating the size, position, or course of the boat. There is no evidence in the record that he had a spotlight on board, which would have shone light on the path in front of him.

---

[3] Although in the administrative record LINA disclaimed any responsibility for the plan's summary description booklet, a responsibility of the plan's administrator, LINA does not challenge that it is considered a plan administrator for these policies on appeal.

[O]perating any type of vehicle while under the influence of alcohol or any drug, narcotic or other intoxicant including any prescribed drug for which the Covered Person has been provided a written warning against operating a vehicle while taking it. Under the influence of alcohol, for purposes of this exclusion, means intoxicated, as defined by the law of the state in which the Covered Accident occurred.

B. Procedural History

LINA initially denied Plaintiffs' claims for three reasons: (1) Green's death was not a "Covered Accident" because he operated a vehicle while intoxicated; (2) Green's death was not a "Covered Accident" because he operated a boat at night without the aid of lights; and, (3) Green was legally intoxicated and the policies excluded recovery for any injury caused by operating a vehicle under the influence of alcohol or drugs. Plaintiffs appealed alleging that LINA: (1) misinterpreted Mississippi and federal law, which required foreseeability to be viewed from the standpoint of the insured; (2) misinterpreted the policy's definition of vehicle; (3) ignored Green's cause of death; and (4) relied on an invalid blood sample. After notifying Plaintiffs that [—4—] they would require an extension to address Plaintiffs' arguments, LINA denied this appeal nearly three months later. LINA reiterated that Green intentionally operated his boat while intoxicated, making the risk of injury or death substantially certain, foreseeable, and not independent of all causes. Separately, LINA relied on the policies' exclusion of coverage for any accident involving the operation of a vehicle while intoxicated.

On June 3, 2011, Plaintiffs filed suit in federal district court seeking recovery. Throughout the discovery process, LINA was reluctant to provide certain documents. The magistrate judge issued an order compelling discovery but later modified it. The district court affirmed this decision. Both parties filed motions for summary judgment. The district court granted LINA's motion for summary judgment and denied Plaintiffs'. Plaintiffs timely appealed both the modified discovery order and grant of summary judgment to LINA. We address each in turn.

DISCUSSION

A. Discovery Order

The magistrate judge reconsidered and modified the original discovery order after LINA demonstrated that the order would require a review of 25,000 claims. The modified order required LINA to produce: (1) any policies or procedures which could have been utilized but limited to current and past policies and procedures for three years prior to the incident; and, (2) claims demonstrating LINA's interpretation of Northrop Grumman plans' intoxication exclusion for participants similarly situated to Green since 2007. The AD&D guide, policies, and manuals Plaintiffs sought had not been used since 2002 and, because outdated policies and procedures were irrelevant under ERISA, *see* 29 C.F.R. § 2560.503–1(m)(8), the magistrate judge did not order their production. The district court affirmed this decision. [—5—]

We review a district court's decision to limit discovery for abuse of discretion. *Crosby v. La. Health Serv. & Indem. Co.*, 647 F.3d 258, 261 (5th Cir. 2011). A district court abuses its broad discretion when its decision is based on an erroneous view of the law, but we will only vacate a court's judgment if it affected the substantial rights of the appellant. *Id.* The appellant must prove both abuse of discretion and prejudice. *Id.* We have instructed district courts to "monitor discovery closely" in ERISA cases and to limit discovery if "the burden or expense of the proposed discovery outweighs its likely benefit, considering the needs of the case, . . . and [*inter alia*] the importance of the discovery in resolving the issues." *Id.* at 264 (internal quotation marks and citations omitted). Given these considerations, we hold that there was no error in modifying this discovery order.

B. The Policies

1. Standard of Review

"Standard summary judgment rules control in ERISA cases." *Cooper v. Hewlett–Packard Co.*, 592 F.3d 645, 651 (5th Cir. 2009) (internal quotation marks omitted). We review a "district court's grant of summary judgment de novo, applying the same standards as the district court." *Id.* Summary judgment is appropriate when "there is no genuine dispute as to any material fact and the movant is entitled to judgment as a matter of law." Fed. R. Civ. P. 56(a). "When parties file cross-motions for summary judgment, we review each party's motion independently, viewing the evidence and inferences in the light most favorable to the nonmoving party." *Duval v. N. Assur. Co. of Am.*, 722 F.3d 300, 303, 1 Adm. R. 270, 271 (5th Cir. 2013) (internal quotation marks omitted).

If the plan gives the administrator discretionary authority to determine eligibility for benefits or to construe the plan's terms, we review a decision to deny benefits only for abuse of discretion. *Atkins v. Bert Bell/Pete Rozelle NFL [—6—] Player Ret. Plan*, 694 F.3d 557, 566 (5th Cir. 2012). If there is no such grant of discretion, our review is de novo. *Id.* "Whether the district court employed the appropriate standard in reviewing an eligibility determination made by an ERISA plan administrator is a question of law" that we review de novo. *Ellis v. Liberty Life Assur. Co. of Bos.*, 394 F.3d 262, 269 (5th Cir. 2004). However, "with or without a discretion clause, a district court rejects an administrator's factual determinations in the course of a benefits review only upon the showing of an abuse of discretion." *Dutka ex rel. Estate of T.M. v. AIG Life Ins. Co.*, 573 F.3d 210, 212 (5th Cir. 2009).

Plaintiffs argue that the district court erred when it reviewed LINA's determination for abuse of discretion only. The district court relied on language in the summary plan description ("SPD") to grant LINA discretion to interpret the policy's terms. Plaintiffs argue that this was improper in light of the Supreme Court's decision in *CIGNA Corp. v. Amara*, 131 S. Ct. 1866 (2011) and our decision in *Koehler v. Aetna Health Inc.*, 683 F.3d 182 (5th Cir. 2012). LINA contends that the plan does confer discretion when read as a whole, specifically relying on the language in both the SPD and in the "claims provisions" section of the plan. The "claims provisions" section contains a "proof of loss" subsection, which states "[w]ritten or authorized electronic proof of loss satisfactory to Us must be given . . . ." Plaintiffs respond that there is a circuit split over whether this "satisfactory to Us" language is sufficient to confer discretion and that it is not sufficient in this case.[4] *See Gross v. Sun [—7—] Life Assur. Co. of Can.*, 734 F.3d 1, 12–13 (1st Cir. 2013) (discussing at length the circuit split on this issue); *see also Cosey v. Prudential Ins. Co. of Am.*, 735 F.3d 161, 168 & n.3 (4th Cir. 2013) (holding that

---

[4] Plaintiffs also argue that LINA's conflict of interest, failure to comply with ERISA procedures, such as denying the appeal outside of the 60 day window, and per se policy against covering alcohol-related incidents demand a de novo standard of review. These arguments are unavailing. This court and the Supreme Court have been clear that a conflict of interest does not change the standard of review but affects only the amount of deference given under an abuse of discretion standard of review. *Metro. Life Ins. Co. v. Glenn*, 554 U.S. 105, 115–19 (2008); *Firman v. Life Ins. Co. of N. Am.*, 684 F.3d 533, 539 (5th Cir. 2012). The same is true for the procedural irregularities and LINA's alleged per se practices. *See Glenn*, [—7—] 554 U.S. at 118–19; *Firman*, 684 F.3d at 539. Further, LINA adequately refutes Plaintiffs' allegations and establishes its compliance with ERISA. To the extent Plaintiffs rely on a Tenth Circuit case, *LaAsmar v. Phelps Dodge Corp. Life Accidental Death & Dismemberment and Dependent Life Ins. Plan*, 605 F.3d 789 (10th Cir. 2010), for the proposition that a delay in deciding an appeal justifies a de novo standard of review, the reasoning from that case is inapplicable here. LINA complied with ERISA regulations for seeking an extension and informed Plaintiffs of the delay. In any event, this court rejects "arguments to alter the standard of review based on procedural irregularities in ERISA benefit determinations, such as delays in making a determination," without a showing of "potential wholesale or flagrant violations that evidence an utter disregard of the underlying purpose of the plan." *Atkins v. Bert Bell/Pete Rozelle NFL Player Ret. Plan*, 694 F.3d 557, 567 (5th Cir. 2012) (internal quotation marks omitted).

the court "now join[s] the circuits that decline to impose an abuse-of-discretion standard of review" based on this language, and therefore, disagreeing with the "minority of circuits" that have concluded that the language does confer discretion).

We need not decide this issue because even under a de novo standard of review Plaintiffs' claims are unavailing. Therefore, we assume without deciding that the standard of review for these policies is de novo.

2. Green's Accident

LINA determined that the circumstances of Green's death were not covered by the policies on two separate grounds: (1) the policies' exclusion precluded coverage for an accident occurring while an insured operated a vehicle while intoxicated; and (2) the accident was not a "Covered Accident" as defined by the policies because it was a foreseeable result of Green's actions. Because we conclude that LINA properly applied the policy exclusion we need not address whether the accident was a "Covered Accident" as defined by the policies.

Plaintiffs argue that this case is identical to *Firman* and that because LINA applied a per se policy excluding coverage for any death involving [—8—] alcohol, regardless of any policy exclusions, they should be able to recover. Plaintiffs' argument misses the mark. This case is not identical to *Firman*. First, Green's plan included an explicit exclusion for alcohol-related deaths whereas the plan in *Firman* did not. The application of such an exclusion does not amount to a per se practice or abuse of discretion. Second, unlike the plan in *Firman*, Green's policy clearly defined a "Covered Accident." A major point of contention in *Firman* was that LINA interpreted "accident" to mean "unforeseeable," which the court concluded was a broader definition than necessary. 684 F.3d at 542–43. Here, the definition in the policies included the term "unforeseeable." Finally, unlike *Firman* there is evidence in addition to Green's blood alcohol content that supports the denial of benefits. This additional evidence includes the toxicologist's report and Green's actions the night of the accident,

which include operating a boat at night without lights. Therefore, we conclude that *Firman* is distinguishable from this case and does not dictate the result.

Plaintiffs next argue that the exclusion is inapplicable because it requires the operation of a "vehicle" while intoxicated and "vehicle" is a term that does not unambiguously include a boat—which is what Green was operating when the accident occurred. Plaintiffs urge that "vehicle" must be defined according to Mississippi law, and because it is ambiguous, it must be construed in favor of Green. Plaintiffs note that under Mississippi law, a vehicle is something that must be used "upon a highway," and therefore, cannot include a boat. *See* Miss. Code Ann. § 63-3-103(a). Additionally, Plaintiffs assert that Mississippi also clearly distinguishes between "vehicles" and "watercrafts." *See* Miss. Code Ann. § 63-3-103(b). Finally, Plaintiffs argue that federal law recognizes that a "vessel" is not a "vehicle," and therefore, LINA's conclusion that the exclusion applies is erroneous. [—9—]

"Federal common law governs rights and obligations stemming from ERISA-regulated plans, including the interpretation" of policy provisions at the heart of this dispute. *Provident Life & Accident Ins. Co. v. Sharpless*, 364 F.3d 634, 641 (5th Cir. 2004).[5] "When construing ERISA plan provisions, courts are to give the language of an insurance contract its ordinary and generally accepted meaning if such a meaning exists." *Id.* We "interpret the contract language in an ordinary and popular sense as would a person of average intelligence and experience, such that the language is given its generally accepted meaning if there is one." *Wegner v. Standard Ins. Co.*, 129 F.3d 814, 818 (5th Cir. 1997) (internal quotation marks omitted). "Only if the plan terms remain ambiguous after applying ordinary principles of contract interpretation are we compelled to apply the

---

[5] "[W]e may draw guidance from analogous state law," however, such guidance can only be used "to the extent that it is not inconsistent with congressional policy concerns." *Wegner v. Standard Ins. Co.*, 129 F.3d 814, 818 (5th Cir. 1997) (internal quotation marks omitted).

rule of *contra proferentum* and construe the terms strictly in favor of the insured." *Id.*

Mississippi law does not apply to the interpretation of "vehicle" as utilized in Green's policies' exclusion. The exclusion explicitly states that benefits will not be paid "for any Covered Injury or Covered Loss, which, directly or indirectly, in whole or in part, is caused by or results from the following . . . operating any type of vehicle while under the influence of alcohol . . . ." The next sentence of this exclusion states: "[u]nder the influence of alcohol, for purposes of this exclusion, means intoxicated, as defined by the law of the state in which the Covered Accident occurred." Contrary to Plaintiffs repeated assertions, this does not mean that Mississippi law applies to the interpretation of the word "vehicle." Mississippi law very clearly applies to interpret "intoxicated" and not "vehicle." [—10—]

We hold that the plain meaning of the word "vehicle" as used in Green's policies is unambiguous and broad enough to encompass a boat. The common and generally accepted meaning of "vehicle" is that it is "a means of carrying or transporting something." *See Webster's Third New International Dictionary* 2538 (2002);[6] *see also Black's Law Dictionary* 1693 (9th ed. 2009) (defining vehicle as "an instrument of transportation or conveyance" and "any conveyance used in transporting passengers or things by land, water, or air"). The usage of the word "vehicle" in the policies unambiguously reinforces this generally accepted meaning of "vehicle." The exclusion explicitly refers to "*any type* of vehicle," evidencing a clear intent for the broadest definition of this term to apply. (emphasis added). The general definitions section defines an "[a]ircraft" as "a vehicle." In another section the policies refer to an "Automobile" and define it extensively as "a self-propelled, private passenger motor vehicle with four or more wheels which is a type both designed and required to be licensed for use on the highway of any state or country." If the word "vehicle" was to have the interpretation

Plaintiffs desire—namely as a device that may be transported on a highway—then there was no reason to include this definition for "Automobile." Simply referring to it as a "vehicle" would have sufficed. An ordinary person reading this exclusion provision in these specific policies would conclude that the term "vehicle" encompasses a boat.

Plaintiffs are correct that Mississippi and federal law define "vehicle" and "motor vehicle" differently in other contexts.[7] However, this fails to create ambiguity concerning the term "vehicle" as used in these policies. In the ERISA context, this court is not bound to construe the terms in favor of the [—11—] insured unless there is ambiguity. *See Wegner*, 129 F.3d at 818. Because there is no ambiguity here and the plain meaning of "vehicle" includes a boat, LINA correctly interpreted "vehicle" to include a boat. Therefore, we hold that LINA properly denied coverage to Plaintiffs as Green's death fell within the policies' explicit exclusion for accidents involving the operation of a vehicle while intoxicated.

CONCLUSION

For the aforementioned reasons, we AFFIRM the district court's grant of summary judgment to LINA and its denial of summary judgment to Plaintiffs. We also AFFIRM the modification of the discovery order.

---

[6] Webster's cites as examples: a locomotive, airplane, and submarine. *See id.*

[7] Specifically, Plaintiffs cite *In re Greenway*, 71 F.3d 1177, 1180 (5th Cir. 1996) (per curiam), 1 U.S.C. § 4, and Miss. Code Ann. § 63-3-103(a).

United States Court of Appeals
for the Fifth Circuit

No. 13-20512

INDEMNITY INS. CO. OF N. AM.
vs.
W&T OFFSHORE, INC.

Appeal from the United States District Court for the
Southern District of Texas

Decided: June 23, 2014

Citation: 756 F.3d 347, 2 Adm. R. 250 (5th Cir. 2014).

Before **HIGGINBOTHAM, CLEMENT,** and **HIGGINSON,** Circuit Judges.

[—2—] CLEMENT, Circuit Judge:

W&T Offshore ("W&T")—an energy exploration and development company—sustained significant damage to its operations as a result of Hurricane Ike. Anticipating that W&T would seek recovery for its Removal of Debris ("ROD") expenses under its Umbrella / Excess Insurance Policies ("Umbrella Policies"), the four Umbrella Insurers Underwriters ("Underwriters") sought a declaratory judgment that they were not liable for W&T's ROD damages. In their motion for summary judgment, Underwriters argued that the Umbrella policies only take effect if W&T's underlying / primary insurance is exhausted by claims that would be covered by the Umbrella Policies. Because W&T's underlying insurance was admittedly exhausted by claims not covered by the Umbrella Policies, the insurers argued that they have no liability. In its cross-motion for summary judgment, W&T argued that the Umbrella Policies takes effect once all underlying insurance is exhausted, regardless of how that exhaustion occurred. The district court granted summary judgment in favor of Underwriters, holding that the plain [—3—] terms of the Umbrella Policies state that it only takes effect if the underlying policies are exhausted by claims that would be covered under the Umbrella Policies themselves. We reverse and render summary judgment in favor of W&T.

FACTS AND PROCEEDINGS

W&T purchased three types of insurance policies to indemnify itself against hurricanes: (1) a commercial general liability policy (MS-S-2773) (the "Primary Liability" policy); (2) five Energy Package Policies ("Energy Package"); and (3) four Umbrella / Excess Liability Policies. Plaintiff-Appellant Underwriters provided the Umbrella Policies, which are identical in all relevant aspects. The Umbrella Policies are the only policies at issue.

The key difference between the Umbrella Policies and the Energy / Primary Liability policies is that the Umbrella Policies do not cover (1) property damage or (2) operators' extra expenses ("OOE") that are incurred by W&T itself; they cover only claims against W&T by a third-party. All relevant policies have been endorsed to cover ROD claims.

On September 12, 2008, Hurricane Ike struck the Gulf of Mexico, allegedly causing damage to over 150 offshore platforms in which W&T had an interest. Braemer Steege—the loss adjuster for W&T's claims—submitted over $150 million in claims for OOE and property damage under the Energy Package. The Energy Package contains a $10 million self-insured retention ("SIR"), which W&T has to exhaust prior to submitting any claims. Once that threshold is met, coverage proceeds in order through five policies, which provide a total of $150 million in coverage over-and-above the $10 million SIR. Because submitted expenses for OOE and property damage exceeded $150 million, Braemer Steege forecasted that W&T would submit all of its ROD claims—estimated to exceed $50 million—to the Umbrella Policies. [—4—]

In anticipation of these claims, Underwriters filed separate suits seeking declaratory judgments that W&T's claims are not covered under the Umbrella Policies because the Retained Limit of those policies had not been exhausted. The "Retained Limit" is the triggering mechanism for the "Coverage" provision of the Insuring Agreement, which provides:

INSURING AGREEMENTS

I. COVERAGE

We will pay on behalf of the **Insured** those sums in excess of the Retained limit that the Insured becomes legally obligated to pay by reason of liability imposed by law or assumed by the Insured under an **Insured Contract** because of **Bodily Injury, Property Damage, Personal Injury** or **Advertising Injury** that takes place during the Policy Period and is caused by an **Occurrence** happening anywhere in the world. The amount we will pay for damages is limited as described in **INSURING AGREEMENT III, LIMITS OF INSURANCE.**

The "Retained Limit" is defined in Insuring Agreement § III.E:

E. Retained Limit

We will be liable only for that portion of damages in excess of the **Insured's** Retained Limit which is defined as the greater of either:

1. The total of the applicable limits of the underlying policies listed in the **SCHEDULE OF UNDERLYING INSURANCE** and the applicable limits of any other underlying insurance providing coverage to the **Insured**; or

2. The amount stated in the **SPECIAL DECLARATIONS** as Self Insured Retention as a result of any one **Occurrence** not covered by the underlying policies listed in the **SCHEDULE OF UNDERLYING INSURANCE** nor by any other underlying insurance providing coverage to the Insured;

And then up to an amount not exceeding the Each Occurrence Limit as stated in the **SPECIAL DECLARATIONS. [—5—]**

Underwriters argue that the Retained Limit of the coverage has not been met because W&T exhausted its underlying policies, (*i.e.*, the "total of the applicable limits of the underlying policies"), using claims that are not covered by the Umbrella Policies, (*i.e.*, the $150 million of OOE and property damage claims). In support, Underwriters cite § III.D, which provides:

D. Subject to **B.** and **C.** above, whichever applies, the Each Occurrence Limit is the most we will pay for the sum of damages covered under **INSURING AGREEMENT [§] I** because of all **Bodily Injury, Property Damage, Personal Injury** and **Advertising Injury** arising out of any one **Occurrence.**

If the applicable limits of insurance of the policies listed in the **SCHEDULE OF UNDERLYING INSURANCE** or of other insurance providing coverage to the **Insured** are reduced or exhausted by payment of one or more claims that would be insured by our Policy we will:

1. In the event of reduction, pay in excess of the reduced underlying limits of insurance; or

2. In the event of exhaustion of the underlying limits of insurance, continue in force as underlying insurance.

W&T argues that this section does not govern the circumstances under which the Retained Limit is depleted, but rather describes the Underwriter's duties and obligations *if* the underlying insurance policies "are reduced or exhausted by payment of one or more claims that would be insured by our Policy." Because the "total of the applicable limits of the underlying policies listed in the **SCHEDULE OF UNDERLYING INSURANCE** and the applicable limits of any other underlying insurance providing coverage to the **Insured**" has been exhausted, W&T argues that Underwriters are liable "for that portion of damages in excess of the **Insured's** Retained Limit."

The district court granted Underwriters' motion for summary judgment, finding that the "underlying insurance can only be exhausted by claims that [—6—] are also covered by the Excess Liability policies themselves." Because W&T exhausted the underlying policies with its OOE and property damage claims, the court held that "coverage under the Excess Liability policies has not been triggered and there is no coverage for the costs for removal of wreck or debris."

W&T appeals, raising the same arguments it did in the court below.

STANDARD OF REVIEW

"We review de novo the district court's grant of summary judgment." *Greenwood 950, L.L.C. v. Chesapeake Louisiana, L.P.*, 683 F.3d 666, 668 (5th Cir. 2012). "Summary judgment is appropriate when there is no genuine dispute as to any material fact and the moving party is entitled to judgment as a matter of law." *Id.* "As part of that analysis, we review de novo the district court's interpretation of the contract, including the question of whether the contract is ambiguous." *Id.*

"Under Texas law, insurance policies and indemnity agreements are contracts, and the general rules of contract interpretation apply." *Travelers Lloyds Ins. Co. v. Pac. Emp'rs Ins. Co.*, 602 F.3d 677, 681 (5th Cir. 2010). "[A] court construing a contract must read that contract in a manner that confers meaning to all of its terms, rendering the contract's terms consistent with one another." *Tittle v. Enron Corp.*, 463 F.3d 410, 419 (5th Cir. 2006). "In doing so, courts should examine and consider the entire writing in an effort to harmonize and give effect to all the provisions of the contract so that none will be rendered meaningless. No single provision taken alone will be given controlling effect; rather, all the provisions must be considered with reference to the whole instrument." *Id.* (internal quotation marks, emphasis, and ellipses omitted).

If, after reading the terms of the policy and giving meaning to all provisions, the terms "are unambiguous, the court must enforce the policy according to its plain meaning." *Travelers Lloyds*, 602 F.3d at 681. "An [—7—] insurance policy's terms are unambiguous if they have definite and certain legal meaning." *Id.* "The parties' disagreement regarding the extent of coverage does not create an ambiguity." *Id.* However, if the terms of the contract are ambiguous, the court should adopt the interpretation that is most favorable to the insured. *Grain Dealers Mut. Ins. Co. v. McKee*, 943 S.W.2d 455, 458 (Tex. 1997).

DISCUSSION

Although Underwriters' argument— embraced by the district court—has force at first glance, a careful reading of the contract unambiguously precludes Underwriters' interpretation. W&T's interpretation fits neatly with (1) the plain text of the Coverage provision, (2) the definition of a Retained Limit, and (3) other contract provisions relating to coverage and payment. Further, W&T's interpretation explains § III.D in a way that is not only consistent with its own language and the contract as a whole, but also sheds light on the nuances of Underwriters' coverage obligations. By contrast, Underwriters' argument relies entirely on the text of § III.D, which is insufficiently specific to carry the burden of a similar provision in *Westchester Fire Ins. Co. v. Stewart & Stevenson Services, Inc.*, 31 S.W.3d 654 (Tex. App.—Houston [1st Dist.] 2000, pet. denied).[1] Further, Underwriters' interpretation of § III.D would render it nonsensical when applied to other portions of the contract. We reverse the judgment of the district court and

---

[1] As will be discussed in Section I.B below, Underwriters' contention that § III.D "mean[s] the same" thing as the provision in *Westchester* because "[o]ne provision is the converse of the other" is a logical fallacy. *See* Liberty Mutual Br. 25. Whereas the provision in *Westchester* stated that exhaustion "by reason of payment of losses not covered by this policy" would result in applying the policy as if "such aggregate limit [had] not been reduced or exhausted," Underwriters' Policies dictate what will happen *if* the underlying policies are exhausted by claims that would be covered by the Umbrella Policies.

render summary judgment in favor of W&T. [—8—]

I. Plain Language of Agreement

The logical place to begin when determining whether W&T's ROD claims are covered by the Umbrella Policies is the "Coverage" provision, which provides:

INSURING AGREEMENTS

I. COVERAGE

We will pay on behalf of the **Insured** those sums in excess of the Retained limit that the Insured becomes legally obligated to pay by reason of liability imposed by law or assumed by the Insured under an **Insured Contract** because of **Bodily Injury, Property Damage, Personal Injury** or **Advertising Injury** that takes place during the Policy Period and is caused by an **Occurrence** happening anywhere in the world. The amount we will pay for damages is limited as described in **INSURING AGREEMENT III, LIMITS OF INSURANCE.**

By its terms, this provision (1) obligates Underwriters to pay "those sums in excess of the Retained limit that the Insured becomes legally obligated to pay by reason of liability imposed by law," and (2) provides that the "amount we will pay for damages is limited" as described in "Insuring Agreements § III – Limits of Insurance." We address these provisions in turn.

A. Retained Limit

Under the Coverage provision, Underwriters are only obligated to pay (1) "sums in excess of the Retained limit" that (2) "the Insured becomes legally obligated to pay by reason of liability imposed by law"[2] because

---

[2] The clause "becomes legally obligated to pay by reason of liability imposed by law" is why Underwriters are not liable for the damages W&T sustained to its own property; the Umbrella Policies indemnify against third-party claims, not first-party claims. This is not disputed.

of (3) an event covered by the policy.[3] Because Underwriters will only pay "sums in excess of the Retained limit," the definition of that term is essential to understanding [—9—] the policy. The "Retained Limit" is defined in Insuring Agreement § III.E, which states that the Retained Limit is defined as the greater of (1) the amount of underlying insurance or (2) the amount of SIR that is not covered by the underlying insurance. The greater amount here is the "total of the applicable limits of the underlying policies listed," which amounts to $161 million in coverage.

Taking the text of the Coverage provision on its face, Underwriters are obligated to pay "sums in excess of" the "total of the applicable limits of the underlying policies listed," *i.e.*, sums in excess of the $161 million of underlying coverage. Nothing in the text of the Coverage provision or the definition of the Retained Limit specifies how the $161 million "limit[] of the underlying policies" must be reached or states that the Retained Limit refers exclusively to sums covered by the Umbrella Policy.

The plain text of the Coverage provision states that Underwriters are liable for any damages in excess of the Retained Limit that are covered by the contract. Because the Retained Limit has been exhausted, this suggests that Underwriters are liable for W&T's ROD damages.

B. Damages Limited by Insuring Agreement § III

"Section I – Coverage" also provides that the "amount we will pay for damages is limited" as described in "Insuring Agreement § III – Limits of Insurance." "Section III – Limits of Insurance" outlines "the most [Underwriters] will pay" under various scenarios; it makes no claims about the breadth of coverage or requirements for exhausting the Retained Limit. Section III.B, for example, states that the "General Aggregate Limit is the most we will pay for all damages *covered under* **Insuring Agreement**

---

[3] Although ROD damages are not mentioned in this provision, they were incorporated by endorsement.

[§] I." (italics added, bold in original). Section III.D—the basis of Underwriters' argument—begins with a similar provision, stating that the "Each Occurrence Limit is the most we will pay for the sum of damages *covered under* **Insuring Agreement** [—10—] *[§] I*." (italics added, bold in original). The "sum of damages covered under **Insuring Agreement [§] I**," as just discussed, are those damages in excess of the Retained Limit, *i.e.*, the "total of the applicable limits of the underlying policies." In context, the "applicable limits of the underlying policies" must refer to the Each Occurrence Limits of those polices. Thus, Underwriters are liable to pay sums in excess of the total "Each Occurrence Limits" of the underlying policies, up to their own Each Occurrence Limit.

If, however, the applicable limits of insurance—*i.e.*, the Each Occurrence limits of the underlying policies—are reduced or exhausted *by payment of one or more claims that would be insured by [the] policy*," Underwriters undertake additional obligations. If the Each Occurrence Limits of the underlying policies are reduced by payments of one or more claims that would be insured by the policy, Underwriters must "pay in excess *of the reduced underlying limits* of the insurance," rather than the standard payment in excess *of the Retained Limit.*

If the underlying policies are exhausted by claims that would be insured by the policy, however, Underwriters undertake an even greater obligation. Whereas Underwriters are generally only obligated to "pay . . . sums," complete exhaustion of the underlying policies by claims that would be insured by the policy requires Underwriters to "continue in force as underlying insurance," which, in addition to making payments as the underlying insurance, requires Underwriters to defend against any suit claiming damages covered by the policy.

The correctness of this interpretation is reflected in "Insuring Agreement § II.A.1 – Defense," which states that when the "Limits of Insurance of the underlying policies . . . have been exhausted by payment of claims to which this Policy applies," Underwriters "shall have the right and duty to defend any claim or **suit** seeking damages covered by the terms and conditions of this [—11—] Policy." Note the specificity with which the defense provision refers to the claims *requiring* Underwriters to defend: those where the "underlying policies . . . have been exhausted by payment of claims *to which this Policy applies*." Those claims require that Underwriters mount a defense on behalf of W&T; given that the usual obligation is simply to "pay . . . sums" on W&T's behalf, the clear implication is that there are some claims which Underwriters must pay where the underlying policies have *not* been exhausted by claims that would be covered by the policy. *See* Insuring Agreements § II.C ("In all other instances except **A.** above, we will not be obligated to assume charge of the investigation, settlement or defense of any claim made, **suit** brought or proceeding instituted against the **Insured**. We will, however, have the right and shall be given the opportunity to participate in the defense and trial of any claims, **suits** or proceedings relative to any **Occurrence** which, in our opinion, *may create liability on our part under the terms of this policy*.") (italics added).

Other provisions discussing the payment of sums under the contract support this interpretation. "Section VI.P – When Loss Is Payable," states that "Coverage under this Policy will not apply unless and until the **Insured** or the **Insured's** Underlying Insurer is obligated to pay the Retained Limit. When the amount of loss has finally been determined, we will promptly pay on behalf of the **Insured** the amount of loss falling within the terms of this Policy." This provision is instructive for several reasons. First, it again refers to the Retained Limit as the triggering mechanism for the Umbrella Policy. Second, it states that its obligation begins when the Underlying Insurance "is obligated to pay the Retained Limit." It does not qualify how the Retained Limit must be paid or that it must be met with claims covered under the Umbrella Policy; it simply states that it must be met. This stands in stark contrast to the next sentence, which explicitly refers to the Umbrella Policies' coverage provisions and states that Underwriters "will promptly pay

. . . the amount of loss falling [—12—] within the terms of this Policy." So while the Retained Limit must simply be met, payments on claims will only be made if they fall under the terms of the policy. If the terms of the Umbrella Policy also governed how the Retained Limit must be exhausted, one would expect to find similar language to that effect.

In fact, that is precisely what occurred in *Westchester*, 31 S.W.3d 654, which was relied upon by both the district court opinion and Underwriters' briefing. The policy in *Westchester* provided that if the aggregate limit of the underlying policies was exhausted "by reason of payment of losses not covered by this policy," Westchester would apply the policy as if "such aggregate limit [had] not been reduced or exhausted."[4] By its explicit terms, the *Westchester* policy notified the beneficiary that its underlying insurance would not be considered exhausted unless it was exhausted by claims covered under the policy. This is far more explicit than the provision at issue here, which merely outlines what will happen *if* the underlying insurance is entirely exhausted by claims covered under the policy; it says nothing about what will happen if the Retained Limit is exhausted by non-covered claims.

Underwriters' contend that § III.D "mean[s] the same" thing as the provision in *Westchester* because "[o]ne provision is the converse of the other." This is a logical fallacy.[5] Whereas the *Westchester* provision

lays out a [—13—] limitation on coverage—if *not* reduced or exhausted by covered claims, then no coverage—the Umbrella Policies explain two potential scenarios—if reduced or exhausted by covered claims, then either (1) pay in excess of reduced limit limit or (2) act as primary insurer. The two policies are not identical, and *Westchester*, rather than helping Underwriters' argument, provides an excellent example of the type of provision that would be included if the policy meant what Underwriters claim it means.

Thus, the Umbrella Policies provide coverage in four ways. First, if the Retained Limit is met, Underwriters pay sums for covered damages in excess to that limit. Second, if the underlying policies are reduced by claims covered under the policy, Underwriters pay sums—not in excess of the Retained Limit—but in excess of the reduced limit of the underlying policies. Third, if the underlying policies are exhausted by covered claims, Underwriters act as the underlying insurers and are obligated to defend against covered claims. And finally, if Underwriters provide the only coverage, they again must act as the underlying insurers and defend against covered claims. Because these scenarios are clear from the face of the policy, we reverse the district court and render judgment in favor of W&T.

CONCLUSION

For the reasons stated, we REVERSE the district court and RENDER SUMMARY JUDGMENT in favor of W&T Offshore.

---

[4] 31 S.W.3d at 658 ("In the event of the reduction or exhaustion of the Aggregate Limits of Liability of the "Underlying Insurance" by reason of payment of losses not covered by **this** policy; this policy shall apply in the same manner it would have applied had such aggregate limit not been reduced or exhausted.").

[5] If A = "underlying policies exhausted by covered claims" and B = "coverage," the provisions work as follows:

Westchester Policy:
Not A → Not B (alternatively, B → A).

Underwriters' Policy:
A → B (alternatively, Not B → Not A). [—13—]

Underwriters are arguing that B → A is the same as A → B. This is the "affirming the consequent" fallacy, and is simply incorrect.

United States Court of Appeals
for the Fifth Circuit

No. 10-20767

NATIONAL LIAB. & FIRE INS. CO.
vs.
R&R MARINE, INC.

Appeal from the United States District Court for the
Southern District of Texas

Decided: June 30, 2014

Citation: 756 F.3d 825, 2 Adm. R. 256 (5th Cir. 2014).

Before **HIGGINBOTHAM, OWEN,** and **GRAVES,** Circuit
Judges.

[—1—] OWEN, Circuit Judge:

This case arises out of the sinking of a vessel owned by Hornbeck Offshore Service (Hornbeck) while at R&R Marine's (R&R) shipyard for repairs. R&R's liability insurer, National Liability & Fire Insurance Company (National), initiated this suit to disclaim liability under its policy. Hornbeck counterclaimed that the policy obligated National to cover all sums for which R&R became [—2—] obligated to pay and cross-claimed against R&R to assert that R&R's negligence caused the sinking of its vessel. The district court found that R&R was negligent and that National was liable for the ensuing damage. National and R&R appeal. We affirm in part, reverse in part, and remand for entry of judgment consistent with this opinion.

I

Hornbeck engaged R&R to repair and refit two vessels: the Erie Service, and the Superior Service. Only the repair of the Erie Service is at issue here. R&R was to perform the work at its shipyards on Lake Sabine in Port Arthur, Texas, subject to the terms of the Shipyard Repair and Drydock Agreement (Agreement). Under this Agreement, "[t]he Vessel(s) [were] deemed accepted into the 'Custody' of the Shipyard when the Vessel(s), with prior notice to the Shipyard, arrive[d] afloat ready to be moored." The Erie Service was afloat upon delivery and R&R was aware of and anticipated its arrival. It is undisputed that the Erie Service was in R&R's custody as of June 2007.

Prior to arrival, much of the vessel's deck plating and bulwarks had been removed in order for R&R to replace deteriorated steel. From June through September, only R&R performed the overhaul work on the Erie Service. Under the Agreement, however, Hornbeck retained access to its vessel so that it could inspect the work and ensure compliance with specifications. To that end, Hornbeck maintained two on-site project managers at R&R's facilities. If these managers observed an issue with or objected to an aspect of R&R's performance, they had the authority to give, and R&R was obligated to follow, orders. Hornbeck's on-site managers also monitored the subcontractors on the Erie Service who were performing work unrelated to R&R's responsibilities.

On September 12, it began to rain and R&R sent its workers home at approximately 9:00 a.m. R&R notified Hornbeck by email of this decision, requesting an extension due to weather delay. At 10:00 a.m., the National [—3—] Hurricane Center (Center) advised the public that Tropical Depression No. 9 had formed and issued a tropical storm warning for an area that included Port Arthur. This meant that sustained winds within the range of 39 to 73 miles per hour could be expected within 24 hours or less. R&R promptly forwarded this warning to Hornbeck to substantiate its request for an extension. In response, one of Hornbeck's project managers asked what actions R&R would be taking for "water entry issues." R&R responded at 10:49 a.m. that the dock was "monitored around the clock everyday" and that it kept "pumps on hand to pump out rain water when required."

By 1:00 p.m., Tropical Depression No. 9 had intensified into Tropical Storm Humberto. Though the Center changed the warning area's boundaries throughout the day, Port Arthur always remained, and in fact became more centered within, the region of concern. Nevertheless, all R&R personnel left the shipyard at 5:00 p.m. without taking any precautions. A hurricane warning did not issue until 12:15 a.m. on September 13. When R&R employees arrived that morning, the Erie Service was listing severely and sinking. Sometime before 7:00 a.m., the Erie Service sank. The parties have stipulated that the Erie Service sank because rainfall and waves from Lake Sabine caused water to enter through the vessel's openings.

Hornbeck received several salvage bids for its vessel, including a "no cure, no pay" option, pursuant to which Hornbeck would have paid $298,000 for a successful salvage. Hornbeck, however, accepted a time-and-materials bid, which cost $245,000 but was subject to unlimited increase if the job proved more difficult than anticipated. The salvage company initially dispatched two derrick barges, but it was necessary to use a third. The salvage work ultimately cost $627,324.64. Hornbeck and R&R demanded that National, R&R's insurer, pay these salvage costs directly. [—4—]

Shortly thereafter, National commenced this litigation against both R&R and Hornbeck to seek a declaratory judgment that it was not required to pay for the salvage costs under a commercial marine liability policy that National had issued to R&R. Hornbeck filed a counterclaim against National asserting, among other things, that "the Policy provide[d] coverage for all sums, including salvage, for which R&R bec[ame] obligated to pay for damage to the ERIE SERVICE while in the care, custody, or control of R&R." Hornbeck also filed a cross-claim asserting that R&R's negligence proximately caused the sinking of the Erie Service.

After eight hearings and two trials, the district court issued a final judgment, which held, in relevant part, that R&R was negligent in failing to secure the Erie Service and protect her from damage by the storm, and that National was required to pay Hornbeck $1,076,843.09 for losses to the Erie Service and additionally to pay to Hornbeck 18 percent interest on this amount, plus $213,683.95 in attorney's fees.

Appeals by National and R&R followed.

II

We first address National and R&R's assertion that the district court erred in finding that R&R's negligence caused the sinking of the Erie Service. Negligence and proximate cause are factual findings that we review for clear error.[1] "A finding is clearly erroneous when, although there is evidence to support it, the reviewing court, based on all of the evidence, is left with a definite and firm conviction that a mistake has been made."[2] But "[i]f the district court's finding is plausible in light of the record as a whole, [this court] cannot reverse [—5—] even though, if sitting as the trier of fact, it would have weighed the evidence differently."[3]

R&R argues that it never had full custody of the Erie Service and alternatively, Hornbeck failed to meet its burden of proof. We conclude that the district court did not clearly err in finding that R&R was negligent.

A

Bailment law governs where, as here, a vessel is left in the shipyard's custody for repairs.[4] Bailment imposes a duty of ordinary care upon the bailee.[5] While the "burden of proof of negligence is on the bailor," by showing that the "vessel was delivered to the bailee in good condition and damaged while in his possession, the bailor makes out a prima facie case of negligence; and the duty then devolves upon the bailee to go forward with the evidence and show affirmatively that he exercised ordinary care."[6]

Here, the district court determined that Hornbeck had established a prima facie case

---

[1] *Bertucci Contracting Corp. v. M/V Antwerpen*, 465 F.3d 254, 258 (5th Cir. 2006) ("Because this case was decided by the district court without a jury, we review the district court's factual findings for clear error." (citing FED. R. CIV. P. 52(a)(6))).

[2] *Stolt Achievement, Ltd. v. Dredge B.E. Lindholm*, 447 F.3d 360, 363 (5th Cir. 2006).

[3] *Bertucci*, 465 F.3d at 258.

[4] *See, e.g., Buntin v. Fletchas*, 257 F.2d 512, 513 (5th Cir. 1958).

[5] *Stegemann v. Miami Beach Boat Slips, Inc.*, 213 F.2d 561, 564 (5th Cir. 1954).

[6] *Id.*

of negligence because it found that the Erie Service was delivered to R&R afloat, R&R had full custody of the vessel, and the vessel sank while under R&R's care. Therefore, the court imposed a presumption of negligence that R&R was required to rebut. R&R, however, contends that such a presumption was erroneous because only a limited bailment was created. It argues that Hornbeck's agents' unconditional access to the Erie Service to oversee R&R's performance, authority to give orders to R&R, and the presence of other subcontractors on the Erie Service undermine the finding that R&R had full custody. [—6—]

A bailment becomes limited "[w]here the delivery of the thing is not complete, as when the owner remains with the thing or has an independent agent or employee responsible for it or for certain aspects of its care."[7] A limited bailment occurs when exclusivity of control over the bailed object is compromised.[8] However, neither the presence and authority of Hornbeck's agents to ensure compliance nor the presence of other subcontractors affected R&R's exclusive control over the Erie Service, its movement within R&R's shipyard, or most importantly, its integrity during the storm. As the district court found, R&R's stipulation to full custody in the Agreement,[9] its control over the worksite, and R&R's responsibility for disaster preparation were all indicators of full custody, at least during the period leading up to and through the Erie Service's sinking.

This finding of full custody is not clearly erroneous in light of the record as a whole. The initial exchange of emails shows that both Hornbeck and R&R understood R&R to be responsible for protecting the vessel. Furthermore, R&R alone had control over when, where, and how to moor the vessel. R&R stated [—7—] during trial that if it had had more time, it would have moved the Erie Service to another shipyard. R&R even had a plan in place for Hurricane Dean—which occurred one month before Hurricane Humberto—to move the Erie Service to another shipyard. There was also testimony establishing a shipyard's general responsibility to handle all mooring of vessels. The record shows that R&R shouldered responsibility for and was in control of protecting the Erie Service from inclement weather. It was not clearly erroneous for the district court to conclude that R&R had full custody of the Erie Service.[10]

B

R&R argues that even if it had full custody of the vessel, it overcame the presumption of negligence and Hornbeck subsequently failed to affirmatively prove R&R's negligence. We do not reach this argument, however, because the district court's finding that R&R had not overcome the presumption of negligence was not clearly erroneous.

---

[7] *Id.* at 565.

[8] *See Chi., St. L. & N.O.R. Co. v. Pullman S. Car Co.,* 139 U.S. 79, 94-96 (1891) (limited bailment where bailor made separate repairs in a separate shop under its exclusive control and to which the bailee had no access); *Goudy & Stevens, Inc. v. Cable Marine, Inc.,* 924 F.2d 16, 19 (1st Cir. 1991) (limited bailment where bailor's agent was making the same repairs alongside the bailee's employees); *Sisung v. Tiger Pass Shipyard Co.,* 303 F.2d 318, 322 (5th Cir. 1962) ("While it is our opinion that the exercise of ordinary care required appellee, as the one in possession of the vessel as bailee or during delivery to have ascertained if the vessel would be left overnight, and to move it to a place of safety in the event it was to be left overnight . . ., where the owner maintains some dominion over the vessel, as Sisung did by *selecting the place of mooring,* there is a corresponding limitation on the duty of the bailee . . . ." (emphasis added) (citing *Stegemann,* 213 F.2d 561)); *City Compress & Warehouse Co. v. U.S.,* 190 F.2d 699, 701-03 (4th Cir. 1951) (limited bailment where vessel owner was responsible for mooring his own ship).

[9] *See T.N.T. Marine Serv., Inc. v. Weaver Shipyards & Dry Docks, Inc.,* 702 F.2d 585, 588 (5th Cir. 1983) (defining a bailment as a "delivery of goods . . . by one person to another . . . beneficial either to the bailor or bailee or both, and *upon a contract,* express or implied . . . ." (emphasis added) (quoting BLACK'S LAW DICTIONARY 129 (5th ed. 1979)).

[10] Though R&R also argues that Hornbeck should be found comparatively negligent, this assertion is foreclosed by our affirmance of the district court's conclusion that R&R had full custody of the Erie Service.

As discussed above, a prima facie case for negligence shifts the burden to the bailee to demonstrate that it exercised ordinary care. This court's precedent suggests two views on how a bailee satisfies this burden.[11] One view requires that a bailee "show only that the loss was caused by some act consistent with due care on his part, such as an act of God."[12] The other view is that the bailee must "show affirmative[] acts which constitute due care."[13] Though the latter [—8—] view is more often expressed,[14] we need not address which is the more appropriate since under either, R&R's explanation fails to establish that it exercised ordinary care.

To rebut the presumption of negligence, R&R argued that the unexpected severity of Hurricane Humberto rendered its inaction reasonable. The district court found, however, that R&R could not "verify that the storm ever reached hurricane-strength at the yard." The district court found, therefore, that R&R had failed to demonstrate the unexpected severity of the weather was an act of God.[15] This finding is plausible in light of the record as a whole. The sustained winds did not reach hurricane force in Port Arthur but were within the range of tropical storm force winds. Nor did the rainfall exceed what was predicted when a tropical storm warning was first issued. The actual weather conditions experienced in Port Arthur were those that had been projected at 10:00 a.m. on September 12—the projection that R&R

forwarded to Hornbeck. Nor did R&R satisfy its burden under the second view of bailment law. As R&R concedes on appeal, the district court correctly found that R&R could not point to any affirmative acts R&R took that constituted due care.

III

R&R contends that even if it was negligent, it is not liable for the full-invoiced salvage amount because Hornbeck's choice between salvage bids was unreasonable and the salvage company's negligence caused the increased cost of salvage. We are unpersuaded. [—9—]

A

"The burden of showing that the victim of tortious conduct failed to minimize his damages rests with the wrongdoer."[16] The tortfeasor must show "(1) that the conduct [of the victim] was unreasonable, and (2) that it had the consequence of aggravating the harm."[17] R&R argues that Hornbeck's selection of the time-and-materials bid was unreasonable because it was against common industry practice and because Hornbeck should have known that the vessel's fragile condition made the salvage operation more complex. The district court held that Hornbeck's selection of the time-and-materials bid was reasonable.

Again, we review for clear error. In doing so, we emphasize that "reasonableness" here does not require "infallibility or exactness of mathematical formula."[18] We "will allow the injured party a wide latitude in determining how best to deal with the situation" because "the necessity for decision-making was thrust upon him by the defendant, and judgments made at times of crisis are subject to human error."[19] In light of this deferential standard, the district court's finding that Hornbeck acted reasonably was not clearly erroneous. "[T]he fact that [an injured party's] efforts

[11] *Buntin v. Fletchas*, 257 F.2d 512, 514 (5th Cir. 1958).

[12] *Id.*

[13] *Id.*

[14] *Chicopee Bank v. Phila. Bank*, 75 U.S. 641, 650 (1869); *CFC Fabrication, Inc. v. Dunn Const. Co.*, 917 F.2d 1385, 1389 (5th Cir. 1990); *Sisung v. Tiger Pass Shipyard Co.*, 303 F.2d 318, 322 (5th Cir. 1962); *Valley Line Co. v. Musgrove Towing Serv., Inc.*, 654 F. Supp. 1009, 1011 (S.D. Tex. 1987).

[15] *See also Valley Line*, 654 F. Supp. at 1012 ("[Defendant] was unaware that the tidal surge which accompanied the hurricane would be so severe and so rapid . . . . On that point, the Court notes that the area around the Musgrove fleet experienced winds in excess of 113 miles per hour and there is some evidence that tornadoes were present in the area.").

[16] *Tenn. Valley Sand & Gravel v. M/V Delta*, 598 F.2d 930, 933 (5th Cir. 1979).

[17] *Id.*

[18] *Id.*

[19] *Id.*

turn[ed] out to be unsuccessful and actually increase[d] the loss does not preclude recovery for all expenses incurred in the process."[20] R&R presents no relevant evidence of common industry practice; nor does the condition of the vessel remove Hornbeck's bid selection from the "range [—10—] of reason."[21] Accordingly, the district court did not err by finding R&R liable for the full-invoiced amount.

B

Alternatively, R&R argues that it is not liable for the additional salvage cost because it was caused by the salvage company's negligence. Although there was testimony at the damages hearing that the salvage company should have known better than to first attempt the operation with the two barges, testimony as to the salvage company's reasonableness was also presented. As discussed above, when reviewing for clear error, this court cannot reverse even if, sitting as a trier of fact, we would have weighed the evidence differently.[22] In any event, even if the salvage company had been negligent, R&R would remain fully liable because this negligence was a foreseeable consequence of R&R's own negligence.[23]

IV

The district court held that National was required by the terms of its policy to pay the amount of damages that R&R owed to Hornbeck as a consequence of R&R's negligence in causing the sinking of the Erie Service. National concedes that if R&R was negligent, it must pay up to its policy limits to Hornbeck for R&R's negligence once a final judgment is entered against R&R. However, National contends no final judgment was entered against R&R as a [—11—] necessary predicate to National's liability. National contends that Hornbeck lacked standing as a third-party claimant to bring its counterclaim. We review a district court's standing decision de novo.[24] Texas law governs the parties' substantive rights.

As an initial argument, National asserts that Hornbeck did not adequately raise a third-party claim in the district court. We disagree. The record reflects that National had fair notice under the liberal pleading standard,[25] and National's pre-trial conduct and communications demonstrate that it was fairly notified that Hornbeck intended to bring a third-party claim.[26]

National is correct, however, that as a general proposition, Texas law requires that when an insured damages the property of a third party, the insurer is not obligated to pay the damages on behalf of its insured until there is a final judgment rendered against the insured or a settlement agreement. Because "Texas is not a direct action state," "a tort claimant has no direct cause of action against the tortfeasor's liability insurer until the insured-tortfeasor is adjudged liable to the claimant."[27] Texas courts have construed this

---

[20] Id.

[21] See Ellerman Lines, Ltd. v. The President Harding, 288 F.2d 288, 290 (2d Cir. 1961); see also Malcolm v. Marathon Oil Co., 642 F.2d 845, 863 & n.30 (5th Cir. Unit B 1981).

[22] See Reich v. Lancaster, 55 F.3d 1034, 1045 (5th Cir. 1995) ("Rule 52(a) also requires that we give due regard to the opportunity of the trial court to judge the credibility of the witnesses. The trial judge's unique perspective to evaluate the witnesses and to consider the entire context of the evidence must be respected." (internal quotation marks omitted)).

[23] See Exxon Co., U.S.A. v. Sofec, Inc., 517 U.S. 830, 832-35 (1996) (holding Sofec was not liable for its negligence in permitting Exxon's tanker to become unmoored because the captain's subsequent navigational decisions were so "extraordinarily" negligent, they were not foreseeable and were therefore the superseding and sole proximate cause of the damage).

---

[24] Delta Commercial Fisheries Ass'n v. Gulf of Mex. Fishery Mgmt. Council, 364 F.3d 269, 272 (5th Cir. 2004).

[25] FED. R. CIV. P. 8(a); Wampler v. S.W. Bell Tel. Co., 597 F.3d 741, 744 (5th Cir. 2010).

[26] See Sundstrand Corp. v. Standard Kollsman Indus., Inc., 488 F.2d 807, 811 (7th Cir. 1973) (citing State Farm Mut. Auto. Ins. Co. v. Scott, 198 F.2d 152, 153 (5th Cir. 1952)).

[27] Ohio Cas. Ins. Co. v. Time Warner Entm't Co., 244 S.W.3d 885, 888-89 (Tex. App.—Dallas 2008,

to be a rule of standing[28] and thus consider whether a final liability judgment existed at the [—12—] time a claim was filed.[29] National is correct that under Texas law, Hornbeck had no "standing" at the time it filed its counterclaim because there was no final judgment establishing R&R's liability. Hornbeck counters that it was "forced" to assert its counterclaim against National when National sued Hornbeck for a declaratory judgment because Hornbeck's counterclaim was "compulsory" within the scope of the Federal Rules.

Under the *Erie* doctrine,[30] "federal courts sitting in diversity apply state substantive law and federal procedural law."[31] Because "[c]lassification of a law as 'substantive' or 'procedural' for *Erie* purposes is sometimes a challenging endeavor," *Erie* and its progeny provide a multi-step inquiry.[32] However, "[w]hen a party has alleged a direct conflict between the Federal Rules and state law, [] an additional step precedes the *Erie* analysis."[33] "The initial step is to determine whether, when fairly construed, the scope of [the Rule] is sufficiently broad to cause a direct collision with the state law or, implicitly, to control the issue before the court, thereby leaving no room for the operation of that law."[34] "In determining whether the Rule covers a particular issue, we look to the plain meaning

of the Rule's language."[35] We also look to judicial interpretations of [—13—] that language.[36] If a direct collision exists, we must apply the Federal Rule as long as it does not violate either the Constitution or the Rules Enabling Act.[37]

Having already determined that state law would otherwise bar the timing of Hornbeck's counterclaim, we next consider whether the filing was compulsory under federal law. The plain language of Rule 13 defines a counterclaim as "compulsory" if it (1) "arises out of the transaction or occurrence that is the subject matter of the opposing party's claim" and (2) "does not require adding another party over whom the court cannot acquire jurisdiction."[38] We also employ the logical relation test to "further define when a claim and counterclaim arise from the same transaction."[39] "The logical relation test is a loose standard which permits a broad realistic interpretation in the interest of avoiding a multiplicity of suits."[40] A logical relationship exists "when the counterclaim arises from the same 'aggregate of operative facts' in that the same operative facts serve[] as the basis of both claims or the aggregate core of facts upon which the claim rests activates additional legal rights, otherwise dormant, in the defendant."[41]

Hornbeck's counterclaim was compulsory within the scope of Rule 13(a). First, the counterclaim arises out of the same occurrence—damage to the Erie Service—that is the subject matter of National's declaratory action. The counterclaim does not require adding another party since National brought its [—14—] initial action against both R&R

---

pet. denied); *see also Great Am. Ins. Co. v. Murray*, 437 S.W.2d 264, 265 (Tex. 1969); *Seaton v. Pickens*, 87 S.W.2d 709, 710 (Tex. 1935); *Sun Oil Co. v. Emp'rs Cas. Co.*, 550 S.W.2d 348, 349 (Tex. App.—Dallas 1977, no writ); *Morris v. Allstate Ins. Co.*, 523 S.W.2d 299, 301 (Tex. App.—Texarkana 1975, no writ).

[28] *See, e.g., Ohio Cas.*, 244 S.W.3d at 888.

[29] *Owens v. Allstate Ins. Co.*, 996 S.W.2d 207, 208-09 (Tex. App.—Dallas 1998, pet. denied) (holding that insurance company lacked standing to bring interpleader action "because [the insured-tortfeasor] was not legally responsible to pay for any of the defendants at the time of the interpleader petition").

[30] *Erie R.R. Co. v. Tompkins*, 304 U.S. 64 (1938).

[31] *Gasperini v. Ctr. for Humanities, Inc.*, 518 U.S. 415, 427 (1996).

[32] *Id.*

[33] *All Plaintiffs v. All Defendants*, 645 F.3d 329, 333 (5th Cir. 2011) (citing *Hanna v. Plumer*, 380 U.S. 460, 469-70 (1965)).

[34] *Id.* (internal quotation marks omitted).

[35] *Id.*

[36] *See id.* at 333-34 (discussing Supreme Court precedent in determining the scope of Rule 23(e) under the Federal Rules of Civil Procedure).

[37] *Id.; Douglas v. NCNB Tex. Nat'l Bank*, 979 F.2d 1128, 1130 (5th Cir. 1992).

[38] FED. R. CIV. P. 13(a)(1)(A), (B).

[39] *Plant v. Blazer Fin. Servs., Inc. of Ga.*, 598 F.2d 1357, 1360 (5th Cir. 1979).

[40] *Id.* at 1361 (internal quotation marks omitted).

[41] *Id.* (quoting *Revere Copper & Brass, Inc. v. Aetna Cas. & Sur. Co.*, 426 F.2d 709, 715 (5th Cir. 1970)).

and Hornbeck. There is a logical relationship between National's disclaimer of liability and Hornbeck's counterclaim that National *is* liable since the same facts underlie both causes. A "direct collision" between state and federal law exists because Hornbeck could not have complied with both state and federal law as to when to assert its counterclaim.

We must, therefore, apply Rule 13(a) so long as it does not violate either the Constitution or the Rules Enabling Act. No constitutional rights are implicated here. Neither does the application of 13(a) violate the Rules Enabling Act because the timing of Hornbeck's counterclaim does not "abridge, enlarge or modify any substantive right" under Texas law.[42] Furthermore, applying 13(a) vindicates "[o]ne of the shaping purposes of the Federal Rules," which is "to bring about uniformity in the federal courts . . . . This is especially true of matters which relate to the administration of legal proceedings, an area in which federal courts have traditionally exerted strong inherent power, completely aside from the powers Congress expressly conferred in the Rules."[43] Rule 13(a) relates to the "administration of legal proceedings" because it was "designed to prevent multiplicity of actions and to achieve resolution in a single lawsuit of all disputes arising out of common matters."[44] Here, it permitted the district court to efficiently address all disputes arising from this litigation. Rule 13(a) merely "alters the *mode* of enforcing state-created rights," and governs the timing of Hornbeck's counterclaim; to hold otherwise "would be to disembowel either the [—15—] Constitution's grant of power over federal procedure or Congress' attempt to exercise that power in the Enabling Act."[45]

---

[42] 28 U.S.C. § 2072(b); *cf. Douglas*, 979 F.2d at 1130 (denying application of Rule 13(a) despite likelihood that state-law claims were compulsory because forcing defendants to counterclaim would have deprived them of non-judicial remedies under Texas law).

[43] *Hanna v. Plumer*, 380 U.S. 460, 472-73 (1965) (quoting *Lumbermen's Mut. Cas. Co. v. Wright*, 322 F.2d 759, 764 (5th Cir. 1963)).

[44] *S. Const. Co. v. Pickard*, 371 U.S. 57, 60 (1962) (per curiam).

[45] *Hanna*, 380 U.S. at 473-74 (emphasis added).

In sum, Rule 13(a) is valid and controls in this case. Consequently, Hornbeck had standing to bring its counterclaim, and the district court properly ruled on that claim after deciding R&R's liability.[46]

V

National challenges the damages award, the award of attorney's fees to Hornbeck, and the assessment of 18% interest on the damage award under the Texas Insurance Code. We conclude that the district court erred in the amount of damages that it awarded and in applying an 18% interest rate.

The district court found that the loss to Hornbeck resulting from R&R's negligence in the sinking of the Erie Service was $1,076,843.09. The judgment against National in favor of Hornbeck included this entire amount. However, it is undisputed that National's policy limit was $1,000,000. The district court erred in awarding Hornbeck in excess of National's policy limits. The award of $1,076,843.09 in damages is accordingly reduced to $1,000,000.

National argues that this amount should be further reduced because it expended in excess of $150,000 in defending R&R against Hornbeck's claim of negligence. The policy provides that defense costs are included within the $1,000,000 policy limit, and therefore, defense costs would "erode" this coverage. However, National did not plead for or prove its defense costs in the district court. It argues in its briefing in our court that it never had the opportunity to do so. This argument is without merit. There was ample opportunity for National to raise and to have the trial court resolve this issue during the lengthy course of the litigation that National itself initiated. National could not rely on [—16—] its argument that Hornbeck had no standing to seek to be paid from the proceeds of R&R's policy until there was a final judgment against R&R as an excuse for failing to raise the issue of defense costs and to prove those costs in the district court.

---

[46] *See* Fed. R. Civ. P. 13(i), 42(b).

The district court awarded attorney's fees from National to Hornbeck in the amount of $213,683.95. Whether National was entitled to recover attorney's fees is determined under state law,[47] unless attorney's fees were imposed as a sanction. Though the district court's order did not express the basis for the grant of attorney's fees, the court's discussion during the fees hearing suggests at least three bases. First, the court may have relied on section 542.060 of the Texas Insurance Code, which provides that an insurer is liable to a beneficiary for "reasonable attorney's fees" should the insurer fail to promptly pay a claim.[48] The court explicitly tied National's obligation to pay attorney's fees to the Texas Insurance Code but also stated that Hornbeck was due these fees "because of National's irrationally prolonging the litigation." Or the court may have granted attorney's fees pursuant to section 38.001(8) of the Texas Civil Remedies and Practice Code, which provides for reasonable attorney's fees if the claim is under an oral or written contract.

The attorney's fees cannot be upheld under section 542.060 of the Texas Insurance Code. Section 542.053 of that Code expressly provides that chapter 542 "does not apply to . . . marine insurance," which is defined as covering "a marine builder or repairer risk."[49] Nor can the award be upheld as sanctions. [—17—] There were no findings or proceedings that would support the imposition of sanctions.

It appears, however, that attorney's fees are recoverable under section 38.001 of the Texas Civil Practice and Remedies Code, even though section 38.006(2) of that Code provides that "[t]his chapter does not apply to a contract issued by an insurer that is subject to the provisions of . . . Chapter 541, Insurance Code."[50] National appears to be subject to the provisions of Chapter 541. The Supreme Court of Texas has held that notwithstanding what might seem to be the clear language of section 38.006, an "insurer is liable for reasonable attorney's fees incurred in pursuing the breach-of-contract action under section 38.001 unless the insurer is liable for attorney's fees under another statutory scheme."[51] The remaining question is whether Hornbeck may sue for breach of the insurance contract even though it is not a party to National's and R&R's contract. The parties have not cited, and we have been unable to find, a decision from a Texas court that squarely addresses the issue. The Supreme Court of Texas has held that "only a third party beneficiary who could enforce a contract to which she is not a party would also be able to sue for attorney's fees under the contract provision of [what is now section 38.001]," and that "the key to determining [the third party's] eligibility for an attorney's fee award . . . requires an analysis of their possible standing as third party beneficiaries to the . . . automobile liability insurance contract."[52] In that case, Childress was injured in an automobile collision with Booth and after obtaining a judgment against Booth, sued Booth's insurer to recover the damages he had [—18—] been awarded from Booth.[53] The Supreme Court reasoned that "[t]here is no claim that either Dairyland [the insurer] or Booth [the insured] contemplated that Childress would become [a] claimant[] of the insurance policy in question. This fact might be determinative of the question but for the statutory scheme that made it incumbent upon Booth, as a driver, to have liability insurance in the first place."[54] Similarly, in the present case, there is no claim that National and R&R contemplated that Hornbeck specifically, as distinguished from R&R's clients generally, would become a claimant under the insurance policy. There is no statute in Texas requiring a ship repairer to carry liability insurance. Accordingly, the Supreme Court's decision in *Dairyland* does not resolve the question.

---

[47] *See INA of Tex. v. Richard*, 800 F.2d 1379, 1381 (5th Cir. 1986) (per curiam) (noting that the award of attorney's fees in disputes involving marine insurance policies is governed by state law).

[48] Tex. Ins. Code Ann. § 542.060.

[49] Tex. Ins. Code Ann. §§ 542.053, 1807.001.

[50] Tex. Civ. Prac. & Rem. Code Ann. § 38.006(2).

[51] *Grapevine Excavation, Inc. v. Md. Lloyds*, 35 S.W.3d 1, 5 (Tex. 2000).

[52] *Dairyland Cnty. Mut. Ins. Co. of Tex. v. Childress*, 650 S.W.2d 770, 775 (Tex. 1983).

[53] *Id.* at 772.

[54] *Id.* at 775.

A Texas court of appeals said in *dicta* that "[a] party who is injured by an insured is considered a third-party beneficiary of a liability insurance policy,"[55] but neither of the cases the decision cited for this proposition[56] supported the statement, and the statement was entirely unnecessary to the court of appeals' holding because the third party had not obtained a judgment against or settled with the insured at the time she sued the insurer and therefore could not proceed against the insurer at that time.[57]

However, a court of appeals permitted Ischy, the widow of a worker killed on the job in an airplane crash, to recover attorney's fees from her deceased [—19—] husband's employer's workers' compensation carrier.[58] The workers' compensation carrier had paid benefits to Ischy and was obligated to pay future compensation benefits to her at the time that she sued and then settled with the operator of the aircraft in which her husband perished.[59] The workers' compensation carrier was entitled to recover from the settlement proceeds the amounts that it had paid to Ischy, and as a result of the settlement, the carrier was relieved from its obligation to pay future benefits.[60] Ischy sued the carrier to obtain attorney's fees under Tex. Rev. Civ. Stat. Ann. art. 8307, §6a for the services rendered by her attorney that benefitted the carrier in her suit against the aircraft operator.[61] Ischy prevailed on that claim under art. 8307, §6a, then sought to obtain her attorney's fees incurred in bringing the suit against the workers' compensation carrier.[62] The court of appeals held that "[a]lthough Ischy is not suing to enforce the contract, we have concluded that this suit is founded upon a contract for purposes of §38.001 attorney's fees. It is undisputed that Ischy was a potential beneficiary of the contract."[63]

Although Texas law is not clear, we make an *Erie* guess[64] and conclude that the Texas courts would construe section 38.001 as allowing Hornbeck to recover attorney's fees from National. Accordingly, the district court did not err [—20—] in awarding attorney's fees. National does not challenge the amount of those fees.

However, the district court did err in the rate of interest that it determined was to be applied. The district court's judgment awarded Hornbeck interest from National on $1,076,843.09 at the rate of 18% per year, citing section 542.060 of the Texas Insurance Code. First, the amount subject to interest must be reduced to $1,000,000, for the reasons considered above. We also conclude that the 18% rate of interest was contrary to Texas law. "We review de novo the district court's determination of state law."[65] Section 542.060 of the Texas Insurance Code "does not apply to . . . marine insurance," which is defined as covering "a marine builder or repairer risk."[66] Because National's policy with R&R falls directly within this exception, the district court erred in awarding interest under the Texas Insurance Code. The pre-judgement rate of interest on the $1,000,000 damage award is modified to 6.0%.

* * *

For the foregoing reasons, we AFFIRM the district court's judgment in part, REVERSE that judgment in part, and remand for the entry of judgment and the appropriate assessment of interest on that judgment in accordance with this opinion.

---

[55] *Rust v. Tex. Farmers Ins. Co.*, 341 S.W.3d 541, 547 (Tex. App.—El Paso 2011, pet. denied).

[56] *State Farm Cnty. Mut. Ins. Co. of Tex. v. Ollis*, 768 S.W.2d 722, 723 (Tex. 1989); *Great Am. Ins. Co. v. Murray*, 437 S.W.2d 264, 265 (Tex. 1969).

[57] *Rust*, 341 S.W.3d at 551-52.

[58] *Ischy v. Twin City Fire Ins. Co.*, 718 S.W.2d 885, 888 (Tex. App.— Austin 1986, writ ref'd n.r.e.).

[59] *Id.* at 885-86.

[60] *Id.* at 886.

[61] *Id.* at 887-88 (citing TEX. REV. CIV. STAT. ANN. art. 8307, § 6a (West Supp. 1986)).

[62] *Id.* at 888 ("The third point of error requests attorney's fees for the prosecution of this lawsuit.").

[63] *Id.*

[64] *Erie R.R. Co. v. Tompkins*, 304 U.S. 64 (1938).

[65] *Great Am. Ins. Co. v. AFS/IBEX Fin. Servs., Inc.*, 612 F.3d 800, 804 (5th Cir. 2010).

[66] TEX. INS. CODE ANN. §§ 542.053, 1807.001.

**United States Court of Appeals
for the Fifth Circuit**

No. 12-11012

TRINITY INDUS., INC.
vs.
UNITED STATES

Appeal from the United States District Court for the
Northern District of Texas

Decided: July 2, 2014

Citation: 757 F.3d 400, 2 Adm. R. 265 (5th Cir. 2014).

Before **OWEN**, **SOUTHWICK**, and **GRAVES**, Circuit Judges.

[—1—] **OWEN**, Circuit Judge:

Trinity Industries, Inc. (Trinity) designed and built vessels during the taxable years ending March 1994 and March 1995 (the claim years). On its amended tax returns, Trinity claimed research tax credits under Internal Revenue Code (I.R.C.) § 41 based on several of these vessel projects. The I.R.S. denied these claims. Trinity then filed this tax refund action in federal court, seeking research tax credits based on the projects. After a two-phase bench trial, the district court held that the tax credit due Trinity was $135,787.60 for 1994 and $0 for 1995. Trinity now appeals, asserting that it is entitled to a tax credit of $1,808,832.53 for 1994 and $2,712,977.00 for 1995. We affirm in part and vacate and remand in part. [—2—]

I

Trinity's amended tax returns for 1994 and 1995 claimed that it was entitled to a research tax credit because its claim year expenses in developing certain vessels constituted qualified research expenses (QREs). As discussed more fully below, I.R.C. § 41 generally provides a 20% credit for claim year QREs that exceed what the taxpayer spent on research in an earlier comparison period (the base amount).[1] The base amount, in turn, is a "fixed base percentage" multiplied by the

company's average annual gross receipts for the four years preceding the claim year.[2] In calculating its research tax credit, Trinity's amended tax returns reported a fixed base percentage (the ratio of base period QREs over base period gross receipts[3]) of 1.3152% for the taxable year ending March 1994 and 1.3125% for the year ending March 1995. The tax returns themselves do not report the base period QREs or the base period gross receipts used to calculate the fixed base percentage. The I.R.S. denied these claims in a 2001 claim disallowance letter.

Trinity subsequently filed this tax refund action in federal court. Before trial began, Trinity retained James Bennett as an expert. Bennett submitted a report finding that the "consistency rule" under I.R.C. § 41(c)(6)—which requires that claim year QREs and base period QREs be computed on a consistent basis[4]—was satisfied on Trinity's amended tax returns. Bennett noted only one caveat to this conclusion: the records available for the claim years were more complete than those available for the base period years, so he [—3—] estimated certain costs for the base period. Based on documentation provided by Trinity, Bennett also provided specific calculations of the base period QREs, the base period gross receipts, and the fixed base percentage. Bennett calculated the overall base period QREs as $49,483,136. Dividing this base period QRE figure by the base period gross receipts ($3,851,683,536) yielded a fixed base percentage of 1.2847%, which was slightly lower than the fixed base percentages reported in the amended tax returns. Although Bennett based his calculations on the same records used to complete the amended tax returns, it is not clear why his fixed base percentage figure was slightly lower.

The district court conducted a two-phase bench trial. In Phase I, the court considered claimed tax credits for six vessel development

---

[1] I.R.C. § 41(a)(1) (codified at 26 U.S.C. § 41(a)(1)).

[2] *Id.* § 41(c)(1).

[3] *Id.* § 41(c)(3)(A).

[4] *Id.* § 41(c)(6)(A) ("[T]he [QREs] taken into account in computing [the fixed base] percentage shall be determined on a basis consistent with the determination of [QREs] for the credit year.").

projects. In its order following Phase I, the court decided that Trinity was wrongly denied credits for only two of the six projects it considered because these two projects (the Mark V and the Dirty Oil Barge) met all four requirements for constituting QREs.[5] According to the court, the other four vessels (the XFPB, the T-AGS 60, the Crew Rescue Boat, and the Hurley Dredge) did not meet the fourth QRE requirement: that substantially all of the research activities in developing the project (i.e., 80% or more) were part of a process of experimentation.[6]

In reaching these conclusions, the court explained that the "shrinking-back rule" in the Treasury regulations ordinarily allows taxpayers to show that smaller subcomponents of a given project satisfy the process-of-experimentation test even if the entire project does not.[7] For instance, if a [—4—] whole vessel project does not satisfy the test, perhaps the development of the vessel's engine is sufficiently experimental. In this case, however, the court noted that "Trinity took an all or nothing approach" because it did not offer proof of its claim year expenses at the subcomponent level. Trinity was unable to offer evidence of its expenses at a more specific level partly because Hurricane Katrina destroyed many of its records. The court thus made its determination on the fourth QRE requirement based on whether, considering each of the six claim year projects as a whole, 80% of the costs incurred in the development of each project were part of a process of experimentation. It did not apply the shrinking-back rule in analyzing the claim year QREs.

In Phase II of the trial, two other vessel projects (the Queen of New Orleans and the Penn Tugs), as well as the method of calculating Trinity's base period QREs were at issue. With regard to its base period QRE calculation, Trinity called as a witness Phil Nuss, Trinity's former Vice President of Engineering. Nuss first confirmed that the ten vessels identified by Bennett in his report were the vessels used in computing the base period QREs on the amended tax returns. Trinity's counsel then asked Nuss whether he believed expenses related to those ten vessels should still be counted as QREs given the district court's Phase I order holding that certain claim year vessel expenses were not QREs. Nuss answered that expenses relating to four of the ten base period vessels should no longer be counted. According to Nuss, two of the base period vessels—the LSV and the North Carolina Auto Ferry—were similar to the Hurley Dredge, one of the claim year vessels held not to be qualified research in Phase I, since they all involved Trinity constructing a vessel based on a design provided to Trinity by a third party. In addition, Nuss believed that another base period vessel—the Cajun Queen—was like the Crew Rescue Boat, a claim year vessel held not to be qualified research in Phase I, since the Cajun Queen was also not a complicated technological boat to build. Finally, [—5—] Nuss testified that a fourth base period vessel—the Ecuador—was like the XFPB, which the district court held was not qualified research in Phase I, since the Ecuador similarly had some experimental features but not enough to satisfy the QRE test. Nuss thus concluded that these four base period vessels should no longer be included in the base period QRE figure, though the other six base period vessels still should be. There was also similar testimony from Sam Charters, Trinity's former Chief Project Engineer, that the LSV was similar, in terms of the amount of experimentation involved, to the Hurley Dredge held not to constitute qualified research.

After Phase II of the trial concluded, the parties submitted briefing addressing whether the two vessel projects at issue constituted QREs, as well as the proper base period QRE

---

[5] See id. § 41(d)(1) (providing that to constitute QREs, (1) the expenses must be deductible under I.R.C. § 174; (2) the research must be for the purpose of discovering technological information; (3) the application of that information must be intended to be useful in the development of a new or improved business component; and (4) substantially all of the research must constitute elements of a process of experimentation).

[6] Id. § 41(d)(1)(C); Treas. Reg. § 1.41-4(a)(6) (codified at 26 C.F.R. § 1.41-4(a)(6)).

[7] See Treas. Reg. § 1.41-4(b)(2).

figure under the consistency rule. Trinity made two distinct arguments about the consistency rule. Its first was that it had followed the consistency rule on its amended tax returns by calculating both its claim year QREs and its base period QREs using an all-or-nothing approach. In making this argument, Trinity acknowledged that it did not use the shrinking-back rule in computing its base period QREs on its returns:

> On the Amended Returns, Trinity sought a tax credit for only certain vessels that could be considered prototypes. In presenting its claim, Trinity took an "all or nothing" approach—*i.e.*, it did not seek shrink-back credit for any subcomponents of any vessels constructed in the Claim Years. *To be consistent with this determination of Claim Year expenditures, Trinity included in the Base Period only expenditures for those vessels that it believed were sufficiently experimental such that the entire vessel constituted qualified research.* Consistent with the manner in which it determined QREs for the Claim Years, *Trinity did not shrink-back to subcomponents of any vessels in the Base Period.* [—6—]

In taking this position, Trinity was not asking the court to allow it to recalculate its base year QREs; it was simply defending how it originally calculated its base period QREs on its amended tax returns.

Trinity then made a second, distinct argument regarding the consistency rule. Relying primarily on the testimony of Nuss but also citing Charters's testimony, Trinity asserted it should be able to remove four vessels from its base period QREs as calculated on its amended tax returns, since those vessels were similar, in terms of how much experimentation was involved, to the four vessels held not to be claim year QREs in Phase I:

> In *Trinity I* the Court articulated a different standard for "prototype" than Trinity applied on the Amended Return.

The Court's holding defined the universe of QREs allowable in the Claim Years. . . . With respect to four of the projects claimed by Trinity, the Court found that the integration of subsystems did not rise to the level required for the cost of developing and constructing the entire vessel to qualify.

> Given this standard, pursuant to [the consistency rule] Trinity's Base Period QREs must be reevaluated in light of the uncontroverted evidence to ensure they are determined consistent with the QREs in the Claim Years. Mr. Nuss . . . considered whether any of the vessels originally included in the Base Period would no longer be considered prototypes under the standard articulated in *Trinity I.* . . . Mr. Nuss testified that expenditures on four vessel projects in the Base Period should not be treated as QRE[s] . . . . For each of these vessels, Mr. Nuss testified that the identification, configuration and integration of the components of the vessels were not sufficiently complex for the vessels to constitute prototypes under the Court's standard.

Trinity contended that, after removing the four base period vessels from the base period QRE figure of $49,483,136 provided by Bennett's report, the base period QRE figure would total $26,706,987. Trinity's second consistency rule argument thus asked the district court to allow it to reduce its base period QRE [—7—] figure by over $20 million, which in turn would reduce its fixed base percentage and increase its overall research tax credit.

In its Phase II order, the district court concluded that Trinity was wrongly denied tax credit for the Queen of New Orleans but was correctly denied credit for the Penn Tugs. According to the court, the Penn Tugs did not meet the fourth QRE requirement. With respect to the consistency rule, the court only addressed the merits of Trinity's first consistency rule argument—Trinity's defense of its use of an all-or-nothing, "entire project" approach in both the base period years and the claim years:

> Trinity now argues that, in view of the consistency rule, its base period QREs should include only projects that were overall 80% or more research. The Court disagrees. . . . Here the Court applied the 80% rule only to entire projects due to a lack of evidence to permit application of the "shrinkback rule." This . . . simply reflects the absence of evidence of costs incurred on a subset of an entire vessel . . . . Accordingly, the Court will not exclude from the base period QREs any QREs incurred that were less than 80% of an entire project.

The court accordingly rejected the merits of Trinity's first argument but failed to address the merits of Trinity's second argument based on Nuss's testimony. The court also failed to acknowledge that Trinity did not use the shrinking-back rule in calculating the base period QREs in its amended tax returns, and therefore the base period QREs *already* excluded any QREs incurred that were less than 80% of an entire project. The same order provided that "[o]ther than Trinity's consistency argument, the Court credits the testimony of Trinity's witnesses and finds Trinity's calculation to be a reasonable estimate of the base amount."

After additional briefing, the district court issued its final judgment holding that Trinity was entitled to $135,787.60 in tax credit for 1994 and $0 for 1995. Trinity now appeals. [—8—]

II

"The standard of review for a bench trial is well established: findings of fact are reviewed for clear error and legal issues are reviewed de novo."[8] A fact finding "is clearly erroneous if it is without substantial evidence to support it, the court misinterpreted the effect of the evidence, or this court is convinced that the findings are against the preponderance of credible testimony."[9] Mixed questions of law and fact are also reviewed de novo.[10]

III

Trinity first contends that the district court erred in applying the consistency rule in calculating its base period QREs. We begin with an overview of the research tax credit calculation and the consistency rule, and then consider Trinity's position regarding the consistency rule.

A

Under I.R.C. § 41, companies can claim a 20% credit for QREs that exceed what they spent in an earlier comparison period.[11] Using the terminology of the I.R.C., the research tax credit is calculated as follows:

- Research credit = the lesser of: 20% x (claim year QREs – base amount), and 20% x (50% x claim year QREs);[12]

- Base amount = fixed base percentage x average annual gross receipts for the four years preceding claim year;[13] [—9—]

- Fixed base percentage = aggregate base period QREs / aggregate base period gross receipts, where base period here = taxable year ending 3/31/1985 through taxable year ending 3/31/1989.[14]

The research tax credit can be summarized in the following formula:

---

[8] *Coe v. Chesapeake Exploration, L.L.C.,* 695 F.3d 311, 316 (5th Cir. 2012) (quoting *Preston Exploration Co. v. GSF, L.L.C.,* 669 F.3d 518, 522 (5th Cir. 2012)).

[9] *Petrohawk Props., L.P. v. Chesapeake La., L.P.,* 689 F.3d 380, 388 (5th Cir. 2012) (quoting *French v. Allstate Indem. Co.,* 637 F.3d 571, 577 (5th Cir. 2011)).

[10] *Id.* (citing *Dickerson v. Lexington Ins. Co.,* 556 F.3d 290, 294 (5th Cir. 2009)).

[11] I.R.C. § 41(a)(1).

[12] *Id.* § 41(a)(1), (c)(2).

[13] *Id.* § 41(c)(1).

[14] *See id.* § 41(c)(3)(A).

To constitute QREs, four requirements must be met:

(1) the expenses must be of the type deductible under I.R.C. § 174; (2) the research must be undertaken "for the purpose of discovering information . . . which is technological in nature;" (3) the application of that information must be "intended to be useful in the development of a new or improved business component of the taxpayer;" and (4) substantially all of the research activities must "constitute elements of a process of experimentation."[15]

Under Treasury regulations, the fourth requirement is met if 80% or more of the research activities constitute elements of a process of experimentation.[16]

This four-part QRE test is to be applied separately to each business component of the taxpayer, which is defined to include any product held for sale, lease, or license, or used by the taxpayer in its trade or business.[17] If, [—10—] however, each of the four requirements is not met with respect to an entire business component, the shrinking-back rule under Treasury Regulation § 1.41-4(b)(2) is implicated. Under the shrinking-back rule, these four requirements "are to be applied first at the level of the discrete business component," but "[i]f these requirements are not met at that level, then they apply at the most significant subset of elements of the product."[18] "This shrinking back of the product is to continue until either a subset of elements of the product that satisfies the requirements is reached, or the

most basic element of the product is reached and such element fails to satisfy the test."[19] Accordingly, the rule "is applied only if a taxpayer does not satisfy the [four requirements] with respect to the overall business component."[20]

The consistency rule also plays a role in computing QREs. The rule ensures that the research tax credit due is not overstated or understated because the taxpayer inconsistently compares QREs in the base period years and the claim year. The rule provides that "the [QREs] taken into account in computing [the fixed base] percentage shall be determined on a basis consistent with the determination of [QREs] for the credit year."[21] The corresponding Treasury regulation uses similar language.[22] [—11—]

B

On appeal, Trinity challenges the district court's application of the consistency rule in calculating its base period QREs, and it presents two distinct arguments as to why the rule was violated. The first argument is that the district court violated the consistency rule by applying the shrinking-back rule in the base period years but not applying it in the claim years. This argument hinges on the assumption that the district court used a shrink-back analysis for the base period QREs, so that if expenses related to the entire vessel did not constitute qualified research, expenses related to subcomponents of the vessel were still counted as qualified research. The Government has not contested Trinity's understanding of the facts, so the parties argue over whether, as a legal matter, when the shrinking-back rule could not be applied

---

[15] *United States v. McFerrin*, 570 F.3d 672, 676 (5th Cir. 2009) (alteration in original) (quoting I.R.C. § 41(d)(1)).

[16] Treas. Reg. § 1.41-4(a)(6).

[17] I.R.C. § 41(d)(2).

[18] Treas. Reg. § 1.41-4(b)(2).

[19] *Id.*

[20] *Id.*

[21] I.R.C. § 41(c)(6)(A).

[22] Treas. Reg. § 1.41-3(d)(1) ("[QREs] and gross receipts taken into account in computing a taxpayer's fixed-base percentage and a taxpayer's base amount must be determined on a basis consistent with the definition of [QREs] and gross receipts for the credit year, without regard to the law in effect for the taxable years taken into account in computing the fixed-base percentage or the base amount.").

in calculating the claim year QREs because of a lack of evidence, the base period QREs also had to be calculated on an all-or-nothing, "whole ship" basis.

There is a significant issue, however, regarding the facts assumed in much of the briefing in our court: the briefs assumed that the shrinking-back rule was applied by the district court, while the record reflects that it *was not* applied in the district court's calculation of the base period QREs. In fact, neither Trinity's amended tax returns, nor Bennett's report, nor the district court judgment based on Bennett's report used the shrinking-back rule in computing Trinity's base period QREs. Trinity's briefing before the district court acknowledged that it did not use the shrinking-back rule in its amended tax returns. Moreover, Bennett's report confirms that neither Trinity's amended tax returns nor his report could have used the shrinking-back rule in computing Trinity's base period QREs. For one, Bennett's report stated that he calculated the base period QREs "based on 100% of the wages, supplies and contract labor costs, less overhead costs" for the ten vessel projects in the base period. Including *all* of the projects' expenses shows that *entire* projects were [—12—] considered qualified research, not just "subcomponents" of the projects like the vessels' engines. Second, Bennett noted that Trinity's records for the base period years were even less detailed than the records for the claim years, in which Trinity was unable to avail itself of the shrinking-back rule because records were lacking. This further establishes that neither Bennett's report nor Trinity's amended returns applied the shrinking-back rule in the base period.

The district court's order also did not employ the shrinking-back rule in computing the base period QREs. In its final judgment, the district court held Trinity was entitled to $135,787.60 for 1994 and $0 for 1995. These figures are the same as those in Trinity's post-trial briefing, which asked the court to adopt the base amount figures from Bennett's report. This means that the base amounts used in the final judgment were calculated using the fixed base percentage, including the base period QREs, used in Bennett's report,

and Bennett's report did not employ the shrinking-back rule in calculating the base period QREs. As a result, the district court's judgment incorporated a base period QRE figure calculated using an all-or-nothing approach, thereby excluding any QREs incurred that were less than 80% of an entire project, even though it held that it would "not exclude from the base period QREs any QREs incurred that were less than 80% of an entire project." Trinity's attorney at oral argument acknowledged that the district court did not apply a shrink-back analysis in calculating the base period QREs.

In short, the district court did not use the shrinking-back rule in calculating Trinity's base period QREs. Trinity argues that the district court should have applied a "whole ship" methodology in calculating its base period QREs, but this is exactly what the district court did by calculating the base amount based on Bennett's report. Moreover, any argument—from either party—about whether the shrinking-back rule should have been applied in the [—13—] base period years need not be addressed as the lack of records from the base period years apparently would have precluded the shrinking-back rule from being applied in the base period. Trinity's first consistency rule argument therefore entitles it to nothing more than what the district court awarded it.

C

Trinity presents a second argument as to why the consistency rule was violated and why it is therefore entitled to a lower base period QRE figure of $26,706,987. The $26,706,987 amount is the base period QRE used in the Bennett report *less* the QREs attributable to the four base period vessels Nuss testified would not constitute qualified research under the standard articulated by the district court in Phase I of trial.

Nuss testified that he did not believe that four base period vessels—the LSV, the North Carolina Auto Ferry, the Cajun Queen, and the Ecuador—involved the level of experimentation necessary to constitute QREs since they were similar, in terms of how much experimentation was involved, to the claim year vessels the district court held not to be QREs after Phase I. In other words, if the district court found that certain claim year vessels—including the XFPB, the T-AGS 60, the Crew Rescue Boat, and the Hurley Dredge—did not satisfy the QRE test, then four of the base period vessels should not have satisfied the QRE test, either. As discussed above, Nuss testified that two of the base period vessels—the LSV and the North Carolina Auto Ferry—were similar to the Hurley Dredge, since they all involved Trinity constructing a vessel based on a design provided to Trinity by a third party. There was also testimony from Charters that the LSV was comparable to the Hurley Dredge since both were based in part on an existing design. Nuss believed that another base period vessel—the Cajun Queen—was like the Crew Rescue Boat, another claim year vessel held not to be qualified research, since the Cajun Queen was also not a complicated technological boat to build. Finally, Nuss testified that [—14—] a fourth base period vessel—the Ecuador—was like the XFPB, which the district court held was not qualified research, since the Ecuador similarly had some experimental features but not enough to satisfy the QRE test. Nuss testified that to calculate the QREs on a consistent basis, the four base period vessels should be removed from the base period QRE calculation.

Though much of Trinity's briefing on appeal focused on its first consistency rule argument concerning the shrinking-back rule, Trinity has adequately raised its second argument based on Nuss's testimony. In its opening brief, Trinity argued that, under a proper application of the consistency rule, this court should calculate its base period QREs as $26,706,987: the base period QRE amount used in the Bennett report *less* the QREs attributable to the four vessels Nuss said would not satisfy the district court's Phase I QRE standard. Trinity's reply brief again referenced Nuss's testimony, noting that "[b]ased on the District Court's ruling in Phase I, [Nuss and Charters] identified four comparable vessels, out of the [ten] submitted by Trinity in the base years, that similarly would not qualify for research credit as whole

ships under the Court's analysis." Trinity also contended that the panel could reverse and render judgment in its favor based on "Nuss's testimony of why four ships from the base years . . . should be removed under the consistency rule" and referred to "Nuss's and Charters's testimony on removing four partial ships from the base years." At oral argument, Trinity's counsel again urged that if the district court disqualified certain claim year vessels, it should have also disqualified the four base period vessels, which involved a similar level of experimentation, as not satisfying the process-of-experimentation test. Trinity therefore sufficiently raised this argument on appeal.

Assuming the district court would credit Nuss's and Charters's testimony, we agree with Trinity that if certain base period vessels are just as [—15—] experimental as claim-year vessels held not to be qualified research, those base period vessels should not be counted as qualified research for purposes of the base period QRE calculation. I.R.C. § 41 allows a taxpayer to claim a tax credit for claim year research expenses that exceed the research expenses spent in an earlier comparison period, the base period years.[23] To equitably measure the increase in qualified research spending between the two periods, the same standard should be applied in determining whether certain projects pursued in the two periods are sufficiently experimental to be qualified research.

The consistency rule addresses this very issue: it aims to ensure that the research tax credit due is not overstated or understated because the taxpayer inconsistently compares QREs in the base period years and the claim year. The rule provides that the QREs "taken into account in computing [the fixed-base] percentage shall be determined on a basis consistent with the determination of [QREs] for the credit year."[24] The corresponding Treasury regulation uses language very similar to the consistency rule itself but adds the word "definition":

---

[23] I.R.C. § 41(a)(1).
[24] *Id.* § 41(c)(6)(A).

[QREs] . . . taken into account in computing a taxpayer's fixed-base percentage and a taxpayer's base amount must be determined on a basis consistent with the definition of [QREs] . . . for the credit year, without regard to the law in effect for the taxable years taken into account in computing the fixed-base percentage or the base amount.[25]

The regulation then provides two illustrations. In the first, for a hypothetical taxpayer, the statutory definition of QRE for its first two base period years (1984 and 1985) is different than a revised QRE definition applicable in its last [—16—] three base period years (1986, 1987, and 1988) and in its claim year (2001).[26] To compute the credit for 2001, the taxpayer must apply the new QRE definition to its 1984 and 1985 base period years "to reflect the change in the definition of qualified research" beginning in 1986.[27] The second illustration following the regulation shows another slightly different application of the consistency rule. It states that if the taxpayer counts "a certain type of expenditure"—such as the wages of its research assistants—as QREs in the claim year, it must also count "similar expenditures" as QREs in its base period years.[28] In sum, the consistency rule calls for consistent application of the QRE definition across the base period years and the claim year, including the types of expenditures the taxpayer treats as QREs.

The consistency rule is equally applicable to a case like this one. Here, the district court decided that certain claim year projects were not sufficiently experimental to pass the fourth QRE requirement—that 80% or more of the research activities involved in the project

constitute elements of a process of experimentation[29]—and Trinity simply asked the court to consider whether four of its base period projects were also not sufficiently experimental to pass that same test. If, for instance, the Ecuador and the XFPB projects involved exactly the same level of experimentation, then it would violate the consistency rule (and understate Trinity's tax credit) not to count the XFPB as qualified research in the claim year but to count the Ecuador as qualified research in [—17—] the base period years. Trinity is entitled to have a consistent QRE test applied to projects in the base period years and the claim years.

The only matter still unsettled is whether the district court would credit Nuss's and Charters's testimony that the four base period vessels were similar to the four claim year vessels held not be qualified research, in terms of how much experimentation was involved. In its order after Phase II of the trial, the district court stated that, "[o]ther than Trinity's consistency argument, the Court credits the testimony of Trinity's witnesses and finds Trinity's calculation to be a reasonable estimate of the base amount." But again, though Trinity raised in the district court the second consistency rule argument based on Nuss's and Charters's testimony, the district court did not address this issue, so it is unclear whether the district court credited those witnesses' testimony on the four base period vessels.

We therefore remand to the district court for a limited purpose: making a factual finding as to whether to credit the testimony of Nuss and Charters that the four base period vessels were as experimental as (or less experimental than) the four claim year vessels held not to satisfy the fourth QRE requirement. If the district court credits this testimony against any possible conflicting testimony or evidence, then those four base period vessels should be removed from the base period QRE calculation, and the resulting base period QRE figure would be $26,706,987. If the district court finds that the four base period

---

[25] Treas. Reg. § 1.41-3(d)(1).

[26] *Id.* § 1.41-3(d)(2) (Example 1).

[27] *Id.*

[28] *Id.* (Example 2); *see also Union Carbide Corp. v. Comm'r*, 97 T.C.M. (CCH) 1207, T.C. Memo 2009-50, at *75 (2009) ("[T]he taxpayer must include the same types of activities from the credit year and the base period when identifying qualified research activities and include the same types of costs as QREs for the credit year and the base period."), *aff'd*, 697 F.3d 104 (2d Cir. 2012).

[29] *See* I.R.C. § 41(d)(1); Treas. Reg. § 1.41-4(a)(6).

vessels (or some of them) were more experimental than the four claim year vessels and were sufficiently experimental to qualify as QREs, then the base period QRE figure should include the expenses associated with those vessel projects. We thus vacate the district court's holding as to the consistency rule and remand for findings as to whether, in light of the district court's Phase I order, the four base period vessels at issue are sufficiently experimental to constitute qualified research. [—18—]

IV

Trinity also challenges the district court's conclusion that its research expenses in developing the Penn Tugs did not satisfy the fourth QRE requirement and therefore did not constitute claim year QREs. Trinity first argues that because the I.R.S. already determined that the Penn Tugs met the fourth QRE requirement, the Government was either conclusively or presumptively bound by that decision in this litigation. When the I.R.S. issued its claim disallowance letter, it incorporated a revenue agent report stating that, with respect to the Penn Tugs, the fourth requirement—the process-of-experimentation test—was satisfied, even though two other QRE requirements were not. Even if the Government is not conclusively bound by the conclusion in Trinity's favor on the fourth QRE requirement, Trinity argues it is entitled to a presumption of correctness, so the Government bore the burden of rebutting it by affirmative evidence.

We disagree. The district court correctly held that the report's conclusion, though admissible evidence,[30] was neither binding nor entitled to a presumption of correctness. In tax refund actions, the district court reviews de novo the Commissioner's decision regarding a taxpayer's tax liability.[31] The

taxpayer has the burden of proving by a preponderance of the evidence that the Commissioner's assessment—its final determination of the taxpayer's liability—was erroneous, since the assessment is presumed to be correct.[32] [—19—] While the assessment itself is entitled to a presumption of correctness, the "reasons for the Commissioner's determination are not relevant for the Court does not review those reasons."[33] Accordingly, here, while the I.R.S.'s ultimate determination of Trinity's tax liability is presumptively correct, the revenue agent report's subsidiary conclusion that the Penn Tugs met the process-of-experimentation test is neither binding on the Government nor presumptively correct.

Trinity's second contention is that, even if the conclusions in the revenue agent report are not binding or presumptively correct in this litigation, the district court erred in deciding that the Penn Tugs did not satisfy the process-of-experimentation test under the fourth QRE requirement. Under this requirement, substantially all (i.e., 80%) of the taxpayer's research activities, "measured on a cost or other consistently applied reasonable basis," must constitute elements of a process of experimentation.[34] As the Treasury

---

[30] See FED. R. EVID. 801(d)(2)(D).

[31] See Clapp v. Comm'r, 875 F.2d 1396, 1403 (9th Cir. 1989) ("In tax cases . . . [the] United States District Court review[s] the Commissioner's decision on the merits de novo."); Int'l Paper Co. v. United States, 36 Fed. Cl. 313, 320 (1996) (recognizing the "de novo nature of tax refund

proceedings in the Court of Federal Claims (as well as in the district courts)").

[32] Carson v. United States, 560 F.2d 693, 695-96 (5th Cir. 1977) ("The burden and the presumption, which are for the most part but the opposite sides of a single coin, combine to require the taxpayer always to prove by a preponderance of the evidence that the Commissioner's determination was erroneous.") (citing United States v. Janis, 428 U.S. 433, [—19—] 440 (1976)); see also Cook v. United States, 46 Fed. Cl. 110, 113-14 (2000) (discussing the presumption of correctness and the taxpayer's burden in tax refund suits).

[33] Int'l Paper Co., 36 Fed. Cl. at 320 (quoting Pierson v. United States, 428 F. Supp. 384, 390 (D. Del. 1977)); see also MICHAEL I. SALTZMAN & LESLIE BOOK, IRS PRACTICE AND PROCEDURE ¶ 1.05[2][a] (explaining that in a tax refund suit in federal court, "any 'record' made in the Service, including the reasons for its assessment, is irrelevant" and that the "action involves a de novo determination of the correct tax and is not a review of the administrative processing of the case").

[34] I.R.C. § 41(d)(1)(C); Treas. Reg. § 1.41-4(a)(6).

regulations elaborate, a "process of experimentation"

involves three steps: (1) "the identification of uncertainty concerning the development or improvement of a business component," (2) "the identification of one or more alternatives intended to eliminate that uncertainty," and (3) "the identification and the conduct of a process of evaluating the alternatives [—20—] (through, for example, modeling, simulation, or a systematic trial and error methodology)."[35]

Case law applying the Treasury regulations explains that the process-of-experimentation test is not satisfied when the taxpayer uses "a method of simple trial and error to validate that a process or product change meets the taxpayer's needs."[36] Instead, at a minimum, the research activities must involve a "systematic trial and error methodology"[37]—"a methodical plan involving a series of trials to test a hypothesis, analyze the data, refine the hypothesis, and retest the hypothesis so that it constitutes experimentation in the scientific sense."[38]

The Penn Tugs were each designed to connect to a barge by an articulating arm (the "Intercon coupler") so that the tugboat and the barge could function as a single ship with high horsepower. In this tug-coupler-barge combination, or articulated tug barge (ATB), "the tug functioned as the propeller for the barge, rather than as a traditional tug that pulls another vessel." Trinity designed the Penn Tugs to avoid the Coast Guard's requirement that large cargo ships have a 20-person crew with advanced licenses. Instead of

treating the ATB as a cargo ship, the Coast Guard would certify the vessel as a tug and a barge, so it could be manned by a smaller crew with simpler licenses, resulting in cost savings for the operator. [—21—]

In addressing the Penn Tugs, the district court first noted that the Intercon coupler part of the ATB was invented, developed, and built by other companies. The court then considered the first Penn Tug and noted that, in designing it, Trinity modified an existing hull design. The court acknowledged this modification involved assessing "the structural integrity of the tug-coupler combination" since "portions of the tug can be 'hanging' from the Intercon coupler, depending on wave action on the barge." The court nonetheless concluded that less than 80% of the costs were incurred in a process of experimentation "because third parties designed and manufactured the coupler system itself and the first Penn Tug was only a modification of an existing design."

The district court then separately addressed the second Penn Tug. Trinity made the elevated pilot house on the first Penn Tug out of aluminum to save weight, but due to changes in Coast Guard fire regulations, Trinity was required to make the pilot house on the second Penn Tug out of steel. Although the heavier steel pilot house required other design changes, the district decided that "the only process of experimentation between the first and second Penn Tugs was the change to the composition of the pilot house." The district court concluded that the second Penn Tug also failed the process-of-experimentation test.

This determination on the Penn Tugs is best characterized as a mixed question of law and fact, since the underlying facts and applicable legal standard are basically undisputed, and the question is whether those facts satisfy the legal standard.[39] We therefore

---

[35] *United States v. McFerrin*, 570 F.3d 672, 677 (5th Cir. 2009) (quoting Treas. Reg. § 1.41-4(a)(5)(i)).

[36] *Union Carbide Corp. v. Comm'r*, 97 T.C.M. (CCH) 1207, T.C. Memo 2009-50, at *81 (2009), *aff'd*, 697 F.3d 104 (2d Cir. 2012); *see United States v. Davenport*, 897 F. Supp. 2d 496, 506 (N.D. Tex. 2012) (same).

[37] Treas. Reg. § 1.41-4(a)(5)(i).

[38] *Union Carbide Corp.*, T.C. Memo 2009-50, at *81; *see Davenport*, 897 F. Supp. 2d at 506 (same).

[39] *See Ornelas v. United States*, 517 U.S. 690, 696-97 (1996) (explaining that for mixed questions of law and fact, "historical facts are admitted or established, the rule of law is undisputed, and the issue is whether the facts satisfy the [relevant

review any underlying fact findings [—22—] for clear error, but we review the legal conclusion that the Penn Tugs failed the process-of-experimentation test de novo.[40] In addition, Trinity had the burden of proof, including the burden of going forward with evidence and the burden of persuasion, that 80% of its Penn Tugs research activities constituted a process of experimentation.[41]

Trinity has not established that 80% of the research activities for the Penn Tugs constituted elements of a process of experimentation. Trinity argues that modifying the existing hull design involved some systematic trial and error—"[f]inding a working hull design required testing and retesting, including computer modeling and at least four design revisions"—and has cited testimony to support this assertion. However, Trinity has failed to establish which other aspects of its research involved the sort of systematic trial and error required under the process-of-experimentation test. For instance, in arguing that changing the composition of the pilot house involved a process of experimentation, Trinity says it "experimented" with an aluminum tower and pilothouse but does not allege that designing the tower involved the sort of systematic trial and error that the hull design involved. While designing the hull involved some systematic experimentation, Trinity has not shown that substantially all of its Penn Tugs research activities involved the type of systematic experimentation courts have required.[42] [—23—]

Moreover, since the coupler was not designed by Trinity, the district court correctly focused on research activities with respect to the tugs only. Trinity does not dispute that it did not invent, design, or build the coupler; it only claims it "had to work alongside the company manufacturing the coupler to design the support structure required for it to work within this prototype." While Trinity had to consider how the tugs would support the coupler, it did not design the coupler itself.

The district court also did not err in finding that, even if aspects of designing the hull involved a process of experimentation, the hull's design was still based on an existing hull design to some extent. Although there was testimony that Trinity had "to start over from scratch with a different hull," the testimony also established that designing the new hull involved "modifications" of old hulls, and that the ultimate hull design had similarities to existing hulls. Additionally, it was not error to consider the two Penn Tugs "separately and sequentially," as Trinity argues. Trinity cites no authority requiring the court to treat the tugs together, and even if Trinity had, Trinity has not shown how the 80% threshold would be surpassed by doing so. Accordingly, the district court did not err in its analysis of the Penn Tugs.

* * *

For the foregoing reasons, the judgment of the district court is AFFIRMED in part, and VACATED and REMANDED in part for proceedings consistent with this opinion.

statutory standard]") (internal quotation marks and citation omitted).

[40] See Dunn v. Comm'r, 301 F.3d 339, 348 (5th Cir. 2002) (holding that the "determination of fair market value" of common stock under Treasury regulations is a mixed question of fact and law, and that the factual premises of mixed questions are reviewed for clear error and the legal conclusions are reviewed de novo).

[41] Int'l Paper Co. v. United States, 36 Fed. Cl. 313, 322 (1996).

[42] See Union Carbide Corp., T.C. Memo 2009-50, at *7, *85-86 (holding that substantially all of the research activities in connection with an "anticoking project" (a project aimed at reducing the build-up of carbon in the taxpayer's furnaces) constituted elements of a process of

experimentation because the project involved collecting and analyzing data to compare existing technologies with alternatives and ultimately refining the process to improve it overall); see also Davenport, 897 F. Supp. 2d at 514-15 (holding that the taxpayer's [—23—] project "did not involve a process of experimentation or the type of systematic plan involving a series of trials to test a hypothesis, analyze the data, refine the hypothesis, and retest the hypothesis; nor did it involve a series of experiments with one or more alternatives to develop the [project]") (internal quotation marks and citation omitted).

United States Court of Appeals
for the Fifth Circuit

No. 13-30888

FIRST AM. BANK
vs.
FIRST AM. TRANSP. TITLE INS. CO.

Appeal from the United States District Court for the
Eastern District of Louisiana

Decided: July 16, 2014

Citation: 759 F.3d 427, 2 Adm. R. 276 (5th Cir. 2014).

Before **BARKSDALE, CLEMENT,** and **OWEN,** Circuit Judges.

[—1—] OWEN, Circuit Judge:

On remand from this court, the district court conducted a bench trial to determine the extent of First American Transportation Title Insurance Company's (FATTIC) liability to First American Bank (First American) under certain vessel title insurance policies. First American appeals the district court's final judgment, asserting that the court erred in calculating the amount due under the policies by using the wrong date of valuation, miscalculating the value of one of the insured vessels, and improperly making certain deductions. First American also challenges the district court's conclusion that FATTIC did not act in bad faith under Louisiana law. We affirm. [—2—]

I

This case is before our court for the second time.[1] Titan Cruise Lines, Inc. (Titan) defaulted on loans obtained from First American. As we previously recounted, First American loaned Titan $28,000,000 to finance its operation of a gaming vessel known as the Ocean Jewel. The loan was secured by a ship mortgage on the Ocean Jewel as well as mortgages on the Emerald Express (Emerald) and the Sapphire Express (Sapphire), two high speed catamarans that transported customers to and from the Ocean Jewel.

---

[1] *See First Am. Bank v. First Am. Transp. Title Ins. Co.,* 585 F.3d 833 (5th Cir. 2009).

FATTIC issued two title insurance policies to First American, one for the Ocean Jewel and one for the Emerald and Sapphire (collectively, the Shuttles). Both policies provide that FATTIC is liable for "actual loss or damage . . . sustained or incurred by [the Insured] by reason of" nineteen enumerated risks. Relevant to the issues before us, those risks include:

Lack of priority of the Mortgage insured hereunder over any statutory lien for Necessaries (as that term is defined in 46 U.S.C. § 31301 or its equivalent under the law of [the vessels' country of registration]) provided to the Vessel[s] prior to or after the Date of Policy whether or not the statutory lien for Necessaries arises prior to or after the Date of Policy.

Section 7(a) of the policies provides the extent of FATTIC's liability. It states, in relevant part, that the company's liability shall not exceed:

(iii) The difference between the value of the Title as insured and the value of the Title subject to the defect, lien or encumbrance insured against by this policy . . . .

Titan's operations were unsuccessful and the company filed for bankruptcy in August 2005. At that time, the Ocean Jewel and Shuttles were encumbered by necessaries liens resulting from debts owed to suppliers of necessaries for the vessels. Shortly after Titan's filing, First American hired [—3—] Norman Dufour, a qualified marine surveyor and appraiser, to appraise the three vessels. Dufour concluded that, as of August 2005, the Ocean Jewel had a fair market value of $10,800,000; the Sapphire had a value of $2,000,000; and the hull of the Emerald, which was under repair, was worth $200,000.

The bankruptcy court approved an agreement for Tampa Bay Shipbuilding & Repair Company (TBSR) to provide berthing and related services to Titan's vessels. As security for payment, the court granted TBSR perfected first-priority liens on each of the berthed vessels. The court also approved a motion by Titan's estate to sell the Ocean Jewel and the Sapphire. Before the sale could be completed, however, the Sapphire sank at her moorings. The estate negotiated with the purchaser to reduce the purchase price by $500,000 and to exclude the Sapphire from the sale. The bankruptcy court approved this agreement, and the Ocean Jewel was sold for $6,450,000. With First American's consent, the bankruptcy court ordered $1,110,000 of the sale proceeds carved out for the benefit of the estate. Of the remaining balance that was left after certain further payments, $1,162,815 was distributed to holders of necessaries liens, leaving $4,172,215 to First American.

The bankruptcy court subsequently approved the estate's abandonment of the Sapphire. TBSR then filed an *in rem* action against the vessel in federal court, asserting that it had a maritime lien as a result of providing necessaries. Following the court's entry of a default judgment against the Sapphire, the U.S. Marshal seized the vessel and sold it at a public auction to TBSR for a $99,227 credit-bid. Eastern Shipbuilding Group, Inc. (Eastern), meanwhile, purchased the Emerald's hull following that vessel's abandonment for a $10,000 credit-bid.

First American filed suit against FATTIC under the Shuttles policy after the insurer claimed that its liability under that policy was limited to the amounts paid to TBSR and Eastern in the foreclosure sales. Following several [—4—] months of litigation, the district court granted FATTIC's motion for partial summary judgment. The court held that First American was not entitled to recover consequential damages and that FATTIC's liability was limited to the amount by which the payments to necessaries lienholders reduced First American's recovery, thus confining the covered loss to the amount bid at the foreclosure sales.

On interlocutory appeal, we affirmed in part and reversed in part.[2] We agreed that First American was not entitled to consequential damages and that its recovery

was limited to the "difference between the value of First American's ship mortgages when unencumbered and the value of First American's ship mortgages subject to the necessaries liens."[3] Nonetheless, we held that this difference could not be ascertained solely by reference to the proceeds from the foreclosure sale. Rather, Louisiana law required that "the finder-of-fact . . . take into consideration all other relevant information when valuing loss under a title insurance policy," including "any appraisals, the foreclosure proceeds, and other market data."[4] Accordingly, we remanded to the district court to determine the difference in value as well as "the proper date of valuation."[5]

While the first appeal was pending, First American filed suit under the Ocean Jewel policy. After negotiating or settling necessaries claims on First American's behalf, FATTIC had tendered $1,162,287 to the Bank, the approximate amount paid to the necessaries lienholders out of the revenue from the Ocean Jewel. FATTIC asserted that sum constituted the full amount [—5—] due under the Ocean Jewel policy. First American disagreed, claiming that its covered losses exceeded the amount received by the necessaries lienholders.

On remand from this court, the district court consolidated the cases and permitted discovery. During discovery, the parties learned that Eastern had sold the Emerald's hull for $500,000 on the open market. After making deductions for the expenses Eastern incurred in preparing the hull for sale, FATTIC remitted $450,139.50 to First American under the Shuttles policy. The parties also discovered that the Sapphire had been sold for $500,000. FATTIC, however, only paid First American $10,515.38, claiming that amount represented the difference between the bank's mortgage as unencumbered and as subject to covered necessaries liens.

After a bench trial, the district court issued findings of fact and conclusions of law. The

---

[2] *Id.* at 839.

[3] *Id.* at 837-39.
[4] *Id.* at 838.
[5] *Id.*

court first concluded that the policies unambiguously required the vessels to be valued as of the date of their judicial sales. Based on those dates, the court found that the Ocean Jewel was worth the amount for which it had sold at the foreclosure sale; accordingly, First American incurred an insured loss of $1,162,287 under the Ocean Jewel policy. The court concluded, however, that the Emerald's foreclosure sale price was not a strong indicator of that vessel's value. Instead, it found that First American had incurred an insured loss of $445,137.50, the amount of Eastern's net proceeds from the resale of the vessel's hull on the open market. The court likewise determined that the $500,000 resale price was the best evidence of the Sapphire's value. However, it held that First American was not entitled to recover that amount; rather, the bank's insured loss was limited to $411,288 because $88,712 of TBSR's credit-bid consisted of uninsured "superpriority claims."

Prior to making its calculations, the district court concluded that this court's holding from the first appeal regarding the appropriate method of [—6—] calculation under the Shuttles policy also applied to the Ocean Jewel. Accordingly, in calculating the value of the three vessels, the district court "note[d] for the record that it considered all available relevant evidence." However, it stated that it did not consider First American's appraisals relevant because they were conducted well in advance of the vessels' sales.

Lastly, the court concluded that FATTIC did not act in bad faith. This appeal followed.

II

Following a bench trial, "a district court's findings of fact are reviewed for clear error and its conclusions of law *de novo*."[6] The court's interpretation of a contract, including whether the contract is ambiguous, "is a matter of law reviewable *de novo*."[7] The parties agree that Louisiana law governs the policies in this case.

III

First American challenges the district court's calculation of FATTIC's liability on several grounds. First, it argues that the court erred in determining the appropriate date of valuation. It contends that the policy is ambiguous on this question and therefore should be construed against FATTIC or, in the alternative, that the policy unambiguously requires valuation as of the date the title defects were discovered.

Louisiana law provides that "[a]mbiguous policy provisions are generally construed against the insurer and in favor of coverage."[8] Such ambiguity only exists if the "policy provision is susceptible to two or more *reasonable* [—7—] interpretations."[9] By contrast, "[i]f the policy wording at issue is clear and unambiguously expresses the parties' intent, the insurance contract must be enforced as written."[10] A contract's silence on an issue does not establish ambiguity if there is only one reasonable interpretation of the parties' intent.[11]

The policies at issue do not specify a date of valuation. The district court concluded, however, that the policies unambiguously require valuation of the vessels as of the date of the foreclosure sales. We agree.

Although Louisiana courts have not addressed this issue, a majority of courts from other jurisdictions have held that, in the absence of specific policy language, a title insurer's liability to a mortgagee should be measured using the foreclosure date.[12] These

---

[6] *McLane Foodservice, Inc. v. Table Rock Rests., L.L.C.*, 736 F.3d 375, 377 (5th Cir. 2013).

[7] *Am. Totalisator Co. v. Fair Grounds Corp.*, 3 F.3d 810, 813 (5th Cir. 1993).

[8] *Cadwallader v. Allstate Ins. Co.*, 2002-1637, p. 4 (La. 6/27/03); 848 So. 2d 577, 580; *see also* LA. CIV. CODE ANN. art. 2056 (2008).

[9] *Cadwallader*, 848 So. 2d at 580 (emphasis in original).

[10] *Id.*

[11] *See, e.g.*, *Sims v. Mulhearn Funeral Home, Inc.*, 2007-0054, pp. 14-15 (La. 5/22/07); 956 So. 2d 583, 593.

[12] *See* JOYCE D. PALOMAR, 1 TITLE INS. LAW § 10:16 (2013-14 ed.); Christopher B. Frantze, *Equity Income Partners LP v. Chicago Title Insurance Co. and Recovery Under a Lender's Title Insurance Policy in a Falling Real Estate Market*, 48 REAL PROP. TR. & EST. L.J. 391, 396 (2013); *see*

courts have reasoned that this date is appropriate because the foreclosure is when the insured actually incurs a covered loss.[13] While a handful of courts have opted to use other dates in [—8—] calculating the amount due a mortgagee, none has used the date of discovery.[14] Rather, they have generally used the date the loan was made and have involved fact patterns in which there was a total failure of title.[15] The use of the loan date has been justified in such instances on the ground that the insured would not have made the loan if it had known the mortgage would be unenforceable or valueless.[16] That rationale is not applicable to a case like this in which the insured mortgagee could reasonably anticipate that its mortgage would be

encumbered by some necessaries liens. Although date-of-discovery is the majority rule for owners' policies, its use is generally justified on the ground that the owner of property suffers a loss immediately upon discovery of a defect, a rationale that is also not applicable to mortgagees.[17]

As First American notes, however, some courts have held that language practically identical to that at issue in this case is ambiguous.[18] We find these cases unpersuasive and, making an *Erie* guess, conclude that the Louisiana Supreme Court would adopt the majority view.[19] "A title insurance policy [—9—] provides for indemnity 'only to the extent that [the insured's] security is impaired and to the extent of the resulting loss that it sustains.'"[20] It does not "guarantee either that the mortgaged premises are worth the amount of the mortgage or that the mortgage debt will be paid."[21] As we recently held, a mortgagee does not suffer a loss under a title insurance policy governed by Louisiana law until its title actually fails.[22] This is so even when an impairment prevents the insured from taking actions that could ultimately mitigate its

---

also Associated Bank, N.A. v. Stewart Title Guar. Co., 881 F. Supp. 2d 1058, 1066 (D. Minn. 2012); *First Internet Bank of Ind. v. Lawyers Title Ins. Co.*, No. 1:07-CV-0869, 2009 WL 2092782, at *6 (S.D. Ind. July 13, 2009); *RTC Mortg. Trust 1994 N-1 v. Fidelity Nat. Title Ins. Co.*, 58 F. Supp. 2d 503, 535 (D.N.J. 1999); *Marble Bank v. Commonwealth Land Title Ins. Co.*, 914 F. Supp. 1252, 1254 (E.D.N.C. 1996).

[13] *See, e.g., First Internet*, 2009 WL 2092782, at *6 ("First Internet bargained to have perfect title in the event of a default and foreclosure, so the time of default and foreclosure is when damages should be measured."); *Marble Bank*, 914 F. Supp. at 1254 ("In the court's view, plaintiff did not suffer a loss until it foreclosed on the project. Since a lender suffers loss only if the note is not repaid, the discovery of an insured-against lien does not trigger recognition of that loss. Only the completion of foreclosure signifies that a lender will not collect on its note." (citation omitted)); PALOMAR, *supra* note 12, § 10:16; Frantze, *supra* note 12, at 394-95 (citing *RTC Mortg. Trust*, 58 F. Supp. 2d at 535).

[14] *See* STEVEN PLITT ET AL., 12 COUCH ON INS. § 185:77 (3d ed. 2014); *see also Citicorp Sav. of Ill. v. Stewart Title Guar. Co.*, 840 F.2d 526, 530 (7th Cir. 1988); *Equity Income Partners LP v. Chi. Title Ins. Co.*, No. CV-11-1614-PHX-GMS, 2012 WL 3871505, at *4 (D. Ariz. Sept. 6, 2012); *G & B Invs., Inc. v. Henderson (In re Evans)*, 460 B.R. 848, 895-900 (Bankr. S.D. Miss. 2011).

[15] *See, e.g., Citicorp Sav.*, 840 F.2d at 527-28; *Equity Income*, 2012 WL 3871505, at *1; *Evans*, 460 B.R. at 895-900.

[16] *See, e.g., Citicorp Sav.*, 840 F.2d at 530 ("As a practical matter, Citicorp would not have extended $27,000 credit to Robinson on the basis of a voidable mortgage. No lender would do so."); *Equity Income*, 2012 WL 3871505, at *3.

[17] PALOMAR, *supra* note 12, at § 10:16; Frantze, *supra* note 12, at 396; *see also Allison v. Ticor Title Ins. Co.*, 907 F.2d 645, 652 (7th Cir. 1990); *Hartman v. Shambaugh*, 630 P.2d 758, 762 (N.M. 1981); *Overholtzer v. N. Cntys. Title Ins. Co.*, 253 P.2d 116, 125 (Cal. 1953).

[18] *See, e.g., First Internet Bank*, 2009 WL 2092782, at *5; *G&B Invs.*, 460 B.R. at 896.

[19] *Howe ex rel. Howe v. Scottsdale Ins. Co.*, 204 F.3d 624, 627 (5th Cir. 2000) ("If the Louisiana Supreme Court has not ruled on this issue, then this Court must make an 'Erie guess' and 'determine as best it can' what the Louisiana Supreme Court would decide." (quoting *Krieser v. Hobbs*, 166 F.3d 736, 738 (5th Cir. 1999))).

[20] *Gibraltar Sav. v. Commonwealth Land Title Ins. Co.*, 905 F.2d 1203, 1205 (8th Cir. 1990) (alteration in original) (quoting *Diversified Mortg. Inv. v. U.S. Life Title Ins. Co. of N.Y.*, 544 F.2d 571, 574 n.2 (2d Cir. 1976)).

[21] *Blackhawk Prod. Credit Ass'n v. Chi. Title Ins. Co.*, 423 N.W.2d 521, 525 (Wis. 1988).

[22] *Amzak Capital Mgmt. v. Stewart Title of La. (In re West Feliciana Acquisition, L.L.C.)*, 744 F.3d 352, 358 (5th Cir. 2014).

losses.[23] It would therefore be an unreasonable interpretation of the policies to say that they provide for valuation as of the date of the discovery since no loss occurs at that point. The most appropriate date to use in calculating First American's losses is the date of the foreclosure sales, as that is when First American incurred covered losses. Accordingly, the district court did not err in selecting that date as the appropriate date of valuation.

IV

First American next argues that the district court erred in calculating the value of the Ocean Jewel, even as of the date of foreclosure, because the court failed to consider all available evidence of the vessel's worth. As First American concedes, the district court specifically stated for the record that it considered "all relevant evidence" of the Ocean Jewel's fair market value in calculating damages. Nonetheless, First American asks us to examine what [—10—] the court did, rather than what it said. First American contends that, notwithstanding the district court's statements, it did not actually measure the Ocean Jewel's fair market value based on all available evidence since the district court disregarded the testimony of First American's expert appraisers and relied exclusively on the price the vessel commanded at the foreclosure sale.

As mentioned, we held during the first appeal that Louisiana law required the district court to calculate the value of the Shuttles based on "all . . . relevant information," including "any appraisals, the foreclosure proceeds, and other market data."[24] We did not address, however, whether Louisiana law requires the same method to be used to calculate the value of a vessel when the sale proceeds *exceed* the amount of necessaries liens. Nor need we decide the question in this case, for even assuming that the district court was required to consider "all relevant evidence," it engaged in that analysis and made a factual finding supported by the record.

Under our precedent, "the trier of fact is not bound by expert testimony."[25] While the court is not "at liberty to disregard arbitrarily the unequivocal, uncontradicted and unimpeached testimony of an expert witness," it may "weigh the credibility of the witness" and "substitute its own common-sense judgment for that of the experts."[26] The district court rejected First American's appraisers' valuations on the ground that the appraisals were done "well in advance of the vessel[s'] sales" and that the Ocean Jewel had lost value as a result of "Titan's abysmal business performance and . . . the passage [—11—] of time." This conclusion is certainly reasonable, especially considering that the Sapphire sold on the open market for $500,000, 75% less than the $2 million First American's appraiser claimed it was worth at the time of the bankruptcy. Aside from the appraisals, the only available evidence of the Ocean Jewel's value was the foreclosure sale price. As we made clear in the first appeal, that price is relevant evidence of the vessel's fair market value that the district court must consider.[27] It was not error, much less clear error, to find that the vessel's value equaled its foreclosure sale price under the circumstances.

V

First American next contends that, even if the district court correctly calculated the value of the Ocean Jewel, it erroneously determined the amount due under the policy that insured that vessel. First American argues that the district court should have calculated the amount due under the Ocean

---

[23] *See id.*; *see also First Am. Bank v. First Am. Transp. Title Ins. Co.*, 585 F.3d 833, 838-39 (5th Cir. 2009) (holding that First American may not recover consequential damages, including losses "arising from the results of damage rather than from the damage itself" (quoting Black's Law Dictionary 964 (8th ed. 2004))).

[24] *First Am. Bank*, 585 F.3d at 838.

[25] *Webster v. Offshore Food Serv., Inc.*, 434 F.2d 1191, 1193 (5th Cir. 1970).

[26] *Id.*; *see also Caboni v. General Motors Corp.*, 398 F.3d 357, 361 (5th Cir. 2005) ("The trier of fact . . . is not bound by expert testimony and is entitled to weigh the credibility of all witnesses, expert or lay.").

[27] *First Am. Bank*, 585 F.3d at 838.

Jewel policy by taking the value of the Ocean Jewel ($6,450,000) and subtracting from that figure the amount First American received from the foreclosure sale ($4,172,215). This calculation, First American asserts, would have yielded a figure of $2,277,785, an amount well in excess of the $1,162,287 to which the district court held First American was entitled.

As we have discussed, the Ocean Jewel policy does not provide for FATTIC to pay First American the difference between the value of the ship and the amount First American received from the foreclosure. Instead, the policy lists nineteen covered risks and provides that the insurer's liability shall not exceed "[t]he difference between the value of the Title as insured and the value of the Title subject to the defect, lien or encumbrance *insured against by this policy*." [—12—]

Although the Ocean Jewel sold for $6,450,000, the bankruptcy court, with First American's consent, ordered that $1,110,000 be carved out for the benefit of the estate and that certain further funds be used to pay other creditors. First American has not explained how this carve-out or the other payments fall into one of the nineteen covered risks or were otherwise insured under the policy.

VI

As its last challenge to the district court's calculations, First American asserts that the court erroneously deducted $88,712 from the value of the Sapphire in calculating the amount due under the Shuttles policy. The district court subtracted that sum on the ground that it equaled the extent of TBSR's credit-bid that "was designated as superpriority claims by the bankruptcy court." Such claims, the court reasoned, were not covered under the policy if they were created after the policy's date of issuance.

First American does not dispute that the bankruptcy court granted TBSR a "superpriority" lien on the Sapphire or that such a lien is excluded from coverage. It argues, however, that TBSR did not use the

"superpriority" lien to obtain the vessel but instead relied on its maritime lien resulting from the provision of necessaries. Because the policies cover such necessaries liens, the argument proceeds, the district court's deduction of $88,712 from the Sapphire's value was in error.

Based on our review of the record, TBSR does not appear to have asserted its "superpriority" lien in the *in rem* action against the Sapphire. Rather, in its pleadings, TBSR consistently stated that it had a claim to the vessel by virtue of its maritime lien from the provision of necessaries. Likewise, when it requested permission to bid on the Sapphire, it asked to be permitted to bid "in the amount of its maritime lien claims, $99,227.38." Nevertheless, even if the claims TBSR asserted against the Sapphire stemmed [—13—] from its maritime liens, that does not mean that the district court's finding as to the value of First American's covered loss is clearly erroneous.

As we have discussed, First American is due "the difference between the value of First American's ship mortgages when unencumbered and the value of First American's mortgages subject to the [covered] necessaries liens."[28] Because of the bankruptcy court's order, TBSR *could have* levied against the Sapphire on the basis of its first-priority lien. The value of First American's mortgages as unencumbered (by covered defects) was thus not the full value of the Sapphire since First American would not have been able to recover that amount. Rather, First American could only recover the full value of the Sapphire minus the extent of the uncovered liens on the vessel. First American does not dispute that TBSR held a first-priority lien for $88,712. Accordingly, the district court did not commit reversible error in deducting that figure to determine the amount due under the Shuttles policy.

VII

In addition to challenging the district court's calculation of damages, First American

---

[28] *Id.* at 837.

argues that the court erred in finding that FATTIC did not act in bad faith in violation of Louisiana Revised Statutes § 22:1892. First American asserts that FATTIC acted arbitrarily in the processing of First American's claims because it did not remit payment under the Shuttles policy until months after this court's ruling in the first appeal.

Under Louisiana law, "A cause of action for penalties . . . requires a showing that (1) an insurer has received satisfactory proof of loss, (2) the insurer fails to tender payment within thirty days of receipt thereof, and (3) [—14—] the insurer's failure to pay is arbitrary, capricious or without probable cause."[29] "The phrase 'arbitrary, capricious, or without probable cause' . . . describe[s] an insurer whose willful refusal of a claim is not based on a good-faith defense."[30] As the Louisiana Supreme Court has clarified, "an insurer need not pay a disputed amount in a claim for which there are substantial, reasonable and legitimate questions as to the extent of the insurer's liability or of the insured's loss."[31] Whether an insured's conduct is arbitrary or capricious "depends on the facts known to the insurer at the time of its action. . . . Because the question is essentially a factual issue, the trial court's finding should not be disturbed on appeal absent manifest error."[32]

The district court found that "FATTIC fulfilled most of its obligations under the policies to the Bank, and that it did so in as timely a fashion as could be expected in a case as complex as this." This finding is not manifestly erroneous. When Titan filed for bankruptcy, FATTIC promptly hired counsel to represent First American's interests. After counsel negotiated and settled the necessary lien claims on the Ocean Jewel down to approximately $1,162,287, FATTIC remitted that sum to First American. The payments for the Shuttles took longer, but that delay was due to the greater factual and legal uncertainty regarding the extent of coverage. Indeed, within three months of learning that the Emerald had generated net proceeds of approximately $445,137.50, FATTIC tendered that amount to the bank. That timeline was [—15—] not arbitrary considering FATTIC paid the sum only fifteen days after discovery concluded. Although FATTIC refused to tender $500,000 to First American for the Sapphire, that refusal was based on good-faith claims regarding the extent of First American's coverage and the actual value of the vessel. Accordingly, the district court did not commit manifest error in finding that First American was not due any penalties under § 22:1892.

* * *

For the foregoing reasons, the judgment of the district court is AFFIRMED.

---

[29] *Levy Gardens Partners 2007, L.P. v. Commonwealth Land Title Ins. Co.*, 706 F.3d 622, 635 (5th Cir. 2013) (alteration in original) (quoting *La. Bag Co. v. Audubon Indem. Co.*, 2008-0453, pp. 11-12 (La. 12/2/08); 999 So. 2d 1104, 1112-13).

[30] *Id.* (alteration in original) (quoting *La. Bag Co.*, 999 So. 2d at 1114).

[31] *La. Bag Co.*, 999 So. 2d at 1116.

[32] *Levy Gardens*, 706 F.3d at 635 (alteration in original) (quoting *Reed v. State Farm Mut. Auto. Ins. Co.*, 2003-0107, p. 14 (La. 10/21/03); 857 So. 2d 1012, 1021).

United States Court of Appeals
for the Fifth Circuit

No. 13-30358

UNITED STATES
vs.
AMERICAN COMMERCIAL LINES, L.L.C.

Appeal from the United States District Court for the
Eastern District of Louisiana

Decided: July 16, 2014

Citation: 759 F.3d 420, 2 Adm. R. 283 (5th Cir. 2014).

Before **JOLLY**, **GARZA**, and **HIGGINSON**, Circuit
Judges.

[—1—] HIGGINSON, Circuit Judge:

Following an oil spill, responsible party American Commercial Lines ("ACL") contracted with Environmental Safety & Health Consulting Services Inc. ("ES&H") and United States Environmental Services, L.L.C. ("USES") to provide cleanup services. After ACL failed to pay the full outstanding amounts owed to ES&H and USES within the 90-day period mandated by the Oil [—2—] Pollution Act of 1990 ("OPA"), the United States paid the balance out of the Oil Spill Liability Trust Fund (the "Fund") and filed suit against ACL to recover its payment. ACL sought to join ES&H and USES as third party defendants, or alternatively hold ES&H and USES directly liable to ACL to the extent ACL was found liable to the United States. The district court joined both parties but dismissed ACL's claims against ES&H and USES as displaced by OPA.[1] We AFFIRM.

---

[1] The district court used the term "preemption" in its "Order and Reasons." "Preemption" and "displacement" are often used interchangeably. *See, e.g., Conner v. Aerovox, Inc.*, 730 F.2d 835, 841 (1st Cir. 1984) (using "preempt" and "displace" interchangeably in concluding that the Federal Water Pollution Control Act displaced federal maritime law). Technically, however, preemption refers to whether federal statutory law supersedes state law, while "displacement" applies when, as here, a federal statute governs a question previously governed by federal common law. Although in the preemption scenario, we assume that "the historic police powers of the States were not to be superseded by [federal law] unless that

FACTUAL BACKGROUND

This case involves an oil spill in the Mississippi River near New Orleans, Louisiana. On July 23, 2008, the M/V TINTOMARA, an ocean-going tanker, collided with DM 932, an unmanned barge carrying slightly less than 10,000 barrels of fuel oil, which was towed by the tug M/V MEL OLIVER. The collision substantially damaged the barge, and a large quantity of oil spilled into the river. ACL owned the tug and barge. D.R.D. Towing, L.L.C. ("DRD") provided the crew for the tug towing the barge under a bareboat charter between ACL and DRD. *Gabarick v. Laurin Maritime (America) Inc. v. D.R.D. Towing Company, L.L.C.*, 2014 WL 2118621, at *1, 2 Adm. R. 228 (5th Cir. May 21, 2014).

Under the Clean Water Act ("CWA"), also known as the Federal Water Pollution Control Act ("FWPCA"), 33 U.S.C. §§ 1321, as amended by OPA, the Coast Guard has primary overall responsibility for directing oil spill cleanup [—3—] in the coastal zone. *See* 33 U.S.C. § 1321(d)(2)(C); 40 C.F.R. § 300.145. However, under OPA, the Coast Guard identifies "responsible part[ies]" who must pay for oil spill cleanup in the first instance,[2] typically "any person owning, operating, or demise chartering the vessel." 33 U.S.C. § 2701(32). Responsible parties may then

---

was the clear and manifest purpose of Congress," displacement analysis assumes that "it is for Congress, not the federal courts, to articulate the appropriate standards to be applied as a matter of federal law." *City of Milwaukee v. Illinois*, 451 U.S. 304, 316-17 (1981). Accordingly, we use the term "displacement" throughout this opinion.

[2] Responsible parties are strictly liable for cleanup costs and damages and first in line to pay any claims for removal costs or damages that may arise under OPA. *See* 33 U.S.C. § 2702(a) ("Notwithstanding any other provision or rules of law. . . each responsible party. . . is liable for the removal costs and damages."); *id.* § 2713(a) ("[A]ll claims for removal costs or damages shall be presented first to the responsible party. . . ."). Hence each responsible party must establish and maintain evidence of its ability to make significant, immediate payments to spill responders and other claimants. *See id.* § 2716(a).

contract with spill responders to execute the oil spill cleanup.

The Coast Guard's National Pollution Funds Center ("NPFC") administers the Fund. The Fund is authorized both (1) to pay outstanding cleanup costs and damages when a responsible party can limit its liability or establish a complete defense (or when no responsible party is ever identified), *see id.* § 2712(a)(4); and (2) to guarantee that particular OPA claimants, including spill responders, are paid quickly, *see id.* § 2713. Claimants must first present their claims to the responsible party, *see id.* § 2713(a), but if the responsible party has not paid the claim within 90 days, "the claimant may elect to commence an action in court against the responsible party . . . or to present the claim to the Fund." *Id.* § 2713(c)(2); *see also* 33 C.F.R. § 136.103(c)(2). The Fund will reimburse only those removal costs that are necessary and reasonable, and that adhere to the relevant statutory criteria for Fund payments. *See* 33 C.F.R. §§ 136.105, 136.201, 136.203, 136.205. When the Fund has made payments to cover the immediate costs of oil spill cleanup, it can recoup those payments from other entities, including the responsible party. "[P]ayment of any claim or obligation by the Fund" results [—4—] in "the United States Government acquiring by subrogation all rights of the claimant . . . to recover from the responsible party." 33 U.S.C. § 2712(f); *see also* 33 C.F.R. § 136.115(a) (compensation from the Fund includes an assignment to the government of the claimant's rights against third parties).

Following the spill, the Coast Guard investigated and determined that, as the owner of the barge DM-932 and tug M/V OLIVER, ACL was a responsible party under OPA and therefore liable for "removal costs and damages" resulting from the incident. *See* 33 U.S.C. § 2702(a). ACL then entered into a contract with spill responders and Third Party Defendants ES&H and USES to provide cleanup services for the oil spill. The spill responders invoiced ACL for their services, but ACL disputed some of the claims and did not pay the full outstanding amounts owed to ES&H and USES for removal and cleanup costs within the 90-day time frame mandated

by OPA.[3] *See id.* § 2713(c)(2). Instead, ACL paid ES&H approximately $10.6 million and withheld $3.9 million; it paid USES approximately $14 million and withheld $4.4 million. At that point, OPA allowed ES&H and USES to "elect" one of two options: (1) sue ACL for payment; or (2) submit a claim for uncompensated removal costs to the Fund. Both spill responders filed claims with the Fund. After requesting "documentation deemed necessary" to pay a claim, *see* 33 C.F.R. § 136.105(a), the Fund paid $3,071,222.83 to ES&H and $1,519,564.74 to USES.[4] *See* 33 U.S.C. § 2713(a)-(d). [—5—]

The United States, in turn, sued ACL to recover the Fund's payment to ES&H and USES, as well as a penalty under the CWA and statutory damages under OPA. In response, ACL contended, *inter alia*, that ES&H and USES failed to provide adequate documentation for the amounts billed to and paid out by the Fund.[5] Consequently, ACL sought to join ES&H and USES as third party defendants to the United States' claims in the proceedings below. Alternatively, ACL sought to hold ES&H and USES directly liable to

---

[3] Specifically, ACL claims that ES&H and USES (1) failed to produce the federally required I-9s establishing legal entitlement to work; (2) failed to produce the Hazardous Waste Operations and Emergency Response ("HAZWOPER") certificates needed to establish that its labor force had received the required training for oil spill cleanup; (3) requested payment for phantom labor and equipment that was never supplied during the cleanup of the oil spill; and (4) sought rates applicable for properly trained, legal workers for laborers who were in fact either not properly trained or not legally entitled to work, or both.

[4] Neither ES&H nor USES challenged the final amounts paid by the United States out of the Fund in response to their claims under OPA, though the payments were less than invoiced.

[5] As indicated in its brief, "ACL understands that the NPFC did not require ES&H or USES to provide either training certificates or the federally required I-9 forms for the laborers but rather relied upon questionable affidavits from ES&H and USES that all of the laborers were properly trained, legal workers. . . If ES&H's and USES's affidavits were false and ES&H and USES in fact had supplied untrained illegal laborers, then ES&H and USES must reimburse either ACL or the United States directly."

ACL to the extent that ACL was found liable to the United States. The United States, ES&H, and USES opposed the joinder of ES&H and USES, and each filed motions to dismiss ES&H and USES as third party defendants to the United States' action against ACL. The district court held that ACL's joinder of ES&H and USES was proper under Fed. R. Civ. P. 14(c) and our decision in *Luera v. M/V Alberta*, 635 F.3d 181, 188-189 (5th Cir. 2011). However, citing *Exxon Shipping Co. v. Baker*, 554 U.S. 471 (2008), and *In re Oil Spill by the Oil Rig "Deepwater Horizon" in the Gulf of Mexico*, 808 F. Supp. 2d 943 (E.D. La. 2011), the district court granted the government's Rule 12(b)(6) motion to dismiss ACL's claims against ES&H and USES because OPA displaces these claims. The district court explained in its Order and Reasons that "[t]he proper procedural vehicle to litigate defects in the claim payment process is as a defense against the Fund under the 'arbitrary and capricious' standard of the Administrative Procedure Act, as ACL acknowledges."

ACL filed the instant appeal. On appeal, ACL concedes that when OPA explicitly sets a rule of law it displaces federal common law and general [—6—] maritime law, and that, as the designated responsible party, ACL was strictly liable under OPA for costs of cleanup. ACL asserts, however, that the district court erred in holding that OPA displaced its federal common law and general maritime law claims against ES&H and USES because "OPA does not 'explicitly' do so."

STANDARD OF REVIEW

A district court's dismissal of a complaint under Rule 12(b)(6) is a question of law that we review *de novo. Torch Liquidating Trust ex rel. Bridge Assoc. LLC v. Stockstill*, 561 F.3d 377, 384 (5th Cir. 2009).

DISCUSSION

Our inquiry presents the question of whether OPA provides the exclusive source of law for an action involving a responsible party's liability for removal costs governed by OPA. For the following reasons, we find that it

does, and accordingly we hold that ACL does not have a cause of action against the spill responders who exercised their statutory right to file claims with the Fund after ACL failed to timely pay their claims.

We have previously held that, in enacting OPA, Congress intended to build upon the Clean Water Act to "'create a single Federal law providing cleanup authority, penalties, and liability for oil pollution.' . . . OPA prescribes a supplemental, comprehensive federal plan for handling oil spill responses, allocating responsibility among participants, and prescribing reimbursement for cleanup costs and injuries to third parties." *In re: Deepwater Horizon*, 745 F.3d 157, 168, 2 Adm. R. 171, 177 (5th Cir. 2014) (quoting S. Rep. No. 101-94, at 9 (1989), *reprinted in* 1990 U.S.C.C.A.N. 722, 730).

More generally, when Congress enacts a carefully calibrated liability scheme with respect to specific remedies, "the structure of the remedies suggests that Congress intended for th[e] statutory remedies to be exclusive." *United States v. M/V BIG SAM*, 681 F.2d 432, 441 (5th Cir. 1982) (internal [—7—] quotation marks and citation omitted) (construing the analogous FWPCA, whose liability standard and limited recovery of removal costs OPA borrows). Indeed, "we are to conclude that federal common law has been preempted as to every question to which the legislative scheme spoke directly, and every problem that Congress has addressed." *Id.* at 442 (quoting *In re Oswego Barge Corp.*, 664 F.2d 327, 344 (2d Cir. 1981)).[6] Here, OPA provides that "[n]otwithstanding any other provision or rule of law . . . each responsible party . . . is liable for the removal costs and damages specified in subsection (b) of this section that result from" an oil spill. 33 U.S.C. § 2702(a). Claimants must first present their claims to the responsible party, *see id.* § 2713(a), but if the responsible party has not paid the claim within 90 days, the claimant may elect to bring suit against the responsible party or seek repayment from the Fund for those removal expenses that are necessary and

---

[6] *See supra* note 1 (noting that "preemption" and "displacement" are often used interchangeably).

reasonable, and that adhere to the relevant statutory criteria for United States payments. *See* id. § 2713(c)(2); *see also* 33 C.F.R. § 136.103(c)(2), 136.105, 136.201, 136.203, 136.205. The Fund may then seek recoupment from the responsible party, having acquired by subrogation all rights of the claimant against the responsible party. *See* 33 U.S.C. § 2712(f); 33 C.F.R. § 136.115(a). The responsible party may then assert defenses to limit its liability for reimbursement, including establishing that the Fund's payments to the claimants were "arbitrary and capricious." *See Buffalo Marine Servs, Inc. v. United States*, 663 F.3d 750, 753 (5th Cir. 2011) ("The Administrative Procedure Act ('APA') allows a federal court to overturn an agency's ruling only if it is arbitrary, capricious, an abuse of discretion, not in accordance with law, or unsupported by substantial evidence on the record taken as a whole." [—8—] (internal quotation marks omitted)). As found by the district court, "OPA directly speaks to the claims asserted by ACL." Hence we hold that this "balanced and comprehensive remedial scheme" provides the exclusive remedy for a claimant to recover statutory removal costs from a responsible party and forecloses a responsible party from bringing a third-party complaint against a spill responder that has chosen to submit claims to the Fund after 90 days without payment. *See M/V BIG SAM*, 681 F.2d at 441.

In the present case, ES&H and USES both presented their claims to the Fund, rather than bringing suit against ACL. Nothing in OPA authorizes a responsible party to bring a third-party complaint against a claimant that has chosen, under § 2713(c)(2), to submit claims to the Fund after 90 days without payment. As the district court noted, such a third-party complaint would risk "avoid[ing] the strict liability that OPA places on responsible parties to pay the cleanup and removal costs," and frustrate the statutory scheme and its goal of providing rapid cleanup and claim resolution.

Contrary to ACL's assertion, OPA's savings clause at 33 U.S.C. § 2751(e) does not apply. OPA's savings clause provides:

Except as otherwise provided in this Act, this Act does not affect—

(1) admiralty and maritime law; or
(2) the jurisdiction of the district courts of the United States with respect to civil actions under admiralty and maritime jurisdiction, saving to suitors in all cases all other remedies to which they are otherwise entitled.

Id. § 2751(e). Statutory construction begins with the language of the statute, and, in the absence of ambiguity, often ends there. *Hardt v. Reliance Standard Life Ins. Co.*, 560 U.S. 242, 251 (2010). We have previously held that "savings clauses must be read with particularity" and should not be interpreted to [—9—] "disrupt the ordinary operation of conflict preemption."[7] *In re Deepwater Horizon*, 745 F.3d at 171, 2 Adm. R. at 180 (rejecting application of OPA savings clause codified at § 2718(c)); *see also Int'l Paper Co. v. Ouellette*, 479 U.S. 481, 492-93 (1987) (rejecting application of two savings provisions of the CWA). The savings clause here begins "except as otherwise provided." 33 U.S.C. § 2751(e). OPA provides a procedure for submission, consideration, and payment of cleanup expenses by the Fund when the responsible party fails to settle such claims within 90 days—the situation presented here. As OPA did "otherwise provide[]," ACL's claims against ES&H and USES for return of payments made by the Fund under OPA cannot be saved by this clause. To interpret § 2751(e) as ACL proposes would be to supersede OPA, and courts cannot, without any textual warrant, expand the operation of savings clauses to modify the scope of

---

[7] While *In re Deepwater Horizon* addressed the preemption of state law claims, rather than the displacement of federal common law claims, the showing required for displacement is less than that for preemption as no evidence of "clear and manifest congressional purpose" to displace need be found. *See City of Milwaukee*, 451 U.S. at 316-17. Hence our holding that "a savings clause does not disrupt the ordinary operation of conflict preemption" is especially true in the displacement context. *In re Deepwater Horizon*, 745 F.3d at 171, 2 Adm. R. at 180.

displacement under OPA.[8]   *See In re Deepwater Horizon*, 745 F.3d at 173, 2 Adm. R. at 181–82.

While we find that OPA displaces ACL's alternative causes of action against ES&H and USES, we note that both ACL and the United States contemplate that ACL may raise its contentions in the district court in defense to the United States' OPA recoupment action. Should ACL establish that the [—10—] Fund's payments to ES&H and USES were unnecessary, unreasonable, or not in compliance with the relevant statutory criteria for Fund payments and hence were "arbitrary and capricious," it may pursue reduction of its liability to the Fund for reimbursement. Regardless of the outcome of the United States' action against ACL, however, ACL may not seek indemnification from ES&H and USES as the United States "acquir[ed] by subrogation all rights of the claimant" and hence stands in for ES&H and USES in any related action. *See* 33 U.S.C. § 2712(f); 33 C.F.R. § 136.115.

CONCLUSION

For the reasons set forth above, we AFFIRM the district court's dismissal of ACL's claims against ES&H and USES as displaced under OPA.

---

[8] Invoking 33 U.S.C. § 2710, ACL further asserts that OPA does not displace its implied indemnity claims against ES&H and USES. *See id.* § 2710(a) ("Nothing in this Act prohibits any agreement to insure, hold harmless, or indemnify a party to such agreement for any liability under this Act."). "Indemnification" is "[t]he action of compensating for loss or damage sustained." Black Law's Dictionary 38 (9th ed. 2009). Holding aside the government's plausible contention that § 2710 concerns liability for the spill itself, rather than liability for cleanup, ES&H and USES have caused no loss or damage to ACL that could form the basis of an indemnity claim. ACL did not actually pay ES&H and USES for any of the disputed material or labor expenses, nor has it yet been required to pay the government such amounts.

United States Court of Appeals
for the Fifth Circuit

No. 13-30712

CELTIC MARINE CORP.
vs.
JAMES C. JUSTICE COMPANIES, INC.

Appeal from the United States District Court for the
Eastern District of Louisiana

Decided: July 29, 2014

Citation: 760 F.3d 477, 2 Adm. R. 288 (5th Cir. 2014).

Before **HIGGINBOTHAM, JONES,** and **PRADO,** Circuit Judges.

[—1—] **PRADO,** Circuit Judge:

Celtic Marine Corp. ("Celtic Marine") filed suit against James C. Justice Companies, Inc. ("Justice") in this maritime dispute for breach of contract. The parties reached two settlement agreements. The parties entered into the second agreement after the first was not fulfilled. After the second settlement agreement was also not timely fulfilled, Celtic Marine moved for summary judgment to enforce an acceleration clause, contained in the second settlement agreement, for all payments due under the first settlement agreement. Celtic Marine also moved under Federal Rule of Civil Procedure 60(b)(6) to reopen the case. The district court granted both motions, granted leave for Celtic Marine to amend its complaint, and later denied Justice's motion to reconsider. [—2—] We affirm summary judgment and dismiss Justice's appeal of the district court's Rule 60(b)(6) order.

I. FACTUAL AND PROCEDURAL BACKGROUND

The action below arises out of a maritime dispute involving Celtic Marine, Kentucky Fuel Corp. ("KFC"), and KFC's guarantor, Justice. In February 2011, KFC entered into a service agreement and spot contract with Celtic Marine (the "2011 Contract"). Therein, Celtic Marine agreed to arrange for the transportation of metallurgical coal on a number of barges. Under a Guarantor's Agreement, Justice guaranteed all obligations KFC owed to Celtic Marine under the 2011 Contract.

On December 7, 2011, Celtic Marine filed suit against Justice for breach of the Guarantor's Agreements. Celtic Marine alleged that KFC failed to fulfill its obligations under the 2011 Contract and, thus, Justice, as guarantor, was responsible for past due freight, shortfall, liquidated damages, demurrage, and other costs.

On February 1, 2012, Celtic Marine, KFC, and Justice executed a settlement agreement settling all claims (the "February Settlement Agreement"). KFC agreed to pay Celtic Marine all continuing demurrage incurred on the loaded barges until the cargo was unloaded. Justice agreed to guarantee KFC's payment of this continuing demurrage and also agreed to pay to Celtic Marine a lump sum of $4,687,215. As additionally required under the February Settlement Agreement, KFC entered into another service agreement and spot contract with Celtic Marine for the transportation of coal (the "2012 Contract"). Justice guaranteed the 2012 Contract as well.

In light of the February Settlement Agreement, the district court entered an order of dismissal "without prejudice . . . within 120 days, to seek summary judgment enforcing the compromise." Later, a dispute arose regarding KFC's compliance with the February Settlement Agreement and the 2012 Contract. [—3—] On May 24, 2012, Celtic Marine moved for an extension of time to enforce the settlement, contending that the cargo had yet to be unloaded and the demurrage charges remained unpaid. The district court granted the motion and extended the deadline to enforce the February Settlement Agreement an additional 120 days until October 4, 2012.

In October 2012, the parties announced a subsequent settlement agreement (the "October Settlement Agreement"), and the district court granted Celtic Marine's motion for an extension of time to enforce settlement and extended its dismissal order until January 12, 2013. Under the October

Settlement Agreement, Justice and KFC agreed to jointly pay Celtic Marine the sum of $2,200,000.00, payable in four installments: (1) $1,925,000.00 to be paid October 5, 2012, the date of the agreement; (2) $91,666.66 to be paid by October 12, 2012; (3) $91,666.66 to be paid by November 1, 2012; and (4) $91,666.66 to be paid by December 1, 2012. In exchange, "Celtic Marine agree[d] to release Justice and KFC upon Celtic Marine's full and irrevocable receipt of the sum of [these payments] from Justice and/or KFC." Clause Three provides: "In the event that any of the installments . . . are not timely received, Celtic Marine reserves the right to seek payment in full for the total amounts owed to it by KFC and Justice under the [February Settlement Agreement and 2012 Contract] as of the date that particular late installment was due . . . and unpaid" ("Clause 3" or "the acceleration clause"). The October Settlement Agreement also incorporated both Justice's guaranty and KFC's guaranty of the "prompt payment and performance" of each other's obligations to Celtic Marine under the October Settlement Agreement.

In the months that ensued, Celtic Marine's chief executive officer Michael O'Connor ("O'Connor") and Justice's Executive Vice President James C. Justice III ("James") exchanged a series of emails concerning Justice's installment payments. There is no dispute that Justice paid all installments [—4—] to Celtic Marine, and that each payment was late. For example, Justice made the first installment payment three weeks late on October 26, 2012 and in the wrong amount of $1,000,000.

Upon receipt of the third installment, O'Connor emailed James on November, 21, 2012: "Check received with thanks. Pls [sic] confirm the last payment of 91,666.66 will be paid Dec. 3rd per agreement." Over the next several weeks, O'Connor repeatedly inquired about the status of the last payment, *inter alia*: "Jay, please confirm the payment will be completed on time"; "Still no payment 91,666.66?"; "Let's get payment completed for [overnight] check"; "Why haven't we been paid the last payment of $ 91,666.66?" James responded in the following email exchange:

O'Connor: January 5, 2013	Are we being paid the $91,666.66 to settle this once and for all? I have lost faith in this agreement from your side.
O'Connor: January 7, 2013	Are you paying us the $91,666.66 today?
James: January 7, 2013	Fri
O'Connor: January 7, 2013	o/n check correct and can't u do it Thurs for Friday devl?

No further emails were exchanged. The final installment payment of $91,666.66 was made that Thursday on January 10, 2013, nearly six weeks past the original due date.

On January 11, 2013, Celtic Marine moved for summary judgment to enforce the acceleration clause and demand all payments due under the February Settlement Agreement. Celtic Marine also moved under Federal Rule of Civil Procedure 60(b)(6) to reopen the case in order to enforce the settlement and to allow it to amend and supplement its claims. The district court found that Celtic Marine maintained the right to invoke the acceleration [—5—] clause and granted its motion for summary judgment. The district court also granted Celtic Marine's Rule 60(b)(6) motion in order to determine the actual amount that Justice owes Celtic Marine. Justice timely appeals both rulings.

II. JURISDICTION

The district court had jurisdiction over this maritime dispute pursuant to 28 U.S.C. § 1333, as well as on the basis of diversity of citizenship under 28 U.S.C. § 1332.

This Court has jurisdiction over interlocutory orders "determining the rights and liabilities of the parties to admiralty cases in which appeals from final decrees are allowed." 28 U.S.C. § 1292(a)(3). Because interlocutory appeals are disfavored, however, this Court has "tended to construe [§ 1292(a)(3)] rather narrowly." *In re Ingram Towing Co.*, 59 F.3d 513, 516 (5th Cir. 1995). Indeed, "[o]rders which do not determine parties' substantive rights or liabilities . . . are not appealable under section 1292(a)(3), even if those orders have important procedural consequences." *Francis v. Forest Oil Corp.*, 798 F.2d 147, 150 (5th Cir. 1986) (citation omitted). Rather, the order appealed must "finally determine the rights or liabilities of either party to this dispute." *In re Patton-Tully Transp. Co.*, 715 F.2d 219, 222 (5th Cir. 1983). "As a general rule, whenever an order in an admiralty case dismisses a claim for relief on the merits it is appealable under section 1292(a)(3)." *Francis*, 798 F.2d at 149.

Here, § 1292(a)(3) grants this Court jurisdiction over Justice's interlocutory appeal of the district court's order granting summary judgment because it had "determin[ed] the rights and liabilities of the [present] parties." *See* 28 U.S.C. § 1292(a)(3); *Bank One, La. N.A. v. Dean*, 293 F.3d 830, 832 (5th Cir. 2002) ("Because the grant of summary judgment disposed of BargeCarib's case on the merits, we have jurisdiction [pursuant to § 1292(a)(3)] even without Rule 54(b) certification."). Section 1292(a)(3) does not, however, grant this Court jurisdiction over the district court's Rule 60(b) order. The district court [—6—] did not finally determine the rights or liabilities of either party to this dispute. Rather, as Justice concedes in its letter brief, the reopening of the case merely "allow[ed] Celtic [Marine] to pursue . . . relief." In other words, the order reopening the case was simply procedural, permitting Celtic Marine to pursue its claims, and was thus not appealable under § 1292(a)(3). *See, e.g., Patton-Tully Transp. Co.*, 715 F.2d at 222 ("While a determination that a plaintiff is not a Jones Act seaman is appealable . . . because it effectively terminates the suit, that portion of an interlocutory order determining that plaintiff is a Jones Act seaman merely allows him to pursue his claim in the hope of obtaining a final judgment against defendant.").

Accordingly, we dismiss for want of jurisdiction Justice's appeal of the Rule 60(b)(6) order, and only address its appeal of summary judgment.

III. STANDARD OF REVIEW

This Court reviews the district court's ruling on summary judgment de novo, applying the same standard as the district court in the first instance. *Turner v. Baylor Richardson Med. Ctr.*, 476 F.3d 337, 343 (5th Cir. 2007) (citation omitted). Summary judgment is appropriate only if "the movant shows that there is no genuine dispute as to any material fact and the movant is entitled to judgment as a matter of law." Fed. R. Civ. P. 56(a). A genuine dispute of material fact exists when the "'evidence is such that a reasonable jury could return a verdict for the nonmoving party.'" *Royal v. CCC & R Tres Arboles, L.L.C.*, 736 F.3d 396, 400 (5th Cir. 2013) (quoting *Anderson v. Liberty Lobby, Inc.*, 477 U.S. 242, 248 (1986)).

"[A] party seeking summary judgment always bears the initial responsibility of informing the district court of the basis for its motion, and identifying those portions of [the record] which it believes demonstrate the absence of a genuine issue of material fact." *Celotex Corp. v. Catrett*, 477 U.S. 317, 323 (1986). Where the nonmoving party bears the burden of proof at trial, [—7—] the moving party satisfies this initial burden by demonstrating an absence of evidence to support the nonmoving party's case. *Id.* at 325. The burden then shifts to "the nonmoving party to go beyond the pleadings and by her own affidavits, or by the 'depositions, answers to interrogatories, and admissions on file,' designate 'specific facts showing that there is a genuine issue for trial.'" *Id.* at 324. The Court must "draw all reasonable inferences in favor of the nonmoving party" and "refrain from making credibility determinations or weighing the evidence." *Turner*, 476 F.3d at 343 (citation and internal quotation marks omitted). A party cannot "defeat summary judgment with conclusory allegations, unsubstantiated assertions, or 'only a scintilla of evidence.'" *Id.* (quoting *Little v. Liquid Air Corp.*, 37 F.3d 1069, 1075 (5th Cir. 1994)).

IV. DISCUSSION

Justice contends that the district court erred when it granted summary judgment. In support, Justice argues that the parties amended the installment payment deadlines such that its payments were not late. In the alternative, Justice argues that Celtic Marine waived its right to enforce Clause 3. We reject each argument in turn below.

A. Amendment of the October Settlement Agreement

The email exchange between O'Connor and James did not amend the October Settlement Agreement. Under Louisiana law,[1] "[a] settlement agreement is a contract" and "[t]he rules of construction applicable to contracts are therefore used." *Doré Energy Corp. v. Prospective Inv. & Trading Co.*, 570 F.3d 219, 225 (5th Cir. 2009) (citing *Trahan v. Coca Cola Bottling Co. United, Inc.*, 2004-0100, p. 14 (La. 3/2/05); 894 So. 2d 1096, 1106; *see* La. Civ. Code Ann. [—8—] art. 3071). "A compromise shall be made in writing . . . ." La. Civ. Code Ann. art. 3072. Under the Louisiana Uniform Electronic Transactions Act ("LUETA"), La. Rev. Stat. Ann. §§ 9:2601–2620, a "writing" may include electronic communications and electronic signatures. LUETA "applies only to transactions between parties, each of which has agreed to conduct transactions by electronic means." *Id.* § 9:2605(B)(1); *see also id.* § 9:2608(A)(1); *EPCO Carbon Dioxide Prods., Inc. v. JP Morgan Chase Bank, NA*, 467 F.3d 466, 469–70 (5th Cir. 2006). In this regard, "[t]he context and surrounding circumstances, including the conduct of the parties, shall determine whether the parties have agreed to conduct a transaction by electronic means." La. Rev. Stat. Ann. § 9:2605(B)(2). Additionally, "[t]here must be a showing that the signer intended to do a legally significant act." *Regions Bank v. Cabinet Works, L.L.C.*, 11-748 p. 15 (La. App. 5 Cir. 4/10/12); 92 So. 3d 945, 956. If LUETA applies, then "[e]-mail can fulfill the requirement of [article 3072] as a writing." *Id.*

---

[1] The October Settlement Agreement provides that it "shall be governed, construed, and enforced under the laws of the State of Louisiana."

Justice argues that the parties' email exchange leading up to its January 10, 2013 payment creates a genuine dispute of material fact whether the parties intended to amend the payment deadlines of the October Settlement Agreement. In support, Justice primarily focuses on O'Connor's request for the final payment "to settle this for once and all." Justice also offers the affidavit of its Executive Vice President, James, who participated in the email exchange. In his affidavit, James claims that the parties intended to amend the payment date. Justice contends that the affidavit of Celtic Marine's chief financial officer, Robert Bayham ("Bayham"), does not constitute competent summary judgment evidence because it was self-serving and lacked personal knowledge. Bayham, Justice continues, "was not a party to, or even privy to, the relevant e-mail exchanges, and . . . had no personal knowledge of them or of the intent of Mr. Justice and Mr. O'Connor in the exchanges"; essentially, [—9—] Celtic Marine "presented no factual basis for the affiant's competency to attest to the contents of the e-mail exchanges or to the intent of the participant drafters."

Celtic Marine responds that it never agreed to modify or amend any terms of the October Settlement Agreement by electronic means. Bayham attested that "[a]t no time has Celtic Marine ever agreed to modify or amend any terms or portions of the February Settlement Agreement or October Settlement Agreement through an email communication." Regarding Bayham's competency, Celtic Marine argues that the statements within Bayham's affidavit demonstrate his personal knowledge of "the details of the agreements between the parties, the course of conduct between the parties, and the amounts which Justice owes." Celtic Marine further notes that all contracts and agreements between the parties—the two settlement agreements, all contracts, and all guaranties—were typed agreements physically signed by authorized representatives of the parties. Conversely, according to Celtic Marine, "[e]mails have never amended the settlement agreements between the parties," and there is no evidence that "Celtic Marine 'intended to do a legally significant act' by sending repeated emails insisting upon payment of the installments owed by Justice.'"

Celtic Marine is correct; there is no evidence that the parties agreed to amend the settlement agreement, electronically or otherwise. Justice focuses only on the email exchange but neglects to establish, as it must, that the parties ever agreed to conduct transactions by electronic means. *See, e.g.*, La. Rev. Stat. Ann. § 9:2605(B)(1) (providing that LUETA applies only where each party "has agreed to conduct transactions by electronic means"). In contrast, Celtic Marine notes, and Justice does not dispute, that the two settlement agreements and all contracts and guaranties between the parties had been typed and physically signed by authorized representatives of the parties. **[—10—]** Moreover, Bayham attested that Celtic Marine had never agreed to modify or amend either settlement agreement by email communication. His personal knowledge of the email exchange is not an issue—Justice does not dispute his competence to attest to the parties' dealing outside of that email exchange, including whether the parties had ever agreed that email communications may amend or modify the agreements. There is no evidence that, prior to the email exchange at issue here, the parties agreed to conduct a transaction by email.

As to the email exchange itself, its plain language establishes that the parties did not intend to amend the October Settlement Agreement. *See Clovelly Oil Co., LLC v. Midstates Petrol. Co., LLC*, 2012-2055, p. 5 (La. 3/19/13); 112 So. 3d 187, 192 ("When the words of a contract are clear and explicit and lead to no absurd consequences, no further interpretation may be made in search of the parties' intent." (citation and internal quotation marks omitted)). Justice harps upon the email in which O'Connor asked "[a]re we being paid the $ 91,666.66 to settle this for once and all?" Justice contends that because the email asked for payment "to settle this for once and all" and James later responded "Fri[day]," the parties thereby amended the October Settlement Agreement such that the final payment, though tardy, would entitle Justice to "a full and irrevocable release."

In the context of the email exchange as a whole, however, O'Connor's request for payment "to settle this for once and all" was simply *one* of Celtic Marine's *fifteen* demands for Justice's final installment payment. Celtic Marine repeatedly asked, for example, "R u [sic] paying us or not?"; "[Last] payment past due per settlement terms and why?"; "Still no payment 91,666.66?". The one-sided nature of Celtic Marine's repeated demands for payment—in contrast to Justice's infrequent and sparse responses—speaks volumes. In fact, the email exchange demonstrates that James never responded to O'Connor's "to settle this for once and all" email, much less **[—11—]** accepted the alleged amendment proposal. Rather, James only responded once O'Connor asked, "[a]re you paying us the $91,666.66 today?" To which James answered, "Fri." Overall, a common-sense reading of the parties' email exchange shows no evidence of an intent to amend the October Settlement Agreement. *See Clovelly Oil Co.*, 2012-2055 at p. 6; 112 So. 3d at 192 ("[A] contract must be interpreted in a common-sense fashion, according to the words of the contract their common and usual significance." (citation and internal quotation marks omitted)). There is no genuine dispute that the email exchange did not amend the October Settlement Agreement.

B. Waiver of the Acceleration Clause

Celtic Marine did not waive its ability to enforce the acceleration clause. In Louisiana, under *Standard Brewing Co. v. Anderson*, 46 So. 926 (La. 1908):

> There is a well[-]established rule . . . that where payments are due in installments, if the payee customarily permits payments to be made after the day on which they are due, [then] there is thereby established a course of conduct from which it is proper to say that the payee by acquiescence therein has waived the right to demand that the acceleration or any similar clause be enforced.

Rex Credit Co. v. Kirsch, 4 So. 2d 797, 798 (La. Ct. App. 1941) (citations omitted). "The purpose for the rule is to prevent an obligee from lulling an obligor into a false sense of security by accepting late payments over an extended period. Fairness requires that the obligee make known his intent to discontinue acceptance of late payments." *Nolan J. Cunningham Apartments, Inc. v. Dupre*, 428 So. 2d 1046, 1047 (La. Ct. App. 1983) (citing *Standard Brewing Co.*, 46 So. 926; *Sternberg v. Mason*, 339 So. 2d 373 (La. Ct. App. 1976)).

This well-established rule, however, applies only if the obligor is ready to pay but delayed only because of the impression, created by the obligee, that a late payment is acceptable. As the Louisiana Supreme Court summarized: [—12—]

> It is perfectly evident from the evidence as a whole that plaintiff never expressly or otherwise waived his right to be paid his rent promptly; and that, if prompt payment was not exacted, it was because of an unwilling and forced indulgence on his part.

> To such a situation the doctrine of the case of *Standard Brewing Co. v. Anderson* is totally inapplicable. That doctrine can obtain only where the tenant is ready to pay the rent promptly and needs no indulgence, but delays in paying simply because he is under the impression, produced by the lessor's past conduct, that it is a matter of no moment whether the payments be made promptly or a few days late.

Briede v. Babst, 59 So. 106, 107 (La. 1912) (citation omitted).

Justice argues that Celtic Marine waived the right to enforce the acceleration clause because Celtic Marine established a course of conduct wherein it accepted late payments without seeking to enforce the acceleration clause. By doing so, according to Justice, Celtic Marine lulled Justice into a false sense of security, only to seek additional money after Justice had made all payments. Celtic Marine purportedly bolstered this false sense of security when it asked for the final payment to "settle this for once and all."

Celtic Marine responds that waiver does not apply because it did not acquiesce in Justice's late payments, but "did all that it could to force Justice to make each payment timely." In other words, in Celtic Marine's view, its "repeated requests" for payment "amount to nothing more than an unwilling or forced indulgence." *See Rex Credit*, 4 So. 2d at 800; *Sternberg v. Mason*, 339 So. 2d 373, 376 (La. App. 1 Cir. 1976).

Briede resolves the parties' dispute here. Justice does not attempt to offer any evidence that it was "ready to pay the [installment] promptly and need[ed] no indulgence" such that the *Standard Brewing* doctrine may obtain under *Briede. See Briede*, 59 So. at 107. On the contrary, James stated in the email exchange that, in regards to paying Celtic Marine, Justice was "scraping the money together" and that "[t]hings are really tough." [—13—]

Moreover, there is no evidence that it was a "matter of no moment [to Celtic Marine] whether the payments be made promptly or a few days late." *See Briede*, 59 So. at 107. In regard to Justice's late payments, O'Connor responded to James that it was "the same for us very tough" and that Celtic Marine "cannot continue to [receive] vague answers." O'Connor also incessantly asked for payment, noting that the late payments presented a "terrible situation" and that he "lost faith in this agreement from [Justice's] side." In response, Justice relies only on the fact that Celtic Marine accepted its late payments. Amidst numerous emails demanding payment, Justice again narrowly focuses on just one—requesting payment "to settle this for once and all"—but does not offer any other evidence that Celtic Marine's acceptance of the late payments was not "because of an unwilling and forced indulgence." At best, this single email amounts to a mere "scintilla of evidence" that cannot defeat summary judgment. *Turner*, 476 F.3d at 343. Accordingly, Justice has not identified a genuine dispute of material fact whether there was a course of conduct establishing a waiver of Celtic Marine's right to exercise the acceleration clause.

In sum, the parties did not amend the October Settlement Agreement, and Celtic Marine did not waive its right to exercise the acceleration clause. The district court did not err in granting summary judgment.

V. CONCLUSION

Justice's appeal of the district court's order on the Rule 60(b)(6) motion is DISMISSED for want of jurisdiction, and the district court's order granting Celtic Marine's summary judgment motion is AFFIRMED.

United States Court of Appeals
for the Fifth Circuit

No. 13-20622

IN RE TMT PROCUREMENT CORP.

Appeals from the United States District Court for the Southern District of Texas and the United States Bankruptcy Court for the Southern District of Texas

Decided: September 3, 2014

Citation: 764 F.3d 512, 2 Adm. R. 295 (5th Cir. 2014).

Before HIGGINBOTHAM, DAVIS, and HAYNES, Circuit Judges.

[—2—] PER CURIAM:

Vantage Drilling Company ("Vantage") appeals three orders from the district court and two orders from the bankruptcy court. The orders were entered during the course of the Chapter 11 proceedings of twenty-one shipping companies. Their combined effect was to place certain shares of Vantage stock *in custodia legis* with the clerk of the court. Because we find that both courts below lacked subject-matter jurisdiction, we VACATE and REMAND.

I

A

In 2012, Vantage, an offshore drilling company, brought an action in Texas state court against Hsin-Chi Su, also known as Nobu Su, alleging breach of fiduciary duty, fraud, fraudulent inducement, negligent misrepresentation, and unjust enrichment (the "Vantage Litigation"). In its original petition, Vantage alleged that Su made material misrepresentations to induce Vantage to contract with companies controlled by Su for the acquisition of certain offshore drilling rigs and drillships. Vantage alleges that, in exchange, it issued approximately 100 million shares of Vantage stock to F3 Capital, an entity solely owned and wholly controlled by Su, and granted Su three seats on Vantage's board of directors, including a seat for himself. According to Vantage, the

subsequent disclosure of Su's misrepresentations placed Vantage [—3—] in severe financial duress, threatening its ability to obtain necessary financing and its ability to perform on several critical contracts. Vantage alleges that Su leveraged Vantage's financial crisis to extract additional Vantage stock and other benefits. Among other relief, Vantage sought a "[j]udgment imposing a constructive trust upon all profits or benefits, direct or indirect, obtained by Su."

Su removed the Vantage Litigation pursuant to 28 U.S.C. § 1446 to the United States District Court for the Southern District of Texas, alleging diversity jurisdiction.[1] Vantage moved to remand, which the district court denied.[2] On appeal, this Court reversed and remanded the Vantage Litigation to the district court with instructions to remand the case to state court.[3]

B

Meanwhile, in 2013, twenty-three foreign marine shipping companies, each owned directly or indirectly by Su, filed voluntary petitions for relief under Chapter 11 of the United States Bankruptcy Code in the United States Bankruptcy Court for the Southern District of Texas.[4] Certain creditors of the shipping companies moved to dismiss the

---

[1] *See* Notice of Removal, *Vantage Drilling Co. v. Su*, No. 4:12-CV-03131 (S.D. Tex. Oct. 22, 2012), Dkt. No. 1.

[2] *See* Opinion on Remand, *Vantage Drilling Co. v. Su*, No. 4:12-CV-03131 (S.D. Tex. Apr. 3, 2013), Dkt. No. 43.

[3] *Vantage Drilling Co. v. Su*, 741 F.3d 535, 539 (5th Cir. 2014).

[4] The shipping companies were: (1) A Whale Corporation; (2) B Whale Corporation; (3) C Whale Corporation; (4) D Whale Corporation; (5) E Whale Corporation; (6) G Whale Corporation; (7) H Whale Corporation; (8) A Duckling Corporation; (9) F Elephant Corporation; (10) F Elephant Inc.; (11) A Ladybug Corporation; (12) C Ladybug Corporation; (13) D Ladybug Corporation; (14) A Handy Corporation; (15) B Handy Corporation; (16) C Handy Corporation; (17) B Max Corporation; (18) New Flagship Investment Co., Ltd.; (19) RoRo Line Corporation; (20) Ugly Duckling Holding Corporation; (21) Great Elephant Corporation; (22) TMT Procurement Corporation; and (23) TMT USA Shipmanagement LLC.

bankruptcy actions, arguing, among other things, that: (a) the shipping companies had filed the petitions in bad [—4—] faith to delay or withhold any recovery by the creditors; (b) the shipping companies had manufactured jurisdiction to stay the creditors' collection efforts; and (c) there was not a reasonable likelihood of rehabilitating the shipping companies.

The bankruptcy court held an evidentiary hearing on the motion to dismiss. At the hearing, Su offered to place approximately 25 million shares of Vantage stock held by F3 Capital into an escrow to be administered by the bankruptcy court to secure the shipping companies' compliance with court orders and to serve as collateral for post-petition borrowing or working capital. The bankruptcy court denied the motion to dismiss, except with respect to F Elephant Corporation and TMT USA Shipmanagement LLC. In its order (the "Dismissal Order"), the bankruptcy court ordered that the twenty-one remaining shipping companies (the "Debtors") "must cause non-estate property (the 'Good Faith Property') with a fair market value of $40,750,000 to be provided to the Estates," and that, if the Good Faith Property was not provided in cash, then it "must include at least 25,000,000 shares of the common stock of" Vantage. The bankruptcy court provided that the Good Faith Property would be used to, among other things: (a) ensure compliance with court orders; (b) pay sanctions; (c) serve as collateral for working capital loans; and (d) satisfy any amounts arising under § 507(b) of the Bankruptcy Code.

The Debtors moved the bankruptcy court to approve a proposed escrow agreement, by which F3 Capital would deposit 25 million shares of Vantage stock with the clerk of the court to be held *in custodia legis* for the benefit of the Debtors.[5] In that motion, F3 Capital and Su represented and warranted that they could "enter into the Share Escrow Agreement and deliver the Good [—5—] Faith Property to the Court without violating any requirements of, or injunctive relief granted in, the [Vantage Litigation]."

---

[5] The Debtors later filed an amended motion.

Vantage responded in two ways. First, Vantage filed an application for a preliminary injunction with the district court in the Vantage Litigation, requesting that Su be enjoined from "transferring, selling, pledging or otherwise encumbering any of the Vantage stock . . . obtained as a result of his fraud and breaches of fiduciary duty to [Vantage], including by placing the shares into escrow to serve as collateral in an unrelated bankruptcy recently initiated by twenty-three insolvent foreign companies that are wholly-owned and controlled by Su."[6] In response, the district court entered an order in which it stated: (a) "[c]omplaints about the encumbrance of [Vantage's] stock arising out of the bankruptcy must be addressed to the bankruptcy court," and (b) Su "may not otherwise sell, transfer, pledge, or encumber his Vantage stock without court permission."[7]

Second, Vantage also appeared as a "party in interest" before the bankruptcy court and opposed the Debtors' motion to approve the proposed escrow agreement. The bankruptcy court held a hearing on the Debtors' motion, at which it concluded that:

> [T]he shares owned by F3 Capital are not subject to a constructive trust as a matter of law and, therefore, may be placed *in custodia legis* without complaint by any other party who has claimed ownership of the shares. . . .
>
> . . . .
>
> I find that this is a due process issue and that an entity that is not a party to a lawsuit, which is the [—6—] situation with F3 Capital in [the Vantage Litigation], may not be deprived of its property in a suit in which, (a) it is not a party, and (b) it received the assets prior to the commencement of the lawsuit.

---

[6] Vantage Drilling Co.'s Application for Preliminary Injunction and Motion for Expedited Discovery at 1, *Vantage Drilling Co. v. Su*, No. 4:12-cv-03131 (S.D. Tex. Aug. 14, 2013), Dkt. No. 75.

[7] Order on Stock Encumbrance at 1, *Vantage Drilling Co. v. Su*, No. 4:12-cv-03131 (S.D. Tex. Aug. 14, 2013), Dkt. No. 79.

The bankruptcy court entered an order (the "Escrow Order") in which, among other things, it: (a) authorized the deposit of 25,107,142 shares of Vantage stock with the clerk of the court *in custodia legis*; (b) provided that the deposited shares of Vantage stock would be used for the same reasons enumerated in the Dismissal Order; (c) required F3 Capital to deposit an additional 900,000 shares of Vantage stock; (d) provided that F3 Capital would retain its voting rights in the deposited shares of Vantage stock; and (e) required F3 Capital to transfer to the Debtors "all of its interests in any chose of action arising against [Vantage], its officers, agents or directors." Vantage filed an interlocutory appeal of the Escrow Order with the United States District Court for the Southern District of Texas.

C

The district court withdrew the reference to the bankruptcy court and denied leave to appeal. It then set a hearing to reconsider, among other issues, Vantage's objections to the Escrow Order. Before the hearing, the Debtors filed an emergency motion in which they requested permission to borrow up to $20 million in post-petition financing (the "DIP Facility"), including up to $6 million on an interim basis pursuant to an attached term sheet. The district court approved in principle the emergency motion and entered an order (the "Interim DIP Order"), which authorized an initial loan of $6 million under the DIP Facility. The Interim DIP Order granted Macquarie Bank Limited (the "DIP Lender") a first priority lien and security interest in the deposited shares of Vantage stock. The Interim DIP Order further provided that the DIP Lender's interests in the deposited shares of Vantage stock "shall not be [—7—] withdrawn, modified, abridged, compromised, stayed, reprioritized or otherwise affected in any matter by any subsequent order [of] the Bankruptcy Court . . . in the Chapter 11 [actions] or that [the District Court] might enter in either the Chapter 11 [actions] or in [the Vantage Litigation]." It also provided that the DIP Lender had extended financing to the Debtors in good faith and was entitled to "the full protections of sections 363(m) and 364(e) of the Bankruptcy Code." It further ordered

that "[i]f any or all of the provisions of [the Interim DIP Order] are hereafter reversed, modified, vacated or stayed, that action will not affect . . . the validity and enforceability of any lien . . . authorized or created hereby or pursuant to [the term sheet], including . . . the special provisions concerning [the deposited shares of Vantage stock]."

The next day, the district court entered an order (the "DIP Addendum"), in which it ordered F3 Capital to deposit an additional 4 million shares of Vantage stock (together with the 25,107,142 shares of Vantage stock originally deposited, the "Vantage Shares") with the clerk of the court to be held *in custodia legis*. The district court also entered another order (the "Order Affirming Escrow"), which provided that the Vantage Shares would "remain under the control" of the bankruptcy court. The district court then re-referred the action to the bankruptcy court. Vantage timely appealed these three district court orders to this Court.[8]

D

After holding hearings, the bankruptcy court entered two orders (the "Final DIP Order" and the "Cash Collateral Order") over the objections of Vantage. The Final DIP Order approved the remaining $14 million in post-petition financing under the DIP Facility requested by the Debtors on terms [—8—] substantially identical to those memorialized in the Interim DIP Order. Like the Interim DIP Order, the Final DIP Order granted the DIP Lender a first priority lien and security interest in the Vantage Shares. The Final DIP Order also provided that the "DIP Lender [was] extending financing to the [Debtors] in good faith and in express reliance upon the protections afforded by sections 363(m) and 364(e) of the Bankruptcy Code and the DIP Lender is entitled to the benefits of the provisions of sections 363(m) and 364(e) of the Bankruptcy Code."[9] The Cash Collateral

---

[8] The appeal was filed under Case No. 13-20622.

[9] The bankruptcy court also reiterated its finding twice that the DIP Lender had negotiated in good faith and "should be deemed a good faith lender in accordance with the Bankruptcy Code" on the record at the hearing.

Order granted the Debtors' pre-petition lenders a first priority lien in the 4 million shares of Vantage stock deposited pursuant to the DIP Addendum "to secure any rights, claims or grants that were given to the [pre-petition lenders] in any prior order" of the bankruptcy court. Among other things, it also provided that "[a]ny rights in [the Vantage Shares] are fully subordinated to the rights granted in [the Final DIP Order] to the DIP Lender."

Vantage timely appealed these two bankruptcy court orders. The bankruptcy court certified the appeal for direct review by this Court. This Court accepted that direct appeal[10] and consolidated it with the prior pending appeal of the district court orders.

II

In reviewing the rulings of the bankruptcy court on direct appeal and the district court sitting in bankruptcy, we review findings of fact for clear error [—9—] and conclusions of law *de novo*.[11] We review mixed questions of law and fact *de novo*.[12]

III

The Debtors assert that Vantage's appeal of all the orders is moot under 11 U.S.C. § 363(m) and 11 U.S.C. § 364(e). The Bankruptcy Code contains statutory mootness provisions in § 363(m) and § 364(e). Section 363(m) provides:

> The reversal or modification on appeal of an authorization under subsection (b) or (c) of this section of a sale or lease of property does not affect the validity of a sale or lease under such authorization to an entity that purchased or leased such property in good faith, whether or not such entity knew of the pendency of the appeal, unless such authorization and

such sale or lease were stayed pending appeal.[13]

Section 364(e) provides:

> The reversal or modification on appeal of an authorization under this section to obtain credit or incur debt, or of a grant under this section of a priority or a lien, does not affect the validity of any debt so incurred, or any priority or lien so granted, to an entity that extended such credit in good faith, whether or not such entity knew of the pendency of the appeal, unless such authorization and the incurring of such debt, or the granting of such priority or lien, were stayed pending appeal.[14] [—10—]

As noted by the Ninth Circuit, § 364(e) was modeled after § 363(m).[15] A failure to obtain a stay of an authorization under these sections moots an appeal of that authorization where the purchaser or lender acted in good faith.[16] It is undisputed that Vantage did not seek or obtain a stay of any of the orders. Vantage argues that this appeal is not statutorily moot for several reasons.

We begin first with Vantage's assertion that the appeal is not moot under either § 363(m) or § 364(e) because § 363 and § 364 only authorize actions in connection with "property of the estate,"[17] and the Vantage Shares are not "property of the estate." This is essentially a statutory attack, but with undertones of subject-matter jurisdiction. This is because whether something is "property of the estate" is an inquiry also relevant to

---

[10] The appeal was filed under Case No. 13-20715.

[11] *See In re Vitro S.A.B. de CV*, 701 F.3d 1031, 1042 (5th Cir. 2012); *In re Martinez*, 564 F.3d 719, 725–26 (5th Cir. 2009).

[12] *In re ASARCO, L.L.C.*, 702 F.3d 250, 257 (5th Cir. 2012).

[13] 11 U.S.C. § 363(m).

[14] *Id.* § 364(e).

[15] *In re Adams Apple, Inc.*, 829 F.2d 1484, 1489 (9th Cir. 1987).

[16] *See In re Pac. Lumber Co.*, 584 F.3d 229, 240 n.15 (5th Cir. 2009); *In re Gilchrist*, 891 F.2d 559, 560–61 (5th Cir. 1990); *In re First S. Sav. Ass'n*, 820 F.2d 700, 704 (5th Cir. 1987).

[17] *See* 11 U.S.C. § 363(b)(1) ("The trustee . . . may use, sell, or lease . . . property of the estate . . . ."); *Id.* § 364(c) ("[T]he trustee . . . may authorize the obtaining of credit or the incurring of debt . . . secured by a lien on property of the estate . . . or secured by a junior lien on property of the estate . . . .").

determining subject-matter jurisdiction.[18] Consistent with our precedent, we do not reach the issue of whether the Vantage Shares are "property of the estate" before deciding the statutory mootness issue because of Vantage's failure to obtain a stay pending appeal.[19] For the same reason, even though Vantage raises a challenge to subject-matter jurisdiction, we do not reach that issue before deciding the statutory mootness issue.[20] [—11—]

We next turn to Vantage's argument that the appeal is not moot under either § 363(m) or § 364(e) because the DIP Lender did not act in "good faith."[21] The Debtors contend that we should not reach the issue of "good faith" because Vantage failed to contest that issue below and is only raising it for the first time on appeal. "It is well established that we do not consider arguments or claims not presented to the bankruptcy court."[22] Vantage argues that it sufficiently raised the issue before the courts below by repeatedly asserting that F3 Capital had fraudulently obtained the Vantage Shares; Vantage had an adverse claim to the Vantage Shares; and Vantage's right to assert a constructive trust

over the Vantage Shares would survive any attempt to pledge, sell, or transfer the Vantage Shares to a purchaser or lender who was on notice of Vantage's adverse claim, including the DIP Lender. We agree. Vantage sufficiently raised the issue of the DIP Lender's "good faith" so as to pursue this issue on appeal. Therefore, we must determine whether the DIP Lender acted in "good faith" within the meaning of § 363(m) and § 364(e).

The proponent of "good faith" bears the burden of proof.[23] Both the district court sitting in bankruptcy and the bankruptcy court held that the DIP Lender was acting in good faith. Whether a determination by a lower court [—12—] that a party acted in "good faith" should be review de novo or under clear error is a matter of some confusion in our circuit.[24] However, under either standard of review, we find that the determination of good faith does not pass muster.

The Bankruptcy Code does not explicitly define "good faith." In the context of § 363(m), we have defined the term in two ways. On the one hand, we have defined a "good faith purchaser" as "one who purchases the assets for value, in good faith, and without notice of adverse claims."[25] On the other hand, we have

---

[18] See infra Part IV(B).

[19] See In re Gilchrist, 891 F.2d 559, 561 (5th Cir. 1990); In re Ginther Trusts, 238 F.3d 686, 689 (5th Cir. 2001).

[20] See In re Gilchrist, 891 F.2d at 561; In re Ginther Trusts, 238 F.3d at 689.

[21] Because we find Vantage's "good faith" argument persuasive, we do not address the two additional reasons offered against mootness. First, Vantage argues that only the Interim DIP Order and the Final DIP Order refer to § 363(m) or § 364(e); authorize post-petition financing; or contain an explicit finding of "good faith." Because the Order Affirming Escrow, the DIP Addendum, and the Cash Collateral Order do not refer to § 363(m) or § 364(e), do not authorize a sale, lease, or post-petition financing, and do not contain an explicit finding of "good faith," Vantage argues that the appeal is not moot as to these orders. Second, Vantage asserts that the protections enumerated in § 363(m) do not apply because none of the orders authorizes "a sale or lease of property" pursuant to § 363.

[22] In re Gilchrist, 891 F.2d at 561 (refusing to address the appellant's challenge to the buyer's good faith under § 363(m) because it had not been raised before the bankruptcy court); see also In re Ginther Trusts, 238 F.3d 686, 689 (5th Cir. 2001).

[23] In re M Capital Corp., 290 B.R. 743, 747 (B.A.P. 9th Cir. 2003).

[24] On the one hand, we have stated that when a district court hearing a bankruptcy appeal dismisses an appeal from the bankruptcy court as moot, we review that dismissal de novo. In re Ginther Trusts, 238 F.3d at 688. Similarly, the Sixth Circuit has held that "good faith" is a mixed question of law and fact. In re Revco D.S., Inc., 901 F.2d 1359, 1366 (6th Cir. 1990) (reviewing finding of "good faith" under § 364(e)). This would suggest that the good faith determinations by the lower courts are subject to a de novo determination. On the other hand, we have previously reviewed a bankruptcy court's "good faith" determination under § 363(m) for clear error. In re Beach Dev. LP, No. 07-20350, 2008 WL 2325647, at *2 (5th Cir. Jun. 6, 2008). District courts in our circuit have done the same. In re Camp Arrowhead, Ltd., 429 B.R. 546, 550–52 (W.D. Tex. 2010).

[25] Hardage v. Herring Nat'l Bank, 837 F.2d 1319, 1323 (5th Cir. 1988) (quoting In re Willemain, 764 F.2d 1019, 1023 (4th Cir. 1985)); see also SEC v. Janvey, 404 F. App'x 912, 916 (5th Cir. 2010) (applying the "good faith" standard set forth in

noted that "the misconduct that would destroy a purchaser's good faith status . . . involves fraud, collusion between the purchaser and other bidders or the trustee, or an attempt to take grossly unfair advantage of other bidders."[26] Here, there is no suggestion of fraud, collusion, or an attempt to take grossly unfair advantage by the DIP Lender. Rather, Vantage only argues that the DIP Lender was on notice of Vantage's adverse claim to the Vantage Shares.

Before we turn to whether the DIP Lender had notice of an adverse claim, however, we must address a threshold argument. Essentially, the [—13—] Debtors want us to discard one of the definitions of "good faith." The Debtors argue that knowledge of an adverse claim should not preclude a finding of "good faith" because this requirement would undermine the purposes of § 363(m) and § 364(e). We acknowledge that there is some power in this argument. The purpose of § 363(m)'s stay requirement "is in furtherance of the policy of not only affording finality to the judgment of the bankruptcy court, but particularly to give finality to those orders and judgments upon which third parties rely."[27] Similarly, the purpose of § 364(e) is "to overcome a good faith lender's reluctance to extend financing in a bankruptcy context by permitting reliance on a bankruptcy judge's authorization."[28] Thus, both § 363(m) and § 364(e) contemplate situations where the good faith purchaser or lender has knowledge of the pendency of an appeal. Yet the good faith purchaser or lender "does not forfeit the protections of the statute," "even though such

knowledge implies the further knowledge that there are objections to the order."[29] "[I]t is clear as we have said that knowledge that there are objections to the transaction is not enough to constitute bad faith."[30] We do not disagree with this accent on the meaning of "good faith." But we think it is irrelevant here. There is a difference, as demonstrated by this case, between simply having knowledge that there are objections to the transaction and having knowledge of an adverse claim. Having knowledge that there are objections to the transaction usually involves those situations in which "some creditor is objecting to the transaction and is trying to get the district court or the court [—14—] of appeals to reverse the bankruptcy judge."[31] Having knowledge of an adverse claim requires something more. That is why the former does not preclude a finding of good faith, whereas the latter does. Here, the DIP Lender's knowledge was not simply limited to objections by creditors of the Debtors. The DIP Lender had knowledge that a third-party, entirely unrelated to the bankruptcy proceedings, had an adverse claim to the Vantage Shares. On these facts, the DIP Lender does not qualify as a good faith purchaser or lender. To our eyes, both definitions have to be applied.[32]

We turn our attention, then, to whether the DIP Lender had notice of an adverse claim. The Bankruptcy Code does not provide a definition of "adverse claim." But it defines "claim" broadly to include a right to payment or a right to equitable remedy.[33] The Debtors

---

Hardage); see also Jeremiah v. Richardson, 148 F.3d 17, 23 (1st Cir. 1998) ("A 'good faith' purchaser is one who buys property in good faith and for value, without knowledge of adverse claims." (internal quotation marks omitted) (emphasis in original)).

[26] In re Bleaufontaine, Inc., 634 F.2d 1383, 1388 n.7 (5th Cir. 1981) (quoting In re Rock Indus. Mach. Corp., 572 F.2d 1195, 1198 (7th Cir. 1978)).

[27] In re Sax, 796 F.2d 994, 998 (7th Cir. 1986) (internal quotation marks omitted).

[28] In re Adams Apple, 829 F.2d at 1488; see also In re W. Pac. Airlines, Inc., 181 F.3d 1191, 1195 (10th Cir. 1999); In re Saybrook Mfg. Co., 963 F.2d 1490, 1493 (11th Cir. 1992); In re EDC Holding Co., 676 F.2d 945, 947 (7th Cir. 1982).

[29] In re EDC Holding Co., 676 F.2d at 947.

[30] Id.

[31] Id.

[32] See In re Rock Indus. Mach. Corp., 572 F.2d at 1197–98 (defining "good faith purchaser" as "one who purchases the assets for value, in good faith, and without notice of adverse claims" while also noting that "the misconduct that would destroy a purchaser's good faith status at a judicial sale involves fraud, collusion between the purchaser and other bidders or the trustee, or an attempt to take grossly unfair advantage of other bidders").

[33] 11 U.S.C. § 101(5). A claim means a "right to payment, whether or not such right is reduced to judgment, liquidated, unliquidated, fixed, contingent, matured, unmatured, disputed, undisputed, legal, equitable, secured, or

assert that there was no "adverse claim" because F3 Capital, the owner of the Vantage Shares, was not a named defendant in the Vantage Litigation. But Vantage instituted the Vantage Litigation to, among other things, recover the Vantage Shares and has repeatedly asserted before the bankruptcy court and the district court that F3 Capital had fraudulently obtained the Vantage Shares and that Vantage had an adverse claim to the Vantage Shares. We find that this was enough: the DIP Lender had adequate notice of the adverse claim, and the DIP Lender does [—15—] not come within the meaning of "good faith" as envisioned by § 363(m) and § 364(e). The statutory mootness provisions are not applicable here, and Vantage may challenge the orders issued by the bankruptcy court and the district court.

IV

Vantage argues that the district court and the bankruptcy court erred in entering the orders because they lacked subject-matter jurisdiction over both the Vantage Shares and the Vantage Litigation.[34]

A

Jurisdiction for bankruptcy cases is defined by 28 U.S.C. § 1334.[35] Under § 1334, district courts have exclusive jurisdiction of "all cases under title 11,"[36] including over "all the property, wherever located, of the debtor as of the commencement of such case, and of property of the estate."[37] Districts courts also

have "original but not exclusive jurisdiction of all civil proceedings arising under title 11, or arising in or related to cases under title 11."[38] The district court can refer cases to the bankruptcy court,[39] whose jurisdiction is more limited.[40] [—16—]

Because § 1334(b) defines jurisdiction conjunctively, "a district court has jurisdiction over the subject matter if it is at least related to the underlying bankruptcy."[41] A matter is "related to" the bankruptcy if "the outcome of that proceeding could *conceivably* have any effect on the estate being administered in bankruptcy."[42]

B

Vantage first asserts that the district court and the bankruptcy court lacked jurisdiction over the Vantage Shares because they are not property of the Debtors or "property of the estate."

Although the Bankruptcy Code does not define "property of the debtor," the meaning of the term "property of the estate" is outlined in 11 U.S.C. § 541. Under § 541(a)(1), "property of the estate" includes "all legal or equitable interests of the debtor in property as of the commencement of the case."[43] Under § 541(a)(6), it includes "[p]roceeds, product, offspring, rents, or profits from property of the estate."[44] Finally, under § 541(a)(7), it also includes "[a]ny interest in property that the

---

unsecured." *Id.* Similarly, a claim means "right to an equitable remedy for breach of performance if such breach gives rise to a right to payment, whether or not such right to an equitable remedy is reduced to judgment, fixed, contingent, matured, unmatured, disputed, undisputed, secured, or unsecured." *Id.*

[34] *See In re Querner*, 7 F.3d 1199, 1201 (5th Cir. 1993) ("Where a federal court lacks jurisdiction, its decisions, opinions, and orders are void.").

[35] *In re Walker*, 51 F.3d 562, 568 (5th Cir. 1995).

[36] 28 U.S.C. § 1334(a).

[37] 28 U.S.C. § 1334(e)(1); *see also Kane Enters. v. MacGregor (USA) Inc.*, 322 F.3d 371, 374 (5th Cir. 2003) ("The district in which a chapter 11 petition is filed has exclusive jurisdiction over the property of the estate.").

[38] *See* 28 U.S.C. § 1334(b).

[39] 28 U.S.C. § 157(a).

[40] Bankruptcy judges "may hear and determine all cases under title 11 and all core proceedings arising under title 11, or arising in a case under title 11" and "enter appropriate orders and judgment." 28 U.S.C. § 157(b); *In re Wood*, 825 F.2d 90, 95 (5th Cir. 1987). In contrast to core proceedings, bankruptcy judges have the limited power to "hear a proceeding that is not a core proceeding but that is otherwise related to a case under title 11" and to "submit proposed findings of fact and conclusions of law to the district court," subject to *de novo* review. 28 U.S.C. § 157(c); *In re Wood*, 825 F.2d at 95.

[41] *In re Querner*, 7 F.3d at 1201.

[42] *In re Wood*, 825 F.2d at 93.

[43] 11 U.S.C. § 541(a)(1).

[44] *Id.* § 541(a)(6).

estate acquires after the commencement of the case."[45] "The party seeking to include property in the estate bears the burden of showing that the item is property of the estate."[46]

To begin, it is undisputed that the Debtors had no legal or equitable interest in the Vantage Shares at the commencement of the case. The Vantage Shares thus could not have been "property of the estate" under § 541(a)(1). Similarly, they could not be "[p]roceeds, product, offspring, rents, or profits [—17—] from property of the estate" under § 541(a)(6). Therefore, they could not be considered "property of the estate" under these provisions.

But the Debtors assert that the Vantage Shares are "property of the estate" under § 541(a)(7) because they are "interest[s] in property that the estate acquire[d] after the commencement of the case." Specifically, the Debtors assert that they acquired an interest in the Vantage Shares after the Vantage Shares were deposited *in custodia legis* pursuant to the orders. Vantage asserts that the Vantage Shares are not property of the estate under § 541(a)(7) for several reasons.

Vantage contends that the Debtors never acquired an interest in the Vantage Shares. "Property interests are created and defined by state law," in this case Texas law.[47] The Escrow Order required the Debtors to deposit "*non-estate property*" with the clerk of the court. F3 Capital deposited the Vantage Shares *in custodia legis*; however, F3 Capital continues to retain title to the Vantage Shares and control their voting rights. Moreover, the deposit of the Vantage Shares is neither a loan nor a gift. The Debtors also did not acquire the right to control or retain the Vantage Shares.[48] As a result, Vantage argues that the Debtors have not acquired any cognizable interest. The Debtors reply that they acquired an interest in the Vantage Shares because they can use the Vantage Shares as collateral to secure loans from the DIP Lender pursuant to the Escrow Order. But Vantage correctly notes that courts have consistently [—18—] held that other forms of collateral do not constitute "property of the estate" under § 541.[49] Vantage therefore asserts that the Debtors did not acquire an interest in the Vantage Shares simply by using them as collateral to secure lending from the DIP Lender.

We need not decide this question of state law, however. Even assuming *arguendo* that the Debtors acquired an interest, Vantage asserts that the Vantage Shares are not property of the estate under § 541(a)(7) because that provision is limited to property interests that are themselves traceable to "property of the estate" or generated in the normal course of the debtor's business. We agree. As we previously recognized in *In re McLain*,[50] "Congress enacted § 541(a)(7) to clarify its intention that § 541 be an all-embracing definition and to ensure that property interests created with or by property of the estate are themselves property of the estate."[51] Other courts have adopted similar reasoning.[52] Thus, the Vantage Shares are

---

[45] *Id.* § 541(a)(7).

[46] *In re Klein-Swanson*, 488 B.R. 628, 633 (B.A.P. 8th Cir 2013).

[47] *In re Swift*, 129 F.3d 792, 795 & n.12 (5th Cir. 1997); *In re Klein-Swanson*, 488 B.R. at 633.

[48] *See In re IFS Fin. Corp.*, 669 F.3d 255, 262 (5th Cir. 2012) (noting that, under Texas law, "control over funds in an account is the predominant factor in determining an account's

ownership"); *see also In re Kemp*, 52 F.3d 546, 551–53 (5th Cir. 1995) (per curiam) (holding that funds held in escrow are "property of the estate" only to the extent of the debtor's independent right to that property); *In re Missionary Baptist Found. of Am., Inc.*, 792 F.2d 502, 505–06 (5th Cir. 1986) (same).

[49] *In re Stonebridge Techs., Inc.*, 430 F.3d 260, 269 (5th Cir. 2005) (per curiam) ("It is well-established in this circuit that letters of credit and the proceeds therefrom are not property of the debtor's bankruptcy estate."); *see also In re Lockard*, 884 F.2d 1171, 1178 (9th Cir. 1989) ("[W]e conclude that the surety bond at issue in this case is not 'property of the estate,' within the meaning of 11 U.S.C. § 541.").

[50] 516 F.3d 301 (5th Cir. 2008).

[51] *Id.* at 312 (internal quotation marks omitted).

[52] *In re Trinity Gas Corp. (Reorganized)*, 242 B.R. 344, 350 (Bankr. N.D. Tex. 1999) ("[T]he obvious purpose of § 541(a)(7) is to include property and rights which are acquired in the estate's normal course of business in property of the estate."); *In re Doemling*, 116 B.R. 48, 50 (Bankr.

not "property of the estate" [—19—] under § 541(a)(7) because they were not created with or by property of the estate, they were not acquired in the estate's normal course of business, and they are not traceable to or arise out of any prepetition interest included in the bankruptcy estate.

The Debtors do not assert that they have an interest in the Vantage Shares that was created with or by other "property of the estate" or that arose in the normal course of business. But they assert that these tracing limitations apply to individual debtors in Chapter 7 or Chapter 11 bankruptcies, not to corporate debtors in Chapter 11 bankruptcies. For corporate debtors in Chapter 11 bankruptcies, the Debtors assert that § 541(a)(7) covers ""[a]ny interest in property that the estate acquires after the commencement of the case."[53] But the Debtors cite no case standing for the proposition that these restrictions on the application § 541(a)(7) do not apply to the estate of a corporate debtor in a Chapter 11 proceeding, and we refuse to adopt such a holding.

Finally, Vantage points out that the Debtors cannot rely on the orders as the means by which the Vantage Shares became "property of the estate" because the bankruptcy court and the district court had no authority to issue the orders unless the Vantage Shares were already "property of the estate." The bankruptcy court and the district court could not manufacture *in rem* jurisdiction over the Vantage Shares by issuing orders purporting to vest the Debtors with a post-petition interest in the Vantage Shares.[54] We agree. The [—20—] Debtors cannot use the orders as "jurisdictional bootstrap[s]" to allow the district court and bankruptcy court to "exercise jurisdiction that would not otherwise exist."[55]

For these reasons, we conclude that the Vantage Shares are not property of the Debtors or "property of the estate."[56] Therefore, the district court and the bankruptcy court lacked jurisdiction on this basis.

C

Vantage next asserts that the district court and bankruptcy court lacked jurisdiction to adjudicate Vantage's claim in the Vantage Litigation because it is not "related to" the Debtors' Chapter 11 proceedings. A matter is "related to" a bankruptcy proceeding if "the outcome of the proceeding could conceivably affect the estate being administered in bankruptcy."[57] Certainty, therefore, is "unnecessary; an action is 'related to' bankruptcy if the outcome could alter, positively or negatively, the debtor's rights, liabilities, options, or freedom of action or could influence the administration of the

---

W.D. Pa. 1990) ("Relatively few courts have been called upon to determine whether a property interest which was acquired postpetition in a Chapter 11 case qualifies as property of the estate pursuant to § 541(a)(7). The following principle can, however, be extracted from certain of those cases: a property interest acquired postpetition during the pendency of a Chapter 11 case qualifies as property of the estate, for purposes of § 541(a)(7), only if said property interest is traceable to (or arises out of) some prepetition property interest which already is included in the bankruptcy estate."); *see also Segal v. Rochelle*, 382 U.S. 375, 380 (1966) (holding that whether property is included in an estate depends on whether it "is sufficiently rooted in the pre-bankruptcy past and so little entangled with the bankrupts' ability to make an unencumbered fresh start").

[53] 11 U.S.C. § 541(a)(7) (emphasis added).

[54] *See Celotex Corp. v. Edwards*, 514 U.S. 300, 327 (1995) (holding that a bankruptcy court could not use "jurisdictional bootstrap[s]" to "exercise jurisdiction that would not otherwise exist"); *In re Guild & Gallery Plus, Inc.*, 72 F.3d 1171, 1182 (3d Cir. 1996) (holding that a consent order purporting to exert jurisdiction over non-estate property cannot "be utilized to support a finding of subject matter jurisdiction over claims that otherwise could not be heard in bankruptcy court").

[55] *Celotex*, 514 U.S. at 327.

[56] Because we conclude that the Vantage Shares are not "property of the estate," the Interim DIP Order and the Final DIP Order were not authorized under § 364 which only authorizes the imposition of liens on "property of the estate." *See* 11 U.S.C. § 364(c)(2)–(3), (d)(1).

[57] *In re TXNB Internal Case*, 483 F.3d 292, 298 (5th Cir. 2007).

bankrupt estate."[58]   But "'related to' jurisdiction cannot be limitless."[59]

Vantage asserts that the bankruptcy court and the district court lacked jurisdiction to interfere with its rights in the Vantage Shares, which are the subject of the Vantage Litigation, because the outcome of that proceeding could not conceivably affect the Debtors' estates. We agree. This Court has previously held that bankruptcy jurisdiction does not extend to state law [—21—] actions between non-debtors over non-estate property.[60] The Supreme Court in *Celotex* read the "related to" prong more broadly to cover non-debtor actions involving non-estate property that nonetheless affect the estate:

> [T]he 'related to' language of § 1334(b) must be read to give district courts (and bankruptcy courts under § 157(a)) jurisdiction over more than simple proceedings involving the property of the debtor or the estate. We also agree . . . that a bankruptcy court's 'related to' jurisdiction cannot be limitless.[61]

However, even under *Celotex*'s broad reading, there is no justifiable basis for exercising jurisdiction over the Vantage Litigation. The only discernable link between the Vantage Litigation and the Debtors' Chapter 11 proceedings is that F3 Capital and the Debtors' have a common owner. This is not enough. The resolution in the Vantage Litigation would not have had any effect on the bankruptcy. As a result, the bankruptcy court and the district court improperly

interfered with the Vantage Litigation by ordering that the Vantage Shares be deposited *in custodia legis* with the clerk of the court; that no subsequent orders in the Vantage Litigation could impair the DIP Lender's interest in the Vantage Shares; that any rights in the Vantage Shares, including those of Vantage, are subordinated to those of the DIP Lender; and that the Vantage Shares are not subject to a constructive trust as a matter of law. [—22—]

The Debtors maintain that the bankruptcy court and the district court had jurisdiction to enter the orders because the orders deal with core proceedings involving the administration of the estate, the acquisition of credit, and the use of property, including cash collateral.[62] This argument muddies the water somewhat because before a court can decide whether an action is a core or a non-core proceeding, it must first determine whether subject-matter jurisdiction under § 1334 even exists.[63] But in any event, we can reject this argument without much explanation. The Vantage Litigation does not fall within the meaning of core proceedings. Our sister circuits have previously rejected this kind of argument in cases where bankruptcy courts adjudicated a non-debtor's right in non-estate property.[64] Similarly, in *In re Wood*,[65] we held that the term "core proceedings" under 28 U.S.C. § 157 did not cover unrelated and independent state court proceedings, such as the Vantage Suit:

> We hold, therefore, that a proceeding is core under section 157 if it invokes a substantive right provided by title 11 or if it is a proceeding that, by its nature,

---

[58] *Id.*

[59] *Celotex*, 514 U.S. at 308.

[60] *See In re Paso Del Norte Oil Co.*, 755 F.2d 421, 424 (5th Cir. 1985) ("A court of bankruptcy has no power to entertain collateral disputes between third parties that do not involve the bankrupt or its property, nor may it exercise jurisdiction over a private controversy which does not relate to matters pertaining to bankruptcy." (citations omitted)); *see also In re Vitek, Inc.*, 51 F.3d 530, 533–38 (5th Cir. 1995).

[61] 514 U.S. at 308; *see also In re Prescription Home Health Care, Inc.*, 316 F.3d 542, 547 (5th Cir. 2002) ("It is well-established that, to be 'related to' a bankruptcy, it is not necessary for the proceeding to be against the debtor or the debtor's property.").

[62] *See* 28 U.S.C. § 157(b)(2)(A), (D) & (M).

[63] *In re Wood*, 825 F.2d at 92–95.

[64] *See In re Guild & Gallery Plus*, 72 F.3d at 1180 ("Since the Summertime painting was not part of the bankrupt estate, then *a fortiori* this matter cannot fall within § 157(b)(2)(A), which can only be applied to matters concerning the administration of the bankrupt estate. . . . The plain language of § 157(b)(2)(A) applies only to property of the bankrupt estate."); *Howell Hydrocarbons, Inc. v. Adams*, 897 F.2d 183, 190 (5th Cir. 1990) ("Whatever else a core proceeding must be, it must involve a decision that ultimately affects the distribution of the debtor's assets.").

[65] 825 F.2d 90 (5th Cir. 1987).

could arise only in the context of a bankruptcy case. The proceeding before us does not meet this test and, accordingly, is a non-core proceeding. The plaintiff's suit is not based on any right created by the federal bankruptcy law. It is based on state created rights. Moreover, this suit is not a proceeding that could arise [—23—] only in the context of a bankruptcy. It is simply a state contract action that, had there been no bankruptcy, could have proceeded in state court.[66]

But as explained above, not only was the Vantage Litigation not a core proceeding, it was not even a non-core proceeding because there is no "related to" jurisdiction in this case. Simply put, the Debtors confuse the argument by putting the matter of placement of jurisdiction (core versus non-core proceedings) before the matter of the existence of subject-matter jurisdiction.

The Debtors also assert that the orders did not interfere with or impair the Vantage Litigation or Vantage's claim to the Vantage Shares. They note that the bankruptcy court and the district court expressed no views on the collateral estoppel effect of their rulings in the Vantage Litigation. This argument fails to persuade because the orders authorized the imposition of liens on the Vantage Shares, subordinated Vantage's rights in the Vantage Shares to those of the DIP Lender, prevented the district court in the Vantage Litigation from impairing the DIP Lender's interest in the Vantage Shares, and held that the Vantage Shares were not subject to a constructive trust as a matter of law. Finally, the Debtors contend that, in any event, Vantage's right to due process under the Fifth Amendment was not infringed because it had the opportunity to be heard at every stage of the proceedings that resulted in the orders.[67] This argument misses the mark—the question is whether the bankruptcy court and the district court had jurisdiction to enter the orders, not whether Vantage's right to due process was violated. [—24—]

For these reasons, we conclude that Vantage's claim in the Vantage Litigation was not "related to" the Debtors' Chapter 11 proceedings. Before the district court and the bankruptcy court exercised jurisdiction over the Vantage Shares, the outcome of the Vantage Litigation could not have had any conceivable effect on the Debtors' estate. In essence, the Debtors have again attempted to use the orders as "jurisdictional bootstrap[s]" by arguing that the Vantage Litigation is "related to" the Debtors' Chapter 11 proceedings because the orders have linked them.[68] This we cannot allow.

V

We conclude that the appeals are not moot, that the Vantage Shares are not "property of the estate," and that the Vantage Litigation is not "related to" the bankruptcy proceedings. The district court and the bankruptcy court had no subject-matter jurisdiction to enter the orders. The orders of the district court and the bankruptcy court are VACATED and this case is REMANDED for proceedings consistent with this opinion. Accordingly, the Debtors' Motion to Dismiss Appeals is DENIED.

---

[66] *Id.* at 97.

[67] *See Mathews v. Eldridge*, 424 U.S. 319, 333 (1976) ("The fundamental requirement of due process is the opportunity to be heard at a meaningful time and in a meaningful manner." (internal quotations omitted)).

[68] *See Celotex*, 514 U.S. at 327.

United States Court of Appeals
for the Fifth Circuit

No. 13-20243

UNITED STATES
vs.
TRANSOCEAN DEEPWATER DRILLING INC.

Appeal from the United States District Court for the
Southern District of Texas

Decided: September 18, 2014

Citation: 767 F.3d 485, 2 Adm. R. 306 (5th Cir. 2014).

Before **REAVLEY, JONES,** and **GRAVES,** Circuit
Judges.

[—1—] REAVLEY, Circuit Judge:

Transocean Deepwater Drilling, Inc. appeals from the district court's order enforcing administrative subpoenas issued by the Chemical Safety and Hazard Investigation Board in connection with an investigation following the disaster on the *Deepwater Horizon* drilling unit in the Gulf of Mexico. Transocean contends that the subpoenas should have been quashed because the Board lacks authority to investigate the incident. We AFFIRM the district court's judgment.

I.

On April 20, 2010, a blowout, explosion, and fire occurred during drilling operations at the Macondo lease site in the Gulf of Mexico. The Macondo well was being drilled by the *Deepwater Horizon*, a mobile offshore drilling unit [—2—] ("MODU") tasked to the job by Transocean. As a result of the incident, eleven people were tragically killed, a large volume of flammable gas, oil, and other hazardous substances were released into the water and ambient air, and substantial property damage occurred.

Numerous governmental agencies responded to the disaster, including the Chemical Safety and Hazard Investigation Board ("CSB" or "the Board"). Established by the Clean Air Act Amendments of 1990 and modeled after the National Transportation Safety Board ("NTSB"), the CSB serves a public safety mission by investigating accidental releases of hazardous substances into the ambient air and by reporting to the public its findings and recommendations for preventing and minimizing the risk of industrial chemical accidents.

As part of its investigation into the incident at the Macondo well, the CSB issued five administrative subpoenas to Transocean. The subpoenas sought answers to interrogatories and the production of relevant records, including documents generated by Transocean's own internal investigation. Transocean took the position that the CSB lacked authority to investigate the incident, and it therefore failed to comply fully with the CSB's subpoenas.

The United States filed a petition on behalf of the CSB to enforce the administrative subpoenas, while Transocean moved to quash them and to dismiss the petition. Transocean argued that the CSB was not authorized to conduct an investigation because, *inter alia*, the incident was a marine oil spill over which the CSB lacks jurisdiction, and the incident did not occur on a stationary source.

The district court denied Transocean's motion and ordered enforcement of the subpoenas. The district court held that the CSB was investigating only the release of airborne gases from the blowout and explosion and was not investigating the subsequent oil spill from the well. The court further [—3—] determined that the CSB would lack authority to investigate an incident involving a marine oil spill only if the NTSB was authorized to investigate. The court held that the NTSB was not authorized to investigate this incident, however, because the incident was located fifty miles off the coast of the United States on the Outer Continental Shelf and did not involve a "vessel of the United States," and because the incident was not transportation related. The court also concluded that the *Deepwater Horizon* and its subsea riser comprised a drilling installation that satisfied the statutory requirement of a "stationary source" from which the accidental release of gases the CSB was authorized to investigate.

The district court therefore held that the CSB had authority to investigate the incident and to issue the administrative subpoenas. Transocean now appeals.

II.

Administrative subpoenas issued in aid of an investigation will generally be enforced judicially if "(1) the subpoena is within the statutory authority of the agency; (2) the information sought is reasonably relevant to the inquiry; and (3) the demand is not unreasonably broad or burdensome." *See Burlington N. R. Co. v. Office of Inspector Gen., R.R. Ret. Bd.*, 983 F.2d 631, 638 (5th Cir. 1993); *see also United States v. Powell*, 379 U.S. 48, 57-58, 85 S. Ct. 248, 255 (1964) (holding that enforcement of administrative subpoenas requires a showing "that the investigation will be conducted pursuant to a legitimate purpose, that the inquiry may be relevant to the purpose, that the information sought is not already within the [agency's] possession, and that the administrative steps required by [statute] have been followed"). The Government bears the initial burden to show that these criteria have been met, although the burden to make a prima facie case is "minimal." *United States v. Tex. Heart Inst.*, 755 F.2d 469, 474 (5th Cir. 1985), *overruled on other grounds by United States v. Barrett*, 837 F.2d 1341 (5th Cir. 1988) (en banc). Once the [—4—] Government has made a prima facie case, the burden of going forward shifts to the party opposing the subpoenas. *Id.*

In this case, Transocean focuses its arguments on appeal on the authority of the CSB to issue the subpoenas. We review the district court's factual findings underlying its decision on this issue for clear error and its conclusions of law de novo. *Burlington*, 983 F.2d at 638, 641.

III.

Transocean contends that the CSB had no authority to issue the administrative subpoenas because the CSB lacked jurisdiction to investigate the incident at the Macondo well. An administrative agency's authority is necessarily derived from the statute it administers and may not be exercised in a manner that is inconsistent with the administrative structure that Congress has enacted. *See FDA v. Brown & Williamson Tobacco Corp.*, 529 U.S. 120, 125, 120 S. Ct. 1291, 1297 (2000); *see also Texas v. United States*, 497 F.3d 491, 500-01 (5th Cir. 2007). Here, as noted above, the CSB is an independent federal investigative agency established by the Clean Air Act Amendments of 1990. *See* Pub. L. No. 101-549, Title III, sec. 301, 104 Stat. 2399 (Nov. 15, 1990). The Board is authorized to "investigate (or cause to be investigated), determine and report to the public in writing the facts, conditions, and circumstances and the cause or probable cause of any accidental release resulting in a fatality, serious injury or substantial property damages." 42 U.S.C. § 7412(r)(6)(C)(i). An "accidental release" is "an unanticipated emission of a regulated substance or other extremely hazardous substance into the ambient air from a stationary source." § 7412(r)(2)(A). A "stationary source" is defined as "any buildings, structures, equipment, installations or substance emitting stationary activities (i) which belong to the same industrial group, (ii) which are located on one or more contiguous properties, (iii) which are under the control of the same person (or persons [—5—] under common control), and (iv) from which an accidental release may occur." § 7412(r)(2)(C).

A.

Transocean argues first that the CSB lacked jurisdiction to investigate the incident at the Macondo well because the *Deepwater Horizon* is not a "stationary source" as that term is contemplated by the statute. Transocean reasons that because the word "stationary" in the term "stationary source" is not defined, the word must be construed as commonly understood, which Transocean contends means a fixed and unchanging object rather than something that is moveable. Transocean argues that the *Deepwater Horizon* was not only moveable but also was a "vessel in navigation." It reasons, therefore, that the drilling unit could not be a stationary source. We disagree with Transocean's reasoning.

Transocean is correct that similar mobile offshore drilling units and other structures, and even the *Deepwater Horizon* itself, have been held to be vessels under maritime law. *See, e.g., Demette v. Falcon Drilling Co.*, 280 F.3d 492, 498-99 (5th Cir. 2002), *overruled in part on other grounds by Grand Isle Shipyard, Inc. v. Seacor Marine, LLC*, 589 F.3d 778 (5th Cir. 2009) (en banc). For example, in *Demette*, we noted that "special-purpose moveable drilling rigs, including jack-up rigs, are vessels within the meaning of admiralty law." *Demette*, 280 F.3d at 498 n.18. It is also well-established that "special-purpose structures" may remain vessels under the Jones Act while engaged in drilling operations. *See, e.g., Offshore Co. v. Robison*, 266 F.2d 769, 776 (5th Cir. 1959). And under Supreme Court precedent a "watercraft practically capable of maritime transportation" is considered to be a "vessel" under the Longshore and Harbor Workers' Compensation Act regardless of its purpose or state of transit at a particular moment. *Stewart v. Dutra Constr. Co.*, 543 U.S. 481, 497, 125 S. Ct. 1118, 1129 (2005). Indeed, the Supreme Court held that a [—6—] watercraft does not "pass in and out of Jones Act coverage depending on whether it was moving at the time of the accident." *Id.* at 495-96, 125 S. Ct. at 1128. Based on the foregoing authority, the district court in the multi-district litigation spawned from the Macondo well incident held that the *Deepwater Horizon* was a vessel under general maritime law. *See In re Oil Spill by the Oil Rig "DEEPWATER HORIZON" in the Gulf of Mexico, on April 20, 2010*, 808 F. Supp. 2d 943, 950 (E.D. La. 2011); *see also In re Deepwater Horizon*, 745 F.3d 157, 164, 2 Adm. R. 171, 174 (5th Cir. 2014) (noting the vessel status of the drilling unit).

Nevertheless, in this case we are not dealing with the application of, or definitions under, the Jones Act and general maritime law. The fact that the *Deepwater Horizon* may be a vessel for purposes of maritime law does not answer the question whether it meets the specific statutory definition of a "stationary source" under the Clean Air Act.

The phrase "stationary source" is expressly defined by the Clean Air Act. When Congress provides a specific definition of a term, we must accept that meaning and limit our analysis to the prescribed definition. *See Stenberg v. Carhart*, 530 U.S. 914, 942, 120 S. Ct. 2597, 2615 (2000) ("When a statute includes an explicit definition, we must follow that definition, even if it varies from that term's ordinary meaning."); *cf. Hamilton v. United Healthcare of La., Inc.*, 310 F.3d 385, 391 (5th Cir. 2002) ("A fundamental canon of statutory construction instructs that *in the absence of a statutory definition*, we give terms their ordinary meaning." (emphasis added)); *see also United States v. Crittenden*, 372 F.3d 706, 711 (5th Cir. 2004) (Dennis, J., concurring in part and dissenting in part) ("[W]hen context dictates that a term has a particular definition, that definition will apply instead of the plain meaning of the term."). We therefore must apply the definition of "stationary source" provided within § 7412(r)(2)(C). [—7—]

We find nothing within the definition of "stationary source" found in § 7412(r)(2)(C) that precludes a vessel from satisfying the statutory requirements for a stationary source. Indeed, counsel for Transocean conceded during oral argument that a vessel could be stationary, but he argued that the drilling unit here was in constant motion over the well because of the unit's stabilizing thrusters. The amicus makes the same argument, contending that under Coast Guard regulations the *Deepwater Horizon* was a vessel considered to be underway.

Of course, the whole point of the stabilizing thrusters is to keep the drilling unit largely stationary over the well so that it can perform its drilling operation, a "stationary activity." *See* § 7412r(2)(c). Regardless whether the unit is considered to be underway, the *Deepwater Horizon* was "dynamically-positioned" and "employed a satellite global positioning device and complex thruster technology *to stabilize itself.*" *In re Oil Spill by the Oil Rig "DEEPWATER HORIZON" in the Gulf of Mexico, on April 20, 2010*, 808 F. Supp. 2d 943, 950 (E.D. La. 2011) (emphasis added). Its eight directional thrusters were used to keep the rig in place over the wellhead during drilling. National Commission on the BP Deepwater Horizon Oil Spill and Offshore Drilling, Macondo: The Gulf Oil Disaster, *Chief Counsel's Report* 29 (2011), available at http://www.eoearth.org/files/164401_164500/1 64423/full.pdf (hereinafter "Chief Counsel's Report").

It is true that the *Deepwater Horizon* was capable of propulsion. However, this propulsion ability is an advancement in drilling technology that has allowed these units to arrive and remain at different drilling locations, making it easier for the oil and gas industry to drill for oil in deeper water. *See* Chief Counsel's report at 12. This is because "[i]n water depths greater than about 1,000 feet, it is increasingly impractical to conduct production operations from structures that are supported by the ocean floor, and floating facilities [—8—] and subsea production systems dominate." *Id.* at 7. This economic advantage to the oil and gas industry does not mean, however, that the activity of the mobile drilling units cannot come under the CSB's jurisdiction as a stationary source if other statutory conditions are met, even though the drilling unit is also a vessel. "Once moved onto location, a [dynamically positioned] rig holds itself in place above a drilling location using satellite positioning technology and directional thrusters." *Id.* at 12-13; *see also id.* at 26 ("Dynamically positioned MODUs utilize dynamic satellite positioning technology connected to powerful directional thrusters to maintain themselves in place over a subsea wellhead."). In this case, the *Deepwater Horizon* was deployed to the Macondo well site in February 2010 and had remained in place at the site for approximately two months.[1] *See id.* [—9—]

---

[1] The amicus urges that the *Deepwater Horizon* could not be a stationary source because under Coast Guard regulations it is considered to be a vessel "underway" and not "on location." It posits that if a vessel is not "on location" it cannot also be a "stationary source." In support of this argument the amicus relies on a Coast Guard investigation report of the *Deepwater Horizon* incident that discussed the status of the drilling unit. *See* U.S. Coast Guard, *Report of Investigation into the Circumstances Surrounding the Explosion, Fire,*

The Government urges, and the district court essentially found, that the Macondo drilling installation as a whole was a stationary source. We agree. At the time of the blowout and explosion the drilling operations occurred at a fixed, specific point in the Gulf of Mexico—the Macondo lease site—and the *Deepwater Horizon* was physically connected (though not anchored) at that site and maintained a fixed position. The drilling installation as a whole included the drilling unit, along with its casing, wellhead, riser, and related apparatus. The blowout preventer alone was more than five stories tall and weighed more than 300 tons sitting atop the wellhead on the ocean floor. Chief Counsel's Report at 29-30. The *Deepwater Horizon* was then connected to the wellhead by 5000 feet of drill pipe. *See In re Oil Spill by the Oil Rig "DEEPWATER HORIZON,"* 808 F. Supp. 2d at 950. As noted above, a stationary source includes "*any* buildings, structures, equipment, installations or substance

Sinking, and Loss of Eleven Crew Members Aboard the MOBILE OFFSHORE DRILLING UNIT DEEPWATER HORIZON in the Gulf of Mexico April 20–22, 2010, at I-10, available at https://www.hsdl.org/?view&did=6700 (hereinafter "Coast Guard Report"). The terms "on location" and "underway" have specific statutory definitions, however, that do not affect whether the vessel may be a "stationary source" for purposes of the Clean Air Act. For example, "on location" means merely that the drilling unit is anchored. *See* 46 C.F.R. § 10.107 ("On location means that a mobile offshore drilling unit is bottom bearing or moored with anchors placed in the drilling configuration."). Because the *Deepwater Horizon* was a dynamically positioned, anchor-less MODU, it could not satisfy the regulatory definition of "on location" and was therefore considered to be "underway." *See* Coast Guard Report at I-5. The Coast Guard Report notes that whether a vessel is "on location" or "underway" determines the navigation rules that the vessel must follow, such as for minimum manning and operational requirements. *See id.* at I-5. That status alone does not indicate whether the vessel is a "stationary source" because a vessel may be "underway" but not "making way." *Id.* at I-5-6. The Coast Guard Report specifically recognizes that even though a vessel does not meet the statutory definition for being "on location," it may nevertheless be "essentially maintaining a fixed position" through the use of its dynamic positioning system. *Id.* at I-6. That was the case with the *Deepwater Horizon.*

emitting stationary activities." § 7412(r)(2)(C) (emphasis added). The drilling installation here satisfied this definition.[2]

Transocean raises a question in its reply brief about the terms of the stationary source definition, namely that the source "belong to the same industrial group," be "located on one or more contiguous properties," be "under the control of the same person," and be something "from which an accidental release may occur." § 7412(r)(2)(C). Transocean has never, in the district court, or its initial brief, raised this argument. Because we do not consider arguments raised for the first time in a reply brief, we decline to address this issue. *See DePree v. Saunders*, 588 F.3d 282, 290 (5th Cir. 2009). [—10—]

B.

Transocean next argues that the CSB lacked jurisdiction to investigate the Macondo well incident because Congress specifically denied the CSB authority over this type of incident. Its argument is essentially two-fold: first, it contends that the Macondo well incident was a marine oil spill, and the Clean Air Act specifically precludes the CSB from investigating all marine oil spills; second, it contends that even if the statute does not preclude the CSB from investigating all marine oil spills, the CSB could not investigate this incident because the NTSB had jurisdiction to investigate.

Transocean's argument is based on the following provision of the Clean Air Act:

> The Board shall coordinate its activities with investigations and studies conducted by other agencies of the United States having a responsibility to protect public health and safety. The Board shall enter into a memorandum of understanding with the National

Transportation Safety Board to assure coordination of functions and to limit duplication of activities which shall designate the National Transportation Safety Board as the lead agency for the investigation of releases which are transportation related. *The Board shall not be authorized to investigate marine oil spills, which the National Transportation Safety Board is authorized to investigate.* The Board shall enter into a memorandum of understanding with the Occupational Safety and Health Administration so as to limit duplication of activities. In no event shall the Board forego an investigation where an accidental release causes a fatality or serious injury among the general public, or had the potential to cause substantial property damage or a number of deaths or injuries among the general public.

§ 7412(r)(6)(E) (emphasis added). [—11—]

Transocean argues that the above italicized language shows that the CSB is not authorized to investigate marine oil spills and that, instead, the NTSB is authorized to investigate all of those incidents.[3]

The district court held that the marine oil spill exclusion did not apply to the CSB's investigation of the Macondo well incident because the CSB was not investigating the marine oil spill associated with the disaster but rather was investigating the release of gases and the explosion that preceded the release of oil. We agree with the district court's conclusion.[4]

---

[2] Again, that the drilling unit itself was capable of propulsion and could and did use its thrusters to counter-act wave activity in order to remain in place over the well does not negate the fact that the drilling operation of the *Deepwater Horizon* was, at the very least, a "stationary activity." *See* § 7412(r)(2)(C).

---

[3] Transocean refers to the emphasized language as the "marine oil spill exclusion." For ease of reference we use the same terminology. We also refer to the clause beginning with the word "which" as the "comma-*which*" clause.

[4] The Coast Guard Report found as follows:

As the well control incident unfolded, an uncontrolled volume of gas flowed up from the wellhead to the MODU and onto the Drill Floor and Main Deck. Gas samples collected by Woods Hole Oceanographic Institute on July 27, 2010 show that the composition of the uncontrolled gas discharged from the

Although Transocean argues that the primary environmental disaster resulting from the Macondo well incident was the massive oil spill, it also concedes in its brief that the blowout, explosion, and fire, followed by the collapse of the *Deepwater Horizon*, involved the release of airborne gases. That release was the triggering of the CSB's authority to investigate. *See* § 7412(r)(2)(A) (authorizing CSB investigations of accidental releases, which are defined as "unanticipated emissions[s] . . . into the ambient air"). Transocean argues, however, that because the CSB's jurisdiction always depends on a release of gases, the marine oil spill exclusion (1) necessarily [—12—] contemplates an accidental release that would otherwise be within the CSB's jurisdiction but is merely incidental to a marine event, and (2) expressly excludes that event from CSB's investigatory authority. A contrary conclusion, Transocean argues, would render the marine oil spill exclusion surplusage. Transocean's argument assumes, however, that the CSB may not investigate *any* release of gases associated with a marine oil spill. As we explain, we disagree.

Transocean's argument is textual, and it is primarily based on the statutory provision noted above that the CSB "shall not be authorized to investigate marine oil spills, which the National Transportation Safety Board is authorized to investigate." *See* § 7412(r)(6)(E). According to Transocean's reading of that sentence, the statute precludes the CSB from investigating *all* marine oil spills insofar as the NTSB has jurisdiction over those occurrences.

---

well was primarily methane (69.9%), with lesser amounts of ethane (6.9%) and propane (4.5%). The remainder of the gas consisted of a mixture of various weight hydrocarbons. Several minutes after the start of the release of gas from the wellhead, a gas cloud within the flammable range formed over large areas on several decks. The explosions likely occurred when gas from this cloud encountered one or more ignition sources on the Drill Floor or elsewhere on the MODU.

Coast Guard Report, 5-6.

We agree with the district court, however, that the CSB is not precluded from investigating all marine oil spills, but rather only those "spills, which" the NTSB may investigate. In other words, the CSB may be precluded from investigating those marine-related incidents that the NTSB is authorized to investigate. This interpretation of the statute reads "which" to mean "that," and it comports with the statutory scheme as a whole.

Transocean contends, however, that based on the rules of grammar and punctuation the word "which" preceded by a comma creates a nonrestrictive, descriptive clause so that the declarative portion of the sentence in § 7412(r)(6)(E)—precluding investigation of marine oil spills—is controlling. *See, e.g.,* William Strunk, Jr. & E.B. White, *The Elements of Style* 3-4 (3d ed. 1979) (hereinafter "Strunk & White") (explaining that nonrestrictive clauses introduced by "which" add nonessential parenthetic information and are set off by commas). If we were reading the sentence in isolation we might agree. But while the rules of grammar are not irrelevant, we should not "be guided by a [—13—] single sentence or member of a sentence;" rather, we must "look to the provisions of the whole law, and to its object and policy." *U.S. Nat'l Bank of Oregon v. Indep. Ins. Agents of Am., Inc.,* 508 U.S. 439, 455, 113 S. Ct. 2173, 2182 (1993) (internal quotation marks and citation omitted); *cf. United States v. Flora,* 362 U.S. 145, 149, 80 S. Ct. 630, 633 (1960) (noting that a court "does not review congressional enactments as a panel of grammarians").

We note first that reading the comma-*which* clause to mean "that" is consistent with subsection (E) as a whole and the subsection's other uses of the word "which." In addition to the comma-*which*, the statute twice uses the word "which" in the previous sentence, reading thusly: "The Board shall enter into a memorandum of understanding with the National Transportation Safety Board to assure coordination of functions and to limit duplication of activities *which* shall designate the National Transportation Safety Board as the lead agency for the investigation of releases *which* are transportation related." § 7412(r)(6)(E) (emphasis added). The first "which" in this sentence refers to the "memorandum of understanding" while the second "which" refers to "releases." It is clear that each "which" in this sentence should be read as "that" because the clauses are restrictive, i.e. they give essential meaning about the preceding nouns (the "memorandum of understanding" and the "releases"). Although Congress is presumed to know the rules of grammar, *see United States v. Goldenberg*, 168 U.S. 102-03, 18 S. Ct. 3, 4 (1897), this grammatical oversight is understandable, as "[u]sing *which* for *that* is perhaps the most common blunder with these words." Bryan A. Garner, *Garner's Dictionary of Legal Usage* 889 (3d ed. 2011); *see also* Strunk & White at 59 ("The use of *which* for *that* is common in written and spoken language.").

If we read the first two uses of "which" in subsection (E) to mean "that," it would be natural to construe the comma-*which* to also mean "that." *See Powerex Corp. v. Reliant Energy Servs., Inc.*, 551 U.S. 224, 232, 127 S. Ct. 2411, [—14—] 2417 (2007) ("[I]dentical words and phrases within the same statute should normally be given the same meaning."); *see also U.S. Nat'l Bank of Oregon*, 508 U.S. at 460, 113 S. Ct. at 2185. Of course, the difference between the first two uses of the word "which" in subsection (E) and the comma-*which* clause is the presence of the comma, and in isolation the comma could be significant. But "a purported plain-meaning analysis based only on punctuation is necessarily incomplete and runs the risk of distorting a statute's true meaning." *Id.* at 454, 113 S. Ct. at 2182; *see Costanzo v. Tillinghast*, 287 U.S. 341, 344, 53 S. Ct. 152, 153 (1932) ("It has often been said that punctuation is not decisive of the construction of a statute."). Construing the words in context, as we must, we strive to "interpret the statute 'as a symmetrical and coherent regulatory scheme.'" *Brown & Williamson Tobacco Corp.*, 529 U.S. at 133, 120 S. Ct. at 1301 (citation omitted). Here, we must consider the "comma-*which*" clause along with the entire provision as part of "'a holistic endeavor.'" *U.S. Nat'l Bank of Oregon*, 508

U.S. at 455, 113 S. Ct. at 2182 (citation omitted). We will "'disregard the punctuation, or repunctuate, if need be, to render the true meaning of the statute.'" *Id.* at 462, 113 S. Ct. at 2186 (citation omitted).

Subsection (E) contemplates that the CSB is not the only government agency charged with a public safety mission and may not be the only investigating agency; indeed, it expressly directs the CSB to "coordinate its activities with investigations and studies by other agencies" with responsibility to protect public health and safety. § 7412(r)(6)(E). Even more specifically, the statute directs the CSB to "enter into a memorandum of understanding" with the NTSB in order to coordinate activities, limit duplication of efforts, and designate the NTSB as the lead agency if an accidental release is transportation related. *Id.* We agree with the district court that this provision must mean there is a category of marine oil spills that are non-transportation related and over which the NTSB lacks exclusive authority. If the comma-[—15—] *which* clause of the marine oil spill exclusion simply precluded the CSB from investigating all marine oil spill incidents there would be no need for the requirement that CSB coordinate with the NTSB or other government agencies to avoid duplication of efforts. In context, the structure of the statute, including the prior uses of the word "which," indicates an intent that the comma-*which* clause was not meant to be non-restrictive.

Moreover, the statute expressly directs the CSB to investigate any time an accidental release causes a fatality or serious injury to the general public. *See id.* ("*In no event shall the Board forego an investigation* where an accidental release causes a fatality or serious injury among the general public, or had the potential to cause substantial property damage or a number of deaths or injuries among the general public." (emphasis added)). This must mean that for especially serious incidents involving either grave injury or the risk of injury, including marine oil spills, the CSB could have concurrent investigative authority with other agencies.[5] And again, the CSB would be required to coordinate its efforts with any other agencies. This provision adds further support to the conclusion that the marine oil spill exclusion is not the all-encompassing prohibition that Transocean urges.

We believe that looking at the full text of the statute, rather than one isolated clause, along with the statute's structure and its public safety purpose shows that the comma-*which* clause was not intended to preclude the CSB from investigating all incidents involving marine oil spills. *See U.S. Nat'l Bank of* [—16—] *Oregon*, 508 U.S. at 455, 113 S. Ct. at 2182 (eschewing isolated words or sentences in favor of "a statute's full text, language as well as punctuation, structure, and subject matter"). This reading of the statute best comports with the overall regulatory scheme. *See Brown & Williamson Tobacco Corp.*, 529 U.S. at 133, 120 S. Ct. at 1301; *see also U.S. Nat'l Bank of Oregon*, 508 U.S. at 461 n.10, 113 S. Ct. at 2186 n.10 (searching for "the best reading of the Act, despite the punctuation marks"). We conclude, therefore, that the statute did not categorically preclude the CSB from investigating all incidents that happen to include a marine oil spill.

Transocean contends that even if the CSB could otherwise investigate the incident at the Macondo well, it was precluded from doing so in this case because the NTSB was authorized to investigate. Transocean relies solely on 49 U.S.C. § 1131(a)(1)(F), which grants the NTSB authority to investigate, *inter alia*, "catastrophic" accidents that are "related to the transportation of individuals or property." It asserts that the Macondo well incident was

catastrophic and that the disaster was related to transportation because the *Deepwater Horizon* was a vessel in navigation.

However, when the blowout occurred on April 20, 2010, the *Deepwater Horizon* was dynamically positioned and physically attached to the seabed, having been on site and engaged in drilling operations for a number of months. The district court held that this fact was crucial to the determination that the incident was not transportation related. Transocean cites no contrary authority. Merely because a disaster involves a vessel does not mean that the disaster was necessarily related to transportation. Although the drilling unit may have been capable of transportation, it was not involved in transporting either individuals or property at the time of the blowout, explosion, and fire. *See* § 1131(a)(1)(F). In other words, although the *Deepwater Horizon* possessed characteristics associated with transportation, those characteristics played no [—17—] role in the disaster, and the accident was not related to transportation. We agree with the district court that § 1131(a)(1)(F) is inapplicable and that the NTSB lacked jurisdiction to investigate the incident under that provision, meaning that the CSB was authorized to act.

IV.

For the reasons stated above, we conclude that the CSB had jurisdiction to investigate the incident at the Macondo well and to issue the administrative subpoenas. The district court's judgment ordering enforcement of the subpoenas is therefore AFFIRMED.

(Reporter's Note: Dissenting opinion on p. 314).

---

[5] Transocean argues that this provision of subsection (E) is inapplicable here because the Macondo well incident was incapable of causing death or injury to members of the general public insofar as the disaster occurred fifty miles off the coast of the United States. First, this argument is inapposite to whether the CSB is precluded from investigating all marine oil spills in the first place. Second, the offshore location of the disaster does not preclude the *potential* for injury to persons on shore since it cannot be denied that airborne hazardous substances could migrate and cause injury on land.

[—18—] JONES, Circuit Judge, dissenting:

I respectfully disagree with the majority opinion, which assists the United States Chemical Safety Board ("CSB") in expanding its jurisdiction into novel territory disallowed by Congress. This is the first time, in twenty years after CSB was ordained, that the agency has sought to investigate in connection with an offshore oil spill.[1] The majority's interpretation of the Clean Air Act disregards the plain meaning of words and grammar and the most fundamental maritime concept, which is the definition of a vessel. To summarize my view: the Mobile Offshore Drilling Unit Deepwater Horizon was a vessel, not a "stationary source" pursuant to 42 U.S.C. § 7412(r)(2)(C), and the Macondo Well blowout caused a "marine oil spill," 42 U.S.C. § 7412(r)(6)(E), which excluded the blowout from CSB jurisdiction either *in toto* or because the NTSB was empowered to investigate.

Because the majority opinion aptly describes the background of this controversy, only a bit need be repeated here. Transocean objects to administrative subpoenas served by CSB when the agency instituted an investigation following the Deepwater Horizon oil spill disaster. The standard for challenging an administrative subpoena is strict: courts may only interfere with the process in a limited number of circumstances, one of which arises when the agency plainly lacks jurisdiction. *See Burlington N. R. Co. v. Office of Inspector Gen., R.R. Ret. Bd.*, 983 F.2d 631, 638 (5th Cir. 1993); *see also United States v. Powell*, 379 U.S. 48, 57–58, 85 S. Ct. 248, 255 (1964). CSB was created as a Clean Air Act counterpart to the National Traffic Safety Board ("NTSB") and charged with investigating unanticipated releases of hazardous substances into the ambient air from "stationary sources." 42 U.S.C. § 7412(r)(2)(C) (defining the term "accidental release" found in 42 U.S.C. [—19—] § 7412(r)(6)(C)(i)). The term "stationary sources," includes "any buildings, structures, equipment, installations or substance emitting stationary activities. . . ." 42 U.S.C. § 7412(r)(2)(C). The Board may follow up an

investigation by recommending regulatory measures to avert future releases into the air. NTSB, in contrast, investigates "transportation-related" aviation, highway, rail, marine or pipeline accidents and also makes regulatory recommendations to improve safety. 49 U.S.C. § 1131(a)(1)(F). Not only CSB and NTSB, but numerous other agencies either routinely or at special request investigate accidents with significant public impact. As a result, the statute that created CSB requires this agency to cooperate with or take a second seat to such agencies:

> The Board shall coordinate its activities with investigations and studies conducted by other agencies of the United States having a responsibility to protect public health and safety. The Board shall enter into a memorandum of understanding with the National Transportation Safety Board to assure coordination of functions and to limit duplication of activities which shall designate the National Transportation Safety Board as the lead agency for the investigation of releases which are transportation related. The Board shall not be authorized to investigate marine oil spills, which the National Transportation Safety Board is authorized to investigate. The Board shall enter into a memorandum of understanding with the Occupational Safety and Health Administration so as to limit duplication of activities. In no event shall the Board forego an investigation where an accidental release causes a fatality or serious injury among the general public, or had the potential to cause substantial property damage or a number of deaths or injuries among the general public.

42 U.S.C. § 7412(r)(6)(E).

Under this provision, if the Deepwater Horizon was not a stationary source, CSB lacked the authority to investigate. Likewise, if the disaster was a marine oil spill, or by even the majority's construction a marine oil spill that [—20—] NTSB was authorized to investigate, CSB lacks authority. I will discuss

---

[1] *Inside OSHA*, Vol. 17, No. 13, at 6 (June 29, 2010).

each of these limits on CSB's authority in turn.

1. Can a vessel be a "stationary source"?

This question seems to answer itself. A "vessel," as defined in federal law, is a device capable of providing transportation on water. 1 U.S.C. § 3; *Stewart v. Dutra Construction Co.*, 543 U.S. 481, 495, 125 S. Ct. 1118, 1128 (2005). "Stationary" means "fixed in a station, course or mode; unchanging, stable, static." Webster's Third New International Dictionary 2229 (1986). Not only does "stationary" modify all of the following terms, but the following illustrations of "stationary sources" are inherently fixed and immobile ("buildings, structures, equipment, installations . . ."). A vessel capable of transportation is not comparable to these illustrated sources and cannot be a stationary source of emissions. To so conclude erases the line between stationary and mobile sources.

But the majority determines otherwise. First, the majority opinion acknowledges that the Deepwater Horizon is a vessel according to Coast Guard regulations, Supreme Court authority, longstanding case law in this circuit, and multiple decisions relating to this oil spill disaster. However, the majority contends, what is good law for maritime purposes does not govern the Clean Air Act's statutory definition. Alternatively, the majority holds, the Deepwater Horizon was in fact "stationary" when the blowout and oil spill occurred, because its dynamic positioning devices kept the unit essentially in place without anchors securing it to the ocean floor while it engaged in drilling operations. Finally, the majority posits that the "Macondo drilling installation as a whole," allegedly encompassing the drill string, riser, blowout preventer, wellhead and casing, all of which stretch over a mile down and into the Outer Continental Shelf seabed, maintained a stationary position. [—21—]

The majority's fundamental error lies in distorting "stationary" from its ordinary meaning, as required by the tools of statutory interpretation, *Castro v. Collecto, Inc.*, 634 F.3d 779, 786 (5th Cir. 2011). The Deepwater

Horizon was a "vessel" from a common sense standpoint. Technically, it was a "dynamically-positioned semi-submersible drilling vessel" that was afloat and under movement at the time of the blowout. *See In re Oil Spill by the Oil Rig Deepwater Horizon in the Gulf of Mexico, on April 20, 2010*, 808 F. Supp. 2d 943, 950 (E.D. La. 2011), *aff'd sub nom. In re Deepwater Horizon*, 745 F.3d 157, 2 Adm. R. 171 (5th Cir. 2014). It navigated, transported personnel and equipment, and continued navigating in order to hold its position in the sea against currents and waves. That it was able to employ advanced technology to accomplish its purpose, rather than sails or rudders, does not detract from its status as a vessel; hence, its status as a "mobile" offshore drilling unit. At all times, it had a navigational crew in addition to a drilling crew. The issue here is not so much whether the Clean Air Act definition must slavishly follow the course of maritime law, but also whether calling this "mobile" offshore drilling a "vessel" conflicts with the ordinary meaning of a "stationary source."

Virtually every opinion of this court relating to the Deepwater Horizon oil spill disaster has referred to the MODU as a "vessel,"[2] and in so doing we have followed a path charted in this court for decades. *See, e.g., Trico Marine Operators, Inc. v. Falcon Drilling Co.*, 116 F.3d 159, 161 (5th Cir. 1997); *Dougherty v. Santa Fe Marine, Inc.*, 698 F.2d 232, 234 (5th Cir. 1983); *Offshore Co. v. Robison*, 266 F.2d 769, 779 (5th Cir. 1959). Our decisions reflect how [—22—] maritime activities have evolved in the last fifty years to include new and ever-more-sophisticated watercraft. The Supreme Court has also defined "vessels" expansively as "any watercraft practically capable of maritime transportation." *Stewart v. Dutra Constr. Co.*, 543 U.S. 481, 497, 125 S. Ct. 1118, 1128 (2005). Also compelling is the Coast Guard's responsibility for regulating mobile offshore drilling units, which recently led it to conclude

---

[2] *See, e.g., In re Deepwater Horizon*, 753 F.3d 570, 571, 2 Adm. R. 233, 233 (5th Cir. 2014); *In re Deepwater Horizon*, 745 F.3d 157, 164, 2 Adm. R. 171, 174 (5th Cir. 2014); *In re Deepwater Horizon*, 739 F.3d 790, 796, 2 Adm. R. 140, 140 (5th Cir. 2014) (labeling the MODU as a vessel).

that if anything, their status as vessels should be fortified. Memorandum from S.D. Poulin, U.S. Coast Guard, to CG-5, Potential Legal Issues Associated With Vessels Employing Dynamic Positioning Systems 10 (Feb. 11, 2011). Why, in the face of ordinary meaning and this body of consistent authority, should a court be able to hold that the Deepwater Horizon, although a "vessel," was a "stationary source"? This is like holding a pig is a pony. The language of the statute is broad but it isn't limitless. Either "stationary" means something related to immobility, or judges are making up a new meaning.

The majority's other reasons for holding that the Deepwater Horizon was a "stationary source" also defy common sense. The majority's description of the sophisticated dynamic positioning system used by Mobile Offshore Drilling Units like the Deepwater Horizon is flawed and, worse, leads to the possibility that CSB jurisdiction will turn on fact-specific determinations of "stationary" versus "mobile" sources. Factually, it is true that the thrusters operated by the MODU's navigational crew kept the unit positioned substantially over the wellhead, but the unit continues at all times to move with the wave motions. Essentially, the thrusters permit the unit to tread water. Anyone treading water, however, is constantly in motion, and so was the Deepwater Horizon. Likewise, a helicopter may hover in place over the ground, but it is always in motion, and I suppose even CSB would not contend it is a "stationary source."

Even more unfortunate is the resort to fact-specific reasoning to determine that this vessel is a "stationary source." Since the statute draws a [—23—] dichotomy between the CSB's responsibility for "stationary source" accidental air releases and NTSB's jurisdiction over "transportation-related" disasters, the CSB's aggressive attempt to blur the dichotomy is at odds with the statute itself. (As will be seen, CSB is horning into the primary jurisdiction of NTSB by urging this court to narrow NTSB's scope as well.) Of course, the statute contemplates splitting duties between NTSB and CSB in appropriate cases, and in such cases requiring CSB to yield to NTSB, but one can easily envision

overlaps without CSB's having to mutilate the definition of "stationary." For instance, if a chemical tank exploded at a rail yard and emitted hazardous fumes, there could be a question whether the cause was transportation-related or due to a stationary source nearby. Similarly, toxic substances or fuel used in connection with aircraft and aircraft maintenance might ignite at an aviation center, emitting hazardous air pollutants. The cause of either accident could be "stationary" or "transportation-related." In the Deepwater Horizon disaster, however, CSB contends that the vessel itself was the "stationary source" because it was dynamically positioned. Henceforth, the same argument could result in fully overlapping CSB/NTSB authority whenever a vehicle, aircraft, or vessel happens to be temporarily moored at the time of an unanticipated toxic air emission.

The majority's final rationale for calling this mobile offshore drilling unit a "stationary source" is to embed it in an "installation as a whole" encompassing the Macondo well and the well's casing[3] and wellhead,[4] which [—24—] are located underneath or at the level of the seabed. This bottom-up logic is erroneous for two reasons.

First, common sense tells us that the five thousand feet of drill string, plus riser and blowout preventer leading from the MODU to the well hardly created a stationary island 50 miles off the United States coast in the Gulf of Mexico. The MODU Deepwater Horizon and its appurtenances are connected to the seabed.[5] But it is quite inconsistent to say

---

[3] *Casing*, SCHLUMBERGER OILFIELD GLOSSARY, (last visited Sept. 16, 2014), http://www.glossary.oilfield.slb.com/en/Terms/c/casing.aspx ("Large-diameter pipe lowered into an openhole and cemented in place.").

[4] *Wellhead*, SCHLUMBERGER OILFIELD GLOSSARY, (last visited Sept. 16, 2014), http://www.glossary.oilfield.slb.com/en/Terms/w/wellhead.aspx ("The system of spools, valves and assorted adapters that provide pressure control of a production well.").

[5] The majority's bottom-up logic is hard to square with a recent opinion of this Court that referred to the blowout preventer and riser as "appurtenances" of the vessel Deepwater Horizon,

that the "installation" is stationary when the only reason for its being stationary is that the vessel uses dynamic positioning thrusters and is constantly in motion to maintain stability over the wellhead. Broadening the term "installation" to denominate the Macondo well and the Deepwater Horizon a "stationary source" is nothing more than rhetorical legerdemain designed to obfuscate the limits on CSB's jurisdiction.

Second, both statutory law and well settled case law have distinguished between fixed and mobile drilling platforms and offshore devices for decades. The Outer Continental Shelf Lands Act distinguishes between "artificial islands" and vessels in order to demarcate between the application of federal or state law and admiralty law. *See* 43 U.S.C. § 1333(1) (distinguishing between artificial islands subject to the choice of law provisions of 43 § 1333(2)(A) and vessels not subject to such provisions); *see also Herb's Welding, Inc. v. Gray*, 470 U.S. 414, 421–23, 105 S. Ct. 1421, 1426–27 (1985) (outlining the division between artificial islands subject to "borrowed state [—25—] law" and other areas subject to maritime law). Artificial islands are drilling or production platforms attached to the seabed in some way and thus fully immobile, while other special purpose structures "such as jack-up rigs, submersible drilling barges, derrick barges, spud barges, and others are vessels as a matter of law." *Manuel v. P.A.W. Drilling & Well Service, Inc.*, 135 F.3d 344, 347 (5th Cir. 1998). It is bedrock that "[w]e assume that Congress is aware of existing law when it passes legislation." *Miles v. Apex Marine Corp.*, 498 U.S. 19, 32 (1990); *see also Goodyear Atomic Corp. v. Miller*, 486 U.S. 174, 184–85, 108 S.Ct. 1704, 1712 (1988) ("We generally presume that Congress is knowledgeable about existing law pertinent to the legislation it enacts."). Setting aside the "marine oil spill exclusion" discussed next, the

---

and the vessel and its appurtenances as separate from the well. *In re Deepwater Horizon*, 753 F.3d 570, 571, 2 Adm. R. 233, 233 (5th Cir. 2014); *Jerome B. Grubart, Inc. v. Great Lakes Dredge & Dock Co.*, 513 U.S. 527, 535, 115 S. Ct. 1043, 1049 (1995) ([M]aritime law ... ordinarily treats an "appurtenance" attached to a vessel in navigable waters as part of the vessel itself.").

CSB's jurisdiction over artificial islands as "stationary" sources fits comfortably within the OCSLA dichotomy and background law. Just as clearly, characterizing the MODU Deepwater Horizon with or without the Macondo well as "stationar" does not. The majority's deviation from background law violates the ordinary interpretive presumption as well as the facts.

2. Can the "marine oil spill exclusion" be excluded?

It is unnecessary to wade into the parties' "comma, which" dispute to reach a sensible interpretation of 42 U.S.C. § 7412(r)(6)(C)(i), which excludes marine oil spills from CSB's investigative authority. This provision as a whole expresses Congress's recognition that other agencies have regulatory jurisdiction over hazardous releases into the ambient air. Consequently, CSB has to cooperate and coordinate with such agencies in furtherance of public health and safety. Foreseeing significant potential overlaps, Congress paid particular attention to the interrelation of CSB with two agencies: the OSHA and NTSB. NTSB, relevant here, is deemed the lead agency for releases "which" are "transportation related." We know from the Supreme Court that [—26—] "related-to" language is enabling in the broadest sense. *Ingersoll-Rand Co. v. McClendon*, 498 U.S. 133, 138–39, 111 S. Ct. 478, 482–83 (1990) (discussing the breadth of the "related-to" pre-emption language in § 514(a) of ERISA). The CSB, moreover, "shall not be authorized to investigate marine oil spills, which the National Transportation Safety Board is authorized to investigate." Nevertheless, "[i]n no event shall the [CSB] forego an investigation where an accidental release causes a fatality or serious injury among the general public or had the potential to cause substantial property damage or a number of deaths or injuries among the general public." I part company with the majority on the applicability of the "marine oil spill exclusion" and their interpretation of the "danger to the public" catchall language.

Taking the "marine oil spill exclusion" first, even if this language is read holistically and narrowly to exclude CSB from only those marine oil spills "that" the NTSB may investigate, *this* marine oil spill was "related to" transportation through the movement of hydrocarbons from the well through the drill string to the Deepwater Horizon[6] and by virtue of the vessel's constant movement. On the face of the provision, where NTSB was authorized to investigate, CSB must recede. Curiously, however, to expand CSB jurisdiction, at the expense of the NTSB, the majority accepted two of CSB's propositions: this oil spill disaster, the largest in American history, was not within the "marine oil spill exclusion," and even if it was, NTSB lacked jurisdiction. These arguments are wrong. The first one would eviscerate the "marine oil spill exclusion" completely. The second erroneously limits NTSB's authority.

Holding that the "marine oil spill exclusion" does not apply if hazardous substances were incidentally released into the air during a "marine oil spill" [—27—] turns the exclusion on its head and renders it a nullity.[7] Virtually any offshore crude oil spill involves the emission of fumes, because petroleum produced from wells is "oil," more technically, "[a] complex mixture of naturally hydrocarbon compounds found in rock. . . . [T]he term is generally used to refer to liquid crude oil. Impurities, such as sulfur, oxygen and nitrogen are common in petroleum." *Petroleum*, SCHLUMBERGER OILFIELD GLOSSARY, (last visited Sept. 16, 2014), www.glossary.oilfield.slb.com/en/Terms/p/petr oleum.aspx. The lighter hydrocarbons and impurities in crude oil readily evaporate into the air; as we all know, there is no smoking at gas pumps because of the volatility of hydrocarbons in "oil." CSB's attempt to separate these mixed hydrocarbons temporally from the oil spill disaster, by purporting to focus its investigation on the emission of fumes that ignited and exploded at the platform, is unrealistic. How unrealistic is confirmed by the scope of the agency's

subpoena at issue here: CSB called for all of the documents that Transocean turned over to all of the other investigating agencies concerning the blowout, explosion and oil spill. Why? Because the liquid and gaseous hydrocarbons all spewed from the well due to the same errors during the drilling process. The investigation cannot be limited to ambient air releases apart from the events that triggered the marine oil spill. This position is factually unsupportable.

Equally untenable is the holding that NTSB lacked authority to investigate this disaster. NTSB has jurisdiction over "any other accident related to the transportation of individuals or property when the [NTSB] decides—

(i) the accident is catastrophic;
(ii) the accident involves problems of a recurring [—28—] character; or
(iii) the investigation of the accident would carry out this chapter.

49 U.S.C. § 1131(a)(1)(F). The majority fall back on their faulty conclusion that the oil spill disaster was not "transportation related."[8] Remarkably, the majority must conclude that "[m]erely because a disaster involves a vessel does not mean that the disaster was necessarily related to transportation." I have already explained why the MODU's status as a vessel is dispositive of the "stationary source" argument; the factual and legal points made there apply even more clearly to this argument. The logical implication of the majority's interpretation forbids NTSB to operate in its area of expertise when certain catastrophic disasters involve a temporarily immobile vehicle, airplane, train, vessel or pipeline activity. The settled legal interpretation of "related" forbids this artificial constraint.

---

[6] Recall that NTSB is also charged to investigate pipeline disasters.

[7] It is an established principle of statutory interpretation that "[w]here possible, every word in a statute should be given meaning." *G.M. Trading Corp. v. C.I.R.*, 121 F.3d 977, 981 (5th Cir. 1997).

[8] The present case involves an accident on the Outer Continental Shelf and is therefore unlike *NTSB v. Carnival Cruise Lines, Inc.*, 723 F. Supp. 1488, 1493 (S.D. Fla. 1989), which dealt with an "extraterritorial investigation" outside of U.S. territory. Since 43 U.S.C. § 1331(a) makes clear that the Outer Continental Shelf is under U.S. law, any investigation would not be extraterritorial.

Finally, the majority erroneously relies on CSB's catchall investigative power over fatalities, serious injuries or property damages to "the general public." 42 U.S.C. § 7412(r)(6)(E). The Deepwater Horizon's crew were specialized oilfield or marine employees covered by OSHA, not "the general public." To be sure, this catchall is an empowering provision, just as Section 1131(a)(1)(F) is empowering to the NTSB. Unlike the NTSB provision, which empowers transportation "related" investigations, CSB's provision covers actual or potential injuries, fatalities or property damage to "the general public." On the facts of this case, the provision is clearly inapplicable. CSB posits its jurisdiction only over the explosion on the MODU Deepwater Horizon [—29—] that was occasioned by the release of volatile hydrocarbons from the well. The Macondo well was located 50 miles offshore of Louisiana. No one has ever claimed that injury occurred to "the general public" onshore from releases into the ambient air. The term "public" is defined to mean "of, relating to, or affecting the people as an organized community." Webster's Third New International Dictionary 1836 (1986); *see also Black's Law Dictionary* 1264 (8th ed. 1999) (defining public as "[r]elating or belonging to an entire community"). The workers who tragically lost their lives in the vessel's explosion are not, under this definition, "the general public." Congress could have easily described CSB's catchall jurisdiction by referring to "individuals" or "any person," but it chose a different term.

Conclusion

This case strictly and properly concerns an agency's statutory authority to issue subpoenas and conduct an investigation. The much broader ramifications of the decision should not, however, be overlooked. First, when Congress has delineated agency authority against clear background principles and with easily defined terms, the agency itself should not play havoc with the statute to expand its authority; an agency has a duty to follow its mandate but go no further. For the sake of maintaining limited government under the rule of law, courts must be vigilant to sanction improper administrative overreach.

See, e.g., Util. Air Regulatory Grp. v. E.P.A., 134 S. Ct. 2427, 2449 (2014) (holding that the EPA exceeded its statutory authority). Second, contrary to some fears expressed about the consequences of holding CSB unable to investigate the Deepwater Horizon disaster, there were at least seventeen investigations, including major reports by a Presidential Commission and the Coast Guard. *See* Exec. Order No. 13,543, 75 Fed. Reg. 29,397 (May 21, 2010) (establishing the National Commission on the BP Deepwater Horizon Oil Spill and Offshore Drilling). The Coast Guard, in fact, was required to "make an [—30—] investigation and public report on each major fire and each major oil spillage occurring as a result of" exploration, development and production of minerals from the OCS. 43 U.S.C. § 1348(d)(1). There is no dearth of proper investigation to protect public safety. Third, as a result of being deemed by this opinion "stationary sources," nearly all non-standard offshore vessels involved in oil and gas production on the OCS will become subject to Clean Air Act regulation and reports in addition to "all of the regulatory requirements of 'traditional' vessels" imposed by the Coast Guard. *See* 42 U.S.C. § 7412(r)(7)(B)(iii); Memorandum from S.D. Poulin, U.S. Coast Guard, to CG-5, Potential Legal Issues Associated With Vessels Employing Dynamic Positioning Systems 10 (Feb. 11, 2011).

For all these reasons, I respectfully dissent.

United States Court of Appeals
for the Fifth Circuit

No. 12-30714

McBRIDE

vs.

ESTIS WELL SERVICE, L.L.C.

Appeal from the United States District Court for the
Western District of Louisiana

Decided: September 25, 2014
Revised: October 24, 2014

Citation: 768 F.3d 382, 2 Adm. R. 320 (5th Cir. 2014).

Before **STEWART**, Chief Judge, and **JOLLY, DAVIS, JONES, SMITH, BARKSDALE**,* **DENNIS, CLEMENT, PRADO, OWEN, ELROD, SOUTHWICK, HAYNES, GRAVES**, and **HIGGINSON**, Circuit Judges.**

* Judge **BARKSDALE** was a member of the original panel and sat with the full Court for rehearing en banc.

** Circuit Judge **COSTA** was not a member of the Court when this case was submitted for rehearing en banc and did not participate in this decision.

[—2—] **DAVIS**, Circuit Judge:

We took this case en banc to decide whether the seaman plaintiffs in this case, both the injured seamen and the personal representative of the deceased seaman, can recover punitive damages under either the Jones Act or the general maritime law. We affirm the district court and conclude that this case is controlled by the Supreme Court's decision in *Miles v. Apex Marine Corp.*,[1] which holds that the Jones Act limits a seaman's recovery to pecuniary losses where liability is predicated on the Jones Act or unseaworthiness. Because punitive damages are non-pecuniary losses, punitive damages may not be recovered in this case.

FACTS AND PROCEEDINGS

These consolidated cases arise out of an accident aboard Estis Rig 23, a barge supporting a truck-mounted drilling rig operating in Bayou Sorrell, a navigable waterway in the State of Louisiana. The truck right toppled over, and one crew member, Skye Sonnier, was fatally pinned between the derrick and mud tank, and three others, Saul Touchet, Brian Suire, and Joshua [—3—] Bourque,[2] have alleged injuries. At the time of the incident, Estis Well Service, L.L.C. ("Estis") owned and operated Rig 23, and employed Sonnier, Touchet, Suire, and Bourque (collectively, the "crew members").

Haleigh McBride, individually, on behalf of Sonnier's minor child, and as administratrix of Sonnier's estate, filed suit against Estis, stating causes of action for unseaworthiness under general maritime law and negligence under the Jones Act and seeking compensatory as well as punitive damages under both claims. The other crew members filed separate actions against Estis alleging the same causes of action and also requesting compensatory and punitive damages. Upon the crew members' motion, the cases were consolidated into a single action. Estis moved to dismiss the claims for punitive damages, arguing that punitive damages are not an available remedy as a matter of law where liability is based on unseaworthiness or Jones Act negligence. Treating it as a motion for judgment on the pleadings under Federal Rule of Civil Procedure 12(c), the court granted the motion and entered judgment dismissing all claims for punitive damages. Recognizing that the issues presented were "the subject of national debate with no clear consensus," the court granted plaintiffs' motion to certify the judgment for immediate appeal under 28 U.S.C. § 1292(b). This interlocutory appeal followed.

The panel, in a scholarly opinion, concluded that the Supreme Court's recent opinion in *Atlantic Sounding Co., Inc. v. Townsend*[3] controlled this case. The panel acknowledged that the *Townsend* court was presented with the limited issue of whether a seaman can recover punitive damages from his employer for willful failure to pay maintenance and cure. That case did not involve a claim for punitive damages under either the Jones Act or the general [—4—] maritime law. The

---

[1] 498 U.S. 19, 111 S. Ct. 317, 112 L. Ed. 2d 275 (1990).

[2] Bourque has settled.

[3] 557 U.S. 404, 129 S. Ct. 2561, 174 L. Ed. 2d 382 (2009).

panel, however, reasoned that the implication of *Townsend*'s holding is broader and teaches that because the unseaworthiness cause of action and the punitive damages remedy pre-existed the Jones Act and the Jones Act did not address either, then both the cause of action and remedy of punitive damages are available to injured seamen and the survivors of deceased seamen.

We granted rehearing en banc to determine whether the Supreme Court's decision in *Miles*, holding that the Jones Act limits a seaman's recovery for unseaworthiness under that Act or the general maritime law to "pecuniary losses," is still good law and whether that holding precludes plaintiffs' claims for punitive damages.

STANDARD OF REVIEW

Whether punitive damages are an available remedy under the Jones Act and general maritime law to seamen or their survivors is a question of law we review de novo.[4]

DISCUSSION

I.

A. Background

Appellants' arguments are founded primarily on their claim under general maritime law. A brief discussion of the legal and historical background of the general maritime law as it relates to the plaintiffs' case is therefore in order.

We start from the bedrock premise that the "[j]udicial power, in all cases of admiralty and maritime jurisdiction, is delegated by the Constitution to the Federal Government in general terms,"[5] reflecting "the adoption by all [—5—] commercial nations (our own included) of the general maritime law as the basis and groundwork of all their maritime

regulations."[6] Once general maritime law was embedded in federal law, however, the question arose as to which branch of government had the authority to modify the maritime law. Over 160 years ago, the Supreme Court declared that the maritime law was subject to regulation by Congress: "The power of Congress to change the mode of proceeding in this respect in its courts of admiralty, will, we suppose, hardly be questioned."[7] The Court later summarized: "[I]t must now be accepted as settled doctrine that, in consequence of these provisions, Congress has paramount power to fix and determine the maritime law which shall prevail throughout the country."[8]

In 1886, the Court, in *The Harrisburg*,[9] held that no action for wrongful death "will lie in the courts of the United States under the general maritime law." That remained the law of the land until the Supreme Court overruled *The Harrisburg* in *Moragne v. States Marine Lines, Inc.* in 1970.[10]

B. The Jones Act and FELA

In 1920, Congress enacted the Jones Act, 46 U.S.C. § 30104, and extended to seamen the same negligence remedy for damages afforded to railroad workers under the Federal Employers' Liability Act ("FELA").[11] This provided a remedy to seamen and their survivors to sue for compensation for personal injury and wrongful death based on the negligence of the seamen's employer. Because Congress imported FELA into the Jones Act, we must begin our analysis with FELA. [—6—]

Under 45 U.S.C. §§ 51-59, FELA provides that a carrier is liable for its negligence,

---

[4] *See Atl. Sounding Co., Inc. v. Townsend*, 496 F.3d 1282, 1284 (11th Cir. 2007), *aff'd*, 557 U.S. 404 (2009).

[5] *The St. Lawrence*, 66 U.S. 522, 526, 17 L. Ed. 180 (1861).

[6] *The Lottawanna*, 88 U.S. 558, 572-73, 22 L. Ed. 654 (1874).

[7] *The Genesee Chief*, 53 U.S. 443, 459-60, 13 L. Ed. 1058 (1851).

[8] *S. Pac. Co. v. Jensen*, 244 U.S. 205, 215, 37 S. Ct. 524, 61 L. Ed. 1086 (1917).

[9] 119 U.S. 199, 213, 7 S. Ct. 140, 30 L. Ed. 358 (1886).

[10] 398 U.S. 375, 90 S. Ct. 1772, 26 L. Ed. 2d 339 (1970).

[11] *Miles*, 498 U.S. at 23-24.

although the employee's recovery is reduced if he was negligent.[12] The compensation allowed for the employee's recovery is simply "in damages."[13] The damages allowed under FELA were defined by the Supreme Court in *Michigan Central Railroad Co. v. Vreeland*.[14] In construing FELA, the Court stated with respect to damages in this wrongful death action: "It is a liability for the loss and damage sustained by relatives dependent upon the decedent. It is therefore a liability for the pecuniary damage resulting to them and for that only."[15]

The *Vreeland* Court stated that the damages under FELA "are such as flow from the deprivation of the pecuniary benefits which the beneficiaries might have reasonably received if the deceased had not died from his injuries."[16] As there must be "some reasonable expectation of pecuniary assistance or support of which they have been deprived" the Court held that "[c]ompensation for such loss manifestly does not include damages by way of recompense for grief or wounded feelings."[17] Similarly, the term "pecuniary" "excludes, also, those losses which result from the deprivation of the society and companionship, which are equally incapable of being defined by any recognized measure of value."[18] Because the jury instruction on damages in *Vreeland* was not "confined to a consideration of the financial benefits which might reasonably be expected from [the decedent] in a pecuniary way," the Court reversed the judgment entered on the verdict.[19] [—7—]

With this background, we turn to the Supreme Court's unanimous opinion in *Miles* in 1990, which we conclude controls this appeal.

II.

A. *Miles*

The facts in *Miles* are on all fours with Ms. McBride's wrongful death action. In both cases, the personal representative of a deceased seaman sued the employer for wrongful death under the Jones Act and general maritime law. No maintenance and cure action was presented in either case. In both cases the seaman met his death in the service of his ship in state waters. The Supreme Court made three significant holdings relevant to this case. The Court held that:

(1) Before the Court's decision in *Moragne v. States Marine Lines, Inc.* in 1970,[20] the general maritime law provided no recovery for wrongful death.[21]

(2) The Court then recognized the anomaly created by the Court's *Moragne* decision, which granted to survivors of longshoremen killed in state waters the right to sue for unseaworthiness under the general maritime law, yet afforded no similar right to the seaman's survivors to sue for wrongful death under the general maritime law. The Court then expressly extended the rule established in *Moragne* to the seaman's survivors, recognizing for the first time their right to assert a general maritime law cause of action for wrongful death.[22]

(3) Finally, the Court considered the issue presented directly in this case: the scope of the survivor's recovery in her general maritime law/unseaworthiness action for wrongful death. The Court, after extended [—8—] discussion and analysis, limited the survivors in *Miles* to recovery of their

---

[12] 45 U.S.C. §§ 51, 53.
[13] *Id.* § 51.
[14] 227 U.S. 59, 33 S. Ct. 192, 57 L. Ed. 417 (1913).
[15] *Id.* at 69.
[16] *Id.* at 70.
[17] *Id.*
[18] *Id.* at 71 (internal quotation marks omitted).
[19] *Id.* at 73-74.

---

[20] 398 U.S. 375 (1970).
[21] *See Miles*, 498 U.S. at 23-24; *see also The Harrisburg*, 119 U.S. 199; Kenneth G. Engerrand & Scott R. Brann, *Troubled Waters for Seamen's Wrongful Death Actions*, 12 J. Mar. L. & Com. 327, 335 (1981).
[22] *Miles*, 498 U.S. at 30.

"pecuniary losses." The Court therefore denied recovery for damages for loss of society.[23]

In considering this element of damages, the *Miles* Court began its analysis by discussing its decision in *Mobil Oil Corp. v. Higginbotham*,[24] in which the Court had considered the scope of a survivor's recovery under the Death on the High Seas Act ("DOHSA") for a person killed on the high seas. The Court noted that in *Higginbotham*, it had rejected a claim for loss of society because Congress, in DOHSA, expressly limited recovery to "pecuniary losses." It therefore declined to supplement the statute and allow more expansive damages. The Court emphasized the important language it relied on from *Higginbotham*: "But in an 'area covered by the statute, it would be no more appropriate to prescribe a different measure of damages than to prescribe a different statute of limitations, or a different class of beneficiaries.'"[25]

The Court then reasoned that its logic in *Higginbotham* controlled its decision in *Miles*. The Court first acknowledged that unlike the statutory language in DOHSA, neither the Jones Act nor FELA made explicit the "pecuniary loss" limitation. The Court concluded, however, that the limitation applied:

When Congress passed the Jones Act, the *Vreeland* gloss on FELA, and the hoary tradition behind it, were well established. Incorporating FELA unaltered into the Jones Act, Congress must have intended to incorporate the pecuniary limitation on damages as well. We assume that Congress is aware of existing [—9—] law when it passes legislation. There is no recovery for loss

of society in a Jones Act wrongful death action.

The Jones Act also precludes recovery for loss of society in this case. The Jones Act applies when a seaman has been killed as a result of negligence, and it limits recovery to pecuniary loss.[26]

The Court therefore squarely held that the recovery of the deceased seaman's survivors under the Jones Act is limited to pecuniary losses. The Court then turned to the scope of the survivor's recovery for unseaworthiness under the general maritime law. As the Court explained, our place in the constitutional scheme does not permit us

to sanction more expansive remedies in a judicially created cause of action in which liability is without fault than Congress has allowed in cases of death resulting from negligence. We must conclude that there is no recovery for loss of society in a general maritime action for the wrongful death of a Jones Act seamen.[27]

Thus, the *Miles* court established "a uniform rule applicable to all actions for the wrongful death of a seaman, whether under DOHSA, the Jones Act or the general maritime law."[28]

In summary, *Miles* decided in a wrongful death case completely indistinguishable from Ms. McBride's case that Congress, by incorporating FELA as the predicate for liability and damages in the Jones Act to seamen and their survivors, intended to import into the Jones Act the *Vreeland* [—10—] "pecuniary limitation on damages as

---

[23] *Id.* at 30-33. In *Miles*, the deceased seaman's mother sought compensation for both the loss of support and services and loss of society, but the jury was instructed she could only recover for loss of society if she had been financially dependent on him.
[24] 436 U.S. 618, 98 S. Ct. 2010, 2014, 56 L. Ed. 2d 581 (1978).
[25] 498 U.S. at 31 (quoting *Higginbotham*, 436 U.S. at 625).

[26] *Id.* at 32 (citation omitted).
[27] *Id.* at 32-33. In other words, because nonpecuniary damages are not available under the Jones Act (a fault-based scheme) even in cases of egregious conduct, it would not make sense to permit such damages under an unseaworthiness claim, which has not required any showing of fault since the Supreme Court's decision in *Mahnich v. Southern S.S. Co.*, 321 U.S. 96, 64 S. Ct. 455, 88 L. Ed. 561 (1944), several decades before *Miles* was decided.
[28] *Miles*, 498 U.S. at 33.

well."[29] Just as in *Higginbotham*, the Court did not "pause to evaluate the opposing policy arguments" because "Congress has struck the balance for us. It has limited survivors to recovery of their pecuniary losses."[30] The Court did not limit its holding to claims under the Jones Act. Rather, the Court held that the damages available under the general maritime law cause of action for wrongful death—which cause of action the Court recognized for the first time in *Miles*—were likewise limited to recovery of pecuniary losses.

The Jones Act applies to both injured seamen and those killed through the negligence of their employer. Even though *Miles* was a wrongful death action, no one has suggested why its holding and reasoning would not apply to an injury case such as those asserted by Messrs. Suire and Touchet.[31] No case under FELA has allowed punitive damages, whether for personal injury or death.[32] Because the Jones Act adopted FELA as the predicate for liability and damages for seamen, no cases have awarded punitive damages under the Jones Act.[33] It

follows from *Miles* that the same result flows when a general maritime [—11—] law personal injury claim is joined with a Jones Act claim. So *Miles*'s conclusion that regardless of opposing policy arguments, "Congress has struck the balance for us" in determining the scope of damages, applies to the personal injury actions as well as Ms. McBride's wrongful death action.

Although Congress and the courts both have a lawmaking role in maritime cases, "Congress has paramount power to fix and determine the maritime law which shall prevail throughout the country."[34] Even if a general maritime law remedy for wrongful death had been available to seamen in 1920, when Congress enacted the Jones Act,[35] the Supreme Court's interpretation of the Jones Act in *Miles* must control, and it resolves the question presented in this appeal.

B. *Townsend*

Appellant argues that the decision of the Supreme Court in *Atlantic Sounding Co. v. Townsend* overrules or severely undermines *Miles* so that it does not control today's case. But instead of overruling *Miles*, the *Townsend* Court carefully distinguished its facts from *Miles* and reaffirmed that *Miles* is still good law.

In *Townsend*, the Court considered a seaman's claim for punitive damages for the willful failure to pay maintenance and cure. In distinguishing its maintenance and cure case from *Miles*'s wrongful death action, the Court in *Townsend* recognized that "a seaman's action for maintenance and cure is 'independent' and 'cumulative' from other claims such as negligence and that the maintenance and cure right is 'in no sense inconsistent with, or an alternative of, the right to recover compensatory damages [under

---

[29] *Id.* at 32.

[30] *Higginbotham*, 436 U.S. at 623.

[31] Indeed, we recognized just such a rule in *Murray v. Anthony J. Bertucci Constr. Co., Inc.*, 958 F.2d 127 (5th Cir. 1992), in which we applied *Miles* to an injury case and barred nonpecuniary loss of society damages to the spouse of the plaintiff seaman asserting an unseaworthiness claim coupled with a Jones Act negligence claim.

[32] *See Miller v. Am. President Lines, Ltd.*, 989 F.2d 1450, 1457 (6th Cir. 1993) ("It has been the unanimous judgment of the courts since before the enactment of the Jones Act that punitive damages are not recoverable under the Federal Employers' Liability Act." (citing *Kozar v. Chesapeake & O. Ry. Co.*, 449 F.2d 1238, 1240-43 (6th Cir. 1971)); *Wildman v. Burlington N. R.R. Co.*, 825 F.2d 1392, 1395 (9th Cir. 1987) ("[P]unitive damages are unavailable under the FELA.").

[33] *See Bergen v. F/V St. Patrick*, 816 F.2d 1345, 1347 (9th Cir. 1987), *opinion modified on reh'g*, 866 F.2d 318 (9th Cir. 1989) ("Punitive damages are non-pecuniary damages unavailable under the Jones Act. . . . Punitive damages are therefore also unavailable under DOHSA." (citing *Kopczynski v. The Jacqueline*, 742 F.2d 555, 561 (9th Cir. 1984)); *Miller*, 989 F.2d at 1457 ("Punitive damages are not

therefore recoverable under the Jones Act." (citing *Kopczynski*, 742 F.2d at 560-61)).

[34] *Jensen*, 244 U.S. at 215.

[35] Again, until *The Harrisburg* was overruled by *Moragne* in 1970, no action for wrongful death was recognized under the general maritime law. *Miles*, 498 U.S. at 23-24.

the Jones [—12—] Act].'"[36] The Court agreed that "both the Jones Act and the unseaworthiness remedies are additional to maintenance and cure: the seaman may have maintenance and cure and also one of the other two."[37] Unlike the seaman's remedy for damages based on negligence and unseaworthiness, "the Jones Act does not address maintenance and cure or its remedy."[38] Thus, in contrast to the action for damages based on unseaworthiness, in an action for maintenance and cure it is "possible to adhere to the traditional understanding of maritime actions and remedies without abridging or violating the Jones Act; unlike wrongful-death actions, this traditional understanding is not a matter to which 'Congress has spoken directly.'"[39]

The *Townsend* court expressly adopted *Miles*'s reasoning by recognizing that "Congress' judgment must control the availability of remedies for wrongful-death actions brought under general maritime law."[40] The Court could not have been clearer in signaling its approval of *Miles* when it added: "The reasoning of *Miles* remains sound."[41]

C. Pecuniary Losses

Appellants argue finally that even if their recovery on their general maritime law action is limited to pecuniary loss, punitive damages should be [—13—] characterized as pecuniary losses. Appellants have no legal authority whatever to support this argument.

We start with FELA because that is the statutory source of the *Vreeland* pecuniary loss limitation. Every circuit court case on the subject holds that punitive damages are not recoverable under FELA because those losses are non-pecuniary.[42] The description of pecuniary losses in Supreme Court cases belie the argument that punitive damages could be characterized as pecuniary. In *Gulf, Colorado & Santa Fe Railway v. McGinnis*, which came out shortly after *Vreeland*, the Supreme Court reiterated the rule announced therein:

> [T]he act [FELA] in this aspect has been construed as intended only to *compensate* the surviving relatives of such a deceased employee for the *actual pecuniary loss* resulting to the particular person or persons for whose benefit an action is given. The recovery must therefore be limited to *compensating* those relatives for whose benefit the administrator sues as are shown to have sustained some *pecuniary loss*.[43]

The message that pecuniary loss is designed to compensate the plaintiff for an actual loss suffered comes through loud and clear. The statement in *Miles* itself describing the covered losses stated that in "[i]ncorporating FELA unaltered into the Jones Act, Congress must have intended to incorporate the pecuniary limitation on damages as well."[44] At least two circuit cases have held that punitive damages under the Jones Act are not recoverable because they are

---

[36] *Townsend*, 557 U.S. at 423 (alteration in original, quoting *Pacific S.S. Co. v. Peterson*, 278 U.S. 130, 138-39, 49 S. Ct. 75, 73 L. Ed. 220 (1928)). This language reflects the *Townsend* Court's understanding that the negligence/unseaworthiness actions are alternative, overlapping actions derived from the same accident and look toward the same recovery. The Court explicitly contrasted these actions with the independent maintenance and cure action. *See Baltimore S.S. Co. v. Phillips*, 274 U.S. 316, 47 S. Ct. 600, 71 L. Ed. 1069 (1927) (reasoning that the negligence and unseaworthiness actions are alternative causes of action, so closely related that judgment on one is res judicata of the other).

[37] *Townsend*, 557 U.S. at 424 (quoting G. Gilmore & C. Black, THE LAW OF ADMIRALTY § 6–23, p. 342 (2d ed. 1975)).

[38] *Id.* at 420.

[39] *Id.* at 420-21 (quoting *Miles*, 498 U.S. at 31).

[40] *Id.* at 419 (citing *Miles*, 498 U.S. at 32-36).

[41] *Id.* at 420.

[42] *See, e.g., Miller*, 989 F.2d at 1457; *Wildman*, 825 F.2d at 1395.

[43] 228 U.S. 173, 175 (1913) (emphasis added) (citing *Vreeland*, 227 U.S. 59, and *Am. R. Co. of Porto Rico v. Didricksen*, 227 U.S. 145, 33 S. Ct. 224, 57 L. Ed. 456 (1913)).

[44] 498 U.S. at 32.

non-pecuniary.[45] Furthermore, interpreting *Miles*, at least one circuit case [—14—] has held that punitive damages are barred for an unseaworthiness claim under general maritime law because such damages are nonpecuniary.[46] No circuit cases are to the contrary.

Indeed, before *Townsend*, respected commentary unequivocally stated: "The Jones Act precludes punitive damages because they are non-pecuniary in nature. The seaman may not use a general maritime law claim to recover damages that would be unavailable under the Jones Act; thus punitive damages are properly denied in such seamen's cases."[47] This is consistent with the black letter law courts routinely include in jury charges, e.g.: "*In addition to actual damages*, the law permits a jury, under certain circumstances, to award the injured person punitive and exemplary damages in order to punish the wrongdoer for some extraordinary misconduct and to serve as an example or warning to others not to engage in such conduct."[48] Punitive damages simply do not fit under the case law as a subset of pecuniary losses.

III. Conclusion

In the words of the Supreme Court, "Congress has struck the balance for us."[49] On the subject of recoverable damages in a wrongful death case under the Jones Act and the general maritime law, it has limited the survivor's recovery to pecuniary losses. Appellants have suggested no reason this holding [—15—] and analysis would not apply equally to the plaintiffs asserting claims for personal injury.

The Supreme Court, in *Townsend*, did not overrule *Miles*. Rather, it took pains to distinguish that maintenance and cure case from *Miles* and confirmed that "[t]he reasoning of *Miles* remains sound."[50]

Based on *Miles* and other Supreme Court and circuit authority, pecuniary losses are designed to compensate an injured person or his survivors. Punitive damages, which are designed to punish the wrongdoer rather than compensate the victim, by definition are not pecuniary losses.

Punitive damages are not recoverable by the plaintiffs in these actions. The judgment of the district court is AFFIRMED.

(Reporter's Note: Concurring opinion on p. 327).

---

[45] *See Bergen*, 816 F.2d at 1347 ("Punitive damages are non-pecuniary damages unavailable under the Jones Act. . . . Punitive damages are therefore also unavailable under DOHSA." (citing *Kopczynski*, 742 F.2d at 561)); *Miller*, 989 F.2d at 1457 ("Punitive damages are not therefore recoverable under the Jones Act." (citing *Kopczynski*, 742 F.2d at 560-61)).

[46] *See Wahlstrom v. Kawasaki Heavy Indus., Ltd.*, 4 F.3d 1084, 1094 (2d Cir. 1993) ("We are in general agreement with the view that plaintiffs who are not allowed by general maritime law to seek nonpecuniary damages for loss of society should also be barred from seeking nonpecuniary punitive damages.").

[47] Thomas J. Schoenbaum, Admiralty & Mar. Law § 5-18 (5th ed.) (footnotes omitted).

[48] Kevin F. O'Malley, Jay E. Grenig & Hon. William C. Lee, 3 Federal Jury Practice and Instructions § 128:81 (6th ed. 2013) (emphasis added). *See also* Fifth Circuit Pattern Jury Instruction No. 4.10, which provides, in relevant part: "The purpose of an award of punitive damages is to punish the defendant and to deter him and others from acting as he did."

[49] *Higginbotham*, 436 U.S. at 623.

[50] *Townsend*, 557 U.S. at 420.

[—16—] CLEMENT, Circuit Judge, concurring, joined by JOLLY, JONES, SMITH, and OWEN, Circuit Judges:

While I join the majority opinion, I write separately to further explain the historical background mandating this result.

I.

McBride's argument in favor of punitive damages largely requires establishing that punitive damages were historically available in pre-Jones Act unseaworthiness cases. To establish this, McBride relies on three main points:

- First, the Supreme Court's discussions in *Townsend* and *Baker* indicating that punitive damages were available in at least some maritime law cases before the Jones Act.

- Second, this Circuit's post-Jones Act, pre-*Miles* case law approving of punitive damages in unseaworthiness cases. *See, e.g.*, *In re Merry Shipping, Inc.*, 650 F.2d 622, 626 (5th Cir. Unit B 1981).

- Third, pre-Jones Act unseaworthiness cases that McBride claims awarded punitive damages.

When examined closely, none of these arguments establish McBride's ultimate contention. To the contrary, decades of maritime practice, along with the Supreme Court's discussions of unseaworthiness liability in *The Osceola*, 189 U.S. 158 (1903), as well as the Court's subsequent clarification in *Pacific Steamship Co. v. Peterson* that unseaworthiness plaintiffs are "entitled to . . . [an] indemnity by way of *compensatory* damages," 278 U.S. 130, 138 (1928), demonstrate that punitive damages were not available for unseaworthiness. [—17—]

A. Supreme Court Jurisprudence Does Not Require Punitive Damages In Unseaworthiness Cases.

As a matter of law and common sense, *Exxon Shipping Co. v. Baker*, 554 U.S. 471 (2008), does not resolve the question before us. As for the law, *Baker* only addressed whether the Clean Water Act preempted the punitive damages supposedly available at general maritime law—not whether punitives were available in unseaworthiness actions. *See, e.g.*, *id.* at 490. And as for common sense, the narrowness of *Baker* explains why the *Townsend* Court actually had to address the issue of punitive damages in maintenance and cure cases rather than simply saying that they had already addressed the issue in *Baker*.[1]

That leaves McBride with the thin strand of *Townsend*. But *Townsend*, as a maintenance and cure case,[2] offers minimal

---

[1] McBride counters strenuously that the result in *Baker* makes no sense unless seamen—the wards of admiralty—are given the same exact remedy as third parties injured in a maritime context. But McBride's argument focuses too much on the magnitude of a seaman's recovery, and not enough on the probability of a seaman's recovery. That a seaman is a ward of admiralty has not traditionally meant that a seaman must always be granted every possible litigation advantage under the general maritime law. *Compare, e.g.*, *The Osceola*, 189 U.S. at 175 (noting that a seaman is "not allowed to recover an indemnity for the negligence of the master"), *with Leathers v. Blessing*, 105 U.S. 626, 630 (1881) (recognizing a negligence recovery under the general maritime law), *and Atl. Trans. Co. of W. Va. v. Imbrovek*, 234 U.S. 52, 63 (1914) (same).

Rather, a seaman's special status brings with it a specialized set of rights that both provides advantages in some regards and disadvantages in other regards. Accordingly, there is nothing inherently incongruous with the special status of seamen for seamen to have lesser remedies in some instances when they also are granted a unique right—backed up by the specter of punitive damages—to a virtually guaranteed maintenance and cure remedy. *See also infra* note 12 (noting better policy reasons for permitting punitive damages for a wrongful failure to provide maintenance and cure than in unseaworthiness cases).

[2] *See Atl. Sounding Corp. v. Townsend*, 557 U.S. 404, 407 (2009).

support given the significant differences between maintenance and cure actions and unseaworthiness actions. While McBride's counsel dismissed these differences in his arguments to this court, his prior academic writings recognized them as reasonable:

> [D]istrict judges . . . reason[ed] roughly as follows: the Jones Act and unseaworthiness actions are Siamese twins. Therefore, once one . . . takes *Miles* to mean that punitive damages are unavailable [—18—] under the Jones Act, further extending *Miles* to mean that punitive damages are also unavailable in unseaworthiness actions is virtually unavoidable. But the action for damages for withholding maintenance and cure is completely separate and independent from the Jones Act and unseaworthiness claims. . . . In contrast with the perceived situation with the Jones Act and unseaworthiness actions, there is no extensive legislation from Congress with respect to maintenance and cure. Congress has left to the courts the task of writing the rules on maintenance and cure. Moreover, the availability of punitive damages to penalize the wrongful withholding of maintenance and cure is intimately tied to the special solicitude for the welfare of seamen and their families, and peculiar role of maintenance and cure in providing a seaman with food and lodging when he becomes sick or injured in the ship's service.

The distinction drawn by the district courts between the law of maintenance and cure and the Jones/unseaworthiness "Siamese twins" was *historically and analytically sound* . . . .[3]

Moreover, the Supreme Court has likewise agreed that the basis for unseaworthiness liability is different than the basis for maintenance and cure liability.[4]

The differences between maintenance and cure and unseaworthiness actions make maintenance and cure cases a poor guide for determining unseaworthiness remedies. Whereas a seaman's right to maintenance and [—19—] cure is "ancient"[5] and made its first appearance in English maritime law in 1338,[6] unseaworthiness is actually an American doctrinal innovation that only began to take shape as an independent action during the 1870s,[7] and did not crystallize until well into the mid-twentieth century. To be sure, cases before the 1870s recognized the shipowner had a duty to furnish a seaworthy ship. But that duty generally did not give rise to an independent action for damages.[8] Instead, unseaworthiness acted as an excuse for non-performance by seamen and insurance companies. So, for example, unseaworthiness excused a seaman from performing his contract,[9] and rendered an insurance contract

---

[3] David W. Robertson, *Punitive Damages in American Maritime Law*, 28 J. Mar. L. & Comm. 73, 147-48 (1997) (emphasis added) (internal quotation marks and footnotes omitted); *see also* 1 Thomas J. Schoenbaum, Admiralty and Maritime Law § 5-18, at 330 (5th ed. 2011) ("[P]unitive damages may not be awarded in a seaman's personal injury or death case either under the Jones Act or unseaworthiness."); David Robertson, *Punitive Damages in American Maritime Law:*

Miles, Baker, and Townsend, 70 La. L. Rev. 463, 464 (2010) ("Historically, conceptually, and functionally, the unseaworthiness and Jones Act tort actions are 'Siamese twins.' The much older maintenance and cure action does not derive from tort principles and is something like a first cousin to the other two."); *cf. id.* at 499 ("[O]pen questions in the tort realm include the availability of punitive damages in unseaworthiness actions . . . .").

[4] *See, e.g., Aguilar v. Standard Oil Co. of N.J.*, 318 U.S. 724, 730 & n.8 (1943) (noting that maintenance and cure liability is "unlike" liability for unseaworthiness and the Jones Act).

[5] *Calmar S.S. Corp. v. Taylor*, 303 U.S. 525, 527 (1938).

[6] *See* John B. Shields, *Seamen's Rights To Recover Maintenance and Cure Benefits*, 55 Tul. L. Rev. 1046, 1046 (1981). Indeed, the right to maintenance and cure dates back to at least the laws of Oleron, which were promulgated during the twelfth century. *See The Osceola*, 189 U.S. 158, 169 (1903).

[7] *See, e.g., The Osceola*, 189 U.S. at 175.

[8] *See, e.g., Reed v. Canfield*, 20 F. Cas. 426, 429 (C.C.D. Mass. 1832) (Story, J.).

[9] *See, e.g., The Heroe*, 21 F. 525, 528 (D. Del. 1884) ("It is not denied that unseaworthiness releases a crew, and that they become entitled to their full wages for the month or for the voyage . . .

void.[10] Thus, once American courts began permitting recovery for unseaworthiness, thereby "allowing an *indemnity* beyond the expense of maintenance and cure," those cases represented a "departure" from the Continental maritime tradition.[11] And notwithstanding the American courts' judicial creativity, unseaworthiness was "an obscure and relatively little used remedy" until it became a strict liability action during the 1940s.[12] [—20—]

These distinctions matter. If *Miles v. Apex Marine Corp.* stands for anything, it at the very least signals that all damages are not automatically available in all maritime cases.[13] Accordingly, even though we are bound by *Townsend's* determination that

---

."). Unseaworthiness also operated as a defense to criminal charges for refusing to obey the master's orders. *See, e.g., United States v. Nye,* 27 F. Cas. 210, 211 (C.C.D. Mass. 1855); *United States v. Ashton,* 24 F. Cas. 873, 874-85 (C.C.D. Mass 1834).

[10] Charles Abbott, A Treatise of the Law Relative to Merchant Ships and Seamen: In Four Parts 181 (London 1802).

[11] *The Osceola,* 189 U.S. at 175 (emphasis added).

[12] *Miles v. Apex Marine Corp.,* 498 U.S. 19, 25 (1990) (quoting Grant Gilmore & Charles L. Black Jr., The Law of Admiralty 383 (2d ed. 1975)); *see also Mahnich v. S. S.S. Co.,* 321 U.S. 96 (1944). As a matter of incentives, there is a greater economic need for punitive damages in the maintenance and cure context than in the unseaworthiness context. Whereas the shipowner has just about every economic incentive to dump an injured seaman [—20—] in a port and abandon him to his fate, a ship owner who agrees to put to sea with an unseaworthy vessel risks (1) abandonment by his crew and his insurers, (2) significant liability to the merchants whose cargo the ship is carrying, and (3) the uninsured loss of a significant asset. And beyond these severe economic consequences, there are potential criminal consequences as well. *See* 46 U.S.C. § 10908 ("A person that knowingly sends or attempts to send, or that is a party to sending or attempting to send, a vessel of the United States to sea, in an unseaworthy state that is likely to endanger the life of an individual, shall be fined not more than $1,000, imprisoned for not more than 5 years, or both."); *see also* Note, *Punitive Damages Stow Away in the Fifth Circuit:* McBride v. Estis Well Service, L.L.C., 38 Tul. Mar. L.J. 649, 663 (2014).

[13] *See* 498 U.S. at 31-33.

punitive damages were available in maintenance and cure cases, we cannot blithely assume that because they are available in a wholly different type of maritime action that pre-dates the Magna Carta they are necessarily available in a maritime action that (1) was first embraced by the Supreme Court in 1903, (2) was described early on as providing an indemnity for *compensatory* damages,[14] and (3) did not take its modern form until well after the passage of the Jones Act. Instead, we need to examine post-Jones Act unseaworthiness cases awarding punitive damages to see whether they provide persuasive authority one way or the other.

B. *Merry Shipping* And Its Ilk Are Poor Guides

In *In re Merry Shipping, Inc.,* this court held, as a matter of first impression, that punitive damages were available to unseaworthiness plaintiffs. 650 F.2d at 626. But *Merry Shipping* primarily relied on (1) non-seaworthiness cases speaking to the damages available under general maritime law for maintenance and cure and trespass, and (2) then-contemporaneous court cases reaching the same result. *See id.* at 624 n.9. [—21—]

Neither source establishes that punitive damages were actually available in unseaworthiness cases prior to the Jones Act. The novel nature of unseaworthiness actions makes other more established maritime actions (such as maintenance and cure cases) poor guides to the availability of such damages in unseaworthiness cases. And nearly all of the contemporaneous cases cited in *Merry Shipping* address the issue in passing and merely assume the availability of punitive damages in some other appropriate case.[15] Only *Baptiste v. Superior Court,* 106

---

[14] *Pac. S.S. Co.,* 278 U.S. at 137-38.

[15] *See, e.g., In re Marine Sulphur Queen,* 460 F.2d 89, 105 (2d Cir. 1972); *U.S. Steel Corp. v. Fuhrman,* 407 F.2d 1143 (6th Cir. 1969); *Phillip v. U.S. Lines Co.,* 355 F.2d 25 (3d Cir. 1966); *Kwak Hyung Rok v. Cont'l Seafoods, Inc.,* 462 F. Supp. 894, 899 (S.D. Ala. 1978); *Renner v. Rockwell Int'l Corp.,* 403 F. Supp. 849, 852 (C.D. Cal. 1975), *rev'd*

Cal. App. 3d 87 (Cal. Ct. App. 1980) and *In re Den Norske Amerikalinje A/S*, 276 F. Supp. 163 (N.D. Ohio 1967), appear to analyze the question before this court, and in the end those cases rely on the proposition that punitive damages are available in other areas of American law and in some other maritime cases, and therefore, there is no reason not to recognize punitive damages in unseaworthiness cases. Throughout all these sources, one searches in vain for actual authority establishing that pre-Jones Act unseaworthiness plaintiffs were entitled to an award of punitive damages. Rather, the primary authority supporting punitive damages in unseaworthiness cases appears to be a collective judicial "oh, hell, why not" principle that holds that because punitive damages are available in many other types of actions they should also be available in unseaworthiness cases.

Now, to be sure, courts rely on presumptions all the time. For example, we regularly rely on the presumption that there should be no right without a remedy. *See, e.g., Bivens v. Six Unknown Named Agents of Fed. Bureau of Narcotics*, 403 U.S. 388 (1971); *Ex Parte Young*, 209 U.S. 123 (1908). But even though we recognize a general principle that there should be no right without [—22—] a remedy, that does not mean that every plaintiff that establishes a legal wrong is entitled to relief. *See, e.g., Marbury v. Madison*, 5 U.S. (1 Cranch) 137 (1803). Similarly, even though punitive damages are available in many other types of actions, and indeed in some maritime cases, that does not mean that unseaworthiness plaintiffs are entitled to punitive damages when such an award runs contrary to historical maritime practice and the instructions of the Supreme Court in *The Osceola* and *Pacific Steamship*. I turn to that issue now.

C. The Historical Evidence Strongly Suggests That Punitive Damages Were Not Available In Unseaworthiness Actions.

From the way this case has been presented, one would expect to find a plethora of pre-Jones Act unseaworthiness cases awarding punitive damages. But a review of the cases cited in the briefs and at oral argument suggests the existence of only a single potential unseaworthiness case awarding punitive damages—*The Rolph*—which does not even pre-date the Jones Act.[16] *See* 293

---

[16] McBride also mentions the cases of *The City of Carlisle*, *The Troop*, *Swift v. The Happy Return*, *The Noddleburn*, and *The Childe Harold* as standing for the proposition that punitive damages were traditionally available in unseaworthiness cases. But these cases do not involve the award of a punitive damages for unseaworthiness.

The City of Carlisle is a maintenance and cure case that began when a sixteen-year-old apprentice seaman was injured while working on a ship. *See* 39 F. 807 (D.C. Ore. 1889). While lowering the sail, the boy was struck by a "clew-iron," fracturing and depressing his skull. *Id.* at 810. Bedridden for weeks with limited personal attention, the boy was thereafter forced to work despite his partial paralysis. *Id.* at 810-11. When the ship reached port, "[t]he master failed and neglected to procure or provide any medical aid or advice for the boy . . . and was contriving and intending to get rid of him as easily as possible." *Id.* at 812. Nor did the master send the boy home at the ship's expense. *Id.* Accordingly, the key issue at trial was the negligence of the boy during the operation with the sail, because negligence of a "gross character" would "forfeit [an injured seaman's] right to be kept and cured at the expense of the vessel": maintenance and cure. The court found that the boy's negligence was not of such a character and described his treatment on the ship as a "grievous wrong." *Id.* at 815. Reinforcing that *The City of Carlisle* concerns maintenance and cure, the court assessed damages for medical care and wages "until his return home." *Id.* at 817.

The Troop is another maintenance and cure case. *See* 118 F. 769 (D.C. Wash. 1902). A sailor fell from high on a ship, severely fracturing the bones of his left arm and right thigh. *Id.* at 769. Although the ship was only six miles off shore, it did not return to port for the seaman's medical care, but continued on its journey for 36 days. *Id.* The captain applied splints himself, put the seaman in a bed too small for his injuries to heal properly, and [—23—] assigned the ship's steward to look after

---

587 F.2d 1030 (9th Cir. 1978); *Mpiliris v. Hellenic Lines, Ltd.*, 323 F. Supp. 865, 894 (S.D. Tex. 1969).

[—23—] F. 269 (N.D. Cal. 1923), aff'd 299 F. 52 (9th Cir. 1924). And even if we leave aside the temporal impossibility of Congress deciding to leave the remedy set out in a 1923 unseaworthiness case untouched in a 1920 statute, *The Rolph* hardly stands out as providing a clear award of punitive damages.

---

the man, a crewman too busy to look in more than every other day. *Id.* at 769-70. The court rejected causes of action based on unseaworthiness or negligence. "I hold that no liability, except for expenses and wages, attaches to the ship or owners for a personal injury to a seaman happening while he is in the service of a British ship, in consequence of the negligence of the captain . . . ." *Id.* at 770. Damages were available based on the "sixth article of the laws of Oleron," which sets out the obligation of maintenance and cure, not unseaworthiness. *Id.* at 771.

Nor do *Swift v. The Happy Return*, 23 F. Cas. 560 (D. Pa. 1799) (No. 13,697), *The Noddleburn*, 28 F. 855 (D. Or. 1886) or *The Childe Harold*, 5 F. Cas. 619 (S.D.N.Y. 1846) (No. 2676), save the day for McBride. *Swift*, which arose long before courts recognized an independent cause of unseaworthiness, deals with a claim for wages. 23 F. Cas. at 561. The discussion of "atrocious" food in *Swift* that McBride points to examines when the ship has an obligation to pay a seaman's boarding expenses in a foreign port, and the later discussion of the need to provide medical care to a seaman again examines the ship's obligations since the Laws of Oleron to provide maintenance and cure. *Id.* at 561 & n.2. *The Noddleburn* concerns a claim by a British seaman against a British vessel and applies British law to analyze whether the fellow servant rule (or the vice principal exception to the fellow servant rule) applies when a seaman falls from a defective rope that the ship's officer was aware of. 28 F. at 855-57. Moreover, a punitive damages claim was not awarded, and the court's only discussion of a possibly enhanced remedy came in the context of poor medical care after the injury. *Id.* at 860. Finally, *The Childe Harold* centered around a crew that claimed violation of a *statutory* requirement to sail with sufficient amounts of "wholesome ship-bread" for a voyage. 5 F. Cas. at 619. The statute provided recovery only if the ship had set sail with insufficient amounts of good bread, not if the bread subsequently rotted on the voyage. For the latter, sailors were "left to their legal remedies, as in other cases of maltreatment, not provided for by statute." *Id.* at 620. And what kind of damages could be recovered for these non-statutory claims? They could leave the ship without penalty and the owner would have to pay them wages for the voyage. *Id.*

The Rolph concerns a brutally violent first mate. The first mate blinded one sailor, deafened another, and ordered yet another to his near-certain death on a heavy sea. *Id.* at 270-72. But *The Rolph* is not a case about punitive damages. The damages the court ordered were based on the testimony of medical witnesses and witnesses concerning "the expectation of life and earnings of these men." *Id.* at 272.[17] If this case is the great proclamation of [—24—] the historical availability of punitive damages for unseaworthiness, one wonders (1) why the *Rolph* court felt it necessary to shroud its award in language that is patently compensatory, and (2) why the Supreme Court observed just five years later in *Pacific Steamship*—which cited the Ninth Circuit's *Rolph* opinion—that an injured seaman who elects to bring a unseaworthiness claim is "entitled to . . . [an] indemnity by way of *compensatory* damages," 278 U.S. at 138 (emphasis added).

Moreover, assuming *arguendo* that *The Rolph* awarded punitive damages, we should not rely on one dust-covered case to establish that punitive damages were generally available in unseaworthiness cases. In the first instance, it would be a one-way ratchet of the worst sort if all we had to do to justify punitives was to pluck out a single court decision awarding such damages. But more importantly, courts can err—particularly given the complexity of maritime law—and so

---

[17] McBride places undue emphasis on the two sailors who garnered $500 recoveries for "claimed assaults, but did not claim any personal injury." 293 F. at 269, 272. The Ninth [—24—] Circuit's decision on appeal explains that the ship owner's liability was for the "injuries appellees received," which suggests that all of the sailors were, in fact, injured. 299 F. at 55; *see also id.* at 53 (noting that the "interveners were also injured"). Further, the district court offered no independent explanation for the two sailors' award in the opinion: the district court's explanation is grouped with the compensatory reasoning that justified the award to the other sailors. And, in any case, whatever awards the sailors may, or may not, have persuaded the district court judge to award, those awards should be read in light of the Supreme Court's compensatory damages gloss provided in *Pacific Steamship* five years later. 278 U.S. at 138.

generalizing a supposed national understanding from one or even a handful of cases is a perilous task.

Worse, the myopic focus on engaging in a close literary analysis of a handful of unseaworthiness cases overlooks some of the strongest evidence that punitive damages were not available in unseaworthiness cases. After the passage of the Jones Act, controlling case law required a seaman to elect whether he wished to pursue an unseaworthiness or a Jones Act claim.[18]   **[—25—]**   Assuming, therefore, that (1) plaintiffs were clever enough to pursue the cause of action that would maximize their recovery, and (2) punitive damages were not available in Jones Act cases,[19] the 1920-1950 explosion of Jones Act cases, when set against the dearth of unseaworthiness cases,[20] suggests that punitives were not available in unseaworthiness actions. Otherwise plaintiffs would have filed more unseaworthiness cases in search of a larger remedy.

McBride offers *no* explanation for this disparity,[21] and his attacks on the *Miles*

uniformity principle do not otherwise rebut the point. We know that unseaworthiness and Jones Act negligence actions had largely the same remedies available even before we consider the *Miles* uniformity principle because injured seamen voluntarily chose to file Jones Act actions over unseaworthiness actions.

Of course, the obvious disparity between Jones Act and unseaworthiness cases does not explain *why* punitive damages were understood as not being available in unseaworthiness cases. That answer is contained within *The Osceola* and *Pacific Steamship*. When describing unseaworthiness, the *Osceola* Court observed: **[—26—]**

> That the vessel and her owner are, both by English and American law, *liable to an indemnity* for injuries received by seamen in consequence of the unseaworthiness of the ship, or a failure to supply and keep in order the proper appliances appurtenant to the ship.

189 U.S. at 175 (emphasis added).

What does it mean to be "liable to an indemnity"? The specific phrase itself appears to have originated in *The Osceola*, and so it is only so helpful on its own. But *Pacific Steamship* helps to clarify that *The Osceola*'s unseaworthiness remedy is an "indemnity by way of compensatory damages." 278 U.S. at 138.[22] And that reading is, in turn, further bolstered by a broader review of damages decisions, which suggests that many

---

[18] The election requirement is no longer good law. *See McAllister v. Magnolia Petroleum Co.*, 357 U.S. 221, 222 n.2 (1958).

[19] *See, e.g., Miller v. Am. President Lines. Ltd.*, 989 F.2d 1450, 1457 (6th Cir. 1993); *Kopczynski v. The Jacqueline*, 742 F.2d 555, 560-61 (9th Cir. 1984); *see also Townsend*, 557 U.S. at 426-28 (Alito, J., dissenting); *cf. Pac. S.S. Co.*, 278 U.S. at 135 (describing a Jones Act negligence action as "an action for compensatory damages, on the ground of negligence").

[20] Gilmore & Black at 327 ("The great period for Jones Act litigation was from 1920 until approximately 1950: during that period the Act was the vehicle for almost all seamen's personal injuries and death actions.").

[21] Nor, short of establishing punitive damages were available in Jones Act negligence actions, could he. Though *part* of the disparity can likely be explained by (1) the lower proximate causation requirement in Jones Act actions, (2) differences in coverage between Jones Act negligence actions and unseaworthiness actions after the Jones Act's passage, and (3) a few other litigation advantages enjoyed by the plaintiff in Jones Act cases, *see, e.g., id.*, the full breadth of the disparity—particularly given the perils of the sea and the undoubted existence of easy unseaworthiness cases—seems

implausible if punitives were supposedly available in unseaworthiness cases, particularly given that a seaman's maintenance and cure claim would backstop (and therefore encourage pursuing) the somewhat riskier unseaworthiness claim.

[22] The quoted *Pacific Steamship* language also suggests that the quantum of damages available in an unseaworthiness action was identical to a Jones Act negligence case. *See Pac. S.S. Co.*, 278 U.S. at 138 ("[W]hether or not the seaman's injuries were occasioned by the unseaworthiness of the vessel or by the negligence of the master or members of the crew . . . there is but a single legal wrongful invasion of his primary right of bodily safety . . . for which he is entitled to but one indemnity by way of compensatory damages.").

contemporaneous courts understood the plaintiff's "indemnity" as being limited to compensatory damages. For example, the Supreme Court explained in *Milwaukee & St. Paul Railway v. Arms* that a court goes "beyond the limit of indemnity" when it awards "exemplary," (*i.e.*, punitive), damages. 91 U.S. 489, 493-94 (1875).[23] Multiple lower courts made similar observations on multiple occasions.[24] [—27—] Given the widespread

---

[23] *See also Arms*, 91 U.S. at 492 ("It is undoubtedly true that the allowance of any thing more than an adequate pecuniary indemnity for a wrong suffered is a great departure from the principle on which damages in civil suits are awarded. But although, as a *general rule*, the plaintiff recovers merely such indemnity, yet the doctrine is too well settled now to be shaken, that exemplary damages may in certain cases be assessed.").

[24] *See, e.g., Post Pub. Co. v. Peck*, 199 F. 6, 15 (1st Cir. 1912) ("There are cases in which a jury may award damages going beyond actual indemnity, going beyond actual injury, for the sake of punishing the defendant, and marking their sense of the wrong which he has committed. This is not a case of that kind."); *Christensen Eng'g Co v. Westinghouse Air Brake Co.*, 135 F. 774, 782 (2d Cir. 1905) ("It is obvious that a fine exceeding the indemnity to which the complainant is entitled is purely punitive, and, notwithstanding the foregoing precedents to the contrary, we think that when it is imposed by way of indemnity to the aggrieved party it should not exceed his actual loss incurred . . . ."); *Huber v. Teuber*, 10 D.C. 484, 489-90 (1879) ("Vindictive, punitive, or exemplary damages are sometimes allowable, not as [—27—] compensation to the plaintiff for his indemnity, but, over and beyond that, as punishment . . ."), *abrogated on other grounds, King v. Nixon*, 207 F.2d 41, 41 n.1 (D.C. Cir. 1953); *The America*, 1 F. Cas. 604, 605 (C.C.S.D.N.Y. 1874) ("It is not like the allowance of punitive damages in actions of slander, assault and battery, and like cases. It gives indemnity only."); *Jay v. Almy*, 13 F. Cas. 387, 389 (C.C.D. Mass. 1846); *Taber v. Jenny*, 23 F. Cas. 605, 609 (D. Mass 1856); *New Union Coal Co. v. Walker*, 31 S.W.2d 753, 755 (Ark. 1930); *Burt v. Shreveport Ry. Co.*, 142 La. 308, 317 (1917); *Hall v. Paine*, 112 N.E. 153, 156 (Mass. 1916); *McHargue v. Calchina*, 153 P. 99, 101 (Or. 1915); *Ill. Cent. R. C. v. Outland's Adm'x*, 170 S.W. 48, 52 (Ky. 1914); *Cudlip v. N.Y. Evening J. Pub. Co.*, 66 N.E. 662, 664 (N.Y. 1903); *Am. Credit Indem. Co v. Ellis*, 59 N.E. 679, 683 (Ind. 1901); *Socialistic Co-Operative Pub. Ass'n v. Kuhn*, 58 N.E. 649, 650 (N.Y. 1900); *Odin Coal Co. v. Denman*, 57 N.E. 192, 195 (Ill. 1900); *Jacob Tome*

---

treatment of the term indemnity as excluding punitive damages, we reach the right result today by taking the *Osceola* and *Pacific Steamship* Courts at their word—as contemporaneous plaintiffs did when they filed Jones Act cases rather than unseaworthiness cases—unseaworthiness defendants are liable for an indemnity by way of compensatory damages and nothing more.

II.

But let's assume for the moment that the foregoing is wrong, and unseaworthiness plaintiffs were entitled to punitive damages before the Jones Act. And let's also assume, contrary to the view of the majority opinion, that the narrower reading of *Miles* is right such that the remedies awarded in post-Jones Act judicial expansions of general maritime law actions should not [—28—] exceed the remedies available in a Jones Act claim if, prior to the judicial expansion, the plaintiff would have only had a Jones Act claim. Would that mean that we should take a split-the-baby approach and make punitive damages available to an injured seaman plaintiff but only compensatory damages available to a wrongful death plaintiff on the theory that,

---

Inst. Of Port Deposit v. Crothers, 40 A. 261, 267 (Md. 1898); *Parker v. Forehand*, 28 S.E. 400, 401 (Ga. 1896); *Snow v. Snow*, 43 P. 620, 621-22 (Utah 1896); *U.S. Trust Co. of N.Y. v. O'Brien*, 38 N.E. 266, 267 (N.Y. 1894); *Little Pittsburg Con. Min. Co. v. Little Chief Con. Min. Co.*, 17 P. 760, 763 (Colo. 1888); *Phila., Wilmington, & Balt. R.R. Co. v. Hoeflich*, 62 Md. 300, 312 (1884) (Bryan, J., dissenting); *Hart v. Bostwick*, 14 Fla. 162, 184 (1872); *Sheffield v. Ladue*, 16 Minn. 388, 393-94 (1871); *Woodman v. Nottingham*, 49 N.H. 387, 394 (1870); *Sturges v. Keith*, 57 Ill. 451, 458 (1870); *Rose's Ex'r v. Bozeman*, 41 Ala. 678, 682 (1868); *Merchants' Bank of New Haven v. Bliss*, 35 N.Y. 412, 416 (1866); *Harrison v. Swift*, 95 Mass. 144, 144-46 (1886); *Arthur v. Wheeler & Wilson Mfg. Co.*, 12 Mo. App. 335, 341-42 (1882). To be sure, such usage was not universal, but the view of treating punitive damages as something greater than an indemnity appears to have been the majority view, *see, e.g., Louisville & N.R. Co. v. Roth*, 114 S.W. 264, 266 (Ky. 1908), and the proper one in the unseaworthiness context, *see, e.g., Pac. S.S. Co.*, 278 U.S. at 138 (noting that unseaworthiness plaintiffs are entitled to an "indemnity by way of compensatory damages").

before the Jones Act, the injured seaman would have had an unseaworthiness claim for punitive damages under general maritime law whereas the wrongful death plaintiff would have had only a Jones Act claim for compensatory damages?

No. Even if punitive damages were available in unseaworthiness actions before the Jones Act, and the Jones Act did not narrow those remedies, returning to the *Merry Shipping* rule for injured seamen plaintiffs still poses a significant *Miles* problem. Notably, the *Merry Shipping* rule does not account for the post-Jones Act expansion of unseaworthiness liability.

Congress passed the Jones Act in the wake of *The Osceola* to permit a seaman to recover for negligence. *See Miles*, 498 U.S. at 29. But at the time of the Jones Act's passage there was a degree of separation between actions cognizable in a general maritime law unseaworthiness action and a Jones Act negligence action. To be sure, though unseaworthiness actions included a "certain species of negligence" at the time the Jones Act was passed, the new Jones Act negligence claim also "include[d] several additional species [of negligence] not embraced" by a general maritime law unseaworthiness claim. *Pac. S.S. Co.*, 278 U.S. at 138. For example, *The Osceola* itself—where the plaintiff would have only had a negligence claim if such a claim were permitted under the general maritime law—demonstrates one such separation between a Jones Act negligence claim and a general maritime law unseaworthiness claim. The separations that existed at the time of the Jones Act's passage create a fatal problem for advocates of the *Merry Shipping* rule. [—29—]

Since the passage of the Jones Act, courts have steadily eroded the separations between unseaworthiness claims and Jones Act negligence claims by enlarging unseaworthiness actions far beyond unseaworthiness's pre-Jones Act state. That expansion goes far beyond merely permitting wrongful death actions for unseaworthiness. *See, e.g., Miles*, 498 U.S. at 30 (confirming the availability of wrongful death actions for unseaworthiness). Rather, unseaworthiness has been transformed into a strict liability action, and then systematically expanded in scope so that it would now award an unseaworthiness recovery to an injured seaman who would have traditionally only had a Jones Act negligence action.[25] And despite some fleeting judicial attempts to recabin unseaworthiness liability,[26] unseaworthiness claims and Jones Act claims can now largely be said to be "Siamese twins."[27]

This post-Jones Act expansion of unseaworthiness liability creates a *Miles* problem if punitive damages are awarded in cases where the plaintiff would have originally had only a Jones Act negligence action. As our sister [—30—] circuits have concluded, the Jones Act prohibits the recovery of punitive

---

[25] *See, e.g., Dresser Indus., Inc. v. Webb*, 429 U.S. 1121, 1121 (1977) (Powell, J., dissenting from the denial of certiorari) ("The doctrine of 'seaworthiness,' on which this recovery was predicated, has been extended beyond all reason."); *Pope & Talbot Inc. v. Hawn*, 346 U.S. 406, 418 (1953) (Frankfurter, J., concurring) ("Since unseaworthiness affords . . . recovery without fault and has been broadly construed by the courts . . . it will be rare that the circumstances of an injury will constitute negligence but not unseaworthiness."); *Mahnich v. S. S.S. Co.*, 321 U.S. 96 (1944); George H. Chamlee, *The Absolute Warranty of Seaworthiness: A History and Comparative Study*, 24 Mercer L. Rev. 519, 542 (1973) (noting that "there is no genuine historical relationship" between modern seaworthiness doctrine and the pre-Jones Act cases); Note, *The Doctrine of Unseaworthiness in the Federal Courts*, 76 Harv. L. Rev. 819, 820 (1963) ("An unseaworthy condition can be found in almost anything, no matter how trivial, that causes injury.").

[26] *See Usner v. Luckenbach Overseas Corp.*, 400 U.S. 494 (1971); *see also id.* at 504 (Harlan, J, dissenting) ("Much as I would welcome a thoroughgoing reexamination of the past course of developments in the unseaworthiness doctrine, I fear that the Court's action today can only result in compounding the current difficulties of the lower courts with this area of the law.")

[27] Gilmore & Black at 383; *see also id.* at 382 (noting that the Supreme Court has "made Jones Act negligence irrelevant in seamen's personal injury actions by its development of the unseaworthiness doctrine.").

damages in a seaman's negligence suit.[28] Accordingly, under the prevailing understanding of unseaworthiness when the Jones Act was passed, at least a set of injured seamen would have had only a recovery for compensatory damages under the Jones Act (and not a general maritime law unseaworthiness claim).[29] Now, however, given the expansion of unseaworthiness liability, a sizeable subset of that set of seamen would also have an unseaworthiness claim that they could pursue. Awarding punitive damages in unseaworthiness cases to that subset of sailors under the logic of *Merry Shipping* would make a mockery of even the narrowest reading of *Miles*.

We should not, in light of *Miles*, disregard Congress's chosen remedy for negligence-type cases by expanding unseaworthiness liability into the realm of negligence, thereby permitting plaintiffs who would have had (1) no recovery at the time of *The Osceola*, and (2) only a compensatory Jones Act recovery at the time of the Jones Act, to all of a sudden recover punitive damages in unseaworthiness. Therefore, without a way to exclude modern unseaworthiness cases that would have only been cognizable as Jones Act negligence claims at the time the Jones Act was passed, the split-the-baby solution that makes punitive damages available to injured seamen but not wrongful death plaintiffs is no solution at all. We cannot simply return to the *Merry Shipping* rule for injured seamen as long as "[t]he reasoning of *Miles* remains strong." *Townsend*, 557 U.S. at 420. [—31—]

III.

Finally, we have good reason to be cautious before signing off on an aggressive expansion of punitive damages in the unseaworthiness context. The availability of insurance for punitive damages varies from jurisdiction to jurisdiction,[30] and simple logic suggests that any increased costs on shippers will be eventually passed along to consumers. Given the sizeable percentages of the world's goods that travel on ships, and the fact that the prices of the remainder of the world's goods are indirectly influenced by the prices of the goods that do travel on ships (*e.g.*, oil prices ultimately affect the price of a vast range of items), the decision in this case needs to have only the minutest impact on shipping prices to have a significant aggregate cost for consumers. In light of the potentially sizable impact, this court should not venture too far and too fast in these largely uncharted waters without a clear signal from Congress.

(Reporter's Note: Concurring opinion on p. 336).

---

[28] *See Miller*, 989 F.2d at 1457; *Kopczynski*, 742 F.2d at 560-61. Admittedly, this is an open question in the Fifth Circuit.

[29] *See, e.g.*, *Pac. S.S. Co.*, 278 U.S. at 135 (describing a Jones Act negligence action as "an action for compensatory damages, on the ground of negligence").

[30] *See, e.g.*, Michael A. Rosenhouse, Annotation, *Liability Insurance Coverage as Extending to Liability for Punitive or Exemplary Damages*, 16 A.L.R.4th 11 (Westlaw 2014).

[—32—] HAYNES, Circuit Judge, joined by ELROD, Circuit Judge, concurring:

I concur in the judgment of the en banc court affirming the district court. I also concur in the reasoning expressed in the majority opinion with respect to the wrongful death and associated claims of Ms. McBride arising out of the death of Skye Sonnier. *Miles* commands this result.

The majority opinion concludes that the outcome for the Sonnier family dictates the outcome for the surviving seamen remaining in this case (Touchet and Suire). I disagree with that conclusion. An action for wrongful death (in general) did not exist at common law. *See Atl. Sounding Co. v. Townsend*, 557 U.S. 404, 420 (2009) (explaining that there was no general common-law doctrine providing a wrongful death action); 2 BENEDICT ON ADMIRALTY § 81(a) (Joshua S. Force ed., 2013); W. PAGE KEETON ET AL., PROSSER & KEETON ON THE LAW OF TORTS § 127, at 945 (5th ed. 1984). In the relevant context, *Miles* explains that it was Congress, not the courts, that created this remedy previously unavailable to the family of the deceased seaman. *See Miles v. Apex Marine Corp.*, 498 U.S. 19, 23–27 (1990) (explaining that the Court originally "held that maritime law does not afford a cause of action for wrongful death"; then "Congress enacted two pieces of legislation [(the Jones Act and DOHSA)] creating a wrongful death action for most maritime deaths"; then the Court followed suit by "creat[ing] a general maritime wrongful death cause of action"). The *Miles* Court then explained that it was limited in providing remedies to wrongful death beneficiaries under general maritime law (and not simply in unseaworthiness actions) because Congress had placed limits on the recovery that these claimants could receive: "DOHSA, by its terms, limits recoverable damages *in wrongful death suits* to *pecuniary* loss sustained by the persons for whose benefit the suit is brought. This explicit limitation forecloses recovery for nonpecuniary loss, such as loss of society, *in a general maritime* [—33—] action." *Id.* at 31 (first and third emphasis added; second emphasis in original) (citation and internal quotation marks omitted); *see also Townsend*,

557 U.S. at 420 ("[I]t was only because of congressional action that a general federal cause of action for wrongful death on the high seas and in territorial waters even existed . . . . As a result, to determine the remedies available under the common-law wrongful-death action, 'an admiralty court should look primarily to these legislative enactments for policy guidance.'" (quoting *Miles*, 498 U.S. at 27)). Thus, unlike common law remedies which evolve through the courts, this remedy is one specifically designed and fashioned by the legislature. It is therefore entirely logical as a matter of legal history (though not as a matter of social policy) that the family of a deceased seaman might not be able to recover punitive damages for his death, while the surviving injured seamen could.

That said, I cannot join the dissenting opinions with respect to the surviving seamen. It is a tautology that "[f]ederal courts are courts of limited jurisdiction." *Kokkonen v. Guardian Life Ins. Co.*, 511 U.S. 375, 377 (1994).[1] That reality results in a recognition that "[t]here is no federal general common law." *Erie R.R. Co. v. Tompkins*, 304 U.S. 64, 78 (1938); *see also Sosa v. Alvarez-Machain*, 542 U.S. 692, 729 (2004) ("[W]e now adhere to a conception of limited judicial power first expressed in reorienting federal diversity jurisdiction . . . that federal courts have no authority to derive 'general' common law." (citation omitted)).

Aside from "gap-filling" (as opposed to general) common law permitted by Congress, there are few exceptions to this rule and they come in "those [instances] in which a federal rule of decision is necessary to protect uniquely [—34—] federal interests." *See Tex. Indus. v. Radcliff Materials, Inc.*, 451 U.S. 630, 640 (1981) (citations and internal quotation marks omitted). Because admiralty law is one of the "narrow areas" that presents "uniquely federal interests," federal courts have developed common law in this area. *Id.* at 640–41.

---

[1] I do not contend that we lack jurisdiction here. I note only that, unlike state courts with broad, general judicial power, federal courts are inherently limited in their reach.

Such general development of the federal common law by the only unelected branch of our federal government should be done (if at all) with great restraint, as we recognized when we decided the case that became *Miles*. *See Miles v. Melrose*, 882 F.2d 976, 986 (5th Cir. 1989) ("While the liberality of admiralty proceedings informs the development of maritime jurisprudence, it does not license courts to create causes of action whenever they see fit."), *aff'd sub nom. Miles v. Apex Marine Corp.*, 498 U.S. 19 (1990); *see also Am. Elec. Power Co. v. Connecticut*, 131 S. Ct. 2527, 2536 (2011) ("[T]he Court remains mindful that it does not have creative power akin to that vested in Congress."); *Miles*, 498 U.S. at 27 (espousing a principle of vigilant judicial restraint and deference to Congress that is to guide the exercise of federal common law authority in the maritime context). The authority to address "uniquely federal interests" should not be exercised without sufficient justification and analysis. *See, e.g.*, Daniel Stanton, Comment, *Between a Rock and a Hard Place: Maintenance and Cure in the Wake of* Atlantic Sounding, 10 LOY. MAR. L.J. 471, 481 (2012) (recognizing the dearth of legal analysis by courts that have addressed maintenance-and-cure restitution and the need to justify the remedy "with additional legal theories"). Recognition of new rights and remedies in maritime law, where appropriate at all, is appropriate only after a thorough analysis of legal, historical, and policy considerations. *See, e.g.*, *Townsend*, 557 U.S. at 409–25 (recognizing availability of punitive damages for seamen whose employers willfully fail to pay maintenance and cure only after a historical analysis of maintenance and cure and punitive damages, as well as considering the possibility of statutory preemption); *Cooper* [—35—] *Stevedoring Co. v. Fritz Kopke, Inc.*, 417 U.S. 106, 110–15 (1974) (weighing ancient admiralty doctrine and policy considerations in approving a federal right to contribution among joint tortfeasors). Additionally, here the parties have not sought and have not briefed a different treatment of one category of claimant from the other, and we should be reluctant to address such differences *sua sponte*. Considering this fact, the need to exercise restraint, and the historical context in which

seamen generally have not recovered punitive damages for unseaworthiness, I think it is inappropriate for a federal intermediate appellate court to extend the law here.

As such, I conclude that Congress is the more appropriate forum to weigh competing policy concerns about the punitive damage remedy against a backdrop of hard facts and searching investigation. *See Boyle v. United Techs. Corp.*, 487 U.S. 500, 531 (1988) (Stevens, J., dissenting) ("When judges are asked to embark on a lawmaking venture, I believe they should carefully consider whether they, or a legislative body, are better equipped to perform the task at hand."); Zachary M. VanVactor, Comment, *Three's a Crowd: The Unhappy Interplay Among the New York Convention, FAA, and McCarran-Ferguson Act*, 36 TUL. MAR. L.J. 313, 336 (2011) (observing a "notion of judicial restraint" in maritime law such that "any decision of . . . magnitude or that resembles legislation by the courts should instead rest with the elected legislature"); *cf. Sosa*, 542 U.S. at 724–27 (cautioning, in law-of-nations context, that federal courts should exercise "a restrained conception of . . . discretion . . . in considering a new cause of action" and that such a decision "is one better left to legislative judgment in the great majority of cases"). As emphasized in *Miles*, "[w]e no longer live in an era when seamen and their loved ones must look primarily to the courts as a source of substantive legal protection from injury and death; Congress and the States have legislated [—36—] extensively in these areas." 498 U.S. at 27. It is Congress, not the courts, that "retains superior authority in these matters." *Id.*

The primary dissenting opinion is grounded in the view that the law already provides for this remedy pursuant to *Townsend*. *Townsend* addressed only maintenance and cure. The opinions filed in this en banc case state a scholarly basis for the analogies or lack thereof between maintenance and cure on the one hand and the causes of action at bar on the other, but no one contends they are identical. Thus, allowing recovery of punitive damages would be an expansion of a remedy, a subject best left to Congress. If a federal court is the right place to extend remedies in this area, I submit that federal court is the United States Supreme Court, not this one. The differing opinions of this court highlight the apparent tension among Supreme Court maritime precedents (primarily, *Miles* and *Townsend*), as well as the varied implications that learned jurists may draw from the relevant historical and policy considerations. This tension is between (at least) two Supreme Court precedents; ultimately, then, definitive resolution of this tension can come only from that Court, not ours. For these reasons, I join the judgment of the court expressed in the majority opinion, although, as to the remaining surviving seamen, not its reasoning.

(Reporter's Note: Dissenting opinion on p. 339).

[—37—] **HIGGINSON,** Circuit Judge, dissenting, joined by **STEWART,** Chief Judge, **BARKSDALE, DENNIS, PRADO,** and **GRAVES,** Circuit Judges:

The question presented by this case is whether seamen may recover punitive damages for their employer's willful and wanton breach of the general maritime law duty to provide a seaworthy vessel. Because the Supreme Court has said that they can, and Congress has not said they can't, I would answer in the affirmative, and REVERSE.

FACTS AND PROCEEDINGS

The consolidated cases arise out of an accident aboard Estis Rig 23, a barge supporting a truck-mounted drilling rig operating in Bayou Sorrell, a navigable waterway in Iberville Parish, Louisiana. As crew members were attempting to straighten the monkey board—the catwalk extending from the derrick—which had twisted the previous night, the derrick pipe shifted, causing the rig and truck to topple over. One crew member, Skye Sonnier, was fatally pinned between the derrick and mud tank, and three others, Saul Touchet, Brian Suire, and Joshua Bourque, have alleged injuries. At the time of the incident, Estis Well Service, L.L.C. ("Estis") owned and operated Rig 23, and employed Sonnier, Touchet, Suire, and Bourque (collectively, the "crew members").

Haleigh McBride, individually, on behalf of Sonnier's minor child, and as administratrix of Sonnier's estate, filed suit against Estis, stating causes of action for unseaworthiness under general maritime law and negligence under the Jones Act and seeking compensatory as well as "punitive and/or exemplary" [—38—] damages.[1] The other crew members filed separate actions against Estis alleging the same causes of action and requesting the same relief. Upon the crew members' motion, the cases were consolidated into a single action over which a Magistrate Judge presided with the parties' consent.[2] Estis moved to dismiss the claims for punitive damages, arguing that punitive damages are not an available remedy for unseaworthiness or Jones Act negligence as a matter of law. Treating it as a motion for judgment on the pleadings under Federal Rule of Civil Procedure 12(c), the Magistrate Judge granted the motion, and correspondingly entered judgment dismissing all claims for punitive damages. Recognizing that the issues presented were "the subject of national debate with no clear consensus," the court granted plaintiffs' motion to certify the judgment for immediate appeal under 28 U.S.C. § 1292(b). This interlocutory appeal followed.

STANDARD OF REVIEW

Whether punitive damages are an available remedy under maritime law is a question of law reviewed de novo. *See Atl. Sounding Co., Inc. v. Townsend,* 496 F.3d 1282, 1284 (11th Cir. 2007) (citations omitted), *aff'd,* 557 U.S. 404 (2009). [—39—]

BACKGROUND

I. Sources of maritime law

There are two primary sources of federal maritime law: common law developed by federal courts exercising the maritime authority conferred on them by the Admiralty Clause of the Constitution ("general maritime law"), and statutory law enacted by Congress exercising its authority under the Admiralty Clause and the Commerce Clause ("statutory maritime law"). *See* U.S. CONST. art. III, § 2, cl. 1 (extending the judicial power of the United States "to all [c]ases of admiralty and maritime [j]urisdiction"); *Romero v. Int'l Terminal Operating Co.,* 358 U.S. 354, 360–61 (1959) (explaining that the Admiralty Clause "empowered the federal courts in their exercise of the admiralty and maritime jurisdiction which had been conferred on

---

[1] "Punitive damages" and "exemplary damages" are synonymous. They reflect two principal purposes of such damages: to *punish* the wrongdoer and thereby make an *example* of him in the hopes that doing so will deter him and others from wrongdoing. David W. Robertson, *Punitive Damages in American Maritime Law,* 28 J. MAR. L. & COM. 73, 82–83 (1997). For ease of reference, I refer to all such damages as "punitive damages."

[2] In March 2012, Bourque settled his claims against Estis.

them, to draw on the substantive law 'inherent in the admiralty and maritime jurisdiction,' [] to continue the development of this law within constitutional limits[,]" and "empowered Congress to revise and supplement the maritime law within the limits of the Constitution") (citation omitted).[3]

II. Causes of action under maritime law

Traditionally, general maritime law afforded ill and injured seamen two causes of action against shipowners and employers. If a seaman became ill or injured while in the service of the ship, the seaman's employer and the ship's owner owed the seaman room and board ("maintenance") and medical care ("cure") without regard to fault, and, if not provided, the seaman had a claim [—40—] against them for "maintenance and cure." If a seaman was injured by a ship's operational unfitness, the seaman had a cause of action for "unseaworthiness." General maritime law did not provide seamen with a separate cause of action for personal injury resulting from employer negligence, *The Osceola*, 189 U.S. 158, 175 (1903), nor did it permit wrongful death or survival claims on behalf of seamen killed during the course of their employment, *The Harrisburg*, 119 U.S. 199, 204–14 (1886), *overruled by Moragne v. States Marine Lines, Inc.*, 398 U.S. 375 (1970).

To remedy those perceived gaps in general maritime law, which, until then, had been filled by a patchwork of state wrongful death statutes,[4] Congress in 1920 enacted the Jones Act and the Death on the High Seas Act ("DOHSA"), which created causes of action for employer negligence in navigable waters and on the high seas, respectively, and authorized survival and wrongful death remedies. *See* 46 U.S.C. § 688 (1920) (codified as amended at 46 U.S.C. § 30104 (2006));[5] 46 U.S.C. §§ 761–68 (1920) (codified as amended at 46 U.S.C. §§ 30301–08 (2006)).[6] The Supreme Court has since recognized a [—41—] parallel cause of action under general maritime law for employer negligence resulting in injury or death. *See Norfolk Shipbuilding & Drydock Corp. v. Garris*, 532 U.S. 811, 818–20 (2001) (citing *Moragne*, 398 U.S. at 409).

III. Punitive damages under maritime law

"Historically, punitive damages," though not always designated as such,[7] "have been

---

[3] For a discussion of the division of maritime rulemaking authority between Congress and the federal courts, see David W. Robertson, *Our High Court of Admiralty and Its Sometimes Peculiar Relationship With Congress*, 55 St. Louis U. L.J. 491, 494–513 (2011).

[4] "These statutes were often unwieldy and not designed to accommodate maritime claims; moreover, because they varied from state to state, the representatives of similarly situated deceased seamen might be awarded widely varying sums based on the fortuity of whether the accident occurred within or without the three-mile limit and, if it were within that limit, based on the laws of the particular state where the casualty occurred." *Ivy v. Security Barge Lines, Inc.*, 606 F.2d 524, 527 (5th Cir. 1979).

[5] The Jones Act provides, in pertinent part:

> A seaman injured in the course of employment or, if the seaman dies from the injury, the personal representative of the seaman may elect to bring a civil action at law, with the right of trial by jury, against the employer. Laws of the United States regulating recovery for personal injury to, or death of, a railway employee apply to an action under this section.

46 U.S.C. § 30104.

[6] DOHSA provides, in pertinent part: [—41—]

> When the death of an individual is caused by wrongful act, neglect, or default occurring on the high seas beyond 3 nautical miles from the shore of the United States, the personal representative of the decedent may bring a civil action in admiralty against the person or vessel responsible. The action shall be for the exclusive benefit of the decedent's spouse, parent, child, or dependent relative.

46 U.S.C. § 30302.

[7] *See Townsend*, 557 U.S. at 414 n.3 (citing awards of punitive damages in early maritime cases and pointing out that "[a]lthough these cases do not refer to 'punitive' or 'exemplary' damages, scholars have characterized the awards authorized by these decisions as such"); Robertson, *Punitive Damages in American Maritime Law*, supra, at 88 (noting that eighteenth and nineteenth century

available and awarded in general maritime actions." *Townsend*, 557 U.S. at 407; *see also id.* at 414 (citing as examples of early punitive damages awards *The City of Carlisle*, 39 F. 807, 817 (D. Or. 1889) (adding $1,000 to plaintiff's damages award for "gross neglect and cruel maltreatment"), and *The Troop*, 118 F. 769, 770–771, 773 (D. Wash. 1902) (concluding that $4,000 was a reasonable award because the captain's "failure to observe the dictates of humanity" and obtain prompt medical care for an injured seaman constituted a "monstrous wrong")). In the early nineteenth century, Justice Story spoke of maritime punitive damages as "the proper punishment which belongs to [] lawless misconduct." *The Amiable Nancy*, 16 U.S. (3 Wheat.) 546, 558 (1818).

Over the next century and a half, the availability of punitive damages for unseaworthiness claims arising under general maritime law was largely [—42—] unquestioned. In *Complaint of Merry Shipping, Inc.*, 650 F.2d 622, 623 (5th Cir. Unit B Jul. 1981), our court confirmed the prevailing view that "punitive damages may be recovered under general maritime law upon a showing of willful and wanton misconduct by the shipowner in the creation or maintenance of unseaworthy conditions." Our court based its holding on the historical availability of punitive damages under general maritime law, the public policy interests in punishing willful violators of maritime law and deterring them from committing future violations, and the uniformity of contemporary courts on the issue. *Id.* at 624–26.[8] After *Merry Shipping*,

the Ninth and Eleventh Circuits followed suit. *See Evich v. Morris*, 819 F.2d 256, 258 (9th Cir. 1987) ("Punitive damages are available under general maritime law for claims of unseaworthiness.") (citations omitted); *Self v. Great Lakes Dredge & Dock Co.*, 832 F.2d 1540, 1550 (11th Cir. 1987) ("Punitive damages should be available in cases where the shipowner willfully violated the duty to maintain a safe and seaworthy ship . . . .").

In *Miles v. Melrose*, 882 F.2d 976, 989 (5th Cir. 1989) (citations omitted), we reiterated that "[p]unitive damages are recoverable under the general maritime law 'upon a showing of willful and wanton misconduct by the [—43—] shipowner' in failing to provide a seaworthy vessel[,]" but held, for the first time, that loss of society damages were not available to nondependent parents in a general maritime cause of action for the wrongful death of a Jones Act seaman.[9] Judge Rubin, speaking for the court, was guided by the "twin aims of maritime law": "achieving uniformity in the exercise of admiralty jurisdiction and providing special solicitude to seamen." *Id.* at 987. It would be anomalous, the court reasoned, if a wrongful death claimant were permitted to recover for loss of society damages under general maritime law even though the claimant was barred from recovering such damages under statutory maritime law. *Id.* at 987–88. And the goal of providing special solicitude to seamen, the

---

maritime courts used a variety of terms to designate damages intended to punish and deter).

[8] At the time *Merry Shipping* was decided, the Second and Sixth Circuits had held that punitive damages were available in unseaworthiness actions, and no circuit court had ruled otherwise. *See In re Marine Sulphur Queen*, 460 F.2d 89, 105 (2d Cir. 1972) (noting, in the unseaworthiness context, that "the award of punitive damages is discretionary with the trial court[,]" and "[a] condition precedent to awarding them is a showing by the plaintiffs that the defendant was guilty of gross negligence, or actual malice or criminal indifference which is the equivalent of reckless and wanton misconduct") (citations omitted); *U.S. Steel*

Corp. v. Fuhrman, 407 F.2d 1143, 1148 (6th Cir. 1969) (noting that punitive damages are recoverable against a ship owner for the actions of a master if "the owner authorized or ratified the acts of the master" or "the owner was reckless in employing him") (citations omitted).

[9] A "Jones Act seaman" is "a master or member of a crew of any vessel," *Stewart v. Dutra Const. Co.*, 543 U.S. 481, 488 (2005) (internal quotation marks omitted) (citations omitted), as distinguished from a "*Sieracki* seaman," which refers to a longshoreman or harborworker who is injured on a vessel while performing traditional work of a seaman and, by virtue of *Seas Shipping Co. v. Sieracki*, 328 U.S. 85 (1946), may bring a claim for unseaworthiness, *Burks v. Am. River Transp. Co.*, 679 F.2d 69, 71, 71 n.1 (5th Cir. 1982), *abrogated on other grounds by Lozman v. City of Riviera Beach, Fla.*, 133 S. Ct. 735, 1 Adm. R. 2 (2013).

wards of admiralty, "would not be furthered in any meaningful way by allowing nondependent parents to recover for loss of society." *Id.* at 988; *see also id.* ("Admiralty cannot provide the parents solicitude at a voyage's outset when their right to recover for loss of society is dependent on the fortuity that the deaths occur in territorial waters and are caused by unseaworthiness." (quoting *Sistrunk v. Circle Bar Drilling Co.*, 770 F.2d 455, 460 (5th Cir. 1985)) (emphases omitted).

The Supreme Court affirmed in a decision most significant for its announcement of a new age of maritime law:

> We no longer live in an era when seamen and their loved ones must look primarily to the courts as a source of substantive legal [—44—] protection from injury and death; Congress and the States have legislated extensively in these areas. In this era, an admiralty court should look primarily to these legislative enactments for policy guidance. We may supplement these statutory remedies where doing so would achieve the uniform vindication of such policies consistent with our constitutional mandate, but we must also keep strictly within the limits imposed by Congress. Congress retains superior authority in these matters, and an admiralty court must be vigilant not to overstep the well-considered boundaries imposed by federal legislation. These statutes both direct and delimit our actions.

Miles v. Apex Marine Corp. ("*Miles*"), 498 U.S. 19, 27 (1990); *see also id.* at 36 ("We sail in occupied waters. Maritime tort law is now dominated by federal statute, and we are not free to expand remedies at will simply because it might work to the benefit of seamen and those dependent upon them."). Analyzing the issue presented with this guiding principle in mind, the Court reasoned that because DOHSA, by its terms, limits damages recovery to "pecuniary loss," *id.* at 31 (citation omitted), and the same limitation had been incorporated into the Jones Act, *id.* at 32,[10] non-pecuniary damages, such as loss of society damages, should not be recoverable in a parallel cause of action [—45—] for the wrongful death of a Jones Act seaman under general maritime law, *id.* at 33. "It would be inconsistent with our place in the constitutional scheme," the Court in *Miles* concluded, "were we to sanction more expansive remedies in a judicially created cause of action in which liability is without fault than Congress has allowed in cases of death resulting from negligence." *Id.* at 32–33.

Miles addressed the availability of loss of society damages to non-seamen under general maritime law, not punitive damages, but the general principle asserted in its analysis— that if a category of damages is unavailable under a maritime cause of action established by statute, it is similarly unavailable for a parallel claim brought under general maritime law—began to be extended by lower courts to cover punitive damages claims by seamen. *See, e.g., Miller v. Am. President Lines, Ltd.*, 989 F.2d 1450, 1454–59 (6th Cir. 1993).

Similarly applying the "*Miles* uniformity principle," as it came to be known, our court, sitting en banc, held that *Miles* "effectively

---

[10] This pecuniary-loss limitation arose out of the Jones Act's incorporation of the remedial provisions of the Federal Employers' Liability Act ("FELA"), 46 U.S.C. § 30104 ("Laws of the United States regulating recovery for personal injury to, or death of, a railway employee apply to an action under this section."), which, at the time the Jones Act was enacted, had been interpreted by the Supreme Court to limit recovery to compensation for "pecuniary" damages, *Mich. Cent. R.R. Co. v. Vreeland*, 227 U.S. 59, 68 (1913) ("[FELA limits] liability [to] the loss and damage sustained by relatives dependent upon the decedent. It is therefore a liability for the pecuniary damage resulting to them, and for that only."). *But see Atl. Sounding Co. v. Townsend*, 557 U.S. 404, 424 fn.12 (2009) ("Because we hold that *Miles* does not render the Jones Act's damages provision determinative of respondent's remedies, we do not address the dissent's argument that the Jones Act, by incorporating the provisions of the Federal Employers' Liability Act, see 46 U.S.C. § 30104(a), prohibits the recovery of punitive damages in actions under that statute.").

overruled" *Merry Shipping*, concluding that "punitive damages [are not] available in cases of willful nonpayment of maintenance and cure under the general maritime law." *Guevara v. Maritime Overseas Corp.*, 59 F.3d 1496, 1513 (5th Cir. 1995) (en banc), *abrogated by Atl. Sounding Co. v. Townsend*, 557 U.S. 404 (2009). The court reasoned that because punitive damages, which are "rightfully classified as non-pecuniary," are not an available remedy for personal injury to a seaman under the Jones Act, they likewise are not an available remedy for personal injury to a seaman, including injury resulting from a maintenance and cure violation, under the general maritime law. *Id.* at 1506–07, 1510–12.[11] The court [—46—] in *Guevara* did not address the availability, post-*Miles*, of punitive damages in unseaworthiness actions; it restricted its discussion to the availability of such damages in the maintenance and cure context. *Id.* at 1499. But it was perceived by some to "portend[] the disappearance of punitive damages from the entire body of maritime law." Robertson, *Punitive Damages in American Maritime Law, supra*, at 154 (collecting cases).

Momentum in that direction was sea-tossed by *Atlantic Sounding Co., Inc. v. Townsend*, 557 U.S. 404, 424 (2009), which explicitly abrogated *Guevara* and restored the availability of punitive damages for maintenance and cure claims under general maritime law. The Supreme Court reasoned that "punitive damages have long been an accepted remedy under general maritime law," including for egregious maintenance and cure violations, and concluded, contrary to

Guevara, that "nothing in the Jones Act altered this understanding." *Id.* at 424. The Jones Act, the Court reminded, "created a statutory cause of action for negligence, but it did not eliminate pre-existing remedies available to seamen for the separate common-law cause of action based on a seaman's right to maintenance and cure." *Id.* at 415–16. Importantly, Justice Thomas writing for the Court reminded that "[i]ts purpose was to enlarge [seamen's] protection, not to narrow it." *Id.* at 417 (citations omitted). Indeed, the Court noted, the Jones Act specifically preserved the seaman's right to "elect" between the remedies provided by the Jones Act and [—47—] those recoverable under pre-existing general maritime law; "[i]f the Jones Act had been the only remaining remedy available to injured seamen, there would have been no election to make." *Id.* at 416.[12]

The Supreme Court clarified that its interpretation of *Miles* did *not* represent an "'abrup[t]' change of course." *Id.* at 422 n.8, 418–22. Rather, the Court explained, reliance on the *Miles* uniformity principle to bar punitive damages recovery under general maritime causes of action would read *Miles* "far too broad[ly]." *Id.* at 418–19. *Miles*, which addressed loss of society damages in maritime wrongful death actions, presented an issue of a different nature than the one presented in *Townsend*, which addressed punitive damages in the maintenance and cure setting:

> Unlike the situation presented in *Miles*, both the general maritime cause of action (maintenance and cure) and the remedy (punitive damages) were well established before the passage of the Jones Act. Also unlike the facts presented by *Miles*, the Jones Act does not address maintenance and cure or its remedy. It is therefore possible to adhere to the traditional understanding

---

[11] The court in *Guevara* went on to hold, in addition, that punitive damages are not available for the willful and wanton refusal to pay maintenance and cure even when personal injury does not result. *Id.* at 1512. The court noted that it was not constrained by the *Miles* [—46—] uniformity principle in its second inquiry because there was no overlap between statutory and general maritime law: neither the Jones Act nor DOHSA, as does the general maritime law, provides for a cause of action for maintenance and cure not resulting in personal injury. *Id.* The court nevertheless exercised its maritime authority to bar punitive damages in such actions as a matter of policy. *Id.* at 1513.

[12] As further evidence that punitive damages "remain[ed] available in maintenance and cure actions after the [Jones] Act's passage," the Court pointed out that in *Vaughan v. Atkinson*, 369 U.S. 527, 529–31 (1962), it "permitted the recovery of attorneys' fees [as a punitive sanction] for the 'callous' and 'willful and persistent' refusal to pay maintenance and cure." *Townsend*, 557 U.S. at 417.

of maritime actions and remedies without abridging or violating the Jones Act; unlike wrongful-death actions, this traditional understanding is not a matter to which "Congress has spoken directly." Indeed, the *Miles* Court itself acknowledged that "[t]he Jones Act evinces no general hostility to recovery under maritime law," and noted that statutory remedy limitations "would not necessarily deter us, if recovery . . . were more consistent with the general principles of maritime tort law." The availability of punitive damages for maintenance and cure actions is entirely faithful to these "general **[—48—]** principles of maritime tort law," and no statute casts doubt on their availability under general maritime law.

Id. at 420–21 (citations omitted). Thus, it concluded more generally, "[t]he laudable quest for uniformity in admiralty does not require the narrowing of available damages to the lowest common denominator approved by Congress for distinct causes of action." *Id.* at 424.[13]

---

[13] This shift from *Miles* to *Townsend* was foreshadowed in *Exxon Shipping Co. v. Baker*, 554 U.S. 471 (2008), which presented the issue of whether the Clean Water Act ("CWA") implicitly preempted maritime causes of action by fishermen, Alaska Natives, and others with property rights in the resources of the ocean. 554 U.S. at 484–89. The Court concluded that the CWA did not preempt plaintiffs' claims, reasoning: "we find it too hard to conclude that a statute expressly geared to protecting 'water,' 'shorelines,' and 'natural resources' was intended to eliminate *sub silentio* oil companies' common law duties to refrain from injuring the bodies and livelihoods of private individuals." *Id.* at 488–89. In so ruling, the Court sounded a different tune on statutory displacement of general maritime law:

> To be sure, "Congress retains superior authority in these matters," and "[i]n this era, an admiralty court should look primarily to these legislative enactments for policy guidance." *Miles v. Apex Marine Corp.*, 498 U.S. 19, 27 (1990). But we may not slough off our responsibilities for common law remedies because Congress has not made a first move, and the absence of federal legislation constraining punitive damages does not

DISCUSSION

The crux of this dispute lies in the parties' competing theories of statutory displacement of general maritime law.

The crew members read *Miles* and *Townsend* as providing, narrowly, that federal courts, in exercising their maritime lawmaking authority, cannot authorize a more expansive remedy for a general maritime cause of action than exists for a parallel statutory maritime cause of action if, at the time the **[—49—]** statutory cause of action or remedy was enacted, the parallel cause of action or remedy did not exist under general maritime law. Applying that principle, they urge that punitive damages remain available as a remedy for the general maritime law cause of action for unseaworthiness because, as Justice Thomas highlighted for the Court in *Townsend*, like maintenance and cure, unseaworthiness was established as a cause of action before the passage of the Jones Act, courts traditionally awarded punitive damages under general maritime law, and the Jones Act does not address unseaworthiness or purport to limit its remedies.

Estis reads those cases as providing, more broadly, that where claimants seek redress for a type of harm compensable under both general and statutory maritime law, they are limited in their recovery to the class of damages authorized by the Jones Act and DOHSA regardless of the claim's history and without need for explicit Congressional recalibration. That is, punitive damages are available only where there is no remedial overlap between past general and never displaced statutory maritime claims because according to Estis, "the Jones Act and unseaworthiness claims constitute a single

---

imply a congressional decision that there should be no quantified rule.

Id. at 508 n.21 (citation omitted). This sentiment was echoed in *Townsend*: "Although 'Congress . . . is free to say this much and no more,' *Miles*, 498 U.S., at 24, 111 S. Ct. 317 (internal quotation marks omitted), we will not attribute words to Congress that it has not written." *Townsend*, 557 U.S. at 424.

cause of action with a single set of remedies." In Estis's view, punitive damages were available in *Townsend*, but not *Miles*, because the *Miles* plaintiffs sought redress for physical injury and wrongful death, harms now compensable only under statutory maritime law, whereas the *Townsend* plaintiffs sought redress for harm caused by wrongful deprivation of maintenance and cure that did not result in physical injury, a type of harm compensable under general maritime law but not under statutory maritime law, which does not separately provide for a cause of action for maintenance and cure or a remedy for its deprivation. Applying that reasoning here, Estis argues that because the crew members [—50—] seek redress for wrongful death and personal injuries arising from a maritime accident—types of harm compensable under statutory maritime law—and punitive damages are not available under statutory maritime law, punitive damages are not available in the present action.

1.

To start, Estis's argument that Jones Act claims and unseaworthiness claims are but one collides with the Supreme Court's decision in *Usner v. Luckenbach Overseas Corp.*, which explained:

A major burden of the Court's decisions spelling out the nature and scope of the cause of action for unseaworthiness has been insistence upon the point that it is a remedy separate from, independent of, and additional to other claims against the shipowner, whether created by statute or under general maritime law.

400 U.S. 494, 498 (1971) (footnotes omitted) (emphasis added); *see also Brunner v. Maritime Overseas Corp.*, 779 F.2d 296, 298 (5th Cir. 1986) (recognizing in section of opinion entitled "Separate Causes of Action" that "[t]he history of the unseaworthiness claim shows that it developed independently of Jones Act negligence and has been treated as a separate cause of action ever since").

To the extent that Estis's focus is on the case's factual setting and not the specific cause of action alleged, Estis's proposed test for determining whether the *Miles* uniformity principle limits the damages recoverable in a maritime case mirrors the one previously adopted by our en banc court in *Guevara*:

In order to decide whether (and how) *Miles* applies to a case, a court must first evaluate the factual setting of the case and determine what statutory remedial measures, if any, apply in that [—51—] context. If the situation is covered by a statute like the Jones Act or DOHSA, and the statute informs and limits the available damages, the statute directs and delimits the recovery available under the general maritime law as well.

59 F.3d at 1506 (emphasis omitted). Estis highlights this congruity and argues that although *Guevara*'s holding that punitive damages are unavailable in actions for maintenance and cure was overruled by *Townsend*, *Guevara*'s guidance on how to apply the *Miles* uniformity principle remains intact.

I would disagree. *Townsend* abrogated *Guevara*'s holding because of *Guevara*'s interpretation of *Miles*, not in spite of it. The petitioners in *Townsend* urged the Supreme Court to adopt the factual setting approach of *Guevara*, but the Court in *Townsend* declared that reading was "far too broad." 557 U.S. at 419. That approach, the Court went on, "would give greater pre-emptive effect to the Act than is required by its text, *Miles*, or any of this Court's other decisions interpreting the statute." *Id.* at 424–25. Indeed, the Court noted, it had already rejected that view in *Norfolk Shipbuilding & Drydock Corp. v. Garris*, 532 U.S. 811, 818 (2001), an intervening case holding that a wrongful death remedy is available under general maritime law for the death of a harborworker attributable to negligence, even though "neither the Jones Act (which applies only to seamen) nor DOHSA (which does not cover territorial waters) provided such a remedy." *Townsend*, 557 U.S. at 421 (citations omitted). The broader point made in *Townsend*, which I would heed today, is that "[t]he laudable quest for uniformity in admiralty does not require the narrowing of available damages to the lowest common denominator approved by Congress for distinct causes of action." *Id.* at 424.

To give effect to that principle, *Townsend* established a straightforward rule, fully faithful to its earlier *Miles* decision: if a general maritime law cause [—52—] of action and remedy were established before the passage of the Jones Act, and the Jones Act did not address that cause of action or remedy, then that remedy remains available under that cause of action unless and until Congress intercedes.[14] Estis did not dispute that the rule's premises are satisfied in this case: the cause of action (unseaworthiness) and the remedy (punitive damages) were both established before the passage of the Jones Act, and that statute did not address unseaworthiness or its remedies; indeed, the Supreme Court has been clear that the Jones

---

[14] *Id.* at 414–15 ("The settled legal principles discussed above establish three points central to resolving this case. First, punitive damages have long been available at common law. Second, the common-law tradition of punitive damages extends to maritime claims. And third, there is no evidence that claims for maintenance and cure were excluded from this general admiralty rule. Instead, the pre-Jones Act evidence indicates that punitive damages remain available for such claims under the appropriate factual circumstances. As a result, respondent is entitled to pursue punitive damages unless Congress has enacted legislation departing from this common-law understanding. As explained below, it has not.") (footnote omitted); *id.* at 420 ("Unlike the situation presented in *Miles*, both the general maritime cause of action (maintenance and cure) and the remedy (punitive damages) were well established before the passage of the Jones Act. Also unlike the facts presented by *Miles*, the Jones Act does not address maintenance and cure or its remedy. It is therefore possible to adhere to the traditional understanding of maritime actions and remedies without abridging or violating the Jones Act.") (citations and footnote omitted); *id.* at 424 ("Because punitive damages have long been an accepted remedy under general maritime law, and because nothing in the Jones Act altered this understanding, such damages for the willful and wanton disregard of the maintenance and cure obligation should remain available in the appropriate case as a matter of general maritime law.").

Act enlarged seamen's protection.[15] Seeking to avoid the conclusion that follows, Estis attempts to distinguish *Townsend*. [—53—]

---

[15] To the extent that Estis does argue that historically, punitive damages have been unavailable as a remedy for unseaworthiness, it misses the point of *Townsend*. *Townsend* established that "the common-law tradition of punitive damages extends to maritime claims." *Townsend*, 557 U.S. at 414; *see also id.* at 424 ("Because punitive damages have long been an accepted remedy under general maritime law, and because nothing in the Jones Act altered this understanding . . . ."). Just as in *Townsend*, Estis provides no evidence that claims for unseaworthiness "were excluded from this general admiralty rule." *Id.* at 415. At best, Estis's historical review matches that of the dissent in *Townsend*. In *Townsend*, however, Justice Thomas dismissed historical ambiguity in a footnote worth reproducing here: [—53—]

> The dissent correctly notes that the handful of early cases involving maintenance and cure, by themselves, do not definitively resolve the question of punitive damages availability in such cases. However, it neglects to acknowledge that the general common-law rule made punitive damages available in maritime actions. Nor does the dissent explain why maintenance and cure actions should be excepted from this general rule. It is because of this rule, and the fact that these early cases support-rather than refute-its application to maintenance and cure actions, that the pre-Jones Act evidence supports the conclusion that punitive damages were available at common law where the denial of maintenance and cure involved wanton, willful, or outrageous conduct.

Id. at 414 n.4 (internal citations omitted). Accordingly, *Townsend* makes clear that in the face of historical dispute, the default rule of punitive damages applies.

The Concurring Opinion of 5 colleagues ("Concurring Op."), however, finds *Townsend* to be a "thin strand" offering only "minimal support." Concurring Op. 2. But Justice Thomas did not limit his historical review to maintenance and cure claims; the Court instead clarified that "[t]he general rule that punitive damages were available at common law extended to claims arising under federal maritime law." *Id.* at 411 (section "II.B" of the opinion). Respectfully, the Concurring Opinion's criticism that I should not "blithely

Estis contends, and the Majority Opinion accepts, that finding punitive damages available would overrule *Miles*. This view overbroadly construes *Miles* to require uniform displacement even as to preexisting causes of action or remedies without clear statutory language or intent.[16] This was an [—54—] expansion taken in *Guevara*, then constrained by the Supreme Court in *Townsend*. The Supreme Court did not touch punitive damages in *Miles*; indeed, our court asserted the *availability* of punitive damages for unseaworthiness claims yet the Supreme Court *certiorari* grant and opinion did not encompass or alter that holding. *See Miles*, 882 F.2d at 989. Indeed, the Court in *Miles* itself noted that a plaintiff may recover for pain and suffering, damages framed as

---

assume" that punitive damages were available for claims arising under the general maritime law is directed at Section II.B of Justice Thomas's majority opinion, a point he deemed "central to resolving this case." *Id.* at 414-15; Concurring Op. at 5.

[16] The Majority Opinion frames *Miles* as involving a "wrongful death" action. Maj. Op. 7. This framing, however, misplaces "wrongful death" in *Townsend*'s analysis, which asks whether the cause of action and the remedy were well established before the Jones Act. *Townsend*, 557 U.S. at 420–21. Unseaworthiness is the underlying *cause of action* relevant to *Townsend*'s analysis. The Majority Opinion acknowledges this when describing *Miles*'s holding: "the Court considered the issue presented directly in this case: the scope of the survivor's recovery in her *general maritime law/unseaworthiness action* for wrongful death." Maj. Op. 7-8 (emphasis added). I agree with this description of *Miles*: the general maritime cause of action is unseaworthiness (an action that no one disputes was well established before the Jones Act), and the question remains as to what remedies are available to a plaintiff who brings an unseaworthiness claim. As to the remedy in this case, punitive damages, *Townsend* announced the default rule that punitive damages are available for actions under the general maritime law (such as unseaworthiness). Decisively, *Townsend* dismissed the argument that "[*Miles*] limited recovery in maritime cases *involving death* or personal injury to the remedies [—54—] available under the Jones Act and the Death on the High Seas Act (DOHSA)," as reading *Miles* "far too broad[ly]." *Townsend*, 557 U.S. at 418 (emphasis added).

nonpecuniary. *Miles*, 498 U.S. at 22.[17] Moreover, *Townsend* declined to reach whether punitive damages are available under the Jones Act:

> Because we hold that *Miles* does not render the Jones Act's damages provision determinative of respondent's remedies, we do not address the dissent's argument that the Jones Act, by incorporating the provisions of the Federal Employers' Liability Act, see 46 U.S.C. § 30104(a), prohibits the recovery of punitive damages in actions under that statute.

557 U.S. at 424 n.12. If Estis's argument adopted in the Majority Opinion is correct that *Miles* directly forecloses the availability of punitive damages for unseaworthiness claims, then *Miles* would have closed the same question as applied to Jones Act claims without need for this exact qualification.

Estis attempts to distinguish *Townsend* on the ground that it involved a maintenance and cure claim, as opposed to an unseaworthiness claim. It is true that unseaworthiness claims are more closely related to negligence claims than they are to maintenance and cure claims. But as we noted in *Guevara*—the primary case upon which Estis relies—the displacement analysis for [—55—] unseaworthiness claims is "wholly applicable to maintenance and cure cases as well." *Guevara*, 59 F.3d at 1504. Indeed, if the decisive paragraph in *Townsend* were amended by replacing "maintenance and cure" with "unseaworthiness," it would retain its persuasive force:

> Unlike the situation presented in *Miles*, both the general maritime cause of action ([unseaworthiness]) and the remedy (punitive damages) were well established before the passage of the Jones Act. Also unlike the facts presented by *Miles*, the Jones Act does not address [unseaworthiness] or its remedy. It is therefore possible to

---

[17] We recognized this in our opinion as well. *Miles*, 882 F.2d at 985.

adhere to the traditional understanding of maritime actions and remedies without abridging or violating the Jones Act; unlike wrongful-death actions, this traditional understanding is not a matter to which "Congress has spoken directly." Indeed, the *Miles* Court itself acknowledged that "[t]he Jones Act evinces no general hostility to recovery under maritime law," and noted that statutory remedy limitations "would not necessarily deter us, if recovery . . . were more consistent with the general principles of maritime tort law." The availability of punitive damages for [unseaworthiness] actions is entirely faithful to these "general principles of maritime tort law," and no statute casts doubt on their availability under general maritime law.

Townsend, 557 U.S. at 420–21 (citations omitted).

Estis argues also that the "chronological" framework announced in *Townsend* is inapt because of the evolution of claims of unseaworthiness. Unlike maintenance and cure, which has remained unchanged in substance for centuries, the claim of unseaworthiness has evolved over the years. Although it was well established before the passage of the Jones Act, it did not become a strict liability claim until 1944, *Mahnich v. Southern S.S. Co.*, 321 U.S. 96, 100 (1944), and was not available to seamen killed during the course of their employment until 1970, *Moragne*, 398 U.S. at 409. [—56—]

I agree that this case differs from *Townsend* in that respect. That is, punitive damages for the willful violation of the duty to provide maintenance and cure appear to have been available, if sparingly awarded, during the pre-Jones Act era. *See Townsend*, 557 U.S. at 414 (citing *The City of Carlisle*, 39 F. at 809, 817 and *The Troop*, 118 F. at 770–71, 773). It is less clear whether punitive damages were awarded for unseaworthiness violations during that period. *See supra* note 15. The parties did not brief this point to the panel, perhaps respectful of the Supreme Court's determination of the issue in *Townsend*. *See*

Townsend, 557 U.S. at 408–15 (section II of the Court's opinion). This distinction, if factually supported and not foreclosed by the Supreme Court, would change the inquiry: the question would not be whether the Jones Act was intended to displace existing remedies, but whether it was meant to foreclose future remedies. But the outcome would be the same.

Our task is not to reconstruct maritime law as it existed in 1920, but to assess whether Congress, in passing the Jones Act and DOHSA, intended to displace pre-existing maritime remedies or foreclose them going forward. *See Townsend*, 557 U.S. at 419–25. Let us assume for the sake of argument, contrary to *Townsend*, that maritime courts during the pre-Jones Act era had taken no position on the propriety of punitive damages in unseaworthiness actions; that Congress in 1920 was painting on a blank canvas. Had Congress "spoken directly" on the matter, then I would follow its guidance. *Townsend*, 557 U.S. at 420–21; *Miles*, 498 U.S. at 27, 32–33. But the Jones Act does not mention unseaworthiness or its remedies nor has any legislative history to that effect been urged or identified to us. 46 U.S.C. § 30104. And "a remedial omission in the Jones Act is not evidence of considered congressional policymaking that should command our adherence in analogous contexts." *Am.* [—57—] *Export Lines, Inc. v. Alvez*, 446 U.S. 274, 283–84 (1980); *see also id.* at 282 ("Nor do we read the Jones Act as sweeping aside general maritime law remedies."). Similarly, "no intention appears that [DOHSA] ha[d] the effect of foreclosing any nonstatutory federal remedies that might be found appropriate to effectuate the policies of general maritime law." *Moragne*, 398 U.S. at 400. Given that "the absence of federal legislation constraining punitive damages does not imply a congressional decision that there should be no quantified rule," *Baker*, 554 U.S. at 508 n.21, it follows that the matter remained open after the Jones Act and DOHSA. We resolved it in *Merry Shipping* when we held that punitive damages *were* an appropriate remedy to effectuate the policies of general maritime law, *see Merry Shipping*, 650 F.2d at 625–26, a view shared then and since by other circuit courts. *See, e.g.*, cases cited *supra* note 8. The

Majority Opinion strongly implies but never asserts directly that the Jones Act did in fact address unseaworthiness and its remedies. The Majority Opinion distinguishes *Townsend* because "[u]nlike the seaman's remedy for damages based on negligence *and unseaworthiness*, 'the Jones Act does not address maintenance and cure or its remedy.'" Maj. Op. 12 (emphasis added). As discussed, no party has taken the position that the Jones Act addresses unseaworthiness or its remedies, likely because this interpretation of the Jones Act lacks support and, indeed, contradicted by the Supreme Court in *Usner. See Chisholm v. Sabine Towing & Transp. Co., Inc.*, 679 F.2d 60, 62 (5th Cir. 1982); *Usner*, 400 U.S. at 498; *Brunner*, 779 F.2d at 298.

Estis goes on to argue that allowing seamen to recover punitive damages under general maritime law would create a number of anomalies. Though one acknowledged function of maritime courts is to reconcile anomalies that present themselves in the law, *e.g., Moragne*, 398 U.S. at 395–409 (overruling [—**58**—] *The Harrisburg*, 119 U.S. at 205 to remedy three maritime law anomalies), I perceive no anomalies.

Estis argues that this approach would allow plaintiffs to circumvent the pecuniary damages limitation in the Jones Act by pleading a claim for unseaworthiness. This is not an anomaly, as the Supreme Court has highlighted; it is a traditional feature of maritime law designed to protect seamen, the wards of admiralty.[18] By design, seamen have always had the "right to choose among overlapping statutory and common-law remedies" for their injuries. *Townsend*, 557 U.S. at 423 (citation omitted); *see also Cortes v. Baltimore Insular Lines*, 287 U.S. 367, 374–75 (1932) (A seaman's "cause of action for personal injury created by the [Jones Act] may

have overlapped his cause of action for breach of the maritime duty of maintenance and cure, just as it may have overlapped his cause of action for injury caused through an unseaworthy ship. In such circumstances it was his privilege, in so far as the causes of action covered the same ground, to sue indifferently on any one of them.") (citations omitted); *Hlodan v. Ohio Barge Line, Inc.*, 611 F.2d 71, 75 (5th Cir. 1980) ("[A] Jones Act claim may be joined with a wrongful death claim for nonpecuniary damages based on general maritime law, where the incident does not arise on the high seas, and that nonpecuniary damages may be recovered under the unseaworthiness claim.") (citations omitted). That a violation of the unseaworthiness duty "may also give rise to a Jones Act claim [—**59**—] is significant only in that it requires admiralty courts to ensure against double recovery." *Townsend*, 557 U.S. at 423 n.10 (citation omitted).

Estis argues, similarly, that it would be anomalous for the law to allow different remedies for what amounts to the same cause of action. It is crucial to reiterate, however, that although similar, the Supreme Court has demonstrated that Jones Act negligence and unseaworthiness are "separate and distinct" claims with different elements and standards of causation. *Chisholm*, 679 F.2d at 62 (citation omitted); *see also Usner*, 400 U.S. at 498; *Brunner*, 779 F.2d at 298. Plaintiffs often bring claims for both causes of action, and the same act that results in liability for one will often result in liability for the other, but that is a common feature of the law. Relatedly, Estis argues that it would make little sense to permit the recovery of punitive damages for unseaworthiness, which imposes liability without regard to fault, while denying such relief on a Jones Act claim, which requires a finding of negligence. *See Merry Shipping*, 650 F.2d at 626. This argument especially overlooks that punitive damages recovery always requires a high culpability finding of willful and wanton conduct, whether the cause of action is for maintenance and cure or unseaworthiness. *See id; see also Stowe v. Moran Towing Corp.*, No. 13-0390, 2014 WL 247544, at *7 (E.D La. Jan. 22, 2014) (relying on *McBride* to note that "[o]f course, punitive

---

[18] Seamen have long been characterized as "wards of admiralty" deserving special protection under maritime law. *See, e.g., Townsend*, 557 U.S. at 417 (noting that seamen are "peculiarly the wards of admiralty"); *Robertson v. Baldwin*, 165 U.S. 275, 287 (1897) ("The ancient characterization of seamen as 'wards of admiralty' is even more accurate now than it was formerly.").

damages are available as a remedy to seamen under the general maritime law claim of unseaworthiness" but dismissing the claim because the finding of willful and wanton conduct was "missing on this record").[19] Punitive damages differ in that [—60—] way from other types of non-pecuniary damages, such as the loss of society damages addressed in *Miles*. In light of that distinction, we previously have rejected this argument against allowing punitive damages recovery under general maritime law. *Id.* ("It does not follow . . . that if punitive damages are not allowed under the Jones Act, they should also not be allowed under general maritime law [because] recovery of punitive damages is restricted to where there is willful and wanton misconduct, reflecting a reckless disregard for the safety of the crew, a much higher standard of culpability than that required for Jones Act liability."). The central concern of *Miles*—that it would be inappropriate to "sanction more expansive remedies in a judicially created cause of action in which liability is without fault than Congress has allowed in cases of death resulting from negligence"—thus, is not present here. 498 U.S. at 32–33.

2.

The Majority Opinion's emphasis on the deceased plaintiff in *Miles* risks the broadening error committed by the losing party in *Townsend*, corrected by the Supreme Court: "In *Miles*, petitioners argue, the Court limited recovery in maritime cases *involving*

death or personal injury to the remedies available under the Jones Act and the Death on the High Seas Act (DOHSA)." *Townsend*, 557 U.S. at 418 (emphasis added). The Court explained that "[p]etitioners' [—61—] reading of *Miles* is far too broad." But even accepting Estis's broad view that a case involving death is so limited, this reasoning would lose all force as applied to personal-injury plaintiffs raising unseaworthiness claims. As to them, *Townsend* applies straightforwardly: *Townsend* described the availability of punitive damages as a "general admiralty rule" applicable to "maritime claims," *id.* at 414–15, and no party has argued that the Jones Act addressed unseaworthiness, let alone that it excepted unseaworthiness from the general maritime rule.[20] *See e.g.*, *In re Asbestos Prods. Liab. Litig.*, MDL No.875, 2014 WL 3353044, at *2–11 (E.D. Pa. July 9, 2014) ("In sum, a general maritime claim of unseaworthiness can support a punitive damages award when brought directly by an injured seaman, but not when brought by a seaman's personal representative as part of a wrongful death or survival action. Put simply, the remedy of punitive damages exists as it did prior to the passage of the Jones Act, and thus does not survive a seaman's death.").

Moreover, the Supreme Court in *Townsend* explained that its general rule applies

---

[19] To the extent that Estis argues that the availability of punitive damages is disruptive, it may be noted that (1) punitive damages were available under *Merry Shipping*, (2) punitive damages are the rule with respect to maintenance and cure, (3) the Supreme [—60—] Court has rejected the argument that punitive damages unduly impact settlement negotiations, *see Baker*, 544 U.S. at 498 n.15 ("One might posit that ill effects of punitive damages are clearest not in actual awards but in the shadow that the punitive regime casts on settlement negotiations and other litigation decisions. But here again the data have not established a clear correlation. (internal citations omitted)), (4) courts can sanction parties if punitive damages are frivolously alleged, and, crucially, (5) Congress can always withdraw their availability.

---

[20] As discussed, *Townsend* stressed the default availability of punitive damages for general maritime causes of action, referring to this "rule" three times in one footnote:

> However, [the dissent] neglects to acknowledge that the general common-law rule made punitive damages available in maritime actions. Nor does the dissent explain why maintenance and cure actions should be excepted from this general rule. It is because of this rule, and the fact that these early cases support—rather than refute—its application to maintenance and cure actions, that the pre-Jones Act evidence supports the conclusion that punitive damages were available at common law where the denial of maintenance and cure involved wanton, willful, or outrageous conduct.

Id. at 414 n.4 (internal citations omitted).

undiminished even when a general maritime claim is, as the Majority Opinion writes, "joined with" or "predicated on" a Jones Act claim. Maj. Op. 2, 11. "The fact that, in some cases, a violation of the duty of [—62—] maintenance and cure may also give rise to a Jones Act claim, is significant *only in* that it requires admiralty courts to ensure against double recovery." *Townsend*, 557 U.S. at 423 n.10 (emphasis added). Under the Majority Opinion's view, however, that an unseaworthiness claim is "joined with" a Jones Act claim is significant in another respect unidentified by the Supreme Court in *Townsend*: it precludes seamen from invoking the general maritime rule providing for punitive damages. Only by contravening *Townsend*'s established rule, then, can Estis offer its position, adopted by the Majority Opinion, that *Miles* forecloses the availability punitive damages in an unseaworthiness injury case. The Majority Opinion concludes otherwise because "no one has suggested why [*Miles*'s] holding and reasoning would not apply to an injury case." Maj. Op. 10. This analysis has no post-*Townsend* support and, instead contravenes the Supreme Court's instruction by inappropriately placing the burden on the seamen to demonstrate that the general maritime rule announced in *Townsend* has been extinguished. As the Supreme Court in *Townsend* instructed, the burden squarely is on Congress: "respondent is entitled to pursue punitive damages unless Congress has enacted legislation departing from this common-law understanding." *Townsend*, 557 U.S. at 415. Congressional silence therefore is oppositely dispositive, and even under the Majority Opinion's broadened interpretation of *Miles*, reversal would be warranted as to the injured seamen, Suire and Touchet.

CONCLUSION

Like maintenance and cure, unseaworthiness was established as a general maritime claim before the passage of the Jones Act, punitive damages were available under general maritime law, and the Jones Act does not address [—63—] unseaworthiness or limit its remedies. I would conclude that punitive damages remain available to seamen as a remedy for the general maritime law claim of unseaworthiness until Congress says they do not. *See Townsend*, 557 U.S. 404.[21]

(Reporter's Note: Dissenting opinion on p. 352).

---

[21] Having so concluded, like the Supreme Court, I would decline to revisit whether punitive damages are available to seamen bringing claims for negligence under the Jones Act. *See Townsend*, 557 U.S. at 424 n.12 (declining to decide whether punitive damages are available to a seaman in a cause of action for negligence under the Jones Act after ruling that such damages are available to a seaman in a cause of action for maintenance and cure).

[—64—] **GRAVES**, Circuit Judge, dissenting, joined by **DENNIS**, Circuit Judge:

I join Judge Higginson's dissent in full, and fully agree with its reasoning and conclusions. I write in support and amplification of the dissent's observation that extending the *Miles* pecuniary damages limitation to the injured crew members in this case compounds the error in the majority opinion.

Even under the majority's view that *Miles v. Apex Marine*, 498 U.S. 19 (1990) is the controlling case, the majority extends *Miles* much too far. There are four plaintiffs in this case: Haleigh McBride, as administratrix of the estate of Skye Sonnier, a seaman who was killed in the accident, and Saul Touchet, Brian Suire, and Joshua Bourque, seamen who were injured in the accident. All four assert causes of action based on unseaworthiness under general maritime law and negligence under the Jones Act. The majority concludes that punitive damages are unavailable for all four of the plaintiffs because, under the *Miles* approach, recovery for death or injury predicated on the Jones Act or unseaworthiness is limited to "pecuniary" damages, and punitive damages are non-pecuniary.

However, read with its proper scope, the pecuniary damages limitation recognized in *Miles* applies only to the wrongful death causes of action brought by McBride. It does not apply to Touchet, Suire, and Bourque, who are seamen asserting Jones Act negligence and general maritime law unseaworthiness causes of action on their own behalf. The pecuniary damage limitation was created in the context of wrongful death statutes, and by statute, history and logic, it applies only to survivors asserting wrongful death claims. This distinction is inherent in the text of the Jones Act itself, which allows a survivor or personal representative to sue in wrongful death only if the seamen dies from the injury. 46 U.S.C § 30104; *see Sistrunk v. Circle Bar Drilling Co.*, 770 F.2d 455, 457 (5th Cir. 1985) (summarizing the actions available in [—65—] maritime death and injury cases). If the seaman survives, he must bring his own action, and the pecuniary damages limitation created by wrongful death statutes and case law should be inapplicable.

It is well-recognized that the original source of the pecuniary damages limitation in maritime law is the Federal Employee Liability Act (FELA), which was incorporated into the Jones Act at its passage. *Miles*, 498 U.S. at 32. However, the FELA limitation of recovery to "pecuniary" damages originally applied only to survivors bringing wrongful death claims, and did not apply to plaintiffs asserting claims for their own injury. In *Michigan Central R. Co. v. Vreeland*, 227 U.S. 59 (1913), the Supreme Court explained that the language of FELA is "essentially identical" to the first wrongful death statute, Lord Campbell's Act, 9 & 10 Vict. ch. 93 (1846), which did not explicitly limit available damages, "but that Act and the many state statutes that followed it consistently had been interpreted as providing recovery only for pecuniary loss." *Miles*, 498 U.S. at 32; *Vreeland*, 227 U.S. at 69-71. The *Miles* Court stated that "[w]hen Congress passed the Jones Act, the *Vreeland* gloss on FELA, and the hoary tradition behind it, were well established. Incorporating FELA unaltered into the Jones Act, Congress must have intended to incorporate the pecuniary limitation on damages as well." *Miles*, 498 U.S. at 32. The majority, however, misinterprets the scope of the pecuniary damages limitation recognized in *Miles*, and historically recognized in FELA and Jones Act cases.

Supreme Court case law discussing FELA and the Jones Act show that the statutory limitation of recovery to "pecuniary" damages applies only to wrongful death claims brought by survivors. Prior to the passage of the Jones Act in 1920, the Supreme Court repeatedly held that FELA's pecuniary damages limitation applied to survivors asserting wrongful death claims, and distinguished those claims from claims brought by injured employees [—66—] themselves. In *Vreeland*, the Court explained that the FELA wrongful death cause of action is independent of any cause of action which the decedent had, and includes no damages which he might have recovered for his injury if he had survived. It is one beyond that which the decedent had,—one proceeding upon altogether different principles. It is a liability for the loss and damage sustained by relatives dependent upon the decedent. It is therefore a liability for the pecuniary damage resulting to them, and for that only.

227 U.S. at 69. In *St. Louis, I.M. & S. Ry. Co. v. Craft,* the Court again distinguished between the employee's own rights and that of his survivors. The Court explained that FELA

invests the injured employee with a right to such damages as will compensate him for his personal loss and suffering,—a right which arises only where his injuries are not immediately fatal. And where his injuries prove fatal, either immediately or subsequently, it invests his personal representative, as a trustee for designated relatives, with a right to such damages as will compensate the latter for any pecuniary loss which they sustain by the death.

237 U.S. 648, 656 (1915) (internal citation omitted) (citing *Vreeland,* 227 U.S. at 68; *Louisville, E. & St. L. R. Co. v. Clarke,* 152 U.S. 230, 238 (1894); *see also Gulf, C. & S.F. Ry. Co. v. McGinnis,* 228 U.S. 173, 175-76 (1913). In *Van Beeck v. Sabine Towing Co.,* the Court adopted this same proposition under the Jones Act. The Court explained that under FELA, as incorporated by the Jones Act,

the personal representative does not step into the shoes of the employee, recovering the damages that would have been his if he had lived. On the contrary, by section 1 of the statute a new cause of action is created for the benefit of survivors or dependents of designated classes, the recovery being limited to the losses sustained by them as contrasted with any losses sustained by the decedent.

300 U.S. 342, 346 (1937). The *Van Beeck* Court went on to explain the effect of an amendment to FELA, which provided that the decedent's own claims, including for pain and suffering, survived his death: [—67—]

However, with the adoption of an amendment in 1910, a new aspect of the statute emerges into view. Section 2 as then enacted continues any cause of action belonging to the decedent, without abrogating or diminishing the then existing cause of action for the use of his survivors. Although originating in the same wrongful act or neglect, the two claims are quite distinct, no part of either being embraced in the other. One is for the wrong to the injured person, and is confined to his personal loss and suffering before he died, while the other is for the wrong to the beneficiaries, and is confined to their pecuniary loss through his death.

Id. at 347 (citations and internal quotation omitted).[1]

---

[1] In *Ivy v. Sec. Barge Lines, Inc.,* this court stated: "In the 66 years since the Vreeland decision, its principle that recovery under the F.E.L.A. is limited to pecuniary damages has remained a constant roadbed for railway workers suits. The same principle has uniformly been adopted with respect to Jones Act death action." 606 F.2d 524, 526 (5th Cir. 1979) (en banc). Every single case cited for these propositions in *Ivy* is a wrongful death action brought by survivors, in the FELA context, *id.* at 526 n.4 (citing *Chesapeake & O. Ry. Co. v. Kelly,* 241 U.S. 485, 487 (1916); *Am. R. Co. of Porto Rico v. Didricksen,* 227 U.S. 145, 149 (1913); *Stark v. Chicago, N. Shore & Milwaukee Ry. Co.,* 203 F.2d 786, 788 (7th Cir. 1953); *Mobile & O.R. Co. v. Williams,* 129 So. 60, 66 (Ala. 1930); *Atl. Coast Line R. Co. v. Daugherty,* 157 S.E.2d 880, 888 (Ga. 1967); *Simmons v. Louisiana Ry. & Nav. Co.,* 96 So. 12 (La. 1923); *Torchia v. Burlington N., Inc.,* 568 P.2d 558, 565 (Mont. 1977)), and in the Jones Act context, *id.* at 526 n.5 (citing *In re of M/V Elaine Jones,* 480 F.2d 11, 31 (5th Cir. 1973); *Cities Serv. Oil Co. v. Launey,* 403 F.2d 537, 540 (5th Cir. 1968); *Igneri v. Cie. de Transports Oceaniques,* 323 F.2d 257, 266 (2d Cir. 1963); *Sabine Towing Co. v. Brennan,* 85 F.2d 478, 481 (5th Cir. 1936) *rev'd sub nom. Van Beeck v. Sabine Towing Co.,* 300 U.S. 342 (1937); *United States v. Boykin,* 49 F.2d 762, 763 (5th Cir. 1931); *Thompson v. Offshore Co.,* 440 F.

These cases make it exceedingly clear that, at the time the Jones Act was passed, wrongful death claims that could be brought by a survivor were distinguished from an employee's own claims for his own injuries under FELA, and the pecuniary damages limitation applied only to the former. *See Van Beeck*, 300 U.S. at 346-47; *St. Louis, I.M.*, 237 U.S. at 656; *Vreeland*, 227 U.S. at 69-71; *see also Cook v. Ross Island Sand & Gravel Co.*, 626 F.2d 746, 749 (9th Cir. 1980) ("Yet, while the Jones Act arguably may apply a pecuniary loss [—68—] restriction to the personal losses of a decedent's beneficiaries, the Act does not apply a pecuniary loss restriction to the injuries of a decedent himself."); *Deal v. A.P. Bell Fish Co.*, 728 F.2d 717, 718 (5th Cir. 1984) (citing *Cook* for the proposition that "the pain and suffering of a drowning seaman is a compensable injury in a wrongful death action under the Jones Act").

Likewise, *Miles* is solely a wrongful death case, and its recognition of a pecuniary damage limitation applies to survivors asserting wrongful death claims. *Miles* itself explained that the plaintiff could not recover loss of society because "[t]he Jones Act applies *when a seaman has been killed* as a result of negligence, and it limits recovery to pecuniary loss." *Miles*, 498 U.S. at 32 (emphasis added). Indeed, all of the reasoning in *Miles* is applicable to survivors bringing wrongful death actions, rather than injured seamen seeking recovery for their own injuries. The *Townsend* Court's discussion of *Miles* makes this clear.

The Court in *Miles* first concluded that the "unanimous legislative judgment behind the Jones Act, DOHSA, and the many state statutes" authorizing *maritime wrongful-death actions*, supported the recognition of a general maritime action for wrongful death of a seaman. Congress had chosen to limit,

however, the damages available for *wrongful-death actions* under the Jones Act and DOHSA, such that damages were not statutorily available for loss of society or lost future earnings. The Court thus concluded that Congress' judgment must control the availability of remedies *for wrongful-death actions* brought under general maritime law.

Atl. Sounding Co., Inc. v. Townsend, 557 U.S. 404, 419 (2009) (citations omitted and emphases added) (quoting *Miles*, 498 U.S. at 24). This is logical, at least pre-*Townsend*, given that the wrongful death cause of action was originally a creation of statutes that have long been read to limit survivors' recovery to their pecuniary losses. *See Miles*, 498 U.S. at 32; *Vreeland*, 227 U.S. at 69-71. But *Miles* says nothing indicating that it intended to recognize a pecuniary [—69—] damage limitation that applies more broadly than the pre-Jones Act FELA limitation.

There is no similar statute, history, or logic limiting seamen's own recovery to their pecuniary losses. No authority indicates that when the Jones Act incorporated FELA, it expanded the pecuniary damage limitation to injured seamen asserting their own claims for their own injuries. Indeed, with this law as background, the *Miles* Court's recognition that "Incorporating FELA unaltered into the Jones Act, Congress must have intended to incorporate the pecuniary limitation on damages as well," *Miles*, 498 U.S. at 32, means something far more limited than the majority recognizes.[2]

Supp. 752, 762 (S.D. Tex. 1977); *In re of Risdal & Anderson, Inc.*, 291 F. Supp. 353, 358 (D. Mass. 1968); *In re of S. S S Co.*, 135 F. Supp. 358, 360 (D. Del. 1955); *Am. Barge Line Co. v. Leatherman's Adm'x*, 206 S.W.2d 955, 957 (Ky. 1947); *Standard Products, Inc. v. Patterson*, 317 So. 2d 376, 378 (Miss. 1975)).

[2] The majority opinion cites only *Murray v. Anthony J. Bertucci Const. Co., Inc.*, 958 F.2d 127 (5th Cir. 1992), as justification for extending the Miles pecuniary damages to an injury case. But of course, in *Murray*, the court held that the spouse of an injured seaman could not recover for loss of society. *Id.* at 128; *but see Am. Exp. Lines, Inc. v. Alvez*, 446 U.S. 274, 276 (1980) (holding that spouse of longshoreman injured in territorial waters could recover loss of society in general maritime law action). That case may provide justification for limiting the recovery of a spouse or dependent in an injury case to pecuniary loss, but provides no justification for extending the pecuniary damage limitation to seamen seeking recovery for their own injuries.

The contrast between the limited "pecuniary" damages that, under the majority's approach, are recoverable in wrongful death actions under FELA and the Jones Act, and the categories of damages that have always been available to seamen, further reveals the error in the majority opinion. The majority briefly implies that "pecuniary" damages are broadly equivalent to "compensatory" damages, which allows the opinion to reason that the pecuniary damage limitation bars recovery of non-pecuniary punitive damages. Although some courts have in the past sporadically discussed them as if they are coextensive, see *Kozar v. Chesapeake & O. Ry. Co.*, 449 F.2d 1238, 1243 (6th Cir. 1971), the relevant statutes and case law, including *Miles* itself, [—70—] do not conflate pecuniary damages with compensatory damages. Instead, "pecuniary" damages are understood to be far narrower.

Miles adopted the Death on the High Seas Act (DOHSA) limitation of damages to "pecuniary loss sustained by the persons for whose benefit suit is brought." *Miles*, 498 U.S. at 31; see also *Mobil Oil Corp. v. Higginbotham*, 436 U.S. 618, 620 (1978). Both *Miles* and *Higginbotham* considered claims for loss of society damages brought by survivors in statutory wrongful death actions, and denied recovery because loss of society damages are non-pecuniary. *Miles*, 498 U.S. at 31-32; *Higginbotham*, 436 U.S. at 623-24. However, neither case provides a definition of "pecuniary," beyond excluding loss of society. DOHSA restricts recovery to "a fair and just compensation for the pecuniary loss sustained by the persons for whose benefit the suit is brought." *Higginbotham*, 436 U.S. at 620; 46 U.S.C. § 30303. This DOHSA limitation, however, applies only to "the decedent's spouse, parent, child, or dependent relative." 46 U.S.C. § 30302; see *Bodden v. Am. Offshore, Inc.*, 681 F.2d 319, 331 (5th Cir. 1982) (explaining that DOHSA "apportions recovery of fair and just compensation for the pecuniary loss sustained by the persons for whose benefit the suit is brought, and that those injuries are "unique to the decedent's dependents and could not accrue until the decedent's death"). The statute does not provide that the pecuniary loss is equivalent

to "fair and just" compensation for all losses, but merely provides for compensation for "pecuniary" losses in an action brought by a decedent's specified beneficiaries. 46 U.S.C. § 30303; see *Higginbotham*, 436 U.S. at 623 (noting that DOHSA "has limited survivors to recovery of *their* pecuniary losses" (emphasis added)); see also *Dooley v. Korean Air Lines Co., Ltd.*, 524 U.S. 116, 123 (1998) (explaining that DOHSA "authorize[es] only certain surviving relatives to recover damages," and "limit[s] damages to the pecuniary losses sustained by those relatives"). [—71—]

Similarly, *Vreeland*—which again is the original source of the FELA limitation of recovery to pecuniary damages—defined "pecuniary" damages far more narrowly than the majority does, explaining that

> A pecuniary loss or damage must be one which can be measured by some standard. It is a term employed judicially, not only to express the character of that loss to the beneficial plaintiffs which is the foundation of their right of recovery, but also to discriminate between a material loss which is susceptible of a pecuniary valuation, and that inestimable loss of the society and companionship of the deceased relative upon which, in the nature of things, it is not possible to set a pecuniary valuation.

227 U.S. at 71 (citation and quotation omitted). This understanding of "pecuniary" damages refers to whether a relative's or beneficiary's loss itself is a financial one that is estimable in monetary terms. In light of *Vreeland's* recognition that this pecuniary damage limitation applied only to survivors, *id.* at 68, this narrow definition is also quite logical. The survivors in *Miles* and *Higginbotham* could not recover loss of society because loss of society, unlike loss of support, is not primarily a financial loss. *Miles*, 498 U.S. at 31; *Higginbotham*, 436 U.S. at 623. With respect to survivors' own recovery, the law had chosen to draw a line between monetary losses and other, more intangible losses. See *Vreeland*, 227 U.S. at 71.

It seems illogical that this principle would be extended to injured seamen seeking recovery for their own injuries. For example, pain and suffering is not a financial loss and is difficult to reduce to a monetary amount; thus it is not a pecuniary damage according to the definition incorporated into FELA. *See id.* Yet there can be no question that injured seamen can seek recovery for their own pain and suffering under the Jones Act and the general maritime law. *E.g., Douse v. Global Pipelines Plus*, 253 F. App'x 342 (5th Cir. 2007) (in Jones Act case, agreeing that injured seamen properly recovered "maintenance and cure through the present, future maintenance and cure, past and future pain [—72—] and suffering, and past and future economic losses"); *Deal*, 728 F.2d at 718; *Crador v. Louisiana Dep't of Highways*, 625 F.2d 1227, 1230 (5th Cir. 1980) (noting that in Jones Act case, "In addition to loss of income the jury could award damages for pain and suffering and impact on one's normal life routines."). Indeed, in *Miles* itself, the plaintiff estate recovered for the pre-death pain and suffering of the decedent seamen. *Miles*, 498 U.S. at 22. By contrast, if we accept the majority's unexplained implication that pecuniary damages must be equivalent to compensatory damages, it is not clear why loss of society would not have been recoverable in *Miles* or *Higginbotham*, as it is not at all clear why loss of society damages are any less compensatory in nature than damages for pain and suffering. *See Sea-Land Servs., Inc. v. Gaudet*, 414 U.S. 573, 586 (1974) (noting that "[u]nquestionably, the deprivation of [society] by wrongful death is a grave loss to the decedent's dependents," and that the case law which barred recovery for loss of society did so on the basis of it being non-pecuniary). When loss of society is not recoverable in wrongful death actions, it is because it is non-pecuniary, not because it is not compensatory. *See id.*

The original view of the pecuniary damages limitation expressed in cases like *Vreeland* must be understood as the definition incorporated into the Jones Act and accepted by the *Miles* Court. *See Miles*, 498 U.S. at 31-32. Thus, even if the *Miles* analysis is applied in this case, *Miles's* recognition of FELA's pecuniary damage limitation is simply adherence to this case law distinguishing between a survivor's wrongful death claims and ability to recover and the rights and recovery of an injured employee or seaman himself.

There is no justification for applying the pecuniary damage limitation, a creature of wrongful death statutes and case law, to injured seamen seeking recovery for their own injuries. Even if the pecuniary damage limitation is applicable in this case, it must apply only to McBride, a survivor of a decedent [—73—] seaman asserting wrongful death claims, and not to Touchet, Suire, and Bourque, who assert unseaworthiness and Jones Act claims based on their own injuries. With *Miles's* pecuniary damage limitation inapplicable to the injured seamen, the dissent's *Townsend*-based approach is the correct analysis of the availability of punitive damages for Touchet, Suire, and Bourque.

United States Court of Appeals
for the Fifth Circuit

No. 12-30883

IN RE DEEPWATER HORIZON

UNITED STATES
vs.
BP EXPLORATION & PROD., INC.

Appeals from the United States District Court for the
Eastern District of Louisiana

Decided: November 5, 2014

Citation: 772 F.3d 350, 2 Adm. R. 357 (5th Cir. 2014).

Before **KING**, **BENAVIDES**, and **DENNIS**, Circuit
Judges.

[—1—] PER CURIAM:

Appellants B.P. Exploration & Production, Inc. ("BP") and Anadarko Petroleum Corporation ("Anadarko") have filed petitions for en banc rehearing of our judgment affirming the lower court's grant of partial summary judgment. The en banc petitions remain pending. Although the parties have not filed separate petitions for panel rehearing, BP has "request[ed] that the panel reconsider its analysis." BP Pet. Reh'g 9. We have done so, and we have also considered the arguments raised by Anadarko, which contends, *inter alia*, that the panel opinion is "likely to sow error in the ongoing trial below." [—2—] Anadarko Pet. Reh'g 13. We disagree with this characterization of our opinion, but, for the sake of clarity, we address some of the arguments raised in the petitions for rehearing en banc. For the reasons discussed below, Appellants' arguments fail to persuade us that we erred or need to alter our decision to affirm the district court's grant of partial summary judgment.

This case involves the federal government's civil enforcement action under Section 311 of the Clean Water Act (CWA), 33 U.S.C. § 1321(b)(7)(A), stemming from the 2010 *Deepwater Horizon* oil spill in the Gulf of Mexico. Section 311, a strict liability provision, mandates the assessment of fines on the owners or operators of any vessel or facility "from which oil or a hazardous substance is discharged." *Id.* In the panel opinion, we affirmed summary judgment on the issue of Appellants' liability under that provision. Interpreting the CWA according to its plain terms, we held that "a vessel or facility is a point 'from which oil or a hazardous substance is discharged' if it is a point at which controlled confinement is lost." *In re Deepwater Horizon*, 753 F.3d 570, 573, 2 Adm. R. 233, 235 (5th Cir. 2014) (quoting 33 U.S.C. § 1321(b)(7)(A)). We further determined that BP and Anadarko, as co-owners of the Macondo Well (the "well"), are liable under Section 311 because there was no dispute of material fact that controlled confinement of oil was lost in the well.

Appellants' various arguments challenging this holding can be grouped into two categories: those based on purported factual errors in the panel opinion, and those based on purported errors in the panel opinion's legal analysis. We address each in turn.

I. Purported Factual Errors in the Panel Opinion

Anadarko first contends that the panel opinion was premised on a mistake of fact, pointing to the following sentence in the opinion's statement of facts: "As part of this preparation [for the *Deepwater Horizon*'s departure from the well site], the well had been lined and sealed with cement." *In re Deepwater* [—3—] *Horizon*, 753 F.3d at 573, 2 Adm. R. at 233. Anadarko argues that, "[c]ontrary to the assumption of the Panel, all parties to this appeal agree that the cement never sealed off the well from the oil and gas in the rock formation beneath it." Anadarko Pet. Reh'g 2. Anadarko further contends that this purported factual error has created, and will continue to create, issues in the proceedings before the lower court. Anadarko Pet. Reh'g 13.

We are doubtful that the panel opinion has created any confusion on this issue. Nevertheless, we here clarify that the above statement was not intended to imply that the cement created a *successful* seal in the well. Anadarko is correct that all parties agree—

and the record is clear—that the cement job failed to prevent hydrocarbons—e.g., oil—from migrating into the wellbore. Indeed, in the sentence following the one at issue, we stated that, "[b]efore the *Deepwater Horizon* departed, this cement failed, resulting in the high-pressure release of gas, oil, and other fluids." *In re Deepwater Horizon*, 753 F.3d at 571, 2 Adm. R. at 233. In any event, this issue is a red herring. Whether the cement initially sealed the well was immaterial to the panel opinion's holding. As discussed in more detail below, it is only the fact that the cement in the well ultimately failed to stop the flow of oil (regardless of whether the cement at any prior point functioned as expected), and that control was therefore lost in the well, that prompted our determination that the well was a point "from which oil or a hazardous substance [was] discharged." 33 U.S.C. § 1321(b)(7)(A).

Anadarko also argues that the panel's holding has effectively denied it its Seventh Amendment right to a jury trial, as Anadarko was not permitted to put forward evidence regarding where controlled confinement was lost. However, the lower court placed no limit on the admissible evidence Anadarko could put forward in opposition to the Government's motion for summary judgment, and in support of its cross-motion for summary judgment, on the issue of Anadarko's Section 311 liability. Moreover, in its summary judgment [—4—] briefing, Anadarko conceded that there were no disputes of material fact with respect to this issue. *See* No. 2:10-MD-2179, Doc. 5113-2.[1] Undoubtedly aware of this concession, Anadarko now contends that it could not have anticipated either the lower court's or the panel's "unprecedented" interpretations of Section 311—finding liability based on where "the uncontrolled movement of oil began," *In re Oil Spill by Oil Rig Deepwater Horizon in Gulf of Mexico, on Apr. 20, 2010*, 844 F. Supp. 2d 746, 758 (E.D. La. 2012), and where "controlled confinement [was] lost," *In re Deepwater Horizon*, 753 F.3d at 573, 2 Adm.

R. at 235, respectively. But in its summary judgment briefing before the lower court, Anadarko was aware that "control" of the oil might be at issue. In support of its argument that the oil was discharged from the *Deepwater Horizon*, Anadarko stated, "the owners and operators of the vessel . . . failed to *maintain control* of the Macondo Well, and as a result of that failure, hydrocarbons discharged from the vessel and its appurtenances into the Gulf of Mexico." No. 2:10-MD-2179, Doc. 5113-2, at 4 (emphasis added).[2]

In any event, there are no additional facts that would alter our conclusion that controlled confinement was lost in the well. As we stated in the panel opinion, the only facts material to this analysis are undisputed. First, there is no question that Anadarko and BP are co-owners of the well. Nor do Appellants dispute that, as a result of the cement's failure, oil flowed into the well and, eventually, into the Gulf of Mexico. Before the lower court, in their responses to the Government's statement of undisputed facts, Appellants conceded for the purposes of summary judgment that "the cement [—5—] job failed to prevent hydrocarbons in the formation from migrating into the wellbore." No. 2:10-MD-2179, Doc. 5113-3, at 5–6; *see also* Doc. 5124-1, at 2. Appellants further conceded that "[t]he Macondo well cement job was critical for maintaining *well control*." No. 2:10-MD-2179, Doc. 5124-1, at 2 (emphasis added); *see also* Doc. 5113-3, at 5 (stating that the "cement job was a means of maintaining well control").[3] Even in their petitions for rehearing, Appellants do not dispute these facts. However, Anadarko now argues that, because the cement never properly sealed the well, the

---

[1] Anadarko did note that there may be disputed facts warranting a jury trial regarding the issue of whether Anadarko is an "owner, operator or person in charge" under 33 U.S.C. § 1321(b)(7)(A). *See* No. 2:10-MD-2179, Doc. 5113-2, at 2 n.2; Doc. 5280, at 10 n.7. But that issue was never before us.

[2] Indeed, Anadarko deemed this "factor . . . crucial to the resolution of these motions [for summary judgment]." No. 2:10-MD-2179, Doc. 5113-2, at 4.

[3] We note that federal regulations not at issue here, but addressed in subsequent proceedings in this case, require that well owners "take necessary precautions to keep wells under control at all times." 30 C.F.R. § 250.401; *see also* 30 C.F.R. § 250.420(a) (requiring that well owners' "casing and cementing programs . . . [p]revent the direct or indirect release of fluids from any stratum through the wellbore into offshore waters").

well "could not have been the 'point at which controlled confinement' of oil was 'lost' because oil was never confined in the well to start."[4] Anadarko Suppl. Br. in Supp. of Pet. Reh'g 7. But that the cement—undisputedly placed in the well—failed to perform its function as a barrier to the flow of oil only underscores that controlled confinement was lost in the well.[5]

Both BP and Anadarko attempt to shift the focus to the *Deepwater Horizon* and its appurtenances (owned by the Transocean entities), arguing that control was lost either (1) when the blowout preventer failed, or (2) when the drilling mud (which Anadarko contends is an appurtenance of the Transocean vessel) was displaced with seawater, causing oil to enter the well. But, as discussed in more detail below, our determination that controlled confinement was lost in the well does not preclude the possibility that [—6—] controlled confinement was also lost elsewhere, an issue that we did not need to rule on. Further, with respect to the drilling mud, there is no dispute that its removal "allowed oil to escape from the formation" and *into the well*. Anadarko Suppl. Br. in Supp. of Pet. Reh'g 7. Again, the focus is on the well, and we come back to the loss of controlled confinement in the well. Moreover, the blowout preventer was not the first and only barrier to the discharge of oil. Rather, in BP's own words, "a [blowout preventer] . . . 'operates as a failsafe device designed to stop a blowout from *progressing* and, *in the event of loss of control*, seal the well and stop the flow of oil.'" BP Blue Br. 11–12 (emphasis added) (quoting *Bricklayers & Masons Local Union No. 5 Ohio Pension Fund v. Transocean Ltd.*, 866 F. Supp. 2d 223, 230–31 (S.D.N.Y. 2012)).

---

[4] It is worth noting that this argument would foreclose Appellants' separate argument, discussed below, that the blowout preventer—which also failed to perform its function of containing oil in the well—was a point at which controlled confinement was lost.

[5] Although Anadarko argues that "[a]t the temporary abandonment stage of a well, the well is not intended to 'control' or 'confine' oil," Anadarko Suppl. Br. in Supp. of Reh'g 6, it is nonetheless undisputed that the cement placed in the well was intended to do so.

Thus, as BP implies, a blowout preventer becomes necessary only when control of the oil has already been lost. Indeed, by contending that the court erred in determining "that controlled confinement of oil was *irretrievably* lost in the well," BP Suppl. Br. in Supp. of Pet. Reh'g 8, BP appears to concede that controlled confinement was *initially* lost in the well.

Therefore, Appellants' contention that controlled confinement was not lost in the well is belied by the undisputed facts in the record and by Appellants' own admissions.

II. Purported Legal Errors in the Panel's Opinion

Appellants also challenge the panel's legal conclusion that "a vessel or facility is a point 'from which oil or a hazardous substance is discharged' if it is a point at which controlled confinement is lost." *In re Deepwater Horizon*, 753 F.3d at 573, 2 Adm. R. at 235 (quoting 33 U.S.C. § 1321(b)(7)(A)).

As an initial matter, BP suggests that the panel "realized" that "only one instrumentality can bear [CWA] liability for a discharge of a given quantum of oil," BP Pet. Reh'g 10, and that the opinion's "logic . . . suggests that Transocean . . . could not be held liable at all," BP Pet. Reh'g 2. Although Appellants would [—7—] perhaps have preferred that the court adopt its "single instrumentality" theory, we did no such thing. *See In re Deepwater Horizon*, 753 F.3d at 573, 2 Adm. R. at 235 ("[A] vessel or facility is *a* point 'from which oil or a hazardous substance is discharged' if it is *a* point at which controlled confinement is lost" (emphasis added)). The opinion makes clear that "any culpability on the part of the *Deepwater Horizon*'s operators does not exempt the well owners from the liability at issue here." *Id.* at 575, 2 Adm. R. at 237. Because the Transocean entities settled, we did not need to consider whether the oil discharged from the well might also have constituted a "discharge" from the *Deepwater Horizon*. Nor did we need to decide for purposes of other hypothetical scenarios not at issue here precisely under what circumstances civil penalty liability attaches for the owners and operators of vessels or facilities "upstream" and "downstream" from the facility or vessel at which controlled confinement was lost.

Appellants also attempt to distinguish the cases we relied upon in support of our holding. Anadarko points to the fact that there is "no reported decision in which the owner of a facility has been held liable for penalties after a discharge from a vessel connected to the facility." Anadarko Pet. Reh'g 7. BP similarly argues that "the cases on which the panel relied . . . . address the different situation where oil is discharged from a *single* instrumentality into the environment and it simply happens to flow across property owned by third parties (who bear no coequal legal responsibility as rig owners and operators to keep the oil confined) before reaching water." BP Pet. Reh'g 11. These arguments may be true so far as they go,[6] but only because no prior reported [—8—] cases have presented facts that are directly analogous to those in the present case. Moreover, Appellants' attempt to distinguish these cases is rooted in an assumption that only one instrumentality may be held liable for a given discharge, an issue that we explicitly did not reach. *See* BP Pet. Reh'g 11 ("[T]he cases on which the panel relied . . . do not speak at all to the real problem of assigning [CWA] liability between one of two mutually exclusive instrumentalities.").

As explained in the panel opinion, our holding is consistent both with the caselaw interpreting Section 311 and with its history of enforcement. The panel opinion points to

several cases and agency decisions where owners of facilities received fines under Section 311 for oil that was released from their facility, even though that oil subsequently flowed through conduits or over property owned by third parties before entering navigable water. *See Pepperell Assocs. v. EPA*, 246 F.3d 15, 20 (1st Cir. 2001); *Pryor Oil Co., Inc. v. United States*, 299 F. Supp. 2d 804, 806 (E.D. Tenn. 2003); *Union Petroleum Corp. v. United States*, 651 F.2d 734, 56, 61–62 (Ct. Cl. 1981); *In re D & L Energy, Inc.*, V–W–13 C–006 (EPA ALJ Feb. 27, 2013); *In re Phila. Macaroni Co.*, CWA–III–187 (EPA ALJ May 28, 1998).[7] Anadarko argues that these cases do not involve penalties under Section 311(b). This contention may be technically true, but it is of little consequence. Although *Pepperell* involved an appeal from an administrative determination that an onshore facility failed to prepare a [—9—] spill response plan under Section 311(j), the ALJ had also previously determined that the facility violated Section 311(b)(3), the provision at issue in this case. 246 F.3d at 20–22. Similarly, while *Union Petroleum* concerned cleanup costs under Section 311(i), rather than civil penalties under Section 311(b)(3), *see* 651 F.2d at 741, Section 311(i) applies "where an owner or operator of a vessel or an onshore facility or an offshore facility *from which oil or a hazardous substance is discharged in violation of subsection (b)(3)* of this section acts to remove such oil or substance," 33 U.S.C. § 1321(i) (emphasis added).

BP also argues that the court failed to address BP's argument "that the location of the discharge depends on the instrumentality

---

[6] Some of the cases cited in the panel opinion may very well have involved instances in which oil discharged from one facility traversed through a second facility, both of which could have been subject to liability under Section 311. For example, in *Pepperell Associates v. EPA*, 246 F.3d 15 (1st Cir. 2001), which involved oil that spilled from a factory, through a sewer, and ultimately into a creek, *id.* at 20, the sewer, in addition to the factory, may have been considered an "onshore facility," *see* 33 U.S.C. § 1321(a)(10) (defining "onshore facility" [—8—] broadly as "any facility (including, but not limited to, motor vehicles and rolling stock) of any kind located in, on, or under, any land within the United States other than submerged land").

[7] Anadarko challenges the panel opinion's citation to the two EPA administrative orders which, according to Anadarko, are "inapposite and [have] no precedential significance." Anadarko Pet. Reh'g 9, 10 n.4. But the panel never contended that these decisions were binding precedent. Rather, they were cited as *relevant* to rebut Appellants' argument that their Section 311 liability was precluded by the fact that the property traversed by the oil was owned by a third party. *See In re Deepwater Horizon*, 753 F.3d at 574, 2 Adm. R. at 236. Anadarko cites no authority rendering a statute's administrative enforcement irrelevant in this context.

from which oil *escapes confinement*." BP Pet. Reh'g 8. According to BP, "when oil simply moves from one confined instrumentality to another without escaping, no Clean Water Act violation can possibly occur." BP Pet. Reh'g 9. Along those same lines, Anadarko asserts that "[c]ommonsense dictates that the movement of oil from a facility into a vessel does not retroactively become a 'discharge' within the meaning of Section 311(b)(7) because the oil later exits the vessel's confinement into the environment." Anadarko Pet. Reh'g 6; *see also* Anadarko Suppl. Br. in Supp. of Pet Reh'g 5. This argument—which, prior to the petitions for rehearing, was raised in a single sentence in BP's opening brief, *see* BP Blue Br. 61[8]— lacks merit. The opinion nowhere suggests that the mere act of moving oil from a facility into a vessel constitutes a discharge. Such an act does not result in oil entering navigable waters and does not necessarily denote a loss of controlled confinement. But it does not follow from this that when the [—10—] controlled confinement of oil in a facility is lost such that it enters a vessel and then navigable waters, only the vessel is liable. Neither the CWA nor "commonsense" dictate otherwise.

Appellants further argue that it was improper for the Panel to include a "control" element in defining a "discharge" under the CWA. Anadarko asserts that, "[i]n its transitive form, the verb 'discharge' is defined as '[t]o release, as from confinement . . . .' [and i]n its intransitive form, the verb 'discharge' is defined, in part, as '[t]o pour forth, emit, or release contents.'" Anadarko Pet. Reh'g 5 n.1 (quoting The American Heritage Dictionary of the English Language 530 (3d ed. 1992)). But as Anadarko's own definitions suggest, the term "discharge" focuses not only on a loss of confinement but on the act of "releas[ing]." This connotes a loss of control. BP argues that inclusion of a "control" element to the test improperly "smuggles [into the case] negligence concepts" inconsistent with "the

statute's strict liability, locational test." BP Suppl. Br. in Supp. of Pet. Reh'g 6–10. However, the inquiry the panel engaged in— determining whether the well was a point at which controlled confinement was lost (without regard to which party, if any, was responsible for the loss of control)—is entirely consistent with such a test. Anadarko contends that including a control element is also problematic because it would mean that "controlled discharges would not be prohibited" by Section 311. Anadarko Pet. Reh'g 5. This argument is unpersuasive. It appears that Anadarko is arguing that the control element would preclude CWA liability in situations when a party *intended* to discharge oil and other hazardous substances. But this confuses the terms "control" and "intent." There is no reason, under our construction of discharge, why a party would not be liable when it intentionally gives up control of oil that had been confined within a facility or vessel that it owned or operated. [—11—]

Anadarko also attacks the panel opinion's standard for determining the point from which oil is discharged as "unworkable." Anadarko hypothesizes "a system where 24 separately owned and operated wells connect to a vessel, which connects to a pipeline, which connects to a floating platform, which interconnects with an interstate pipeline, which interconnects with an onshore facility dozens of miles away," and asks: "How could a fact-finder find the precise point where 'controlled confinement is lost' within that system?" Anadarko Pet. Reh'g 8. Anadarko, however, fails to give any reasons explaining why it would be difficult to determine where controlled confinement is lost in an interconnected system. In this case, for instance, it was not difficult to determine that the controlled confinement of oil was lost in the well. Second, Anadarko's hypothetical again assumes that there may only be a single point at which controlled confinement is lost, an issue we did not rule on.

Both BP and Anadarko also contend that the panel should have applied the rule of lenity or the anti-penalty canon to construe Section 311 narrowly so as not to apply to

---

[8] The sentence reads: "It is undisputed that the only oil ever to escape confinement and reach water escaped from the *Deepwater Horizon* and its appurtenances and that only oil that reaches water is capable of . . . trigger[ing] Section 1321(b)(7) liability." BP Blue Br. 61.

them. However, such presumptions are warranted only "if, after considering text, structure, history, and purpose, there remains a grievous ambiguity or uncertainty in the statute, such that the Court must simply guess as to what Congress intended." *Barber v. Thomas*, 560 U.S. 474, 488 (2010) (internal citation and quotation marks omitted). Here, because the text of Section 311, and the history of its application, clearly demonstrate that a vessel or facility is a point "from which oil or a hazardous substance is discharged," 33 U.S.C. § 1321(b)(7)(A), if it is a point at which controlled confinement is lost, we decline Appellants' appeals to the rule of lenity and the anti-penalty canon.

Finally, BP argues that it is not, "as the panel thought, attempting to introduce concepts of 'third-party fault' into the strict-liability scheme of the [—12—] [CWA]." BP Pet. Reh'g 14. But this argument is contradicted by Appellants' briefing in this case, both before the panel and before the lower court. At multiple times in the course of this litigation, Appellants have attempted to shift liability to Transocean on the grounds that they were not at fault for the spill, but that Transocean was at fault.

III. Conclusion

For the reasons given in the panel opinion, as supplemented hereby, the panel continues to hold that the district court judgment was correct.

United States Court of Appeals
for the Fifth Circuit

No. 13-30731

BLESSEY MARINE SERVICES, INC.
vs.
JEFFBOAT, L.L.C.

Appeal from the United States District Court for the
Eastern District of Louisiana

Decided: November 10, 2014

Citation: 771 F.3d 894, 2 Adm. R. 363 (5th Cir. 2014).

Before **STEWART**, Chief Judge, and **WIENER** and
COSTA, Circuit Judges.

[—1—] **WIENER**, Circuit Judge:

A district court jury granted the breach of warranty claim of Plaintiff-Appellant Blessey Marine Services, Inc. ("Blessey"), but denied its breach of contract claim. Blessey now appeals the district court's denial of two motions: one for partial summary judgment and the other *in limine*. Blessey's primary claim on appeal is that the district court should have entered judgment as a matter of law against Defendant-Appellee Jeffboat, L.L.C. ("Jeffboat"), once the court found the disputed portion of the contract ambiguous. Blessey also urges that the district court erred by admitting parol and extrinsic evidence. We do not reach the merits of either contention because we conclude that (1) we lack jurisdiction to review the district court's denial of Blessey's motion for [—2—] partial summary judgment, and (2) Blessey waived its right to challenge the district court's admission of extrinsic evidence.

I.

FACTS AND PROCEEDINGS

A. Background

Over the course of their twenty-year business relationship, Jeffboat, an inland boat and barge builder located in Indiana, sold more than fifty barges to Blessey, a provider of transport services for goods through inland waterways. In April 2009, Blessey and Jeffboat entered into a contract in which Jeffboat agreed to build a barge for Blessey at a base unit price of $3,325,000 ("Original Contract"). This price was calculated on the assumption that Jeffboat would procure the steel to build the barge at an average cost of $800 per ton, but the price of the barge was subject to some adjustments. Significant to this case, Article III of the Original Contract specified that the adjusted unit price would depend on the "actual average cost per ton . . . for all steel plate and structural steel used in the construction of the barge to be escalated/de-escalated," but in no event would the cost per ton exceed $800 for purposes of calculating the ultimate price.

Jeffboat and Blessey subsequently negotiated for additional barges. In July 2009, they executed a "First Amendment" to the Original Contract, which stated, in relevant part:

> Article III is amended in part to add the additional terms and conditions as follows . . . . [t]he Base Unit Contract Price for each Hot Oil Vessel and the Clean Service Vessel may be adjusted by reason of: 1. The increase or decrease resulting from alterations pursuant to Article V of the Contract, 2. The increase or decrease resulting from changes in taxes pursuant to Article VI of the Contract. [—3—]

That amendment also stated that "[e]xcept for the steel escalation as provided in Article III of the Contract, the terms and conditions of the Contract shall apply to the Hot Oil Vessels and Clean Service Vessel of this Amendment."

Jeffboat maintains that, by virtue of the parties' execution of the Amendment, Blessey elected to purchase additional barges at a "fixed" price of $525 per ton for steel, rather than the "market" price contemplated in the Original Contract. Blessey read the terms differently and sued Jeffboat for breach of contract, insisting that the invoice for the barges did not reflect the de-escalation of the price of steel. (Blessey later added a breach of warranty claim on the grounds that two of the delivered vessels were not fit for their intended use.)

B. District court proceedings

Both parties moved for summary judgment on whether the "steel escalation" comprehended in the Amendment applied to the prices of the five barges that Jeffboat sold to Blessey thereunder. Jeffboat took the position that the Amendment unambiguously excluded the steel *de-escalation* provision. Blessey too maintained that the Amendment was unambiguous, but insisted that it was the steel *escalation* provision in the Original Contract that was explicitly excluded by the Amendment. Blessey argued alternatively that if the district court were to find the Amendment ambiguous, it would have to enter judgment against Jeffboat because Indiana law requires that any ambiguity be construed against the drafter. The district court denied both parties' motions for summary judgment, and ruled that "[t]he amended contract's terms are sufficiently ambiguous as to preclude summary judgment for either side, even when considered in light of the extrinsic evidence the parties have presented."

The parties submitted a joint pretrial order that identified contested questions of law, including whether Indiana law compels the entry of judgment [—4—] against the drafter of an ambiguous contract. Blessey also filed a motion *in limine,* in which it asked the court to exclude parol and extrinsic evidence of the parties' intent, arguing that Indiana law bars such evidence when the contract includes an integration clause. The district court disagreed with Blessey's characterization of Indiana law, concluding that the cases Blessey cited actually compel admitting the evidence, not excluding it. Noting that it had already determined in its summary judgment order that the Amendment was ambiguous, the district court likewise denied Blessey's motion *in limine* on the grounds that "[r]esolution of the ambiguity will require the jury to hear and weigh relevant extrinsic evidence."

Following a three day trial, the jury rejected Blessey's breach of contract claim, but found in favor of Blessey on its breach of warranty claim. Blessey does not appeal any aspect of the jury's verdict; rather, its sole challenge is to the district court's denial of its motions for partial summary judgment and *in limine.*

II.

ANALYSIS

A. Denial of summary judgment motion

Before reaching the merits of Blessey's appeal, we consider whether we have jurisdiction to review the district court's denial of Blessey's motion for partial summary judgment. The general rule in this Circuit is that "an interlocutory order denying summary judgment is not to be reviewed when final judgment adverse to the movant is rendered on the basis of a full trial on the merits."[1] We recognized a narrow exception to this rule in *Becker v. Tidewater, Inc.,* holding that if the appellant seeks review of "the district [—5—] court's legal conclusions in denying summary judgment, *and* the case was a bench trial," we have jurisdiction to review the denial of summary judgment.[2]

Blessey seeks our review of the district court's disposition of a question of law, but its appeal does not fit the *Becker* exception because the district court conducted a jury trial. Although we acknowledge that other circuits will review purely legal issues decided on summary judgment without considering the kind of trial conducted, we are bound by *Becker.*[3]

---

[1] *Black v. J.I. Case Co.,* 22 F.3d 568, 570 (5th Cir. 1994).

[2] 586 F.3d 358, 365 n.4 (5th Cir. 2009) (emphasis supplied); *see also May v. Miss. Dep't of Corr.,* 531 F. App'x 464, 468 (5th Cir. 2013) (per curiam) ("Underlying our approach in *Becker* was our recognition that, because motions for judgment as a matter of law are not required to be made following a *bench* trial, it is appropriate to review the court's denial of summary judgment in this context." (emphasis supplied) (internal quotation marks and citation omitted)).

[3] *United States v. Short,* 181 F.3d 620, 624 (5th Cir. 1999) ("[We] are bound by the precedent of previous panels absent an intervening Supreme

Neither are we persuaded by the two other theories advanced by Blessey in support of appellate jurisdiction: (1) It is appealing the district court's "repeated misinterpretation" of Indiana law, rather than simply the denial of summary judgment; and, (2) we should excuse its failure to make a Rule 50 motion because the district court denied Jeffboat's Rule 50 motion. First, although the district court might have consistently rejected Blessey's position that Indiana law requires entry of judgment against the known drafter of an ambiguous contract in its pretrial and trial orders, Blessey only seeks our review of that court's denial of its motions for summary judgment and *in limine*. Second, Blessey's contention that we should excuse its failure to make a Rule 50 motion fares no better. Part of our reasoning in *Becker* was that we have jurisdiction over a denial of summary judgment on a purely legal issue, but only when the district court conducted a bench trial, in part "because Rule [—6—] 50 motions for judgment as a matter of law are not required following a bench trial."[4] The inverse of this principle suggests that we would have jurisdiction to hear an appeal of the district court's legal conclusions following a *jury* trial, but only if the party restated its objection in a Rule 50 motion.[5] In this case, however, Blessey did not make a Rule 50 motion for judgment as a matter of law on the issue it now seeks to appeal. Accordingly, we will not speculate whether we would have jurisdiction to review a denial of summary judgment if the legal issue were preserved in a Rule 50 motion, regardless of the type of trial conducted—bench or jury. We merely conclude that, under *Becker*, we do not have jurisdiction to review the district court's denial of

Blessey's motion for partial summary judgment.[6]

Furthermore, even if we were to assume *arguendo* that we do have such jurisdiction, we would affirm the district court's denial of partial summary judgment on the merits. The thrust of Blessey's appeal is that the district court should have entered judgment in its favor once the court determined that the contract language was ambiguous because "Indiana law, unlike the law of many other states, establishes that if a contract is truly ambiguous . . . then it *must* be construed against the drafter (if there is one)." Although it is true that, as a general rule, Indiana law requires that ambiguous terms be construed against a known drafter, Blessey overreaches in contending that [—7—] Indiana law contemplates entering judgment against the drafter of an ambiguous contract in every case.[7]

We acknowledge that "Indiana *arguably* applies the rule of construing ambiguities against the drafter more liberally, and the Indiana Supreme Court has *occasionally* applied the rule without considering whether extrinsic evidence would clarify the parties' intent."[8] This does not mean, however, that Indiana law mandates that *every* ambiguous contract be construed against a known drafter, which is Blessey's position. Rather, "[w]hen a contract's terms are ambiguous or uncertain and its interpretation requires extrinsic evidence, its construction is a matter for the fact-finder."[9] Thus, if we had

---

Court case explicitly or implicitly overruling that prior precedent . . . .").

[4] *Becker v. Tidewater, Inc.*, 586 F.3d 358, 365 n.4 (5th Cir. 2009) (citing *Colonial Penn Ins. v. Mkt. Planners Ins. Agency, Inc.*, 157 F.3d 1032, 1037 n.3 (5th Cir. 1998)).

[5] The First and Fourth Circuits adhere to this rule. *See Ji v. Bose Corp.*, 626 F.3d 116, 128 (1st Cir. 2010) ("[O]ur rule is that even legal errors cannot be reviewed unless the challenging party restates its objection in a motion for JMOL."); *Chesapeake Paper Prods. Co. v. Stone & Webster Eng'g Corp.*, 51 F.3d 1229, 1235 (4th Cir. 1995).

[6] *See Becker*, 586 F.3d at 365 n.4.

[7] *See Holiday Hospitality Franchising, Inc. v. AMCO Ins. Co.*, 983 N.E.2d 574, 577-578 (Ind. 2013) ("Where contractual language is ambiguous, we generally resolve those ambiguities in favor of the [draftee], but will not do so if such an interpretation fails to harmonize the provisions of a contract as a whole." (citations omitted)).

[8] *See BKCAP, LLC v. CAPTEC Franchise Trust 2000-1*, 572 F.3d 353, 361 (7th Cir. 2009) (emphasis supplied).

[9] *Johnson v. Johnson*, 920 N.E.2d 253, 256 (Ind. 2010) (citation omitted). The district court's jury instruction on the ambiguity question aligned with Indiana law: "If, after considering those additional factors, doubt still remains as to a contract provision's meaning, you should consider that

B. Denial of motion *in limine*

Blessey also seeks to appeal the district court's denial of its motion *in limine*, arguing that the court erred in doing so because the Amendment contained the following integration clause: "All prior verbal and written offers relating to this First Amendment are hereby terminated." Blessey submits that, under Indiana law, "[w]hen two parties have made a contract and expressed it in a writing to which they have both assented as the complete and [—8—] accurate integration of that contract," extrinsic evidence is not admissible "for the purpose of varying or contradicting the writing."[10] Jeffboat disputes that this language operates as an integration clause, asserting that its intended purpose is to foreclose any future attempts by Blessey to purchase additional barges under the terms of the Amendment.

We do not need to address the merits of this issue either. By adducing some of the same extrinsic evidence at trial that it had sought to exclude in its motion *in limine*, Blessey waived its right to challenge the district court's admission of that evidence.[11] In *Ohler v. United States*, the United States Supreme Court held that "a party introducing evidence cannot complain on appeal that the evidence was erroneously admitted."[12] Not only did it introduce evidence that it now complains the district court erroneously admitted at trial, Blessey also referred to such evidence in its opening statement, advising the jury that "[i]n the negotiations and the e-mails, you'll see references to the same terms and conditions as the original contract; you'll see e-mails that reference firm and fixed prices; you'll see emails that reference barges that were never built."

Although Blessey insists that application of *Ohler* would have placed it in an "untenable" position at trial because its witnesses would not have been able to rely on extrinsic evidence to explain their testimony, this argument [—9—] actually weighs in favor of admission.[13] We are not persuaded by Blessey's contention that Federal Rule of Evidence 103(b) supports holding that its objection was preserved by the filing of its motion *in limine*. The Advisory Notes accompanying the 2000 Amendment to Rule 103 make clear that this rule "*does not* purport to answer whether a party who objects to evidence that the court finds admissible in a definitive ruling, and who then offers the evidence to 'remove the sting' of its anticipated prejudicial effect, thereby waives the right to appeal the trial court's ruling."[14] We conclude that, by introducing extrinsic evidence, Blessey waived its right to appeal the district court's denial of its motion *in limine* to exclude just such evidence.

III.

CONCLUSION

The district court's denial of Blessey's motions for partial summary judgment and *in limine* is AFFIRMED.

---

jurisdiction to consider the district court's denial of Blessey's motion for partial summary judgment, we would affirm it.

---

provision against the party that is responsible for drafting the contract or choosing the terms whose meaning is unclear and in favor of the other party."

[10] *See Dicen v. New Sesco, Inc.*, 839 N.E.2d 684, 688 (Ind. 2005).

[11] *See Ohler v. United States*, 529 U.S. 753, 755 (2000); *see also Clarett v. Roberts*, 657 F.3d 664, 671 (7th Cir. 2011) ("The logic of *Ohler* applies with equal force in both criminal and civil cases . . . . We note that every circuit to have addressed the question has applied *Ohler* in civil cases.").

[12] 529 U.S. at 755; *see also United States v. Fluker*, 698 F.3d 988, 998 (7th Cir. 2012); *United States v. Newburn*, 58 F. App'x 358, 358 (9th Cir. 2003) (rejecting challenge when the appellant "registered his objection to the introduction of the images prior to trial, [but] he chose to mention them in his own direct testimony").

[13] *See Canny v. Dr. Pepper/Seven-Up Bottling Grp.*, 439 F.3d 894, 904 (8th Cir. 2006) (noting that a civil litigant "cannot avoid the consequence of its own trial tactic by arguing it was forced to introduce the evidence during the direct examination . . . to diminish the prejudice").

[14] FED. R. EVID. 103(b) advisory committee's note (emphasis supplied).

United States Court of Appeals
for the Fifth Circuit

No. 13-20144

COFFIN
vs.
BLESSEY MARINE SERVICES, INC.

Appeal from the United States District Court for the
Southern District of Texas

Decided: November 13, 2014

Citation: 771 F.3d 276, 2 Adm. R. 367 (5th Cir. 2014).

Before **JOLLY, HIGGINBOTHAM,** and **SOUTHWICK,**
Circuit Judges.

[—1—] **JOLLY,** Circuit Judge:

Blessey Marine Services, Inc. ("Blessey")
brings this interlocutory appeal
challenging the district court's denial of
its motion for summary judgment. The district
court declined to decide as a matter of law
whether nine individual plaintiffs (collectively
the "Plaintiffs"), former vessel-based
tankermen on Blessey barges, who brought
suit under the Fair Labor Standards Act
("FLSA") seeking overtime pay, were exempt
from the FLSA as seamen.[1] Although the
[—2—] district court conditionally certified a
class action, only eleven individuals joined,
and the parties decided to proceed
individually.

Blessey produced extensive evidence
during discovery suggesting that the
Plaintiffs' loading and unloading duties were
done as part of the vessel crew and aided the
seaworthiness of the vessel, and at the close of
discovery it moved for summary judgment. In
response, the Plaintiffs largely ignored
responding to Blessey's evidence and
arguments, and countered that loading and
unloading a vessel is nonseaman work as a
matter of law, a question that was decided by
our opinion in *Owens v. SeaRiver Maritime,
Inc.,* 272 F.3d 698 (5th Cir. 2001). The
Plaintiffs argued that *Owens* forecloses any

factual inquiry into the nature and character
of loading and unloading duties. The district
court accepted this interpretation of *Owens*
and concluded that loading and unloading the
vessel was in and of itself, without regard to
attachment to a specific vessel as seamen for
other purposes, nonseaman work as a matter
of law. It set the case for trial so that a jury
could determine whether those duties were a
substantial amount of the Plaintiffs' overall
work.

Our review of the applicable law and record
evidence leads us to a contrary conclusion; we
believe that the district court misapplied
Owens. Furthermore, the record establishes
that these vessel-based tankermen performed
only seaman work, making them exempt from
the FLSA's overtime provisions. Accordingly,
we VACATE the district court's denial of
summary judgment and REMAND the case to
the district court for entry of judgment in
favor of Blessey.

I.

We begin with a discussion of the relevant
facts, which are largely undisputed. Blessey's
business primarily consists of shipping liquid
cargo along inland and oceanic waterways.
Blessey uses a system of equipment [—3—]
called a unit tow, which consists of a towboat
and two tank barges, to ship the liquid. The
towboat contains the navigation controls,
machinery space, and propulsion, and it
pushes the barges through the waterway.
Meanwhile, the barges are connected to the
towboat through a series of lines and wires.
Each Blessey barge consists of several
separate tanks that can be used for storing
liquid, and loading and unloading such a
barge is a complex process.

The unit tow is manned by a crew that
lives and works on the towboat for a
designated period of time (called a hitch).
Typically, crew members work for 20 days on
a unit tow followed by 10 days off (called a 2-
for-1 day hitch). Each day, a crew member
generally works two six-hour shifts. Crew
sizes may vary from as few as four to as many
as ten people.

---

[1] The appeal is properly before us because the
district court certified its order for immediate
appeal, and we subsequently granted Blessey's
petition for leave to appeal. *See* 28 U.S.C. § 1292(b).

The crew consists of a "wheelman," a pilot, tankermen, and deckhands. The "wheelman" is usually a captain or relief captain, and all members of the crew work at his or her direction. A "tankerman" has gained deckhand experience and received required training in the loading and unloading of liquid cargo from a barge. Blessey's tankermen are vessel-based and share the nineteen duties that deckhands perform along with various additional tasks related both to the maintenance of the barges and the loading and unloading process. The parties agree that most of these tasks are seaman work.[2] Relevant here, Blessey requires its tankermen to perform the loading and unloading process for the unit tow. Thus, the tankermen both load and unload [—4—] the barges and perform other tasks related to the loading and unloading process.[3] The Plaintiffs argue that *these* categories of duties are nonseaman work, while acknowledging their many other duties are seaman work.

The Plaintiffs typically worked as seamen aboard a vessel for approximately 84 hours

during a seven-day period and were paid a "day rate," or a flat daily sum. They were not paid overtime for any work, as is customary and lawful with respect to seamen.

II.

A.

We review the district court's decision to deny summary judgment de novo and apply the same standards as the district court. *Lawyers Title Ins. Corp. v. Doubletree Partners, L.P.*, 739 F.3d 848, 856 (5th Cir. 2014). Summary judgment is appropriate "if the movant shows that there is no genuine dispute as to any material fact and the movant is entitled to judgment as a matter of law." Fed. R. Civ. P. 56(a). We may consider the record evidence before the district court, but we may not assess credibility or weigh evidence. *Lawyers Title Ins. Corp.*, 739 F.3d at 856. The motion for summary judgment in this case is based on the FLSA exemption for seamen, and the "ultimate determination of whether an employee is exempt . . . is properly characterized as a conclusion of law, subject to plenary review." *Dalheim v. KDFW–TV*, 918 F.2d 1220, 1226 (5th Cir. 1990).

B. [—5—]

To decide whether the Plaintiffs are exempt seamen, we turn to the relevant statutory and regulatory language setting out obligations with respect to the FLSA. The FLSA generally forbids employing workers for a workweek longer than forty hours "unless such employee receives compensation for his employment . . . at a rate not less than one and one-half times the regular rate at which he is employed." 29 U.S.C. § 207(a)(1). An employee is not protected by this broad prohibition, however, if he falls within an exemption from statutory coverage. *Meza v. Intelligent Mexican Mktg., Inc.*, 720 F.3d 577, 580–81 (5th Cir. 2013). Relevant here, the FLSA exempts from overtime "any employee employed as a seaman." 29 U.S.C. § 213(b)(6). Congress did not define "seaman," and it is left to us to interpret the term to resolve this appeal.

---

[2] Tankermen have nineteen deckhand duties, and the parties agree that all of them are seaman work: (1) cleaning, (2) handling lines, (3) standing watch, (4) making locks, (5) putting out lights, (6) handling running lights, (7) cooking, (8) changing engine filters, (9) radio communications, (10) repairing lines, (11) troubleshooting barge engines, (12) troubleshooting boat engines, (13) painting, (14) changing oil in engines, (15) purchasing supplies, (16) chipping, (17) changing oil in generators, (18) tying off to docks, and (19) building tow. Similarly, the parties agree that three tankerman duties are also seaman work: (1) pumping out bilge water, (2) fueling the vessels, and (3) adding lube oil.

[3] The Plaintiffs identified a number of these related tasks. Tankermen are responsible for "lubing the barge," which requires: (1) oiling grease-fittings on the barges, (2) changing the oil and oil-filters on the barge engines, (3) cleaning the barges of oil spots and debris, (4) making sure all hatches and dogs are tightly secured, and (5) doing an overall readiness inspection of the barge. Additionally, the tankermen must (1) check pressure gauges for heated fuel, (2) check outgoing or incoming temperature of heating oil, (3) maintain the generator, (4) drain water from the expansion tank, and (5) fuel the barge. Tankermen also perform a variety of other tasks related to loading and unloading while the barge is docked.

For guidance, we turn primarily to the Department of Labor ("DOL") regulations, which we have held to be "entitled to great weight." *Dole v. Petroleum Treaters, Inc.*, 876 F.2d 518, 521 (5th Cir. 1989) (citing *Tony & Susan Alamo Found. v. Sec'y of Labor*, 471 U.S. 290, 297 (1985)). Generally, a vessel's crew members are seamen, so long as they meet the criteria in 29 C.F.R. § 783.31. 29 C.F.R. § 783.32. Section 783.31 outlines these criteria as follows:

> [A]n employee will ordinarily be regarded as "employed as a seaman" if he performs, as master or subject to the authority, direction, and control of the master aboard a vessel, service which is rendered primarily as an aid in the operation of such vessel as a means of transportation, provided he performs no substantial amount of work of a different character.

Id. § 783.31. The regulations provide that work other than seaman work becomes substantial "if it occupies more than 20 percent of the time worked by the employee during the workweek." *Id.* § 783.37.

The use of the word "ordinarily" in § 783.31 evinces that the FLSA eschews a fixed meaning of the term seaman. The regulations emphasize [—6—] flexibility, indicating that the term's "meaning is governed by the context in which it is used and the purpose of the statute in which it is found." *Id.* § 783.29(c). Similarly, we must evaluate an employee's duties based "upon the character of the work he actually performs and not on what it is called or the place where it is performed." *Id.* § 783.33. As we have recognized, the FLSA as a whole is "pervaded by the idea that what each employee actually does determines its application to him." *Walling v. W. D. Haden Co.*, 153 F.2d 196, 199 (5th Cir. 1946). Accordingly, the application of the seaman exemption generally depends on the facts in each case. *See McLaughlin v. Bos. Harbor Cruise Lines, Inc.*, 419 F.3d 47, 51–52 (1st Cir. 2005) (recognizing that application of the seaman exemption is a fact-intensive question that can be answered in many cases only after a trial).

III.

With this framework guiding us, we will address both categories of duties at issue in this suit, beginning with the loading and unloading duties and concluding with those responsibilities related to loading and unloading.

A.

1.

The district court concluded, and the Plaintiffs urge on appeal, that our decision in *Owens* establishes that loading and unloading a vessel is *always* nonseaman work. We consider this reading of *Owens* to be erroneous.

First, *Owens* involves significantly different facts from this case. The plaintiff in *Owens* only sought overtime pay for his work loading and unloading barges as a member of SeaRiver's land-based Strike Team. Although he had previously worked as a vessel-based tankerman, he did not pursue any overtime for that work. We emphasized that during the relevant time period Owens was *not* a crew member of a tow and *not* tied to a particular vessel for a voyage. 272 F.3d at 700. Similarly, Owens worked "on unattended or 'tramp' [—7—] barges that were neither towed by SeaRiver boats nor attended by SeaRiver crews." *Id.* By contrast, the Plaintiffs here *were* members of a unit tow crew, *were* assigned to particular vessels for a voyage, and *were* expected to perform work on barges that were towed by Blessey's boats and crews.

Although the Plaintiffs contend that these factual differences are irrelevant, this contention is inconsistent with our analysis in *Owens*. The Plaintiffs point to several DOL regulations that purportedly suggest that loading and unloading duties are not seaman work. *See* 29 C.F.R. § 783.32 (suggesting that loading and unloading freight is nonseaman work but may not change a seaman's classification if the work is insubstantial); 29 C.F.R. § 783.36 (explaining that barge tenders who primarily or substantially load and unload cargo are not seamen). We acknowledged such language in *Owens*, but we noted with some caution that "[w]orkers who are primarily concerned with loading and unloading cargo are not, *generally speaking*, seamen within the meaning of the FLSA." 272 F.3d at 704 (emphasis added). Our inclusion of the words "generally speaking" is significant because we explicitly acknowledged through this language that we *always* consider the factual context when deciding whether an employee is exempt. While the DOL regulations suggest that in many cases loading and unloading duties are nonseaman work, we recognized that such a rule cannot be categorical in the light of the DOL's crucial qualification that the application of the seaman exemption "depends *upon the character of the work* [an employee] actually performs and not on what it is called or the place where it is performed." 29 C.F.R. § 783.33 (emphasis added).

We also recognized in *Owens* that the character of loading and unloading duties might change when a member of a vessel-based crew performs such duties. In a footnote, we indicated that rigid application of the DOL's twenty percent rule, which it uses to determine whether nonseaman work is [—8—] substantial or insubstantial, could create an absurd result where an employee works primarily at sea but is a nonseaman for a brief period when he loads or unloads at port. 272 F.3d at 702 n.5. This footnote further underscores the limits of our decision in *Owens*, as we left open the question of loading and unloading duties for vessel-based employees.

Finally, the Plaintiffs contend that we rejected in *Owens* the type of evidence that Blessey relies upon today, to wit, evidence connecting loading and unloading duties to the navigational integrity of the unit tow. SeaRiver argued, as Blessey argues now, that improper loading or unloading of a barge could render it unsafe or cause it to break apart. We concluded that the duties in that case only prepared the vessel for navigation but did not actually aid its operation. *Id.* at 704. Our primary concern, though, was that accepting such evidence as *dispositive* would expand the definition of seaman to encompass many land-based personnel. Again in a footnote, we expounded that "[f]or example, a *land-based worker* who installs navigation equipment on vessels would be a seaman, as would a worker *at a refueling dock.*" *Id.* at 704 n.6 (emphasis added). Although the evidence in *Owens* was insufficient to suggest that loading and unloading assisted the vessel's operation, we did not categorically reject the relevance of such evidence in other cases, particularly when the work in question is performed by a member of the vessel's crew.

We conclude that the district court erred when it determined that *Owens* required it to hold that loading and unloading duties performed by vessel-based tankermen were nonseaman duties as a matter of law.

2.

Instead, our review of the relevant law and undisputed facts leads us to the conclusion that loading and unloading was seaman work when done by these vessel-based Plaintiffs. We turn first to § 783.31, which provides that an employee is a seaman if two criteria are met: (1) the employee is "subject to the [—9—] authority, direction, and control of the master;" and (2) the employee's service is primarily offered to aid the "vessel as a means of transportation," provided that the employee does not perform a substantial amount of different work. 29 C.F.R. § 783.31. Both parties agree that the Plaintiffs were subject to the master's control. As to the second prong, the Seventh Circuit persuasively notes that this provision "just means that the employee must be a (more or less) full-time member of the marine crew, that is, the crew that is responsible for operating the ship." *Harkins v. Riverboat Servs., Inc.*, 385 F.3d 1099, 1104 (7th Cir. 2004). This reading is consistent with our own precedent in which we attempt to give the term seaman "its ordinary meaning." *Dole*, 876 F.2d at 523.

We have early-on recognized that vessel-based barge tenders who maintain and service a barge are exempt seamen under the FLSA. *Gale v. Union Bag & Paper Corp.*, 116 F.2d 27, 29 (5th Cir. 1940). In *Gale*, the plaintiffs slept on the barges and attended the lines, put out running and mooring lines, pumped out bilge water, and performed other tasks. We concluded that they were exempt seamen and reasoned that "[t]hey were necessary for the operation, welfare and safety of the barges" and that they performed many duties "necessary and usual to the navigation of the barges." *Id.* at 28. We recognized, for example, "[i]f the tow line had parted at any time on a voyage the barge would have been helpless and might have become a total loss if the barge tender was not there to drop the anchor and otherwise look out for its safety." *Id.* In *Owens*, we cited to *Gale* and emphasized that the workers in *Gale* "worked, ate, and slept on board their assigned barges." 272 F.3d at 701.

In our view, the reasoning of *Gale* controls this case. It is undisputed that the Plaintiffs ate, slept, lived, and worked aboard Blessey's towboats. They were members of the crew and worked at the direction of the captain. As [—10—] to the loading and unloading duties, the district court recognized that the "Plaintiffs do not contest [Blessey's] argument that improper loading and unloading can compromise the seaworthiness of the barge." *Coffin v. Blessey Marine Servs., Inc.*, No. 4:11–214, 2013 WL 244918, at *3 (S.D. Tex. Jan. 22, 2013). Martin Creel, a Blessey captain, and James Clendenon, a Blessey executive, both submitted declarations evincing that proper loading and unloading is essential to the efficient, safe movement of the unit tow. The Plaintiffs also testified that safe loading and unloading contributed to the efficient movement of the barge.

We note that *Gale* applied to barge tenders, and the DOL has also promulgated a regulation regarding such employees and categorized them as exempt seamen in many cases. That regulation also provides, however:

[T]here are employees who, while employed on vessels such as barges and lighters, are primarily or substantially engaged in performing duties such as loading and unloading or custodial service which do not constitute service performed primarily as an aid in the operation of these vessels as a means of

transportation and consequently are not employed as "seamen."

29 C.F.R. § 783.36. Although the Plaintiffs urge us to interpret this statement to preclude any finding that loading or unloading duties are seaman work, we do not interpret the regulation so narrowly. As we noted above, we already rejected such a categorical rule in *Owens*. *See* 272 F.3d at 704 (emphasizing that workers who primarily load and unload barges are *generally speaking* not seamen under the FLSA). Moreover, this statement appears merely to recognize the presumption that loading and unloading duties are nonseaman work because those duties are usually performed by harbor-based personnel who have little to no role in the barge's navigational mission. *See McCarthy v. Wright & Cobb Lighterage Co.*, 163 F.2d 92 (2d Cir. 1947) (concluding that a shore-based bargee was not a seaman because his maritime duties consumed [—11—] only a few minutes of his day and he primarily supervised and facilitated the loading or unloading of cargo); *see also Anderson v. Manhattan Lighterage Corp.*, 148 F.2d 971 (2d Cir. 1945) (determining that workers were not seamen when they transferred cargo in New York Harbor and were rarely on board the vessel during the tow).

By contrast, in this case vessel-based tankermen performed the loading and unloading duties as members of a unit tow's crew. The Plaintiffs' presence aboard the vessels naturally affected the nature of their loading and unloading duties.[4] Critically, the

---

[4] Of course, we recognize that an employee is not a seaman merely because he works on a boat. *See* 29 C.F.R. § 783.33. Indeed, we have recognized that employees on a dredge boat may aid in the operation of the vessel while still performing primarily nonseaman duties. *Walling v. W. D. Haden Co.*, 153 F.2d 196, 199 (5th Cir. 1946). Our decision in *W. D. Haden* is readily distinguishable from this case, however, because we concluded there that the workers on the dredge boat were employed primarily in industry because they harvested shells from the ocean. Here, the Plaintiffs worked on a vessel that shipped cargo on inland and oceanic waterways. Their work on the water was fundamentally seaman work, and their

context in which work is done can affect whether it is seaman or nonseaman work. *See Martin v. Bedell*, 955 F.2d 1029, 1035 (5th Cir. 1992). In *Martin*, the Secretary of Labor brought suit to compel a company to pay overtime to cooks who worked aboard boats that provided offshore maintenance to oil companies. We recognized that a vessel-based "cook is *usually* a seaman because he usually cooks *for* seamen." 955 F.2d at 1036. We remanded that case for further factual findings, however, so that the district court could determine whether the cooks spent a significant amount of time preparing food for nonseamen. *Id.* Our distinction underscores the important point that food preparation is neither inherently seaman nor nonseaman work, and its character depends on the context in which it is performed.

In *Martin*, we were aided by a DOL regulation providing that "[t]he term 'seaman' includes members of the crew such as . . . cooks . . . if, as is the usual [—12—] case, their service is of the type described in § 783.31." 29 C.F.R. § 783.32. The presumption that members of the crew are seamen is not limited to cooks, as the regulation includes the broad terms "includes" and "such as" to indicate that the enumerated positions are exemplary, not exclusive. *See Christopher v. SmithKline Beecham Corp.*, 132 S. Ct. 2156, 2170 (2012) (explaining in the context of another FLSA regulation that use of the verb "includes" indicates "that the examples enumerated in the text are intended to be illustrative, not exhaustive"). As with § 783.36, this provision indicates that a crew member does not lose his status "simply because, as an incident to such employment, he performs some work not connected with operation of the vessel as a means of transportation, such as assisting in the loading or unloading of freight at the beginning or end of a voyage." 29 C.F.R. § 783.32. Again, the Plaintiffs urge us to decide that this statement means that loading and unloading duties are never seaman work.

It appears to us that this statement only means that in some, perhaps in many,

situations and circumstances involving loading and unloading duties, the work is nonseaman. Blessey's evidence demonstrates that the loading or unloading of its liquid cargo requires precision so that the barge can operate safely. Naturally, when an individual lives aboard the vessel that he or she loads or unloads, this living situation will affect the character of his or her duties. In *Owens*, the tankerman duties were divorced from the subsequent navigation of the barge. *See* 272 F.3d at 704 (noting that the plaintiff did not move or moor the barge and only prepared it for navigation). By contrast, the Plaintiffs here recognized that their loading and unloading duties were integrated with their many other duties. Indeed, the plaintiff in *Owens* chose not to sue for the time he was a tankerman in navigation. *Id.* at 700. For example here, Plaintiff Joshua Fox testified that he would regularly walk his barge to make certain that the barge was level because doing his job improperly [—13—] could mean that the barge would get stuck when traveling down a river or canal. Eric Jones and Zachary Latiolais, two other Plaintiffs, testified that performing their loading and unloading duties effectively made their jobs and the captain's job easier. Thus, the Plaintiffs are instead seamen because, like a cook, they are a member of the crew and perform work that meets the definition of § 783.31.

We conclude that Blessey's tankermen *are* seamen while loading and unloading the vessel because these duties were integrated within their many other duties. Inquiries into FLSA exempt status "remain[] intensely factbound and case specific," and we have cautioned that "[e]ach case must be judged on its own peculiar facts." *Dalheim*, 918 F.2d at 1226–27. The DOL applies this principle to the seaman exemption, emphasizing that the exemption's application "depends upon the character of the work." 29 C.F.R. § 783.33. Blessey has produced undisputed evidence evincing that these vessel-based tankermen performed their loading and unloading duties with an eye toward navigation *and* were required to perform such duties safely so that the vessel could safely operate on inland and oceanic waterways. We see no basis for distinguishing their loading and unloading

---

presence on the water was not incidental to the primary purpose of their employment.

duties from the many other duties the vessel-based barge tenders performed in *Gale*.[5] *See Jordan v. Am. Oil Co.*, 51 F. Supp. 77, 78–79 (D.R.I. 1943) (applying the seaman exemption to vessel-based tankermen based on our decision in *Gale*). [—14—]

Finally, we consider that the policies of the FLSA support our decision today. The FLSA's exemptions were designed to apply to

a kind of work that was difficult to standardize to any time frame and could not be easily spread to other workers after 40 hours in a week, making compliance with the overtime provisions difficult and generally precluding the potential job expansion intended by the FLSA's time-and-a-half overtime premium.

Christopher, 132 S. Ct. at 2173 (internal quotation marks omitted). As the American Waterways Operators explained in its amicus brief, generally speaking, tankermen devote varying amounts of time to loading and unloading on each hitch. On some hitches, workers may spend as little as ten percent of their time loading and unloading, while others may spend fifty percent or more. Thus, a tankerman could be a seaman on some hitches and not on others, making it disruptive and disputatious on the vessel. *See Owens*, 272 F.3d at 702 n.5. Similarly, Blessey's tankermen work aboard a vessel with limited space for other workers, making the unit tow an environment where "working more than 40 hours a week is an appropriate work norm." *Harkins*, 385 F.3d at 1102. Thus, the policy objectives of the FLSA support this decision.

---

[5] The Plaintiffs contend that cases like *Gale* and *Jordan* are inapposite because they were decided before the DOL adopted the twenty percent rule used to determine whether nonseaman duties are substantial. This argument is unavailing for two reasons. First, we continue to recognize *Gale* in cases concerning the seaman exemption. *See Owens*, 272 F.3d at 701. Second, we cautioned in *Owens* against the rigid application of the twenty percent rule. *Id.* at 702 n.5. It appears to us that a careful evaluation of the nature and character of the work in question assuages our concerns in *Owens*.

For these reasons, we conclude that loading and unloading duties are seaman work when performed by these vessel-based tankermen.

B.

We briefly note that the Plaintiffs also argued a number of tasks related to their loading and unloading duties were also nonseaman work for FLSA purposes. They explain in their brief that the district court did not address these categories of work and urge that the work is not part of this appeal. This work *is* part of this appeal, though, both because Blessey has briefed the issue and because we may affirm the district court for any reason supported by the [—15—] record, even if the district court did not rely on that reason. *United States v. Gonzalez*, 592 F.3d 675, 681 (5th Cir. 2009).

This argument gives us little pause, though, as the activities related to loading and unloading were also clearly seaman work. As Blessey notes, many of these readiness duties are part of the basic maintenance of a barge. The basic maintenance of a vessel is almost always seaman work for FLSA purposes. *See Louviere v. Standard Dredging Corp.*, 239 F.2d 164, 164–65 (5th Cir. 1956) (recognizing that a deckhand's routine maintenance work on a tug constituted seaman duties for FLSA purposes). As we discussed in detail above, the loading and unloading process is connected with the Plaintiffs' many seaman duties as members of the crew.

Additionally, our interpretation of the FLSA regulations above would also control this issue in this appeal. We have held that the loading and unloading is *itself* seaman work for FLSA purposes, and by extension the work related to loading and unloading is also seaman work under the FLSA.

IV.

In sum, we have focused on the totality of the facts presented in this appeal, and we have held that loading and unloading duties along with any related duties constitute seaman work when performed by vessel-based tankermen. Consequently, the district court erred when it denied Blessey's motion for summary judgment on this issue. The tankermen performed duties crucial to the mission and purpose for the unit tow and were at all times engaged in work regarding the safe and efficient operation of a "vessel as a means of transportation" under § 783.31. This holding is in harmony with our precedent, the relevant DOL regulations, and the spirit and purpose of the FLSA.

VACATED, and REMANDED,
for entry of judgment in favor of Blessey.

United States Court of Appeals
for the Fifth Circuit

No. 13-30299

IN RE LOUISIANA CRAWFISH PRODUCERS

Appeal from the United States District Court for the
Western District of Louisiana

Decided: November 24, 2014

Citation: 772 F.3d 1026, 2 Adm. R. 375 (5th Cir. 2014).

Before **SMITH, BARKSDALE,** and **HAYNES,** Circuit
Judges.

[—1—] PER CURIAM:

The Louisiana Crawfish Producers Association–West and some of its [—2—] members, commercial fishermen operating in the Atchafalaya Basin in Louisiana, sued a number of oil and gas companies and their insurers, claiming aspects of the companies' pipeline activities impeded water flows and commercial navigation, causing economic damages. The plaintiffs appeal a dismissal for failure to state a claim in favor of two defendants, Dow Intrastate Gas Company ("DIGC") and Willbros RPI, Inc. ("Willbros"). We affirm.

I.

The plaintiffs sued in Louisiana state court under state law and general maritime law. After dismissal of the state-law claims, one of the defendants removed to federal court. That court denied a Rule 12(b)(6) motion to dismiss maritime tort claims against the defendants alleged to have engaged in dredging. It dismissed maritime tort claims against the defendants alleged to have engaged in oil and gas exploration but not dredging, which included DIGC and Willbros. The court declined to dismiss successor-in-interest claims against most of the defendants alleged to be successors of entities that had engaged in dredging. Inconsistently with its treatment of some other defendants, however, the court did not discuss successor-in-interest claims against DIGC even though the complaint claimed that DIGC is the successor to Dow Chemical Company ("Dow"), a defendant alleged to have engaged in dredging. Nevertheless, having dismissed the maritime tort claims against DIGC, the court dismissed DIGC as a defendant.

The plaintiffs appealed. While the appeal was pending, most of the dismissed defendants settled. The only defendants that remain parties to the appeal are DIGC and Willbros.

The specific allegations against DIGC and Willbros fall into two categories. First, the plaintiffs claim DIGC and Willbros engaged in activities that constitute maritime torts. They allege DIGC placed cement mats on exposed [—3—] sections of an existing pipeline, impeding water flows and commercial navigation. They claim Willbros built a pipeline on an existing spoil bank that it had leveled using bulldozers, obstructing gaps in the spoil bank and thereby impeding water flows and commercial navigation. In the plaintiffs' view, both defendants' activities violated the applicable Army Corps of Engineers ("Army Corps") permits. The plaintiffs do not contend DIGC or Willbros used vessels in any of these projects.

Second, the plaintiffs claim that Dow is the "predecessor" to DIGC and that DIGC operated under an Army Corps permit originally issued to Dow. Plaintiffs provide no further information about the relationship between DIGC and Dow, but the defendants acknowledge in their brief that Dow and DIGC have a corporate parent-subsidiary relationship.

II.

We review *de novo* a dismissal for failure to state a claim, "accepting all well-pleaded facts as true and viewing those facts in the light most favorable to the plaintiff." *Stokes v. Gann*, 498 F.3d 483, 484 (5th Cir. 2007) (per curiam). The plaintiff must plead "enough facts to state a claim to relief that is plausible on its face." *Bell Atl. Corp. v. Twombly*, 550 U.S. 544, 570 (2007). "Factual allegations must be enough to raise a right to relief above the speculative level on the assumption that all the allegations in the complaint are true (even if doubtful in fact)." *Id.* at 555 (footnote and citations omitted). Mere "labels and conclusions" or "a formulaic recitation of the elements of a cause of action" are insufficient. *Id.*

III.

To state a claim for a maritime tort, the plaintiff must allege facts [—4—] sufficient to satisfy the "location test" and "connection test."[1] The location test is satisfied if the tort occurred on navigable waters or if the injury occurred on land but was caused by a vessel on navigable waters. *Grubart*, 513 U.S. at 534. The tort "occurred on" navigable waters if the harm "took effect" there. *Egorov, Puchinsky, Afanasiev & Juring v. Terriberry, Carroll & Yancey*, 183 F.3d 453, 456 (5th Cir. 1999) (per curiam). The connection test is satisfied if two conditions are met. *Grubart*, 513 U.S. at 534. First, "the general features of the type of incident involved" must have "a potentially disruptive impact on maritime commerce." *Id.* (quoting *Sisson v. Ruby*, 497 U.S. 358, 363, 364 n.2 (1990)). The court uses "a description of the incident at an intermediate level of possible generality," *id.* at 538, that is neither too broad to distinguish among cases nor too narrow to recognize potential effects on maritime commerce, *id.* at 538–39. Second, "the general character of the activity giving rise to the incident" must show "a substantial relationship to traditional maritime activity." *Id.* at 534 (quoting *Sisson*, 497 U.S. at 365, 364 & n.2) (internal quotation marks omitted). The court considers "whether a tortfeasor's activity, commercial or noncommercial, on navigable waters is so closely related to activity traditionally subject to admiralty law that the reasons for applying special admiralty rules would apply in the suit at hand." *Id.* at 539–40.

The location test is easily satisfied: The plaintiffs allege the defendants' activities impeded water flows and commercial navigation, meaning the harm "took effect" on navigable waters. *See Egorov*, 183 F.3d at 456. Likewise, the [—5—] first prong of the connection test is met: "[T]he general feature[] of the type of incident involved," *Grubart*, 513 U.S. at 534 (quoting *Sisson*, 497 U.S. at 363), is the obstruction of water flows. Although such obstruction does not always disrupt maritime commerce, it has the potential to do so, which is all that is required. *See id.*

The plaintiffs have not alleged facts sufficient to satisfy the second prong of the connection test, however. The key issue is the appropriate level of generality at which to describe "the general character of the activity giving rise to the incident," *id.* (quoting *Sisson*, 497 U.S. at 365, 364) (internal quotation marks omitted). The plaintiffs urge the general character of the activity is "negligent/intentional construction activity resulting in the obstruction of navigable waters with spoil," while the defendants maintain it is "pipeline construction and repair," as the court found.

The latter description is the better one. The plaintiffs' characterization conflicts with *Sisson*'s instruction, 497 U.S. at 364, "that the relevant 'activity' is defined not by the particular circumstances of the incident, but by the general conduct from which the incident arose," and warning not "to focus more particularly on the causes of the harm," *id.* at 365. Plaintiffs' description is merely a statement of the cause of the harm. Were we to use the characterization "negligent/intentional construction activity resulting in the obstruction of navigable waters with spoil," there would be no more specific cause.[2] As a result, "the general character of the activity

---

[1] *See Jerome B. Grubart, Inc. v. Great Lakes Dredge & Dock Co.*, 513 U.S. 527, 534 (1995) (announcing test for admiralty jurisdiction); *May v. Transworld Drilling Co.*, 786 F.2d 1261, 1265 (5th Cir. 1986) ("The test to determine the existence of a cause of action in maritime tort is identical with that applied to determine jurisdiction in admiralty."). Jurisdiction is not at issue here: One of the original defendants removed under the Convention on the Recognition and Enforcement of Foreign Arbitral Awards, *see* 9 U.S.C. § 203, so there is jurisdiction regardless of whether there would be admiralty jurisdiction over the claims against DIGC and Willbros.

[2] *Cf. Exec. Jet Aviation, Inc. v. City of Cleveland, Ohio*, 409 U.S. 249, 268–74 (1972) (finding that general character was air travel, not aircraft crashing into navigable waters).

giving rise to the incident"[3] is "pipeline construction and repair."[4] [—6—]

The only remaining issue is whether "pipeline construction and repair" shows "a substantial relationship to traditional maritime activity."[5] The caselaw shows it does not,[6] so the plaintiffs have failed to state a claim for a maritime tort against DIGC and Willbros.

IV.

The general rule of corporate-successor liability is that a corporation that purchases another corporation "is not responsible for the seller's debts or liabilities, except where (1) the purchaser expressly or impliedly agrees to assume the obligations; (2) the purchaser is merely a continuation of the selling corporation; or (3) the transaction is entered into to escape liability." *Golden State Bottling Co. v. NLRB*, 414 U.S. 168, 182 n.5 (1973). We have not addressed which test should govern corporate-successor liability in maritime-tort cases, but the plaintiffs have offered no reason to depart from the *Golden State* rule,[7] [—7—] and other courts considering the issue have used that general approach.[8] Accordingly, we adopt the *Golden State* rule where a defendant is alleged to be a corporate successor to a maritime tortfeasor but is not accused of having engaged in tortious conduct.

The plaintiffs' allegations that Dow is the "predecessor" to DIGC and that DIGC operated under an Army Corps permit originally issued to Dow do not show that an exception to *Golden State*'s default rule of nonliability plausibly applies. Without more, they have failed to state a claim for successor liability against DIGC.

AFFIRMED.

---

[3] *Grubart*, 513 U.S. at 534 (quoting *Sisson*, 497 U.S. at 365, 364) (internal quotation marks omitted).

[4] The only case the plaintiffs cite in support, *Apache Corp. v. Global Santa Fe Drilling* [—6—] *Co.*, 832 F. Supp. 2d 678 (W.D. La. 2010), *aff'd sub nom. Apache Corp. v. Global Santa Fe Drilling Co.*, 435 F. App'x 322 (5th Cir. 2011) (per curiam), is distinguishable. There, the plaintiff alleged the defendant had negligently secured its drilling rig during a hurricane, causing it to allide with the plaintiff's platform. *Id.* at 682–83. The court described the general character of the activity as "the activities necessary to secure a vessel during a storm," not "oil and gas activities." *Id.* at 688. That characterization was appropriate because the oil and gas activity did not "giv[e] rise to the incident." *Grubart*, 513 U.S. at 534 (quoting *Sisson*, 497 U.S. at 364) (internal quotation marks omitted). The outcome would have been the same had the rig been, say, a fishing vessel. In the instant case, the oil and gas activity was a link in the causal chain even though it was not the ultimate cause of the harm.

[5] *Grubart*, 513 U.S. at 534 (quoting *Sisson*, 497 U.S. at 364 n.2) (internal quotation mark omitted).

[6] *See Herb's Welding, Inc. v. Gray*, 470 U.S. 414, 425 (1985); *cf. Hufnagel v. Omega Serv. Indus., Inc.*, 182 F.3d 340, 352 (5th Cir. 1999) (platform construction and repair).

[7] The plaintiffs' reliance on *Sperry Rand Corp. v. Radio Corp. of Am.*, 618 F.2d 319 (5th Cir. 1980), is misplaced. There, the owners of a vessel involved in a grounding and collision caused by a defective steering system sued its manufacturer, Sperry Rand, which then sued the manufacturers of component parts. *Id.* at 320. There were no claims based on corporate-successor liability. The owners brought a tort claim against Sperry Rand, whose claim against the manufacturers was based on an express indemnification agreement. *See id.*

[8] *See Lyons v. Rienzi & Sons, Inc.*, 863 F. Supp. 2d 213, 225–26 (E.D.N.Y. 2012), *reconsidered in part*, No. 09-CV-4253, 2012 WL 1339442 (E.D.N.Y. Apr. 17, 2012); *Royal Ins. Co. v. Smatco Indus. Inc.*, 201 B.R. 755, 757 (E.D. La. 1996).

United States Court of Appeals
for the Fifth Circuit

No. 14-40326

IN RE RLB CONTRACTING, INC.

Appeal from the United States District Court for the
Southern District of Texas

Decided: December 3, 2014

Citation: 773 F.3d 596, 2 Adm. R. 378 (5th Cir. 2014).

Before **DAVIS** and **HAYNES**, Circuit Judges.*

*This opinion is being entered by a quorum of this
Court pursuant to 28 U.S.C. § 46.

[—1—] PER CURIAM: [—2—]

etitioner-Appellant RLB Contracting, Inc. ("RLB") filed this action under the Limitation of Liability Act ("Limitation Act" or "Act"), 46 U.S.C. § 30501 *et seq.*, seeking to limit its liability to $750,000, the value of the dredge vessel, "Jonathan King Boyd" (the "Vessel"), after a fatal allision between a fishing boat and the Vessel's dredge pipe. Claimants-Appellees Mark Butler, Joseph Sigle, and Linda Butler (collectively, "the Butlers"), occupants or representatives of occupants of the fishing boat, had previously sued RLB in Texas state court for personal injuries and property damage, and for the wrongful death of one occupant, Butler's twelve-year-old daughter Sammi ("S.B."). In response to RLB's limitation action, the Butlers contended that RLB had missed the Limitation Act's six-month jurisdictional deadline for invoking the protections of the Act.[1] After examining a series of letters exchanged between counsel for the parties, the district court agreed that, more than six months before RLB filed the limitation action, it had received written notice of a potential claim which had a "reasonable possibility" of exceeding the value of the dredge. The court therefore granted the Butlers' motion for summary judgment and dismissed RLB's action as time-barred. Reviewing the district court's ruling *de novo*, we affirm.

I. FACTS AND PROCEEDINGS

A. Fishing boat accident

On July 1, 2011, the Vessel was engaged in dredging operations near Anahuac in Chambers County, Texas. A fishing boat carrying Mark Butler, his son Joseph Sigle, Sigle's son B.S., and Butler's daughter S.B., collided with a floating dredge pipe associated with the Vessel. All occupants of the fishing [—3—] boat were thrown overboard, suffering various physical injuries, and S.B. was killed. The Butlers contend that the dredge pipe was inadequately marked and that RLB had negligently failed to post warnings of ongoing dredging operations. The Coast Guard initiated an investigation shortly after the accident.

B. Legal proceedings

Mark Butler filed suit against RLB in Texas state court on June 14, 2012, and RLB was served with the state court petition on July 2.[2] RLB filed its limitation of liability action in federal district court on December 28, 2012, seeking to limit its liability to the $750,000 value of the Vessel.

The Butlers filed a motion to dismiss the limitation action as untimely, contending that RLB had received written notice of the claim more than six months prior to the time it filed the limitation action. According to the Butlers, their counsel had sent RLB's counsel numerous emails between July 26, 2011, and June 14, 2012, each of which addressed the Butlers' pending claim.

The case was referred to a magistrate judge who issued a Report and Recommendation ("R&R") which concluded that, on the basis of those emails, RLB had received the required notice and thus missed the six-month window

---

[1] *See* 46 U.S.C. § 30511(a) (2013) ("The owner of a vessel may bring a civil action in a district court of the United States for limitation of liability under this chapter. The action must be brought within 6 months after a claimant gives the owner written notice of a claim.").

[2] Sigle joined the suit on October 24, 2012, on his own behalf and as next friend of B.S., and Linda Butler, S.B.'s mother, joined the suit as an additional plaintiff on December 12, 2012.

for filing a limitation action. The district court, after converting the Butlers' motion to dismiss to a motion for summary judgment, adopted the R&R, granted summary judgment to the Butlers, and dismissed the limitation action as time-barred.

C. Pre-suit correspondence

At the heart of this dispute is a series of letters, mostly exchanged via email, between RLB's two lawyers, Andrew Schulz and Wayne Pickering, and [—4—] Butler's counsel, Frank Daniel. On July 26, 2011, a few weeks after the accident, Daniel sent Schulz a letter via fax, informing him that Daniel had been retained by the Butlers.[3] He asked Schulz for "any information [he] or [RLB] may have regarding the cause of the accident, in addition to all witnesses and interested parties." He also made an overture toward settlement, informing Schulz that Daniel "would welcome the opportunity to discuss with [Schulz] [his] thoughts moving forward." Finally, Daniel wrote that "[t]his letter will also serve as notice to your client to preserve all evidence as listed in the attached notice." An attachment to the letter, titled "Notice to RLB Contracting, Inc.," gave Schulz and RLB "notice not to destroy, conceal or alter any paper or electronic files or other data." The attachment further noted that "failure to comply with this notice can result in severe sanctions being imposed by the Court {and liability in tort} for spoliation of evidence or potential evidence." Daniel advised that he expected to obtain this evidence "[t]hrough discovery."

Schulz responded to Daniel the same day via email. In it, he stated that because "the investigation [was] ongoing, . . . any substantive information w[ould] remain part of [his firm's] work product until the investigation [was] complete." These references to "the investigation" meant the Coast Guard investigation of the accident.

On August 19, 2011, Daniel sent Schulz an email stating that "it might behoove [them] to seriously consider mediation before any lawsuit." Daniel expressly based this recommendation on information that he had gathered about "the nature of the injuries, bystander claims, graphic photos, [and] the PTSD claims" of his clients and other witnesses, as well as from a meeting with [—5—] Linda Butler's attorney. Daniel referenced the additional pain that his clients would have to endure "if [they] are forced to litigate and go through depositions."

On August 24, 2011, Schulz wrote to Daniel, rejecting his proposal to mediate and noting that "any attempt to evaluate the case would be futile" until the Coast Guard investigation was complete. Daniel wrote back the next day, reiterating that mediation was their "best option" as "investigations will only tell us so much." Schulz responded: "Okay. But I cannot imagine a carrier just throwing out your number of $3M, without more, just to your clients." He added that they could "keep the dialogue going." There was another exchange of emails on October 28, primarily dealing with preservation of the fishing boat for any future litigation.

The record reflects no correspondence for the next seven months. Then, on May 30, 2012, Daniel sent one last mediation offer to Schulz, noting that, as the Coast Guard investigator had released his report, Daniel "wanted to check with [Schulz] one last time about pre-suit mediation." Schulz replied that he would check with Pickering and the "carrier" (presumably, RLB's insurance carrier). Later that day, Daniel wrote to Schulz requesting an RLB safety manual and a witness's name in preparation for any possible mediation. He also advised Schulz that he would be taking a statement from a boater who had allided with the dredge pipe on the same day as had his client. Finally, Daniel's email addressed possible state and federal venues for the lawsuit.

On June 8, 2012, Schulz received an email from Daniel that he had been instructed to file suit.[4] On June 14, Daniel wrote to Schulz and

---

[3] Schulz represents all claimants except Linda Butler, who is represented by Darwin Seidel.

[4] The Butlers claim that RLB can be presumed to have received service on June 22, as a notice of suit to RLB from the Chambers County clerk's

Pickering, [—6—] advising them that the lawsuit would be heard "in the 253rd with Judge Cain" and indicating that he would send a "courtesy copy of the file-stamped petition." (There is no evidence in the record that Daniel actually sent the petition before RLB was served on July 2, 2012.)

II. ANALYSIS

A. Standard of Review

A party who contends that a limitation action was not timely filed challenges the district court's subject matter jurisdiction.[5] We review *de novo* dismissals under Federal Rule of Civil Procedure 12(b)(1) for lack of subject matter jurisdiction.[6] On issues involving jurisdiction, the district court may consider evidence outside the pleadings and resolve factual disputes.[7] We review purely factual findings for clear error and mixed questions of law and fact *de novo*.[8] RLB, as

the party asserting jurisdiction, has the burden of proof.[9]

Both parties relied on evidence outside the pleadings, so the district court converted Butler's motion to dismiss into a motion for summary judgment under Federal Rule of Civil Procedure 12(d). We review summary [—7—] judgment rulings *de novo*, viewing evidence in the light most favorable to the nonmoving party.[10] Summary judgment is warranted when there is no genuine issue of material fact, and the moving party is entitled to judgment as a matter of law.[11]

We have made the general observation that Rule 12(b)(1) and Rule 56 diverge in their treatment of factual disputes. In this case, however, neither the magistrate judge in the R&R, nor the district court in adopting it, made any relevant factual findings. Furthermore, a review of the record reveals no material factual disputes. Thus, the Rule 12(b)(1) and Rule 56 standards converge, and a straightforward *de novo* review applies.

B. Limitation of Liability Act

The Limitation Act "allows a vessel owner to limit liability for damage or injury . . . to the value of the vessel or the owner's interest in the vessel."[12] To invoke the protections of the Act, the vessel owner must bring an action in district court "within 6 months after a claimant gives the owner written notice of a claim."[13] This requirement is jurisdictional.[14]

We have said that a communication qualifies as "written notice" if it "reveals a 'reasonable possibility' that the claim will

---

office appears to state a mailing date of June 19. According to the Butlers, in Texas state court, service is complete as of mailing and may be presumed after "the three day grace period" in Federal Rule of Civil Procedure 6(d). This reasoning is unconvincing. The Butlers conflate *service* under the state [—6—] and federal rules of civil procedure with *notice* under the Limitation Act. They cite no case holding that presumptive notice, rather than actual notice, is sufficient under that Act. More importantly, the Butlers did not press this theory before the district court, and therefore may raise it for the first time on appeal. *See Kinash v. Callahan*, 129 F.3d 736, 739 n.10 (5th Cir. 1997) ("As a general rule, this Court does not review issues that are raised for the first time upon appeal.").

[5] *In re Eckstein Marine Serv. L.L.C.*, 672 F.3d 310, 315 (5th Cir. 2012).

[6] *See id.* at 314.

[7] *See Freeman v. United States*, 556 F.3d 326, 334 (5th Cir. 2009); *see also Williamson v. Tucker*, 645 F.2d 404, 413 (5th Cir. 1981) ("[N]o presumptive truthfulness attaches to plaintiff's allegations, and the existence of disputed material facts will not preclude the trial court from evaluating for itself the merits of jurisdictional claims.").

[8] *In re Eckstein*, 672 F.3d at 314; *Complaint of Tom-Mac, Inc.*, 76 F.3d 678, 682 (5th Cir. 1996).

[9] *See In re Eckstein*, 672 F.3d at 314.

[10] *See Flock v. Scripto-Tokai Corp.*, 319 F.3d 231, 236 (5th Cir. 2003).

[11] *Id.*

[12] *Lewis v. Lewis & Clark Marine, Inc.*, 531 U.S. 438, 446 (2001). A limitation action essentially establishes a limited fund equal to the value of the vessel and consolidates all potential claims before one federal district court. *See id.* at 448.

[13] 46 U.S.C. § 30511(a) (2013). This provision was previously codified at 46 U.S.C. app. § 185.

[14] *In re Eckstein*, 672 F.3d at 315.

exceed the value of the vessel."[15] This standard evokes two inquiries: (1) whether the writing [—8—] communicates the *reasonable possibility* of a claim, and (2) whether it communicates the *reasonable possibility* of damages in excess of the vessel's value. Answering these questions requires a "fact-intensive inquiry into the circumstances of the case."[16]

The purpose of the "reasonable possibility" standard is to place the burden of investigating potential claims on the vessel owner:

> The Limitation Act provides generous statutory protection to the vessel owners who reap all of its benefits. When there is uncertainty as to whether a claim will exceed the vessel's value, the reasonable possibility standard places the risk and the burdens associated with that risk on the owner. In other words, if "doubt exists as to the total amount of the claims or as to whether they will exceed the value of the ship the owner will not be excused from satisfying the statutory time bar since he may institute a limitation proceeding even when the total amount claimed is uncertain."[17]

Assigning the risk of uncertainty to the vessel owner fits the purpose of the six-month limitation, which is "to require the shipowner to act promptly to gain the benefit of the statutory right to limit liability."[18] Thus, "[o]nce a reasonable possibility has been raised, it becomes the vessel owner's responsibility to initiate a prompt investigation and determine whether to file a

limitation action."[19] We emphasize that the standard is a reasonable *possibility*, not a reasonable *probability*. Although this standard "is not toothless, it is also not particularly stringent."[20]

We have said less about what a communication must contain to qualify as such a written notice under the Act. A state court complaint clearly gives [—9—] notice of the claim itself. A demand need not express a specific quantum of damages so long as there is a reasonable possibility that a claim's value will exceed the value of the vessel.[21] This court has not, however, addressed what is required for a written communication that is *not* a filed complaint to qualify as notice.

C. Written Notice

As a threshold matter, to the extent that we have never explicitly held that a written communication may serve as notice under the Act in lieu of a filed complaint, we do so today.[22] In this case, that presents three issues: (1) whether a series of letters, none of which constitutes notice on its own, may be considered together to find notice in the

---

[15] *Id.* at 317. RLB relies on the multifactor test from *Matter of Loyd W. Richardson Const. Co.*, 850 F. Supp. 555, 557 (S.D. Tex. 1993). However, we have consistently used the "reasonable possibility" test, and continue to do so here. *See In re Eckstein*, 672 F.3d at 317; *Billiot v. Dolphin Servs., Inc.*, 225 F.3d 515, 518 (5th Cir. 2000); *Complaint of Tom-Mac, Inc.*, 76 F.3d 678, 683 (5th Cir. 1996).

[16] *In re Eckstein*, 672 F.3d at 317.

[17] *Id.* at 317–18 (quoting *Complaint of Morania Barge No. 190, Inc.*, 690 F.2d 32, 34 (2d Cir. 1982)).

[18] *Exxon Shipping Co. v. Cailleteau*, 869 F.2d 843, 846 (5th Cir. 1989).

[19] *In re Eckstein*, 672 F.3d at 317.

[20] *Id.*

[21] *See id.* at 317–19 ("[A] claimant need not prove or even specifically allege that his damages will exceed the value of the vessel in order to trigger the six month deadline. So long as the reasonable possibility standard has been met by the claimant's allegations, the vessel owner bears the risk even if the total value of the claim is uncertain." *Id.* at 319.). Thus, although a claimant who affirmatively demands a lower amount does not trigger the six-month period until he later amends his complaint to demand a higher figure, a vessel owner who has reason to know of "*other* claims . . . arising out of the same occurrence [that] may exceed the value of his ship" is still on notice from the start. *Id.* at 319 (emphasis added) (quoting *Exxon Shipping*, 869 F.2d at 846; *see also, e.g.*, *Complaint of Morania Barge*, 690 F.2d at 34–35.

[22] *See In re Marquette Transp. Co., L.L.C.*, 524 F. App'x 989, 992–93 (5th Cir. 2013) (per curiam) (unpublished); *see also Complaint of Beesley's Point Sea-Doo, Inc.*, 956 F. Supp. 538, 540 (D.N.J. 1997)) ("It is well settled that letters sent by claimants to vessel owners may, in some circumstances, constitute notice sufficient to trigger the six-month rule under the Act.").

aggregate, (2) whether Daniel's letters convey a "reasonable possibility" of a potential claim, and (3) whether those letters establish a "reasonable possibility" that the amount of the claim might exceed the value of the Vessel.

1. Aggregate Notice

The Butlers urge us to consider counsel Daniel's letters "bundled together" and to evaluate the entire body of correspondence under the Act's "written notice" requirement. The statutory text does not foreclose the [—10—] possibility of aggregate notice; it only requires the claimant to give "the owner written notice," not *a* written notice.[23] In fact, some district courts, including one in this circuit, have considered a body of correspondence rather than each of its individual constituent parts in a vacuum.[24]

Moreover, from a practical standpoint, it makes sense to do so. In situations like this one, in which the vessel owner and the putative claimant corresponded over time, it is natural for individual letters to focus narrowly on specific subjects and for later letters to assume knowledge of the contents of previous letters. Considering the correspondence as a whole better approximates what the vessel owner, as the recipient of *all* of the writings, should have thought was a "reasonable possibility" of a potential claim and its value.

Furthermore, it would be an artificial exercise to require a claimant who did engage in a lengthy correspondence to designate the single most favorable writing from the series as *the* written notice. Far better for the record to reflect what actually occurred and for the district court to make its ruling accordingly. Thus, we shall consider whether the entire series of letters satisfies the "reasonable possibility" requirement.

2. "Reasonable Possibility" of Potential Claim

We have not previously addressed the issue of what a writing must contain to give a vessel owner notice of a potential claim. Both RLB and the Butlers analogized to district court cases (primarily from courts outside this circuit) and emerge with two different methodologies for analyzing the facts at hand. RLB starts with an idea of what proper notice of a claim would look like and searches through Daniel's emails for statements matching that standard. [—11—] RLB states that notice must "refer to the cause of [claimants'] injuries or the types of injuries sustained . . . and clearly assert blame on the petitioner." RLB also tries to disqualify Daniel's emails for "provid[ing] no details regarding the claims, injuries, or causes of injuries" and for not mentioning any "demand of a right, specific blame for damage, or call upon something due." RLB asserts that, even though Daniel's emails might have obliquely referred to a potential lawsuit, absent the magic words it sought, RLB "was never put on notice that [the Butlers] would be seeking a claim based on RLB's alleged negligence in connection with the vessel." RLB also claims that it had serious doubts as to the viability of the potential claim because of Butler's alleged contributory negligence. The Butlers point out that RLB cannot simultaneously disclaim knowledge of a pending claim and assert knowledge of a potential defense to that claim. Furthermore, the issue here is the "reasonable possibility" that a claim *exists*, not probability of success on the merits.[25]

In contrast, the Butlers' approach is to start with the letters themselves, then consider whether together those letters reveal the reasonable possibility of a pending claim. Daniel's first letter instructed RLB "to preserve evidence as if a suit had been initiated"; his email of August 19, 2011, mentioned the evidence he had already

---

[23] 46 U.S.C. § 30511(a) (2013).

[24] *See Complaint of Beesley's*, 956 F. Supp. at 541; *Matter of Oceanic Fleet, Inc.*, 807 F. Supp. 1261, 1263 (E.D. La. 1992).

[25] *Cf. In re Hawaiian Watersports, LLC*, No. 07-00617, 2008 WL 3065381, at *5 (D. Haw. Feb. 29, 2008) ("Plaintiff would not be excused from being on notice if it believed it had some other compelling defense to the claim, such as no negligence on its part." (citations omitted)).

gathered and requested mediation "before any lawsuit"; his email on May 30 of the following year discussed state and federal venues for the suit and again requested mediation; finally, his emails of June 8 and 14, 2012, explicitly bring up filing the lawsuit and service of process. According to the Butlers, these statements, when taken together, paint a picture of a pending claim. [—12—]

The Butlers' approach is more compatible with the reasonable-possibility test's fact-intensive nature, as it starts with the actual facts rather than a predefined factual pattern. This finds support from the Second Circuit, which does not require "exacting specificity in a notice of claim to a vessel owner."[26] Rather, that court uses "a broad and flexible standard of review—reading letters of notice in their entirety and considering their 'whole tenor'— when determining if sufficient notice was given."[27]

In its favor, RLB's position does invoke the benefits of a bright-line rule: A clear list of required statements and demands would provide guidance to future claimants and vessel owners alike. In addition to being less fact-focused, however, there are two additional problems with this approach. First, regarding damages, we have held that the risk of uncertainty lies with the vessel owner. It would be inconsistent to reverse that risk when it comes to notice of a potential claim. Second, mandating that written notice contain "magic words" or specific elements might well impose a requirement not found in the statutory text.

As the Butlers' analytical approach appears to be more compatible with our precedent, and as it is factually inconceivable that RLB had no notice of a claim after almost a year of emails discussing the case—culminating in the June 14 missive informing RLB that Butler had actually filed suit—we hold that by June 14, 2012, at the latest, RLB had notice of the Butlers' claim. This is obviously more than six months prior to the December 28, 2012, filing date of RLB's limitation action. [—13—]

3. "Reasonable Possibility" of Damages in Excess of Vessel's Value

To the same extent that RLB had notice of the Butlers' potential wrongful death suit, it had notice that there was a reasonable possibility of damages in excess of $750,000, even though Daniel's emails never gave a specific number. Our recent decision in *In re Eckstein Marine Service L.L.C.* addressed almost precisely this same issue.[28] In that case, the state court plaintiff alleged permanent and disabling injuries, but did not provide a specific damages figure. We rejected the vessel owner's contention that, without a dollar amount or certainty as to the extent and permanence of the plaintiff's injuries, the period for filing a limitation action could not start.[29] We concluded that, in light of the severity of the injuries, a vessel owner should have realized the potential for damages in excess of its vessel's value (coincidentally, also $750,000), and that any uncertainty was the owner's burden to resolve.[30] That is the reason for a six-month grace period. The analogy to this case is clear.[31]

The $3 million figure and dispute surrounding it are red herrings. RLB attacks the district court's conclusion that RLB "certainly knew" of the $3 million value of the claim, and seeks to rely on the fact that this settlement offer never appeared in *Daniel's* letters, only in Schulz's rejection. However, RLB has no reply to the district court's

---

[26] *Doxsee Sea Clam Co. v. Brown*, 13 F.3d 550, 554 (2d Cir. 1994).

[27] *Id.*

[28] 672 F.3d 310 (5th Cir. 2012).

[29] *Id.* at 317.

[30] *Id.* at 317–18; *see also Paradise Divers, Inc. v. Upmal*, 402 F.3d 1087, 1091 (11th Cir. 2005); *Doxsee*, 13 F.3d at 554–55.

[31] We note further that in *In re Eckstein*, the vessel owner had actually done some legal research to find that juries typically awarded about $335,000 for injuries similar to those suffered by the state court plaintiff, demonstrably less than the boat's value of $750,000. We still did not excuse the untimely filing of the limitation action, however, stating that "[w]hile this finding might have made it less *probable* that [the state court plaintiff's] claim would exceed $750,000, in light of the other evidence available to [the vessel owner] it did not make the *possibility* of such an award unreasonable." *In re Eckstein*, 672 F.3d at 318 (emphases added).

primary reasoning: RLB should have [—14—] realized that an action involving the death of a child would easily exceed $750,000 in potential damages. We are satisfied that more than six months prior to filing its limitation action, RLB had notice of a potential claim the value of which had the reasonable possibility of exceeding the value of its vessel.

III. CONCLUSION

The Butlers have established that the pre-suit writings from their counsel to RLB's counsel conveyed the reasonable possibility that RLB faced a claim exceeding $750,000, the value of the Vessel. RLB thus had written notice under the Limitation Act earlier than six months before it filed its limitation action. The district court's dismissal of RLB's complaint as time-barred is AFFIRMED.

United States Court of Appeals
for the Fifth Circuit

No. 13-20572

SAVANT
vs.
APM TERMINALS

Appeal from the United States District Court for the
Southern District of Texas

Decided: December 5, 2014

Citation: 776 F.3d 285, 2 Adm. R. 385 (5th Cir. 2014).

Before **HIGGINBOTHAM, CLEMENT,** and **HIGGINSON,**
Circuit Judges.

[—1—] **HIGGINSON,** Circuit Judge:

F loyd L. Savant appeals the district court's grant of summary judgment in favor of his employer, Universal Maritime Service Corp. ("Universal Maritime"),[1] dismissing his claim under the Age Discrimination in Employment Act ("ADEA"), 29 U.S.C. § 621 et seq. For the following reasons, we AFFIRM. [—2—]

FACTS AND PROCEEDINGS

Until October 2009, Savant worked as a yard tractor[2] operator at one of Universal Maritime's port terminal facilities. Universal Maritime is a member of the West Gulf Maritime Association ("West Gulf"), a multi-employer trade association that negotiates and administers multi-employer collective bargaining agreements with the International Longshoremen's Association ("ILA" or the "Union") and its affiliated local unions. Savant, who was born in 1934, has been a member of the ILA Local No. 24 for over twenty years.

A collective bargaining agreement ("CBA") governed Savant's employment at Universal

Maritime. The South Atlantic and Gulf Coast District ("SAGC District") had negotiated this agreement with West Gulf on behalf of the Union. The CBA states that its grievance procedure and arbitration "shall be the exclusive remedy with respect to any and all disputes arising between the Union or any person working under the Agreement . . . and the Association or any company acting under the Agreement." In addition to the CBA, the SAGC District and West Gulf also negotiated a Memorandum of Understanding ("MOU") to supplement the CBA's terms. The MOU states that "[a]ny complaint that there has been a violation of any employment law, such as . . . [the] ADEA, . . . shall be resolved solely by the grievance and arbitration provisions of the collective bargaining agreement." The MOU also states that its procedure "shall be a worker's sole remedy for a violation of any anti-discrimination or employment law."

In October 2009, while Savant was operating a yard tractor, he was involved in an accident with an over-the-road driver who ran through a stop sign. Both vehicles were damaged. As required under the applicable Occupational Safety and Health Administration ("OSHA") regulations and an [—3—] OSHA industry settlement agreement, Universal Maritime referred Savant to a refresher training and evaluation for operating powered industrial trucks ("PITs"). See 29 C.F.R. § 1910.178(l)(4)(ii)(B). A PIT operator who does not pass this evaluation will not be recertified and will not be permitted to operate PIT equipment until he successfully completes the PIT refresher training. Under West Gulf's training policies, a PIT operator who fails the evaluation three times in one year must wait one year before he will be permitted to attend the training again.

Savant attended PIT refresher training three times during the year following the October 2009 accident, and Universal Maritime contends that he failed the evaluation each time. As a result, he is no longer allowed to operate PIT equipment at Universal Maritime. Savant has nevertheless continued working at Universal Maritime's facilities in different job classifications,

---

[1] Universal Maritime claims that Savant erroneously sued "APM Terminals," the Appellee named in the case caption. Universal Maritime also does business as APM Terminals.

[2] A yard tractor is a truck that is used to haul large shipping containers.

earning the same hourly rate that he made as a PIT operator. Instead of filing a grievance through the Union challenging his evaluation results, Savant filed this lawsuit in federal court, alleging age discrimination in violation of the ADEA.

In the district court, Universal Maritime filed a motion for summary judgment, arguing that Savant lacked standing because he failed to exhaust the CBA and MOU's grievance and arbitration procedures.[3] The district court granted the motion for lack of standing and entered judgment in favor of Universal Maritime. This appeal timely followed.

STANDARD OF REVIEW

This court reviews a district court's grant of summary judgment de novo, applying the same standards as the district court. *Rogers v. Bromac Title* [—4—] *Servs., L.L.C.*, 755 F.3d 347, 350 (5th Cir. 2014). Summary judgment is appropriate "if the movant shows that there is no genuine dispute as to any material fact and the movant is entitled to judgment as a matter of law." Fed. R. Civ. P. 56(a). A genuine issue of material fact exists if "the evidence is such that a reasonable jury could return a verdict for the nonmoving party." *Anderson v. Liberty Lobby, Inc.*, 477 U.S. 242, 248 (1986). In deciding whether a fact issue exists, courts must view the facts and draw reasonable inferences in the light most favorable to the nonmoving party. *Scott v. Harris*, 550 U.S. 372, 378 (2007). This court is "not limited to the district court's reasons for its grant of summary judgment and may affirm the district court's summary judgment on any ground raised below and supported by the record." *Rogers*, 755 F.3d at 350 (internal quotation marks omitted).

DISCUSSION

The district court held that Savant lacked standing to bring his ADEA claim in federal court because he had failed to exhaust the grievance and arbitration remedies under the

CBA and MOU. A plaintiff is ordinarily "required to attempt to exhaust any grievance or arbitration remedies provided in [a] collective bargaining agreement" before seeking relief in federal court. *See DelCostello v. Int'l Bhd. of Teamsters*, 462 U.S. 151, 163 (1983); *Harris v. Chem. Leaman Tank Lines, Inc.*, 437 F.2d 167, 170 & n.3 (5th Cir. 1971). This principle applies even when a plaintiff is alleging employment discrimination in violation of a federal statute. In *14 Penn Plaza LLC v. Pyett*, the Supreme Court clarified that, in the absence of statutory language to the contrary, a union may agree with an employer to submit employees' statutory claims exclusively to arbitration or another non-judicial grievance procedure. 556 U.S. 247, 256–58, 274 (2009). For that agreement to be enforceable, however, the CBA must "clearly and unmistakably require[] union members to arbitrate." *Id.* at 274. In *Penn Plaza*, the Court held that this "clear and unmistakable" [—5—] standard was satisfied when an anti-discrimination provision explicitly referenced the ADEA and stated that "[a]ll such claims shall be subject to the grievance and arbitration procedures . . . as the sole and exclusive remedy for violations." *Id.* at 252, 260.

This court applied *Penn Plaza*'s test in *Ibarra v. United Parcel Service*, 695 F.3d 354 (5th Cir. 2012). The court agreed with other circuits that have concluded that, "for a waiver of an employee's right to a judicial forum for statutory discrimination claims to be clear and unmistakable, the CBA must, at the very least, identify the specific statutes the agreement purports to incorporate or include an arbitration clause that explicitly refers to statutory claims." *Id.* at 359–60. In *Ibarra*, the court concluded that the CBA did not require an employee to submit her Title VII claim to the grievance process because the CBA only stated generally that "any controversy, complaint, misunderstanding or dispute arising as to interpretation, application or observance of any of the provisions of this Agreement" must be submitted to the grievance process. *Id.* at 356–57.

---

[3] Universal Maritime argued in the alternative that, even if Savant had standing, his ADEA claim nevertheless failed on the merits. The district court did not reach this argument.

This dispute therefore turns on whether the district court properly concluded that there was no genuine issue of fact as to whether the MOU and the CBA, when read together, clearly and unmistakably waived union members' right to a judicial forum for ADEA and other statutory discrimination claims. When interpreting a collective bargaining agreement, federal law governs. *See Int'l Ass'n of Machinists & Aerospace Workers v. Masonite Corp.*, 122 F.3d 228, 231 (5th Cir. 1997); *see also Textile Workers Union v. Lincoln Mills of Ala.*, 353 U.S. 448, 456–57 (1957). Nevertheless, "courts may draw upon state rules of contractual interpretation to the extent that those rules are consistent with federal labor policies." *Nichols v. Alcatel USA, Inc.*, 532 F.3d 365, 377 (5th Cir. 2008) (internal quotation marks omitted). "However, the construction and application of a collective bargaining [—6—] agreement's terms cannot be strictly confined by ordinary principles of contract law." *United Paperworkers Int'l Union v. Champion Int'l Corp.*, 908 F.2d 1252, 1256 (5th Cir. 1990). "The provisions of a labor contract may be more readily expanded by implication than those of contracts memorializing other transactions." *Id.* Moreover, "[w]hen several documents represent one agreement, all must be construed together in an attempt to discern the intent of the parties, and the court should attempt to give effect to every contractual provision." *Id.*

Here, the CBA, by itself, is not clear and unmistakable. It states:

> This grievance procedure and arbitration shall be the exclusive remedy with respect to any and all disputes arising between the Union or any person working under the Agreement . . . and [West Gulf] or any company acting under the Agreement . . . and no other remedies shall be utilized, except those remedies specifically provided for under this Agreement.

Like the CBA in *Ibarra*, the CBA governing Savant's employment does not specifically identify the ADEA, and it does not state that statutory discrimination claims are subject to its grievance and arbitration procedures. Therefore, the CBA alone cannot bar Savant from filing suit under the ADEA.

The MOU, however, is clear and unmistakable. It states: "Any complaint that there has been a violation of any employment law, such as . . . [the] ADEA, . . . shall be resolved solely by the grievance and arbitration provisions of the collective bargaining agreement." The MOU further clarifies that its procedure "shall be a worker's sole remedy for a violation of any anti-discrimination or employment law." Although *Penn Plaza* and *Ibarra* only addressed the clarity of arbitration clauses in CBAs, Savant has not articulated a reason not to extend the rule from those cases to clauses in an MOU or other agreement that is binding on the union and the employer. In other words, for an arbitration agreement to be enforceable as to statutory [—7—] claims, either the CBA or an ancillary agreement binding the union and the employer must satisfy the "clear and unmistakable" rule. *See Anglin v. Ceres Gulf Inc.*, 503 F. App'x 254, 255 (5th Cir. 2012) (noting that if an MOU between the union and employer bound the employee, the employee would not have been able to bring her statutory claims in federal court because "[t]he MOU specifically identifie[d] Title VII" and indicated that "complaints brought under that statute are subject to the CBA's grievance and arbitration provisions"). Therefore, here, given the MOU's explicit references to the ADEA and other statutory discrimination claims, the district court properly concluded that the MOU satisfies the *Ibarra* requirement.

On appeal, Savant argues that the district court erred because the MOU was voluntary, but not binding on the Union. First, Savant emphasizes that West Gulf and the Union never signed the MOU. This fact, however, is not dispositive. "An employer can in writing obligate itself to follow portions of a collective bargaining agreement without signing the collective bargaining agreement itself." *D.E.W., Inc. v. Local 93, Laborers' Int'l Union*, 957 F.2d 196, 201 (5th Cir. 1992); *see also NLRB v. Beckham, Inc.*, 564 F.2d 190, 194

(5th Cir. 1977) ("Once an agreement has been reached, . . . it is an unfair labor practice for a party to refuse to sign the written contract.").[4] Indeed, a CBA need not even be reduced to writing. "Instead, what is required is conduct [—8—] manifesting an intention to abide by the terms of an agreement." *NLRB v. Haberman Constr. Co.*, 641 F.2d 351, 356 (5th Cir. 1981).

The evidence in the record supports the district court's conclusion that the parties intended to be bound by the MOU. First, with no objection from Savant's counsel, Savant admitted at his deposition that the MOU was an agreement between his local union and West Gulf on how statutory discrimination claims would be resolved. He also admitted that he had authorized the Union to enter into these types of agreements on his behalf. Universal Maritime also submitted an affidavit from the current president of West Gulf stating that the MOU procedures had been applied to the ILA locals and have been used since at least 2004. Indeed, the former president of West Gulf had sent the unions a letter confirming that the local unions would be bound by the MOU, and there is no evidence in the record that Savant's local union tendered an objection to that letter. Next, legal representatives of West Gulf, the SAGC District, and ILA Local No. 24 (Savant's local union) gave a presentation in

May 2008 about the MOU's grievance and arbitration procedure, describing it as "a worker's sole remedy for any violation of anti-discrimination laws." Finally, at least four grievance reports were filed between July 2008 and April 2011 by ILA locals, including one from Savant's local union, adjudicating discrimination claims using the MOU's grievance and arbitration procedures.

Resisting the conclusion that the MOU is binding on the parties, Savant contends that the Union rejected the MOU.[5] Savant, however, fails to cite any evidence in the summary judgment record that supports this assertion. For one, there is no indication in the record that the Union's constitution, bylaws, [—9—] or rules and regulations required the Union to submit proposed agreements or MOUs to the union membership for approval. Without such a requirement, the Union could have agreed to the MOU without ever consulting the local unions and union membership. *See O'Neill v. Air Line Pilots Ass'n, Int'l*, 886 F.2d 1438, 1447 (5th Cir. 1989) ("The [Labor Management Reporting Disclosure Act, 29 U.S.C. § 411(a)(1),] does not require submission of proposed agreements or any segments thereof to the membership; nor grant members the right to vote on negotiating, executing and approving contracts."), *rev'd on other grounds*, 499 U.S. 65 (1991); *see also White v. White Rose Food*, 237 F.3d 174, 182 (2d Cir. 2001) ("Federal labor law does not require rank-and-file ratification of employer-union agreements. Such ratification is required only if the union's constitution or by-laws or the agreement itself so provides." (citations omitted)). Moreover, in his application for membership in the Union, Savant signed a statement agreeing to "ratify and approve any collective bargaining agreement entered into on [his] behalf by the Union."

Finally, finding no support in the summary judgment record of this lawsuit, Savant relies instead on this court's unpublished opinion in

---

[4] Our sister circuits have reached similar conclusions. *See, e.g.*, *Bricklayers Local 21 of Ill. Apprenticeship & Training Program v. Banner Restoration, Inc.*, 385 F.3d 761, 767 (7th Cir. 2004) ("[A] signature to a collective bargaining agreement is not a prerequisite to finding an employer bound to that agreement."); *Brown v. C. Volante Corp.*, 194 F.3d 351, 352, 354–56 (2d Cir. 1999) (holding that the conduct of an employer who did not sign two CBAs, but paid contributions and wages at the rates agreed to in the agreements, manifested an intent to adopt the unsigned agreements); *Trs. of Wyo. Laborers Health & Welfare Plan v. Morgen & Oswood Constr. Co. of Wyo.*, 850 F.2d 613, 622 (10th Cir. 1988) (concluding that the parties had reached an agreement even though the Union had not yet signed a "Laborers Compliance Agreement"); *NLRB v. Deauville Hotel*, 751 F.2d 1562, 1569 n.10 (11th Cir. 1985) ("The[] act of signing [the CBA] was nothing more than ministerial.").

[5] In an interrogatory response, Savant also claimed that "[t]here are not any memoranda of agreement or understanding that has [sic] been approved by the union and its members."

Anglin v. Ceres Gulf Inc. In *Anglin*, the court considered a similar set of characters—the ILA, the SAGC District, and West Gulf—and the same CBA and MOU. 503 F. App'x at 254–55. Martha Anglin, the plaintiff, had filed a Title VII lawsuit against her employer and West Gulf, and West Gulf, in turn, similarly argued that Anglin was required to pursue her discrimination claim through the grievance and arbitration procedure. *Id.* at 255. Savant argues that *Anglin* "established" that "the union has rejected the MOU." But that is a mischaracterization of the court's holding: *Anglin* reversed the grant of summary judgment against Anglin because "[t]here remain[ed] a factual question as to whether [the MOU] is binding on Anglin." *Id.* As the court explained, Anglin's uncontroverted testimony was that "the MOU was rejected **[—10—]** by local union members." *Id.* Anglin, however, belonged to a different ILA local union (Local No. 1351) than the local union that represents Savant (Local No. 24). *Id.* at 254. Therefore, Anglin's testimony about Local No. 1351's rejection of the MOU does not create a genuine issue of fact as to whether Savant's Local No. 24 rejected or approved the MOU.[6] And as discussed above, the summary judgment record in this case supports the district court's conclusion that the MOU bound Savant's local union.

Having resolved that the parties in this case have a valid agreement to arbitrate Savant's ADEA claim, the court concludes that the arbitration provisions in the CBA and MOU must be enforced. Because Savant did not exhaust the CBA's grievance procedures, he lacks standing to pursue his ADEA claim in federal court. The court therefore will not address the merits of his age discrimination claim.

CONCLUSION

For the foregoing reasons, we AFFIRM the district court's grant of summary judgment in favor of Universal Maritime.

---

[6] Savant's reliance on an affidavit from Martha Anglin that he filed in his own lawsuit is similarly misplaced because it discusses Anglin's local union, not Savant's. Moreover, the district court struck the Anglin affidavit, and Savant does not challenge the district court's ruling on the motion to strike on appeal. *See St. Paul Mercury Ins. Co. v. Williamson*, 224 F.3d 425, 445 (5th Cir. 2000) ("Generally, we deem abandoned those issues not presented and argued in an appellant's initial brief . . . .").

United States Court of Appeals
for the Fifth Circuit

No. 13-31301

UNITED STATES
vs.
BOLLINGER SHIPYARDS, INC.

Appeal from the United States District Court for the
Eastern District of Louisiana

Decided: December 23, 2014

Citation: 775 F.3d 255, 2 Adm. R. 390 (5th Cir. 2014).

Before **DAVIS, DeMOSS,** and **ELROD,** Circuit Judges.

[—1—] **DAVIS,** Circuit Judge:

The United States of America appeals from the district court's final judgment in which the court granted the defendants-appellees' motion to dismiss its False Claims Act case under FED. R. CIV. P. 12(b)(6). We conclude that the United States alleged sufficient facts in its complaint to allow a factfinder to infer that the defendants-appellees either knew that their statements were false or had a reckless disregard of their truth or falsity. We therefore REVERSE and REMAND for further proceedings consistent with this opinion.[1] [—2—]

I. FACTS

The United States filed this action under the False Claims Act ("FCA"), 31 U.S.C. §§ 3729 et seq., alleging that Bollinger Shipyards, Inc., Bollinger Shipyards Lockport, L.L.C., and Halter Bollinger Joint Venture, L.L.C. (collectively, "Bollinger") knowingly submitted false statements and false claims for payment to the government in relation to a government contract under which Bollinger was to modify eight vessels owned by the United States Coast Guard ("Coast Guard"). After allowing the United States to replead once, the district court granted Bollinger's second Rule 12(b)(6) motion to dismiss,

holding that the United States failed to satisfy the plausibility and particularity requirements of the Federal Rules of Civil Procedure concerning Bollinger's knowledge under the FCA. The United States appeals this dismissal.

Because this case comes up on the grant of a motion to dismiss under Rule 12(b)(6), we review the district court's ruling de novo.[2] Generally, we "must assess whether the complaint contains sufficient factual matter, accepted as true, to state a claim for relief that is plausible on its face under *Bell Atlantic Corp. v. Twombly*, 550 U.S. 544, 570, 127 S.Ct. 1955, 167 L.Ed.2d 929 (2007), and *Ashcroft v. Iqbal*, 556 U.S. 662, 678, 129 S.Ct. 1937, 173 L.Ed.2d 868 (2009)."[3]

The facts as stated in the United States' First Amended Complaint are as follows: In 1999, the Coast Guard began a program called Deepwater to upgrade or replace its aging fleet of vessels, aircraft, and electronics systems. One of the contractors competing for the project was Integrated Coast Guard Ship Systems ("ICGS"). ICGS's proposal included converting existing 110-foot [—3—] Coast Guard patrol boats into 123-foot patrol boats to extend the service life of the boats by adding a 13-foot extension to the hulls, among other changes. Under this proposal, the conversion of the 110-foot boats would be subcontracted to Bollinger, which had originally built the boats.

In September 2000, the Coast Guard expressed concerns to Bollinger about the feasibility of converting the vessels and questioned whether the hulls of the converted vessels would have adequate structural integrity. In response, Bollinger prepared a longitudinal strength analysis describing the modified boats' projected "section modulus," a measure of longitudinal strength. Bollinger performed its calculation of the section modulus using the Midship Section Calculator ("MSC") program, which uses as inputs a number of components, including the

---

[1] The district court had federal question jurisdiction under 28 U.S.C. §§ 1331 and 1345, and we have jurisdiction over this appeal from a final judgment under 28 U.S.C. § 1291.

[2] *Scanlan v. Texas A&M Univ.*, 343 F.3d 533, 536 (5th Cir. 2003).

[3] *Spitzberg v. Hous. Am. Energy Corp.*, 758 F.3d 676, 683 (5th Cir. 2014) (footnote omitted).

structural geometry of the ship's hull, the physical and engineering properties of the hull, and shell plate material and thickness. Bollinger advised the Coast Guard that the minimum section modulus required by the American Bureau of Shipping ("ABS"), an independent organization that develops standards for shipbuilding, was 3,113 cubic inches, and the calculated section modulus for the proposed modified boats would be 7,152. As was later discovered, Bollinger reached this calculated section modulus by inputting a thicker hull plating than existed in the 110-foot boats. Bollinger did not advise the Coast Guard that it used a thicker hull plating in its calculations, and its proposal did not include a provision for replacing or thickening the hull in the boats. In August of 2001, Bollinger was notified that the Coast Guard would require Bollinger to certify compliance with ABS structural standards.

In June 2002, the Coast Guard then selected ICGS as the contractor for the Deepwater program and entered into a contract with ICGS. The contract required ICGS and its subcontractors, including Bollinger, to provide the Coast [—4—] Guard with a "CDRL S012-11," a Hull and Load Strength Analysis, to verify that the 123-foot boat design met the program and contract requirements. The contract also required Bollinger to obtain ABS certification of compliance with ABS structural standards.

In August 2002, the Coast Guard issued the first of four delivery task orders under the contract for the design and modification of the 123-foot patrol boats. On August 26, 2002, Bollinger's chief executive officer, Boysie Bollinger, sent an email to other Bollinger officials stating that an ABS official had offered to provide a confidential assessment of the structural analysis of the converted vessels. Boysie Bollinger sought advice on whether to accept the offer. T.R. Hamblin, Bollinger's vice president, recommended declining the offer, reflecting concern that the review would find that the design required additional structural support. Boysie Bollinger replied:

I'm concerned that [ABS] sells CG on the fact that they need this review. . . . [ABS] would love the additional responsibility from the CG and as we both know, adverse results could cause the entire 123 to be an un-economical solution if we had to totally rebuild the hull. . . . MY CONCERN—we don't do anything—ABS gets CG to require it without our input, and the result is we BLOW the program.

The same day this email exchange occurred, Bollinger found that the actual section modulus, without an increase in hull plating thickness, was less than the 7,152 cubic inches it reported to the Coast Guard. Bollinger ran the MSC application at least three times that day, changing the input data each time, and obtaining results of 2,836, 3,037, and 5,232 cubic inches. Each calculation used some incorrect inputs, with the 5,232 calculation having one input that was 16,000 times greater than the correct input value. A few days later, for internal purposes, Bollinger used the 3,037 value in its draft version [—5—] of the CDRL S012-11. However, in an initial CDRL S012-11 sent to the Coast Guard on September 4, 2002, Bollinger submitted a section modulus of 5,232 cubic inches and certified that the section modulus met ABS requirements.

On October 9, 2002, Bollinger met with Coast Guard officials during a Preliminary Design Review meeting. To address the Coast Guard's concerns regarding the validity of the 5,232 cubic inch section modulus calculation in light of Bollinger's original calculation of 7,152, Bollinger told the Coast Guard that it would have ABS review the calculation and the vessels' longitudinal strength. Nonetheless, Bollinger never requested ABS review of the midship section modulus calculation and longitudinal strength, and ABS never performed this review. Bollinger submitted its final version of the CDRL S012-11 to the Coast Guard on December 16, 2002, reporting that the section modulus was 5,232 cubic inches and again certifying that the section modulus met ABS requirements. On December 18, 2002, during a Critical Design Review meeting with the Coast Guard,

Bollinger represented that it had engaged ABS to review compliance with ABS standards; however, the ABS never reviewed the section modulus calculation.

In March 2004, the first 123-foot boat, the Matagorda, was delivered to and accepted by the Coast Guard. In September 2004, it was discovered that the Matagorda had suffered a structural casualty, including buckling of the hull. An investigation by the Coast Guard and a recalculation of the section modulus by Bollinger revealed that the true section modulus of the completed ship was 2,615 cubic inches, well below the ABS minimum of 3,113 cubic inches required by the contract and also below any figure Bollinger reported to the Coast Guard prior to delivery.

Before the Coast Guard realized that the section modulus number was incorrect, it had accepted delivery of four modified patrol boats. For vessels five [—6—] through eight, the Coast Guard and ICGS pursued structural modifications to increase the section modulus, and made two structural modifications to the vessels. In reliance on the feasibility of the modifications, the Coast Guard accepted delivery of vessels five through eight. Ultimately, the structural modifications were inadequate, and the Coast Guard removed all eight boats from service. On May 17, 2007, the Coast Guard revoked its acceptance of the boats.

II. PROCEDURAL HISTORY

The United States brought suit against Bollinger under the FCA, alleging that Bollinger knowingly presented or caused to be presented false or fraudulent claims for payment to the United States and knowingly made statements material to false or fraudulent claims for payment or approval by the United States in violation of 31 U.S.C. § 3729(a)(1). The district court granted Bollinger's initial motion to dismiss with leave to amend the FCA claims. However, while granting leave to amend the FCA claims, the court applied the "government knowledge defense" to foreclose all FCA claims for payments made after the Coast Guard was made aware that the section modulus calculation was incorrect.

After the United States filed an amended complaint, the district court granted Bollinger's second motion to dismiss and entered final judgment in the case. The district court held that the United States failed to plead plausibly and with particularity that Bollinger acted "knowingly" in making false statements or claims for payment. The court again ruled that the "government knowledge defense" foreclosed the United States' claims for those payments made after the Coast Guard became aware that the section modulus calculation was incorrect. The United States timely appealed the final judgment dismissing its claims. [—7—]

III.   LAW AND ANALYSIS

A. The United States Properly Pleaded Knowledge.

The primary issue on appeal is whether the district court correctly held that the United States failed to sufficiently plead Bollinger's scienter. The resolution depends on the Rule 12(b)(6) standard set out above, the elements of an FCA claim, and the pleading requirements set out in FED. R. CIV. P. 8 and 9(b). On de novo review, we disagree with the district court's holding and conclude that the United States adequately pleaded Bollinger's scienter.

B. Applicable Law

A violation of the FCA occurs when (1) "there was a false statement or fraudulent course of conduct; (2) made or carried out with the requisite scienter; (3) that was material; and (4) that caused the government to pay out money or to forfeit moneys due (i.e., that involved a claim)."[4] To meet the "requisite scienter" requirement, the United States must plead that Bollinger acted with knowledge of

---

[4] *United States ex rel. Longhi v. Lithium Power Techs., Inc.*, 575 F.3d 458, 467 (5th Cir. 2009) (quoting *United States ex rel. Wilson v. Kellogg Brown & Root, Inc.*, 525 F.3d 370, 376 (4th Cir. 2008)).

the falsity of the statement, which is defined, at a minimum, as acting "in reckless disregard of the truth or falsity of the information."[5]

To state a claim under the FCA, the plaintiff must meet both the plausibility pleading standard of Fed. R. Civ. P. 8 and the heightened pleading standard of Fed. R. Civ. P. 9(b).[6] Thus, the United States must (1) plead "enough facts [taken as true] to state a claim to relief that is plausible on its face,"[7] and (2) plead "with particularity the circumstances constituting fraud [—8—] or mistake," although "[m]alice, intent, knowledge, and other conditions of a person's mind may be alleged generally."[8]

A claim is plausible if "the plaintiff pleads factual content that allows the court to draw the reasonable inference that the defendant is liable for the misconduct alleged. The plausibility standard is not akin to a 'probability requirement,' but it asks for more than a sheer possibility that a defendant has acted unlawfully."[9] The plausibility standard "does not give district courts license to look behind [a complaint's] allegations and independently assess the likelihood that the plaintiff will be able to prove them at trial."[10] The particularity standard of Rule 9(b) generally requires the plaintiff to plead the time, place, and contents of the false representation and the identity of the person making the representation.[11] However, an FCA claim can meet Rule 9(b)'s standard if it alleges "particular details of a scheme to submit false claims paired with reliable indicia that lead to a strong inference that claims were actually submitted."[12] Knowledge need not be pled with particularity under Rule

9(b); it need only be pled plausibly pursuant to Rule 8.[13]

C. The District Court Erred in Imposing a Higher Pleading Standard for Bollinger's State Of Mind.

As an initial matter, the district court erred by requiring the United States to plead the FCA's knowledge element with particularity under Rule 9(b).[14] The United States asserted in its First Amended Complaint that, [—9—] because Bollinger ran three different section modulus calculations with false inputs and submitted the highest to the United States, "it can be reasonably inferred that Bollinger knowingly input false data into the MSC application to obtain a false section modulus result high enough to avoid further Coast Guard scrutiny and ABS review of the vessel's structural integrity." This allegation complies with Rule 9(b)'s requirement that Bollinger's intent and knowledge be pled only generally, as well as Rule 8's requirement that the allegation be plausible.

The district court erroneously concluded that the fact "that Bollinger reported only the highest of the three section modulus figures to the Coast Guard does not indicate that it acted with the requisite scienter" because the United States failed to allege that Bollinger knew the correct section modulus figure and therefore concealed the true calculation.[15] Furthermore, the district court stated:

> There is no allegation that any relevant document—and the United States has had access to hundreds of thousands in this litigation—suggests any particular reason why Bollinger chose one figure over another, much less that the reason

---

[5] 31 U.S.C. § 3729(b)(1)(A)(iii).

[6] *See United States ex rel. Grubbs v. Kanneganti*, 565 F.3d 180, 185 (5th Cir. 2009).

[7] *Id.* (quoting *Twombly*, 550 U.S. at 570) (alteration in original).

[8] FED. R. CIV. P. 9(b).

[9] *Ashcroft v. Iqbal*, 556 U.S. 662, 678 (2009) (citation and internal quotation marks omitted).

[10] *Harold H. Huggins Realty, Inc. v. FNC, Inc.*, 634 F.3d 787, 803 n.44 (5th Cir. 2011).

[11] *Grubbs*, 565 F.3d at 190.

[12] *Id.*

---

[13] *See* FED. R. CIV. P. 9(b); *Iqbal*, 556 U.S. at 686-87.

[14] *See United States v. Bollinger Shipyards, Inc.*, 979 F. Supp. 2d 721, 731 (E.D. La. 2013) ("Because the United States has not alleged with particularity, pursuant to Rule 9(b), that Bollinger made material false statements *with the requisite scienter*, its theory of FCA [—9—] liability cannot survive Bollinger's motion to dismiss." (emphasis added)).

[15] *Id.* at 731.

was to choose a false number that was higher than the minimum ABS requirement.[16]

The FCA does not require the United States to show that Bollinger knew the *correct* figure. The FCA is satisfied if the plaintiff alleges the defendant either knew that the figure was false or acted with reckless disregard of its truth or falsity. The facts alleged by the United States support the inference that Bollinger, at a minimum, acted with reckless disregard of the truth or [—10—] falsity of the section modulus figures, including the highest figure it submitted to the Coast Guard. Equally significant, in rejecting the United States' argument for why Bollinger submitted the highest of three false figures to the United States, the district court did not consider the circumstantial evidence and general allegations of Bollinger's knowledge and intent. Therefore, the district court failed to apply the correct standard for pleading knowledge under Rules 8 and 9(b).

D. The District Court Erred In Drawing Inferences Against The United States And In Favor Of Bollinger.

Given that knowledge may be pled generally, we conclude the United States did plead facts making it more than a sheer possibility that Bollinger acted with knowledge.[17] The First Amended Complaint, viewed in the light most favorable to the United States, states a claim under the FCA. The district court erred by viewing the facts in the light most favorable to Bollinger and drawing inferences against the United States.

The complaint clearly alleges that all of the factors that Bollinger entered into the MSC to calculate the section modulus were within Bollinger's knowledge and control as the designer and builder of both the original 110-foot boats and the modified 123-foot boats. The complaint states that Bollinger realized on August 27, 2002, that with the correct hull-plate thickness, the ships did not meet the original projected section modulus value of

7,152 that it gave to the Coast Guard. Bollinger ran three section modulus calculations that produced results of varying section modulus strength. Bollinger used a lower figure internally and then submitted a higher figure to the United States. [—11—]

The United States also pointed to an email exchange from around the same time between Bollinger's CEO, Boysie Bollinger, and vice president, T.R. Hamblin, regarding an offer by ABS's Robert Kramer to perform a confidential structural analysis of a converted vessel. Mr. Hamblin recommended that Mr. Bollinger decline ABS's offer to conduct the analysis because, the United States contends, he was concerned that the ABS analysis would find that the design required additional structural support. Mr. Bollinger agreed with Mr. Hamblin and declined ABS's offer. In an email between Mr. Bollinger and Mr. Hamblin, Mr. Bollinger stated that "[ABS] would love the additional responsibility from the [Coast Guard] and as we both know, adverse results could cause the entire [conversion] to be an uneconomical solution if we had to totally rebuild the hull. . . . MY CONCERN—we don't do anything—ABS gets CG to require it without our input, and the result is we BLOW the program." The United States alleged this email implied that the vice president "should take steps to avoid ABS review of the design of the complete hull, a review likely to have exposed the inadequacy of the structural integrity of the hull." We agree that this is a permissible interpretation of the emails which would arguably support an inference that Bollinger was attempting to conceal the inadequate structural integrity of the hulls.

Bollinger eventually submitted the highest of three calculations (5,232) to the Coast Guard, while employing in its internal documents the middle calculation (3,037). The 5,232 figure submitted to the Coast Guard used one input value 16,000 times greater than the value that had been used in the other two calculations. Finally, even after the Coast Guard expressed concern over the section modulus of 5,232 and Bollinger represented that it would have ABS review the calculation, Bollinger did not have ABS do so. [—12—]

---

[16] *Id.*

[17] *See Iqbal*, 556 U.S. at 678.

On these facts, the district court improperly drew inferences in favor of Bollinger and focused on the fact that the United States failed to include certain facts in its complaint, none of which was necessary in this case which depends so much on circumstantial evidence. First, the district court found that Mr. Bollinger's email does not "on its face" say anything "about taking steps to avoid ABS review, much less falsifying figures."[18] The letter need not explicitly state that; indeed, the complaint alleged that the letter "indicated" it. The district court did not view the letter, including its potential implications, in the light most favorable to the United States.

Second, concerning Mr. Bollinger's concern that Bollinger might "BLOW the program" if ABS reviewed the converted vessel at the Coast Guard's request, the court found, "His email *reads most naturally* as expressing a desire that Bollinger be involved in any ABS review, to answer questions and provide information or insights that could help ABS evaluate the design."[19] The district court found the United States' allegations concerning the 2002 email exchange "simply not reasonable."[20] With respect to the three false calculations noted above, the district court declined to draw the reasonable inference urged by the United States: "The United States argues simply that three incorrect calculations suggest an effort to fabricate. This is unpersuasive. . . . Further, the allegation that one of the incorrect values in the reported calculation was 16,000 times greater than the correct input is of little significance without knowing the context and nature of these inputs."[21] [—13—]

We conclude the district court erred by improperly weighing the evidence, by focusing on facts the United States did not plead rather than the inferences that the pleaded facts supported, and by viewing the facts in the light most favorable to Bollinger. Rule 12(b)(6) does not require the United States to present its best case or even a particularly *good* case,

only to state a plausible case. The First Amended Complaint satisfies that minimum standard and sets out facts sufficient to support a claim under the FCA. Whether or not the United States may prevail on its claim in later stages of this proceeding, it has at least stated enough to survive this facial challenge.

Based on the facts set out in the complaint, one may reasonably infer that Bollinger acted "in reckless disregard of the truth or falsity" of the measurements.[22] A key factor is Bollinger declining outside review of a critical calculation while expressing concern that such review might reveal problems in hull strength—the exact problem with the section modulus calculation that ultimately caused the boats to be decommissioned. Relatedly, Bollinger falsely certified that the boats had been reviewed for unrestricted service by a representative of an independent agency, when Bollinger had not had any independent agency review them. Similarly, one could reasonably infer that Bollinger acted, at a minimum, recklessly in regard to the truth or falsity of the section modulus number because it calculated three different incorrect values (one of which included a value overinflated by 16,000 times) and submitted only the highest one to the United States. Viewed in the light most favorable to the United States, these facts state a claim under the FCA. [—14—]

E. The District Court Applied the Government Knowledge Defense Prematurely.

Because we conclude the United States has sufficiently pleaded knowledge, we must address whether some of the United States' claims are subject to dismissal under the "government knowledge defense" because the Coast Guard continued to make payments and accept delivery of the ships after it was aware of the incorrect section modulus calculation. "The inaptly-named 'government knowledge defense'" is the principle "that under some circumstances, the government's knowledge of the falsity of a statement or claim can defeat FCA liability on the ground that the claimant

---

[18] 979 F. Supp. 2d at 732.
[19] *Id.* (emphasis added).
[20] *Id.* at 733.
[21] *Id.* at 731.

[22] 31 U.S.C. § 3729(b)(1)(A)(iii).

did not act 'knowingly,' because the claimant knew that the government knew of the falsity of the statement and was willing to pay anyway."[23] "This defense is inaptly named because it is not a statutory defense to FCA liability but a means by which the defendant can rebut the government's assertion of the 'knowing' presentation of a false claim."[24] Under this principle, "[w]here the government and a contractor have been working together, albeit outside the written provisions of the contract, to reach a common solution to a problem, no claim arises."[25]

The question is whether the government knowledge defense may be applied at the motion to dismiss stage. Research discloses only one district court case where it has been applied at this stage rather than at the summary judgment or trial stage.[26] All circuit

court authorities suggest that the defense [—15—] should not be applied at this stage because it serves simply as a factor weighing against the defendant's knowledge, as opposed to a complete negation of the knowledge element.[27]

We agree with our sister circuits. The government knowledge defense is not appropriate at the motion to dismiss stage, which requires us to draw all [—16—] inferences in favor of the United States. It is more proper at the summary judgment or trial stage as "a means by which the defendant can rebut the government's assertion of the 'knowing' presentation of a false claim."[28]

---

[23] *United States v. Southland Mgmt. Corp.*, 326 F.3d 669, 682 (5th Cir. 2003) (en banc) (Jones, J., specially concurring) (citation and internal quotation marks omitted).

[24] *Id.* at 682 n.8 (Jones, J., specially concurring).

[25] *Id.* at 682 (Jones, J., specially concurring) (citations omitted).

[26] *See United States ex rel. Marquis v. Northrop Grumman Corp.*, No. 09-C-7704, 2013 WL 951095 (N.D. Ill. Mar. 12, 2013). Even though the district court in *Marquis* granted the motion to dismiss based in part on the government knowledge defense, it noted that the underlying facts might not actually support the defense: [—15—]

> Based upon such facts, Marquis has alleged that the Government paid Northrop under the Contract after acquiring knowledge of and investigating the purported Contract violations. Thus, Marquis has failed to state a valid FCA claim. *The court notes that the facts alleged in the complaint leave open the possibility that a claim or claims may have been presented for payment before the Government received notice of the purported Contract violations.* However, the complaint does not sufficiently allege that such was the case, which leads the court to the second deficiency in the complaint, Marquis' failure to plead with the particularity required of Federal Rule of Civil Procedure Rule 9(b) (Rule 9(b)).

2013 WL 951095 at *2 (emphasis added). Even if it is proper to address the government knowledge defense at the motion to dismiss stage, the district

court's conclusion in *Marquis* seems suspect, given Rule 12(b)(6)'s requirement that a court construe the facts in the light most favorable to the plaintiff.

[27] In *United States ex rel. Hagood v. Sonoma Cnty. Water Agency*, 929 F.2d 1416 (9th Cir. 1991), the Ninth Circuit reasoned:

> [T]he knowledge possessed by officials of the United States may be highly relevant. Such knowledge may show that the defendant did not submit its claim in deliberate ignorance or reckless disregard of the truth. But this comforting conclusion for the Water Agency cannot be reached by mere inspection of Hagood's complaint. Only at the stage of trial or summary judgment will it be possible for a court to say, for example, that the Water Agency did merely what the Corps bid it do, that the Water Agency had no knowledge that its contract was based on what Hagood has alleged was false information.

Id. at 1421; *see also United States ex rel. Burlbaw v. Orenduff*, 548 F.3d 931, 952 (10th Cir. 2008) ("[The government knowledge defense] is only an inference. It does not *automatically* preclude a finding of scienter." (citation omitted)); *Southland*, 326 F.3d at 682 n.8 (Jones, J., specially concurring) (describing the defense as "a means by which the defendant can rebut the government's assertion of the 'knowing' presentation of a false claim"); *United States ex rel. Kreindler & Kreindler v. United Techs. Corp.*, 985 F.2d 1148, 1156 (2d Cir. 1993) ("[W]e agree with *Hagood* that the statutory basis for an FCA claim is the defendant's knowledge of the falsity of its claim, which is not automatically exonerated by any overlapping knowledge by government officials." (citation omitted)).

[28] *Southland*, 326 F.3d at 682 n.8 (Jones, J., specially concurring).

IV. CONCLUSION

Because we conclude that the complaint alleges sufficient facts to state a claim, we REVERSE and REMAND for further proceedings consistent with this opinion.[29]

---

[29] On appeal, Bollinger asserted four alternative grounds for dismissal which we decline to adopt, including its contention that the First Amended Complaint should be dismissed because it refers only generally to "Bollinger" and fails to allege with particularity the specific acts taken by each of the three defendants. The United States argues that its ability to plead the acts of each defendant with greater particularity depends on discovery of facts within Bollinger's control, and Bollinger has not provided that information in discovery. The district court has not yet addressed this issue, but in the event the district court finds some merit in Bollinger's argument on remand, it may consider less drastic alternatives to dismissal, including leave to amend, perhaps after additional discovery. *See* FED. R. CIV. P. 15(a)(2); *Grubbs*, 565 F.3d at 192 & n.36.

United States Court of Appeals
for the Fifth Circuit

No. 14-30510

IN RE ROLLS ROYCE CORP.

Petition for a Writ of Mandamus to the United States
District Court for the Western District of Louisiana

Decided: December 30, 2014

Citation: 775 F.3d 671, 2 Adm. R. 398 (5th Cir. 2014).

Before **HIGGINBOTHAM, JONES,** and **PRADO,** Circuit
Judges.

[—1—] **HIGGINBOTHAM,** Circuit Judge:

This mandamus petition brings the question of who—the parties or the court—determines in which judicial district a civil action is to proceed. In *Atlantic Marine Construction Company*,[1] the Supreme Court held that when all parties have entered into a forum selection contract, that contract controls, except in exceptional circumstances, and the district court must transfer the action to the agreed-upon district.[2] Here, we must address a related issue—what should a district court do when some, but not all, litigants are subject to a forum selection clause, and one of the parties to the clause files a motion to sever and transfer its claims to the forum chosen in the contract.

Faced with this situation, the district court refused to sever and transfer the party claiming the benefit of the forum selection clause. We respectfully [—2—] disagree, persuaded that on these facts the forum selection contract must be enforced and GRANT the petition for mandamus.

I.

The underlying litigation concerns the liability stemming from a helicopter crash in the Gulf of Mexico. A Bell 407 helicopter owned by Petroleum Helicopters, Inc. ("PHI")

allegedly suffered a failure of its number two engine bearing, forcing the pilot to make an emergency landing in the Gulf. During the landing, the pilot inflated the helicopter's skid-mounted emergency pontoon floats, which were designed to keep the helicopter from sinking. While the pontoon bags worked long enough to allow a safe evacuation of passengers and crew, one of the pontoons eventually failed, and the helicopter flipped, rendering the aircraft a total loss.

PHI brought suit in Louisiana state court against three parties: (1) Rolls Royce Corporation ("Rolls Royce"), which designed and manufactured the engine bearing, (2) Apical Industries, Inc. ("Apical"), which designed, manufactured, and sold the pontoon flotation system, and (3) Offshore Helicopter Support Services, Inc. ("OHS"), which repaired and reworked the float system before the crash. The defendants timely removed on the basis of diversity jurisdiction.

Once in federal court, Rolls Royce moved to sever PHI's claims against the company, and to transfer those claims to the Southern District of Indiana.[3] [—3—] It relied on a forum selection clause in a warranty to which the engine bearing was subject, which stated, in relevant part:

> Any controversy or claim arising out of or relating to this Limited Warranty or breach thereof shall be litigated only in

---

[1] *Atl. Marine Const. Co., Inc. v. U.S. Dist. Ct. W.D. Tex.*, 134 S. Ct. 568 (2013).

[2] *See id.* at 582.

---

[3] The motion to sever was filed pursuant to Federal Rule of Civil Procedure ("Rule") 21 and the motion to transfer was filed pursuant to 28 U.S.C. § 1404(a).

These motions were the second set of motions filed in this case. Rolls Royce had originally filed a motion to dismiss under Rule 12(b)(3) or, in the alternative, to transfer pursuant to 28 U.S.C. § 1404 or § 1406. The district court denied this motion without prejudice, pending the Supreme Court's release of its decision in *Atlantic Marine*, which resolved a circuit split about whether a transfer motion pursuant to a forum selection clause ought be brought pursuant to section 1404, section 1406, or Rule 12(b)(3). After *Atlantic Marine* ruled that section 1404 was the proper vehicle, 134 S. Ct. at 580, Rolls Royce renewed its motion—and that motion is the one at issue in this case.

the Circuit or Superior Courts of Marion County, Indiana or of the United States District Court for the Southern District of Indiana, Indianapolis Division. In connection with the foregoing, the Purchaser consents to the jurisdiction and venue of such courts and expressly waives any claims or defenses of lack of jurisdiction or proper venue by such courts.

Apical and OHS, neither of whom were subject to a forum selection clause, opposed the severance and transfer, as did PHI.

The district court denied the motion.[4] First, it determined that the entire action could not be transferred to Indiana.[5] Second, the court turned to the issue of whether severance under Federal Rule of Civil Procedure ("Rule") 21 was warranted. The court articulated five factors that district courts had used in analyzing a severance motion, and concluded that each weighed against [—4—] severance.[6] As a result, there

was no basis for a transfer.[7] Finally, the district court considered whether the Supreme Court's decision in *Atlantic Marine* mandated transfer. It held that it did not. The district court determined that key difference between this case and *Atlantic Marine* was that not all parties to the litigation had signed a forum selection contract. Reading *Atlantic Marine* to mandate severance and transfer of the party to the contract, the district court reasoned, "would not further the Supreme Court's stated goal in *Atlantic Marine* of not disrupting the expectations of parties who bargained for litigation in a particular forum but would, instead, potentially inconvenience and prejudice parties having absolutely no relationship to a forum-selection clause they had no part in conferring."[8]

Following the denial of its severance-and-transfer motion, Rolls Royce petitioned this court for mandamus relief.[9]

II.

A writ of mandamus is an "extraordinary remedy,"[10] and may only issue if three criteria are met:

First, the party seeking issuance of the writ [must] have no other adequate means to attain the relief he desires, a condition designed to ensure that the writ will not be used as a substitute for the regular appeals process. Second, the petitioner must satisfy the burden of showing that [his] right to issuance of the writ is clear and indisputable. Third, even if the first two prerequisites have been met, the issuing court, in the exercise of its discretion, [—5—] must be

---

[4] The district court originally referred this motion to a magistrate judge, who recommended denying transfer. *PHI, Inc. v. Apical Indus.*, No. 13-CV-00015, 2014 WL 1820717 (W.D. La. Mar. 7, 2014). The district court adopted the magistrate judge's report, with only minor clarifications. *Petroleum Helicopters, Inc. v. Apical Indus., Inc.*, No. 13-CV-0015, 2014 WL 1820859 (W.D. La. May 6, 2014). We refer to both decisions together as "the district court."

[5] *See PHI*, 2014 WL 182, at *2-4. The court could not transfer the case pursuant to 28 U.S.C. § 1404(a) because that section allows transfer only to a district in which the action could have been brought, or where all parties consent. The court assumed that the Indiana district court would lack personal jurisdiction over OHS, and so the action could not have been originally brought in that district. *See Hoffman v. Blaski*, 363 U.S. 335, 343-44 (1960). Furthermore, only Rolls Royce consented to transfer. *PHI*, 2014 WL 1820717, at *4.

Nor could the court transfer the case pursuant to 28 U.S.C. § 1406(a), since that statute allows transfer only when the action was brought "in the wrong division or district," 28 U.S.C. § 1406(a), and here, the Western District of Louisiana was the proper district. *PHI*, 2014 WL 1820717, at *4.

[6] *PHI*, 2014 WL 1820717, at *5 ("Numerous district courts in the Fifth Circuit have held that the following factors should be considered when

deciding whether a claim should be severed under Rule 21: (1) whether the claims arose out of the same transaction or occurrence, (2) whether the claims present common questions of law or fact, (3) whether settlement or judicial economy would be promoted, (4) whether prejudice would be averted by severance, and (5) whether different witnesses and documentary proof are required.").

[7] *See id.* at *7.

[8] *Id.* at *10.

[9] It did not seek certification for an interlocutory appeal under 28 U.S.C. § 1292(b).

[10] *Will v. United States*, 389 U.S. 90, 95 (1967).

satisfied that the writ is appropriate under the circumstances.[11]

"These hurdles, however demanding, are not insuperable."[12] We consider each in turn.

A.

First, Rolls Royce must show that mandamus is its exclusive vehicle to seek relief. It does. Our court, in accord with our sister circuits, has held "mandamus is an appropriate means of testing a district court's [section] 1404(a) ruling."[13] Other means for review are unavailable. Rolls Royce cannot appeal an adverse final judgment under 28 U.S.C. § 1391, because it "would not been able to show that it would have won the case," had the action been litigated in its desired forum.[14] While the Supreme Court has crafted a narrow exception to the final order doctrine, termed the "collateral order doctrine" or "*Cohen* exception,"[15] we have previously held that transfer orders do not fall within the scope of this doctrine.[16] Nor can Rolls Royce bring an interlocutory appeal under 28 U.S.C. § 1292(b), as our circuit precedent forecloses reviews of transfer orders under that statute.[17] Apical and OHS argue otherwise, saying that certification is available, because the district court's order contained a [—6—]

cognizable "controlling question of law."[18] We have, though, squarely rejected this conclusion, holding that "[t]he Congressional policy against piecemeal appeals, as expressed in the final judgment rule, to which [section] 1292(b) is a narrow exception, is eroded by permitting review of exercise of the judge's discretion under [section] 1404(a) as a 'controlling question of law.'"[19]

There is one complication—the district court did not rule on a transfer motion, but a joint transfer and severance motion. While we have previously held that the denial of a standalone Rule 21 severance motion can be challenged through an appeal of a final judgment,[20] we believe that the combination of transfer and severance inquiries dictates a different response. As the Federal Circuit, addressing whether mandamus was available to review the denial of a transfer and severance motion, concluded:

> With regard to the 'no other means' requirement, there is no meaningful distinction between a petitioner's seeking review of an order denying transfer because the district court clearly abused its discretion in applying the [section] 1404(a) factors and a petitioner's seeking review of an order denying a motion to transfer because the district court clearly abused its discretion by not severing the claims as a predicate to determining whether to transfer. In either case, a defendant would not have an adequate remedy for an improper failure to transfer or sever . . . .[21]

---

[11] *Cheney* v. *U.S. Dist. Ct. for Dist. of Columbia*, 542 U.S. 367, 380-81 (2004) (alterations in original) (citations and internal quotation marks omitted).

[12] *In re Volkswagen of Am., Inc.*, 545 F.3d 304, 311 (5th Cir. 2008) (en banc) (quoting *Cheney*, 542 U.S. at 381).

[13] *Id.* at 309.

[14] *Id.* at 319 (quoting *In re Nat'l Presto Indus, Inc.*, 347 F.3d 662, 663 (7th Cir. 2003)).

[15] *Cohen* v. *Beneficial Indus. Loan Corp.*, 337 U.S. 541, 546 (1949). "To fall within *Cohen's* collateral order doctrine, an 'order must (1) conclusively determine the disputed question, (2) resolve an important issue completely separate from the merits of the action, and (3) be effectively unreviewable on appeal from a final judgment." *Henry* v. *Lake Charles Am. Press, L.L.C.*, 566 F.3d 164, 171 (5th Cir. 2009) (quoting *Coopers & Lybrand* v. *Livesay*, 437 U.S. 463, 468 (1978)).

[16] *See Brinar* v. *Williamson*, 245 F.3d 515, 517 (5th Cir. 2001).

[17] *See Volkswagen.* 545 F.3d at 319 (citing *Garner* v. *Wolfinbarger*, 433 F.2d 117, 120 (5th Cir. 1970)).

[18] 28 U.S.C. § 1292(b).

[19] *Garner,* 433 F.2d at 120 (citing 28 U.S.C. § 1292(b)). Our court, sitting en banc, reaffirmed this conclusion in *Volkswagen.* 545 F.3d at 319.

[20] *See United States* v. *O'Neill*, 709 F.2d 361, 371-72 (5th Cir. 1983); *see also Amie* v. *City of Jennings*, 217 F. App'x 338, 338-39 (5th Cir. 2007) (unpublished). These decisions do not discuss the potential of mandamus review under such circumstances.

[21] *In re EMC Corp.*, 677 F.3d 1351, 1354-55 (Fed. Cir. 2012).

We agree. Because the transfer order is unreviewable except through mandamus, and because the severance inquiry is, as will be discussed later, inextricably linked to the transfer analysis, we conclude that there are no other means for review of the district court's order but through mandamus. [—7—]

B.

We turn now to whether Rolls Royce's right to mandamus relief is "clear and indisputable."[22] We look to whether there has been a "clear abuse of discretion," which, under our circuit precedent, includes situations where the district court "relies on erroneous conclusions of law" which "produce a patently erroneous result."[23]

We conclude that, in this instance, the district court erred in refusing to transfer Rolls Royce in accordance with its forum selection clause and in light of the Supreme Court's decision in *Atlantic Marine*. This said, we do not read *Atlantic Marine* to mandate severance and transfer of a party bearing a forum selection clause in all multiparty cases, regardless of countervailing considerations of judicial economy.

1.

By the light of *Atlantic Marine*,[24] we analyze a transfer motion brought by a party seeking to enforce a forum-selection cause pursuant to 28 U.S.C. § 1404.[25] Section 1404, in turn, provides that "[f]or the convenience of parties and witnesses, in the interest of justice, a district court may transfer any civil action to any other district or division where it might have been brought or to any district or division to which all parties have consented."[26]

We begin with the purpose of section 1404, by which Congress granted to the federal district court the power to allocate cases and controversies among federal district courts.

The Supreme Court made plain that this grant of authority was intended to afford a powerful tool to bring forth efficient judicial case management among the various federal courts. The statute "should be [—8—] regarded as a federal judicial housekeeping measure, dealing with the placement of litigation in the federal courts and generally intended, on the basis of convenience and fairness, simply to authorize a change of courtrooms."[27] These factors, in turn, are measured across two dimensions: the interests of the litigants, and the interests of the public and judicial system writ large.[28]

Animating the former are considerations governing the cost and ease of litigation.[29] Animating the latter are a broader set of concerns, ranging from the interest in having a case involving local disputes and local law resolved by a local court,[30] to facilitating judicial economy and avoiding duplicitous

---

[22] *Volkswagen*, 545 F.3d at 311.

[23] *Id.* at 310.

[24] *Atl. Marine Const. Co., Inc. v. U.S. Dist. Ct. W.D. Tex.*, 134 S. Ct. 568 (2013).

[25] *Id.* at 579-80.

[26] 28 U.S.C. § 1404(a).

[27] *Van Dusen v. Barrack*, 376 U.S. 612, 636-37 (1964).

[28] *See Atl. Marine*, 134 S. Ct. at 581; *see also* Wright & Miller, Fed. Prac. & Proc. § 3854 (4th ed. 2014) ("[I]t has long been clear that the interest of justice is a factor (albeit an amorphous and somewhat subjective one) to be considered on its own and that is very important.").

[29] *See, e.g., Atl. Marine*, 134 S. Ct. at 581 n.6 ("Factors relating to the parties' private interests include 'relative cost of access to sources of proof; availability of compulsory process for attendance of unwilling, and the cost of obtaining attendance of willing witnesses . . . and all other practical problems that make trial of a case easy, expeditious and inexpensive.") (quoting *Piper Aircraft Co. v. Reyno*, 454 U.S. 235, 241 n.6 (1981)).

[30] *See id.* ("Public-interest factors may include 'the administrative difficulties flowing from court congestion; the local interest in having localized controversies decided at home; [and] the interest in having the trial of a diversity case in a forum that is at home with the law.") (quoting *Piper Aircraft*, 454 U.S. at 241 n.6) (brackets in original).

The *Atlantic Marine* court was careful to note that these factors are illustrative, not exhaustive. We have held the same. *See In re Volkswagen of Am., Inc.*, 545 F.3d 304, 315 (5th Cir. 2008) (en banc) (holding that the *Piper Aircraft* factors "are not necessarily exhaustive or exclusive"); *Action Indus. Inc. v. U.S. Fid. & Guar. Co.*, 384 F.3d 337, 340 (5th Cir. 2004) (holding that no single *Piper Aircraft* factor "can be said to be of dispositive weight").

litigation.[31] This inquiry necessarily requires the district court to "balance a number of case-specific factors," and the Supreme Court has [—9—] cautioned that a section 1404 transfer inquiry requires an "individualized, case-by-case consideration of convenience and fairness."[32]

When the parties hold a valid forum selection clause, *Atlantic Marine* alters the normal section 1404 analysis. As is most relevant here, the district court cannot independently weight the parties' private interests, but must deem such interests to weigh in favor of the preselected forum, the parties having struck that balance by their selection contract.[33] Accordingly, only the public-interests may weigh against transfer, and "[b]ecause those factors will rarely defeat a transfer motion, the practical result is that the forum-selection clauses should control except in unusual cases."[34]

2.

For cases where all parties signed a forum selection contract, the analysis is easy: except in a truly exceptional case, the contract controls. But not so where, as here, not all parties to the lawsuit have entered into a forum selection agreement. The petitioner urges, as does our colleague in concurrence, that the analysis—and the result—follow pari passu with *Atlantic Marine*. With respect, we believe the answer is more complicated.

a.

In terms of the party who signed the agreement, *Atlantic Marine* is clear—the court cannot consider private-interest factors that counsel against [—10—] transfer to the agreed-upon forum. But the analysis differs when there are parties who have not entered into any forum-selection contract. First, *Atlantic Marine* was premised on the fact that the parties had agreed in advance where their private litigation interests lie, and the reviewing court had no cause to disturb those expectations.[35] A litigant not party to such a contract did not, of course, make any such advance agreements and *their* private interests must still be considered by the district court.[36] As such, the section 1404 analysis, modified by *Atlantic Marine*, might point in the direction of one judicial district for the forum-selection clause parties, and in another direction for the parties without a preexisting agreement.

---

[31] *See, e.g., Cont'l Grain Co.* v. *The FBL-585*, 364 U.S. 19, 26 (1960) ("To permit a situation in which two cases involving precisely the same issues are simultaneous pending in different District Courts leads to the wastefulness of time, energy and money that [section] 1404 was designed to prevent."); *In re Volkswagen of Am., Inc.*, 566 F.3d 1349, 1351 (Fed. Cir. 2009) (highlighting the importance of judicial economy when determining a section 1404 transfer).

[32] *Stewart Org.* v. *Ricoh Corp.*, 487 U.S. 22, 29 (1988) (quoting, second, *Van Dusen* v. *Barrack*, 376 U.S. 612, 622 (1964)).

[33] *See Atl. Marine*, 134 S. Ct. at 582 ("When parties agree to a forum-selection clause, they waive the right to challenge the preselected forum as inconvenient or less convenient for themselves or their witnesses, or for their pursuit of the litigation. A court accordingly must deem the private-interest factors to weigh entirely in favor of the preselected forum.").

[34] *Id.* The Court held that the presence of a forum-selection clause wrought two additional changes to the section 1404 analysis: first, that "the plaintiff's choice of forum merits no weight," and, second, that "when a party bound by a forum-selection clause flouts its contractual obligation and files suit in a different forum, a [section] 1404(a) transfer of venue will not carry with it the original venue's choice-of-law rules—a factor that in some circumstances may affect public-interest considerations." *Id.* at 581-82.

[35] *See id.* at 582 ("When the parties agree to a forum-selection clause, they waive the right to challenge the pre-selected forum . . . .").

[36] *Atlantic Marine* is premised on the idea that a forum selection clause is a contract between two parties, and that that contract must be honored. *See, e.g., id.* at 581-82 (concluding that "the *plaintiff's* choice of forum merits no weight," and that the private interests are not relevant because "[w]hen *parties agree* to a forum selection clause, they waive the right to challenge the *preselected forum*") (emphasis added). The Court is silent with respect to situations where, as here, there are third-party externalities at play—specifically the presence of objecting defendants who have not signed any forum selection agreement.

A properly conducted section 1404 inquiry may well require a district court to send different parties to pursue the same suit in different districts, implicating concerns attending parallel lawsuits not present in *Atlantic Marine*. While *Atlantic Marine* noted that public factors, standing alone, were unlikely to defeat a transfer motion,[37] the Supreme Court has also noted that section 1404 was designed to minimize the waste of judicial resources of parallel litigation of a dispute.[38] The tension between these centrifugal [—11—] considerations suggests that the need—rooted in the valued public interest in judicial economy—to pursue the same claims in a single action in a single court can trump a forum-selection clause.

b.

There is more. To transfer the claims of the forum-clause defendant, the district court would first have to sever those claims from the claims of the non-forum clause defendants, which remain in the original district. The petitioner's answer is that *Atlantic Marine* vitiates the traditional severance analysis in multiparty cases. This is not so clear.

A district court has wide discretion to sever a claim against a party into separate cases,[39] in vindication of public and private factors.[40]

[37] *Id.* at 582.

[38] *See Cont'l Grain Co. v. The FBL-585*, 34 U.S. 19, 26 (1960); *see also U.S.O. v. Mizuho Holding Co.*, 547 F.3d 749, 750 (7th Cir. 2008) (holding, in the *forum non conveniens* context, that parallel litigation concerns justified dismissing a case filed in a domestic court, as "[t]here is no reason for identical suits to be proceeding in different courts"); *Coady v. Ashcraft & Gerel*, 223 F.3d 1, 10-11 (1st Cir. 2000) (concluding that the goal of avoiding parallel litigation justified transferring all cases to a single judicial district).

[39] *See Applewhite v. Reichold Chems., Inc.*, 67 F.3d 571, 574 (5th Cir. 1995); *Burnet v. United Gas Pipeline Co.*, 15 F.3d 500, 505 (5th Cir. 1994).

[40] While our circuit has not formally adopted a severance test, our district courts have settled on a standard which accords with that used in other circuits. *See, e.g., Paragon Office Servs., LLC v. UnitedHealthcare Ins. Co., Inc.*, No. 3:11-CV-2205-D, 2012 WL 4442368, at *1 (N.D. Tex. Sept. 26, 2012) (defining Rule 21 factors as "(1) whether the claims arise out of the same transaction or

Though we have not squarely addressed the issue, our jurisprudence suggests that the severance inquiry is different—and more focused on judicial efficiency—when it is combined with a section 1404 motion to transfer than when the severed case would remain in the original judicial district. In *Liaw Su Teng v. Skaarup Shipping Corporation*,[41] addressing the situation where a court could transfer [—12—] some but not all parties,[42] we suggested that when considering a severance-and-transfer motion, the inquiry collapsed into an inquiry into the relative merits of convenience versus judicial economy. We held that when addressing a severance-and-transfer request:

> [T]he court must weigh carefully whether the inconvenience of splitting the suit outweighs the advantages to be gained from the partial transfer. It should not sever if the defendant over whom jurisdiction is retained is so involved in the controversy to be

occurrence; (2) whether the claims present some common questions of law or fact; (3) whether settlement of the claims or judicial economy would be facilitated; (4) whether prejudice would be avoided if severance were granted; and (5) whether different witnesses and documentary proof are required for the separate claims.") (quoting *Morris v. Northrop Grumman Corp.*, 37 F. Supp. 2d 55, 580 (S.D.N.Y. 1999)); *see also* Wright & Miller, Fed. Prac & Proc. § 1689 (3d ed. 2004) ("Even when venue is proper to all defendants, the court may sever a claim against a party and transfer it to a more convenient forum or sever an unrelated claim and give it separate treatment when doing so would be in the interest of some or all of the parties. On the other hand, severance will be refused if the court believes that it only will result in delay, inconvenience, or added expense.").

[41] 743 F.2d 1140 (5th Cir. 1984), *overruled on other grounds, In re Air Crash Disaster Near New Orleans, La. on July 9, 1982*, 821 F.2d 1147 (5th Cir. 1987).

[42] At the time, as per *Hoffman v. Blaski*, 363 U.S. 335, 343-44 (1960), a court could transfer an action only to a judicial district in which the court could have properly exercised personal jurisdiction and venue over the defendant. Under the current version of section 1404, a federal district court may now transfer a case to any "district or division to which all parties have consented." 28 U.S.C. § 1404(a).

transferred that partial transfer would require the same issue to be litigated in two cases. That being the situation here, the district court should not have severed the claims if there were any alternative. Manifestly, the plaintiffs will suffer some inconvenience if they are forced to litigate their claims in two courts, half the world apart from each other, with not only the consequent added expense and inconvenience but also the possible detriment of inconsistent results. A single forum is also most suitable for determining possible counter- and cross-claims. The public also has an interest in facilitating a speedy and less-expensive determination in one forum of all of the issues arising out of one episode.[43]

Several of our sister circuits have also collapsed the severance-and-transfer analysis into a single inquiry into judicial economy. In *White* v. *ABVO Engineering Corporation*,[44] the Third Circuit held that a severance motion is distinct from, and precedes, a transfer motion, but that "[b]efore effecting such a severance, a judge should weigh the convenience to the parties requesting transfer against the potential inefficiency of litigating the same facts in two [—13—] separate forums."[45] The court did note that the analytical question was essentially whether "the interests of judicial economy dictated . . . a severance and transfer."[46] The Second Circuit has similarly held that "where the administration of justice would be materially advanced by severance and transfer, a district court may properly sever the claims against one or more defendants for the purpose of permitting the transfer of the action against the other defendants."[47] While judicial economy is not the sole consideration for a district court facing a severance-and-transfer motion, it retains a cardinal role.

It is true that *Atlantic Marine* does not speak directly to the issue of severance. Yet, its principal conclusion that a reviewing court cannot consider the private interests of a party who entered into a forum selection clause remains relevant to a severance-and-transfer inquiry.[48] We are persuaded that the severance-and-transfer inquiry in situations where some but not all parties have entered into a forum selection clause ought go as follows: First, pursuant to *Atlantic Marine*, the private factors of the parties who have signed a forum agreement must, as matter of law, cut in favor of severance and transfer to the contracted for forum. Second, the district court must consider the private factors of the parties who have *not* signed a forum selection agreement as it would under a Rule 21 severance and section 1404 transfer analysis. Finally, it must ask whether this preliminary weighing is outweighed by the judicial economy considerations of having all claims determined in a single lawsuit. In so determining, the district court should consider whether there are procedural mechanisms that can reduce the costs of severance, such as common pre-trial procedures, video depositions, [—14—] stipulations, etc. Such practices could echo those used by judges in cases managed pursuant to multidistrict litigation statutes.[49]

This is necessarily a fact-sensitive analysis, and while we agree that *Atlantic Marine* informs the analysis, we cannot conclude that it categorically requires severance-and-transfer in all situations. By failing to properly consider the impact of *Atlantic Marine* in considering the severance and transfer motion, we conclude that the district court erred in its construction of law, and thus mandamus is appropriate.[50]

c.

We recognize that that a large percentage of the federal judiciary's business is conducted

---

[43] *Liaw Su Teng*, 743 F.2d at 1148-49.
[44] 199 F.3d 140 (3d Cir. 1999).
[45] *Id.* at 144.
[46] *Id.* at 145.
[47] *Wyndham Assoc.* v. *Bintliff*, 398 F.2d 614, 618 (2d. Cir. 1968).

[48] *Atl. Marine Const. Co.*, 134 S. Ct. at 582.
[49] *See, e.g.*, Sean J. Griffith & Alexandra D. Lahav, *The Market for Preclusion in Merger Litigation*, 66 Vand. L. Rev. 1053, 1134 (2013).
[50] *See In re Volkswagen of Am., Inc.*, 545 F.3d 304, 310 n.4 (5th Cir. 2008) (en banc).

through the use of the multidistrict litigation process.[51] Strictly speaking, *Atlantic Marine* does not implicate transfer decisions by the Panel on Multidistrict Litigation. Those decisions are made pursuant to 28 U.S.C. § 1407, while *Atlantic Marine*, by its terms, only speaks to transfer motions brought under section 1404(a).[52] Nonetheless, because Congress set similar considerations to guide treatment of transfer motions in both contexts,[53] we believe that *Atlantic Marine*'s reasoning informs MDL practice.

Whether a case is to be transferred to an MDL docket is not our decision to make.[54] We note, however, that judicial economy is of significant concern to [—15—] a MDL transfer decision and often parallels private interests—more so than for the mine-run transfer—and so while *Atlantic Marine* may counsel against such consolidation in a marginal case, its independent force is much dissipated in the world of MDL.

d.

Our concurring colleague posits that we have misconstrued *Atlantic Marine*. We must respectfully disagree. In our view, as we said earlier, the Supreme Court's central teaching in *Atlantic Marine* is that when parties contractually agree on a choice of forum clause, that agreement dictates the result of any "private factor" inquiry under a transfer, or as here, severance motion. At the same time, the Supreme Court made plain that

public interest factors are to be considered when present. In day-to-day operation the public interest factors will seldom impede enforcement. *Atlantic Marine* signifies that of the universe of federal multiple-party, multiple-district civil cases, few will be affected by this decision. A significant percentage of multi-party cases, representing about 40 percent of the federal civil case load, are managed through MDL dockets.[55] These cases are to be transferred back to their original forum for trial; a right only reinforced by the presence of a contracted- [—16—] for forum.[56] The choice of law implicit in that contract would also be assured.[57] The multi-party cases not in need of MDL management by definition present a much weaker call upon the public interest. And, as here, careful pre-trial management will allow the district courts to sever and transfer the contracting litigant while minimizing prejudice to the remaining parties. Nor do we suggest that merely joining a party to the suit will defeat a severance

---

[51] *See* U.S. Judicial Panel on Multidistrict Litigation: Pending MDLS, http://www.jpml.uscourts.gov/pending-mdls-0 (reporting that, as of December 15, 2014, 127,105 pending district court cases have been consolidated into 289 MDL dockets).

[52] *See Atl. Marine Const. Co.*, 134 S. Ct. at 579.

[53] *Compare* 28 U.S.C. § 1404(a) (a district court may transfer a case "[f]or the convenience of parties and witnesses, in the interest of justice"), *with* 28 U.S.C. § 1407(a) (the multidistrict panel may transfer cases "for the convenience of parties and witnesses and [if it] will promote the just and efficient conduct of such actions").

[54] *See* 28 U.S.C. § 1407(a) (judicial panel on multidistrict litigation is responsible for transferring cases to a consolidated multidistrict panel).

[55] A word about how we calculated this statistic. According to the Judicial Panel on Multidistrict Litigation, as of September 30, 2014, there were 127,704 civil actions currently pending and assigned to an MDL docket. *See* U.S. Judicial Panel on Multidistrict Litigation, Statistical Analysis of Multidistrict Litigation, Fiscal Year, 2014, http://www.jpml.uscourts.gov/sites/jpml/files/JPML _Statistical_Analysis_of_Multidistrict_Litigation-2014_0.pdf. As per the Administrative Office of the U.S. Courts, as of June 30, 2014, the last time period for which data was available, there were 334,141 civil cases pending in the federal district courts, of which 287,801 were private civil actions. *See* Table C-1, Statistical Tables for the Federal Judiciary, http://www.uscourts.gov/uscourts/Statistics/Statisti calTablesForTheFederalJudiciary/2014/june/C01Ju n14.pdf. Assuming that the pending MDL case load was similar in June 2014 and September 2014, MDL cases would represent approximately 38% of all civil cases and 44% of all private civil cases.

[56] *See* 28 U.S.C. § 1407(a) ("Each action so transferred shall be remanded by the panel at or before the conclusion of such pretrial proceedings to the district from which it was transferred . . . .").

[57] *See In re Air Disaster at Ramstein Air Base, Germany, on 8/29/90*, 81 F.3d 570, 576 (5th Cir. 1996) ("When a transferee court presides over several diversity actions consolidated under the multidistrict rules, the choice of law rules of each jurisdiction in which the transferred actions were originally filed must be applied.").

motion pursuant to a valid forum contract—certainly not when joined in a transparent effort to defeat the transfer. Our district judges are best situated to balance the competing interests and prudently exercise their judgment in determining how the business of the federal courts is to be allocated, giving the contracted-for choice of forum its due. Such management is indeed their hallmark.

C.

Here, the district court erred in not considering Rolls Royce's forum-selection clause when conducting its severance-and-transfer analysis.[58] Moreover, there is no evidence in the record indicating special administrative difficulties with severance, or that the interests of the defendants not privy to the clause would be significantly threatened. It remains that such interests can be secured by the hand of an experienced federal trial judge with such devices as common discovery among separated cases and sequencing of any dispositive motions or trials. As we recognized in *Volkswagen* "writs of [—17—] mandamus are supervisory in nature and are particularly appropriate when the issues also have an importance beyond the immediate case."[59]

III.

The mandamus petition is GRANTED. The judgment of the district court is REVERSED and this case is REMANDED with instructions to sever and transfer the claims against Rolls Royce.

(Reporter's Note: Concurring opinion on p. 407).

---

[58] *See Phi, Inc.* v. *Apical Indus., Inc.*, No. 6:13-CV-00015, 2014 WL 1820717, at *5-6 (W.D. La. Mar. 7, 2014).

[59] *Volkswagen*, 545 F.3d at 319 ("Because venue transfer decisions are rarely reviewed, the district courts have developed their own tests, and they have applied these tests with too little regard for consistency of outcomes.").

[—18—] **JONES**, Circuit Judge, specially concurring:

Although I agree that mandamus was warranted in this matter, I respectfully cannot subscribe to the majority's limiting the scope of *Atlantic Marine* to two-party disputes (or, as the majority somewhat misleadingly puts it, disputes where "all parties" have signed a contract with a forum selection clause). *Atlantic Marine Construction Co., Inc. v. U.S. Dist. Court*, ___ U.S. ___, 134 S. Ct. 568 (2013). This the majority accomplishes by holding, in a case where one of three defendants has had a longstanding forum selection agreement with the plaintiff, that the defendant's motion to seek severance (Fed. R. Civ. P. 21) reintegrates "private interest" factors into a district court's decision whether to enforce the clause. *Atlantic Marine* cannot be so cabined, in my view or in the view of numerous other courts whose decisions are not even cited by the majority opinion.[1]

The Supreme Court spoke at length in *Atlantic Marine* about the importance of enforcing valid forum-selection clauses. It explained that these provisions represent "the parties' agreement as to the most proper forum," and [—19—] that giving them effect protects the "legitimate expectations" of the parties and "furthers vital interests of the justice system." 134 S. Ct. at 581. "When parties have contracted in advance to litigate disputes in a particular forum," the Court continued, "courts should not unnecessarily disrupt the parties' settled expectations." *Id.* at 584. Although *Atlantic Marine* was a two-party case, the Court's opinion is explicitly premised on the importance of upholding the legitimate expectations of the parties to a forum-selection clause. The Court thus holds that "private interest" factors[2] relevant to a 28 U.S.C. § 1404(a) transfer motion cannot defeat a valid forum-selection clause, nor is it even likely that "public interest" factors[3] can militate against transfer. 134 S. Ct. at 582.

The majority here deviate from *Atlantic Marine* because two of the defendants were not parties to the forum-selection clause and because Fed. R. Civ. P. 21, authorizing severance, must be applied to effectuate the clause. Rule 21 involves essentially the same "private interest" factors that the Court rejected in *Atlantic Marine*.[4] [—20—]

---

[1] Since *Atlantic Marine*, numerous district courts have ruled on motions to transfer in multi-defendant cases subject to a forum-selection clause, and none has deployed Rule 21 to thwart transfer. 14-30510. *See, e.g., Carmouche Ins., Inc., v. Astonish Results, L.L.C.*, No. 14-cv-00061, 2014 WL 2740464, at *6-7 (M.D. La., June 17, 2014) (explaining that Rule 21 factors including inconvenience and prejudice to party opposing severance are irrelevant under *Atlantic Marine*); *Valspar Corp. v. E.I. DuPont de Nemours & Co.*, No. 13-cv-3214, 2014 WL 1607584 (D. Minn. Apr. 21, 2014), at *2-3 (same); *Excentus Corp. v. Giant Eagle, Inc.*, No. 13-cv-178, 2014 WL 923520 (W.D. Pa. Mar. 10, 2014), *at 10 (same); *1-Stop Fin. Serv. Centers of Am., LLC v. Astonish Results, LLC*, No. 13-cv-961, 2014 WL 279669 (W.D. Tex. Jan. 23, 2014), at *10 (same); *Monje v. Spin Master, Inc.*, No. 09-cv-1713, 2013 WL 6498073, at *4 (D.Ariz. Dec. 11, 2013) (noting that in these circumstances, "[s]everance is a necessary precursor to . . . transfer, and it is justified by the same reason [s]"). Moreover, the district courts that have not enforced forum-selection clauses in multi-defendant cases have not done so on the basis of Rule 21. *In re TFT-LCD (Flat Panel) Antitrust Litig.*, MDL No. 1827, 2014 WL 1477748 (N.D. Cal. Apr. 14, 2014), at *2 (determining that public-interest considerations weighed against transfer); *Aquila v. Fleetwood, R.V., Inc.*, No. 12-cv-3281, 2014 WL 1379648 (E.D.N.Y. Mar. 27, 2014), at *4-5 (same).

[2] Private interest factors include "relative ease of access to sources of proof; availability of compulsory process for attendance of unwilling, and the cost of obtaining attendance of willing, witnesses; possibility of view of premises, if view would be appropriate to the action; and all other practical problems that make trial of a case easy, expeditious and inexpensive." *Piper Aircraft Co. v. Reyna*, 454 U.S. 235, 241, n.6, 102 S. Ct. 252, 70 L.Ed. 2d 419 (1981) (internal quotation marks omitted).

[3] Public interest factors include "the administrative difficulties flowing from court congestion; the local interest in having localized controversies decided at home; [and] the interest in having the trial of a diversity case in a forum that is at home with the law." *Id.* at 581 n.6 (quoting *Piper Aircraft v. Reyna*, 454 U.S. 235, 241 n.6, 102 S. Ct. 252, 258 n.6 (1981).

[4] The Rule 21 factors include "(1) whether the claims arose out of the same transaction or occurrence, (2) whether the claims present common questions of law or fact, (3) whether settlement or

Yet, according to the majority's new three-factor test (if I understand it correctly), after allowing *Atlantic Marine* to "cut in favor" of one defendant's severance/transfer to the agreed forum, a court may permit the "private interest factors" of the non-forum selection clause defendants to overcome that clause in favor of "the judicial economy considerations of having all claims determined in a single forum."[5] The majority concludes that *Atlantic Marine* cannot "categorically" require severance-and-transfer in all cases. Sadly, the party who negotiated for a specific forum in which to resolve its disputes with a plaintiff is back at square one if the plaintiff joined another defendant.[6]

While I understand the complications that could arise in multiparty litigation where one, or even more than one, forum-selection clause exists, I find it hard to believe that the unanimous Supreme Court might not have been equally percipient. Simple two-party disputes are near a vanishing breed of litigation. It seems highly unlikely that the Supreme Court granted certiorari and awarded the extraordinary relief of mandamus simply to proclaim that a forum selection clause must prevail only when one party sues one other party. The Court is not naive about the nature of litigation today. Further, the Court's reasoning emphasizes the "settled expectations" of parties who have agreed to a forum selection clause. When private parties have chosen *ex ante* to protect themselves by selecting a forum, this is no different from their selection of arbitration for dispute resolution. Arbitration clauses, of course, cannot be rendered unenforceable in multiparty litigation. Finally, the majority's

view sacrifices the clarity of *Atlantic Marine* to easy manipulation, [—21—] because, if it is correct, any clever party to a lawsuit can readily join another party or individual in an attempt to avoid the forum selection clause.

For these reasons, I believe the majority have erroneously and confusingly diminished the scope of *Atlantic Marine*. I concur in the judgment only.

---

judicial economy would be promoted, (4) whether prejudice would be averted by severance, and (5) whether different witnesses and documentary proof are required." *PHI, Inc.*, 2014 US Dist. LEXIS 63352, at*15.

[5] Because the majority indiscriminately refer to both types of defendants in terms of "private interest" factors, I interpret the holding as best I can.

[6] A defendant unfortunate enough to be involved in a case sent to the Judicial Panel on Multidistrict Litigation is even behind square one, according to the majority's totally impertinent *dicta*, which have no place in this case.

United States Court of Appeals for the Sixth Circuit

United States Court of Appeals
for the Sixth Circuit

No. 12-6118

CNA INS. CO.
vs.
HYUNDAI MERCHANT MARINE CO., LTD.

Appeal from the United States District Court for the
Western District of Kentucky at Louisville

Decided: March 26, 2014

Citation: 747 F.3d 339, 2 Adm. R. 410 (6th Cir. 2014).

Before **BATCHELDER**, Chief Judge; **COOK** and
O'MALLEY, Circuit Judges.*

* The Honorable Kathleen M. O'Malley, Circuit Judge
for the United States Court of Appeals for the Federal
Circuit, sitting by designation.

[—2—] **BATCHELDER**, Chief Judge:

At its core, this appears to be a simple case: Corning hired Hyundai to transport cargo overseas, Hyundai's subcontractors accidentally destroyed the cargo during transit, and nobody wants to pay for it. After some significant legal decisions and a jury trial, the district court found Hyundai and the subcontractors liable to CNA for the loss, though it refused CNA's request for prejudgment interest. Both sides appeal and, as one might expect, this is not nearly as simple as it would seem. Based on the reasoning that follows, we AFFIRM in part, REVERSE in part, and REMAND for reconsideration consistent with this opinion.

I.

The Corning facility in Harrodsburg, Kentucky, makes 4-foot by 4-foot sheets of very thin fusion-drawn flat-glass for use in LCD flat-screen televisions and computer monitors.[1] Corning packs these sheets into custom-made wooden crates, each holding approximately 500 sheets. These crates are sized so that exactly 12 (three across and four deep) fit into a standard 20-foot steel intermodal shipping container leaving only negligible space (less than four inches). This is called "cubing out" the shipping container and eliminates the need for additional packing or securing.

Corning ships its glass, in these containers, to Corning Display Technologies in Tainan, Taiwan (an entirely separate company), which buys all the glass that Corning can produce and also buys more from other vendors. Consequently, Corning ships as many containers per day as it can fill, usually several, and has been doing so for years. Despite the expected fragility of such thin glass and the high volume of shipments, Corning has had virtually no problems with shipping by rail and the damage rate has been extremely low (estimated at one or two sheets for every few crates). [—3—]

As of 2006, Corning and Hyundai Merchant Marine had for several years been parties to a Service Contract in which Corning agreed to ship and Hyundai agreed to carry Corning's cargo from certain locations in the United States to certain locations in Asia: specifically, as relevant here, from Harrodsburg to Tainan for the shipment of the aforementioned glass (and the return shipment of the empty crates).[2] Corning dealt exclusively with Hyundai as the sole carrier for a through shipment; Corning had no role in selecting or contracting with any other carriers in the chain; and Corning made a single payment to only Hyundai. The Service Contract contained other pertinent provisions:

4.A. "[Hyundai] shall be deemed an independent contractor with respect to [Corning] and nothing herein contained shall be construed to be inconsistent with that relationship or status. . . ."

---

[1] Each sheet is actually 1300 mm x 1340 mm, or approximately 4'3" x 4'5". And each sheet is 0.635 mm thick, or 0.025 inches thick, which is thinner than typical posterboard (which is 1/32 inch, or 0.03125 inches, thick).

[2] While the fact that the contract includes return carriage of the crates from Tainan to Harrodsburg could affect the analysis that follows, we find that it does not affect the outcome of this decision so we will not discuss it further.

9.A. "Indemnification — [Hyundai] shall indemnify and hold [Corning] harmless from any and all liability, expense (including reasonable attorney's fees), cause of action, suit, claim or judgment . . ."

13.A "Choice of Law — This Agreement shall be, insofar as relevant, governed by the terms of the Shipping Act of 1984, and otherwise by the laws of the State of New York and of the United States of America."

15.C. Incorporates Hyundai's Regular Form Bill of Lading provisions, unless they conflict, in which case the terms of the Service Contract control. (The only relevant conflict here is that this Service Contract expressly deems Hyundai as Corning's independent contractor, whereas the Hyundai Regular Form Bill of Lading attempts to deem Hyundai as Corning's agent). [—4—]

The Hyundai Regular Form Bill of Lading[3] contains certain pertinent provisions as well:

2(B). Clause Paramount — extending COGSA[4] to cover all times "when

the goods are in the custody of [Hyundai]."

4. Subcontracting —

(B) "[Hyundai] shall be entitled to subcontract on any terms the whole or any part of the handling, storage[,] or carriage of the Goods and any duties undertaken by [Hyundai] in relation to the Goods."

(C) "[Corning] warrants that no claim shall be made against any of [Hyundai]'s Subcontractors or any Subcontractor's Subcontractor, except Carriers where otherwise appropriate, . . . If any such claims should nevertheless be made, [Corning] shall indemnify [Hyundai]. . . ."

(D) Himalaya Clause — "Without prejudice to the foregoing, in regard [to a claim] against a Subcontractor regarding handling, storage[,] or carriage of the Goods, every such Subcontractor shall have the benefit of all provisions in this Bill of Lading as if such provisions were expressly for the Subcontractor's benefit."

5. Responsibility for Loss or Damage—

(B)(2) "If [Corning] establishes that [Hyundai] is liable for the . . . damage to . . . the Goods, and subject to the provisions of this Bill of Lading, including Article 21; . . . [then] with respect to . . . damage caused during the handling, storage, or carriage of the Goods by [Hyundai]'s Subcontractor, such liability shall be to the extent to which such Subcontractor would have been liable to [Corning] if it had made a direct and separate

---

[3] The record contains two slightly different versions of Hyundai's Regular Form Bill of Lading. We are using the version used by the district court, as the parties expressed no objection to that choice in either the district court or here. More importantly, the differences in the versions do not change the substance of the agreement as pertinent here.

[4] COGSA is the Carriage of Goods by Sea Act, 46 U.S.C. § 30701. The key feature of COGSA, as it pertains here, is that it allows the ocean carrier to limit its liability and even sets out a default limitation of liability of $500 per package while the cargo is on the ship ("between the tackles"). COGSA also allows the ocean carrier to extend this limitation of liability to the overland portions of the journey ("beyond the tackles") with a properly written Clause Paramount in the bill of lading. This feature of COGSA makes the Clause Paramount particularly important.

contract with [Corning] in respect of such handling, storage, or carriage." [—5—]

21. Limitation of Liability for Loss or Damage –

(A) "Subject to subpart (B) below, for the purpose of determining the extent of [Hyundai]'s liability for . . . damage to the Goods, [Corning] agrees that the sound value of the Goods is [Corning]'s net invoice cost, plus freight and insurance premium, if paid. [Hyundai] shall not be liable for any loss of profit or any consequential loss."

(B) "Insofar as . . . damage to . . . the Goods was caused during the part of the custody or carriage to which the applicable version of the Hague Rules applies:

(1) "Neither [Hyundai] nor the Vessel shall be liable for . . . damage in an amount exceeding the minimum allowable limit per package . . . , which [under] COGSA . . . is U.S. $500 per package, . . . unless the value (and nature) of the Goods higher than this amount has been declared in writing by [Corning] before receipt of the Goods by [Hyundai] and inserted on the face of this Bill of Lading, and extra freight has been paid as required. . . ."

(2) "Where the Goods have been packaged into a container . . . by or on behalf of [Corning], it is expressly agreed that the number of such containers . . . shall be considered to be the number

of packages . . . for the . . . application of th[is] limitation of liability. . . ."

It is undisputed that this Service Contract governs the claims in this case.

Based on this Service Contract—which anticipated the shipment of multiple 20-foot-standard shipping containers, every weekday, from the Corning facility in Harrodsburg, Kentucky, to Corning Display Technologies in Tainan, Taiwan—Hyundai coordinated or performed each of the six (6) legs of this journey, as an intermodal shipment via a single through bill of lading.

Hyundai subcontracted with a motor carrier (DHL) to pick up the containers at Corning's facility in Harrodsburg and drive them to the railhead in Louisville. A single truck would carry a single container, and Corning would provide the driver with a "straight" bill of lading for the journey to Louisville, as verification that the cargo in the [—6—] sealed container departed in good condition. The truck driver did not issue a bill of lading to Corning, in its own right or on behalf of Hyundai.

Hyundai subcontracted with a rail carrier (Norfolk Southern Railway Co., pursuant to an "Intermodal Transportation Agreement," which incorporates Norfolk Southern's Rules, including an option to select Carmack-based liability[5] at a higher price, which Hyundai did not select[6]) to unload the containers from the

---

[5] The Carmack, 49 U.S.C. § 11706, liability scheme, particular to road and rail carriers under the jurisdiction of the United States Surface Transportation Board (STB), is central to this appeal and is introduced in Section II.A, *infra*.

[6] This is noteworthy because the Surface Transportation Board has permitted rail carriers to avoid Carmack liability for container carriage, so long as the carrier offers Carmack coverage (even at a higher price) to the shipper and the shipper declines. *See Babcock & Wilcox Co. v. Kan. City S. R.R.*, 557 F.3d 134, 142 n.6 (3d Cir. 2009) (relying on 49 U.S.C. § 10502(e) and § 11706). Here, both rail carriers offered Carmack coverage to Hyundai (at a higher price) and Hyundai declined—but neither rail carrier nor Hyundai ever offered a Carmack coverage option to Corning.

truck at the Louisville railhead, load them onto a flatcar, and carry the containers by train to Chicago. It is noteworthy that standard flatcar loading for such containers provides for three (3) containers per flatcar: two (2) 20-foot containers placed on the flatcar with their "noses" (closed ends) touching in the middle so that their doors are exposed at either end, and a 40-foot container placed on top of the two 20-foot containers. All containers remain sealed. Norfolk Southern did not issue any bill of lading, either in its own right or on behalf of Hyundai.

Hyundai subcontracted with another rail carrier (Burlington Northern Santa Fe Railway Co., "BNSF," pursuant to an "International Transportation Agreement," which incorporates BNSF's Rules and also offers the option to select Carmack liability at a higher price, which Hyundai did not select) to take possession of the flatcar in Chicago and carry the containers by train to the railhead in Tacoma, Washington. The containers were not removed from the flatcar; the entire flatcar was transferred into BNSF's custody (a "steel wheel" interchange). It is noteworthy that both Norfolk Southern and BNSF maintain detailed records, via computer, of the handling of the trains and railcars, including movement on the line and at the terminal, coupling and decoupling, and any [—7—] rough handling. BNSF did not issue any bill of lading, either in its own right or on behalf of Hyundai.

Hyundai had a third rail carrier (Tacoma Municipal Beltline Railway, "TMBR," apparently a wholly-owned subsidiary of Hyundai) take possession of the flatcar at the railhead in Tacoma and carry the containers by train to the Washington United Terminal (WUT) seaport. Because TMBR operates over two hundred miles of rail in and around the Tacoma railhead and seaport, it appears that this was necessary carriage and not merely a switching service. TMBR did not issue any bill of lading, either in its own right or on behalf of Hyundai.

Hyundai, an ocean carrier, would unload the containers from the railcars at the WUT seaport and load them onto a ship for sea carriage to the seaport in Kaohsiung, Taiwan. It is at this point that Hyundai would issue a bill of lading specific to the cargo at hand. This was an "ocean" bill.

Hyundai subcontracted with a motor carrier (not named in the record, and terms unknown) to pick up the containers at the Kaohsiung seaport and carry them by truck to Corning Display Technologies in Tainan, Taiwan.[7] Nothing in the record suggests that this motor carrier issued any bill of lading, either in its own right or on behalf of Hyundai. To summarize the six legs of the journey:

1. DHL motor carriage (truck) – Harrodsburg to Louisville;

2. Norfolk Southern rail carriage (train) – Louisville to Chicago;

3. BNSF rail carriage (train) – Chicago to Tacoma;

4. TMBR rail carriage (train) – Tacoma to WUT seaport;

5. Hyundai sea carriage (ship) – WUT to Kaohsiung, Taiwan, seaport;

6. Unknown motor carriage (truck) – Kaohsiung to Tainan.

This journey would take weeks to complete, door-to-door from Harrodsburg to Tainan. [—8—]

On February 21, 2006, Corning shipped several standard 20-foot containers, as it had done every weekday for years, but unlike those thousands of other shipments, two of these containers (identified as HMDU2347259 and HMDU2262167) were damaged on the way to Tainan.

As was usual, Corning prepared its own straight bill of lading for each container. Each

---

[7] It is suggested in the record that Hyundai did not subcontract this part of the trip, and that either Corning or Corning Display Technologies contracted with this motor carrier directly. Either way, it is not relevant to the analysis herein.

truck driver signed the Corning straight bill upon accepting the container, thus acknowledging that he had received the container from Corning in good condition. Neither truck driver issued Corning a bill of lading; in fact, no carrier ever issued a bill of lading for any cargo at any point during this shipment. Correspondingly, Corning never declared a value for this cargo prior to shipment.

The truck drivers transferred the containers to Norfolk Southern in Louisville on that same day, February 21, 2006. Norfolk Southern placed both containers on the same flatcar, presumably—because the record contains no evidence to the contrary—with noses touching in the middle and a 40-foot container set on top. Norfolk Southern did not record or report any damage to either container at that point. Norfolk Southern transferred the flatcar to BNSF in Chicago on February 26, 2006. BNSF did not record or report any damage to either container at that point. BNSF transferred the flatcar to TMBR in Tacoma on March 4, 2006. TMBR did not record or report any damage to either container at that point. These containers were intended to be loaded onto the Hyundai vessel "Hyundai Duke" for overseas shipment to Taiwan.

On March 5, 2006, Hyundai unloaded the containers from the flatcar onto the dock. Sometime thereafter, a WUT employee observed that the two containers were visibly damaged; the front (nose) end of each container was "bulging," or buckled outward. When the containers were opened for inspection, it was discovered that some of the wooden crates were visibly damaged and some of the glass within had broken. There was no report of any damage to any other container on any other car from this train (including the 40-foot container presumably set atop these two).

On March 7, 2006, Marc Cash, the "Assistant Manager for Outbound Trouble Shooting" for Hyundai, sent an email to Corning, to inform Corning of the situation: [—9—]

Good afternoon, please note that the below 2 units arrived via the rail into WUT and the container were bulging, which is an indicator that the cargo may not have been properly secured.

HDMU2347259

HDMU2262167

. . .

Upon consultation with HMMA/Claims,[8] we are arranging a survey and Transload to take place tomorrow, Wednesday March 8th approximately 1:00 PM. I will be speaking with the surveyor directly after the initial viewing, and will be able to provide further evidence of the cause. Since the commodity is shown as 'Flat Glass', it is possible there may be some cargo damage.

Hyundai contracted Craig Burgess of Cullen Maritime Services, Inc. (Seattle, Washington), to perform an on-site survey of the damage. Burgess confirmed that both containers and four (4) of the crates within were visibly damaged and speculated that the damage was due to aggressive "humping" during the rail carriage. Humping is a means of moving and connecting rail cars during transfer or interchange in which the cars come to a sudden stop. Burgess also opined that the loading and packing of the crates within the containers, by Corning in Harrodsburg, appeared to have been satisfactory. The record does not contain a written report by Burgess or Cullen Maritime.

On March 10, 2006, Marc Cash sent a follow-up email to John Wagner of Corning to report on the information obtained from Burgess:

Good afternoon John, pleasure to speak with you today.
As per our telecon, the Transload and Survey took place 3/9, and the results

_____

8 "HMMA/Claims" refers to the Hyundai Merchant Marine of America, Inc. Claims Department.

were that in the opinion of the surveyor the bulging of the nose of the 2 containers was due to aggressive humping of the Flatcars by the rail carriers. The surveyor found no issue with your loading and stowage of the cargo in the containers.

Apparently, Cash sent photos of the damage (both containers and crates) to Wagner sometime thereafter and, on March 14, 2006, Wagner responded to Cash via email: [—10—]

Marc:
I have shared the photos of the damaged crates with our plant in Harrodsburg, KY. The amount of force the product was subjected to in the humping incident has likely damaged the glass. There is reason to suspect that any or all of the crates have damage from the shock, not just the four where you found the external splintering of the wood. I would like both containers returned to origin for inspection at no cost to Corning.
Please advise arrangements and ETA so we can plan for the inspection. If damage is found we will be processing a claim.

Note that, at this point, both Cash (Hyundai) and Wagner (Corning) had accepted that a rail carrier's humping of the flatcars caused the damage. But later (much later, it turns out), Norfolk Southern and BNSF disproved this assumption by producing logs to show that no humping or rough handling had occurred during the carriage of these two containers. Cash replied to Wagner that same day:

Good afternoon John, please note the we will make immediate arrangements to return these 2 containers to Harrodsburg, KY for further examination.
Please note that I have spoken to, and added to this distribution, personnel from our National Claims Dept. for further coordination and direction from this point forward to ensure smooth handling of any concerns. The contact person for HMMA Claims is as follows:
Mr. Todd Frare
. . .
I will advise once cargo is railbilled and scheduled to depart Tacoma for Harrodsburg, KY.

Hyundai unloaded the 24 crates from the damaged containers, loaded them into two different containers, and shipped them back to Harrodsburg, via the same route by which they had arrived. Meanwhile, Corning filed an insurance claim with its insurer, CNA. When the cargo arrived back in Harrodsburg, CNA scheduled its own survey of the crates to fully assess the damage.

Mark Ohlson of Riverlands Marine Surveyors and Consultants, Inc. (Louisville, Kentucky), conducted a survey on March 31 and April 6, 2006, and prepared a written report dated April 19, 2006 (Riverlands Report), for CNA. In the Riverlands Report, Ohlson noted that Robert Craig, a Marine Surveyor representing Hyundai, was also [—11—] present. When Corning opened the containers and removed the crates, Ohlson found that all but four (4) of the 24 crates exhibited visible damage to the crate itself or the glass inside. When they opened two (2) of the apparently undamaged crates for inspection, both revealed damaged glass. Ohlson attributed the damage to the likelihood of "humping" during the rail transport, but this was almost certainly based not on any evidence but on Burgess's speculation during the initial on-site survey in Tacoma and Cash's adoption and repetition of that assertion in his email to Corning. Ohlson also opined that Corning's method of stowing and packing had been suitable for the shipping.[9] Finally, Ohlson declared the shipment a total loss and recommended that the glass be disposed of and the crates returned to their manufacturer for refurbishment.

---

[9] Given that Hyundai personnel had loaded the crates into new containers in Tacoma for return shipment, this assertion was based either on Corning's standard practices or the statement from the initial on-site survey in Tacoma.

CNA paid Corning $664,679.88 on the claim and was subrogated to Corning's right to sue for recovery. On September 27, 2006, CNA filed suit in the Southern District of New York, naming three defendants: Hyundai, Norfolk Southern, and BNSF (hereinafter "the Carriers"). CNA claimed breach of the Service Contract, liability for bailment, and negligence. CNA cited the Carmack Amendment, 49 U.S.C. § 11706, in the opening paragraph (jurisdiction section) of its complaint.

The Carriers moved to transfer venue to the Eastern District of Kentucky, arguing that it would have been an appropriate venue originally and would be more convenient for the parties and any witnesses, given that the carriage began at the Corning facility in Harrodsburg, in the Eastern District of Kentucky. CNA opposed the transfer and moved, in the alternative, for a transfer to the Western District of Washington, where the damage was discovered. The animosity between the attorneys, if not the parties, became clear immediately. The court "granted" the Carriers' motion and transferred the case, not to the Eastern District as requested, but to the Western District of Kentucky, specifically Louisville. While this appears to have been a mistake, the parties proceeded in the Western District of Kentucky, and any objection or error has long since been waived. [—12—]

The Carriers moved for summary judgment on three bases: (1) that CNA had not pled Carmack claims, so the absence of contractual privity prevented CNA from suing the rail carriers; (2) that the Service Contract's[10] Subcontracting Clause prohibited CNA from suing the rail carriers; and (3) that the Carriers were entitled to enforcement of the $500-per-package COGSA limitation of liability, arguing for a limit of $12,000 for the 24 crates.[11] The district court rejected the

Carriers' argument that CNA had not pled Carmack claims, found that CNA had done so, and held that the case would proceed solely under Carmack, apparently on the basis that the damage had undisputedly occurred while the cargo was in the possession of a rail carrier.[12] The court next [—13—] explained

limitation of liability provision (Form Bill of Lading § 21(B)(2), as incorporated into the Service Contract) specifically states that a "package" is a "container" packed by Corning, which at least implies that there were actually only two such "packages" damaged here. Thus, under a strict reading, Hyundai would have been liable for only $1,000 on this shipment.

[12] On appeal here, the Carriers argue that CNA "withdrew" or "waived" its breach-of-contract, bailment, and negligence causes of action in the district court, and chose instead to proceed solely on its Carmack cause of action. This contention mischaracterizes the district court proceedings on this issue and is ultimately unsupportable and untrue.

In their motion for summary judgment, filed July 1, 2008, the Carriers stated near the end of their argument that CNA "ha[d] not asserted a cause of action under the Carmack Amendment." R. 78 at p. 25. This was a reasonable contention, given that CNA's complaint contained three express causes of action (breach of contract, bailment, and negligence) and only referred to Carmack in the jurisdiction section, not as a cause of action. R. 38 (Complaint). In its response memorandum, dated August 1, 2008, CNA answered that it had raised three causes of action *under* Carmack:

"It is acknowledged that [CNA]'s claims for breach of contract, negligence, and bailment are *encompassed* and preempted by the Carmack Amendment, and *as such*, [CNA] has no state law claims against [the Carriers], but rather one *comprehensive* claim *under* the Carmack Amendment."

R. 84 at 11 (emphasis added). In their sur-reply, dated August 15, 2008, the Carriers did not contend that CNA had withdrawn or waived the three common-law causes of action but instead reiterated their belief that CNA had not pled Carmack and argued, in the alternative, for summary judgment on the common-law causes of action because Carmack preempted them. R. 88 at 12. In ruling on the motion, the district court held that Carmack encompassed the claims:

---

[10] Unless specified, any reference to the Service Contract includes reference to the Form Bill of Lading, which was specifically incorporated therein, except for provisions that conflicted with the Service Contract itself.

[11] It is unclear why the Carriers' attorney sought $500 per crate ($12,000) when the

that the Subcontracting Clause did not make the rail carriers "immune from suit"; instead, it merely "obligate[ed] Corning to indemnify Hyundai for any resultant claims by any Subcontractor against Hyundai arising out of these same facts." Finally, the court explained that because the Clause Paramount, as it is written in the Service Contract, does not expressly extend COGSA's $500-per-package limit of liability to the subcontractor rail carriers, it does not apply to them; and

> "CNA alleges causes of action against [the Carriers] sounding in breach of contract, bailment, and negligence, as encompassed by the Carmack Amendment. . . . Generally, and in part, the Carmack Amendment imposes liability for the actual loss or injury to property caused by rail carriers. It is undisputed that the Cargo was damaged while in the possession of one or both Rail [Carriers]."

R. 102 at 3 (Memorandum Opinion, March 16, 2009). The district court also included a footnote in this passage:

> "While [the Carriers] argue preliminarily that CNA has failed to explicitly plead claims [under] the Carmack Amendment, the court is satisfied that CNA's Complaint clearly alleges comprehensive claims under the Carmack Amendment as opposed to individual [—13—] common law causes of action."

R. 102 at 3 n.2 (quotation marks and citations omitted). Thus, CNA did not withdraw or waive its breach-of-contract, bailment, or negligence causes of action in the district court, but rather sought to preserve these causes of action as encompassed within the Carmack claim. Even if it could be said that CNA withdrew or waived these causes of action, CNA did so only on the understanding that Carmack preempted them and the case would proceed under Carmack. There is simply no basis to conclude, as the Carriers would have us do, that if the district court had deemed Carmack inapplicable at the summary judgment stage and left CNA with only the common law causes of action, that CNA would have nonetheless still withdrawn or waived those causes of action, i.e., that it would have dismissed its case altogether. Instead, as CNA has made clear throughout, CNA would have pursued these three common-law causes of action under diversity jurisdiction, as alleged in its complaint. *See also* fn.13 and fn. 14, *infra*.

because it applies only to damage occurring to inland cargo while that cargo is in Hyundai's custody, it does not apply to Hyundai in these circumstances. Consequently, the court denied the Carriers' attempts to limit their liability.

CNA had also moved for summary judgment, seeking to strike the Carriers' limitation-of-liability defenses on two theories: (1) that the Indemnification Clause in the Service Contract provided for full remuneration for the loss of the cargo; and (2) that the Carmack Amendment barred the rail carriers from any attempted limitation of liability.[13] The court rejected CNA's first theory, explaining that the Indemnification

---

[13] CNA moved for summary judgment on July 1, 2008, the same day the Carriers had filed their motion (see forgoing footnote), and argued that Carmack governed "by force of law." R. 79 at 16. The Carriers replied:

> "With respect to the provisions of the Carmack Amendment applicable to rail carriers, it is notable that the Carmack Amendment does not 'govern' claims of breach of contract, bailment[,] and negligence; rather, the Carmack Amendment completely preempts such causes of action."

R. 85 at 23; *see also* R. 85 at 25 ("If the Carmack Amendment is applicable to the instant matter, then all of the claims pled by [CNA] are preempted."). CNA disagreed in its sur-reply, insisting that "these causes of action are found to be *authorized by* the Carmack Amendment and do not constitute 'state law causes of action.'" R. 87 at 12 (relying on *Travelers Prop. Cas. Co. v. A.D. Transp. Express, Inc.*, No. 04-5830, 2007 WL 2571957, *2 n.3 (D.N.J. Aug. 31, 2007) (holding the same)). As noted in the foregoing footnote, CNA did not withdraw or waive its breach-of-contract, bailment, or negligence causes of action in the district court. The Carriers contention that CNA did so is unfounded and untrue.

As an aside, we find it irritating and somewhat troubling that we had to explore this non-issue in such depth solely because the Carriers' counsel misrepresented it to us in his brief and at oral argument. To be sure, this was a complicated case with a lengthy procedural history and we will assume that counsel [—14—] was merely mistaken and not duplicitous in his contentions. Nevertheless, we encourage him to be more thorough and cautious in the future.

[—14—] Clause obligates Hyundai to indemnify Corning against third-party claims, but "has no bearing on Hyundai's liability to Corning for the loss of the Cargo." The court did not specifically decide the Carmack argument, but instead granted the motion based on its finding that the Service Contract's limitations of liability did not apply to any of the Carriers.

The case proceeded to a jury trial under a single Carmack cause of action.[14] CNA proved its Carmack prima facie case (i.e., the cargo was tendered in good condition, it arrived in damaged condition, and actual damages were quantified), so the burden shifted to the Carriers' to demonstrate one of the five excepted causes.[15] The Carriers attempted to prove that the damage was due to Corning's "improper" stowing and packing, inasmuch as it had left three inches of space (in the 20-foot container) between the crates and the end wall. CNA easily rebutted this contention. The real mystery was how the damage actually occurred—the railroads demonstrated that there had been no "humping," as had been speculated, nor was that even a plausible cause given that the containers had likely been positioned on the flatcar nose-to-nose. Also, the railroads demonstrated that no other containers on that train had been damaged. It appears likely that the containers were damaged after being removed from the flatcar, but the case was neither presented nor defended that way.

The jury found for CNA, holding the Carriers jointly and severally liable for $498,509.91 (which is exactly 75% of the $664,679.88 claim, to the penny). Notably, there is no provision under Carmack for contributory negligence or a partial award, and the court did not instruct the jury that it

could issue a partial award, so this appears to have been improper. But CNA did not protest the verdict to the district court or appeal [—15—] it here. CNA did move for pre-judgment interest under New York law (9%) or, alternatively, federal law, but the district court denied that motion.

Meanwhile, the Carriers moved for judgment as a matter of law, arguing (1) that Carmack did not apply to Hyundai because it is not a rail carrier; (2) that the Surface Transportation Board had exempted intermodal rail transportation from Carmack unless the shipper selects it and pays extra for it, which Corning did not do; and (3) that Carmack does not permit lawsuits by Corning, the shipper, against Norfolk Southern or BNSF, because they are mere connecting carriers under Carmack. Because the district court had already considered and rejected these arguments in its summary judgment decisions, the Carriers relied on an intervening Supreme Court decision to raise these issues anew, namely *Kawasaki Kisen Kaisha Ltd. v. Regal-Beloit Corp.*, 561 U.S. --, 130 S. Ct. 2433 (June 21, 2010). The district court denied the motions, explaining:

> [T]he court finds that [*Kawasaki*] *Kisen* . . . does not preclude the liability of Hyundai [] under the Carmack Amendment in this case. The [*Kawasaki*] case is inapplicable herein. The court further finds that the evidence supports the jury's award of damages against all three defendants for the full value of the freight.

The Carriers appealed. CNA cross-appealed, contesting the court's denial of prejudgment interest.

II.

The preliminary and overriding question in this appeal concerns the meaning and application of the Carmack Amendment. That is, we must determine whether Carmack actually applies here.

---

[14] As a final comment on the Carriers' contention that CNA withdrew or waived its breach-of-contract cause of action, we note that CNA actually sought to argue its breach-of-contract theory at trial. The district court refused, holding that this was an "either/or" proposition in which CNA was barred from arguing breach of contract by proceeding under Carmack.

[15] *See* Section II.A, *infra*, which presents Carmack's burden-shifting framework.

A.

The Carmack Amendment to the Interstate Commerce Act, originally enacted in 1906 and currently codified at 49 U.S.C. § 11706, states in pertinent part:

(a)　A rail carrier providing transportation or service subject to the jurisdiction of the [Surface Transportation] Board under this part [—16—] shall issue a receipt or bill of lading for property it receives for transportation under this part.

That rail carrier and any other carrier that delivers the property and is providing transportation or service subject to the jurisdiction of the [Surface Transportation] Board under this part are liable to the person entitled to recover under the receipt or bill of lading.

The liability imposed under this subsection is for the actual loss or injury to the property caused by - -

(1)　the receiving rail carrier;

(2)　the delivering rail carrier; or

(3)　another rail carrier over whose line or route the property is transported in the United States or from a place in the United States to a place in an adjacent foreign country when transported under a through bill of lading.

Failure to issue a receipt or bill of lading does not affect the liability of a rail carrier.

A delivering rail carrier is deemed to be the rail carrier performing the line-haul transportation nearest the destination but does not include a rail carrier providing only a switching service at the destination.

(b)　The rail carrier issuing the receipt or bill of lading under subsection (a) of this section or delivering the property for which the receipt or bill of lading was issued is entitled to recover from the rail carrier over whose line or route the loss or injury occurred the amount required to be paid to the owners of the property, as evidenced by a receipt, judgment, or transcript, and the amount of its expenses reasonably incurred in defending a civil action brought by that person.

(c)(1)　A rail carrier may not limit or be exempt from liability imposed under subsection (a) of this section except as provided in this subsection. A limitation of liability . . . in a receipt, bill of lading, contract, or rule in violation of this section is void.

49 U.S.C. § 11706 (certain paragraph breaks added). These provisions also apply to motor carriers, *see* 49 U.S.C. § 14706(a)(1) (virtually identical for motor carriers), and [—17—] freight forwarders.[16] *See Royal & Sun*

---

[16] There are no "freight forwarders" in this case, although both parties have, at times, improperly suggested that there are. Simply put, "[f]reight forwarders consolidate less than [a] carload [of] freight into carloads for shipment." *Chicago, Milwaukee, St. Paul & Pac. R.R. v. Acme Fast Freight*, 336 U.S. 465, 467 (1949); *see also id.* at n.2. That did not happen here. More specifically: "Freight forwarders generally make arrangements for the movement of cargo at the request of clients and are vitally different from carriers, such as vessels, truckers, stevedores[,] or warehouses, which are directly involved in transporting the cargo. Unlike a carrier, a freight forwarder does *not* issue a bill of lading, and is therefore not liable to a shipper for anything that occurs to the goods being shipped." *Prima U.S. Inc. v. Panalpina, Inc.*, 223 F.3d 126, 129 (2d Cir. 2000); *see also Norfolk S. R.R. v. Kirby*, 543 U.S. 14, 18 (2004) ("A freight forwarding company arranges for, coordinates, and facilitates cargo transport, but does not itself transport cargo.").

Alliance Ins. v. Ocean World Lines, Inc., 612 F.3d 138, 145 (2d Cir. 2010).

Though it might not be obvious from the text, "Carmack's original premise is that the [initial] receiving carrier is liable for damage caused by the other [subsequent] carriers in the delivery chain," *Kawasaki*, 130 S. Ct. at 2446. The current version of Carmack makes the final, or "delivering," carrier liable to the shipper as well. So, the aggrieved shipper need only sue the initial ("receiving") or final ("delivering") carrier and need not seek out the carrier actually at fault, nor must the plaintiff-shipper determine the circumstances by which the loss or damage actually occurred.

In a Carmack claim, the Supreme Court has set out a burden-shifting framework, in which the shipper may establish a prima facie case with a showing of three basic elements:

(1) that the initial ("receiving") carrier received the cargo in good condition,

(2) that the cargo was lost or damaged, and

(3) the amount of actual loss or damages.

Thereupon, the burden shifts to the defendant-carrier to show both that it was not negligent and that the damage was instead due to one of five excepted causes: (1) an act of God; (2) an act of terrorism or war; (3) an act of the shipper itself; (4) an act of public authority; or (5) the inherent vice or nature of the goods. *Missouri Pac. R.R. v. Elmore & Stahl*, 377 U.S. 134, 137-38 (1964). [—18—]

If the defendant-carrier meets this burden, it wins. If not, then the shipper prevails based on its establishing the—very low threshold—prima facie case. Recall that this named defendant-carrier (either the receiving or delivering carrier, or both) may attempt to recover any judgment from the intermediate carrier that was actually at fault for the loss or damage. 49 U.S.C. § 11706(b).

B.

"Common carrier liability" at common law was "of an extraordinary character, and cover[ed] every risk that the property c[ould] be subject to, except a loss by the act of God or by an unavoidable accident, [or] by the public enemy." *St. Louis, I. M. & S. R.R. v. Knight*, 122 U.S. 79, 88 (1887). The carrier's alternative was to limit its liability by contract with the shipper, which, due to the "extraordinary liability which the law impose[d]," almost every carrier chose to do. *See id.* As a result, there was no uniform law for carrier liability, but instead, every case was dependent on the contract between the carrier and the shipper, typically embodied in a bill of lading.

It also bears mention that, pre-Carmack, there were hundreds of rail carriers operating their own rail lines as part of a massive, interconnected, nationwide system. So a shipment from Harrodsburg, Kentucky, to Tacoma, Washington, might pass through a half-dozen or more carriers, each of whom would operate under the contract (bill of lading) that the shipper had formed with the initial carrier, even though the shipper, and possibly even the initial carrier, had no knowledge of who these subsequent carriers might be. This made it very difficult, if not impossible, for the shipper to locate the carrier actually responsible for loss or damage to the cargo during transit.

As enacted in 1906, the Carmack Amendment partially codified the common law by adopting a form of common-carrier liability, and restricted the carrier's right to limit that liability by contract. In *Atlantic Coast Line R.R. v. Riverside Mills*, 219 U.S. 186 (1911), the Supreme Court considered an early challenge to Carmack and clarified that the Amendment placed full liability on the initial "receiving" carrier and prohibited any attempt to contractually limit that liability: [—19—]

Reduced to the final results, the Congress has said that a receiving [i.e., initial] carrier, in spite of any stipulation to the contrary, shall be deemed, when it receives property in one state, to be transported to a point in another, involving the use of a connecting carrier for some part of the way, to have adopted such other carrier as its agent, and to incur carrier liability throughout the entire route, with the right to reimbursement for a loss not due to his own negligence.

Id. at 205. The Court portrayed this as an agency construct: "The liability of the [initial] receiving carrier which results in such a case is that of a principal for the negligence of his own agents [i.e., the subsequent connecting or delivering carriers]." *Id*. at 206. Otherwise stated:

In substance[,] Congress has said to such [initial] carriers: 'If you receive articles for transportation from a point in one state to a place in another, beyond your own terminal, you must do so under a contract to transport to the place designated. If you are obliged to use the services of independent carriers in the continuance of the transit, you must use them as your own agents, and not as agents of the shipper.'. . . The [initial] receiving carrier is, as principal, liable not only for its own negligence, but for that of any agency it may use, although, as between themselves, the company [i.e., carrier] actually causing the loss may be primarily liable.

Id. at 206-07. The Court rejected statutory and constitutional challenges. The Court's underlying, though unstated, premise is that there is a single contract for the shipment of the goods—either an actual contract, such as in a bill of lading, or a constructive contract based on Carmack's governing regulation—and that contract is between the shipper and only the initial (receiving) carrier.

Two years later, in *Adams Express Co. v. Croninger*, 226 U.S. 491, 505-06 (1913), the Court explained that Congress had, with the Carmack Amendment, fully preempted state law concerning the liability of interstate rail and road carriers. The Court also restated and clarified:

The significant and dominating features of th[e] [Carmack] [A]mendment are these: [—20—]

First. It affirmatively requires the initial carrier to issue a receipt or bill of lading therefor, when it receives property for transportation from a point in one state to a point in another.

Second. Such initial carrier is made liable to the lawful holder thereof for any loss, damage, or injury to such property caused by it.

Third. [The initial carrier] is also made liable for any loss, damage, or injury to such property caused by any common carrier, railroad, or transportation company to which such property may be delivered, or over whose line or lines such property may pass.

Fourth. It affirmatively declares that no contract, receipt, rule, or regulation shall exempt such [initial] common carrier, railroad, or transportation company from the liability hereby imposed.

Id. at 504 (quotation marks omitted); *see also Norfolk & W. R.R. v. Dixie Tobacco Co.*, 228 U.S. 593, 594-95 (1913) (explaining that Carmack "requires any common carrier receiving property for transportation from a point in one state to a point in another to issue a receipt or bill of lading for the same; makes the [initial] receiving carrier liable for loss caused by any common carrier *in transitu*; and provides that no contract shall exempt it from the liability thus imposed").

Note that an actual or tangible bill of lading is not necessary to impose liability on the initial carrier under Carmack's plain terms, 49 U.S.C. § 11706(a) ("Failure to issue a receipt or bill of lading does not affect the liability of a rail carrier."), or *Atlantic Coast Line*'s constructive-contract premise, 219 U.S. at 206 ("If you receive articles for transportation . . . , you must do so under a contract to transport to the place designated."), and that *Adams Express*, 226

U.S. at 504, treats "contract, receipt, rule, or regulation" as equally powerless to limit the carrier's liability. Thus, Carmack's requirement that the initial carrier issue the shipper a bill of lading is not a requirement to form an actual contract, though that is certainly acceptable and typically anticipated; it is a requirement that the initial carrier issue the shipper a receipt for the cargo as acknowledgment of the constructive contract making that carrier solely liable to the shipper for the entire carriage. [—21—]

Because the shipper's contract (actual or constructive), as embodied in or symbolized by the initial carrier's bill of lading to the shipper, is the sole agreement governing the duration of the carriage and is between the shipper and only the initial carrier, making subsequent carriers mere agents of the initial carrier, any overlapping bill(s) of lading issued by any subsequent carriers are void. *Missouri, K & T R.R. v. Ward*, 244 U.S. 383, 387 (1917). That is:

> For the purpose of fixing the liability, the several carriers must be treated, not as independent contracting parties, but as one system; and the connecting lines become in effect mere agents [of the initial carrier], whose duty it is to forward the goods under the terms of the contract made by their principal, the initial carrier.

Id. at 387-88. Thus, in *Missouri, K & T*, the Court upheld the shipper's suit against two subsequent rail carriers under the terms of the initial shipper's bill of lading (contract) and voided a subsequent, overlapping bill of lading. *See also Texas & Pac. R.R. v. Leatherwood*, 250 U.S. 478, 481 (1919).

Note that the *Missouri, K & T* Court allowed the shipper to sue and recover from subsequent rail carriers, despite the absence of contractual privity between the shipper and those carriers:

> While the receiving carrier is . . . responsible for the whole carriage, each connecting [carrier] may still be sued [by the shipper] for damages occurring on

its line; and the liability of such participating carrier is fixed by the applicable valid terms of the original bill of lading.

Missouri, K & T, 244 U.S. at 387. This is an expansion of Carmack beyond its terms: here, the subsequent carriers are not acting as agents for the initial carrier to complete the carriage; rather the initial carrier is made the agent for the subsequent carriers to bind them to a contract with the shipper.

Ten years later, in *Missouri Pacific R.R. v. Porter*, 273 U.S. 341 (1927), the Court considered an overseas export of goods shipped under a single through bill of lading (albeit separated into two sub-parts: one for rail transport from Arkansas to Georgia and another for sea transport from Georgia to England). The emphasis in *Porter* [—22—] was the Court's holding that Congress had occupied the entire field regulating interstate bills of lading, thereby invalidating any coincident state laws.[17] In its analysis, however, the Court opined (perhaps in dicta) that the Carmack Amendment would not apply to the domestic overland part of an international, overseas shipment under a through bill of lading:

> The question is whether Congress has entered upon the regulation of provisions in bills of lading affecting liability of railroads for loss of property received by them for transportation over an interstate inland route to a seaport for delivery to a foreign vessel for ocean carriage to a nonadjacent foreign country. . . . The defendants . . . rightly say that the Carmack Amendment . . . does not apply to such a shipment.

Id. at 345; *see also Reider v. Thompson*, 339 U.S. 113, 120 (1950) (Frankfurter, J., dissenting) (asserting that "[t]he conclusion of the *Porter* case" was "that the Carmack Amendment does not apply to an unbroken

---

[17] Recall that the Court had already established, in *Adams Express*, 226 U.S. at 505, that the Carmack Amendment fully preempted state law concerning the liability of interstate rail and road carriers.

transaction of commerce with a nonadjacent foreign country"). Ultimately, the Court held that the situation presented was governed by the general statute concerning bills of lading and the federal courts' interpretation and application of that statute (i.e., federal common law).

If this passage were a legal holding, then Carmack plainly would not apply to the domestic portion of an overseas export under a through bill of lading, even if the initial receiving carrier otherwise fell within Carmack's coverage. But the Court has, since then, expressly limited this as a holding and has treated this issue as an open question, so it is likely dicta.

In *Mexican Light & Power Co. v. Texas Mexican R.R.*, 331 U.S. 731 (1947), the Court considered a shipment of cargo under two overlapping bills of lading, as in *Missouri, K & T*, and again found the second bill void. The first bill (from the initial carrier, Pennsylvania R.R.) covered carriage from Pennsylvania to Laredo, Texas, for export to El Oro, Mexico, with a caveat that the purchaser's agent would meet the shipment in Laredo, presumably to arrange for border crossing. *Id.* at 732-33. More [—23—] importantly, the shipper had paid Pennsylvania R.R. for shipment all the way to the Mexican border; i.e., through Laredo, but not actually out of the country (so not technically an export). When the subsequent ("connecting") carrier (Texas Mexican R.R.) stopped in Laredo, it issued another bill of lading, for the trip from Laredo to El Oro. But because Pennsylvania R.R. had paid Texas Mexican R.R. to deliver the shipment all the way to the border, Texas Mexican did not receive any further payment for the second bill of lading. At the border, the shipment was transferred to the National Railway of Mexico, in whose custody it was later damaged. The shipper sued Texas Mexican R.R. under Carmack, as the putative initial (receiving) carrier on the second bill of lading. The Court rejected Carmack liability for Texas Mexican, explaining:

[U]nless the connecting carrier has received a consideration for the bill of lading in addition to that which flowed under the bill of lading issued by the initiating carrier, the Carmack Amendment makes such second bill of lading void. It can neither enlarge the liability of the connecting carrier nor contract that of the initiating carrier.

. . .

[Because] the so-called bill of lading [issued by Texas Mexican R.R.] did not evidence any new and independent undertaking, when judged by the rigid requirements by which bills of lading are valid under the Carmack Amendment, . . . the shipment over the Texas-Mexican [R.R. line] legally moved only under the original bill of lading[;] the Pennsylvania [R.R.] was never displaced as the initial carrier[;] and . . . therefore the Texas-Mexican [R.R.] was not liable for damage that occurred on the Mexican [National] Railroad.

Id. at 734-35. Note that this exclusion of Texas Mexican R.R. because it was merely a subsequent connecting carrier is a reversal from *Missouri, K & T*, 244 U.S. at 387, in which the Court permitted the shipper to sue two subsequent rail carriers. This is peculiar because the Court cited to, quoted from, and relied on *Missouri, K & T* in holding that the subsequent bill of lading was void.

In *Reider v. Thompson*, 339 U.S. 113 (1950), the Court considered an overseas import of goods shipped under two non-overlapping bills of lading; one for the sea transport from Buenos Aires to New Orleans and another for the rail transport from New [—24—] Orleans to Boston. The Court held that the absence of a through bill meant that the trip comprised two separate journeys, each covered by its own separate bill of lading, the second of which (the overland, rail portion) fell under Carmack, even though the first (overseas) part would not. The Court explained:

There was no through bill of lading from Buenos Aires to Boston. . . . The contract for ocean transportation terminated at New Orleans. Having terminated, nothing of it remained for the new, separate, and distinct domestic contract of carriage to 'supplement' [i.e., overlap]. . . . If the various parties dealing with this shipment separated the carriage into distinct portions by their contracts, it is not for courts judicially to meld the portions into something they are not. The test is not where the shipment originated, but where the obligation of the carrier as receiving carrier originated. Thus it is not significant that the shipment in this case originated in a foreign country, since the foreign portion of the journey terminated at the border of the United States. The obligation as receiving carrier originated when respondent [railroad] issued its original through bill of lading at New Orleans. That contract of carriage was squarely within the provisions of the statute.

Id. at 117 (citations omitted). Because there were two independent contracts, the Court put the first (oversea) contract aside and considered only the second (entirely domestic, overland) contract individually. In this light, the Court was not considering "an unbroken transaction of commerce with a nonadjacent foreign country," *id.* at 120 (Frankfurter, J., dissenting), and it distinguished *Missouri Pacific R.R. v. Porter*, 273 U.S. at 345 (which had stated that Carmack would not apply to the "inland route to a seaport" as part of an overseas shipment in foreign commerce):

> The Court [in *Missouri Pacific R.R. v. Porter*] briefly alluded to the coverage of the Carmack Amendment. But the sole issue in [that] case was whether federal regulation of bills of lading had covered the field to the exclusion of state regulation of the same subject matter. The Court's discussion of the Carmack Amendment [in that case] does not control our decision in this case.

Reider, 339 U.S. at 116 n.1.

Nonetheless, the *Reider* Court's reasoning implied that the use of a through bill (from Buenos Aires to Boston) would have altered the outcome, suggesting that its [—25—] outcome could have been consistent with *Porter*, or at least not inconsistent with it. That is, had the shipper and ocean carrier entered a single through contract, from Buenos Aires to Boston, with the rail carrier at New Orleans a mere subcontractor to the ocean carrier, then the "obligation of the carrier as receiving carrier" *vis-a-vis* the shipper would have originated with the ocean carrier in Buenos Aires, and that carrier would not be subject to Carmack. Thus the shipper would have no grounds to invoke Carmack, either against the ocean carrier as the "receiving" carrier or against the rail carrier, a mere "connecting" carrier under the single through contract.

One lingering question would be whether Carmack applied separately to the rail component of the journey; that is, whether the rail carrier in New Orleans would have been a Carmack "receiving carrier" *vis-a-vis* the ocean-carrier-as-shipper, under the view that its obligation began in New Orleans.[18] Likely not. In *Reider*, 339 U.S. at 118, the Court found it important that, because "the shipment in this case could not have moved an inch beyond New Orleans under the ocean bill[,] the Carmack Amendment required [the rail carrier] to issue a . . . bill of lading for the carriage from New Orleans to Boston." Applying that reasoning the other way, under a through bill the shipment would certainly continue through New Orleans under the ocean bill, so the rail carrier would not have needed to issue a bill of lading to continue the carriage to Boston. Moreover, because the rail carrier would receive no additional consideration for the second bill of lading beyond that already paid by the ocean carrier under the through bill, that second bill would have been void under the Carmack analysis in *Mexican Light & Power*, 331 U.S. at 734. Regardless, the Court has since rejected this ocean-carrier-as-shipper argument expressly. *See Kawasaki*, 130 S. Ct. at 2445 ("A carrier does not become a [Carmack] receiving carrier simply by accepting goods for further

---

[18] This theory was one of Justice Sotomayor's contentions in her dissent in *Kawasaki*, 130 S. Ct. at 2455.

transport from another carrier in the middle of an international shipment under a through bill.").

Thus, though far from definitive, a composite of the Court's Carmack case law as of *Reider* reasonably appeared to hold that Carmack: (1) fully preempted state law [—26—] as to an interstate rail carrier's liability; (2) mandated a single contract for carriage (i.e., the receiving carrier's bill of lading), such that any subsequent and overlapping contract would be void; (3) either allowed or disallowed a shipper's lawsuit against a "connecting" carrier, without clear explanation; and (4) would likely not apply to an overseas through contract, i.e., "an unbroken transaction of commerce with a nonadjacent foreign country." Unfortunately, the Court's ensuing cases concerning the Carmack Amendment confused as much as, or more than, they clarified.

In *Norfolk Southern R.R. v. Kirby*, 543 U.S. 14 (2004), the Court did not discuss or even mention the Carmack Amendment, but its analysis affects our Carmack analysis nonetheless. *Kirby* involved two overlapping bills of lading (i.e., contracts), both of which were through bills for an import of goods from Australia to Alabama via the port at Savannah, Georgia. The shipper (Kirby) hired an intermediary (ICC) to arrange the carriage; ICC hired an ocean carrier (Hamburg Sud) to perform the through carriage; and Hamburg Sud hired a rail carrier (Norfolk Southern) to complete the overland portion. ICC issued a bill of lading directly to Kirby; Hamburg Sud issued a second bill to ICC, without Kirby's knowledge. Each bill contained a Clause Paramount, extending COGSA's terms to cover the overland portions of the carriage, and a Himalaya Clause, extending the bills' limitations of liability to the subcontractors. Norfolk Southern operated under these two bills and did not issue any bill of its own. When the train derailed, Kirby sued Norfolk Southern for breach of contract and negligence. Norfolk Southern invoked the limitations of liability in the bills of lading. The Eleventh Circuit held that neither bill limited Norfolk Southern's liability to Kirby: the Hamburg Sud bill did not bind Kirby, and

the ICC bill did not reach Norfolk Southern. But the Supreme Court disagreed and—interpreting the bills (contracts) under federal maritime law—reversed, holding that both bills limited Norfolk Southern's liability to Kirby. *Id.* at 36.

For our purposes, the most critical aspect of the opinion is the Court's complete omission of any reference to Carmack, which is particularly odd given that (1) it is a rail-carrier-liability case concerning the defendant rail carrier's attempt to limit its liability to the shipper, i.e., at the very core of Carmack; (2) the Court framed its first issue as a [—27—] conflict between federal and state law, *id.* at 22,[19] even though Carmack fully preempts state law concerning rail carrier liability,[20] (3) at least one *amicus* brief—the United States, acting on the Court's invitation—expressly brought the potential Carmack applicability to the Court's attention;[21] and (4) Carmack came up again at

---

[19] *See Kawasaki*, 130 S. Ct. at 2438-39 ("*Kirby* held that bill of lading provisions permissible under COGSA can be invoked by a domestic rail carrier, despite contrary state law.").

[20] *See Missouri Pacific R.R. v. Porter*, 273 U.S. at 345; *Adams Express*, 226 U.S. at 505.

[21] The United States Solicitor General, accepting the Court's invitation to submit an *amicus curiae* brief, noted the potential applicability of the Carmack Amendment and advised that "[i]t is unsettled whether the Carmack Amendment applies to land transport under international, multimodal through bills of lading, such as the bills in this case." Brief of Amicus Curiae United States, *Norfolk Southern R.R. v. Kirby*, 2003 WL 22762727 at *11.

The Solicitor General further suggested that Kirby may have waived the Carmack issue when it "was not raised in the lower courts or in [its] brief in opposition." *Id.* Kirby replied that it had not waived the Carmack issue but, rather, had argued only the issues decided by the district court on summary judgment and raised to the circuit court on interlocutory appeal. Brief of Respondent Kirby, *Norfolk Southern R.R. v. Kirby*, 2003 WL 22977857 at *9 n.11.

It is questionable whether Kirby could have waived Carmack if it were, in fact, the controlling law. But assuming, *arguendo*, that Kirby could and did waive Carmack, even though it applied, it is unlikely that the Court would omit the controlling

oral argument, albeit as merely a passing reference.[22] There can be little doubt that if Carmack applied it would significantly alter the analysis and outcome (e.g., prohibiting Norfolk Southern from limiting its liability by contract, voiding the overlapping Hamburg Sud bill of lading, and applying its burden-shifting framework to resolve Kirby's merits analysis). Con-sequently, the most reasonable explanation for the Court's omission is that it determined, *sub silentio*, that Carmack did not apply.

Instead, the Court applied COGSA in assessing the rail carrier's liability. The Court acknowledged that COGSA would not apply to the rail carrier "by its terms," unless the parties extended it by contract, and explained that the parties had done just that in the bills of lading:

> By its terms, COGSA governs bills of lading for the carriage of goods from the time when the goods are loaded on [to the ship] to the time [—28—] when they are discharged from the ship. For that period, COGSA's 'package limitation' operates as a default rule. But COGSA also gives the option of extending its rule by contract. As COGSA permits, [ICC and] Hamburg Sud in [their] bill[s] of lading chose to extend the [COGSA] default rule to the entire period in which the machinery would be under [their] responsibility, including the period of the inland transport. [They] would not enjoy the efficiencies of the default rule if the liability limitation [they] chose did not apply equally to all legs of the journey for which [they] undertook responsibility. And the apparent

purpose of COGSA, to facilitate efficient contracting in contracts for carriage by sea, would be defeated.

Id. at 29 (citations and certain quotation marks omitted). That is, to the extent that Carmack would have applied to the rail carriage in this case, the two "extension" clauses in the bills of lading—the Clause Paramount (contractually extending COGSA to the overland portions of the carriage) and the Himalaya Clauses (contractually extending COGSA to the rail carrier subcontractor)—trumped Carmack, rendered it wholly inapplicable (to the point of omission), and replaced it with COGSA.

Put another way, parties to a maritime contract for intermodal through carriage (i.e., ocean carriage containing a rail leg) can contract for COGSA coverage throughout, and exclude Carmack entirely, with a properly written Clause Paramount and Himalaya Clause. This premise begets three questions, which—not coincidentally—are the three questions the Court answered in *Kirby*: (1) what is a maritime contract; (2) what is a sufficient Himalaya Clause; and (3) can an intermediary really limit the subcontractor's liability to the shipper without the shipper's knowledge or consent.

The Court emphasized its "conceptual approach" to identifying maritime contracts: "so long as a bill of lading requires *substantial* carriage of goods by sea . . . it is a maritime contract [but] . . . [i]f a bill's *sea* components are *insubstantial*, then the bill is not a maritime contract." *Id.* at 27 (emphasis added). Most pertinent for our purposes here, this test draws no distinction between imports and exports, and actually rejects "a rule . . . that depends solely on geography." *Id.* As written, even if the *Kirby* shipment had left Alabama bound for Australia via the port at Savannah, one would expect the Court to have employed the same test and reached the same result. [—29—]

Next, the Court held that Himalaya Clauses that are written broadly (i.e., covering "any" servant or contractor) must also be read broadly, to include any foreseeable

---

law without explanation. It is more likely that the Court found that Carmack did not apply.

[22] *See* Oral Argument Transcript, *Norfolk Southern R.R. v. Kirby*, No. 02-1028, 2004 WL 2348277 at *24. *See also* Wm. Baldwin, Comment, *Land Versus Sea; Carmack v. COGSA: Why the Carmack Amendment Should Not Apply to Inland Portions of Multimodal Shipments*, 82 Tul. L. Rev. 731, 743 (2007) (finding it peculiar that the *Kirby* Court ignored the Carmack aspect of the case "even though the issue was mentioned briefly during oral arguments").

subcontractors as intended beneficiaries, thus rejecting a rule of "linguistic specificity or privity." *Id.* at 31. That is, despite the parties' failure to specifically include a rail carrier in the Himalaya Clause, the term "any" and the necessity of rail carriage to complete the journey established the rail carrier's inclusion:

> Thus, the parties must have anticipated that a land carrier's services would be necessary for the contract's performance. It is clear to us that a railroad like Norfolk was an intended beneficiary of the ICC bill's broadly written Himalaya Clause. Accordingly, Norfolk's liability is limited by the terms of that clause.

Id. at 32. This was a direct reversal of the Eleventh Circuit's rule.

Finally, the Court held that the intermediary can act as the shipper's agent for the single, limited purpose of binding the shipper "to the liability limitations it negotiates with downstream carriers." *Id.* at 34. The shipper is not without recourse, however, as the shipper may sue the intermediary for any loss that exceeds the limit to which the intermediary bound the shipper. *Id.* at 35.

So *Kirby* appears to contain two of our recurring, underlying, but often unstated premises. The first would be that Carmack does not apply to an unbroken transaction of commerce with an overseas foreign country. The other is that a shipper may sue a subsequent carrier under a through contract (here a subcontractor's subcontractor), despite the absence of express contractual privity between the shipper and that carrier. *See Kawasaki*, 130 S. Ct. at 2456 n.8 (Sotomayor, J., dissenting) ("In *Kirby*, . . . we took as a given that the shipper could sue the inland rail carrier, even though the shipper was not a party to the rail carrier's bill of lading with an intermediary.").

In its most recent case, *Kawasaki Kisen Kaisha Ltd. v. Regal-Beloit Corp.*, 561 U.S. --, 130 S. Ct. 2433, 2438-39 (2010), the Court considered this same scenario again—an overseas import of goods shipped under a through bill of lading—but this time addressed the Carmack issue. This case involved an import from China to [—30—] Oklahoma via the port at Long Beach, California.[23] The shipper (Regal-Beloit) hired an ocean carrier (Kawasaki Kisen, a.k.a. K-Line) to perform the through carriage, and K-Line hired a rail carrier (Union Pacific R.R.) to complete the overland portion. K-Line issued a through bill of lading to Regal-Beloit; Union Pacific did not issue any bill of lading. The K-Line bill of lading contained five pertinent provisions: (1) a Himalaya Clause, extending limitations of liability to K-Line's subcontractors (e.g., Union Pacific); (2) a Subcontracting Clause, authorizing K-Line to subcontract at its discretion; (3) a Clause Paramount, extending COGSA's terms to cover the entire journey, including the overland portions; (4) a Choice of Law Clause, designating Japanese law; and (5) a Forum Selection Clause, designating the Tokyo District Court.

When the train derailed in Oklahoma, Regal-Beloit sued K-Line and Union Pacific in California state court, and the case was removed immediately to federal district court. After the district court dismissed based on the Tokyo Forum Selection Clause (premised on its underlying holding that the Clause Paramount extended the COGSA bill of lading to the rail portion of the journey and the Himalaya Clause extended it to cover Union Pacific), the Ninth Circuit reversed, holding that "the Carmack Amendment . . . trumped the [COGSA-based contract, and its] forum-selection clause." *Id.* at 2440. On certiorari, the Court said "[t]he forum selection provision . . . gives rise to the dispute here," but framed the issue far more broadly as "whether Carmack applies to the inland segment of an overseas import shipment under a through bill of lading." *Id.* And:

> The instant cases present a question neither raised nor addressed in *Kirby*. It

---

[23] There were actually four shippers, with four bills of lading, to four different locations in the Midwestern United States. But because all relevant aspects are identical, we will treat this as one shipper and one shipment.

is whether the terms of a through bill of lading issued abroad by an ocean carrier can apply to the domestic part of the import's journey by a rail carrier, despite prohibitions or limitations in another federal statute. That statute is known as the Carmack Amendment and it governs the terms of bills of lading issued by domestic rail carriers. 49 U.S.C. § 11706(a). [—31—]

Id. at 2439. The Court chose not to explain why this question was left unaddressed in *Kirby*, despite expressly acknowledging the similarity of the fact patterns, *id.* at 2438, and asserting that "[m]uch of what the Court said in *Kirby* applies to the present case[]," *id.* at 2442. Moreover, the Court did not pick up or begin where *Kirby* left off, with the preeminence of maritime contracts.

The Court began by deconstructing the text of the Carmack statute, saying: "Carmack divides the realm of rail carriers into three parts: (1) receiving rail carriers; (2) delivering rail carriers; and (3) connecting rail carriers." *Id.* at 2442. A "receiving rail carrier" is the initial carrier to receive the cargo from the shipper "at the journey's point of origin" and the only carrier that must issue a bill of lading pursuant to Carmack's requirements; a "delivering rail carrier" is the last carrier to deliver the cargo; and a "connecting carrier" is any and every carrier in between. *Id.* at 2443. The Court emphasized that the term "receiving rail carrier" is a statutory term of art, as defined above, not just "any rail carrier that in the colloquial sense 'received' the property from another carrier." *Id.*

The Court then pivoted on the "receiving rail carrier" term, explaining that this term not only categorizes a particular carrier under Carmack (for purposes of identifying the liable carrier and the carrier responsible for the bill of lading), but also determines whether Carmack even applies to a shipment. The Court held that Carmack applies only to shipments for which there is a receiving carrier required to issue a Carmack bill of lading—meaning, a road or rail carrier that is *both* subject to STB jurisdiction *and* receiving cargo from the shipper at the journey's point

of origin. *Id.* at 2443. No "receiving carrier" means no Carmack bill of lading, which means no Carmack applicability (despite the involvement of carriers that would qualify as "connecting" or "delivering" rail carriers). *Id.*; *see also id.* at 2449 (concluding that "[b]ecause the journey included no receiving rail carrier that had to issue bills of lading under Carmack, [—32—] Carmack does not apply"). This was a novel approach in that no court had previously assessed Carmack's applicability quite this way.[24]

So Carmack's threshold question is whether the carriage begins with an as-defined "receiving rail carrier"; i.e., as the Court put it, "ascertaining the shipment's point of origin is critical to deciding whether the shipment includes a receiving rail carrier," *id.* at 2443. The analysis, to which we have added some bracketed explanatory language, follows:

> [F]or Carmack's provisions to apply the journey must begin with a receiving rail carrier, which would have to issue a Carmack-compliant bill of lading. It follows that Carmack does not apply if the property is received [from the shipper, and the journey begins] at an overseas location under a through bill that covers the transport into an inland location in the United States. In such a

---

[24] The dissent contested the majority's point-of-origin requirement for "receiving" carriers and insisted that Carmack applies to *any* carrier under the STB's jurisdiction, essentially any road or rail carrier in the United States:

Once a first domestic rail carrier subject to the [Surface Transportation] Board's jurisdiction receives property in the United States, Carmack attaches, regardless of where the property originated. Carmack then applies to any other rail carrier subject to the Board's jurisdiction in the chain of transportation, no matter whether the ultimate destination of the property is in the United States or elsewhere, for the period the carrier is traveling within the United States.

Id. at 2451 (Sotomayor, J., dissenting; joined by Stevens and Ginsburg, JJ.).

case, there is no . . . rail carrier [subject to the jurisdiction of the STB] that receives the property [directly from the shipper to begin the journey in the form of] domestic rail transportation, and thus no carrier that must issue a Carmack-compliant bill of lading. The initial carrier in that instance receives the property at the shipment's [overseas] point of origin[, which is not subject to the jurisdiction of the United States STB,] for overseas multimodal import transport, not for domestic rail transport. . . .

The present cases illustrate the operation of these principles. Carmack did not require K Line to issue bills of lading because K Line was not a . . . rail carrier [hence, not subject to the United States STB's jurisdiction]. K Line[, an ocean carrier,] obtained the cargo [from Regal-Beloit, at the journey's point of origin] in China for overseas transport across an ocean [by ship] and then to inland destinations in the United States [by rail, via subcontractor Union Pacific]. K Line shipped this property under COGSA-authorized through bills of lading. That K Line chose to use rail transport to complete one segment of the journey under these <u>essentially maritime contracts</u> does not put K Line within [—33—] Carmack's reach and thus does not require [K Line] to issue Carmack bills of lading [as a Carmack-defined 'receiving carrier'].

As for Union Pacific, it was also not a receiving rail carrier under Carmack. The cargo owners conceded at oral argument that, even under their theory, Union Pacific was a mere delivering carrier, which did not have to issue its own Carmack bill of lading. This was a necessary concession.[25] A carrier does not become a receiving carrier simply by accepting goods for further transport from another carrier in the middle of an international shipment under a through

bill. After all, Union Pacific was not the 'initial carrier' for the carriage [from the point of origin].

Id. at 2444-45 (quotation marks and citations omitted; paragraph break and emphasis added).[26]

Despite the included reference to "essentially maritime contracts" and the associated allusion to *Kirby*, this Carmack-focused analysis is clearly different from *Kirby*'s "conceptual approach" to maritime-contract-applicability analysis, *see Kirby*, 543 U.S. at 27. Under *Kirby*'s "conceptual approach," one would consider the entire journey described in the through bill as a single journey and decide whether that journey contained "substantial" sea carriage, thereby making the through bill a "maritime contract" and invoking the predominant interest in the uniform application of maritime law over conflicting interests (or laws). *Id.* at 28-29. Reciprocally, if the journey contained only "insubstantial" sea carriage, the through bill would be some other type of contract, *see id.* at 27 ("If a bill's *sea* components are insubstantial, then the bill is not a maritime contract."), perhaps a railroad contract if rail carriage were the predominant portion of the journey. But under the analysis from the forgoing passage from *Kawasaki*, 130 S. Ct. at 2444-45, Carmack can *never* apply to a through carriage originating overseas, no matter how "insubstantial" the sea portion of the carriage might [—34—] be or how overwhelming the rail portion of the carriage might be,[27] because carriage originating

---

[25] The inclusion of this sentence is curious, and both its basis and purpose are unexplained.

[26] It is perhaps noteworthy that the Court's express designation of Union Pacific as the Carmack-defined "delivering" carrier did not alter the analysis, which is based entirely on the Carmack receiving carrier.

[27] Consider, for example, an import from Havana, Cuba, destined for Tacoma, Washington, via the Port of Miami. Under the "conceptual approach" in *Kirby*, 543 U.S. at 27, the 230-mile sea portion would appear insubstantial in relation to the 3,300-mile overland portion, thereby signifying a railroad contract and not a maritime contract. Because numerous cases (from *Adams Express* to *Kirby*) have held that federal law (specifically Carmack) preempts state law, while *Kirby* would preclude federal maritime law and *Kawasaki* would

overseas could not satisfy *Kawasaki*'s requirement for a receiving rail carrier.

At this point in its opinion, the Court had answered the question before it (as the Court had framed it), holding that Carmack does not apply to the inland segment of an overseas import shipped under a through bill of lading because there is no "receiving carrier." And the Court announced that it "need not address the instance where goods are received at a point in the United States for export." *Id.* at 2444. The Court, however, continued:

> If a [rail] carrier like Union Pacific . . . w[ere] . . . a receiving carrier under Carmack, this would in effect outlaw through shipments under a single bill of lading. This is because a carriage like the one in the present case would require two bills of lading: one that the overseas carrier (here, K Line) issues . . . under COGSA, and a second one that the first domestic rail carrier (here, Union Pacific) issues . . . under Carmack. *Kirby* noted the popularity of through bills of lading, in which cargo owners can contract for transportation across oceans and to inland destinations in a single transaction. The Court sees no reason to read COGSA and Carmack to outlaw this efficient mode of international shipping by requiring these journeys to have multiple bills of lading.

Id. at 2445. So, although expressly declining to decide whether Carmack applies to overseas exports that begin with a rail carrier (i.e., a Carmack receiving rail carrier), the Court nonetheless offered this bit of reasoning, which is as applicable here to exports as it is to imports.

Further, the Court declared that "the interpretation of Carmack the Court now adopts attains the most consistency between Carmack and COGSA." *Id.* at 2447. The Court's discussion is confined to *imports*, but it is difficult if not impossible to [—35—]

---

preclude Carmack, it appears that some type of federal common law would govern this situation.

distinguish an *export* situation when viewed in light of these policy arguments. Consider this part of the discussion, which includes bracketed language relative to exports:

> Applying two different bill of lading regimes to the same through shipment would undermine COGSA and international, container-based multi-modal transport. As *Kirby* explained, the international transportation industry clearly has moved into a new era—the age of multimodalism, door-to-door transport based on efficient use of all available modes of transportation by air, water, and land.

> If Carmack applied to an inland segment of a shipment [to or] from overseas under a through bill, then one set of liability and venue rules would apply when cargo is damaged at sea (COGSA) and another almost always would apply when the damage occurs on land (Carmack). Rather than making claims by cargo owners easier to resolve, a court would have to [first] decide where the damage occurred to determine which law applied. As a practical matter, this requirement often could not be met; for damage to the content of containers can occur when the contents are damaged by rough handling, seepage, or theft, at some unknown point. Indeed, [such an] approach would seem to require rail carriers to open containers at the port to check if damage has been done during the sea voyage [or, reciprocally, require sea carriers to open the containers at the port to check if damage had been done during the rail carriage]. This disruption would undermine inter-national container-based transport. The Court will not read Congress' non-substantive recodification of Carmack in 1978 to create such a drastic sea change in practice in this area.

> Applying Carmack's provisions to international import [or export] shipping transport would also undermine the purpose of COGSA, to facilitate efficient

contracting in contracts for carriage by sea. Th[is] case[] provide[s] an apt illustration. The sophisticated cargo owner[] here [i.e., Regal-Beloit] agreed to maritime bills of lading that applied to the inland segment through the Himalaya Clause and authorized K Line to subcontract for that inland segment on any terms whatsoever. [Regal-Beloit] thus made the decision to select K Line as a single company for [its] through transportation needs, rather than contracting for rail services [itself]. The through bills provided the liability and venue rules for the foreseeable event that the cargo was damaged during carriage. Indeed, [Regal-Beloit] obtained separate insurance to protect against any excess loss. . . .

. . .

Congress has decided to allow parties engaged in international maritime commerce to structure their contracts, to a large extent, as they [—36—] see fit. It has not imposed Carmack's regime, textually and historically limited to the carriage of goods received for domestic rail transport, onto what are essentially maritime contracts.

Id. at 2447-49 (paragraph break inserted; editorial marks, quotation marks, and citations omitted) (language relative to "exports" added in brackets). Clearly, the validity of these points does not turn on whether the shipment was an import or an export.

Thus, in light of the foregoing, the rule of *Kawasaki* appears to be that Carmack does not apply to the overseas shipment of goods— import or export—shipped under a single through bill of lading. This is consistent with the Court's prior dicta and outcomes. *See Missouri Pacific R.R. v. Porter*, 273 U.S. at 345; *Reider*, 339 U.S. at 117; *id*. at 120 (Frankfurter, J., dissenting) ("the Carmack Amendment does not apply to an unbroken transaction of commerce with a nonadjacent foreign country"); *Kirby*, 543 U.S. at 29. And lower courts are coming to that same view.

C.

The courts that have considered whether Carmack applies to the inland segment of an overseas export have come down on both sides of the question; some initially applying Carmack based on the existence of the receiving carrier (i.e., a rail carrier that is *both* subject to STB jurisdiction *and* receiving cargo from the shipper at the journey's point of origin), but more recently rejecting it based on the arguments and rationale favoring COGSA and maritime contracts.

In the only Sixth Circuit case of significance on this issue, *American Road Service Company v. Consolidated Rail Corporation*, 348 F.3d 565, 568 (6th Cir. 2003), we held that Carmack "does not extend to a shipment under a through bill of lading unless a domestic segment of the shipment is covered by a separate domestic bill of lading." Because this opinion concerned an import, predated *Kirby* and *Kawasaki*, and included reasoning that has since been rejected, it is of limited value for our present purposes, even though it is generally consistent with *Kirby* and *Kawasaki*. [—37—]

Since *Kawasaki*, the Southern District of New York has issued conflicting opinions on Carmack's applicability to the rail leg of an overseas export under a through bill. In *American Home Assurance Co. v. Panalpina, Inc.*, No. 07-cv-10947, 2011 WL 666388 (S.D.N.Y. Feb. 6, 2011), the court considered an export of forklifts, from Illinois to Australia via a California port, under a single through bill (containing a Himalaya Clause, a Clause Paramount, and COGSA coverage). When the train derailed, the shipper sued the rail carrier (BNSF) and the court relied on *Kawasaki*'s "receiving rail carrier" analysis, holding that "Carmack applies when the first rail carrier in the chain of transportation accept[s] the cargo at the shipment's point of origin" and that "Carmack provides the default legal regime governing the inland leg of a multimodal shipment originating within the United States and traveling on a through bill of lading." *Id*. at *4. This was not appealed. In *Hartford Fire Insurance Co. v. Expeditors International*, No. 10-cv-5643, 2012

WL 2861433 (S.D.N.Y. July 9, 2012), the court considered an export of solar panels, from Massachusetts to France via a New York port, under a single through bill, and granted summary judgment to a connecting carrier based on *Kawasaki*'s receiving-carrier analysis. The court added some reasons for rejecting Carmack:

> There are two additional reasons why Carmack does not apply in this instance.
>
> First, [the] plaintiff sued based upon the Bill of Lading issued by [the receiving carrier] and thus, is bound by its terms. The Bill of Lading clearly states that COGSA applies to [the receiving carrier] and its subcontractors.
>
> Second, . . . Congress has not imposed Carmack's regime onto what are essentially maritime contracts. Where a bill of lading requires substantial carriage of goods by sea, its purpose is to effectuate maritime commerce—and thus it is a maritime contract. The Bill of Lading—and the undisputed facts regarding the transport—evidence that a substantial part [of the contract] depended [on] carriage of the goods to France via sea.
>
> For all of those reasons, the [c]ourt finds that COGSA, not the Carmack Amendment, applies to the question of liability before the [c]ourt. [—38—]

Id. at *6 (quotation marks and citations omitted). This was not appealed. Finally, in *Royal & Sun Alliance Insurance v. Service Transfer, Inc.*, No. 12-cv-97, 2012 WL 6028991 (S.D.N.Y. Dec. 4, 2012), the court considered the export of human plasma, from Kentucky to Austria via a Virginia port, under a single through bill, and rejected Carmack applicability even though the initial carrier (a truck, not a train) was subject to STB jurisdiction and putatively subject to Carmack, explaining:

> Being the first carrier does not necessarily make [initial-carrier] STI the 'receiving' carrier for the purposes of Carmack coverage. Instead, the 'receiving' carrier is the 'principal' party to the contract governing the subject shipment and is responsible for the whole carriage. In other words, it is the carrier which holds unity of responsibility for the transportation to [the] destination. . . .
>
> . . .
>
> Here, it is undisputed that STI was not the carrier responsible for the entire course of the shipment. [The shipper] signed the single Waybill and paid [the coordinating carrier] a single 'all-in' through rate to handle the shipment of goods from Kentucky through to its final destination in Austria. Therefore, STI did not function as a 'receiving' carrier, and the Carmack Amendment does not apply.
>
> This outcome is consistent with the Supreme Court's emphasis on efficiency in international maritime trade.

Id. at *4 (footnote and certain quotation marks omitted) (citing *Missouri K & T v. Ward*, 244 U.S. at 388, and *Mexican Light & Power*, 331 U.S. at 734). While this proposition is somewhat difficult to reconcile with *Kawasaki*, the court did rely on *Kawasaki* for a follow-up (broader) proposition:

> Although the Supreme Court has not addressed the present circumstances, where goods are received at a point in the United States for export, the same reasoning [the Court used in rejecting Carmack in *Kawasaki*] applies to those contracts which create a single transaction for shipments across inland segments to overseas destinations.

Id. This case was not appealed. Based on these cases, the Southern District of New York seems to have done a turnabout on this, from applying Carmack originally to now rejecting it outright. [—39—]

In *Norfolk Southern Railway v. Sun Chemical*, 735 S.E.2d 19 (Ga. Ct. App. 2012), the Georgia Court of Appeals considered an export of ink from Kentucky to Brazil via a port in Savannah, Georgia, under a through bill issued by the ocean carrier (subcontracting the rail carrier, Norfolk Southern). When the train derailed, Sun Chemical sued Norfolk Southern under Carmack. The Georgia court relied on *Kirby* to construe the bill of lading as a maritime contract, thereby precluding Carmack. *Id.* at 27. The court also opined that while *Kawasaki* had expressly excluded the export scenario from its decision, it had nonetheless "also answered the broader question" and rejected Carmack applicability "in a case involving a through bill of lading for land and sea transit of goods, [in which] a domestic rail carrier not in privity with the owner of the goods . . . ha[d] made alternate contractual arrangements with the owner's agent." *Id.* at 25. Finally, the court discussed in some detail the aforementioned cases from the Southern District of New York, concluding:

> We think that the Southern District of New York's more recent decision in *Expeditors* implements *Kirby*'s and *Kawasaki Kisen*'s objectives of promoting efficient maritime contracting more effectively than the earlier *Panalpina* decision, and that federal law requires us to uphold the bargained-for terms of the through bill of lading before us, including its binding of Sun to its downstream agent Riss's refusal of the Carmack liability offered by Norfolk Southern.

Id. at 27. The end result, then, was the denial of Carmack applicability in this export case.

D.

This brings our attention back to the predominant question in the present case. Does Carmack apply to the road and rail legs of an overseas *export* shipped under a single through bill? Although the Supreme Court left this question unanswered, it nonetheless provided guidance for future decisions, from

which the prevailing trend is that Carmack does not apply to this situation. [—40—]

Under the *Kirby* "conceptual approach," 543 U.S. at 27-29, we must first determine whether the shipping contract (bill of lading) at issue is a maritime contract[28] and, if so, enforce that contract under maritime law,[29] over any conflicting interests or laws. Here, the Service Contract governs the carriage from Harrodsburg to Tainan, a journey which contains substantial sea carriage,[30] making the Service Contract a "maritime contract." *See id.* As a maritime contract, it would effectively preempt any Carmack applicability and instead govern by its own terms. *Id.* There can be little doubt that this theory comports with *Kirby*'s grand view, in general, of maritime contracts.

Any doubt would come from *Kawasaki*, particularly if we invert *Kawasaki*'s holding mechanistically to fit it to our facts, fail to follow it all the way through, and perhaps add language that is not actually there. This presents a beguiling conclusion to which at least one court appears to have leapt, while

---

[28] "Conceptually, so long as a bill of lading requires *substantial* carriage of goods by sea, its purpose is to effectuate maritime commerce—and thus it is a maritime contract." *Kirby*, 543 U.S. at 27 (emphasis added).

[29] The application of federal maritime law actually requires a "two-step analysis." *Kirby*, 543 U.S. at 23. In the first step, the contract must be a "maritime contract." *Id.* at 23-27. In the second, the case must not "so implicate local interests as to beckon interpretation by state law." *Id.* at 27-29. There are no local interests in the present case, certainly none more pervasive than those in *Kirby*, and therefore this second step is easily satisfied here.

[30] The sea carriage portion of this journey, from Tacoma to Kaohsiung, is approximately 6,225 miles across the Pacific Ocean, which is undoubtedly "substantial." This is not in dispute, nor is it open to reasonable dispute. For comparison purposes, the overland portions of this journey total approximately 2,500 miles. Having said that, we do not read *Kirby* as holding, nor do we hold here, that distances (alone or relative) are determinative of whether the sea portion of the journey is "substantial"; *Kirby* leaves the definition of "substantial" open to future consideration.

overlooking the logical chasm beneath. *See Panalpina*, 2011 WL 666388 at *4.

Under the *Kawasaki* "receiving-carrier approach," 130 S. Ct. at 2442-45, we determine whether the carriage begins with a Carmack-defined "receiving carrier"[31] and, *if not*, then disregard Carmack and enforce the contract on its terms. *See also id.* at 2449 ("Because the journey included no receiving rail carrier that had to issue bills of lading under Carmack, Carmack does not apply."). But what of our present facts—when the [—41—] carriage *does* begin with a Carmack-defined receiving carrier? It is tempting simply to say that *Kawasaki* requires the result that Carmack *does* apply when carriage *does* begin with a Carmack-defined receiving carrier. But *Kawasaki* does not hold that, expressly or otherwise. In fact, *Kawasaki* expressly declined to so hold. *Id.* at 2444 ("Today's decision need not address the instance where goods are received at a point in the United States for export."). The opinion does state that "for Carmack's provisions to apply the journey must begin with a receiving rail carrier," *id.*, but even that is actually a limitation on Carmack, not an assertion of Carmack applicability. Following the *Kawasaki* opinion all the way through—including the discussion of *Kirby* and COGSA—the inverse of the holding is almost as clear as the holding, albeit not as easily stated as a bright-line rule: when the journey does begin with a Carmack-defined receiving carrier, Carmack may still not apply to a multimodal through bill with a substantial sea component, for all the reasons set out in *Kirby*, such as the practical benefits of through shipments under a single bill of lading, the nuisance or dilemma that a disputed question of fact (i.e., the actual location of the loss or damage) could dictate the determination of the governing law concerning liability or venue, the inefficiencies

of encouraging carriers to open the containers at transfer, and the power of congressional intent in drafting COGSA. *Id.* at 2447-49.

Here, the Service Contract governs the carriage from Harrodsburg to Tainan, a journey which does begin with a Carmack-defined receiving road carrier, but which also implicates all of the *Kirby*-based concerns articulated in *Kawasaki*. Because this is a through carriage under a single contract, applying Carmack to the road and rail portions[32] would cut the through bill into separate components (land and sea), effectively "outlawing" the use of the through bill. *See Kawasaki*, 130 S. Ct. at 2445. In this case, the containers never made it on to the ship, so the court was not presented with a contested question of fact concerning the location of the damage (land or sea) as a predicate to its foremost legal decision, but this would have been a significant issue if a Kaohsiung port employee had discovered the damage rather than the Tacoma [—42—] employee. Even under the present facts, the Carriers dwelled on CNA's inability to prove where the damage actually occurred.[33] And, just as *Kirby* and *Kawasaki* portend, under a scheme in which venue, choice of law, liability, etc., depend on the particular location of the loss or damage, the carriers proceeding with this on-going Service Contract would be well advised to open the sealed containers at transfer to protect their individual interests. Consequently, applying Carmack to the road and rail portions of this single, intermodal journey would undermine the benefits that Congress sought under COGSA and the parties sought in the Service Contract. *See id.* at 2449 ("Congress has decided to allow parties engaged in international maritime commerce to structure their contracts, to a large extent, as they see fit.").

---

[31] Recall that a Carmack-defined "receiving carrier" is a road or rail carrier that is *both* subject to the jurisdiction of the United States Surface Transportation Board *and* receiving the cargo from the shipper at the journey's point of origin, such that it is required under Carmack to issue a Carmack bill of lading. *Kawasaki*, 130 S. Ct. at 2443.

[32] Note that Carmack, by its own terms, applies to road and rail and would not apply to the oversea portion.

[33] In fact, the Carriers' begin their appellate brief to this court with these two sentences: "This case is about a shipment of freight that was damaged at some point in transit. It has not been established how the freight was damaged, where the freight was damaged, or exactly when it was damaged." And this is *after* a jury trial.

As a result, based on the foregoing analysis, considered in light of the aggregation of Supreme Court case law, particularly *Kirby* and *Kawasaki*, as well as our general agreement with the post-*Kawasaki* federal and state court decisions, we hold that the Carmack Amendment does not apply to the road or rail leg of an intermodal overseas export shipped under a single through bill of lading.[34] Therefore, the district court erred by applying Carmack in this case as it did.

We also recognize, however, that the district court's initial decision in March 2009 was prior to *Kawasaki*, and its post-*Kawasaki* decision in September 2012 was without the benefit of the developing decisions from other courts.[35] While we must nonetheless conclude that the district court's decision was in error, we will also consider, [—43—] based on the peculiar facts and circumstances of this case, whether some portion of that error was ultimately harmless. That is, whether it would be prudent to affirm some portion of the judgment in the context of a proper analysis.

III.

In its complaint, CNA asserted three causes of action, purportedly arising under Carmack: breach of contract, bailment, and negligence. In ruling on the summary judgment motions, the district court held that because Carmack applied, it encompassed and preempted these separate causes of action and the case would proceed as a single Carmack cause of action.[36] As explained in the foregoing section, this was in error; Carmack did not apply by its own terms. Instead, the district court should have disregarded Carmack and enforced the Service Contract on its terms.[37]

Meanwhile, because it had applied Carmack and preempted the individual causes of action, the district court did not address the Carriers' motions for summary judgment on CNA's tort-based causes of action, bailment and negligence. The Carriers had argued that CNA could not maintain causes of action in tort because their duties arose solely by contract and, therefore, inasmuch as the Service Contract controlled the case, the only viable claim was for breach of that contract.

Under either federal maritime law or New York law,[38] a plaintiff cannot maintain a tort cause of action based on a defendant's breach of duties that arose solely out of [—44—] their contract. *Int'l Ore & Fertilizer Corp. v. SGS Control Servs., Inc.*, 38 F.3d 1279, 1283 (2d

---

[34] In the district court, CNA had asserted, and the court had relied upon, Carmack as the basis for federal jurisdiction. But in its complaint, CNA also properly asserted diversity jurisdiction. 28 U.S.C. § 1332. Therefore, the inapplicability of Carmack does not divest this case of federal subject matter jurisdiction. And we would perhaps be remiss if we overlooked the fact that, because this is a maritime contract, federal jurisdiction exists pursuant to federal maritime law. *See Wilburn Boat Co. v. Fireman's Fund Ins. Co.*, 348 U.S. 310, 313 (1955) ("Since the [contract] here sued on is a maritime contract the Admiralty Clause of the Constitution brings it within federal jurisdiction.").

[35] Note, for example, how the Southern District of New York did a complete reversal, from applying Carmack in February 2011, *Panalpina*, 2011 WL 666388, to rejecting it in December 2012, *Royal & Sun*, 2012 WL 6028991.

[36] *See* footnotes 12, 13, and 14, *supra*, for the background and particulars of this decision. *See also* Section II.A, *supra*, for Carmack's burden-shifting framework. At trial, CNA proved its Carmack prima facie case (i.e., the cargo was tendered in good condition, it arrived in damaged condition, and actual damages were quantified), so the burden shifted to the Carriers to demonstrate one of the five excepted causes. The Carriers attempted to prove that the damage was due to Corning's "improper" stowing and packing. CNA rebutted this contention and the jury found for CNA, awarding $498,509.91 in damages. The court awarded post-judgment interest, but denied pre-judgment interest.

[37] One term in particular bears mention and some clarification. The Choice of Law provision, § 13.A, dictates that New York state law and federal law govern. Of course, we just established in Section II.D., *supra*, that the Service Contract is a maritime contract pursuant to *Kirby*, 543 U.S. at 27-29, and therefore maritime law governs here. But we relegate this discrepancy to a footnote because "New York law . . . also requires application of federal maritime law to maritime cases." *Sundance Cruises Corp. v. Am. Bureau of Shipping*, 7 F.3d 1077, 1081 (2d Cir. 1993).

[38] The Service Contract specifies either federal or New York law in its choice of law provision.

Cir. 1994) (citing *East River S.S. Corp. v. Transam. Delaval Inc.*, 476 U.S. 858, 872-73 (1986) (federal maritime), and *Clark-Fitzpatrick, Inc. v. Long Island R.R.*, 516 N.E.2d 190 (N.Y. 1987) (New York)); *see also Fireman's Fund Ins. Co. v. Orient Overseas Container Line Ltd.*, 763 N.Y.S.2d 427, 432 (N.Y. Civ. Ct. 2003). The plaintiff's cause of action against such defendant lies in breach of contract.

It is undisputed here that the Carriers' duties arose out of the Service Contract; this case contains no duty (nor breach of any duty) that was not anticipated by and included in the Service Contract. Consequently, we conclude as a matter of law that CNA cannot maintain any actions in bailment or negligence against the Carriers; its cause of action is limited to breach of the Service Contract. Therefore, the district court's denial of these tort causes of action—effectively dismissing them—was ultimately correct and we can affirm this part of the judgment. *See Schlaud v. Snyder*, 717 F.3d 451, 459 n.6 (6th Cir. 2013) (noting that we may affirm on any basis supported by the record).

CNA's sole colorable cause of action is for breach of the Service Contract. Had the district court denied Carmack applicability and dismissed the tort claims, it would have been left with CNA's breach of contract claim and the Carriers' defenses thereto. It is noteworthy that the only two parties to the Service Contract are CNA[39] as the shipper and Hyundai as the carrier. The rail carriers are unnamed "subcontractors" who neither negotiated nor signed the Service Contract. Due to their differing circumstances, we analyze the breach of contract claims against each differently.[40] [—45—]

---

[39] Because CNA, as subrogee, is prosecuting this case as if it were Corning, we will refer to CNA as the merchant- or shipper-side party to the Service Contract, even though Corning is the actual party to the contract.

[40] Throughout the proceedings, the Carriers have had joint representation. More than once, the district court asked counsel whether separate representation was warranted. Each time, counsel (and the Carriers' representatives) answered that the co-defense posed no conflict of interest and that

A.

The rail carriers, Norfolk Southern and BNSF, are Hyundai's "subcontractors"; they are not parties to the Service Contract and, therefore, not in privity with CNA. But, as explained in *Kirby*, 543 U.S. at 32, because the journey contained substantial overland carriage, CNA and Hyundai "must have anticipated that a land carrier's services would be necessary for the contract's performance," thereby making Norfolk Southern and BNSF "intended beneficiaries."

"[T]o the extent a third-party qualifies as an intended beneficiary, it may enforce contract terms in its favor." *In re M/V Rickmers Genoa Litig.*, 622 F. Supp. 2d 56, 72 (S.D.N.Y. 2009) (citing Restatement 2nd of Contracts § 304) (footnote omitted). Thus, in *Kirby*, the rail carrier's status as an intended beneficiary (along with the "broadly written Himalaya Clause" in that case) allowed that rail carrier to invoke that contracts' limitation of liability clauses. *Kirby*, 543 U.S. at 32.

But, more to the point here, "qualifying as an intended beneficiary in no way *creates* contractual obligations on the part of the intended beneficiary." *In re M/V Rickmers*, 622 F. Supp. 2d at 72 (emphasis in original) (citing *Stein Hall & Co. v. S.S. Concordia Viking*, 494 F.2d 287, 291 (2d Cir. 1974) ("While the carrier and the shipper can extend certain contractual protections, such as the limitation on damages, to . . . third-party beneficiaries, they cannot contract to bind an unconsenting third party.")). The "methods for actually binding an intended beneficiary to a bill of lading are [1] showing that the third party exhibited acceptance to be so bound and [2] through an agency relationship with one of the contracting parties. Absent such a showing, contractual obligations cannot be imposed on an intended beneficiary." *Id.* (internal citation omitted).

---

they were satisfied with the joint representation. Consequently, we proceed from the premise that the Carriers have waived any contention that their individual interests are inconsistent or that their defenses diverge in any significant way. The Carriers received the defense they wanted.

Neither Norfolk Southern nor BNSF exhibited any agreement to be bound by the Service Contract (or the Hyundai Regular Form Bill of Lading incorporated therein). To the contrary, each contracted with Hyundai independently, under its own standard transportation agreement. Moreover, the Service Contract, § 4.A, expressly disclaims an agency relationship that would allow Hyundai to act as an agent on behalf of CNA, [—46—] asserting instead that "[Hyundai] shall be deemed an independent contractor with respect to [CNA]."[41] To be sure, *Kirby*, 543 U.S. at 33-34, holds that an intermediary (such as Hyundai) necessarily acts as an agent for the shipper (here, CNA) in relation to the subcontractors (here, Norfolk Southern and BNSF), but not "in the classic sense." Rather, the intermediary acts as the shipper's "agent for a *single, limited* purpose: when [the intermediary] contracts with subsequent carriers for limitation on liability." *Id.* at 34 (emphasis in original). That is, Hyundai was not CNA's agent for purposes of binding Norfolk Southern or BNSF.[42]

---

[41] Of course, merely labeling Hyundai an "independent contractor" does not necessarily make it so. *See, e.g., Langfitt v. Fed. Marine Terminals, Inc.*, 647 F.3d 1116, 1121 (11th Cir. 2011) (discussing the factors commonly employed to distinguish an agent from an independent contractor). Corning hired Hyundai to conduct the entire carriage, paid Hyundai a flat rate, and had no control over any aspect of Hyundai's performance. Hyundai had complete control over the manner and means of performance; the selection, terms, payment, and right to terminate subcontractors; its equipment and materials; and the opportunity to profit. Corning hired Hyundai to perform the predetermined carriage and paid the rate that Hyundai charged for completion of that carriage. This was not an agency relationship.

[42] In Section II.B, *supra*, we acknowledged that the Supreme Court in *Missouri, K & T*, 244 U.S. at 387, treated the initial carrier as an agent for the subsequent carriers to bind them to the contract with the shipper, and accordingly upheld the shipper's lawsuit against them. But that was a Carmack case—and an outlier in the Carmack line of cases at that—while this is a straight breach of contract without Carmack considerations. Given the arm's length transactions between the rail carriers and Hyundai, including the rail carriers' transportation agreements on which their relationships are based, there is no basis to hold

More importantly, *Kirby*, 543 U.S. at 31, held that "contracts for carriage of goods by sea must be construed like any other contracts: by their terms and consistent with the intent of the parties." Here, the Service Contract evinces the parties' clear intent *not* to bind subcontractors (such as Norfolk Southern and BNSF) to CNA, nor to hold them directly liable to CNA for damage to the cargo. As just mentioned, the Service Contract deems Hyundai an independent contractor, and reiterates that "nothing herein contained shall be construed to be inconsistent with that relationship or status." This intent to bind only Hyundai is also evident in the Form Bill of Lading. Section 4(B) allows Hyundai to subcontract at its complete discretion. In Section 4(C), "[Corning] warrants that no claim shall be made against any of [Hyundai]'s Subcontractors or any Subcontractor's Subcontractor." And Section 5(B)(2) specifically provides for Hyundai's liability for damage to the cargo by a subcontractor. Considering these terms [—47—] in this Service Contract as being indicative of the intent of the parties, we find that these subcontractors are not directly liable to CNA.

We conclude as a matter of law that CNA cannot maintain a breach of contract action against the rail carrier defendants, Norfolk Southern and BNSF, in this case. The district court erred by denying their motion for summary judgment on this ground. We reverse the district court's decision and vacate the ensuing judgments against these two defendants, Norfolk Southern and BNSF.

B.

Hyundai is a party to the Service Contract and is in privity with CNA.[43] This is a straight forward breach-of-contract action in which we analyze the Service Contract, pursuant to federal maritime law, to

---

that Hyundai was acting as an agent for the rail carriers in this case.

[43] Again, because CNA, as subrogee, is prosecuting this case as if it were Corning, we refer to CNA as the merchant- or shipper-side party to the Service Contract, even though Corning is the actual party to the contract.

determine the parties' agreed-upon liability scheme as applied to the present circumstances. For example, the contracts at issue in *Kirby* contained "broadly written" Clauses Paramount and Himalaya Clauses (as specifically worded in those contracts) that excluded Carmack, extended COGSA throughout the carriage, and even extended the contracts' provisions to the subcontractor's subcontractor despite the absence of contractual privity. Correspondingly, we must consider the specific clauses as written in the Service Contract and apply them appropriately.

We consider first the Clause Paramount, Form Bill of Lading § 2(B), which extends COGSA inland (beyond the tackles) "when the goods are in the custody of [Hyundai]." The district court held that because the cargo was in the custody of a rail carrier subcontractor when damaged, the Clause Paramount did not apply, inasmuch as, [—48—] by its terms, it applies only to damage occurring to cargo in Hyundai's custody.[44] The district court was correct in this interpretation.

We are further persuaded that this is correct upon consideration of the next provision at issue, which provides for Hyundai's liability when the goods are in the custody of a subcontractor:

> [W]ith respect to . . . damage caused during the handling, storage, or carriage of the Goods by [Hyundai]'s Subcontractor, such liability shall be to the extent to which such Subcontractor would have been liable to [CNA] if it had made a direct and separate contract with [CNA] in respect of such handling, storage, or carriage.

Form Bill of Lading § 5(B)(2). That is, Hyundai proposed (in its Regular Form Bill of Lading), and the parties agreed to, a separate scheme to govern Hyundai's liability for damage to the cargo under circumstances in which a subcontractor, such as a road or rail carrier, damaged the goods.[45]

So pursuant to this provision, Hyundai is liable "to the extent to which [a road or rail carrier] would have been liable to [the shipper] if it had made a direct and separate contract with [the shipper]" for that carrier's portion of the journey. Of course, if a road or rail carrier made a separate contract with the shipper for carriage, it would be subject to Carmack. *See, e.g., Reider,* 339 U.S. at 117. Under Carmack, it would be unable to limit its liability by contract.[46] 49 U.S.C. § 11706(c)(1); *Adams Express,* 226 U.S. at [—49—] 504. And the court would ultimately determine the liability pursuant to Carmack's burden-shifting framework. *See Missouri Pac. R.R.,* 377 U.S. at 137-38.

Based on the foregoing, we conclude as a matter of law and pursuant to the terms of the Service Contract, that CNA's claim for breach

---

[44] In so doing, the district court further concluded *as a matter of contract interpretation* that the Service Contract's limitation-of-liability provisions did not apply in the present circumstances. That is, even though the district court applied Carmack as the overriding law and CNA had moved to deny the limitation of liability on the basis that Carmack prohibits such limitations, *see* 49 U.S.C. § 11706(c)(1), the district court did not base this decision on Carmack.

[45] At oral argument, the Carriers' counsel speculated that this provision was merely a means by which CNA could sue the subcontractors directly, thus governing the subcontractors' liability. We do not read this provision that way. Moreover, because, in § 4(C), "[CNA] warrant[ed] that no claim shall be made against any of [Hyundai]'s Subcontractors," we must conclude that § 5(B)(2) governs *Hyundai's* liability for the subcontractors' conduct.

[46] Certainly, a rail carrier may avoid Carmack liability for container carriage if it offers Carmack coverage to the shipper and the shipper declines. *See Babcock & Wilcox,* 557 F.3d at 141 n.6 (relying on 49 U.S.C. § 10502(e) and § 11706). Because Hyundai stands in the shoes of the rail carrier here, Hyundai could have either been compensated for or avoided Carmack liability by offering Carmack coverage to the shipper, Corning/CNA. But because Hyundai did not offer any Carmack coverage option, Hyundai cannot avoid Carmack liability on this basis. Moreover, the district court determined as a matter of contract [—49—] interpretation that the Service Contract's limitations of liability did not apply to the present circumstances, regardless of Carmack. We agree and affirm that portion of the district court's decision.

of contract by Hyundai for "damage caused during the handling, storage, or carriage of the Goods by [Hyundai]'s Subcontractor"—be it DHL, Norfolk Southern, BNSF, or TMBR— must be resolved under Carmack. Because the district court proceeded on the theory, which the jury later confirmed by its verdict, that the damage occurred while the cargo was in the custody of either Norfolk Southern or BNSF, the court was ultimately correct in its application of Carmack to determine Hyundai's liability and we can affirm this portion of the decision. *See Schlaud*, 717 F.3d at 459 n.6 (we may affirm on any basis supported by the record).

While the district court erred by applying Carmack to this case as a general principle, that error was ultimately harmless because the court would have properly applied Carmack under a straight forward breach-of-contract action. *See* Fed. R. Civ. P. 61 (instructing that "[a]t every stage of the proceeding, the court must disregard all errors and defects that do not affect any party's substantial rights"); 28 U.S.C. § 2111 ("On the hearing of any appeal or writ of certiorari in any case, the court shall give judgment after an examination of the record without regard to errors or defects which do not affect the substantial rights of the parties."); *see also Rosencrantz v. Lafler*, 568 F.3d 577, 588-92 (6th Cir. 2009) (discussing harmless error). We affirm the district court's judgment against Hyundai, in favor of CNA, on the jury award of $498,509.91 in damages.

IV.

CNA contends that the district court erred by denying its motion for prejudgment interest. In its denial, the district court's stated rationale was that "[t]he verdict was [—50—] rendered in this case on the Carmack Amendment claim only [and] [t]he Carmack Amendment does not specifically provide for the recovery of pre-judgment interest . . . ." As explained in the foregoing sections, the district court erred by applying Carmack to this case as a general principle; this case is properly decided on the Service Contract and the applications of the pertinent provisions therein. Therefore, the decision is not based

on "the Carmack Amendment claim only," and this aspect of the district court's rationale for denying prejudgment interest is insupportable. The Service Contract controls.

We are also unpersuaded by the court's additional rationale that "this is not a case in which one party has had the use of the other party's money." By failing to reimburse Corning for the cost of the damaged glass at the time of the accident (and thereby forcing Corning to file a claim with CNA), Hyundai did have the use of Corning's (or CNA's) money during that time. Having said that, the award of prejudgment interest is a matter of discretion, *see Werner Enters. v. Westwind Maritime Int'l*, 554 F.3d 1319, 1328 (11th Cir. 2009), and additional factors may affect the determination.

We necessarily remand this case for reconsideration of the question of prejudgment interest in light of the pertinent provisions of the Service Contract as applied to the present decision. We also direct the court's attention to *In re ClassicStar Mare Lease Litigation*, 727 F.3d 473, 494-97 (6th Cir. 2013), which amplifies our current view of prejudgment interest.

V.

Based on the foregoing, we **AFFIRM** the judgment against defendant Hyundai, **REVERSE** and **VACATE** the judgments against defendants Norfolk Southern and BNSF, and **REMAND** this case to the district court so that it may reconsider the question of prejudgment interest.

(Reporter's Note: Dissenting opinion, in part, on p. 440).

[—51—] O'MALLEY, Circuit Judge, dissenting in part:

I agree with most of the findings in the thorough and thoughtful majority opinion. Specifically, I agree that the Carmack Amendment does not apply to the road or rail leg of an intermodal overseas export shipped under a single through bill of lading. I also agree that CNA cannot maintain actions in bailment or negligence against the carriers, and that its cause of action is limited to a claim for breach of the Service Contract. Finally, I agree that CNA's breach of contract action is available only against Hyundai, not the rail carrier defendants. And, I agree that Hyundai is liable, by contract, for the subcontractor's conduct. It is the next conclusion—the one set forth in section III.B. of the majority opinion—with which I cannot agree.

I do not believe that Hyundai's contractual liability to Corning (and, hence to CNA) "must be resolved under Carmack" as the majority holds. Instead, because Hyundai was authorized as Corning's agent to limit the subcontractor's liability, and did so by and on behalf of Corning, I believe Hyundai's liability is limited to that same extent. Because I believe the majority misreads Form Bill of Lading § 5(B)(2) and improperly construes the extent of Hyundai's liability, I respectfully dissent from the majority's conclusion that Hyundai is liable to CNA to the full extent of the liability specified in the Carmack Amendment.

Form Bill of Lading § 5(B)(2) states that, "with respect to . . . damage caused during the handling, storage, or carriage of the Goods by [Hyundai]'s Subcontractor, such liability shall be to the extent to which such Subcontractor would have been liable to [Corning] if it had made a direct and separate contract with [Corning] in respect of such handling, storage, or carriage."[1] Based on this provision, the majority finds Hyundai liable to CNA to the extent of liability imposed by the Carmack Amendment. The majority finds that, if the rail carriers had separately and directly contracted with [—52—] Corning, those contracts would have been subject to the Carmack Amendment because the subcontractors are domestic rail carriers. Maj. Op. at 48–49. As such, the majority concludes that these rail carriers would have been unable to limit their liability by contract in the absence of an express waiver by Corning, and that Hyundai also may not limit its pass-through liability. *Id.* The majority reaches this conclusion based on the proposition that "a rail carrier may avoid Carmack liability for container carriage if it offers Carmack coverage to the shipper and the shipper declines." *Id.* at 51 n.46 (citation omitted). Because it finds that "Hyundai stands in the shoes of the rail carrier here," the majority concludes that Hyundai cannot avoid Carmack liability on this basis because "Hyundai did not offer [Corning] any Carmack coverage option." *Id.* What the majority fails to recognize, however, is that the rail carriers *did* offer Carmack coverage to Corning, through its agent, and that Corning affirmatively waived that coverage. While Hyundai must fulfill the carrier's obligations to Corning, it actually stood in Corning's shoes for purposes of defining the scope of that liability.

The Service Contract states that "[p]arties agree to allow [Hyundai] to contract or *establish agency* as may be necessary to provide inland transportation or door to door services in international commerce if called for in the rates spelled out in Appendix C." Service Contract, RE:78-6, Page ID #496 at ¶ 2(A) (emphasis added). Then, section 4(B) of the Form Bill of Lading provides Hyundai with the authority to "subcontract *on any terms* the whole or any part of the handling, storage[,] or carriage of the Goods and any duties undertaken by [Hyundai] in relation to the Goods." (emphasis added). Further, Form Bill of Lading § 5(A) states that "[Hyundai], in making arrangements for transportation . . . or handling before loading or after discharge acts only as [Corning's] agent and assumes no responsibility therefor." These provisions, taken together, allowed Hyundai to *establish agency* for purposes of entering into agreements with other carriers *on any terms*. And Hyundai, acting as Corning's agent as

---

[1] The Service Contract incorporates Hyundai's Form Bill of Lading.

outlined in section 5(A), proceeded to subcontract the rail portions of the shipment. Hyundai, fully within its authority, then refused full Carmack liability from the subcontractors, and, accordingly, limited the liability of the subcontractors. Consequently, the analysis should end here, as we know the amount of liability Corning set for the subcontractors through its agent, [—53—] Hyundai. Although Hyundai is ultimately accountable for that liability, it was also authorized to limit its terms.

While the majority points out that Hyundai is defined at places in the Service Contract as an independent contractor, nothing precluded Hyundai from acting as *both* an independent contractor and an agent, depending upon the activity in question. "[N]othing about the title independent contractor invariably precludes someone from being an agent under appropriate circumstances." *United States v. Hudson*, 491 F.3d 590, 595 (6th Cir. 2007) (citing Restatement (Second) of Agency § 2(3) ("An independent contractor . . . may or may not be an agent.")); *Eyerman v. Mary Kay Cosmetics, Inc.*, 967 F.2d 213, 219 (6th Cir. 1992) (noting that "a person may be both an independent contractor and an agent"). Thus, the fact that Hyundai acted as an independent contractor who could not bind the carriers to a direct contract with Corning—pursuant to its express authorization to do so in both the Service Contract and the Form Bill of Lading—does not conflict with Hyundai's ability to act as the agent of Corning for purposes of limiting the scope of the carriers' liability. Hyundai can and did properly limit the subcontractor's liability on behalf of Corning.[2]

In this regard, I specifically disagree with the majority's conclusion that Form Bill of Lading § 5(B)(2) placed Hyundai in the "shoes" of the rail carriers. Section 5(B)(2)

states that Hyundai's "liability shall be *to the extent* to which the *Subcontractor* would have been liable to [Corning] if it had made a direct and separate contract with [Corning] in respect of such handling, storage, or carriage." (emphases added). This provision does not actually place Hyundai in the subcontractor's shoes, it only holds Hyundai liable *to the extent* the *subcontractor* would have been liable to Corning under such circumstances. As such, the hypothetical analysis called for under § 5(B)(2) should not consider whether Hyundai itself offered Corning any Carmack coverage option; it should look to what the *subcontractor* offered to Corning through its agent. It appears, moreover, that the purpose of this provision was to assist Hyundai in segmenting liability [—54—] among the subcontractors in circumstances where the parties could assess the damage to the goods against a *particular* subcontractor; the majority reads far too much into it.

For these reasons, I believe that Hyundai is contractually liable to CNA to the extent, and only to the extent, acting on behalf of Corning, it held the carriers liable: to the tune of $10,000.00, and no more. *See* BNSF Rules, RE: 79-12 at Item 64, Page ID #769; NS Rules, RE: 78-14 at Item 8.6.2, Page ID #591. I note, moreover, that, even if we were to assume that Hyundai did not act as Corning's agent when limiting the carriers' liability, we could not, as the majority does, assume that Corning would not have waived Carmack liability if it had contracted directly with the rail carriers. I believe that we would need to remand for a determination of the amount of liability Corning *would have contracted for* with the subcontractors based upon a consideration of all relevant evidence. On this point, the agreement between Corning and Hyundai is highly relevant. Of particular note, Corning did not request full liability under COGSA by declaring the full value, despite having the option of receiving a greater scope of liability in return for payment of a higher fee. Instead, Corning purchased additional insurance through CNA to cover this difference in liability coverage, opting to pay lower freight costs. Thus, it seems likely Corning would have taken the same approach in a direct and separate contract with the

---

[2] While it may seem odd that Corning would give Hyundai the authority to limit its *own* liability by limiting that of the carriers, that is precisely the arrangement Corning chose. Notably, this is consistent with Corning's overall choices—waiving liability in return for lower shipping charges and choosing, instead, to buy insurance from CNA to cover any damages to the goods transported.

subcontractors vis-à-vis its option for Carmack liability, with its attendant higher cost, by declining full Carmack liability.

For the foregoing reasons, I respectfully dissent from the majority's finding that Hyundai is liable to CNA under the Carmack Amendment; I would limit Hyundai's liability to $10,000.

United States Court of Appeals
for the Sixth Circuit

No. 13-3970

UNITED STATES
VS.
KUMAR

Appeal from the United States District Court for the
Northern District of Ohio at Cleveland

Decided: April 22, 2014

Citation: 750 F.3d 563, 2 Adm. R. 443 (6th Cir. 2014).

Before **ROGERS, McKEAGUE,** and **WHITE,** Circuit Judges.

[—2—] McKEAGUE, Circuit Judge:

After pleading guilty to making a false report of a boat in distress, in violation of 14 U.S.C. § 88(c), defendant Danik Shiv Kumar was sentenced to three months in prison and ordered to pay restitution in the total amount of $489,007.70. In this appeal, he challenges the restitution order on three grounds. Finding no error, we affirm the judgment of sentence.

I

Defendant Danik Kumar was nineteen years old in March 2012 and was enrolled in his first year in the Aviation Technology Program at Bowling Green State University in northwestern Ohio. A licensed pilot, Kumar was given the assignment of flying alone at night from Wood County Airport near Bowling Green to Burke Lakefront Airport in Cleveland, and then back again, after 10:00 p.m. on March 14, 2012. The flight plan required him to fly over a portion of Lake Erie. The first leg of the flight was uneventful. On the return trip, Kumar observed what he believed to be a flare rising from a boat on the lake below. When he reported this sighting to Cleveland Hopkins International Airport, he was instructed to fly lower for a closer look. As he did so, Kumar could not see a boat. Yet, fearful of sounding stupid and hurting his chances of one day becoming a Coast Guard pilot, he reported that he saw additional flares going up. He described a 25-foot fishing vessel with four people aboard wearing life jackets with strobe lights activated.

Kumar's detailed report of four mariners in distress prompted a massive search and rescue mission by the United States Coast Guard, with help from the Canadian Armed Forces. During the next twenty-one hours, four vessels and two aircraft participated in the search, including the *Thunder Bay*, a 140-foot Coast Guard cutter with a crew of about twenty; three smaller rescue boats, each with a crew of four; a 65-foot search and rescue helicopter with a crew of four; and the Canadian CC130 Hercules airplane with a crew of seven. Over a month later, on [—3—] April 25, Kumar admitted to a Coast Guard investigator that his report of a boat in distress had been false.

Kumar was indicted on the charge of making a false distress call, a class D felony per 14 U.S.C. § 88(c)(1). Under § 88(c)(3), one who makes such a false distress call to the Coast Guard is "liable for all costs the Coast Guard incurs as a result of the individual's actions." Kumar pleaded guilty on January 17, 2013. He was sentenced on August 16, 2013 to a prison term of three months and a three-year term of supervised release, and was ordered to pay restitution in the amounts of $277,257.70 to the United States Coast Guard, and $211,750.00 to the Canadian Armed Forces. On appeal, Kumar contends the district court was without authority to order restitution to the Canadian Armed Forces and erred in its calculation of costs incurred by the Coast Guard as a result of his actions.

II

Whether imposition of restitution is permissible under the circumstances is reviewed de novo, but the amount of restitution is reviewed for abuse of discretion. *United States v. Boring*, 557 F.3d 707, 713 (6th Cir. 2009). An abuse of discretion occurs when a ruling is based on an error of law or a clearly erroneous finding of fact, or when the reviewing court is otherwise left with the definite and firm conviction that the district court committed a clear error of judgment.

United States v. Clay, 667 F.3d 689, 693 (6th Cir. 2012); *United States v. Batti*, 631 F.3d 371, 379 (6th Cir. 2011).

A. "All Costs Incurred as a Result"

Prior to imposing sentence, the district court received briefing from the parties on the restitution issues and conducted two hearings. At the first hearing, each side presented the testimony of a financial expert. The government called Commander Kevin Mohr, Chief of Financial Analysis for the Coast Guard. Commander Mohr testified about the Coast Guard's reimbursable standard rates, adopted pursuant to Office of Management and Budget Circular No. A-25 ("OMB A-25") and generally applicable to all Coast Guard units across the nation.

OMB A-25 establishes federal policy regarding fees assessed for government resources. The objective of the policy, consistent with 31 U.S.C. § 9701(a), is to "ensure that each service, [—4—] sale, or use of Government goods or resources provided by an agency to specific recipients be self-sustaining." R. 28-3, OMB A-25 § 5.a, Page ID # 416. It provides that "user charges will be sufficient to recover the full cost to the Federal Government . . . of providing the service, resource or good." *Id.* at § 6.a.2(a), Page ID # 417. "'Full cost' includees all direct and indirect costs to any part of the Federal Government of providing a good, resource, or service." *Id.* at § 6.d.1. These costs include direct and indirect personnel costs, physical overhead, management and supervisory costs, and costs of enforcement, collection and research. *Id.* The Coast Guard's standard reimbursable rates are designed to implement these purposes. They are set forth in Commandant Instruction 7310.1M. R. 28-1, Page ID # 390.

Commander Mohr testified that the standard reimbursable rates are used for budget formulation and for obtaining reimbursement—from federal and non-federal agencies and from responsible parties—for use of or damage to Coast Guard assets. Mohr said the standard rates are also used in seeking restitution in cases like this. The standard rates represent determinations of the hourly costs of using various Coast Guard assets and personnel. The rates are comprised of various components, including direct costs (e.g., labor, employee benefits, fuel, maintenance); support costs (e.g., support activities received from area commands, districts, groups); general and administrative costs (e.g., legal services, payroll processing); pension benefit adjustment (e.g., retirement pay and medical expenses); operating asset depreciation; and operating asset cost of capital. *Id.*, Encl. (1), Page ID # 393.

Mohr explained that the costs Kumar is liable for are determined by multiplying the respective hourly rates by the number of hours the Coast Guard assets and personnel involved in this 21-hour search and rescue operation were deployed. This sum, $277,257.70, Mohr testified, represents the "full cost" sustained by the Coast Guard as a result of Kumar's false report. In Mohr's opinion, this "full cost," as defined in OMB A-25 and implemented by Commandant Instruction 7310.1M, represents "all costs" Kumar is liable for under 14 U.S.C. § 88(c).

Kumar contends this approach places too much emphasis on "all costs" while ignoring the "as a result" limitation. He argues that § 88(c) creates a restitution remedy and that the "as a result" language operates to limit recovery to actual losses proximately caused by his false report. Kumar contends he is liable under § 88(c) only for those costs directly attributable to his [—5—] actions, not for the "indirect costs" included in Commander Mohr's calculation, i.e., support costs, general and administrative costs, pension benefit adjustment, operating asset depreciation, operating asset cost of capital. According to his expert, forensic accountant Dennis S. Medica, when the Coast Guard's costs are limited to "operating costs" (i.e., by deducting from the Coast Guard's estimate all fixed costs that would have been incurred irrespective of Kumar's actions), the recovery is reduced to $118,216.

At the sentencing hearing, the district court confirmed that neither side objected to the other's mathematics. Nor did Kumar challenge any particular items of indirect costs claimed by the Coast Guard. The dispute, then and now, is essentially a legal one, revolving around interpretation of § 88(c). The question is whether "all costs incurred as a result" limits the Coast Guard's recovery to direct costs or also includes indirect costs associated with the deployment of resources as a result of Kumar's false report. R. 44, Sent. tr. at 120-23, page ID # 742-45.

There appears to be little published case law directly on point. The government argues that its position here mirrors the approach uniformly taken in courts across the country in enforcing § 88(c). *See e.g., United States v. Sanders*, 511 F. App'x 463 (6th Cir. 2013) (8-hour search with helicopter involving 38 personnel; restitution of $53,316); *United States v. Emil*, 56 F.3d 65, 1995 WL 322455 (6th Cir.) (restitution of $5,177.28); *United States v. James*, 986 F.2d 441 (11th Cir. 1993) (holding "all costs" includes costs associated with search and rescue mission and subsequent apprehension); *United States v. Crockett*, No. 3:09-cr-345 (N.D. Ohio 2010) (restitution of $112,735.70); *United States v. Haun*, No. 5:06-cr-18 (N.D. Fla. 2006) (holding "all costs" means full reimbursement; restitution of $140,279). The restitution amounts ordered in these cases are less than what the Coast Guard claims in this case, but the government contends this is simply due to the fact that Kumar's false report, detailed and credible as it was, triggered a massive and more expensive response.

Kumar cites other case law showing that, traditionally, restitution has been employed not to punish the wrongdoer, but to restore the victim, whose recovery is therefore limited to actual losses proximately caused by the wrongdoing. *See Hughey v. United States*, 495 U.S. 411, 416 (1990); *United States v. Gamble*, 709 F.3d 541, 546 (6th Cir. 2013); *United States v. Evers*, 669 F.3d 645, 659 (6th Cir. 2012). Kumar is right, and this argument has strong appeal. [—6—] However, none of these cases addressed the law we must construe, 14 U.S.C. § 88(c). As the Court noted in *Hughey*, "in all cases involving statutory interpretation, we look first to the language of the statute itself." *Hughey*, 495 U.S. at 415.

Section 88(c) does not mention "restitution." Yes, it functions in a manner akin to restitution, and Kumar's judgment of sentence refers to restitution, but the statutory language we interpret does not. Nor does it limit the Coast Guard's recovery to its "losses." It makes one who gives a false report liable for *all costs* incurred by the Coast Guard as a result of his actions.

There is no dispute that Kumar's false report proximately caused the mobilization of one Coast Guard aircraft and four vessels, together with their crews and related onshore personnel during a 21-hour period. Nor is there any dispute about the full cost of these resources to the Coast Guard, as measured in hourly reimbursable rates in accordance with accounting standards adopted by the Federal Accounting Standard Advisory Board. Nor is there any dispute that these accounting standards define "full cost" as the total amount of resources used to produce the product or service, including direct and indirect costs. R. 28-5, Statement of Federal Financial Accounting Standards 4, ¶ 89, Page ID # 452. This definition is consistent with the policy established by 31 U.S.C. § 9701(a) and OMB A-25, § 6, discussed above.

Commander Mohr conceded on cross-examination that Kumar's false report did not result in increased indirect costs to the Coast Guard, but recovery under § 88(c) is not limited to increased costs. Section 88(c) renders Kumar liable for *all costs* associated with resources mobilized as a result of his false report. We therefore find no error in the district court's ruling that Kumar is liable under § 88(c) for the full cost of the service rendered by the Coast Guard, $277,257.70.[1] This is an onerous burden to place on the shoulders of a young man, but it is consonant with Congress's manifest intent to deal harshly with such hoaxes, in order to deter

---

[1] As indicated above, Kumar did not challenge below and has not challenged on appeal any particular items of indirect costs claimed by the Coast Guard, and our opinion should not be construed as meaning that "all costs" necessarily entitles the Coast Guard to recovery of all claimed indirect costs in every case.

the diversion of critical resources away from true emergencies. [—7—]

B. Authority to Order Restitution to Canadian Armed Forces

The judgment of sentence also orders Kumar to pay restitution in the amount of $211,750 to the Receiver General for Canada for the Canadian Armed Forces' contribution to the search and rescue mission. In making this order, the district court recognized that 14 U.S.C. § 88(c) does not confer authority to order reimbursement to any party other than the United States Coast Guard. Accordingly, after receiving supplemental briefing from the parties, the district court ruled that it had discretion under 18 U.S.C. § 3583(d) to order restitution as a condition of supervised release. Kumar challenges this ruling, contending that 14 U.S.C. § 88(c), specifically addressing the circumstances under which liability for costs resulting from a false report may be imposed, controls over the more general provision of 18 U.S.C. § 3583(d).

"One of the most basic canons of statutory interpretation is that a more specific provision takes precedence over a more general one." *United States v. Perry*, 360 F.3d 519, 535 (6th Cir. 2004). Yet, canons of construction are resorted to as guides only where there is an apparent conflict between laws, *see id.* (citing *United States v. Castro-Rocha*, 323 F.3d 846, 851 (10th Cir. 2003)), or some other ambiguity that requires the court to go beyond the plain meaning of a statute's text to discern legislative purpose. Again, "in all cases involving statutory interpretation, we look first to the language of the statute itself." *Hughey*, 495 U.S. at 415.

Here, there is neither conflict nor ambiguity in the language of these statutes. Section 88(c) is a very specific statute rendering the one who knowingly and willfully makes a false report liable for all costs incurred by the Coast Guard. It clearly and unambiguously limits this entitlement to the Coast Guard only. This case presents a dispute about the meaning of "all costs," but the scope of the entitlement is otherwise clear:

no victim other than the Coast Guard is entitled to all costs under § 88(c).

Section 3583(d) is, in material respects, similarly clear, albeit wordier. It gives the sentencing court discretion to prescribe, as a condition of supervised release, any condition that may be prescribed as a condition of probation under 18 U.S.C. § 3563(b) (i.e., including restitution under 18 U.S.C. § 3556) or any other condition it considers to be appropriate, so long as it is reasonably related to the sentencing factors prescribed in 18 U.S.C. § 3553(a), involves no [—8—] greater deprivation of liberty than is reasonably necessary, and is consistent with any pertinent policy statements issued by the Sentencing Commission.

Clearly, the Canadian Armed Forces is a victim of Kumar's offense, and Kumar does not challenge the "appropriateness" of the district court's exercise of discretion to order restitution under the above paraphrased language. Rather, Kumar's challenge is limited to the notion that the district court's broad discretionary authority under § 3583(d) is trumped or preempted by the more specific § 88(c). Yet, there being no conflict between the two statutes and no material ambiguity in their language, there is no reason why the two statutes cannot be deemed to coexist and co-operate. There is no support for the notion that § 88(c) reflects a congressional purpose to exclude victims other than the Coast Guard from recovery of losses caused by a false report. We find no error in the district court's determination that it had authority under § 3583(d) to order Kumar to pay restitution to the Canadian Armed Forces.

C. Amount of Restitution

Finally, Kumar contends that even if the district court had authority to order him to pay restitution, the court abused its discretion by doing so based on an inadequate record. He contends the written communications from the Canadian Armed Forces presented by the government lack sufficient indicia of reliability to support the order of restitution. Indeed, no witness testified to the Canadian Armed Forces' losses at the sentencing hearing. While there is no dispute that the Canadian Armed Forces contributed a CC130 Hercules aircraft with seven-man crew to the search and rescue mission for some 12 hours, the record of its losses is less than ideal. It consists of several letters and copies of e-mail messages.

In the first of these, a letter dated December 7, 2012, Major Marty Zimmer claimed the cost associated with operating the CC130 aircraft in this particular search and rescue mission was $211,750. R. 25-11, Page ID # 349. Subsequent communications purported to clarify that this figure was limited to operating costs (i.e., fuel, maintenance, parts, crew and ground and administrative support) based on an hourly rate of $17,500. *See e.g.*, R. 31-5, Sworn Letter, Maj. Zimmer, dated August 8, 2013, Page ID # 587. When additional support costs were added, pursuant to Department of National Defence policy, to determine the "full cost" of the mission, [—9—] the hourly rate increased to $30,792, and the total costs sought to be recovered rose to $372,583 (CAD). *Id.*

It thus appears that the Canadian Armed Forces, like the U.S. Coast Guard, classifies reimbursable rates variously, as either "direct operating costs" or "full cost." Faced with these two figures submitted in support of the Canadian claim, $211,750 and $372,583, the district court ordered Kumar to pay the lesser amount, finding the government had not carried its burden of proving the Canadian Armed Forces' entitlement to the larger amount, full cost, by a preponderance of the evidence.

Kumar contends this order is not supported by sufficient reliable evidence. He acknowledges that a district court may consider hearsay evidence in sentencing, *see Elson*, 577 F.3d at 732, but he argues he was denied fair opportunity to refute it inasmuch as no witness was presented by the government. Also, he argues that the wide discrepancy between the estimates offered indicates the evidence lacks the "minimal indicia of reliability" required to meet due process. *Id.*

The district court found the discrepancy between the two figures submitted by Major Zimmer adequately explained. We agree. That is, the discrepancy does not undermine the reliability of the information presented. Properly understood, the Canadian cost-calculating methodology is similar to the methodology employed by the Coast Guard. Kumar did not challenge the Coast Guard's methodology. It is thus not readily apparent how the lack of a live witness to explain the Canadian methodology materially prejudiced Kumar's opportunity to refute it. Kumar's challenge to the Coast Guard's claimed costs went strictly to the legal question of whether all costs were recoverable or only those costs directly attributable to his false report. Under 14 U.S.C. § 88(c), as explained above, the Coast Guard is entitled to all costs. However, the Canadian Armed Forces cannot recover under § 88(c). Its recovery is limited to restitution, i.e., recovery of actual losses proximately caused by Kumar's wrongdoing. The $211,750 figure adopted by the district court reflects "the cost directly related to employing this aircraft on this particular SAR incident." R. 25-11, Maj. Zimmer letter dated Dec. 7, 2012, Page ID # 349. The $211,750 figure, confirmed by Major Zimmer's sworn letter of August 8, 2013, thus appears to be a reasonable and reliable approximation of the Canadian Armed Forces' actual [—10—] losses directly resulting from Kumar's false report. We therefore find no abuse of discretion in the district court's order of restitution in this amount.

III

Accordingly, defendant Kumar's claims of error are denied and the district court's judgment of sentence is **AFFIRMED**.

(Reporter's Note: Concurring opinion, in part, and Dissenting opinion, in part, on p. 448).

[—11—] WHITE, Circuit Judge, concurring in part and dissenting in part:

I concur in the majority's determinations that the district court had authority to order restitution in favor of the Canadian Armed Forces and that the amount is adequately supported by the record. I dissent from the affirmance of the amount of the obligation imposed under 14 U.S.C. § 88(c).

The question is whether 14 U.S.C. § 88(c), which imposes liability for "all costs the Coast Guard incurs as a result of" a false distress message, contemplates the use of the standard reimbursable rates ("user charges") adopted pursuant to 31 U.S.C. § 9701 and Office of Management and Budget Circular No. A-25. I do not believe it does.

As noted by the majority, OMB A-25 directs that user charges include "an appropriate share of" both direct and indirect costs, including items such as management and supervisory costs, consulting, an annual rate of return, costs of establishing standards, any required environmental impact statements, physical overhead, utilities, depreciation of buildings, costs of supplies, insurance, and unfunded retirement costs. In short, OMB A-25 requires an agency such as the Coast Guard to compute for the open market the "full cost" of its services, which includes all the direct and indirect costs that go into running, maintaining, housing, improving and managing the Coast Guard.

14 U.S.C. § 88(c), enacted in 1990, long after § 9701 became law, is a specific statute speaking directly to the penalties to be imposed on a person who makes a false report to the Coast Guard. Its clear purpose is to require the offender to pay all costs resulting from the false report. Had Congress intended that those costs include general overhead and indirect costs of the type included in user charges established under § 9701 it would have been a simple matter for Congress to refer to § 9701, or any schedule of user charges promulgated pursuant to that provision. However, § 9701 is not cross referenced and user charges are not

mentioned. Instead, the focus of § 88(c) is all costs *resulting* from the false report. [—12—]

Indirect costs and overhead are appropriately included in calculating the "full cost" of a benefit or service for the purpose of calculating a figure that approximates what that benefit or service might cost on the open market, which is the purpose of § 9701. However, these indirect costs are not what one would normally associate with "all costs the Coast Guard incurs as a result of" the false report. Overhead and administrative costs related to research, headquarters, payroll processing, environmental impact studies, building maintenance, and other similar expenses are hardly costs incurred as a result of Kumar's false report.

Further, I find little guidance in the cases cited by the majority. *United States v. Sanders*, 511 F. App'x 463, 465 (6th Cir. 2013), an unpublished opinion, simply states that the defendant was ordered to pay $53,306 in restitution to the Coast Guard. The amount assessed was not a subject of the appeal, and the opinion includes no discussion of how that amount was calculated. Nor does the district court record in that case support the majority's position. The $53,306 figure is found in a spreadsheet attachment to the sentencing transcript as Exhibit B. This spreadsheet lists the personnel involved in the search, the number of hours they were involved, their pay grade, and the hourly rate. It also provides an hourly rate for equipment. There is no information regarding the source of the hourly rates.

United States v. Emil, 56 F.3d 65, No. 94-1871, 1995 WL 322455, at *1 (6th Cir. May 26, 1995), too, is an unpublished opinion that simply states the amount of restitution ordered by the district court, $5,177.28, without any discussion. *United States v. Crockett*, No. 3:09-cr-345 (N.D. Ohio Jan. 19, 2010), is a district court case in which restitution of $112,735.70 was imposed under § 88(c), but nothing in the record indicates how the amount was calculated.

United States v. James, 986 F.2d 441 (11th Cir. 1993), does address the amount of restitution ordered. But the issue there was whether the district court properly included costs associated with locating James' boat after the Coast Guard realized that his distress reports were a hoax. James argued that the additional amounts were not properly assessed because § 88(c) by its terms is limited to costs the Coast Guard incurs when attempting "to save lives and property when no help is needed," and § 89, which deals with law enforcement, has no provision for the repayment of costs incurred as a result of law enforcement efforts. The court rejected James' argument, concluding that § 88(c) "requires that James be held liable for all costs the Coast [—13—] Guard incurred in responding to James' false distress message." *James*, 986 F.2d at 444. The court continued, "*but for* James' actions, the Coast Guard would not have expended any resources on a search and rescue mission and subsequent apprehension," and observed that the line between search and rescue on the one hand and law enforcement on the other may be blurred as a mission develops the sense that there may be a hoax, but continues to search and verify that no one is in danger before terminating a search. *Id.* (emphasis in original). *James* has no relevance to the question whether user charges calculated pursuant to § 9701's all-inclusive approach are properly used to determine the costs incurred as a result of a false distress message.[1]

United States v. Haun, No. 5:06-cr-18-001/RS (N.D. Fla. Aug. 16, 2006), a northern district of Florida case, did involve user charges established pursuant to § 9701. However, in that case the defendant challenged the use of "outside government" rates rather than the lesser "in government" rates. The district court determined that "all

costs" properly included the pension and other costs that were in the outside-government rate but not the in-government rate. The threshold question whether it is proper to the use § 9701 rates to determine amounts owed under § 88(c) was assumed, but not addressed.

Section 88(c) speaks of all costs incurred as a result of the false report; in contrast, § 9701 and OMB A-25 speak of including all costs, direct and indirect, in an effort to price a good or service as it would be priced on the open market and account for all overhead costs that are necessary to run the overall operation but do not result from the fact that the particular good or service was produced or rendered. User charges calculated pursuant to the latter provisions include elements that are not related to a false distress signal and produce an inflated cost figure. I would remand for an adjustment of the penalty imposed under § 88(c).

---

[1] I note also that the *James* court stated that § 88(c) has "no recorded legislative history." However, in the Congressional Record, Representative Studds of Massachusetts, the sponsor of the bill, stated: "If you make a hoax call to the Coast Guard, and the Coast Guard sends out a helicopter or a patrol boat in response, you will be liable for every penny of the Coast Guard's increased operating expenses resulting from the call." 136 Cong. Rec. 7270 (daily ed. Sept. 10, 1990) (H7269-02, H7270).

This page intentionally left blank

United States Court of Appeals for the Seventh Circuit

United States Court of Appeals
for the Seventh Circuit

No. 13-1686

CROMPTON
vs.
BNSF RY. CO.

Appeal from the United States District Court for the
Southern District of Illinois

Decided: March 12, 2014

Citation: 745 F.3d 292, 2 Adm. R. 452 (7th Cir. 2014).

Before **WOOD**, Chief Judge, and **BAUER**, and
EASTERBROOK, Circuit Judges.

[—1—] **BAUER**, Circuit Judge:

Brian Crompton ("Crompton") brought suit against BNSF Railway Company ("BNSF") under the Federal Employment Liability Act, 45 U.S.C. §§ 51-60 and the Locomotive Inspection Act, 49 U.S.C. § 20701. He alleges that he was knocked off a train due to negligence on the part of BNSF. BNSF moved for summary judgment on both counts; the district court denied its motion and allowed the case to [—2—] proceed to a jury. The jury found BNSF liable and awarded damages to Crompton. BNSF now appeals to this Court. The issue before us is whether the evidence presented at trial was sufficient for a jury to conclude that BNSF was negligent. We find that it was and affirm.

I. BACKGROUND

Crompton began work as a railroad conductor for BNSF in 2001. On April 24, 2011, he worked on BNSF 5695, a General Electric AC4400 series locomotive, which was set to travel from Paducah, Kentucky, to Centralia, Illinois. Before the train departed, Bruce Yancey ("Yancey"), a BNSF engineer, performed the required daily inspection. Yancey found no defects with the locomotive, including its doors and latches. During the trip, Crompton exited the front cab door several times, and found nothing wrong with the door or its latch. As the train approached Neilson Junction, it was traveling downhill. Crompton exited the front cab door of the

locomotive to throw a switch so that the train would continue towards Centralia. He asserts that he closed and latched the front cab door before he stepped out onto the platform. The door remained closed for fifty-one seconds, and then it suddenly flew open, knocking Crompton off the train and to the ground. He suffered injuries to his head, neck, and back.

Crompton brought suit against BNSF under both the Locomotive Inspection Act ("LIA") and the Federal Employment Liability Act ("FELA"), claiming that BNSF failed to keep the locomotive and its parts in good working order, and that he was injured due to BNSF's negligence. [—3—]

A. BNSF's Motion for Summary Judgment

BNSF moved for summary judgment on both counts. In response, Crompton attached the depositions of BNSF engineer Yancey, BNSF engineer Lindell David Perry, Jr. ("Perry"), and BNSF machinist Francis Ferry ("Ferry"). Yancey testified that he had ridden on similar model AC 4400 locomotives when the front cab door came open on its own without being opened or operated by a crew member. He also stated that doors coming open were common problems found on AC 4400 locomotives, and that BNSF's management was aware that the front cab doors come open improperly. He stated that he once attended a safety meeting that was called and conducted by BNSF company management due to another employee's injury that was caused by a locomotive's front door coming unlatched and opening. Perry stated that he had been on locomotives similar to BNSF 5695 where the front cab door came open on its own without being opened by a crew member as well, and said that BNSF was well aware of this problem. Ferry inspected BNSF 5695 after the accident, and commented that if the front cab door had been latched by Crompton, it would not have come open absent some sort of defect.

The district court denied BNSF's motion for summary judgment, explaining that a reasonable jury could conclude that the latch was defective. The court found that the evidence, taken in the light most favorable to

Crompton, was sufficient for the case to proceed to a jury. [—4—]

B. The Trial

At trial, Crompton presented the testimony of BNSF engineers Yancey and Perry. Both men testified that they had been on locomotives similar to BNSF 5695 where the front cab door had come open on its own without being unlatched by a crew member. They also asserted that BNSF was aware of this issue. Crompton testified as well, saying he was certain that he had closed and latched the door before he exited the locomotive as the train approached Neilson Junction. He also pointed out that the door remained closed for 51 seconds after he latched it even though the train was traveling downhill. He presented evidence of other types of latches that BNSF could have employed on the front cab door, which he claims would have better secured the door.

BNSF then presented evidence that Yancey conducted a pre-trip inspection of BNSF 5695 on the morning of the accident, but found no defects with the door or its latch; he certified that everything was working properly. Yancey inspected the locomotive again after the accident, and found no defects with the door or its latch. BNSF also presented the expert testimony of machinist Clifford Bigelow ("Bigelow"). Bigelow inspected BNSF 5695 after the accident, and confirmed the absence of a defect in the latch. He stated that he "saw no plausible explanation for that door unlatching by itself without some outside manipulation." Bigelow explained that the handle would have had to move nearly 45 degrees to disengage the door from the door frame, and testified that vibration alone would not be something that could have manipulated the handle open. [—5—]

BNSF also relied on Crompton's testimony. Crompton had used the latch on the front cab door of BNSF 5695 several times during the trip from Paducah to Centralia on April 24, 2011, and testified that he found nothing wrong with the door or its latch. He also acknowledged that he did not notice any excess vibration or any rough spots as the train approached Neilson Junction, and admitted that he did not know why the latch came open.

In addition, BNSF presented evidence that the latch on the front cab door of BNSF 5695 had a perfect safety inspection record. Dana Maryott ("Maryott"), the director of BNSF's maintenance and inspection policies, testified that every locomotive is required to undergo a calendar day safety inspection, which must be recorded in BNSF's database. He explained that if defects are noted during the inspection, those issues are reported to the mechanical desk, which enters the information into the database. Maryott reviewed the maintenance records of BNSF 5695, and found no reports of any defects with its doors or latches. Maryott also presented the daily inspection reports for all BNSF locomotives in the 4400 series, those with doors and latches similar to those on BNSF 5695, and found no reports of any defective doors or latches between January 2002 and March 2012.

After weighing the evidence, the jury found BNSF negligent and Crompton contributorily negligent. The jury allotted 70% of the fault to BNSF and 30% to Crompton. The jury determined that BNSF violated both the FELA and the LIA, a strict liability statute, so BNSF was required to pay 100% of Crompton's damages. The jury awarded $1.6 million to Crompton. [—6—]

BNSF moved for judgment as a matter of law and then moved for a new trial. BNSF argued that since Crompton had produced no evidence of a defect with the door or its latch, the evidence presented was legally insufficient to support a finding of liability. The district court, however, denied BNSF's motions, finding that there was "sufficient evidence from which a jury could conclude that the latch was defective and that BNSF had notice of the defect." The district court explained, "Crompton's testimony that he latched the door coupled with the jury's conclusion that the latch was intended to keep the door closed could reasonably lead the jury to conclude that the door was defective when the door opened after Crompton had latched it." BNSF now appeals.

II. DISCUSSION

This Court reviews sufficiency of the evidence challenges *de novo*, viewing the evidence in the light most favorable to the nonmoving party and drawing all inferences in its favor. *Wis. Alumni Research Found. v. Xenon Pharm. Inc.*, 591 F.3d 876, 885–86 (7th Cir. 2010). We defer to the credibility determinations of the jury, *United States v. Perez*, 612 F.3d 879, 885 (7th Cir. 2010), and will overturn a jury verdict "only when there is a complete absence of probative facts to support the conclusion reached." *Lavender v. Kurn*, 327 U.S. 645, 653 (1946); *Lynch v. Ne. Reg'l Commuter R.R. Corp.*, 700 F.3d 906, 911 (7th Cir. 2012).

A. The FELA

Crompton brought suit against BNSF under the FELA. The FELA imposes on railways a general duty to provide a safe workplace. *McGinn v. Burlington N. R.R. Co.*, 102 F.3d 295, 300 (7th Cir. 1996). It states: [—7—]

> every common carrier by railroad … shall be liable in damages to any person suffering injury while he is employed by such carrier … for such injury or death resulting in whole or in part from the negligence of any of the officers, agents, or employees of such carrier, or by reason of any defect or insufficiency, due to its negligence, in its cars, engines, appliances, machinery, track … or other equipment.

49 U.S.C. § 51.

The FELA provides a "broad federal tort remedy for railroad workers injured on the job," *Williams v. Nat'l R.R. Passenger Corp.*, 161 F.3d 1059, 1061 (7th Cir. 1998), and should be construed liberally to effectuate congressional intent. *Atchison, Topeka & Santa Fe Ry. Co. v. Buell*, 480 U.S. 557, 562 (1987). While a plaintiff must prove "the common law elements of negligence [to prevail in a FELA case], including foreseeability, duty, breach, and causation," *Fulk v. Illinois Cent. R.R. Co.*, 22 F.3d 120, 124 (7th Cir.

1994), a "relaxed standard of causation applies under FELA." *CSX Transp., Inc. v. McBride*, 131 S.Ct. 2630, 2636 (2011). The FELA "vests the jury with broad discretion to engage in common sense inferences regarding issues of causation and fault." *Harbin v. Burlington N. R.R. Co.*, 921 F.2d 129, 132 (7th Cir. 1990). "Courts are not free to reweigh the evidence and set aside the jury verdict merely because the jury could have drawn different inferences or conclusions or because judges feel that other results are more reasonable." *Tennant v. Peoria & Pekin Union Ry. Co.*, 321 U.S. 29, 35 (1944). [—8—]

B. The LIA

Crompton brought suit against BNSF under the LIA as well. The LIA provides that a locomotive and its parts must be "in proper condition and safe to operate without unnecessary danger of personal injury." 49 U.S.C. § 20701(1). The LIA does not create a right to sue, but merely establishes a safety standard; a failure to comply with that standard is negligence per se under the FELA. *Urie v. Thompson*, 337 U.S. 163, 188–89 (1949).

C. Sufficiency of the Evidence

The parties present competing theories of causation in this case: Crompton argues that the latch on the front cab door was defective in some way, which caused the door to come open, while BNSF contends that Crompton never properly latched the door, which is the reason it came open. When faced with alternative theories of causation, it is not our job to decide which theory is more plausible; instead, as long as facts exist to support the jury's conclusion, its verdict must stand. BNSF may not "relitigate the factual dispute" in this court. *Lavender v. Kurn*, 327 U.S. at 652.

The Supreme Court's opinion in *Lavender v. Kurn* proves instructive. Haney, a railroad employee, was operating a switch one evening so that a train could reenter the station. *Id.* at 647. After the train passed the switch, Haney was found on the ground nearby, unconscious. *Id.* at 648. He had been struck in the back of the head by "some fast moving small round object." *Id.* A doctor testified that the object may have been attached to a slow-moving train, but also admitted that Haney's skull fracture may have been caused by a blow from [—9—] a pipe or a similar object. *Id.* at 649. The parties presented conflicting theories of causation: the plaintiff asserted that Haney was struck in the back of the head by a hook that protruded from the side of the rail car, whereas the railroad theorized that Haney was murdered for his money by one of the "tramps and hoboes" who frequented the area. *Id.* If the first theory was accurate, then the railroad was liable for Haney's death. The hook was affixed to the train at a height about a foot taller than Haney. *Id.* However, if Haney had been standing on a mound of dirt located near the track at just the right moment, he may have been sufficiently tall enough for the hook to have struck him in the head. *Id.* Other evidence, supporting the railroad's theory, showed that Haney's pistol was found loose under his body, and that his empty wallet was recovered about a block away. *Id.* at 650. The jury found the railroad liable, but the Missouri supreme court reversed. *Id.* at 651. The Supreme Court then reinstated the jury's verdict. *Id.* at 652. The Court explained that even though the evidence tended to indicate that it was "physically and mathematically impossible for the hook to strike Haney," this evidence was irrelevant upon appeal, since there was a "reasonable basis in the record for inferring that the hook struck Haney." *Id.* The Court stated that "it would be an undue invasion of the jury's historic function to weigh the conflicting evidence, judge the credibility of witnesses and arrive at a conclusion opposite from the one reached by the jury." *Id.* at 652–53.

In *Ellis v. Union Pac. R. Co,* 329 U.S. 649 (1947), the Supreme Court reasoned along similar lines. A railroad employee was crushed between a train car and a building. *Id.* at 650. A jury reached a verdict in favor of the employee, but the state [—10—] Supreme Court reversed, finding the evidence insufficient to support a finding of negligence. *Id.* The Supreme Court reinstated the jury's verdict, stating:

The choice of conflicting versions of the way the accident happened, the decision as to which witness was telling the truth, the inferences to be drawn from uncontroverted as well as controverted facts, are questions for the jury. Once there is a reasonable basis in the record for concluding that there was negligence which caused the injury, it is irrelevant that fair-minded men might reach a different conclusion. For then it would be an invasion of the jury's function for an appellate court to draw contrary inferences or to conclude that a different conclusion would be more reasonable. And where, as here, the case turns on controverted facts and the credibility of witnesses, the case is peculiarly one for the jury. *Id.* at 653.

In *Lynch,* we explained that a jury can "make reasonable inferences based on [] circumstantial evidence even where conflicting inferences are also appropriate and where no direct evidence establishes which inference is correct." 700 F.3d at 917. We reasoned that as long as it was "'possible to tell a story' that involve[d] employer negligence," summary judgment was improper. *Id.* at 918 (quoting *Coffey v. Ne. Illinois Reg'l Commuter R.R. Corp. (METRA),* 479 F.3d 472, 476 (7th Cir. 2007).

Here, the case turns on whether it was possible to tell a story, based on the evidence presented, that the latch on the front cab door of BNSF 5695 was defective in some way, which caused it to come open. The latch at issue was a counterweighted door latch, which works using gravity. The door's [—11—] handle acts as a counterweight; when properly latched, it holds the door closed. The latch could fail only if (1) the door frame was warped, (2) friction prevented the handle from turning enough to allow it to properly latch, (3) jostling or vibration added enough energy to overcome the force of gravity and to turn the latch upward, allowing the door to come open, or (4) the door was never properly latched in the first place.

Crompton does not argue that the door frame was warped or that friction prevented the handle from turning. Instead, he asserts that the front cab door must have been defective in some way, since he is certain that he latched the door, and the door stayed closed for almost a minute before suddenly flying open. He theorizes that the slowing of the train as it traveled downhill, coupled with the train's vibration, must have jostled the door handle enough to cause the door to come unlatched. To support this theory, Crompton presented evidence from several BNSF employees, who testified that they had seen similar train doors come open on their own in the past, without being unlatched by a crew member. The jury chose to believe Crompton's theory of causation and ruled in his favor.

As a matter of physics, Crompton's theory is implausible, since the door's counter-weighted handle would have had to move upwards against gravity in order to unlatch the door. BNSF's expert explained that the door handle would have had to engage in a "very significant amount of rotation to disengage it from the door frame" and posited that he didn't "see [vibration] having nearly [the] amplitude required to rotate the handle out of position, to the open position." The front cab door potentially could have come unlatched if the train hit a hole or encountered excessive vibration, but the record does [—12—] not support such a finding. Yancey, the train's engineer, testified that he noticed no rough spots or jolts as the train approached Neilson Junction. Crompton agreed, and could point to no rough spots or jolts to explain the sudden opening of the door.

Though we may find Crompton's theory improbable as far as the laws of physics are concerned, BNSF has produced no evidence to prove his theory impossible. The record contains ample evidence to support Crompton's version of events as well as the jury's inference that the front cab door of BNSF 5695 must have been defective in some way. Several BNSF employees testified that doors with a latch just like the one on the front cab door of BNSF 5695 came open from time to time without any outside manipulation. They also testified that BNSF was aware of these doors coming open, and held at least one meeting to discuss the issue. Crompton testified that on April 24, 2011, as the train approached Neilson Junction, he was

sure that he latched the door; afterwards, the door stayed closed for almost a minute before it flew open and knocked him from the train. When "there is an evidentiary basis for the jury's verdict, the jury is free to discard or disbelieve whatever facts are inconsistent with its conclusion." *Lavender v. Kurn*, 327 U.S. at 653. Here, the jury chose to believe Crompton's version of events, and there was a reasonable basis in the record for it to do so. Since BNSF presented no evidence on appeal sufficient to disprove Crompton's theory of causation, we will not disturb the jury's verdict. [—13—]

III. CONCLUSION

The evidence presented at trial was sufficient for a jury to conclude that BNSF was negligent. Accordingly, we AFFIRM the jury's verdict.

United States Court of Appeals
for the Seventh Circuit

No. 13-2102

BROWN

vs.

BURLINGTON N. SANTA FE RY. CO.

Appeal from the United States District Court for the
Central District of Illinois

Decided: August 29, 2014

Citation: 765 F.3d 765, 2 Adm. R. 457 (7th Cir. 2014).

Before **ROVNER, WILLIAMS**, and **TINDER**, Circuit Judges.

[—1—] **TINDER**, Circuit Judge:

Shannon Brown appeals the dismissal of his lawsuit against the Burlington Northern Santa Fe Railway Company ("BNSF"), which he filed under the Federal Employers' Liability Act ("FELA"), 45 U.S.C. § 51 *et seq.* The sole issue he disputes on appeal is the district [—2—] court's[1] decision to exclude the testimony of his expert witness, David Fletcher, M.D. We conclude that the district court did not abuse its discretion and therefore affirm its grant of summary judgment.

I. Background

At the time of this appeal, Brown was a 36-year-old man residing in Knoxville, Illinois. He began his employment with BNSF in 1996 as a member of the Maintenance of Way Department. From 2006 to 2009 he progressed through a variety of job duties as a foreman, track inspector, and machine operator. In 2007 a family physician diagnosed Brown with carpal tunnel syndrome in both wrists and cubital tunnel syndrome in his left elbow.[2] On

October 25 of that year, [—3—] Brown allegedly injured his right shoulder after lifting heavy angle bars at work.[3] He reported the alleged injury only after increasing pain prompted him to visit an emergency room. His family physician could not detect any injury despite conducting tests, and instead sent Brown to physical therapy. By December 3rd of 2007, Brown reported that his shoulder was pain free, and his doctor cleared him to return to work with no restrictions.

The day following his official return date, however, Brown had surgery on his right wrist to relieve his carpal tunnel syndrome. Surgery on the other wrist followed on January 22, 2008. He returned to work on March 24 without any restrictions. He had surgery on his left elbow in October of 2009 to treat his cubital tunnel syndrome, and he was cleared to return to work on January 4, 2010. Brown's surgeon for both of his wrist surgeries and his elbow surgery informed him that all three procedures were successful and resolved his symptoms. Brown would remain employed at BNSF without medical restriction until September 28, 2011, at which point he no longer worked at the company.

---

impinged, or pinched, numbness, tingling, and sometimes pain of the affected fingers and hand may occur and radiate into the forearm." At its most severe, the condition may result in "permanent deterioration of muscle tissue and loss of hand function." *Carpal Tunnel Syndrome,* http://www.webmd.com/pain-management/carpal-tunnel/carpal-tunnel-syndrome (last visited Aug. 25, 2014). Similarly, "[c]ubital tunnel syndrome … is caused by increased pressure on the ulnar nerve, which passes close to the skin's surface in the area of the elbow commonly known as the 'funny bone.'" Symptoms of cubital tunnel syndrome include "[p]ain and numbness in the elbow," "[t]ingling, especially in the ring and little fingers," "[w]eakness affecting the ring and little fingers," and "[d]ecreased ability to pinch the thumb and little finger." *Cubital and Radial Tunnel Syndrome,* [—3—] http://www.webmd.com/pain-management/cubital-radial-tunnel-syndrome(last visited Aug. 25, 2014).

[3] Some disagreement persists in the record as to what exactly Brown claims to have been lifting when the alleged injury occurred, but that issue is irrelevant for our purposes.

---

[1] The parties consented to a referral of this case to a magistrate judge, who excluded Brown's proposed expert testimony and granted summary judgment. For simplicity we will refer to the judge as the district court.

[2] According to WebMD, "[c]arpal tunnel syndrome occurs when the median nerve is compressed because of swelling of the nerve or tendons or both. … When this nerve becomes

Before returning from his elbow surgery in 2009, Brown sued BNSF under FELA, alleging that the railway negligently caused cumulative trauma to his wrists, elbow, and shoulder. According to Brown, his duties at the railroad re- [—4—] quired him to use vibrating tools that either caused or aggravated his wrist conditions. He further alleges that, in September of 2009, he was required to work excessive hours without proper equipment while BNSF was short-staffed; he maintains that this exertion triggered or exacerbated the cubital tunnel syndrome in his left elbow, prompting his surgery the next month.

Discovery commenced, and Brown retained Dr. Fletcher to examine him and provide expert medical testimony. Dr. Fletcher's expertise in diagnosing railway work injuries and identifying their cause is unchallenged. He is licensed to practice medicine in Illinois, and is a full-time physician. He graduated from Rush Medical College in Chicago and holds a Master's Degree in Public Health from the University of California, Berkeley. Dr. Fletcher is a Fellow of the American College of Occupational and Environmental Medicine and has been appointed Clinical Assistant Professor at the University of Illinois and Southern Illinois University. In 2012 he was one of two doctors chosen to serve on the Illinois Workers" Compensation Commission. He is also the medical director of SafeWorks, Illinois, a private occupational health clinic. Starting in 1985 and continuing through his 2012 deposition, Dr. Fletcher occasionally served as an independent contractor with two railroad companies, the Norfolk Southern Corporation and the Canadian National Railway Company. In that capacity he treated work-related injuries and performed physicals, tested employees" fitness for duty, and conducted some ergonomic evaluations. He has served as an expert witness in past FELA cases.

Dr. Fletcher eventually submitted four expert reports on Brown's behalf, although the last was excluded as untimely [—5—] in a ruling that Brown does not challenge. The first report discussed Brown's medical records and his independent medical evaluation that Dr. Fletcher conducted on August 2, 2011. Dr. Fletcher reported that Brown had no history of smoking, diabetes, or other common health risk factors. He noted that Brown reported a needle-like sensation in the palms of both hands that was minimal and easy to ignore. Brown also told Dr. Fletcher that his shoulder was "97%" better and caused him no pain. Dr. Fletcher inquired as to Brown's employment, and Brown told him that his job required him to lift 100 pounds from the floor and 50 pounds overhead. He further reported that he worked between 12 and 16 hours a day, repeatedly lifting between 35 and 40 pounds and using hydraulic and vibratory tools. He informed Dr. Fletcher that as a foreman he commonly had to repair track, shovel dirt, drive spikes, use sledge hammers, and lift heavy metal bars.

Dr. Fletcher's first report also relayed the results of his physical examination of Brown. The report notes atrophy and loss of muscle strength in his left elbow. Dr. Fletcher conducted a Tinel's test on the elbow, which revealed nerve irritation. An elbow compression test similarly uncovered signs of injury. Dr. Fletcher also indicated impingement of Brown's right shoulder, but his report goes on to contradict that finding by reporting that "impingement signs were negative bilaterally." The report states that an MRI would be necessary to reach a "formal diagnosis" of any shoulder injury, but it notes that Brown could not undergo that test because he had a pacemaker in his chest. Dr. Fletcher recommended an arthroscopic procedure to identify any problems, but no such surgery was performed. Brown has not pointed out any other test confirming an injury to his shoulder. Nev- [—6—] ertheless, Dr. Fletcher attributed Brown's wrist, elbow, and shoulder injuries to his work at BNSF.

Dr. Fletcher's second report was an update on Brown's progress, issued on January 3, 2012, after he had examined him a second time. Brown reported pins and needles in his left elbow and numbness in his left hand, and Dr. Fletcher concluded that he required another elbow surgery. He also stated that Brown "had incurred permanent loss" of function and required "[p]ermanent job restrictions." Again Dr. Fletcher attributed these medical problems to Brown's job.

In his third report, dated February 27, 2012, Dr. Fletcher more closely examined the cause of Brown's condition. After summarizing Brown's health concerns, he stated that he suffered from a "cumulative trauma disorder" caused by his work on the railroad. Carpal tunnel syndrome and cubital tunnel syndrome are both examples of cumulative trauma disorder because they result from repeated applications of force over time rather than one discrete event. Dr. Fletcher stated that he came to this conclusion by the process of differential etiology. "[I]n a differential etiology, the doctor rules in all the potential causes of a patient's ailment and then by systematically ruling out causes that would not apply to the patient, the physician arrives at what is the likely cause of the ailment." *Myers v. Ill. Cent. R.R. Co.*, 629 F.3d 644, 644 (7th Cir. 2010).

As we have noted, to conduct his method of differential etiology, Dr. Fletcher's third report states that he employed a "job site analysis," which consists of "traveling to the literal worksite with the patient and reviewing his or her job duties; measuring frequency and force required for various job tasks; videotaping and photographing job task activities for [—7—] further analysis"; identifying "variances in the written job description as compared to the actual duties performed; using scientific measuring tools, such as a Chatillon gauge, which constitutes an objective measure of force; assessing push/pull job function factors; and evaluating the level of force exertion required to perform a job task." Through the job site analysis, Dr. Fletcher could "rule in" Brown's railroad work as a cause of his injury.

BNSF deposed Dr. Fletcher, and his accounting of his etiological investigation in this case differed considerably from the typical methodology described in his reports. Instead of going to Brown's work site and making scientific measurements and records, Dr. Fletcher simply photographed Brown holding various work tools at the BNSF rail yard. He testified that the railroad did not allow him to observe Brown or a similarly situated employee perform representative work tasks. (Brown did not, however, move to compel BNSF's cooperation on this point.) Instead, Dr. Fletcher based his opinion on observations he has made as an independent contractor since 1985. But when pressed for specifics, he recounted occasional memories of railroad work he witnessed ten years ago on a different site from the one Brown worked on. Dr. Fletcher also admitted that he never learned how long Brown would have used certain equipment each day, and he acknowledged that Brown's work varied over the course of a day and from one day to the next. He also stated that he did not consider how Brown's responsibilities changed as he progressed at his job to track inspector and then to foreman.

Moreover, Fletcher's report did not discuss a number of potential alternative causes for Brown's ailment. During his deposition, Dr. Fletcher stated that he had been aware of [—8—] some, but not all, of the relevant information surrounding these potential alternative causes. For example, Brown was a volunteer firefighter. Fletcher testified that he knew this but that he did not know how long Brown had worked as a firefighter. He never observed Brown's volunteer work there or learned his job duties. Brown also had a family history of cumulative trauma disorder, which Dr. Fletcher recognized but discounted. Although the doctor acknowledged that the "higher the [individual's body mass index or "BMI"] the more likely obesity could be an independent risk factor," he dismissed this potential cause because Brown's BMI was "[b]orderline" and he was not "morbidly obese." Dr. Fletcher did know that Brown regularly rode a motorcycle during the relevant time period, but he did not know the frequency or duration of the rides, or the type of motorcycle he owned. He concluded that any effect from the motorcycle would be minor because, he stated, Brown spent considerably more time working than riding. Finally, although Dr. Fletcher reported that Brown had no history of smoking, Brown himself admitted in his deposition that he had quit smoking only two or three years earlier.

The district court excluded Dr. Fletcher's reports and testimony under Federal Rules of Evidence 702 and 703. The court held that Dr. Fletcher's methods were unreliable because he deviated substantially from the recognized scientific practices that he described in his reports. As to Brown's shoulder, the district court doubted whether Brown had even sustained an injury because Dr. Fletcher had conceded that no formal diagnosis was possible without an MRI. More broadly, the district court reasoned that Dr. Fletcher was offering an ergonomic opinion as to the relation between Brown's job duties and his injury, and that such opinions re- [—9—] quired a sound job site analysis of the type Dr. Fletcher mentions in his report. But because Dr. Fletcher never actually performed a job site analysis or observed Brown at work, his opinion lacked a reliable, testable basis. Moreover, Dr. Fletcher claimed that he was applying the method of differential etiology to "rule out" other potential causes, but the district court found that he failed to meaningfully consider or investigate several such possible risk factors for Brown's condition, such as his motorcycle riding, volunteer firefighting, obesity, smoking, and family history of cumulative trauma disorders. In other words, Dr. Fletcher had failed both to "rule out" several possible causes and also to properly "rule in" Brown's job as a cause of his condition. Because Dr. Fletcher did not adhere to his own stated methods for performing a job site analysis or differential etiology, the district court found that he in fact adhered to no reliable method, but instead impermissibly relied on his own subjective experience and untestable assumptions.

Brown's case for establishing his work conditions as a cause of his injury depended on Dr. Fletcher's testimony, so the district court dismissed his FELA claim. This appeal followed.

II. Discussion

Congress enacted FELA in the first decade of the twentieth century in response to "the physical dangers of railroading that resulted in the death or maiming of thousands of workers every year." *Consol. Rail Corp. v.*

Gottshall, 512 U.S. 532, 542 (1994). The Act requires a plaintiff to prove all the elements of a negligence claim against his employer, but courts have "liberally construed" the statute "to further FELA's humanitarian purposes." *Id.* at 542–43. In particular, [—10—] a FELA claim is judged according to "a relaxed standard of causation" whereby a plaintiff must prove only that the employer's "negligence played any part, even the slightest, in producing the injury or death for which damages are sought." *Id.* at 543 (quoting *Rogers v. Mo. Pac. R.R. Co.*, 352 U.S. 500, 506 (1957)).

The relaxed causation standard is simple enough to meet in cases involving readily understood injuries, *e.g.*, those that result from being hit by a train. "But when there is no obvious origin to an injury and it has multiple potential etiologies, expert testimony is necessary to establish causation." *Myers*, 629 F.3d at 643 (citation and quotation marks omitted). In particular, "[f]or most cumulative trauma injuries, courts follow the general principle that a layman could not discern the specific cause and thus they have required expert testimony about causation." *Id.* Brown contends that he has suffered cumulative trauma injuries to his wrists and elbows, along with a shoulder injury, and he concedes that he was required to provide admissible expert testimony to establish causation for each. We are not so sure about that. Brown allegedly injured his shoulder performing a discrete act of lifting that could be readily understood by a layman. And in *Myers* we noted dicta in the Sixth Circuit case *Hardyman v. Norfolk & Western Railway, Co.*, 243 F.3d 255 (6th Cir. 2001), indicating that "general causation testimony is enough to send the case to a jury for carpal tunnel syndrome." *Myers*, 629 F.3d at 643. We do not know whether summary judgment will always be appropriate in the absence of expert testimony where the plaintiff has alleged such discrete, easily comprehensible injuries. Nevertheless, Brown chose to pursue a standard cumulative trauma theory and has not argued that his case could survive summary [—11—] judgment without expert testimony. Nor does he point to sufficient lay evidence in the record to support a finding of fault for his shoulder injury. Therefore, we agree with the parties that we may reverse the district court's grant of summary judgment only if we also reverse its decision to exclude Dr. Fletcher's testimony.

A district court's decision to exclude expert testimony is governed by Federal Rules of Evidence 702 and 703, as construed by the Supreme Court in *Daubert v. Merrell Dow Pharmaceuticals, Inc.*, 509 U.S. 579 (1993). Rule 702(c) requires that an expert's testimony be "the product of reliable principles and methods." Similarly, Rule 703 requires the expert to rely on "facts or data," as opposed to subjective impressions. *Daubert* laid out four factors by which courts can evaluate the reliability of expert testimony: (1) whether the expert's conclusions are falsifiable; (2) whether the expert's method has been subject to peer review; (3) whether there is a known error rate associated with the technique; and (4) whether the method is generally accepted in the relevant scientific community. 509 U.S. at 593–94.

Dr. Fletcher sought to offer a differential etiology in this case. "Differential diagnosis is an accepted and valid methodology for an expert to render an opinion about the identity of a specific ailment." *Myers*, 629 F.3d at 644. So is differential etiology, which focuses on the cause, not just the identity, of an ailment. *Id.* But an expert still must faithfully apply the method to the facts at hand. A differential etiology, like a differential diagnosis, "satisfies a *Daubert* analysis if the expert uses reliable methods. … Determining the reliability of an expert's differential diagnosis is a case-by-case determination." *Ervin v. Johnson & Johnson, Inc.*, 492 F.3d 901, [—12—] 904 (7th Cir. 2007); *see also Myers*, 629 F.3d at 644. The party offering the expert testimony bears the burden of proving its reliability. *Lewis v. CITGO Petroleum Corp.*, 561 F.3d 698, 705 (7th Cir. 2009).

In reviewing the district court's decision to exclude expert testimony, this court "first undertakes a *de novo* review of whether the district court properly followed the framework set forth in *Daubert* … ." *United States v. Hall*, 165 F.3d 1095, 1101 (7th Cir. 1999). If

the court properly understood its role therein, we then review its ultimate decision to exclude expert testimony for an abuse of discretion. *Kumho Tire Co. v. Carmichael*, 526 U.S. 137, 152 (1999). This deference is in keeping with the district court's vital "gatekeeping" role in ensuring that only helpful, legitimate expert testimony reaches the jury. *Daubert*, 509 U.S. at 597.

Brown first contends that the district court "exceeded the scope of its gatekeeping function" under *Daubert* by nitpicking Dr. Fletcher's factual observations and gainsaying his conclusions—both of which are properly roles for the jury—rather than simply determining whether he used a reliable method. Appellant's Br. at 36. Second, Brown argues that Dr. Fletcher did properly adhere to his method of differential etiology and that the district court abused its discretion in finding otherwise. We take both arguments in turn.

The district court properly understood the *Daubert* framework. It noted that "[t]he court's role as gatekeeper is strictly limited to an examination of the expert's methodology." *Brown v. Burlington N. Santa Fe Ry. Co.*, No. 09-1380, 2013 WL 1729046 at *8 (C.D. Ill. Apr. 22, 2013). Brown responds that the district court's reasoning belies that acknowledgement. Specifically, the district court faulted Dr. [—13—] Fletcher for apparently relying on Brown's recitation of his medical history to conclude that he did not smoke when it appears that he did. The court also noted that Dr. Fletcher's report did not describe Brown's family history of cumulative trauma disorder. Brown's failure to accurately relay his medical history should not have led the court to impugn Dr. Fletcher's methods. "Medical professionals reasonably may be expected to rely on self-reported patient histories." *Walker v. Soo Line R.R. Co.*, 208 F.3d 581, 586 (7th Cir. 2000) (citing *Cooper v. Carl A. Nelson & Co.*, 211 F.3d 1008, 1019–21 (7th Cir. 2000)). Likewise, the district court doubted Brown's self-reporting of his job duties to Dr. Fletcher, in particular his claims that he worked 12-16 hours a day. The court also discounted Dr. Fletcher's diagnosis of Brown's shoulder injury because he was not able to perform an MRI. Finally, the district court accused Dr. Fletcher of misidentifying a track jack as an iron angle bar, which would be a significant error because the two items are quite distinct. Brown argues that the district court's findings on these points amount to improperly quibbling with factual details of the expert's report. After all, even experts make mistakes, and imperfections in their presentations are supposed to be tested by opposing counsel and put before the jury.

Although the district court did observe factual deficiencies in Dr. Fletcher's reports, it clearly stated that it was excluding the doctor's testimony because he failed to follow a reliable method; indeed, he deviated from his own stated description of a job site analysis and of differential etiology in general. Dr. Fletcher entirely failed to personally observe Brown's working conditions, obtain a written work description, or perform scientific tests. He also failed to investigate several possible causes of Brown's health problems. The fac- [—14—] tual deficiencies or discrepancies the district court identified are the result of Dr. Fletcher's faulty methods and lack of investigation. The district court used the gaps in Dr. Fletcher's analysis as illustrative examples of the perils inherent in applying subjective experience instead of a proper scientific approach. The district court did not exceed its role under *Daubert*.

Brown's remaining argument is that the district court abused its discretion in finding that Dr. Fletcher failed to apply a reliable method. We have recognized that there is "nothing controversial" about using differential etiology to establish legal cause. *Schultz v. Akzo Nobel Paints, LLC*, 721 F.3d 426, 433 (7th Cir. 2013). However, an expert must do more than just state that she is applying a respected methodology; she must follow through with it. In deciding whether an expert employed a reliable method, the district court has discretion to consider "'[w]hether the expert has adequately accounted for obvious alternative explanations.'" *Id.* at 434 (quoting Fed. R. Evid. 702 (2000) Committee Note). The expert need not exclude all alternatives with certainty, however. *See Gayton v. McCoy*, 593

F.3d 610, 619 (7th Cir. 2010) ("[A]n expert need not testify with complete certainty about the cause of an injury; rather he may testify that one factor could have been a contributing factor to a given outcome.").

The district court did not abuse its discretion in finding that Brown's motorcycle riding and volunteer firefighting were obvious potential alternative causes for his injuries. The causal link Dr. Fletcher drew between Brown's job and his injuries lay in the presence of vibratory and other types of equipment that can harm elbows, wrists, and shoulders [—15—] over time. But the handlebars of a running motorcycle obviously vibrate, and firefighters must frequently struggle with heavy equipment. Brown is correct that under FELA he need only prove that BNSF's negligence was a cause, not the sole cause, of his injury. But without performing an investigation, Dr. Fletcher could not rule out either activity as the sole cause of Brown's condition. And although Brown's weight, history of smoking, and family medical history were each not likely the sole cause of his ailments, these risk factors combined with either the volunteer firefighting or motorcycle riding (or both) could have been wholly responsible for Brown's condition. We do not know how likely this possibility is because Dr. Fletcher did not meaningfully consider it.

Brown insists that Dr. Fletcher did consider these obvious alternative causes, but the record shows otherwise. The doctor disregarded Brown's motorcycle riding as a factor because he assumed Brown worked for longer periods than he rode. But as BNSF rightly points out, the proper question is how long he rode the motorcycle as compared to how long he used vibratory or similarly taxing tools at work. And Dr. Fletcher could not possibly answer that question in a systematic, testable fashion because he did not know the duration and frequency of Brown's motorcycle riding. Even worse, he did not know the duration or frequency of Brown's exposure to vibrations at work. He did not have enough information to conclude that one value was higher than the other, or even to doubt that the former overwhelmingly exceeded the latter. Comparing two unknown, potentially wide-ranging variables is not a scientific exercise. There is no known error rate attached to such a calculation, nor is such guesswork widely accepted in the scientific community. *See Daubert*, 509 U.S. at 593–94. Similarly, Dr. [—16—] Fletcher did not know what hours Brown worked as a firefighter, or what his responsibilities were. These were not merely factual oversights; they are flatly inconsistent with differential etiology. That method does not establish a cause for an injury directly, through observation or factual reconstruction. Rather, it relies on the process of elimination by ruling out other alternatives. The failure to rule out obvious potential alternative causes is therefore fatal to Dr. Fletcher's testimony.

Dr. Fletcher's failure to consider Brown's motorcycle riding and volunteer firefighting distinguishes this case from *Schultz*, 721 F.3d 426, which Brown cites in support of his argument. In that case, the plaintiff had smoked in the past, but the expert explicitly stated that exposure to benzene was known to pose an even greater risk. This meant, in the expert's opinion, that the benzene was a "substantial factor" in his cancer. *Id.* at 433–34. Here, Dr. Fletcher did not reliably weigh the risks posed by Brown's job-related exertion as compared to his other activities. This case is also quite different from *Hardyman*, in which the expert "took an extensive history of Plaintiff's non-occupational work activities." 243 F.3d at 261 (discussing the plaintiff's bowling, golf, and other recreational activities).

Not only did Dr. Fletcher fail to investigate and systematically rule out two obvious potential causes, but it is not clear that he ruled out any serious alternative. It is true that Brown apparently does not have diabetes, which could be a risk factor. Dr. Fletcher also determined that Brown's weight was not likely not a problem, because his BMI was "[b]orderline." But even this is difficult to square with his observation during his deposition that "[t]he higher the BMI [—17—] the more likely that obesity could be an independent risk factor" for carpal tunnel syndrome. He did not explain at all why this

positive relationship would exist only for the "morbidly obese." Brown's weight could have made it more likely that his motorcycle riding or volunteer firefighting was solely responsible for his condition. Of course, we can only speculate because Dr. Fletcher did not adequately investigate this possibility.

As the district court correctly observed, Dr. Fletcher's failure to rule out obvious potential causes was only half the problem. He also failed to reliably "rule in" Brown's workplace activity as a potential cause of Brown's condition. Dr. Fletcher failed to consider that Brown's job duties changed considerably as he progressed, beginning in 2006, from maintenance-of-way work to different roles as a foreman, track inspector, and machine operator. More fundamentally, Dr. Fletcher noted that his method required him to conduct a "job site analysis." This involved "traveling to the literal worksite with the patient and reviewing his or her job duties; measuring frequency and force required for various job tasks; videotaping and photographing job task activities for further analysis"; identifying "variances in the written job description as compared to the actual duties performed; using scientific measuring tools, such as a Chatillon gauge, which constitutes an objective measure of force; assessing push/pull job function factors; and evaluating the level of force exertion required to perform a job task." Observing Brown's actual working conditions was important in order to avoid "ruling in" risk factors that were not actually present at his job. The use of videotape and photography to record Dr. Fletcher's observations would have been crucial to ensuring that his conclusions could be objectively tested, [—18—] peer reviewed, and reproduced. The same applies to the use of scientific tools that provide recorded measurements and the written job description that could offer an objective comparison with the doctor's observation. Dr. Fletcher also testified that he usually had a professional ergonomist conduct much of this investigation, but he did not use his services in this case. All of these steps are designed so that the expert can rely not on his own subjective experience or bias but on reliable scientific methods. Dr. Fletcher noted that the above safeguards were important in his own report, yet he failed to follow them. This again distinguishes Brown's case from *Hardyman*, where the plaintiff's ergonomics expert "conducted an extensive investigation of Plaintiff's work conditions." 243 F.3d at 263. Without a legitimate investigation, Dr. Fletcher could not reliably ascertain whether Brown's work was even a contributing factor to his injury.

In response, Brown contends that precise measurements of the duration and frequency of his exposure to vibratory and other potentially damaging tools are unnecessary because no precise relationship between the frequency and duration of exposure and a particular cumulative trauma injury is known. Indeed, it likely varies from patient to patient. But because Brown was exposed to multiple sources of continued vibration and other trauma, Dr. Fletcher had to have some reliable basis for opining that Brown's work activities played at least a small role in his injury. Data comparing the relative duration and frequency of exposure could have provided that basis; perhaps there were other ways. But Dr. Fletcher did not pursue any of them. Brown also argues that BNSF's experts also did not perform frequency and duration tests of its equipment either, but pointing out deficiencies in the defendant's expert testimony cannot help Brown, who [—19—] bears the burden of proving negligence and demonstrating the reliability of his own expert.

Brown claims that Dr. Fletcher was prevented from conducting the type of job site analysis described in his reports because BNSF would not cooperate by, for example, allowing him to test its tools or providing him with a written job description. But that is a matter that should have been brought to the district court's attention during discovery. A party cannot enter into evidence unhelpful expert testimony on the grounds that the other side made them do it. If Brown felt that BNSF was unreasonably constraining his expert's investigation, he should have raised that issue and then, if unsuccessful, pressed it on appeal.

Nor did Dr. Fletcher follow his own advice in diagnosing Brown's alleged shoulder injury. In his first report he noted that a "formal diagnosis" would not be possible without an MRI. The district court did not abuse its discretion in holding Dr. Fletcher to that representation. And if Dr. Fletcher failed to follow his own stated methods, the court could reasonably conclude that he had failed to follow any reliable method. Brown has not shown that Dr. Fletcher's actual approach, as opposed to what he claimed to have done, was generally accepted in the scientific community. His process could not produce falsifiable results or survive peer review, and it is impossible to put an error rate on his guesswork. *See Daubert*, 509 U.S. at 593–94.

No one disputes that Brown's injuries could have been caused by frequent or long-lasting vibrations, or that his job exposed him to a significant amount of vibration over the years. But if that were sufficient to establish causation, expert testimony would be unnecessary in this case. Any lay- [—20—] man can understand that connection. Brown wishes to use Dr. Fletcher's quarter-century of experience in the field to rule out other potential causes. But experience without reliable, testable methodology is not sufficient. *See Gen. Elec. Co. v. Joiner*, 522 U.S. 136, 146 (1997) ("[N]othing in either *Daubert* or the Federal Rules of Evidence requires a district court to admit opinion evidence that is connected to existing data only by the *ipse dixit* of the expert."). Moreover, Dr. Fletcher's application of his own experience is itself suspect. At his deposition he was forced to rely on his memory of "spen[ding] half an hour, 40 minutes ... a decade ago" at a different rail yard to describe the type of maintenance-of-way work that Brown performed. The vagueness of this testimony is a good illustration of why mere expertise and subjective understanding are not reliable scientific evidence. The district court did not abuse its discretion by concluding that opinions based on this sort of recollection would be no help to the jury.

III. Conclusion

Because the district court did not abuse its discretion in excluding Dr. Fletcher's expert testimony, its grant of summary judgment is AFFIRMED.

This page intentionally left blank

United States Court of Appeals for the Eighth Circuit

United States Court of Appeals
for the Eighth Circuit

No. 13-2313

NEW YORK MARINE AND GEN. INS. CO.
vs.
CONTINENTAL CEMENT CO., LLC

Appeal from the United States District Court for the
Eastern District of Missouri – St. Louis

Decided: July 17, 2014

Citation: 761 F.3d 830, 2 Adm. R. 468 (8th Cir. 2014).

Before **WOLLMAN, MURPHY,** and **GRUENDER,** Circuit Judges.

[—2—] MURPHY, Circuit Judge:

The Mark Twain, a cement barge owned by Continental Cement Company, LLC and Summit Materials, LLC (Continental Cement), sank in the Mississippi River at St. Louis on the morning of February 7, 2011. Insurers for the barge, Starr Indemnity & Liability Company and New York Marine & General Insurance Company (Starr Indemnity), investigated the sinking and declined coverage for both the loss of the hull and the expense of removing the barge from the river. The insurers then brought this action in the district court seeking a determination of their rights and obligations under Continental Cement's insurance policies. Continental Cement counterclaimed for breach of contract and vexatious refusal to pay under Missouri law.

The insurers later located a survey of the Mark Twain from 2008 which indicated that the barge had not been watertight at the time Continental Cement obtained its policies. On the grounds that Continental Cement had breached its duty of utmost good faith by withholding this survey from its insurance application, Starr Indemnity amended its complaint to assert that the insurance policies were void. Continental Cement responded with a motion for partial summary judgment, asserting in part that this circuit had not recognized the defense of utmost good faith in

maritime insurance cases. The district court[1] disagreed, concluded that the defense was "entrenched" federal law, and denied the summary judgment motion. The case proceeded to trial, and the jury returned a general verdict in favor of the insurers. The district court entered a corresponding final judgment, and Continental Cement appeals. We affirm. [—3—]

I.

On this appeal we view the facts in the light most favorable to the insurers because the jury ruled in their favor. *Friedman & Friedman, Ltd. v. Tim McCandless, Inc.,* 606 F.3d 494, 496 (8th Cir. 2010). Summit Materials is the majority owner of Continental Cement Co., a cement manufacturing company. Continental Cement had been using five barges to transport cement from its manufacturing facility in Hannibal, Missouri down the Mississippi River to its distribution facility in St. Louis. The Mark Twain was among these barges. Built in the 1920s, the Mark Twain was a steel hulled barge with riveted construction. It had ten compartments along the perimeter, each separated by a bulkhead. These bulkheads were intended to be watertight to protect the vessel from sinking should a leak develop in any one compartment.

In 2008 Continental Cement considered retiring the Mark Twain as a transport barge to use as a stationary dock barge. It hired marine engineer Wade McGrady to survey the barge for its fitness for this purpose. McGrady inspected the barge and prepared a "General Condition Survey" summarizing his findings. In his survey McGrady noted that while there were no active hull leaks, "numerous rivets appeared to have been leaking in the past." He also observed that some of the bulkheads were no longer watertight because they were missing rivets. He also inspected the bilge system, which is designed to pump water out of the ship, and testified at trial that it was "not even close" to functioning. The system was in such a "deteriorated state" that water

---
[1] The Honorable John A. Ross, United States District Judge for the Eastern District of Missouri.

could flow through it and between compartments in the event of a leak. McGrady's survey ended with ten recommendations, including "further subdivision" of the perimeter compartments to isolate water from a leak, and repairs to the bilge system "to prevent progressive flooding." After reviewing this survey, Continental Cement decided not to convert the Mark Twain into a dock barge, and instead put it back into transport service without making any repairs. [—4—]

On November 4, 2010 Continental Cement applied to Starr Indemnity for a marine insurance policy for all five of the company's barges, including the Mark Twain. Starr Indemnity's form application stated that "QUOTES ARE SUBJECT TO SATISFACTORY CONDITION & VALUATION SURVEYS; USUALLY AT THE EXPENSE OF THE APPLICANT / ASSURED" and requested that the applicant "PLEASE INCLUDE RECENT SURVEYS, IF AVAILABLE." Continental Cement attached to its application an "Appraisal Report" from 2006 that listed the value of each barge but did not list any problems with the Mark Twain. Continental Cement did not attach McGrady's 2008 "General Condition Survey" of the Mark Twain. Starr Indemnity issued the company a primary marine insurance contract and an excess policy that went into effect on December 31, 2010. The underwriter later testified in the district court that he was not aware of the 2008 survey when he reviewed the company's application. If the survey had been provided, he indicated it would have raised in his mind "a serious issue of seaworthiness."

The Mark Twain was at Continental Cement's dock in St. Louis when it sank on the morning of Monday, February 7, 2011. Evidence presented at trial indicates that Continental Cement employees noticed the barge was sitting low in the water three days before it sank, but they conducted only a cursory inspection, performed limited pumping, and left the barge unattended from Saturday afternoon until the barge went under at 6 a.m. on Monday. Shortly after the barge sank, Continental Cement reprimanded

its terminal manager for his "lack of proper judgment and supervision (not notifying any of your superiors, nor staffing and pumping the Mark Twain with Continental [Cement] personnel until the known leak was repaired)." Continental Cement did not share either this communication or the 2008 survey with Starr Indemnity.

After Starr Indemnity conducted an independent investigation into why the barge sank, it sent a letter on May 9, 2011 declining insurance coverage for the loss of the Mark Twain's hull, as well as for wreck removal expenses. With respect to hull [—5—] coverage, Starr Indemnity's claims agent stated that Continental Cement had not identified a peril covered by the policy that caused the barge to sink, and asserted that "the loss appears to have been due to a lack of due diligence" by Continental Cement. As to wreck removal, the claims agent stated that in the absence of a governmental order requiring Continental Cement to remove the sunken barge, removal was unnecessary and unwarranted under the policy. That same day Starr Indemnity filed an action in federal court seeking a declaration of its rights and obligations under the insurance policies.

During the discovery process Starr Indemnity learned about the 2008 survey, and on August 14, 2012 it filed a fourth amended complaint that added two affirmative defenses. Starr Indemnity argued (1) that by withholding the 2008 survey from its insurance application, Continental Cement had breached its duty of utmost good faith, and (2) that the Mark Twain was unseaworthy at the time Continental Cement applied for insurance and the company thus breached its absolute warranty of seaworthiness. If these arguments were proven, either or both of the affirmative defenses could void the insurance policies.

Continental Cement filed its answer and counterclaim on August 30, 2012, alleging breach of the insurance contract and vexatious refusal to pay. Continental Cement then brought several motions for partial summary judgment. In one of its motions Continental Cement argued that the Eighth Circuit does not recognize the defense of utmost good faith in maritime insurance cases. In denying the motion, the district court concluded that the doctrine of utmost good faith is "entrenched" federal law and that it was a question for the jury whether Continental Cement had violated its duty by withholding the 2008 survey.

The case went to trial. At the close of evidence Continental Cement moved for judgment as a matter of law, partially based on Starr Indemnity's utmost good faith defense. Continental Cement argued (1) that withholding the 2008 survey was at most [—6—] an innocent omission and thus there was insufficient evidence to submit the defense to the jury, and (2) that Starr Indemnity had waived this defense by not including it in its initial letter declining coverage. After this motion was denied, Continental Cement challenged the jury instruction on utmost good faith "for the same reasons stated in Continental [Cement]'s motion for judgment as a matter of law." The court rejected this challenge.

The parties disputed whether special interrogatories or a general verdict should be submitted to the jury. The insurers proposed a series of special interrogatories, but the district court decided these would be "more confusing than beneficial to the jury." The district court instead offered to edit a general verdict form so the jury could "identify which affirmative defense they had found," but Starr Indemnity declined this option. Among the district court's instructions to the jury was one instructing it to find insurance coverage for the removal expenses of the wrecked barge unless it found the policies void from their inception on either of Starr Indemnity's affirmative defenses. On May 1, 2013 the jury returned a general verdict in favor of the insurers. The district court accordingly entered judgment in favor of Starr Indemnity, stating that "based upon the verdicts of the jury, the insurance policies for the barge the MARK TWAIN have been voided at their inception."

Continental Cement appeals, arguing that the district court erred by applying the federal doctrine of utmost good faith instead of Missouri state law. In the alternative the company asserts that the district court erred by denying both its motion for judgment as a matter of law and its challenge to the jury instruction on the duty of utmost good faith. [—7—]

II.

We first address Starr Indemnity's contention that Continental Cement waived its appeal. The insurers argue that Continental Cement cannot challenge the validity of only one of its two independent affirmative defenses—breach of the duty of utmost good faith and breach of the absolute warranty of seaworthiness—when these two alternative bases for the jury's general verdict resulted in identical damages and when the company failed to object to the use of the general verdict form. We disagree.

A federal trial court has discretion to submit a case to the jury with either a general or special form of verdict. *Davis v. Ford Motor Co.*, 128 F.3d 631, 633 (8th Cir. 1997) (citing Fed. R. Civ. P. 49). A general verdict cannot be upheld if the jury might have based that verdict "in whole or in part on an invalidly submitted theory of liability." *Friedman*, 606 F.3d at 502 (citing *Sunkist Growers, Inc. v. Winckler & Smith Citrus Prod. Co.*, 370 U.S. 19, 29–30 (1962)). We have recognized that any such error would be harmless if a valid alternative theory would result in the same damages as any invalidated theory. *See, e.g., Tioga Pub. Sch. Dist. v. U.S. Gypsum Co.*, 984 F.2d 915, 921 (8th Cir. 1993); *Robertson Oil Co., Inc. v. Phillips Petroleum Co.*, 871 F.2d 1368, 1376 (8th Cir. 1989). We have applied this harmless error rule only when the jury's verdict clearly showed that it had found for the plaintiff on both theories. *See id.* That rule would not apply here. If Continental Cement were to succeed on its claim that the doctrine of utmost good faith was unavailable, the final judgment would have to be reversed because "there is no way to know that the invalid claim . . . was not the sole basis for the verdict." *United N.Y. & N.J. Sandy Hook Pilots Ass'n v. Halecki*, 358 U.S. 613, 619 (1959).

Finally, Continental Cement's failure to object to the general verdict form also does not waive this appeal, as we "have not necessarily required an objection at trial in order to address problems arising from the way in which [a] case was submitted." *Friedman*, 606 F.3d at 501 n.4. [—8—]

III.

We next address the merits of the appeal. Continental Cement's claim is that the district court erred by applying the federal doctrine of utmost good faith. A dispute arising under a marine insurance contract is "governed by state law, unless an established federal admiralty rule addresses the issue raised." *Assicurazioni Generali S.P.A. v. Black & Veatch Corp.*, 362 F.3d 1108, 1111 (8th Cir. 2004) (citing *Wilburn Boat Co. v. Fireman's Fund Ins. Co.*, 348 U.S. 310, 316–21 (1955)). In its fourth amended complaint, Starr Indemnity asserted that a controlling federal admiralty rule governs this case. Under the federal common law doctrine of utmost good faith or *uberrimae fidei*, "a failure by the insured to disclose conditions affecting the risk, of which he is aware, makes the contract voidable at the insurer's option." *Stipcich v. Metro. Life Ins. Co.*, 277 U.S. 311, 316 (1928). Based on this doctrine Starr Indemnity alleged that its insurance policies for Continental Cement were void. Continental Cement did not disclose to the insurers that the 2008 study had revealed flaws in its barge, and Starr Indemnity asserts that it thereby suppressed evidence material to the insurers' decision to underwrite the risk.

In its motion for partial summary judgment, Continental Cement disputed the claim that the federal doctrine of utmost good faith is an established federal admiralty rule. It argued instead that Missouri law applies, thereby requiring Starr Indemnity to show an additional element of fraud. In support of its position Continental Cement cites a Fifth Circuit opinion, *Albany Insurance Co. v. Anh Thi Kieu*, 927 F.2d 882 (5th Cir. 1991). In *Anh Thi Kieu*, the Fifth Circuit named three factors to consider in determining whether a federal maritime rule controls an issue: "(1) whether the federal maritime rule constitutes

entrenched federal precedent; (2) whether the state has a substantial and legitimate interest in the application of its laws; (3) whether the state's rule is materially different from the federal maritime rule." *Id.* at 886 (internal citations omitted). That court concluded that in *Anh Thi Kieu* all three factors favored [—9—] the application of state law, noting "with some hesitation," that "the *uberrimae fidei* doctrine is entrenched no more." *Id.* at 889.

Here, the district court concluded that the doctrine of utmost good faith remains "entrenched federal precedent" and that the case of *Anh Thi Kieu* was an aberration. The district court pointed out that numerous other circuits have recognized the doctrine of utmost good faith as entrenched and noted that the Eighth Circuit applied the doctrine in 2003 in an ERISA case. *See Shipley v. Ark. Blue Cross and Blue Shield*, 333 F.3d 898, 903 (8th Cir. 2003). The district court denied summary judgment to Continental Cement after concluding that there remained issues of fact regarding whether it had violated its duty of utmost good faith. Continental Cement now appeals the district court's choice of law determination.

A.

Before we reach the merits of the choice of law question, we must first consider whether it has been properly preserved. *Lopez v. Tyson Foods, Inc.*, 690 F.3d 869, 875 (8th Cir. 2012) ("This court is unable to address [] arguments . . . not preserve[d] . . . for appeal."). At the close of evidence when Continental Cement moved for entry of judgment as a matter of law on Starr Indemnity's utmost good faith defense, it argued only that (1) the evidence submitted was insufficient to support the defense, and (2) Starr Indemnity had waived the defense of utmost good faith by omitting it from its declination letter. At this point Continental Cement did not renew the argument made in its partial motion for summary judgment that Missouri law, rather than federal common law, should govern this issue. Starr Indemnity now asserts that Continental Cement's failure to renew its choice of law argument in a Rule 50 motion at trial renders this argument unavailable at this point.

It is generally true that a denial of summary judgment is interlocutory in nature and not appealable after trial and judgment. *Johnson Int'l Co. v. Jackson Nat'l Life* [—10—] *Ins. Co.*, 19 F.3d 431, 434 (8th Cir. 1994). Once a case proceeds to trial, "the question of whether a party has met its burden must be answered with reference to the evidence and the record as a whole, rather than by looking to the pretrial submissions alone." *Id.* Thus, the proper redress for an argument denied at summary judgment is not through appeal of that denial, "but through subsequent motions for judgment as a matter of law and appellate review of those motions if they were denied." *White Consol. Indus., Inc. v. McGill Mfg. Co.*, 165 F.3d 1185, 1189 (8th Cir. 1999) (internal quotation marks omitted).

At least seven circuits examining this rule have carved out an exception for arguments made at summary judgment that are "purely legal" in nature. *See Feld v. Feld*, 688 F.3d 779, 781–82 (D.C. Cir. 2012) (citing cases). These circuits have concluded that "[t]he rationale for requiring a Rule 50 motion does not apply to purely legal questions," because "[n]o changed facts or credibility determinations at trial could alter" the court's analysis on a pure question of law. *Id.* at 782. At least two circuits have disagreed, having concluded that a Rule 50 motion is required to preserve any legal or factual issue for appeal if it was first denied in a summary judgment motion. *Id.* at 782–83. The circuits in the latter group have emphasized the difficulty of "determining the bases on which summary judgment is denied and whether those bases are legal or factual." *Chesapeake Paper Prods. Co. v. Stone & Webster Eng'g Corp.*, 51 F.3d 1229, 1235 (4th Cir. 1995) (internal quotation marks omitted); *see also Ji v. Bose Corp.*, 626 F.3d 116, 127–28 (1st Cir. 2010).

Our own case law on this subject is conflicting. *See Lopez*, 690 F.3d at 875. In *Metropolitan Life Insurance Co. v. Golden Triangle*, 121 F.3d 351, 355 (8th Cir. 1997), we firmly rejected any "dichotomy[] between a summary judgment denied on factual grounds

and one denied on legal grounds [as] both problematic and without merit." Two years later, however, another panel took the opposite approach. In *White Consolidated Industries*, 165 F.3d at 1189–90, the court determined without discussing *Metropolitan Life* that "when . . . denial of summary judgment is based on [—11—] the interpretation of a purely legal question, such a decision is appealable after final judgment." *White Consol. Indus.*, 165 F.3d at 1190. Faced with this inter panel conflict, we concluded in Lopez that under our circuit rules "*Metropolitan Life*'s earlier holding is the law in this circuit." *Lopez*, 690 F.3d at 875.

A closer examination of our opinion in *Metropolitan Life* reveals that we did not indiscriminately foreclose all appeals taken from the denial of an issue raised at summary judgment. In a footnote we recognized a distinction between the denial of a summary judgment motion involving the merits of a claim and one involving preliminary issues, such as a statute of limitations, collateral estoppel, or standing. *Metro. Life*, 121 F.3d at 355 n.6 (internal citations omitted). Nevertheless, *Metropolitan Life* "d[id] not require us to determine whether a denial of a summary judgment motion on an issue preliminary to the merits can be reviewed after trial where no motion for judgment as a matter of law has been made." *Id.* That issue remains open.

A choice of law question is generally preliminary to determination of the merits in a case, and we conclude such a question can be reviewed on appeal if it has been denied in a summary judgment motion. We have even reviewed a choice of law argument decided on a motion for summary judgment *after* a full trial on the merits. *Collins v. State Farm Mut. Auto. Ins. Co.*, 902 F.2d 1371, 1372–73 (8th Cir. 1990). *Collins* predated *Metropolitan Life*, but its examination of the choice of law issue was consistent with the exception later discussed in *Metropolitan Life* dealing with issues preliminary to the merits. That discussion was based on prior circuit opinions which examined issues such as statutory time bars, collateral estoppel, or standing after a full trial. *Metro. Life*, 121 F.3d at 355 n.6. We agree with the Seventh Circuit that a "choice of law decision is sufficiently independent of the ultimate summary judgment inquiry . . . to warrant [appellate] review." *Gramercy Mills, Inc. v. Wolens*, 63 F.3d 569, 572 (7th Cir. 1995); *see also* 15B Wright & Miller, Fed. Pract. & Proc. Juris. §3914.28 n.26 (2d ed.). [—12—]

B.

Whether the federal doctrine of utmost good faith or Missouri law applies to this dispute about maritime insurance coverage is a question of law subject to de novo review. *Assicurazioni*, 362 F.3d at 1111. In *Wilburn Boat Co. v. Fireman's Fund Insurance Co.*, 348 U.S. 310 (1955), the Supreme Court acknowledged the conflicting interests in this area of law: maritime disputes are traditionally governed by federal law, but insurance disputes are generally determined by state law. Striking a balance between the two in *Wilburn Boat*, the Court determined that courts should apply state law to maritime insurance disputes unless there is a judicially established federal admiralty rule governing the issue. 348 U.S. at 314, 316–21; *see also Assicurazioni*, 362 F.3d at 1111; *Cargill, Inc. v. Commercial Union Ins. Co.*, 889 F.2d 174, 178 (8th Cir. 1989).

We conclude that the doctrine of utmost good faith is such a judicially established federal admiralty rule. The Supreme Court has long recognized the doctrine. See *McLanahan v. Universal Ins. Co.*, 26 U.S. (1 Pet.) 170, 185 (1828) ("The contract of insurance has been said to be a contract *uberrimae fidei*, and the principles which govern it, are those of an enlightened moral policy."); *Phoenix Mut. Life Ins. Co. v. Raddin*, 120 U.S. 183, 189 (1887); *Stipcich*, 277 U.S. at 316. In fact, by the time of the Court's *Stipcich* decision in 1928, the doctrine was referred to as a "traditional" aspect of insurance law. 277 U.S. at 316. Acknowledging this tradition in insurance law, we discussed the doctrine in the context of a fire insurance case in 1931. *Springfield Fire & Marine Ins. Co. v. Nat'l Fire Ins. Co.*, 51 F.2d 714, 719 (8th Cir. 1931). In *Springfield*, we explained that the doctrine of *uberrimae fidei* was a "cardinal rule of

insurance contracts . . . early adopted as to marine insurance contracts." *Id.* Other circuits have long acknowledged this doctrine in the maritime insurance context as well. *See, e.g., Ingersoll Milling Mach. Co. v. M/V Bodena*, 829 F.2d 293, 308 (2d Cir. 1987); *E. Coast Tender Serv., Inc. v. Robert T. Winzinger, Inc.*, [—13—] 759 F.2d 280, 284 n.3 (3d Cir. 1985); *Kilpatrick Marine Piling v. Fireman's Fund Ins. Co.*, 795 F.2d 940, 942 (11th Cir. 1986).

Although the Fifth Circuit rejected the doctrine of utmost good faith in favor of state law in *Albany Insurance Co. v. Anh Thi Kieu*, 927 F.2d 882 (1991), a number of circuits which have addressed the question since then, including our own, have concluded that the doctrine remains established federal precedent. In *Shipley v. Ark. Blue Cross and Blue Shield*, we recognized in 2003 that "insurance policies are traditionally contracts *uberrimae fidei*," in upholding a right of rescission where material information had been withheld on a health insurance application governed by ERISA. 333 F.3d at 903 (quoting *Stipcich*, 277 U.S. at 316). The Ninth Circuit pointedly rejected the approach of the Fifth Circuit while deciding a maritime insurance case, explaining that "in the face of 200 years of precedent, it takes more than a single circuit case and spotty citation in recent years to uproot an entrenched doctrine." *Certain Underwriters at Lloyds, London v. Inlet Fisheries, Inc.*, 518 F.3d 645, 653 (9th Cir. 2008). Appellate courts in the Second Circuit, Third Circuit, and Eleventh Circuit have reached a similar conclusion in the maritime context. *See AGF Marine Aviation & Transp. v. Cassin*, 544 F.3d 255, 262–63 (3d Cir. 2008); *N.Y. Marine & Gen. Ins. Co. v. Tradeline*, 266 F.3d 112, 123 (2d Cir. 2001); *HIH Marine Serv., Inc. v. Fraser*, 211 F.3d 1359, 1362–63 (11th Cir. 2000).

Based on its lengthy history, we conclude that "no rule of marine insurance is better established tha[n] the utmost good faith rule." *Inlet Fisheries*, 518 F.3d at 653–54 (quoting Thomas J. Schoenbaum, *The Duty of Utmost Good Faith in Marine Insurance Law: A Comparative Analysis of American and English Law*, 29 J. Mar. L. & Com. 1, 11

(1998)). We thus decline to follow the approach adopted by a single circuit in *Anh Thi Kieu* or to fashion a new rule based on policy considerations urged by Continental Cement. Under the Supreme Court's longstanding framework in *Wilburn Boat*, "[o]ur only task is to determine whether *uberrimae fidei* is already an [—14—] established rule of federal maritime law," and we conclude that it is. *Inlet Fisheries*, 518 F.3d at 654.

IV.

Continental Cement argues in the alternative that the district court erred by denying its motion for judgment as a matter of law on Starr Indemnity's utmost good faith defense. We must first consider whether this argument was properly preserved for appeal. Upon examining the record, we conclude that it was not. A party cannot challenge the sufficiency of the evidence if it failed to file a postverdict motion under Rule 50(b) after the district court denied its Rule 50(a) motion. *See, e.g., S.E.C. v. Das*, 723 F.3d 943, 948 (8th Cir. 2013). Continental Cement asserts that it is raising legal issues and therefore was not required to renew its motion after trial. *See Linden v. CNH Am., LLC*, 673 F.3d 829, 832–34 (8th Cir. 2012). The record does not support that argument.

The specific issues raised by Continental Cement in its motion for judgment as a matter of law involved questions of fact: namely, (1) whether the withheld survey was an innocent omission or a material concealment and (2) whether Starr Indemnity had notice of the existence of the survey at the time it sent its declination letter. To the extent Continental Cement is challenging the denial of its motion for judgment as a matter of law on any grounds other than those raised in its motion at trial, such arguments would be similarly unavailable. *Browning v. President Riverboat Casino-Missouri, Inc.*, 139 F.3d 631, 636 (8th Cir. 1998) ("A party is required to have raised the reason for which it is entitled to judgment as a matter of law in its Rule 50(a) motion before the case is submitted to the jury and reassert that reason in its Rule 50(b) motion after trial."). Based on this record we conclude

that Continental Cement waived its appeal of the denial of its motion for judgment as a matter of law on Starr Indemnity's utmost good faith defense. [—15—]

V.

Finally, Continental Cement argues that the district court erred by failing to instruct the jury that it must determine whether its nondisclosure of the 2008 survey was material to the risk insured by Starr Indemnity. In order "to preserve an argument concerning a jury instruction for appellate review, a party must state distinctly the matter objected to and the grounds for the objection on the record." *Dupre v. Fru-Con Eng'g, Inc.*, 112 F.3d 329, 334 (8th Cir. 1997). At the jury instruction conference in the district court Continental Cement objected to the utmost good faith defense instruction solely on the grounds that "there is no evidence to support submitting on the doctrine of the duty of utmost good faith." Continental Cement did not object at the trial stage to the wording of the instruction on the basis it raises on appeal, namely the purported failure to instruct on materiality.

Moreover, quite apart from the issue of waiver, the district court did not abuse its discretion in submitting instruction No. 8 on the defense of utmost good faith. *Friedman*, 606 F.3d at 499. Even when "a portion of a jury instruction is assigned as error," we must "look to the instructions as a whole" to determine whether such error is prejudicial. *Villanueva v. Leininger*, 707 F.2d 1007, 1009–10 (8th Cir. 1983). The relevant instruction stated that "[t]he doctrine of utmost good faith requires policy holders to disclose facts to an insurer that *are material* to a calculation of the insurance risk," and defined materiality as "something which would have influenced the judgment of a prudent underwriter in calculating the insurance risk and/or setting terms or conditions of coverage." (Emphasis added). While this language appeared in the introductory part of the instruction given by the district court rather than in the verdict directing paragraph, "[n]o prejudicial error resulted, because the court adequately covered the subject area." *Id.* at 1010. We conclude that "taken as a whole" this instruction "fairly and adequately presented . . . the applicable law to a jury." *Id.* [—16—]

VI.

Accordingly, we affirm the judgment of the district court.

This page intentionally left blank

United States Court of Appeals for the Ninth Circuit

United States Court of Appeals
for the Ninth Circuit

No. 12-73385

COLUMBIA RIVERKEEPER
VS.
UNITED STATES COAST GUARD

On Petition for Review of an Order of the United
States Coast Guard

Decided: August 5, 2014

Citation: 761 F.3d 1084, 2 Adm. R. 478 (9th Cir. 2014).

Before **ALARCÓN, TASHIMA,** and **IKUTA,** Circuit
Judges.

[—3—] **IKUTA,** Circuit Judge:

This appeal addresses one of the several administrative proceedings in which Columbia Riverkeeper, Columbia-Pacific Common Sense, and Wahkiakum Friends of the River (collectively Riverkeeper) have attempted to intervene in an effort to prevent LNG Development Company, LLC (doing business as Oregon LNG), from constructing a liquefied natural gas facility and pipeline along the Columbia River in Oregon. As part of the lengthy terminal siting process, the Coast Guard provided the Federal Energy Regulatory Commission (FERC) with a letter of recommendation (sometimes referred to as a LOR) regarding the suitability of the waterway for vessel traffic associated with the proposed facility. Riverkeeper petitions for review of the Coast Guard's issuance of the letter of recommendation, contending that we have jurisdiction under 15 U.S.C. § 717r(d)(1), which authorizes judicial review of agency orders and actions that "issue, condition, or deny any permit, license, concurrence, or approval." Because the letter of recommendation is not such an order or action, we conclude we lack jurisdiction and dismiss the petition for review. [—4—]

I

Liquefied natural gas (LNG) is natural gas that has been "supercooled into liquid form" and "reheated back into gas form at natural gas terminals" for transport to customers.

Wash. Gas Light Co. v. FERC, 532 F.3d 928, 929 n.1 (D.C. Cir. 2008). Although the process for liquefying natural gas has been known since the 19th Century and used commercially since the 1950s, interest in transporting LNG for commercial use increased first in the 1970s due to declines in gas reserves, and again more recently. *See* Jacob Dweck, David Wochner, & Michael Brooks, *Liquefied Natural Gas (LNG) Litigation After the Energy Policy Act of 2005: State Powers in LNG Terminal Siting*, 27 Energy L.J. 473, 473 (2006). The supercooling process reduces the volume of the natural gas to 1/600th of natural gas in vapor form, and, according to the Coast Guard, makes transporting liquefied natural gas "the most economical way to import natural gas from overseas." Once natural gas has been liquefied, it can be transported in an LNG tanker to an LNG import terminal, which receives, stores and processes the LNG. These facilities are "typically sited in coastal areas with shipping access." *AES Sparrows Point LNG, LLC v. Smith*, 527 F.3d 120, 124 (4th Cir. 2008). Because activities involving LNG have a potential for explosions, fires, and spills, federal, state, and local governments have taken steps to regulate the siting and operation of LNG terminal facilities.

A

To understand the role of the Coast Guard's letter of recommendation in the regulatory process, it is necessary to review the historical development of the legal framework for siting LNG terminal facilities. Prior to 2005, different federal [—5—] agencies allocated responsibility for regulating LNG terminal facilities amongst themselves by means of interagency agreements, with little guidance from Congress. The Natural Gas Act of 1938 (NGA) authorized FERC's predecessor agency (the Federal Power Commission) to approve the import and export of natural gas, 15 U.S.C. § 717b (1938), and the extension and improvement of transportation facilities, 15 U.S.C. § 717f (1938), but did not reference LNG terminal facility siting responsibility. Beginning in 1968, Congress enacted a series of pipeline safety statutes that gave the Department of

Transportation (DOT) authority to issue minimum safety standards for siting new liquefied natural gas pipeline facilities, 49 U.S.C. § 60103. DOT and FERC ultimately entered into an interagency agreement to allocate their respective responsibilities. *See* Memorandum of Understanding between the Department of Transportation and the Federal Energy Regulatory Commission regarding Liquefied Natural Gas Transportation Facilities (1985).

In addition, the Coast Guard asserted authority over siting decisions affecting the safety and security of port areas and navigable waterways under the Ports and Waterways Safety Act, 33 U.S.C. §§ 1221–1236, the Magnuson Act of 1950, 50 U.S.C. § 191, and Executive Order No. 10173, 15 Fed. Reg. 7005 (Oct. 18, 1950). In early 1978, the Coast Guard and a DOT subagency (the Office of Pipeline Safety Operation of the Materials Transportation Bureau) entered into a memorandum of understanding regarding the division of regulatory responsibility over LNG terminals. Believing that the agreement gave it broad regulatory authority, the Coast Guard commenced a rulemaking proceeding and proposed regulations that would require any person siting an LNG facility to obtain a "use permit" from the Coast Guard. Liquefied Natural Gas Facilities, 43 Fed. Reg. 34362, 34365 [—6—] (Aug. 3, 1978) (proposed 33 C.F.R. § 126.2012). After further congressional action suggested that the Coast Guard's view of its regulatory authority was too broad, the Coast Guard reduced its ambition. Pursuant to a revised memorandum of understanding with DOT, signed in 1986, the Coast Guard proposed revised regulations replacing its proposed "use permit" requirement with a requirement that a project proponent merely secure a letter of recommendation from the Coast Guard. Liquefied Natural Gas Waterfront Facilities, 53 Fed. Reg. 3370, 3377 (Feb. 5, 1988) (proposed 33 C.F.R. § 127.009).

Beginning in the 1990s, there was a rapid increase in efforts to site LNG import terminals. In response to growing safety and environmental concerns, a number of states claimed authority to regulate LNG facilities under specific state LNG statutes or under general environmental, zoning, or construction laws. *See* Parfomake & Vann, Congressional Research Service, *Liquefied Natural Gas (LNG) Import Terminals: Siting, Safety, and Regulation*, at 16–17 (Dec. 14, 2009); *see also, e.g., Weaver's Cove Energy, LLC v. R.I. Coastal Res. Mgmt. Council*, 589 F.3d 458, 472–73 (1st Cir. 2009); *AES Sparrows Point LNG*, 527 F.3d at 124. California also asserted exclusive authority to regulate LNG facilities that did not impact interstate commerce, claiming that FERC lacked authority under the NGA to regulate such sites. *See, e.g., Re: Sound Energy Solutions*, Notice of Intervention and Protest of the Public Utilities Commission of the State of California, at 7–9, FERC Docket No. CP04-58-000 (Feb. 23, 2004).

In 2004, FERC, the Coast Guard, and a DOT subagency (the Research and Special Programs Administration) responded to the terrorist events of September 11, 2001 by [—7—] entering into another interagency agreement to divide regulatory responsibility for the safety and security review of waterfront LNG facilities. This agreement confirmed that FERC had lead regulatory authority for the siting and construction of onshore LNG facilities. The agencies also agreed that FERC would be the lead agency for preparing an environmental impact statement (EIS) under the National Environmental Policy Act (NEPA),[1] 42 U.S.C. §§ 4321–4370h.

In 2005, consistent with this 2004 interagency agreement, the Coast Guard issued a "Navigation and Vessel Inspection

---

[1] For all "major Federal actions significantly affecting the quality of the human environment" the responsible official must conduct environmental analyses pursuant to NEPA. 42 U.S.C. § 4332(C). Such analysis must include a "full and fair discussion of [the action's] significant environmental impacts and shall inform decisionmakers and the public of the reasonable alternatives which would avoid or minimize adverse impacts or enhance the quality of the human environment." 40 C.F.R. § 1502.1. "Major federal actions" include "projects and programs entirely or partly financed, assisted, conducted, regulated, or approved by federal agencies." 40 C.F.R. § 1508.18(a).

Circular," NVIC 05-05, providing guidance for persons "seeking a permit to build and operate a shore-side LNG terminal." The circular confirmed that FERC was responsible for authorizing the siting and construction of onshore LNG facilities, and was the lead agency for the NEPA process. The circular stated that the Coast Guard would serve as a cooperating agency under NEPA, *see* 40 C.F.R. § 1501.6, and would provide FERC with a letter of recommendation (as required in the Coast Guard's 1988 regulations) that set forth its formal evaluation of the suitability of the waterway for LNG marine traffic. According to the Coast Guard, issuing such a letter of recommendation was a "federal action which [—8—] requires compliance with NEPA" to the same extent as FERC's authorization for construction and operation of an LNG facility.

Just a few months later, Congress enacted the Energy Policy Act (EPAct) of 2005, Pub. L. No. 109-58, 119 Stat. 594, which finally clarified Congress's intent regarding the division of responsibility for siting and operating LNG terminal facilities. The EPAct resolved a number of important issues. First, the Act amended the applicable section of the Natural Gas Act to give FERC "the *exclusive* authority to approve or deny an application for the siting, construction, expansion, or operation of an LNG terminal," *id.*, § 311, 119 Stat. at 686, codified at 15 U.S.C. § 717b(e)(1) (emphasis added), thereby precluding other federal or state agencies from asserting such authority.

Second, in response to the states' interest in having some control over LNG import terminals within their jurisdiction, Congress took a compromise position. Although Congress's grant of "exclusive authority" to FERC in siting decisions precluded the states' imposition of state law requirements, the EPAct preserved the states' authority under several federal environmental laws to require project proponents to obtain a state compliance certification. *Id.*, § 311, 119 Stat. at 686, codified at 15 U.S.C. § 717b(d). But to prevent states from using this authority to block LNG projects completely, *see* Dweck, Wochner, & Brooks, *supra,* at 483–85 (examining Connecticut's successful efforts to

block the Islander East pipeline project using its water quality certification authority under the CWA), the EPAct allowed for federal judicial review of an order or action of a "State administrative agency acting pursuant to Federal law to issue, condition, or deny any permit, license, concurrence, or approval," Pub. L. No. 109- [—9—] 58, § 313, 119 Stat. at 689–90, codified at 15 U.S.C. § 717r(d)(1); *see Islander E. Pipeline Co. v. Conn. Dep't of Envtl. Prot.*, 482 F.3d 79, 85 (2d Cir. 2006) (stating that legislative history confirms that this provision was enacted to allow expedited federal judicial review of a state's denial of a required federal permit); *see also* Dweck, Wochner, & Brooks, *supra,* at 482–83 (noting that the conflict between Islander East and Connecticut led Congress to enact § 717r(d)).

Finally, the EPAct confirmed that FERC was the "lead agency for the purposes of coordinating all applicable Federal authorizations and for the purposes of complying with" NEPA. Pub. L. No. 109-58, § 313, 119 Stat. at 689, codified at 15 U.S.C. § 717n(b)(1). It required FERC to promulgate regulations for NEPA compliance that require a pre-filing of LNG import terminal siting applications. *Id.*, § 311, 119 Stat. at 687, codified at 15 U.S.C. § 717b-1(a).

Although the EPAct did not speak directly to the Coast Guard's role in siting LNG facilities, after the EPAct's enactment, the Coast Guard revisited its internal procedures, and issued a new "Navigation and Vessel Inspection Circular," NVIC 05-08, on December 22, 2008. Now understanding that its letter of recommendation was not a final decision, but rather mere advice to FERC (the agency with exclusive authority to make all siting decisions under the EPAct), the Coast Guard determined its letter of recommendation did not "constitute a permitting action and must not impose requirements or conditions mandated by the Coast Guard." Accordingly, the Coast Guard no longer deemed its letter of recommendation to require separate compliance with NEPA. In 2010, Congress confirmed this approach. In § 813 of the Coast Guard Authorization Act of [—10—] 2010, Congress required "the Secretary of the department in which the

Coast Guard is operating" to "make a recommendation, after considering recommendations made by the States, to the Federal Energy Regulatory Commission as to whether the waterway to a proposed waterside liquefied natural gas facility is suitable or unsuitable for the marine traffic associated with such facility." Pub. L. No. 111-281, § 813, 124 Stat. 2905, 2999. This language confirmed Congress's intent to limit the Coast Guard's role in licensing LNG facilities to issuing letters of recommendation.

B

Accordingly, by 2009 (the year the Coast Guard issued the letter of recommendation in this case), the regulatory framework for a party seeking to site an LNG facility was as follows. FERC was the exclusive siting authority and "lead agency" under NEPA. 15 U.S.C. § 717n(b)(1). FERC required an applicant to engage in a pre-filing procedure before filing an application. *See* 18 C.F.R. §§ 153.12, 157.21 (2009). Among other pre-filing steps, the applicant had to file a letter of intent and waterway suitability assessment with the captain of the port[2] of the zone in which the facility would be located, pursuant to 33 C.F.R. § 127.007 (2009) and 18 C.F.R. § 157.21 (2009). After reviewing the letter of intent and accompanying assessment, the captain of the port would issue a letter of recommendation regarding the proposed facility. 33 C.F.R. § 127.009 (2009). Under Coast Guard regulations, a person "directly affected" by the letter of recommendation could "request reconsideration by the Coast Guard officer responsible," *id.* § 127.015(a) (2009), and [—11—] pursue two additional levels of administrative review, *id.* § 127.015 (2009).[3]

---

[2] A "captain of the port" is the officer so designated by the Commandant of the Coast Guard. 14 U.S.C. § 634(a).

[3] In 2012, the Coast Guard amended its regulations to provide that the letter of recommendation is not appealable because it "is a recommendation from the [captain of the port] to the agency having jurisdiction" and "does not constitute agency action for the purpose of § 127.015 or the Administrative Procedure Act." 33

After the project proponent filed an application with FERC, FERC would undertake an extensive review and consultation process with various federal, state, and local agencies, as well as private parties, and also convene public hearings. *See* 15 U.S.C. §§ 717b(e)(2)(B), 717b-1. This process included the work necessary to comply with NEPA. Other state and federal cooperating agencies assist FERC in preparing an EIS. The project proponent was required to obtain all necessary permits and approvals from state and other federal bodies, and could challenge the denial of any permits or approvals required under federal law in a federal court of appeals. *See id.* § 717r(d)(1). Once this process was completed, FERC could issue a final decision approving or denying the application. *See id.* § 717b(e)(2). FERC could approve the application "in whole or part, with such modifications and upon such terms and conditions" as it found necessary and appropriate. *Id.* § 717b(e)(3).

Upon FERC's issuance of the order, any person could apply for rehearing within 30 days. *Id.* § 717r(a). Within 60 days of FERC's order on the application for rehearing, an aggrieved party could obtain review of the order in the court [—12—] of appeals "wherein the natural-gas company to which the order relates is located" by filing a written petition. *Id.* § 717r(b).

II

We now turn to the facts of this case. In 2007, Oregon LNG began the pre-filing process: It made an initial filing with FERC and filed a letter of intent and a preliminary waterway suitability assessment with the captain of the port for Portland for a proposed LNG terminal and pipeline. The letter stated that Oregon LNG intended to construct an LNG facility on the East Skipanon Peninsula, near the confluence of the Skipanon and the Columbia River in Warrenton, Oregon. In August 2007, FERC published a notice of intent to prepare an EIS for the East Skipanon LNG terminal. LNG Development Company, LLC and Oregon Pipeline

---

C.F.R. § 127.009(b) (2012). That regulation does not apply retroactively. *See id.* § 127.009(e) (2012).

Company; Notice of Intent, 72 Fed. Reg. 50356 (Aug. 31, 2007).

Oregon LNG filed its formal application for the East Skipanon LNG terminal with FERC in October 2008, prompting FERC to issue a notice of application. LNG Development Company, LLC (d/b/a Oregon LNG); Oregon Pipeline Company, LLC; Notice of Applications, 73 Fed. Reg. 65301 (Nov. 3, 2008). Riverkeeper and other environmental organizations intervened in the FERC proceedings pursuant to 18 C.F.R. § 385.214 on November 17, 2008.[4]

On April 24, 2009, the captain of the port issued the letter of recommendation at issue in this case, and the accompanying analysis for Oregon LNG's East Skipanon [—13—] LNG terminal, pursuant to 33 C.F.R. § 127.009. The letter stated the captain's determination "that the applicable portions of the Columbia River and its approaches are not currently suitable, but could be made suitable for the type and frequency of LNG marine traffic associated with this project." The letter of recommendation included the following statement:

> While this letter has no enforcement status, the determinations, analysis, and ultimate recommendation as to the suitability of this waterway, as contained in this letter, would be referenced in concert with a Captain of the Port Order, should an LNG transit be attempted along this waterway without full implementation of the risk mitigation measures.

The analysis accompanying the letter listed additional mitigation measures that were recommended "to responsibly manage the safety and security risks" of the project, while acknowledging that the specifics of each suggested mitigation measure would require "further development through the creation of an Emergency Response Plan as well as a Transit Management Plan."

On May 22, 2009, Riverkeeper and other intervenors requested reconsideration of the letter of recommendation under 33 C.F.R. § 127.015(a) (2009), on the ground that the Coast Guard had failed to comply with NEPA and the [—14—] Endangered Species Act (ESA),[5] 16 U.S.C. §§ 1531–44. The captain of the port denied the motion for reconsideration on July 9, 2009, and Riverkeeper filed an administrative appeal, see 33 C.F.R. § 127.015(b)(1) (2009), which was denied by a district commander on December 2, 2010.

Thereafter, an assistant commandant denied Riverkeeper's second administrative appeal, see 33 C.F.R. § 127.015(c), on August 25, 2012. In his August 25th decision letter, the assistant commandant stated that issuance of the letter of recommendation was not an agency action under the ESA or Administrative Procedure Act (APA), or a "major federal action" under NEPA, because its issuance "carries no legal significance in and of itself," The letter of recommendation was "not a condition precedent for and does not bar FERC" from authorizing the East Skipanon LNG terminal without adopting the captain of the port's recommendations or incorporating any of the mitigation measures. The letter does not "impose any legal requirement on any party to comply with" its recommendations; it is not legally binding on the Coast Guard, any other government agency, or Oregon LNG. Nor does the letter have an impact on vessel traffic, because "[t]he issuance of an LOR neither authorizes, nor prohibits, an LNG carrier from conducting a transit of the waterway" and vessels are not required to obtain Coast Guard transit permits. Rather, the issuance of a captain of the port letter "is separate and distinct from the [—15—] recommendations provided in an LOR, which are not enforceable, and the [captain of the port] is not bound by the recommendations contained in the LOR."

---

[4] The FERC proceedings are ongoing.

[5] The ESA requires each federal agency to "insure that any action authorized, funded, or carried out by such agency . . . is not likely to jeopardize the continued existence of any endangered species or threatened species or result in the destruction or adverse modification of habitat of such species which is determined by the Secretary." 16 U.S.C. § 1536(2).

Riverkeeper then filed a petition for review here, challenging the letter of recommenddation and the August 25, 2012 decision pursuant to 15 U.S.C. § 717r(d)(1) of the Natural Gas Act. Oregon LNG intervened in the proceedings.

III

As a threshold matter, we must determine whether § 717r(d)(1) gives us jurisdiction to review Riverkeeper's challenge to the letter of recommendation and the Coast Guard's final denial of Riverkeeper's administrative appeal. Riverkeeper contends that in enacting § 717r(d)(1), Congress intended to create an exception to the general rule that "review of agency action is typically located in the district courts under the APA absent a specific statutory provision to the contrary," *Cal. Energy Comm'n v. Dep't of Energy*, 585 F.3d 1143, 1148 (9th Cir. 2009). We review questions regarding our jurisdiction de novo. *Sandoval-Luna v. Mukasey*, 526 F.3d 1243, 1245 (9th Cir. 2008) (per curiam). "It is to be presumed that a cause lies outside [of federal courts'] limited jurisdiction, and the burden of establishing the contrary rests upon the party asserting jurisdiction." *Kokkonen v. Guardian Life Ins. Co. of Am.*, 511 U.S. 375, 377 (1994) (citations omitted).

A

We begin with the text of the jurisdictional statute, which provides in relevant part: [—16—]

The United States Court of Appeals for the circuit in which a facility subject to section 717b of this title . . . is proposed to be constructed, expanded, or operated shall have original and exclusive jurisdiction over any civil action for the review of an order or action of a Federal agency (other than the Commission) or State administrative agency acting pursuant to Federal law to issue, condition, or deny any permit, license, concurrence, or approval (hereinafter collectively referred to as "permit") required under Federal law . . . .

15 U.S.C. § 717r(d)(1).

The statute does not define the terms "order or action" or "permit, license, concurrence, or approval," and so we interpret these words according to "their ordinary, contemporary, common meaning." *Transwestern Pipeline Co. v. 17.19 Acres of Prop. Located in Maricopa Cnty.*, 627 F.3d 1268, 1270 (9th Cir. 2010) (internal quotation marks omitted). In making this interpretation, we give due consideration to the context of these words "with a view to their place in the overall statutory scheme." *Satterfield v. Simon & Schuster, Inc.*, 569 F.3d 946, 953 (9th Cir. 2009) (internal quotation marks omitted).

Neither we nor our sister circuits have defined the phrase "order or action" in § 717r(d)(1). In interpreting statutes authorizing judicial review of agency decisions, however, the Supreme Court has held that "[t]he strong presumption is that judicial review will be available only when agency action becomes final." *Bell v. New Jersey*, 461 U.S. 773, 778 (1983) [—17—] (holding that a statute allowing judicial review of "any action" by the Secretary of Education gives federal courts jurisdiction only over orders or actions that are final); *see also FPC v. Metro. Edison Co.*, 304 U.S. 375, 383–84 (1938) (holding that the word "order" in a section of the Federal Power Act substantially identical to § 717r(b) refers only to final orders). This long-standing rule of construction reflects the Supreme Court's inference that Congress generally does not intend to "afford[] opportunity for constant delays in the course of the administrative proceeding," such as would arise if courts could review every interim agency order or action. *Metro. Edison*, 304 U.S. at 383.

Nothing in § 717r(d)(1) overcomes this "strong presumption." *Bell*, 461 U.S. at 778. Congress's intent to authorize judicial review over only final orders or actions is strongly supported by the language of § 717r(d)(1), which limits judicial review to those agency decisions that "issue, condition, or deny any permit, license, concurrence, or approval," the sort of final decisions that occur at the conclusion of an administrative process. Further, reading § 717r(d)(1) as limiting judicial review to final agency decisions is consistent with the long-standing interpretation of § 717r(b), a related section of the same statute. Although § 717r(b) permits federal court review of "an order" issued by FERC, the Supreme Court (as well as our sister circuits and our own precedents) read this language as authorizing judicial review only over final orders. *See Consol. Gas Supply Corp. v. FERC*, 611 F.2d 951, 958 (4th Cir. 1979) (considering § 717r(b)); *Atlanta Gas Light Co. v. FPC*, 476 F.2d 142, 147 (5th Cir. 1973) (same); *cf. Metro. Edison Co.*, 304 U.S. at 383–84 (considering language in the Federal Power Act, 16 U.S.C. § 825*l*(b), which is substantially identical to § 717r(b)); *The Steamboaters v. FERC*, 759 F.2d 1382,[—18—] 1387–88 (9th Cir. 1985) (same); *Papago Tribal Util. Auth. v. FERC*, 628 F.2d 235, 238 (D.C. Cir. 1980) (same). In adding § 717r(d)(1) to § 717r when it enacted the EPAct, Congress did not give any sign it intended federal courts to exercise a broader scope of review over non-FERC decisions than over FERC decisions. Finally, the presumption that Congress intended to authorize judicial review over only final agency decisions is supported by the same considerations relied on by the Supreme Court in *Metropolitan Edison Co.*: construing § 717r(d)(1) as allowing judicial review of every interim action of a state or federal agency would "do violence to the manifest purpose of the provision," 304 U.S. at 384, which was to expedite siting decisions, *see Islander E. Pipeline Co.*, 482 F.3d at 85. Accordingly, we conclude that § 717r(d) authorizes judicial review only over orders or actions that are "final."[6] An action or order is

---

[6] In construing the language of the Federal Power Act, which is substantially identical to § 717r(b), *Papago*, 628 F.2d at 245, we imposed additional requirements for judicial review, holding that a FERC order is subject to judicial review under the Federal Power Act only if "(1) the order is final; (2) the order, if unreviewed, would inflict irreparable harm on the party seeking review; and (3) judicial review at this stage of the process would not invade the province reserved to the discretion of the agency," *City of Fremont v. FERC*, 336 F.3d 910, 913–14 (9th Cir. 2003). We need not address here whether these requirements are also applicable in the § 717r context.

"final when it imposes an obligation, denies a right, or fixes some legal relationship." *City of Fremont*, 336 F.3d at 914 (internal quotation marks omitted); *see also Or. Natural Desert Ass'n v. U.S. Forest Serv.*, 465 F.3d 977, 986–87 (9th Cir. 2006) (same); *Atlanta Gas*, 476 F.2d at 147 (noting an order reviewable under § 717r(b) must be "unambiguous in legal effect" and have "some substantial effect on the parties which cannot be altered by subsequent administrative action"). [—19—]

Section 717r(d)(1) limits our review not only to final actions and orders, but also to those that "issue, condition, or deny any permit, license, concurrence, or approval (hereinafter collectively referred to as 'permit') required under Federal law." Although the statute does not define "permit, license, concurrence, or approval," it collectively refers to these terms as "permit," indicating that Congress intended to capture the type of agency determination that grants or denies permission to take some action. *See United States v. Stevens*, 559 U.S. 460, 474 (2010) (applying *noscitur a sociis* canon). The dictionary definition of permit is "a written warrant or license granted by one having authority," Merriam-Webster's Collegiate Dictionary 923 (11th ed. 2003), which is similar to the definitions of the other statutory terms.[7] Indeed, the terms are often defined by one another. *See, e.g.*, Black's Law Dictionary 1176 (8th ed. 2003) (defining "permit" as "a certificate evidencing permission; a *license*" (emphasis added)); *id.* at 938 (defining "license" as "[a] *permission*, usu. revocable, to commit some act" (emphasis added)).

Accordingly, Congress contemplated that an order or action reviewable under § 717r(d)(1) would be (1) a final agency action or order (2) issuing, conditioning or denying

---

[7] *See* Merriam-Webster's Collegiate Dictionary 717 (11th ed. 2003) (defining "license" as "a permission to act"; "a permission granted by competent authority to engage in . . . an activity otherwise unlawful"); *id.* at 259 (defining "concurrence" as "an agreement or union in action"); *id.* at 61 (defining "approval" as "an act or instance of approving" and defining "approve" as "to give formal or official sanction to").

(3) an agency determination (of a sort analogous to a permit) that has the legal effect of granting or denying permission to take some action. [—20—]

B

Applying this interpretation, the letter of recommendation for the East Skipanon LNG terminal is not a permitting action or order under § 19 of the Natural Gas Act.

On its face, the Coast Guard's letter of recommendation for this terminal is not an agency determination granting or denying permission to take some action. As early as 1986, the Coast Guard recognized that its siting authority was limited and retreated from its position that it was authorized to issue a "use permit" for LNG terminal facilities. Instead, it promulgated regulations allowing it to issue only a letter of recommendation. Congress's express grant of exclusive siting authority to FERC, *see* 15 U.S.C. § 717b(e)(1), further clarified that the Coast Guard lacks authority over siting decisions. Congress is assumed to know existing law, and Congress did not require FERC to obtain or comply with the Coast Guard's letter of recommendation, even though the Coast Guard had begun issuing such letters long before the EPAct was enacted. *See Goodyear Atomic Corp. v. Miller*, 486 U.S. 174, 184–85 (1988) ("We generally presume that Congress is knowledgeable about existing law pertinent to the legislation it enacts.").

Congress subsequently confirmed that the Coast Guard's only obligation was to "make a recommendation" to FERC as to the suitability of the waterway. Pub. L. No. 111-281, § 813, 124 Stat. at 2999.[8] Because "recommendation" is not [—21—] defined, we assume Congress adopted the common meaning of the term "recommendation," which is a suggestion or advisement without decisive

---

[8] Congress passed the 2010 Coast Guard Authorization Act after the Coast Guard issued the letter of recommendation for the East Skipanon LNG terminal but before the final administrative appeal denial. The parties do not dispute that the 2010 statute applies here.

authority, *see* Merriam-Webster's Collegiate Dictionary 1039 (11th ed. 2003) (defining "recommendation" as "the act of recommending"); *id.* (defining "recommend" as "to present as worthy of acceptance . . . . ; to endorse as fit worthy or competent . . . ; advise"). Because nothing in the EPAct or the Coast Guard Authorization Act suggests that the Coast Guard's "recommendation" is anything more than expert advice which FERC will use to inform its decision of whether to approve the proposed facility, we conclude the Coast Guard's letter of recommendation for the East Skipanon LNG terminal does not have any conclusive legal effect.[9] *Cf.* Revision of LNG and LHG Waterfront Facility General Requirements, 75 Fed. Reg. 29420, 29423 (May 26, 2010) ("Recommendations expressed in the [letter of recommendation] represent the Coast Guard's professional input and are provided in the context of the Federal, State, or local jurisdictional agency's proceedings, which provide for participation and public comments."). Because a letter is not a "permit, license, concurrence, or approval," for purposes of § 717r(d)(1), it is therefore not subject to judicial review. [—22—]

Riverkeeper raises several arguments against this interpretation. First, Riverkeeper suggests that if § 717r(d)(1) applies only to final actions relating to permits, and does not apply to the Coast Guard's letter of recommendation, it will do no work in the statutory regime. Since we are to interpret statutes to avoid making any provision superfluous, *Corley v. United States*, 556 U.S. 303, 314 (2009), Riverkeeper argues that such an interpretation cannot be correct. We

---

[9] To the extent Riverkeeper argues that the final administrative appeal denial was a "final agency action" based on language in 33 C.F.R. § 127.015(d) (2009), we reject this argument, because nothing in the record indicates that the Coast Guard's final decision had the effect of issuing, conditioning, or denying a permit, *see* 15 U.S.C. § 717r(d)(1). Because Riverkeeper did not appeal the action in district court asserting jurisdiction under the APA, which provides for judicial review of final agency actions, *see* 5 U.S.C. § 704, we need not address whether Riverkeeper could have asserted a claim for relief in that context.

disagree. The main purpose of § 717r(d)(1) was to allow judicial review of state agencies' denial of certifications required under federal environmental laws. *See Islander E. Pipeline Co.*, 482 F.3d at 85–88 (reviewing state order denying petitioner's application for a Water Quality Certificate). Moreover, the NGA itself makes clear that certain federal agency actions are subject to judicial review under this section; for instance, FERC must "obtain the *concurrence* of the Secretary of Defense before authorizing the siting, construction, expansion, or operation of liquefied natural gas facilities affecting the training or activities of an active military installation." 15 U.S.C. § 717b(f)(3) (emphasis added).

Second, Riverkeeper argues that the term "letter of recommendation" is misleading, and as a practical matter, such a letter constitutes a final agency action or order under § 717r(d)(1). We agree that an agency's characterization of its action as being provisional or advisory is not necessarily dispositive, and courts consider whether the practical effects of an agency's decision make it a final agency action, regardless of how it is labeled. Under the APA, for instance, even if the agency does not label its decision or action as final, it may be reviewable if it "has the status of law or comparable legal force" or if "immediate compliance with its terms is expected." *Or. Natural Desert Ass'n*, 465 F.3d at [—23—] 987. In *Bennett v. Spear*, 520 U.S. 154 (1997), the Supreme Court concluded that a biological opinion issued by the Fish and Wildlife Service pursuant to the ESA was an appealable final agency action under the APA because it effectively authorized a federal agency to take endangered species if it complied with the prescribed conditions. *Id.* at 177–78. While styled as an "opinion," the biological opinion had "direct and appreciable legal consequences." *Id.* at 178. Likewise, a document styled as a "guidance document" may amount to a final agency action when it "reflect[s] a settled agency position which has legal consequences." *Appalachian Power Co. v. EPA*, 208 F.3d 1015, 1023 (D.C. Cir. 2000). By contrast, an agency determination that certain property contains wetlands subject to the Clean Water Act is not a reviewable action under the APA, because that decision does not determine rights or obligations from which legal consequences will flow. *Fairbanks N. Star Borough v. U.S. Army Corps of Eng'rs*, 543 F.3d 586, 593–94 (9th Cir. 2008). We have followed the same approach in the NEPA and ESA contexts as well. *See Ramsey v. Kantor*, 96 F.3d 434, 444 (9th Cir. 1996) (concluding an agency's incidental take statement was the functional equivalent of a permit and therefore constituted a "major Federal action" triggering NEPA obligations); *cf. Karuk Tribe of Cal. v. U.S. Forest Serv.*, 681 F.3d 1006, 1021–23 (9th Cir. 2012) (en banc) (concluding the Forest Service's decision authorized rather than advised proposed mining activity and therefore triggers ESA requirements), *cert. denied*, 133 S. Ct. 1579 (2013).

Relying on these precedents, Riverkeeper maintains that the Coast Guard's letter of recommendation for the East Skipanon LNG terminal is the functional equivalent of a permit because either (1) the letter of recommendation is in practice a necessary prerequisite for siting of a facility or [—24—] (2) the letter of recommendation will effectively regulate vessel traffic along the waterway after the facility's construction. We disagree with both assertions.

First, the record does not establish that obtaining the Coast Guard's approval of the proposed site for an LNG terminal is a necessary prerequisite for siting an LNG facility. Here, the Coast Guard has no enforcement authority over FERC's siting decision, and its letter of recommendation does not produce legal consequences. In *Bennett* and *Appalachian Power*, by contrast, the agency action had a "virtually determinative effect" on the project proponent. *Bennett*, 520 U.S. at 169; *see also id.* at 178 (stating that the Fish and Wildlife Service's biological opinion "alter[ed] the legal regime" to which the federal agency was subject and had the power to preclude the federal agency's ability to go forward with its water reclamation project); *Appalachian Power*, 208 F.3d at 1023 (stating that "through the Guidance, EPA has given the States their 'marching orders'").

Nor does the record support Riverkeeper's argument that, as a practical matter, FERC always complies with the Coast Guard's letter of recommendation, which effectively gives it the force of law. In making this claim, Riverkeeper relies primarily on the First Circuit's decision in *City of Fall River v. FERC*, 507 F.3d 1 (1st Cir. 2007). But Riverkeeper's reliance on *Fall River* is misplaced because in that case FERC gave the person seeking to construct an LNG terminal facility a conditional approval that was subject to the Coast Guard's approval of a vessel transportation plan. *Id.* at 3–5. Under these circumstances, the Coast Guard's approval did have binding effect, because FERC had the plenary authority to make a siting order subject to such a requirement. *See* 15 U.S.C. § 717b(e). But nothing in *Fall River* suggests that [—25—] FERC has a firm internal policy to condition its approval upon the Coast Guard's decision, and there is no evidence in the record before us suggesting that FERC has such an entrenched policy generally or imposed such a condition here.

Second, we reject Riverkeeper's claim that the Coast Guard's letter of recommendation will effectively regulate vessel traffic along the waterway after the facility's construction. For this claim, Riverkeeper relies on the captain of the port's statement in the letter of recommendation that "should an LNG transit be attempted along this waterway without full implementation of the risk mitigation measures" the Coast Guard would reference the letter of recommendation's "determinations, analysis, and ultimate recommendation as to the suitability of this waterway" in a "Captain of the Port Order." On its face, this language suggests that the Coast Guard intends to prevent the East Skipananon LNG facility from receiving vessels unless the project proponent complies with the letter's requirements. But the record establishes that the Coast Guard has not taken this position. Most important, the Coast Guard's final administrative decision, dated August 25, 2012, states that mitigation measures in the letter of recommendation are not binding on the captain of the port, and that as a practical matter, the Coast Guard does not and could not regulate the waterways

by preventing vessel transit to LNG terminals that failed to obtain an approval letter. In considering the effect of the letter of recommendation, we are bound by the final determination at the higher level of the agency. *Cf. Nat'l Ass'n of Home Builders v. Defenders of Wildlife*, 551 U.S. 644, 659 (2007) ("[T]he fact that a preliminary determination by a local agency representative is later overruled at a higher level within the agency does not render the decisionmaking process arbitrary and capricious."); *Bechtel v. Admin. Review* [—26—] *Bd., U.S. Dep't of Labor*, 710 F.3d 443, 449 (2d Cir. 2013) (concluding ALJ's error was "beside the point" where the Administrative Review Board recognized the error and explained that it did not affect the case's outcome).[10] Accordingly, we conclude that the letter of recommendation is not in practice a final agency action.[11]

C

Although the record does not establish that the Coast Guard's letter of recommendation is a final agency order or action "to issue,

---

[10] The Coast Guard press release and public relations documents, which also state that Oregon LNG must implement the risk mitigation measures in the Coast Guard's letter of recommendation, merely track the language of the letter, and so do not provide any additional support for Riverkeeper's interpretation. The April 13, 2009 "Executive Brief" cited in Riverkeeper's reply suffers from the same infirmity.

[11] Riverkeeper points to two other documents to support its interpretation of the import of the letter of recommendation, but its arguments are meritless. First, Riverkeeper claims that language in the Bradwood project's final environmental impact statement indicates that LNG tankers must comply with mitigation measures set forth in the Coast Guard's letter of recommendation. Even if we interpreted the Bradwood environmental documents as Riverkeeper urges, the Coast Guard analyzed the Bradwood project under its pre-EPAct guidance document (NVIC 05-05), which is no longer applicable here. Riverkeeper's reliance on a May 2009 letter from the Coast Guard to FERC is likewise misplaced; that letter merely explains that the Coast Guard, not FERC, has jurisdiction over design and equipment requirements on vessels. Nothing in the Coast Guard's letter indicates that the advice contained in a letter of recommendation is binding.

condition, or deny any permit, license, concurrence, or approval" required under Federal law, 15 U.S.C. § 717r(d)(1), this does not mean that the Coast Guard's recommendations are immune from judicial review. [—27—] Rather, any Coast Guard recommendation adopted by FERC in its final order, or any failure to adopt such a recommendation, would be reviewable under 15 U.S.C. § 717r(b). In addition, any final orders regarding vessel traffic issued by the Coast Guard pursuant to its own independent authority will be subject to judicial review as final agency action. *See, e.g., Wong v. Bush,* 542 F.3d 732, 735 (9th Cir. 2008) (considering challenges to rule establishing security zone); *Wilmina Shipping AS v. U.S. Dep't of Homeland Sec.,* 934 F. Supp. 2d 1, 4, 19 (D.D.C. 2013) (considering challenge to a captain of the port's order). But because Riverkeeper has not carried its burden of showing that the letter of recommendation for the East Skipanon LNG terminal is a final agency order or action to issue a permit we lack jurisdiction to consider it or the August 25, 2012 decision affirming the letter.

DISMISSED.

United States Court of Appeals
for the Ninth Circuit

No. 12-35936

LOWER ELWHA KLALLAM INDIAN TRIBE
vs.
LUMMI NATION

Appeal from the United States District Court for the
Western District of Washington

Decided: August 19, 2014

Citation: 763 F.3d 1180, 2 Adm. R. 489 (9th Cir. 2014).

Before **HAWKINS, RAWLINSON,** and **BEA,** Circuit
Judges.

[—3—] **BEA,** Circuit Judge:

This appeal involves a fishing territory dispute between two sets of Indian tribes: the Lower Elwha S'Klallam Tribe, the Jamestown S'Klallam Tribe, and the Port Gamble S'Klallam Tribe ("the Klallam") on the one hand, and the Lummi Nation Tribe ("the Lummi") on the other. The appeal [—4—] arises from a proceeding brought by the Klallam pursuant to the continuing jurisdiction of a 1974 decree issued by the U.S. District Court for the Western District of Washington ("Boldt Decree"), and it involves a dispute over the geographic scope of the Lummi's "usual and accustomed fishing grounds" ("U&A"). We must decide if a prior Ninth Circuit opinion has already decided whether the waters immediately to the west of northern Whidbey Island are a part of the Lummi's U&A such that the question is controlled by law of the case. We conclude that the question has not yet been determined and therefore reverse and remand.

Factual and Procedural Summary

This case arises from a request for determination brought by the Klallam in 2011 to determine the fishing rights of the Lummi under the 1855 Treaty of Point Elliott. The Klallam initiated this subproceeding for a determination of rights, declaratory relief, and to prohibit the Lummi from fishing in certain waters.

On January 22, 1855, the Lummi entered into the Treaty of Point Elliott with the United States. 12 Stat. 927 (1855). This treaty "secured" to the Lummi "[t]he right of taking fish at usual and accustomed grounds and stations." *Id.* at 928. The "usual and accustomed grounds and stations" is abbreviated throughout this opinion as "U&A."

In 1970 the United States, as trustee for all the treaty tribes including the Klallam and the Lummi, filed suit in the Western District of Washington to obtain an interpretation of the Treaty of Point Elliott and an injunction protecting treaty fishing rights from interference by Washington State. Both the Klallam and the Lummi intervened as plaintiffs. In 1974, [—5—] Judge Boldt issued extensive findings of fact, conclusions of law, and a permanent injunction. *United States v. Washington,* 384 F. Supp. 312 (W.D. Wash. 1974) ("Boldt Decree").

The Boldt Decree defined the Treaty of Point Elliott's reference to "usual and accustomed grounds and stations" as meaning "every fishing location where members of a tribe customarily fished from time to time at and before treaty times, however distant from the then usual habitat of the tribe, and whether or not other tribes then also fished in the same waters[.]" *Id.* at 332.

The Boldt Decree discussed the Lummi in particular. *Id.* at 360–62. Judge Boldt found that the Lummi fished using reef nets "on Orcas Island, San Juan Island, Lummi Island and Fidalgo Island, and near Point Roberts and Sandy Point." *Id.* at 360. In addition, Judge Boldt found that the Lummi "trolled the waters of the San Juan Islands for various species of salmon." *Id.* Moreover, "[i]n addition to the reef net locations listed above, the [U&A] of the Lummi Indians at treaty times included the marine areas of Northern Puget Sound from the Fraser River south to the present environs of Seattle[.]" *Id.* at 360.

Judge Boldt also reserved the "continuing jurisdiction" to hear future subproceedings regarding "the location of any of a tribe's

[U&A] not specifically determined by" the Boldt Decree. *Id.* at 419.

1. Subproceeding 89-2

On March 3, 1989, in response to the Lummi's continued fishing of certain disputed waters, the Klallam invoked this [—6—] continuing jurisdiction of the Western District of Washington to initiate Subproceeding 89-2. In this Subproceeding, the Klallam filed a request for determination that "the [U&A] of the Lummi Tribe does not include the Strait of Juan de Fuca, Admiralty Inlet and/or the mouth of Hood Canal."

On February 15, 1990, Judge Coyle of the Western District of Washington granted summary judgment to the Klallam. ("Coyle Decision"). Judge Coyle, after examining the Boldt Decree and the evidence on which it was based, found that "the Lummis' [U&A] were not intended to include the Strait of Juan de Fuca. The court is further persuaded that the mouth of the Hood Canal would not be an area which Judge Boldt would have intended to include in the Lummis' [U&A]." Further, Judge Coyle concluded that "Judge Boldt did not intend Admiralty Inlet to be part of the Lummis' [U&A]."

Judge Coyle, however, did not enter final judgment. *United States v. Lummi Indian Tribe*, 235 F.3d 443, 447–48 (9th Cir. 2000). The Lummi filed a cross-request for determination, and both parties continued to litigate. *Id.* The Lummi's cross-request sought determination that:

> the [U&A] of the Lummi Indian tribe include the waters of the Strait of Juan de Fuca east from the Hoko River to the mouth of the Puget Sound, *the waters west of Whidbey Island*, Admiralty Inlet, the waters south of Whidbey Island to the present environs of Seattle, and the waters of Hood Canal south from Admiralty Inlet to a line drawn from Termination Point due East across Hood Canal. [—7—]

(emphasis added). The Lummi filed a motion to dismiss and a motion for summary judgment; the Klallam filed a cross-motion to dismiss.

On September 4, 1998, Judge Rothstein, to whom the subproceeding had been reassigned, denied the Lummi's motions and granted the Klallam's cross-motion to dismiss. ("Rothstein Decision"). She held that "the court can discern no difference between" the area covered by the Klallam's request for determination before Judge Coyle (*i.e.* the Strait of Juan de Fuca, Hood Canal, and the Admiralty Inlet) and the Lummi's cross-request for determination before her (which included "the waters west of Whidbey Island)." Although "[t]he Lummi's request is worded differently from the [Klallam's] original request[,] . . . [it] covers essentially the same areas." Judge Rothstein also held that, even though Judge Coyle did not enter final judgment, the Coyle Decision was law of the case. Therefore, she adopted the Coyle Decision's finding that "Judge Boldt did not intend to include the Strait of Juan de Fuca, Admiralty Inlet or the mouth of the Hood Canal in the Lummi" U&A. Judge Rothstein accordingly denied the Lummi's cross-request for determination and granted the Klallam's cross-motion to dismiss.

The Lummi appealed Judge Rothstein's order to the Ninth Circuit. *Lummi Indian Tribe*, 235 F.3d at 445. The panel held, first, that the Coyle Decision was not final because Judge Coyle never entered final judgment. *Id.* at 448–49. Because it was not final, the panel continued, the Coyle Decision merged into the Rothstein Decision. *Id.* at 449. Therefore, the panel concluded, both the Coyle Decision and the Rothstein Decision were before the panel in the appeal. *Id.* [—8—]

As the panel framed the issue:

> The question before Judge Coyle was whether the Lummi's [U&A], as expressed in Finding of Fact 46 of *Decision I* [*i.e.* of the Boldt Decree]—"the marine areas of Northern Puget Sound from the Fraser River south to the present environs of Seattle"—included the disputed areas [*i.e.* the Strait of Juan de Fuca, Hood Canal, and the

Admiralty Inlet]. The phrase used by Judge Boldt is ambiguous because it does not delineate the western boundary of the Lummi's [U&A].

Id. The panel analyzed the evidence that was before Judge Boldt and concluded that Judge Boldt had not intended to include either the Strait of Juan de Fuca or the Hood Canal in the Lummi's U&A, because Judge Boldt commonly distinguished between the Puget Sound, where the Lummi fished, and the Strait of Juan de Fuca and Hood Canal, where other tribes fished. *Id.* at 450–52. The panel held that "It is clear that Judge Boldt viewed Puget Sound and the Strait of Juan de Fuca as two distinct regions, with the Strait lying to the west of the Sound." *Id.* at 451–52. The panel also concluded that Judge Boldt did intend for the Admiralty Inlet, *i.e.* "[t]he waters to the west of Whidbey Island, separating that island from the Olympic Peninsula[,]" to be included in the Lummi's U&A, because, "[g]eographically," the Admiralty Inlet

would likely be a passage through which the Lummi would have traveled from the San Juan Islands in the north to the "present environs of Seattle." If one starts at the [—9—] mouth of the Fraser River (a Lummi [U&A], see Findings of Fact 45 & 46) and travels past Orcas and San Juan Islands (also Lummi [U&A], see Finding of Fact 45), it is natural to proceed through Admiralty Inlet to reach the "environs of Seattle."

Id. at 452 (*quoting* the Boldt Decree, 384 F. Supp. at 360). The panel thus affirmed in part and reversed in part. *Id.* at 453.

After *Lummi Indian Tribe* was decided, the Lummi Natural Resources Commission, a tribal body, interpreted the decision as including in the Lummi U&A "Haro Strait and Admiralty Inlet and the waters between the two." In April, 2009, the Klallam moved for the district court in Subproceeding 89-2 to hold the Lummi in contempt for violating the court orders regarding the extent of the Lummi's U&A. The Lummi moved to dismiss, arguing that Subproceeding 89-2 was closed,

and the issue should be addressed in a new subproceeding. The district court, Judge Martinez, granted the Lummi's motion to dismiss and denied the Klallam's motion without prejudice so it could be renewed as a new subproceeding.

2. Subproceeding 11-02

On November 4, 2011, the Klallam initiated Subproceeding 11-02 by filing a request for determination that the Lummi's U&A do not include "the eastern portion of the Strait of Juan de Fuca or the waters west of Whidbey Island (excepting Admiralty Inlet)." In particular, the Klallam defined the "case area" at dispute as follows: [—10—]

Lummi is impermissibly fishing i[n] the marine waters northeasterly of a line running from Trial island near Victoria, British Columbia, to Point Wilson on the westerly opening of Admiralty Inlet, bounded on the east by Admiralty Inlet and Whidbey Island, and bounded on the north by Rosaria Strait, the San Juan Islands, and Haro Strait.

The Klallam then moved for summary judgment.

On October 11, 2012, Judge Martinez granted summary judgment to the Klallam. He concluded that "[t]he law of the case holds that the Lummi U&A does not include the Strait of Juan de Fuca or the waters west of Whidbey Island that were named in the Lummi Cross-request for determination. That issue has been finally determined and may not be re-litigated." The district court came to this conclusion because the Rothstein decision determined that there was no difference between "the Strait of Juan de Fuca, Hood Canal, and the Admiralty Inlet" and a list of locations that included "the waters west of Whidbey Island." The district court also quoted extensively from a report on traditional U&A of Indian tribes, including the Lummi, by Dr. Lane, on which Judge Boldt had relied in making his findings of facts. This report stated that "Lummi fishermen were accustomed, at least in historic times, and probably earlier, to visit fisheries as distant as the Fraser River in the north and Puget Sound in the south." The district court found that this statement would not compel the conclusion that the waters west of northern Whidbey Island should be included in the Lummi U&A because "the Lummi have pointed to no facts before Judge Boldt which would support the conclusion that he intended to include all the marine waters in between." [—11—]

The Lummi moved for reconsideration on the ground that the district court's decision was overbroad because it interpreted the Lummi's U&A as not including waters off the southern coast of the San Juan Islands. The district court denied the motion, but did clarify that "the Lummi U&A should include nearshore waters immediately to the south of San Juan Island and Lopez Island." The Lummi appealed both the district court's original decision and its denial of their motion for reconsideration.

Standard of Review

The parties disagree over what standard of review we should apply in analyzing the district court's conclusion that the law of the case holds that the Lummi U&A does not include the waters west of northern Whidbey Island. The Klallam argue that the correct standard of review is abuse of discretion, and that there are only five circumstances under which a district court abuses its discretion in applying the law of the case, none of which applies here. *See Lummi Indian Tribe*, 235 F.3d at 452–53 (holding that application of the doctrine of law of the case is "discretionary" and that a district court abuses its discretion "in applying the law of the case doctrine only if: (1) the first decision was clearly erroneous; (2) an intervening change in the law occurred; (3) the evidence on remand was substantially different; (4) other changed circumstances exist; or (5) a manifest injustice would otherwise result").

Abuse of discretion, however, is the standard when it is clear that the law of the case doctrine applies. Here, on the other hand, the parties dispute whether the doctrine applies at all, *i.e.* whether the issue has

already "been decided explicitly or by necessary implication." *Id.* at 452. This is a question [—12—] of law and therefore we review *de novo* this threshold question of whether the issue is controlled by law of the case at all.

Analysis

"The law of the case doctrine is a judicial invention designed to aid in the efficient operation of court affairs." *Lummi Indian Tribe*, 235 F.3d at 452. "Under the doctrine, a court is generally precluded from reconsidering an issue previously decided by the same court, or a higher court in the identical case." *Id.* "For the doctrine to apply, the issue in question must have been decided explicitly or by *necessary implication* in the previous disposition." *Id.* (internal quotation marks and brackets omitted) (emphasis added).

In their request for determination here, the Klallam assert that "Subproceeding 89-2 [has] determined that the Lummi's U&A does not include the eastern portion of the Strait of Juan de Fuca or the waters west of Whidbey Island (excepting Admiralty Inlet)." The Klallam state that they "do not seek to relitigate Lummi's [U&A] but, rather, seek to demonstrate that [these] waters . . . have already been found by th[e district c]ourt and the Ninth Circuit Court of Appeals to be outside of Lummi's U&A." The Lummi acknowledge that it is clear law of the case that Judge Boldt did not intend to include the Strait of Juan de Fuca in the Lummi's U&A. The Lummi argue, however, that no prior proceeding has established precisely the eastern boundary of the Strait of Juan de Fuca, and that this eastern boundary is somewhere to the west of the western shores of northern Whidbey Island. The Klallam, on the other hand, argue that the eastern boundary of the Strait of Juan de Fuca is the western shores of northern Whidbey Island. [—13—]

No court has yet *explicitly* determined the eastern boundary of the Strait of Juan de Fuca. Thus, the question before the panel is, has a prior judicial decision in Subproceeding

89-2 already established, by *necessary implication*, the eastern boundary of the Strait of Juan de Fuca such that future litigation of the question in this case is controlled by law of the case.

The district court found that earlier decisions in Subproceeding 89-2 had already established that the Strait of Juan de Fuca's eastern boundary was the western shores of northern Whidbey Island. In reaching this conclusion, the district court relied on Judge Rothstein's statement in Subproceeding 89-2 that she could "discern no difference" between the geographical area comprising "the Strait of Juan de Fuca, Admiralty Inlet, and the Hood Canal," as the Klallam defined the case area in their request for determination in Subproceeding 89-2, and "the waters of the Strait of Juan de Fuca east from the Hoko River to the mouth of Puget Sound, the waters west of Whidbey Island, Admiralty Inlet, the waters south of Whidbey Island to the present environs of Seattle, and the waters of Hood Canal, south of Admiralty Inlet to a line drawn from termination Point due east across Hood Canal," as the Lummi defined the case area in their cross-request for determination in the same Subproceeding. To the district court, this statement demonstrated that the Rothstein Decision held that "the Strait of Juan de Fuca" and "the waters west of Whidbey Island" were not different regions, but rather the "waters" were included in the "Strait." Moreover, the district court determined that, while it is true that the Ninth Circuit reversed the Rothstein Decision with regard to the Admiralty Inlet, finding that the Inlet was a part of the Lummi's U&A, it affirmed the rest of the Rothstein Decision. Therefore, the [—14—] district court held, it is law of the case that the eastern boundary of the Strait of Juan de Fuca is the western shores of northern Whidbey Island.

This reasoning suggests it has already been determined by necessary implication that the waters immediately west of northern Whidbey Island are part of the Strait of Juan de Fuca and hence not a part of the Lummi's U&A. The Rothstein Decision determined that "the Strait of Juan de Fuca, Admiralty Inlet, [and] the mouth of the Hood Canal" and the "waters

west of Whidbey Island" were not different regions, but rather the latter was a subset of the former. The Rothstein Decision also determined that the Strait of Juan de Fuca was not included in the Lummi's U&A. *Lummi Indian Tribe* affirmed the second of these findings, namely that the Strait of Juan de Fuca was not included in the Lummi's U&A. 235 F.3d at 450–52. This finding at least suggests that it also affirmed the first finding that the "waters west of Whidbey Island" are a subset of the Strait of Juan de Fuca, and therefore are not included in the Lummi's U&A.

Other language in *Lummi Indian Tribe*, however, contains reasoning that would suggest just the opposite, namely that the waters immediately to the west of Whidbey Island *are* included in the Lummi's U&A. The reason the 2000 Ninth Circuit panel reversed the Rothstein Decision to find that the Admiralty Inlet *was* included in the Lummi's U&A was that the Admiralty Inlet "would likely be a passage through which the Lummi would have traveled" from the Fraser River, south through the San Juan Islands, to the present environs of Seattle. *Id.* at 452. Applying that reasoning here, the "passage through which the Lummi would have traveled" from the San Juan Islands to the Admiralty Inlet would have been the waters directly to the west of Whidbey Island. Thus, [—15—] this reasoning suggests that the waters immediately to the west of northern Whidbey Island would be included within the Lummi's U&A.

Both the district court and the Klallam on appeal argue that applying this reasoning here would violate "the oft-quoted principle that transit through an area does not, without more specific evidence of fishing, lead to inclusion of an area in a tribe's U&A." This principle comes from the Boldt Decree, which stated

> Marine waters were also used as thoroughfares for travel by Indians who trolled en route. Such occasional and incidental trolling was not considered to make the marine waters traveled thereon the usual and accustomed

fishing grounds of the transiting Indians.

384 F. Supp. at 353 (internal citations omitted). The Ninth Circuit, however, in interpreting the Boldt Decree's language ("the [U&A] of the Lummi Indians at treaty times included the marine areas of Northern Puget Sound from the Fraser River south to the present environs of Seattle," *id.* at 360), concluded that this language meant the Admiralty Inlet was included in the Lummi's U&A, because "it is natural to proceed through Admiralty Inlet to reach the 'environs of Seattle.'" *Lummi Indian Tribe*, 235 F.3d at 452. This suggests that the Ninth Circuit had concluded that the Lummi's use of "the marine areas of Northern Puget Sound from the Fraser River south to the present environs of Seattle" was more than mere "occasional and incidental trolling." If to "proceed through Admiralty Inlet" rendered Admiralty Inlet a part of the Lummi U&A, then to proceed from the [—16—] southern portions of the San Juan Islands to Admiralty Inlet would have the same effect: to render the path a part of the Lummi U&A, just like Admiralty Inlet. This implicit conclusion would suggest that the *Lummi Indian Tribe* panel interpreted the Boldt Decree's language to mean that the Lummi had a continuous and unbroken U&A connecting Fraser River to Seattle. This would further suggest that it has already been determined by necessary implication that the waters immediately west of northern Whidbey Island *are* a part of the Lummi's U&A.

Thus, each of *Lummi Indian Tribe*'s two holdings implies a different result. Therefore, we conclude that *Lummi Indian Tribe* is ambiguous regarding whether the waters immediately to the west of northern Whidbey Island are included within the Lummi U&A, and accordingly that this issue has not yet been decided explicitly or by necessary implication.

The law of the case doctrine applies only when the issue was "decided explicitly or by necessary implication in the previous disposition." *Id.* (internal quotation marks and brackets omitted); *see United Steelworkers of Am. v. Ret. Income Plan For Hourly-Rated*

Employees of ASARCO, Inc., 512 F.3d 555, 564 (9th Cir. 2008) (holding that "law of the case acts as a bar only when the issue in question was actually considered and decided by the first court"). We hold that no prior decision in this case has yet explicitly or by necessary implication determined whether the waters immediately west of northern Whidbey Island are a part of the Lummi's U&A. [—17—] Therefore, the district court erred in concluding that the issue was controlled by law of the case.[1]

Conclusion

Therefore, we **REVERSE** the district court's grant of the Klallam's motion for summary judgment and **REMAND** to the district court for further proceedings consistent with this opinion.

(Reporter's Note: Dissenting opinion follows on p. 495).

---

[1] We agree with Judge Rawlinson that *Lummi Indian Tribe*, 235 F.3d 443, by affirming Judge Rothstein's decision that the Strait of Juan de Fuca is not within the Lummi U&A, implied that it was also affirming Judge Rothstein's conclusion that the waters west of northern Whidbey Island were not a part of the Lummi U&A. The dissent, however, does not address the reasoning implicit in the panel's reversal of Judge Rothstein's conclusion regarding the Admiralty Inlet. That reasoning implied that the Lummi U&A contains an unbroken swath from Fraser River south to the present environs of Seattle, thereby including at least the waters immediately west of Whidbey Island. Because these two implications point in opposite directions, the Ninth Circuit opinion cannot have "necessar[il]y impli[ed]" one way or the other whether the Lummi U&A contain any waters west of northern Whidbey Island.

[—17—] **RAWLINSON**, Circuit Judge, dissenting:

I respectfully dissent from the majority's conclusion that no court has determined whether the "usual and accustomed [fishing] grounds and stations" (U&A) for the Lummi Nation Tribe (Lummi) included the waters west of northern Whidbey Island. [—18—]

In my view, the answer to this question is contained in our prior opinion, *United States v. Lummi Indian Tribe*, 235 F.3d 443 (9th Cir. 2000). That case also addressed a challenge to Judge Rothstein's adherence to Judge Coyle's previous determination that neither the Strait of Juan de Fuca, Admiralty Inlet nor the mouth of the Hood Canal were within the Lummi's usual and accustomed fishing areas. *See id.* at 447. Judge Rothstein's adherence to Judge Coyle's decision followed her application of the law of the case doctrine. *See id.*

As the district court noted, Judge Rothstein was quite detailed in her description of the areas sought to be included by the Lummi in its U&A:

> This request [the Lummi Cross-Request for Determination][1] sought a declaration that the Lummi U&A included the waters of the Strait of Juan de Fuca east from the Hoko River to the mouth of Puget Sound, *the waters west of Whidbey Island* to the present environs of Seattle and the waters of Hood Canal. . . . *The Lummi have not asserted that their cross-request covers a different area covered by the Four Tribes' initial request and by Judge Coyle's decision.* Rather, they argue that Judge Coyle's decision is not final and is of no precedential value. The court can discern no difference between the two requests for [—19—] determination, nor have the Lummi convincingly argued that there is a difference. Thus, this

order is intended to resolve both requests for determination.

United States v. Washington, Nos. CV 70-9213 RSM, 11-SP-02, 2012 WL 4846239 at *6 (W.D. Wash., Oct. 11, 2012) (emphases added).

Judge Rothstein's ruling encompassed the following facts:

1. The Four Tribes filed an initial proceeding seeking to exclude the waters west of Whidbey Island from the Lummi U&A. *See id.* at 2.

2. Judge Coyle granted summary judgment in favor of the Four Tribes, but never reduced his order to judgment. *See id.*

3. The Lummi subsequently filed a "Cross-Request For Determination" seeking to include within its U&A the waters west of Whidbey Island. *See id.*

4. Judge Rothstein viewed the initial proceeding filed by the Four Tribes seeking to exclude the waters west of Whidbey Island and the cross-request for determination filed by the Lummi seeking to include the waters west of Whidbey Island as the one and the same request—to determine if the waters west of Whidbey Island were included in the Lummi U&A. *See id.* at 6.

5. Judge Rothstein interpreted Judge Coyle's decision as law of the case that the disputed areas, including the [—20—] waters west of Whidbey Island, were not within the Lummi U&A. *See Lummi*, 235 F.3d at 447.

On appeal of Judge Rothstein's ruling, we reversed only to the extent that her ruling excluded Admiralty Inlet from the Lummi U&A. In doing so, we described Admiralty Inlet as "consist[ing] of the waters to the west of Whidbey Island, separating that island from the Olympic Peninsula. . . ." *Id.* at 452. It stands to reason that any other portion of the

---

[1] The Lummi's Cross-Request for Determination sought to include the same areas that competing tribes described as the Four Tribes sought to have excluded in the initial petition before Judge Coyle. *See Lummi*, 235 F.3d at 446–47.

waters west of Whidbey Island that were not included in our description remain excluded from the Lummi U&A. In *Lummi,* we had no difficulty "concluding that Judge Rothstein properly applied the law of the case doctrine."

I continue in the belief that our prior conclusion is correct, and that the law of the case doctrine precludes further expansion of the Lummi U&A. I would affirm the district court.

United States Court of Appeals
for the Ninth Circuit

No. 13-35854

LACANO INVESTMENTS, LLC
vs.
BALASH

Appeal from the United States District Court for the
District of Alaska

Decided: August 28, 2014

Citation: 765 F.3d 1068, 2 Adm. R. 497 (9th Cir. 2014).

Before **WALLACE, WARDLAW,** and **CHRISTEN,** Circuit Judges.

[—3—] **WALLACE,** Circuit Judge:

Plaintiffs-Appellants Lacano Investments, LLC, Nowell Avenue Development, and Ava L. Eads, allege that they hold land patents that were issued by the federal government many years before Alaska entered the Union. The patents give title to certain streambeds in Alaska. In 2010 and 2011, the Alaska Department of Natural Resources determined that the waterways above these streambeds were navigable in 1959, the year Alaska was admitted to the Union, and remain navigable. Under the Submerged Lands Act of 1953, all land beneath such waterways belongs to the State of Alaska. *See* 43 U.S.C. § 1311(a) ("[i]t is determined and declared to be in the public interest that (1) title to and ownership of the lands beneath navigable waters within the boundaries of the respective States . . . are, subject to the provisions hereof, recognized, confirmed, established, and vested in and assigned to the respective States"); Act to Provide for the Admission of the State of Alaska into the Union, Pub. L. No. [—4—] 85-508, 72 Stat. 339, 343 § 6(m) (1958) ("[t]he Submerged Lands Act of 1953 shall be applicable to the State of Alaska and the said State shall have the same rights as do existing States thereunder"). The Department sent letters to Plaintiffs with the navigability determinations and its conclusion that the streambeds are "state-owned."

According to Plaintiffs, Alaska's determination that the waterways have been navigable since 1959 does not disturb the title to the land that was granted to them by the federal patents. Plaintiffs sued the Alaska officials who made the navigability determinations in federal court. Plaintiffs allege that they retain title to the disputed lands because, under the Submerged Lands Act, streambeds that had already been patented by the federal government were not granted to Alaska upon its statehood. *See* 43 U.S.C. § 1301(f) ("[t]he term 'lands beneath navigable waters' [that belongs to the states] does not include the beds of streams in lands . . . if such streams were not meandered in connection with the public survey of such lands under the laws of the United States and if the title to the beds of such streams was lawfully patented or conveyed by the United States"). Plaintiffs sought a declaratory judgment that the navigability determinations, and thus the conclusions that the streambeds were state-owned, violated 43 U.S.C. § 1301(f), as well as an injunction prohibiting Defendants from claiming title to the lands beneath the waterways.

The state officials moved to dismiss the complaint under Federal Rule of Civil Procedure 12(b)(1), for lack of subject matter jurisdiction. The district court agreed, and dismissed the action with prejudice. [—5—]

Plaintiffs filed a timely notice of appeal. We review a district court's decision to grant a motion to dismiss for lack of subject matter jurisdiction de novo. *Colony Cove Props., LLC v. City of Carson*, 640 F.3d 948, 955 (9th Cir. 2011). We review the district court's denial of leave to amend for abuse of discretion. *Airs Aromatics, LLC v. Opinion Victoria's Secret Stores Brand Mgmt., Inc.*, 744 F.3d 595, 598 (9th Cir. 2014). We have jurisdiction under 28 U.S.C. § 1291, and affirm.

I.

The state officials moved to dismiss the complaint. The "jurisdictional attack" in their motion was "facial," which means that the state officials "assert[] that the allegations contained in [the] complaint are insufficient on their face to invoke federal jurisdiction," but the officials do not "dispute[] the truth of the allegations." *Safe Air for Everyone v. Meyer*, 373 F.3d 1035, 1039 (9th Cir. 2004). In this facial attack, we must accept all of the factual allegations in the complaint as true. *Wolfe v. Strankman*, 392 F.3d 358, 362 (9th Cir. 2004).

Plaintiffs argue that because we must accept all of their factual allegations as true, we must reverse the district court, insofar as the complaint alleges that the lands are by definition not submerged, state-owned, lands under federal law. In other words, Plaintiffs argue that because we accept the allegations in the complaint as true, at this stage of the litigation we must conclude that Alaska has no interest in the lands under Plaintiffs' complaint, which means that it was error to dismiss the complaint for lack of subject matter jurisdiction. [—6—]

While we do accept all of the *factual* allegations in the complaint as true, *id.*, we do not accept *legal conclusions* in the complaint as true, even if "cast in the form of factual allegations." *Doe v. Holy See*, 557 F.3d 1066, 1073 (9th Cir. 2009) (citation omitted). Plaintiffs' complaint does not include factual allegations that the streambeds are privately owned under the Submerged Lands Act. Instead, the complaint contains only legal conclusions to that effect: "[t]he Alaska Statehood Act delineates the terms under which statehood was granted" and thus Plaintiffs' lands are "exempted from the Submerged Lands Act"; "Plaintiff Lacano is the fee simple owner of record . . ."; "Plaintiff Nowell is the fee simple owner of record . . ."; "Plaintiff Eads is the fee simple owner . . . ".

Further, we also "may look beyond the complaint and consider extrinsic evidence." *Warren v. Fox Family Worldwide, Inc.*, 328 F.3d 1136, 1141 n.5 (9th Cir. 2003). Attached to the complaint are the letters sent by the Department of Natural Resources, upon which the complaint relies to explain the basis of Plaintiffs' action. Those letters demonstrate Alaska's claim of ownership to the disputed properties.

Thus, Plaintiffs cannot avoid a motion to dismiss under Rule 12(b)(1) merely because they asserted in their complaint that Alaska does not own the streambeds. *See, e.g., W. Mohegan Tribe and Nation v. Orange Cnty.*, 395 F.3d 18, 20, 23 (2d Cir. 2004) (dismissing a complaint for lack of subject matter jurisdiction despite "accepting the factual allegations contained in the complaint as true" where the complaint asserted that the plaintiffs, rather than the State of New York, held title to disputed lands). [—7—]

II.

We next consider whether state sovereign immunity bars Plaintiffs' action. The Eleventh Amendment bars federal courts from hearing certain "suit[s]" filed by individual citizens against a state without the consent of the state. U.S. Const. amend. XI; *see generally Hans v. Louisiana*, 134 U.S. 1 (1890). But that Amendment does not bar actions when citizens seek only injunctive or prospective relief against state officials who would have to implement a state law that is allegedly inconsistent with federal law. *See generally Ex parte Young*, 209 U.S. 123 (1908). "The *Ex parte Young* doctrine is founded on the legal fiction that acting in violation of the Constitution or federal law brings a state officer into conflict with the superior authority of the Constitution, and he is in that case stripped of his official or representative character and is subjected in his person to the consequences of his individual conduct." *Cardenas v. Anzai*, 311 F.3d 929, 935 (9th Cir. 2002) (internal quotation marks omitted) (citing *Young*, 209 U.S. at 159–60). Not all actions that solely seek prospective relief against state officials fall within the *Young* exception, however. *See Idaho v. Coeur d'Alene Tribe of Idaho*, 521 U.S. 261 (1997).

A.

In *Coeur d'Alene*, the Coeur d'Alene Tribe sued the State of Idaho and state officers who enforced Idaho law in federal court, alleging an interest under federal law in lands submerged under navigable waterways within the original boundaries of the Coeur d'Alene Reservation. *Id.* at 264–65. Those lands had been "long deemed by [Idaho] to be an integral part of its territory." *Id.* at 282. The Tribe brought title claims, sought a declaratory judgment to establish its [—8—] right to use and occupy the lands, and sought an injunction prohibiting Idaho from infringing upon its rights to the land. *Id.* at 265. The "underlying dispute" was "[w]hether the Coeur d'Alene Tribe's ownership extends to the banks and submerged lands of [] [L]ake [Coeur d'Alene] and various . . . rivers and streams [within the boundaries of the Coeur d'Alene Reservation] . . . or instead ownership is vested in the State of Idaho." *Id.* at 264.

Idaho moved to dismiss the complaint on Eleventh Amendment sovereign immunity grounds. *Id.* at 265. When the case reached the Supreme Court, a five-Justice majority agreed that the Eleventh Amendment barred the action. *Id.* at 288; *id.* at 296–97 (O'Connor, J., concurring).

Justice Kennedy's principal opinion was joined in part by four other members of the Supreme Court. The principal opinion recognized that "[a]n allegation of an ongoing violation of federal law where the requested relief is prospective is ordinarily sufficient to invoke the *Young* fiction." *Coeur d'Alene*, 521 U.S. at 281. But the case was "unusual in that the Tribe's suit [was] the functional equivalent of a quiet title action which implicates special sovereignty interests." *Id.* According to the principal opinion, the parties (and the Court) agreed "that the Tribe could not maintain a quiet title suit against Idaho in federal court, absent the State's consent." *Id.*

Although the Tribe was not actually seeking quiet title relief, the Court concluded that the declaratory and injunctive relief the Tribe sought was "close to the functional equivalent of quiet title." *Id.* at 282. This similarity to a quiet title action was "especially troubling when coupled with the far-reaching and invasive relief the Tribe seeks," which if successful [—9—] "would bar the State's principal officers from exercising their governmental powers and authority over the disputed lands and waters" because the Tribe had independent sovereign authority. *Id.* The Court looked to "the realities of the

relief the Tribe demand[ed]." *Id.* Because of the historical and legal importance of submerged lands to state sovereignty, the Court held that "if the Tribe were to prevail, Idaho's sovereign interest in its lands and waters would be affected in a degree fully as intrusive as almost any conceivable retroactive levy upon funds in its Treasury." *Id.* at 287. Thus, "[t]he dignity and status of its statehood allow[ed] Idaho to rely on its Eleventh Amendment immunity," and the Court ordered the Tribe's action dismissed. *Id.* at 287–88.

Justices O'Connor, Scalia and Thomas joined in the portions of *Coeur d'Alene* described above, and joined in full a separate partial concurrence written by Justice O'Connor. Although this was only a partial concurrence, we analyze it along with the principal opinion in which only two Justices concurred to determine what part of the principal opinion was agreed upon by the five-Justice majority of the Court. *See Agua Caliente*, 223 F.3d at 1046 (discussing both the principal opinion and concurrence of *Coeur d'Alene*). In her concurrence, Justice O'Connor agreed that "[t]his case is unlike a typical *Young* action," and thus barred by the Eleventh Amendment, for two reasons. 521 U.S. at 289 (O'Connor, J., concurring). First, the Tribe's action was "the functional equivalent of an action to quiet [the Tribe's] title to the bed of Lake Coeur d'Alene," which was not acceptable under the Eleventh Amendment because "[a] federal court cannot summon a State before it in a private action seeking to divest the State of a property interest." *Id.* Second, "the Tribe does not merely seek to possess [the] land . . . [but] seeks to eliminate altogether the State's regulatory power over the [—10—] submerged lands at issue." *Id.* Justice O'Connor concluded that these distinctions from the "typical *Young* action" meant that "the Tribe's suit must be dismissed." *Id.* at 291.

B.

Here, Plaintiffs' action implicates precisely the same sovereignty interests as in *Coeur d'Alene* itself. In their complaint, Plaintiffs allege they are "fee simple owners" of the streambeds beneath the navigable waters, seek to lift the "cloud" from their properties, and request that a federal court return "full use and enjoyment of their property." The relief Plaintiffs request "is close to the functional equivalent of quiet title." *Id.* at 282. The lands at issue are streambeds beneath navigable waters, which are "lands with a unique status in the law and infused with a public trust." *Id.* at 283. If the court were to rule in Plaintiffs' favor, the "benefits of ownership and control would shift from the State" to Plaintiffs. *Id.* at 282. Thus, the Eleventh Amendment bars this action.

Coeur d'Alene provides only a "unique" and "narrow" exception to *Young*, and does not "bar all claims that affect state powers, or even important state sovereignty interests." *Agua Caliente*, 223 F.3d at 1048. But when an action implicates the "exact issues" of *Coeur d'Alene* itself, namely "navigability of waters or the state's control over submerged lands," federal courts lack jurisdiction to hear the case. *Anderson-Tully Co. v. McDaniel*, 571 F.3d 760, 763 (8th Cir. 2009). This case presents the same issues as *Coeur d'Alene*.

Although we affirm the district court's judgment that it lacked jurisdiction over this action, we do not affirm its reasoning. Guided by the parties, the district court made a [—11—] good-faith effort to determine whether Alaska has a sufficient interest in the lands to assert Eleventh Amendment immunity, and did so by analogizing to other circumstances in which a government entity claims title to property. But that attempt to assess the interest in the property held by the state is not necessary under *Coeur d'Alene*. The approach we take instead is "functional": we compare the relief sought by Plaintiffs to a quiet title action, and dismiss because it was "close to the functional equivalent" of such an action, as the lands at issue are submerged lands beneath navigable waters, which have a "unique status in the law" insofar as "[s]tate ownership of them has been considered an essential attribute of sovereignty." 521 U.S. at 282–83 (internal quotation marks and citation omitted); *see also Agua Caliente*, 223 F.3d at 1046 ("[t]he challenge posed by *Coeur d'Alene* is to figure out whether the Tribe's claims

here are of the same character as those in *Coeur d'Alene*").

C.

We next turn to Plaintiffs' counter-arguments.

1.

Plaintiffs first suggest that *Coeur d'Alene* is no longer good law. They assert that we should instead follow the Supreme Court's more recent guidance, that "[i]n determining whether the doctrine of *Ex parte Young* avoids an Eleventh Amendment bar to suit, a court need only conduct a 'straightforward inquiry into whether [the] complaint alleges an ongoing violation of federal law and seeks relief properly characterized as prospective.'" *Verizon Md., Inc. v. Pub. Serv. Comm'n of Md.*, 535 U.S. 635, 645 (2002) (quoting *Coeur d'Alene*, 521 U.S. at 296). [—12—]

But *Coeur d'Alene* remains binding upon us. *Verizon* did not overrule *Coeur d'Alene*, and in fact the Court quoted language from the earlier opinion. Moreover, the Court recently affirmed *Coeur d'Alene*'s core holding that the Eleventh Amendment bars actions that are "the functional equivalent of a quiet title suit" against a state. *Va. Office for Prot. and Advocacy v. Stewart*, 131 S. Ct. 1632, 1639–40 (2011) (quoting *Coeur d'Alene*, 521 U.S. at 282). To the extent there is some tension between the "straightforward inquiry" recognized in *Verizon* and the "unique" and "narrow" circumstances of *Coeur d'Alene*, we must follow *Coeur d'Alene*, "which directly controls, leaving to [the Supreme] Court the prerogative of overruling its own decisions." *Agostini v. Felton*, 521 U.S. 203, 237 (1997) (citation omitted).

2.

Plaintiffs next argue that this case is "the exact opposite factual situation" of *Coeur d'Alene*, because here Alaska sought to divest Plaintiffs of their alleged longstanding title, whereas in *Coeur d'Alene*, it was the plaintiffs who sought to divest the state of its longstanding title. But that is not a proper distinction of *Coeur d'Alene*. The majority opinion was not predicated upon the length of the state's claim to title. Instead, it was based upon the "principle that [submerged lands beneath navigable waters] are tied in a unique way to sovereignty," regardless of when the state determined that the waters were navigable. 521 U.S. at 286; *see also Anderson-Tully*, 571 F.3d at 761 (dismissing under *Coeur d'Alene* despite the recency of the state's title claim to the submerged lands). [—13—]

3.

Finally, Plaintiffs attempt to distinguish their action from that in *Coeur d'Alene* because there, if the tribe were to have been awarded the property, it would have deprived the State of Idaho of "all regulatory power" over the submerged lands. This is true: federally-recognized tribes are themselves sovereigns. *See, e.g., Coeur d'Alene*, 521 U.S. at 268 (stating that "Indian tribes . . . should be accorded the same status as foreign sovereigns"). If the Coeur d'Alene Tribe were awarded title, Idaho may not have had any regulatory authority at all over the disputed lands. Because Plaintiffs in this case are not a separate sovereign, they argue that "Alaska would remain free to exercise lawful regulatory jurisdiction over Landowners' property as they do over other private lands." According to Plaintiffs, this case is distinguishable from *Coeur d'Alene* because there is no threat that "all regulatory power" would be divested from Alaska.

This is not a sufficient distinction of *Coeur d'Alene*. Both the principal opinion and Justice O'Connor's concurrence mention tribal sovereignty as a consideration to support the conclusion that the action should be dismissed. But neither opinion considered this determinative.

The principal opinion discussed the Tribe's sovereign character, which meant its action sought "far-reaching and invasive relief" that was "in effect, a determination that the lands in question are not even within the regulatory jurisdiction of the State." *Id.* at 282. At that point in the opinion, however, the majority

had already concluded that "Eleventh Amendment would bar" "a quiet title suit against Idaho" or relief that "is close to the functional equivalent of quiet title" in federal court. *Id.* at 281–82. The fact that the [—14—] plaintiff was a federally recognized tribe only made the Tribe's action "especially troubling" in its impact on state sovereignty. *Id.* at 282.

Similarly, Justice O'Connor had two bases for distinguishing the case from a typical *Young* action that could be heard in federal court. *Id.* at 289 (O'Connor, J., concurring). First, "the suit is the functional equivalent of an action to quiet [the plaintiff's] title to the bed of Lake Coeur d'Alene." *Id.* "A federal court cannot summon a State before it in a private action seeking to divest the State of a property interest." *Id.* It was only her second basis that discussed the tribe's attempt to divest Idaho of all regulatory power. Even in that context, she continued to make clear that "[c]ontrol of [submerged lands] is critical to a State's ability to regulate use of its navigable waters." *Id.* Thus, in Justice O'Connor's view, states must possess actual control over submerged lands in order to regulate properly the use of navigable waters. Because the tribe sought "in effect[] to invoke a federal court's jurisdiction to quiet title to sovereign lands," Justice O'Connor concluded that the action had to be dismissed. *Id.* at 296.

Thus, we conclude that the identity of plaintiffs is not dispositive in cases that implicate the *Coeur d'Alene* exception to *Ex parte Young*. *See also Anderson-Tully Co.*, 571 F.3d at 763 (ordering dismissal of an action filed by a private party under *Coeur d'Alene*); *MacDonald*, 164 F.3d at 972 (same). Federal courts lack jurisdiction over all actions where a plaintiff seeks relief that is "close to the functional equivalent of quiet title" over submerged lands that have a "unique status in the law" and which are "infused with a public trust." *Coeur d'Alene*, 521 U.S. at 282–83. [—15—]

III.

Finally, Plaintiffs argue that the district court erred in denying them leave to amend their complaint. But this was not an abuse of discretion. As should be clear, any amendment would be futile. No set of facts pleaded by Plaintiffs would allow their complaint to proceed, given *Coeur d'Alene.*

AFFIRMED.

United States Court of Appeals
for the Ninth Circuit

No. 13-36165

STURGEON
vs.
MASICA

Appeal from the United States District Court for the
District of Alaska

Decided: October 6, 2014

Citation: 768 F.3d 1066, 2 Adm. R. 503 (9th Cir. 2014).

Before **FARRIS, NELSON,** and **NGUYEN,** Circuit Judges.

[—6—] NGUYEN, Circuit Judge:

John Sturgeon ("Sturgeon") challenges the National Park Service's ("NPS") enforcement of a regulation banning the operation of hovercrafts on the Nation River, part of which falls within the Yukon-Charley Rivers National Preserve. The ban prevented Sturgeon from using his personal hovercraft on his moose hunting trips on the Nation River. The State of Alaska intervened, challenging NPS's authority to require its researchers to obtain a permit before engaging in studies of chum and sockeye salmon on the Alagnak River, part of which falls within the boundaries of the Katmai National Park and Preserve.

Sturgeon and Alaska present the same legal argument: § 103(c) of the Alaska National Interest Lands Conservation Act ("ANILCA") precludes NPS from regulating activities on state-owned lands and navigable waters that fall within the boundaries of National Park System units in Alaska. The district court granted summary judgment in favor of the federal appellees. Because we find that Sturgeon's interpretation of § 103(c) is foreclosed by the plain text of the statute, we affirm as to Sturgeon. We hold that Alaska lacks standing to bring this challenge, and thus vacate and remand with instructions that Alaska's case be dismissed. **[—7—]**

I.

The facts are straightforward and largely undisputed. Since 1971, Sturgeon has hunted moose on an annual basis on the Nation River.[1] The lower six miles of the Nation River lie within the Yukon-Charley Rivers National Preserve ("Yukon-Charley"), which is a unit of the National Park System. In 1990, Sturgeon purchased a small, personal hovercraft, which he used on his hunting excursions. In September 2007, while repairing his hovercraft on a gravel bar adjoining the river, Sturgeon was approached by three NPS law enforcement employees. They informed him that NPS regulations prohibited the operation of hovercrafts within the Yukon-Charley and issued him a verbal warning. Sturgeon protested that the NPS regulations were inapplicable because he was operating his hovercraft on a state-owned navigable river. Sturgeon contacted his attorney via satellite phone, who in turn contacted Andee Sears, a Regional Law Enforcement Specialist with NPS. Sears told Sturgeon's attorney that the hovercraft must be removed from the Yukon-Charley. Sturgeon complied.

Later, Sturgeon followed up with Sears over the phone and met with him in Anchorage. Sears advised Sturgeon that even though Alaska might own the submerged land beneath the river, the hovercraft ban was nonetheless in force within **[—8—]** the boundaries of the Yukon-Charley. Sears warned Sturgeon that he risked criminal liability if he operated his hovercraft within the Yukon-Charley. In response to these warnings, Sturgeon refrained from using his hovercraft during the 2008 to 2010 moose hunting seasons and has not been able to hunt

---

[1] The Nation River is a tributary of the Yukon River. While Sturgeon's complaint also mentions his hunting excursions on the Yukon River, part of which also falls within the Yukon-Charley Rivers National Preserve, he failed to raise a separate claim for the Yukon River. Thus, the district court found that only the applicability of the regulation to the Nation River was before the court. *Sturgeon v. Masica*, No. 3:11-CV-0183-HRH, 2013 WL 5888230, at *6 (D. Alaska Oct. 30, 2013). Sturgeon does not challenge that finding on appeal.

on the portions of the Nation River that fall within the boundaries of the Yukon-Charley.

Although Sturgeon sent a letter to then-Secretary of the Interior, Ken Salazar, petitioning for repeal or amendment of the NPS regulations restricting his access to navigable waters located within national park boundaries, he did not receive a response. He then sued in federal district court, seeking an order declaring that NPS's regulations violated ANILCA, as applied to him on state-owned lands and waters, and enjoining the federal defendants from enforcing these regulations.

Alaska intervened, raising the same argument that the application and enforcement of NPS regulations on state-owned lands and waters violated ANILCA. Specifically, Alaska challenged NPS regulations that required employees of the Alaska Department of Fish and Game to obtain a scientific research and collecting permit before engaging in genetic sampling of chum and sockeye salmon on the Alagnak River. These regulations purportedly harmed Alaska "in the form of increased staff time and expense in complying with NPS procedures and in the form of delays in implementing the project." Alaska further argued that NPS's actions both interfered with its sovereign right to manage and regulate its lands and waters and chilled its citizens' ability to enjoy the rights and benefits flowing from its management of state resources. [—9—]

On summary judgment, the district court ruled in favor of the federal appellees. *Sturgeon v. Masica*, No. 3:11-CV-0183-HRH, 2013 WL 5888230, at *9 (D. Alaska Oct. 30, 2013). The district court found that Sturgeon's and Alaska's interpretation of ANILCA § 103(c) lacks support in the plain language of the statute. *Id.* at *8–*9. This appeal followed.

II.

We review questions of law resolved on summary judgment de novo, and the district court's factual findings for clear error. *Al Haramain Islamic Found., Inc. v. U.S. Dep't of Treasury*, 686 F.3d 965, 976 (9th Cir. 2012).

III.

As an initial matter, the federal appellees contend that we lack jurisdiction over this appeal because Sturgeon and Alaska have failed to establish standing. Even though the federal appellees did not present these arguments to the district court below, they may nonetheless do so for the first time on appeal. The constitutional requirements for standing under Article III are jurisdictional, cannot be waived by any party, and may be considered sua sponte. *City of Los Angeles v. Cnty. of Kern*, 581 F.3d 841, 845 (9th Cir. 2009). The oft-repeated "irreducible constitutional minimum of standing contains three elements." *Lujan v. Defenders of Wildlife*, 504 U.S. 555, 560 (1992). "First, the plaintiff must have suffered an 'injury in fact,'" which is both concrete and particularized, as well as actual or imminent. *Id.* "Second, there must be a causal connection between the injury and the conduct complained of," meaning that the injury must be "fairly traceable to the challenged action of the defendant." [—10—] *Id.* (quoting *Simon v. Eastern Ky. Welfare Rights Org.*, 426 U.S. 26, 41–42 (1976) (quotation mark and alterations omitted)). Third, it must be likely that a favorable decision would redress the injury identified. *Id.* at 561.

Apart from these constitutional concerns, "there exists a body of 'judicially self-imposed limits on the exercise of federal jurisdiction'" that forms the prudential standing doctrine. *Cnty. of Kern*, 581 F.3d at 845 (quoting *Allen v. Wright*, 468 U.S. 737, 751 (1984)); *see also Sprint Commc'ns Co., L.P. v. APCC Servs., Inc.*, 554 U.S. 269, 289–90 (2008). Because these considerations are nonconstitutional in nature, they may be deemed waived if not previously raised before the district court. *Cnty. of Kern*, 581 F.3d at 845.

A.

We find that Sturgeon has established standing. The federal appellees argue that Sturgeon has failed to show probable or imminent enforcement of the NPS regulations to meet the first requirement of an injury-in-fact. The federal appellees' view, however, cannot be reconciled with the Supreme Court's recent decision in *Susan B. Anthony List v. Driehaus*, 134 S. Ct. 2334 (2014), where the Court emphasized that *threatened* enforcement actions may suffice to create Article III injuries. "When an individual is subject to such a threat, an actual arrest, prosecution, or other enforcement action is not a prerequisite to challenging the law." *Id.* at 2342. Thus, "a plaintiff satisfies the injury-in-fact requirement where he alleges 'an intention to engage in a course of conduct arguably affected with a constitutional interest, but proscribed by a statute, and there exists a credible threat of prosecution thereunder.'" *Id.* [—11—] (quoting *Babbitt v. Farm Workers Nat'l Union*, 442 U.S. 289, 298 (1979)).

Sturgeon has satisfied the injury-in-fact requirement. He has alleged an intention to use his hovercraft, and has contacted both NPS and the Department of the Interior regarding the applicability and enforcement of the regulation to his hovercraft use. Sturgeon's inability to use his hovercraft for moose-hunting purposes arguably implicates his right under the Privileges or Immunities Clause of the Fourteenth Amendment "to use the navigable waters of the United States, however they may penetrate the territory of the several States." *The Slaughter-House Cases*, 83 U.S. 36, 79 (1872); *see also Courtney v. Goltz*, 736 F.3d 1152, 1160, 1 Adm. R. 428, 432–33 (9th Cir. 2013) (interpreting the Privileges or Immunities Clause to encompass "a right to *navigate* the navigable waters of the United States"). Sturgeon thus alleges "an intention to engage in a course of conduct arguably affected with a constitutional interest." *Susan B. Anthony List*, 134 S. Ct. at 2342 (quoting *Babbitt*, 442 U.S. at 298).

Further, there is no dispute that his intended conduct is proscribed by NPS regulation. *See* 36 C.F.R. § 2.17(e) (stating that "[t]he operation or use of hovercraft is prohibited" within NPS-administered lands and waters, which include the Yukon-Charley). Finally, "there exists a credible threat of prosecution thereunder." *Susan B. Anthony List*, 134 S. Ct. at 2342 (quoting *Babbitt*, 442 U.S. at 298). The federal

appellees concede that Sturgeon received a verbal warning not to use the hovercraft, that Special Agent Sears told Sturgeon's lawyer that Sturgeon "should remove the hovercraft from the preserve," and that Sears later indicated that Sturgeon "[might] be subject to criminal liability if he [—12—] operated a hovercraft in the preserve."[2] These facts are sufficient to show a credible threat of enforcement against Sturgeon.

Next, the federal appellees argue that any injury-in-fact identified by Sturgeon is not "fairly traceable" to actions of NPS. We disagree. The regulation was promulgated by NPS and enforcement has been threatened by NPS employees. Therefore, Sturgeon's injuries are "fairly traceable" to actions of NPS. Finally, a favorable decision would redress Sturgeon's identified injury-in-fact, and the federal appellees do not contend otherwise.

In addition to contending that Sturgeon lacks Article III standing, the federal appellees argue that prudential considerations of ripeness and adverseness militate against a finding of standing. However, the federal appellees failed to raise these arguments before the district court. We thus find them waived, as prudential standing arguments "can be deemed waived if not raised in the district court" due to their nonconstitutional nature.[3] *Cnty. of Kern*, 581 F.3d at 845 (quoting *Bd. of Natural Res. v. Brown*, 992 F.2d 937, 946 (9th Cir. 1993)) (internal quotation marks omitted). [—13—]

B.

The State of Alaska, on the other hand, lacks standing. Alaska offers three bases to support its standing: (1) harm "in the form of

---

[2] Indeed, if Sturgeon violated NPS's hovercraft ban, he would risk incurring a fine and imprisonment for up to six months. *See* 36 C.F.R. § 1.3(a).

[3] Moreover, it may be that the "Article III standing and ripeness issues in this case 'boil down to the same question'"—namely, whether a sufficient injury-in-fact exists to render the case ripe. *Susan B. Anthony List*, 134 S. Ct. at 2341 n.5 (quoting *MedImmune, Inc. v. Genentech, Inc.*, 549 U.S. 118, 128 n.8 (2007)).

increased staff time and expense" in obtaining and complying with the terms of a scientific research and collecting permit; (2) injuries to Alaska's sovereign right to control its lands and waters; and (3) the Secretary of the Interior's denial of its petition for administrative proceedings that would repeal or amend the regulations at issue. We address each of the proffered bases in turn.

With regard to Alaska's chum and sockeye salmon study, the increased burdens to Alaska as a result of NPS's permit requirement clearly constitute injuries-in-fact. It is undisputed that NPS employees informed Alaska's Department of Fish and Game ("DFG") that a scientific research and collecting permit was required before it engaged in the study. The scientific research and collecting permit that DFG actually obtained and the General Conditions and Park Specific Guidance that accompanied it– all of which are part of the record– demonstrate that DFG was forced to comply with numerous obligations and limitations under the terms of the permit. To name just a few, DFG was not allowed to destroy research specimens without NPS's prior authorization, was obligated to catalogue collected specimens into NPS's Interior Collections Management System and label such specimens with NPS accession and catalog numbers, and was required to submit an Investigator's Annual Report and copies of other final reports and publications resulting from the study within a year of publication. The record thus amply supports Alaska's allegation of harm in the form of increased staff time and expense. [—14—]

But while Alaska may have suffered cognizable injuries, a favorable ruling would not redress these injuries. Alaska's complaint sought a declaration that the NPS regulations were invalid and void as applied to state-owned lands and waters and an injunction barring future enforcement of the regulations on state-owned lands and waters. Such relief would not remedy injuries relating to DFG's chum and sockeye salmon study in 2010, which have already been incurred and suffered. At oral argument, Alaska represented that DFG's chum and sockeye

salmon study is complete, and the record offers no indication that related studies or efforts are pending or forthcoming. In the absence of evidence showing how the requested relief would redress its identified injuries, Alaska may not rely on activities relating to the 2010 study of chum and sockeye salmon to establish standing. *Cf. Lujan*, 504 U.S. at 564 ("Past exposure to illegal conduct does not in itself show a present case or controversy regarding injunctive relief . . . if unaccompanied by any continuing, present adverse effects." (alteration in original) (quoting *Los Angeles v. Lyons*, 461 U.S. 95, 102 (1983)) (internal quotation marks omitted).

The second basis proffered by Alaska presents a closer question. Alaska argues that the NPS regulations violate its "sovereign[]" and "proprietary interests" in its lands and waters, and interfere with its "authority and ability to manage its property in accordance with the Alaska Constitution and state law." States certainly possess sovereign and proprietary interests that may be pursued via litigation. *Alfred L. Snapp & Son, Inc. v. Puerto Rico ex rel. Barez*, 458 U.S. 592, 601–02 (1982); *see also, Pennsylvania v. New Jersey*, 426 U.S. 660, 665 (1976) ("It has . . . become settled doctrine that a State has standing to sue only when its sovereign or quasi-sovereign interests are implicated . . . ."). However, we [—15—] conclude that Alaska's arguments are unavailing for purposes of establishing standing under the circumstances of this case.

To begin with, Alaska failed to meet the requirement that its purported injuries be "actual or imminent." *Lujan*, 504 U.S. at 560 (quoting *Whitmore v. Arkansas*, 495 U.S. 149, 155 (1990)) (internal quotation mark omitted). Because Alaska did not identify any actual conflict between NPS's regulations and its own statutes and regulations, we are left with only a vague idea of how exactly NPS's permitting requirement infringes on the state's sovereign and proprietary interests in its lands and waters, or how the requirement interferes with the state's control over and management of those lands and waters. In the absence of such a conflict, Alaska's purported injuries are too "conjectural or hypothetical" to constitute injuries-in-fact. *Id.* (quoting *Whitmore*, 495 U.S. at 155) (internal quotation marks omitted).

Alaska has cited no case that finds standing based simply on purported violations of a state's sovereign rights. Rather, evidence of actual injury is still required. For example, in *Massachusetts v. EPA*, 549 U.S. 497 (2007), the Supreme Court found that Massachusetts had standing to challenge the EPA's denial of a rulemaking petition requesting regulation of greenhouse gas emissions under the Clean Air Act. *Id.* at 510–11, 526. The Court noted that the state was due "special solicitude in [the] standing analysis" based on two factors: (1) Massachusetts sought to vindicate a procedural right, which eliminated the need under Article III to demonstrate redressability and immediacy, and (2) Massachusetts's status as a "sovereign State." *Id.* at 517–20; *see also Washington Envtl. Council v. Bellon*, 732 F.3d 1131, 1144–45 (9th Cir. 2013) (distinguishing *Massachusetts v. EPA*). Even in light [—16—] of this special solicitude, however, the Court specifically found that "[b]ecause the Commonwealth 'own[ed]' a substantial portion of the state's coastal property,' it ha[d] alleged a particularized injury in its capacity as a landowner" due to rising global sea levels. *Massachusetts*, 549 U.S. at 522 (citation omitted).

Similarly, in *Oregon v. Legal Services Corp.*, 552 F.3d 965 (9th Cir. 2009), Oregon contended that a private, nonprofit corporation established by the United States to provide federal funds to local legal assistance programs "thwart[ed] [its] efforts at policy making with regards to Oregon's Legal Service Program." *Id.* at 973. We rejected Oregon's claim because "there [was] no dispute over Oregon's ability to regulate its legal services program, and no claim that Oregon's laws ha[d] been invalidated as a result of the [corporation's] restrictions." *Id.* Because Oregon was able "to regulate its legal service programs as it desire[d]," there was thus "no judicially cognizable injury." *Id.* at 974.

Finally, *Nevada v. Burford*, 918 F.2d 854 (9th Cir. 1990), is also illustrative. Nevada challenged the Bureau of Land Management's decision to grant a right-of-way over state-owned land to the Department of Energy. *Id.* at 855. Because Nevada's complaint was "silent as to how [the Bureau's] alleged violations . . . resulted in injury to Nevada," in the absence of demonstrated injury, its claim "'constitute[d] a generalized grievance that the [Bureau] [was] not acting in . . . accordance' with federal laws" and was thus "insufficient to demonstrate standing." *Id.* at 856–57 (first, third, and fourth alterations added, second alteration in original) (quoting *Nevada v. Burford*, 708 F. Supp. 289, 295 (D. Nev. 1989)). *See also Table Bluff Reservation (Wiyot Tribe) v. Philip Morris, Inc.*, 256 F.3d [—17—] 879, 883 (9th Cir. 2001) (finding no injury-in-fact where twenty Native American tribes challenged a Master Settlement Agreement between Philip Morris, Inc. and forty-six states, five territories, and the District of Columbia because the tribes identified no tribal regulations or contracts that would be affected by the Agreement).

Similarly, here, Alaska's claims regarding its sovereign and proprietary interests lack grounding in a demonstrated injury. While Alaska alleges that NPS regulations "have directly interfered with Alaska's ability as a sovereign to manage and regulate its land and waters," Alaska identifies no conflict between NPS regulations and its own state statutes and regulations.[4] Any injury to Alaska's sovereign and proprietary interest is pure conjecture and thus insufficient to establish standing.

The third and final basis upon which Alaska relies to establish standing is the Secretary of the Interior's denial of its petition

---

[4] Alaska also alleges that the NPS regulations have had "a chilling effect" on Alaskans' use and enjoyment of state-owned lands and waters. But "a state does not have standing 'to protect her citizens from the operation of federal statutes.'" *Oregon v. Legal Servs. Corp.*, 552 F.3d 965, 971 (9th Cir. 2009) (quoting *Massachusetts v. EPA*, 549 U.S. 497, 520 n.17 (2007)). And "the State must articulate an interest apart from the interests of particular private parties." *Id.* (quoting *Alfred L. Snapp & Son, Inc. v. Puerto Rico ex rel. Barez*, 458 U.S. 592, 607 (1982)) (internal quotation mark omitted). Alaska has failed to do so.

for new administrative proceedings. A plaintiff possesses standing to enforce procedural rights "so long as the procedures in question are designed to protect some threatened concrete interest of his that is the ultimate basis of his standing." *Lujan*, 504 U.S. at 573 n.8. As discussed above, Alaska fails to identify any "threatened concrete [—18—] interest." Alaska cannot rely on the Secretary's denial of its petition because "[p]articipation in agency proceedings is alone insufficient to satisfy judicial standing requirements." *Gettman v. Drug Enforcement Admin.*, 290 F.3d 430, 433 (D.C. Cir. 2002) (quoting *Fund Democracy, LLC v. SEC*, 278 F.3d 21, 27 (D.C. Cir. 2002)) (internal quotation marks omitted). Alaska's "right to petition the agency does not in turn 'automatic[ally]' confer Article III standing when that right is deprived." *Id.* (alteration in original) (quoting Pet'rs' Br.).

Therefore, we hold that Alaska has failed to establish standing to challenge the NPS regulations. We vacate the district court's judgment as to Alaska and remand with instructions that Alaska's case be dismissed for lack of jurisdiction.

IV.

We now turn to the merits of Sturgeon's challenge. Sturgeon contends that § 103(c) of ANILCA bars the application and enforcement of NPS's hovercraft ban on the Nation River,[5] which he contends is state-owned land. According to Sturgeon, the plain text of the statute, its legislative history, and our decision in *City of Angoon v. Marsh*, 749 F.2d 1413 (9th Cir. 1984), support his view. [—19—] Before explaining why we find Sturgeon's contentions unpersuasive, we offer a bit of background.

---

[5] Many of Sturgeon's arguments resemble a facial challenge to NPS's general regulatory authority over nonfederal land within conservation system units. However, the district court's finding that Sturgeon had pleaded an as-applied challenge, *Sturgeon*, 2013 WL 5888230, at *1, is not contested on appeal, and we therefore limit our consideration to the regulation as applied to Sturgeon.

A.

ANILCA, enacted in 1980, offered new "protection[s] for the national interest in the scenic, natural, cultural and environmental values on the public lands in Alaska, and at the same time provide[d] adequate opportunity for satisfaction of the economic and social needs of the State of Alaska and its people." 16 U.S.C. § 3101(d). Summarized succinctly, "ANILCA is generally concerned with the designation, disposition, and management of land for environmental preservation purposes." *Stratman v. Leisnoi, Inc.*, 545 F.3d 1161, 1165 (9th Cir. 2008). To this end, Congress "set aside approximately 105 million acres of federal land in Alaska for protection of natural resource values by permanent federal ownership and management." *Nat'l Audubon Soc'y v. Hodel*, 606 F. Supp. 825, 827–28 (D. Alaska 1984). Portions of those lands were used to expand existing units of the National Park System and create new units, which were to be administered by the Secretary of the Interior. 16 U.S.C. § 410hh; *id.* § 410hh-1. Such units included national parks, preserves, and monuments. *See* 16 U.S.C. § 410hh; *id.* § 410hh-1. ANILCA refers to units of the National Park System situated in Alaska as "conservation system unit[s]" ("CSUs"). 16 U.S.C. § 3102(4).

Not all lands that lie within the boundaries of a CSU are owned by the federal government. Where possible, Congress drew unit boundaries "to include whole ecosystems and to follow natural features," and was thus cognizant of the fact that state, Native, or private-owned land could fall within the boundaries of CSUs. *Marsh*, 749 F.2d at 1417 (quoting [—20—] 125 Cong. Rec. 9905 (1979)). The presence of both federal-owned and nonfederal-owned land lying within CSUs led Congress to clarify two things: first, what land would actually comprise the CSUs, and second, more generally, how land falling within a CSU's boundaries–whether federally owned or not–could be regulated. *See id.* (discussing the House version of ANILCA and the "Tsongas substitute" in the Senate).

Such clarification came in ANILCA § 103(c). The full text of that subsection reads as follows:

Only those lands within the boundaries of any conservation system unit which are public lands (as such term is defined in this Act) shall be deemed to be included as a portion of such unit. No lands which, before, on, or after December 2, 1980, are conveyed to the State, to any Native Corporation, or to any private party shall be subject to the regulations applicable solely to public lands within such units. If the State, a Native Corporation, or other owner desires to convey any such lands, the Secretary may acquire such lands in accordance with applicable law (including this Act), and any such lands shall become part of the unit, and be administered accordingly.

16 U.S.C. § 3103(c).

Section 103(c) thus contains three separate instructions regarding the composition and regulation of CSUs. First, only "public lands" lying within the boundaries of a CSU are "deemed to be included as a portion of such unit." *Id.* Under [—21—] ANILCA, "public lands" are "[f]ederal lands" (including "lands, waters, and interests therein") in which the United States holds title after December 2, 1980. *Id.* § 3102(1)–(3). The first sentence of § 103(c) makes clear that the boundaries of CSUs "do[] not in any way change the status of that State, native, or private land" lying within those boundaries. 125 Cong. Rec. 11158 (1979).

The second sentence of § 103(c) declares that state, Native, and private-owned land shall not be subject to "regulations applicable solely to public lands within such units." 16 U.S.C. § 3103(c). Accordingly, under § 103(c)'s plain text, only public land lying within a CSU's boundaries may be subjected to *CSU-specific regulations*—nonfederal land is expressly made exempt from such regulations. As the 1979 Senate Report on ANILCA makes clear, nonfederal land would not be "subject to the management regulations which may be

adopted to manage and administer any national [CSU] *which is adjacent to, or surrounds, the private or non-federal public lands.*" S. Rep. No. 96-413, at 303 (1979), *reprinted in* 1980 U.S.C.C.A.N. 5070, 5247 (emphasis added). Importantly for purposes of this case, in contrast to CSU-specific regulations, "[f]ederal laws and regulations of general applicability to both private and public lands" are "unaffected," and "would be applicable to private or non-federal public land holdings within [CSUs]." *Id.*

Finally, § 103(c)'s third sentence provides that the Secretary of the Interior may acquire nonfederal land lying within a CSU's boundaries; such land would then "become part of the unit" and may "be administered accordingly." 16 U.S.C. § 3103(c). Once acquired, what was previously nonfederal land would no longer be free from "regulations applicable solely to public lands within [CSUs]." *Id.*; *see* [—22—] *also* 126 Cong. Rec. 21882 (1980) (noting that "if the [Native-] corporations ever decide to dispose of their property, [it] could become part of the [CSU]").

B.

With this background in mind, we easily resolve Sturgeon's appeal. Sturgeon argues that the plain language of ANILCA § 103(c) removes nonfederal lands from the reach of federal regulations promulgated to manage public lands. Thus, his argument goes, NPS may not enforce the hovercraft ban on the lower portion of the Nation River that falls within the Yukon-Charley because the water and submerged land of that river is owned by the state of Alaska.

While we agree with Sturgeon that § 103(c) is unambiguous, we find that it unambiguously forecloses his interpretation. The plain text of § 103(c) only exempts nonfederal land from "regulations applicable *solely* to public lands within [CSUs]." 16 U.S.C. § 3103(c) (emphasis added). The regulation at issue, banning hovercraft use in the Yukon-Charley, is not so limited.

In 1976, Congress vested the Secretary of the Interior with the authority to "[p]romulgate and enforce regulations concerning boating and other activities on or relating to waters located within areas of the National Park System, including waters subject to the jurisdiction of the United States." 16 U.S.C. § 1a-2(h). Pursuant to this grant of authority, the Secretary promulgated a number of regulations to "provide for the proper use, management, government, and protection of persons, property, and natural and cultural resources within areas under the jurisdiction of the National Park Service." 36 C.F.R. § 1.1(a). Within the chapter of the [—23—] Code of Federal Regulations containing those regulations, parts 1 through 5 "apply to all persons entering, using, visiting, or otherwise within" federally owned lands and waters administered by NPS and "[w]aters subject to the jurisdiction of the United States located within the boundaries of the National Park System, including navigable waters." 36 C.F.R. § 1.2(a)(1), (3). The hovercraft ban is located within part 2 of that chapter. *See* 36 C.F.R. § 2.17(e).

In short, then, the hovercraft ban is not one that "appli[es] solely to public lands within [CSUs]" in Alaska. 16 U.S.C. § 3103(c). Rather, this regulation applies to all federal-owned lands and waters administered by NPS nationwide, as well as all navigable waters lying within national parks. Thus, even assuming (without deciding) that the waters of and lands beneath the Nation River have been "conveyed to the State" for purposes of § 103(c), that subsection does not preclude the application and enforcement of the NPS regulation at issue. Because of its general applicability, the regulation may be enforced on both public and nonpublic lands alike within CSUs. Though Sturgeon might prefer a more robust regulatory exemption, we "must presume that a legislature says in a statute what it means and means in a statute what it says." *Barnhart v. Sigmon Coal Co., Inc.*, 534 U.S. 438, 461–62 (2002) (quoting *Conn. Nat'l Bank v. Germain*, 503 U.S. 249, 253–54 (1992)).[6] [—24—]

---

[6] Because we resolve this case based on the plain text of the statute, we need not address whether our decisions in *John v. United States (Katie John III)*, 720 F.3d 1214 (9th Cir. 2013), *John v. United States (Katie John II)*, 247 F.3d

C.

Sturgeon acknowledges that § 103(c)'s language exempts nonfederal lands from regulations applicable "solely" to public lands, but argues that overreliance on the word "solely" leads to a result contrary to the express legislative purpose of restricting federal authority over nonfederal land within CSUs. "When confronted with a statute which is plain and unambiguous on its face, we ordinarily do not look to legislative history as a guide to its meaning." *Tennessee Valley Auth. v. Hill*, 437 U.S. 153, 184 n. 29 (1978); *see also Balen v. Holland Am. Line Inc.*, 583 F.3d 647, 653 (9th Cir. 2009) (quoting *North Dakota v. United States*, 460 U.S. 300, 312 (1983)) (internal quotation mark omitted) (stating that when statutory language is clear, its "language must ordinarily be regarded as conclusive"). But even if we consider the legislative history of ANILCA, we find no support for Sturgeon's claim. Rather, the legislative records from the House and Senate contain numerous statements supporting the plain language of the statute. The sponsor of § 103(c) in the House offered the view that his amendment "restate[d] and ma[de] clear" that nonfederal lands within CSUs would not be "subject to regulations which are applied to public lands which, in fact, are part of the unit." 125 Cong. Rec. 11158 (1979). The primary sponsor of ANILCA in the House declared that nonfederal land would not be constrained by "regulations applicable to the public lands within the specific conservation system unit." 125 Cong. Rec. 9905 (1979). The House Concurrent Resolution that added § 103(c) to ANILCA specified that "only public lands (and not State or private lands) are to be subject to the [CSU] regulations applying to public lands." 126 Cong. Rec. 30498 (1980). Finally, the Senate Report notes that § 103(c) would exempt nonfederal land from "regulations which may be [—25—] adopted to manage and administer any [CSU] which is adjacent to, or surrounds, the private or non-Federal public lands." S. Rep. No. 96-413, at 303 (1979), *reprinted in* 1980 U.S.C.C.A.N.

1032 (9th Cir. 2001) (en banc) (per curiam), or *State of Alaska v. Babbitt (Katie John I)*, 72 F.3d 698 (9th Cir. 1995) supply an alternative basis for affirming the district court.

5070, 5247.[7] Rather than help Sturgeon, the legislative history confirms that ANILCA § 103(c) did not purport to exempt nonfederal lands within CSUs from generally applicable federal laws and regulations like the hovercraft ban.

D.

Next, Sturgeon argues that our decision in *City of Angoon v. Marsh*, 749 F.2d 1413 (9th Cir. 1984), supports his interpretation. Sturgeon's reliance on *Marsh*, however, is misplaced. *Marsh* involved the interaction between two subsections of ANILCA § 503. The first, § 503(b), established the Admiralty Island National Monument, which was composed of 921,000 acres "of public lands." *Id.* at 1416 (emphasis omitted) (quoting ANILCA, Pub. L. No. 96-487, § 503(b), 94 Stat. 2371 (1980)). The second, § 503(d), stated that "[w]ithin the Monument[], the Secretary shall not permit the sale of [sic] harvesting of timber." *Id.*

Reading these two subsections in conjunction, we held that the district court erred in finding that "all lands within the boundaries of a National Forest System Monument"– **[—26—]** including private lands–"come within the harvesting prohibition of section 503(d)." *Id.* (emphasis omitted). We pointed out that under § 503(b), the Admiralty Island National Monument, "by definition, consists solely of public or federally owned lands." *Id.* Thus, § 503(d)'s use of the phrase "[w]ithin the Monument" was inapplicable "to *private lands* which are within the boundaries of a national forest conservation system unit." *Id.* (emphasis added and omitted).

---

[7] Sturgeon also claims that until 1996, NPS did not purport to have regulatory authority over state-owned lands and waters within CSUs, but in July 1996, NPS reversed course. Even if so, NPS's current view comports with the text of the statute, and to the extent Sturgeon believes that NPS's purported change in position militates against deference, "[a]gency inconsistency is not a basis for declining to analyze the agency's interpretation under the *Chevron* framework." *Nat'l Cable & Telecomms. Ass'n v. Brand X Internet Servs.*, 545 U.S. 967, 981 (2005).

Marsh clearly is inapposite to the present dispute. First, *Marsh*'s discussion of § 103(c) is largely dicta because that subsection was inapplicable to the timber harvesting ban at issue. While ANILCA § 103(c) refers to "regulations applicable solely to public lands within such units," § 503(d) imposes a statutory prohibition against timber harvesting. At most, *Marsh* drew inferences from § 103(c) for the purpose of determining the reach of § 503(d). *See id.* at 1418 (noting that the court examined sections 102, 103(c), 503(d), and 506(c) "harmoniously" to determine Congressional intent regarding the ban on timber harvesting). Second, *Marsh* offers little guidance in Sturgeon's case because, if promulgated as a regulation, § 503(d)'s ban on timber harvesting would fall under § 103(c)'s exception to the application of regulations applying solely to public lands, while NPS's hovercraft ban does not. Section 503(d) specifically refers to activities taking place "[w]ithin the Monument[]," and thus only limits conduct taking place on *public lands* within a specific CSU. For that reason, if promulgated as an agency regulation, its harvesting ban would qualify as a "regulation[] applicable solely to public lands within [CSUs]," and would be unenforceable on state, Native, or private-owned land under ANILCA § 103(c). As we noted above, NPS's hovercraft ban is not so constrained, and it applies to federally owned lands and waters **[—27—]** administered by NPS nationwide, as well as navigable waters within national parks.

V.

We reject two additional arguments asserted by Sturgeon, that the Secretary of the Interior exceeded her statutory authority in promulgating the regulation at issue and that her action raises serious constitutional concerns.

A.

The 1976 Park Service Administration and Improvement Act ("1976 Act") grants the Secretary of the Interior broad authority over boating and water-related activities within the National Park System. That authorization provides as follows:

> [T]he Secretary of the Interior is authorized . . . [to] [p]romulgate and enforce regulations concerning boating and other activities on or relating to waters located within areas of the National Park System, including waters subject to the jurisdiction of the United States: *Provided*, That any regulations adopted pursuant to this subsection shall be complementary to, and not in derogation of, the authority of the United States Coast Guard to regulate the use of waters subject to the jurisdiction of the United States.

16 U.S.C. § 1a-2(h). Sturgeon contends that the latter portion of this subsection restricts the Secretary's regulatory power [—28—] and does not permit her to regulate any and all activities on waters within national parks.

However, the plain text of the 1976 Act merely requires that any regulations promulgated by the Secretary *complement*, and not *derogate*, Coast Guard authority over waters subject to federal jurisdiction. It does not, as Sturgeon argues, limit the Secretary's regulatory authority to that enjoyed by the Coast Guard. The Oxford English Dictionary defines "complement" to mean "to supply what is wanting," 3 *Oxford English Dictionary* 610 (2d ed. 1989), and "derogate" to mean to "diminish," *id*. at 504. Thus, under the 1976 Act, the Secretary may regulate boating and other water-related activities taking place within the National Park System and its navigable waters so long as those regulations supplement and do not diminish the Coast Guard's authority.[8]

Indeed, the legislative history of the 1976 Act makes this clear. The concern regarding the regulatory authority of the Coast Guard was first raised by the Secretary of the Interior in a letter to the House Committee on Interior and Insular Affairs.[9] H.R. Rep. No. 94-1569, at 13 (1976), *reprinted in* [—29—] 1976 U.S.C.C.A.N. 4290, 4299. The Secretary noted that the Coast Guard possessed existing authority to "promulgate and enforce regulations for the promotion of *safety of life and property on* . . . waters subject to the jurisdiction of the United States." *Id*. (alteration in original) (emphasis added) (quoting 14 U.S.C. § 2(3)). Because many waters within the National Park System were navigable, the Secretary noted that his agency would "exercise authority concurrent with the Coast Guard in many instances," and thus recommended an amendment clarifying that the bill's grant of regulatory authority would "not diminish the Coast Guard's authority under existing law to regulate boat design and safety." *Id*. The remainder of the bill would still, however, grant her the authority "to regulate *recreational, commercial and other uses and activities* relating to all waters of the National Park System." *Id*. (emphasis added).

The statute reflects just such a clarifying amendment. *See* 16 U.S.C. § 1a-2(h). Thus, both the plain text and the legislative history of the 1976 Act make clear that Sturgeon's argument that the Secretary of the Interior exceeded her statutory authority is without merit.

B.

Finally, Sturgeon contends that the Secretary's exercise of her regulatory authority under the 1976 Act implicates "serious constitutional concerns." Specifically,

---

[8] Moreover, ANILCA § 1319 provides that "[n]othing in [the statute] shall be construed as . . . superseding, modifying, or repealing, except as specifically set forth in this Act, existing laws applicable to the various Federal agencies which are authorized to . . . *exercise licensing or regulatory functions in relation thereto*." 16 U.S.C. § 3207 (emphasis added).

[9] The Secretary of Transportation also submitted a letter to the House Committee "strongly object[ing]" to the fact that the bill as drafted "would authorize the Secretary of the Interior to promulgate and enforce boating regulations which relate to construction, performance, and equipment standards"– responsibility for which had been previously delegated to "the Secretary of the department in which the Coast Guard is operating." H.R. [—29—] Rep. No. 94-1569, at 24 (1976), *reprinted in* 1976 U.S.C.C.A.N. 4290, 4310.

he raises the specter of potential violations of the Property and Commerce Clauses, though without offering any specifics as to how or why the NPS regulations contravene those clauses. We [—30—] therefore decline to invalidate NPS's hovercraft ban on constitutional grounds because "[w]hatever the extent of the State's proprietary interest in [its] river[s], the pre-eminent authority to regulate the flow of navigable waters resides with the Federal Government." *New England Power Co. v. New Hampshire*, 455 U.S. 331, 338 n.6 (1982); *see also Alaska v. United States*, 545 U.S. 75, 116–17 (2005) (Scalia, J., concurring in part and dissenting in part) ("If title to submerged lands passed to Alaska, the Federal Government would still retain significant authority to regulate activities in the waters of Glacier Bay by virtue of its dominant navigational servitude, other aspects of the Commerce Clause, and even the treaty power.").

VI.

We hold that even assuming that the waters of and lands beneath the Nation River have been "conveyed to the State" for purposes of ANILCA § 103(c), NPS's hovercraft ban is not a regulation that applies solely to public lands within CSUs in Alaska. Therefore, as to Sturgeon, we affirm the district court's grant of summary judgment in favor of the federal appellees. Because Alaska cannot establish standing on this record, we vacate the district court's judgment as to Alaska and remand with instructions that Alaska's action be dismissed for lack of subject matter jurisdiction.

AFFIRMED IN PART, VACATED AND REMANDED IN PART.

United States Court of Appeals
for the Ninth Circuit

No. 13-35835

SHELL GULF OF MEXICO INC.
vs.
CENTER FOR BIOLOGICAL DIVERSITY, INC.

Appeal from the United States District Court for the
District of Alaska

Decided: November 12, 2014

Citation: 771 F.3d 632, 2 Adm. R. 514 (9th Cir. 2014).

Before **FARRIS**, **NELSON**, and **NGUYEN**, Circuit
Judges.

[—3—] **NELSON**, Circuit Judge:

The Beaufort and Chukchi Seas lie on
Alaska's Arctic coast. This area contains
a bountiful ecosystem that supports a
wide array of life, but it is also rich in natural
resources, specifically, oil and gas. Shell Gulf
of Mexico, Inc. and Shell Offshore, Inc.
(collectively Shell) have invested heavily in
the exploration and development of oil and gas
resources in the Beaufort and Chukchi Seas.

To carry out its operations, Shell sought
and obtained approval from the Bureau of
Safety and Environmental Enforcement (the
Bureau) of two oil spill response plans
required by the Oil Pollution Act. Shortly after
obtaining approval, Shell filed a lawsuit under
the Declaratory Judgment Act against several
environmental organizations, seeking a
declaration that the Bureau's approval did not
[—4—] violate the Administrative Procedures
Act (APA). Shell claimed that it needed a swift
determination of the legality of the approval
so it could conduct exploratory drilling
without worrying that the environmental
groups would seek to overturn the Bureau's
approval of the spill response plans.

Shell's lawsuit represents a novel litigation
strategy, whereby the beneficiary of agency
action seeks to confirm its lawfulness by suing
those who it believes are likely to challenge it.
We must decide whether this strategy runs
afoul of Article III's case or controversy
requirement. We hold that it does. Shell does

not have legal interests adverse to the Bureau
under the APA, and it may not file suit solely
to determine who would prevail in a
hypothetical suit between the environmental
groups and the Bureau. Consequently, we lack
jurisdiction.

I. Background

Many environmental organizations and
citizen activists, including the defendants in
this case, vehemently oppose Shell's Arctic oil
and gas exploration activities. In addition to
making public statements condemning Shell's
plans, several organizations have filed
lawsuits challenging regulatory approval of
Shell's activities. Some of these organizations
have proclaimed litigation to be a particularly
effective tool for achieving their goal of
stopping oil and gas exploration in the Arctic,
and have stated their intentions to continue
resisting Shell's plans in court.

A recent Arctic drilling dispute concerns
Shell's compliance with the Oil Pollution Act,
33 U.S.C. § 1321(j). Under the Oil Pollution
Act, Shell must file an oil spill response plan
with the Bureau and obtain the Bureau's
[—5—] approval for that plan prior to
handling, storing, or transporting oil. *See id*.
§ 1321(j)(5)(F). Shell filed oil spill response
plans with the Bureau for its operations in the
Beaufort and Chukchi Seas, which the Bureau
approved.

Weeks after obtaining the Bureau's
approval, Shell filed a lawsuit against the
environmental groups seeking a declaration
that the Bureau's approval did not violate the
APA. In its complaint, Shell alleged that the
environmental groups were engaged in an
ongoing campaign to prevent Shell from
drilling for oil in the Arctic, and that some of
the environmental groups had threatened to
bring litigation challenging the Bureau's
approval of the oil spill response plans. Shell
alleged that the environmental groups' history
of opposing Shell's activities through
litigation, coupled with their public criticism,
made it virtually certain that they would file
litigation challenging the Bureau's approval.
Shell asserted that it needed to accelerate
resolution of the allegedly inevitable challenge

to the Bureau's action in order to protect its investments and conduct exploratory drilling without the threat of judicial intervention.

The environmental groups moved to dismiss Shell's complaint, arguing, *inter alia*, that Shell's lawsuit did not satisfy Article III's case or controversy requirement. The district court denied the motion to dismiss. Eventually, some, but not all, of the environmental groups filed a lawsuit challenging the Bureau's approval of Shell's oil spill response plans. *See Alaska Wilderness League v. Jewell*, No. 13-35866 (9th Cir. filed Sept. 17, 2013).[1] This case was consolidated with the case against the Bureau, and the district [—6—] court entered summary judgment against the environmental groups. The environmental groups now appeal the district court's denial of their motion to dismiss.

II. Legal Standard

We review the existence of subject matter jurisdiction de novo. *United States v. Peninsula Commc'ns, Inc.*, 287 F.3d 832, 836 (9th Cir. 2002).

III. Discussion

The Declaratory Judgment Act provides that "any court of the United States . . . may declare the rights and other legal relations of any interested party seeking such declaration." 28 U.S.C. § 2201(a). This statute does not create new substantive rights, but merely expands the remedies available in federal courts. *Countrywide Home Loans, Inc. v. Mortgage Guar. Ins. Corp.*, 642 F.3d 849, 853 (9th Cir. 2011). Congress created this remedy, in part, to allow potential defendants to file preemptive litigation to determine whether they have any legal obligations to their potential adversaries. *Seattle Audubon Soc. v. Mosely*, 80 F.3d 1401, 1405 (9th Cir. 1996). Filing a preemptive declaratory judgment action benefits potential defendants by relieving them "from the Damoclean threat of impending litigation which a harassing

adversary might brandish[.]" *Hal Roach Studios, Inc. v. Richard Feiner and Co., Inc.*, 896 F.2d 1542, 1555 (9th Cir. 1990) (quoting *Societe de Conditionnement v. Hunter Eng'g Co.*, 655 F.2d 938, 943 (9th Cir.1981)).

While the Declaratory Judgment Act therefore created a new procedural mechanism for removing the threat of impending litigation, it did not expand the jurisdiction of [—7—] federal courts. *Skelly Oil Co. v. Phillips Petroleum Co.*, 339 U.S. 667, 671 (1950). In particular, a federal court may only grant a declaratory judgment in "controversies which are such in the constitutional sense." *Aetna Life Ins. Co. of Hartford, Conn. v. Haworth*, 300 U.S. 227, 240 (1937). To determine whether a declaratory judgment action presents a justiciable case or controversy, courts consider "whether the facts alleged, under all the circumstances, show that there is a substantial controversy, between parties having adverse legal interests, of sufficient immediacy and reality to warrant the issuance of a declaratory judgment." *Md. Cas. Co. v. Pac. Coal & Oil Co.*, 312 U.S. 270, 273 (1941).

Shell contends that this case is justiciable because the parties have adverse legal interests and have been mired in a substantial, real, and immediate controversy over the lawfulness of its Arctic oil and gas explorations. Shell points out that it brought this lawsuit to solve the precise problem the Declaratory Judgment Act is meant to address. Shell asserts that it needs a quick resolution of any challenge to the Bureau's approval before continuing its exploratory drilling, and that in the absence of a preemptive lawsuit, it fears the environmental groups would wait until the eve of the drilling season to file litigation at the most inconvenient moment. Shell further claims that adverse legal interests are present in this case because Shell and the environmental groups have opposing legal positions regarding the lawfulness of the Bureau's approval of Shell's oil spill response plans, and because Shell would suffer economic harm if the environmental groups' view prevailed in court.

---

[1] Defendants Northern Alaska Environmental Center and The Wilderness Society are not parties to the lawsuit against the Bureau.

We need not address whether there is a substantial controversy present in this case, because we hold that Shell and the environmental groups do not have "adverse legal [—8—] interests." *Md. Cas. Co.*, 312 U.S. at 273. To determine whether the parties to a declaratory judgment action have adverse legal interests, we first identify the law underlying the request for a declaratory judgment. *Mylan Pharm., Inc. v. Thompson*, 268 F.3d 1323, 1330 (Fed. Cir. 2001); *Collin Cnty., Tex. v. Homeowners Ass'n for Values Essential to Neighborhoods, (HAVEN)*, 915 F.2d 167, 171 (5th Cir. 1990) ("A party's legal interest must relate to an actual 'claim arising under federal law that another asserts against him[.]'" (quoting *Lowe v. Ingalls Shipbuilding, A Div. of Litton Sys., Inc.*, 723 F.2d 1173, 1179 (5th Cir.1984))). It is necessary to first examine the underlying law because the Declaratory Judgment Act only creates new remedies, and therefore, the adverse legal interests required by Article III must be created by the authority governing the asserted controversy between the parties. When identifying the adverse legal interests arising from the law underlying the request for declaratory relief, courts examine both the persons who can assert rights under that law and those who have obligations under it. *See Collin Cnty.*, 915 F.2d at 171 ("Since it is the underlying cause of action of the defendant against the plaintiff that is actually litigated in a declaratory judgment action, a party bringing a declaratory judgment action must have been a proper party had the defendant brought suit on the underlying cause of action.").

The law underlying Shell's request for a declaratory judgment is the APA, and we therefore consider the rights and obligations created by that law. The APA allows a person "aggrieved" by agency action to seek judicial review. 5 U.S.C. § 702. Actions under the APA may be brought only against federal agencies. *City of Rohnert Park v. Harris*, 601 F.2d 1040, 1048 (9th Cir. 1979). A claim under the APA cannot be asserted against a private party. *W. State Univ. of [—9—] S. Cal. v. Am. Bar Ass'n*, 301 F. Supp. 2d 1129, 1133 (C.D. Cal. 2004). Thus, with respect to declaratory judgment claims arising out of the APA, the relevant

"adverse legal interests" are held by a federal agency and a person aggrieved by that agency's action.

Turning to the facts before us, it follows that the only entities with adverse legal interests are the Bureau and the environmental groups. The environmental groups were "aggrieved" by the approval of Shell's oil spill response plans, and the Bureau is the federal agency responsible for their approval. Since the APA therefore allows the environmental groups to file suit against the Bureau, adverse legal interests exist between those parties. Shell, by contrast, does not have legal interests under the APA that are adverse to either the Bureau or the environmental groups. Because its plans were approved, Shell was not "aggrieved" by the Bureau's actions. Moreover, since Shell is not a federal agency, it cannot possibly have any legal obligations under the APA to the environmental groups. Put simply, the Bureau lies at the center of the underlying controversy and is the locus of the adverse legal interests created by the APA. Without its participation, no case or controversy can exist.

Indeed, since it is the Bureau, and not Shell, that can be sued under the APA, it would be odd to conclude that a case or controversy exists merely because Shell seeks to know who would prevail if the environmental groups asserted an APA claim against the Bureau. Were we to conclude that jurisdiction exists, our holding would create several unusual consequences, two of which are particularly noteworthy. First, it would allow a district court to declare the Bureau's actions unlawful under the APA in a judgment that is not binding on the Bureau itself. After all, the Bureau need not [—10—] participate in this lawsuit, and it would therefore not be bound by any judgment. *Taylor v. Sturgell*, 553 U.S. 880, 884 (2008). Thus, a district court entertaining Shell's lawsuit would be potentially unable to enter a judgment resolving the very question Shell seeks to litigate. Second, absent agency intervention, such a lawsuit would allow the lawfulness of agency action to be adjudicated without hearing the agency's own justification for its actions. We conclude, therefore, that it would be unwise to exercise jurisdiction over a dispute concerning agency action while potentially omitting the critically important perspective of the agency itself.

Shell emphasizes the sincerity of its legal disagreement with the environmental groups and the substantial economic effects it would suffer from a judgment against the Bureau, but these alone do not create a justiciable case or controversy. It is axiomatic that differing views of the law are not enough to satisfy Article III. *Hollingsworth v. Perry*, 133 S. Ct. 2652, 2661 (2013) ("The presence of a disagreement, however sharp and acrimonious it may be, is insufficient by itself to meet Art. III's requirements." (quoting *Diamond v. Charles*, 476 U.S. 54, 62 (1986))). Moreover, Shell's economic interest in the outcome of a lawsuit between the Bureau and the environmental groups is not a legal interest merely because it relates to a lawsuit. "A party's legal interest must relate to an actual claim arising under federal law that another asserts *against him.*" *Collin Cnty.*, 915 F.2d at 171 (internal quotation marks omitted) (emphasis added). Lawsuits affect a vast range of persons, and an Article III case or controversy does not exist wherever an individual possibly, probably, or even certainly affected by litigation asks a federal court to resolve a legal question. Thus, it is not enough for a declaratory judgment plaintiff to assert, as Shell does here, a practical interest in the outcome of a lawsuit [—11—] between other parties. Instead, Article III requires the existence of adverse legal interests arising from a legal claim, and that is absent from this case.

The Fifth Circuit has also concluded that a practical interest in the outcome of a lawsuit is not necessarily a legal interest capable of satisfying the case or controversy requirement. In *Collin County v. HAVEN*, HAVEN, a homeowner's organization, stated publicly that it intended to file a lawsuit challenging the Federal Highway Administration's approval of an environmental impact statement (EIS) drafted for a proposed state highway. 915 F.2d at 172. Fearing delay in the highway's construction, Collin County sued HAVEN under the

Declaratory Judgment Act, seeking a declaration that the EIS was sufficient as a matter of law. The Fifth Circuit held that there was no justiciable controversy because HAVEN "could not have sued Collin County or any of the other plaintiffs over the sufficiency of the EIS." *Id.* at 171. The Fifth Circuit acknowledged that the county had strong practical interests in the completion of the highway, but reasoned Collin County had no legal interests adverse to HAVEN because it faced "no actual liability for any deficiency in the EIS." *Id.* Like the plaintiffs in *Collin County*, Shell merely has a practical interest in the outcome of a lawsuit between the Bureau and the environmental groups, and that is not enough to satisfy the case or controversy requirement.[2] [—12—]

Thus, because no adverse legal interests exist between the environmental groups and Shell, this case is not justiciable, and we therefore lack jurisdiction. We reverse and remand for further proceedings consistent with this opinion.

REVERSED AND REMANDED.

---

[2] Shell contends that *Collin County* is distinguishable because Shell was able to intervene in the APA action that was eventually brought against the Bureau, whereas the plaintiffs in *Collin County* had no right to intervene. *See Collin County*, 915 F.2d at 171. In its discussion of whether one of the plaintiffs could have been added to an affirmative suit brought by HAVEN, however, the Fifth Circuit made clear that its decision rested on the premise that the plaintiffs "could not have been [—12—] sued directly on account of any alleged deficiency in the final EIS." *Id.* Thus, the holding in *Collin County* did not rest on the plaintiffs' inability to intervene, but on the lack of any claim against them.

United States Court of Appeals
for the Ninth Circuit

No. 12-35266

INSTITUTE OF CETACEAN RESEARCH
vs.
SEA SHEPHERD CONSERVATION SOC'Y

On a Motion for Contempt

Decided: December 19, 2014

Citation: 774 F.3d 935, 2 Adm. R. 518 (9th Cir. 2014).

Before **KOZINSKI**, **TASHIMA**, and **SMITH**, Circuit Judges.

[—4—] **SMITH**, Circuit Judge:

Institute of Cetacean Research (Cetacean), Kyodo Senpaku Kaisha, Ltd., Tomoyuki Ogawa, and Toshiyuki Miura (collectively, Plaintiffs) filed this contempt proceeding against Sea Shepherd Conservation Society (Sea Shepherd US), its founder Paul Watson, its administrative director Susan Hartland, and six volunteer members of the Sea Shepherd US board (collectively, Defendants). The Plaintiffs allege that the Defendants violated our injunction prohibiting Sea Shepherd US, Watson, and "any party acting in concert with them" from physically attacking or coming within 500 yards of the Plaintiffs' whaling and fueling vessels on the open sea. [—5—]

After we handed down our injunction, the Defendants adopted what they called the "separation strategy." Pursuant to the strategy, they ceded control of the Operation Zero Tolerance (OZT) campaign, designed to thwart the Plaintiffs' whaling activities in the Southern Ocean, to foreign Sea Shepherd entities. The Defendants knew those entities would use assets transferred to them by the Defendants in the OZT campaign, and that there was a "very high risk" the entities would violate our injunction. It is undisputed that these foreign entities repeatedly committed acts against the Plaintiffs' whaling ships during the OZT campaign that would have violated the injunction if performed by the Defendants.

In this opinion, we consider whether the Defendants violated our injunction when they implemented the "separation strategy." The Plaintiffs contend that the strategy was aimed at evading our injunction and ensuring that the OZT campaign proceeded unabated, despite the issuance of the injunction. In support of their contention, the Plaintiffs point to undisputed evidence that the Defendants provided substantial assistance to the OZT campaign after our injunction issued. The Defendants contend, on various grounds, that they should not be held liable for the acts of entities they did not control and whose violations they could not prevent.

Our thorough review of the record in this case, and the concessions of counsel at oral argument, compel us to hold Sea Shepherd US, Watson, and Sea Shepherd US's volunteer board members in contempt for violating our injunction. [—6—]

FACTUAL AND PROCEDURAL BACKGROUND

Plaintiff Cetacean is a Japanese research foundation that has for many years received permits from the Japanese government authorizing it to take whales for research purposes. The International Convention for the Regulation of Whaling, to which the United States, Japan, and 87 other nations are signatories, authorizes whale hunting when conducted in compliance with a research permit issued by a signatory. *See* Int'l Conv. for the Regulation of Whaling, art. VIII, § 1, Dec. 2, 1946, 62 Stat. 1716, 161 U.N.T.S. 74. Japan issued such a permit to Cetacean that authorized it to take whales in the Southern Ocean during the period December 20, 2012 to March 31, 2013.

For several years, Sea Shepherd US and its founder, Watson, have opposed Cetacean's whale hunting efforts in the Southern Ocean. Sea Shepherd US is organized as an Oregon nonprofit corporation with tax-exempt status under section 501(c)(3) of the Internal Revenue Code. It is governed by an unpaid board of volunteer directors. Several current and former directors of the organization are respondents in this contempt proceeding.

In addition to Sea Shepherd US, there exist a number of foreign Sea Shepherd entities, including those organized and governed under the laws of Australia, Belgium, France, Germany, the Netherlands, and the United Kingdom. We sometimes refer to Sea Shepherd US and the other Sea Shepherd entities collectively as "Sea Shepherd."

Since 2004, Sea Shepherd has mounted a yearly campaign to prevent Cetacean from killing whales in the Southern Ocean. Sea Shepherd's tactics have included throwing smoke [—7—] bombs and glass containers of acid at the Plaintiffs' vessels; dragging metal-reinforced ropes in the water to damage the vessels' propellers and rudders; throwing safety flares with metal hooks at nets hung from the Plaintiffs' vessels in the hope that they will set fire to the vessels; and shining high-powered lasers at the Plaintiffs' vessels to annoy the crew. *See Inst. of Cetacean Research v. Sea Shepherd Conservation Soc'y*, 860 F. Supp. 2d 1216, 1223–24 (W.D. Wash. 2012), *rev'd*, 725 F.3d 940, 1 Adm. R. 406 (9th Cir. 2013). Sea Shepherd has piloted its vessels in ways that make collisions with the Plaintiffs' vessels highly likely; in fact, collisions have occurred on several occasions. *Id.* Hoping to prevent Sea Shepherd's dangerous interference with its whaling activities, the Plaintiffs brought an action for injunctive relief in the United States District Court for the Western District of Washington. After the district court denied their request for a preliminary injunction, 860 F. Supp. 2d 1216, *rev'd*, 725 F.3d 940, 1 Adm. R. 406, the Plaintiffs appealed. We reversed. *Inst. of Cetacean Research v. Sea Shepherd Conservation Soc'y*, 725 F.3d 940, 1 Adm. R. 406 (9th Cir. 2013).

We issued an injunction pending appeal against Sea Shepherd US and Watson on December 17, 2012. The injunction provided in relevant part:

Defendants Sea Shepherd Conservation Society and Paul Watson, and any party acting in concert with them (collectively "defendants"), are enjoined from physically attacking any vessel engaged by Plaintiffs the Institute of Cetacean

Research, Kyodo Senpaku Kaisha, Ltd., Tomoyuki Ogawa or Toshiyuki Miura in the Southern Ocean or any person on any such vessel (collectively [—8—] "plaintiffs"), or from navigating in a manner that is likely to endanger the safe navigation of any such vessel. In no event shall defendants approach plaintiffs any closer than 500 yards when defendants are navigating on the open sea.

This injunction remains in effect pending further order of court. *Inst. of Cetacean Research*, 725 F.3d at 947, 1 Adm. R. at 410.

At the time our injunction was handed down, Sea Shepherd US was organizing and preparing in earnest for OZT, its ninth annual whale defense campaign against the Plaintiffs. Prior to the issuance of our injunction, Sea Shepherd US, as in previous years, had taken the lead administrative role in preparing for the campaign. It recruited both volunteer and paid crew, and outfitted and fueled four vessels for the campaign: the *Bob Barker*, *Steve Irwin*, *Sam Simon*, and *Brigitte Bardot*. Sea Shepherd US had already spent over 2 million dollars on the campaign when our injunction issued.

Watson received a copy of our injunction on December 18, 2012, the day after it issued. At that time, Watson was in the Southern Ocean serving as campaign leader, just as he had in previous years. Over the next several days, Watson and other members of Sea Shepherd devised a plan that would come to be known as the "separation strategy." Pursuant to the strategy, Sea Shepherd US would turn over control of OZT and transfer assets it owned to foreign Sea Shepherd entities, including Sea Shepherd Australia. Sea Shepherd Australia is an Australian public company limited by guarantee and registered under the laws of Australia. For each of the previous whale defense campaigns, Sea Shepherd [—9—] Australia has provided an operations base for the four vessels as well as logistical support. Watson was a member of the boards of both Sea Shepherd US and Sea Shepherd Australia when the injunction issued. As part of the separation strategy, Watson would step down from the boards of both entities, and a new OZT campaign leader would assume Watson's responsibilities. Watson, however, would remain on board the *Steve Irwin* as an "observer" during the campaign.

The members of Sea Shepherd US's board learned of the injunction by email on December 18, 2012. When the injunction was handed down, the board was composed of Watson, who was also the paid Executive Director of Sea Shepherd US, and volunteer members Lani Blazier, Marnie Gaede, Bob Talbot, Robert Wintner, Ben Zuckerman, and Peter Rieman, all of whom are respondents in this proceeding.

Gaede, the board's vice president, called a telephonic board meeting for December 20, 2012, during which Sea Shepherd US's attorneys discussed the significance of the injunction and advised the board members on how to respond. All of the board members were present, along with another respondent in this proceeding, Susan Hartland, Sea Shepherd US's Administrative Director. The board discussed the separation strategy and agreed to implement it. Shortly after the board meeting, members of Sea Shepherd US and Sea Shepherd Australia began working together to facilitate the transfer of operational control of OZT to Sea Shepherd Australia. On December 22, 2012, Jeff Hansen, a board member of Sea Shepherd Australia, emailed Watson and Hartland regarding plans for Sea Shepherd Australia to "take [—10—] over," and for Bob Brown, a former Australian senator and decorated environmentalist, to lead the campaign.

Watson chaired a telephonic board meeting of Sea Shepherd Australia on December 27, 2012, in which the board unanimously resolved to assume responsibility for running OZT. Thereafter, Watson submitted his resignation from the Sea Shepherd Australia board and Brown became a member. On December 31, 2012, the Sea Shepherd Australia board resolved that Brown and Hansen would be the new leaders of OZT.

Despite its plan to separate from OZT, Sea Shepherd US's financial support for the campaign did not end immediately after the injunction was issued. Sea Shepherd US paid $163,405 in OZT-related expenses that were invoiced after the injunction was handed down. The majority of this money was spent to refuel the *Steve Irwin* and pay the credit card expenses of OZT ship captains.

On or about December 27, 2012, several of the Plaintiffs' whaling ships departed Japan for the Southern Ocean. Watson informed the Sea Shepherd US board of this development by email on December 27, 2012. Watson's email stated: "All four Sea Shepherd ships and their crew will be ready to greet the Japanese whalers when they arrive. They intend to kill whales and Sea Shepherd's objective is to see that not a single whale is slain. . . . It appears that the hunt is on and we intend to hunt whalers."

On December 28, 2012, Watson formally resigned from his various roles in Sea Shepherd US and as campaign leader for OZT, effective December 31, 2012. He surrendered command of the *Steve Irwin* to Siddharth Chakravarty, a [—11—] citizen of India, but remained on board the ship. Other Sea Shepherd US employees participating in OZT also tendered their resignations to the board. Although Sea Shepherd US stopped paying independent contractors serving as captains and crew members of OZT, Watson helped arrange for the crew to be paid by foreign Sea Shepherd entities.

There is evidence that Watson was not a mere passive participant in OZT after he resigned his leadership positions. During the OZT campaign, Watson appeared by phone on a radio show in March of 2013. His answers to questions posed during the show indicate that he believed himself to be a participant in OZT, not just an observer. He said, for instance, "*we're* chasing the Japanese factory ship *Nisshin Maru* and keeping it from killing whales." When asked about the atmosphere aboard the ship, Watson said, "Oh, everybody's very upbeat on our ship because *we've* managed to make sure they don't kill many whales this year." (emphases added).

Watson was also consulted for guidance on how to proceed with certain aspects of the campaign. For instance, on December 28, 2012, Chakravarty emailed a New Zealand customs official seeking permission to anchor the *Brigitte Bardot* off the New Zealand coast. He learned that the ship would require a hull inspection. Peter Hammarstedt, the captain of the *Bob Barker*, emailed Chakravarty that "[t]his will have to be Paul's decision. Sid, please check with him and let us know ASAP." After being asked by email for his "decision," Watson replied "[y]es proceed with this option." Watson was consulted for advice about logistical aspects of the campaign on several other occasions after the injunction was issued. [—12—]

In a December 30, 2012 meeting, the Sea Shepherd US board accepted Watson's resignation and elected new board leadership consisting of Gaede as president, Wintner as vice president, Blazier as secretary, and Rieman as treasurer. The board formally voted to sever all financial and other forms of support to OZT in a series of emails exchanged between January 8 and 9, 2013. The board also voted to ratify a series of grants of property for no consideration to Sea Shepherd entities participating in OZT. Specifically, Sea Shepherd US granted ownership of the *Bob Barker* to Sea Shepherd Netherlands, and gave equipment to both Sea Shepherd Australia and Sea Shepherd Netherlands. The vessel and the equipment Sea Shepherd US granted had original purchase prices totaling over two million dollars.

On January 29, 2013, in violation of our injunction, the *Brigitte Bardot* approached within 20.25 yards of the *Yushin Maru 3*, one of the Plaintiffs' ships, while it was navigating on the open sea. Several additional violations of our injunction occurred on February 15, 17, 18, 19, 20, 24, 25, 27, and 28. Most violations involved incursions of the 500-yard safety perimeter established by the injunction, but collisions occurred on February 20 and 25 in the course of efforts by Sea Shepherd to prevent one of the Plaintiffs' ships from refueling. Watson was on board the *Steve Irwin* when these collisions occurred.

On February 11, 2013, the Plaintiffs filed a motion to find Sea Shepherd US in contempt and asked us to appoint a special master to conduct contempt proceedings. The basis of the motion was the January 29 incident in which the *Brigitte Bardot* approached within 500 yards of one of the Plaintiffs' vessels. On February 21, 2013, we referred the contempt motion to the Appellate Commissioner. The [—13—] Plaintiffs later amended their motion to allege additional acts of contempt, and to include Watson, the six volunteer directors, and Hartland as respondents to the contempt proceedings. The Appellate Commissioner held a contempt hearing in Seattle from October 28, 2013 to November 6, 2013. The parties stipulated that actions had occurred at sea that, if performed by enjoined parties, would violate our injunction, and testimony about those events was limited. The hearing focused on how Sea Shepherd US, Watson, the volunteer directors, and Hartland responded to our injunction, and their relationship to the persons and entities leading OZT after Sea Shepherd US's withdrawal from the campaign.

The Appellate Commissioner issued his Report and Recommendation on January 31, 2014. He recommended we find that none of the Defendants had committed an act of contempt, as he believed they had "adopted a 'separation' strategy and took reasonable steps to carry out that strategy in order to guarantee their own compliance with the injunction." The Commissioner determined that the Defendants had not directly violated the injunction and could not be held in contempt for the actions of the non-parties leading OZT.

The Plaintiffs and the Defendants each filed objections to the Commissioner's Report and Recommendation.

JURISDICTION AND STANDARD OF REVIEW

In our February 25, 2013 order, we retained jurisdiction over "any further appeals or writs" in this case. *Inst. of Cetacean Research*, 725 F.3d at 948, 1 Adm. R. at 410. We have "inherent power" to initiate contempt proceedings. *See Young v. United States ex rel. Vuitton et Fils S.A.*, 481 U.S. 787, 795 (1987) (citing *Michaelson v. United States ex rel. Chicago*, [—14—] *St. P., M., & O.R. Co.*, 266 U.S. 42, 45 (1924)). We also have statutory authority to punish both civil and criminal contempt pursuant to 18 U.S.C. § 401.

The parties disagree regarding the standard of review applicable to the Appellate Commissioner's findings of fact in his Report and Recommendation. The Defendants argue that the Commissioner acted as a special master, and thus that we should review his findings of fact for clear error. The Plaintiffs, however, maintain that we should review the Commissioner's findings of fact de novo.

We need not resolve which standard of review applies to the Commissioner's findings of fact because our decision rests on grounds the Commissioner incorrectly rejected because of errors of law. Specifically, the Commissioner wrongly concluded that the Defendants could not be held liable for aiding and abetting others to violate the injunction. The Commissioner also wrongly concluded that the volunteer directors' purported good faith reliance on advice of counsel was relevant to whether they violated the injunction. Even if clear error review applied, it would still be appropriate to correct factual findings predicated on a misunderstanding of the governing rules of law. *See Bose Corp. v. Consumers Union of United States, Inc.*, 466 U.S. 485, 501 (1984) (citing *Pullman-Standard v. Swint*, 456 U.S. 273, 287 (1982); *Inwood Labs., Inc. v. Ives Labs., Inc.*, 456 U.S. 844, 855 n.15 (1982)).

DISCUSSION

The Plaintiffs contend that the Defendants violated our injunction by aiding and abetting non-parties, including Sea Shepherd Australia, to commit acts prohibited by the [—15—] injunction. The Plaintiffs argue that the purpose of the "separation strategy" was not to ensure compliance with our injunction, but to ensure that OZT proceeded unabated. In addition, the Plaintiffs contend that Watson violated the injunction by personally coming within 500 yards of one of the Plaintiffs' ships.

The Defendants argue that they implemented the separation strategy in a good faith effort to comply with the injunction. They further contend that they lacked control over the other Sea Shepherd entities and cannot be held accountable for the actions of these entities.

The volunteer board members point to their reliance on the advice of counsel as proof of their good faith in responding to the injunction, and argue that even if they would otherwise be liable for contempt, they are protected from liability by the Volunteer Protection Act, 42 U.S.C. § 14503. Rieman argues that he should not be held in contempt because he resigned from the Sea Shepherd US board shortly after learning that a Sea Shepherd vessel had come within 500 yards of one of the Plaintiffs' ships. Hartland, Sea Shepherd US's Administrative Director, argues that she should not be held in contempt because she was not a member of the board and did not vote to ratify the separation strategy.

We address these arguments in turn.

I. Sea Shepherd US's Contempt Liability

"Civil contempt . . . consists of a party's disobedience to a specific and definite court order by failure to take all reasonable steps within the party's power to comply." *In re* [—16—] *Dual-Deck Video Cassette Recorder Antitrust Litig.*, 10 F.3d 693, 695 (9th Cir. 1993). A party may also be held liable for knowingly aiding and abetting another to violate a court order. *See Regal Knitwear Co. v. NLRB*, 324 U.S. 9, 14 (1945) ("defendants may not nullify a decree by carrying out prohibited acts through aiders and abettors, although they were not parties to the original proceeding"). "The party alleging civil contempt must demonstrate that the alleged contemnor violated the court's order by 'clear and convincing evidence,' not merely a preponderance of the evidence." *Dual-Deck*, 10 F.3d at 695 (citing *Vertex Distrib., Inc. v.*

Falcon Foam Plastics, Inc., 689 F.2d 885, 889 (9th Cir. 1982)).

The Plaintiffs argue that Sea Shepherd US's separation strategy aided and abetted Sea Shepherd Australia and other Sea Shepherd entities to perform acts that would have violated the injunction if done by parties bound by it. We agree, and hold Sea Shepherd US in contempt on this basis.

Sea Shepherd US's separation strategy effectively nullified our injunction by ensuring that OZT proceeded unimpeded, in part by using former Sea Shepherd US assets. Sea Shepherd US ceded control over OZT to Sea Shepherd Australia and other Sea Shepherd entities it believed to be beyond the injunction's reach, knowing these entities were virtually certain to violate the injunction. At the same time, Sea Shepherd US continued to provide financial and other support for OZT after the injunction by, among other things, transferring for no consideration a vessel and equipment worth millions of dollars to Sea Shepherd Australia and other entities. [—17—]

A. Sea Shepherd US's Withdrawal from OZT

Sea Shepherd US chose to implement the separation strategy because it believed that doing so would allow OZT to proceed. There was clear and convincing evidence that Sea Shepherd US was highly motivated to see the OZT campaign completed. Shortly after the injunction issued, Watson emailed the captains of various Sea Shepherd vessels and Hartland. He wrote: "The Japanese whalers are coming. There is no doubt about that. The question is how do we stop them now? If we back down to the 9th [Circuit] Court, the whales will die." The same day, Watson emailed his attorney a proposed press release stating, in part:

> The Sea Shepherd position is clear: Our ships, officers and crew are 100% committed to achieving a zero kill quota on whales. This is Operation Zero Tolerance and the 120 crew from 26 nations are prepared to risk their lives

to defend endangered and protected whales in the Southern Ocean Whale Sanctuary.

Both Sea Shepherd US and Sea Shepherd Australia recognized that the injunction would hinder Sea Shepherd US's ability to lead OZT. Shortly after the injunction was issued, Hansen, a board member of Sea Shepherd Australia, emailed Watson and Hartland stating: "As the injunction that has been put in place by the US Federal court impedes SSCS's ability to save the lives of whales, we need another body other than SSCS to step in and take over for whales."

Sea Shepherd US ceded control of OZT to Sea Shepherd Australia on the belief that Sea Shepherd Australia was not bound by the injunction. Shortly after the injunction issued, [—18—] Watson wrote a proposal to Sea Shepherd US's board stating in part:

> The decision by the other organizations to comply with the injunction rests with the Board of Directors of the Sea Shepherd organizations registered under the laws of their respective nations. The orders of the 9th U.S. [Circuit] Court cannot possibly restrict them and this especially so with Sea Shepherd Australia where the Japanese fleet is seen to be operating in direct defiance of the Australian Federal Court and is presently in contempt of this court ruling.

Sea Shepherd Australia also believed that it was not bound by the injunction. In the weeks following the issuance of the injunction, Sea Shepherd Australia board member John McMullan, an attorney, and Melbourne barrister Debbie Mortimer, with whom he consulted, concluded that the injunction did not bind the organization. Both believed that Australian courts were unlikely to enforce the injunction because of an Australian federal court order enjoining the Plaintiffs from conducting whaling operations in the Southern Ocean Whale Sanctuary. In the early days after the injunction was handed down, Bob Brown, who would soon assume leadership over OZT, visited one of the OZT ships to reassure the crew that the injunction would not impede Sea Shepherd Australia's ability to proceed with OZT.

Sea Shepherd US's board knew it was highly likely that Sea Shepherd Australia and other entities would commit acts that violated the injunction during OZT. This was conceded by counsel at oral argument when he stated that Sea Shepherd [—19—] US board members "knew [the *Bob Barker*, which the board granted to Sea Shepherd Netherlands for no consideration,] would be used in OZT, and there was a very high risk it would violate the injunction."

When the injunction issued on December 17, 2012, Sea Shepherd US was leading OZT with Watson serving as the campaign leader and captain of the *Steve Irwin*. Yet, Sea Shepherd US did not respond to the injunction by attempting to prevent people and equipment under its control from participating in the campaign. Watson, as Executive Director of Sea Shepherd US, did not use his authority to withdraw the *Steve Irwin* from OZT after the injunction issued. Instead, he remained in charge of the campaign and captain of the *Steve Irwin* until late December, when he turned the campaign over to Sea Shepherd Australia. In his testimony before the Appellate Commissioner, Watson conceded that he could have remained in control of the OZT vessels after the injunction and tried to make sure that they complied. Sea Shepherd US had a number of employees working on OZT when the injunction issued, including Peter Hammarstedt, the Director of Marine Operations and captain of the *Bob Barker*. Sea Shepherd US did not order these employees to leave the ships. Nor did it order them to withdraw the ships from the OZT campaign. It would have been perfectly reasonable for Sea Shepherd US to do so in order to ensure that these vessels and employees did not subsequently violate the injunction. *Cf. In re Transamerica Corp.*, 184 F.2d 319 (9th Cir. 1950) (bank held in contempt for failing to countermand instructions to acquire bank branches, even though all necessary steps had been taken prior to injunction); *see also* 2 James L. High & Shirley T. High, *A Treatise on the Law of Injunctions* 1448 (4th ed. 1905) ("It is the clear duty of one who is enjoined from the commission of a particular act not [—20—] only to refrain from doing the act in person, but also to restrain his employees from doing the thing forbidden, and a mere passive and personal obedience to the order will not suffice.").

Sea Shepherd US eventually stopped paying the salaries of crew members participating in OZT, but many of them, including Hammarstedt, continued to participate in the OZT campaign. Sea Shepherd US gave Hammarstedt and two other former employees participating in OZT three months of "severance" pay after they resigned. Importantly, after Watson resigned from his roles with Sea Shepherd US, he requested that arrangements be made for the crew aboard the ships to be paid by other Sea Shepherd entities. Rather than instruct its employees to help prevent OZT, Sea Shepherd US effectively shifted these employees to its affiliates' payrolls to ensure continued participation in a campaign it knew was very likely to result in violations of the injunction.

In sum, Sea Shepherd US wanted OZT to continue; knew that the injunction would prevent it from leading the OZT campaign effectively; believed that Sea Shepherd Australia was beyond the reach of the injunction; and knew that Sea Shepherd Australia held the same belief. It also knew that there was a high risk that other Sea Shepherd entities would violate the terms of the injunction if OZT proceeded as planned. Sea Shepherd US's decision to withdraw from OZT, relinquishing any ability to take reasonable steps to prevent other Sea Shepherd entities from violating the injunction, must be viewed with these background facts in mind. Sea Shepherd US did not so much withdraw from OZT as turn the campaign and millions of dollars of assets over to entities it knew would do what the injunction forbade Sea Shepherd US and Watson from doing directly. [—21—]

B. Sea Shepherd US's Post-Injunction Assistance to OZT

Despite the ample evidence that Sea Shepherd US withdrew from OZT to ensure that it proceeded unhindered, our decision to hold Sea Shepherd US in contempt does not rest solely on its failure to take steps to prevent violations of our injunction. Our decision is primarily compelled instead by the undisputed evidence noted *infra* that Sea Shepherd US continued to provide material support to OZT after the injunction issued, confident that the entities it assisted would likely violate the injunction.

A party "may not nullify a decree by carrying out prohibited acts through aiders and abettors, although they were not parties to the original proceeding." *Regal Knitwear Co.*, 324 U.S. at 14. As a result, a party to an injunction who assists others in performing forbidden conduct may be held in contempt, even if the court's order did not explicitly forbid his specific acts of assistance. *See NLRB v. Deena Artware, Inc.*, 361 U.S. 398, 413 (1960) (Frankfurter, J., concurring) (observing that "[e]very affirmative order in equity carries with it the implicit command to refrain from action designed to defeat it"); *United States v. Shipp*, 214 U.S. 386, 422–23 (1909) (holding sheriff in contempt for failing to prevent lynching and observing that he "in effect aided and abetted it"); *Roe v. Operation Rescue*, 919 F.2d 857, 871 (3d Cir. 1990) ("The law does not permit the instigator of contemptuous conduct to absolve himself of contempt liability by leaving the physical performance of the forbidden conduct to others. As a result, those who have knowledge of a valid court order and abet others in violating it are subject to the court's contempt powers."); *NLRB v. Laborers' Int'l Union of N. Am., AFL-CIO*, 882 F.2d 949, 954 (5th Cir. 1989) [—22—] ("One need not commit an unlawful act in order to be liable for conspiring to evade a judgment of a court: it is contempt to act solely for the purpose of evading a judgment.").

1. Post-Injunction Payments for OZT Expenses

Sea Shepherd US incurred substantial expenses related to OZT after the injunction issued. $348,565 of those expenses were for orders placed before the injunction was issued, but paid afterwards. Sea Shepherd US took no steps to rescind the orders, divert delivery to a third party, or charge for their use. Moreover, other OZT-related expenses were both ordered and paid for after the injunction issued on December 17, 2012. For instance, an order of $106,830 in fuel for the *Steve Irwin* was invoiced on December 31, 2012, paid for by Sea Shepherd US that day, and delivered in January of 2013. Between January 1 and 16, 2013, Sea Shepherd US paid $16,373 in credit card charges of the captains of vessels involved in OZT. In all, Sea Shepherd US paid $163,405 in OZT-related expenses that were invoiced and paid for by Sea Shepherd US after the issuance of the injunction. Sea Shepherd US and the individual board members confirmed through their counsel at oral argument the accuracy of the $163,405 figure.

2. Donations to OZT

Watson helped facilitate donations to OZT after the injunction issued. On December 28, 2012, Watson wrote an email to a Sea Shepherd US fundraiser, stating:

> You can continue to fund raise for Sea Shepherd USA but not to ask for funds for Operation Zero Tolerance. If people wish to [—23—] restrict a donation to Operation Zero Tolerance they can do so but it will have to be made out to Sea Shepherd Australia and there can be no tax receipt.
>
> Rob Holden has a 501(c)(3) organization called Blue Rage and if need be donations can be made to Blue Rage and Blue Rage can send it on toe [sic] Sea Shepherd Australia.

Thus, even though Sea Shepherd US was unable to collect tax-deductible charitable donations for use in OZT, Watson proposed

3. Asset Grants to OZT for No Consideration

Sea Shepherd US's most troubling post-injunction support for OZT came in a series of substantial grants of property it made to various Sea Shepherd entities participating in the OZT campaign. In January of 2013, the Sea Shepherd US board authorized a series of grants to Sea Shepherd Australia and Sea Shepherd Netherlands. Specifically, Sea Shepherd US gave equipment aboard the *Brigitte Bardot* to Sea Shepherd Australia for no consideration. This equipment had an original purchase price of more than $175,000. Sea Shepherd US also gave equipment aboard the *Steve Irwin* to Sea Shepherd Netherlands, again for no consideration. This equipment had an original purchase price of several hundreds of thousands of dollars. Most significantly, Sea Shepherd US also transferred ownership of its vessel, the *Bob Barker*, to Sea Shepherd Netherlands for no consideration. As noted earlier, the *Bob Barker* and the transferred equipment had a total original purchase price of nearly two million dollars. [—24—] The *Brigitte Bardot*, *Steve Irwin*, and *Bob Barker* all participated in OZT. Each vessel was involved in at least one violation of the injunction; the *Bob Barker* was involved in several.

The Sea Shepherd US board knew that these items would be used in OZT when it voted to grant them to Sea Shepherd Australia and Sea Shepherd Netherlands. The email asking the board members to vote on the grants stated "[p]lease consider this grant *in conjunction with Operation Zero Tolerance*." Sea Shepherd US board member Robert Wintner testified that he understood this email to mean that the granted items would be used for OZT. And, if this evidence leaves any doubt, Sea Shepherd US and the individual board members conceded at oral argument through their counsel that the board knew that the equipment would be used in OZT, and that there was a "very high risk" that the *Bob Barker* would violate the injunction.

In light of this undisputed evidence, we hold that Sea Shepherd US violated the injunction by giving others it knew were highly likely to violate the injunction the means to do so. The fact that the injunction's terms did not specifically forbid Sea Shepherd US's acts of assistance does not immunize Sea Shepherd US from liability. "In deciding whether an injunction has been violated it is proper to observe the objects for which the relief was granted and to find a breach of the decree in a violation of the spirit of the injunction, even though its strict letter may not have been disregarded." *John B. Stetson Co. v. Stephen L. Stetson Co.*, 128 F.2d 981, 983 (2d Cir. 1942); *see Prang Co. v. Am. Crayon Co.*, 58 F.2d 715 (3d Cir. 1932); *Cal. Fruit Growers Exch. v. Sunkist Drinks, Inc.*, 25 F. Supp. 401 (S.D.N.Y. 1938); *see also Salazar v. Buono*, 559 U.S. 700, 762 (2010) [—25—] (Breyer, J., dissenting) (citing *Stetson Co.*, 128 F.2d at 983). Our objective in issuing the injunction was to stop Sea Shepherd from attacking the Plaintiffs' vessels. Sea Shepherd US thwarted that objective by furnishing other Sea Shepherd entities with the means to do what it could not after the issuance of the injunction.

It has long been settled law that a person with notice of an injunction may be held in contempt for aiding and abetting a party in violating it. *See Peterson v. Highland Music, Inc.*, 140 F.3d 1313, 1323–24 (9th Cir. 1998) (citing *NLRB v. Sequoia Dist. Council of Carpenters*, 568 F.2d 628, 633 (9th Cir. 1977)); *Laborers' Int'l Union of N. Am., AFL-CIO*, 882 F.2d at 954; *Max's Seafood Cafe ex rel. Lou-Ann, Inc. v. Quinteros*, 176 F.3d 669, 674 (3d Cir. 1999). Much of the applicable case law addresses the issue of when it is fair to hold non-parties to an injunction liable for aiding and abetting a party's violation of the injunction. *See, e.g., Regal Knitwear Co.*, 324 U.S. at 14; *Levin v. Tiber Holding Corp.*, 277 F.3d 243, 250–51 (2d Cir. 2002); *Goya Foods, Inc. v Wallack Mgmt. Co.*, 290 F.3d 63, 75 (1st Cir. 2002); *Highland Music*, 140 F.3d at 1323–24; *Illinois v. U.S. Dep't of Health & Human Servs.*, 772 F.2d 329, 332 (7th Cir. 1985); *Waffenschmidt v. MacKay*, 763 F.2d 711, 717 (5th Cir. 1985); *Alemite Mfg. Corp. v. Staff*, 42 F.2d 832, 832–33 (2d Cir. 1930). It is clear to us that if a non-party to an injunction may be held in contempt for aiding and abetting violations of an injunction, a party to an injunction may be as well. We therefore hold that a party may be held in contempt for giving a non-party the means to violate an injunction, if the party knows it is highly likely the non-party will use those means to violate the injunction. [—26—]

Under such circumstances, the party giving assistance need not affirmatively desire to cause a violation of the injunction; it is enough that the party know a violation is highly likely to occur. In so ruling, we are guided by common law rules of fault-based liability. "Tort law ordinarily imputes to an actor the intention to cause the natural and probable consequences of his conduct." *DeVoto v. Pacific Fidelity Life Ins. Co.*, 618 F.2d 1340, 1347 (9th Cir. 1980) (citing Restatement (Second) of Torts § 8A (1965)). "Intent is not . . . limited to consequences which are desired. If the actor knows that the consequences are certain, or substantially certain, to result from his act, and still goes ahead, he is treated by the law as if he had in fact desired to produce the result." Restatement (Second) of Torts § 8A(b) (1965). We have adopted a similar definition of intent outside the common law tort context. For instance, we employed it when we defined the elements of contributory infringement of copyright in *Perfect 10, Inc. v. Amazon.com, Inc.*, 508 F.3d 1146, 1170–71 (9th Cir. 2007), where we observed that "common law principles establish that intent may be imputed." *See also Metro-Goldwyn-Mayer Studios Inc. v. Grokster Ltd.*, 545 U.S. 913, 934–35 (2005) (endorsing the use of "rules of fault-based liability derived from the common law" in assessing liability for contributory infringement). Under these circumstances, we find it appropriate to impute to Sea Shepherd US an intent to cause a violation of the injunction, regardless of whether Sea Shepherd US affirmatively desired that a violation occur.

We also find it relevant that Sea Shepherd US's acts of assistance proximately caused violations of the injunction. We are once again guided by principles derived from common law rules of fault-based liability. The Supreme Court recently summarized the principles of proximate [—27—] causation in *Paroline v. United States*, 134 S. Ct. 1710, 1719 (2014). "As a general matter, to say one event proximately caused another is a way of making two separate but related assertions. First, it means the former event caused the latter. This is known as actual cause or cause in fact." *Id.* Second, it means the former event was "not just any cause, but one with a sufficient connection to the result." *Id.*

We begin this portion of our analysis by asking whether Sea Shepherd US's assistance actually caused violations of the injunction. "The concept of actual cause 'is not a metaphysical one but an ordinary, matter-of-fact inquiry into the existence . . . of a causal relation as laypeople would view it.'" *Id.* (quoting 4 F. Harper, F. James, & O. Gray, Torts § 20.2, p. 100 (3d ed. 2007)). We need not assess whether Sea Shepherd US's acts caused each and every violation of the injunction. At a minimum its transfer of ownership and control of the *Bob Barker* to Sea Shepherd Netherlands caused the violations involving the *Bob Barker*. The foreign Sea Shepherd entities could not have used the vessel to violate the injunction if they did not control it.

We next inquire whether Sea Shepherd US's conduct had a "sufficient connection to" violations of the injunction. *See Paroline*, 134 S. Ct. at 1719. In applying this "flexible concept," *id.* (internal quotation marks omitted), we are mindful of its purpose: "A requirement of proximate cause . . . serves, *inter alia*, to preclude liability in situations where the causal link between conduct and result is so attenuated that the consequence is more aptly described as mere fortuity." *Id.* (citing *Exxon Co., U.S.A. v. Sofec, Inc.*, 517 U.S. 830, 838–39 (1996)). For this reason, "[p]roximate cause is often explicated in terms of foreseeability or the scope of the risk created by the predicate conduct." *Paroline*, [—28—] 134 S. Ct. at 1719 (citing 1 Restatement (Third) of Torts: Liability for Physical and Emotional Harm § 29, p. 493 (2005)).

We have no trouble finding a sufficient causal connection between Sea Shepherd US's intentional conduct and violations of the injunction. Sea Shepherd US knew that there was a very high risk that foreign Sea Shepherd entities would use the *Bob Barker* to violate the injunction. It was clearly foreseeable that transferring the ownership and control of the vessel to Sea Shepherd Netherlands in order that it participate in OZT would result in violations of our injunction.

The fact that the foreign Sea Shepherd entities had a more direct role in causing the violations than Sea Shepherd US does not negate the causal connection between Sea Shepherd US's acts and the violations of our injunction. An event may have multiple proximate causes. *See id.* ("Every event has many causes . . . and only some of them are proximate, as the law uses that term."); *Sheridan v. United States*, 487 U.S. 392, 406 (1988) (Kennedy, J., concurring) ("It is standard tort doctrine that a reasonably foreseeable injury can arise from multiple causes, each arising from a breach of a different duty and each imposing liability accordingly."); *see also Lillie v. Thompson*, 332 U.S. 459, 461–62 (1947) (per curiam). As we have observed in applying California tort law, "the fact that the actor's conduct becomes effective in harm only through the intervention of new and independent forces for which the actor is not responsible is of no importance." *Bank of N.Y. v. Fremont Gen. Corp.*, 523 F.3d 902, 910 (9th Cir. 2008) (quoting *Tate v. Canonica*, 180 Cal. App. 2d 898, 907 (1960)). "[N]o consideration is given to the fact that . . . the actor's conduct has created a situation harmless unless acted [—29—] upon by other forces for which the actor is not responsible." *Tate*, 180 Cal. App. 2d at 907 (internal quotation marks omitted). By analogy, a party who acts knowing that his conduct is highly likely to cause a violation of an injunction may not avoid liability simply because another person outside his immediate control actually carried out the violation.

We are mindful that the contempt power, like other "inherent powers" of the judiciary, "must be exercised with restraint and discretion." *See Roadway Express, Inc. v. Piper*, 447 U.S. 752, 764–65 (1980) (citing *Gompers v. Bucks Stove & Range Co.*, 221 U.S. 418, 450–51 (1911); *Green v. United States*, 365 U.S. 165, 193–94 (1958) (Black, J., dissenting)). Nevertheless, "[t]he purpose of contempt proceedings is to uphold the power of the court," *Bessette v. W.B. Conkey Co.*, 194 U.S. 324, 327 (1904), and to ensure that the court's vindication of litigants' rights is not merely symbolic. Our orders would have little practical force, and would be rendered essentially meaningless, if we were unable to prevent parties bound by them from flagrantly and materially assisting others to do what they themselves are forbidden to do.

The Defendants argue that to hold them in contempt for aiding and abetting we must find them "indirectly liable," because "[t]he alleged acts of contempt were committed by third parties." The Defendants contend that this requires a clear and convincing showing that they "incited" or "controlled" the third-party acts of contempt. This argument is without merit.

While the record amply supports the inference that Sea Shepherd US, and Watson in particular (discussed *infra*), "incited" others to violate the injunction, a showing of [—30—] incitement or control is not required to hold Sea Shepherd US in contempt. It is not necessary to impute the acts of others to Sea Shepherd US to hold it in contempt; we hold Sea Shepherd US in contempt for the acts *it* committed after the injunction issued. *See Laborers' Int'l Union of N. Am., AFL-CIO*, 882 F.2d at 954 ("One need not commit an unlawful act in order to be liable for conspiring to evade a judgment of a court: it is contempt to act solely for the purpose of evading a judgment."); *John B. Stetson Co.*, 128 F.2d at 983 (holding that courts may "find a breach of the decree in a violation of the spirit of the injunction, even though its strict letter may not have been disregarded"). As a party to the injunction, Sea Shepherd US is liable because it intentionally furnished cash payments, and a vessel and equipment worth millions of dollars, to individuals and entities it knew would likely violate the injunction.

The out-of-circuit cases Sea Shepherd US cites in support of its incitement and control argument are plainly irrelevant to the issues presented here. Sea Shepherd US cites a Federal Circuit patent case, *Tegal Corp. v. Tokyo Electron Co., Ltd.*, 248 F.3d 1376, 1378 (Fed. Cir. 2001). But *Tegal* held only that a party enjoined from "facilitating" infringement of a patent cannot be held in contempt merely for failing to prevent another's infringement, absent an affirmative act of facilitation. *Id.* at 1378–80. This holding is not relevant to our facts, which *do* involve affirmative acts.

Sea Shepherd US's citation to *National Organization for Women, Inc. v. Scheidler*, 267 F.3d 687 (7th Cir. 2001), *rev'd on other grounds*, 537 U.S. 393 (2003), is also unavailing. The injunction in *Scheidler* explicitly prohibited the defendants from "aiding, abetting, inducing, directing, or inciting" others to violate the injunction. *Id.* at 705. The [—31—] *Scheidler* defendants argued that the injunction exposed them to liability for the conduct of persons they did not control, and whose actions they did not authorize. *Id.* at 706. The Seventh Circuit disagreed, finding that "[n]othing in the order purports to hold the defendants liable for actions they do not direct, incite, or control." *Id.* at 707. Even if *Scheidler*'s narrow holding about the specific terms of one injunction could be construed broadly as a holding about the general law of contempt for aiding and abetting, and it clearly cannot, the holding would not apply here. We do not purport to hold any of the Defendants liable for actions they did not direct, incite, or control. Rather, we hold them liable only for their own intentional acts in furtherance of OZT. A party bound by an injunction may not provide a non-party with the means to violate it, knowing the non-party will be likely to do so.

Sea Shepherd US also argues that contempt for aiding and abetting requires a showing that a third-party's violations were "for the benefit of, or to assist" Sea Shepherd US. But the out-of-circuit case Sea Shepherd US cites in support of this argument is clearly inapposite. *See Goya Foods, Inc.*, 290 F.3d at 75. *Goya Foods* addresses when a *non-party* to an injunction may be held in contempt for

conduct that would violate the injunction if performed by a party bound by it. *Id.* The First Circuit held that, to be liable for civil contempt, a non-party's "challenged action must be taken for the benefit of, or to assist, a party subject to the decree." *Id.* This requirement, like Rule 65's requirement that a person cannot be bound by an injunction unless he is in "active concert or participation with" a party, is animated partly by due process concerns raised when courts seek to bind a non-party. *See* Fed R. Civ. P. 65(d)(2)(C); *Max's Seafood Cafe ex rel. Lou-Ann, Inc.*, 176 F.3d at 674. Holding Sea Shepherd US in contempt for violating an injunction to which it is a party [—32—] raises no analogous due process concerns. Sea Shepherd US's liability for intentionally assisting non-parties to violate an injunction by which it is clearly bound does not depend on whether the non-parties violated the injunction for Sea Shepherd US's benefit, or their own, or for no reason at all.

The Defendants also argue that they should not be held in contempt because the so-called "separation strategy" was based on a reasonable and good faith interpretation of the injunction. We reject this argument.

It is true that we have recognized a narrow "good faith" exception to the general rule that intent is irrelevant in civil contempt proceedings. *See Vertex*, 689 F.2d at 889. We held in *Vertex* that "if a defendant's action appears to be based on a good faith and reasonable interpretation of (the court's order), he should not be held in contempt." *Id.* (internal quotation marks omitted). By its terms, the *Vertex* exception only applies where a defendant's interpretation is "reasonable." Parties who act on the unreasonable advice of counsel risk being held in contempt if their actions violate a court's order.

The facts of this case, however, do not require a *Vertex* inquiry into the reasonableness of the Defendants' interpretation of our injunction. The principle announced in *Vertex* was based on the well-established rule that a "vague" order may not be enforced. *See id.* (citing *Int'l Longshoremen's Ass'n, Local 1291 v. Phila.*

Marine Trade Ass'n, 389 U.S. 64, 76 (1967) (reversing a civil contempt judgment founded upon a decree too vague to be understood)). In *Vertex*, the parties disputed whether the words "includes" and "incorporating" in the consent judgment were impermissibly vague. 689 F.2d at 890. The [—33—] case thus involved a "semantic battle" about the meaning of allegedly vague terms in the language of the judgment. *See id.*

No such "semantic battle" is at issue here. The meaning of the text of the injunction is not disputed by any of the parties. No one contends that the injunction's text states, in so many words, that Sea Shepherd US may not donate millions of dollars of equipment to entities it knows are likely to violate the injunction. And no one contends that the text states that Sea Shepherd US may not continue to fund OZT, knowing that violations of the injunction were likely to occur if the campaign proceeded unabated. The *language* of the injunction itself is not ambiguous. What the Defendants claim is ambiguous, however, is whether they could avoid liability by hewing to the narrow letter of the injunction while simultaneously ignoring its spirit by giving substantial assistance to OZT. *Vertex* is not relevant to resolving such an "ambiguity."

Even if the *Vertex* exception were applicable here, we would find that the Defendants unreasonably resolved the "ambiguity." In making this determination, we are guided by the Supreme Court's commentary in *McComb v. Jacksonville Paper Co.*, 336 U.S. 187 (1949). In *McComb*, the Court reversed a district court's decision declining to enforce an injunction that prohibited a party from violating the Fair Labor Standards Act. *Id.* at 194. Both the district court and the court of appeals found that the alleged contemnor's specific conduct did not violate the injunction's general prohibition against violations of the FLSA. *Id.* at 190–91. Noting that the respondents "acted at their peril" when they "undertook to make their own determination of what the decree meant," *id.* at 192, the Court reasoned: [—34—]

It does not lie in their mouths to say that they have an immunity from civil contempt because the plan or scheme which they adopted was not specifically enjoined. Such a rule would give tremendous impetus to the program of experimentation with disobedience of the law which we condemned in *Maggio v. Zeitz*[1] . . . . The instant case is an excellent illustration of how it could operate to prevent accountability for persistent contumacy. Civil contempt is avoided today by showing that the specific plan adopted by respondents was not enjoined. Hence a new decree is entered enjoining that particular plan. Thereafter the defendants work out a plan that was not specifically enjoined. Immunity is once more obtained because the new plan was not specifically enjoined. And so a whole series of wrongs is perpetrated and a decree of enforcement goes for naught.

Id. at 192–93.

To find the Defendants' self-serving interpretation of their obligations under our injunction reasonable would be to invite "experimentation with disobedience." The schemes available to those determined to evade injunctions are many and varied, *see, e.g., Deena Artware, Inc.*, 361 U.S. at 398; *Laborers' Int'l Union of N. Am., AFL-CIO*, 882 F.2d at 954; *Parker v.* [—35—] *United States*, 126 F.2d 370 (1st Cir. 1942), and no injunction can explicitly prohibit every conceivable plan designed to defeat it. Though they had every opportunity, the Defendants did not seek clarification of their obligations. *See McComb*, 336 U.S. at 192 (noting that the respondents could have avoided appeal by simply petitioning for "modification, clarification or construction of the order"). By construing their obligations narrowly to include only refraining from acts specifically enumerated in the injunction, and not acts likely to nullify the injunction, the Defendants assumed the

---

[1] 333 U.S. 56, 69 (1948) (observing in different context that "[t]he procedure to enforce a court's order commanding or forbidding an act should not be so inconclusive as to foster experimentation with disobedience").

risk that their attempts at technical compliance would prove wanting. We accordingly reject the Defendants' good faith argument, and hold Sea Shepherd US in civil contempt.

II. Volunteer Board Members

The Plaintiffs have also moved for contempt against Sea Shepherd US's volunteer board members based on their ratification of the separation strategy, and their approval of transfers of ownership of valuable property, for no consideration, to Sea Shepherd entities participating in OZT. At the time the injunction issued, the volunteer board members were Lani Blazier, Marnie Gaede, Bob Talbot, Robert Wintner, Ben Zuckerman, and Peter Rieman. Having found Sea Shepherd US liable for civil contempt, we also hold the board members just named in civil contempt.

The law is clear that those who control an organization may be held liable if they fail to take appropriate action to ensure compliance with an injunction:

> A command to the corporation is in effect a command to those who are officially responsible for the conduct of its affairs. If [—36—] they, apprised of the writ directed to the corporation, prevent compliance or fail to take appropriate action within their power for the performance of the corporate duty, they, no less than the corporation itself, are guilty of disobedience, and may be punished for contempt.

Wilson v. United States, 221 U.S. 361, 376 (1911). There is no dispute that the individual board members knew of the injunction and voted to implement the separation strategy, including the transfer of property for no consideration to Sea Shepherd Australia and Sea Shepherd Netherlands.

The Appellate Commissioner made much of the volunteer directors' reliance on the advice of counsel, and the Defendants urge us to do the same. But the Commissioner's conclusion that the volunteer directors intended to comply with the injunction is at odds with Sea Shepherd US's subsequent concession at oral argument that the board knew there was a "very high risk" the vessel and equipment it provided would be used to violate the injunction. Under the circumstances, it is simply not credible that the volunteer directors believed they were complying with the injunction when they agreed to grant, for no consideration, millions of dollars of equipment and materials needed to carry out OZT to entities they believed would be highly likely to use those materials to violate the injunction.

Moreover, even if we were to assume, *arguendo*, that the volunteer directors truly acted in reliance on counsel's advice, that reliance is largely irrelevant. There is "no basis in law" for a "'good faith' exception to the requirement of obedience to a court order." *In re Crystal Palace Gambling Hall, Inc.*, [—37—] 817 F.2d 1361, 1365 (9th Cir. 1987). A party's good faith reliance on the advice of counsel does not excuse the violation of a court's order. *See Steinert v. United States*, 571 F.2d 1105, 1108 (9th Cir. 1978) (holding that "[d]isobedience of a valid court order does not cease to be willful when done in good faith reliance on the advice of a tax accountant"); *Eustace v. Lynch*, 80 F.2d 652, 656 (9th Cir. 1935) (holding that the "advice of an attorney is not a defense to an act of contempt"); *see also United States v. Asay*, 614 F.2d 655, 661 (9th Cir. 1980) (holding that defiance of summonses was "willful despite the advice of counsel" (citing *Steinert*, 571 F.2d at 1108)). As we observed in *Steinert*, "[t]o hold otherwise would make stultification of a court order impermissibly easy. In litigation frequently the client must assume the risks of his advisor's errors." 571 F.2d at 1108. Accordingly, the volunteer directors may be held liable for contempt.

A. Peter Rieman

Peter Rieman stands in a somewhat different position than the other named board members. Rieman resigned from the board on February 11, 2013, following the first alleged violation of the injunction on January 29, 2013. Rieman was concerned that he had no control over the actions of those involved in OZT and was worried that he faced personal exposure for subsequent violations of the injunction.

The Appellate Commissioner concluded correctly that "[i]f SSCS's actions (and inactions) put it in contempt, then [Rieman] is as liable as the other Volunteer Directors." It is true that Rieman lacked control over Sea Shepherd US after he resigned in February 2013. But by that time, he had already voted to ratify and implement the separation strategy, [—38—] and an OZT vessel had already breached the safety perimeter imposed by our injunction. Rieman's resignation therefore does not immunize him from liability for contempt.[2]

B. Volunteer Protection Act

The volunteer directors argue that the provisions of the Volunteer Protection Act (VPA), 42 U.S.C. § 14503, immunize them from a finding of contempt. We reject this argument, and hold that the VPA does not affect the power of federal courts to impose civil fines to redress contempt.

Under some circumstances, the VPA immunizes volunteers from liability for harm caused by actions taken within the scope of their volunteer responsibilities. The VPA provides in relevant part:

[N]o volunteer of a nonprofit organization or governmental entity shall be liable for harm caused by an act or omission of the volunteer on behalf of the organization or entity if–

(1) the volunteer was acting within the scope of the volunteer's responsibilities in the nonprofit organization or governmental entity at the time of the act or omission;

[and] . . . [—39—]

(3) the harm was not caused by willful or criminal misconduct, gross negligence, reckless misconduct, or a conscious, flagrant indifference to the rights or safety of the individual harmed by the volunteer . . . .

42 U.S.C. § 14503(a).

The Plaintiffs raise a host of arguments why the volunteer directors do not qualify for immunity under the VPA. The Plaintiffs contend that the attorney's fees they seek are not "harm" under § 14503(a); that the board members' misconduct was willful under § 14503(a)(3); and that they did not act within the scope of their responsibilities under § 14503(a)(1) when they ratified the separation strategy. We need not address these arguments, for we hold that the VPA does not affect our power to hold those bound by our injunction in contempt.

We find it highly improbable that when Congress passed the VPA, it intended to prohibit federal courts from finding volunteer board members liable for their acts of contempt.[3] The text of the VPA does not specifically mention courts' equity jurisdiction or their contempt powers. Nor does the VPA's legislative history provide support for the conclusion that Congress's purposes included curbing the judicial power [—40—] to enforce orders through contempt. The Committee on the Judiciary's report observed that "H.R. 911, as amended, immunizes a volunteer from liability for harm caused by *ordinary negligence.*" H.R. Rep. 105-101(I) at 5 (emphasis added). The committee report also speaks of the "litigation craze" and "[o]ur 'sue happy' culture." *Id.* It explains that the VPA is

---

[2] This finding of contempt as to Rieman does not, however, preclude the taking into account of his early resignation by way of mitigation when appropriate remedial sanctions are considered under Part V, below.

[3] The parties largely focus their arguments on whether the VPA applies to federal causes of action, in addition to state causes of action. But whether the VPA applies to federal causes of action is not directly relevant to whether the VPA circumscribes federal courts' contempt power, and the cases cited are inapposite. *See Armendarez v. Glendale Youth Ctr., Inc.*, 265 F. Supp. 2d 1136, 1140 (D. Ariz. 2003); *Nunez v. Duncan*, 2004 WL 1274402, at *1 (D. Or. June 9, 2004); *Am. Produce, LLC v. Harvest Sharing, Inc.*, 2013 WL 1164403, at *3 (D. Colo. Mar. 20, 2013).

"intended to remove a significant barrier—the fear of *unreasonable* legal liability—to inducing individuals to volunteer their time to charitable endeavors." *Id.* (emphasis added). These references indicate that the VPA's purpose was to curb lawsuits against volunteers, not to curb courts' contempt power.

The importance of the power of courts to punish for contempt makes it highly unlikely that Congress would curtail that power without explicitly indicating its intention. "[T]he power of courts to punish for contempts is a necessary and integral part of the independence of the judiciary, and is absolutely essential to the performance of the duties imposed on them by law." *Gompers v. Buck's Stove & Range Co.*, 221 U.S. 418, 450 (1911). This power is "inherent in all courts." *Michaelson*, 266 U.S. at 65. We acknowledge that Congress may limit lower federal courts' exercise of the contempt power. *See, e.g., Bessette v. W. B. Conkey Co.*, 194 U.S. 324 (1904); *Ex Parte Robinson*, 86 U.S. 505 (1873). "Nevertheless, 'we do not lightly assume that Congress has intended to depart from established principles' such as the scope of a court's inherent power." *Chambers v. NASCO, Inc.*, 501 U.S. 32, 47 (1991) (quoting *Weinberger v. Romero–Barcelo*, 456 U.S. 305, 313 (1982)); *see also Link v. Wabash R.R. Co.*, 370 U.S. 626, 631–32 (1962). Absent a "much clearer expression of purpose," *see Link*, 370 U.S. at 631–32, we will not assume that Congress intended to limit our inherent power to punish contempt. [—41—]

We accordingly hold that the VPA does not reach federal courts' power to find volunteer board members in contempt of their orders. Accordingly, the VPA does not immunize Sea Shepherd US's volunteer board members from liability for contempt.

III. Watson

In addition to holding Watson in contempt as the Executive Director of Sea Shepherd US, we hold him in contempt for personally violating the injunction by coming within 500 yards of one of the Plaintiffs' vessels.

Unlike the other individual respondents, Watson was present in the Southern Ocean aboard the *Steve Irwin* during the entire OZT campaign. Watson claimed to believe that he could stay on the *Steve Irwin*, acting as an observer, and remain in compliance with the injunction. Chakravarty, the captain of the *Steve Irwin*, assured Watson that the ship would not approach within 500 yards of the whaling vessels. The two developed a contingency plan in the event that the *Steve Irwin* looked like it might breach the 500-yard safety perimeter. Under the plan, Chakravarty would transfer Watson to the *Brigitte Bardot* prior to any encounter. This plan proved unworkable in practice. Chakravarty abandoned the plan to transfer Watson in mid-February when he and the other captains attempted a blockade to prevent one of the Plaintiffs' vessels from refueling. As a result, Watson personally came within 500 yards of the Plaintiffs' whaling vessel while on board the *Steve Irwin*.

Watson testified that he did not disembark the *Steve Irwin* because he believed that he risked detention or extradition if he did so in Australia or New Zealand, the only two countries [—42—] within 1000 miles of the *Steve Irwin*'s position. When the injunction issued, Watson was subject to an INTERPOL red notice for criminal charges he faced in Japan. But there was strong evidence that Watson was unlikely to be extradited from Australia, and that he knew it. Sea Shepherd was very popular in Australia, and Watson's Australian attorney had advised him that the risk of arrest and extradition by Australia was remote.

We find that Watson failed to take all reasonable steps within his power to comply with the injunction. A reasonable person in Watson's position would not have tried to evade a warrant for his arrest while also risking being held in contempt. To hold otherwise would be to condone as reasonable Watson's attempt to evade the criminal charges he was facing. We accordingly hold Watson in civil contempt for coming within 500 yards of Plaintiffs' vessels.

IV. Hartland

The Plaintiffs also request that Hartland, Sea Shepherd US's Administrative Director, be held in contempt. Hartland is in a different position than the other individual respondents. She was not a member of Sea Shepherd US's board, and accordingly did not vote to ratify the separation strategy. As the Appellate Commissioner found, "[t]here is no evidence that Hartland took any action in response to the injunction that was not authorized by the SSCS board." This alone does not immunize Hartland from contempt, for our injunction explicitly bound not just Sea Shepherd US and Watson, but those acting "in concert" with them. However, unlike the volunteer board members, Hartland could only have complied with the injunction by resigning from her paid employment. Under the specific circumstances of this case, [—43—] we conclude that it would not be equitable to hold Hartland in contempt.

V. Appropriate Remedial Sanctions

The Plaintiffs request three forms of relief to redress the Defendants' contempt: (1) attorney's fees and costs as compensation for bringing the Defendants' acts of contempt to the attention of the court; (2) bonded, suspended sanctions in the amount of $2 million or such amount the court deems appropriate; and (3) an order directing that the Defendants may purge themselves of contempt by seeking in good faith to revoke their grants of property to Sea Shepherd entities.

We hold that the Plaintiffs are entitled to recover attorney's fees and costs incurred in bringing and prosecuting these contempt proceedings. "[T]he cost of bringing the violation to the attention of the court is part of the damages suffered by the prevailing party and those costs would reduce any benefits gained by the prevailing party from the court's violated order." *Perry v. O'Donnell*, 759 F.2d 702, 705 (9th Cir. 1985). At a minimum, the Plaintiffs shall recover their fees and costs against Sea Shepherd US and Watson. The Plaintiffs are also entitled to compensation for any actual damages suffered and resources (such as fuel and personnel costs) that were wasted as a result of the Defendants' contumacious acts interfering with the Plaintiffs' mission. We will re-refer this matter to the Appellate Commissioner to determine the appropriate amount of attorney's fees and costs as well as compensatory damages to award. The Commissioner shall determine whether the volunteer directors should also be held liable, and the extent to which each of them should be held liable, jointly and/or severally. [—44—]

The Plaintiffs' requests for coercive sanctions and an order to compel compliance should be directed to the district court. Our opinion of February 25, 2013, as amended May 24, 2013, provided that the preliminary injunction "will remain in effect until further order of this court." *Inst. of Cetacean Research*, 725 F.3d at 947, 1 Adm. R. at 410. However, we issued our mandate on June 7, 2013, at which time the district court assumed supervision over the Defendants' present compliance with the preliminary injunction. While we retain jurisdiction to order remedial relief for acts of contempt that took place prior to the issuance of our mandate, because these coercive sanctions are forward-looking, we believe that policing the Defendants' continuing compliance with the preliminary injunction is better left to the district court, subject to our review on appeal. This panel retains jurisdiction over all appeals in this case.

CONCLUSION

We hold Sea Shepherd Conservation Society, Paul Watson, Lani Blazier, Marnie Gaede, Bob Talbot, Robert Wintner, Ben Zuckerman, and Peter Rieman in civil contempt. We do not hold Susan Hartland in contempt. We re-refer this matter to the Appellate Commissioner for further proceedings in a separate order filed contemporaneously.

IT IS SO ORDERED.

United States Court of Appeals for the Eleventh Circuit

United States Court of Appeals
for the Eleventh Circuit

No. 13-11092

OFFSHORE OF THE PALM BEACHES, INC.
vs.
LYNCH

Appeal from the United States District Court for the
Southern District of Florida

Decided: February 3, 2014

Citation: 741 F.3d 1251, 2 Adm. R. 536 (11th Cir. 2014).

Before **MARCUS, FAY,** and **WALKER***, Circuit Judges.

*Honorable John Walker, Jr., United States Circuit Judge for the Second Circuit, sitting by designation

[—1—] MARCUS, Circuit Judge: [—2—]

In this admiralty action, a boat owner, Offshore of the Palm Beaches, Inc. ("Offshore"), appeals from a district court order that permitted a lone claimant, Lisa Lynch, to pursue personal injury claims in state court after Offshore had invoked the Limitation of Liability Act ("Limitation Act"), 46 U.S.C. § 30501 (2006). Offshore argues that its forum selection should control because Lynch lost the race to the courthouse. Our case precedent instructs us that we have jurisdiction to review the district court's order as one dissolving or modifying an injunction pursuant to 28 U.S.C. § 1292(a)(1). On the merits, we affirm. The district court did not abuse its considerable discretion in determining that Lynch may proceed first in state court with her tort claim before the district court adjudicates the boat owner's efforts to limit its liability to the value of the vessel.

I.

On October 13, 2011, Offshore owned and maintained a 2008 Everglades 27CC, a twenty-six foot vessel used as part of Offshore's Freedom Boat Club. Lynch and her husband, Michael, were members of the Club. That day the couple took the boat to sea off Palm Beach County, Florida, where, five-hundred yards from shore, they struck the wake of another craft. The concussion threw Lynch from the bow bench into the air. Gravity brought her back to the boat, with an impact she claims caused catastrophic physical injury. Specifically, Lynch alleges [—3—] that Offshore's negligence was to blame for damages well in excess of the vessel's $95,000 value.

A few months after the incident, on February 6, 2012, attorney Darryl Kogan wrote Offshore a letter noting his representation of Lynch and requesting the company's liability insurance information. Six months later, on August 6, 2012, Offshore sued in the United States District Court for the Southern District of Florida seeking exoneration or limitation of its liability to the value of the vessel pursuant to the Limitation Act. Soon thereafter, the district court enjoined any other cause of action against Offshore or the vessel relating to the incident.

In her answer, Lynch asserted a claim for her extensive injuries based on Offshore's failure to exercise reasonable care. On October 22, she moved to dismiss, stay, or lift the injunction to allow her to proceed in state court and try her common law tort claim to a jury, invoking the single claimant exception to exclusive federal admiralty jurisdiction otherwise reposed in the district court under the Limitation Act. Following unambiguous case precedent, she included in her motion a set of detailed stipulations designed to protect Offshore's right to litigate any limitation of liability in federal district court:

Stipulations of Claimant in Support of Claimant's Motion to Dismiss, Stay And/or Lift the Injunction in this Matter and Permit the Claimant to Proceed in State Court

Provided the Court lifts its Monition and Injunction of August 10, 2012 (D.E. 6) and stays this action to permit the single Claimant to [—4—] proceed against the Petitioner in a state court action for personal injury, the single Claimant, LISA LYNCH, stipulates and agrees as follows:

1. That the Petitioner, OFFSHORE, has the right to litigate the issue of whether it is entitled to limit its liability under the provisions of the Limitation of Liability Act, 46 U.S.C. § [30501] et seq., in this Court, and this Court has exclusive jurisdiction to determine that issue.

2. That the Petitioner has the right to have this Court determine the value and the Petitioner's interest in the vessel Model year 2008, Everglades 27CC, Bearing Hull Identification No.: PJDB1043B708 and any other vessel determined by this Court to be a proper part of the limitation fund, such value and interest to be the value and interest in the vessel(s) as provided by the applicable federal law immediately following the incident at issue, and this Court has exclusive jurisdiction to determine that issue.

3. That the Claimant will not seek a determination of the issues set forth in paragraphs (1) and (2) above in any state court, or any other forum outside of this limitation proceeding, and consents to waive any res judicata or issue preclusion effect the decisions, rulings or judgments of any state court, or any other forum outside of this limitation proceeding, might have on those issues.

4. That the Claimant will not seek to enforce any judgment rendered in any state court, or any other forum outside of this limitation proceeding, against the Petitioner that would expose the Petitioner to liability in excess of the limitation fund to be determined by this Court, until such time as this Court has adjudicated the Petitioner's right to limit that liability. In the event this Court determines that the Petitioner is entitled to limit its liability, the Claimant agrees that it will not seek to enforce any judgment that would require the Petitioner to pay damages in excess of the limitation fund to be determined by this Court.

On February 12, 2013, the district court entered a final default as to all persons who did not file a timely claim or answer against the vessel. In fact, [—5—] Lynch was the only claimant who had filed a claim with the court. On February 20, the district court entered an order (the one at issue today) that lifted the injunction and stayed the federal proceeding in order to allow Lynch to litigate Offshore's liability in a Florida forum. The court directed the clerk to close the case for administrative purposes. Offshore filed a timely notice of appeal. The district court denied Offshore's motion to stay its order pending appeal.

II.

Offshore asserts that we have appellate jurisdiction to review the court's action as a final order pursuant to 28 U.S.C. § 1291,[1] or as a non-final order determining "the rights and liabilities of the parties to admiralty cases" under § 1292(a)(3).[2] Lynch disagrees. Our case precedent instead compels the conclusion that we have jurisdiction under §1292(a)(1) to review the trial court's order modifying or dissolving an injunction.[3]

Early Fifth Circuit case-law held that parties could not appeal admiralty orders that modified injunctions in limitation actions under the precursors to any of [—6—] the three provisions—§§ 1291, 1292(a)(1), or 1292(a)(3).[4] *See Postal S.S. Co. v. Int'l*

---

[1] "[T]he courts of appeals . . . shall have jurisdiction of appeals from all final decisions of the district courts of the United States . . . ." 28 U.S.C. § 1291.

[2] "[T]he courts of appeals shall have jurisdiction of appeals from: . . . (3) Interlocutory decrees of such district courts or the judges thereof determining the rights and liabilities of the parties to admiralty cases in which appeals from final decrees are allowed." *Id.* § 1292(a).

[3] "[T]he courts of appeals shall have jurisdiction of appeals from: (1) Interlocutory orders of the district courts of the United States . . . granting, continuing, *modifying*, refusing or *dissolving* injunctions, or refusing to dissolve or modify injunctions . . . ." *Id.* (emphasis added).

[4] In *Bonner v. City of Prichard*, 661 F.2d 1206, 1209 (11th Cir. 1981) (en banc), we adopted as binding all Fifth Circuit precedent handed down before October 1, 1981.

Freighting Corp., 133 F.2d 10, 11 (5th Cir. 1943); *Stark v. Tex. Co.*, 88 F.2d 182, 183 (5th Cir. 1937). Applying a dated distinction between the law, equity, and admiralty sides of a federal district court's jurisdiction, these cases concluded that interlocutory admiralty appeals fall within the explicit admiralty provision of § 1292(a)(3).[5] *See Stark*, 88 F.2d at 183 ("Appeals from interlocutory decrees in admiralty . . . are allowed only when the interlocutory decree determines rights and liabilities of the parties."). In reaching this result, the early cases relied on *Schoenamsgruber v. Hamburg America Line*, 294 U.S. 454, 457-58 (1935), which held that federal jurisdiction to review orders affecting injunctions (§ 1292(a)(1)) "extends only to suits in equity" because the inclusion of the specific admiralty provision of § 1292(a)(3) "indicates that Congress did not intend to make appealable any other interlocutory decrees in admiralty." In other words, the specific admiralty grant in § 1292(a)(3) governed to the exclusion of the general injunction provision in § 1292(a)(1). Moreover, because a stay in a limitation action did not determine "the rights and liabilities of the parties," the specific admiralty provision in §1292(a)(3) did not provide jurisdiction. *See Postal S.S.*, [—7—] 133 F.2d at 11. Therefore, an appellate court could not review a district court order modifying an injunction in a limitation action.

In 1960, however, a panel of the Fifth Circuit in binding precedent held that the Supreme Court had abrogated the Circuit's earlier cases, *Postal S.S.* and *Stark*. *See Pershing Auto Rentals, Inc. v. Gaffney*, 279 F.2d 546, 547-48 (5th Cir. 1960). *Pershing* concluded that, in light of the Supreme Court's decision in *Lake Tankers Corp. v. Henn*, 354 U.S. 147 (1957), appellate jurisdiction existed under § 1292(a)(1) to review a modification to a Limitation Act injunction. 279 F.2d at 547-48. ("For accepting our prior decisions, *Stark* [and] *Postal S.S.*, as holding to the contrary, we think that *Lake Tankers*, in this context at least, requires that

we no longer adhere to them." (citations omitted)).

After *Pershing*, a series of Circuit cases permitted § 1292(a)(1) interlocutory review of admiralty injunctions. Thus, for example, when a trial court enjoined salvage operations at a wreck site, the former Fifth Circuit cited *Pershing* in hearing an appeal that challenged the injunction:

> We do not . . . believe that § 1292(a)(3) provides the exclusive authorization for *interlocutory* appeals in admiralty. In admiralty cases where injunctive orders are entered which would be appealable under § 1292(a)(1) if entered in the course of an ordinary civil proceeding, interlocutory appeals will properly lie under that statutory provision. Prior to the unification of the admiralty rules with the federal civil rules it was generally presumed that the admiralty judge lacked the chancellor's power to order injunctive relief; therefore, the question whether appeals could be taken from such orders in admiralty cases under § 1292(a)(1) was seldom posed. The question [—8—] did, however, arise in the context of injunctions entered in limitation of liability proceedings which barred prosecution of other actions while the limitation action proceeded. We held that such injunctions, and orders modifying them, were appealable under § 1292(a)(1).

Treasure Salvors, Inc. v. Unidentified Wrecked & Abandoned Sailing Vessel, 640 F.2d 560, 564-65 (5th Cir. Mar. 1981) (emphasis added). *Treasure Salvors* also cited approvingly to Wright and Miller, who thought it "plain that application of § 1292(a)(1) should depend on whether the district court has in fact issued or denied an injunction, not on whether the proceedings are designated as in admiralty. The policies permitting appeal are completely unaffected by the historic distinction between law, equity, and admiralty jurisdiction." *Id.* at 565 (quoting 16 Charles Alan Wright et al., *Federal Practice and Procedure* 113 (1977)); *see also* 16 Charles Alan Wright et al., *Federal Practice and Procedure* § 3927 (2d ed. 1996 &

---

[5] At the time of these decisions, § 1292(a)(3) was codified at 28 U.S.C. § 227.

Supp. 2013) (opining that, in the context of §1292(a)(1), "any residual distinctions between admiralty and other civil actions are irrelevant").

Still other binding Circuit cases in the Limitation Act context have likewise found appellate jurisdiction under § 1292(a)(1). *See Complaint of Mucho K, Inc.*, 578 F.2d 1156, 1157 (5th Cir. 1978) ("[W]e find the order independently appealable as the granting, refusal, or modification of an injunction under § 1292(a)(1) . . . . *See Pershing*." (citation omitted)); *Beal v. Waltz*, 309 F.2d 721, 723 (5th Cir. 1962) (citing *Pershing* and accepting § 1292(a)(1) jurisdiction to review denial of a motion to modify an injunction in a limitation action); *see also* **[—9—]** *Beiswenger Enters. Corp. v. Carletta*, 86 F.3d 1032 (11th Cir. 1996) (accepting jurisdiction without discussion when both parties on appeal cited §1292(a)(1)). However, two cases—one from the old Fifth Circuit and the other from this Court—continued to apply *Postal S.S.* and *Stark* as barring § 1292(a)(1) interlocutory jurisdiction, without mentioning *Pershing*. *See State Establishment for Agric. Prod. Trading v. M/V Wesermunde*, 770 F.2d 987, 990 (11th Cir. 1985); *Austracan, (U.S.A.) Inc. v. M/V Lemoncore*, 500 F.2d 237, 240 (5th Cir. 1974).

Under our prior precedent rule, we are bound to follow a binding precedent in this Circuit "unless and until it is overruled by this court en banc or by the Supreme Court." *United States v. Martinez*, 606 F.3d 1303, 1305 (11th Cir. 2010) (quoting *United States v. Vega-Castillo*, 540 F.3d 1235, 1236 (11th Cir. 2008)). We inherited this rule from the old Fifth Circuit, which had similarly deferred to prior precedent. *See, e.g.*, *Davis v. Estelle*, 529 F.2d 437, 441 (5th Cir. 1976). Therefore, when faced with an intracircuit split, we look to the *earliest* case not abrogated by the Supreme Court or by this Court sitting en banc. *See Morrison v. Amway Corp.*, 323 F.3d 920, 929 (11th Cir. 2003) ("[W]hen circuit authority is in conflict, a panel should look to the line of authority containing the earliest case, because a decision of a prior panel cannot be overturned by a later panel." (quoting *Walker v. Mortham*, 158 F.3d 1177, 1188 (11th Cir. 1998))). By holding that the Supreme Court

had abrogated the old Fifth Circuit decisions limiting § 1292(a)(1) **[—10—]** interlocutory appeals in admiralty actions, *Pershing* in 1960 became the earliest case to decide the issue we face today for purposes of measuring prior precedent. Notwithstanding that some subsequent Circuit decisions overlooked *Pershing*, we are obliged to follow it. We have § 1292(a)(1) jurisdiction.[6]

III.

Turning then to the merits, we review a district court's decision to stay a limitation action arising under the Limitation Act and to modify a related injunction for abuse of discretion. *Lewis v. Lewis & Clark Marine, Inc.*, 531 U.S. 438, 440 (2001); *Garrido v. Dudek*, 731 F.3d 1152, 1158 (11th Cir. 2013). A ruling based on an error of law is an abuse of discretion. *Young v. New Process Steel, LP*, 419 F.3d 1201, 1203 (11th Cir. 2005).

The Limitation Act plainly allows a vessel owner to limit its liability to the value of the vessel for any claim arising from a maritime incident that occurred "without the privity or knowledge of the owner." 46 U.S.C. § 30505.[7]

---

[6] Because *Pershing* makes clear that we have appellate jurisdiction under § 1292(a)(1), we need not address whether we also might have jurisdiction under §§ 1291 or 1292(a)(3). Thus, we have no occasion to consider whether the holdings in *Postal S.S.* and *Stark* concerning these sections remain binding precedent in this Circuit.

[7] The Limitation Act provides in relevant part:

(a) . . . [T]he liability of the owner of a vessel for any claim, debt, or liability described in subsection (b) shall not exceed the value of the vessel and pending freight. . . .

(b) . . . Unless otherwise excluded by law, claims, debts, and liabilities subject to limitation under subsection (a) are those arising from any embezzlement, loss, or **[—11—]** destruction of any property, goods, or merchandise shipped or put on board the vessel, any loss, damage, or injury by collision, or any act, matter, or thing, loss, damage, or forfeiture, done, occasioned, or incurred, without the privity or knowledge of the owner.

46 U.S.C. § 30505.

An owner [—11—] may bring a limitation action in federal district court within six months of receiving written notice of a claim. *Id.* § 30511. The owner must deposit with the district court an amount (or an approved security) equal to the value of the vessel. *Id.* When the complaint and the deposit are submitted, "all claims and proceedings against the owner related to the matter in question shall cease." *Id.* The court then is directed to issue notice to all persons asserting claims against the vessel arising from the incident. Fed. R. Civ. P. Supp. R. F(4). The court may subsequently enter a default against any potential claimants who have not submitted timely filings. Those who do assert claims form a *concursus* that allows the district court to determine the liability of the owner to each individual in a single proceeding, constraining the total liability to the value of the vessel. *See, e.g., Beiswenger,* 86 F.3d at 1036 ("If the vessel owner is found liable, but limitation is granted, the admiralty court distributes the limitation fund among the damage claimants in an equitable proceeding known as a *concursus.*"). The Act thus provides the federal courts with "exclusive admiralty jurisdiction to determine whether the vessel owner is entitled to limited liability." *Id.* [—12—]

However, as our courts have long observed, this exclusivity of admiralty jurisdiction rubs up against the "saving to suitors" clause, which grants to the district courts original jurisdiction over admiralty cases, "saving to suitors in all cases all other remedies to which they are otherwise entitled." 28 U.S.C. § 1333; *see Lewis,* 531 U.S. at 448 ("Some tension exists between the saving to suitors clause and the Limitation Act."). This clause "embodies a presumption in favor of jury trials and common law remedies in the forum of the claimant's choice." *Beiswenger,* 86 F.3d at 1037. The Supreme Court has limited the tension between the Limitation Act and the "saving to suitors" clause by carving out an *exception* when a vessel owner faces only a single claimant. *See Langnes v. Green,* 282 U.S. 531, 542 (1931) (approving of a district court's conclusion "that, where there was only a single claim, there was no need for the adoption of the peculiar and exclusive jurisdiction of the admiralty court; and that

an answer setting up the limitation of liability would give the shipowner the relief to which he was entitled"); *see also Lewis,* 531 U.S. at 451 ("[T]he Courts of Appeals have generally permitted claimants to proceed with their claims in state court where there is only a single claimant, as in *Langnes,* or where the total claims do not exceed the value of the limitation fund, as in *Lake Tankers.*"). In a single claimant case, the district court may, at its discretion, order a stay of the limitation action to allow the claim to be tried in another forum. *See Lewis,* 531 U.S. at 448-51. [—13—] Before a stay may issue, however, the claimant must enter a series of stipulations that "effectively guarantee that the vessel owner will not be exposed to competing judgments in excess of the limitation fund." *Beiswenger,* 86 F.3d at 1038. This bifurcated procedure is far from novel. Indeed, the single claimant exception has been applied for over a century. *See Langnes,* 282 U.S. at 542 (citing *The Lotta,*150 F. 219, 222 (D.S.C. 1907)).

Offshore's arguments on appeal misunderstand the nature of this framework. Offshore first claims that it, not Lynch, was the relevant "suitor" entitled to its forum of choice because it initiated the limitation action. In essence, Offshore calls for a race to the courthouse, where the first party to file assumes "suitor" status and secures its forum of choice. The Limitation Act provides no such weapon to vessel owners. Lynch is the only § 1333 "suitor" in this case because she held the personal injury claim at issue. *See, e.g., Lake Tankers,* 354 U.S. at 153 (equating Limitation Act "claimants" with § 1333 "suitors": "Congress not only created the limitation procedure for the primary purpose of apportioning the limitation fund among the *claimants* where that fund was inadequate to pay the claims in full, but it reserved to *such suitors* their common-law remedies" (emphases added)). Offshore, a vessel owner that sought only to use the Act to cabin its liability in anticipation of Lynch's lawsuit, does not qualify. [—14—]

Moreover, a first-to-file rule would conflict with the narrow nature of the Act, which serves to protect vessel owners' rights to limited liability, not to give them a choice of forum for defending claims. *See Lewis*, 531 U.S. at 450-51; *see also Lake Tankers*, 354 U.S. at 152-53 ("The Act is not one of immunity from liability but of limitation of it and we read no other privilege for the shipowner into its language over and above that granting him limited liability."). We feel no urge to expand in this way a statute our cases deem "hopelessly anachronistic." *Hercules Carriers, Inc. v. Claimant State of Fla., Dep't of Transp.*, 768 F.2d 1558, 1564 (11th Cir. 1985); *Univ. of Tex. Med. Branch at Galveston v. United States*, 557 F.2d 438, 441 (5th Cir. 1977). Offshore asks that we do what the Supreme Court forbids: "transform the Act from a protective instrument to an offensive weapon by which the shipowner could deprive suitors of their common-law rights." *Lake Tankers*, 354 U.S. at 152. We decline the invitation. Though Lynch had not filed a "suit" before Offshore sought refuge under the Act in the district court, the single claimant exception and the "saving to suitors" clause protect her choice of forum.

Finally, to the extent Offshore argues that Lynch cannot escape federal admiralty jurisdiction because Lynch elected that forum by filing her claim in the district court Limitation Act proceedings, we remain unpersuaded. Submitting a claim in a limitation action initiated by a vessel owner does not amount to an [—15—] election that precludes a claimant from seeking a state forum. *See, e.g., Beiswenger*, 86 F.3d at 1037-38 (explaining how those who file claims in a limitation action may pursue state remedies). A party's election to bring its case in admiralty pursuant to Rule 9(h) can create a binding selection of federal admiralty jurisdiction.[8] *See St. Paul Fire & Marine Ins.*

Co. v. Lago Canyon, Inc., 561 F.3d 1181, 1187 (11th Cir. 2009). But, as the district court found, Lynch filed a claim in the limitation action "premised on Florida common law." Lynch made no Rule 9(h) election. When a vessel owner initiates a limitation action and an injured party submits a claim, the single claimant exception may still be available to allow suit in an alternate forum.

Offshore waived its remaining arguments on appeal by failing to raise them before the district court. *See Access Now, Inc. v. Sw. Airlines Co.*, 385 F.3d 1324, 1331 (11th Cir. 2004) ("[A]n issue not raised in the district court and raised for the [—16—] first time in an appeal will not be considered by this court." (quoting *Walker v. Jones*, 10 F.3d 1569, 1572 (11th Cir. 1994))).[9] Offshore contends that the

---

[8] In full, Rule 9(h) reads:

(h) Admiralty or Maritime Claim.

(1) *How Designated.* If a claim for relief is within the admiralty or maritime jurisdiction and also within the court's subject-matter jurisdiction on some other ground, the pleading may designate the claim as an admiralty or maritime claim for purposes of Rules 14(c), 38(e), and 82 and the Supplemental Rules for Admiralty or Maritime Claims and Asset Forfeiture Actions. A claim cognizable only in the admiralty or maritime jurisdiction is an admiralty or maritime claim for those purposes, whether or not so designated.

(2) *Designation for Appeal.* A case that includes an admiralty or maritime claim within this subdivision (h) is an admiralty case within 28 U.S.C. § 1292(a)(3).

Fed. R. Civ. P. 9.
[9] None of the recognized exceptions to our waiver rule apply here:

First, an appellate court will consider an issue not raised in the district court if it involves a pure question of law, and if refusal to consider it would result in a miscarriage of justice. Second, the rule may be relaxed where the appellant raises an objection to an order which he had no opportunity to raise at the district court level. Third, the rule does not bar consideration by the appellate court in the first instance where the interest of substantial justice is at stake. Fourth, a federal appellate court is justified in resolving an issue not passed on below . . . where the proper resolution is beyond any doubt. Finally, it may be appropriate to consider an issue first raised on appeal if that issue presents significant questions of general impact or of great public concern.

single claimant exception does not apply because Lynch's daughter may also have suffered injuries and, as a minor, she could avoid procedural default. But at no time did Offshore bring this issue to the attention of the district court, which found as an uncontested matter that Lynch was the only claimant. As a result, Offshore has waived its objection to the court's determination of single claimant status. *See id.*

Offshore also voices displeasure—for the first time on appeal—about the sufficiency of Lynch's stipulations, complaining both that they did not fully protect Offshore's rights and that they were never filed with the district court. In section II of her motion seeking relief from the injunction, Lynch stipulated in detail, as we have noted, that Offshore had the right to litigate the limitation of liability and the [—17—] value of the vessel in the district court, and that Lynch would not seek to enforce a state court judgment before the district court had the opportunity to adjudicate Offshore's effort to limit its liability. Again, this issue has been waived on appeal because Offshore never disputed in any way the sufficiency of the stipulations or the method by which they were entered before the district court. *See id.*

AFFIRMED.

Access Now, 385 F.3d at 1332 (alteration in original) (quoting *Wright v. Hanna Steel Corp.,* 270 F.3d 1336, 1342 (11th Cir. 2001)).

United States Court of Appeals
for the Eleventh Circuit

No. 12-13647

UNITED STATES
vs.
CAMPBELL

Appeal from the United States District Court for the
Southern District of Florida

Decided: February 20, 2014

Citation: 743 F.3d 802, 2 Adm. R. 543 (11th Cir. 2014).

Before **PRYOR, JORDAN,** and **FAY,** Circuit Judges.

[—1—] **PRYOR,** Circuit Judge:

Two changes in law—a statutory change and a decisional change—require us to reconsider whether the admission of a certification of the Secretary of State to establish extraterritorial jurisdiction for a prosecution of drug trafficking on the [—2—] high seas violates a defendant's right to confront the witnesses against him at trial. U.S. Const. Amend. VI. In *United States v. Rojas*, we held that the admission at trial of a certification to establish jurisdiction over a Panamanian vessel laden with cocaine and seized on the high seas did not violate the Confrontation Clause of the Sixth Amendment. 53 F.3d 1212, 1216 (11th Cir. 1995). After we decided *Rojas*, Congress amended the Maritime Drug Law Enforcement Act to provide that "jurisdictional issues arising under this chapter are preliminary questions of law to be determined solely by the trial judge," and that the "[j]urisdiction of the United States with respect to a vessel subject to this chapter is not an element of an offense." Pub. L. 104-324, § 1138, 110 Stat. 3901, 3988-89, (1996) (codified as amended 46 U.S.C. § 70504(a)). Also after we decided *Rojas*, the Supreme Court overruled its decision in *Ohio v. Roberts*, 448 U.S. 56, 100 S. Ct. 2531 (1980), and held that the Confrontation Clause bars the admission of a testimonial statement by "a witness who did not appear at trial unless he was unavailable to testify, and the defendant had had a prior opportunity for cross-examination." *Crawford v. Washington*, 541 U.S. 36, 53–54, 124 S. Ct. 1354, 1365 (2004). In the light of these changes in law, we reach the same decision we reached in *Rojas*, but for a different reason. Because the certification proves jurisdiction, as a diplomatic courtesy to a foreign nation, and does not prove an element of a defendant's [—3—] culpability, we conclude that the pretrial admission of the certification does not violate the Confrontation Clause.

I. BACKGROUND

On October 26, 2011, the United States Coast Guard observed a vessel in the international waters off the eastern coast of Jamaica. While the Coast Guard was pursuing the vessel, the three individuals aboard the vessel discarded dozens of bales into the water, which the Coast Guard later determined to be approximately 997 kilograms of marijuana. The vessel lacked all indicia of nationality: it displayed no flag, port, or registration number. Glenroy Parchment identified himself as the master of the vessel and claimed the vessel was registered in Haiti. The Coast Guard then contacted the Republic of Haiti to inquire whether the vessel was of Haitian nationality. The government of Haiti responded that it could neither confirm nor deny the registry. The other two individuals aboard the vessel, Christopher Patrick Campbell and Pierre Nadin Alegrand, as well as Parchment later admitted that they knew they were illegally transporting marijuana.

After a federal grand jury indicted Campbell, Alegrand, and Parchment under the Maritime Drug Law Enforcement Act, 46 U.S.C. § 70501 *et seq.*, for conspiracy to possess and for possession with intent to distribute 100 kilograms or more of marijuana, *id.* §§ 70503(a)(1), 70506(a), 70506(b); 21 U.S.C. [—4—] § 960(b)(2)(G), Campbell filed a motion to dismiss for lack of jurisdiction on three grounds: (1) that admission of a certification of the Secretary of State to prove a response to a claim of registry, *see* 46 U.S.C. § 70502(d)(2), would violate Campbell's right under the Confrontation Clause and that there was insufficient evidence to prove that Campbell was aboard a vessel subject to the jurisdiction of the United States; (2) that the Act violated Campbell's right to due process of law under the Fifth Amendment because he had no contacts with the United States; and (3) that Congress exceeded its constitutional power to define and punish felonies committed on the high seas when it enacted the Act. Campbell conceded that our precedents foreclosed his last two arguments, but he stated his intent to preserve his objections for further review.

The district court referred the motion to a magistrate judge, who held a hearing about whether the certification of the Secretary of State established jurisdiction. At the hearing, the United States introduced into evidence the certification of the Secretary of State, which included the statement of Commander Daniel Deptula of the United States Coast Guard that he had contacted the Republic of Haiti to inquire whether the vessel was registered there and that Haiti responded that it could neither confirm nor deny the registry of the vessel. Campbell objected to the admission of the certification on the ground that it [—5—] violated his right under the Confrontation Clause, but the magistrate judge overruled the objection because the certification was "self-authenticating" and "whether there should be further proof beyond the State Department document is really a separate question and does not go to the admissibility of the certification." The magistrate judge issued a report and recommendation that the certification of the Secretary of State established extraterritorial jurisdiction over the vessel and that the Act was constitutional both on its face and as applied to Campbell. The district court adopted the report and recommendation.

Campbell waived his right to a trial by jury in a written statement signed by him, his counsel, the prosecutor, and the district court judge, and at a bench trial, the parties stipulated to the material facts. But Campbell maintained at trial that the stipulation about the communication between Commander Deptula and Haiti proved only the representation by the Coast Guard that a Haitian official could neither confirm nor deny the registration of the vessel and not that the

communication from a Haitian official actually occurred. Campbell acknowledged that the district court had already determined its jurisdiction based only on the certification of the Secretary of State, but he argued "that there was nobody from Haiti that actually signed a certificate or provided any documents." The district court found Campbell guilty on both the conspiracy and possession counts. [—6—]

II. STANDARDS OF REVIEW

We review questions of law *de novo* and findings of fact for clear error. For example, we review "*de novo* a district court's interpretation and application of statutory provisions that go to whether the court has subject matter jurisdiction. . . . The district court's factual findings with respect to jurisdiction, however, are reviewed for clear error." *United States v. Tinoco*, 304 F.3d 1088, 1114 (11th Cir. 2002) (internal quotation marks omitted). "We review *de novo* the legal question of whether a statute is constitutional." *Id.* at 1099. And we review constitutional objections *de novo*. *United States v. Brown*, 364 F.3d 1266, 1268 (11th Cir. 2004).

III. DISCUSSION

The Constitution empowers Congress "[t]o define and punish Piracies and Felonies committed on the high Seas, and Offences against the Law of Nations." U.S. Const. Art. I, § 8, cl. 10. The Supreme Court has interpreted that Clause to contain three distinct grants of power: to define and punish piracies, to define and punish felonies committed on the high seas, and to define and punish offenses against the law of nations. *United States v. Bellaizac–Hurtado*, 700 F.3d 1245, 1248 (11th Cir. 2012). This appeal involves a conviction for an offense defined by an act of Congress under the second grant of power. [—7—]

Congress enacted the Maritime Drug Law Enforcement Act to prohibit any person from "knowingly or intentionally . . . possess[ing] with intent to manufacture or distribute, a controlled substance on board . . . a vessel subject to the jurisdiction of the United States." 46 U.S.C. § 70503(a)(1). In 1996, Congress amended the Act to provide that "[j]urisdiction of the United States with respect to a vessel subject to this chapter is not an element of an offense." 46 U.S.C. §70504(a). The section continues that "[j]urisdictional issues arising under this chapter are preliminary questions of law to be determined solely by the trial judge." *Id.*

The Act declares "a vessel without nationality" as subject to the jurisdiction of the United States and defines a stateless vessel as including "a vessel aboard which the master or individual in charge makes a claim of registry and for which the claimed nation of registry does not affirmatively and unequivocally assert that the vessel is of its nationality." *Id.* § 70502(c)(1)(A), (d)(1)(C). Congress made clear that the Act "applies even though the act is committed outside the territorial jurisdiction of the United States." *Id.* § 70503(b). The Act permits several methods for obtaining a response from a foreign nation to a claim of registry and provides that a certification of the Secretary of State is conclusive proof of a response to a claim of registry by a foreign nation: "The response of a foreign nation to a claim [—8—] of registry under paragraph (1)(A) or (C) may be made by radio, telephone, or similar oral or electronic means, and is proved conclusively by certification of the Secretary of State or the Secretary's designee." *Id.* § 70502(d)(2) (emphasis added). The Act does not require the certification of the Secretary of State to include the details of how an official received or from whom the official received the response to a claim of registry from a foreign nation.

Campbell challenges his convictions on five grounds, four of which attack the constitutionality of the Act. First, Campbell argues that the admission of the certification of the Secretary of State to establish extraterritorial jurisdiction violated his right under the Confrontation Clause. Second, Campbell contends that the pretrial determination of jurisdiction under the Act violated his rights under the Fifth and Sixth Amendments to have a jury determine that

issue. Third, Campbell argues that the certification of the Secretary of State provided insufficient evidence for the district court to determine that it had jurisdiction. Fourth, Campbell argues that Congress lacked the power under the Felonies Clause to define his conduct as a criminal offense. Fifth, Campbell argues that his conviction violated his right to due process under the Fifth Amendment because he had no contacts with the United States. These arguments fail. [—9—]

A. The Confrontation Clause Does Not Bar the Admission of a Certification of the Secretary of State To Establish Extraterritorial Jurisdiction.

Campbell argues that the admission of the certification of the Secretary of State without the ability to cross-examine a Haitian witness violated his right under the Confrontation Clause, but that argument fails. The Confrontation Clause does not bar the admission of hearsay to make a pretrial determination of jurisdiction when that hearsay does not pertain to an element of the offense. Because the stateless nature of Campbell's vessel was not an element of his offense to be proved at trial, the admission of the certification did not violate his right to confront the witnesses against him.

The Confrontation Clause provides that "[i]n all criminal prosecutions, the accused shall enjoy the right . . . to be confronted with the witnesses against him . . . ." U.S. Const. Amend. VI. In *Crawford*, the Supreme Court ruled that the Confrontation Clause bars the admission of a testimonial statement by "a witness who did not appear *at trial* unless he was unavailable to testify, and the defendant had had a prior opportunity for cross-examination." 541 U.S. at 53–54, 124 S. Ct. at 1365 (emphasis added). The Supreme Court explained that a testimonial statement "is typically a solemn declaration or affirmation made for the purpose of establishing or proving some fact," such as an affidavit, custodial examination, or prior testimony at a preliminary hearing. *Id.* at 51, 124 S. Ct. at 1364 (internal [—10—] quotation marks omitted). But the Supreme Court has never extended the reach of the Confrontation

Clause beyond the confines of a trial. *See Bullcoming v. New Mexico*, --- U.S. ---, 131 S. Ct. 2705, 2713 (2011) ("As a rule, if an out-of-court statement is testimonial in nature, it may not be introduced against the accused *at trial* unless the witness who made the statement is unavailable and the accused has had an opportunity to confront that witness." (emphasis added)); *Michigan v. Bryant*, --- U.S. ---, 131 S. Ct. 1143, 1162 (2011) ("[W]hen a court must determine whether the Confrontation Clause bars the admission of a statement *at trial*, it should determine the primary purpose of the interrogation by objectively evaluating the statements and actions of the parties to the encounter, in light of the circumstances in which the interrogation occurs." (emphasis added) (internal quotation marks omitted)); *Pennsylvania v. Ritchie*, 480 U.S. 39, 52, 107 S. Ct. 989, 999 (1987) (opinion of Powell, J.) ("The opinions of this Court show that the right to confrontation is a *trial* right, designed to prevent improper restrictions on the types of questions that defense counsel may ask during cross-examination."); *California v. Green*, 399 U.S. 149, 157, 90 S. Ct. 1930, 1934–35 (1970) ("Our own decisions seem to have recognized at an early date that it is this literal right to 'confront' the witnesses *at the time of trial* that forms the core of the values furthered by the Confrontation Clause." (emphasis added)); *Barber v. Page*, 390 [—11—] U.S. 719, 725, 88 S. Ct. 1318, 1322 (1968) ("The right to confrontation is basically a *trial* right." (emphasis added)).

In *Rojas*, we rejected a challenge, under the Confrontation Clause, to the introduction of a certification of the Secretary of State under the Act, 53 F.3d at 1216, but we decided that issue before Congress made the determination of extraterritorial jurisdiction a pretrial issue of law for the district court and before the Supreme Court decided *Crawford*. Our decision in *Rojas* relied on the pre-*Crawford* standard that permitted the admission of hearsay if it was sufficiently reliable. *Id.; Roberts*, 448 U.S. at 66, 100 S. Ct. at 2539, *abrogated by Crawford*, 541 U.S. at 61–62, 124 S. Ct. at 1370–71. And Congress amended the Act to provide that extraterritorial jurisdiction is "not an element of an offense,"

but is instead a "preliminary question[] of law to be determined solely by the trial judge." 46 U.S.C. § 70504(a).

Although these changes in law mean that *Rojas* no longer controls this issue, the admission of the certification of the Secretary of State did not violate Campbell's right under the Confrontation Clause. In *United States v. Tinoco*, we held that Congress was entitled to remove the jurisdictional requirement from consideration by the jury because that requirement "does not raise factual questions that traditionally would have been treated as elements of an offense under the [—12—] common law," such as the actus reus, causation, and the mens rea elements. 304 F.3d at 1108. Instead, the jurisdictional requirement serves as a "diplomatic courtesy to foreign nations and as a matter of international comity." *Id.* Proof of jurisdiction "does not affect the defendant's blameworthiness or culpability, which is based on the defendant's participation in drug trafficking activities, not on the smoothness of international relations between countries." *Id.* at 1109; *see also United States v. Rendon*, 354 F.3d 1320, 1327 (11th Cir. 2003) (reiterating that extraterritorial jurisdiction is not an element of the offense). And, unlike some federal crimes in which the jurisdictional element provides Congress with the authority to proscribe the offense under Article I, the Act makes the determination of jurisdiction a discretionary "statutory hurdle[] to a court's subject matter jurisdiction." *Tinoco*, 304 F.3d at 1104 n.18; *see also id.* at 1110 n.21 (explaining that many federal criminal statutes, such as the Hobbs Act, 18 U.S.C. § 1951(a), and the Travel Act, *id.* § 1952(a), "require[] a particularized, case-by-case factual finding that some product or activity of the defendant relate in some way to interstate commerce"). This jurisdictional requirement "is unique because it is not meant to have any bearing on the individual defendant, but instead is meant to bear only on the diplomatic relations between the United States and foreign governments." *Id.* at 1109. The Confrontation Clause protects a defendant's trial [—13—] right to confront testimony offered against him to establish his guilt, and the Supreme Court has never extended the reach of the Confrontation Clause beyond the confines of a trial. And, because a pretrial determination of extraterritorial jurisdiction does not implicate the Confrontation Clause, we need not decide whether the certification of the Secretary of State is testimonial in nature. *Cf. United States v. Mitchell–Hunter*, 663 F.3d 45, 52 (1st Cir. 2011) (expressing doubt that a certification of the Secretary of State is testimonial hearsay because "an objective State Department designee would not expect that the certifications would be used at trial, as they are relegated by statute to the pretrial jurisdiction determination"); *United States v. Angulo–Hernández*, 565 F.3d 2, 12 (1st Cir. 2009) (questioning whether a certification of the Secretary of State under the Act is testimonial within the meaning of the Confrontation Clause).

Our analysis aligns with other authorities too. For example, faced with the same issue raised by Campbell, the First Circuit held that, "in this non-trial context, where evidence does not go to guilt or innocence, the Confrontation Clause does not apply." *United States v. Nueci–Peña*, 711 F.3d 191, 199 (1st Cir. 2013) (internal quotation marks omitted); *see also Mitchell–Hunter*, 663 F.3d at 51. And both this Court and other courts have declined to extend the right to confront witnesses to other pre- and post-trial proceedings that do not concern the [—14—] adjudication of a defendant's guilt or innocence. *See, e.g., United States v. Powell*, 650 F.3d 388, 392–93 (4th Cir. 2011) (holding that the Confrontation Clause does not apply at sentencing and noting that all other federal circuit courts that hear criminal appeals agree); *United States v. Cantellano*, 430 F.3d 1142, 1146 (11th Cir. 2005) (holding that, even after *Crawford*, the confrontation right does not apply at a non-capital sentencing hearing); *United States v. Smith*, 79 F.3d 1208, 1210 (D.C. Cir. 1996) (holding that the confrontation right does not apply at a pretrial detention hearing because the purpose is to determine whether accused may remain at large, and it "is neither a discovery device for the defense nor a trial on the merits"); *United States v. Andrus*, 775 F.2d 825, 836 (7th Cir. 1985) (holding that the Sixth Amendment does not provide a

confrontation right at a preliminary hearing); *LaChappelle v. Moran*, 699 F.2d 560, 564–65 (1st Cir. 1983) (holding that the confrontation right does not apply at an in camera conference to determine the reason a witness refuses to answer a question because such a judicial proceeding "is not a stage of the trial at which an accused must be present"); *United States v. Harris*, 458 F.2d 670, 677–78 (5th Cir. 1972), (holding that the confrontation right does not apply at a preliminary hearing); *see also Wolff v. McDonnell*, 418 U.S. 539, 567–68, 94 S. Ct. 2963, 2980 (1974) ("[Confrontation and cross-examination] are essential in criminal trials where the accused, if found [—15—] guilty, may be subjected to the most serious deprivations. . . . But they are not rights universally applicable to all hearings[,] . . . and it does not appear that confrontation and cross-examination are generally required in [disciplinary hearings in prisons]."); *cf. United States v. Clark*, 475 F.2d 240, 247 (2d Cir. 1973) (holding that the confrontation right applies at a pretrial suppression hearing because "the suppression hearing centers upon the validity of the search for and seizure of evidence which the government plans to use later in seeking to prove guilt"). We need not decide whether the Confrontation Clause could ever apply to a pretrial determination and conclude only that it does not apply to this pretrial determination of jurisdiction where the certification does not implicate either the guilt or innocence of a defendant charged with an offense under the Act.

B. The Pretrial Determination of Jurisdiction Does Not Violate the Fifth or Sixth Amendment.

Campbell argues that the Fifth and Sixth Amendments require a jury to determine whether extraterritorial jurisdiction exists, but Campbell's argument fails for two reasons. First, Campbell waived his right to a jury trial in a signed, written filing. Second, as explained in the preceding section, we have rejected the argument that a jury must determine jurisdiction under the Act. *See Rendon*, 354 F.3d at 1327; *Tinoco*, 304 F.3d at 1109–10. Campbell acknowledges that these precedents foreclose his argument. After all, the Supreme Court long ago held, in a [—16—] case about a ship seized at sea for carrying contraband (liquor during Prohibition), that a district court could decide before trial the jurisdictional issue about the location of the vessel without submitting that issue to a jury. *Ford v. United States*, 273 U.S. 593, 606, 47 S. Ct. 531, 535 (1927). The Supreme Court explained that the issue of jurisdiction "was necessarily preliminary to th[e] trial" because "[t]he issue whether the ship was seized within the prescribed limit did not affect the question of the defendants' guilt or innocence. It only affected the right of the court to hold their persons for trial." *Id.*

C. The District Court Did Not Err When It Determined It Had Jurisdiction Based on the Certification of the Secretary of State.

Campbell argues that the district court erred when it determined that extraterritorial jurisdiction existed. He argues that the certification of the Secretary of State lacked details about the communications between the Coast Guard and Haiti and that the United States did not offer any testimony to corroborate the certification. The district court did not err.

Campbell stipulated to the admission of the representations by the Coast Guard in the certification, and the Act provides that the certification is conclusive proof of a response to a claim of registry. The certification contained the statements of Commander Deptula, who explained that he had asked the Haitian government whether the suspect vessel was registered in Haiti and that Haiti [—17—] responded that it could neither confirm nor deny the registry. The certification therefore provided conclusive proof that the vessel was within the jurisdiction of the United States under the Act.

D. The Act Is a Constitutional Exercise of Congressional Power under the Felonies Clause.

Campbell argues that Congress exceeded its authority under the Felonies Clause when it enacted the Act because his drug trafficking offense lacked any nexus to the United States and because drug trafficking was not a capital offense during the Founding era, but he acknowledges that his arguments are foreclosed by our precedents. "[W]e have always upheld extraterritorial convictions under our drug trafficking laws as an exercise of power under the Felonies Clause." *See Bellaizac–Hurtado*, 700 F.3d at 1257. And we have long upheld the authority of Congress to "extend[] the criminal jurisdiction of this country to any stateless vessel in international waters engaged in the distribution of controlled substances." *United States v. Marino–Garcia*, 679 F.2d 1373, 1383 (11th Cir. 1982). Moreover, in *United States v. Estupinan*, we rejected an argument "that Congress exceeded its authority under the Piracies and Felonies Clause in enacting the [Maritime Drug Law Enforcement Act]." 453 F.3d 1336, 1338 (11th Cir. 2006).

We also have recognized that the conduct proscribed by the Act need not have a nexus to the United States because universal and protective principles [—18—] support its extraterritorial reach. *See United States v. Saac*, 632 F.3d 1203, 1209–11 (11th Cir. 2011); *Estupinan*, 453 F.3d at 1338 ("[T]his circuit and other circuits have not embellished the [Act] with the requirement of a nexus between a defendant's criminal conduct and the United States." (internal quotation marks and alterations omitted) (quoting *Rendon*, 354 F.3d at 1325)). The Felonies Clause empowers Congress to punish crimes committed on the high seas. *Saac*, 632 F.3d at 1210. And "inasmuch as the trafficking of narcotics is condemned universally by law-abiding nations, we see no reason to conclude that it is 'fundamentally unfair' for Congress to provide for the punishment of persons apprehended with narcotics on the high seas." *Estupinan*, 453 F.3d at 1339 (internal quotation marks omitted). Congress "may assert extraterritorial jurisdiction over vessels in the high seas that are engaged in conduct that 'has a potentially adverse effect and is generally recognized as a crime by nations that have reasonably developed legal systems.'" *Tinoco*, 304 F.3d at 1108 (quoting *United States v. Gonzalez*, 776 F.2d 931, 939 (11th Cir. 1985)). And "[t]he protective principle does not require that there be proof of an actual or intended effect inside the Unites States." *Gonzalez*, 776 F.2d at 939. Congress also may assert extraterritorial jurisdiction because "the law places *no restrictions* upon a nation's right to subject stateless vessels to its jurisdiction." *United States v. Ibarguen–Mosquera*, 634 F.3d 1370, 1379 (11th Cir. [—19—] 2011) (internal quotation marks omitted). Stateless vessels, such as the one Campbell boarded, are "international pariahs" that have "no internationally recognized right to navigate freely on the high seas." *Marino–Garcia*, 679 F.2d at 1382; *see also United States v. Perlaza*, 439 F.3d 1149, 1161 (9th Cir. 2006) (discussing that for stateless vessels, no proof of nexus is required); *Rendon*, 354 F.3d at 1325 ("Because stateless vessels do not fall within the veil of another sovereign's territorial protection, all nations can treat them as their own territory and subject them to their laws." (internal quotation marks omitted)).

Campbell argues that Congress cannot proscribe drug trafficking on the high seas under the Felonies Clause because only capital crimes were considered felonies at the Founding, but we disagree. Although we have recognized that "there is a dearth of authority interpreting the scope of Congress's power under the [Felonies] Clause," *Saac*, 632 F.3d at 1209, the First Congress understood its power under the Felonies Clause to include proscribing criminal conduct on the high seas that did not warrant capital punishment. In the Crimes Act of 1790, the First Congress made it a crime at sea to "entertain or conceal any such pirate or robber, or receive or take into his custody any ship, vessel, goods or chattels, which have been by any such pirate or robber piratically and feloniously taken" and punished that conduct with "imprison[ment] not exceeding three years," Ch. 9, [—20—] § 11, 1 Stat. 112, 114; imposed a three-year maximum sentence, if convicted, for "any seaman or other person [who] commit[s] manslaughter upon the high seas," *id.* § 12, 1 Stat. at 115; and imposed a seven-year maximum sentence for intending to "maim or disfigure" a person "upon the high seas, *id.* § 13.

At the time of the Founding, there was "ambiguity in the meaning of [a] felony." Will Tress, *Unintended Collateral Consequences: Defining Felony in the Early American Republic*, 57 Clev. St. L. Rev. 461, 465 (2009). "At common law, [a felony was] an offense for which conviction result[ed] in forfeiture of the defendant's lands or goods (or both) to the Crown, regardless of whether any capital or other punishment [was] mandated." *Black's Law Dictionary* 651 (8th ed. 2004); *see also* 4 William Blackstone, *Commentaries* *94 (1769) ("Felony, in the general acceptation of our English law, comprize[d] every species of crime, which occasioned at common law the forfeiture of lands or goods."); Giles Jacob, *A New Law Dictionary* (10th ed. 1782) (listing types of punishment for felonies at common law, including death, loss of inheritance, and forfeiture of goods and lands). "By the late seventeenth century, felony had come to mean any very serious crime, especially those punishable by death." Eugene Kontorovich, *The "Define and Punish" Clause and the Limits of Universal Jurisdiction*, 103 Nw. U. L. Rev. 149, 160 (2009) (quoting Blackstone, *supra*, at *94); *see also* Jacob, *supra* [—21—] ("*Felony* is diftinguifhed from lighter offences, in that the punifment of it is death: but not always, for petit larceny is *felony*, . . . yet it is not punifhed by death, though it be lofs of goods . . . ."). And at the time of the Founding, felony was "a multi-definitional term" with "so many meanings from so many parts of the common law[] and so many statutes . . . that it is impossible to know precisely in what sense we are to understand this word." Tress, *supra*, at 463, 465 (quoting 6 Nathan Dane, Digest of American Law 715 (1823)); *see* 2 Timothy Cunningham, *A New and Complete Law Dictionary* (3d ed. 1783) (explaining that, "by the law at this day," felonies included treason, murder, homicide, burning of houses, burglary, robbery, rape, chance-medley, and petit larceny and that punishments for felonies ranged from death and forfeiture of goods and chattels to terms of imprisonment and hard labor). As James Madison explained, in defense of the power of Congress to define felonies on the high seas, the term "felony" has a "loose signification." *The Federalist No. 42*, at 262 (James Madison) (Clinton Rossiter ed., 1961); *see also United States v. Smith*, 18

U.S. (5 Wheat.) 153, 159 (1820) (acknowledging the "indeterminate" definition of felony under the Felonies Clause). Campbell's argument that only capital crimes were felonies at the time of the Founding fails because the Founding generation would have understood the term to include a broader range of crimes. [—22—]

Campbell cites *United States v. Palmer*, 16 U.S. (3 Wheat.) 610, (1818), to support his argument that Congress may punish only capital offenses under the Felonies Clause, but *Palmer* did not address this issue. In *Palmer*, the Supreme Court upheld a law enacted by Congress under the Piracies and Felonies Clause that prohibited "murder or robbery, or any other offence, which, if committed within the body of a county, would by the laws of the United States, be punishable with death." *Id.* at 626–27. But the Court explained that "punishable with death" served solely to identify which other crimes were included in the statute even though not particularly recited. *Id.* at 628. *Palmer* did not address whether Congress could exercise its power, under the Felonies Clause, to proscribe conduct not punishable by death. Although *Palmer* did not address this issue, we have repeatedly held that Congress has the power, under the Felonies Clause, to proscribe drug trafficking on the high seas. *See, e.g., Estupinan*, 453 F.3d at 1339; *Rendon*, 354 F.3d at 1326.

E. Campbell's Conviction Did Not Violate His Right to Due Process.

Campbell argues that his convictions violated his right to due process because his offense of drug trafficking lacked a nexus to the United States, but he concedes that our precedents foreclose this argument too. We held in *Rendon* that the Due Process Clause of the Fifth Amendment does not prohibit the trial and [—23—] conviction of an alien captured on the high seas while drug trafficking, because the Act provides clear notice that all nations prohibit and condemn drug trafficking aboard stateless vessels on the high seas. 354 F.3d at 1326. And "this [C]ircuit and other circuits have not embellished the [Act] with the requirement of

a nexus between a defendant's criminal conduct and the United States." *Estupinan*, 453 F.3d at 1338 (internal quotation marks and alternations omitted). Campbell's conviction did not violate his right to due process under the Fifth Amendment.

IV. CONCLUSION

We **AFFIRM** Campbell's judgment of convictions.

United States Court of Appeals
for the Eleventh Circuit

No. 12-15164

MARTINEZ
vs.
CARNIVAL CORP.

Appeal from the United States District Court for the
Southern District of Florida

Decided: February 24, 2014

Citation: 744 F.3d 1240, 2 Adm. R. 551 (11th Cir. 2014).

Before **MARCUS, DUBINA,** and **WALKER,*** Circuit
Judges.

*Honorable John Walker, Jr., United States Circuit
Judge for the Second Circuit Court of Appeals, sitting by
designation

[—1—] DUBINA, Circuit Judge: [—2—]

Appellant Melvin Gualberto Medina Martinez ("Martinez") appeals the district court's order compelling arbitration of his claims pursuant to the Convention on the Recognition and Enforcement of Foreign Arbitral Awards ("CREFAA"), 9 U.S.C. §§ 201–208. Martinez argues his claim of Jones Act negligence, 46 U.S.C. § 30104, does not fall within his employment contract ("Seafarer's Agreement") with Carnival Cruise Lines, Inc. ("Carnival") and, therefore, is not within the scope of the contract's arbitration clause. We agree with the district court that arbitration is required, and therefore, we affirm the district court's order compelling arbitration.

I.

Martinez is a Honduran citizen who suffered a back injury while employed as a mason aboard Carnival's vessel, the Fascination. Martinez worked ten hours per day, seven days a week, and was required to lift and transport boxes of tiles and cement and heavy rolls of carpet. During his employment, Martinez developed back pain, which he reported to his supervisor. After his condition worsened, and he began to feel pain not only in his back but also in his lower extremities, Martinez sought further medical care.

Martinez had back surgery in Panama, performed by Carnival's selected physician, Dr. Avelino Gutierrez. After the surgery, Martinez continued to experience serious orthopedic and neurological problems, including numbness in [—3—] both legs, difficulty urinating, need for a catheter, sexual dysfunction, and psychological problems. Carnival sent Martinez to Miami, where he continued to receive medical treatment.

The Seafarer's Agreement, which covered the terms of Martinez's employment, included an arbitration clause stating that, except for wage disputes, "any and all disputes arising out of or in connection with this Agreement, including any question regarding its existence, validity, or termination, or Seafarer's service on the vessel, shall be referred to and finally resolved by arbitration." [R. DE 1-1 at 6, ¶ 7.]

After his injury, Martinez filed suit against Carnival in Florida state court, asserting claims of Jones Act negligence, unseaworthiness, and failure to provide adequate maintenance and cure. In his Jones Act claim, Martinez alleged that the physician chosen and paid by Carnival negligently performed his back surgery. Carnival removed the case to the federal district court and filed a motion to compel arbitration. The district court granted the motion, dismissed as moot all other pending motions, and closed the case for administrative purposes. Martinez then timely appealed.

II. [—4—]

"We review the district court's interpretation of [an] arbitration clause de novo." Hemispherx Biopharma, Inc. v. Johannesburg Consol. Invs., 553 F.3d 1351, 1366 (11th Cir. 2008).

III.

As we must, we first address our jurisdiction to hear this case. Carnival contends that we lack jurisdiction because the district court's order compelling arbitration was a non-appealable interlocutory order, not a final appealable decision. We are unpersuaded.

The Federal Arbitration Act provides that a party may appeal "a final decision with respect to an arbitration." 9 U.S.C. § 16(a)(3). A final decision "is a decision that ends the litigation on the merits and leaves nothing more for the court to do but execute the judgment." *Green Tree Fin. Corp.-Ala. v. Randolph*, 531 U.S. 79, 86, 121 S. Ct. 513, 519 (2000) (internal quotation marks omitted). Yet, a party may not appeal "an interlocutory order . . . compelling arbitration." 9 U.S.C. §16(b)(3).[1] Thus, a district court order compelling arbitration and dismissing a plaintiff's claim is a final decision within the meaning of § 16(a)(3). *Hill v. Rent-A-* [—5—] *Center, Inc.*, 398 F.3d 1286, 1288 (11th Cir. 2005). In contrast, a district court order compelling arbitration and staying the proceedings before the court is an interlocutory order that cannot be appealed. *Am. Express Fin. Advisors, Inc. v. Makarewicz*, 122 F.3d 936, 939 (11th Cir. 1997). Carnival essentially argues that because the district court simply granted the motion to compel and closed the case for administrative purposes, but did not dismiss the case, its order was more akin to a stay of the proceedings; thus, the district court's decision was an interlocutory order that may not be appealed under § 16(b)(3).

The Supreme Court has adopted a functional test for finality, examining what the district court has done, and has reiterated that a decision is final if it "ends the litigation on the merits and leaves nothing for the court to do but execute the judgment." *Ray Haluch Gravel Co. v. Cent. Pension Fund of the Int'l Union of Operating Eng'rs & Participating Emp'rs*, ___ U.S. ___, 134 S. Ct. 773, 779

(2014); *Green Tree*, 531 U.S. at 86, 121 S. Ct. at 519; *Catlin v. United States*, 324 U.S. 229, 233, 65 S. Ct. 631, 633 (1945). Our court has applied the same test for finality, *see, e.g., W.R. Huff Asset Mgmt. Co. v. Kohlberg, Kravis, Roberts & Co.*, 566 F.3d 979, 984 (11th Cir. 2009); *Pitney Bowes, Inc. v. Mestre*, 701 F.2d 1365, 1368 (11th Cir. 1983), and looks to the practical effect of the district court's order, not to its form. [—6—] *See Thomas v. Blue Cross & Blue Shield Ass'n*, 594 F.3d 823, 829 (11th Cir. 2010) ("In making [§ 1291 finality] determinations, 'we take a functional approach, looking not to the form of the district court's order, but to its actual effect.'" (quoting *Birmingham Fire Fighters Ass'n 117 v. Jefferson Cnty.*, 280 F.3d 1289, 1293 (11th Cir. 2002)). In *Young v. Prudential Insurance Co. of America*, 671 F.3d 1213 (11th Cir. 2012), looking to the substance of the district court's order, we held that it was not final even though it dismissed the case on the merits because the order had remanded part of the case, but "in substance," left unresolved whether the plaintiff was entitled to relief. *Id.* at 1215.

The pertinent question we address in this case is not whether the district court's administrative closure is the functional equivalent of a dismissal, but rather, whether the district court's order, on the record before us, ended the litigation on the merits and left nothing more for the district court to do but execute the judgment. The district court granted Carnival's motion to compel, dismissed as moot all other motions, and administratively closed the case. Notably, the district court's order did not stay the proceedings, nor did it contemplate any further action on this case. Although the district court did not dismiss the case, the court's order left all [—7—] further merits determinations to the arbitrator.[2] Thus, the order effectively "end[ed] the litigation on the merits and [left] nothing more for the [district] court to do but execute the judgment." *Green Tree*, 531 U.S. at 86, 89, 121 S. Ct. at 519, 521 (internal quotation marks omitted)

---

[1] Though Chapter 1 of the Federal Arbitration Act, which includes 9 U.S.C. § 16, does not directly apply to this case, *see id.* § 1 ("[N]othing herein contained shall apply to contracts of employment of seamen . . . ."), the jurisdictional issue is evaluated under the framework of 9 U.S.C. § 16 because the CREFAA incorporates the provisions of Chapter 1 that do not conflict with it. *Id.* § 208.

[2] Indeed, both parties conceded at oral argument that there were no other issues for the district court to resolve after it compelled arbitration.

(determining that an order of the district court compelling the parties to arbitrate and dismissing all the claims before it was a final and appealable decision).

We acknowledge that administratively closing a case is not the same as dismissing a case. *See Fla. Ass'n for Retarded Citizens, Inc. v. Bush*, 246 F.3d 1296, 1298 (11th Cir. 2001) (per curiam) (stating that a "closed" case does not prevent the district court from reactivating a case). Moreover, an administrative closure is not dispositive of finality. However, our focus is not on the district court's label, but rather, on the effect of the district court's order. *See Thomas*, 594 F.3d at 829. When the district court compels arbitration and disposes of all pending motions, it leaves the court with nothing more to decide, and it effectively and functionally has issued a decision that "ends the litigation on the merits." *Ray Haluch*, ___ U.S. at ___, 134 S. Ct. at 779. [—8—]

In a prior case, we addressed the finality of an administratively closed case. *See Brandon, Jones, Sandall, Zeide, Kohn, Chalal & Musso, P.A. v. MedPartners, Inc.*, 312 F.3d 1349 (11th Cir. 2002) (per curiam), *abrogated by Ray Haluch*, ___ U.S. ___, 134 S. Ct. 773. In *Brandon*, we determined that the district court order was not final even though it administratively closed the case because the district court explicitly retained jurisdiction to award attorneys' fees. *Id.* at 1355. The district court in *Brandon*, unlike the district court in the present case, acknowledged that it still had other matters to resolve. *Id.* at 1353. Our court even noted that in most cases when a district court "rule[s] on all the relief requested," and "close[s]" the case in its order, "that conduct would lead us to conclude that the order was final." *Id.* at 1354. Thus, even under the analysis utilized in *Brandon*, the district court order in the present case would be final because it disposed of all pending motions and did not retain jurisdiction to confirm the arbitration award or to award attorneys' fees associated with the arbitration. *See also Emp'rs Ins. of Wausau v. Bright Metal Specialties, Inc.*, 251 F.3d 1316, 1321 (11th Cir. 2001) ("[G]enerally speaking, a decision of the district court is final when it disposes of all the issues framed by the litigation and leaves nothing for the district court to do but execute the judgment."). [—9—]

The slight distinction between an administratively closed case and a dismissed case does not resolve the question of finality. What matters is whether the case, in all practicality, is finished. In this case, the district court not only administratively closed the case, but it also denied all pending motions as moot and compelled arbitration. The district court's order was a functionally final and appealable decision because it left nothing more for the court to do but execute the judgment. Accordingly, we conclude that the order compelling Martinez to arbitrate his claims was "a final decision with respect to an arbitration," and we have appellate jurisdiction. 9 U.S.C. § 16(a)(3). *See also Montero v. Carnival Corp.*, 523 F. App'x 623, 625 (11th Cir. 2013) (per curiam) (holding that the district court order compelling arbitration was a final appealable decision even though the order closed rather than dismissed the case).

IV.

Martinez argues the district court erred in compelling arbitration because the Seafarer's Agreement terminated before this dispute arose.

The termination provision of the Seafarer's Agreement between Martinez and Carnival states, in relevant part:

This Agreement shall automatically terminate without notice immediately upon Seafarer's unscheduled disembarkation of the assigned vessel if Seafarer disembarks the vessel for any reason, [—10—] including but not limited to unscheduled personal leave, illness or injury, for more than one full voyage. This Agreement shall also terminate without notice immediately upon Seafarer being unfit or unable to serve in his or her stated position at the commencement of a new voyage.

[R. 4-1 ¶ 2.] Under this language, the Seafarer's Agreement terminated when Martinez disembarked from the cruise ship to seek treatment for his back injury which was preventing him from doing his job.

The Seafarer's Agreement's arbitration clause does not expressly state whether it survives the termination of the Seafarer's Agreement, but its unambiguous language suggests viability. The provision states in relevant part:

> Except for a wage dispute governed by [Carnival]'s Wage Grievance Policy and Procedure, any and all disputes arising out of or in connection with this Agreement, including any question regarding its existence, validity, or termination, or Seafarer's service on the vessel, shall be referred to and finally resolved by arbitration . . . .

[R. 4-1 ¶ 7.] Clearly, the parties contemplated some circumstances in which the arbitration clause would survive the termination of the Seafarer's Agreement.

"[P]arties can agree to arbitrate 'gateway' questions of 'arbitrability,' such as whether the parties have agreed to arbitrate or whether their agreement covers a particular controversy." *Rent-A-Center, W., Inc. v. Jackson*, 561 U.S. 63, ___, 130 S. Ct. 2772, 2777 (2010). Thus, a court may [—11—] conclude that the parties agreed to arbitrate the very issue of "arbitrability" where "there is clear and unmistakable evidence that they did so." *Id.* at ___, 130 S. Ct. at 2783 (internal quotation marks omitted). Because parties can agree to arbitrate the very question of arbitrabililty, they can also agree to arbitrate disputes about contract termination. In this case, the district court did not err in refusing to determine whether the Agreement had terminated because the question of termination has remained in dispute and the "clear and unmistakable" language of the contract indicates that the parties intended for just such a dispute to be decided by

arbitration and not the court. *See id.* at ___, 130 S. Ct. at 2783.[3]

Martinez also argues that even if the arbitration provision survives the termination of the agreement, his claim for medical negligence falls outside the scope of the arbitration clause in his employment contract because it did not arise under the Seafarer's Agreement. He asserts that the language requiring arbitration pursuant to the Agreement does not include claims that arise from shoreside medical negligence. [—12—]

There is a "federal policy favoring arbitration of labor disputes." *Granite Rock Co. v. Int'l Bhd. of Teamsters*, 561 U.S. 287, ___, 130 S. Ct. 2847, 2857 (2010) (internal quotation marks omitted). When parties agree to arbitrate some matters pursuant to an arbitration clause, the "law's permissive policies in respect to arbitration counsel that any doubts concerning the scope of arbitral issues should be resolved in favor of arbitration." *Id.* at ___, 130 S. Ct. at 2857 (internal quotation marks omitted). Courts apply the presumption of arbitrability "only where a validly formed and enforceable arbitration agreement is ambiguous about whether it covers the dispute at hand," and "where the presumption is not rebutted." *Id.* at ___, 130 S. Ct. at 2858–59.

In determining whether a dispute arises out of a contract, "the focus is on whether the tort or breach in question was an immediate, foreseeable result of the performance of contractual duties." *Doe v. Princess Cruise Lines, Ltd.*, 657 F.3d 1204, 1218 (11th Cir.

---

[3] Martinez also contends Carnival is equitably estopped from enforcing the arbitration provision because Carnival took the inconsistent position of treating the Seafarer's Agreement as terminated when it stopped paying his wages but as not terminated for the purpose of arbitrating his claim. Martinez is incorrect. Carnival's assertion that the arbitration provision survives termination of the Seafarer's Agreement is not inconsistent with treating the Seafarer's Agreement as terminated. Thus, equitable estoppel does not apply. *See Sea Byte, Inc. v. Hudson Marine Mgmt. Servs., Inc.*, 565 F.3d 1293, 1304 (11th Cir. 2009) (stating that equitable estoppel applies only when a party adopts a position that is contrary to an earlier position).

2011) (internal quotation marks omitted). In *Doe*, we held that claims arising under the Jones Act "are dependent on [the plaintiff's] status as a seaman employed by the cruise line and the rights that [the plaintiff] derives from that employment status." *Id.* at 1221. *See also O'Boyle v. United States*, 993 F.2d 211, 213 (11th Cir. 1993) ("[I]n order to recover damages under the Jones Act, [a plaintiff] must have [—13—] the status of a seaman."). Although the Jones Act dictates Carnival's duty of care, that duty extends to Martinez only because he was employed by Carnival as a seaman under the contract. In addition, the terms of the Agreement, which specifically reference Carnival's obligation to provide medical treatment aboard the vessel or ashore, contemplated that Carnival would provide shoreside medical care for injuries Martinez sustained while on the job. Accordingly, we conclude that Martinez's dispute with Carnival clearly arose out of or in connection with the Seafarer's Agreement and is subject to arbitration.

V.

For the foregoing reasons, we affirm the district court's order compelling arbitration.

AFFIRMED.

United States Court of Appeals
for the Eleventh Circuit

No. 12-16433

SKYE
vs.
MAERSK LINE, LTD.

Appeal from the United States District Court for the
Southern District of Florida

Decided: May 15, 2014

Citation: 751 F.3d 1262, 2 Adm. R. 556 (11th Cir. 2014).

Before **PRYOR, JORDAN,** and **FAY,** Circuit Judges.

[—1—] **PRYOR,** Circuit Judge:

This appeal requires us to decide whether a seaman can recover money damages under the Jones Act, 46 U.S.C. § 30104, for an injury stemming from [—2—] excessive work hours and an erratic sleep schedule. William Skye, formerly the chief mate of the *Sealand Pride*, a commercial vessel, suffers from left ventricular hypertrophy, which he complained that his employer, Maersk Line Limited Corporation d/b/a Maersk Line Limited, caused when it negligently saddled him with "excessive duties and duty time" such that he was "overworked to the point of fatigue." At trial, the jury found Maersk liable to Skye, who the jury found suffered damages of $2,362,299.00, which the district court reduced to $590,574.75 to account for Skye's comparative negligence. Maersk moved for a judgment as a matter of law on the ground that the decision of the Supreme Court in *Consolidated Rail Corp. v. Gottshall*, 512 U.S. 532, 114 S. Ct. 2396 (1994), barred Skye's complaint. The district court denied that motion and entered judgment in favor of Skye. We **REVERSE** the denial of the motion for a judgment as a matter of law and **RENDER** judgment in favor of Maersk because Skye's complaint of an injury caused by work-related stress is not cognizable under the Jones Act, which concerns injuries caused by physical perils. *See Gottshall*, 512 U.S. at 558, 114 S. Ct. at 2411–12.

I. BACKGROUND

Between 2000 and 2008, William Skye worked on the *Sealand Pride* as chief mate. The *Sealand Pride* was first chartered and later operated by Maersk. Skye's job duties required him to work overtime, which adversely affected his [—3—] health because of fatigue, stress, and lack of sleep. Skye regularly worked between 90 and 105 hours per week for 70 or 84 days at a time. At sea, Skye worked 12 hours; in port, he might have worked "round the clock."

In 2000, Skye's cardiologist diagnosed him with a benign arrhythmia and recommended that Skye change his diet and rest more. In 2003, Skye returned to his cardiologist, who said his diagnosis had not changed. Skye's symptoms worsened in 2004 when Maersk began directly managing the *Sealand Pride* and increased his duty time. Skye worked 12 to 15 percent more overtime hours. And his working hours were replete with arduous duties: logging in cargo carrying hazardous material at various ports for eight hours at a time; inspecting roughly 144 "reefers," which are refrigerated containers, to ensure they were keeping cargo cold; repairing "cell guides," which hold cargo containers; and descending six stories via ladders and manholes into the hull of the *Sealand Pride* to inspect and repair the interior of the ballast tanks, which hold water to balance the ship.

By 2008, Skye was experiencing headaches, a sore back, and a burning sensation in his chest in addition to his arrhythmia, so Skye returned to his cardiologist, who diagnosed him with left ventricular hypertrophy, a thickening of the heart wall of the left ventricle, which his cardiologist attributed to hypertension. Skye's cardiologist concluded that Skye's "continued physical stress related to his job, with long hours and lack of sleep" caused his labile [—4—] hypertension—intermittent high blood pressure while on the job—which, in turn, caused his left ventricular hypertrophy. The cardiologist advised Skye to stop working on the vessel.

In 2011, Skye filed a complaint against Maersk for negligence under the Jones Act.

Skye alleged that his working conditions caused his left ventricular hypertrophy and that Maersk was negligent when it failed to provide him with reasonable working hours, an adequate crew, and adequate rest hours and instead "overworked [him] to the point of fatigue." He alleged that these working conditions led to "physical damage to [his] heart."

At trial, Skye and his cardiologist testified that his excessive hours and resulting stress were the most likely causes of his injury. Skye testified that his arduous work schedule and his lack of sleep had an adverse effect on his health. His cardiologist testified that Skye's working conditions "were a substantial contribution" to his left ventricular hypertrophy. The cardiologist opined that Skye developed labile hypertension because of the "stress of his job as chief mate" and "the lack of regular sleep," which in turn "caused the left ventricular hypertrophy." The cardiologist explained that "people who live under constant physical stress secrete large amounts of adrenaline" as part of a "fight or flight response." And when "adrenaline is secreted for long periods of the day, that has a deleterious effect on their health." He continued, "Long working hours and stress can lead to [—5—] this fight or flight response, and that, in turn, can lead to left ventricular hypertrophy."

At the conclusion of trial, Maersk moved for a directed verdict on the grounds that Skye could not recover for money damages for an injury caused by work-related stress and, alternatively, that the statute of limitations barred his claim. Maersk argued that *Gottshall*, in which the Supreme Court held that plaintiffs could not recover for work-related stress under the Federal Employers' Liability Act, barred Skye's claim as a matter of law. The district court denied the motion.

Before the jury deliberated, the court instructed the jury as follows that it must decide whether Skye's injury and its causes were physical or emotional:

The law holds that a seaman such as the plaintiff cannot receive compensation for a purely emotional injury. A purely emotional injury is an injury that has no physical causes, but, rather was solely caused by the injured person's perception of a nonphysical stress. The injured person, however, may receive compensation for an injury caused in any part by physical stress. You will need to determine whether plaintiff's injury is a physical one or an emotional one. If you determine it is an emotional one, in order to recover, plaintiff has the burden of proving by a preponderance of the evidence that his injury was sustained as a result of his fear for his own physical safety or incurred while in a zone of immediate physical danger.

The district court provided the jury with a special verdict form that required it to decide whether Skye's injury was "physical" or "emotional." [—6—]

The jury returned a verdict finding that Skye sustained a physical injury, but that Skye was 75 percent at fault for his injuries. It found that Skye suffered damages of $2,362,299.00, which the district court reduced to $590,574.75 to account for Skye's comparative negligence. After the verdict, Maersk moved for a judgment as a matter of law, which the district court denied.

II. STANDARD OF REVIEW

We review the denial of a motion for a judgment as a matter of law *de novo* and apply the same standards as the district court. *Ash v. Tyson Foods, Inc.*, 664 F.3d 883, 892 (11th Cir. 2011). We will reverse the denial of a motion for a judgment as a matter of law "only if the facts and inferences point overwhelmingly in favor of one party, such that reasonable people could not arrive at a contrary verdict." *Id.* (internal quotation mark omitted). "We will not second-guess the jury or substitute our judgment for its judgment if its verdict is supported by sufficient evidence." *Lambert v. Fulton Cnty., Ga.*, 253 F.3d 588, 594 (11th Cir. 2001). "We view all the evidence and draw all inferences from it in the light most favorable to . . . the nonmoving party." *Ash*, 664 F.3d at 892.

III. DISCUSSION

The Jones Act provides a cause of action in negligence for "a seaman" personally injured "in the course of employment," 46 U.S.C. § 30104, in the same way that the Federal Employers' Liability Act provides a cause of action in [—7—] negligence for injured railroad employees against their employers, 45 U.S.C. §§ 51–60. The Jones Act incorporated the remedial scheme of the Federal Employers' Liability Act, and case law interpreting the latter statute also applies to the Jones Act. 46 U.S.C. § 30104 ("Laws of the United States regulating recovery for personal injury to, or death of, a railway employee apply to an action under this section."); *see also O'Donnell v. Great Lakes Dredge & Dock Co.*, 318 U.S. 36, 38–39, 63 S. Ct. 488, 490 (1943).

Not all work-related injuries are cognizable under the Federal Employers' Liability Act and, by extension, the Jones Act. *See Gottshall*, 512 U.S. at 555–56, 114 S. Ct. at 2410–11. The Supreme Court has made clear that these statutes are "aimed at ensuring 'the security of the person from *physical invasions* or menaces.'" *Id.* (emphasis added) (quoting *Lancaster v. Norfolk & W. Ry. Co.*, 773 F.2d 807, 813 (7th Cir. 1985)). For employers to be liable, the employees' injuries must be "caused by the negligent conduct of their employers that threatens them imminently with physical impact." *Id.* at 556, 114 S. Ct. at 2411.

Skye's injury is not cognizable under the Jones Act even when we draw all inferences from the evidence presented to the jury in the light most favorable to him and assume that his work schedule caused him to develop left ventricular hypertrophy. The Jones Act does not allow a seaman to recover for injuries caused by work-related stress because work-related stress is not a "physical peril[]." *Id.* at [—8—] 555, 114 S. Ct. at 2410. The district court erred when it denied the motion of Maersk for a judgment in its favor as a matter of law.

Skye's complaint fails for the same reason that plaintiff Alan Carlisle's complaint failed in *Gottshall*. In *Gottshall*, the Supreme Court ruled that injuries caused by the long-term effects of work-related stress are not cognizable under the Federal Employers' Liability Act because they are not caused by any physical impact or fear from the threat of physical impact. 512 U.S. at 558, 114 S. Ct. at 2411–12. Carlisle sued his employer after suffering from insomnia, headaches, depression, weight loss, and a nervous breakdown attributable to "work[ing] 12- to 15-hour shifts for weeks at a time." *Id.* at 539, 114 S. Ct. at 2402. Carlisle alleged that his employer failed to provide him with a safe workplace "by forcing him to work under unreasonably stressful conditions" and that its failure "resulted in foreseeable stress-related health problems." *Id.* The Supreme Court adopted the zone-of-danger test for injuries not caused by a physical impact; Carlisle's injuries were compensable only if Carlisle was injured when he was within the zone of danger of a physical impact caused by his employer's negligence. *Id.* at 556, 114 S. Ct. at 2410–11 ("[A] worker within the zone of danger of physical impact will be able to recover for emotional injury caused by fear of physical injury to himself, whereas a worker outside the zone will not."). The Supreme Court held that "Carlisle's work-stress-related claim plainly does not fall within the common law's [—9—] conception of the zone of danger, and Carlisle makes no argument that it does. . . . [W]e will not take the radical step of reading [the Federal Employers' Liability Act] as compensating for stress arising in the ordinary course of employment." *Id.* at 558, 114 S. Ct. at 2411–12; *see also Smith v. Union Pac. R.R. Co.*, 236 F.3d 1168, 1173–74 (10th Cir. 2000) ("[A] work schedule is not the physical peril against which [the Federal Employers' Liability Act] protects."); *Szymanski v. Columbia Transp. Co.*, 154 F.3d 591, 594–95 (6th Cir. 1998) (en banc) (holding that the estate of a seaman could not recover under the Jones Act for a fatal heart attack allegedly induced by excessive work hours); *Crown v. Union Pac. R.R. Co.*, 162 F.3d 984, 985 (8th Cir. 1998) (refusing recovery for extreme weight gain, carpal tunnel syndrome, knee joint problems, cough syncope syndrome, sleep apnea, diabetes, various addictions, and a nervous breakdown, all of which were attributable to excessive work hours).

Under *Gottshall*, Skye's complaint is not cognizable under the Jones Act. His complaint parallels Carlisle's complaint of an injury induced by overwork. Skye complained that he was "injured while aboard the vessel" because "[r]educed manning and other conditions caused excessive duties and duty time." And Skye alleged that Maersk was negligent when it "[f]ail[ed] to provide [him] with reasonable working hours," "adequate personnel, time, and equipment," and "adequate rest hours," and "overworked [him] to the point of fatigue." [—10—]

As the Supreme Court explained in *Gottshall*, the "central focus" of the Federal Employers' Liability Act, and the Jones Act by extension, is "on physical perils." 512 U.S. at 555, 114 S. Ct. at 2410. An arduous work schedule and an irregular sleep schedule are not physical perils. That Skye developed a "physical injury" is no matter; the *cause* of his injury was work-related stress. *See Szymanski*, 154 F.3d at 594–95. Carlisle too had physical injuries—weight loss and headaches—but a physical injury is not enough. *Gottshall*, 512 U.S. at 539, 558, 114 S. Ct. 2402, 2411–12. Compensating Skye for his injury would potentially lead to, in the words of the Supreme Court, "a flood of trivial suits, the possibility of fraudulent claims . . . and the specter of unlimited and unpredictable liability" because there is no way to predict what effect a stressful work environment— compared to a physical accident such as an exploding boiler—would have on any given employee. *See id.* at 557, 114 S. Ct. at 2411. Skye's complaint of a physical injury caused by work-related stress is foreclosed by binding precedent of the Supreme Court, and the judgment in his favor cannot stand as a matter of law. *Id.* at 558, 114 S. Ct. at 2411– 12. Because we decide that Skye's complaint is not cognizable under the Jones Act, we need not decide whether the statute of limitations bars his claim. [—11—]

IV. CONCLUSION

We **VACATE** the judgment awarding Skye $590,574.75. We **REVERSE** the denial of the motion of Maersk for a judgment as a matter of law and **RENDER** judgment in favor of Maersk.

(Reporter's Note: Concurring opinion on p. 560).

[—12—] FAY, Circuit Judge, concurring specially:

I concur in the court's opinion, because we are bound by the decision of the Supreme Court in *Consolidated Rail Corp. v. Gottshall*, 512 U.S. 532, 114 S. Ct. 2396 (1994). In my view, however, the majority opinion in that case is contrary to the language, purpose, and spirit of the Federal Employers' Liability Act ("FELA"), 45 U.S.C. § 51 *et seq.*, and the Jones Act, 46 U.S.C. § 30104, concerning a seaman's recovery of damages for a job-related injury. The core purpose of both is to provide covered employees with a safe place to work. Being required to work 90 and 105 hours per week for 70 or 84 days at a time is hardly being given a safe place to work. I fail to see the difference between being given a defective piece of equipment and being required to work outrageous hours, in determining whether or not the workplace was safe. Surely, an employer is no less negligent in doing either.

Most respectfully, my hope is that the Supreme Court will revisit this area of the law. As Justice Ginsburg stated in her dissent in *Gottshall*: "Instead of the restrictive 'zone' test that leaves severely harmed workers remediless, however negligent their employers, the appropriate FELA claim threshold should be keyed to the genuineness and gravity of the worker's injury." *Gottshall*, 512 U.S. at 572, 114 S. Ct. at 2419 (Ginsburg, J., dissenting).

(Reporter's Note: Dissenting opinion on p. 561).

[—13—] JORDAN, Circuit Judge, dissenting:

With respect, I dissent.

William Skye alleged, and proved to the satisfaction of a jury, that he suffered physical damage to his heart as a result of Maersk forcing him to work for an excessive number of hours (about 16 hours a day on average) without providing him adequate periods of rest. Like the district court, I do not think that Mr. Skye's claim under the Jones Act, 46 U.S.C. § 30104, constituted a claim for negligent infliction of emotional distress, i.e., "mental or emotional harm (such as fright or anxiety) that is caused by the negligence of another that is not directly brought about by a physical injury, but may manifest itself in physical symptoms." *Consolidated Rail Corp. v. Gottshall*, 512 U.S. 532, 544 (1994).

The verdict form asked the jury whether Mr. Skye sustained a "physical injury" or an "emotional injury." The jury specifically found that Mr. Skye sustained *only* a physical injury due to Maersk's negligence, and characterized this injury as "left ventricular hypertrophy," a thickening of the heart wall which can affect the pumping of blood in the ventricle and lead to congestive heart failure. *See* Verdict Form, D.E. 158 at 1, 2; Trial Tr., D.E. 166 at 606. We owe "great deference" to the jury's factual findings, *Grant v. Preferred Research, Inc.*, 885 F.2d 795, 798 (11th Cir. 1989), and I do not believe we can say, as a matter of law on this record, that Mr. Skye's injury was purely emotional. *See also Quality* [—14—] *Foods, Inc. v. U.S. Fire Ins. Co.*, 715 F.2d 539, 543 (11th Cir. 1983) ("We cannot over emphasize [*sic*] the great weight and deference which must be given to jury verdicts."). As a result, the zone of danger test articulated in *Gottshall* does not apply. *See Gottshall*, 512 U.S. at 547-48 (adopting zone of danger test to "limit[ ] recovery for emotional injury to those plaintiffs who sustain a physical impact as a result of a defendant's negligent conduct, or who are placed in immediate risk of physical harm by that conduct").

I recognize that federal and state courts are divided about the scope of *Gottshall*. Some courts have read *Gottshall* more broadly, as the majority does, while others have interpreted it more narrowly, as I do. *Compare, e.g., Szymanski v. Columbia Transp. Co.*, 154 F.3d 591, 594-95 (6th Cir. 1998) (10-3 en banc decision), *and Capriottti v. Consolidated Rail Corp.*, 878 F. Supp. 429, 432-33 (N.D.N.Y. 1995), *with, e.g., Walsh v. Consolidated Rail Corp.*, 937 F.Supp. 380, 387-89 (E.D. Pa. 1996), *and Duncan v. Am. Commercial Barge Line, LLC*, 166 S.W.3d 78, 83-84 (Mo. App. E.D. 2004). As I see it, the more constrained reading of *Gottshall* is supported by the Supreme Court's more recent decision in *Norfolk & Western Railway Co. v. Ayers*, 538 U.S. 135, 157 (2003), which distinguished *Gottshall* and held that "an asbestosis sufferer [can] seek compensation for fear of cancer as an element of his asbestosis-related pain and suffering damages." In the words of *Ayers*, "[t]he plaintiffs in *Gottshall* and [*Metro-North Commuter Railroad* [—15—] *Co. v. Buckley*, 521 U.S. 424 (1997)] grounded their suits on claims of negligent infliction of emotional distress. The claimants before us, in contrast, complain of a negligently inflicted physical injury (asbestosis) and attendant pain and suffering." *Id.* at 148. Like the claimants in *Ayers*, Mr. Skye is complaining of a negligently inflicted physical injury—left ventricular hypertrophy.

Congress enacted the Jones Act "for the benefit and protection of seamen who are peculiarly the wards of admiralty." *Atl. Sounding Co. v. Townsend*, 557 U.S. 404, 417 (2009) (internal quotation marks omitted). Given that purpose, and absent definitive indication from the Supreme Court, I would not read the Jones Act to preclude liability for an employer who makes a seaman work so hard and so continuously that he suffers physical injury in the form of heart disease, heart attack, organ failure, seizure, or stroke.

United States Court of Appeals
for the Eleventh Circuit

No. 13-11765

SABO
vs.
CARNIVAL CORP.

Appeal from the United States District Court for the
Southern District of Florida

Decided: August 12, 2014

Citation: 762 F.3d 1330, 2 Adm. R. 562 (11th Cir. 2014).

Before **MARCUS,** Circuit Judge, and **PROCTOR,** * and
EVANS, ** District Judges.

* The Honorable R. David Proctor, United States
District Judge for the Northern District of Alabama,
sitting by designation.

** The Honorable Orinda D. Evans, United States
Senior District Judge for the Northern District of Georgia,
sitting by designation.

[—2—] **PROCTOR,** District Judge:

Today, we consider whether Carnival
Corporation & PLC, which is a dual-
listed company—i.e., a corporate
structure that joins separate corporations in a
common economic enterprise, while allowing
the corporations to maintain their individual
legal identities—is properly suable under the
laws of Florida in this action. After careful
review and with the benefit of oral argument,
we conclude that it is not. We therefore affirm
the district court's dismissal of this lawsuit.

I. The Pleadings and Dismissal Below

From time immemorial, there have been
those who have made their living on the sea, a
long tradition joined by Zolt Sabo, Ilija Janev,
and Stefan Vidojkovic, all of whom worked
aboard Cunard Line cruise ships.
Unfortunately, their careers were not without
interruption, as all of them sustained back
injuries that required land-based rest and
recuperation. Injured sea workers are entitled
by law to certain medical and unemployment
benefits, commonly referred to as
"maintenance and cure," and Sabo, Janev, and
Vidojkovic (hereinafter sometimes referred to
as "the [—3—] Seafarers") each collected such

benefits, with each receiving three months of
wages and two months of medical expenses.
Those are the benefits that these and other
employees agreed to in their contracts with
Cunard Celtic Hotel Services, Ltd., a company
that operates under the corporate umbrella of
Carnival Corporation & PLC—the dual-listed
company ("DLC") comprised of Carnival
Corporation (a Panamanian corporation
headquartered in Miami, FL) and Carnival
PLC (a British corporation headquartered in
Southampton, England). However, the
Seafarers became unsatisfied with the extent
of their maintenance and cure, believing that
their contracts impermissibly limited their
compensation.

On July 18, 2012, Plaintiffs Sabo, Janev,
and Vidojkovic filed a class action complaint
against Defendants Carnival Corporation and
Carnival PLC alleging failure to provide
maintenance and cure in accordance with
general United States maritime law and the
Jones Act, a federal statute that provides legal
remedies not otherwise guaranteed under
general maritime law. Defendants responded
by filing a Motion to Dismiss, arguing, among
other things, that the Seafarers' claims were
due to be dismissed because (1) the district
court lacked *in personam* jurisdiction over
Carnival PLC, (2) Carnival Corporation was
an improper party to the case (as it was
adequately shielded from liability by its
corporate form), and (3) the Complaint failed
to meet federal pleading standards. [—4—]

The Seafarers' Response made clear that
they only intended to sue one defendant,
Carnival Corporation & PLC,[1] completely reorienting the focus of the case and making
Plaintiffs' ability to bring suit against a DLC
the operative issue. In its subsequent Order,
the district court addressed the Seafarers'
newly articulated position, and wholly

---

[1] Response in Opposition to Motion to Dismiss
at 1-2, *Sabo v. Carnival Corp.*, No. 12-22653 (S.D.
Fla. Sept. 17, 2012) ("First and foremost, Plaintiffs
have sued one entity and one entity only: The dual-
listed company known as Carnival Corporation &
PLC. Plaintiffs have not sued Carnival Corporation
in its individual corporate capacity. Plaintiffs
likewise have not sued Carnival PLC in its
individual corporate capacity.").

rejected the notion that it could exercise jurisdiction over a DLC, including Carnival Corporation & PLC:

> [The] Class Action Complaint fails to convince the Court that the enterprise formed through the dual-listed company structure overcomes the individual corporate identity of Carnival Corporation and Carnival PLC to give the Court jurisdiction over the dual-listed company Carnival Corporation and PLC.[2]

The district court did not completely foreclose the possibility that a DLC could be haled into court, but noted that "the case or controversy would have to arise from said corporate structure (i.e., the shared assets or investments [of the DLC])."[3] Dismissing their complaint without prejudice, the district court gave the Seafarers ten days to file an amended complaint. [—5—]

The Seafarers filed an amended class action complaint that named Carnival Corporation & PLC as the sole defendant. The amended complaint closely resembled the initial complaint, but devoted greater space to describing the nature of the DLC, in an apparent attempt to demonstrate the corporate structure's amenability to suit in the Southern District of Florida. However, the amended complaint failed to directly address the district court's initial misgivings about the legal status of DLCs, an omission that would prove fatal to the Seafarers' case. Indeed, the district court bluntly rebuffed their creative attempt to amend their pleading, writing:

> Plaintiffs, by amending their Class Action Complaint to name the dual-listed corporation Carnival Corporation and PLC as the sole defendant, have ignored the Court's prior determination that the dual-listed corporation was not a proper entity . . . The Amended Class Action Complaint contains the same allegations as the original Class Action

Complaint. The Court declines to delineate from its previous position that this action does not arise from the structure of the dual-listed corporation. Therefore, the Court does not have personal jurisdiction over the dual-listed corporation Carnival Corporation and PLC.[4]

The Seafarers appealed the district court's Order, presenting the question that we answer today: based upon the record before us and the laws of Florida, was Carnival Corporation & PLC, a DLC, subject to suit as a corporation, according to [—6—] the doctrine of estoppel, or under a joint venture theory of liability? We conclude it was not.

II. Standard of Review

In evaluating the district court's decision to dismiss a case for lack of personal jurisdiction pursuant to Federal Rule of Civil Procedure 12(b)(2), we review the legal conclusions of the district court *de novo*. *See Meier ex rel. Meier v. Sun Int'l Hotels, Ltd.*, 288 F.3d 1264, 1268 (11th Cir. 2002).

III. Discussion

A dual-listed company (DLC) is a corporate structure that binds two separate corporations into a unified economic enterprise, but allows the participating entities to maintain their individual legal identities. The arrangement is established through the execution of an equalization agreement, a contract that defines and governs the relationship between the two companies. Such a structure bears many merger-like qualities, such as common ownership of assets and integrated management, but also exhibits some hallmarks of corporate independence, such as separate stock exchange listings. Almost always utilized by corporations of disparate national origin, DLCs are employed for a variety of reasons, including the advantages they potentially offer in the areas of tax, investor/public relations, and regulatory oversight. Carnival Corporation and Carnival

---

[2] Order Granting Defendants' Motion to Dismiss at 5, *Sabo v. Carnival Corp.*, No. 12-22653 (S.D. Fla. Nov. 29, 2012).

[3] *Id.* at 6.

[4] Order Granting Defendants' Second Motion to Dismiss at 5-6, *Sabo v. Carnival Corp.*, No. 12-22653 (S.D. Fla. March 18, 2013).

PLC (formerly P&O Princess Cruises) chose to dual list (rather than merge) because it allowed them to [—7—] gain access to multiple financial markets (both the New York Stock Exchange and the London Stock Exchange), avoid divestment from British institutional investors (many of whom are restricted from holding shares in foreign-owned companies), and maintain their distinct, individual brands.

Just as the creation of Carnival Corporation & PLC involved significant tactical considerations, so too did the Seafarers' decision to sue the DLC rather than its different corporate components. Instead of pursuing a complicated, convoluted case against Carnival Corporation & PLC, the Seafarers could have asserted claims against Cunard Celtic Hotel Services, Ltd. (their direct, contractual employer) or Carnival PLC (Cunard Celtic's parent company). However, in this matter the Seafarers have charted a course less traveled, making the tactical choice to focus their suit on the DLC in hopes of reaping greater rewards. By suing the DLC, the Seafarers apparently hoped to (a) invoke U.S. maritime law, which affords injured seamen more extensive maintenance and cure than that provided under the Seafarers' U.K.-based contracts, and (b) tap into a larger pool of potential class members, opening the class not only to workers from the Seafarers' own Cunard Line, but also to employees from Carnival Corporation & PLC's entire fleet. Indeed, the Seafarers took a gamble in solely pursuing the DLC, one that could pay off in broader, more viable claims, but only if they could demonstrate that a DLC is a properly suable entity. [—8—]

Throughout this litigation, the Seafarers have primarily advanced three theories[5] as to why Carnival Corporation & PLC—despite its status as a DLC—is a suable entity. First, they assert that Carnival Corporation & PLC is, in reality, a corporation and, thus, can be sued like one. Second, they aver that Carnival Corporation & PLC is subject to the doctrine of corporation by estoppel, arguing that it cannot avoid being sued as a corporation after holding itself out as a corporate-like entity. Third and finally, they contend that Carnival Corporation & PLC is essentially a joint venture between the participating corporations, making the DLC suable pursuant to Florida's law of joint ventures. These theories are addressed in turn below.

A. Carnival Corporation & PLC is Not Suable as a Corporation

The Seafarers focus much of their briefing efforts on demonstrating the unified, integrated nature of Carnival Corporation & PLC in an attempt to persuade the court that the DLC should be treated like any other stand-alone corporation. Indeed, they claim that "Carnival Corporation & PLC operate[s] as a single enterprise sufficient to establish personal jurisdiction over both entities as a single operation."[6] Although the Seafarers are correct in their assertion that Carnival [—9—] Corporation & PLC resembles a corporation in many ways, their simplistic argument badly misses the mark.

Indeed, regardless of whether an entity exhibits qualities common to corporations, it is not properly subject to treatment as a corporation absent incorporation, the fundamental act of corporate creation and the dividing line between corporations and non-corporations.[7] In order for Carnival

---

[5] To be clear, the Seafarers' arguments are not so precisely delineated in their briefing. Nevertheless, the court has discerned these as the primary arguments made in support of reversal.

[6] Brief of Appellants at 15, *Sabo v. CCL*, No. 13-11765 (11th Cir. June 10, 2013); *see also id.* at 10 ("[W]hen those two aforesaid entities[,] Carnival Corporation and P&O Princess Cruise Line . . .[,] merged in 2003, it formed one entity, whether incorporated or not, called [—9—] Carnival Corporation & PLC[,] the Appellee herein. Assuredly, if Appellee can use this singular brand to retain stockholders in either of the two markets in which it list[s] its stocks, to sign contracts, to make decisions regarding cruise operations and/or advertise to consumers, that same entity can be held liable for their tortious acts in a court of law.")).

[7] *See, e.g.*, Florida Business Corporation Act, Fla. Stat. § 607, et seq., which defines a corporation as "a corporation for profit . . . *incorporated* under or subject to the provisions of this act." Fla. Stat. § 607.01401(5) (emphasis added).

Corporation & PLC to assume the characteristics of a corporation (particularly the ability to sue and be sued),[8] it must be incorporated, an action which the Seafarers at least implicitly acknowledge has not occurred, neither in Florida, nor in any of the other forty-nine states. Accordingly, despite their best efforts, the Seafarers cannot maintain a suit against Carnival Corporation & PLC on the basis of its corporate-like qualities.

B. Carnival Corporation & PLC is Not Estopped from Denying that it is a Corporation [—10—]

The Seafarers also argue that Carnival Corporation & PLC should be estopped from denying that it is a corporation because it has publicly promoted itself as a single entity. Indeed, they contend that Carnival Corporation & PLC "should not be allowed to argue the lack of formal creation of its DLC when it represents itself as a singular company. . . . Appellee should be estopped from denying this company's existence as a defense."[9] Corporation by estoppel is a recognized theory in the state of Florida, having been codified at Section 617.1904:

> No body of persons acting as a corporation shall be permitted to set up the lack of legal organization as a defense to an action against them as a corporation, nor shall any person sued on a contract made with the corporation or sued for an injury to its property or a wrong done to its interests be permitted to set up the lack of such legal organization in his or her defense.

Fla. Stat. § 617.1904 (1997). However, the theory is utilized infrequently, and when it is, it is applied to far different circumstances than those found here. A prime example of such circumstances exists in *Harry Rich Corp.*

v. Feinberg, 518 So.2d 377 (Fla. 3d DCA 1987), where a creditor sought to hold both a corporation and a corporate representative liable for a disputed contract. When the creditor and representative negotiated the contract in question, the corporation—unbeknownst to either the creditor or the representative—had yet to be incorporated, creating a question as to who the creditor could pursue for the failed contract. *Harry Rich*, [—11—] 518 So.2d at 378. The precise issue on appeal was whether the creditor could maintain an action against the corporate representative, but the appellate court also extensively discussed the doctrine of corporation by estoppel, which dictated that the corporation be held liable on the contract despite its non-existence at the time of contracting. *Id.* at 379-81. As the *Harry Rich* court explained, "[f]airness dictates that a creditor dealing with what it believes to be a corporation should be able to recover from that entity. . . . The doctrine of corporation by estoppel . . . provides the creditor with that opportunity." *Id.* at 381. In other words, the doctrine of corporation by estoppel is most appropriately used to maintain the expectations of parties to a contract, allowing a "corporation [to] sue and be sued as if it existed if the parties to the contract behaved as if it existed." *Id.* at 379.

A starkly different situation is before us here. The Seafarers entered into employment contracts with Cunard Celtic Hotel Services, Ltd., but now bring suit against Carnival Corporation & PLC, an entity which had no apparent involvement in the formation of their contracts. Indeed, the Seafarers have not alleged that they had reason to believe either that they were contracting with Carnival Corporation & PLC, or that Carnival Corporation & PLC was a legal entity capable of being sued. Absent such expectations, the Seafarers may not hold Carnival Corporation & PLC liable by way of corporation by estoppel. The doctrine is simply inapplicable to the facts alleged here. [—12—]

---

[8] *See, e.g.*, Fla. Stat. § 607.0302 ("[E]very corporation . . . has the same powers as an individual to do all things necessary or convenient to carry out its business and affairs, including without limitation power: (1) To sue and be sued, complain, and defend in its corporate name.").

[9] Reply Brief of Appellants at 4 & 6, *Sabo v. CCL*, No. 13-11765 (11th Cir. August 19, 2013).

C. Carnival Corporation & PLC is Not Suable as a Joint Venture

Finally, the Seafarers argue that DLCs are analogous to joint ventures, and attempt to graft the law of joint ventures onto DLCs, including Carnival Corporation & PLC. Specifically, the Seafarers latch onto the notion—articulated in cases such as *Sutton v. Smith*, 603 So.2d 693, 699 (Fla. 1st DCA 1992)—that all the parties to a joint venture are subject to personal jurisdiction in a forum state when the joint venture contemplates and actually performs within that state. In particular, the Seafarers contend as follows:

> Since a DLC is like a joint venture, but the parties to the DLC have an actual partnership and share everything they own, not just a single project, it stands to incontrovertible reason that a DLC which involves operating, conducting, engaging in, or carrying on the business of the DLC in Florida as comprehensively as Carnival Corporation & PLC does, places the DLC within the ambit of Fla. Stat. § 48.193(1)(a), satisfies due process requirements, and confers personal jurisdiction on the DLC's members.[10]

However, their joint venture argument is plagued by two major flaws.

First, despite the simple allure of their portrayal of the DLC as "a joint venture on steroids,"[11] the Seafarers' theory fails because a DLC simply does not equate to a joint venture. In its most basic form, a Florida joint venture is "an association of persons or legal entities to carry out a *single business enterprise* for [—13—] profit." *Florida Tomato Packers, Inc. v. Wilson*, 296 So.2d 536, 539 (Fla. 3d DCA 1974) (emphasis added). However, as the Seafarers themselves readily admit,[12] DLCs are more global and all-encompassing in purpose than are joint ventures. Consequently, a DLC cannot be deemed a joint venture for jurisdictional purposes. And it is of no consequence that the DLC and the joint venture are both collaborative in nature; the scopes of the two structures are diametrically distinct, thereby rendering inappropriate the application of Florida's joint venture laws to Carnival Corporation & PLC.

Second, even assuming *arguendo* that a DLC is properly treatable as a joint venture, the Seafarers would still only be able to reach the joint venture participants (i.e., Carnival Corporation and Carnival PLC) as a result of the joint venture's contacts with the state of Florida. This is because the rule set forth in *Sutton*—which forms the basis of the Seafarers' joint venture theory—stands only for the proposition that the *members* of a joint venture, not the joint venture itself, are subject to a forum state's exercise of personal jurisdiction over them if the joint venture contemplates and actually involves performance in that state. *Sutton*, 603 So.2d at 698 ("We conclude that the sponsorship agreement, wherever made, created a joint business venture between Appellees and Sutton that contemplated [—14—] and in fact involved significant performance in Florida and thereby subjected all *parties to that joint venture*, including Appellees, to personal jurisdiction by Florida courts in respect to causes of actions arising out of the joint venture activities in Florida.") (emphasis added). This analysis makes sense, because a joint venture is not an independent legal entity, but rather a vehicle for limited collaboration between individual entities. *See Florida Tomato Packers, Inc.*, 296 So.2d at 539 ("A joint venture has been defined as a special combination of two or more persons, who, in some specific venture, seek a profit jointly *without the existence between them of any actual partnership, corporation, or other business entity*.") (emphasis added). In other words, a joint venture itself is not an entity that is properly subject to suit, which ultimately renders the Seafarers' joint venture

---

[10] Brief of Appellants at 11, *Sabo v. CCL*, No. 13-11765 (11th Cir. June 10, 2013).

[11] Response in Opposition to Motion to Dismiss at 8, *Sabo v. Carnival Corp.*, No. 12-22653 (S.D. Fla. Sept. 17, 2012).

[12] Brief of Appellants at 11, *Sabo v. CCL*, No. 13-11765 (11th Cir. June 10, 2013) ("A DLC is

---

somewhat like a joint venture, but the two parties share everything they own, not just a single project.").

argument meaningless as it relates to the question of whether Carnival Corporation & PLC is a properly suable entity.

IV. Conclusion

Our ruling today—that Carnival Corporation & PLC is not properly suable in this action—may appear, at first glance, to produce a harsh and unfair result. However, the Seafarers could have pressed their claims against another entity. Indeed, it seems abundantly clear that the Seafarers could have brought an action against Carnival PLC (the Cunard Line's parent company), but chose not to, instead making a tactical decision to pursue potentially broader claims against [—15—] Carnival Corporation & PLC. The Seafarers rolled the dice in targeting Carnival Corporation & PLC exclusively in this case; unfortunately for them, that roll did not pay off.

AFFIRMED.

United States Court of Appeals
for the Eleventh Circuit

No. 13-15520

JURICH
vs.
COMPASS MARINE, INC.

Appeal from the United States District Court for the
Southern District of Alabama

Decided: August 22, 2014

Citation: 764 F.3d 1302, 2 Adm. R. 568 (11th Cir. 2014).

Before **CARNES**, Chief Judge, **JORDAN**, and **ROSENBAUM**, Circuit Judges.

[—2—] PER CURIAM:

This consolidated appeal arises out of a claim for wages brought under the general maritime law by four seamen—Nickolas Jurich, Jesse Gann, Charles Wood, and Wilbur Smith. The seamen asserted their claims against two maritime employment agencies—Compass Marine, Inc., and Seaport Marine, Inc.—that they retained to help them find jobs. Smith also asserted the same claim against Odyssea Marine, Inc., a maritime transport company that hired him based on a referral from Seaport Marine.

When the seamen retained the employment agencies' services, they signed a series of agreements assigning to the agencies the right to collect a portion of their [—3—] first six to ten paychecks if they accepted a job as a result of the employment agencies' efforts. One of the documents they signed, a "Paycheck Mailing Agreement," provided that each seaman would have his employer send his paychecks directly to the employment agency while his debt was still outstanding. Under the agreement, the agency would take its agreed upon share of the wages and forward the balance of the paycheck to the seaman. Once the debt had been fully repaid, the employer would begin sending the seaman his paychecks directly. The agreement also stated that it was "irrevocable" until the seaman's debt had been repaid.

Compass and Seaport Marine eventually found jobs for the four seamen, and those two agencies collected a portion of their wages, following the procedure agreed upon in the Paycheck Mailing Agreements. It is undisputed that the agencies fully performed under the contracts and that they obtained their fees through the assignment of the seamen's wages made under the Paycheck Mailing Agreements.

The four seamen eventually brought suit, asserting a claim for wages under the general maritime law. In their complaints, they alleged that the wage assignments they had signed were invalid under 46 U.S.C. § 11109(b), which states that a seaman's "assignment . . . of wages . . . made before the payment of wages does not bind the party making it." 46 U.S.C. § 11109(b); see also Wilder [—4—] v. Inter-Island Steam Navigation Co., 211 U.S. 239, 247, 29 S.Ct. 58, 61 (1908) (interpreting the predecessor statute to 46 U.S.C. § 11109). Based on that statutory provision and the special protection that courts typically afford seamen under the "wards of admiralty" doctrine, they claimed that they were entitled to a full refund of the wages that had been collected under the Paycheck Mailing Agreements by Compass and Seaport Marine. After discovery, the district court granted the defendants summary judgment on the plaintiffs' claims, and the seamen now appeal those decisions.

We review de novo a district court's grant of summary judgment, viewing all facts and reasonable inferences in the light most favorable to the nonmoving party. Allison v. McGhan Med. Corp., 184 F.3d 1300, 1306 (11th Cir. 1999). Summary judgment is appropriate where there is no genuine issue as to any material fact and the moving party is entitled to judgment as a matter of law. Id.

After reviewing the record, reading the parties' briefs, and hearing oral argument, we affirm the judgment of the district court for the reasons set out in its two well-reasoned and well-written orders, which were filed on November 4, 2013, and November 7, 2013. See Smith v. Seaport Marine, Inc., 981 F. Supp. 2d 1188 (S.D. Ala. 2013); Jurich v. Compass

Marine, Inc., No. 1:12-cv-00176-WS-B, 2013 WL 5960899 (S.D. Ala. Nov. 7, 2013). We adopt those orders as our opinion with the same effect as if we had written them ourselves. In doing so, we emphasize [—5—] that Compass' and Seaport's inclusion of the word "irrevocable" in the Paycheck Mailing Agreements was improper and contrary to the plaintiffs' clear statutory right under § 11109(b), which provides that the seamen were not bound by those agreements.

As a final point, we note that the district court's summary judgment orders addressed only the plaintiffs' claims for wages that were brought under the general maritime law and predicated on a violation of § 11109(b). The dismissal of any other claims before those two summary judgment orders was not appealed to this Court, and we express no opinion on the validity of those claims or of any claim other than one for wages brought under the general maritime law and based on a violation of § 11109(b). That means that if Compass and Seaport continue using the word "irrevocable" in their Paycheck Mailing Agreements, they may do so at their eventual peril.

AFFIRMED.

United States Court of Appeals
for the Eleventh Circuit

No. 13-10107

WINTHROP-REDIN
VS.
UNITED STATES

Appeal from the United States District Court for the
Middle District of Florida

Decided: September 23, 2014

Citation: 767 F.3d 1210, 2 Adm. R. 570 (11th Cir. 2014).

Before **HULL, MARCUS,** and **BLACK,** Circuit Judges.

[—1—] **MARCUS,** Circuit Judge:

For his role as a boat crew member in an international drug-smuggling operation, Wilson Daniel Winthrop-Redin pled guilty to a federal charge of [—2—] conspiracy to possess five kilograms or more of cocaine with the intent to distribute and was sentenced to 168 months in prison. Two years after entering his plea, Winthrop-Redin sought postconviction relief under 28 U.S.C. § 2255, claiming that his plea was coerced by death threats from the boat's captain and that his counsel provided ineffective assistance by instructing him not to report the threats to the district court. We affirm the district court's rejection of the claims without an evidentiary hearing. Because Winthrop-Redin put forward only implausible and conclusory allegations, "the motion and the files and records of the case conclusively show that the prisoner is entitled to no relief" without a hearing. 28 U.S.C. § 2255(b); *see Aron v. United States*, 291 F.3d 708, 715 n.6 (11th Cir. 2002).

I.

A plea agreement signed by Winthrop-Redin contained the following essential facts. Winthrop-Redin, a Panamanian national, and other codefendants agreed to participate in a maritime drug-smuggling scheme and received advance payment of several thousand dollars. In November 2009, Winthrop-Redin and his codefendants left Panama aboard the St. Vincent-registered Motor Vessel (M/V)

Olympiakos bound for Barranquilla, Colombia. In Colombia, the M/V Olympiakos received a load of coal, a "cover load" of legitimate cargo to conceal the smuggling mission. Shortly before the M/V Olympiakos left port, three armed [—3—] individuals boarded the boat to protect the drug shipment. On December 1, 2009, the M/V Olympiakos met a go-fast boat off the Colombian coast. Ninety bales of cocaine were moved from the go-fast boat to the M/V Olympiakos. The crew of the M/V Olympiakos, including Winthrop-Redin, concealed the cocaine in a hidden compartment. On December 2, 2009, the United States Coast Guard approached, boarded, and inspected the Olympiakos in international waters. The Coast Guard discovered the hidden compartment and seized the ninety bales of cocaine, which weighed over 2,000 kilograms. With the consent of the government of St. Vincent, Winthrop-Redin and his codefendants were brought to the United States, with their first point of entry in the Middle District of Florida. Winthrop-Redin and seven others[1] were indicted on two counts: (1) conspiring to possess with the intent to distribute and to distribute five kilograms or more of cocaine while on board a vessel subject to the jurisdiction of the United States, 21 U.S.C. § 960(b)(1)(B)(ii); 46 U.S.C. §§ 70503(a), 70506(a)-(b), as well as (2) possessing with intent to distribute five kilograms or more of cocaine on board a vessel subject to the jurisdiction of the United States, 21 U.S.C. § 960(b)(1)(B)(ii); 46 U.S.C. §§ 70503(a), 70506(a). [—4—]

Each of the codefendants pled guilty. Winthrop-Redin entered into a written plea agreement that provided he would plead guilty to conspiracy, the first count of the indictment, in exchange for the dismissal of the second count, possession. Winthrop-Redin initialed each page of the agreement and signed its last page. In the plea agreement, Winthrop-Redin expressly waived his right to appeal his sentence, except on the grounds

---

[1] Joffre Alouso Plaza-Arevalo, Javier Enrique Castillo-Romero, Luis Nunez Reyes-Serrano, Clemente Bautista-Silva, Gustavo Adolfo de Poll-Noriega, Paulo Andres Molina-Roja, and Jorge Anres Molina-Molina.

that the sentence violated the Eighth Amendment or exceeded the statutory maximum penalty or the applicable Guidelines range determined by the district court. Section B.8 of the agreement, "Voluntariness," provided that Winthrop-Redin "acknowledges that [he] is entering into this agreement and is pleading guilty freely and voluntarily . . . without threats, force, intimidation, or coercion of any kind." Petitioner also voluntarily agreed to cooperate fully with the United States in all relevant matters.

Before the plea was accepted, a magistrate judge questioned Winthrop-Redin under oath and at length at a hearing to ensure he pled knowingly and voluntarily. Among other things, the plea colloquy included the following exchange:

THE COURT: Mr. Winthrop, has anybody promised you anything other than what is set out in your plea agreement to get you to plead?

MR. WINTHROP-REDIN: No.

THE COURT: Has anybody promised you a particular sentence?

MR. WINTHROP-REDIN: No. [—5—]

THE COURT: Has anybody threatened you or a member of your family in any way to get you to plead?

MR. WINTHROP-REDIN: No.

THE COURT: Do you feel like anybody is forcing you into this decision?

MR. WINTHROP-REDIN: No.

THE COURT: You've been represented here by Mr. Gottfried. Do you have any complaints about anything your lawyer has done?

MR. WINTHROP-REDIN: None.

The magistrate judge concluded that Winthrop-Redin and his codefendants were coherent and understood the allegations and potential punishment, and that a factual basis existed to support the allegations. The court specifically found that none of defendants had been threatened, forced, or coerced into pleading guilty: "From everything that appears to me today, gentlemen, your pleas are being entered freely and voluntarily with an understanding of the consequences and I will so find and recommend the matter proceed to sentencing." Thereafter, the district court accepted the plea and sentenced Winthrop-Redin to 168 months imprisonment to be followed by 60 months of supervised release. That sentence reflected a two-level firearms enhancement related to the possession of firearms by co-conspirators, but Winthrop-Redin received a two-level "safety valve" reduction pursuant to Sentencing Guidelines § 5C1.2 as a less-culpable defendant who [—6—] agreed to provide information about the offense to law enforcement. *See United States v. Brownlee*, 204 F.3d 1302, 1304 (11th Cir. 2000).

Winthrop-Redin filed a direct appeal from the final judgment, arguing that the district court erred by denying him a minor role reduction and by imposing the firearms possession enhancement. This Court, however, dismissed the appeal due to the appeal waiver.

In March 2012, more than two years after signing the plea agreement and entering his guilty plea, Winthrop-Redin filed a pro se motion to vacate his sentence pursuant to 28 U.S.C. § 2255. Inter alia, he argued that his plea was involuntarily entered because he and his family received death threats, and that he received ineffective assistance of counsel when deciding to plead guilty.[2] In an affidavit accompanying the motion, Winthrop-Redin said that he had been hired by Alexis Hernandez-Soto, "the captain / chief master"

---

[2] Winthrop-Redin also argued that his appeal waiver was entered involuntarily, and that the government breached the plea agreement by recommending a firearm-possession sentencing enhancement but not recommending he receive a downward departure for substantial assistance. The certificate of appealability we issued in this case does not include these claims.

of M/V Olympiakos, for a trip from Panama to Colombia. The United States concedes that Hernandez-Soto was an informant for the Drug Enforcement Administration. According to Winthrop-Redin, after a dispute, Hernandez-Soto ordered the assassination of a Colombian crew member. When Winthrop-Redin confronted him, Hernandez-Soto said that he and his cohorts would kill Winthrop-Redin and his family if he told the [—7—] authorities or the crew member's family about the murder of the Colombian. Subsequently, Winthrop-Redin said, he was forced to stay in the vessel under death threats. Winthrop-Redin also claimed that Hernandez-Soto and two other crew members working as informants for the United States government "coerc[ed] me to plead guilty under death threats." Notably, however, he did not offer where, when, or why he was coerced to plead guilty. All he said was that he "did not have a choice other than to comply with [Hernandez-Soto's] orders." Winthrop-Redin admitted, as he had to, that he swore under oath at the sentencing hearing that his guilty plea was entered knowingly and voluntarily and that he had not been coerced or threatened to do so. He claimed, nevertheless, at the highest order of abstraction, that he pled out of fear. And he claimed that, but for the threats against him and his family, he would have proceeded to trial.

Winthrop-Redin further claimed that he received ineffective assistance of counsel. He alleged that his attorney advised him not to say anything to the district court or anyone else about Hernandez-Soto having killed the Colombian crew member because doing so would complicate the case. Winthrop-Redin also claimed that, despite his request, his attorney did not contact the Panamanian Consulate to get legal help and did not contact the Colombian Consulate to notify them of the crew member's killing. [—8—]

In response, the United States told the district court that the alleged threats concerning the murder happened on the vessel before Winthrop-Redin was arrested (and before he was charged with anything), and that Winthrop-Redin had not alleged any threats regarding his decision to enter a guilty plea or proceed to trial. Winthrop-Redin replied that "Hernandez-Soto made direct threats to his family and movant while movant was detained ready to proceed to trial." Again notably, Winthrop-Redin did not offer when the threats had been made and did not explain where, how, or why. Winthrop-Redin claimed only that his family told him "that Hernandez-Soto and other cohorts of him were calling them with death threats if movant proceeded to trial or testified in court about the assassination of the crew member."

The district court refused relief because it found that the record showed Winthrop-Redin knowingly and voluntarily entered his guilty plea. The district court noted that Winthrop-Redin's claim that he was directly threatened while he "was detained ready to proceed to trial" was factually impossible: Hernandez-Soto was never charged in the case and thus never detained, and therefore could not have directly threatened Winthrop-Redin to force him to plead guilty. The court also found claims about threats to Winthrop-Redin's family members to be without merit because Hernandez-Soto told the United States about the death on the vessel and had no reason to silence Winthrop-Redin. The district court did not conduct an [—9—] evidentiary hearing on this or any of Winthrop-Redin's other § 2255 claims, which it also rejected. The court declined to issue a certificate of appealability.

Winthrop-Redin filed a timely notice of appeal, and we granted a certificate of appealability on one issue: "Whether Winthrop-Redin is entitled to an evidentiary hearing on his claim that his guilty plea was not knowing or voluntary due to threats that he received and ineffective assistance of plea counsel."

II.

We review the district court's denial of an evidentiary hearing in a § 2255 proceeding for abuse of discretion. *Aron*, 291 F.3d at 714 n.5. "A district court abuses its discretion if it applies an incorrect legal standard, applies the law in an unreasonable or incorrect manner, follows improper procedures in making a determination, or makes findings of fact that are clearly erroneous." *Citizens for Police Accountability Political Comm. v. Browning*, 572 F.3d 1213, 1216-17 (11th Cir. 2009) (per curiam). We liberally construe *pro se* filings, including *pro se* applications for relief pursuant to § 2255. *Aron*, 291 F.3d at 715; *Mederos v. United States*, 218 F.3d 1252, 1254 (11th Cir. 2000).

Section 2255 permits a federal prisoner to bring a collateral challenge by moving the sentencing court to vacate, set aside, or correct the sentence. 28 U.S.C. § 2255(a). Once a petitioner files a § 2255 motion, "[u]nless the motion and the files and records of the case conclusively show that the prisoner is entitled to no [—10—] relief, the court shall . . . grant a prompt hearing thereon, determine the issues and make findings of fact and conclusions of law with respect thereto." *Id.* § 2255(b). A petitioner is entitled to an evidentiary hearing if he "alleges facts that, if true, would entitle him to relief." *Aron*, 291 F.3d at 715 (quoting *Holmes v. United States*, 876 F.2d 1545, 1552 (11th Cir. 1989)). "[A] petitioner need only allege—not prove—reasonably specific, non-conclusory facts that, if true, would entitle him to relief." *Id.* at 715 n.6. However, a district court need not hold a hearing if the allegations are "patently frivolous," "based upon unsupported generalizations," or "affirmatively contradicted by the record." *Holmes*, 876 F.2d at 1553 (quoting *Guerra v. United States*, 588 F.2d 519, 520-21 (5th Cir. 1979)[3]); *see, e.g., Lynn v. United States*, 365 F.3d 1225, 1239 (11th Cir. 2004) ("Because the . . . affidavits submitted by Lynn amount to nothing more than mere conclusory allegations, the district court was not required to hold an evidentiary hearing on the issues and correctly denied Lynn's § 2255 motion.").

"A guilty plea, if induced by promises or threats which deprive it of the character of a voluntary act, is void. A conviction based upon such a plea is open to collateral attack." *Machibroda v. United States*, 368 U.S. 487, 493 (1962). At the same time, plea bargaining retains its benefits of certainty and efficiency

"only [—11—] if dispositions by guilty plea are accorded a great measure of finality." *Blackledge v. Allison*, 431 U.S. 63, 71 (1977); *see id.* ("To allow indiscriminate hearings in federal postconviction proceedings . . . for federal prisoners under 28 U.S.C. § 2255 . . . would eliminate the chief virtues of the plea system—speed, economy, and finality."). While § 2255 exists "to safeguard a person's freedom from detention in violation of constitutional guarantees," the Court observed that "[m]ore often than not a prisoner has everything to gain and nothing to lose from filing a collateral attack upon his guilty plea." *Id.* at 71-72. As a result, "the representations of the defendant, his lawyer, and the prosecutor at [a plea] hearing, as well as any findings made by the judge accepting the plea, constitute a formidable barrier in any subsequent collateral proceedings." *Id.* at 73-74; *see id.* at 80 n.19 (explaining that if the record reflects the procedures of plea negotiation and includes a verbatim transcript of the plea colloquy, a petitioner challenging his plea will be entitled to an evidentiary hearing "only in the most extraordinary circumstances"). "The subsequent presentation of conclusory allegations unsupported by specifics is subject to summary dismissal, as are contentions that in the face of the record are wholly incredible." *Id.* at 74.

The district court did not abuse its considerable discretion in declining to hold a § 2255(b) evidentiary hearing because Winthrop-Redin's involuntary plea claim is based only on conclusory and incredible allegations. We say so for a [—12—] number of reasons. For starters, the record contains powerful evidence from Winthrop-Redin himself indicating that his guilty plea was knowing and voluntary. Winthrop-Redin initialed and signed the plea agreement, which specified that he had decided to plead knowingly and voluntarily, without threats, force, intimidation, or coercion. Winthrop-Redin then testified under oath and in detail that his plea had not been induced by threats or force leveled against him or his family. *See* Fed. R. Crim. P. 11(b)(2) ("Before accepting a plea of guilty . . . , the court must address the defendant personally in open court and

---

[3] In *Bonner v. City of Prichard*, 661 F.2d 1206, 1209 (11th Cir. 1981) (en banc), we adopted as binding precedent all decisions of the former Fifth Circuit handed down before October 1, 1981.

determine that the plea is voluntary and did not result from force [or] threats . . . ."). Such "[s]olemn declarations in open court carry a strong presumption of verity." *Blackledge*, 431 U.S. at 74; *accord United States v. Gonzalez-Mercado*, 808 F.2d 796, 800 n.8 (11th Cir. 1987) ("While Rule 11 is not insurmountable, there is a strong presumption that the statements made during the colloquy are true."). Indeed, because Winthrop-Redin made statements under oath at a plea colloquy, "he bears a heavy burden to show his statements were false." *United States v. Rogers*, 848 F.2d 166, 168 (11th Cir. 1988) (per curiam).

In the second place, Winthrop-Redin waited more than two years after he pled guilty, and only after all other avenues for relief from his sentence were exhausted, to say anything to the district court about alleged threats. Then, to counter his "directly inconsistent former testimony," Winthrop-Redin "tendered [—13—] only his own affidavit." *Bryan v. United States*, 492 F.2d 775, 779-80 (5th Cir. 1974) (en banc). The former Fifth Circuit noted in dicta that "the allegations of [a § 2255] petitioner accompanied by his own affidavit are insufficient to mandate an evidentiary hearing in the face of a Rule 11 record detailing statements by the petitioner that his plea was not induced by any threats or coercion." *Matthews v. United States*, 533 F.2d 900, 902 (5th Cir. 1976). While this clear-cut principle does not bind our decision because, in prior precedent, the Fifth Circuit explained that under § 2255(b) "[n]o per se rule can be applied, for in the final analysis, the issue becomes one of fact," it does inform our analysis. *Bryan*, 492 F.2d at 778; *see United States v. Vega-Castillo*, 540 F.3d 1235, 1236 (11th Cir. 2008) (per curiam) ("Under the prior precedent rule, we are bound to follow a prior binding precedent 'unless and until it is overruled by this court en banc or by the Supreme Court.'" (quoting *United States v. Brown*, 342 F.3d 1245, 1246 (11th Cir. 2003))). The fact that Winthrop-Redin presented only his own affidavit bears on whether the record conclusively shows he is entitled to no relief. *See Bryan*, 492 F.2d at 780 (warning against a system where "the number of hearings which a wilful affiant could provoke as to a single

conviction would be limitless, for each time he could swear that someone at the last preceding hearing suborned false testimony from him"). In addition, we observe that Winthrop-Redin nowhere alleged what evidence he intended to adduce at an evidentiary hearing. The district court is [—14—] entitled to discredit a defendant's newly-minted story about being threatened when that story is supported only by the defendant's conclusory statements.

Moreover, Winthrop-Redin did not put forward "specific and detailed factual assertions" that, if true, would entitle him to relief. *Id.* at 779. Winthrop-Redin's affidavit states that Hernandez-Soto ordered the killing of a crew member and threatened Winthrop-Redin not to say anything about the murder. But Winthrop-Redin was charged with, and pled guilty to, conspiracy to possess cocaine with the intent to distribute, not murder. Winthrop-Redin's allegations in no way connect the threats concerning disclosure of the killing with the decision to plead guilty, which occurred substantially later in time. As a result, even if it were true that Hernandez-Soto told Winthrop-Redin to say nothing about the murder, that fact would not establish that the guilty plea on the drug conspiracy charge was involuntary. If anything, pleading guilty, which required Winthrop-Redin to tell the government and the district court about the smuggling operation and all related matters, created far more risk of divulging details about the alleged murder than proceeding to trial. After all, in the plea agreement Winthrop-Redin "agree[d] to cooperate fully with the United States," to testify "fully and truthfully" in any federal court proceeding connected with "the charges in this case and other matters," and to make "a full and complete disclosure of all relevant information." Winthrop-Redin does not explain how Hernandez-Soto's alleged command *not* to [—15—] divulge the murder coerced him into entering a plea agreement that involved cooperating *with* the government and disclosing all relevant facts.

Besides the threats tied to the crew member killing, Winthrop-Redin puts forward no specific facts in support of his conclusory claim that he "was intimidated and coerced into pleading guilty by codefendants in my case who threatened to kill me and my family members." Notably, he does not offer how Hernandez-Soto conveyed threats urging him to plead guilty, when, where, or how often they were made, or even why Hernandez-Soto wanted him to plead. He argues nevertheless that his allegations are sufficiently specific for a hearing because they include "(1) the naming, or description, of persons involved; (2) an account of the relevant acts or conduct of such persons; (3) an account of the time and place where such acts or conduct took place; and (4) a statement of how such acts or conduct prejudiced the petitioner." *Diamond v. United States*, 432 F.2d 35, 40 (9th Cir. 1970). But Winthrop-Redin flunks his own test. He offers no account of the time, place, or acts involved in the threats he says pressured him into a guilty plea. Alone, the conclusory assertion that he pled guilty because of death threats from Hernandez-Soto is not enough to warrant a § 2255 hearing in the face of this full record, including Winthrop-Redin's prior testimony that he pled guilty [—16—] knowingly and voluntarily.[4] The district court was not required to allow a fishing-expedition based only on Winthrop-Redin's incredible allegations. *See Machibroda*, 368 U.S. at 495 ("The language of [§ 2255(b)] does not strip the district courts of all discretion to exercise their common sense.").

Winthrop-Redin also alleges in his affidavit that he told his attorney that he wanted to tell the district court about the threats from Hernandez-Soto, but that "counsel misadvised [him] not to say anything about it to the judge,

the prosecutor, or anyone else and that is was better to keep it that way or things would get much more complicated in the case." On appeal, Winthrop-Redin argues that he is entitled to an evidentiary hearing on his claim that counsel was ineffective for advising him not to tell the district court about the threats and for allowing him to plead guilty under duress.

"During plea negotiations defendants are 'entitled to the effective assistance of counsel.'" *Lafler v. Cooper*, 132 S. Ct. 1376, 1384 (2012) (quoting *McMann v. Richardson*, 397 U.S. 759, 771 (1970)). To establish ineffective assistance, a defendant must show deficient performance and prejudice. *Strickland v.* [—17—] *Washington*, 466 U.S. 668, 687 (1984). On the first prong, "counsel is strongly presumed to have rendered adequate assistance and made all significant decisions in the exercise of reasonable professional judgment." *Id.* at 690. To establish prejudice, a defendant must show "there is a reasonable probability that, but for counsel's unprofessional errors, the result of the proceeding would have been different." *Id.* at 694. "A reasonable probability is a probability sufficient to undermine confidence in the outcome." *Id.* Where, as here, the petitioner challenges his guilty plea based on his counsel's alleged deficient performance, he can show prejudice only if "there is a reasonable probability that, but for counsel's errors, he would not have pleaded guilty and would have insisted on going to trial." *Hill v. Lockhart*, 474 U.S. 52, 59 (1985).

Winthrop-Redin is not entitled to a § 2255(b) evidentiary hearing because he does not specifically allege that he told his attorney he had been threatened with death unless he pled guilty. Instead, as he explained in his district court Memorandum of Law, Winthrop-Redin claimed that he told his attorney "the details of how Hernandez-Soto ha[d] killed the Colombian crew member in the vessel and that he had threatened to kill movant and his family if he did not keep his mouth shot [sic]." Even if this allegation were true, Winthrop-Redin would not be entitled to relief. We cannot say that counsel would have exceeded the bounds of reasonable professional

---

[4] In an unverified Reply filed in support of his motion, Winthrop-Redin claimed that his family told him "that Hernandez-Soto and other cohorts of him were calling them with death threats if movant proceeded to trial or testified in court about the assassination of the crew member." Winthrop-Redin does not argue on appeal that statements in the Reply entitle him to a hearing. And the Reply still fails to allege specific facts. It does not describe which "other cohorts" conveyed the threats, how many times they did so, when the threats were made, which family members received them, what the threatening parties actually said, or why Hernandez-Soto and "other cohorts" wanted him to plead guilty.

judgment by advising a client not to tell the judge about [—18—] a separate incident unconnected to the client's decision to plead guilty. Moreover, as the government points out, counsel's alleged advice might even have protected his client's interests. If the district court considered murder of the crew member to be reasonably foreseeable relevant conduct, the court could have increased Winthrop-Redin's sentencing level under the Guidelines. *See* U.S. Sentencing Guidelines Manual §§ 2A1.1(a), 2D1.1(d)(1) (2009). Nor did Winthrop-Redin allege prejudice sufficient to warrant a hearing because he did not claim in his § 2255 motion or his supporting affidavit that his decision to plead guilty was affected by his attorney's advice not to tell the judge about threats related to the crew member's murder.[5]

Finally, Winthrop-Redin claims that his counsel was deficient for failing to contact the Consulates of Panama and Colombia to inform them of the crew member's murder and to obtain legal assistance. But Winthrop-Redin does not say what help, if any, the Consulates could have provided. He certainly does not allege that the failure to contact them had any effect on his decision to plead guilty. [—19—] Without specific allegations supporting his *Strickland* claim, Winthrop-Redin is not entitled to a § 2255(b) evidentiary hearing.

AFFIRMED.

---

[5] In his district court Reply, Winthrop-Redin first stated that "[h]ad counsel rendered an undivided and loyal defense to movant, movant would have testified *in camera* about the assassination case, he would have proceeded to trial and he would have never pleaded guilty . . . ." Again, Winthrop-Redin does not argue on appeal that statements made for the first time in the Reply entitle him to a hearing. And even if Winthrop-Redin had properly presented it to the district court, the conclusory allegation would not warrant a hearing. Winthrop-Redin still alleges no specific facts connecting his attorney's advice about the death of the crew member with the decision to plead guilty.

United States Court of Appeals
for the Eleventh Circuit

No. 13-13519

EQUAL EMPLOYMENT OPPORTUNITY COMM'N
VS.
ROYAL CARIBBEAN CRUISES, LTD.

Appeal from the United States District Court for the
Southern District of Florida

Decided: November 6, 2014

Citation: 771 F.3d 757, 2 Adm. R. 577 (11th Cir. 2014).

Before **CARNES,** Chief Judge, and **RESTANI,*** Judge,
and **MERRYDAY,*** * District Judge.

* The Honorable Jane A. Restani, United States Court
of International Trade Judge, sitting by designation.

** The Honorable Steven D. Merryday, United States
District Judge for the Middle District of Florida, sitting by
designation.

[—2—] PER CURIAM:

The Equal Employment Opportunity
Commission ("the EEOC" or "the
Commission") appeals the district court's
denial of the EEOC's application for
enforcement of its administrative subpoena
issued to Royal Caribbean Cruises, Ltd.
("RCCL"). After careful consideration and with
the benefit of oral argument, we affirm.[1]

BACKGROUND

In June 2010, Jose Morabito, an
Argentinean national who was employed by
RCCL as an assistant waiter on one of its
cruise ships, filed a charge of discrimination
with the EEOC. Mr. Morabito alleged that
RCCL violated the Americans with
Disabilities Act ("ADA"), 42 U.S.C. § 12112,
when RCCL refused to renew his employment
contract after he was diagnosed with a
medical condition. Mr. Morabito had been
diagnosed with HIV and Kaposi Sarcoma, but
he had been declared fit for duty by his
physician.

RCCL responded to the charge with a
position statement contending that (1) the
ADA was inapplicable because Mr. Morabito
was a foreign national who was employed on a
ship flying the flag of the Bahamas and (2)
because RCCL's ships are registered under
the law of the Bahamas, RCCL was required
to follow the Bahamas Maritime Authority
("BMA") medical standards for seafarers,
which [—3—] allegedly disqualified Mr.
Morabito from duty at sea.

After receiving RCCL's position statement,
the EEOC requested a list of all employees
discharged by RCCL since 2010 pursuant to
the BMA medical standards. RCCL objected,
asserting that the ADA did not cover foreign
nationals working on foreign-flagged ships
and that the information sought was not
relevant to Mr. Morabito's charge.

The EEOC ultimately issued an
administrative subpoena, which included
requests for the following information[2]:

(1) List all employees who were
discharged or whose contracts were
not renewed [from August 25, 2009,
through present[3]] due to a medical
reason . . . .

(2) For each employee listed in response
to request number 1, include
employee's name, citizenship,
employment contract, position title,
reason for and date of discharge, a
copy of the separation notice and the
last known contact information for
each individual.

(3) For each employee listed in response
to request number 1, include their
employment application and related
correspondence, any interview notes,

---

[1] The district court had jurisdiction pursuant to
42 U.S.C. § 2000e-9 (2012) and 29 U.S.C. § 161(2).
We exercise jurisdiction pursuant to 28 U.S.C.
§ 1291.

---

[2] The subpoena also requested information
pertaining to RCCL's general hiring and firing
practices and its business operations in Miami,
Florida. RCCL fully responded to these requests.

[3] The EEOC's original subpoena requested
information from January 1, 2008, through present.
The EEOC modified the relevant timeframe so that
the information was limited to August 25, 2009,
through present.

the identity of the person who hired the employee, how the employee obtained the position (i.e. online, in person, recruiter), the location where the employee was interviewed, and the identity and location of the person who made the final hiring decision. [—4—]

(4) List all persons who applied for a position but were not hired within the relevant period due to a medical reason . . . .

(5) For each employee listed in response to request number 4, include their citizenship, employment application and related correspondence, any interview notes, the identity of the person [who] hired the employee, how the employee learned of the position (i.e. online, in person, recruiter), the location where the employee was interviewed, and the identity and location of the person who made the final hiring decisions.

RCCL partially complied by providing records for employees or applicants who were United States citizens. The EEOC sought to compel enforcement of the requests for the remaining records regarding non-U.S. citizens who had been discharged or denied employment because of a medical condition.

The magistrate judge recommended that the petition to enforce the subpoena be denied on the grounds that the information sought was not relevant to Mr. Morabito's charge and that compliance with the disputed portions of the subpoena would be unduly burdensome. The EEOC filed objections with the district court. The district court rejected the EEOC's contentions and affirmed and adopted the magistrate judge's report and recommendation. The EEOC appeals.

DISCUSSION

In investigating allegations of unlawful employment practices, the EEOC is entitled to inspect and copy "any evidence of any person being investigated or proceeded against that relates to unlawful employment practices . . . and is relevant to the charge under investigation." 42 U.S.C. § 2000e-8(a) (2012). Although [—5—] "courts have generously construed the term 'relevant' and have afforded the Commission access to virtually any material that might cast light on the allegations against the employer," the Supreme Court has cautioned against construing the EEOC's investigative authority so broadly that the relevancy requirement is rendered "a nullity." EEOC v. Shell Oil Co., 466 U.S. 54, 68–69 (1984). A district court also "may weigh such equitable criteria as reasonableness and oppressiveness in issuing a subpoena for documents." EEOC v. Packard Elec. Div., Gen. Motors Corp., 569 F.2d 315, 318 (5th Cir. 1978).[4]

"The 'relevance' of documents in an administrative proceeding is a mixed question of law and fact, which implies that our standard of review of such determinations should look either to 'legal error' or to 'clear error,' depending on the circumstances." Id. at 317–18. We review the district court's balancing of the relative hardships and benefits of enforcement for abuse of discretion. Id. at 318. We find no error in the district court's opinion.

As the district court noted, the record below makes clear that the disputed portions of the subpoena are aimed at discovering members of a potential class of employees or applicants who suffered from a pattern or practice of discrimination, rather than fleshing out Mr. Morabito's charge. Although statistical and comparative data in some cases may be relevant in determining whether unlawful [—6—] discrimination occurred, the EEOC was required to make some showing that the requested information "bears on the subject matter of the[] individual complaint[]." Id.

The arguments presented by the EEOC on this point amounted to simply parroting the Supreme Court's statement that the

---

[4] All decisions of the Fifth Circuit issued prior to the close of business on September 30, 1981, are binding precedent. Bonner v. City of Prichard, 661 F.2d 1206, 1209 (11th Cir. 1981).

information "might cast light on the allegations" against RCCL. *Shell Oil*, 466 U.S. at 69. It is not immediately clear, however, why company-wide data regarding employees and applicants around the world with any medical condition, including conditions not specifically covered by the BMA medical standards or similar to Mr. Morabito's, would shed light on Mr. Morabito's individual charge that he was fired because of his HIV and Kaposi Sarcoma diagnoses. This is especially so as RCCL admits that Mr. Morabito was terminated because of his medical condition, which RCCL alleges was required by the BMA medical standards. This does not appear to be a case where statistical data is needed to determine whether an employer's facially neutral explanation for the adverse employment decision is pretext for discrimination. We cannot say based on the record before us that the district court clearly erred in determining the interrelation, or lack thereof, between the information sought and the allegations in Mr. Morabito's charge. *See Packard*, 569 F.2d at 318 (holding that district court's finding that facility-wide statistical data was not relevant to individual charges of discrimination was not clearly erroneous); *EEOC v. United [—7—] Air Lines, Inc.*, 287 F.3d 643, 654–55 (7th Cir. 2002) (holding that world-wide company information regarding employees who had taken medical leave of absence or had been laid off and benefits they received was not relevant to resolving individual flight attendant's charge that employer unlawfully failed to make contributions to French social security system on behalf of Americans employed or domiciled in France).

The EEOC focused most of its efforts before the district court, and in its briefs before us, on its argument that the EEOC is entitled to expand the investigation to uncover other potential violations and victims of discrimination on the basis of disability. According to the EEOC, this information is relevant because it is the same type of discrimination alleged in Mr. Morabito's charge and RCCL's reliance on the BMA standards suggests that others might have been discriminated against. We do not construe the relevancy standard so broadly. It

might be that this information is related to Mr. Morabito's individual charge, but the standard by which the EEOC's subpoena power is governed is *"relevant* to the charge under investigation." 42 U.S.C. § 2000e-8(a) (emphasis added). The relevance that is necessary to support a subpoena for the investigation of an individual charge is relevance to the contested issues that must be decided to resolve that charge, not relevance to issues that may be contested when and if future charges are brought by others. Because RCCL has admitted that the reason [—8—] that it refused to renew Mr. Morabito's contract is his medical condition, whether it refused to renew other employee's contracts for the same reason is irrelevant to his charge. That issue is settled. Although eradicating unlawful discrimination and protecting other as-yet undiscovered victims are laudatory goals and within the Commission's broad mandate, the EEOC must still make the necessary showing of relevancy in attempting to enforce its subpoena. We agree with the magistrate judge and the district court that the broad company-wide information sought by the EEOC here has not been demonstrated to be relevant to the only contested issues that remain from those that arose as a result of the individual charge brought by Mr. Morabito.

Even if the information sought has some tenuous relevance to the charge filed by Mr. Morabito, we find no error in the district court's holding that compliance with the subpoena would be unduly burdensome to RCCL. As explained, the information sought by the EEOC is at best tangentially relevant to Mr. Morabito's individual charge of discrimination. The only issues in dispute regarding Mr. Morabito's individual charge are whether the EEOC has jurisdiction over his claim, as he is a foreign national who was employed on a foreign-flagged ship, and whether the BMA standards provide a valid justification for RCCL's employment decision. RCCL already has provided the EEOC with information regarding its corporate [—9—] structure, its hiring and firing practices, the BMA standards, and the circumstances surrounding Mr. Morabito's termination. The EEOC failed to present a cogent argument as to how the additional information sought, which pertains to employees and applicants from around the world suffering from *any* medical condition, in the light of the information the EEOC already possesses, would further aid the Commission in resolving the issues in dispute regarding Mr. Morabito's charge.

To the extent that the EEOC desires this information so that it may advocate on behalf of other potential victims of employment discrimination, the need for the subpoenaed information is relatively low. The Commission has the ability to file a Commissioner's charge alleging a pattern and practice of discrimination that could support a request for that information. *See* 42 U.S.C. § 2000e-5(b) (2012) (providing that a discrimination charge may be filed "by or on behalf of a person claiming to be aggrieved, or by a member of the Commission"). In any case, the EEOC may not enforce a subpoena in the investigation of an individual charge merely as an expedient bypass of the mechanisms required to file a Commissioner's charge.

In contrast to the limited need for the subpoenaed information to resolve Mr. Morabito's claim, the burden on RCCL in complying with the subpoena would be significant. RCCL would be required to manually [—10—] review and cross-reference paper documents relating to thousands of former employees. Additionally, RCCL would be required to collect records from independent hiring partners concerning thousands of applicants who were not hired. To supply the information sought, RCCL estimated that it would need to divert five to seven employees from their usual tasks for forty hours a week for two months. As the EEOC has little, if any, need for the requested information to resolve Mr. Morabito's charge, this burden is unwarranted.

Moreover, RCCL has raised a legitimate question regarding whether the EEOC has jurisdiction over the claims of foreign nationals on foreign-flagged ships, like Mr. Morabito, when doing so likely would interfere with the internal order of the vessels. *See Spector v. Norwegian Cruise Line Ltd.*, 545 U.S. 119, 125 (2005) ("Our cases hold that a

clear statement of congressional intent is necessary before a general statutory requirement can interfere with matters that concern a foreign-flag vessel's internal affairs and operations . . . ."); *Lobo v. Celebrity Cruises, Inc.*, 704 F.3d 882, 888 & n.10, 1 Adm. R. 440, 442 & n.10 (11th Cir. 2013) (holding that the Labor Management Relations Act and National Labor Relations Act do not apply to wage disputes between foreign-flagged ship and its foreign crew, even when ship enters U.S. waters). Although we need not decide at this time whether the EEOC lacks [—11—] jurisdiction over claims of foreign nationals employed on foreign-flagged ships, *see EEOC v. Kloster Cruise Ltd.*, 939 F.2d 920, 922–23 (11th Cir. 1991), the district court was justified in considering this potential jurisdictional hurdle in weighing the potential benefits and hardships of enforcing the EEOC's wide-ranging subpoena in this case.

In an attempt to challenge the district court's analysis, the EEOC cites cases from other Courts of Appeals that suggest that a party seeking to avoid enforcement of an EEOC administrative subpoena must show that compliance would interfere with its normal business operations. *See* Appellant's Br. 43–44 (citing *EEOC v. Bay Shipbuilding Corp.*, 668 F.2d 304, 313 (7th Cir. 1981); *EEOC v. Citicorp Diners Club, Inc.*, 985 F.2d 1036, 1040 (10th Cir.1993); *EEOC v. Randstad*, 685 F.3d 433, 452 (4th Cir. 2012)). According to the EEOC, RCCL has not even attempted to show that devoting five to seven employees for two months would disrupt its normal business operations when RCCL employs over 50,000 people and is a multi-billion dollar business.

We reject such a rigid rule in the burdensomeness analysis. The court in *Packard* stated that a district court is authorized to "weigh such equitable criteria as reasonableness and oppressiveness" and that "this rubric impl[ies] a balancing of hardships and benefits." 569 F.2d at 318. The use of [—12—] "such . . . criteria" and the plural of "hardship" and "benefit" clearly indicates that a district court may consider a number of factors in this analysis, rather than requiring specific types of evidence on a single factor. *See also United Air Lines*, 287 F.3d at 653 (noting that cases such as *Bay Shipbuilding* have suggested a party must show that compliance would threaten normal business operations but explaining "that scenario is more illustrative than categorical" and "[w]hat is unduly burdensome depends on the particular facts of each case and no hard and fast rule can be applied to resolve the question" (internal quotation marks omitted)); *EEOC v. Ford Motor Credit Co.*, 26 F.3d 44, 47 (6th Cir. 1994) ("Essentially, this court's task is to weigh the likely relevance of the requested material to the investigation against the burden to Ford of producing the material.").

We conclude that the district court's weighing of the burden to RCCL, which certainly was not trivial, and the likely irrelevance of the information to Mr. Morabito's charge was not an abuse of discretion, especially in the light of the jurisdictional issues raised by RCCL.[5] [—13—]

CONCLUSION

For the foregoing reasons, the district court's denial of the EEOC's application to enforce the administrative subpoena is

AFFIRMED.

---

[5] We decline the EEOC's invitation to modify the scope of the subpoena. First, the possibility of modification was not presented to the district court in the objections to the magistrate judge's report and recommendation. Additionally, under the EEOC's proposed modification, RCCL would still be required to supply information regarding all applicants who were denied employment because of a medical condiction and all terminated employees who had worked on ships that entered U.S. waters. It is unclear how much this modification would reduce the burden on RCCL in reviewing the documents necessary to compile that information, and the relevancy and jurisdictional issues described above remain.

United States Court of Appeals
for the Eleventh Circuit

No. 13-13067

FRANZA
vs.
ROYAL CARIBBEAN CRUISES, LTD.

Appeal from the United States District Court for the
Southern District of Florida

Decided: November 10, 2014

Citation: 772 F.3d 1225, 2 Adm. R. 582 (11ᵗʰ Cir. 2014).

Before **MARCUS** and **ANDERSON**, Circuit Judges, and
GOLDBERG,* Judge.

* Honorable Richard W. Goldberg, United States
Court of International Trade Judge, sitting by
designation.

[—2—] MARCUS, Circuit Judge:

In this maritime negligence dispute, an elderly cruise ship passenger fell and bashed his head while the vessel, the "Explorer of the Seas," was docked at port in Bermuda. The injured traveler, Pasquale Vaglio, was wheeled back onto the ship, where he sought treatment from the onboard medical staff in the ship's designated medical center. Over the next few hours, Vaglio allegedly received such negligent medical attention that his life could not be saved. In particular, the ship's nurse purportedly failed to assess his cranial trauma, neglected to conduct any diagnostic scans, and released him with no treatment to speak of. The onboard doctor, for his part, failed even to meet with Vaglio for nearly four hours. Tragically, Vaglio died about a week later. Now, Vaglio's daughter, appellant Patricia Franza, seeks to hold the cruise line, Royal Caribbean Cruises, Ltd. ("Royal Caribbean"), vicariously liable for the purported negligence of two of its employees, the ship's doctor and its nurse, under one of two theories: actual agency (also termed respondeat superior) or apparent agency.

Franza commenced this suit against Royal Caribbean in the United States District Court for the Southern District of Florida under 28 U.S.C. § 1333 and the general maritime law, but the district court dismissed her complaint in its entirety. First, in disposing of Franza's actual agency claim, the trial court applied a longstanding rule set forth most prominently in *Barbetta v. S/S Bermuda Star*, 848 [—3—] F.2d 1364 (5th Cir. 1988). Although the general maritime law of the United States has long embraced the principles of agency law, the so-called *"Barbetta* rule" immunizes a shipowner from respondeat superior liability whenever a ship's employees render negligent medical care to its passengers. The rule confers this broad immunity no matter how clear the shipowner's control over its medical staff or how egregious the claimed acts of negligence. Separately, the trial court dismissed Franza's apparent agency claim as inadequately pled.

On appeal, Franza raises two questions of first impression. No binding precedent in this Court or in its predecessor, the former Fifth Circuit Court of Appeals, decided whether a passenger might invoke the principles of actual agency, or those of apparent agency, to impute to a cruise line liability for the medical negligence of its onboard nurse and doctor. After thorough review, we hold that both theories are available in this case. We have repeatedly emphasized that vicarious liability raises fact-bound questions, and we can discern no sound reason in law to carve out a special exemption for all acts of onboard medical negligence. Much has changed in the quarter-century since *Barbetta*. As we see it, the evolution of legal norms, the rise of a complex cruise industry, and the progression of modern technology have erased whatever utility the *Barbetta* rule once may have had. We thus decline to adopt the *Barbetta* rule, and find that the complaint in this case plausibly establishes a claim against Royal Caribbean under [—4—] the doctrine of actual agency, as well as a claim under the principles of apparent agency. Accordingly, we reverse and remand for further proceedings consistent with this opinion.

I.

When we review a dismissal granted under Federal Rule of Civil Procedure 12(b)(6) for failure to state a claim, we accept the well-pled allegations in the complaint and construe

specific types of evidence on a single factor. *See also United Air Lines*, 287 F.3d at 653 (noting that cases such as *Bay Shipbuilding* have suggested a party must show that compliance would threaten normal business operations but explaining "that scenario is more illustrative than categorical" and "[w]hat is unduly burdensome depends on the particular facts of each case and no hard and fast rule can be applied to resolve the question" (internal quotation marks omitted)); *EEOC v. Ford Motor Credit Co.*, 26 F.3d 44, 47 (6th Cir. 1994) ("Essentially, this court's task is to weigh the likely relevance of the requested material to the investigation against the burden to Ford of producing the material.").

We conclude that the district court's weighing of the burden to RCCL, which certainly was not trivial, and the likely irrelevance of the information to Mr. Morabito's charge was not an abuse of discretion, especially in the light of the jurisdictional issues raised by RCCL.[5] [—13—]

CONCLUSION

For the foregoing reasons, the district court's denial of the EEOC's application to enforce the administrative subpoena is

AFFIRMED.

---

[5] We decline the EEOC's invitation to modify the scope of the subpoena. First, the possibility of modification was not presented to the district court in the objections to the magistrate judge's report and recommendation. Additionally, under the EEOC's proposed modification, RCCL would still be required to supply information regarding all applicants who were denied employment because of a medical condiction and all terminated employees who had worked on ships that entered U.S. waters. It is unclear how much this modification would reduce the burden on RCCL in reviewing the documents necessary to compile that information, and the relevancy and jurisdictional issues described above remain.

United States Court of Appeals
for the Eleventh Circuit

No. 13-13067

FRANZA
vs.
ROYAL CARIBBEAN CRUISES, LTD.

Appeal from the United States District Court for the
Southern District of Florida

Decided: November 10, 2014

Citation: 772 F.3d 1225, 2 Adm. R. 582 (11ᵗʰ Cir. 2014).

Before **MARCUS** and **ANDERSON,** Circuit Judges, and
GOLDBERG,* Judge.

* Honorable Richard W. Goldberg, United States
Court of International Trade Judge, sitting by
designation.

[—2—] **MARCUS,** Circuit Judge:

In this maritime negligence dispute, an elderly cruise ship passenger fell and bashed his head while the vessel, the "Explorer of the Seas," was docked at port in Bermuda. The injured traveler, Pasquale Vaglio, was wheeled back onto the ship, where he sought treatment from the onboard medical staff in the ship's designated medical center. Over the next few hours, Vaglio allegedly received such negligent medical attention that his life could not be saved. In particular, the ship's nurse purportedly failed to assess his cranial trauma, neglected to conduct any diagnostic scans, and released him with no treatment to speak of. The onboard doctor, for his part, failed even to meet with Vaglio for nearly four hours. Tragically, Vaglio died about a week later. Now, Vaglio's daughter, appellant Patricia Franza, seeks to hold the cruise line, Royal Caribbean Cruises, Ltd. ("Royal Caribbean"), vicariously liable for the purported negligence of two of its employees, the ship's doctor and its nurse, under one of two theories: actual agency (also termed respondeat superior) or apparent agency.

Franza commenced this suit against Royal Caribbean in the United States District Court for the Southern District of Florida under 28 U.S.C. § 1333 and the general maritime law, but the district court dismissed her complaint in its entirety. First, in disposing of Franza's actual agency claim, the trial court applied a longstanding rule set forth most prominently in *Barbetta v. S/S Bermuda Star,* 848 [—3—] F.2d 1364 (5th Cir. 1988). Although the general maritime law of the United States has long embraced the principles of agency law, the so-called "*Barbetta* rule" immunizes a shipowner from respondeat superior liability whenever a ship's employees render negligent medical care to its passengers. The rule confers this broad immunity no matter how clear the shipowner's control over its medical staff or how egregious the claimed acts of negligence. Separately, the trial court dismissed Franza's apparent agency claim as inadequately pled.

On appeal, Franza raises two questions of first impression. No binding precedent in this Court or in its predecessor, the former Fifth Circuit Court of Appeals, decided whether a passenger might invoke the principles of actual agency, or those of apparent agency, to impute to a cruise line liability for the medical negligence of its onboard nurse and doctor. After thorough review, we hold that both theories are available in this case. We have repeatedly emphasized that vicarious liability raises fact-bound questions, and we can discern no sound reason in law to carve out a special exemption for all acts of onboard medical negligence. Much has changed in the quarter-century since *Barbetta.* As we see it, the evolution of legal norms, the rise of a complex cruise industry, and the progression of modern technology have erased whatever utility the *Barbetta* rule once may have had. We thus decline to adopt the *Barbetta* rule, and find that the complaint in this case plausibly establishes a claim against Royal Caribbean under [—4—] the doctrine of actual agency, as well as a claim under the principles of apparent agency. Accordingly, we reverse and remand for further proceedings consistent with this opinion.

I.

When we review a dismissal granted under Federal Rule of Civil Procedure 12(b)(6) for failure to state a claim, we accept the well-pled allegations in the complaint and construe them in the light most favorable to the plaintiff. *Chaparro v. Carnival Corp.*, 693 F.3d 1333, 1335 (11th Cir. 2012) (per curiam). Viewed through this lens, the facts as pled and the procedural history are straightforward.

On July 23, 2011, Pasquale Vaglio was a passenger aboard the "Explorer of the Seas," a cruise ship owned and operated by Royal Caribbean. Compl. ¶¶ 9; 8. Together with his wife and family, *id.* ¶¶ 11, 13, Vaglio traveled with Royal Caribbean to a port-of-call in Bermuda. After the ship docked in Bermuda early in the morning, Vaglio fell while boarding a trolley "at or near the dock" and suffered a severe blow to the head. *Id.* ¶ 10. Although Vaglio "could have easily been referred ashore for . . . examination, evaluation and treatment," *id.* ¶ 44, he was instead "taken in a wheelchair to the ship's infirmary," *id.* ¶ 11. In fact, notwithstanding other treatment options, Vaglio allegedly "was *required* to go to the ship's medical center to be seen for his injuries." *Id.* ¶ 35 (emphasis added). [—5—]

Vaglio first entered the ship's infirmary at about 10:00 a.m. *Id.* ¶ 11. No physician examined him at that time; rather, Racquel Y. Garcia, a nurse allegedly employed full-time by Royal Caribbean, performed the first relevant medical evaluation. *Id.* Nurse Garcia knew about the trolley accident, and indeed she observed a lump and an abrasion on Vaglio's head. *Id.* Nevertheless, without administering or even recommending any diagnostic scans, Nurse Garcia advised Vaglio and his wife that Vaglio "was fine to return to his cabin." *Id.* ¶ 11. Cautioning only "that [Vaglio] might have a concussion," the nurse instructed Vaglio's wife to keep an eye on her husband's condition. *Id.* Vaglio received no "further care or treatment" during this first visit to the ship's infirmary. *Id.* Instead, "relying on the advice of the ship's medical personnel," the Vaglios returned to their cabin at around 10:45 a.m. *Id.* ¶ 12.

Ninety minutes later, at about 12:15 p.m., Vaglio's son and daughter-in-law "noted a deterioration in [Vaglio's] status." *Id.* ¶ 13. Concerned, his daughter-in-law called 911,

but it took approximately twenty minutes for "someone [to] arrive[ ] with a wheelchair to transport Mr. Vaglio to the infirmary." *Id.* According to the complaint, Vaglio then encountered another delay: the onboard medical staff would not examine Vaglio until the ship's personnel obtained credit card information. *Id.* ¶ 14. [—6—]

At about 1:45 p.m., nearly four hours after his first visit to the ship's infirmary, Vaglio was finally evaluated by the "ship's physician," Dr. Rogelio Gonzales. *Id.* ¶¶ 7, 15. Like Nurse Garcia, Dr. Gonzales was allegedly an employee of Royal Caribbean. *Id.* ¶ 7. During his examination, Dr. Gonzales started a Mannitol drip and ordered that Vaglio be transferred to King Edward Memorial Hospital in Bermuda "for further care and treatment." *Id.* ¶ 15. Vaglio arrived at the Bermudian hospital at approximately 4:22 p.m., about two-and-a-half hours after his only meeting with Dr. Gonzales, and more than six hours after he was first examined by Nurse Garcia. *Id.* ¶ 16. By that time, Vaglio's life was beyond saving. Id. On July 24, 2011, the day after his deadly fall, Vaglio was airlifted to Winthrop-University Hospital in Mineola, New York. *Id.* ¶ 17. There he remained in intensive care until he died one week later.

On January 10, 2013, Patricia Franza, Vaglio's daughter and the personal representative of his estate, initiated this suit under 28 U.S.C. § 1333 and the general maritime laws of the United States.[1] Notably, Franza did not attempt to sue any of the relevant medical personnel directly. Instead, she filed a three-count complaint solely against Royal Caribbean, and she continues to press two of her [—7—] three claims on appeal.[2] Both remaining counts charge Royal

---

[1] In relevant part, 28 U.S.C. § 1333 provides: "The district courts shall have original jurisdiction, exclusive of the courts of the States, of . . . [a]ny civil case of admiralty or maritime jurisdiction, saving to suitors in all cases all other remedies to which they are otherwise entitled."

[2] Franza's complaint contained one count of "negligent hiring, retention[,] and training by [Royal Caribbean]." Compl. ¶¶ 41-46. On appeal, however, Franza has specifically abandoned that claim.

Caribbean with the negligence of its onboard medical personnel, and both counts arise from the same nine categories of allegedly negligent conduct: (1) "failing to properly assess [Vaglio's] condition"; (2) "allowing a nurse to make the initial assessment"; (3) "failing to have a doctor assess [Vaglio]"; (4) "failing to timely diagnose and appropriately treat [Vaglio]"; (5) "failing to order appropriate diagnostic scans to further assess the degree of injury"; (6) "failing to obtain consultations with appropriate specialists"; (7) "failing to properly monitor [Vaglio]"; (8) "failing to evacuate [Vaglio] from the vessel for further care in a timely manner"; and (9) "deviating from the standard of care for patients in Mr. Vaglio's circumstances who had suffered a significant blow to the head." *Id.* ¶ 20.

Franza ascribed this misconduct to Royal Caribbean in two ways. First, Franza invoked the doctrine of actual agency, alleging that Royal Caribbean was negligent "by and through the acts of its employees or agents." *Id.* In the alternative, she argued that Royal Caribbean was liable "under the theory of apparent agency," *id.* ¶ 40, because the cruise line purportedly "manifested to [Vaglio] . . . that its medical staff . . . were acting as its employees and/or actual agents," *id.* ¶ 28, and Vaglio, in turn, "relied to his detriment on his belief that the [—8—] physician and nurse were direct employees or actual agents of [Royal Caribbean]." *Id.* ¶ 38.

On May 30, 2013, the district court granted Royal Caribbean's motion to dismiss. *Franza v. Royal Caribbean Cruises, Ltd.*, 948 F. Supp 2d 1327 (S.D. Fla. 2013). The trial court addressed Franza's actual agency claim separately from the one based on apparent agency. The court dismissed the actual agency count as a matter of law and with prejudice. Specifically, the district court applied the *Barbetta* rule to conclude that Franza's actual agency claim was "predicated on duties of care which are not recognized under maritime law." *Id.* at 1331. Next, although acknowledging that some courts had applied the doctrine of apparent agency in similar cases, the district court dismissed Franza's apparent agency claim as inadequately pled. In particular, the trial court determined that

Franza had not plausibly claimed that Vaglio ever relied on the appearance of an agency relationship. *Id.* at 1332-33.[3] Following the holding in *Barbetta*, the district court had no occasion to address whether Franza had sufficiently alleged the fact of negligence, and did not consider whether Franza had plausibly pled the requisite indicia of control that might have justified imputing liability to Royal Caribbean for its employees' wrongful acts. Franza timely appealed.

II. [—9—]

We review *de novo* the district court's dismissal for failure to state a claim under Rule 12(b)(6), examining Franza's allegations in the light most favorable to the plaintiff. *Hill v. White*, 321 F.3d 1334, 1335 (11th Cir. 2003) (per curiam). "To survive a motion to dismiss, a complaint must contain sufficient factual matter, accepted as true, to 'state a claim to relief that is plausible on its face.'" *Ashcroft v. Iqbal*, 556 U.S. 662, 678, 129 S. Ct. 1937, 1949 (2009) (quoting *Bell Atlantic Corp. v. Twombly*, 550 U.S. 544, 570, 127 S. Ct. 1955, 1974 (2007)). This standard is met "where the facts alleged enable 'the court to draw the reasonable inference that the defendant is liable for the misconduct alleged.'" *Simpson v. Sanderson Farms, Inc.*, 744 F.3d 702, 708 (11th Cir. 2014) (quoting *Iqbal*, 556 U.S. at 678, 129 S. Ct. at 1949). Put differently, "[i]t is sufficient if the complaint succeeds in 'identifying facts that are suggestive enough to render [each required element] plausible.'" *Rivell v. Private Health Care Sys., Inc.*, 520 F.3d 1308, 1310 (11th Cir. 2008) (per curiam) (quoting *Watts v. Fla. Int'l Univ.*, 495 F.3d 1289, 1296 (11th Cir. 2007)).

III.

On appeal, Franza first challenges the dismissal of her actual agency claim. Neither the Supreme Court nor this Court has ever decided, in binding precedent, whether a passenger may hold a shipowner vicariously liable for the medical negligence of the ship's employees. In *De Zon v. American President*

---

[3] Though the district court gave Franza leave to amend her allegations of apparent agency, Franza elected not to do so.

Lines, Ltd., [—10—] the Supreme Court held that a "shipowner was liable in damages for harm suffered as the result of any negligence on the part of the ship's doctor." 318 U.S. 660, 669, 63 S. Ct. 814, 819 (1943). However, the *De Zon* Court cabined this holding to apply only where a ship's doctor breached a shipowner's special duty to a seaman—not a passenger—under the Jones Act. *See id.* at 668 (declining to consider question of liability "in the absence of the Jones Act").[4] Separately, pursuant to repealed Eleventh Circuit Rule 36-1, this Court once affirmed without opinion a dismissal order resembling the order at issue here. *See Nanz v. Costa Cruises, Inc.,* 932 F.2d 977 (11th Cir. 1991) (Table). We are not bound, however, by a table disposition. *See, e.g., U.S. Steel, LLC, v. Tieco, Inc.,* 261 F.3d 1275, 1280 n.3 (11th Cir. 2001) ("An affirmance pursuant to Rule 36-1 has no precedential value.").

A.

We begin with these basic principles. Federal admiralty jurisdiction flows from the Constitution itself, *see* U.S. Const. art. III, § 2 ("The judicial Power shall extend . . . to all Cases of admiralty and maritime Jurisdiction . . . ."), and "[w]ith admiralty jurisdiction comes the application of substantive admiralty law." *E.* [—11—] *River S.S. Corp. v. Transamerica Delaval Inc.,* 476 U.S. 858, 864, 106 S. Ct. 2295, 2298-99 (1986). "Absent a relevant statute, the general maritime law, as developed by the judiciary, applies." *Id.* at 2299. Indeed, the Supreme Court has repeatedly explained in maritime suits that the "Judiciary has traditionally taken the lead in formulating flexible and fair remedies in the law maritime, and 'Congress ha[s] largely

left to [the Supreme] Court the responsibility for fashioning the controlling rules of admiralty law." *United States v. Reliable Transfer Co.,* 421 U.S. 397, 409, 95 S. Ct. 1708, 1715 (1975) (quoting *Fitzgerald v. U.S. Lines Co.,* 374 U.S. 16, 20, 83 S. Ct. 1646, 1650 (1963)); *see Moragne v. States Marine Lines, Inc.,* 398 U.S. 375, 405 n.17, 90 S. Ct. 1772, 1790 (1970) (noting that courts are not barred from announcing maritime rules simply because Congress has "not legislat[ed] on [the] subject"); *Romero v. Int'l Terminal Operating Co.,* 358 U.S. 354, 361, 79 S. Ct. 468, 474 (1959) (explaining that courts are best equipped "to draw on the substantive law 'inherent in the admiralty and maritime jurisdiction'" (quoting *Crowell v. Benson,* 285 U.S. 22, 55, 52 S. Ct. 285, 294 (1932))); *see also* 1 Benedict on Admiralty, Ch. VII, § 110 (2014) (stating that Congress's maritime authority "is impliedly inherent in or derived from the grant of the judicial power").

The Supreme Court has likewise authorized and directed the lower federal courts to shape this law, explaining that the Constitution "empowered the federal [—12—] courts," including "the Tribunals inferior to the Supreme Court," to "develop[ ]" the general maritime law. *Romero,* 358 U.S. at 360-61, 79 S. Ct. at 474 (internal quotation marks omitted); *see, e.g., Transamerica,* 476 U.S. at 865, 106 S. Ct. at 2299 (endorsing maritime theory of products liability first adopted by several circuits); *see also Exxon Shipping Co. v. Baker,* 554 U.S. 471, 508 n.21, 128 S. Ct. 2605, 2630 (2008) (observing that "modern-day maritime cases . . . support judicial action to modify a common law landscape largely of [the courts'] own making"); *Edmonds v. Compagnie Generale Transatlantique,* 443 U.S. 256, 259, 99 S. Ct. 2753, 2756 (1979) ("Admiralty law is judge-made law to a great extent . . . ."). In short, we enjoy considerable latitude in maritime cases because, under the constitutional grant, the "[b]oundaries" of maritime law generally "were to be determined in the exercise of the judicial power." *The Thomas Barlum,* 293 U.S. 21, 43, 55 S. Ct. 31, 38 (1934).

Congress has not imposed vicarious liability where, as here, a passenger seeks

---

[4] Although *De Zon*'s holding clearly applies only to cases involving injuries to seamen, arising under the Jones Act, Royal Caribbean suggests the Supreme Court implicitly approved the principles elaborated in *Barbetta,* since the Court observed that the rule barring suits by passengers had been developed by "judges of great learning, for courts of last resort of states having much to do with maritime pursuits." *De Zon v. Am. Pres. Lines,* 318 U.S. 660, 666 n.2, 63 S. Ct. 814, 818 (1943). This dicta in no way expressed any view about the wisdom or efficacy of the *Barbetta* rule.

recovery from a shipowner for the medical negligence of the ship's employees.[5] Nor has Congress barred the application of vicarious liability in this [—13—] context.[6] Thus, in addressing Franza's claims, we are obliged to exercise our broad discretion in admiralty and maritime to develop this law, just as the Fifth Circuit did in *Barbetta*.

Under the general maritime law, a shipowner traditionally has owed no duty to practice medicine or to carry a physician on board. *See De Zon*, 318 U.S. at 668, 63 S. Ct. at 819 (acknowledging that "there may be no duty to the seaman to carry a physician").[7]

---

[5] In 1882, Congress passed legislation requiring certain passenger ships to carry medical personnel and to furnish "surgical instruments, medical comforts, and medicines proper and necessary for diseases and accidents incident to sea-voyages, and for the proper medical treatment of such passengers during the voyage." Pub. L. No. 47-374, § 5, 22 Stat. 188 (1882) (codified at 46 U.S.C. § 155 (1982)). "[T]he services of such surgeon or medical practitioner [were required to] be promptly given, in any case of sickness or disease, to any of the passengers . . . who . . . need[ed] his services." *Id.* The "master of the vessel" was liable for any [—13—] violation of this statute. *Id.* However, Congress repealed this act in 1983, *see* Pub. L. No. 98-89, § 4(b), 97 Stat. 600 (1983), without ever enacting substitute legislation.

[6] In a few areas of maritime law, Congress has specifically limited the application of agency principles. *See, e.g.*, 33 U.S.C. § 905(b) (2012) (forbidding third-party suits against shipowners under Longshore and Harbor Workers' Compensation Act where injured person was "employed by the vessel to provide stevedoring services" and "the injury was caused by the negligence of persons engaged in providing stevedoring services to the vessel"); *Hurst v. Triad Shipping Co.*, 554 F.2d 1237 (3d Cir. 1977) (tracing Congress's policy rationale for § 905(b) exception); 46 U.S.C. § 30505(b) (2012) (capping certain maritime liability where shipowner lacks "privity or knowledge"); *Paradise Divers, Inc. v. Upmal*, 402 F.3d 1087, 1089-90 (11th Cir. 2005) (per curiam) (explaining Congress's policy rationale for § 30505 limitation). As we have observed, however, no such legislation protects a maritime principal from all vicarious liability in a case like this one.

[7] Franza suggests, however, that new laws now require cruise ships to carry medical personnel. She points specifically to one statute, 46 U.S.C. § 3507 (2012), which mandates that cruise ships provide

---

Therefore, the shipowner is only liable to its passengers for medical negligence if its conduct breaches the carrier's more general duty to [—14—] exercise "reasonable care under the circumstances." *Kermarec v. Compagnie Generale Transatlantique*, 358 U.S. 625, 632, 79 S. Ct. 406, 410 (1959). Franza does not argue that Royal Caribbean violated this duty directly. Rather, she asks us to hold Royal Caribbean vicariously liable under the doctrine of respondeat superior, precisely because the ship's medical employees allegedly failed to treat her father with appropriate care.

Though we have never examined whether the principles of vicarious liability apply to a passenger's claim for onboard medical negligence, the federal courts have been especially active in the general area of maritime torts. *See Exxon*, 554 U.S. at 508 n.21, 128 S. Ct. at 2630 (highlighting "the large part [that courts] have taken in working out the governing maritime tort principles"). In maritime tort cases, the federal courts often have: (1) adopted new theories of tort liability, *see, e.g.*, *Transamerica*, 476 U.S. at 865, 106 S. Ct. at 2299 ("join[ing] [several circuits] in recognizing products liability, including strict liability, as part of the general maritime law"); (2) introduced new causes of action, *see, e.g.*, *Am. Export Lines, Inc. v. Alvez*, 446 U.S. 274, 284-86, 100 S. Ct. 1673, 1679-80 (1980) (recognizing claim for loss of consortium under general maritime law), and *Moragne*, 398 U.S. 375, 90 S. Ct. 1772 (recognizing cause of

---

"medical staff" who possess either a "current physician's or registered nurse's license" to render "medical treatment" to victims of sexual assault. *Id.* § 3507(d). We do not read this codification as creating a broad based obligation that ships carry medical personnel onboard in order to meet the general health needs of their passengers. Franza also argues that many cruise ships are flagged in the Bahamas, where cruise ships must carry a "duly qualified medical practitioner." *See* Bahamian Merchant Shipping Act § 124. But Franza's complaint alleges that Royal Caribbean is a Liberian corporation, Compl. ¶ 5, and does not specify where the "Explorer of the Seas" is flagged. Nor, finally, is it otherwise clear what impact a Bahamian statute would have on a cruise ship's obligations arising under the general maritime law of the United States.

action for wrongful death under general maritime law); and (3) promulgated new remedial rules, *see, e.g., McDermott, Inc. v. AmClyde*, 511 U.S. 202, 114 S. Ct. 1461 (1994) (adopting proportionate-fault [—15—] rule for calculation of nonsettling maritime tort defendants' compensatory liability).

Moreover, across well over a century of maritime tort precedent, the Supreme Court has required maritime principals to answer for the negligence of their onboard agents. *See, e.g., The Kensington*, 183 U.S. 263, 268, 22 S. Ct. 102, 104 (1902) (characterizing as "unjust and unreasonable" any attempt by carriers to contract around "responsibility for the negligence of . . . their servants"); *The J.P. Donaldson*, 167 U.S. 599, 603, 17 S. Ct. 951, 953 (1897) (holding shipowner "responsible for injuries caused to third persons by [the] negligence" of ship's captain). These teachings now permeate the general maritime law. *See, e.g., Langfitt v. Fed. Marine Terminals, Inc.*, 647 F.3d 1116, 1121 (11th Cir. 2011) ("[A]n otherwise non-faulty employer [is] vicariously liable for the negligent acts of its employee acting within the scope of employment."); *Archer v. Trans/American Servs., Ltd.*, 834 F.2d 1570, 1573 (11th Cir. 1988) ("Federal maritime law embraces the principles of agency.").

That maritime law has long incorporated the concept of respondeat superior should come as no surprise. Shipowners, like other principals, exercise real control over their agents. *See, e.g., Barrios v. La. Const. Materials Co.*, 465 F.2d 1157, 1164 (5th Cir. 1972) (detailing maritime principal's "control over the operations [—16—] which resulted in the injury to [plaintiff]").[8] In maritime cases, as elsewhere, we therefore think it "manifestly just" to hold principals responsible for the conduct they command from their employees. *Sony Corp. of Am. v. Universal City Studios, Inc.*, 464 U.S. 417, 437, 104 S. Ct. 774, 786 (1984); *see* Restatement (Second) of Agency § 219 cmt. a ("[F]rom [the acknowledgment of a principal's right of control], the idea of

responsibility for the harm done by the servant's activities follow[s] naturally.").

Thus, we have regularly permitted *passengers* to invoke respondeat superior in maritime negligence suits.[9] In *Suzuki of Orange Park, Inc. v. Shubert*, for example, a passenger in a watercraft was struck by another recreational vessel on a slalom course. 86 F.3d 1060, 1061-62 (11th Cir. 1996). In addressing the question of liability, we observed that the corporate owner of the watercraft could be "vicariously liable under principles of respondeat superior" if the passenger's injury were negligently inflicted by a driver "acting on [the owner's] behalf." *Id.* at 1066 & n.5 (emphasis omitted). In *Gibboney v. Wright*, two minor passengers [—17—] aboard a borrowed racing sloop were injured in a flash fire caused by an improperly secured fuel tank. 517 F.2d 1054, 1055-56 (5th Cir. 1975). There, the former Fifth Circuit discerned "ample basis under familiar maritime principles to impute [the] negligence [of both the vessel's manufacturer and a marine surveyor] to [the shipowner,] so far as liability [for injury to the passengers] [was] concerned." *Id.* at 1059. And in *Ramjak v. Austro-American S.S. Co.*, the former Fifth Circuit found a shipowner vicariously liable where a seaman—"in a spirit of ostentation and bravado"—negligently climbed the ship's mast and fell onto a passenger. 186 F. 417, 418 (5th Cir. 1911); *see also Doe v. Celebrity Cruises, Inc.*, 394 F.3d 891, 908, 913 (11th Cir. 2004) (citing Restatement (Second) of Agency and holding cruise line strictly liable for crew member assaults on passengers). Quite simply, our precedent has long allowed passengers to invoke the doctrine of respon-

---

[8] In *Bonner v. City of Prichard*, 661 F.2d 1206, 1209 (11th Cir. 1981) (en banc), we adopted as binding precedent all Fifth Circuit decisions issued before October 1, 1981.

[9] Additionally, our admiralty precedent is rife with cases holding principals vicariously liable under respondeat superior for injuries negligently inflicted *by* agents *to* agents. *See, e.g., In re Dearborn Marine Serv., Inc.*, 499 F.2d 263, 284-86 (5th Cir. 1974); *Barrios*, 465 F.2d at 1164; *Tri-State Oil Tool Indus., Inc. v. Delta Marine Drilling Co.*, 410 F.2d 178, 187 (5th Cir. 1969). Because liability is sometimes complicated by statutory concerns in this related context, however, we separately collect these cases only to demonstrate the broad salience of respondeat superior in our admiralty precedent.

deat superior in a diverse medley of maritime tort disputes.

We do not stand alone in this. Our sister circuits, too, have generally applied agency principles to impute liability in maritime tort cases. *See Matheny v. Tenn. Valley Auth.*, 557 F.3d 311, 315 (6th Cir. 2009) (accepting concession that tugboat owner was liable for third-party death caused by tugboat captain's negligence); *CEH, Inc. v. F/V Seafarer*, 70 F.3d 694, 705 (1st Cir. 1995) (holding shipowner "vicarious[ly] liabl[e]" where captain was shipowner's "agent" who sabotaged third-party lobstering operation); *McDonough v. Royal Caribbean Cruises, Ltd.*, 48 [—18—] F.3d 256, 258 (7th Cir. 1995) (holding cruise line vicariously liable where steward pushed dolly over passenger's foot); *Jackson Marine Corp. v. Blue Fox*, 845 F.2d 1307, 1310 (5th Cir. 1988) (applying "general agency principles" to impute captain's fraud on third-party to shipowner); *De Los Santos v. Scindia Steam Navigation Co. Ltd.*, 598 F.2d 480, 489 (9th Cir. 1979) (explaining that shipowner could incur liability under respondeat superior if crewmembers knew of allegedly defective condition that injured plaintiff); *Pritchett v. Kimberling Cove, Inc.*, 568 F.2d 570, 579 (8th Cir. 1977) (holding boat owner "vicariously" liable where owner's "agent" negligently entrusted boat to minor who injured passengers in second boat); *Ira S. Bushey & Sons, Inc. v. United States*, 398 F.2d 167, 171-72 (2d Cir. 1968) (holding United States vicariously liable to third-party dry-dock owner after Coast Guardsman negligently caused dry-dock to sink); *see also Landstar Express Am., Inc. v. Fed. Mar. Comm'n*, 569 F.3d 493, 498 (D.C. Cir. 2009) (using "common law agency principles" to interpret Shipping Act of 1984); *Servis v. Hiller Sys. Inc.*, 54 F.3d 203, 207 (4th Cir. 1995) (interpreting Suits in Admiralty Act in light of "basic principles of agency law" and Restatement (Second) of Agency); *Peter v. Hess Oil Virgin Islands Corp.*, 903 F.2d 935, 940 (3d Cir. 1990) (construing Longshore and Harbor Workers' Compensation Act to incorporate "borrowed servant doctrine"); *Bartlett-Collins Co. v. Surinam* [—19—] *Navigation Co.*, 381 F.2d 546, 550 (10th Cir. 1967) (commenting in admiralty case that "existence of an agency is a question to be decided by the trier of the fact").

Thus, even absent any statutory mandate, the Supreme Court and all of the federal circuits have for many years generally applied agency rules across a rich array of maritime cases. Against this dynamic backdrop, Franza makes only a modest request. We can see nothing inherent in onboard medical negligence, when committed by full-time employees acting within the course and scope of their employment, that justifies suspending the accepted principles of agency. Certainly, nothing in our case law creates—or even suggests—a bright-line zone of immunity for the onboard negligence of a cruise ship's medical employees.

We acknowledge, however, that other circuits have long barred vicarious liability in this particular context. *See Barbetta*, 848 F.2d at 1372 ("[G]eneral maritime law does not impose liability under the doctrine of respondeat superior upon a carrier or ship owner for the negligence of a ship's doctor who treats the ship's passengers."); *accord The Great Northern*, 251 F. 826, 832 (9th Cir. 1918); *The Korea Maru*, 254 F. 397, 399 (9th Cir. 1918); *cf. Cummiskey v. Chandris, S.A.*, 895 F.2d 107, 108 (2d Cir. 1990) (per curiam) (citing *Barbetta* and "declin[ing] the invitation to break with maritime precedent" "on the facts before [the court]").[10] In effect, these cases stand for the sweeping proposition that no [—20—] conceivable set of facts could *ever* justify holding a shipowner vicariously liable when a passenger receives negligent medical care aboard its ship. We remain unpersuaded.

Instead, we think it more accurate to say that, absent any statutory mandate to the contrary, the existence of an agency relationship is a question of fact under the

---

[10] Several district courts within this Circuit have extended this principle to protect carriers from [—20—] liability for the actions of ships' nurses, as well as their doctors. *See, e.g., Hajtman v. NCL (Bahamas) Ltd.*, 526 F. Supp. 2d 1324, 1327-28 (S.D. Fla. 2007); *Jackson v. Carnival Cruise Lines, Inc.*, 203 F. Supp. 2d 1367, 1374-76 (S.D. Fla. 2002); *Stires v. Carnival Corp.*, 243 F. Supp. 2d 1313, 1318 (M.D. Fla. 2002).

general maritime law. *See Naviera Neptuno S.A. v. All Int'l Freight Forwarders, Inc.*, 709 F.2d 663, 665 (11th Cir. 1983) ("[T]he existence of an agency relationship is a question of fact."); *accord Garanti Finansal Kiralama A.S. v. Aqua Marine & Trading Inc.*, 697 F.3d 59, 71 (2d Cir. 2012) (same); *Hawkspere Shipping Co., Ltd. v. Intamex, S.A.*, 330 F.3d 225, 236 (4th Cir. 2003) (observing that existence of agency relationship presents "triable issue of fact"); *Chan v. Soc'y Expeditions, Inc.*, 39 F.3d 1398, 1406 (9th Cir. 1994) (noting that existence of agency relationship "is a question of fact"); *Equilease Corp. v. M/V Sampson*, 756 F.2d 357, 363 (5th Cir. 1985) ("The existence of *any* agency relationship is a question of fact . . . ." (emphasis added)); *Bartlett-Collins*, 381 F.2d at 550 ("[T]he existence of an agency is a question to be decided by the trier of the fact."). Thus, as we see it, at the pleading stage, a passenger must allege "sufficient facts to render it facially plausible that . . . an agency relationship [is] . . . present." *Bamert* [—21—] *v. Pulte Home Corp.*, 445 F. App'x 256, 265 (11th Cir. 2011) (citing *Davila v. Delta Air Lines, Inc.*, 326 F.3d 1183, 1185 (11th Cir. 2003)). In cases of medical malpractice, as in other maritime respondeat superior cases, the essential element of the relationship is the principal's control over its agents.

Plainly, under the ordinary rules of agency, the allegations in Franza's complaint support a finding that Nurse Garcia and Dr. Gonzales were agents of Royal Caribbean. According to our unambiguous precedent, an agency relationship requires: "(1) the principal to acknowledge that the agent will act for it; (2) the agent to manifest an acceptance of the undertaking; and (3) control by the principal over the actions of the agent." *Whetstone Candy Co. v. Kraft Foods, Inc.*, 351 F.3d 1067, 1077 (11th Cir. 2003). Franza adequately alleged each of these elements.

For starters, Franza's complaint plausibly established: (1) that Royal Caribbean "acknowledged" that Nurse Garcia and Dr. Gonzales would act on its behalf, and (2) that each "accepted" the undertaking. Most importantly, Franza specifically asserted that

both medical professionals were "employed by" Royal Caribbean, were "its employees or agents," and were "at all times material acting within the scope and course of [their] employment." Compl. ¶¶ 6, 7, 20. Furthermore, the cruise line directly paid the ship's nurse and doctor for their work in the ship's medical center. *Id.* ¶ 28. Third, the medical facility was created, [—22—] owned, and operated by Royal Caribbean, *id.*, whose own marketing materials described the infirmary in proprietary language, *see id.* ("[T]he doctor and nurse both worked at what [Royal Caribbean] describes in its advertising as *its* medical centers[.]" (emphasis added and internal quotation marks omitted)). Fourth, the cruise line knowingly provided, and its medical personnel knowingly wore, uniforms bearing Royal Caribbean's name and logo. *Id.* ¶ 29. And, finally, Royal Caribbean allegedly represented to immigration authorities and passengers that Nurse Garcia and Dr. Gonzales were "members of the ship's crew," *id.* ¶¶ 31, 33, and even introduced the doctor "as one of the ship's Officers," *id.* ¶ 30. Taken as true, these allegations are more than enough to satisfy the first two elements of actual agency liability.

Moreover, the facts alleged in Franza's complaint plausibly demonstrate that Royal Caribbean exercised "control" over the ship's medical personnel. *See Whetstone*, 351 F.3d at 1077. As we have explained, control is the fulcrum of respondeat superior. We have recognized the following considerations as "probative" of control in the maritime context: "(1) direct evidence of the principal's right to or actual exercise of control; (2) the method of payment for an agent's services, whether by time or by the job; (3) whether or not the equipment necessary to perform the work is furnished by the principal; and (4) whether the principal had the right to fire the agent." *Langfitt*, 647 F.3d at 1121. Franza's [—23—] complaint plausibly supports a finding of control under at least three of these four factors.

To begin with, Franza alleged substantial "direct evidence" of Royal Caribbean's "right to control" Nurse Garcia and Dr. Gonzales. *Id.* The onboard medical personnel were: (1)

"employed by" Royal Caribbean, Compl. ¶¶ 6, 7; (2) hired to work in a facility that the cruise line "owned and operated," *id.* ¶ 28; (3) paid directly by the cruise line, *id.*; (4) considered to be members of the ship's "crew," *id.* ¶ 31, 33; and (5) "required" to wear uniforms furnished by Royal Caribbean, *id.* ¶ 29. Additionally, the cruise line "put the ship's physician and nurse *under the command* of the ship's superior officers." *Id.* ¶ 32 (emphasis added). At the pleading stage, these allegations offer considerable "direct evidence" of the cruise line's "right to control" its medical staff.

Franza's specific assertions about the ship's "method of payment" bolster her claim that Royal Caribbean controlled its onboard medical personnel. *See Langfitt,* 647 F.3d at 1121. Franza alleged that Royal Caribbean paid "salaries" to the ship's medical staff. Compl. ¶ 28. This compensation structure normally suggests an agency relationship, since payment is "by time" and not "by the job." *Langfitt,* 648 F.3d at 1121; *see* Restatement (Second) of Agency § 220 cmt. h (observing that "payment by hour or month" indicates "the relation of master and servant"). Additionally, onboard passengers are allegedly "billed directly by [—24—] [Royal Caribbean] through the passengers' Sign and Sail Card." Compl. ¶ 28. Thus, the cruise line exercises complete control over any funds that might otherwise have flowed directly from the passengers to the medical professionals in consideration of treatment rendered.

Finally, Royal Caribbean allegedly "pays to stock the 'medical centers' with all supplies, various medicines and equipment," *id.* ¶ 28, which lends further support to a finding of control by the cruise line. *See Langfitt,* 648 F.3d at 1121 (finding agency more likely where "the equipment necessary to perform the work is furnished by the principal"). Franza did not specifically allege whether Royal Caribbean had the "right to fire" its onboard medical personnel, and thus her complaint does not directly address the fourth factor indicating control under *Langfitt.* Nevertheless, as we have seen, Franza did assert that Nurse Garcia and Dr. Gonzales

were "member[s] of the crew," Compl. ¶ 31, 33, who were "under the command of the ship's superior officers," *id.* ¶ 32. Presumably, the company maintains the authority to fire crewmembers. *See* Robert D. Peltz, *Has Time Passed Barbetta by?,* 24 U.S.F. Mar. L.J. 1, 31 (2012) (noting that "[t]ypical employment agreements give the cruise line the right to terminate the shipboard doctor's employment") [hereinafter Peltz, *Has Time Passed Barbetta by?*].

Royal Caribbean urges us to look beyond the complaint, to Vaglio's passenger ticket contract, which the cruise line attached to its motion to dismiss [—25—] and which purports to limit the ship's liability for onboard medical services. According to Royal Caribbean, the contract makes clear that onboard medical personnel are independent contractors, not employees or agents. At this early stage in the proceedings, however, we decline to consider the passenger ticket contract for three reasons. First, Franza did not attach the ticket contract to the complaint. Second, the complaint makes no mention of the contract. *See Bickley v. Caremark Rx, Inc.,* 461 F.3d 1325, 1329 n.7 (11th Cir. 2006) (permitting court to consider defendant's exhibits *only* if "the plaintiff refers to certain documents in the complaint and those documents are central to the plaintiff's claim" (internal quotation marks and citation omitted)); *Hoffman-Pugh v. Ramsey,* 312 F.3d 1222, 1225 (11th Cir. 2002) (same); *see also Fin. Sec. Assurance, Inc. v. Stephens, Inc.,* 500 F.3d 1276, 1284 (11th Cir. 2007) (considering materials beyond complaint and its exhibits where plaintiff referred to document in complaint, document was central to claim, contents were undisputed, and defendant attached document to motion to dismiss). Finally, even if we were to look to the contract at this stage, we would not consider the nurse and doctor to be independent contractors simply because that is what the cruise line calls them. *See, e.g., Cantor v. Cochran,* 184 So. 2d 173, 174 (Fla. 1966) ("While the obvious purpose to be accomplished by this document was to evince an independent contractor status, such status depends [—26—] not on the statements of the parties but upon all the circumstances of their dealings with each other.").[11]

On balance, then, Franza's complaint unambiguously establishes an agency relationship between the employer, Royal Caribbean Cruises, Ltd., and its full-time employees, Nurse Garcia and Dr. Gonzales. Nothing in the complaint suggests that these medical professionals somehow acted outside the scope and course of their employment or that the requisite control was missing. Thus, applying the standard principles of agency, we are compelled to hold that Franza's complaint sets out a plausible basis for imputing to Royal Caribbean the allegedly negligent conduct of its onboard medical employees.

B.

We decline to adopt the rule explicated in *Barbetta*, because we can no longer discern a sound basis in law for ignoring the facts alleged in individual medical malpractice complaints and wholly discarding the same rules of agency that we have applied so often in other maritime tort cases.[12] No decision of the [—27—] Supreme Court or this Court binds us to the strictures of *Barbetta*, and

though we do not lightly deviate from a rule applied widely and for many years by other federal courts, we are now reluctant to endorse the approach taken by the Fifth, Ninth, and Second Circuits. As Justice Holmes famously put it, we should not follow a rule of law simply because "it was laid down in the time of Henry IV," particularly where "the grounds upon which it was laid down have vanished long since, and the rule simply persists from blind imitation of the past." Oliver Wendell Holmes, *The Path of the Law*, 10 Harv. L. Rev. 457, 469 (1897).[13]

When we exercise our broad admiralty jurisdiction, "our experience and new conditions [sometimes] give rise to new conceptions of maritime concerns." *The Thomas Barlum*, 293 U.S. at 52, 55 S. Ct. at 41-42. Here, the roots of the *Barbetta* rule snake back into a wholly different world. Instead of nineteenth-century [—28—] steamships, *see, e.g., Barbetta*, 848 F.2d at 1369 (citing *O'Brien v. Cunard S.S. Co.*, 28 N.E. 266, 267 (Mass. 1891)), we now confront state-of-the-art cruise ships that house thousands of people and operate as floating cities, complete with well-stocked modern infirmaries and urgent care centers. In place of truly independent doctors and nurses, we must now acknowledge that medical professionals routinely work for corporate

---

[11] Additionally, we note that the ticket contract arguably is internally inconsistent: at one point the contract actually discusses medical personnel and independent contractors in the alternative, *see* Mot. to Dismiss Ex. A, *Franza v. Royal Caribbean Cruises, Ltd.*, 13-20090-CIV (S.D. Fla. Feb. 4, 2013), at 2 ("To the extent Passengers retain the services of medical personnel *or* Independent contractors . . . ." (emphasis added)), seemingly suggesting that medical personnel are *not* independent contractors.

[12] Several courts have already rejected or cast doubt upon the majority rule enunciated by the Fifth Circuit in *Barbetta*. *See, e.g., Huntley v. Carnival Corp.*, 307 F. Supp. 2d 1372, 1374-75 (S.D. Fla. 2004) (declining to apply majority rule); *Nietes v. Am. President Lines, Ltd.*, 188 F. [—27—] Supp. 219, 220-21 (N.D. Cal. 1959) (same); *Mack v. Royal Caribbean Cruises, Ltd.*, 838 N.E. 2d 80, 91(Ill. App. Ct. 2005) (same); *see also Lobegeiger v. Celebrity Cruises, Inc.*, 11-21620-CIV, 2011 WL 3703329 at *9 n.8 (S.D. Fla. Aug. 23, 2011) (noting weakness in majority rule); *Fairley v. Royal Cruise Line, Ltd.*, 1993 A.M.C. 1633 (S.D. Fla. 1993) (same); *Carnival Corp. v. Carlisle*, 953 So. 2d 461, 469-70 (Fla. 2007) (same).

[13] Royal Caribbean argues that we must follow *Barbetta* in order to preserve the uniformity of maritime law. *See* Appellee's Br. at 20-24. Uniformity is a powerful and motivating concern in federal admiralty jurisdiction. *See, e.g., So. Pac. Co. v. Jensen*, 244 U.S. 205, 216, 37 S. Ct. 524, 529 (1917), *superceded by statute*, 69 Pub. L. 803, 44 Stat. 1424 (1927), codified as amended at 33 U.S.C. § 901 et seq., (highlighting "the proper harmony and uniformity of" maritime law). However, the federal admiralty interest in uniformity is not a *stare decisis* command. Moreover, the Supreme Court introduced the principles of uniformity and harmony specifically to prevent undue encroachment upon national maritime law by the several states. *See, e.g., Romero*, 358 U.S. at 373, 79 S. Ct. at 480 ("[S]tate law must yield to the needs of a uniform federal maritime law when this Court finds inroads on a harmonious system."); *see also Mink v. Genmar Indus., Inc.*, 29 F.3d 1543, 1548 (11th Cir. 1994) (characterizing "federal [maritime] interest in uniformity" as "a reverse-*Erie* doctrine").

masters. And whereas ships historically went "off the grid" when they set sail, modern technology enables distant ships to communicate instantaneously with the mainland in meaningful ways. In short, despite its prominence, the *Barbetta* rule now seems to prevail more by the strength of inertia than by the strength of its reasoning. *See United States v. Reliable Transfer Co.*, 421 U.S. 397, 410, 95 S. Ct. 1708, 1715 (1975). In our view, "[t]he reasons that originally led" other courts to adopt "the rule have long since disappeared." *See id.* The rule rests on three basic arguments that a shipowner cannot exercise meaningful control over its medical staff. But as we see it, none withstands close scrutiny. We address each in turn.

1.

The first pillar is the claim that any doctor-patient (or nurse-patient) relationship, whether on land or at sea, precludes vicarious liability by its very "nature." *Barbetta*, 848 F.2d at 1369. Historically, courts have offered two separate arguments to explain why no third-party principal could ever [—29—] meaningfully control the conduct of a medical professional and, therefore, no liability could be vicariously imposed. Nowadays, however, the great majority of American common law courts have disavowed this categorical liability exception and each of the rationales that once compelled it.

a.

Traditionally, courts insulated medical professionals from vicarious liability simply because of the professionals' special skills and independent judgment. Essentially, these courts reasoned that, as a policy matter, highly trained medical practitioners would and should freely use their own best judgment. Thus, the courts decided as a matter of law that employers could not exercise control over doctors to the extent necessary to establish an agency relationship. *See, e.g., Parsons v. Yolande Coal & Coke Co.*, 91 So. 493, 495 (Ala. 1921) (barring vicarious liability because doctor "renders services requiring such training, skill, and experience, the exercise of which must be in accordance

with his best judgment and without interference"); *Schloendorff v. Soc'y of N.Y. Hosp.*, 105 N.E. 92, 94 (N.Y. 1914) (Cardozo, J.) (precluding vicarious liability because medicine was "an independent calling . . . sanctioned by a solemn oath"); *Pearl v. W. End St. Ry. Co.*, 57 N.E. 339, 339 (Mass. 1900) (Holmes, C.J.) (finding "no more distinct calling than that of the doctor, and none in which the employ[ee] is more distinctly free from the control or direction of his employer"); *see also Eads* [—30—] *v. Borman*, 277 P.3d 503, 511 (Or. 2012) (en banc) (noting historical view that medical professionals, "because of the skill and judgment they exercised," were not subject to employer's "control").

Contemporary common law courts, however, have overwhelmingly abandoned this approach. As a fundamental matter, "[t]he rules for determining the liability of the employer for the conduct of both superior servants and the humblest employees are the same," Restatement (Second) of Agency § 220 cmt. a, and employers routinely answer for the misconduct of their skilled employees, *see, e.g., Bing v. Thunig*, 143 N.E.2d 3, 6 (N.Y. 1957) (objecting that "the special skill of other employees (such as airplane pilots, locomotive engineers, chemists, to mention but a few) has never been the basis for denying the application of respondeat superior"). Informed by this general rule, the courts have come to recognize that no principled distinction separates medical skill from other categories of expertise or requires universal immunization from oversight. As one court observed, "consistent application of the proposition [barring vicarious liability for medical negligence based on the degree of skill involved] . . . would require that virtually every professional who is expected to exercise independent judgment . . . would have to be deemed an independent contractor." *McDonald v. Hampton Training Sch. for Nurses*, 486 S.E.2d 299, 303 (Va. 1997). Such wholesale immunity has never been the rule. [—31—]

Moreover, as the medical profession has developed, many courts have come to acknowledge that "an obligation to maintain control of their medical judgment does not . . .

prevent a physician or nurse from becoming a[n] . . . employee." *Arango v. Reyka*, 507 So. 2d 1211, 1214 (Fla. Dist Ct. App. 1987). Unlike "physicians of the past," who often functioned as "distinct independent entities and independent centers of occupation and profession," today's medical practitioners routinely work for major conglomerates, corporations, and other large associations. *Villazon v. Prudential Health Care Plan, Inc.*, 843 So. 2d 842, 854 (Fla. 2003). As the Florida Supreme Court has remarked, "[t]he thought of visiting a private and independent office of a totally independent physician may now be one more of history and cultural conditioning than current reality." *Id.*

The fact is that modern healthcare professionals often participate in diverse agency relationships. They are employed, for example, by hospitals, universities, clinics, other practitioners, and corporations of all kinds. Such principals may powerfully influence the medical judgment and conduct of their employees in many different ways. They might, for instance, restrict the practice of medicine "through hiring criteria, training, formal practice guidelines, hierarchical supervision structures, peer review groups[,] and disciplinary measures." *Harris v. Miller*, 438 S.E.2d 731, 737 (N.C. 1994) (footnote omitted). Even subtler constraints may be enough to establish agency relationships in certain cases. *See,* [—32—] *e.g., Hodges v. Doctors Hosp.*, 234 S.E.2d 116, 118 (Ga. Ct. App. 1977) (finding jury question on issue of agency because hospital required staff physician to perform rotations in emergency room and paid him $100 per day); *Newton Cnty. Hosp. v. Nickolson*, 207 S.E.2d 659, 661-63 (Ga. Ct. App. 1974) (finding jury question on issue of agency because hospital paid physician on hourly basis and set physician's work schedule).

Amidst these broad networks of control, it should come as no surprise that the courts overwhelmingly recognize and apply the principles of vicarious liability in the world of modern medicine. *See, e.g., Univ. of Ala. Health Servs. Found., P.C. v. Bush ex rel. Bush*, 638 So. 2d 794, 799 (Ala. 1994) (recognizing vicarious liability for medical

negligence under Alabama law); *Villazon*, 843 So. 2d at 854-55 (same under Florida law); *Allrid v. Emory Univ.*, 285 S.E.2d 521, 525-26 (Ga. 1982) (same under Georgia law); *see also Eads*, 277 P.3d at 511-12 ("[M]ost jurisdictions now hold that an entity that *employs* a physician is subject to vicarious liability for that physician-employee's malpractice if the negligent act was committed in the course and scope of the employment.").

This does not mean, of course, that every medical practitioner is someone else's agent. The application of the doctrine is plainly fact-specific, and no bright-line rule could fit every circumstance. Again, control of the agent by the principal remains the touchstone of the analysis. Thus, the courts have considered agency [—33—] relationships on a case by case basis, and a wide variety of employers have faced vicarious liability for the medical negligence of their employees. *See, e.g., Univ. of Ala. Health Servs.*, 638 So. 2d at 801-02 (university foundation); *Villazon*, 843 So. 2d at 854 (health maintenance organization); *Allrid*, 285 S.E.2d at 525-26 (hospital); *see also TransCare Md., Inc. v. Murray*, 64 A.3d 887, 889 (Md. 2013) (ambulance transport company); *Cox v. M.A. Primary & Urgent Care Clinic*, 313 S.W.3d 240, 254 (Tenn. 2010) (urgent care clinic); *Rannard v. Lockheed Aircraft Corp.*, 157 P.2d 1, 6 (Cal. 1945) (en banc) (aerospace corporation); *Jones v. Tri-State Telephone & Telegraph Co.*, 136 N.W. 741, 741-42 (Minn. 1912) (telephone company); *Mrachek v. Sunshine Biscuit, Inc.*, 283 A.D. 105, 107-08 (N.Y. App. Div. 1953) (corporate bakery). As a matter of law, we are hard-pressed to see why the principal-agent relationship between a shipowner and a medical professional should be treated any differently—particularly where the shipowner employs a large medical staff, wholly outfits the clinics where its medical employees work, and exercises sufficient control over those personnel.

b.

Separately, we are told that shipowners cannot control onboard medical personnel because the doctor-patient (or nurse-patient) relationship is "under the control of the passengers themselves." *Barbetta*, 848 F.2d at 1369 (quoting [—34—] *O'Brien*, 28 N.E. at 267). The Supreme Judicial Court of Massachusetts put it this way, in a nineteenth-century opinion cited heavily in *Barbetta*:

> [The passengers] may employ the ship's surgeon, or some other physician or surgeon who happens to be on board, or they may treat themselves if they are sick, or may go without treatment if they prefer; and, if they employ the surgeon, they may determine how far they will submit themselves to his directions, and what of his medicines they will take and what reject, and whether they will submit to a surgical operation or take the risk of going without it. The master or owners of the ship cannot interfere in the treatment of the medical officer when he attends a passenger. He is not their servant, engaged in their business, and subject to their control as to his mode of treatment.

O'Brien, 28 N.E. at 267; *accord The Great Northern*, 251 F. at 831-32. Under this rule, the passenger—as patient—always calls the shots.

There are a number of problems with this load-bearing *Barbetta* principle. Most basically, we remain unimpressed by the assumption that a patient always controls his medical relationships as a matter of law. Again, the facts are critical. It makes little sense, for example, to suggest that an unconscious trauma patient meaningfully chooses the emergency treatment he receives. What's more, for some time, the courts have imputed vicarious liability where employers have required their employees or prospective employees to submit to a company doctor's care. *See, e.g., Lockheed Aircraft Corp.*, 157 P.2d at 6; *Tri-State Telephone*, 136 N.W. at 741; *Beadling v. Sirotta*, 176 A.2d 546, 549-50 (N.J. Super. Ct. Law Div. 1961); *Mrachek*, 283 A.D. 105 at 107-08. In such cases, [—35—] vicarious liability attaches in part because the treated person "ha[s] no [medical] choice." *Id.* at 108.

More to the point, we are particularly skeptical of the view that the patient always holds the critical reins in this particular context. With no land on the horizon, a passenger who falls ill aboard a cruise ship has precious little choice but to submit to onboard care. The hard reality is that, at least in the short term, he may have literally nowhere else to go. *See, e.g., Fairley v. Royal Cruise Line Ltd.*, 1993 A.M.C. 1633, 1638 (S.D. Fla. 1993) (characterizing injured or sick passengers as "captive audience" whose "only resort" is onboard medical staff); *Carlisle v. Carnival Corp.*, 864 So. 2d 1, 5 (Fla. Dist. Ct. App. 2003) (rejecting "the unrealistic suggestion that an ailing cruise passenger at sea has some meaningful opportunity to simply forego treatment by the ship's doctor"), *decision quashed* 953 So. 2d 461, 469-70 (Fla. 2007) ("find[ing] merit" in intermediate appellate court's holding but applying *Barbetta* rule because "federal principles of harmony and uniformity" constrain state courts in maritime cases). Moreover, even where resources exist to evacuate passengers to land-based medical facilities, afflicted persons may reasonably be reluctant to seek treatment from an unknown doctor or medical facility in a foreign land. Franza's complaint only underscores these problems, to the extent she claims that Vaglio "was *required* to go to the ship's medical center to be seen for his injuries." Compl. ¶ 35 (emphasis added). [—36—]

In any case, even if we were to assume that a patient *always* controls the treatment he receives, we would not be required to conclude that a patient *exclusively* controls the doctor-patient relationship. As we have recognized elsewhere, "courts have found that a [physician's employer] may be vicariously liable for the negligent acts of physicians even where the [employer] *does not control the manner and method of the physician's work*." *Johns v. Jarrard*, 927 F.2d 551, 556 (11th Cir. 1991) (applying Georgia law) (emphasis added). Modern courts widely acknowledge that a principal "both can, and in fact do[es], significantly control the overall delivery of medical services . . . even if the [principal] does not direct a professional's discrete actions in treating individual patients." *Eads*, 277

P.3d at 511. Notwithstanding a patient's right to opt in or out of treatment, an employer can influence a doctor's (or nurse's) practice of medicine in countless other ways. *See, e.g., Harris*, 438 S.E.2d at 737 (hiring criteria, training, practice guidelines, supervision, peer review, and disciplinary measures); *see also Hodges*, 234 S.E.2d at 118 (scheduling and compensation); *Newton Cnty. Hosp.*, 207 S.E.2d at 661-63 (same).

Again, these mechanisms of control will not always yield a finding of agency. But agency is a question of fact, and we see no sound reason for refusing to apply its principles in this context. The long and the short of it is that, outside the maritime realm, the doctor-patient relationship no longer ineluctably, and as a [—37—] matter of law, bars application of respondeat superior. One by one, American common law courts have responded to seismic shifts in the medical industry by holding principals responsible for the medical negligence of their agents. Given the "wholesale abandonment of the rule in most of the area where it once held sway," *Moragne*, 398 U.S. at 388, 90 S. Ct. at 1781, we are reluctant to cling to these arguments under the general maritime law.

2.

The second pillar on which *Barbetta* rests is the claim that the scope and nature of a cruise line's expertise renders it unable to supervise a medical professional. As many courts have observed, with a note of finality, "[a] ship is not a floating hospital." *Barbetta*, 848 F.2d at 1369 (quoting *Amdur v. Zim Israel Navigation Co.*, 310 F. Supp. 1033, 1042 (S.D.N.Y. 1969)). In other words, since a shipowner is "not in the business of providing medical services to passengers," we are told that no cruise line could "possess the expertise requisite to supervise"—and, by extension, to control—the ship's medical personnel. *Id.* (internal quotation marks omitted). Even if *some* entities might be vicariously liable for medical negligence, the argument goes, a cruise line is no such entity as a matter of law.

Again, we are unpersuaded by the breadth of this immunity-yielding rule of law. In the first place, it seems to us disingenuous for large cruise lines to disclaim [—38—] any medical expertise when they routinely provide access to extensive medical care in the infirmaries they have constructed for this very purpose. Viewing Franza's complaint in a light most favorable to the plaintiff, Royal Caribbean is sufficiently involved in the business of providing medical care to yield the possibility of liability. Thus, for example, the cruise line allegedly owns and operates onboard medical centers, Compl. ¶ 28, which are staffed by doctors and nurses whom the cruise line has hired, trained, outfitted, paid, and controlled, *id.* ¶¶ 6, 7. Moreover, if we credit Franza's claim that Royal Caribbean "pays to stock the 'medical centers' with all supplies, various medicines and equipment," *id.* ¶ 28, we also presume the cruise line knows at least something about its purchases. Taken at face value, these allegations evince at least some institutional knowledge of medicine. In fact, courts recognize the medical knowledge of hospitals on largely the same basis. *See Bing*, 143 N.E.2d at 11 (concluding that hospitals directly "undertake to treat the patient" because they "employ on a salary basis a large staff of physicians, nurses and internes" and "charge patients for medical care and treatment"); *accord Harris*, 438 S.E.2d at 736-37; *Eads*, 277 P.3d at 511.[14] [—39—]

---

[14] What's more, we suspect that Franza's allegations only scratch the surface. We have no difficulty imagining other cases in which additional evidence could demonstrate a cruise line's medical expertise—particularly since, in the public domain, cruise lines routinely claim to possess such knowledge. *See, e.g.*, Peltz, *Has Time Passed Barbetta by?*, at 19 (quoting statement by Director of Princess Cruise Lines Medical Department claiming that "major cruise lines have designed modern medical facilities comprising several ICUs, computerized radiology, and sophisticated laboratories" and "have achieved accreditation to international health care standards and ISO 9001 certification"); *id.* at 14-16 (noting that sixteen major cruise lines [—39—] cooperated with American College of Emergency Physicians to develop and adopt "industry-wide guidelines" addressing "unique needs and limitations of shipboard medical infirmaries"); Adam Goldstein, *Medical Tranquility and Peace of Mind*, Royal Caribbean (Sept. 27, 2010), http://www.royalcaribbean.com/connect/medical-

There can be no dispute, however, that a cruise ship is different from a hospital. Undeniably, the practice of medicine is far more central to hospital operations than to the business of cruising. But under basic agency principles, the scope of an employer's vicarious liability is not limited to negligence arising from its primary business. Instead, common law courts regularly have imputed liability for actions taken "in the scope of [the agent's] authority or employment," *Meyer v. Holley*, 537 U.S. 280, 285, 123 S. Ct. 824, 829 (2003), without further requiring that any such conduct implicate the principal's core business. Therefore, when a person is "employed" to perform medical services, Compl. ¶¶ 6, 7, and where any negligence occurs "within the scope and course of [that] employment," *id.*, vicarious liability is sometimes appropriate—even if the employer is not a primarily medical enterprise. *See, e.g., Lockheed Aircraft Corp.*, 157 P.2d 1 [—40—] (aerospace corporation); *Chi. Rock Island & Pac. Ry. Co. v. Britt*, 74 S.W.2d 398, 403 (Ark. 1934) (railroad); *Tri-State Telephone*, 136 N.W. 741 (telephone company); *Mrachek*, 283 A.D. 105 (corporate bakery); *Ebert v. Emerson Elec. Mfg. Co.*, 264 S.W. 453, 458 (Mo. Ct. App. 1924) (manufacturing plant); *see also Gen. Elec. Co. v. Rees*, 217 F.2d 595, 599 (9th Cir. 1954) (suggesting that malpractice of employee-doctor "might have bound" General

Electric); *Hawksby v. DePietro*, 754 A.2d 1168, 1171-2 (N.J. 2000) (explaining that newspaper company might have been liable for employee-doctor's negligence absent workers' compensation scheme). Against this authority, *Barbetta* stands for the proposition that cruise lines peculiarly lack all medical expertise—so much so that a shipowner, unlike every other class of employer that employs medical staff, can never be held vicariously liable for medical malpractice as a matter of law.

In particular, where the provision of some medical services is incidental to the principal's core business, courts have not hesitated to entertain the possibility of vicarious liability. *See, e.g., Blackburn v. Blue Mountain Women's Clinic*, 286 Mont. 60, 79-80 (Mont. 1997) (reversing district court's dismissal of family planning clinic in suit concerning counselor's negligence); *Speed v. Iowa*, 240 N.W. 2d 901 (Iowa 1976) (affirming judgment against state for medical malpractice occurring at University of Iowa's Student Health Infirmary); *cf. Kleinknecht v. Gettysburg College*, 989 F.2d 1360, 1374-75 (3d Cir. 1993) [—41—] (suggesting college might be vicariously liable for negligence of athletic program trainers during medical emergency); *Santiago v. Archer*, 136 A.D. 2d 290, 292 (N.Y. App. Div. 1988) (reversing district court's grant of summary judgment because union might be vicariously liable for medical malpractice occurring at its clinic).

One example that strikes us as particularly salient is case law addressing whether universities should be exempt from medical malpractice when they choose to open medical clinics that serve their student bodies and members of the community. University clinics are in many ways similar to cruise ship medical centers. Both types of facilities provide an abbreviated menu of treatment and procedure options as compared to a hospital or private physician's office. *Emory Univ. v. Porubiansky*, 282 S.E. 2d 903, 903, 904 (Ga. 1981) (noting that clinic patients agree to treatment that "proceed[s] more slowly" and may not be able to "insist on complete treatment"); *Ash v. N.Y. Univ. Dental Ctr*, 164 A.D. 2d 366, 369 (N.Y. App. Div. 1990) (noting that a clinic might "limit[]

---

tranquility-and-peace-of-mind (touting cruise line's onboard lab equipment, x-ray units, and clot-busting thrombolytics); Press Release, Princess Cruises, Princess Cruises' Medical Departments Earn Unique Distinction with Prestigious Quality Certification and Accreditation (May 6, 2010), http://www.princess.com/news/press_releases/2010/05/Princess-Cruises'-Medical-Departments-Earn-Unique-Distinction-with-Prestigious-Quality-Certification-and-Accreditation.html ("[O]ur medical centers achieve similar quality standards to medical facilities ashore[.]"); Royal Caribbean Cruises Ltd., *2012 Stewardship Report*, 17 (2012), http://media.royalcaribbean.com/content/en_US/pdf/13034530_RCL_2012StwrdshpTwoPgrs_v4.pdf (noting that shipowners supply equipment and provide training to enable onboard blood transfusions). We do not credit as fact any information not pled in the complaint, but we note that another plaintiff could have cited any of this information to rebut the basic assumption that cruise ships are not in the business of providing medical services.

itself to certain types of care or refus[e] to perform certain procedures"). Moreover, neither a cruise line nor a university is in the primary business of providing medical services. Finally, each entity claims to have constructed and maintained its facilities, not for the purpose of entering the medical service business, but as a supplement to its primary business. For the universities, clinics provide basic services to students [—42—] and community members and serve as educational and research tools for their students and professors. *See Tunkl v. Regents of the Univ. of Cali.*, 383 P.2d 441, 442 (Cal. 1963); *Emory Univ.*, 282 S.E. at 905. And for the cruise lines, medical centers allegedly are provided as a convenience to passengers who may become ill at sea.

In the university clinical program context, courts have declined to create sweeping immunity from medical malpractice liability, explaining that these characteristics of clinics do not justify "an exemption from the duty to exercise reasonable care." *Emory Univ.*, 282 S.E. 2d at 905. As the Georgia Supreme Court has observed, clinics, and thus the universities that run them, "engage in the practice of [medicine]" by "offering services." *Id*. This fact, rather than the university's core business or underlying purposes for deciding to provide medical care, is of primary importance when determining whether an exemption from liability is appropriate. *See id.* ("The status of Emory University School of Dentistry as primarily a training institution does not allow for an exemption from the duty to exercise reasonable care."). Additionally, in reponse to a university's argument that it should be immune from vicarious, though not direct, negligence, the California Supreme Court has noted that no feature of clinical programs justified such a departure from general principles of agency. The court observed that "a legion of decisions . . . have drawn no distinction between the corporation's [—43—] own liability and vicarious liability resulting from the negligence of agents," *Tunkl v. Regents of the Univ. of Cali.*, 383 P.2d 441, 448 (Cal. 1963), and that no rationale supported adopting a different rule in the case of university clinics. In our view, blanket immunity from vicarious

liability is similarly unwarranted when cruise ships choose to create, stock, and operate onboard medical centers with their own physicians and nurses. Taking Franza's allegations at face value, Royal Caribbean employed medical personnel who rendered negligent services in the course and scope of their medical employment, onboard a ship outfitted by the principal with a medical infirmary or urgent care center. This seems to us to be sufficient medical knowledge to at least withstand a motion to dismiss for failure to state a claim.

Moreover, no principle from maritime tort law justifies treating shipowners so differently from ordinary employers. On the contrary, shipowners have been held vicariously liable for misconduct that falls at least this far outside the heartland of the cruising business. In *Muratore v. M/S Scotia Prince*, for example, a shipowner's subcontractor's photographer-employees tortiously photographed and harassed a passenger. 845 F.2d 347, 349-50 (1st Cir. 1988). The First Circuit affirmed the shipowner's vicarious liability because the tortfeasors were "part of [the ship's] crew," even though the shipowner was not primarily in the business of photography. *Id.* at 353. If shipowners could be held liable for the photography of [—44—] a subcontractor's employee, we see little reason to suppose they could not be called to answer for the medical negligence of the practitioners they directly employ and control. *Cf. Rogers v. Allis-Chalmers Mfg. Co.*, 92 N.E.2d 677, 683 (Ohio 1950) (acknowledging possibility that machinery manufacturer could be vicariously liable for negligence by employees "engaged in athletic activities," though manufacturer was "not in the business of athletics"); *Strait v. Hale Constr. Co.*, 26 Cal. App. 3d 941, 950 (Cal. Dist. Ct. App. 1972) (affirming farmer's vicarious liability for highway collision caused by on-loan employee-operator of farmer's loaned machine, though farmer was avowedly "not in the business of renting heavy equipment and furnishing an operator").

There are also important policy reasons that inform against broad immunity for cruise lines against any liability for their medical staff's malpractice. Carriers owe their ailing passengers "a duty to exercise reasonable care to furnish such aid and assistance as ordinarily prudent persons would render under similar circumstances." *Barbetta*, 848 F.2d at 1371 (internal quotation marks omitted). By investing in medical infrastructure and hiring skilled medical employees, cruise ships avoid the potentially high cost of providing reasonable care in more expensive ways. *See, e.g., The Iroquois*, 194 U.S. 240, 243 (1904) (explaining that reasonable care depends on, *inter alia*, "the proximity of an intermediate port"). The shipowner, by providing onboard medical resources, will often "avoid[ ] [its] [—45—] sometimes inconvenient and costly duty to change course for the benefit of an ailing passenger." *Nietes*, 188 F. Supp. at 221. Under the *Barbetta* rule, shipowners have access to a liability free method of discharging their duty of care to passengers that is outside the realm of meaningful judicial review. Additionally, beyond any potential for cost avoidance, cruise lines may even profit affirmatively from onboard medical care. For instance, they might charge passengers for treatment rendered. *See* Compl. ¶ 28. And, surely, for at least some ticket-buying customers, the availability of onboard medical facilities is a deal-maker.[15] In short, cruise lines have chosen quite deliberately to enter the business of medicine, often in a large way, and they reap the tangible benefits of this business strategy. Thus, it seems hardly anomalous to require cruise lines to bear the burden of this choice. *See generally* Gregory C. Keating, *The Idea of Fairness in the Law of Enterprise Liability*, 95 Mich. L. Rev. 1266, 1269 (1997).[16] [—46—]

All told, *Barbetta*'s assumption that cruise lines lack any medical expertise is difficult to accept in light of the industry's decision to construct, outfit, and staff medical centers onboard its ships. Moreover, no feature peculiar to cruise lines distinguishes them from other corporate principals which must ordinarily answer for the medical negligence of their employees. Again, we are loath to adopt a principle of law that always immunizes a shipowner without regard to any of the facts.

3.

The final pillar on which *Barbetta* rests is the notion that shipowners never exercise "sufficiently immediate" control over their onboard medical personnel to warrant vicarious liability. *Barbetta*, 848 F.2d at 1371 (quoting *Amdur*, 310 F. Supp. at 1042). At its core, this argument assumes that no shipowner may ever be close enough to control its onboard medical staff, whether the ship is geographically near or distant from the principal's home base. The glaring problem we see with this conclusion is its fact-dependent premise. Put simply, shipowners and their vessels (and their onboard medical staff) are not always far apart. Thus, for example, whenever onboard treatment occurs before a ship [—47—] departs, the owner of the vessel may be very close at hand. Moreover, a ship that has already set sail may still be near its harbor of origin, or a ship may hug the

---

[15] Indeed, in one study, persons over sixty represented nearly thirty percent of all respondents who had ever taken a cruise vacation. Taylor Nelson Sofres, *2011 Cruise Market Profile Study*, Cruise Lines Int'l Assoc., 32 (June 2011), http://www.cruising.org/sites/default/files/pressroo m/Market_Profile_2011.pdf. Considering the likely preferences of this key demographic, we think it very unlikely that cruise lines will respond to their new liability by eliminating onboard medical care.

[16] Several other policy arguments suggest setting aside the *Barbetta* rule. First, as compared with an employee-doctor, a resource-rich cruise line can more readily bear the cost of a plaintiff's injury. *See generally* Prosser & Keeton, *The Law of Torts*

500-01 (5th ed. 1984) (noting that employer is better able to "absorb," "distribute," and "shift" losses caused by employee torts) [hereinafter Prosser & Keeton, *The Law of Torts*]; Guido Calabresi, *Some Thoughts on Risk Distribution and the Law of Torts*, 70 Yale L.J. 499, 527 (1961) (describing "deep pocket" justification for imposing liability on principals). Second, by imposing vicarious liability for employee torts, we encourage profit-seeking employers to minimize the risk of costly tortious [—46—] conduct. *See generally* Richard A. Posner, *A Theory of Negligence*, 1 J. Legal Stud. 29, 43 (1973) (describing respondeat superior as mechanism encouraging employers to "invest until the last cent of [their] investment . . . saves one cent in . . . costs"); Prosser & Keeton, *The Law of Torts*, at 500 (identifying "modern justification for vicarious liability" as "deliberate allocation of risk" (footnote omitted)).

coastline and remain close to land-based medical facilities. And some ships may even be owned by physical persons, whose supervision would certainly be "immediate" whenever they traveled onboard. In short, principals and onboard agents may be physically close together. To the extent that physical separation vitiates control, the relevant questions are fact-based and ill-suited to resolution by a per se rule of law.

Furthermore, as a general rule, the mere fact of physical separation between principals and agents does *not* inevitably defeat respondeat superior—in medical malpractice cases or elsewhere. Again, the facts are everything. *See, e.g., Scott v. SSM Healthcare St. Louis*, 70 S.W.3d 560, 568 (Mo. Ct. App. 2002) ("reject[ing] the notion that [an agency] relationship cannot be found merely because the hospital does not have the right to stand over the doctor's shoulder"); *see also TransCare Md.*, 64 A.3d at 889-90, 903 (suggesting that ambulance company could be vicariously liable for employee-paramedic's negligence aboard helicopter); *Sigmon v. Tompkins Cnty.*, 449 N.Y.S. 2d 621, 623 (N.Y. Sup. Ct. 1982) (suggesting that ambulance company could be vicariously liable for medical malpractice rendered by employee nurse traveling in ambulance); Restatement (Second) of Agency § 220 cmt. d ("[T]he control or right to control needed to [—48—] establish the relation of master and servant may be *very attenuated*." (emphasis added)); *cf. Grigsby v. Coastal Marine Serv. of Tex., Inc.*, 412 F.2d 1011, 1031 (5th Cir. 1969) (implying unseaworthiness liability of "remote owner" where "conduct . . . somehow implicates" that owner).

Even if distance may undercut liability in some cases, we see no need to adopt a one size fits all rule where advanced technology often enables effective communication between shore based principals and onboard medics. We do not have to hypothesize about scenarios to support this point, because cruise lines proudly advertise their own capabilities. Several cruise lines now purport to staff extensive land-based medical departments with expert personnel. *See* Peltz, *Has Time Passed Barbetta by?*, at 20 & n.69 (citing

examples). By many accounts, these and other onshore practitioners meaningfully communicate with a ship's medical employees even while the ship is at sea. *See, e.g., id.* at 21-22 (detailing onboard treatment of passenger's acute-onset stroke "[w]ith clinical and logistical assistance" of shore-based medical team). These communications occur through channels that were unheard of when the Fifth Circuit decided *Barbetta*, long before the advent of widespread cellular and satellite communications. *See, e.g.,* Royal Caribbean Cruises Ltd., *2010 Stewardship Report*, 8 (2010), www.royalcaribbeanpresscenter.com/download-press-release/891/ (highlighting modern cruise line's "teledermatology" partnership with shore based university); [—49—] Holland America Line, *Onboard Medical Services and Facilities*, 1 (2005), http://www.hollandamerica.com/assets/news/PR_Medical.pdf (explaining that "[t]he ship is able to access any medical specialist at [University of Texas Medical Branch] in Galveston" and "radiologists can provide an instant overread of any x-rays done on board). Because, twenty-six years after *Barbetta*, we now think a shipowner could plausibly supervise a ship's medical employees in places near and far, we reject the sweep of the rule's final rationale.

In short, we do not find that the arguments set forth in *Barbetta* justify its broad grant of immunity from vicarious liability in all claims of medical malpractice. Rather, we think we are obliged to follow our own maritime precedent, which demands fact-intensive treatment of agency questions. We cannot accept a legal principle that would erect a categorical exception from this settled practice, and we see no reason to follow an outdated rule that serves no useful purpose in modern maritime law. Thus, we hold that Franza's allegations established a plausible agency relationship between the employer, Royal Caribbean Cruise Lines, Ltd., and its employees, Nurse Garcia and Dr. Gonzales, and that the district court improvidently granted the Rule 12(b)(6) motion to dismiss.

IV. [—50—]

Franza also appeals the dismissal of her claim brought under the alternative theory of apparent agency.[17] We are the first circuit to address whether a passenger may use apparent agency principles to hold a cruise line vicariously liable for the onboard medical negligence of its employees. Like the district court, we conclude that a passenger may sue a shipowner for medical negligence if he can properly plead and prove detrimental, justifiable reliance on the apparent agency of a ship's medical staff-member. However, we part ways with the district court's conclusion that Franza's apparent agency claim was pled inadequately. As we see it, Franza has plausibly alleged all of the elements of apparent agency.

A.

Plainly, actual agency and apparent agency are distinct theories of liability. Unlike actual agency, the doctrine of apparent agency allows a plaintiff to sue a principal for the misconduct of an independent contractor who only reasonably appeared to be an agent of the principal. *See, e.g., Borg-Warner Leasing*, 733 F.2d [—51—] at 836 (Florida law); *Crowe*, 382 F.2d at 688 (Georgia law); *see also* Restatement (Second) of Agency § 267.

These separate doctrines have been applied for quite different reasons and under very different circumstances. While respondeat superior derives from a principal's right to control the conduct of its agents, liability under apparent agency flows from equitable concerns. *See Brown ex rel. Brown v. St. Vincent's Hosp.*, 899 So. 2d 227, 236 (Ala. 2004) (equating apparent agency with agency by estoppel under Alabama law); *Jackson Hewitt, Inc. v. Kaman*, 100 So. 3d 19, 31 (Fla. Dist. Ct. App. 2011) ("[L]iability based on apparent authority is a form of estoppel."); *Capital Color Printing, Inc. v. Ahern*, 661 S.E.2d 578, 585 (Ga. Ct. App. 2008) (noting that "doctrine of apparent agency is predicated on principles of estoppel" (internal quotation marks and alteration omitted)); *accord Primeaux v. United States*, 181 F.3d 876, 879 (8th Cir. 1999) ("[O]stensible agency is no agency at all; it is in reality based entirely on an estoppel." (internal quotation marks and citation omitted)); *Drexel v. Union Prescription Ctrs., Inc.*, 582 F.2d 781, 791 (3d Cir. 1978) (equating apparent agency and agency by estoppel under Pennsylvania law); *Sennott v. Rodman & Renshaw*, 474 F.2d 32, 38 (7th Cir. 1973) (same under Illinois law); *Hill v. St. Clare's Hosp.*, 490 N.E.2d 823, 827 (N.Y. 1986) (same under New York law); *see also Baptist Mem'l Hosp. Sys. v. Sampson*, 969 S.W.2d 945, 947 (Tex. 1998) (noting doctrine's equitable [—52—] foundation); *Morback v. Young*, 113 P. 22, 24 (Or. 1911) (same); *Donnelly v. S.F. Bridge Co.*, 49 P. 559, 560 (Cal. 1897) (same). Essentially, then, liability may be appropriate under apparent agency principles when a principal's conduct could equitably prevent it from denying the existence of an agency relationship.

Because apparent agency does not turn on any notion of control, the *Barbetta* rule does not directly address the question of apparent agency.[18] Apprehending this distinction,

---

[17] Many courts use the terms apparent agency, apparent authority, ostensible agency, and agency by estoppel interchangeably. Though some courts have distinguished apparent agency and apparent authority as theories of liability that require no reliance, we have never recognized that distinction. *See, e.g., Borg-Warner Leasing v. Doyle Elec. Co.*, 733 F.2d 833, 836 (11th Cir. 1984) (requiring "detrimental reliance" to establish "apparent authority" under Florida law); *Arceneaux v. Texaco, Inc.*, 623 F.2d 924, 926-27 (5th Cir. 1980) (requiring "reliance" to establish "apparent authority in tort cases" under Louisiana law); *Crowe v. Hertz Corp.*, 382 F.2d 681, 688 (5th Cir. 1967) (equating "apparent agency" with "agency by estoppel" and requiring "reliance" under Georgia law). In any case, even if we were to acknowledge the possibility of "apparent agency" liability without reliance, Franza's complaint did not allege vicarious liability on any such theory. Accordingly, we intend the term "apparent agency" in the ordinary sense.

[18] A few courts have suggested that, because of *Barbetta*'s prominence, no plaintiff could ever reasonably mistake the agency status of onboard medical personnel "[a]bsent an explicit manifestation by the ship owner countering the settled principle that medical staff [members] are not their agents." *Huang v. Carnival Corp.*, 909 F. Supp. 2d 1356, 1361 (S.D. Fla. 2012); *see also*

many district courts within this Circuit have already recognized a shipowner's apparent agency liability for onboard medical negligence. *See, e.g., Aronson v. Celebrity Cruises, Inc.*, __ F. Supp. 2d ___, No. 12-CV-20129, 2014 WL 3408582, at *12 (S.D. Fla. May 9, 2014); *Lobegeiger v. Celebrity Cruises, Inc.*, 869 F. Supp. 2d 1356, 1361 (S.D. Fla. 2012); *Peavy v. Carnival Corp.*, No. 1:12-CV-20782, 2012 WL 5306353, at *2 (S.D. Fla. Oct. 26, 2012); *Gentry v. Carnival Corp.*, No. 11-21580-CIV, 2011 WL 4737062, at *4-5 (S.D. Fla. Oct. 5, 2011); *Smolnikar v. Royal Caribbean Cruises Ltd.*, 787 F. Supp. 2d 1308, 1324 [—53—] (S.D. Fla. 2011); *Peterson v. Celebrity Cruises, Inc.*, 753 F. Supp. 2d 1245, 1248 (S.D. Fla. 2010); *Ridley v. NCL (Bahamas) Ltd.*, 824 F. Supp. 2d 1355, 1362 (S.D. Fla. 2010); *Rinker v. Carnival Corp.*, No. 09-23154-CIV, 2010 WL 9530327, at *4 (S.D. Fla. June 18, 2010); *Barnett v. Carnival Corp.*, No. 06-22521-CIV, 2007 WL 1746900, at *2 (S.D. Fla. June 15, 2007); *Hajtman v. NCL (Bahamas) Ltd.*, 526 F. Supp. 2d 1324, 1328 (S.D. Fla. 2007); *Suter v. Carnival Corp.*, 2007 A.M.C. 2564 (S.D. Fla. 2007); *Doonan v. Carnival Corp.*, 404 F. Supp. 2d 1367, 1371-72 (S.D. Fla. 2005); *Huntley v. Carnival Corp.*, 307 F. Supp. 2d 1372, 1375 (S.D. Fla. 2004); *Fairley v. Royal Cruise Line Ltd.*, 1993 A.M.C. 1633, 1639-40 (S.D. Fla. 1993).

We agree with this view. As we have noted at some length, the principles of agency permeate the general maritime law, *see Archer*, 834 F.2d at 1573, and apparent agency is no exception. The great weight of admiralty precedent has long allowed

---

Hajtman, 526 F. Supp. 2d at 1328-29 (holding that *Barbetta* rule precluded any reasonable belief that medical staff were agents of shipowner); *Warren v. Ajax Navigation Corp.*, 1995 A.M.C. 2609 (S.D. Fla. 1995) (same). Whatever its merits, this argument does not survive our departure from the traditional rule. Separately, other courts have concluded that the *Barbetta* rule bars apparent agency claims because apparent agency is merely a form of respondeat superior. *See, e.g., Balachander v. NCL (Bahamas) Ltd.*, 800 F. Supp. 2d 1196, 1204 (S.D. Fla. 2011); *Wajnstat v. Oceania Cruises, Inc.*, No. 09-21850-CIV, 2011 WL 465340, at *4 (S.D. Fla. Feb. 4, 2011). We think that view misapprehends the analytical distinction between actual and apparent agency.

plaintiffs to sue shipowners based on the apparent authority of third-parties. *See El Amigo v. Houston Marine Eng'g Works*, 285 F. 868, 870 (5th Cir. 1923) (upholding claim against shipowner because third-party who ordered supplies, repairs, and necessities "ha[d] apparent authority to bind the vessel"); *accord Garanti*, 697 F.3d at 72 (reversing summary judgment in maritime contract dispute because of factual question regarding third-party's "actual *or apparent* authority to act on [shipowner's] behalf" (emphasis added)); *Hawkspere*, 330 F.3d [—54—] at 236 (affirming shipowner's maritime lien because no issue of fact existed "as to whether [third-party] acted as an actual *or apparent* agent for [shipowner]" (emphasis added)); *Lake Charles Stevedores, Inc. v. Professor Vladimir Popov MV*, 199 F.3d 220, 228 (5th Cir. 1999) (affirming denial of maritime lien on theory of "apparent authority" because shipowner did not "undert[ake] actions that caused [plaintiffs] reasonably to believe that [third-party] was its agent"); *Cactus Pipe & Supply Co. v. M/V Montmartre*, 756 F.2d 1103, 1111 (5th Cir. 1985) (absolving shipowner of liability for damaged cargo because third-party did not have "apparent authority" to issue bills of lading); *cf. Marine Transp. Servs. Sea-Barge Grp., Inc. v. Python High Performance Marine Corp.*, 16 F.3d 1133, 1138-39 (11th Cir. 1994) (recognizing doctrine of equitable estoppel in maritime context).

The federal circuits have made only passing references to apparent agency principles in maritime *tort* cases. *See, e.g., Reino de España v. Am. Bureau of Shipping, Inc.*, 691 F.3d 461, 474 n.16 (2d Cir. 2012) (suggesting that maritime principal might have been liable for reckless conduct if alleged agent had possessed "apparent authority" to receive certain notifications); *Kawasaki Kisen Kaisha, Ltd. v. Plano Molding Co.*, 696 F.3d 647, 659 (7th Cir. 2012) (implying that maritime principal might have been liable for negligence under doctrine of "apparent authority" if plaintiffs had established their "belie[f] that [third-party] [—55—] was acting as [principal's] agent"). Nonetheless, given the broad salience of agency rules in maritime law, *see Archer*, 834 F.2d at 1573, and the important role the federal courts play in setting the bounds of maritime torts, *see Exxon*, 554 U.S. at 508 n.21, 128 S. Ct. at 2630, we think apparent agency principles apply in this context. Indeed, the equitable foundations of apparent agency are just as important in tort as in contract. *See Arceneaux*, 623 F.2d at 926 (assuming that Louisiana courts would apply apparent agency in tort cases because they had done so in contract); *see also Drexel*, 582 F.2d 791-92 (concluding under Pennsylvania law that "policies" and "factual issues" support apparent agency in both contract and tort).

Having long applied the principles of apparent agency in maritime cases, we can discern no sound basis for allowing a special exception for onboard medical negligence, particularly since we have concluded that actual agency principles ought to be applied in this setting as well. Outside the maritime realm, many common law courts—including the courts found in all three states of this Circuit—have recognized vicarious liability for the medical negligence of apparent agents. *See, e.g., Brown*, 899 So. 2d at 238 ("see[ing] no reason" in medical malpractice case "to abandon [the Alabama Supreme Court's] rule" of apparent agency); *Roessler v. Novak*, 858 So. 2d 1158, 1162 (Fla. Dist. Ct. App. 2003) (holding principal "vicariously liable for the acts of physicians, even if they are independent [—56—] contractors, if these physicians act with . . . apparent authority"); *Richmond Cnty. Hosp. Auth. v. Brown*, 361 S.E.2d 164, 166-67 (Ga. 1987) (recognizing vicarious liability where principal "represented to [plaintiff] that its emergency room physicians were its employees"); *see also Eads*, 277 P.3d at 514 ("[T]he weight of authority in other jurisdictions is that, in a proper case, a hospital or other entity can be held vicariously liable for a physician's negligence on an apparent authority theory."). Medical negligence triggers the same equitable concerns whether it arises on land or at sea, and, therefore, we think apparent agency liability may be appropriate in both settings.

B.

Under the doctrine of apparent agency, just as in the case of actual agency, vicarious liability turns on the facts presented. When applying the tort and contract law of several states, we have repeatedly observed that apparent agency liability requires finding three essential elements: first, a representation by the principal to the plaintiff, which, second, causes the plaintiff reasonably to believe that the alleged agent is authorized to act for the principal's benefit, and which, third, induces the plaintiff's detrimental, justifiable reliance upon the appearance of agency. *See Borg-Warner Leasing*, 733 F.2d at 836 (Florida law); *Arceneaux*, 623 F.2d at 927 & n.4 (Louisiana law); *Crowe*, 382 F.2d at 688 (Georgia law). [—57—] Applying these general principles to the facts alleged in this case, we conclude that Franza has plausibly and adequately pled all three elements of apparent agency.

In the first place, Royal Caribbean purportedly made a number of salient representations to Vaglio. The cruise line: (1) "promote[d] its medical staff and represent[ed] them as being [cruise line] employees through brochures, internet advertising, and on the vessel," Compl. ¶ 26; (2) publicly described the medical centers in proprietary language, *id.* ¶ 28; (3) billed passengers directly for onboard medical services, *id.* ¶ 28; (4) required its doctors and nurses to wear uniforms bearing the cruise line's name and logo, *id.* ¶ 29; (5) held out Dr. Gonzales and Nurse Garcia as "members of the ship's crew" to passengers and immigration authorities, *id.* ¶¶ 31, 33; and (6) "introduce[d]" Dr. Gonzales to the ship's passengers "as one of the ship's Officers," *id.* ¶ 30.

Second, based on these allegations, Vaglio reasonably could believe that Dr. Gonzales and Nurse Garcia were authorized to render medical services for the cruise line's benefit. Indeed, according to Franza's complaint, Royal Caribbean actually intended that its passengers perceive the ship's medical staff to be agents of the cruise line, insofar as the cruise line encouraged "the idea that the medical staff who work in its 'medical centers' are employed by the cruise line as part of a marketing tool to induce passengers such as [Vaglio] to buy cruises on its ships." *Id.* ¶ 27. [—58—]

Finally, as for the third element, the district court dismissed Franza's apparent agency claim because her complaint "d[id] not state how Vaglio relied on, or changed his position in reliance on, his alleged belief that the doctor and/or nurse was Royal Caribbean's agent." *Franza*, 948 F. Supp. 2d at 1333. We disagree. It is true that "apparent agency [cannot] exist for the benefit of the person injured without reliance upon the apparent holding out of the principal." *Crowe*, 382 F.2d at 688. Moreover, this reliance must be "detrimental," *Borg-Warner Leasing*, 733 F.2d at 836, and "justifiabl[e]," *Arceneaux*, 623 F.2d at 927 n.4 (quoting Restatement (Second) of Agency § 267); *see also Drexel*, 582 F.2d at 791; *Stone v. Palms W. Hosp.*, 941 So. 2d 514, 520 n. 13 (Fla. 4th DCA 2006) (per curiam). However, the complaint alleged precisely such reliance:

> [Vaglio] relied to his detriment on his belief that the physician and nurse were direct employees or actual agents of [Royal Caribbean] in that [Vaglio] followed the advice of the nurse and/or physician who did not seek any further medical testing or evaluation while the ship was in Bermuda, that he relied on the ship's nurse and/or physician, [and] that he did not follow-up with the ship's medical staff as he was told that he did not have any serious injury.

Compl. ¶ 38.

We are hard-pressed to see how this pleading falls short. Indeed, Franza explained that Vaglio (1) "relied to his detriment" (2) "on his belief" (3) that Dr. Gonzales and Nurse Garcia "were direct employees or actual agents of [Royal Caribbean]." Furthermore, through the specifying phrase, "in that," she alleged [—59—] precisely *how* Vaglio relied on the appearance of agency: (1) he "followed the advice of the nurse and/or physician," (2) despite the fact that those medical personnel "did not seek any further medical testing or evaluation while the ship was in Bermuda," and (3) the degree of his reliance was so pronounced "that he did not [even] follow up with the ship's medical staff." At this early stage in the proceeding, one plausible interpretation of Franza's allegations is that Vaglio indeed relied to his profound detriment on the appearance of agency, in that he would not have blindly trusted the advice of unknown medical personnel (who sought no counsel from other medical professionals while the ship was docked) if the ship's doctor and nurse had not borne the imprimatur of a well-known and trusted cruise line. Under these circumstances, and in light of Royal Caribbean's advertised medical expertise, detrimental reliance may have been justifiable.

Of course, we recognize that Franza could have taken her allegations one step further. Thus, she could have specifically claimed that Vaglio would not have followed the advice of the ship's medical personnel had he suspected they were not actually the agents of Royal Caribbean. Effectively, however, that sort of statement would only put Franza's existing message in the negative. We do not require plaintiffs to perform such linguistic gymnastics in order to defeat a motion to dismiss. On these specific allegations, then, we are constrained to reverse the district court's dismissal of Franza's apparent agency claim. [—60—]

V.

Having determined that Franza plausibly alleged two alternative theories of vicarious liability, we turn to a final question: whether the complaint adequately supports a claim of negligence in the first place. We think it does. To plead negligence in a maritime case, "a plaintiff must allege that (1) the defendant had a duty to protect the plaintiff from a particular injury; (2) the defendant breached that duty; (3) the breach actually and proximately caused the plaintiff's injury; and (4) the plaintiff suffered actual harm." *Chaparro*, 693 F.3d at 1336. All four elements are met here.

First, Franza alleged that Royal Caribbean was duty-bound to "provide prompt and appropriate medical care" following Vaglio's severe head injury. Compl. ¶ 19. It is indisputable that cruise lines must treat their passengers with "ordinary reasonable care under the circumstances." *Keefe v. Bahama Cruise Line, Inc.*, 867 F.2d 1318, 1322 (11th Cir. 1989) (per curiam). Implicit in this variable standard is the notion that cruise lines will not always be held to the same standard of care that would guide treatment onshore. This is as it should be, since standards of care typically vary among differently situated healthcare providers. *See, e.g., Jackson v. Pleasant Grove Health Care Ctr.*, 980 F.2d 692, 694 & n.2 (11th Cir. 1993) (recognizing in nursing home negligence case that, under Alabama law, relevant standard of care governs "similarly situated health care [—61—] provider[s]"), *abrogated on other grounds by Weisgram v. Marley Co.*, 528 U.S. 440, 120 S. Ct. 1011 (2000); *see also Cruz-Vázquez v. Mennonite Gen. Hosp., Inc.*, 613 F.3d 54, 56 (1st Cir. 2010) (noting that standard of care depends on "relevant medical circumstances"); *Watson v. United States*, 485 F.3d 1100, 1109-10 & n.7 (10th Cir. 2007) (finding no clear error in determination that ambulatory care clinic was not required under applicable standard of care to stock Mannitol, since evidence suggested that "Mannitol was not a medication normally administered outside of a hospital setting"); *cf.* Fla. Stat. Ann. § 766.102 (2013) (defining standard of care in medical malpractice action "in light of all relevant surrounding circumstances"). Here, the precise contours of Royal Caribbean's duty depend on questions of fact that need not and cannot be answered at this stage. However, Franza's specific allegations suffice.

Second, Royal Caribbean, by and through its medical personnel, purportedly breached its duty in "one or more of the following ways": (1) "failing to properly assess the condition" of Vaglio; (2) "allowing a nurse to make the initial assessment"; (3) "failing to have a doctor assess [Vaglio]"; (4) "failing to timely diagnose and appropriately treat [Vaglio]"; (5) "failing to order appropriate diagnostic scans to further assess the degree of injury";

(6) "failing to obtain consultations with appropriate specialists"; (7) "failing to properly monitor [Vaglio]"; (8) "failing to evacuate [Vaglio] from the vessel for further care in a [—62—] timely manner"; and (9) "deviating from the standard of care for patients in Mr. Vaglio's circumstances who had suffered a significant blow to the head." Compl. ¶ 20. If proven, these allegations could establish a breach of even a modest duty of care, framed by the particular circumstances of the case.

Third, Franza has alleged that, as a "direct and proximate result of [this] negligence," Vaglio's "condition deteriorated to the point that he fell into a coma and died." *Id.* ¶ 22. In fact, had Vaglio "received the appropriate care and treatment," the claim is made that, "more likely than not[,] . . . he would have survived." *Id.* ¶ 23. Finally, Vaglio suffered damages as a result of Royal Caribbean's alleged negligence. Vaglio's estate "has become obligated to pay significant medical bills and other expenses," *id.* ¶ 24, and his "widow . . . has lost his pension, his social security, medical insurance, and the value of his services and incurred expenses for medical care, funeral services[,] and interment," *id.* ¶ 25. Taken in a light most favorable to Franza, these assertions set forth a *prima facie* claim of negligence.

VI.

In sum, the allegations in Franza's complaint plausibly support holding Royal Caribbean Cruises, Ltd., vicariously liable for the medical negligence of its onboard nurse and doctor. Because Franza adequately pled all of the elements of both actual and apparent agency, we hold that Franza may press her claims under [—63—] either or both theories. Accordingly, we reverse and remand for further proceedings consistent with this opinion.

REVERSED AND REMANDED.

United States Court of Appeals
for the Eleventh Circuit

No. 13-11342

ATLANTIC MARINE FLA., LLC
VS.
EVANSTON INS. CO.

Appeal from the United States District Court for the
Middle District of Florida

Decided: December 24, 2014

Citation: 775 F.3d 1268, 2 Adm. R. 605 (11th Cir. 2014).

Before **TJOFLAT, COX,** and **ALARCÓN,** * Circuit
Judges.

* Honorable Arthur L. Alarcón, Senior U.S. Circuit
Judge for the Ninth Circuit, sitting by designation.

[—2—] **TJOFLAT,** Circuit Judge:

In this case, a marine engineering firm purchased an architect's and engineer's professional liability insurance policy, which insured the firm against any liability it might incur in a tort action for the negligent preparation of working drawings used to build an oceangoing passenger vessel. After the vessel was launched and in operation, a tragic accident occurred when the bulkhead door in the vessel's forward engine room malfunctioned, causing the death of the ship's captain. The captain's personal representative, claiming that the engineering firm and the shipbuilder were independently at fault, brought an action against them in state court. Pursuant to the insurance policy, the insurance company provided the engineering firm a defense. The shipbuilder demanded that the insurance company provide it a defense as well, but the insurance company refused to do so on the ground that the policy did not cover the shipbuilder as an insured. The insurance company having denied coverage, the shipbuilder turned to its own insurance company for a defense. Its insurer had issued the shipbuilder a comprehensive [—3—] marine liability policy, which insured the shipbuilder against any liability it might incur in a tort action based on its own negligence.

After the two insurance companies separately settled with the personal representative, the shipbuilder and its comprehensive marine liability insurer brought this declaratory judgment action against the company that insured the engineering firm. The insurer sought reimbursement of the expenses incurred defending the shipbuilder, as well as the settlement monies it paid the personal representative. The District Court concluded that although the shipbuilder was not a named insured under the engineering firm's insurance policy, it was a third-party beneficiary of the insurance the policy provided. Thus, the court held, the shipbuilder was entitled to the same rights the policy afforded the policy's named insured, the engineering firm. The insurance company appeals the judgment. We reverse.

I.

A.

The engineering firm is Guido Perla & Associates ("GPA"). In April 1998, GPA, pursuant to a contract with Delta Queen Steamboat Company ("Delta Queen"), began preparing the specifications and guidance drawings to be used in [—4—] the construction of two passenger vessels, the *Cape May Light* and the *Cape Cod Light*.[1] As this preparation was underway, Delta Queen assigned the contract to Coastal Queen Holdings, LLC ("Coastal Queen"), which then, on May 1, 1999, entered into an agreement with American Marine, Inc. ("AMI")[2] to construct the two vessels in accordance with GPA's guidance drawings.[3] Doc. 56-8, at 3.[4]

---

[1] The vessel involved in the instant case was the *Cape May Light*.

[2] Atlantic Marine Florida, LLC, brought the complaint in this case as successor in interest to Atlantic Marine, Inc.

[3] The Coastal Queen-AMI contract provided that AMI would construct and outfit the vessels, provide design and engineering services as necessary, and complete "all work necessary to construct, test and deliver each Vessel in accordance with the" guidance drawings as prepared by GPA. Doc. 56-8, at 3. The contract referred to GPA as "[AMI]'s engineering subcontractor." Doc. 56-8, at 32. Coastal Queen and AMI agreed that GPA's

On January 12, 2000, AMI entered into a contract with GPA ("the AMI-GPA Agreement" or "the Agreement") under which GPA agreed to complete on behalf of AMI the design and engineering services called for by GPA's contract with Delta Queen. GPA agreed to do so "in a manner . . . consistent with all appropriate professional standards." Doc. 1-2, ¶ 2, at 2. The Agreement required GPA to obtain four separate forms of insurance. Two are relevant here: one [—5—] would provide comprehensive general liability ("CGL") insurance; the other would provide architect's and engineer's professional liability ("A&E") insurance.[5] GPA would be the "named

insured" in both policies, whereas AMI would be designated an "additional insured" in only the CGL policy. GPA obtained a CGL insurance policy from The Hartford Casualty Insurance Company ("Hartford"), but AMI was [—6—] not added as an additional insured.[6] The policy covered GPA for its liability to third parties for personal injuries caused by its negligence.[7] It specifically excluded from coverage, however, liability resulting from its negligence in performing professional services.[8] GPA obtained an A&E insurance policy from Evanston Insurance Company ("Evanston").[9] The policy covered

---

guidance drawings would be revised to conform to the vessels' specifications. *Id.* at 6, 24. As indicated in the following text, AMI then contracted with GPA to provide the design and engineering services required for the construction of both vessels. The record does not indicate whether any of the provisions of GPA's contract with Delta Queen pertaining to specifications and guidance drawings were incorporated by AMI's contract with GPA, or, if so, which provisions were incorporated.

[4] Unless otherwise noted, all docket citations refer to the District Court docket, *Atl. Marine Fla., LLC v. Evanston Ins. Co.*, No. 3:08-cv-00538 (M.D. Fla.).

[5] The full text of the relevant provisions of the AMI-GPA Agreement is as follows:

8. Insurance.

a) GPA shall take out, carry and maintain with insurance company or companies, and in policies of insurance acceptable to AMI, the following insurance with limits not less than indicated for the respective items:

. . . .

(2) Comprehensive General Liability Insurance, including contractual liability, and products completed operations liability with waiver of subrogation in favor of AMI with limits not less than $2,000,000.00 bodily injury and property damage combined, each occurrence and aggregate. *Such insurance must cover AMI as an additional insured* and the policy shall contain the following language: "Naming AMI as an additional insured shall not prevent recovery in any situation in which recovery would have been available had AMI not been named an additional insured."

. . . .

(4) Architect's and Engineer's Professional Liability Insurance from Evanston Insurance Company on a claims made basis with limits

not less than $5,000,000.00 covering both vessels with defense costs in addition to the policy limits and with a $25,000.00 per vessel deductible. . . . Such Architect's and Engineer's Professional Liability Insurance shall contain coverage for breach of contract for errors, omissions or negligent acts. *While GPA will be named insured, AMI agrees to pay the premium for this Architect's and Engineer's Professional Liability Insurance directly to Evanston Insurance Company on behalf of GPA.*

Doc. 1-2, at 5 (emphasis added). Although paragraph (2), unlike paragraph (4) contains no reference to GPA as the "named insured," by specifying that GPA would take out the insurance and that AMI must be covered as a named inured, the parties implicitly agreed that GPA would be the named insured.

[6] The policy's coverage began on April 1, 2001, and was extended retroactively. For business liability, the retroactive date was April 1, 1999. Doc. 1-3, at 5. For employee-benefits liability, it was April 1, 1998—approximately the date GPA began its work under its contract with Delta Queen. *Id.* It appears from the record that AMI was not named an additional insured due to GPA's error.

[7] In the words of the policy, "sums that the insured becomes legally obligated to pay as damages because of 'bodily injury'" caused by "an accident." Doc. 1-3, at 19, 38.

[8] The policy excluded from coverage "'bodily injury' . . . arising out of the rendering or failure to render any professional services by or for [the Named Insured], including (1) [t]he preparing, approving, or failing to prepare or approve . . . designs and specifications; and (2) [s]upervisory, inspection, or engineering services." Doc. 1-3, at 41.

[9] GPA obtained the policy on November 9, 1999, approximately two months before its contract with AMI was finalized. The policy's coverage extended retroactively for claims made on the basis of GPA's

GPA for its liability to third parties for personal injuries caused by its negligence in performing professional services—the coverage the CGL policy specifically excluded.

B.

The *Cape May Light* was christened in Alexandria, Virginia, in April 2001. Later that year, on October 27, the ship was berthed in Green Cove Springs in Clay County, Florida, in anticipation of an extended lay-up period. At approximately [—7—] 4:30 P.M., the ship's captain, Charles Beverly, and the port engineer were in the forward engine room. At one end of the room was a watertight forward bulkhead door, which was designed to shut automatically upon the loss of power. The port engineer left the room to secure the port fueling station, leaving Captain Beverly to cut the ship's power and disconnect its battery terminals. After Captain Beverly did this, he became trapped in the forward bulkhead door in a position that prevented rescuers from accessing its emergency release mechanism. By the time help arrived, he had died from compression asphyxiation.[10]

C.

On October 25, 2002, Captain Beverly's personal representative, Ann Beverly ("Beverly"), filed a wrongful-death action against IMUSA,[11] GPA, and AMI in the Fourth Judicial Circuit Court of Florida.[12] As amended, her complaint alleged that the bulkhead door that caused Captain Beverly's death was designed [—8—] and manufactured by IMSUA and installed by AMI, and that GPA designed the *Cape May Light*, including the system of which the bulkhead door was a part. The complaint contained separate claims of strict liability and negligence against IMUSA (Counts I and II), AMI (Counts III and IV), and GPA (Counts V and VI). The claims of strict liability against IMUSA, AMI, and GPA were materially identical: the bulkhead door, Beverly alleged, was defective and unreasonably dangerous because it had been designed and manufactured so that a person caught or trapped in the door could not reach or activate a release mechanism to disengage or release it.[13] The claims of negligence against the three defendants were also materially identical, except that IMUSA was charged with negligence in designing and manufacturing the door, AMI was allegedly negligent in manufacturing and installing the door, and GPA was allegedly negligent in designing the watertight door and the system of which it was a part so that a person caught or trapped in the door could not activate a release mechanism to disengage or release the door.[14]

In February 2003, AMI demanded that GPA or its insurers, Evanston and [—9—] Hartford, provide it with a defense to the

---

acts, errors, or omissions in the rendering of professional services on or after April 1, 1998. After the AMI-GPA Agreement was finalized, GPA extended the term of the policy as required by the Agreement.

[10] U.S. Coast Guard, Investigation Activity Report, Case No. 138905 (Oct. 27, 2001), *available at* https://cgmix.uscg.mil/iir; *see also* Veronica Chapin, *Law & Disorder: Ortega River Boat Crash Kills Man*, Fla. Times-Union (Oct. 30, 2001), http://jacksonville.com/tu-online/stories/103001/met_7686508.html; *Ship's Master Killed by Door*, Prof. Mariner Mag. (Mar. 2, 2007, 12:00 AM), http://www.professionalmariner.com/March-2007/Ships-master-killed-by-door.

[11] IMUSA is the trade name of Project and Construction Welding, Inc., the manufacturer of the watertight door.

[12] Beverly also sued American Classic Voyages, Co.; Delta Queen Steamboat Company; Delta Queen Coastal Voyages, LLC.; and Cape May Light, LLC. We make no further reference to these defendants because the claims lodged against them are not pertinent here.

[13] Alternatively, the complaint alleged, the bulkhead door was defective and unreasonably dangerous because it either lacked a device to prevent the door from accidentally trapping someone using it, or it lacked adequate warnings. These theories of liability were reproduced in essentially identical form in each count. The complaint extended its allegations of strict liability to GPA on the basis of GPA's designing the *Cape May Light* to include the door.

[14] Each count also alleged that each party was negligent in failing to adequately test, inspect, and post warnings about the dangers of the watertight door.

claims of strict liability and negligence.[15] AMI contended that Evanston was obligated to provide it with a defense under GPA's A&E policy because (1) Beverly's claims were based on GPA's negligence in furnishing the design and engineering services for the *Cape May Light*, and (2) GPA had promised, in the AMI-GPA Agreement, that any liability AMI incurred due to such negligence would be borne by Evanston under the A&E policy. AMI contended that Hartford was obligated to provide it with a defense under the GPA's CGL policy because it was an "additional insured."

Evanston rejected AMI's demand on multiple grounds. First, since AMI was neither a named nor an additional insured in the A&E policy, it was not contract-bound to provide AMI with a defense. Second, AMI was being sued for its own negligence, not GPA's, and the policy did not provide coverage for AMI's negligence. Finally, AMI could not recover under the policy unless and until it obtained a judgment against GPA establishing that GPA's negligent performance [—10—] of professional services caused Captain Beverly's death. Hartford also rejected AMI's demand. Although the record does not disclose the reasons for Hartford's rejection, it appears that Hartford's position was that AMI was neither a named nor an additional insured under GPA's CGL policy; moreover, the policy excluded coverage for GPA's negligent performance of professional services.

Evanston provided a defense for GPA as required by the A&E policy. American Home Assurance Company ("American Home"), AMI's comprehensive marine liability insurer, provided AMI's defense. In their answers to the Beverly complaint, both AMI and GPA denied the allegations of wrongdoing. Then, after the parties had joined issue, AMI moved the court for leave to file a cross-claim against GPA. The proposed cross-claim sought indemnification from GPA for any damages it might have to pay Beverly due to GPA's negligence in designing or engineering the bulkhead door.

The motion was still pending when Evanston and American Home separately settled Beverly's claims against their respective named insureds, GPA and AMI.[16] After learning that American Home was negotiating a settlement of [—11—] Beverly's claims against AMI, *see* Doc. 56-5, at 3, Evanston settled the claims against GPA in June 2007 for approximately $300,000. Soon thereafter, American Home settled the claims against AMI for $325,000.

D.

After these settlements were reached, AMI and American Home brought this declaratory judgment action against Evanston and Hartford.[17] AMI sought a declaration that

---

[15] We note in passing that on November 7, 2001, just weeks after Captain Beverly's death, AMI commenced arbitration proceedings against GPA, alleging breach of contract, breach of implied warranty, and negligence, as well as a right to contractual indemnification arising from the design and manufacture of the *Cape May Light*. Doc. 56-7, at 3. AMI's statement of its claim in the arbitration proceeding appears to be unrelated to Beverly's wrongful-death action. *See* Statement of Claim, *Atl. Marine, Inc. v. Guido Perla & Assocs.*, at 2–4 (Miami Mar. Arb. Council Nov. 7, 2001). After an arbitration panel convened, the arbitration proceedings were held in abeyance. Doc. 56-7, at 3 & n.1. Counsel for GPA noted in an affidavit that the arbitration was eventually dismissed with prejudice. Doc. 56-5, at 2.

[16] *See* Doc. 56-6; *see also* Affidavit of Alan Fiedel ¶ 6, Doc. 56-5 (noting that this motion was never heard); Docket, *Beverly v. Project & Constr. Welding, Inc.*, No. 03-CA-001121 (Fla. 4th Cir. Ct.) (reflecting the same). The record does not disclose whether AMI sought leave to file a cross-claim against IMUSA for indemnification on the ground that [—11—] IMUSA, in manufacturing the bulkhead door, created the defective and unreasonably dangerous condition described in Counts III and IV of Beverly's complaint.

[17] AMI and American Home invoked the District Court's diversity jurisdiction under 28 U.S.C. § 1332, its admiralty and maritime jurisdiction under 28 U.S.C. § 1333, and the Declaratory Judgment Act, 28 U.S.C. § 2201. The District Court had jurisdiction under §§ 1332 and 1333, but not § 2201, because the Declaratory Judgment Act does not provide the federal courts with subject matter jurisdiction. *Stuart Weitzman, LLC v.*

both insurers had a duty to defend it against Beverly's claims; American Home, which provided AMI a defense, sought reimbursement of the expenses it incurred in doing so and the $325,000 it paid Beverly, as well as attorney's fees incurred in prosecuting the complaint in the instant case and costs.[18] [—12—] Evanston, in response, sought contrary declarations, including that (1) the claims Beverly's complaint asserted against AMI were not covered under the A&E policy, and, for that reason, AMI was not entitled to a defense; and (2) American Home, as AMI's subrogee, could not recover under the A&E policy because AMI had not obtained a judgment against GPA based on GPA's negligence in designing the bulkhead door that malfunctioned.

On cross-motions for summary judgment, the District Court found that AMI was a third-party beneficiary under the insurance contract between Evanston and GPA. The policy therefore provided AMI coverage for the claims Beverly asserted against it and obligated Evanston to provide it with a defense against Beverly's claims.[19]

Microcomputer Res., Inc., 542 F.3d 859, 861–62 (11th Cir. 2008).

[18] The complaint also sought a declaration that Evanston breached a contract with AMI when it failed to seek AMI's consent before settling the Beverly estate's claim against GPA. This claim was based on Endorsement No. 7 of the A&E policy, which provided that Evanston

> shall not settle any Claim without the consent of [AMI]. If, however, [AMI] shall refuse to consent to any settlement recommended by [Evanston] and shall elect to contest the Claim or continue any legal proceedings in connection with such Claim, then the Liability of [Evanston] for such Claim shall not exceed the sum of (1) the amount for which such Claim could have been so settled plus (2) Claims Expenses incurred up to the date of such refusal.
> [—12—]

Doc. 1-2, at 20. The District Court held that though Endorsement No. 7 indeed required Evanston to notify and obtain AMI's consent before settling claims, AMI could not succeed in its claim because it failed to adequately plead damages. Doc. 88, at 7–8. AMI has not cross-appealed the court's ruling.

[19] The District Court also held that despite GPA's failure to list AMI as an additional insured

Nonetheless, after an abortive appeal by Evanston to this Court,[20] the District Court denied American Home's claim for reimbursement of the expenses it [—13—] incurred in providing AMI a defense. It did so on the grounds that American Home also had a duty to defend AMI, and that "[c]ontribution is not allowed between insurers incurred in defense of a mutual insured." Doc. 159, at 4–5 (quoting *Argonaut Ins. Co. v. Md. Cas. Co.*, 372 So. 2d 960, 963 (Fla. 3d Dist. Ct. App. 1979).[21] The court ultimately entered judgment for American Home in the amount of $622,131.32. The District Court arrived at this figure by adding the amount American Home paid Beverly in settlement, $325,000; attorney's fees under Florida Statute § 627.428 in the sum of $164,305.26;[22]

---

on the Hartford CGL policy, AMI was an additional insured by virtue of its promise in the AMI-GPA Agreement to obtain CGL insurance. *Id.* at 12–13 & n.3. The court concluded, however, that Hartford had no duty to defend or indemnify AMI under the policy because the policy expressly excluded from its coverage liability for bodily injury resulting from GPA's provision of engineering services. *Id.* at 14–15. AMI has not appealed this ruling.

[20] We dismissed Evanston's prior appeal for want of jurisdiction, *Atl. Marine Fla., LLC v. Evanston Ins. Co.*, No. 10-13458 (11th Cir. July 21, 2011) (per curiam), as we did AMI's associated motion for appellate fees and costs and to transfer to the District Court, *id.* (Dec. 2, 2011).

[21] The court rejected an exception to the *Argonaut* rule that applies "when the obligation to indemnify has been transferred completely from one insurer to another pursuant to an indemnification agreement between the insured parties." Doc. 159, at 5–6 (citing *Cont'l Cas. Co. v. City of S. Daytona*, 807 So. 2d 91, 93 (Fla. 5th Dist. Ct. App. 2002).

[22] Florida Statutes § 627.428 states, in pertinent part:

> (1) Upon the rendition of a judgment or decree by any of the courts of this state against an insurer and in favor of any named or omnibus insured . . . , the trial court . . . shall adjudge or decree against the insurer and in favor of the insured . . . a reasonable sum as fees or compensation for the insured's or beneficiary's attorney prosecuting the suit in which the recovery is had.
>
> . . .
>
> (3) When so awarded, compensation or fees of the attorney shall be included in the judgment or decree rendered in the case.

$132,014.56 in prejudgment interest; and costs in the amount of $811.50. Evanston now appeals the District Court's declaratory judgment and the court's award of attorney's fees [—14—] and costs to American Home.

II.

This appeal presents two issues. The first is whether, under the terms of the A&E policy, including its endorsements, Evanston was obligated to provide AMI a defense in the Beverly lawsuit. Evanston was obligated to do so if the allegations underpinning Beverly's claims came within the coverage the policy provided. *See Jones v. Fla. Ins. Guar. Ass'n*, 908 So. 2d 435, 442–43 (Fla. 2005) ("It is well settled that an insurer's duty to defend its insured against a legal action arises when the complaint alleges facts that fairly and potentially bring the suit within policy coverage.").[23] The second issue is whether the A&E policy obligated Evanston to pay American Home, as AMI's subrogee, the price of its settlement with Beverly.

The amount of attorney's fees consisted of the sum of $125,790 for the period of time prior to the district court's grant of summary judgment in the declaratory judgment action and $38.515.26 for the work completed following its grant of summary judgment. Because of the way we resolve this appeal, we do not address the District Court's holding that AMI was an "omnibus insured" entitled to attorney's fees in this declaratory judgment action pursuant to § 627.428.

[23] The proper interpretation of the A&E policy's insuring agreement or any other relevant policy provision poses a question of law. The parties agree that Florida law governs, and the District Court applied it. Under Florida law, ordinary principles of contract interpretation govern the interpretation of an insurance policy. *Intervest Constr. of Jax, Inc. v. Gen. Fid. Ins. Co.*, 133 So. 3d 494, 497 (Fla. 2014). We read the policy's provisions as a whole, not in isolation, *Harrington v. Citizens Prop. Ins. Corp.*, 54 So. 3d 999, 1004 (Fla. 4th Dist. Ct. App. 2010) (citing, *e.g.*, *Swire Pac. Holdings, Inc. v. Zurich Ins. Co.*, 845 So. 2d 161, 166 (Fla. 2003); *Auto-Owners Ins. Co. v. Anderson*, 756 So. 2d 29, 34 (Fla. 2000)), and we construe terms according to their plain meaning, *Garcia v. Fed. Ins. Co.*, 969 So. 2d 288, 291 (Fla. 2007). We have approached the interpretation of the relevant A&E policy provisions in accordance with these principles.

A.

Evanston was not obligated to provide AMI a defense in the Beverly lawsuit [—15—] unless the A&E policy it issued GPA covered Beverly's clams. We therefore begin our resolution of the first issue by examining the policy's coverage. We then consider whether the facts alleged in Beverly's complaint fell within the ambit of this coverage.

The policy's coverage was set out in Paragraph I of its Insuring Agreements, as follows:

I. Coverage: Claims Made Provision. The Company [Evanston] will pay on behalf of the Named Insured all sums in excess of the deductible amount stated in the Declarations which the Named Insured shall become legally obligated to pay as Damages by reason of any act, error or omission committed or alleged to have been committed by the Named Insured, or any person or organization for whom the Named Insured is legally liable, provided always that:

. . . .

(b) The Named Insured's legal liability arises out of the performance of professional services as described in Schedule 1 for the project described in the Declarations, [the construction of the *Cape May Light* and the *Cape Cod Light*.]

Doc. 1-2, ¶ 1, at 33.[24] [—16—]

---

[24] Schedule 1 is not contained in the record. As indicated in part I.A., *supra*, the AMI-GPA Agreement required GPA to complete the design and engineering services called for by GPA's contract with Delta Queen. AMI conceded, and the District Court found, that GPA was the policy's only named insured. Evanston was obligated to pay a judgment against GPA to the extent the judgment exceeded the policy's deductible of $25,000 per cruise ship and was within the "limit of liability" amount of $5,000,000 for each claim and

Beverly's claims for damages against AMI, Counts III and IV of the wrongful-death complaint, were based on strict liability and negligence, respectively. In Count III, Beverly alleged, essentially, that AMI installed the bulkhead door that caused Captain Beverly's death and that the door was defective and unreasonably dangerous for several reasons, including that a person caught or trapped in the door could not reach or activate a release mechanism to disengage or release the door. The facts underpinning Count IV were that AMI was negligent in installing a bulkhead door containing the defects described in Count III.

It is obvious that these factual allegations did not bring Beverly's claims within the coverage provided by Paragraph I of the Insuring Agreements. AMI concedes as much. This coverage obligated Evanston to satisfy any judgment Beverly might obtain against GPA for negligently designing the bulkhead door, not a judgment recovered against AMI for negligently installing the door. Because the Insuring Agreements provided AMI no coverage, AMI had to find coverage elsewhere in the insurance policy.

AMI points to two endorsements to the policy, Endorsements Nos. 10 and 11, as providing the necessary coverage. Both were issued pursuant to the AMI-GPA Agreement. According to AMI, the endorsements made it a third-party beneficiary of the insurance contract, giving it the status of an insured and the right to a defense at Evanston's expense. The District Court agreed. It found that [—17—] Endorsements Nos. 10 and 11 evidenced Evanston and GPA's intent that the policy primarily benefit AMI and "explicitly extend[ed] coverage to AMI" for Beverly's claims. Doc. 88, at 8–10.[25] Because Florida

law obligates insurers to defend only their insureds, *Nateman v. Hartford Cas. Ins. Co.*, 544 So. 2d 1026, 1027 (Fla. 3d Dist. Ct. App. 1989), the court necessarily held by implication that AMI was an insured.

Endorsement No. 10 amended one of the policy's exclusions, Exclusion I. That exclusion states:

The Insuring Agreements and all other provisions of this policy shall not apply to:

I. Liability assumed by the Named Insured by agreement, whether written or oral, including, but not limited to, hold harmless and indemnity clauses, warranties, guarantees, certifications or penalty clauses, unless such liability arises from an error, omissions or negligent act of the Insured and would have attached in the absence of such agreement. [—18—]

Doc. 1-2, at 34. This form of exclusion is standard in most commercial general liability policies. It omits from coverage the liability of non-insureds assumed by the named insured under an agreement with the non-insured to indemnify or hold harmless the non-insured.[26]

$5,000,000 aggregate. As it turned out, Evanston settled Beverly's claim for a sum within the policy limits prior to trial.

[25] The court also found that AMI's payment of the policy's premium directly to Evanston constituted further evidence that Evanston and GPA intended to make AMI a third-party beneficiary of the policy's coverage. In our view, that finding was immaterial to a proper construction of the policy. As an initial matter,

"[w]here the language in an insurance contract is plain and unambiguous, a court must interpret the policy in accordance with the plain meaning so as to give effect to the policy as written"; extrinsic evidence of the parties' intent is not relevant to the analysis. *Wash. Nat'l Ins. Co. v. Ruderman*, 117 So. 3d 943, 948, 952 (Fla. 2013). Moreover, the payment was part of the contract price AMI paid GPA for performing engineering services. AMI either paid the premium amount to GPA, which would in turn pay Evanston, or AMI would pay Evanston directly. AMI chose the latter option simply to ensure that the premium got paid.

[26] *See* 1 Barry R. Ostrager & Thomas R. Newman, *Handbook on Insurance Coverage Disputes* § 7.05 (16th ed. 2013). This kind of exclusion typically "does not refer to the insured's breaches of its own contracts." *Id.*; *see also, e.g., S. Guar. Ins. Co. v. Zantop Intern. Airlines, Inc.*, 767 F.2d 795, 798 n.3 (11th Cir. 1985); *Auto Owners Ins. Co. v. Travelers Cas. & Surety Co.*, 227 F.

Endorsement No. 10 repeated the language of Exclusion I, and it added a second sentence, emphasized below:

> . . . Liability assumed by the Named Insured by agreement, whether written or oral, including, but not limited to, hold harmless and indemnity clauses, warranties, guarantees, certifications or penalty clauses, unless such liability arises from an error, omissions or negligent act of the Insured and would have attached in the absence of such agreement. *However, this exclusion shall not apply to liability of the Named Insured for a breach of the express contract described below [the AMI-GPA Agreement], but only to the extent that the liability is the result of an act, error, or omission of the Named Insured arising out of the professional services described in the Declarations.*

Doc. 26-2, at 37 (emphasis added).

The first sentence of the endorsement reprinted the language of Exclusion I, which provided AMI no coverage. *See Siegle v. Progressive Consumers Ins. Co.*, 819 So. 2d 732, 740 (Fla. 2002) ("[P]olicy exclusions cannot create coverage where there is no coverage in the first place." (quotation marks omitted)). And the [—19—] second sentence merely clarified the first sentence: if AMI were to bring a breach-of-contract claim against GPA and prevail, GPA would have coverage and Evanston would pay AMI's judgment, provided that GPA's liability for the breach was based on its performance of professional services. In short, Endorsement No. 10 did not transform Exclusion I into an insuring agreement and thereby provide AMI with coverage for its own tortious conduct.

Turning to the second endorsement on which AMI relies, Endorsement No. 11 stated:

> In consideration of the premium charged, such insurance as is afforded by this policy applies to the liability of

others imposed by law, which is assumed by the Named Insured under the contract described below [the AMI-GPA Agreement], but only to the extent that the liability of others is the result of an act, error, or omission of the Insured arising out of the professional services described in the Declarations.

Doc. 1-2, ¶ 1, at 24. AMI contends that although Evanston did not expressly include AMI as an insured under the policy, Evanston intended that Endorsement No. 11—read against the background of Endorsement No. 10—create coverage for the claims Beverly stated in Counts III and IV of her complaint.[27] Consequently, [—20—] AMI argues, Evanston was required to provide it with a defense against those claims. We are not persuaded.

Endorsement No. 11 stated, in essence, that the coverage the A&E policy afforded GPA would apply to AMI, too, if AMI were held liable to Beverly (or anyone else) for an "act, error, or omission" of GPA in its performance of professional services in

---

[27] In its motion for summary judgment, AMI argued that GPA's agreement "to provide the professional services under th[e] [AMI-GPA] Agreement in a manner that is consistent with all appropriate professional standards," Doc. 1-2, ¶ 2, at 2, qualified as "liability of other[s] imposed by law [the law of contract]," Doc. 38, at 7 (second alteration in original). The [—20—] argument was meritless. The phrase "liability imposed by law" does not mean "the law of contract." *See* Ostrager & Newman § 7.01 ("The phrase . . . 'liability imposed by law' refers to the liability of the insured arising from the breach of a duty that exists independent of any contractual relationship between the insured and the injured party.").

AMI has also argued that the phrase "such insurance . . . applies to the liability of others imposed by law" means that "others" are insureds. *See* Appellees'/Cross-Appellants' Br. 15–16. But the phrase "liability of others imposed by law" in Endorsement No. 11 specified the *category* of liability to which insurance extended, not *who qualified* as an insured. In this case, the endorsement would have extended coverage to *GPA* in the event that a third party obtained a judgment against AMI requiring it to pay tort damages because of GPA's professional negligence in designing the *Cape May Light* or the *Cape Cod Light*.

Supp. 2d 1248, 1269–70 (M.D. Fla. 2002); 9 Lee R. Russ & Thomas F. Segalla, *Couch on Insurance 3d* § 129:31 (2005 & Supp. 2014).

connection with AMI's construction of the *Cape May Light*. Thus, had Beverly, in her wrongful-death action, obtained a judgment against AMI based on a finding that GPA's negligence in designing the bulkhead door caused Captain Beverly's death, Evanston would have paid the judgment.[28] But this never came to pass; AMI was never adjudged liable to Beverly due to GPA's negligent design of the bulkhead door. Rather, American Home, for AMI, settled with Beverly prior to trial. [—21—]

AMI's argument seems to be that the fact that it settled Beverly's claims rather than suffer the entry of a judgment of "liability imposed by law" should not matter: as a third-party beneficiary of the insurance contract, the mere possibility that it might have been found liable to Beverly based on GPA's negligent design of the bulkhead door entitled it to a defense. We disagree. After considering what would have transpired had Evanston acceded to AMI's demand to step in and take over its defense, we conclude that AMI was not a third-party beneficiary as the District Court found.

Here is what would have happened had Evanston assumed AMI's defense: In providing both its named insured (GPA) and AMI with a defense to Beverly's claims, Evanston would have found itself in a conflict of interest. To avoid the conflict, instead of selecting counsel to represent the respective parties, thereby maintaining some control over the conduct of their defenses, Evanston would have had to give the parties the funds to employ counsel of their choice and to pay the expenses incurred in their separate defenses. *See* Fla. Stat. § 627.426(2) (requiring insurers, after providing written notice of their reservation of rights, to either refuse to defend, obtain a nonwaiver agreement from, or retain mutually agreeable independent counsel for an insured). The Evanston-funded attorneys for GPA and AMI would have separately answered Beverly's complaint and denied liability for Captain Beverly's death. AMI's attorney would have also filed a cross-

claim [—22—] against GPA, alleging that GPA's negligence in designing the bulkhead door was the sole cause of Captain Beverly's death.

Evanston and GPA could not have intended such an arrangement. True, they agreed that Evanston would indemnify AMI for any liability "imposed" on it "by law" due to GPA's negligent performance of professional services. But they hardly intended that Evanston, at GPA's expense,[29] would finance AMI's cross-claim to establish that GPA's negligence led to such liability. To determine otherwise would require us to assume that GPA agreed to fund suits to establish its own professional negligence—as only a judgment that it was professionally negligent would bring AMI's claim within the A&E policy's coverage. It would also require us to assume that Evanston agreed to fund lawsuits to establish liability resulting in a judgment for which it would be responsible for paying.

In sum, we find no basis for the District Court's third-party-beneficiary finding and set aside the court's determination that Evanston was obligated to provide AMI a defense.

B.

The second issue before us in this appeal is whether the District Court erred in holding Evanston liable for the $325,000 sum American Home paid Beverly to [—23—] settle her claims. The short answer is yes. American Home failed to establish, as required by Endorsement No. 11, that AMI's liability for Captain Beverly's death was the result of an "act, error, or omission of [GPA] arising out of the professional services" it had performed. This feature of Endorsement No. 11 mirrored the procedure required by Florida Statutes § 627.4136, which provides, in relevant part:

> It shall be a condition precedent to the accrual or maintenance of a cause of action against a liability insurer by a person not an insured under the terms of the liability insurance contract that

---

[28] Evanston confirmed at oral argument that it would have paid the judgment to the extent it was within the policy's limits.

[29] *See supra* note 25.

such person shall first obtain a settlement or verdict against a person who is an insured under the terms of such policy for a cause of action which is covered by such policy.

That the A&E policy mirrors this Florida statute should not be surprising, as insurance policies in Florida incorporate the requirements of Florida's insurance code. *E.g.*, *Hassen v. State Farm Mut. Auto. Ins. Co.*, 674 So. 2d 106, 108 (Fla. 1996); *Dep't of Ins. v. Teachers Ins.*, 404 So. 2d 735, 741 (Fla. 1981) (citing *Bd. of Pub. Instruction v. Town of Bay Harbor Islands*, 81 So. 2d 637 (Fla. 1955)).

C.

Because we reverse the District Court's judgment in favor of AMI and American Home and direct the entry of judgment for Evanston, the court's award of attorney's fees under Florida Statute § 627.428 is also reversed. [—24—]

III.

For the foregoing reasons, the judgment of the District Court is REVERSED. On receipt of our mandate, the court is directed to enter judgment for Evanston.

SO ORDERED.

United States Court of Appeals for the District of Columbia Circuit

United States Court of Appeals
for the District of Columbia Circuit

No. 13-7081

BAUER
vs.
MAVI MARMARA

Appeal from the United States District Court for the District of Columbia

Decided: December 19, 2014

Citation: 774 F.3d 1026, 2 Adm. R. 616 (D.C. Cir. 2014).

Before **SRINIVASAN,** Circuit Judge, **EDWARDS,** Senior Circuit Judge, and **SENTELLE,** Senior Circuit Judge.

[—2—] **EDWARDS,** Senior Circuit Judge:

The Neutrality Act ("Act"), 18 U.S.C. § 962, was initially passed in 1794. It "has been generally recognized as the first instance of municipal legislation in support of the obligations of neutrality, and a remarkable advance in the development of International Law." *The Three Friends*, 166 U.S. 1, 52 (1897). The Act makes it unlawful to furnish, fit out, or arm a vessel within the United States with the intent of having the vessel used in the service of a foreign state or people to commit hostilities against another foreign state or people with whom the United States is at peace. Any person who violates the Act "[s]hall be fined . . . or imprisoned not more than three years, or both." 18 U.S.C. § 962. In addition, vessels that are covered by the Act are subject to forfeiture, and persons who give information leading to the seizure of such vessels may recover a bounty, with "one half to the use of the informer and the other half to the use of the United States." *Id.*

On July 11, 2011, appellant, Dr. Alan J. Bauer, filed a complaint in the District Court to pursue a claim under the Neutrality Act. The complaint asserted that Dr. Bauer had informed the United States Government of vessels that had been funded, furnished, and fitted by anti-Israel organizations in the United States, together with violent and militant anti-Israel organizations from other countries, in violation of the Act. The complaint further averred that the vessels were to be employed in the service of Hamas, a terrorist organization in the Gaza Strip, to commit hostilities against Israel. Dr. Bauer claimed that he had the right, as an informer, to condemn the vessels for forfeiture and to share in the bounty.

The District Court dismissed the complaint, on the ground that: [—3—]

18 U.S.C. § 962 lacks an express private cause of action, and the court declines the plaintiff's invitation to imply one. Accordingly, this case must be dismissed for the plaintiff's failure to state a claim upon which relief may be granted.

Bauer v. Mavi Marmara, 942 F. Supp. 2d 31, 43 (D.D.C. 2013). In its brief to this court, the United States ("Government"), appearing as an interested party, agrees that "[a] private individual has no authority to bring an action under Section 962." United States Br. 10. "Moreover," according to the Government, "even assuming a private party can bring a forfeiture action under the statute, the government's participation would be required, and the government here declines to participate in Dr. Bauer's suit." *Id.* During oral argument before this court, Government counsel also argued that Dr. Bauer's suit should be dismissed for lack of standing.

Dr. Bauer concedes that the Neutrality Act does not provide an express cause of action. He insists, however, that a private cause of action may be judicially implied. In support of this position, Dr. Bauer contends that statutes that contain a bounty provision and that do not forbid a private cause of action should be understood to implicitly grant a private cause of action to informers. In his briefs to this court, Dr. Bauer does not directly address standing. He seems to assume that if a party has a private cause of action to sue, he necessarily has standing.

It is well understood that a party who seeks to pursue an action in federal court must first establish Article III standing. As the Supreme Court explained in *Lujan v.*

Defenders of Wildlife, 504 U.S. 555 (1992): [—4—]

[T]he irreducible constitutional minimum of standing contains three elements. First, the plaintiff must have suffered an injury in fact—an invasion of a legally protected interest which is (a) concrete and particularized, and (b) actual or imminent, not conjectural or hypothetical. Second, there must be a causal connection between the injury and the conduct complained of—the injury has to be fairly traceable to the challenged action of the defendant, and not the result of the independent action of some third party not before the court. Third, it must be likely, as opposed to merely speculative, that the injury will be redressed by a favorable decision.

Id. at 560–61 (citations, internal quotation marks, and alterations omitted).

We recognize that when a plaintiff's alleged injury arises solely from a statute, questions concerning standing and the availability of a private cause of action under the statute may be intertwined. Nevertheless, standing and a failure to state a cause of action are not the same.

The question whether a federal statute creates a claim for relief is not jurisdictional. *Nw. Airlines, Inc. v. Cnty. of Kent, Mich.*, 510 U.S. 355, 365 (1994). Therefore, an objection to a party's failure to state a claim upon which relief can be granted can be forfeited if it is not properly raised. *Arbaugh v. Y&H Corp.*, 546 U.S. 500, 507 (2006). On the other hand, standing is jurisdictional and it can never be forfeited or waived. *Steel Co. v. Citizens for a Better Env't*, 523 U.S. 83, 94–95 (1998). "Standing can be raised at any point in a case proceeding and, as a jurisdictional matter, may be raised, *sua sponte*, by the court." *Steffan v. Perry*, 41 F.3d 677, 697 n.20 (D.C. Cir. 1994) (en banc). And "[w]hen there is doubt about [—5—] a party's constitutional standing, the court *must* resolve the doubt, *sua sponte* if need be." *Lee's Summit, Mo. v. Surface Transp. Bd.*, 231 F.3d 39, 41 (D.C. Cir. 2000) (first emphasis added). Given this

mandate, we have carefully focused on the requirements of Article III and concluded that Dr. Bauer's suit must be dismissed for want of standing, not for failure to state a cause of action.

Our decision here is informed by the Supreme Court's decision in *Vermont Agency of Natural Resources v. United States ex rel. Stevens*, 529 U.S. 765 (2000). In *Stevens*, the Court held that bounty hunters like Dr. Bauer have standing to sue only through "the doctrine that the assignee of a claim has standing to assert the injury in fact suffered by the assignor." *Id.* at 773. That case concerned the False Claims Act, 31 U.S.C. §§ 3729–3733, which expressly authorizes private parties who are aware of fraud against the Government to sue on behalf of the Government and collect restitution and penalties from the fraudsters, keeping part of the recovery for themselves. *Id.* § 3730(b)(1). The *Stevens* Court found that

the statute gives the relator himself an interest *in the lawsuit*, and not merely the right to retain a fee out of the recovery. Thus, it provides that "[a] person may bring a civil action for a violation of section 3729 *for the person and for the United States Government*," § 3730(b) (emphasis added); gives the relator "the right to continue as a party to the action" even when the Government itself has assumed "primary responsibility" for prosecuting it, § 3730(c)(1); entitles the relator to a hearing before the Government's voluntary dismissal of the suit, § 3730(c)(2)(A); and prohibits the Government from settling the suit over the relator's objection without a judicial determination of "fair[ness], adequa[cy] and reasonable[ness]," § 3730(c)(2)(B). [—6—]

Stevens, 529 U.S. at 772. In light of these statutory provisions, the Court held that the False Claims Act "can reasonably be regarded as effecting a partial assignment of the Government's damages claim." *Id.* at 773. It reached this conclusion in part because the False Claims Act "gives the relator himself an interest *in the lawsuit,* and not merely the right to retain a fee out of the recovery." *Id.* at 772.

There is no such assignment under the Neutrality Act. An informer under the Neutrality Act has nothing more than an inchoate and conditional interest in a bounty, which hinges on whether the Government pursues a forfeiture action. Therefore, an informer like Dr. Bauer cannot establish either injury-in-fact or redressability and has no standing to pursue this action on his own to enforce the Government's interests in neutrality in foreign affairs.

I. BACKGROUND

A. *The Neutrality Act*

Congress passed the Neutrality Act in 1794. Act of June 5, 1794, ch. 50, 1 Stat. 381. The Act

> was recommended to congress by President Washington in his annual address on December 3, 1793, was drawn by Hamilton, and passed the senate by the casting vote of Vice President Adams. [It] was designed to keep the United States from getting dragged into the conflict between England and France. Thomas H. Lee, *The Safe-Conduct Theory of the Alien Tort Statute,* 106 COLUM. L. REV. 830, 847 (2006) (describing the "young Republic's neutrality crisis" as the Founders precariously navigated "between the Scylla of Britain and the Charybdis of [—7—] France."). Thus, the Act appears to be a legislative enactment of President Washington's warning—made famous in his farewell address—that the young nation should remain free from entangling alliances. George Washington, Farewell Address (Sept. 19, 1796), *reprinted in* S. Doc. No. 106-21 (2000).

Bauer, 942 F. Supp. 2d at 33 (citation and internal quotation marks omitted); *see also The Three Friends,* 166 U.S. at 52–53.

As noted above, the Act criminalizes certain actions committed in the United States that support a foreign state or people against any other foreign state or people with whom the United States is at peace. Though repeatedly amended, and very rarely invoked, much of the original Act remains in force to this day.

The section of the Neutrality Act at issue in this case states:

> Whoever, within the United States, furnishes, fits out, arms, or attempts to furnish, fit out or arm, any vessel, with intent that such vessel shall be employed in the service of any foreign prince, or state, or of any colony, district, or people, to cruise, or commit hostilities against the subjects, citizens, or property of any foreign prince or state, or of any colony, district, or people with whom the United States is at peace; . . . [s]hall be fined under this title or imprisoned not more than three years, or both.

18 U.S.C. § 962. The Act further provides that

> Every such vessel, her tackle, apparel, and furniture, together with all materials, arms, ammunition, and stores [—8—] which may have been procured for the building and equipment thereof, shall be forfeited, one half to the use of the informer and the other half to the use of the United States.

Id.

Bounty statutes such as the Neutrality Act were popular immediately after the ratification of the Constitution.

> Although there is no evidence that the Colonies allowed common-law *qui tam* actions (which . . . were dying out in England by that time), they did pass several informer statutes expressly authorizing *qui tam* suits. Moreover, immediately after the framing, the First Congress enacted a considerable number of informer statutes. Like their English

counterparts, some of them provided both a bounty and an express cause of action; others provided a bounty only.

Stevens, 529 U.S. at 776–77 (citation and footnotes omitted). The Neutrality Act was a "bounty only" statute. As we explain below, no judicial decision of which we are aware has ever construed the Neutrality Act to afford standing to a private party to prosecute an alleged criminal infraction or to independently pursue a forfeiture claim.

B. *The Gaza Flotilla and Dr. Bauer's Lawsuit*

According to Dr. Bauer's complaint, his lawsuit arises from the 2007 rise to power of Hamas, a terrorist organization in the Gaza Strip. After Hamas seized power in Gaza and began carrying out systematic rocket and missile attacks against civilian targets in Israel, Israel imposed a maritime [—9—] blockade to limit Hamas's ability to receive material support that would facilitate the attacks.

Dr. Bauer alleges that, in response to the blockade, anti-Israel organizations in the United States, together with violent and militant anti-Israel organizations from other countries, initiated efforts to breach Israel's blockade, to harm Israeli security, and to support the Hamas-controlled government in the Gaza Strip. These groups allegedly raised money within the United States and through U.S. bank accounts, which they used to "furnish[] and fit[] out and attempt[] to furnish and fit out the Defendant Vessels, with the intent that the Defendant Vessels be employed in the service of a colony, district, or people [Hamas-controlled Gaza], to cruise and commit hostilities against" Israel, "with whom the United States is at peace." Compl. ¶ 18, *reprinted in* App. 6.

On June 13, 2011, Dr. Bauer sent a letter to Attorney General Eric Holder, identifying the alleged violation of the Neutrality Act and providing the names of 14 vessels that were involved. On July 11, he filed a complaint in the District Court, setting out the allegations above and requesting that the court commence forfeiture proceedings against the vessels.

On its own motion, the District Court issued an order to show cause why Dr. Bauer's complaint should not be dismissed for lack of standing. The court also requested, pursuant to 28 U.S.C. § 517, that the Department of Justice file a statement of interest on standing in the case. After receiving submissions from Dr. Bauer and the Government, the District Court dismissed the complaint on the ground that the Neutrality Act did not authorize a private suit for forfeiture and, therefore, Dr. Bauer had failed to state a claim on which relief could be granted. *Bauer*, 942 F. Supp. 2d at 43. Dr. Bauer now appeals. [—10—]

II. ANALYSIS

A. *Introduction – The Critical Threshold Requirement of Article III Standing*

The District Court and the parties have focused on the question whether Dr. Bauer's complaint states a cause of action. To assess the case in these terms is to assume that Dr. Bauer has standing, which is a threshold jurisdictional requirement. We do not accept this assumption. As the Court noted in *Bender v. Williamsport Area School District*, 475 U.S. 534 (1986):

> Federal courts are not courts of general jurisdiction; they have only the power that is authorized by Article III of the Constitution and the statutes enacted by Congress pursuant thereto. For that reason, every federal appellate court has a special obligation to satisfy itself not only of its own jurisdiction, but also that of the lower courts in a cause under review, even though the parties are prepared to concede it. And if the record discloses that the lower court was without jurisdiction this court will notice the defect, although the parties make no contention concerning it. When the lower federal court lacks jurisdiction, we have jurisdiction on appeal, not of the merits but merely for the purpose of correcting the error of the lower court in entertaining the suit.

Id. at 541 (citations, internal quotation marks, and brackets omitted). Under Article III, a party who invokes the court's authority "must have suffered an injury in fact—an invasion of a legally protected interest which is (a) concrete and particularized, and (b) actual or imminent, not conjectural or hypothetical." *Lujan*, 504 U.S. at 560 (citations and internal [—11—] quotation marks omitted). And "it must be likely, as opposed to merely speculative, that the injury will be redressed by a favorable decision." *Id.* at 561 (internal quotation marks omitted). In this case, Dr. Bauer has failed to show that he has suffered or been assigned any injury in fact, and he cannot show that his alleged injury will be redressed by a favorable action of the court. Therefore, we are obliged to dismiss his complaint because we have no jurisdiction to hear it.

Critical to this holding is our finding that a person who claims to be an informer under the Neutrality Act has nothing more than an inchoate and conditional interest in collecting a bounty, which does not ripen unless the Government seeks forfeiture of the vessels identified by the purported informer. By default, a member of the public has no more legal interest in forfeiting property associated with a crime than with prosecuting the crime itself. It is therefore hardly surprising that under the Neutrality Act, as with most criminal statutes, the Government alone determines whether to prosecute offenders. *See Linda R.S. v. Richard D.*, 410 U.S. 614, 619 (1973) (holding that "a private citizen lacks a judicially cognizable interest in the prosecution or nonprosecution of another"). Dr. Bauer does not dispute this. Similarly, although the Act also authorizes a civil action for forfeiture, it does not afford standing to purported informers to pursue forfeiture on their own. An informer like Dr. Bauer can point to no concrete injury. An inchoate, conditional interest in a bounty is not enough to demonstrate injury in support of standing.

Dr. Bauer is also unable to satisfy the redressability prong of Article III standing because the court cannot compel the Government to pursue action to seek forfeiture of the disputed vessels. Without such action by the Government, Dr. Bauer has nothing to claim under the Neutrality Act. An informer may be disappointed if the Government declines to [—12—] pursue forfeiture, but disappointment of this sort is a far cry from the injury and redressability required to prove Article III standing. *See, e.g., Miami Bldg. & Constr. Trades Council v. Sec'y of Def.*, 493 F.3d 201, 202, 205–06 (D.C. Cir. 2007) (holding that "disappointment" at a "lost opportunity" is not enough for standing where the possibility for redress rests in the discretion of a third party who has declined to take action necessary to serve the plaintiff's interests); *see also Lujan*, 504 U.S. at 562 (no standing if an element of standing "depends on the unfettered choices made by independent actors not before the courts and whose exercise of broad and legitimate discretion the courts cannot presume either to control or to predict" (citation and internal quotation marks omitted)).

In the analysis below, we show that the language, purpose, and historical context of the Neutrality Act support our finding that informers have no standing to sue for forfeiture on their own.

B. *The Language and Purpose of the Neutrality Act Show That Private Parties Do Not Have Standing to Pursue Forfeiture on Their Own Under the Neutrality Act*

"It is settled law that an informer can in no case sue in his own name to recover a forfeiture given in part to him, unless the right to sue is accorded by the statute raising the forfeiture. That is why the terms and structure of the particular statute are decisive." *Conn. Action Now, Inc. v. Roberts Plating Co.*, 457 F.2d 81, 84 (2d Cir. 1972) (citation and internal quotation marks omitted). Focusing on the terms and structure of a statute also ensures fealty to the proper judicial role: "Raising up causes of action where a statute has not created them may be a proper function for common-law courts, but not for federal tribunals." *Alexander v. Sandoval*, [—13—] 532 U.S. 275, 287 (2001) (citation and internal quotation marks omitted).

The Neutrality Act was one of many bounty statutes passed in the early days of the

Republic, and many of those statutes explicitly authorized informers to sue. The express inclusion in some statutes of language granting private parties a right to sue certainly suggests that Congress did not intend for such a right to be implied in the absence of express authorization.

For example, a few months before the Neutrality Act was passed, Congress enacted the Slave Trade Act of 1794, which made it illegal to "build, fit, equip, load or otherwise prepare any ship or vessel" within the United States for the purpose of carrying on the slave trade. Act of Mar. 22, 1794, ch. 11, § 1–2, 1 Stat. 347, 347–48. The Slave Trade Act was passed by the same Congress that passed the Neutrality Act, yet the terms of the statutes are very different with respect to whether a private party has standing to pursue a claim. The Slave Trade Act provided, explicitly, that the bounty went to "the use of him or her *who shall sue for and prosecute.*" *Id.* § 2, 1 Stat. at 349 (emphasis added). When Congress passed the Neutrality Act several months later, it did not include any language of this sort. Many other bounty statutes from this era, unlike the Neutrality Act, also explicitly afforded private parties a right to sue to claim bounties allegedly owed to them. *See Stevens*, 529 U.S. at 777 n.6 (collecting examples). The Neutrality Act stands out because of what it does not say.

The absence of any provision in the Neutrality Act affording standing to private parties to pursue actions for forfeiture on their own is unsurprising in light of the Government's primacy in the management of international affairs. *See United States v. Curtiss-Wright Export Corp.*, 299 [—14—] U.S. 304, 320 (1936); *Olivier v. Hyland*, 186 F. 843, 843 (5th Cir. 1911) (per curiam) ("The enforcement of the neutrality laws of the United States is of necessity under the control of the government of the United States . . . ."). As the Supreme Court has reminded us, courts must be "particularly wary of impinging on the discretion of the Legislative and Executive Branches in managing foreign affairs" because of the "potential implications for the foreign relations of the United States." *Sosa v. Alvarez-Machain*, 542 U.S. 692, 727

(2004). And as this court has previously noted in the context of a separate provision of the Neutrality Act (albeit one without a bounty provision), it would "be doubly difficult to find a private damage action within the Neutrality Act, since this would have the practical effect of eliminating prosecutorial discretion in an area where the normal desirability of such discretion is vastly augmented by the broad leeway traditionally accorded the Executive in matters of foreign affairs." *Sanchez-Espinoza v. Reagan*, 770 F.2d 202, 210 (D.C. Cir. 1985) (Scalia, J.) (citation omitted); *see also Smith v. Reagan*, 844 F.2d 195, 201 (4th Cir. 1988) (courts should be wary of "tread[ing] on matters of foreign policy which have long been recognized as the exclusive province of the political branches," and courts "must be especially certain of congressional intent before inferring a private cause of action" in the realm of foreign affairs).

In sum, there is nothing in the language or purpose of the Neutrality Act that supports Dr. Bauer's position in this case. [—15—]

C. *There Is No Case in Which the Supreme Court or Any Federal Appellate Court Has Held That Private Parties Have Standing to Pursue Forfeiture on Their Own Under the Neutrality Act*

Dr. Bauer claims that, despite the absence of any language in the statute to support his standing to pursue a forfeiture action, the Neutrality Act always has been understood to endorse private causes of action by purported informers. This, according to Dr. Bauer, confirms his standing in this case. We can find no creditable evidence to support this view.

Dr. Bauer has not cited a single decision issued by the Supreme Court or any federal appellate court in which a private party has been allowed to prosecute either a criminal action or a forfeiture pursuant to the Neutrality Act. Indeed, historical practice has been manifestly to the contrary. Because "private citizen[s] lack[] a judicially cognizable interest in the prosecution or nonprosecution of another," *Linda R.S.*, 410 U.S. at 619, criminal actions under the Neutrality Act have been pursued only by Government prosecutors. *See, e.g., United States v. Quincy*, 31 U.S. 445 (1832) (Government criminal prosecution for violations of the Neutrality Act); *United States v. Reyburn*, 31 U.S. 352 (1832) (same); *United States v. Trumbull*, 48 F. 99 (S.D. Cal. 1891) (same). Neutrality Act forfeitures have likewise been pursued only by Government officials. *See, e.g., The Three Friends*, 166 U.S. 1 (seizure and forfeiture by the Government); *Gelston v. Hoyt*, 16 U.S. 246, 320 (1818) (noting that only a Government official has the "authority to make the seizure, or to enforce the forfeiture"); *The Laurada*, 98 F. 983 (3d Cir. 1900), *affirming The Laurada*, 85 F. 760 (D. Del. 1898) (action filed on behalf of the United States praying that vessel be condemned and declared forfeited for an alleged violation [—16—] of the Neutrality Act); *The City of Mexico*, 28 F. 148 (S.D. Fla. 1886) (decree of forfeiture issued in favor of the Government).

As the court held in *Olivier*:

> The enforcement of the neutrality laws of the United States is of necessity under the control of the government of the United States. Where a seizure is made on complaint of an informer for violation of [the Neutrality Act], and the United States, through its proper representatives, intervenes, disavows, and declines to ratify the seizure, as in the instant case, the informer can have no such inchoate or other interest as will permit the further prosecution of the case in his behalf.

186 F. at 843.

In an effort to overcome the overwhelming weight of authority against him, Dr. Bauer points to dictum in a footnote in the Supreme Court's decision in *United States ex rel. Marcus v. Hess*, 317 U.S. 537 (1943). The footnote describes *qui tam* actions generally, and then states that "[s]tatutes providing for a reward to informers which do not specifically either authorize or forbid the informer to institute the action are construed to authorize him to sue." *Id.* at 541 n.4 (citing *Adams v. Woods*, 6 U.S. (2 Cranch) 336 (1805)). This dictum has never been applied or otherwise followed by the Supreme Court or any federal appellate court.

It is telling that *Adams v. Woods*, which is the lone citation offered by the Court in *Hess* to support the dictum, includes nothing to support Dr. Bauer's argument. Dr. Bauer suggests that the dictum in *Hess* refers to the *Adams* Court's statement that when "the statute which creates the forfeiture [—17—] does not prescribe the mode of demanding it[,] either debt or information would lie." 6 U.S. (2 Cranch) at 341. We are not convinced of this statement's relevance. Indeed, *Adams* has nothing to do with whether a private party can pursue a forfeiture action under the Neutrality Act. Rather, *Adams* confronted the question of which causes of action were covered by a statute of limitations that applied to, *inter alia*, "forfeiture." 6 U.S. (2 Cranch) at 336–40. The Court read the statute of limitations to apply to all causes of action normally implied by a forfeiture statute: not only the "informations" specifically mentioned by the statute of limitations, but also "actions of debt" that were not mentioned. The Court's statement merely recognized that when a statute provides for forfeiture, the prosecuting party can normally bring *either* an information or an action of debt—two distinct causes of action at common law.

The Court in *Adams* said nothing about *who* could bring these actions. Indeed, that question was not contested: the statute at issue in the case, the Slave Trade Act of 1794, explicitly authorized a private party to sue. § 2, 1 Stat. at 349. Neither does the Court's statement that forfeiture implies an action of debt compel the conclusion that private parties may pursue forfeiture claims on their own under the Neutrality Act. On this score, the Supreme Court has made it clear that the United States itself can bring a civil action of debt to recover forfeited property. *Stockwell v. United States*, 80 U.S. 531, 542–43 (1871).

Given *Adams*'s lack of support for the dictum in *Hess*, it is unsurprising that courts have criticized and declined to follow the cryptic sentence in footnote 4 in *Hess*. *See, e.g., Jacklovich v. Interlake, Inc.*, 458 F.2d 923, 927 n.10 (7th Cir. 1972); *Conn. Action*

Now, Inc., 457 F.2d at 84–85 & n.5; *Bass Anglers Sportsman's Soc. of Am. v. Scholze Tannery, Inc.*, [—18—] 329 F. Supp. 339, 344–45 (E.D. Tenn. 1971) (collecting additional cases rejecting the *Hess* dictum); *see also* Diane D. Eames, Comment, *The Refuse Act of 1899: Its Scope and Role in Control of Water Pollution*, 58 CALIF. L. REV. 1444, 1460–61 & n.106 (1970) ("It is not clear that *Hess* correctly interpreted the *Adams* dicta." *Id.* at 1460.). The Supreme Court itself has noted that the sentence in footnote 4 in *Hess* is merely "dictum," *Stevens*, 529 U.S. at 777 n.7, and the Court has never given it effect in any case.

Dr. Bauer also points to some cases for their dicta regarding an informer's right to *seize* a vessel. Apart from the fact that the right to seize is not at issue here, none of the cases cited stands for the proposition that a Neutrality Act informer can prosecute the forfeiture itself. *See Olivier*, 186 F. at 843 (noting that an informer's "seizure" can be disavowed by the government; not recognizing any informer's right to execute forfeiture); *The Venus*, 180 F. 635, 635 (E.D. La. 1910) ("express[ing] no opinion" as to whether an informer can institute an action of seizure); *The City of Mexico*, 28 F. at 148 (governmental seizure); *see also Gelston*, 16 U.S. at 310, 319–20 (discussing the right of an informer "to seize" a vessel, but distinguishing between seizure and forfeiture).

We end where we started: Dr. Bauer has failed to cite a single decision issued by the Supreme Court or any federal appellate court in which a private party has been afforded standing to prosecute either a criminal action or a forfeiture pursuant to the Neutrality Act. In short, there is no good authority to support Dr. Bauer's standing in this case. [—19—]

D. *The History of Enforcement Actions Brought Pursuant to Informer Statutes Does Not Support Dr. Bauer's Standing in This Case*

The foregoing analysis does not precisely focus on bounty or informer statutes, as such, but it nonetheless makes it plain that Dr. Bauer has failed to meet his burden of proving standing in this case. Because the Neutrality Act is an informer statute, we proceed to explain why the history of enforcement actions brought pursuant to such statutes does not support Dr. Bauer's standing here.

As the Supreme Court has noted, the violation of a law such as the Neutrality Act does not injure the informer directly; the violation injures only the Government. *See Stevens*, 529 U.S. at 771–73 (identifying both "the injury to [the Government's] sovereignty arising from violation of its laws . . . and [any] proprietary injury resulting from the" crime). Therefore, it is clear that Dr. Bauer himself was not directly, concretely, and specifically injured by the acts of the Gaza flotilla organizers that he alleged in his complaint. A bounty may give an informer such as Dr. Bauer a "concrete private interest in the outcome of [the] suit," but such an interest is "unrelated to injury in fact [and] insufficient to give [an informer] standing." *Id.* at 772 (first alteration in original) (citations and internal quotation marks omitted). Because Dr. Bauer suffered no injury to a legally protected right from the alleged violation of the law, he does not have personal standing to bring a claim arising from the asserted violation.

There is more to it, however, because the Court in *Stevens* made it clear that an informer in a *qui tam* action may have standing through "the doctrine that the assignee of a claim has standing to assert the injury in fact suffered by the assignor." *Id.* at 773. Thus, in *Stevens*, the Court held that the [—20—] False Claims Act "effect[ed] a partial assignment of the Government's damages claim" by granting private plaintiffs the right (subject to government control) to bring a *qui tam* action against those who defrauded the government. *See id.* The assignment in the False Claims Act context is "partial" because the Government retains the right in those cases to intervene and dismiss the claim. "Dismissal ends the assignment." *See Swift v. United States*, 318 F.3d 250, 254 n.* (D.C. Cir. 2003). The controlling question in this case, then, is whether the Neutrality Act is a *qui tam* statute comparable to the False Claims Act and other such statutes. That is, does the

Neutrality Act include an assignment of all or a portion of the Government's interest in the statutory bounty sufficient to confer standing on an informer like Dr. Bauer? We hold that it does not.

Since the time of our Nation's founding, Congress has passed numerous informer statutes. As noted above, however, Dr. Bauer has not identified any decision issued by the Supreme Court or a federal appellate court in which a private informer was allowed to pursue forfeiture pursuant to a statute that did not explicitly grant or clearly imply a private cause of action. We can find no such case. Several courts and scholars have extensively surveyed the field and have found near-universal agreement that a statute must clearly indicate a private cause of action, and that language such as that in the Neutrality Act is insufficient. *See, e.g., Conn. Action Now, Inc.*, 457 F.2d at 84 ("All of the past rulings (of which we are aware) upholding a private right to sue turned on language which stated expressly or clearly implied that the informer could begin the proceeding without waiting for governmental action."); *id.* at 84 & n.4 (collecting cases and statutes); *Omaha & R.V.R. Co. v. Hale*, 63 N.W. 849, 850–51 (Neb. 1895) (surveying examples and finding no "serious conflict" on this point); *Drew v. Hilliker*, 56 Vt. 641, 645 (1884) **[—21—]** (discussing typical linguistic formulations that trigger a private cause of action); William H. Rodgers, Jr., *Industrial Water Pollution and the Refuse Act: A Second Chance for Water Quality*, 119 U. PA. L. REV. 761, 787–88 & nn.171–74 (1971) (surveying authorities).

We have found only one, one-hundred-fifty year old, state court decision whose holding appears to support Dr. Bauer's position. *Chi. & Alton R.R. Co. v. Howard*, 38 Ill. 414 (1865). In that case, the Illinois Supreme Court interpreted a state statute with informer language similar to the language in the Neutrality Act, and held that it afforded an informer a right to pursue a *qui tam* action for the recovery of various statutory penalties. Courts and commentators have noted the aberrant nature of the decision, repudiated it, and occasionally even offered theories for how it is consistent with the general rule. Rodgers,

Industrial Water Pollution, supra, at 788 & nn.173–74 (singling *Howard* out as aberrant and repudiated); *Hale*, 63 N.W. at 850–51 (disagreeing with *Howard*); *Conn. Action Now, Inc.*, 457 F.2d at 85 n.6 (characterizing *Howard*'s reasoning as consistent with the general rule). In any event, the decision is neither controlling nor convincing, so it offers no solace to Dr. Bauer here.

CONCLUSION

For the reasons discussed above, we affirm the judgment of the District Court dismissing the complaint. We do so, however, on the ground that Dr. Bauer lacks standing to pursue his action under the Neutrality Act.

So ordered.

United States Court of Appeals for the Federal Circuit

United States Court of Appeals
for the Federal Circuit

No. 13-5073

CENTURY EXPLORATION NEW ORLEANS, LLC
vs.
UNITED STATES

Appeal from the United States Court of Federal
Claims

Decided: March 14, 2014

Citation: 745 F.3d 1168, 2 Adm. R. 626 (Fed. Cir. 2014).

Before **LOURIE, DYK,** and **WALLACH,** Circuit Judges.

[—2—] **DYK,** Circuit Judge:

Appellants Century Exploration New Orleans, LLC (Century) and Champion Exploration, LLC (Champion) appeal from a judgment of the Court of Federal Claims (Claims Court) granting summary judgment to the government on the issue of breach of contract.

Century and Champion are in the business of oil and gas exploration, development, and production. They jointly leased the mineral rights to land on the Outer Continental Shelf from the government. The terms of their lease allowed the government to change existing regulatory requirements under the Outer Continental Shelf Lands Act of 1953 (OCSLA), 43 U.S.C. § 1331 et seq. The appellants argue the government breached their lease because it imposed additional regulatory requirements pursuant to the Oil Pollution Act (OPA), 33 U.S.C. § 2701 et seq. We agree with the Claims Court that the government made these changes pursuant to OCSLA, not OPA, and we affirm. [—3—]

BACKGROUND

Appellants Century and Champion obtained an oil and gas lease from the government for a 5760-acre tract called Block 920, Ewing Bank (EW920) located on the Outer Continental Shelf. They made an initial bonus payment of $23,236,314 to acquire the lease and have paid the government additional rental payments of $9.50 per acre,

per lease year—$54,720 per year—since that initial payment. The lease (Lease No. OCS–G 32293) became effective on August 1, 2008, and had an initial term running through July 31, 2016. Section 1 of the lease provided:

This lease is issued pursuant to the Outer Continental Shelf Lands Act of August 7, 1953, 67 Stat. 462[,] 43 U.S.C. § 1331 et seq., as amended (92 Stat. 629), (hereinafter called the "Act"). The lease is issued subject to the Act; all regulations issued pursuant to the Act and in existence upon the Effective Date of this lease; all regulations issued pursuant to the statute in the future which provide for the prevention of waste and conservation of the natural resources of the Outer Continental Shelf and the protection of correlative rights therein; and all other applicable statutes and regulations.

J.A. 88.

In *Mobil Oil Exploration & Producing Southeast, Inc. v. United States*, the Supreme Court interpreted a lease provision that was nearly identical to the one at issue here. 530 U.S. 604 (2000).[1] In *Mobil Oil* , the question was [—4—] whether certain oil company leases were subject to a new statute, the Outer Banks Protection Act, 33 U.S.C. 2753 (1990), 104 Stat. 555 (repealed 1996), which was enacted after the leases were signed and changed the requirements applicable to the lessees. *Mobil Oil*, 530 U.S. at 611-13. The Court held that the leases were subject to all statutes and regulations in existence as of their effective date, but, as to future regulations, were subject only to OCSLA regulations issued after the effective date of the leases. *Id.* at 615. Thus, the Court concluded that the government's imposition of

---

[1] For the lease language of *Mobil Oil*, see *Conoco Inc. v. United States*, 35 Fed. Cl. 309, 317 (1996), *rev'd sub nom. Marathon Oil Co. v. United States*, 158 F.3d 1253 (Fed. Cir. 1998), *opinion withdrawn and superseded on* [—4—] *reh'g*, 177 F.3d 1331 (Fed. Cir. 1999), *rev'd sub nom. Mobil Oil Exploration & Producing Se., Inc. v. United States*, 530 U.S. 604 (2000), *aff'd sub nom. Marathon Oil Co. v. United States*, 236 F.3d 1313 (Fed. Cir. 2000).

new regulatory requirements pursuant to the Outer Banks Protection Act breached the leases. *Id.* at 620. Here, appellants similarly claim that the government changed regulatory requirements after the effective date of their lease pursuant to OPA, not OCSLA.

On April 20, 2010, an explosion and fire on the Deepwater Horizon oil rig—a semi-submersible drilling rig located in the Gulf of Mexico—killed eleven workers and resulted in an oil spill that lasted several months. Although the rig was equipped with a blowout preventer—a mechanism designed to stop the flow of oil in the event of a blowout—this device failed to function after the accident. By the time the drill operator finally managed to cap the oil well on July 15, 2010, 87 days after the initial blowout, 4.9 billion barrels of crude oil had been released into the gulf. As a result of the spill, the government imposed new regulatory requirements, which the appellants urge increase the cost of their required bond. The question is whether these requirements were imposed under OCSLA or OPA. [—5—]

On January 25, 2011, Century filed a three-count complaint in the Claims Court. In its complaint, Century asserted that, as a result of these new regulations, "the government breached its lease agreement with plaintiffs (Count I); that it effected an uncompensated taking of its private property in violation of the Fifth Amendment (Count II); and that the government's activities may have given rise to other, unspecified causes of action (Count III)." J.A. 23. In support of its breach claim, Century alleged that the government's changes to the applicable regulations violated various sections of the Administrative Procedure Act (APA), 5 U.S.C. §§ 553, 706, were therefore unauthorized, and breached the lease. On September 12, 2011, Champion filed a complaint against the government, adopting the allegations Century set forth in its complaint. Since this appeal is exclusively concerned with the appellants' breach claims, we confine our discussion to that issue.

On July 13, 2012, the government filed a motion for summary judgment on the appellants' breach of contract claims. The government argued that it had not breached the appellants' lease. In the alternative, the government argued that even if it had breached the contract, the sovereign acts doctrine shielded it from liability. The appellants filed a cross-motion for partial summary judgment, seeking a determination that the government was liable for breach of contract.

In response to these motions, the Claims Court granted summary judgment to the government, holding that it did not breach any express term of the lease. The Claims Court also found that the government did not breach its implied duty of good faith and fair dealing. With respect to the appellants' APA challenges, the court held that it did not possess subject matter jurisdiction to hear such claims. In the alternative, the Claims Court held that the government was not liable under the sovereign acts doctrine. The Claims Court entered a final judgment [—6—] under Federal Rule of Civil Procedure 54(b) in favor of the government, dismissing the appellants' breach of contract claims with prejudice.

Century and Champion timely appealed, and we have jurisdiction pursuant to 28 U.S.C. § 1295(a)(3). We review the grant of summary judgment de novo. *United States v. Great Am. Ins. Co. of N.Y.*, 738 F.3d 1320, 1329 (Fed. Cir. 2013). The interpretation of the lease is also an issue of law that we review de novo. *C. Sanchez & Son, Inc. v. United States*, 6 F.3d 1539, 1544 (Fed. Cir. 1993).

DISCUSSION

I. Express Breach

The principal issue presented in this appeal is whether the government breached any express term of Century and Champion's lease. As discussed above, the Supreme Court considered a nearly identical oil lease provision in *Mobil Oil* . The Court held that the lease should be interpreted to protect the lessees from new statutes, new non-OCSLA regulations, and changes to the text of OCSLA itself. *Mobil Oil*, 530 U.S. at 616. But the lessees were required to comply with changes in *OCSLA regulations.* As the Court explained:

> [t]he lease contracts say that they are subject to then-existing regulations and to certain future regulations, those issued pursuant to OCSLA [and certain other statutes] . . . . This explicit reference to future regulations makes it clear that the catchall provision that references "all other applicable . . . regulations," must include only statutes and regulations already existing at the time of the contract, a conclusion not questioned here by the Government.

Id. at 616 (second omission in original) (internal citation omitted). This court followed the Supreme Court's interpretation of the lease language in *Amber Resources Co. v.* [—7—] *United States*, 538 F.3d 1358, 1368 (Fed. Cir. 2008), and held that similar lease language only obligated compliance with future changes to OCSLA regulations. *Id.* at 1362-63, 1368.

A

Initially, some description of OCSLA and OPA is useful. OCSLA provides that the United States, and not the individual states, shall have jurisdiction and control over the submerged lands of the Outer Continental Shelf.[2] 43 U.S.C. § 1332(1); *see Barker v.*

---

[2] OCSLA provides the United States with legal jurisdiction over:

> the subsoil and seabed of the Outer Continental Shelf and to all artificial islands, and all installations and other devices permanently or temporarily attached to the seabed, which may be erected thereon for the purpose of exploring for, developing, or producing resources therefrom, or any such installation or other device (other than a ship or vessel) for the purpose of transporting such resources, to the same extent as if the Outer Continental Shelf were an area of exclusive Federal jurisdiction within a State[.]

43 U.S.C. § 1333(a)(1). OCSLA defines the Outer Continental Shelf as all submerged land that is beyond the outer limits of state jurisdiction (three

Hercules Offshore, Inc., 713 F.3d 208, 213, 1 Adm. R. 206, 207 (5th Cir. 2013) ("OCSLA asserts exclusive federal question jurisdiction over the OCS."). Congress enacted OCSLA to ensure that a "vital national resource reserve held by the Federal Government for the public" would be "made available for expeditious and orderly [—8—] development, subject to environmental safeguards, in a manner which is consistent with the maintenance of competition and other national needs." 43 U.S.C. § 1332(3). In furtherance of this objective, the Department of Interior (Interior Department) enters into mineral leases with private parties. These mineral leases authorize private parties, such as oil companies, to explore the Outer Continental Shelf for oil and natural gas and extract any reserves that are discovered. Thus, the only entities entitled to conduct oil and gas exploration, development, and production on the Outer Continental Shelf are lessees of the federal government. *See id.* §§ 1333(1), 1334. In enacting OCSLA, Congress was careful to stipulate that

> operations in the outer Continental Shelf should be conducted in a safe manner by well- trained personnel using technology, precautions, and techniques sufficient *to prevent or minimize the likelihood of blowouts, loss of well control, fires, spillages, physical obstruction to other users of the waters or subsoil and seabed, or other occurrences which may cause damage to the environment or to property, or endanger life or health.*

Id. § 1332(6) (emphasis added).

OCSLA vests the Secretary of the Interior (Interior Secretary) with the authority to regulate exploration under the oil and gas leases, as well as the resulting development and production activities. *Id.* § 1334. Specifically, OCSLA provides that the Secretary

---

nautical miles from shore) and within the limits of national jurisdiction (200 nautical miles from shore). *See* 43 U.S.C. §§ 1301(a), 1331(a); *Amber*, 538 F.3d at 1362.

shall prescribe such rules and regulations as may be necessary to carry out [the provisions of OCSLA]. The Secretary may at any time prescribe and amend such rules and regulations as he determines to be necessary and proper in order to provide *for the prevention of waste and conservation of the natural resources of the outer Continen-* [—9—] *tal Shelf,* and the protection of correlative rights therein, and, notwithstanding any other provisions herein, such rules and regulations shall, as of their effective date, apply to all operations conducted under a lease issued or maintained under the provisions of this subchapter.

Id. § 1334(a) (emphasis added). Thus, OCSLA "authorize[s] the [Interior Department], by valid regulations, to impose anywhere in the OCS all reasonable development and production conditions it deems necessary to its stewardship of the OCS and administration of OCSLA." *Gulf Restoration Network v. Salazar,* 683 F.3d 158, 169-70 (5th Cir. 2012) (citing 43 U.S.C. §§ 1334, 1351; H.R. Rep. 95–1474, at 115 (1978) (Conf. Rep.), *reprinted in* 1978 U.S.C.C.A.N. 1674). Pursuant to this authority, the Interior Secretary has promulgated regulations and orders that govern a lessee's oil exploration, development, and production activities on the Outer Continental Shelf. *See* 30 C.F.R. pt. 250 (2010).[3]

The Oil Pollution Act, 33 U.S.C. § 2701 et seq., is simultaneously narrower and broader in scope than OCSLA. In 1990, Congress enacted OPA in response to "rising public concern following the Exxon Valdez oil spill." *The Oil Pollution Act Overview,* United States Environmental Protection Agency, http://www.epa.gov/oem/content/lawsregs/opaover.htm (last visited Feb. 10,

2014). This law expanded the federal government's ability to respond to oil spills by imposing strict liability on parties respon- [—10—] sible for releasing oil into navigable waters. *See* 33 U.S.C. §§ 2701- 2713; Thomas J. Wagner, *The Oil Pollution Act of 1990: An Analysis,* 21 J. Mar. L. & Com. 569, 574- 76 (1990). OPA also created the national Oil Spill Liability Trust Fund, which can be used to clean up oil spills when the party responsible is unknown or refuses to pay. *See* 33 U.S.C. § 2712; *Oil Spill Liability Trust Fund,* United States Environmental Protection Agency, http://www.epa.gov/osweroe1/content/learning/oilfund.htm (last visited Feb. 10, 2014) . Thus, unlike OCSLA, which covers all mineral activity on the Outer Continental Shelf pursuant to leases from the United States, 43 U.S.C. §§ 1331-1356, OPA is specifically designed to govern oil spill prevention, clean up, and compensation in all United States navigable waters whatever the source of the exploration, development, and production rights. Inho Kim, *Ten Years After the Enactment of the Oil Pollution Act of 1990: a Success of a Failure,* 26 Marine Pol'y 197, 197 (2002); Wagner, *supra,* at 569; *Oil Pollution Act of 1990 (OPA),* United States Coast Guard, http://www.uscg.mil/npfc/About_NPFC/opa.asp (last visited Feb. 11, 2014). However, the OPA regulations involved here only apply to activities on the Outer Continental Shelf. *See* 30 C.F.R. ch. II, pt. 254, subpt. B.

Oil and gas companies leasing land on the Outer Continental Shelf must comply with both OCSLA and OPA. These statutes contain some overlapping provisions, in particular those relating to the remediation of oils spills. For example, during the relevant period, both OCSLA and OPA regulations required oil companies to submit Oil Spill Response Plans. OCSLA regulation 30 C.F.R. § 250.219 required all Outer Continental Shelf lessees to provide such a plan. *See also* Oil and Gas and Sulphur Operations in the Outer Continental Shelf—Plans and Information, 70 Fed. Reg. 51,478-01 (Aug. 30, 2005). OPA regulation 30 C.F.R. § 254.1 required all owners or operators of oil handling, storage, or transportation facilities [—11—] "located seaward of the coast line" (that is, on the Outer Continental Shelf) to submit a plan. 30 C.F.R. § 254.1.

---

[3] Unless otherwise indicated, this opinion references the version of the Code of Federal Regulations (C.F.R.) that was in effect when appellants acquired their lease. The provisions of the C.F.R. governing Outer Continental Shelf leasing, exploration, and development that are relevant to this opinion have been relocated from Part 250 of Title 30 to Part 550 of that title.

OCSLA and OPA regulations required these plans to ensure that oil and gas companies were prepared to respond to any oil spills that might result from their activities off the United States coastline.

Even prior to the execution of the appellants' lease, OCSLA and its implementing regulations required lessees to submit an exploration plan to the government before commencing any drilling activities. *See* 43 U.S.C. § 1340(c)(1), (e)(2); 30 C.F.R. § 250.201 (2010). Such an exploration plan detailed the lessee's proposed exploration activities on the Outer Continental Shelf and required government approval before the lessee commenced any exploration activity. 30 C.F.R. § 250.201 (2010). Importantly, the regulations required that such an exploration plan include an Oil Spill Response Plan that contained a calculation of the volume of oil that would result from a worst case discharge scenario. *Id.* § 250.219(a)(2)(iv) (2010). A worst case discharge scenario was defined as "the daily rate of an uncontrolled flow of natural gas and oil from all producible reservoirs into the open wellbore"[4] that would result from a blowout, such as the one that triggered the Deepwater Horizon disaster. *Worst Case Discharge Determination*, Bureau of Ocean Energy Management, http://www.boem.gov/Oil-and-Gas-Energy-Program/Resource-Evaluation/Worst-Case-Discharge/Index.aspx (last visited Feb. 11, 2014). Lessees were also required to "demonstrate oil spill financial [—12—] responsibility for facilities proposed in [their exploration plan]," 30 C.F.R. § 250.213(e)(2) (2010), and the appellants elected to comply by posting a bond. *See* 30 C.F.R. § 253.20 (2010) (describing the different methods of demonstrating oil spill financial responsibility). The appellants' bond requirements depended on their worst case discharge volume: the greater the worst case discharge volume, the larger the bond

required to cover their potential liability. *See id.* § 253.13 (2010) (setting out the correspondence between worst case discharge volume and bond requirement).[5]

OPA did not require oil companies to submit an exploration plan; rather, each company was required to submit an Oil Spill Response Plan, which included a worst case discharge scenario. As with the OCSLA requirements, this only applied to Outer Continental Shelf lessees. [—13—]

The OCSLA regulations borrowed and incorporated the OPA regulation's method of calculating worst case discharge volume and the assumptions for that calculation. Thus, Outer Continental Shelf lessees were required to follow § 254.27's methodology when calculating worst case discharge volume for OCSLA purposes, and all oil and gas operators were required to follow § 254.27's methodology when calculating worst case discharge volume for OPA purposes. Finally, § 250.103, an OCSLA regulation, enabled the government to issue Notices to Lessees and Operators (NTLs) that "clarify, supplement, or provide more detail about certain requirements," *id.*, of the OCSLA statute and regulations. As the Interior Department has explained, it "issues NTLs to explain and clarify its regulations." Oil and Gas and Sulphur Operations in the Outer Continental Shelf—Plans and Information, 70 Fed. Reg. 51,478-01, 51,478 (Aug.

---

[4] The wellbore is the hole the lessee or operator has drilled for the purpose of exploring or extracting natural gas or oil from the earth. In the oil production context, reservoirs are subsurface pools of hydrocarbons, such as crude oil or natural gas, contained in porous or fractured rock formations.

---

[5] The appellants also argue that their increased bonding requirements breached Section 8 of the lease. Section 8 reads: "The Lessee shall maintain at all times the bond(s) required by regulation prior to the issuance of the lease and shall furnish such additional security as may be required by the Lessor if, after operations have begun, the Lessor deems such additional security to be necessary." J.A. 89. Section 8 refers to 30 C.F.R. § 250.213(e)(1)'s "appropriate bond" requirement, also known as the performance bond requirement. As the Claims Court accurately explained, "[i]n order to demonstrate a breach of section 8 of the lease, plaintiffs must establish that they are now required to furnish a bond that exceeds the bond required under the regulations in effect when the lease was executed." J.A. 40. Because the appellants' performance bonding requirement has not changed, there has been no breach of Section 8 of the lease.

30, 2005). The OPA statute and the OPA regulations thereunder made no provision for the issuance of NTLs.

The appellants contend that the NTLs in this case are equivalent to new regulations within the meaning of the lease provisions. Even assuming the NTLs are new regulations, however, they were issued pursuant to OCSLA, and thus do not breach the lease.

B

The change at issue here concerns the worst case discharge calculation and the bond requirement that corresponds to that calculation. The government issued Notice to Lessees No. 2010–N06 (NTL-06) and related documents on June 18, 2010, after the effective date of the lease. This order and the various documents explaining it required lessees to make changes to the way they calculated worst case discharge volume. *See infra* Slip. Op. at 14-16. The only identified consequence of this alteration was to alter the lessees' bond requirement. [—14—]

The appellants argue that the government's issuance of NTL-06 breached their lease because: (1) it changed the worst case discharge scenario, thereby imposing additional bonding costs, and (2) the change was made pursuant to OPA, not OCSLA. There appears to be no dispute as to the first question. At oral argument, the appellants clarified that, in their view, NTL-06 resulted in four principal changes to the worst case discharge calculation, which increased their corresponding bond requirement.[6] First, and most importantly, after the effective date of the lease, the government sent an email to Century[7] stating that under NTL-06, the

appellants must "[i]ncrease the length of time [of] the uncontrolled blowout response from 30 to 120 days." J.A. 1432. Prior to NTL-06, the OCSLA regulations, by reference to OPA regulation 30 C.F.R. § 254.47(a)(3), only required oil company lessees to assume that oil would flow from their wells for 30 days [—15—] during a blowout when calculating their worst case discharge volumes. The government email to Century explained that the appellants should revise their OCSLA-mandated exploration plan in light of NTL-06 and now assume that oil would flow from their well for 120 days when calculating the worst case discharge volume.

Second, prior to the issuance of NTL-06, lessees did not have to include all reservoirs that a drilling operator might pass through to reach its intended drilling location in the calculation of the uncontrolled flow that could result from a blowout. The parties do not specify the source of this obligation. However, the frequently asked questions document (FAQ document) accompanying NTL-06 apparently modified this requirement. Under NTL-06, lessees must "consider *all* reservoirs, not just where you're drilling to, but anything you might pass through" when calculating worst case discharge volume. Oral Argument 5:57-6:02, *available at* http://www .cafc.uscourts.gov/oral-argument-recordings/all/century-exploration.html. More specifically, lessees must now "determine the daily rate of an uncontrolled flow from *all producible* reservoirs into the open wellbore." J.A. 663 (emphasis added).

Third, NTL-06 changed assumptions regarding what could be treated as being in the wellbore when calculating worst case discharge volume. Previously, lessees counted the fact that certain equipment, such as

---

[6] In addition to these four principal changes, NTL-06 also rescinded an older order, NTL-08, which had waived certain regulatory requirements for particular lessees. As the appellants conceded at oral argument, the rescission of NTL-08 is not relied on in the complaint. Therefore, we do not discuss NTL-08 here.

[7] The government sent this email to Century directly, instead of both Century and Champion, because Century was the designated lease operator. As the lease operator, Century was in charge of

submitting the appellants' exploration plan, meeting the bond requirements, and applying for permits to drill. *See* 30 C.F.R. § 250.105 (2013) ("Operator means the person the lessee(s) designates as having control or management of operations on the leased area or a portion thereof. An operator may be a lessee, the BSEE-approved or BOEM-approved designated agent of the lessee(s), or the holder of operating rights under a BOEM-approved operating rights assignment."); J.A. 88.

drillpipe, logging tools, and drill bits were in the wellbore, thereby reducing total discharge volume, when they calculated worst case discharge volume. Again, the source of this requirement is unclear. However, the FAQ document explained that lessees "should [now] assume that the wellbore *is free of* drillpipe, logging tools, or other similar equipment." J.A. 665 (emphasis added). Thus, under NTL-06, lessees "no longer consider anything being in the wellbore." Oral Argument 5:47-5:51, *available at* [—16—] http://www.cafc.uscourts.gov/oral-argument-recordings/all/century-exploration.html.

Fourth, NTL-06 prohibits lessees from including the presence of a blowout preventer (the mechanism that failed to contain the Deepwater Horizon blowout) in their worst case discharge calculation. As the appellants explained at oral argument, "for years beforehand you counted the fact that you had a blowout preventer on the well when you determined worst case discharge." *Id.* at 17:52-18:02. Once again, the source of this requirement is not specified. However, the FAQ document stated that lessees should now assume that a blowout preventer is not connected to the wellhead.

Prior to the issuance of NTL-06, the appellants' worst case discharge volume was 1,500 barrels and their corresponding bond requirement amounted to $35 million. The appellants contend, and the government does not contest, that NTL-06 and the various documents explaining that order increased their worst case discharge volume to 142,977 barrels per day and their corresponding bond requirement to $150 million.

C

While not disputing the existence of the changes or their impact, the government urges that the changes were made pursuant to OCSLA, not OPA. The appellants argue that they were made pursuant to OPA. More precisely, appellants argue that because NTL-06 and related documents changed the assumptions lessees must follow when calculating their worst case discharge volume, and the regulation governing the worst case

scenario calculation is an OPA regulation, NTL-06 effectively changed an OPA regulation. In response, the government explains that the OCSLA regulation outlining what oil spill information lessees must include in their exploration plans, § 250.219(a)(2)(iv), simply incorporates the OPA methodology for calculating worst case discharge volume through [—17—] reference. The government points out that NTL-06 did not change the text of the OPA regulation itself. Rather, in the government's view, it altered only OCSLA regulatory requirements.

We agree with the government. Initially, it is important that OCSLA authorized the government to adopt regulations concerning blowout protection and worst case discharge scenarios; the government did not need to act under the authority granted by OPA. Pursuant to Section 1 of the lease, the government could issue new OCSLA regulations which provide for the "prevention of waste and conservation of the natural resources of the Outer Continental Shelf" by the lessees. J.A. 88. This lease provision can be traced directly to § 1334 of OCSLA: "The Secretary may at any time prescribe and amend such rules and regulations as he determines to be necessary and proper in order *to provide for the prevention of waste and conservation of the natural resources* of the outer Continental Shelf, and the protection of correlative rights therein . . . ." 43 U.S.C. § 1334 (emphasis added).

The case law interpreting § 1334 gives a broad scope to the phrase "prevention of waste and conservation of the natural resources," making clear that it extends to environmental protection. *See, e.g., Pauley Petroleum Inc. v. United States*, 591 F.2d 1308, 1325 (Ct. Cl. 1979) (explaining that a new regulation imposing absolute liability on lessees for any pollution resulting from their activities would be "lawful and reasonable" because OCSLA provides "'[t]he Secretary may at any time prescribe and amend such rules and regulations [] in order to provide for the prevention of waste and conservation of the natural resources of the outer Continental Shelf'" (quoting 43 U.S.C. § 1334(a)(1) (1970))); *Get Oil Out! Inc. v. Exxon Corp.*, 586 F.2d 726, 729 (9th Cir. 1978); *Union Oil Co. of*

Cal. v. Morton, 512 F.2d 743, 749-50 (9th Cir. 1975) (stating that the phrase "conservation of the natural resources of the outer Continental Shelf" "encompasses all [—18—] the natural resources of the shelf, not merely the mineral resources" (citations omitted)); *Gulf Oil Corp. v. Morton*, 493 F.2d 141, 145 (9th Cir. 1973) ("[I]n authorizing the Secretary to issue regulations, [OCSLA] speaks of 'conservation of the natural resources of the outer Continental Shelf,' not just of conservation of oil, gas, sulphur and other mineral resources. . . . Its natural meaning would encompass all such resources, not just oil and gas, sulphur and other minerals." (quoting 43 U.S.C. § 1334(a))). Thus, the case law supports a finding that OCSLA endows the government with the authority necessary to regulate worst case discharge scenarios and to require adequate bonding. *See also* 43 U.S.C. § 1337(a)(7)(A) (authorizing the Interior Secretary to require lessees to post a bond in accordance with the applicable regulations).

Nevertheless, the appellants point out that the mere existence of government authority to act under OCSLA does not immunize the government from liability for regulatory changes. To avoid liability for changes, the government must also have acted *pursuant* to OCSLA authority. In *Mobil Oil*, the government argued that, irrespective of the statutory change at issue in that case, the government could have undertaken the exact same action pursuant to OCSLA. 530 U.S. at 615-16. The Supreme Court rejected this argument, recognizing that the new requirements were "created by [the Outer Banks Protection Act], a later enacted statute," *Mobil Oil*, 530 U.S. at 616, not an OCSLA regulation. The court explained that "[t]he fatal flaw in [the government's] argument [] arises out of the Interior Department's own statement—a statement made when citing the Outer Banks Protection Act to explain its approval delay." *Id.* at 617-18. Thus, even though OCSLA may have permitted the government to require the exact same actions the Outer Banks Protection Act required, because the government cited the Outer Banks Protection Act as the [—19—] authority for carrying out these actions, the Court found that the government effectuated

them pursuant to the Outer Banks Protection Act and was liable for breach. In reaching this conclusion, the Supreme Court emphasized the government's *chosen source of authority*: the government cited the Outer Banks Protection Act, not OCSLA regulations. *Id.*

We confirmed this approach in *Amber*. In *Amber*, Congress amended the Coastal Zone Management Act to impose new regulatory requirements. 538 F.3d at 1366. Thus, *Amber* turned on whether these new requirements breached the oil companies' contracts. *Id.* Relying on *Mobil Oil*, we reasoned that "[b]ecause the 1990 [Coastal Zone Management Act] amendments . . . imposed significantly more burdensome requirements for granting lease suspensions, the new statute in this case breached the lease agreements in the same way as the new statute in *Mobil Oil*." *Id.* at 1371. The government argued that it could have undertaken the exact same action pursuant to the OCSLA regulations in effect at that time. *Id.* at 1372. Nevertheless, because the government imposed new requirements based on the *new statutory* changes to the Coastal Zone Management Act, not *existing OCSLA regulations*, we held that these requirements breached the contract. *Id.*

Here, we reach a different conclusion. Although, as discussed above, both the OCSLA and OPA worst case discharge scenario regulations are limited to OCS lessees, we conclude that the government changed the appellants' worst case discharge calculation pursuant to OCSLA. First, NTL-06 itself identified OCSLA regulation § 250.103 as its source of authority. NTL-06 only referenced and discussed OCSLA regulations and requirements. As NTL-06 explains, OCSLA regulations § 250.219 and § 250.250 required "all [OCSLA exploration] plans" to be "accompanied by information regarding oil spills, including calculations of [the lessee's] worst case dis- [—20—] charge scenario." J.A. 657. Although OCSLA regulation § 250.219(a)(2)(iv) instructed lessees to calculate their worst case discharge volume according to the OPA regulation methodology, NTL-06 never mentioned the OPA regulations. NTL-06 simply augmented the factors lessees must consider when calculating their worst case discharge scenario for *OCSLA purposes*.[8]

Second, there has been no showing or even suggestion that the NTL-06 changes applied outside the OCSLA context. Critically, NTL-06 states that it only changes a lessee's worst case discharge scenario "required by [OCSLA regulation] 30 C.F.R. § 250.219(a)(2)(iv)." J.A. 658. NTL-06 did not change the text of the relevant OPA regulation, § 254.47, and nothing suggests that NTL-06 altered any part of the OPA regulation. Indeed, the appellants do not claim that NTL-06 changed the text of relevant OPA regulation. NTL-06 merely changed the way an OCSLA regulation incorporates an OPA calculation. Moreover, for three out of the four alleged alterations to the worst case discharge calculation, it is not even clear that the original requirement was an OPA requirement. A change to an OCSLA regulation does not breach the express terms of the lease language as interpreted by the Supreme Court in *Mobil Oil* and this court in *Amber*.[9] [—21—] [—22—]

---

[8] At oral argument, the appellants also contended that the changes NTL-06 brought about were made pursuant to OPA because a later issued NTL, NTL No. 2012-N06, altered OPA regulation § 254.47(b). Issued on August 10, 2012, after the appellants filed their complaint and after the government moved for summary judgment, NTL No. 2012-N06 is irrelevant to this appeal, and we decline to discuss it. The same is true of NTL 2013-N02.

[9] The appellants suggest that in adopting OCSLA regulation 30 C.F.R. § 250.219, the Interior Department recognized that the worst case discharge calculation was [—21—] included in the OCSLA regulation merely as a "streamlined" means to comply with OPA. Century's Reply Br. 12 (quoting Oil and Gas and Sulphur Operations in the Outer Continental Shelf—Plans and Information, 70 Fed. Reg. at 51,486). This is not correct. The OCSLA regulation in question states that lessees may provide, as an alternative to an individual Oil Spill Response Plan (OSRP), "[r]eference to [an] approved regional OSRP (see 30 C.F.R. 254.3) [that must] . . . include: . . . [1] The calculated volume of your worst case discharge scenario (see 30 C.F.R. 254.26(a)), and [2] a comparison of the appropriate worst case discharge scenario in your approved regional OSRP with the worst case discharge scenario that could result

II. Implied Breach and Administrative Procedure Act Challenges

We have considered the appellants' other arguments and find them to be without merit. Appellants cannot rely on the implied covenant of good faith and fair dealing to change the text of their contractual obligations. As this court recently clarified in *Metcalf Construction, Inc. v. United States*,

the 'implied duty of good faith and fair dealing cannot expand a party's contractual duties beyond those in the express contract or create duties inconsistent with the contract's provisions.' . . . [O]ur formulation means simply that an act will not be found to violate the duty (which is implicit in the contract) if such a finding would be at odds with the terms of the original bargain, whether by altering the contract's discernible allocation of risks and benefits or by conflicting with a contract provision. The implied duty of good faith and fair dealing is limited by the original bargain: it prevents a party's acts or omissions that, though

---

from your proposed exploration activities." 30 C.F.R. § 250.219(a)(2)(iv) (2010).

The comment in the Federal Register on which the appellants rely was directed to the second aspect of the regulation. The Interior Department's summary of the comment reads: "With respect to paragraph (a)(2)(iv), [the Offshore Operators Committee] inquires regarding the purpose of providing a comparison between the site specific worst case discharge and that in the regional OSRP." The Interior Department's response to the comment was similarly limited: "No change. . . . MMS uses the information required under paragraph (a)(2)(iv) as a streamlined means to ensure compliance with requirements of the Oil Pollution Act of 1990." Oil and Gas and Sulphur Operations in the Outer Continental Shelf—Plans and Information, 70 Fed. Reg. 51,478-01, 51,486 (Aug. 30, 2005) (codified at 250.219(a)(1)(iv) (2010)). Neither the comment nor the response concerned the requirement to provide a worst case discharge scenario. *See* Summary of the Offshore Operators Committee's Comments on Subpart B Proposed Regulation at 35-40, Bureau of Safety and Environmental Enforcement (on file with Bureau of Safety and Environmental Enforcement).

not proscribed by the contract expressly, are inconsistent with the contract's purpose and deprive the other party of the contemplated value.

No. 2013-5041, Slip Op. at 10 (Fed. Cir. Feb. 11, 2014) (quoting *Precision Pine & Timber, Inc. v. United States*, 596 F.3d 817, 831 (Fed. Cir. 2010)); *see also Precision Pine*, 596 F.3d at 829-31 (Fed. Cir. 2010) ("The government may be liable for damages when the subsequent government action is specifically designed to reappropriate the benefits the other party expected to obtain from the transaction, thereby abrogating the government's obligations under the contract."); 13 Samuel Williston & Richard A. Lord, A Treatise on the Law of Contracts § 63:22 (4th ed. 2000) ("As a general principle, there can be no breach of the implied promise or covenant of good faith [—23—] and fair dealing where the contract expressly permits the actions being challenged, and the defendant acts in accordance with the express terms of the contract."). We hold that the government has not breached its implied duty of good faith and fair dealing because the lease expressly authorized the government action at issue here: changes to OCSLA regulatory requirements.

We also affirm the Claims Court's holding that it is without subject matter jurisdiction to decide the appellants' APA challenges. *See Lion Raisins, Inc. v. United States*, 416 F.3d 1356, 1370 n.11 (Fed. Cir. 2005) ("Of course, no APA review is available in the Court of Federal Claims.").[10] Because we have found no breach in this case, we need not reach the government's sovereign acts defense.[11]

---

[10] The appellants also argue that the term "other applicable statutes" in Section 1 of the lease should be interpreted to incorporate the APA. Appellant Century's Br. 8, 28. However, as the Claims Court correctly concluded, the APA is not an applicable statute in the sense of the lease language.

[11] In arguing that the government breached its implied duty of good faith and fair dealing, the appellants mention other post-Deepwater Horizon changes to the regulatory requirements such as two separate government-issued moratoria on drilling, a new Drilling Safety Rule, and another NTL (NTL-10). We do not discuss these changes because the appellants have not articulated a theory under which they form a basis for breach liability.

AFFIRMED

This page intentionally left blank

Tables of Authority

This page intentionally left blank

Table of Cases

This page intentionally left blank

Table of Cases [1]

---

[1] Cases named solely after ships, *see, e.g., The Pennsylvania*, 86 U.S. (19 Wall.) 125 (1873), are alphabetized under the letter "T." Cases where the United States is the plaintiff are alphabetized by defendant under the letter "U."

B

C

D

E

F

G

H

I

J

K

L

M

N

O

P

S

T

U

V

W

Y

Z

This page intentionally left blank

Table of Statutes and Rules

This page intentionally left blank

TABLE OF STATUTES AND RULES [1]

PAGE

TREATIES/INTERNATIONAL

FEDERAL

CONSTITUTION

MISCELLANEOUS

---

[1] As cited in the opinions reported.

STATUTES

RULES

REGULATIONS

STATE

This page intentionally left blank

Index

This page intentionally left blank

INDEX

C

D

E

F

J

L

M

N

T

Y

Z

This page intentionally left blank